CONCEPTS AND TECHNIQUES

Rodney J. Anderson, FCA

Partner, Clarkson, Gordon & Co.,
Chartered Accountants

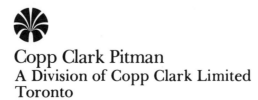

Copp Clark Pitman
A Division of Copp Clark Limited
Toronto

To the late J.R.M. Wilson, FCA

ISBN 0-7730-4222-9

Copp Clark Pitman
517 Wellington Street West
Toronto M5V 1G1

Printed and bound in Canada

Acknowledgements

I am grateful to my partners and to our staff for providing me with the opportunity and the considerable time required to write this book and for helping me in the many aspects of its preparation. So many individuals have been of assistance that any list of acknowledgements is bound to be incomplete. There are a number, however, to whom I am particularly indebted. Under the direction of R.M. Skinner, FCA, the basic framework of the analytical auditing approach, described in Chapters 25 and 26, and a number of the techniques incorporated in the chapters on the financial statement audit were developed more than ten years ago. Having participated in this development under his guidance, I co-authored with him in 1966 the book *Analytical Auditing*. Because of modifications suggested by our staff's experience in its application over the past decade, and because of the evolution of auditing standards during that period, that book is now superseded (at least in its original edition) by the present book. I am also indebted to R.G. Gage, FCA, for a major contribution to the development of the computer auditing procedures now reflected in numerous chapters of this book – later he was involved in implementing computer education programs now widely used throughout the profession. For helping me in many years of struggle with the perplexities of statistical sampling and more recently for the review of Chapters 12, 13 and 22, I am grateful to Professor A.D. Teitlebaum, PhD, of McGill University and D.A. Leslie, CA. In addition, B.W. Simpson, CA, prepared initial drafts of many of the financial statement audit chapters, J.A. Callum, CA, of Chapter 8, J.H. Kearns, CA, of Chapter 14, and D. Neil, CA, of the questions and problems in Volume 1. Other assistance was provided by K.G. Cook, CA, E.A. McGrath, CA, and R.C. Milner, CA. I am grateful for helpful review comments from D.L. Gordon, FCA, K.A. MacKenzie, CA, D.C. Selley, CA, J.M.M. Kirkwood, CA, J.A. Milburn, PhD, CA, and many others. For a review of the legal aspects of Chapter 5 and part of Chapter 4 I am indebted to J.W. Mik and A.J. MacIntosh, QC. W.V. Tovell performed a valuable manuscript review. Mickey Hubbert, Sylvia Ego and Joyce Ferguson processed seemingly endless typing drafts with cheerful efficiency. And my publishers, my partners, and my wife all endured repeatedly missed deadlines on my part with incredible patience.

I am grateful to the Canadian Institute of Chartered Accountants, various inter-provincial committees, the American Institute of Certified Public Accountants, and other bodies for the permission to quote selected excerpts from pronouncements, rules of professional conduct, studies, and other publications and to adapt certain examination material for use in the questions and problems.

Most of all my thanks are due to John A. Davidson, CA. He not only prepared initial drafts of almost half the chapters, but organized and supervised the many stages of the manuscript production, reviewed all the final drafts in detail, caught and corrected large numbers (but no doubt not all) of my errors, and in all ways was my partner in this undertaking of several years.

Finally, I must acknowledge my indebtedness to the late J.R.M. Wilson, FCA. Twenty years ago he persuaded me, an unaccountable chemistry graduate, to enter the accounting profession. His book, *Auditing Procedures, An Introduction For The Student-In-Accounts* was my first exposure to debits and credits. He instigated the writing of this present book. And over the past two years he performed a painstaking content review of all key chapters save a small handful uncompleted at the time of his sudden death. To countless members of our profession, as to me, he was an inspiration. This book is dedicated to him.

Niagara-on-the-Lake
October, 1976   Rodney J. Anderson

Introduction

This book has three major purposes: to serve as a comprehensive explanatory guide and a reference on auditing for practising public accountants, to serve as an auditing textbook for both beginning and advanced students, and to provide a Canadian perspective on auditing and professional practice not readily available in recent literature. To meet the first two objectives adequately the book is necessarily long. For ease of use it has been divided into two volumes. Volume 1 covers principally the *concepts* and *techniques* of auditing; Volume 2 covers the *organization* of, and *procedures* employed in, the typical annual audit. Both volumes should be of use to the practitioner and the advanced student. Volume 1 by itself should be of use to the new student.

The book is directed primarily to the *external audit*, an audit performed by a professional auditor in public practice leading to the expression of an opinion on a set of financial statements. Prospectuses, special purpose reports and unaudited financial statements are also covered because work in these areas is an important part of public practice. Many of the chapters can be of use to internal auditors and government auditors, as methodologies employed and objectives are often similar; however, a comprehensive treatment of their important work is beyond the scope of this book. Also, while an auditor must first be an expert accountant, accounting principles and financial statement presentation are well covered in various accounting texts and need not be repeated here. Nor are detailed tax laws and regulations discussed, though the procedures for verifying tax liabilities and tax provisions are covered. The subject of internal control *is* included, however, because of its inseparable connection with audit planning, verification, and evaluation.

The book has been written from the viewpoint of Canadian practice. The principal references are therefore to Canadian laws, regulations, auditing standards, rules of professional conduct, and authoritative pronouncements. References have been made to standards and pronouncements in other countries (primarily the United States) where these were considered to have an important bearing on Canadian practice. Many of the chapters on concepts, basic techniques and specific procedures are, of course, of general application whatever the nationality of the auditor.

One of the aims of the book has been to relate auditing procedures to a set of logical and coherent underlying concepts. In this day of increasing litigation and public re-examination of auditors' responsibilities, it is not enough to carry out a routine list of audit steps merely because similar steps have been performed before. The auditor must be able to justify the timing, nature and extent of the procedures he performs in terms of their logical consistency with clearly defined auditing objectives and professional and legal standards. For that reason, the two volumes are intended to be used together. Every attempt has been made to give explanations and reasons for the procedures described in Volume 2 and to identify the objectives being served. In many cases, however, the explanations depend on, or are amplified in, the discussion in Volume 1. To facilitate the cross-references, chapters have been numbered in one consecutive series through both volumes and a common index has been included at the end of each volume.

Another aim of the book has been to suggest methods of organizing procedures into an efficient and practical structure for the annual audit. For that reason, considerable attention has been given to planning and to engagement management. One of the difficulties with those subjects is the number of varying and acceptable methods of organizing an audit. Whereas the narrowing of alternatives in *accounting* for similar circumstances is a desirable goal, such uniformity is not essential, nor even desirable, in *auditing*. Several alternative auditing methods may provide equally justifiable means of fulfilling the same audit objective. Space would not permit an explanation of every possible audit structure. And yet, since efficient organization is often half the battle, to omit all examples of specific methods of organization would be poor service to many readers – particularly those students, practitioners, and firms who lack access to comprehensive auditing manuals. The book has attempted, therefore, to provide a general discussion of the various alternative audit approaches and audit techniques and then to offer specific suggestions of particular approaches and techniques which may prove useful. Inevitably, the suggestions reflect the views of the writer. It is hoped, however, that the underlying concepts will be found sufficiently defined in each case that students and practitioners with different preferences as to approach can readily adapt the suggestions to their own style of organization.

Another difficulty in describing auditing procedures is the tremendous diversity of circumstances in individual audits. The formality of audit planning discussed in one chapter may seem to belabour the obvious for the very small audit and yet may prove oversimplified for the very large. Computer-assisted audit techniques described in another chapter may be found too sophisticated for the audit of a rudimentary system while at the same time naive and introductory to specialists experienced in the audit of the most advanced systems. Some effort has been made throughout the book to indicate the effects of these differences in scale and complexity. But the following caveat must be recognized: *no suggested auditing procedure appearing in any textbook can be held out to be necessary on all audits nor necessarily sufficient on any given audit.* The auditor has a responsibility to apply those procedures which in his judgment are necessary to meet generally accepted auditing standards and to comply with rules of professional conduct.

Laws, pronouncements and auditing practices are continually changing. The references in this book are as of October 1, 1976. (They include the effect of Auditing Recommendations in Section 5400, The Auditor's Standard Report, and Section 8100, Unaudited Financial Statements, approved by the CICA Auditing Standards Committee in September 1976 – though a possible renumbering of Handbook sections is under study as this book goes to press.) The reader should refer to laws and pronouncements issued and other developments occurring subsequent to that date. The CICA Handbook extracts quoted include all applicable Recommendations (those which appear in italicized form in the auditing portion of the Handbook) and occasionally additional explanatory comments. For the full set of explanatory comments the reader should refer, of course, to the CICA Handbook itself. Unless already indicated in the text, Handbook excerpts are identified by [CICA Handbook] immediately following the quotation. Detailed references to Handbook paragraphs numbers and the sources of non-Handbook quotations may be found in the notes at the back of each volume.

In referring to the practitioner, auditor, and audit staff member throughout this book, use has been made of the masculine pronoun. It is unfortunate that our language leaves no alternative but to choose between the cumbersome "he or she" or the chauvinistic use of one gender. The fact is, as pointed out in Chapter 21, that while women have represented only a small percentage of the profession in the past, they now make up a significant proportion of new registrants (over 30% in some firms). The overdue addition of this resource to the ranks of the profession, including its senior ranks, will be one of the major changes of the coming two decades.

Some suggestions follow for the use of this book by practitioners, for its use in formal education programs, and for its use by students.

Use by practitioners
While practitioners will be familiar in general with auditing concepts and auditing procedures, recent years have seen a number of dramatic changes and many areas of unresolved controversy. Some of these developments are changes in corporation law, new rules of professional conduct, new definitions of generally accepted auditing standards, expanding legal responsibilities, new approaches to internal control analysis and computer systems, reconsideration of the levels of audit assurance, developments in statistical sampling, controversies over the role of audit materiality, new concepts of compliance testing, methods of integrating conclusions for the audit as a whole, debate over the concept of fairness, problems in reporting on uncertainties, new developments in international reporting, the expanding number of special reports, different types of association with unaudited statements, the question of interim reporting, proposals for association with forecasts, responsibilities with respect to fraud and questionable payments, new methods of receivable confirmation, research in regression analysis, problems with contingent liabilities, the effect of equity accounting on auditing procedures, and the difficulties of auditing related party transactions. The foregoing list is far from complete. The practitioner will find both volumes useful as a timely guide to these new developments as well as a convenient reference for the field as a whole.

For most practitioners, a few of the sections of the early chapters (mainly the first two) are clearly introductory. Nearly all chapters, however, contain material on one or more of the new developments just mentioned. Many chapters assume a familiarity with concepts developed in preceding chapters. In particular, the theory outlined in Chapter 6, the approaches to compliance and substantive verification discussed in Chapters 9 and 11, and the treatment of testing in Chapters 12 and 13 underlie the procedures described throughout the remainder of the two volumes.

Some practitioners may find the book useful as a basis for critically examining their procedures and, in some cases, for updating their own procedure manuals for the effect of recent developments in auditing concepts. Practitioners without procedure manuals may find the book useful either as an on-the-job guide or as a basis for preparing condensed manuals for their own use backed up by the book as a reference.

Use in formal education programs
The book is intended to serve as a flexible and multi-purpose aid to the educator, whether the professor in university, the education director in a pro-

vincial Institute or Order, or the partner in charge of training in a public accounting firm. The following comments are directed primarily to the Canadian profession, though many of the points will have application in other countries.

In Canada, formal education in auditing and professional practice can be classified into five segments – university conceptual courses (or institute equivalent), in-firm basic training (or institute equivalent), advanced technique courses, pre-examination schools and programs, and CICA professional development program.

1. University conceptual course (or institute equivalent).
Most Institutes in Canada recognize university courses in auditing as a prerequisite to the writing of the uniform final examinations. Most, if not all, of the auditing courses presently offered by universities are one-semester courses, with an emphasis on concepts. Volume 1 should be valuable for this type of course. The reading assignments and related lectures for a 13-week one-semester course could conveniently be broken down as shown below. Experimentation with preliminary drafts of the manuscript in a number of university courses has shown that this amount of subject matter can be covered in a reasonably concentrated one-semester course. It is desirable, in such a course, that intermediate financial and management accounting be prescribed as a prerequisite.

Lesson	Chapter
a) Audit objectives and history of the profession	1,2
b) Ethics and public practice	2,3
c) The auditor's responsibilities	4
d) Legal liability	5
e) Audit concepts, assumptions, fraud	6
f) Internal control	7,8*
g) Interim audit procedures	9
h) Evidence and the financial statement audit	10,11
i) Audit testing	12
j) Planning and supervision	15
k) Working papers and review	16
l) Audit reporting	17,18*,19*
m) The future	21
*portions only	

The foregoing list omits statistical sampling (Chapters 13 and 22), computer-assisted audit techniques (Chapter 14) and association with unaudited financial information (Chapter 20) as being likely beyond the scope of a one-semester course if anything but the most superficial coverage were desired. It also suggests inclusion of only selected portions of the computer control chapter (Chapter 8) and some of the reporting chapters (Chapters 18 and 19) since these chapters go into more depth than an initial course would warrant. Obviously, however, alternative course structures would be possible.

In some cases, internal control may be adequately dealt with in a basic management or financial accounting course. In such cases, additional time could be spent on any of the above subject areas or, perhaps, a topic such as statistical sampling could be included.

While there is a growing demand in Canada for formal auditing education beyond the one-semester level, this demand is generally being met by courses outside the university. However, where a two-semester university course is offered, it is suggested that the additional contents of Volume 1 be covered along with selected chapters from Volume 2 to illustrate the practical application of auditing concepts.

2. In-firm basic training (or institute equivalent).
Many public accounting firms provide up to fifteen days of auditing training to new students in their first year. Generally, the prime emphasis is on the "how to" of auditing procedures and the documentation practices followed by the particular firm. Such training is often supplemented by an in-firm audit manual for use on the job. However, even these practice-oriented courses often include explanations of basic auditing concepts and the reasons why various procedures are performed. Possible use of chapters from the book as the basis of lecture material or as pre-reading material follows:

a) Chapters 1, 4 and 10, as pre-reading for an introductory day on auditing,
b) Parts of Chapters 6, 7 and 9 as pre-reading for training in review and evaluation procedures in general,
c) Chapter 25 as pre-reading and study material for a comprehensive flow-charting segment,
d) Chapters 9, 26, and 28 as integrated material for a detailed discussion of interim audit procedures,
e) Chapter 12 as pre-reading or post-reading for testing segments of training programs,
f) Chapters 32 to 42 on a selected basis as pre-reading material for training in specific year-end procedures,
g) Chapters 15, 16, 24, 30, 31 and 44 as pre-reading material for a more advanced course concerned with the planning and supervision of audit engagements.

3. Advanced technique courses.
Advanced technique courses may be offered by universities (as a second semester course in auditing), by firms or by provincial Institutes. The book could be

used as pre-reading or integrated education material for a number of such courses including, for example:

a) Chapters 12, 13 and 22 for an advanced course in audit testing,
b) Chapter 14 for a course in computer-assisted audit techniques,
c) Chapters 8, 9, 25 and 27 for a course in computer controls and computer auditing,
d) Chapter 23 for a course on initial audit engagements,
e) Selected portions of Chapters 32 to 42 for training in the more complex verification areas of the audit.

4. Pre-examination schools and programs.

Some provincial Institutes or groups of provincial Institutes sponsor formal programs to prepare the students for the final examination and to test them in individual subject areas. In addition, a number of pre-examination programs have been developed by large firms and universities for the same purpose. The contents of this book were developed with careful attention to the *Uniform Final Examination Syllabus*. In the past, requirements in the areas of professional ethics, legal liability, professional practice, and computer auditing, among others, have often had to be met by reading material drawn from many different sources. It is hoped that this book will provide an efficient means of reviewing all the important auditing areas in the syllabus.

5. CICA professional development program.

A number of advanced technique courses are incorporated in the CICA professional development program. In addition, much of the CICA program is geared to bringing public practitioners up to date in the new developments in auditing. Since one of the prime purposes of this book has been to cover these new developments, it is hoped that it may be found useful in conjunction with a variety of CICA auditing courses.

Use by students

Use of the material in this book by the student taking formal education programs has already been mentioned. But even the best programs must inevitably omit, or cover only superficially, some subjects. And good procedure manuals must usually limit the space they devote to underlying explanations. In preparing for entry into the profession, a prospective chartered accountant in Canada will wish to be familiar with all the subjects prescribed in the *Uniform Final Examination Syllabus*. It is hoped that all 44 chapters of this book will be found helpful in that preparation.

Table of Contents

Volume 2 –
Organization and Procedures

1

The External Audit

Auditing is the process of examining evidence regarding a report, statement or other assertion to determine its correspondence to established criteria. The audit of a set of financial statements investigates whether these statements reflect underlying business transactions following existing criteria for financial statement preparation. A tax auditor checks a tax return to determine whether it reflects the taxpayer's tax liability in accordance with legislative rules. A government auditor may audit a government departmental report to see whether it properly records that department's authorized activities in accordance with prescribed recording procedures. An internal auditor may examine operational evidence to determine whether the assertion by a corporate department that prescribed operating procedures have been followed is in accordance with the observed facts. A common thread runs through this wide variety of audits. There must be some report, statement or assertion presented by one party – presumably for use by a second party. There must be some established criteria, some yardstick or set of ground rules, known to all parties, as to how such report, statement or assertion is supposed to be prepared. There must be a third party, the auditor, who examines evidence and forms an objective opinion as to whether the report, statement or assertion indeed meets these criteria.

Each of these different types of audit (external, internal, governmental) fulfills a necessary and important social function. The principal subject of this book, however, is the *external audit:* an audit performed by a professional auditor in public practice leading to the expression of opinion (*attestation*) on a set of financial statements. Audited financial statements are financial statements accompanied by an *audit report* containing such opinion. The audit report does *not certify* the statements in the sense of guaranteeing their accuracy; it does, however, express a careful professional opinion which serves the useful function of lending additional credibility to the statements. In Canada, the majority of external audits performed each year are required by companies acts or securities legislation and accordingly are often called *statutory audits*. In addition, a great many non-statutory external audits are performed each year to meet the needs of financial statement users (owners, lenders, or others). These include audits of partnerships, proprietorships and various special purpose engagements.

In this introductory chapter, four different tasks are undertaken: a consideration of the general role of auditing in the modern world, a brief history of the development of audit objectives, an outline of this book in terms of the relationship of audit procedures to general objectives, and an overview of the annual audit. These four separate elements will provide the background necessary for the more specific topics of the chapters which follow.

1.1 The role of accounting information in society

Since the purpose of the external audit is to lend credibility to, and thus enhance the value of, accounting communication, an understanding of the objectives of the external audit must begin with the role of accounting information in society.

1.1.1 Documentation, control and communication

Accounting can be defined as "the process of analyzing and systematically recording, in terms of money or some other unit of measurement, operations or transactions and of summarizing, reporting and interpreting the results thereof."[1] The three key processes of recording, analyzing and reporting in turn imply three uses or functions of accounting.[2]

The simple recording process represents the *documentary* function of accounting. A debt not documented may be forgotten. Self-interest has therefore prompted the recording of commercial transactions as an integral part of man's economic activity since the earliest agricultural barters of Sumeria and Egypt. The analysis process, carried to its fullest extent, implies the *control* function of accounting. Appropriate analysis of accounting data assists the management of an enterprise to make business decisions and thus to control and direct its operations. While these two functions of accounting influence, and are influenced by, the presence of an audit examination, they do not in themselves give rise to the need for an external audit. The reporting process represents the *communication* function of accounting. Accounting provides a medium for communicating to outside interested parties the progress of an enterprise and the stewardship of its management. Because this communication is usually made in the form of financial statements, this aspect of accounting is often called *financial accounting*. It is this communicative aspect of accounting which gives rise to the audit requirement.

1

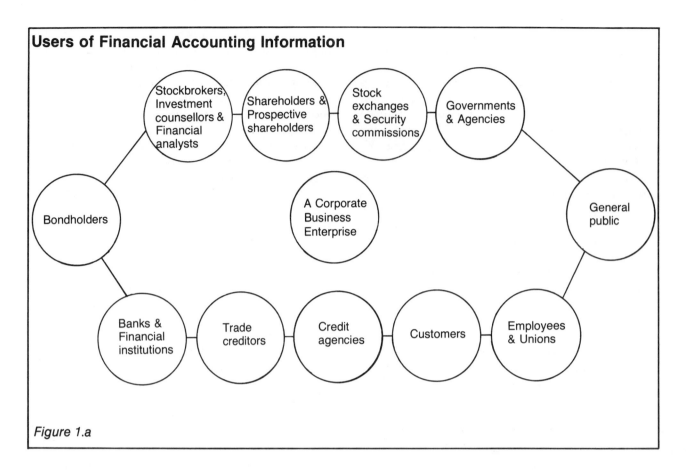

Users of Financial Accounting Information

Stockbrokers, Investment counsellors & Financial analysts

Shareholders & Prospective shareholders

Stock exchanges & Security commissions

Governments & Agencies

Bondholders

A Corporate Business Enterprise

General public

Banks & Financial institutions

Trade creditors

Credit agencies

Customers

Employees & Unions

Figure 1.a

1.1.2 Financial accounting

A central feature of our modern economic system has been the emergence of the corporation as a vehicle for mobilizing capital and human resources. Today large and small corporations in total assemble millions of dollars obtained from thousands of investors and lenders and deploy them in operations extending across the country or as part of international operations around the world. The result has been an increasing separation between owners and lenders on the one hand, and management on the other. For our economic system to function, effective communication between these separated groups is essential. Financial accounting provides this communication. A more user-oriented definition that stresses this communicative role defines accounting as "the process of identifying, measuring, and communicating economic information to permit informed judgements and decisions by users of the information."[3]

1.1.3 Users of financial accounting information

Figure 1.a shows the various uses of financial information for a typical investor-owned corporate enterprise providing goods, services or financing to the general public or to other business enterprises.

Shareholders and prospective shareholders

Before commencing commercial activities the corporation requires capital, often in substantial amounts. This capital is obtained from shareholders who, in exchange for their investment, expect dividends, capital appreciation, or a mixture of both. To induce prospective shareholders to invest, the corporation must provide them with financial and other economic information, usually in the form of a prospectus. Each business unit must obtain its capital in competition with other business units. The investment choice between competing companies is made by a prospective shareholder primarily on the basis of the information received from these companies, either directly or through an analysis of such information by a third party (such as a financial analyst). In either case, it is generally assumed that the more accurate the information received the more efficient will be the market-place allocation of capital resources among competing capital users.

In subsequent periods the business must provide the shareholders with continuing financial accounting information (usually in the form of annual and interim reports) so that they may consider the value of their investment, assess the stewardship of their interests by the company's directors, and re-assess the allocation of their own invested resources.

Stock exchanges and securities commissions

Various groups and institutions exist to aid in the accumulation of equity capital and to assist and protect the investor. Canadian stock exchanges provide a ready market place for the shareholder to buy or sell his investments. The existence of this market facilitates the raising of new capital by corporations. The stock exchanges together with the provincial securities commissions require financial accounting information both for the investors' use and protection and for their own regulation of the market place.

Stockbrokers, investment counsellors and financial analysts

Stockbrokers, investment counsellors and financial analysts are available to give the shareholder or prospective shareholder expert assistance in acquiring or disposing of his investment. To render this assistance they must, in turn, rely on financial accounting information from the business enterprise.

Bondholders and bankers

A corporation may raise capital not only through equity issues but also through bonds and notes. Bondholders and other financial institutions lend the corporation money in exchange for interest payments. The interest rate is set on the basis of the prevailing market for interest rates, the quality of security for the loan, and the loan risk. The loan risk, in turn, must be assessed on the basis of financial accounting information provided by the corporation (for prospective bondholders generally through a prospectus). Similar assessments of loan risks on the basis of financial accounting information must be made by bankers approached for a corporate bank loan. As with shareholders, the bondholders and bankers will also require continuing financial accounting information in subsequent periods so that they may consider the value and security of their investment and re-assess the allocation of their own invested resources.

Trade creditors

In the course of its daily operations, the business will acquire goods and services from other business units in exchange for money. As the exchange is generally not simultaneous, the other business units will be trade creditors for a period of time. In exchange for obtaining trade credit, the business enterprise may have to provide financial accounting information to establish its ability to make eventual payment for the acquired goods and services. Such information may be supplied directly to individual trade creditors or indirectly through credit agencies who in turn will report to their subscribers as to the corporation's credit worthiness.

Government

Various levels of government and their agencies have an interest in the activities of the business enterprise and require financial accounting information from it annually. Certain information (financial statements filed with tax returns) is used by government in the tax assessment and collection process. Other information is used for regulatory and statistical purposes as well as for providing objective data on which the expanding range of national economic policies of government can be based.

Other users

Other users of financial accounting information issued by the enterprise may include employees, unions, customers, and the general public.

1.1.4 The continuing need for financial accounting

The type of financial accounting information which best serves the needs of society is not static; it changes with the changing needs and changing economic structure of society itself. Financial accounting has changed in the past from historical-cash-basis to historical-accrual-basis. The future may well see the introduction of some form of current-value accounting. The orientation of financial accounting has shifted in the past from an emphasis of the balance sheet to an emphasis of the income statement, particularly net income and earnings per share. The future may well see further shifts to encompass human resource accounting and social benefit accounting. Measurements of corporate success in achieving social goals may supplement traditional measurements of profitability as a result of the growing concerns over consumer protection, environment conservation and the quality of life in an increasingly urbanized, technological society. These concerns together with the trend toward increasing government intervention in the economic structure may all affect the criteria deemed appropriate for future decision-making and so the nature of the financial accounting information needed by future decision-makers. The foregoing pattern of information-users (shareholders, bondholders, creditors, government) may also change in many ways.

But some conditions seem likely to persist: the growing complexity, specialization, and interdependence of different components in our economic society. With those conditions, whatever the shape of the future, it seems clear that the need for some form of accounting communication will continue.

1.2 The role of auditing in society

1.2.1 The need for attestation

To be effective, accounting communication must be both accurately prepared by the sender and believed and acted upon by the receiver. To believe and act upon the information received, the receiver or user must have some way of satisfying himself as to its quality. Four conditions preclude many users of accounting information from achieving this satisfaction directly and therefore create the need for an objective audit or attestation upon which they can rely.[4]

The most obvious such condition is *remoteness*. Most users of financial accounting information are remote from the data they are receiving. The remoteness may be physical: an investor living in Vancouver is not able to assess directly the quality of accounting information prepared by a company in Montreal. Or it may be legal: under corporations acts shareholders have no right of access to the books of account of the corporation whose shares they hold. Or it may be economic: although the government has a statutory right of access to a company's records to validate tax information and a lending institution may occasionally have a contractual right of access to validate loan information, in many cases such users will choose to avoid the costs of exercising these rights if objective attestation of the information is available.

A second common condition is *conflict of interest*. Preparers of financial accounting information will frequently have interests which are at variance with those of many of its users. Normal human behaviour includes tendencies both towards integrity, candour, care and a sense of fair play, and towards bias, forgetfulness, deceit, carelessness, the desire to secure advantage by concealment of information, and the wishful thought that bad news will go away if ignored. There is little reason to believe that the preparers of financial accounting information will, on the average, be any better or worse than the rest of us in the blending of these human qualities. Management will be subject to the normal temptations (a) to exaggerate the successes and minimize the failures in their stewardship of the shareholders' interests; (b) to exaggerate the earnings per share upon which shareholders and bondholders make decisions as to whether to provide new capital, or bankers as to whether to call existing loans; or alternatively (c) to minimize present earnings in order to "bank" profits for a rainy day; (d) to minimize the taxable income on which the corporation will have to pay tax; and (e) to exaggerate the reported wage costs from which union negotiators will draw their arguments.

Most preparers of financial accounting information probably resist most of these temptations most of the time. But it would be naive to believe that some bias is not likely to creep in sometime. Wherever users of financial accounting information perceive actual or potential conflicts of interest between themselves and the preparers of the information, they will have a natural reluctance to accept the information without some attestation of its quality by an auditor free from actual or potential conflict.

A third factor is *complexity*. Information systems and the processes of preparing data for financial reports are becoming increasingly complex. With increasing complexity the probability of error, whether unintentional or deliberate, increases. At the same time, the ability of the user to satisfy himself as to the quality of the information, even if he had access to all the underlying records, is diminished substantially. In such cases the user requires someone else, on his behalf, to employ an appropriate level of expertise in assessing and attesting to the quality of the information.

A final factor is the *consequence* of error. If the user is to act upon the information he receives (for example, by buying, retaining, or selling equity interests or by advancing, continuing, or withdrawing credit) an imprudent action based upon poor quality information will be of direct financial consequence to him. The greater the potential consequence, the greater his need for satisfaction (through attestation) as to the quality of the information received.

It has been said that "an objective of financial statements is to serve primarily those users who have limited authority, ability, or resources to obtain information and who rely on financial statements as their principal source of information about an enterprise's economic activities."[5] However, because of the conditions of remoteness, conflict of interest, and complexity and because of the consequence of error, most users are not in a position to satisfy themselves directly as to the quality of the information they receive.

The role of auditing is therefore to add credibility to financial statements and thus to enhance the effectiveness of accounting communication needed by our economic system.

1.2.2 Criteria for judging quality

Since the user is in effect delegating to the auditor the task of achieving satisfaction, on his behalf, as to the quality of the financial accounting information, it follows that there must be some implicit agreement between user and auditor as to what constitutes acceptable quality. Attributes of quality accounting information have been variously defined by different bodies. One such definition suggests the attributes of *relevance* (it must be useful); *verifiability* (qualified investigators would reach similar conclusions about it); *freedom from bias* (it must be impartial); and *quantifiability* (it should be measurable in some way).[6] But the critical point is that there should be some *established criteria* against which the quality of the accounting information can be gauged. Without an agreed yardstick against which the accounting information is to be measured, any opinion as to its quality would be purely subjective and the communication of such subjective opinions would be of doubtful utility to users.

At the beginning of this chapter auditing was defined as the process of examining evidence regarding a report, statement or other assertion to determine its correspondence to established criteria. A more complete definition may now be given:

> Auditing is a systematic process of objectively obtaining and evaluating evidence regarding assertions about economic actions and events to ascertain the degree of correspondence between those assertions and established criteria and communicating the results to interested users.[7]

For the vast majority of financial statements of business enterprises which represent general purpose statements (for use by shareholders, prospective investors, the general public, etc.), established criteria are provided by *generally accepted accounting principles*.

The concepts of generally accepted accounting principles and fair presentation in accordance with such principles will be more fully examined in later chapters.

1.2.3 The short-form auditor's report

For most persons the auditor's report, appended to the annual financial statements, is the only visible evidence of the external auditor's activity. The standard short-form report presently in use in Canada reads as follows:

Auditor's Report[8]

To the Shareholders of
Any Company Limited:
    I have examined the balance sheet of Any Company Limited as at December 31, 1977 and the statements of income, retained earnings and changes in financial position for the year then ended. My examination was made in accordance with generally accepted auditing standards, and accordingly included such tests and other procedures as I considered necessary in the circumstances.

In my opinion these financial statements present fairly the financial position of the company as at December 31, 1977, and the results of its operations and the changes in its financial position for the year then ended in accordance with generally accepted accounting principles applied on a basis consistent with that of the preceding year.

City, date

(Signed) . . . .
Chartered Accountant

1.2.4 Value added by the audit function

The audit process, culminating in the issuance of the short-form auditor's report, enhances the value of accounting information in two ways: by providing *control* and by adding *credibility*.

Control is provided in three ways. First, the audit provides an element of *preventive control*. Employees responsible for the many accounting procedures leading to the ultimate preparation of financial statements are likely to perform their tasks in a more careful manner when they are aware that their results will be checked. Thus, the known presence of the audit function improves the quality of the accounting information. Secondly, the audit provides an element of *detective control*. Material accounting or reporting errors that have inadvertently escaped the attention of management, or that have deliberately been made, have a high probability of being detected by the audit and thus corrected prior to issuance of the financial statements. Indeed, many immaterial errors are commonly caught and corrected as well, although it is not specifically the purpose of the audit to find immaterial errors. Finally, the most important aspect (for outsiders) is the element of *reporting control*. Material errors of measurement, presentation or disclosure detected by the audit but not corrected in the financial statements (whether originally arising through unintentional mistake, through unconscious bias, or through deliberate intent) are disclosed by way of qualifications expressed in the auditor's report. When the auditor's report is issued without qualification, the reader knows that the statements have been subjected to the test of an external objective examination and found acceptable.

Credibility is added by the audit function because the user of the audited accounting information knows that the above controls have been applied to it. As a result, he will place more reliance on audited financial information than on unaudited information. The value to him of the accounting information will have been enhanced by the presence of the accompanying auditor's report and the controls which this report represents.

Control and *credibility* represent the attest values added by the audit function. A proper professional audit, however, should contribute other important values as well. It is unlikely that in the performance of the necessary work to support the opinion expressed in the audit report the auditor will not encounter areas where improvements could be made in his client's systems or controls or where additional matters should be considered in his client's financial and tax planning. Service to his client[9] in these areas is a very important by-product of the external auditor's work. Indeed, in many cases, it is the presence of these collateral services which makes the audit an economical package from management's point of view. The professional auditor must always be alert for opportunities to be of service to his client while at the same time discharging conscientiously his attest responsibilities to the users of the audited financial statements.

This book is primarily concerned with the attest objectives of the audit. It would be a serious omission, however, not to emphasize at the outset that *complete service to the client, within the auditor's sphere of competence, must be a fundamental goal in every audit.* Only in this way can the potential value represented by the audit function be fully achieved.

1.3 The development of audit objectives

1.3.1 Present-day objectives

The value added by the audit function has been described in terms of the enhancement of the value of financial accounting information and the provision of related services to management. The specific objectives of annual external audit examinations of general purpose financial statements in Canada today may be defined as:

Primary objective (mandatory)
To express, on the basis of sufficient appropriate audit evidence, an objective opinion, as to whether the financial statements present fairly the financial position, results of operations and changes in financial position of the organization in accordance with generally accepted accounting principles applied on a consistent basis.

Secondary objective (discretionary)
To identify opportunities and provide timely suggestions for improvements in internal control, systems efficiency, financial or tax planning, and accounting methods to the extent that such identification and provision can be combined conveniently with the procedures required under the primary objective or to the extent that such suggestions are requested by the client.

Obviously, it is important that the two objectives not be confused. No amount of concentration on useful recommendations can make up for inadequacies in fulfilling attest objectives. Conversely, unnecessary extension of attest procedures will not compensate for lost opportunities to provide useful service.

Audits by external auditors can also be conducted for a variety of special purposes, such as determining the price a prospective purchaser should pay for a business, or investigating a discovered fraud. These "special purpose" audits require separate treatment which depends upon the circumstances of the particular case. Most external audits, however, fall into the attest category – the expression of an opinion on the financial statements. Their primary purpose is not the detection of minor defalcations and indeed they are not designed to provide reasonable assurance of catching defalcations unless sufficiently material to distort the fairness of the financial statement presentation. This does not mean that in these audits the auditor can be unmindful of the possibilities of fraud. If, in fact, he encounters any conditions suggestive of fraud he has a duty to investigate until his doubts are resolved.

Sometimes where the basic audit is still one directed at an expression of opinion, its scope may be extended, *at the specific request of the auditor's client,* to include supplementary objectives such as investigation of particular operating results, or performance of an internal audit function. In such cases, of course, additional procedures are necessary.

1.3.2 Objectives determined by society

Auditing objectives are not absolute and unchanging truths. Auditing is utilitarian in purpose; its objectives are therefore those which are perceived to have social utility at a particular point in time. Although the need for auditing will continue as long as the need for accounting communication, specific auditing objectives will not necessarily remain unchanged. That auditing objectives have continuously changed to reflect the perceived needs of society can be seen from a brief review of their development.

1.3.3 The origins of auditing

The practice of auditing commenced on the day that one individual assumed stewardship over another's property. In reporting on his stewardship, the accuracy and reliability of that information would have been subjected to some sort of critical review. Evidence has been found that over two thousand years ago Egyptians, Greeks and Romans all utilized systems of check and counter-check on the accounting of officials to whose care public funds had been entrusted. Indeed, the ancient records of auditing are chiefly confined to public accounts. Those required to account for their handling of public funds attended before a responsible official, known as the auditor, who listened to their accounting (the word "audit" meaning "he hears" in Latin). While modern day practices have rendered obsolete such oral presentation and aural examination of accounts, the terms "audit" and "auditor" have lived on. In 1494 an Italian philosopher, Fra Luca Pacioli, wrote a treatise in which he described the double-entry bookkeeping system, referred to the importance of internal controls, and recommended that the books be audited for internal check.

In England, during the Feudal Age, it was the practice of the government to send auditors on circuit to manors and estates to check the accounting for disbursements and revenues. Historians have attributed in part the stable financial position established in England during the reign of Elizabeth I to the work of auditors appointed by the Crown. These were responsible officials who travelled the realm to maintain a check over funds accruing to and disbursed on behalf of the Crown.

Prior to the Industrial Revolution, auditing was generally concerned with the detection of frauds; accounts when audited were usually checked 100% and, despite Pacioli, the importance of internal control was generally not recognized. Auditing was directed primarily to government accounts. There was, however, a growing trend to audit commercial ventures where the activities took place remote from the owner. The earliest documented examples of non-public audits were the audits of accounts of sailing ships returning from the East and the New World. The Industrial Revolution, however, brought the beginning of large-scale commercial and industrial enterprises and the replacement of the one-time joint venture by the continuing corporation. With this development, the need for non-public audits became even more apparent.

During the seventeenth and eighteenth centuries in England the growth of large numbers of common law corporations and the ensuing development of a highly speculative and unregulated market in corporation stocks led to a number of spectacular financial failures, the most notorious of which was the South Sea 'Bubble' of 1720.

The public outcry following such failures frequently led to investigations which in turn called for the talents of independent accountants. Indeed throughout the latter part of the eighteenth century and the early part of the nineteenth century, it be-came increasingly common to call upon outsiders skilled in record keeping to investigate bankruptcies, settle disputes over counts, and to some extent maintain the records of merchants. Thus, during this period there developed slowly a body of skilled specialists who were ready to meet the legislative requirements of 1844.

1.3.4 The United Kingdom 1844-1930

By 1844, the emergence of the corporation was leading to an increasing number of situations where a few individuals controlled the management of large sums of capital contributed by many shareholders. Recognizing the possible conflicts between these separated interests, the British Parliament passed in that year the Joint Stock Companies Act which stipulated that the directors provide annually to the shareholders a balance sheet setting forth the state of affairs of the company. To ensure that the information furnished to the shareholders would give a fair picture, the Act provided for the appointment of auditors who were empowered to examine the corporate records at all reasonable times throughout the year and were required to report on the propriety and adequacy of the accounts and the balance sheet. A major objective of the audit remained the detection of fraud; the tests were detailed and the importance of internal controls again generally not recognized. Nevertheless, it is from this date that we can trace the development of modern day auditing, for the legislators had recognized that the effectiveness of accounting communication was limited by the quality of the accounting procedures followed and that an auditor's evaluation thereof was accordingly desirable.

Under the 1844 Act the auditor was neither required to be independent of management nor to be a qualified accountant. In most cases he was a shareholder appointed by his fellow members. The involvement of independent public accountants in the audits of public corporations developed slowly from that date. In addition to fraud detection a major objective of these early shareholder audits was to ensure that the balance sheet properly portrayed the company solvency (or insolvency) for the benefit of the company's creditors and bankers.

In 1856, the year after limited liability was granted to registered companies, the general provision for compulsory company audits was repealed. Nevertheless, in the following years compulsory audit provisions were built into individual statutes for railways, banks, and certain other specific industries and in 1862 provisions were added for an 'inspection' of any company if demanded by a group of shareholders. The repeal of the general mandatory provisions, however, proved to be ill-advised. In the last 40 years of the nineteenth century 50 000 companies, out of a total of 90 000 registered, came to an end. This high rate of economic failure together with fraudulent promotion prompted a reconsideration of the desirability of audits to improve the prevention and detection of fraud and error. Moreover, the 1890's had seen a series of landmark court decisions (discussed in Chapter 5) attempting to clarify the duties and responsibilities of auditors, primarily with respect to the detection of fraud. As a result, in 1900, a new Companies Act re-introduced compulsory audits. The 1900 Act did not require the auditor to be a qualified accountant but it did recognize the need for independence. It stipulated that the auditor should not be a director or officer of the company.

The new Act also brought in certain other features unique to company auditing at that time:

    (a) The auditor was to obtain access to all company books and records he required in his auditing work. This right did not limit him merely to accounting books and records but in addition gave him access to minutes, contracts, etc.

    (b) The auditor was to append a certificate to the foot of the audited balance sheet stating that all requirements as an auditor had been complied with.

    (c) In addition to providing this certificate, the company auditor was required to report to the shareholders on the balance sheet stating whether, in his opinion, it conveyed a true and correct view of the state of affairs of the company.

While the 1900 Act was a prominent milestone in the history of company auditing, establishing as it did compulsory audits, auditor independence from the directors, and a standard form of audit report, nevertheless the basic objectives of the audit remained as before. A prominent textbook published in 1905 stated that the object of an audit was threefold: the detection of fraud, the detection of technical errors, and the detection of errors of principle. These objectives were to remain relatively unchanged in the United Kingdom for the next 30 years.

With the foregoing legal and economic developments, it is not surprising that the latter half of the nineteenth century saw the development of public accounting as a profession. In 1854, a society of accountants in Edinburgh, which had been organized to prescribe standards of practice, applied for and was granted a royal charter. Members of the Edinburgh society henceforth became known as "Chartered Accountants". This was the first professional organization of public accountants in the world. Similar organizations were chartered in Glasgow, 1855; and in Aberdeen, 1867. In 1880 a number of accounting bodies amalgamated under

charter to form the Institute of Chartered Accountants in England and Wales. The preamble to that Institute's charter gives some indication of the relative importance of the various accounting activities at that time. Responsibilities were listed in the order: liquidators and receivers, trustees in bankruptcy or arrangements with creditors, various positions of trust under court's justice, and auditing of public companies and of partnerships.

The new breed of professional public accountants in the United Kingdom enjoyed a prominent position among English speaking countries. As a result, audit objectives and procedures in North America were initially derived from English texts. In addition, towards the end of the century many English and Scottish chartered accountants emigrated to North America and were influential in the development of the profession both in Canada and the United States. Transplanted to a new environment, however, auditing was exposed to new influences and the next significant development in audit objectives was therefore to occur in the New World.

1.3.5 Canada 1879-1930

The development of public accounting in Canada sprang from its British antecedents. English and Scottish accountants were prominent among the founders of accounting practices in Canada during the early 1800's. Moreover, with its similarity of corporate legislation it was natural that in Canada the profession should grow very rapidly and along the lines of its U.K. model. The major growth of the American profession, and its consequent influence on Canada, was not to occur until a later date.

In 1879 the first North American association of accountants was formed in Toronto and incorporated in 1883 by provincial statute as the Institute of Chartered Accountants of Ontario. In 1880 a Montreal association was formed and, obtaining its charter somewhat more rapidly in the same year, became the first legally incorporated accounting association on the continent (now the Order of Chartered Accountants of Quebec). In 1902 what is now the Canadian Institute of Chartered Accountants (CICA) was incorporated by federal charter. By the early 1900's provincial institutes had been established in most provinces.

Early corporation legislation generally followed U.K. precedents. An Ontario corporations act in 1897 introduced inspection clauses similar to the U.K. At the turn of the century, audits, though not compulsory by statute, were frequently provided for in a corporation's letters patent or by-laws. With a revised Ontario act in 1907, and partly as a result of the urging of the Ontario Institute, the first general mandatory audit provisions appeared in Canada (following the precedent of the U.K. act of 1900). Ten years later, mandatory audit provisions appeared in a federal act. Neither of these acts, however, required an income statement. Throughout the next two decades, the income statement, if presented, was generally not covered in the auditor's report, although such coverage had been a frequent practice in earlier years. Mandatory balance sheet audit provisions were soon incorporated in most provincial corporation legislation.

In the early 1900's provincial securities legislation began to appear, reflecting the principles of "blue sky laws"[10] developed in the United States. In 1928 the Ontario Securities Act formed the basis for a uniform securities act in most provinces, although subsequent years were to see the erosion of this uniformity.

At the beginning of the century, auditing in Canada, as in the U.K., generally consisted of a detailed checking of the clerical accuracy of record keeping together with an examination of related internal documentary evidence. Over the years, however, as corporations grew in size, detailed checking was replaced by tests of transactions. No longer was it considered necessary to make a detailed examination of every entry, footing, and posting during the year in order to achieve the value which resulted from an audit. By 1930, testing was the norm, and some attention was being given to internal control. Only limited external evidence, however, was examined as part of most audits.

1.3.6 The United States 1887-1930

The development of the accounting profession in the United States likewise began from the traditions established in Scotland and England. The great majority of nineteenth century accountants practising in the United States were trained in the United Kingdom and originally came to North America at the request of British investors who wished to have their interests protected. Large British accounting firms opened American offices, new American firms sprang up, and state societies of accountants were formed. In 1887 the predecessor of the national organization, now the American Institute of Certified Public Accountants (AICPA), was created. In 1896 legal recognition was given to the profession with the passage of the first Certified Public Accountant (CPA) law in New York State. By 1923 all states had passed CPA legislation.

The initial objectives of auditing, with their emphasis on fraud, were gradually modified by the greater concern for fairness of financial statement disclosure. Partly, this change occurred because the American audit arose not from statutory requirements but from the demands of banks and other lenders for some independent check on the creditworthiness reflected in a company's balance sheet. As a result American accountants developed a 'balance-sheet audit' approach in contrast to the clerical checking which had been the starting point of U.K. and Canadian audits. The first major work on auditing in the United States published in 1912 characterized this change to objectives as follows: "In what might be called the formative days of auditing students were taught that the chief objectives of an audit were, (1) detection and prevention of fraud, and (2) detection and prevention of errors, but in recent years there has been a decided change in demand and service. Present day purposes are: (1) To ascertain actual financial condition and earnings of an enterprise; (2) Detection of fraud and errors, but this is a minor objective."[11]

At the turn of the century, the balance sheet had been the preeminent statement as in the United Kingdom, and the auditor's report emphasized it accordingly. Solvency, rather than earning power, was the principal characteristic protrayed by financial statements and conservative valuations of assets were favoured. With the imposition of federal income taxes in 1913 however, a major new field for public accountants was created. Not only were accountants to be involved increasingly in the preparation of tax returns and the provision of tax advice, but the taxability of income brought a new importance to the income statement. Gradually, over the ensuing years, emphasis began to shift to the fairness of presentation of income and earnings per share. Thus, by the 1930's the auditor's report of financial statements began to serve primarily the purpose of adding credibility to the statement assertions rather than providing evidence of absence of fraud.

1.3.7 The profession from 1930 to the present

In 1930 considerable differences existed between the professions in Britain, Canada, and the United States. In Britain and Canada the statutory audit had led to rapid growth of the profession but auditing was founded on the concept of transaction checking only recently reduced from a detailed to a test basis. In the United States development had been somewhat less rapid and the pattern of voluntary audits to meet creditor requests had been the testing of internal evidence as to assets and liabilities (the 'balance sheet audit') rather than transaction testing. 'Balance sheet auditing' had also begun to spread to Canada. With the financial crash of 1929 and the publicity given to corporate failures during the ensuing depression, the pattern in the United States changed abruptly. The growing emphasis on fairness of presentation of financial information was specifically reflected in the enactment of the Securities Act of 1933 and the Securities Exchange Act of 1934, which created the Securities and Exchange Commission (SEC). Companies registered with the SEC were required to file audited financial statements, the auditor's report covering both the balance sheet and the income statement. In contrast, mandatory audit reporting on the income statement did not appear in the U.K. until the Companies Act of 1947, nor in Canada until the CICA Bulletin of 1951 (setting the pattern for the Ontario Corporations Act of 1953 and the federal act of 1964).

From 1930 on, developments in the United States replaced the United Kingdom as the dominant outside influence on the Canadian profession. One of these developments was the greater use of external evidence in the auditor's examination. Many Canadian auditors were already examining some external evidence as a desirable but not mandatory procedure. In 1934 the U.S. profession made the examination of external evidence as to cash and securities a mandatory practice. In 1939, the McKesson and Robbins case (involving fictitious warehouses supposed to contain inventory) led to the extension of U.S. audit procedures to include confirmation of accounts receivable and physical observation of inventory stocktaking. The former was soon general practice in Canada as well, although inventory observation was not required by professional pronouncements until 1959. Likewise the use of these extended procedures gradually increased in Britain and was finally adopted as mandatory in professional pronouncements in 1967 and 1968.

In 1941 the SEC urged the inclusion of a reference to *generally accepted auditing standards* in U.S. auditors' reports and it became necessary for the profession to define such standards. In 1948 auditing objectives, basically as they exist today, were embodied in generally accepted auditing standards adopted by members of the AICPA. In Canada, similar standards were first incorporated in the Quebec Institute code of ethics in the 1960's, subsequently in the rules of ethics of all provincial institutes, and in 1975 in the Auditing Recommendations of the CICA.

The major output of professional pronouncements in the United States during the 1930's and 1940's had a significant impact on the Canadian profession. In 1946 the CICA began its own series of Bulletins. By the 1940's it was clear that the primary objective of the normal audit was to determine the fairness of reported financial statements. Testing was the rule, not the exception, and the degree of testing decided upon was largely dependent on the effectiveness of internal control. With the gradual

addition of external evidence to Canadian audits (following U.S. precedents) and with the gradual addition of transaction testing to U.S. audits (to justify reliance on internal control) the two streams of the profession in North America moved together. In Britain the audit objective also shifted from one of fraud detection to assessment of fair presentation, placing reliance on internal control.

The advent of computers in the 1950's and statistical sampling techniques in the 1960's had significant effects on auditing methods but did not alter auditing objectives. Reliance on control (including computer controls) and the use of testing (including statistical sampling and computerized selection) continued to form part of the auditor's methods of meeting the attest objectives. During these decades as well, a succession of court cases in the United States served to extend the auditor's legal responsibilities to greater numbers of "third parties" and a British case, although not dealing with an audit as such, breached the major defence the auditor had clung to up to that time. This trend likewise has not altered auditing objectives but has significantly affected the consequences of failing to meet these objectives.

1.3.8 Summary of historical development of objectives

In summary, the main focus of auditing has shifted from government accounts (although such audits remain an important feature in our system of government) to the investor-owned enterprises. With respect to investor-owned enterprises the primary objectives of auditing have changed from an investigation of bankruptcies (although the bankruptcy and trustee field continues to be an important field in which a number of chartered accountants specialize) to an examination of financial statements. In auditing such statements, the primary objectives have changed from the detection of fraud to an evaluation of the fairness of presentation (though the auditor cannot be unmindful of the possibility of fraud, particularly if material enough to affect fairness of presentation). In considering fairness of presentation, emphasis has gradually shifted from the balance sheet to the income statement (though both statements remain of importance).

These changes in auditing objectives have reflected the changing nature of economic society: the emergence of the corporation, the growth in size of business enterprise, the advent of corporate and securities legislation, and the recognition of chartered accountancy as a profession. Future changes in society may well require further changes in auditing objectives.

At the same time, changes have occurred in the audit approaches to meeting these objectives. Auditing procedures have shifted from 100% checking to testing based on reliance on a study of internal control. In North America, physical observation of assets and communication with third parties have become standard audit techniques. New techniques to audit computer systems and to utilize statistical sampling concepts have been developed. The auditor's responsibilities to third parties have been extended. Even without changes in auditing objectives, such changes in auditing methods can be expected to continue in the future.

1.4 The audit process (and outline of this book)

1.4.1 The audit environment

The foregoing historical review has indicated the close relationships between the changing needs of *society*, the changing structure of *the law*, the growth of *the accounting profession*, and the development of *auditing objectives*. These factors together with the *needs of the particular user* and the *policies of the individual practitioner or firm* constitute the audit environment within which any given audit is conducted (see Figure 1.b).

1.4.2 Relationship of the audit to the audit environment

The audit environment in turn determines the nature of the audit examination to be conducted and of the audit report to be issued. The relationship of the audit to the audit environment is shown in Figure 1.c. A brief review of this diagram will provide the reader with a preview of the subjects to be discussed in the later chapters of this book.

Needs of society

The basic needs of economic society for credible accounting communication and therefore for objective attestation have already been discussed. These needs in turn have influenced the law and the general objectives of the accounting profession. (Possible future developments are discussed in Chapter 21.)

Legal requirements

The statutes in Canada affecting most directly the work of the external auditor are the Federal and various provincial Business Corporation Acts. These acts require companies incorporated under their jurisdiction to have an annual audit (with certain exemptions for smaller companies), establish the auditor's responsibilites (at least in broad outline), specify certain reporting requirements, and govern most of the activities of business corporations in Canada. Under these acts the auditor is generally appointed to hold office for a particular year and to report on the financial statements for that year. In practice, it is common for the same auditor or firm of auditors to be appointed year after year. This permits a continuous relationship to be built up between auditor and client and enables the auditor to structure his work around the concept of a repeating annual audit. The *statutory audit* (arising out of the incorporating act) is common to most Commonwealth countries. In contrast, in the United States compulsory external audits (except where provided for specifically by the articles of incorporation or by-laws of the company) are not required under corporations acts but arise out of the provisions of the Securities Act of 1933 and the Securities Exchange Act of 1934 governing companies offering securities to the general public. Securities Acts in many provinces of Canada also influence audit and reporting requirements. These statutes, together with the general provisions of business law, the criminal code, and related court cases, as they affect the legal liability of auditors, are discussed in Chapters 4 and 5.

Other statutes govern and protect the practice of public accounting and establish the present professional organizations. These statutes are covered as part of the review of the structure of the profession in Chapter 2.

General professional objectives

The accounting profession in Canada consists of all chartered accountants, their student employees and a number of non-CA licensed practitioners. It is organized into ten provincial Institutes of Chartered Accountants (in the case of Quebec, an Order) as well as a national body, the Canadian Institute of Chartered Accountants (CICA). Each member of a provincial Institute is automatically a member of the CICA. Members of the Institute of Chartered Accountants of Bermuda are also members of the CICA.

Responsive to the needs of society, certain general objectives characteristic of any profession have been recognized by chartered accountants over the years. These include the objectives of: providing competent and honest service to the public; subordinating personal interest to that of the public good; maintaining,

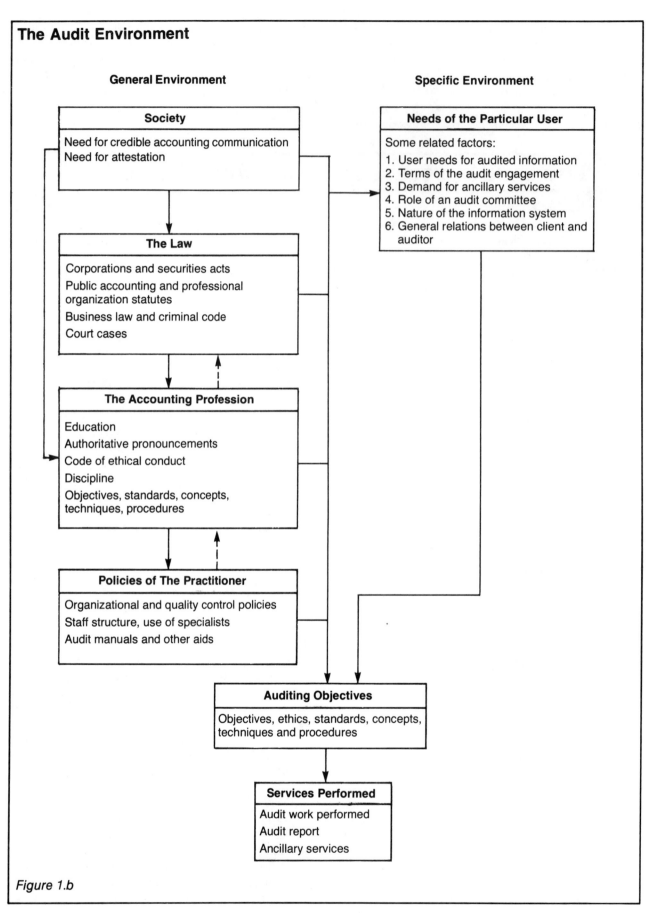

The Audit Environment

General Environment

Specific Environment

Society

Need for credible accounting communication
Need for attestation

Needs of the Particular User

Some related factors:

1. User needs for audited information
2. Terms of the audit engagement
3. Demand for ancillary services
4. Role of an audit committee
5. Nature of the information system
6. General relations between client and auditor

The Law

Corporations and securities acts

Public accounting and professional organization statutes

Business law and criminal code

Court cases

The Accounting Profession

Education

Authoritative pronouncements

Code of ethical conduct

Discipline

Objectives, standards, concepts, techniques, procedures

Policies of The Practitioner

Organizational and quality control policies

Staff structure, use of specialists

Audit manuals and other aids

Auditing Objectives

Objectives, ethics, standards, concepts, techniques and procedures

Services Performed

Audit work performed

Audit report

Ancillary services

Figure 1.b

through education, research, authoritative pronouncements, and discipline, adequate standards throughout the profession to protect the public interest; behaving in an ethical manner towards clients, fellow members of the profession, and students; and enhancing the good name of the profession. These general profession objectives are discussed in Chapter 2.

The general professional objectives in turn have led to the establishment of a code of ethical conduct and have provided the framework in which auditing objectives for the individual engagement are defined.

Rules of professional conduct

All the provincial Institutes have adopted Rules of Professional Conduct which their members must follow. These ethical rules cover standards of conduct affecting the public interest, relations with fellow members, and the organization and conduct of a professional practice. These rules are discussed in Chapter 3.

Auditing objectives

The auditing objectives for a given audit of a set of general purpose financial statements have already been defined in 1.3.1. These objectives, the expression of an informed opinion and the provision of related services, reflect the needs of society as perceived by the profession and as embodied, in part, in the law.

Generally accepted auditing standards

The promulgation of *generally accepted auditing standards* (GAAS) by the AICPA in the United States in 1948 and the by CICA in Canada in 1975 has already been referred to in the historical summary. These standards constitute a definition by the profession of certain fundamental goals that must be achieved in every audit of a set of financial statements in order to meet the foregoing auditing objectives. The *general standard* calls for competence, objectivity and due care; the *field work standards* call for proper planning, execution, and supervision, an organized study of internal control, and sufficient appropriate audit evidence to support the opinion expressed; the *reporting standards* call for an evaluation of the accounting communication in terms of its consistent correspondence to generally accepted accounting principles (GAAP) and a clear explanation of any reservations of opinion. Generally accepted auditing standards are discussed in Chapter 4. The standards overlap in certain respects with the profession's Rules of Professional Conduct and this relationship is likewise discussed in Chapter 4.

Generally accepted auditing standards, in turn, influence the form of audit report required and imply a set of auditing concepts as to how a particular audit program should be structured.

Needs of the particular user

The needs of the particular user of the audited financial information obviously have an influence on the audit work performed and the form of audit report issued. This influence was indicated in Figure 1.b. Of course, certain minimum requirements cannot be altered by the user. For example, in a statutory audit certain reporting requirements and auditing responsibilities are established by law and cannot be waived. The user may, however, request an extension of these services (for example, to include a *long-form report* analyzing and commenting on individual financial statement figures, or to include preparation of tax returns). Specific items discussed in later chapters include the role of engagement letters and audit committees.

Form of audit report required

For most general purpose financial statements, the form of audit report is influenced by generally accepted auditing standards and by legal requirements (the wording of the normal short-form report was given earlier in this chapter). However, in some special purpose audits (for example, an audit of the statements of a business being purchased where the purchaser and vendor have agreed on certain bases of valuation for purposes of these statements) statutory requirements and generally accepted accounting principles may not apply; here the form of audit report will be modified to fit the purpose for which it is intended.

Auditing concepts

Generally accepted auditing standards explicitly introduce certain auditing concepts and implicitly introduce additional ones. Auditing concepts may be classified and named in many different ways. Under the system of classification used in this book, the explicit auditing concepts are: *competence, objectivity, due care, evidence, fairness,* and *generally accepted accounting principles,* while the implicit auditing concepts are: *verification, relevance, reliability, sufficiency, materiality, degree of assurance, inherent risk, control risk, audit risk, reasonable skepticism, judgement, economy,* and *timeliness.* The inter-relationship of these various auditing concepts, one with another and with generally accepted auditing standards, available audit techniques and an efficient structure of the audit, constitutes a *theory of auditing,* which is presented in Chapter 6.

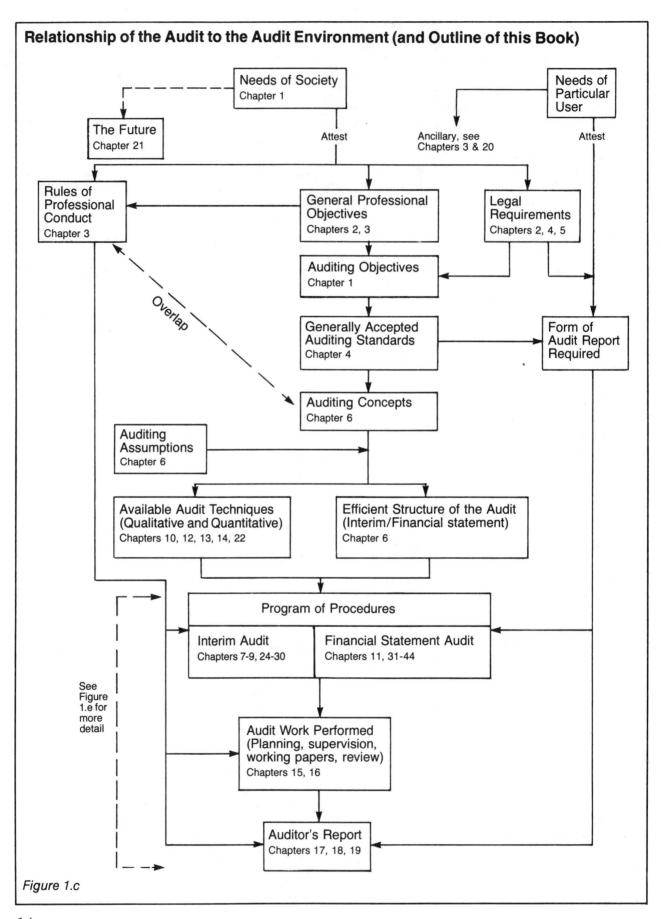

Relationship of the Audit to the Audit Environment (and Outline of this Book)

Needs of Society
Chapter 1

Needs of Particular User

The Future
Chapter 21

Attest

Ancillary, see
Chapters 3 & 20

Attest

Rules of Professional Conduct
Chapter 3

General Professional Objectives
Chapters 2, 3

Legal Requirements
Chapters 2, 4, 5

Overlap

Auditing Objectives
Chapter 1

Generally Accepted Auditing Standards
Chapter 4

Form of Audit Report Required

Auditing Concepts
Chapter 6

Auditing Assumptions
Chapter 6

Available Audit Techniques
(Qualitative and Quantitative)
Chapters 10, 12, 13, 14, 22

Efficient Structure of the Audit
(Interim/Financial statement)
Chapter 6

Program of Procedures

Interim Audit
Chapters 7-9, 24-30

Financial Statement Audit
Chapters 11, 31-44

See Figure 1.e for more detail

Audit Work Performed
(Planning, supervision, working papers, review)
Chapters 15, 16

Auditor's Report
Chapters 17, 18, 19

Figure 1.c

14

Auditing assumptions

Included in any theory of auditing are a certain number of auditing assumptions. Examples are the assumption that external evidence is generally more reliable than internal evidence and the assumption that good internal control inhibits the occurrence of errors. These assumptions are also discussed in Chapter 6.

Available audit techniques

The concept of audit evidence leads to a consideration of the different types of audit evidence available (physical, documentary, third party representation, etc.) and the available audit techniques for gathering such evidence (observation, confirmation, analysis, etc.). Audit evidence and qualitative audit techniques are discussed in Chapter 10 and the subject of computer-assisted audit techniques in Chapter 14. Quantitative audit techniques are discussed in Chapter 12 (audit testing in general) and in Chapters 13 and 22 (the use of statistical sampling).

Efficient structure of the audit

Generally accepted auditing standards themselves imply a division of the audit program into (a) a review and evaluation of internal control together with testing of transactions and (b) a gathering of other evidence to support the audit opinion. In this book the first division is referred to as the *interim audit* and the second as the *financial statement audit.* The basis of this division in terms of auditing theory is discussed in Chapter 6. Different practitioners may divide the total audit program slightly differently or may use other names for the divisions, but it is unlikely that there is any disagreement on the general concepts underlying this division. The primary objectives of the interim audit, the financial statement audit, and the annual audit as a whole are summarized in Figure 1.d. This figure introduces the terms *review* (ascertaining the nature of systems and control), *compliance verification* (checking the degree of compliance with the prescribed system of internal control) and *substantive verification* (substantiating financial statement

---

Primary (Attest) Audit Objectives

Of the whole audit

To express, on the basis of sufficient appropriate audit evidence, an objective opinion as to whether the financial statements present fairly the financial position, results of operations, and changes in financial position of the organization in accordance with generally accepted accounting principles applied on a consistent basis.

Of the interim audit

1. To determine
   (a) through a review and evaluation of the accounting system and other relevant internal controls, and
   (b) through either compliance verification of the existence, effectiveness and continuity of operation of those controls on which reliance is to be placed or substantive verification of internal evidence

   the accuracy and reliability of the accounting records and the appropriateness of accounting methods followed, and thus to provide a basis for planning the timing, nature and extent of the substantive procedures necessary to support an opinion on the financial statements; and

2. To perform those substantive procedures which can most usefully be commenced at an interim date.

Of the financial statement audit

To determine
   (a) on the basis of the interim audit results, and
   (b) through substantive verification of the existence (or occurrence), completeness, ownership (or incidence or propriety), valuation (or measurement), and presentation of assets, liabilities, income components and other financial statement figures,

the appropriate opinion to be expressed in the audit report.

Figure 1.d

figures), which terms will be more fully explained in later chapters.

Programs of interim audit and financial statement audit procedures.

When available audit techniques are organized within this two-stage structure of the audit, the result is a detailed program of interim audit procedures and financial statement audit procedures. Each auditing *procedure* (for example, examining fixed asset purchase invoices) can be thought of as a particular audit *technique* (vouching) applied to a particular type of *evidence* (documentary) to accomplish a particular *objective* (establishing the existence and valuation of fixed assets). With all the possible combinations of types of techniques, evidence, objectives, and financial statement components, the list of common auditing procedures is quite extensive. Accordingly, auditing procedures are described separately in Volume 2 (Chapters 23 to 44), although every attempt is made to indicate their relationship to the conceptual foundations discussed in this volume.

The organization of the interim audit is described in Chapter 9 and the related subject of internal control in Chapters 7 and 8. The program of interim audit procedures, however, is covered in Chapters 24 to 30 of Volume 2. Likewise, the organization of the financial statement audit is described in Chapter 11 while the program of financial statement audit procedures is covered in Chapters 31 to 44.

The structure of the audit program will also be affected by the form of audit report required; a long-form report, commenting separately on numerous specific items within the financial statements, may call for more procedures on certain details than a short-form report.

Audit work performed

The actual audit work performed in any given engagement consists of an appropriate choice of the qualitative and quantitative audit techniques available in both the interim audit and financial statement audit stages. What constitutes an appropriate choice must be decided by the exercise of *professional judgement*.

No suggested auditing procedure appearing in any textbook can be held out to be invariably necessary on all audits nor necessarily sufficient on any given audit. The practitioner has a responsibility to apply those procedures which in his judgement are necessary to meet generally accepted auditing standards and to comply with ethical rules.

The best occasion for the application of this judgement is during the planning process. Planning and supervision of the audit work are discussed in Chapter 15 and documentation of the work (working papers) and review in Chapter 16.

Audit report

The audit report issued will depend upon the results of the audit work performed and the form of audit report required, this form being in turn influenced by reporting standards. In issuing the audit report, relevant ethical rules must also be observed. Audit reporting is discussed in Chapters 17, 18 and 19.

Ancillary services

It has been said earlier that an important part of an auditor's work each year is service beyond the basic attest objective. Many practitioners derive less than 50% of their revenue from attest services. Even those concentrating primarily on auditing, usually find that up to 25% of their chargeable hours are devoted to the rendering of ancillary services. These services may include suggestions for improvements in systems or controls, assistance in preparation of tax returns, tax planning, financial planning, or various types of management consulting. The extent to which such ancillary services are performed will depend upon the needs of the particular user and the competence of the auditor. The manner of offering such ancillary services is also governed by the ethical rules, as is discussed in Chapter 3. Recommendations to management concerning internal control systems and general accounting matters are covered as an integral part of the audit process because most practitioners consider these functions an essential part of normal client service. Because of the technical nature of the income tax area, preparation of tax returns is referred to only in very general terms. Ancillary services involving association with unaudited financial information are discussed in Chapter 20.

1.5 An overview of the annual audit

While the various components of the annual audit are discussed in detail in subsequent chapters, it is useful for the reader at the outset to have a general appreciation of the complete process. This chapter therefore concludes with a brief overview of the typical annual audit.

If, in addition to the two principal divisions, interim audit and financial statement audit, allowance is made for planning, review and reporting, seven distinct stages in the audit process can be identified. These are: planning, interim audit, review and planning, financial statement audit, review, reporting, and post-audit. The relationship of these seven stages to working papers prepared, ancillary services offered and audit staff levels employed is shown in Figure 1.e. Of course, the work of the various staff levels must not be compartmentalized. Rather, as discussed in Chapter 15, all must work together as one coordinated audit team.

Planning

Auditing has been defined as a 'systematic process', which implies that the audit examination is both a purposeful and ordered activity wherein specific procedures will be followed to achieve defined objectives. Proper planning is essential to such a process. Audit planning is required on three levels. First, the practitioner (or firm) must plan for a rational allocation of human resources to meet the requirements of all clients. Second, certain fundamental planning decisions must be made for each individual audit (the approach to the interim audit, materiality, type of testing to be employed, etc.). Third, detailed programming for both the interim and the financial statement audits must be completed (the timing and extent of accounts receivable confirmation, etc.).

The interim audit

The link between financial statement assertions and economic activities on which these assertions report is the enterprise's information system. As economic events become more complex and business operations increase in size, more and more reliance must be placed on the continuing system and less and less on a one-time assembling of data for year-end financial statements. An auditor reporting on one hundred economic events (transactions) is in a position to consider the meaning of each as he reviews the

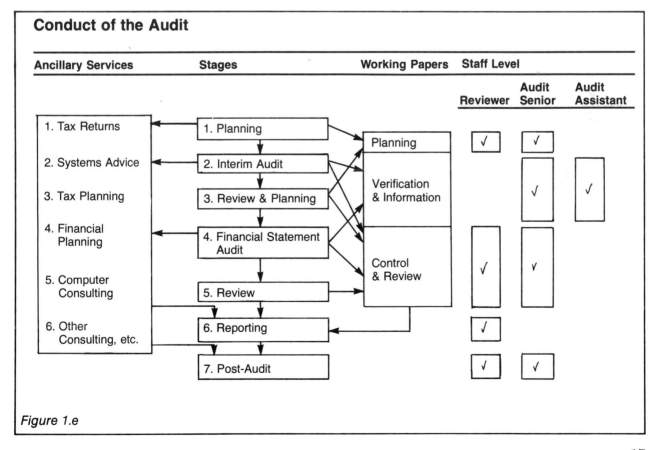

Figure 1.e

compilation of information for the financial statements. The auditor reporting on 100 000 individual economic events cannot.

Similarly, as enterprises increase in size, the auditor must place increased reliance on the information system to produce correct results and proportionately less on the detailed examination of objective evidence supporting individual financial statement assertions. Such reliance on a financial information system can only be placed if it is warranted. Thus, during the interim audit, the auditor must investigate the information system so that he can arrive at an informed judgement as to the accuracy and reliability of the accounting records and procedures. He then will be in a position to determine the further procedures necessary to attest to financial statement assertions. The objectives of the interim audit were summarized in Figure 1.d.

The components of the interim audit for medium and larger enterprises consist of:
• review of systems and preliminary compliance verification,
• evaluation of systems,
• further compliance verification,
• preliminary substantive (dual-purpose) verification,
• evaluation of compliance,
• internal control/management letter.

Review of interim audit and further planning

The interim audit, except to the extent that it may provide useful suggestions for the client, is only a means to an end, the auditor's opinion of the financial statements. It is therefore necessary to review and evaluate the results of the interim audit, first, to ensure that procedures have been executed in accordance with the initial plan and, second, to use the results to modify, refine, or complete the audit planning for the financial statement audit.

The financial statement audit

The financial statement audit is directed specifically to obtaining and evaluating evidence to support individual financial statement assertions for the purpose of formulating and arriving at an opinion on the financial statements in total. The objectives were summarized in Figure 1.d. The nature and extent of evidence gathered bears a direct relationship to the strengths or weaknesses of the system of internal control, the materiality of individual financial statement assertions, the inherent risk of error, availability of evidence and cost of obtaining the evidence.

The components of the financial statement audit consist of:

• pre-year-end substantive verification,
• completion and evaluation of interim audit,
• year-end substantive verification,
• evaluation of substantive verification results,
• additional services (where requested),
• formation of opinon.

Final review

Audit working papers provide an important support for the auditor's opinion as well as documenting the verification procedures performed. This documentation is important so that the adequacy of assistants' work may be reviewed and approved.

Depending on the size of the audit, the nature of the audit team and the policies of the audit practitioner or firm, there may be one, two or three levels of working paper review. Throughout this book the audit team is described in terms of three levels: audit assistant, audit senior, and reviewer (see Figure 1.e.). Of course, for a sole practitioner without staff all three functions are combined in one person, while for a large audit by a large firm the number of distinct levels may be four or five or more. Typically, the audit senior, in charge of the audit field work, will review sections completed by the audit assistants and then present a complete file to the reviewer or reviewers. Normally the review process will result in a number of questions which will necessitate further explanations in the working papers and/or additional audit verification.

Reporting

Upon the conclusion of the audit examination and review process, the audit report (generally drafted at an earlier stage) will be completed. The wording of the short-form audit report was given earlier. However, if the auditor is not completely satisfied with the presentation of the financial statements or with the adequacy of the evidence he has been able to obtain, he must amend the standard short-form wording appropriately. The most common amendments are known as *reservations* of opinion, and may, as required, take the form of a *qualification,* an *adverse opinion,* or a *denial of opinion.* Other amendments may be required with respect to inconsistencies, additional explanations, international reporting considerations, or special purpose reports.

When the financial statements are issued, the final signed audit report will accompany them. In many cases the financial statements themselves will be typed in the auditor's office as a service to management. Nonetheless, the financial statements are the representations of management and management is responsible for their accuracy and fairness of presentation. The auditor's responsibility is the audit report and the appropriateness of the professional opinion expressed therein.

Another important form of audit reporting is the reporting to management of pertinent audit findings (errors discovered, weaknesses observed in the system of internal control, etc.) and useful recommendations with respect to strengthening controls, improving efficiency, improving tax and financial planning, etc. These findings and recommendations are usually incorporated into some form of management letter. Sometimes one such letter is issued at the completion of the interim audit and a further follow-up letter at the completion of the financial statement audit.

Post-audit events

The duties of an auditor commonly extend beyond the date appearing on the audit report. He may be called upon to attend audit committee or board of directors' meetings where the audited financial statements are being approved. Under most corporations acts he has a statutory right to attend the annual general meeting of shareholders, when the audited financial statements are presented. In rare cases, information received subsequent to the issue of the financial statements may provide evidence of material errors in valuation or presentation which require the recalling of such statements and the issuing of amended statements. Other duties after the audit report date may include preparation or assistance in preparation of the corporate tax returns and follow-up of points raised in the management letter.

Finally, in an ongoing engagement the auditor must make plans for the next year's audit. Often the best time for such planning is shortly after the completion of the past year's audit, when relevant information is readily at hand.

1.6 Reference material

The role of accounting information

R.M. Skinner, FCA, *Accounting Principles – A Canadian Viewpoint,* (CICA, 1972).
A Statement of Basic Accounting Theory, American Accounting Association, 1966.
Report of the Study Group on the Objectives of Financial Statements, *Objectives of Financial Statements,* (AICPA, 1973).

History of auditing

John L. Carey, *The Rise of the Accounting Profession,* (AICPA, 1969).
B. Gene Brown, *Changing Audit Objectives and Techniques,* The Accounting Review, October 1962.

1.7 Questions and problems

Review and discussion

1. Compare the roles of external auditing, internal auditing and government auditing in our society.
2. What are the objectives of accounting?
3. Accounting has been described as the process of identifying, measuring and communicating economic information to permit informed judgements and decisions by the users of the information. Give three examples of information needs of users.
4. To utilize accounting information effectively users of financial information must believe the information to be correct. Why do users of financial information require an audit?
5. What are the attributes of quality accounting information? How do these attributes relate to the auditor and his duties?

6. What are the objectives of an external audit? Who is best equipped to carry out these objectives? Why?
7. Audit emphasis has gradually shifted from the balance sheet to the income statement. Discuss the nature of and the reasons for the shift. What are your thoughts as to the proper emphasis in today's economy?
8. Why should an auditor limit his procedures to the "testing of transactions" rather than 100% checking?
9. Seventy-five years ago the detection of fraud was a principal audit objective. What has caused the reduced emphasis of this objective?
10. Give examples of the types of work which might be done during the interim audit and during the financial statement audit.
11. Describe the interrelationship of the interim and

financial statement audits.

12. Give three specific examples of situations where there is a conflict of interest between preparers of financial statements and users.

13. What is your interpretation of the meaning of each of the key phrases in the scope paragraph (first paragraph) of the short-form auditor's report?

14. Describe the useful additional services that an auditor can provide for his client as a result of the information obtained in performing the work necessary to render an unqualified audit opinion.

15. What is the difference between general professional objectives and generally accepted auditing standards?

16. Why is ethical conduct so important to the chartered accountant?

2 The Profession

The *accountancy profession* in Canada consists of the members of various professional accounting organizations. The largest of these is the Canadian Institute of Chartered Accountants (CICA), with over 20 000 chartered accountants (CA's) and many thousand students. Other important professional organizations are the Certified General Accountants' Association of Canada, with several thousand certified general accountants (CGA's), the Society of Industrial Accountants of Canada, with several thousand registered industrial accountants (RIA's)[1] and the Canadian members of the Institute of Internal Auditors. Co-operation among these different organizations has been an important development of recent years. Because the principal subject of this book is the audit performed by professional auditors in public practice, and because most professional auditors are chartered accountants, this chapter will deal with the accountancy profession largely from the viewpoint of the chartered accountant.

Accountancy profession

The purpose of the accountancy profession in Canada is "to achieve and maintain the highest level of professional competence and to carry out with integrity and a high standard of ethics its responsibility to society in the measurement and communication of information pertaining to the efficient allocation and effective use of resources [CICA Handbook]."[2] Members of the Canadian Institute include both those in public practice and those who, while originally trained within the public practice sector, are now employed in industry, government and education. Indeed, slightly more than half of all Institute members are in the latter categories, a much higher proportion than found in some countries. Their important positions in the community, their maintenance of professional standards, and their active participation in Institute committees have always been one of the strengths of the Canadian profession. Most of the discussion in this chapter and in Chapter 3 relates to the accountancy profession as a whole but certain parts relate solely to chartered accountants in the practice of *public accounting*.

Public accounting

A public accountant is defined as:

a person who alone or in partnership with others for reward engages in public practice involving

(i) the performance of services which include causing to be prepared, signed, delivered or issued any financial, accounting or related statement, or

(ii) the issuing of any written opinion, report or certificate concerning such statement

if by reason of the signature, stationery or wording employed or otherwise it is indicated that such individual or partnership acts in relation to said statement, opinion, report or certificate as an independent accountant or auditor, or as an individual having or purporting to have expert knowledge in accounting or auditing matters. Despite the generality of the foregoing, 'Public Accountant' shall not include a person who acts merely as a bookkeeper, cost accountant, or on the installation of bookkeeping, business or cost systems, nor does it include a person who performs accounting or auditing functions in respect of any public authority or any commission, committee or emanation thereof, including a Crown corporation. [CICA Handbook][3]

This definition established by the CICA is included with slight amendment in the public accountancy acts of several of the provinces. In addition to the more than 10 000 chartered accountants in public practice, public accountants in Canada include several hundred CGA's and a number of other non-CA licensed practitioners.

General professional objectives of the accountancy profession

The basic needs of economic society for reliable and credible accounting communication have already been discussed in Chapter 1. Responsive to these needs, certain general professional objectives have been recognized by chartered accountants over the years. These objectives include:

1. providing competent and honest service to the clients and general public;
2. subordinating personal interest to that of the public good;
3. maintaining, through education, research, authoritative pronouncements and discipline, adequate standards throughout the profession to protect the public interest;
4. behaving in an ethical manner towards clients, fellow members of the profession, and students; and
5. enhancing the good name of the profession.

These general objectives have to a certain extent been incorporated in the objects of the CICA and of the provincial Institutes and Order. More specifically they have been built into the Rules of Professional Conduct adopted by each provincial organization.

2.1 Accountancy – a profession

Various criteria have been suggested from time to time as the identifying hallmarks of a profession. One recent statement of such criteria is contained in the foreword to the Uniform Rules of Professional Conduct. In this statement, eight elements are identified as being accepted by the majority of learned authorities and court decisions for purposes of characterizing a profession. These eight distinguishing elements, arranged below in groups purely for ease of subsequent discussion, are as follows:[4]

Mastery of an intellectual skill
1. There is a mastery by the practitioners of a particular intellectual skill, acquired by lengthy training and education;

Public practice and personal service
2. The foundation of the calling rests on public practice – the application of the acquired skill to the affairs of others for a fee;
3. The calling centres on the provision of personal services rather than entrepreneurial dealing in goods;

Objective outlook
4. There is an outlook in the practice of the calling, which is essentially objective;

Subordination of personal interest
5. There is acceptance by the practitioners of a responsibility to subordinate personal interests to those of the public good;

Organization, standards, ethics and co-operation
6. There exists a developed and independent society or institute, comprising the members of the calling, which sets and maintains standards of qualification, attests to the competence of the individual practitioner and safeguards and develops the skills and standards of the calling;
7. There is a specialized code of ethical conduct, laid down and enforced by that society or institute, designed principally for the protection of the public;
8. There is a belief, on the part of those engaged in the calling, in the virtue of interchange of views, and in a duty to contribute to the development of their calling, adding to its knowledge and sharing advances in knowledge and technique with their fellow members.

While each of these characteristics may not be prominent in each profession, any group calling itself a profession should have a majority of them. The following discussion indicates that all of the characteristics indeed apply to accountancy.

2.1.1 Mastery of an intellectual skill

Admission requirements to the CA program vary from province to province but the more common requirements include, (a) a university degree, (b) a recommendation by a practising member that the applicant has good moral character and habits, and (c) the gaining of employment in a practising member's office which meets qualifications set out by the provincial Institute or Order.

The administration of the educational program for C.A. students likewise varies from province to province. Methods range from the granting of credits for specific university courses (advanced standing) to the organization of special correspondence courses and Institute-sponsored classes. Course contents, however, are generally similar, although there are some differences in emphasis. The ultimate objectives in each province are identical: namely, to train a skilled professional with specific knowledge requirements set down in the *uniform final examination syllabus*. All students in Canada must pass a common uniform final examination set by the Inter-provincial Education Committee and based on the syllabus. The Inter-provincial Education Committee, chaired by a representative of the CICA, consists of representatives from each provincial Institute of chartered accountants (in Quebec an Order). The uniform final examination ensures a consistent standard of professional quality across Canada. The examination syllabus, periodically updated by the Inter-provincial Education Committee, calls for basic knowledge of law, economics, the management process, the functional fields of business and the organization of the accounting profession; broad understanding of statistics and regression analysis; and in-depth knowledge of professional ethics and authoritative pronouncements. The other areas of knowledge requirement, with various required levels of understanding, are detailed under six major sub-headings:

1. Financial accounting and reporting
2. Auditing and professional practice
3. Managerial accounting and control
4. Finance
5. Taxation (federal)
6. Electronic data processing

Every student-in-accounts in Canada is well advised to obtain and study the details of this syllabus carefully. Careful analysis of the syllabus will often reveal specific knowledge requirements which lie outside the formal education program in any particular province. It is the responsibility of the student to acquire this knowledge, either through practical experience or through outside reading, prior to writing the final examination.

In addition to the education requirements, each province requires a specific length of *practical experience* either prior to writing the final examination or prior to being granted the CA certificate. In most provinces, the general requirement for persons entering the CA program with little or no advanced standing (for example, arts, sciences and engineering graduates) is three years' practical experience. Students who have significant advanced standing (generally business school graduates with specific course credits) are subject to lower experience requirements. Experience requirements must generally be gained in a practising member's office. Such offices must meet prescribed standards in order for their students' service therein to qualify as required experience.

The satisfactory completion of the education program, experience requirement, and uniform final examination results in the granting of admission to one of the ten provincial Institutes (or Order) of Chartered Accountants in Canada and the right to use the designation "Chartered Accountant" (CA). During this training process the primary intellectual skills which are acquired by students-in-accounts are in the areas of accounting, auditing and taxation. The attainment of the CA certificate does not, however, signify the end of the education of the chartered accountant. Continuing education requirements for chartered accountants, particularly those practising public accounting, are discussed in Chapter 3.

2.1.2 Public practice and personal service

The foundation of the calling of accountancy rests in public practice. All chartered accountants are trained in the public practice sector. The fact that many subsequently accept important positions in industry, government and the academic world does not change this foundation; nor does it mean that those chartered accountants do not continue as full members of the profession.

Public practice means that the practitioner's services are available to all. The clientele of the public accountant may range from the giant corporation to the corner store. Of course, many citizens never directly employ the services of a public accountant as they do those of a personal physician or lawyer. Nevertheless, every person in Canada who has savings invested in the shares of a company listed on a Canadian stock exchange (including those whose savings have been invested through a financial intermediary such as a pension fund or insurance company) is, in effect, utilizing the services of the public accountant who audits the investee's financial statements.

The acquired skills of the public accountant applied in auditing, accounting, tax and consulting engagements represent personal services. The pur-

pose of distinguishing the provision of personal services from entrepreneurial dealing in goods is not to contrast their values (both are of great importance in our economy) but rather to contrast their effects on the consumer. The consumer of goods can assess their quality before he buys. The public, however, is not generally in a position to judge the adequacy of an audit performed by a chartered accountant. The rule of *caveat emptor* (let the buyer beware) is accordingly not practicable in the case of professional services. Clients must generally trust the auditor's competence and integrity rather than their own ability to judge the quality of the services rendered. This in turn places a responsibility on the public accountant and his students, when performing auditing or other services, to carry out their work in a professional manner that justifies this trust.

2.1.3 Objective outlook

A public accountant's work must be carried out in an objective and impartial manner. Whether he is providing accounting services (preparing financial statements) or auditing services (expressing an opinion on financial statements) his work must not be biased in favour of one party to the possible detriment of another. The concept of objectivity as it applies to auditing in particular will be discussed at length in later chapters.

2.1.4 Subordination of personal interest

The professional accountant has a responsibility to subordinate personal interests to those of the public good. This responsibility exists on three levels: moral (a question of conscience), ethical (self-regulated by the profession) and legal (determined by the courts). The concept of subordination of personal interest can be found throughout the rules of professional conduct adopted in each province. Frequently these rules place strictures, in the interests of the public good, on activities which might otherwise appear to be to the short-run advantage of the practising accountant. Of course, in the long run, the interests of all members of the profession are also best served by these strictures. Ethical rules were not created from any holier-than-thou attitude. Without public confidence in his integrity, the earning power of the practitioner would be non-existent. Putting the public first, is a pre-requisite for the successful pursuit of any professional practice.

2.1.5 Organization, standards, ethics and co-operation

Chartered accountants in Canada are organized into ten provincial Institutes (in Quebec, an Order) together with the Canadian Institute of Chartered Accountants. Much of this chapter is devoted to a discussion of these organizations. These Institutes in turn set standards of qualification and enforce a specialized code of ethical conduct designed primarily for the protection of the public and secondarily for the maintenance of orderly and courteous conduct within the profession. These rules of professional conduct are discussed in Chapter 3. In addition, the eleven Institutes, through their numerous committees, serve as a forum for the interchange of ideas, the advancement of accounting and auditing research, the development of new techniques, and many other activities. The public interest demands the efficient dissemination of knowledge throughout any profession. New ideas and techniques developed by individual practitioners or by practising firms are shared with the entire profession through publication in *CA Magazine*, inclusion in published research studies, or incorporation in professional development courses.

In summary, then, by the foregoing criteria, accountancy is indeed a profession which, alongside the more historic professions of law and medicine, enjoys a well earned position in our society.

2.2 Legislation regulating public accounting

As regulation of the professions is primarily a matter of provincial jurisdiction in Canada, each province has evolved its own distinct approach to the regulation of the practice of public accounting. There are, however, many similarities among the methods used in various provinces as there are, to a lesser extent, between these methods and those in use in the United States and the United Kingdom. Two distinct types of provincial legislation bear upon the regulation of public accounting in Canada. First, 'enabling legislation' in all provinces has established professional organizations (the various provincial Institutes and Order of Chartered Accountants) whose members are, at least in part, public accountants. Secondly, more recent 'regulatory legislation' in some provinces specifically controls the persons who practise public accounting or use the name, public accountant. The two types of legislation are interconnected in the sense that the latter may often regulate public accounting in part by reference to membership on standards of the professional organizations created by the former. In some provinces the enabling legislation itself contains certain regulatory elements. In Quebec the two types of legislation are completely combined.

2.2.1 Enabling legislation

Each of the ten provinces in Canada has enacted enabling legislation creating a professional organization; the provincial Institute of Chartered Accountants (in Quebec, the Order of Chartered Accountants). The enabling legislation, which generally follows the pattern established in the United Kingdom, not only incorporates the professional organization but also reserves to it the use of certain professional designations, such as "chartered accountant", invests in the organization a substantial amount of self determination, and grants it varying degrees of control and influence over its members.

The enabling legislation passed in Ontario is typical of that of many of the provinces. The provisions of the Ontario Act include:

1. the objects of the Institute,
2. the minimum size of the governing body,
3. the officers for the Institute,
4. the annual general meeting of the members,
5. authority of the Institute to establish by-laws controlling admittance to the Institute, setting fees to be charged to its members, establishing educational training requirements for its students, and providing for the exercise of disciplinary authority over its members and its students, and authority of the Institute to set rules of professional conduct,
6. categories of membership: Associate (CA) and Fellow (FCA),[5]
7. designation of the terms, chartered accountant, CA and FCA and provision of penalties for the use of these initials or terms by other than members of the Institute.

In some provinces there are further provisions establishing a degree of involvement of the provincial government either by representation on the governing body (as, for example, in British Columbia) or by involvement in the approval of admissions and admission requirements (as, for example, in Alberta). The new legislative pattern in Quebec is outlined in 2.2.3.

All provincial Institutes provide a copy of their incorporating legislation in their member's handbook.

The enabling legislation does not, except in Quebec, restrict the practice of public accounting or the use of the term "public accountant". In several provinces such restrictions are contained in separate regulatory legislation.

2.2.2 Regulatory legislation

Legislation regulating the practice of public accounting has been enacted in a growing number of provinces including Ontario, Quebec, British Columbia, Nova Scotia, and Prince Edward Island. The purpose of regulatory legislation, protection of the public, is achieved by provisions which prohibit an incompetent person from holding himself out as qualified to offer the services rendered by a public accountant. Critics of any profession-regulating legislation sometimes complain that it establishes a monopoly. Public accounting legislation does indeed create a type of monopoly, at least in the 'core activity' of attestation (rendering an opinion on financial statements). However, provided that all competent students are able, as they are, to enrol, write the necessary examinations, and enter the profession, the only exclusiveness of this 'monopoly' is its exclusion of those unable to meet the standards which proper service to the public requires. Of course, the existence of regulatory legislation places a responsibility on the profession to maintain adequate enrolment, proper standards and education, and careful discipline of its members.

In the provinces where regulatory legislation does not exist, it is possible for any non-CA to offer services as a public accountant (though he may not call himself a chartered accountant). Where enabling legislation has incorporated more than one accounting group, the public is faced with the problem of attempting to distinguish between an assortment of designations and qualifications. The maintenance of proper standards for all public accounting services offered to the public is best ensured by a single qualifying professional body. Accordingly, it has been the policy of the chartered accounting profession to seek provincial regulatory legislation "to restrict the practice of public accounting to members of the provincial Institute with appropriate protection, where necessary, to the existing rights of members of other accounting bodies to practice" [CICA Handbook].[6] It is likely that the enactment of regulatory legislation will gradually be extended across Canada.

Regulatory legislation generally provides for either (a) regulation by a board responsible to the provincial government or, less commonly, (b) regulation by an independent self-governing body, the provincial Institute itself.

Regulation by a board responsible to the provincial government

The regulatory legislation in Ontario is typical of that of a number of the provinces. In order for a person to practise as a public accountant in the Province of Ontario, he must hold a licence issued by the Public Accountants Council of Ontario, which council is responsible for administering The Public Accountancy Act. To qualify for this licence a practitioner must either be a member of the Institute of Chartered Accountants of Ontario or else belong to a small 'grandfather' group of non-CA public accountants who were in practice in 1950, the date when the regulatory legislation was passed. The regulatory act does not define the qualifications of chartered accountants, this being left to the Ontario Institute.

In some provinces public accounting licences are granted to others in addition to chartered accountants and a grandfather group. For example, in Nova Scotia, the Public Accountants Board issues licences to qualified members of The Institute of Chartered Accountants of Nova Scotia, qualified members of the Registered Public Accountants Association of Nova Scotia, successful candidates in the Intermediate CA examination, and commerce graduates from a recognized university. In accordance with the regulations established by this Board, any licensed accountant may study the CA course of instruction and/or sit for the CA qualifying examinations after a specified term of experience without entering specific articles for clerkship or employment with a firm of chartered accountants.

In some provinces the licensing board includes official representatives of various organizations. For example, the Auditors Certification Board of British Columbia (established to supplement the provisions of that province's companies act) includes representatives from the B.C. Institute of Chartered Accountants, the CGA's, the RIA's, the Registrar of Companies, and the Superintendent of Brokers.

The licensing of public accountants by a board responsible to the provincial government is analagous to the practice of most states in the United States, where licensing is controlled by state boards. There are, however, important differences. In most states, not only the licensing but complete control over the professional qualifications, in terms of both education and experience requirements, rests with the state boards. The professional degree is granted by the state board of accountancy, which certifies the successful candidate as a "certified public accountant" (CPA). With educational requirements being established by fifty states there is somewhat greater variation in specific requirements than in Canada. However, as in Canada, all candidates must pass a uniform final examination (in the United States set by the American Institute of Certified Public Accountants). While in Canada a chartered accountant derives his CA from his admission into a provincial Institute, in the United States a certified public accountant obtains his CPA from the state and membership in the AICPA or in a state CPA society is voluntary. In practice, however, 80% of the more than 100,000 practising CPA's join such organizations.

Regulation by the provincial Institute

In Prince Edward Island, public accounting licenses are granted directly by the provincial Institute. A similar situation existed prior to 1974 in Quebec.

2.2.3 Professional codes (Quebec 1974)

One of the characteristics of contemporary society is the growth of consumerism: the desire for increased protection of the consumer and increased control of those who supply him goods and services. This desire has been evidenced in many recent pieces of legislation. The professions have not been exempt from this trend. One of the latest examples of this trend was the enactment of the Professional Code in Quebec in 1974. This Code places the overall regulation of over thirty different professions in the hands of a Professional Board, which includes five government representatives. Under this Board, the regulation of each individual profession, including the Order of Chartered Accountants of Quebec, is administered by a separate Bureau, which includes representatives from other professions and from the public as well as from the profession in question. A lawyer must serve as chairman of each profession's Discipline Committee. This pattern of involving outside parties to represent the public interest on the governing body of the provincial professional organization is one that may well spread in future years.

2.3 Provincial organizations of chartered accountants

The enabling legislation enacted by the provinces confirmed the founding of the earliest professional accounting organizations in North America. In 1879, twenty-five years after the first Edinburgh charter, an Ontario association was founded (now The Institute of Chartered Accountants of Ontario) and incorporated in 1883 by provincial statute. In 1880, a Quebec association was founded (now the Order of Chartered Accountants of Quebec). In the same year it obtained its incorporating legislation—the first on the continent. Enabling legislation did not appear in the United States for another sixteen years, nor at the federal level in Canada until the turn of the century. By that time many other provinces had incorporated their own organizations.

Today, each province has an active organization of chartered accountants with reasonably similar objectives, structures and activities. Those of the Ontario Institute are outlined briefly below as typical. Details for all provincial Institutes may be found in their respective Member's Handbooks.

2.3.1 Objectives

The objectives of the Ontario Institute[7] are defined by statute to be:

(a) to promote and increase the knowledge, skill and proficiency of its members and students-in-accounts;
(b) to regulate the discipline and professional conduct of its members and students-in-accounts;
(c) to promote and protect the welfare and interest of the Institute and the accounting profession.

2.3.2 Structure and activities

The activities of each provincial Institute or Order are run by a governing board, bureau or council. In Ontario the Council is elected annually by the membership of the Institute. In some provinces (as in Quebec and Alberta) the governing body in addition contains representatives from government or other bodies. The council generally has the powers to elect or appoint its officers; appoint a registrar to maintain a register of students and CA's in the province; appoint various committees to carry out the ongoing activities of the Institute; authorize the formation of District Associations of Chartered Accountants and District and Provincial Associations of students; and pass by-laws subject to the ratification of the membership at the annual meeting.

The main activities of each provincial Institute centre around the enrolment, education and examination of students; the professional development of members; the promulgation and enforcement of rules of professional conduct; the submission of briefs on proposed provincial legislation in such fields as securities, corporations, and taxation; the organization of annual conferences; and the provision of various services to members and to the public.

Enrolment, education and examination of students

Typically, an Applications Committee considers applications for enrolment. An Education Committee may administer the education program for students and the setting of any examination prior to the uniform final examination. Delegates will be sent to represent the province on the Inter-provincial Education Committee.

Professional development of members

With respect to the continuing professional development of members, courses are administered by the provincial Education Committee, though generally developed by the CICA.

Promulgation and enforcement of rules of professional conduct

The maintenance of high ethical standards is perhaps the most important activity in terms of protection of the general public. The activities of Professional Conduct, Discipline and Appeal Committees are discussed later in the chapter.

Legislation committees

A variety of Legislation, Securities, and Taxation Committees generally submit briefs to the provincial government on proposed provincial legislation or legislative amendments in these areas. Historically, these briefs have played a significant role in forestalling many problems in the increasingly complex structure of modern legislation.

Services to members and to the public

A number of provincial Institutes have established a *practice advisory service* in recent years. In Ontario, for example, such a service was instituted in 1972, staffed on a full-time basis by an experienced professional practitioner, to encourage and assist the public accounting practitioner in maintaining the quality and improving the professional performance of his practice. This service is provided without charge to members of the Institute who request advice in areas of practice management, statement presentation and auditing procedures.

Another common service to members is a *consultation service*. In Ontario, for example, the consultation service is provided for use by sole practitioners and practitioners in small firms with respect to technical accounting and auditing problems where they would welcome the opportunity to check their judgment with an experienced member of the profession. The service is provided on a private, confidential and volunteer basis. The service is free as long as the problem requires only a minimum amount of time by the volunteer consultants. Although many members practice in medium and large firms to obtain the benefits of specialization, research and consultation made possible by larger numbers, the existence of the Institute's consultation service ensures that all practising members of the profession have access to any specialized information they may need to provide competent service to their clients.

One of the services offered to the public is often a *fees mediation service*. In Ontario, for example, when a practitioner and his client are in dispute over fees for services rendered they may, by mutual agreement, submit their problem to the fees mediation panel of the Ontario Institute. The parties to the dispute must both make an undertaking to be bound by the decision of the panel and the volunteer panel assumes no legal liability to either party. This service is provided to members of the Institute and their clients free.

Other activities

Numerous other committees, advisory groups, and task forces are established by various provincial Institutes responsive to the perceived needs of their members or to recent legislative or economic developments. Examples include a municipal audit advisory group reviewing the current standards in this specialized field, an insurance committee responding to a request by a provincial superintendent of insurance, a special committee on accounting engagements, and many others.

Inter-provincial co-ordination

To ensure that the efforts of the profession are not dissipated through duplication or overlapping either between different provinces or between provincial and CICA committees, a Co-ordination Committee was established in 1971. This committee includes representatives from each of the ten provincial Institutes or Order and from the CICA. This committee oversees the appropriate maintenance of three responsibility areas – the agreed functions of the CICA, the agreed functions of the provincial Institutes and the functions which are the joint responsibility of provincial and national associations.

2.4 The Canadian Institute of Chartered Accountants

The Canadian Institute of Chartered Accountants was incorporated by federal charter in 1902 under the name "Dominion Association of Chartered Accountants". This corporation was constituted with the object of providing a body for inter-provincial co-operation and national direction for the profession. The ensuing seven years saw considerable discord between the national organization and the existing provincial Institutes because no clear division of programs had been delineated. In 1909, however, differences between these professional organizations were resolved and it was agreed that members of each provincial Institute would automatically become members of the national organization. This interlocking membership feature has continued to the present day. In consequence, there now exists in Canada a unified and coherent national body for chartered accountants. It was also agreed that the basic role of the Dominion Association would be to improve standards of practice, give efficient service to ' the public and provide assistance to the provincial organizations. In 1949 the name of the Dominion Association was changed to the "Canadian Institute of Chartered Accountants". In 1973 a formal affiliation agreement was entered into between the CICA and the Institute of Chartered Accountants of Bermuda. A more detailed history of the Canadian Institute of Chartered Accountants is contained in the CICA Handbook.

2.4.1 Objectives

The objectives of the CICA may be summarized as follows:

1. to maintain the highest national and international stature as a professional organization,
2. in co-operation with the provincial Institutes, to develop and maintain a body of knowledge and to prepare the uniform final examinations,
3. to develop new knowledge through research and to issue authoritative statements on accounting principles and auditing standards for the guidance of business, government, the public and members,
4. to promote improvements and minimize unwarranted variations in financial reporting practices,
5. to encourage chartered accountants to expand their services to the public,
6. to communicate effectively with the federal government and the public on matters of national concern to the profession,
7. to co-operate with other Canadian organizations of accountants,
8. to promote international harmonization of principles, standards and practices of the profession,
9. to publish a professional journal and other high quality publications.[8]

2.4.2 Structure and activities

The affairs of the Institute are directed by a 23 member Board of Governors, appointed annually on a rotating basis by the provincial Institutes and Order and by the Bermuda Institute, except for the President and the Vice President, who are appointed annually by the other Board Members. Each member of a participating Institute is automatically a member of the Canadian Institute of Chartered Accountants. Each member may make his voice heard in the affairs of the Institute by attending the annual meeting or volunteering to serve on one of the many committees. However, because of the appointment to the Board, control over the Canadian Institute ultimately rests with the provincial organizations.

The Board of Governors meets at least four times a year. Board activities include the appointment of committees, election of an Executive Committee, appointment of the Executive Director, and consideration of policy matters. Direct responsibility for supervision of Institute activities is delegated by the Board to the executive committee and the executive director. Policy decisions made by the Board are implemented by either the executive committee or a relevant sub-committee. The executive director and staff of the CICA have the responsibility of advising the Board and the Committees as to objectives; co-ordinating the work of all committees and Institute programs; and providing clerical and research assistance to committees.

In accordance with the foregoing objectives, the principal activities of the CICA are the conducting of research; the preparation of professional development courses; the publishing of *CA Magazine* (the Institute's journal) and other publications; the submission of briefs on proposed federal legislation; the study of expanded services in the management consulting, taxation, and other fields; the organization of annual conferences, and the maintenance of good public relations.

These activities have in turn dictated the structure of the CICA staff. In 1973 the research department was expanded with the appointment of a General Director of Research supported by a Director of Accounting Research, a Director of Auditing Standards, and a Director of Research Studies, each with a staff of qualified research assistants. In 1974 a *technical advisory bureau* was established within this department to answer technical accounting and auditing queries submitted in writing or by toll-free telephone by chartered accountants or the public across Canada.

The publications department produces, among its many publications, the monthly *CA Magazine*. The editor is assisted by an independent editorial board. Subscription to the magazine, required reading for all students and chartered accountants wishing to keep abreast of professional developments in Canada, is included in the membership fee paid to the provincial Institute. The department also publishes the pronouncements, recommendations and studies of various CICA committees together with such major books as *Accountants and the Law of Negligence, Going Public in Canada*, and *Accounting Principles – A Canadian Viewpoint*. Other important departments are the professional development department and the public relations department.

2.4.3 Committees

As in the provincial Institutes, CICA Committees are staffed on a volunteer basis by chartered accountants in public practice, government, education, and industry, interested in contributing their abilities to further the advancement of their profession. Committees are established by the Board of Governors, which approves their terms of reference and establishes the composition of their members.

Some of the important committees of the CICA are:

1. Administrative and policy committees such as the Executive, Policy Planning, Finance, and Presidential Nominating Committees.
2. Accounting Research and Auditing Standards Committees,
3. Federal Legislation Committee,
4. Professional Development Committee,
5. Management Consultants and Taxation Committees,
6. Public Relations and Annual Conference Committees.

Details of all CICA committees, and their many subcommittees, can be found in the CICA Handbook. The role of the Professional Development Committee is discussed in Chapter 3. Because the work of the Accounting Research and Auditing Standards Committees has a major impact on auditing, the subject of this book, the role of these two committees is discussed briefly below.

Accounting Research and Auditing Standards Committees

Until 1969 the predecessor, Accounting and Auditing Research Committee, issued Bulletins for the guidance of members with respect to both accounting and auditing matters. In that year, the existing Bulletins were consolidated into the CICA Handbook. In 1973, coincident with the expansion of the CICA's research program and staff, the committee was split into the two present committees, and the relevant section of the Handbook divided between *Accounting Recommendations* and *Auditing Recommendations*.

The Board of Governors has granted to these two committees respectively the authority to issue Accounting recommendations and Auditing Recommendations on their own responsibility. Both committees follow a carefully defined set of procedures to ensure that all viewpoints are identified and considered before pronouncements are issued. Projects are initially assigned to a working section of the relevant committee to develop, first, a 'statement of principles' and, second, proposed Handbook wording. After each of these two stages the material must be approved, or modified, by a two-thirds vote of the full committee. The proposed Handbook wording is then normally circulated to all chartered accountants and certain other interested parties as an *exposure draft*. After modifications arising from consideration of comments received, and if approved by a two-thirds vote of the full committee, a final Recommendation is issued for insertion in the CICA Handbook.

The Accounting Research Committee is composed of 22 members including chartered accountants in practice, industry and education as well as appointees of the Financial Executives Institute of Canada, the Certified General Accountants' Associations of Canada, the Society of Industrial Accountants of Canada, and the Financial Analysts Federation (Canadian Affairs Committee). The participation of the latter four organizations reflects the interest of many sectors of Canadian society in the development of appropriate accounting principles and methods of financial statement disclosure. One of the purposes of formulating and promulgating recommendations with respect to accounting principles is to clarify accounting communication by narrowing co-existing alternative methods of accounting for identical situations. The Accounting Recommendations of the committee include recommendations relating to both general accounting matters (e.g., general standards of financial statement presentation, disclosure of accounting policies, business combinations) and specific financial statement items (e.g., inventories, deferred taxes, earnings per share). Over the years, these recommendations have come to be accepted in the profession, business, and government as representing *generally accepted accounting principles*. The role of generally accepted accounting principles in financial reporting, in corporation and securities legislation, and in the auditor's report is discussed in Chapter 17.

The Auditing Standards Committee is composed of 16 members consisting of chartered accountants in public practice and in government. Its practising members cover the spectrum of small, regional and national practices. Auditing Recommendations of the committee include recommendations relating to *generally accepted auditing standards*, to audit reporting, to broad aspects of audit procedures, and to unaudited financial statements.

Committee membership for both committees is for a three year term and involves a substantial commitment of time (approximately 25 meeting-days per year). The agendas of both full committees are organized by their respective steering committees. Beginning in 1974 these steering committees were authorized to issue *Accounting Guidelines* and *Auditing Guidelines* to interpret Recommendations, to express their views on other particular issues of concern when the formal Recommendation process does not apply, or to provide provisional guidance until formal Recommendations can be issued. Guidelines are filed in the CICA Handbook but do not have the authority of Recommendations. In addition, the committees sponsor the preparation of various Research Studies (on accounting, auditing, or both) and Audit Technique Studies in order to provide a detailed review of selected accounting and auditing problems by individual authors or study groups. The responsibility of approving final publication of such studies rests with a Joint Research Steering Committee (a coordinating group for the two full committees) although views expressed in the studies are solely those of their authors.

In 1974 an Accounting Research Advisory Board, consisting of senior representatives of industry and finance, was established. This Advisory Board meets twice a year and provides a broader forum for the business committee to offer advice to the CICA research committees and staff.

2.5 The profession in the United States

The public accounting profession in the United States has always had a great influence on the Canadian profession due to geographical proximity, the number of American subsidiary companies operating in Canada and the affiliation between Canadian and American public accounting firms. When auditing a Canadian subsidiary of an American corporation the Canadian external auditor may often be requested to issue a special audit report to the parent company auditors using the format and standards common in the United States. This has required a thorough knowledge of American accounting practices and auditing standards.

Authoritative pronouncements in new areas of concern to the accounting profession around the world have often been first promulgated in the United States. American pronouncements are in turn given careful consideration by committees of both provincial and Canadian Institutes in Canada, as well as by organizations of public accountants in other countries.

2.5.1 The American Institute of Certified Public Accountants

As described earlier, public accounting in the United States is regulated by Boards of Accountancy that are responsible to state legislatures. While licensing requirements for public accountants vary from state to state, the use of the term certified public accountant (CPA) is restricted to those persons who, among other requirements, have passed a national uniform final examination. Membership in a state CPA society or in the national organization, the American Institute of Certified Public Accountants, is voluntary but most CPA's join such organizations.

The AICPA traces its origins, through predecessor groups, back to 1887. Membership in the AICPA is granted to all accredited CPA's who apply. The purposes of the AICPA are to develop and maintain standards for the examination of candidates who apply for CPA licensing, to promote and maintain high professional and moral standards within the accountancy profession, and to advance accounting research and improve accounting education. As with its Canadian counterpart the principal activities of the AICPA are conducted through its many technical committees. Its monthly magazine, the *Journal of Accountancy*, provides an opportunity for members of the profession to express their views. As with the CICA, one of the primary activities of the AICPA has been the issuing of authoritative pronouncements on accounting and auditing matters.

Accounting pronouncements

During the period from 1938 to 1959 two different technical committees of the AICPA issued Accounting Research and Terminology Bulletins dealing with the controversial accounting issues of the day. In 1959, accounting research was turned over to a new technical committee, the Accounting Principles Board. Members of the Accounting Principles Board were appointed by the council of the AICPA, and as in its CICA counterpart, the members were volunteers. The significant work of the Accounting Principles Board was the publication of Opinions. APB Opinions came to be regarded as authoritative pronouncements on generally accepted accounting principles. In addition, research staff of the Board published research studies which explored new and topical accounting problems.

In 1973, in order to broaden the input base for the research program and to increase its resources, the volunteer Accounting Principles Board was replaced by an independent body of 7 full-time members: the Financial Accounting Standards Board (FASB). Members of the FASB are appointed by the Board of Trustees of a foundation, chosen in turn by the AICPA, the Financial Executives Institute, the National Association of Accountants, the Financial Analysts Federation, and the American Accounting Association. After comprehensive procedures of publishing discussion memoranda, holding public hearings, and circulating exposure drafts, the Board issues final Financial Accounting Standards. Earlier APB Opinions continue in force until modified by such Standards. The AICPA code of ethics identifies FASB pronouncements as being, in effect, authoritative for its members.

With the establishment of the FASB, the committee structure of the AICPA was revised and an Accounting Standards Executive Committee established. One of its principal functions is to present submissions on behalf of the AICPA to assist the FASB in its deliberations.

Auditing pronouncements

During the period from 1939 to 1972 the Committee on Auditing Procedures of the AICPA issued 54 Statements on Auditing Procedures. In 1972 this body was reconstituted as the Auditing Standards Executive Committee. This committee issues Statements on Auditing Standards which are recognized as interpretations of the *generally accepted auditing standards* passed by the AICPA membership in 1948. The AICPA code of ethics requires adherence to generally accepted auditing standards and requires that members be prepared to justify departures from the committee's Statements. Statement on Auditing Standards No. 1 issued in 1973 consolidated all prior statements and, together with the many statements issued since that date, represents today one of the most comprehensive interpretations of auditing standards in the world.

2.5.2 The American Accounting Association

The American Accounting Association is the leading academically oriented accounting organization in the world. Founded in 1916, it has a membership of over 10 000. One-third of the membership, and the most active portion, consists of persons in academic positions. The Canadian region of the American Accounting Association, organized in 1967, has several hundred members.

The objectives of the American Accounting Association are centred primarily in the area of accounting research. The association's journal, *The Accounting Review*, is published quarterly and has been a major vehicle in the development of accounting theory in the United States. In 1976 it began an auditing section. Other publications have included historically important books such as Patton and Littleton's *An Introduction to Corporate Accounting Standards* (1940), and Mautz and Sharaf's *The Philosophy of Auditing* (1961).

2.6 International accounting organizations

With the advent of the multi-national corporation and the growth of international finance it is no longer appropriate or desirable to have national borders separating varying accounting and auditing practices. The movement towards international harmonization within the accounting profession has, until recent years, been slow − but, despite the natural skepticism that greets such endeavours, this movement is surely inexorable.

The International Congress of Accountants

The first forum for the interchange of views among accountants internationally was the International Congress of Accountants, held every five years for the last half century. The big step, however, was taken during the 1972 Congress in Sydney, Australia, when heads of delegations from sixty countries unanimously approved the establishment of a committee with the long-term objective of developing a permanent world-wide professional organization and uniform international standards. This committee is named the International Co-operation Committee for the Accountancy Profession (ICCAP).

The International Co-operation Committee for the Accountancy Profession (ICCAP)

ICCAP has eleven members, each representing the total accounting profession in his country. Canada's delegate represents both the CICA and other Canadian accounting organizations. ICCAP was directed to co-ordinate work leading to recommendations for technical, ethical and educational guidelines for the international profession as well as reciprocal recognition of qualifications. Five subcommittees were established to tackle these projects and a small full-time staff to coordinate activities until the World Congress of 1977.

International Federation of Accountants (IFAC)

As this book goes to press, a proposal for a permanent international organization, to be named the International Federation of Accountants (IFAC), has been prepared for presentation to the 1977 Congress. The proposed organization, with over 100 members and a permanent secretariat, would replace the transitional eleven-member ICCAP. Its activities would include the study of matters such as a minimum code of professional ethics for member bodies, requirements and programs for professional education and training for accountants, accounting and auditing standards and procedures, cost and management information, and management of an accounting practice.

International Accounting Standards Committee (IASC)

The Sydney Congress also recommended the creation of a semi-autonomous body under ICCAP to promulgate international accounting standards. Such a body was formed in 1973: the International Accounting Standards Committee (IASC), with a secretariat located in London, England. The founding members consist of accounting bodies in nine countries, including the CICA for Canada. Each founding member is represented by two delegates. More than thirty additional associate members have since joined. In forming the IASC, the nine founding members agreed:

a) ...to publish in the public interest, basic standards to be observed in the presentation of audited accounts and financial statements and to promote their worldwide acceptance and observance;

b) to support the standards ... ;
c) to use their best endeavours:
   (i) to ensure that published accounts comply with these standards or that there is disclosure of the extent to which they do not ... ;
   (ii) to ensure that the auditors satisfy themselves that the accounts comply with these standards. If the accounts do not comply with these standards the audit report should either refer to the disclosure of non-compliance in the accounts, or should state the extent to which they do not comply;
   (iii) to ensure that ... appropriate action is taken in respect of auditors whose audit reports do not meet the requirements of (ii) above.[9]

It is clear that the commitments undertaken by the signatories to the agreement are both significant and far-reaching.

Pronouncements of the committee are referred to as International Accounting Standards (IAS) and, after exposure in all member countries, require a three-quarters vote of the delegates from the founding members before final issuance. The first IAS standards were issued in 1975. The CICA has undertaken to study all such standards carefully with the expectation that CICA Recommendations will usually be brought into conformity if different. In the rare case where an inconsistency remains it will be noted in the CICA Handbook. CICA Recommendations, while calling for the use of Handbook methods, suggest that it is desirable for international companies to disclose any deviations from IAS pronouncements the disclosure called for in term (c) (i) of the IASC agreement. The Canadian delegates to the IASC maintain a close liaison with the CICA Accounting Research Committee. The International Federation of Stock Exchanges, of which the various Canadian exchanges are members, has passed a resolution supporting standards to be issued by the IASC. It is likely that in the years to come the pronouncements of the IASC will have a profound impact on financial reporting practices around the world. It is proposed that the IASC would continue to function as a semi-autonomous body under IFAC.

Accountants International Study Group (AISG)

Somewhat pre-dating the IASC, a three-nation study group was formed in 1966: the Accountants International Study Group (AISG), consisting of representatives from the United Kingdom, the United States and Canada. This study group has issued many valuable comparative studies as to accounting and auditing thought in the participating countries. The studies are not intended to represent authoritative pronouncements. Whether this group will continue to serve a useful role in the future will no doubt depend on the progress of the IASC.

Regional organization

In addition, over the years, a number of regional organizations have been developed. For example, the CICA regularly sends representatives to the Interamerican Accounting Conference, which includes over twenty member countries in North and South America. Vancouver was chosen as the site for the 1977 conference.

2.7 Regulatory agencies

Paralleling the growth of the accounting profession, and responsive to the need for ensuring the availability of appropriate financial information for investors and prospective investors, has been the growth of regulatory agencies.

2.7.1 Provincial securities commissions

Provincial securities legislation was first introduced in Canada in 1928. Today each province has a Securities Act or a Securities Frauds Preventions Act under which an administrator regulates the securities industry as well as corporations offering securities to the public. Recent years have seen a move toward more uniform legislation. The legislative provisions in Ontario, Quebec, and the four western provinces are now reasonably similar, while a uniform act is under study among the Atlantic provinces. Unlike the United States, no federal securities legislation exists in Canada, although its possibility has been actively discussed in recent years. In 1971, however, the securities administrators of eight provinces formed a national association and promulgated a series of national policies. One of these national policies recognizes the Accounting Recommendations of the CICA as constituting generally accepted accounting principles.

In most provinces (including Ontario, Quebec, and the western four), the securities administrator is a provincial Securities Commission. These commissions have assumed an important role in Canada since the end of the second world war. The Ontario Securities Commission, for example, while founded in 1928, had only the duty of registering securities salesmen until a new Ontario Act in 1945 reorganized it into its present form; further revisions were made in 1966. In a few provinces (for example, New Brunswick and Nova Scotia) the securities administrator is instead a Registrar.

The main functions of the provincial securities commissions are (a) to register those who sell to and advise investors, (b) to ensure 'full, true, and plain disclosure' of all pertinent facts by those whose securities are held by or offered to the public, and (c) to investigate and prosecute offenders. It is the second function, of course, that is of particular interest to the accounting profession. Disclosure requirements include rules with respect to prospectuses accompanying new security issues and rules regarding proxy solicitation, insider trading and reporting, and financial disclosure in both annual audited statements and semi-annual unaudited interim statements.

2.7.2 The Securities and Exchange Commission

The establishment of the Securities and Exchange Commission (SEC) in the United States in 1934 reflected the public concern for fair disclosure following numerous financial failures brought on by the market crash and the ensuing world-wide depression. The SEC was organized as a quasi-judicial agency with responsibility for the registration of companies whose securities were traded on American stock exchanges, for the enforcement of legislation designed to ensure that investors were provided with all relevant material financial information, and for the civil prosecution of parties guilty of misrepresentations, deceit, and other fraudulent acts and practices in the sale of securities in general (whether or not required to be registered). Subsequent legislation and regulation has greatly expanded the scope of activities of the SEC. Currently practically all companies who offer securities to the public in the United States (including all those listed on American stock exchanges) must file with the SEC a number of detailed information returns incorporating financial and other data. Much of this information must be attested to by an external auditor. SEC regulations also require such companies to have an annual independent audit.

In meeting its responsibilities the SEC has been greatly concerned with both accounting principles and auditing standards. With the issuance of Regulation S-X in 1940, the major accounting regulation of the SEC, the Commission prescribed the form and substance of financial statements required to be filed with it. Further publications of the SEC of particular importance to the auditor are the accounting series releases, which include reports on investigations and opinions of the chief accountant of the SEC.

The scope of authority of the SEC is broad, including the power to devise and promulgate generally accepted accounting principles as well as the power to set specific standards concerning the conduct of the audit and the form of the auditor's report. In practice the SEC has usually, but not always, left such principles and standards to be established by the accounting profession (the AICPA and later the FASB). On occasion, SEC pronouncements have led to major changes, such as the extension of auditing procedures to include inventory observation and receivables confirmation following the McKesson & Robbins case. Indeed, many of the current authoritative pronouncements on both accounting and auditing matters can, at least in part, be traced to earlier decisions of the SEC. In this respect the SEC has assumed a much more activist role in the United States than have the provincial securities commissions in Canada. Accountants differ in their views as to the desirability of such a role, but there is no question that it marks a major difference between the accounting environments of the two countries.

The reach of the SEC extends beyond the boundaries of the United States. The Commission applies various rules with respect to the independence of accountants not only to the auditors of a U.S. parent company, but also to the foreign auditors of a consolidated foreign subsidiary. As a result, many chartered accountants in Canada have had to acquire a reasonable familiarity with SEC regulations in order to serve their Canadian clients.

2.7.3 The stock exchanges

In addition to securities commissions, stock exchanges as well impose certain disclosure requirements on listed companies. A corporation listing its shares on a Canadian stock exchange must sign a listing agreement which requires management to disclose prescribed information, including the filing of annual audited financial statements, the filing of quarterly unaudited interim financial statements, and the prompt reporting of any material change in the business or affairs of the corporation. Corporations accept these more stringent reporting obligations in return for the benefits of greater marketability for their securities which listed status confers.

While securities trading began in Canada in the first quarter of the nineteenth century it was not until the 1870's that the first two stock exchanges (Toronto and Montreal) were incorporated. The remaining three Canadian exchanges (Vancouver, Winnipeg and Calgary) were incorporated considerably later. In contrast, in the United States, the New York Stock Exchange dates back to 1817.

Generally the provincial securities acts permit the stock exchanges to exercise considerable self-regulation. However, with the revision of the Ontario Securities Act in 1966, influenced to a degree by the model of the SEC, a number of the surveillance functions previously exercised at the stock exchange level were passed up to the provincial securities commission.

2.8 A concept of ethical conduct

The term *ethics* refers to a philosophy of human conduct with emphasis on the moral question of right and wrong. *Professional ethics* is concerned firstly with principles of proper conduct for a professional person in his personal behaviour and in his relations with the public, his clients and his fellow professionals. Secondly, beyond principles, it is concerned with specific rules for guidance in practical situations. The purpose of professional ethics is to protect the public and to provide assurance to the public of this protection. Such assurance is indispensable to the function of the external auditor because, in the final analysis, his opinion must be accepted as a matter of faith. In most circumstances the reader of the financial statements is in no position to check the veracity of the financial data, the thoroughness of the auditing procedures applied, or the justification for the audit opinion expressed. For the audit report to lend credibility to the financial statements the user must therefore have confidence in the competence and professional integrity of the auditor. The existence of a rigorous code of professional ethics helps to elicit this confidence. A secondary purpose of such a code is to achieve orderly and courteous conduct within the profession.

Fundamental to an understanding of the ethical responsibilities of the external auditor is an understanding of the evolution of his role in society. As discussed in Chapter 1, almost until the twentieth century the external auditor was an agent of management or government sent in to check on the employees of a firm owned by one or a few shareholders. As the number of shareholders involved in an enterprise increased, management was no longer a small group of owners but virtually a self-perpetuating group responsible to a large number of remote shareholders whose ability to look after their collective interests had been greatly diminished. The ethical responsibilities of the auditor include that of fair and impartial treatment of both the management group and all classes of shareholders as well as all other users of the financial statements.

The professional assumption of rigorous ethical standards in turn justifies certain privileges which the profession enjoys. Society has granted the chartered accountant special recognition, special freedoms and in many instances an exclusive licence to render opinions on financial data. In addition, chartered accountants have been provided with a guaranteed market for their services with the compulsory audit provisions of the corporations acts in Canada. Finally, the profession has been granted wide latitude in self-discipline, although in Quebec this responsibility is now shared with other members of the community. Acceptance of these professional privileges demands that the highest level of professional ethics be maintained and enforced.

It is important to remember that the ethical responsibilities of a chartered accountant extend beyond his relationship with clients. It is natural for the student-in-accounts initially to view the client-auditor relationship as the only important one. A review of his provincial code of professional conduct, and of landmark legal decisions relating to the conduct of the external auditor, will quickly disabuse him of this view. A great responsibility extends to all potential readers of his audit report and indeed to society in general.

It is also important for the student and the chartered accountant to recognize that pressures on the chartered accountant to violate his trust to society are very real and ever present. Even though in theory the external auditor is hired by shareholders, in practice his engagement and the approval of the fee for his services are in the hands of management (though, with growing frequency, subject to approval by an audit committee). The external auditor is not, how-ever, an employee or an agent of management, but rather functions as an independent contractor serving many clients. In this role he is nevertheless expected to act as a quasi-public servant in providing assurance to all those who may rely on financial reports prepared by management.

When studying rules of professional conduct it is important to appreciate that these rules are not static. Judgments made during a professional career will be highly influenced both by professional goals and the ideals which have been incorporated in an ethical code. Conversely, professional ideals may be greatly influenced by important practical judgments. In a changing business world, professional ideals will evolve in response to changing needs of society. The changing needs of society are frequently articulated in the form of legal decisions (see Chapter 5) or decisions by regulatory agencies. Such decisions will often occasion a modification in the profession's rules of conduct.

Because specific rules of behaviour are a necessarily imperfect attempt to interpret agreed general principles, most codes of professional ethics, including all of those adopted by each provincial Institute in Canada, indicate that specific rules set a minimum level of behaviour and that it is the general principles embodied in the rules which must, in the final analysis, be used as a pattern of conduct upon which the professional man should model his behaviour.

> ... rules of conduct, which are enforceable by sanctions, cannot by their nature state the most that is expected of members, or students, but simply the least. The rules thus define a minimum level of acceptable conduct; ethical conduct in its highest sense, however, is a product of personal character – an acknowledgement by the individual that the standard to be observed goes beyond that of simply conforming to the letter of a list of prohibitions.[10]

2.9 Enforcing the rules of professional conduct

In Canada the Rules of Professional Conduct are set and enforced by the provincial Institutes. Their powers of discipline are formidable, ranging from reprimand to expulsion (which, in many provinces, means disbarment from the practice of any function of public accounting). The means of enforcing the rules are reasonably similar from province to province. The Ontario pattern is described below as a typical example.

Three different committees of the Institute are appointed by Council to play a role in the enforcement of the rules of professional conduct: the Professional Conduct Committee, the Discipline Committee, and the Appeal Committee. Procedures commence with the receipt of a complaint concerning an individual chartered accountant or a firm of chartered accountants practising in the province. The complaint may be lodged by another chartered accountant or by any member of the general public.

Professional Conduct Committee

The Professional Conduct Committee has the role of investigator and prosecutor in the disciplining process. It receives the complaint, makes an investigation, and at its sole discretion, either lays a formal charge or sets the matter aside. Aside from the power to informally admonish, the Professional Conduct Committee itself has no power to discipline. If a formal charge is laid, it presents the case against a member or firm at a formal hearing of the Discipline Committee.

Discipline Committee

The Discipline Committee conducts formal hearings into the conduct of individual members or firms who are charged with violation of one or more sections of the Rules of Professional Conduct. The member or firm being charged is entitled to be represented by counsel at formal hearings and to question witnesses. The Discipline Committee, Appeal Committee or Council may require the attendance of any member or student as witness and may order the presentation of any books, documents or working papers in the possession of its members. At the conclusion of the formal hearing the Discipline Committee may reprimand the offending member or student, order a fine to be paid to the Institute, suspend the member or student, or expel the member or student from the Institute.

Appeal Committee

The decision of the Discipline Committee may be appealed either by the offending member or firm or by the Professional Conduct Committee. Appeals are considered at a formal hearing of the Appeal Committee. The Appeal Committee, after a formal hear-ing, may confirm, reject or modify the findings and any order of the Discipline Committee.

When the decision of the Appeal Committee is to confirm or order the suspension or expulsion of a student or member, one further route of appeal is open: an appeal directly to the Council of the Institute. Confirmation, rejection or modification of the findings of the Appeal Committee, made by Council, are final within the Institute. There is, of course, always a right of appeal to the courts, although on the few such appeals in the past the decisions have generally not been modified.

Public Accountants Council

In Ontario, the person or persons making complaints against members have an alternative course of action, where the member is a practising public accountant. The Public Accountants Council, responsible for administering The Public Accountancy Act, may hold hearings into the conduct of any licensed public accountant. The result of such hearing may be the revocation of the licence to practise. When a practising member of the Ontario Institute is suspended or expelled by the Institute, the Public Accountants Council then holds its own hearings to decide whether or not that member's licence to practise public accounting should be revoked.

2.10 Reference material

CICA Handbook (Canadian Institute of Chartered Accountants).

Members' handbooks of the various provincial Institutes or Order.

2.11 Questions and problems

Review and discussion

1. What are the objectives of the accounting profession?
2. Is there a need for Uniform Final Examinations? How should final examinations relate to practical experience?
3. Describe the division of powers between the provincial Institutes or Order and the CICA.
4. What are the purposes of the Accounting Research and the Auditing Standards Committees of the CICA?
5. What similarities are there between the CICA and the AICPA? What are the differences?
6. Why must an auditor be objective? In what ways can the auditor enhance this objectivity?

7. How have various security commissions affected the accounting profession (a) in Canada and (b) in the United States?
8. Why does the auditing profession need regulation from an internal governing body and/or external sources?
9. What are professional ethics?
10. Identify the range of services provided by chartered accountants in public practice. What are the potential conflicts in carrying out ancillary services in conjunction with a statutory audit engagement?

Problems

1. Soon after he obtained his CA designation, Herman G. left public accounting to manage his father's cattle ranch near Calgary. Six years later he decided to return to public practice as a sole practitioner.
   a) What problems, if any, exist for Herman related to the provincial rules of professional conduct?
   b) What are your views regarding compulsory education after obtaining the CA designation, in this type of situation?
   c) Would your views differ if Herman had not returned to public practice?

2. Your firm is the auditor for a company called Arc Investments Ltd. During your examination of the share records of the company, you noted that 25% of the outstanding common shares are registered in the name of a partner of your firm. The partner concerned is not directly involved in the audit.
   a) What is your firm's ethical position?
   b) Do you feel that your firm has an "independence" problem in this situation?
   c) As audit senior, what would your course of action be after making this discovery?

3. Hardy Door Inc. is a U.S. company based in Detroit. Its Canadian subsidiary, H.D. Ltd., is located in Windsor, Ontario. Your firm has been appointed auditors of H.D. Ltd. The president of Hardy has requested that you use the AICPA short-form audit report when you issue your opinion on the financial statements.
   a) What problems, if any, does this situation pose to you, a Canadian chartered accountant?
   b) What specific professional bodies or service groups could help in this situation?
   c) What would your response be to the President of Hardy?

4. As an accounting student trying to prepare for the uniform CA examinations, you do not feel your firm is giving you proper on-the-job training. What is your course of action?

5. The various provincial Securities Commissions in Canada and the SEC in the United States play a significant role in the development of financial statement disclosure and developing generally accepted accounting principles. How do you feel the role of these Commissions relates to the objectives of the Canadian Institute of Chartered Accountants?

6. "The law is the lowest form of ethics". How does this quotation relate to you as a Canadian chartered accountant?

7. Mr. L.K. Dalton, a Canadian chartered accountant, was convicted under the criminal code for operating an illegal gambling house. How does and/or how should this conviction affect his standing as a member of the Canadian Institute of Chartered Accountants?

8. What are the advantages and disadvantages of the various means of educating or training students-in-accounts.

9. The Chartered Accountancy Profession and individual chartered accountants have a responsibility to educate the public in their standards of auditing and as to their professional competence. Comment.

10. Identify the current status of regulatory legislation governing the practice of public accounting in your province. Give detailed critical comment on this position.

11. Most Discipline Committees will not hold a hearing into a member's conduct while he or she is before the Courts on the same matter. Comment on the reasons for this policy.

Ethics and
Public Practice

The concept of ethical conduct and the practical enforcement of rules of professional conduct in Canada have already been discussed. The purpose of this chapter is to review the content of the more important rules adopted in Canada by the various Institutes and Order of Chartered Accountants.

3.1 Rules of professional conduct in Canada

While the general principles of codes of ethics adopted by public accountants around the world are similar, specific rules differ from country to country, and, to a minor extent, from province to province. Reference was made in the previous chapter to an inter-provincial Coordination Committee, one of whose functions is to minimize unnecessary differences in professional rules from province to province. In 1975, the Inter-Provincial Committee on Uniform Rules of Ethics (a subcommittee of the Coordination Committee) recommended that a set of Uniform Rules of Professional Conduct, modelled on the Ontario Institute rules, be adopted by all provincial Institutes of Chartered Accountants to replace the previous 1969 uniform code of ethics. As this book goes to press almost all of the provincial Institutes have adopted these Uniform Rules and adoption by other provinces is anticipated. The discussion in this chapter therefore is based upon the Recommended Uniform Rules of Professional Conduct. Some of the rules make reference to specific Institute committees (e.g., professional conduct, discipline and appeal committees) whose titles and functions may differ from province to province. In such cases, the Ontario version of the rules has been used for purposes of illustration in this chapter. The substance of many of the individual rules is also contained in regulations of some of the provincial licensing Boards or Councils.

3.1.1 Structure of the Uniform Rules of Professional Conduct

The Uniform Rules of Professional Conduct are divided into four major classes preceded by a foreword and a definitions section and accompanied by an extensive series of more detailed Interpretations:

A. *Foreword*
  • the distinguishing elements of a profession
  • the basic principles underlying the rules
  • a discussion of these basic principles
B. *Definitions, application, and interpretation*
C. *Rules of professional conduct*
  1. *General rules*
    • compliance and misconduct (101 - 102)
  2. *Standards of conduct affecting the public interest*
    • reputation (201)
    • integrity and due care (202)
    • competence (203)

  • objectivity (204)
  • reporting (205 - 206)
  • client relations and confidentiality (207 - 210)
  • reporting of breaches of conduct (211)
  • trust funds (212)
  • unlawful activities (213)
  • prohibition of tenders, contingent fees, commissions (214 - 216)
  • publicity and advertising (217)
  3. *Relations with fellow members and with non-members engaged in public accounting*
    • non-solicitation of engagements (301)
    • communication with predecessor accountant (302)
    • joint engagements and special assignments (303 - 305)
    • employment practices (306)
  4. *Organization and conduct of a professional practice*
    • firm names (401)
    • practice of public accounting (402 - 407)
    • practice of related functions concurrently with public accounting (408 - 409)
    • practice of related functions exclusively (410)
D. *Interpretations*
  • following general order and numbering of the rules

Because of the inter-relationship between many of the rules their discussion in this chapter is not in strict numerical order. Furthermore, a few of the rules relate to more than one aspect of public practice and are accordingly referred to in more than one section. Figure 3.a indicates the location of the discussion of the various rules in this chapter. A few of the rules and many of the more detailed interpretations are covered only in broad outline. The practitioner or student should refer to the complete text of the rules and interpretations contained in the Members' Handbook of his provincial Institute.

3.1.2 Underlying principles

The foreword to the rules enunciates six underlying principles which are fundamental to the entire structure of the rules and interpretations.

1. A member or student shall conduct himself at all times in a manner which will maintain the good reputation of the profession and its ability to serve the public interest.
2. A member or student shall perform his professional services with integrity and care and accept an obligation to sustain his professional competence by keeping himself informed of, and complying with, developments in professional standards.

Location of Discussion of Rules in This Chapter

Classes of rules (and related interpretations)	Chapter sections where these rules are discussed				
	3.1	3.2	3.3	3.4	3.5
General rules	101-102				
Standards of conduct affecting the public interest		201-211 213, 215-216	214, 217	203-205 212	
Relations with fellow members and non-members engaged in public accounting			306		301-305
Organization and conduct of a professional practice	410		401-407	408-409	

Figure 3.a

3. A member who is engaged to express an opinion on financial statements shall hold himself free of any influence, interest or relationship, in respect of his client's affairs, which impairs his professional judgment or objectivity or which, in the view of a reasonable observer, has that effect.
4. A member or student has a duty of confidence in respect of the affairs of any client and shall not disclose, without proper cause, any information obtained in the course of his duties, nor shall he in any way exploit such information to his advantage.
5. The development of a member's practice shall be founded upon a reputation for professional excellence, and the use of methods commonly characterized as self-promotion or solicitation is not in keeping with this principle.
6. A member shall act in relation to any other member with the courtesy and consideration due between professional colleagues and which, in turn, he would wish to be accorded by the other member.

The soundness of these principles is, for the most part, self-evident. Their substance is included in the discussion of the individual rules in the following sections of this chapter.

3.1.3 Interpretations

The Rules of Professional Conduct themselves are generally adopted within any given provincial Institute in the form of a by-law, which must be approved by the membership. While membership approval is essential for the basic criteria of professional conduct, it would be a cumbersome requirement for every specific detail on which guidance may from time to time be desirable. Accordingly, the large number of Interpretations accompanying the Rules of Professional Conduct are generally passed by resolution of the Council of the provincial Institute. As additional problems or ambiguities are identified by the various provincial Discipline and Professional

Conduct Committees across the country, additions or modifications can then be made to these Interpretations on a timely basis. A preliminary section of the Rules of Professional Conduct states that they are to be read in the light of the Foreword (the underlying principles) and of the Interpretations.

3.1.4 Applicability to non-practitioners and students

Chartered accountants employed in government, education or industry must observe all rules except those clearly relating specifically to public accounting or those granting a specific exception for non-practitioners. Many of the rules in the first two classes (general rules and standards of conduct affecting the public interest) thus apply equally to practitioners and non-practitioners. This broad applicability is based on the concept of a unified profession of which both practising and non-practising chartered accountants are full members and in which the activities of any one member can reflect on all others. Many of the more important rules are also worded expressly to apply as well to students employed by practising chartered accountants.

Chartered accountants engaged in the public practice of management consulting or in the provision of services as trustee in bankruptcy or of electronic data processing services and who are not engaged in or affiliated with a public accounting practice are exempted from certain rules governing public accounting practice. The exemptions include rules relating to contingency fees (215), sharing of fees (216), prohibition of advertising (217), prohibition of solicitation of professional engagements entrusted to another public accountant (301), organization and description of the professional practice (403 – 406), and concurrent practice of related functions (408 – 409).

> **410.1**   A member engaged in the public practice of a function not inconsistent with public accounting, and who is not also engaged in the practice of public accounting, may, in carrying on his practice, conduct his affairs (or his firm's or corporation's affairs) free of the constraints imposed upon members engaged in the practice of public accounting by rules 215, 216, 217, 301, rules 403 to 406 inclusive and rules 408 and 409, but not in such a fashion as to tend to bring disrepute on the profession.

> **410.2**   A member so engaged shall not refer a client for services to another member or firm engaged in the practice of public accounting for a commission or other compensation.

The purpose of these exemptions is to avoid placing such chartered accountants at an unfair disadvantage to their non-CA competitors in these fields.

3.1.5 General rules

The two general rules establish a duty of compliance with all by-laws, rules, regulations, orders and resolutions of the relevant provincial Institute or Order and establish a conviction by a competent Canadian court as sufficient evidence of professional misconduct.

> **101**   Members and students shall comply with the by-laws, rules and regulations and rules of professional conduct of the Institute as they may be from time to time and with any order or resolution of the council or officers of the Institute under the by-laws.

> **102**   Any member or student who has been convicted of any criminal or similar offence may be charged with professional misconduct by the professional conduct committee; in such cases, a certificate of conviction by any competent court shall be sufficient evidence of the conviction and of the commission of the offence.

3.2 Standards of conduct affecting the public interest

The principal rules in this class relate to reputation, integrity and due care, professional competence, objectivity, non-association with false or misleading statements, confidentiality, and avoidance of unlawful activites. The importance of these rules is obvious.

3.2.1 Reputation

> **201**   A member or student shall conduct himself at all times in a manner which will maintain the good reputation of the profession and its ability to serve the public interest.

This rule is, in fact, a general underlying principle (the first of those previously quoted) from which all the rules concerned with standards of conduct of a chartered accountant could theoretically be derived. Based on this rule, practising accountants should not participate in activities inconsistent with the practice of public accounting nor activities which will bring the profession into disrepute. This rule is also important in guiding relations between members, particularly in situations where criticism of a fellow member is necessary.

3.2.2 Integrity and due care

> **202**   A member or student shall perform his professional services with integrity and due care.

A chartered accountant or a CA student should be honest, conscientious and careful in the work he performs for the public. While a duty of due professional care is simple to state, its interpretation in particular circumstances requires considerable judgment.

Due professional care implies the careful application of all the standards of the profession and the observance of all the rules of professional conduct. For example, an auditor offering his services to the public must be competent to perform audit services. Where the persons directly performing the service (e.g., students employed in an audit examination) do not meet all the competence requirements individually, this lack must be compensated for by increased supervision and review – so that the audit team as a whole achieves the level of competence required. Due professional care demands objectivity and impartiality in the performance of the audit and rendering of the opinion. Due professional care demands that the audit examination be carried out in accordance with the profession's field work standards and the audit report prepared in accordance with the profession's reporting standards (as discussed in Chapter 4). Finally, due professional care requires the auditor to give appropriate recognition to all statutory and other legal requirements, to all authoritative professional pronouncements, and to other practices which, while not the subject of legal or professional pronouncements, are in general usage by his colleagues.

3.2.3 Competence

> **203**   A member shall sustain his professional competence by keeping himself informed of, and complying with, developments in professional standards in all functions in which he practises or is relied upon because of his calling.

One of the distinguishing elements of a professional has been identified as the mastery of an intellectual skill acquired by lengthy training and education. While Rule 203 refers solely to the sustaining of professional competence at the member level it, of course, presupposes its acquisition at the student level. Chapter 2 reviewed the contribution of admission requirements, formal education programs and the uniform final examination to the competence of the trained chartered accountant. A number of other factors are also important.

Competence of the CA student

In addition to the formal education programs and Institute-sponsored classes discussed in Chapter 2, practitioners employing students generally supplement their education with extensive in-house training programs. Many firms provide up to several weeks of formal training for their students from the time they join the firm until they obtain their C.A. For smaller firms the development of such an extensive program is difficult and they naturally tend to place greater reliance on Institute programs. To promote equality of professional training some Institutes have developed special supplementary courses. For example, the Ontario Institute, over and above regular course requirements, has a compulsory one-week auditing course for new students lacking a university credit in auditing or adequate in-firm formal training.

Whether formal training is taken within the firm itself or from an outside source, all auditing firms are expected to oversee their students' progress and ensure that the course requirements of the uniform final examination are being met. By far the most important method of acquiring technical proficiency, however, is on-the-job training. All practitioners employing students are responsible to ensure that they receive a reasonable diversity of experience and that they work under the active supervision of audit seniors who can gauge their progress in acquiring on-the-job experience.

Review of a student's progress is important both to him and to his employer. Most firms use some form of appraisal report – some preferring to complete the report at the conclusion of each audit engagement, others on a regular periodic basis such as every six months. Appraisal forms usually rate a student according to personal characteristics that are important to his function as an auditor and according to predetermined levels of proficiency expected. The appraisals generally reflect the collective observations of a number of audit seniors and one or more managers or supervisors for whom he has worked. The objective of such a report is to pinpoint strengths which justify an increase in responsibility and work

level and weaknesses which call for some remedial action. Remedial action may consist of specific job assignments or training programs in the deficient areas, increased direct supervision, transfer to another position or staff within the firm for a change of associates, reclassification to a lower job level, or, in the extreme, termination of employment. It is fundamental to any successful appraisal program that the student appraised achieve an awareness of his own strengths and weaknesses – for in the final analysis, self-improvement is the most effective medicine. For this reason, the counselling aspects of the appraisal process are crucial. The manager or supervisor must discuss a student's performance fairly and candidly, at the same time soliciting the student's views on his own performance. Self-identified shortcomings are always easier to cure than deficiencies alleged by others and perhaps imperfectly understood by the subject.

The skills demanded of a CA student are primarily in the areas of accounting, auditing and taxation, with some minor management ability required where, after one or two years' experience, he is selected as an audit senior, supervising more junior assistants, on a medium-sized engagement. Once the student has obtained his CA degree, however, his proficiency and skill must advance to entirely new levels.

Competence of the chartered accountant

Satisfaction of the requirements for the CA certificate is evidence only of a basic competence in the fields of accounting, auditing and taxation at the time the certificate is granted. At that time, chartered accountants will commonly be judged competent to perform the following types of auditing and related services:

1. To take complete charge of small audit engagements, planning the audit, performing all necessary auditing procedures, drafting financial statements (on his client's behalf), drafting the audit report, and preparing client tax returns. What constitutes a small audit engagement will vary from firm to firm, but many would restrict in-charge assignments of a new CA to annual engagements not exceeding 100 to 200 hours each. Even in audit engagements of this size the new CA will often encounter tax planning areas, contentious accounting matters, systems points, computer service bureau applications, etc., where he requires assistance or advice.
2. To prepare tax returns and provide tax planning service to personal tax clients. On contentious points, however, he will usually require some consultation with a tax specialist.

3. To take charge of the field work as audit senior for medium-sized clients (perhaps up to 500 annual audit hours), supervising assistants on the job, performing most of the necessary audit procedures, drafting financial statements and preparing client tax returns. In these engagements, however, he will normally have to rely on his supervisor or manager (a person with two to six year's experience as a CA) to play an active role in the planning and reviewing of the engagement. In addition, reference to various specialists (tax specialists, computer audit specialists, sampling specialists) will often be required.
4. To take charge, only in exceptional cases, of the field work of the largest clients. Typically, the audit senior on the largest audits (in the thousand hour annual range) has, instead, one or two years' experience as a CA. Even with this greater experience, the active participation of manager, partner and specialists in the planning and review stages is usually important.

The attainment of professional status, the CA certificate, does not in itself justify the accepting of complex engagements without further study and experience. The chartered accountant has a professional obligation to ensure that he has or acquires the competence to perform an engagement he accepts and to decline those engagements for which he does not have or cannot on a timely basis acquire the necessary competence. Many of the ancillary services which chartered accountants perform (discussed later in this chapter) will be beyond the competence of the brand new CA.

Nor does the acquisition of the CA certificate ensure that even basic competence can be maintained without continuing study and effort. Auditing and other professional services offered by the chartered accountant include procedures subject to a high risk of technological obsolescence. Rule 203 makes it clear that a chartered accountant has a professional obligation to keep abreast of all developments in professional standards. This is accomplished in three different ways.

First, the chartered accountant must read and maintain familiarity with all new professional pronouncements (Accounting and Auditing Recommendations, Rules of Professional Conduct, etc.) as well as relevant guidelines (Accounting and Auditing Guidelines) and studies (Research, Audit Technique, and other Studies) as they are issued. With the volume of pronouncements in recent years this is no mean task. One important aid to keeping abreast of new developments is the reading of *CA Magazine*, including its research department. Because of the closeness of Canadian practice to that in the United States most chartered accountants also regularly read the *Journal of Accountancy* and many find it desirable to keep up to date with all authoritative pronouncements of the AICPA and the Financial Accounting Standards Board.

Second, the chartered accountant will improve his competence through continuing practical experience in the provision of auditing, tax and general business services, particularly if he is conscientious in researching and consulting with his colleagues on all new problems encountered.

Third, the chartered accountant must continue to attend courses and training programs related to his area of service. In larger accounting firms many of these programs will be conducted as in-house classes or seminars. A CA will generally receive one to two weeks of in-firm training in his first two years as a CA and additional courses at the manager and partner level will extend thereafter throughout his entire professional career. In other firms, greater reliance will be placed on attendance at professional development seminars sponsored by the provincial Institutes. Such seminars, however, draw their participants from all areas of the profession: small practising firms, large practising firms, education, government, and industry. Some of these seminars are developed by the provincial Institutes themselves, some by individual practitioners or practising firms, and some by the CICA. All, however, are administered by the provincial Institutes. In any given year, courses at various locations and times may be offered in auditing subjects (analytical auditing, audit reporting, computer auditing, sampling, etc.); current research and legislation; financial management; public practice (systems, fees, partnership agreements); mergers, acquisitions, sales and valuations; and taxation; to name only some.

Professional development

In recent years the profession has been giving consideration to various proposals for mandatory professional development. In the United States, sixteen states have mandatory professional development in some form. In Canada, a number of professions have been studying the subject. In 1975, a special CICA committee presented proposals, subsequently referred to the provincial Institutes and Order, calling for approximately 15 days of courses every 3 years, subject to certain exemptions. While those specific proposals were rejected by a number of provincial Institutes (for example, Ontario), the topic itself will undoubtedly continue to attract debate. Some chartered accountants argue that mandatory requirements are inconsistent with professional self-discipline. Other arguments have centered on the applicability of such proposals to non-practising versus practising members, to specialists versus generalists, to formal educational courses versus self-study and voluntary guidelines, to compulsory course attendance versus demonstration of continuing education through compulsory open-book re-examination or through compulsory practice review. Whatever the ultimate resolution of these questions, it is important to realize that they concern only procedures for promoting or insuring compliance with a rule of professional conduct which already exists. Compliance with Rule 203 itself is a professional responsibility of each chartered accountant with or without any formal mechanism for monitoring results.

Specialization and competence

Some chartered accountants choose to specialize for some period of their practising careers. For those who choose a specialty it is often desirable to complete one or two years general audit experience at the CA level first. Common areas of specialty include taxes and computer auditing. In larger firms other specialty areas might be accounting research, auditing methods (including sampling), and staff education. In addition, a chartered accountant may decide to specialize in one of the ancillary services such as bankruptcy work, or management consulting. Each of these specialties involves its own, often quite extensive, training requirements. A chartered accountant offering his services in one of these areas is required by Rule 203 to sustain the necessary professional competence to justify the public's reliance on such services.

3.2.4 Objectivity

> **204**   A member who is engaged to express an opinion on financial statements shall hold himself free of any influence, interest or relationship, in respect of his client's affairs, which impairs his professional judgment or objectivity or which, in the view of a reasonable observer, has that effect.

One of the reasons identified in Chapter 1 as underlying society's need for the attest function was the concern over an actual or perceived conflict of interest between management and the shareholders to whom it reports. It follows that for the attest function to answer this concern, it must be performed by an auditor free from any actual or perceived conflict of interest with the readers of his report. This double responsibility, avoidance of an actual impairment of objectivity and avoidance of the appearance of such impairment, is reflected in the wording of Rule 204. These two aspects of the objectivity rule warrant separate consideration.

Avoiding actual impairment of objectivity

It is fundamental to the practice of public accounting that the chartered accountant must not subordinate his professional judgment to the will of others, and that he express his conclusions honestly and impartially. This is the quality of objectivity. It means a willingness to call a spade a spade regardless of consequence. Of course, objectivity does not mean rigid and arrogant decisions unmindful of the possiblity of alternative, defensible views which the client may have in areas necessarily subject to judgmental valuation. It does mean, however, that if a material misstatement is involved and if there is no alternative, properly defensible interpretation of the facts, then the auditor must not allow his judgment to be influenced (a) by the opposition of members of his client's staff, (b) by the inconvenience or embarrassment of insisting upon the necessary adjustments to the statements, or (c) by a reluctance, failing such adjustments, to qualify his audit report. Similarly, if the auditor has not obtained reasonable audit assurance that a material misstatement is not present, he must not allow his judgment to be influenced by the inconvenience of expanding his audit procedures to the point where he can be satisfied. Persons who do subordinate their judgment to others, perhaps for fear of losing an engagement, do not retain in the long run the respect of their clients, the business community, or their professional colleagues.

Objectivity is important in three aspects of the auditor's work: the designing of the audit program, the performing of the examination, and the preparation of the audit report. We may refer to these three aspects as programming, investigative, and reporting objectivity.

Programming objectivity means that the auditor must exercise complete and impartial control over the selection of audit techniques and procedures and the extent of their application. The audit program is the property of the auditor, not of the client. The client may define overall objectives in broad terms in the case of a non-statutory audit or additional objectives in the case of statutory audit (as long as none of these specified objectives are in conflict with generally accepted auditing standards), but the auditor must exercise his own professional judgment in designing the audit program to achieve those objectives. Most clients readily accept this position and have no desire to interfere in the auditor's choice of procedures. Nonetheless, the auditor must always be alert for the possiblity of attempted interference. Particular care is required when such attempted interference is not overt but takes the subtle form of the alleged impracticality of locating certain documents, the alleged undesirability of communicating with certain third parties, or simply an uncooperative attitude with respect to requested information. The external auditor must equally be suspicious of any attempt by the client's staff to review or to have access to his audit program or working papers. Legal decisions support the importance of programming objectivity by confirming that the audit program and working papers are the property of the auditor.

Investigative objectivity means that the external auditor must have complete control over the selection of areas, economic events, activities, person relationships and company policies which he wishes to examine. This freedom demands direct and free access to all corporate and accounting records; the right to seek information from officers, directors and employees; and the right to communicate, where appropriate, with company solicitors, advisors, suppliers and customers. This does not mean that reasonable requests of the client should not be met. A request that confidential executive payroll records be examined not by the newest student but rather by the audit senior or audit manager is clearly not an attempt to interfere with investigative objectivity but merely a proper desire to preserve the confidentiality of sensitive information.

Audit staff must recognize the dangers of developing too close a personal relationship with client officers or employees. An audit senior who is a close personal friend of a corporate controller may be prone to accept superficial answers to problems which warrant further probing. Maintaining good client relations is of course always important and close friends may happen to work for or join client organizations. Nonetheless, care must be taken to avoid any unconscious bias in performing audit procedures or evaluating audit results. Legislative provisions support the objectivity of the auditor in Canada by giving him statutory right of access to all records and information he requires.

Reporting objectivity means that the external auditor must have complete freedom from control or undue influence in his expression of opinion or in his presentation of recommendations arising as a result of his examination. The external auditor must not feel an obligation to champion the cause of any particular group interested in the results of the financial statements. Rather he must form his opinion impartially so that all conflicting interests can confidently place reliance on his report. The client must recognize in turn that the auditor's report is his own and, while attached to the financial statements, it is a representation of the auditor and not of the client. The importance of the auditor's reporting objectivity is supported by the provisions of all corporations acts in Canada (discussed in the next chapter) and, in recent years, by the advent of audit committees as well.

Avoiding the appearance of impairment of objectivity

Only the auditor himself can ensure that he has in fact maintained his objectivity. But it is also important that the public not perceive any appearance of impaired objectivity. If an auditor appeared to suffer from a conflict of interest, even though in fact, known only to himself, he remained entirely objective, readers would question the reliability of his audit report and the purpose of attestation would thus remain unfulfilled.

It is clearly not possible in the real world to avoid every conceivable possibility of impairment of objectivity that could be alleged. The Rules of Professional Conduct instead appeal to the concept of what a reasonable and knowledgeable observer would consider to be an apparent impairment.

> ... chartered accountants cannot practise their profession and participate in the affairs of their community without being exposed to circumstances that may place pressures upon their objectivity and integrity, and it would be impractical to impose detailed proscriptions intended to cover all conceivable situations. To do so on a rigid basis would be to inhibit the rendering of useful services even when the likelihood of impairment of the chartered accountant's objectivity was relatively remote.
>
> While it may be difficult for a chartered accountant always to appear completely free of any disabling influence, interest or relationship in respect of his client's affairs, pressures upon his objectivity or integrity are subject to powerful countervailing forces and restraints - his liability in law, his responsibility to his profession for his professional actions and, perhaps most importantly, the inbred resistance of a disciplined professional person to any infringement upon his basic impartiality and integrity in the rendering of services.
>
> Since, however, the public must be assured of the chartered accountant's freedom from any conflict of interest, the profession tests its existence against the criterion of whether a reasonable man, having knowledge of all the facts and taking into consideration normal strength of character and normal behaviour under the particular circumstances, would conclude that a specified relationship between a chartered accountant and a client posed an unacceptable threat to the chartered accountant's independence of judgment. Only thus can public confidence in the objectivity and integrity of the chartered accountant be sustained, and it is upon this public confidence that the reputation and usefulness of the profession rest.[1]

The lengthy Interpretation to Rule 204 sets out a number of specific requirements which are considered essential for a reasonable observer to conclude that objectivity has not been impaired.

The most obvious situation which could impair an auditor's objectivity in the view of an observer would be his holding of a direct or indirect financial interest in his client. A banker or a minority shareholder might well question the impartiality of an auditor's report if he, his family or his partners had an investment in the company covered by the report. Accordingly, the Interpretation to Rule 204 prohibits investments directly or indirectly by an auditor, his immediate family, or his partners in shares, bonds, debentures, mortgages, notes or advances of or to a corporate client or any associate thereof. Likewise, an auditor (or any of his partners) is not permitted to be a director, officer or employee of the client organization or any associate for fear that he will not be able to make impartial evaluations of the results of management decisions in which he participated. Immediate family of the auditor (generally those in his household) or of his partners may be employees but not directors or officers of a client organization or associate. A corporate associate for these purposes includes, within certain limits, parent companies, subsidiaries, companies under common control, investor companies which equity-account for their holdings in the client company, and investee companies the investments in which are equity-accounted by the client company.

There are a number of reasonable exceptions to this general prohibition concerning investment in clients or participation in management. Chartered accountants may invest in public mutual funds where they are not auditors of the fund even though the mutual fund invests in securities of their clients. A chartered accountant may enter into normal business transactions with his client (e.g., a mortgage loan from a trust company, and a purchase subject to the normal terms of trade and price from a retail establishment). However, in entering into such transactions the external auditor, his partners or immediate family should not receive any special consideration or preference that is not granted to other customers. The policies of most accounting firms prohibit their employees from receiving special discounts or other favours from clients which would give the appearance of conflict of interest.

It should be remembered that avoiding the appearance of impairment of objectivity is the second of the two requirements imposed by Rule 204. The first, and more important, requirement is the maintenance of that inward quality of objectivity which only the professional person can judge within himself. Objectivity is a positive quality, not just an absence of possible conflicting interests. With the proliferation of procedural criteria focussed on avoidance of apparent conflicts of interest, it is essential that each member of the profession not lose sight of the true goal of objectivity as a state of mind.

Objectivity, independence and fees

The quality of objectivity called for in the Rules of Professional Conduct has often been referred to as 'independence' in legislation and in accounting literature. For example, as discussed in the next chapter, some corporations acts in Canada require the auditor to be 'independent'. AICPA pronouncements in the United States call for an 'independence in mental attitude'.[2] It seems clear that these latter requirements are intended to define the same state of impartiality as is called for in Rule 204 and its accompanying Interpretations.

From time to time, however, suggestions have arisen from some quarters that an auditor's contractual relationship with his client and his receipt of audit fees from his client, is a theoretical impairment of complete independence. According to this view complete independence would require all audits to be conducted by a government bureau or alternatively by practitioners appointed by government and perhaps subject to compulsory rotation every few years. Such an arrangement, however, is subject to three serious objections. First, by breaking the historical auditor-client relationship which permits continuity in planning and conducting recurring annual audits, it could be expected that annual audits, even with the best efforts toward cost control, would become considerably more expensive. Second, by removing management's right to recommend to the shareholders the auditor of its choice to conduct the statutory audit, secondary services to management (recommendations on internal control, income taxes, and financial planning) would undoubtedly receive less attention. Yet it is these secondary services which, integrated with the mandatory attest function, often make the annual audit an economical package from management's point of view. Third, removing management's choice also removes a powerful incentive for the auditor to be cost-conscious in his work; a bureaucracy-run audit function could be expected inevitably to develop inefficiencies adding further to the total cost. Complete independence, in this sense, then, would be hardly in the social interest. What is wanted is not a complete absence of all ties to the real world (which is what an extreme interpretation of the word independence might imply), but rather the maintenance of mental objectivity in planning, performing, and reporting upon the audit work. Accordingly, in the new Uniform Rules of Professional Conduct introduced in 1975 the term objectivity has been used throughout as a more appropriate designation of the quality desired.

Nevertheless, certain inappropriate actions with respect to fees could be argued to impair or give the appearance of impairing an auditor's objectivity. Thus, for example, the Interpretations to Rule 204 prohibit an auditor from accepting commissions or finder's fees from third parties with respect to sales of securities or insurance to a client. Acceptance, without client consent, of finder's fees in connection with arranging client financing or in connection with a purchase or sale of a business by a client are also prohibited. In the rare cases where a practitioner provides advice to and receives fees from two parties to the same transaction, he must inform each of his clients of this relationship. Finally, while not covered in the Rules or Interpretations, common sense suggests that audit and other fees should be billed and collected promptly. The existence of substantial unpaid fees from past years during the conduct of the current year's audit could appear to impair an auditor's objectivity. A conflict of interest could be alleged between the auditor's desire to maintain good relations in order to collect the past debt and his duty to resist inadequate statement presentations whatever the consequence.

Rule 215 prohibits contingent fees:

215 A member engaged in the practice of public accounting shall not offer or agree to render any professional service for a fee contingent on the results of such service, nor shall he represent that he does any service without fee except services of a charitable, benevolent or similar nature.

For example, a chartered accountant could not accept an engagement in which his remuneration was to be based on a percentage of profits. Such an arrangement would create a conflict of interest when the auditor expressed an opinion on these same profits and accordingly might be viewed as impairing his objectivity.

Two additional Rules closely related to Rule 204 and its Interpretations are self-explanatory:

208.1 A member or student shall not, in connection with any transaction involving a client, hold, receive, bargain for, become entitled to or acquire any fee, remuneration or benefit without the client's knowledge and consent.

208.2 A member or student shall not, in connection with any transaction involving his employer, hold, receive, bargain for, become entitled to or acquire any fee, remuneration or benefit without the employer's knowledge and consent.

216 Other than in relation to the sale and purchase of an accounting practice, a member engaged in the practice of public accounting shall not directly or indirectly pay to any person who is not a public accountant a commission or other compensation to obtain a client, nor shall he accept directly or indirectly from any person who is not a public accountant a commission or other compensation for a referral to a client of products or services of others.

Ancillary services

A number of other Rules and Interpretations relating to objectivity and the provision of ancillary services are discussed later in this chapter.

3.2.5 False or misleading statements

205 A member or student shall not sign or associate himself with any letter, report, statement, representation or financial statement which he knows, or should know, is false or misleading, whether or not the signing or association is subject to a disclaimer of responsibility.

Association with false or misleading statements clearly harms the public and damages the good reputation of the profession. Rule 205 applies equally (a) to a chartered accountant in industry preparing financial statements (or other representations), (b) to a practising chartered accountant (or student) preparing unaudited financial statements (accompanied by a disclaimer of opinion) or tax returns as an accounting or tax service, or (c) to a practising chartered accountant (or student) expressing an opinion on financial statements or making recommendations on internal control as an audit service. In ascertaining whether a member or student knew or should have known that an item was false or misleading, a Discipline Committee could refer to current authoritative pronouncements, with which he should be considered familiar, and consider whether in the light of these pronouncements, and the facts of the case, the member or student used due professional care and sound judgment in the circumstances. It is not enough merely to have been ignorant of the falsehood of certain statements; one must not have become associated with them with reckless disregard for whether they might be true or false. A member or student has an obligation to give thoughtful consideration to all the pertinent information he has before signing or associating himself in any way with letters, reports, or financial statements.

3.2.6 Audit reporting

206.1 In expressing an opinion on financial statements examined by him a member shall not
(1) fail to reveal any material fact known to him which is not disclosed in the financial statements, the omission of which renders the financial statements misleading, nor
(2) fail to report any material mis-statement known to him to be contained in the financial statements.

206.2 A member shall not express an opinion on financial statements examined by him
(1) if he fails to obtain sufficient information to warrant an expression of opinion, or
(2) if he has not complied in all material respects with the auditing standards of the profession, or
(3) if the exceptions or qualifications to the opinion are sufficiently material to nullify the value of such opinion.

206.3 Subject to item (3) of rule 206.2 a member shall not express an opinion on financial statements examined by him which are not prepared in accordance with the accounting standards of the profession unless such opinion is suitably qualified; without limiting the generality of the foregoing, if a member expresses an opinion without qualification or exception that financial statements are presented in accordance with generally accepted accounting principles and if such statements depart in any material respect from the recommendations of The Accounting and Auditing Research Committee of The Canadian Institute of Chartered Accountants or its successor(s) [the Accounting Research Committee], such departure must be capable of justification as proper in the particular circumstances.

The key audit provision in this rule is 206.2(2), which prohibits a member from expressing an opinion on financial statements "if he has not complied in all material respects with the auditing standards of the profession". An accompanying Interpretation makes reference to "generally accepted auditing standards". The relationship between the Rules of Professional Conduct and generally accepted auditing standards is discussed in Chapter 4; in brief, if 206.2(2) is read as normally requiring observance of generally accepted auditing standards as set out in the CICA Handbook, subject to any departures justified to the satisfaction of the relevant provincial Institute or Order, then all the other provisions of Rule 206 merely reinforce automatic requirements of those standards: disclosure of material omissions and misstatements, obtaining of sufficient information, and requirement to justify departures from Accounting Recommendations in the CICA Handbook. The significance of this rule for the auditor, then, is that it makes a failure to follow appropriate accounting and auditing standards of the profession a breach of the Rules of Professional Conduct and therefore subject to discipline by the provincial Institutes and Order.

3.2.7 Client relations and confidentiality

207 A member shall inform his client of any business connections, any affiliations, and any interests of which the client might reasonably expect to be informed but this does not necessarily include disclosure of professional services he may be rendering or proposing to render to other clients.

209 A member or student shall not take any action, such as acquiring any interest, property or benefit, in connection with which he makes improper use of confidential knowledge of a client's affairs obtained in the course of his duties.

210.1 A member or student shall not disclose or use any confidential information concerning the affairs of any client except when properly acting in the course of his duties or when such information is required to be disclosed by order of lawful authority or by the council, the professional conduct committee, the discipline committee or the appeal committee in the proper exercise of their duties.

The purpose of Rule 207 is to require full disclosure to the client of relationships whose concealment might be taken to imply a conflict of interest, an impairment of objectivity, or a possible abuse of confidential information. As stated, the responsibility to inform does not necessarily extend to the disclosure of professional services rendered to other clients. For example, the fact that a practitioner renders professional services to six retail stores in direct competition with one another need not necessarily be disclosed; there is no inherent conflict of interest in such a situation as long as the confidentiality of each client's affairs is preserved. However, cases can arise where disclosure is appropriate. For example, where the practitioner is asked by another party (such as a government body or a prospective purchaser) to accept an engagement to investigate or evaluate an organization or industry group which includes audit clients of the practitioner, it would normally first be appropriate to disclose these audit relationships. Likewise, as already explained in the previous section, the client should be informed in those rare cases where a fee is obtained from another party to the same transaction; and the client's consent should be obtained before accepting any finder's fees with respect to arranging financing or in connection with a purchase or sale of a business.

It is fundamental to the audit process of gathering evidence that there be full and frank disclosure of information between client and auditor. As a result, an auditor is bound to accumulate information as to the private financial affairs of his client, the improper disclosure of which might be a serious injury to the client's competitive position. Rules 209 and 210.1 therefore require the auditor to maintain such information in confidence and to refrain from taking any action on the basis of confidential knowledge. Breaches of this confidence would be damaging to the good reputation of the profession and probably fatal to the practice of the public accountant involved. Moreover, without the assurance of confidentiality, client responses to auditor enquiries would be inevitably circumspect - with a resulting decline in audit reliability as well as a probable increase in audit cost (through greater emphasis on alternative means of discovering facts). An Interpretation to Rule 210 points out that banker and other third party requests for information can only be answered with the client's consent.

As discussed earlier, working papers are the property of the auditor and not the client. However, the auditor is not free to do with his papers whatever he pleases. Their confidentiality must be maintained. Thus, when selling a Practice to another public accountant, the chartered accountant must obtain his client's permission before passing on papers containing confidential information.

A particularly subtle problem involving confidentiality can arise when two clients have significant business transactions with one another. For example, client A may have a large account receivable from client B, a private company known by the auditor to have recently suffered large financial losses. On the one hand, the auditor may know the debt is likely to go bad and requires a substantial allowance; on the other, he has a duty to maintain the confidentiality of his information as to client B, and should its improper disclosure precipitate adverse consequences for client B the latter could well have a right of action against the auditor. In such a situation, the confidentiality rule must be observed, but the auditor may decide to delay, if possible, issuing his report on Client A until other non-confidential sources of information as to the collectibility of the debt can be obtained.

Two exceptions to complete confidentiality are provided by Rule 210.1 - disclosure when required by provincial Institute committees concerned with discipline (which committees in turn then have a duty to preserve confidentiality) and disclosure when required by order of lawful authority. With respect to the latter requirements, the communications between client and accountant (unlike client and lawyer) do not enjoy the status of "privileged communication" and must be disclosed upon order of the courts.[3] An Interpretation of Rule 210 makes reference to a 1970 case before the Supreme Court of Ontario in which the judge stated that a professional person has a duty to ask the court for a ruling before divulging at a trial information obtained in a confidential capacity.

3.2.8 Reporting of breaches of conduct

210.2 A member or student shall not disclose or use any confidential information concerning the affairs of his employer except when properly acting in the course of his duties or when such information is required to be disclosed by order of lawful authority or by the council, the professional conduct committee, the discipline committee and the appeal committee in the proper exercise of their duties.

210.3 A member or student shall attend to assist council, the professional conduct committee, the discipline committee and the appeal committee when required and shall produce any book, papers and records in their possession, custody or control which may be required from time to time.

211 Subject to the provisions of Rule 210, a member shall bring to the attention of the professional conduct committee any apparent breach of these rules or any instance involving or appearing to involve doubt as to the competence, reputation or integrity of a member, student or applicant.

It is in the public interest that the Rules of Professional Conduct established by the profession be adhered to by all its members. Enforcement and discipline procedures were described in the previous chapter. However, the task of maintaining high standards throughout the profession cannot be left entirely to formal committees. Every chartered accountant has an obligation not only to conform his own behaviour to the profession's rules but also, under Rule 211, to report apparent breaches of the rules observed in other members of the profession. An unethical action by any one member is a reflection on all others. It would be naive to believe that the accounting profession, as all other walks of life, does not have its share of unscrupulous individuals or others who, despite a good past record, succumb to the temptation to short-cut the stringent demands that professional service imposes. The profession has a responsibility to the public to maintain the most rigorous self-policing.

Students are excluded from the obligation imposed by Rule 211 as it would be unfair to expect of them the experience to assess apparent breaches of the rules appropriately.

It should be noted that the confidentiality requirements in Rule 210 overrule the reporting obligations in Rule 211 in certain circumstances. A member has a duty to maintain the confidentiality of his client's affairs. Thus, while Rule 210.1 requires confidential information to be submitted on demand of appropriate Institute committees (further reinforced by Rule 210.2), it does not permit confidential information to be volunteered when not demanded. Rule 211 does not therefore apply to confidential information, unless the client's consent has been obtained. Thus, a member on a new engagement becoming aware of misconduct on the part of a former auditor should request and obtain the client's consent before reporting the apparent misconduct if it involves confidential information. Furthermore, Rule 210.2 imposes a duty of confidentiality concerning the affairs of one's employer. If a member becomes aware of professional misconduct on the part of his practising employers, he should first attempt to resolve the matter internally within the firm. If the matter is not resolved to his satisfaction, he must use his professional judgment to determine which of the rule of employer confidentiality or the rule of reporting breaches of conduct should guide his further actions.

3.2.9 Unlawful activities

213 A member or student shall not knowingly lend himself, his name or his services to any unlawful activity.

The worth of this rule is self-evident. Its application in practice, however, can be complex. When, for example, a practising chartered accountant becomes aware of a criminal act (for example, bribery of a government official) committed by the management of a client organization, he may have (a) a professional responsibility to maintain the confidentiality of the affairs of the client organization, (b) a professional duty to dissociate himself from the unlawful activity, and (c) conceivably an implied statutory obligation to inform the shareholders of the client organization of the reasons for his dissociation (e.g., resignation). The resolution of these sometimes conflicting duties can call for the most careful professional judgment and, with respect to the legal obligations involved, competent legal advice. It is an area which requires further study by the profession as a whole.

3.2.10 Other matters

The remaining rules under "standards of conduct affecting the public interest" involve the handling of

trust funds, prohibition of tenders and contingent fees, and restrictions on advertising – and are discussed in the following sections of this chapter.

In addition to the Rules of Professional Conduct, the by-laws of the provincial Institutes and Order directly impose certain obligations on their members or make other provisions to protect the public from those not competent to render a proper professional service. For example, the by-laws typically remove from membership persons who become bankrupt, persons who are determined to be mentally ill by a court, and persons certified incompetent and admitted to a mental institution. Once a bankrupt member has been discharged from bankruptcy, a mentally incompetent member declared capable by the courts of managing his own affairs, or a mentally ill person discharged from an institution he may be readmitted to the Institute upon permission being granted by Council.

3.3 Public practice in Canada

Today there are more than 10 000 Canadian chartered accountants in public practice. About an equal number work in industry, government or education. Of those in public practice, about one in ten is a sole practitioner. The rest are partners or employees of local, regional, or national accounting firms. In total the practising component of the profession employs over 6 000 students.

3.3.1 Partnership form of organization

Approximately 90% of the practising profession is organized in the form of partnerships of chartered accountants. Practice in a corporate form is prohibited by the laws of most of the provinces of Canada and generally by most provincial Rules of Professional Conduct, though an exception is made for corporations allowed in another province:

> **407** A member shall not be associated in any way with any corporation engaged in Canada in the practice of public accounting except that a member may associate with a professional corporation engaged in the practice of public accounting in a province other than [this one] if such corporation is recognized and approved for such practice by ' the provincial institute in the province concerned.

Traditionally, members of a profession have been prohibited from incorporating their public practices on the grounds that the limited liability and anonymity of a corporation were inconsistent with personal professional service. Of course, all practising accountants limit their financial liability in any case

through the use of professional liability insurance. Thus, it can be argued that it is the risk not of immediate financial catastrophe but of loss of reputation and consequent loss of business that is today the principal external motivation to maintain high standards – and would remain so if practices were incorporated. In any case, incorporation would not protect a professional man from liability for his own personal professional negligence. It would, however, protect the personal assets of other employees or officers of the corporation who had not personally been negligent. In recent years professional incorporation has been permitted in the United States by the AICPA Code of Professional Ethics and by the laws of several states. Most American practices, however, have continued to date in the traditional partnership form. As this book goes to press, draft legislation to permit professional incorporation is under consideration in Alberta. Whatever the future laws and ethical rules in Canada, it seems likely that the partnership form of practice will continue to be common.

Joining a number of different chartered accountants together in one partnership practice provides a number of important benefits to clients and to the individual partners and employees of the practice:

1. It allows continuity of service to the client by an ongoing professional organization.
2. It allows daily interchange of ideas in the solution of professional and client problems.
3. It allows a degree of specialization by the individual partners and employees.
4. It assembles the personal resources required to

52

perform the audits of national and multi-national companies.

No one individual can expect to maintain a high degree of knowledge and competence in all the disciplines in which chartered accountants provide services. Thus, partnership practices permit a broadening of the range of professional services from that which one individual could offer. At the same time, this diversity of work makes essential the development of specialists and of effective systems of exchanging information between specialists and generalists.

3.3.2 Partners

Within any accounting partnership, the partners by definition constitute the highest level of authority. Partners are individually and collectively responsible for all professional work done by a firm. In professional matters concerning his client the individual audit partner generally has the principal responsibility, though in most partnerships he is required to consult with other partners in defined circumstances. Internally however, as in any organization, there must usually be some structure to ensure the efficient management of the practice as a whole. In a large partnership, for instance, overall administration of the firm may be the responsibility of a management committee of senior partners. They in turn may select a managing partner to run the day-to-day operation of the practice. Partners at all levels in the firm may have a voice in the firm's operations by sitting on various policy or advisory committees having jurisdiction over different professional areas, such as, tax, accounting, auditing, personnel and training.

While some partners may decide to specialize in certain areas (taxes, accounting and auditing research, administration) which separate them to a greater or lesser extent from day to day service to audit clients, by far the vast majority will remain audit or client service partners. The audit partner usually has a direct professional responsibility for a group of clients. He maintains contact with the clients, makes overall audit arrangements, reviews the work of his subordinates and gives final assent to the issue of audit opinions. The partner renders advice to his clients where requested and, like the general medical practitioner, calls on specialists within the firm to assist in rendering additional services as needed.

Generally partners are expected to contribute important amounts of time to civic, professional and educational activities in their communities. Of course, employees of a partnership as well as sole practitioners also make important contributions. Active participation in the activities of the various pro-

vincial Institutes or Order, the CICA, and their respective committees is also important if a practitioner is to contribute his share to the building of the chartered accountancy profession. Contribution of specialized skills in the leadership of professional and other organizations is necessary if the chartered accountant is to do his share in developing the economic and social environment whose benefits he enjoys. An important by-product of involvement in civic activities is contact with other leaders in the community and sometimes with prospective new clients – although the individual who seeks involvement for this motive alone is unlikely to have the dedication which will attract the notice of others.

In large firms there will be managers or supervisors reporting to the audit partner. For firms operating on a staff system, each audit partner may be responsible for one or two managers, each of whom will in turn have responsibility for a staff of from six to ten chartered accountants and students. For firms operating on a pool system, larger groupings of partners, supervisors or managers, chartered accountants and students may form a client service unit.

3.3.3 Specialists

The creation of a group practice allows the development of specialist services. Common specialist groups in larger public accounting practices include tax specialists, accounting research specialists, auditing method specialists (including computer audit specialists and sampling specialists), specialists in trustee in bankruptcy services and management consultants. Often this last group is organized into a separate management consulting partnership affiliated with the public accounting firm.

Specialist may be utilized by the client service team in either or both of two ways. They may act as resource groups with responsibilities for education of professionals on the client service team and to provide consultation on technically difficult matters when required. Alternatively, they may have direct client responsibilities themselves.

3.3.4 Ethical considerations in the organization and conduct of a public accounting practice

Two of the underlying principles previously quoted from the Foreword to the Rules of Professional Conduct are especially relevant to the organization and conduct of a public accounting practice:

1. A member or student shall conduct himself at all times in a manner which will maintain the good repu-

tation of the profession and its ability to serve the public interest.

2. The development of a member's practice shall be founded upon a reputation for professional excellence, and the use of methods commonly characterized as self-promotion or solicitation is not in keeping with this principle.

These general principles are supported by a number of specific Rules and Interpretations, only some of which will be specifically quoted here. The rule prohibiting incorporation of a public accounting practice has already been discussed. Other Rules relate to the practice name and description, membership and licensing requirements, multi-office partnerships, and self-promotion and solicitation.

Practice name and description

401 A member shall not engage in the practice of public accounting, or in the public practice of any function not inconsistent therewith, under a name or style which is misleading as to the nature of the organization (proprietorship, partnership or, where permitted, corporation) or the nature of the functions performed.

Rule 401 prohibits misleading names in general. Rules 402 and 406 specify additional requirements to be observed, some of which are summarized below.

The practice of public accounting should be carried out under a personal name. A sole practitioner, except in unusual circumstances, should practice under his own name. Partnerships should practice under the names of current or previous partners of the firm unless special permission is received from the Institute (for example, many large Canadian firms practise under international names). Where the number of partners in a firm exceeds the number of names in their firm name, the words "& Co." may be added. The descriptive style of the practice should be simply "chartered accountants" or "public accountants" (and not designations such as "specialists in mining audits" or "experts in internal control analysis").

Institute membership and licensing requirements

Rules 402, 403 and 406 contain a number of provisions relating to institute membership and licensing. All partners of public accounting firms using the descriptive style "chartered accountants" must be members of the Canadian Institute of Chartered Accountants. This membership is automatic through membership in one or more of the provincial Institutes or Order. All partners or sole practitioners resident in a given province must similarly be members of the corresponding provincial Institute or Order. If one partner in a public accounting firm was not a

chartered accountant (and member of the CICA), the firm would have to practise under the descriptive style of "public accountants".

The requirement that all members of a partnership using the descriptive style "chartered accountants" be members of the CICA has important implications for international accounting firms. Such firms, if they wish to practise in Canada with the designation of "chartered accountants", must form a separate Canadian partnership, each partner of which is a member of a provincial Institute and of the CICA. While such international firms may share training and other technical materials with affiliated firms in other countries, the requirement for a separate Canadian firm controlled by chartered accountants resident in Canada ensures that the Canadian accounting profession will retain a distinct identity.

If a firm designated as "chartered accountants" is practising in any given province at least one partner of that firm must be a member of that provincial Institute. Thus, larger public accounting firms having a practice office in a given province, but perhaps no partner resident in that province, must arrange for at least one partner to be a member of that provincial Institute. This requirement ensures that the disciplining authority within a given province will have access to a partner should a breach of conduct occur within its boundaries. Many firms in practice go beyond this rule and ensure that one partner is a member of the Institute in any province in which the firm performs services whether or not an office is maintained in that province. A member of a provincial Institute is responsible for any failure of his partners or associates living in other provinces to abide by his Institute's rules with respect to practice in his province.

Multi-office partnerships

It is quite common for practising members or firms to open offices in localities removed from the main office of practice. Rule 403 requires that each such office be under the personal supervision of a member of the Institute who is normally in attendance at that office. This provision ensures that a member of the public dealing with an accounting firm at any location will be dealing with a partner or employee who is a chartered accountant and therefore fully accountable for his professional responsibilities.

404 A member shall not hold out or imply that he has an office in any place where he is in fact only represented by another public accountant or a firm of public accountants and, conversely, a member who only represents a public accountant or a firm of public accountants, shall not hold out or imply that he maintains an office for such public accountant or such firm.

Rule 404 is intended to ensure that where there are agency relationships between members at different locations, the general public does not mistakenly infer that a public accountant is practising directly where in fact he only has an agent.

Self-promotion, competitive bidding and solicitation

A number of the Rules and related Interpretations contain strictures against advertising, against publicly claiming special skills above those possessed by colleagues with equal qualification, against solicitation for engagements, and against responding to tenders. The Foreword to the Uniform Rules of Professional Conduct explains these strictures as preventing "a scrambling for clientele inappropriate to an essentially intellectual calling which emphasizes quality of service".

> It would not be in the public interest, for example, that the selection of a practitioner by a client was a function of the skill of the practitioner's advertising agency and the size of his advertising budget; nor that a practitioner could, publicly, claim for himself professional skills exceeding those of similarly qualified practitioners, in a purely subjective fashion and without let, hindrance or reasonable constraint; nor that quality of service in the important realms of rights and property, in which chartered accountants function, should become secondary to price—for example, a public accounting engagement being tailored to a bid price rather than to the needs of the engagement, as they emerge, in the professional judgment of the chartered accountant; nor that self-promotion replace the building of a reputation for professional competence.[4]

A general prohibition of unprofessional behaviour in obtaining clients is set out in Rule 405:

> **405** A member engaged in the practice of public accounting shall not adopt any method of obtaining or attracting clients which tends to bring disrepute on the profession.

Rule 214 prohibits members from engaging in competitive bidding for public accounting engagements:

> **214** A member shall not respond to any call for tenders for the provision of professional services in respect of the practice of public accounting.

This prohibition reflects the concern that competitive bidding could lead to the extent of an audit program being tailored to the bid price rather than to a professional consideration of the evidence necessary to justify the expression of an opinion on which the public will be relying.

Increasingly, proposals for accounting services are called for by prospective clients. This rule does not prohibit a member from submitting proposals concerning professional appointments which discuss the member's qualification to perform the service, some of the means by which the service will be rendered, an approximation of the time that the service will take, and the standard hourly rates of the personnel. What is prohibited is a firm price bid, for this would disregard unanticipated costs which may later be encountered in providing the required public accounting service. Bids or estimates are not prohibited with respect to services outside the public accounting field.

The AICPA Board of Professional Ethics, prior to 1972, contained a similar prohibition against competitive bidding. This rule was not carried over into the revised code approved in 1972, because of concern that enforcement of this rule could be contrary to U.S. federal anti-trust laws. It is always possible that Rule 214 may at some future date be criticized in Canada on similar grounds. It is all the more important, therefore, that chartered accountants be familiar with the justification of this rule (as summarized in the foregoing quotation from the Foreword to the Rules of Professional Conduct).

Rule 217 prohibits chartered accountants from advertising to obtain clients:

> **217** Except to the extent permitted in any Interpretations adopted and published by the council from time to time interpreting the intent or meaning of this rule, a member engaged in the practice of public accounting shall not advertise.

A prohibition against advertising is common to all professions in our society (though for a short time advertising was allowed in the early days of the American profession). The reason, as already quoted from the Foreword, is that having the selection of auditor by a client a function of the skill of the former's advertising agency or of the size of his advertising budget rather than of the professional competence of the auditor himself would hardly be in the public interest.

A number of exceptions to the general prohibition of advertising are contained in the numerous and detailed Interpretations of Rule 217. Some of the principal ones are the following:

1. A public practitioner or firm may incorporate in his or its letterhead the firm name, business and home telephone numbers, the occupation as chartered accountant or public accountant, the names of partners, reference to other cities where the firm has offices, and reference to other firms acting as representatives. Letterhead for a public accounting practice may also include, if correct, the designation of "trustee in bankruptcy" but should not contain a description of additional activities such as tax consulting, electronic data processing or management consulting. As described

later, separate letterheads may be used for each of the "management consulting" and "electronic data processing" functions if desired.

2. A practitioner or firm may place his or its professional card, containing information generally the same as in the letterhead, in any publication which is open to all members. In addition, the card may incorporate an announcement of a change of address, the opening of a new office, the admission of new partners, a change in the firm name, etc. Such a card containing an announcement may also be circulated directly to clients and close associates.

3. Subject to a number of restrictions, practising members may list their names in the yellow pages of the telephone directory.

4. A public practitioner or firm may advertise for staff either for themselves or on behalf of a client. Advertising for students-in-accounts may also involve the preparation of a recruitment brochure. All such advertising is subject to a number of restrictions. Moreover, in some but not all provinces, Rule 306 provides that a member may not offer employment to the employee of another member, whether in connection with responses to advertisements or otherwise, without first informing that other member.

5. Subject to a number of guidelines, practitioners may publish articles, make speeches, comment to the press on current matters and appear on radio and television.

6. Practitioners or firms may circulate to their clients and close associates tax circulars, newsletters and firm literature on special subjects. They may be sent to non-clients, however, only in response to specific requests.

In recent years the question of advertising restrictions within the professions has attracted some public debate. In 1976, for example, the U.S. Justice Department initiated a lawsuit against the American Bar Association arguing that its prohibition of references to price or description of service in advertising contravenes anti-trust laws. In 1975, professional engineers in British Columbia relaxed their previous restrictions to permit disclosure of information about price and services.

3.4 Ancillary services and related ethical considerations

Services rendered by public practitioners can be briefly classified as follows:

1. Public accounting services
   a) Attest services
      • audits of financial statements, special purpose reports, prospectuses
   b) Other services closely related to the audit function
      • advice on systems and internal control
      • computer systems advice
      • advice on accounting matters
      • financial advice (new financings, government grants, corporate reorganizations)
      • management accounting advice (budgets, cost systems)
      • general business advice
      • preparation on drafting of annual financial statements
   c) Bookeeping services
      • preparation of monthly or annual unaudited financial statements
      • maintenance of books of account—(may overlap with the ancillary service of electronic data processing)
   d) Tax services
      • preparation of tax returns
      • advice on tax planning, estate planning, solution of tax problems
   e) Special investigations
      • investigations re proposed business acquisitions or mergers
      • business valuations

2. Ancillary services
   a) Management consulting
      • advice to management in the areas of organization, systems, computers, facilities, personnel, marketing, engineering, operations research etc.
   b) Trustee in backruptcy
      • services as trustee in bankruptcy, liquidator or receiver
      • consulting services related to credit evaluations and financial reorganization
   c) Electronic data processing
      • processing client data by computer to prepare books of account and periodic financial reports.

Probably about half of the fee revenue of sole practitioners and smaller partnerships is derived from non-attest and ancillary services. In contrast, probably over three-quarters of the fee revenue for larger national firms is derived from attest and attest-related services. But for all practitioners non-attest and ancillary services are at least an important, and often a growing, component of their practice.

The non-attest services listed under the heading of public accounting such as bookkeeping services and tax practice are considered an integral part of the normal activities of all public practitioners and accordingly are subject to all the regular rules for the conduct of public accounting. The three ancillary services, however, are subject to certain additional rules. Ancillary services may be performed in one of three ways:
a) as a department of the public accounting practice,
b) in a separate organization affiliated with the public accounting practice,
c) in a separate organization not affiliated with any public accounting practice.
The Rules of Professional Conduct for ancillary services vary depending on which of these three forms of organization are adopted.

Ancillary services as a department of the public accounting practice

Rule 408 governs ancillary services when integrated with a public accounting practice.

> **408** A member engaged in the practice of public accounting may engage in a business or practice as a department or part of such public accounting practice, in one or more of the following functions, hereinafter sometimes referred to as the related functions:
> 1) management consulting,
> 2) trustee in bankruptcy,
> 3) electronic data processing, and
> 4) such other functions as council may, from time to time, designate,
> subject to the following provisions:...

The remaining provisions of Rule 408 permit the designations of "management consulting", "trustee in bankruptcy" and "electronic data processing" on separate letterheads for each function, permit the "trustee in bankruptcy" designation to be combined, if desired, on the regular public accounting letterhead, but otherwise prohibit reference to the ancillary functions on the letterheads and published professional cards of the public accounting practice. The last prohibition is based on the view that a practitioner's competence in ancillary services should not be paraded as a qualification before prospective clients seeking purely accounting services.

Ancillary services through an affiliated organization

Rule 409 governs ancillary services when offered through a separate organization affiliated with the public accounting practice.

> **409.1** A member engaged in the practice of public accounting may carry on a business or practice through an organization separate from such public accounting practice, either as a proprietor, a partner, or as a director, officer or shareholder of a corporation and may associate with non-members for this purpose, in one or more of the following functions, hereinafter sometimes referred to as the related functions:
> 1) management consulting,
> 2) trustee in bankruptcy,
> 3) electronic data processing, and
> 4) such other functions as council may, from time to time, designate,
> subject to the following provisions: ...

The remaining provisions of Rule 409.1 permit the same designations as Rule 408, prohibit designation of the business as "chartered accountant" or "public accountant", permit the use (subject to council approval) of non-personal firm names for electronic data processing, permit the ancillary practice to be carried on in a corporate form, and prohibit (except for electronic data processing) equity interests by non-CA's other than those active in the business.

The principal departures permitted from public accounting rules are permission of incorporation and association with non-members. The permission to incorporate reflects the fact that practitioners providing ancillary servies must often compete with incorporated non-CA competitors. Nevertheless, most management consulting practices with which chartered accountants are affiliated have retained the partnership form. The permission to associate with non-members recognizes that the provision of consulting and EDP services will generally require a multi-discipline approach going beyond the competence of the average chartered accountant. Without this permission, management consulting firms containing chartered accountants as partners would be unable to invite engineers, psychologists, computer specialists and economists into the partnership. However, where the practice of related functions is affiliated with a public accounting practice, the remaining Rules of Professional Conduct (including the general rules on relationships with other auditors) are enforced.

> **409.2** Before commencing an assignment in any of the related functions from a client of another public accountant who is the duly appointed auditor, a member engaged in the practice of public accounting who is associated with a firm or corporation carrying on a business or practice in any of the related functions shall first notify, or shall ensure that the associated firm or corporation first notifies, such accountant of the assignment.
>
> **409.3** A member engaged in the practice of public accounting who is associated with a firm or corporation carrying on a business or practice in one or more of the related functions, either as principal, partner, director, officer or shareholder, shall be responsible to the Institute for any failure of such firm or corporation to abide

by the rules of professional conduct of the Institute as if such firm or corporation were a member engaged in the practice of public accounting.

Rule 409.3 places the onus of responsibility on the chartered accountant members of organizations practising related functions to ensure that these organizations abide by the Rules of Professional Conduct applicable to all chartered accountants. While such provisions are stringent, their justification is that the practices and procedures of such organizations will, in the public view, always reflect on their affiliated accounting practices.

Ancillary services through a non-affiliated organization

Where ancillary servies are offered through a separate organization not affiliated with any public accounting practice, the CA members of such an organization are exempted from many of the more stringent Rules of Professional Conduct because there is no related public accounting practice on which their conduct will reflect. Rule 410, providing these exemptions, was discussed at the beginning of this chapter.

3.4.1 Tax practice

The implementation of a federal income tax on corporations in 1916 provided a tremendous boost to the practice of public accounting. Businesses which previously maintained inadequate records turned to the public accountant for his assistance in developing systems which could turn out the information needed for income tax returns. In addition, systems and records had to be good enough to bear the scrutiny of inspectors from the Department of National Revenue. Over the years since 1916 tax legislation has grown in complexity and with it the need for expert assistance both in the preparation of tax returns and in tax planning. The introduction of tax reform in Canada in 1972 introduced a further dimension with the imposition of capital gains tax. The growth of multi-national corporations has made it necessary to conduct tax planning on an international basis.

Tax services are not one of the separable "related functions" but rather an integral part of public accounting. All large firms of public accountants maintain separate tax departments staffed by chartered accountants expert in federal and provincial income taxes, federal sales and excise taxes, provincial sales taxes, estate taxes and succession duties, and international taxation. For smaller firms and sole practitioners tax work is also an essential ingredient of the practice. Indeed, many clients of both large and small public accounting firms engage these firms solely or primarily for the provision of tax services. These tax services include:

a) direct assistance in determining tax liability,
b) verification of income and sales tax amounts,
c) preparation of corporate tax and other information returns,
d) preparation of individual tax returns,
e) advice as to tax planning both at the personal and corporate level,
f) assistance in discussing tax assessments.

The provision of these tax services in the larger public accounting firms is divided between the firm's tax group and auditing personnel, the specific allocation depending on individual firm policies. Smaller practices and smaller offices of larger practices usually designate one or two individuals to maintain expertise on tax matters in addition to other client service activities. The sole practitioner will often devote more than one-quarter of his working hours to tax matters. The tax knowledge required by public practitioners is great and goes far beyond the requirements of the uniform final examination syllabus. Indeed, in a large practice, the field of knowledge is so extensive that tax specialists themselves tend to sub-specialize in one or more particular areas of taxation.

The charted accountancy profession has no monopoly in the provision of tax services. Many organizations provide assistance to the general public in the preparation of individual tax returns. Large companies usually prepare their own tax returns although most others have them prepared by the external auditor. Tax planning and the solution of tax problems frequently require the services of a lawyer to interpret the relevant income tax act and related case law as it applies to a client's situation. Chartered accountants must avoid giving legal advice, which is the practice of law and therefore not within their competence. Lawyers, for their part, are quick to make use of the chartered accountant's familiarity with a client's tax affairs, tax planning options, and governmental practices. As a result, a spirit of cooperation has grown up between the legal and accounting professions in Canada, far more than in many other countries. An example is the two professions' joint sponsoring of the Canadian Tax Foundation, a non-partisan organization which, in addition to publishing various tax studies, makes regular submissions to the Federal Government on income tax legislation.

The Rules of Professional Conduct do not contain any separate ethical considerations for a tax practice. There are, however, some distinctions between the provision of tax and auditing services. The practitioner does not express an opinion on the fairness of presentation of tax information as he does on audited financial statements. Accordingly, in the provision of tax services impartiality is not the essential attribute it is for auditing. Rule 204 on objectivity, previously discussed, is not therefore applicable to tax services. Indeed, as an adviser on tax matters, the chartered accountant is advocate not judge. He should seek for his client the most favorable tax position which, assuming full knowledge of all the facts, can properly be considered consistent with the law. The practising chartered accountant is not an agent of the government. Where there is a degree of doubt between two reasonable approaches to the determination of tax, he should properly resolve such doubts in his client's favour, disclosing to his client, however, any reasonable risks of government challenge. This does not mean, of course, that false or misleading statements can be condoned. Rule 205 prohibiting association with false or misleading documents, previously discussed, applies equally to tax practice as to all other aspects of the practitioner's professional services. Whether or not the tax return is signed (as it is in the case of personal tax returns), the practitioner preparing the return is associated with it and must observe the same standards of truthfulness and integrity as is required throughout his professional work. Thus, if in preparing a tax return, the chartered accountant becomes aware that the information is false or misleading, he should refuse to complete the return, insist on client correction of the matter, or else resign the engagement.

One of most difficult ethical questions is the correct action to choose when a deliberate or fraudulent error is observed in the tax returns prepared by the client. Although Rule 205 may not apply (as the practitioner may not be associated with client-prepared returns), the practitioner must consider whether continuation of his engagement constitutes association with unlawful activities. At the same time, Rule 210.1 on confidentiality precludes gratuitous disclosure of the impropriety to the Department of National Revenue. If the practitioner resigns, as most would in such situations, he must consider whether he has any implied statutory responsibility to explain the reasons for his resignation to the shareholders. Once again, the resolution of these sometimes conflicting duties calls for careful professional judgment and, on occasion, legal advice.

3.4.2 Trustee in bankruptcy, liquidator, receiver

Prior to 1900 the trustee in bankruptcy practice of professional accounting firms and sole practitioners occupied a greater proportion of the time than attest and accounting services. Indeed, at the time the first

Institute was chartered in Edinburgh in 1854, the principal activities of accountants were in trustee work, investigations, and the provision of accounting advice to the courts. In Canada, the earliest public accountants were, by training and profession, trustees. Today, as a consequence of the growing importance of the attest function, tax work, and other services, trustee work is no longer the only service provided by public accountants, though it remains an important part of the activities of larger Canadian accounting firms. Among smaller practitioners, some derive a large proportion of their revenue from trustee in bankruptcy services while others, not having the extensive and specialized knowledge required, participate in this activity hardly at all.

The services of chartered accountants engaged in this area of practice include:
a) acting as trustees in bankruptcy
   i) liquidating the estates of bankrupt enterprises and individuals on behalf of creditors,
   ii) managing, on behalf of creditors, insolvent companies that can be restored to financial health,
b) acting as liquidators on behalf of shareholders,
c) acting as receivers or receiver/managers,
d) acting as business advisers with respect to credit evaluations, financial reorganizations, and the negotiating of compromises between companies and their shareholders and creditors.

Frequently, most of the practitioner's work will be in categories (a) (ii) and (d) - that is, rescuing financially sick organizations rather than picking up the pieces after they have collapsed.

As one of the related functions, a trustee practice is permitted to be carried on in corporate form under the Rules of Professional Conduct and a few such practices are incorporated. Where not incorporated, trustee practices are usually carried on in the names of separately licensed individuals. Proposed revisions to federal bankruptcy legislation include permission to incorporate and it can be expected that incorporated practices will become more common in the future.

Rule 204, previously discussed, requires a member engaged to express an opinion on financial statements to avoid any impairment or apparent impairment of objectivity. While this Rule, nominally, relates only to attest services, some of its Interpretations extend the concept of objectivity to trustee services as well. In particular, the Interpretations prohibit a member or his associates from accepting an appointment as trustee in bankruptcy when he or his firm have held the position of auditor for that client during the preceding two years. It is similarly suggested as inadvisable to accept such an appointment when the member has served as accountant (preparing unaudited financial statements) or tax adviser during the preceding two years. The reason for these prohibitions is that a potential conflict of interest could exist or could be thought to exist if, in carrying out his past duties, the practitioner had acquired confidential information concerning his client's affairs which he would now be duty-bound to pass on to the creditors. Such considerations do not, however, according to the Interpretations, preclude acceptance of appointment as liquidator on behalf of the shareholders, or as receiver or receiver/manager, in the absence of statutory prohibitions, provided the practitioner can act with objectivity.

Certain provincial legislation, however, is more restrictive than the foregoing rules. For example, the Ontario Business Corporation Act prohibits a person from being appointed as receiver/manager, or liquidator who has been auditor within the two preceding years.

A member practising as a trustee in bankruptcy, receiver or liquidator customarily must hold and deal with money and property in trust for others (creditors, shareholders, etc.). Rule 212 calls for due observance of the terms of the trust, maintenance of adequate records, and segregation of trust bank accounts.

> **212**   A member or student who handles money or other property in trust shall do so in accordance with the terms of the trust and the general law relating to trusts and shall maintain such records as are necessary to account properly for the money or other property; unless otherwise provided for by the terms of the trust, money held in trust shall be kept in a separate trust bank account or accounts.

Bankruptcy practice is regulated by the federal Superintendent of Bankruptcy and various prescribed examinations and other requirements must be met before a federal appointment as an administrator or trustee in bankruptcy can be obtained.

3.4.3 Bookkeeping and EDP services

The extent of bookkeeping services offered by chartered accountants varies with the location and size of their practices and the size and nature of their clients. Larger client organizations may require primarily audit services and little in the way of bookkeeping assistance. Small clients, on the other hand, may not require attest services but desperately need competent bookkeeping assistance.

In many practices, bookkeeping services provide the first essential contact between the chartered accountant and a new client. Following closely behind are the introduction of management advisory services, preparation of tax returns, and assistance in obtaining financing. Financing arrangements in turn

may lead to the requirement for attest services. Finally, as the client grows, and hires his own accounting assistants, the need for the original external bookkeeping services may disappear. As the starting point of the pattern, bookkeeping services can represent an important practice-building device.

Bookkeeping services sometimes include the maintenance of all books of original entry and sometimes just the preparation of month-end adjusting entries and monthly financial statements. In order to provide these services the chartered accountants usually employ bookkeeping assistants and, where the practice is large, bookkeeping machines (or, as discussed below, EDP equipment) to facilitate high volume processing.

During the 1960's most provincial codes of ethics prohibited the practising member from referring to his position in any way except as chartered accountant, public accountant and trustee in bankruptcy. Thus, if the practitioner provided bookkeeping services he could not indicate the service even on separate letterhead, business cards etc. With the growth of computer technology, however, clients of public accountants were continually approached with proposals that they transfer various of their accounting functions (from invoicing to payrolls to monthly financial statements) to commercial computer data centres. This development had three significant effects on most public accounting practices. First, the practising accountant had to become knowledgeable about such service centres so that he could advise his client on their selection and on contractual arrangements to safeguard the client's interests. Second, the external auditor had to understand the impact of the service centre on his client's system of internal control and the consequent effect on auditing procedures. Third, and most important, many smaller practitioners realized that, unless they entered the data processing field themselves, they would have to accept a diminution in their bookkeeping services and in their clientele.

But entry into the highly competitive EDP field posed two new significant problems. First the public accountant found himself in a poor competitive position because not only did his provincial code of ethics forbid advertising but it also prohibited indications on his letterhead or business cards that he was in the business of data processing. This problem was partially solved by changes introduced in 1969 (and continued in the present Rules of Professional Conduct) which allow public accountants to announce their data processing services on separate letterhead and business cards and which allow them to form separate data processing organizations, which can be incorporated. The general prohibitions against advertising still remain, however, except for those chartered accountants who are not practising public accounting.

The second problem was the fact that a service centre operating its own computer required a high volume operation to make the business pay. To some extent, high volume could be obtained by reaching a broader range of clients than just those who had required manual bookkeeping services in the past. Any client who could not afford an in-house computer became a potential customer for data processing services. Indeed, the breadth of the potential clientele attracted many larger firms who had previously had little interest in providing bookkeeping services. Many other practitioners found that without owning or renting full-time computers they could, by renting block time from larger data centres, still provide a profitable EDP service on a retail basis to their smaller clients.

The range of data services provided by public accountants depends on their individual philosophies of practice. At the one extreme, some public accountants are primarily interested in using their training and experience to provide controllership assistance to clients as an adjunct to monthly computer preparation of books of account, general ledger, financial statements and budgets. Such services are only partially in competition with the raw processing services of commercial data service centres. Other public accounting firms have gone into more direct competition and offer a full range of EDP services from preparation of original documentation, invoices, orders, cheques, payroll etc. to sales analysis, cost distributions, and monthly financial statements.

3.4.4 Management consulting services

The term 'management consulting services' refers to a range of services which public accountants and their affiliates offer to audit clients and in many cases non-audit clients as well, and which go far beyond the traditional areas of public accountancy. The growth of consulting services paralleled the development of highly specialized techniques for managing businesses, controlling costs, managing personnel, selecting marketing strategies, constructing buildings, etc., familiarity with which was generally beyond the scope of any one business enterprise.

The knowledge explosion and the growing needs of business for new and sophisticated techniques has had a dramatic effect on the public accounting profession. All larger accounting firms in Canada have developed extensive management consulting departments, usually organized as separate affiliated firms.

Management services provided by the public accounting and affiliated firms break down into three basic types. First, many services are closely coordinated with the recommendations on internal control, accounting, and financial planning typically arising out of the audit function. Such services are generally provided by the audit personnel directly and indeed service to the client in these areas is a secondary objective of most audit programs (particularly the 'interim audit' component).

Second, many specific services such as special investigations for fraud, investigations for the purchase or sale of a business, major systems design, budgeting and forecasting, computer feasibility studies, design of cost systems, major advice as to financing, while not an integral part of regular audit work, are services which chartered accountants, with some additional specialist training, are well qualified to provide. Such services may be provided either by audit personnel, by a management services department or by a separate affiliated consulting firm. The growth in these services over the past 40 years, has led inevitably to an expanded, third type of service reaching far beyond the scope of accounting as such.

The third level of service led the chartered accountant into collaboration with other disciplines: operations research, engineering, mathematics, economics, marketing, industrial psychology, project management, executive compensation, computer technology, and many others. Services in these areas are generally provided by separate affiliated firms. The work of consulting firms, in approximate order of volume, typically covers general management and organization, computer applications, executive placement, finance and control, personnel services, production, distribution, marketing, and resource development. In Canada such firms are generally members of the Canadian Association of Management Consultants.

The affiliation of a public accounting and a management consulting firm has certain advantages for each of them and for their common client. First, the public accounting firm and the quality of its work are already known to the client through the recurring audit. Second, the regular audit examination already provides a basic familiarity with the client organization, its operations and its problems. Third, the client has the assurance that his continuing relationship with the auditing firm places additional pressure on the affiliated consulting firm to perform services which will stand the test of time – pressure that is not as direct for an independent firm performing a one-time assignment. This does not mean, however, that all consulting clients are audit clients. Indeed, in many affiliated management consulting firms, a significant proportion of the consulting engagements are for organizations (for example, government departments) who are not audit clients.

As already discussed, chartered accountants associated with independent consulting firms and not practising public accounting are, under Rule 410, exempted from several of the Rules of Professional Conduct. However, where practising chartered accountants are associated with consulting firms, as is the more normal case, the principal Rules of Professional Conduct must be observed (although the right to use a separate letterhead and business cards designating the service and the right, not often exercised, of incorporation are granted). Under Rule 409.3 the chartered accountants associated with such consulting firms are responsible for the compliance of their non-CA associates with these Rules.

In particular, it should be remembered that Rule 203 requires a member to sustain his competence in all services he is providing to the public. Attaining a CA does not automatically qualify the chartered accountant to provide the complete range of consulting services. In determining whether he is in a position to undertake a given consulting assignment, the chartered accountant must consider his own background and ability as objectively as possible. If he has not and cannot on a timely basis acquire the necessary competence, he should decline the engagement. He helps his client in such cases if he can recommend someone else who could provide the service desired. Of course, there can be a natural reluctance to refer the work to another public accountant out of fear that the audit engagement itself may be lost. As referrals in such cases, however, are in the public interest, this fear is countered by stringent ethical rules imposed on the firm to whom a referral is made (see the next section).

3.4.5 Objectivity and the provision of ancillary services

Rule 204, previously discussed, requires the auditor to avoid any impairment or apparent impairment of his objectivity. The Uniform Rules of Professional Conduct clearly contemplate that a professional man can provide both audit and ancillary services to the same client without impairing his objectivity (with a few specified exceptions such as the prohibition against simultaneous services as auditor and trustee in bankruptcy).

From time to time, however, there have been critics who have argued that the provision of bookkeeping services or management consulting services impairs a person's objectivity as auditor. The argument is, in the former case, that if an accountant has prepared the books he will have a blind spot when it comes to

judging their accuracy; in the latter case, it is held that if an accountant has advised management to adopt a particular course of action he cannot be objective in evaluating the financial results of that action. In the United States, the Securities and Exchange Commission has ruled that a public accounting firm which kept and posted a client's general ledger (though all other bookkeeping work was performed by the client's employees) had impaired its independence as auditor. As a result, American accounting firms commonly refrain from providing bookkeeping services to any audit clients who must register with the SEC. The effects of this practice may extend to requesting affiliated accounting firms in Canada to refrain from providing bookkeeping services to Canadian audit clients registering with the SEC or affiliated with SEC registrants.

It is to be hoped that further extension of this viewpoint will be strongly resisted by the profession–not because of its effect on the profession but because it is ultimately contrary to the public interest. It is because audit services are closely interrelated with other services, that chartered accountants are able to do a more effective audit, attract better calibre men and women into the profession, and provide a more economical package of services to their clients. Should these services be split apart as a result of the efforts of theoretical purists to isolate auditors in ivory towers, the audit services available to the public in years to come could lose much of their professional stamp and degenerate in the extreme to a rigid and mechanical process performed by clerks unconcerned with the usefulness or the costs of their procedures.

The fact is that the public needs more than just attest services. For many of the ancillary services provided by the public accountant there exists no economical alternative source of supply. For example, if all tax advice by public accountants were to be suddenly outlawed, it would be hard to find other groups with the manpower, training, and experience to fill the vacuum. Should the creation of such groups be forced by law, the cost of tax advice (lacking an audit base) would rise spectacularly. Furthermore, the complete segregation of attestation and ancillary services would put many small practitioners out of business and deny the small businessman in Canada a source of confidential and continuing business advice he needs.

In the final analysis, if an auditor lacks the inner strength to maintain his objectivity, demands that he cease providing non-attest services will not solve the problem. Objectivity is not the mere avoidance of apparent conflicts of interest but an inner discipline which the chartered accountant must have the strength to maintain, whatever the temptation to make convenient exceptions. Indeed it is the conquering of such temptation which is the essence of being a professional.

There is nonetheless some reasonable boundary beyond which the public accountant should not go in providing ancillary services. That boundary lies where the ancillary service ceases being advice and becomes active involvement in the management of the client's operations. Bookkeeping services and preparation of tax returns certainly do not constitute active involvement in management. Nor does the provision of consulting advice. It would be prudent, however, for the public accountant to ensure that his clients recognize this boundary, and that in the end it is client management which makes all final decisions.[5]

3.4.6 Specialization and specialist designations

Reference has already been made to the growth of specialization within the accounting profession: tax practice, accounting research, computer auditing, statistical sampling, business valuations, systems work, etc. No one person can hope to be expert in all of these fields. Specialization and extensive specialist training is already taking place. For example, the training program for chartered accountants who specialize in taxation extends over a period of several years after the CA level and indeed is now splitting into various sub-specialties. Yet, apart from the related functions of trustee in bankruptcy, management consulting, and electronic data processing the Rules of Professional Conduct prohibit any specialist designations. Clearly such prohibitions must be continued as long as there are no objective yardsticks for gauging a chartered accountant's attainment of specialist status. But more and more frequently the question is being asked as to whether such designations and such yardsticks (prescribed qualifications, examination, etc.,) should not be developed.

The medical profession has already crossed this bridge. In Canada and the United States some 20 different medical specialties are formally recognized and controlled. The legal profession, on the other hand, while containing many obvious areas of specialization (corporate law, litigation, criminal law, patent law, constitutional law, etc.) prohibits, like the accounting profession, any specialist designations.

The argument in favour of formalized specialist study and accreditation and the use of specialist designations is that the public would be better protected if the specialists it engages are required to meet defined specialist standards. The arguments against specialist designations include the inevitable complexity of the system, its divisiveness within the profession, and the difficulty of maintaining the definition of specialist qualifications up to date. While all of us probably have a nostalgic longing for a simpler world, increasing complexity and specialization are clearly the trend of the future. It is hard to see how one day the profession will not have to face up to specialist accreditation.

3.5 Relations between public practitioners

The advancement of the public accounting profession as a whole and the maintenance of a high level of service to the public depends to a large extent on a fraternal sense of goodwill and mutual confidence among all chartered accountants. For this reason, the Rules of Professional Conduct contain a number of specific provisions governing relations between members of the profession.

3.5.1 Professional appointments

Rules 301 to 303 prohibit solicitation, require communication with a predecessor accountant, and regulate joint engagements.

Prohibition of solicitation

301   A member engaged in the practice of public accounting shall not directly or indirectly solicit professional engagements which have been entrusted to another public accountant; without limiting the generality of the foregoing, a member shall not seek to secure such an engagement by representing that he is able to carry out the engagement at a lower fee than that of the other public accountant.

Solicitation of professional engagements is prohibited for the same reasons as advertising, competitive bidding, and fee-sharing. The public interest would not be well served by a scrambling for clients in which the fee became more important than the quality of work required by the engagement. The Interpretations to Rule 301 provide guidance to a member approached by a prospective client presently or formerly audited by another member:

301/2   A client in selecting professional advisers is entitled to information which will help him in making his selection. In addition, members have a responsibility to ensure that a transfer of professional work is carried out in an orderly fashion in the best interests of the client.

301/3   When approached by a prospective client about the assumption of work, it is proper for a member to meet with him to discuss his problems. There are, however, inquiries which must be made at the beginning of this discussion:

- Does the prospective client already engage the services of another public accountant?
- If so, has he decided to dispense with the services of the present accountant?
- Has the prospective client notified the present accountant (incumbent) of this intention?

301/4   These inquiries are a matter of professional courtesy and are intended to ensure that the member is fully aware of the relationship existing between the prospective client and any incumbent accountant; having made them, a member is entitled to discuss, with the potential client, his work and its scope.

301/5   The potential client will wish to discuss with the member the services that he is in a position to offer and to obtain some indication of the cost of such services. There is no objection to the member supplying such information. In doing so, however, there are certain things that must be borne in mind.

301/6   A member must avoid giving any indication that he has exclusive knowledge or abilities which are not available from other members of the profession. The member is, however, entitled to give factual information as to his organization and as to the skills available within his organization.

301/7   Normally, professional fees are based on the time required to perform the services undertaken. There is no objection to a member stating what his per diem rates are, based on his standard rates for all clients. A member discussing a new assignment is not in a position to quote a fee or fee range, however, until he has been assured that the client has decided to dispense with the services of the incumbent accountant and has had an opportunity to become fully familiar with the problems which he may encounter in carrying out the assignment, since otherwise he will not know how many days will be required to carry out his professional responsibilities. This is one reason why the rules of conduct provide that a member shall not seek to secure an engagement by representing that he can perform professional services for a lower fee than another public accountant and why responding calls for tenders is prohibited.

Communication with predecessor accountant

302   A member shall not accept an appointment with respect to any function relating to the practice of public accounting, when he is replacing another public accountant, without first communicating with such public accountant and enquiring whether there are any circumstances he should take into account which might influence his decision whether or not to accept the appointment.

The intent of this rule is not to prevent a change in accountant merely on the grounds that the predecessor would prefer to retain the engagement. A client must, after all, be free to have his work performed by the practitioner of his choice. Rather, it is to ensure that a prospective successor has complete knowledge of the circumstances before deciding whether to accept the engagement. For example, should the predecessor be losing his position for objecting to a misleading accounting presentation, the prospective successor who concludes he would have identical objections might well decide that it was inappropriate to accept the appointment. The profession's standards could hardly be maintained if it became a simple matter to 'shop around' for members who were willing to ignore them. Assuming such a motive is not the reason for the prospective change, however, a second purpose of the rule is to ensure that the change proceeds smoothly and with the cooperation of all concerned. This is a matter both of professional courtesy to a colleague and efficient service to the public.

Interpretations set out the following recommended steps to comply with Rule 302: [6]

a) The prospective successor should ask that the predecessor (retiring accountant) first be notified of the proposed change by the client.

b) The successor should then enquire of the predecessor whether there are any circumstances he should take into account which might influence his decision whether or not to accept the engagement.

c) As a matter of professional courtesy the predecessor should respond promptly:

   i)   if there are no circumstances the successor should be made aware of, he need simply say this,

   ii) if there are circumstances the successor should be made aware of, he must consider first the question of confidentiality

   - if confidentiality is not involved, he should merely report the circumstances,
   - if, as is more likely, confidentiality is involved, he should report that such circumstances exist but cannot be disclosed without the client's consent (where confidentiality is in doubt legal advice should be sought).

d) The successor should not commence work until he has received the above response or, so as not to unduly delay the assignment, after a reasonable effort has been made to communicate with the predecessor.

e) The successor should also enquire whether there is any ongoing business of which he should be aware in order to ensure that the client's interests are protected.

f) The predecessor should cooperate with the successor and should be prepared to transfer promptly to the client or, if instructed, to the successor any client books or documents in his possession.

g) The predecessor should be prepared to supply reasonable information to his successor about the work being assumed.

It is common practice for the predecessor accountant, with consent of the client, to allow his successor full access to his working paper files and the right to take extracts therefrom. Such a practice typifies the spirit of cooperation and public service which is the hallmark of any profession.

Joint appointments

303   A member who accepts any appointment jointly with another public accountant shall accept joint and several responsibility for any portion of the work to be performed by either; no member shall proceed in any matter within the terms of such joint appointment without due notice to the other accountant.

The worth of this rule is self-evident.

3.5.2 Special assignments and referrals

When a chartered accountant is asked to provide services that he is not competent to render he has the choice of:

a) acquiring the necessary competence through self-study or professional development courses if this can be done on a timely basis,
b) consulting with another CA, an outside specialist or one of the consultation services of a provincial Institute or the CICA, or
c) referring the work to another chartered accountant, firm of chartered accountants or an independent consultant.

For smaller practices, referral of certain assignments will often be the appropriate choice. Indeed, the identification and referral of a special engagement is in itself a most useful service to a client, much as is the family doctor's diagnosis and a referral of a problem to the appropriate medical specialist.

In order to ensure that referrals are handled in the best interests of the client and at the same time with full protection of the rights for the referring member, Rules 304 and 305 place strict constraints on the member receiving the referral.

304   A member engaged in the practice of public accounting shall, before commencing any special assignment for a client of another public accountant who is the duly appointed auditor, when not limited or restricted by the terms of his assignment, first notify such accountant of the assignment.

305.1   A member who accepts a special assignment, whether by referral or otherwise, from a client of a public accountant who is continuing in his relationship with that client shall not take any action which would tend to impair the position of the other public accountant in his ongoing work with his client.

305.2   A member who receives an engagement for services by referral from another public accountant shall not provide or offer to provide any different services to the referring accountant's client without the consent of the referring accountant; the interests of the client being of overriding concern, the referring accountant shall not unreasonably withhold such consent.

It should be remembered that these rules apply to members not only in public accounting but also those in the related functions (such as management consulting).

On many occasions work will be referred to a chartered accountant by a non-CA, such as a banker or a lawyer. In such cases Rule 216, previously discussed, prohibits the payment of any commission for the referral.

3.5.3 Criticism of a colleague

Rule 201, previously discussed, requires members to conduct themselves in a manner which will maintain the good reputation of the profession. Gratuitous and unjustified criticsm of colleagues is not conducive to the maineneance of this reputation.

Nonetheless, during the course of his professional work a member may find that in serving the best interests of his client he has a responsibility to criticize a professional colleague. Such criticism may be explicit, or it may be implied when a auditor takes over an engagement from another public accountant and decides that material adjustments are required in the client's accounts. A chartered accountant may also become aware of specific examples of noncompliance with the Rules of Professional Conduct which, under Rule 211, are to be reported to the professional conduct committee of the provincial Institute. In any event, there may well be facts or explanations known to the prospective recipient of the criticism which have a bearing on the matter. Accordingly, an Interpretation to Rule 201 calls for a chartered accountant, before criticising a colleague, to submit any proposed criticism to his colleague so that any eventual criticism takes into account all the available information. Occasionally, however, a client may restrict the terms of the engagement so as to prohibit such a submission. In those cases, the chartered accountant should be on record with his client that he has not consulted his colleague.

3.6 Reference material

Recommended Uniform Rules of Professional Conduct (including accompanying Interpretations), Inter-provincial Committee on Uniform Rules of Ethics, 1975.

Rules of Professional Conduct appearing in the Members Handbook of the reader's provincial Institute or Order.

AICPA Statement on Auditing Standards No. 1, Sections 210, 220 and 230, 'Training and proficiency of the independent auditor', 'Independence', and 'Due care in the performance of work'.

AICPA Statement on Auditing Standards No. 7, Communications Between Predecessor and Successor Auditors.

3.7 Questions and problems

Review and discussion

1. Chartered accountants have an internal code of conduct to which all CA's must adhere. Why?
2. Why is a CA required to maintain competence? In what ways can this competence be achieved?
3. Should there be different rules pertaining to competence for CA's in industry, government and specialized areas of practice? Give reasons.
4. What are the limitations of on-the-job training as a method of maintaining a high level of competence?
5. A contractual relationship between an auditor and his client and the collection of fees for services cause an impairment of the auditor's independence. Discuss this statement.
6. During the course of the audit of A Company, you discover an addition error in an invoice from B Company (you are also the auditor of B Company). The extent of the error ($100 000) is material to A Company. What are your responsibilities to A Company and to B Company?
7. Give the reasons for and against carrying on the practice of public accounting in corporate form.
8. Your client, C Company, has asked you to review its accounting system and to recommend an electronic data processing service. Your firm also operates an EDP service bureau. Describe the conflict of interest in answering this request. How can it be resolved? On what basis could you recommend your own service bureau?
9. The following advertisement appeared in the Financial Post:
   "SMITH & JOHNSON – CHARTERED ACCOUNTANTS (Taxation experts)"
   Discuss the merits of this ad.
10. You have been asked by J. T. Smith, President of AB Company, to accept the appointment as auditors for the ensuing year. The audit had previously been done by another firm of chartered accountants. What should happen before this engagement is accepted?

11. Confidential client information becomes known to an auditor during the course of each examination of the accounts of a company. State the conditions which allow an auditor to divulge such information.

Problems

1. The audit of QR, Co. Ltd. had just been completed. Henry Keen, the chief accountant for QR, approached Jim Sharp, the audit senior, with the following proposal. "Why don't you let me copy your audit file? Thus when you come in for next year's audit, I can have the majority of your working papers prepared, vouchers pulled and set aside and we can save both time and money."
   a) What problems, if any, does Henry's proposal pose with respect to independence and to audit evidence?
   b) If you were Jim Sharp, what would your reaction be?
   Remember, you do not want an upset client.

2. Fred Porter, a sole practitioner, was approached by his largest client, ABC Co. Ltd. ABC was about to go public. The president of ABC was concerned that Fred might not be able to provide all the special services that ABC might require. Fred's response was: "Hold on for a day or two; I think I can work something out." Fred then approached John Sloan, senior partner of a large national firm, with the following proposal: "I will bring ABC and the other clients in my firm to you in return for a partnership in your firm." The fee potential for ABC was quite high.
   a) What problems does this situation pose for Fred Porter and for John Sloan?
   b) If Fred's proposal were accepted, do you feel he would have an independence problem?
   c) If Fred's proposal were rejected, and the president of ABC approached John Sloan on

his own, what procedures must be followed by John Sloan and by Fred Porter?

3. JB & Co., a large national firm of chartered accountants, were the auditors of Dream Co. Ltd., a public company which traded on both the Toronto and Vancouver stock exchanges. Gordon Clarke, the partner in charge of the audit, happened to have a very rebellious teenaged son. One day, after a heated argument with his father, Gordon's son went out and purchased 1 000 shares of Dream. After Gordon learned of the facts he was furious. "Our firm could lose the audit because of you."

   a) What independence problems now exist for Gordon Clarke and his firm?

   b) What procedures do you suggest he follow?

4. PCF Ltd. was indebted to Bright, Soulier & Co., Chartered Accountants, for approximately $100 000 representing audit fees and tax advice for the years 1974 and 1975. Bright, Soulier & Co. were appointed auditors for 1976. The partner in charge of the audit told the president (40% owner) of PCF that, until the fees for 1974 and 1975 had been paid, they would not commence the 1976 audit. The president of PCF in his reply stated that the 1976 audit was crucial to the future operations of his company. "If we have an unqualified audit report," he said, "we will be able to receive the additional financing, from the bank and the 30 minority shareholders, that our company requires. Your fees for all three years could then be paid." (Unqualified audit reports were given in both 1974 and 1975.)

   a) Comment on the audit partner's refusal to commence the 1976 audit in light of professional and statutory responsibilities.

   b) What independence problems, if any, exist if the audit partner decides to commence the 1976 audit before the 1974 and 1975 fees have been paid?

5. Sugar, Brooks & Co. were the auditors of a local trust company. Ed Sugar, the senior partner, notices that some of his audit staff are dating members of the client's staff. The next day Ed issued a company policy stating that no staff member shall date a member of the client's staff. He quoted from the rules of professional conduct stating that members of the Institute must not only be independent but also must appear to be independent.

   a) Discuss this policy in relation to your provincial rules of professional conduct.

   b) As a "dating" audit staff member, what course of action would you take in this situation?

6. Bright, Soulier & Co., Chartered Accountants, have resigned as auditors for PCF Ltd. Peak, Wick & Co., Chartered Accountants, have been approached by the president of PCF to accept the appointment as auditors for the 1976 fiscal year. PCF Ltd. is still indebted to Bright, Soulier & Co. for approximately $100 000 (see question 4 above). What are the responsibilities of both audit firms in this situation? If you were the partner of Peak, Wick & Co. making the decision, would you accept the appointment? State your reasons for making this decision.

7. During the examination of the financial statements of the XYZ Company for 1976 (the initial examination of this newly acquired client), you, the audit senior, have progressed sufficiently far in the examination of inventories at both the beginning and the end of 1976 to conclude tentatively that there may be a material overstatement of inventories at the beginning of the year. Your investigation reveals that the possible overage results from the improper pricing of certain work in process which was purchased in a semi-finished condition from another manufacturer for the purpose of being reworked and sold by the company. As the other manufacturer was liquidating his business, the client was able to purchase the inventory for scrap prices, based on the weight of the metal involved. In reflecting this inventory at the end of 1975, the company, with approval of its then auditors, priced this inventory at replacement cost rather than at the actual cost incurred.

   While the prior auditors have made their working papers available, there are indications that they are somewhat disturbed at having lost the engagement. How should this situation be handled?

8. A company operated manufacturing plants in several cities. Except for general policy decisions, control of its operations was decentralized. Greatly increased competition in its business, accompanied by a general business recession, seriously affected the company's sales volume and price structure and, for the first time in many years, it began losing money. The board of directors decided that something had to be done about it and replaced the president.

   The new president concluded that the company's fortunes could be improved by concentrating more control over the various plants at head office and by closing down a number of plants which either were losing money or were only marginally profitable. At the same time a number of the senior officers were replaced, including those responsible for sales and credit and collections. This process commenced in December 1977.

Implementation of the new policy resulted in substantial book losses on sales of plant facilities and on the realization of inventories at certain locations. In addition, the company experienced substantial bad debts and lengthy delays in payment with customers with whom it had previously had no difficulty. The company's new president was naturally much disturbed by all these losses and felt that they must stem from faulty accounting in prior years. As a result, he arranged for an immediate change of auditors, in June 1978, implying that the former ones were either incompetent or had been negligent in their work.

The new auditors recommended providing for additional losses to be expected (a) upon ultimate realization of the fixed assets held for sale, (b) on liquidation of inventories and (c) upon settlement of accounts receivable from trade customers who had previously paid their bills promptly, but were now more than sixty days delinquent.

The losses sustained and those additionally provided for in connection with the closed facilities were together so large that the company decided to exclude them from determination of its net income for 1978 and to show them as special charges against retained earnings. In their report on the company's financial statements for that year, the new auditors stated that, since this was their initial examination and since they did not investigate the status of the pertinent items at the beginning of the year, they were unable to determine what portion of the "net loss and special charges" was attributable to prior years, or whether the accounting principles and practices applied during the year were on a basis consistent with that of the preceding year.

On the basis of the facts as stated above, what points would you expect the former auditors to make, if called upon by the board of directors to explain their position in relation to their unqualified reports of prior years?

9. MD Clinic, a partnership of twenty doctors, has decided that it requires the services of a firm of chartered accountants to comment on accounting systems and controls and to prepare personal tax returns for each partner. They have asked you to bid for this work and ask that, in the bid, you outline the reasons why you are qualified to complete the engagement and the fee you expect to receive.

Prepare a letter, in good form responding to this request. Make any necessary assumptions.

10. CA acts as a "finder" for client A in the acquisition of Business B and charges the client 2% of the acquisition price. He asks you, his student, to research his ethical position. On enquiry you find that the acquired company, Business B, was an audit client that had gone into bankruptcy. CA acted as Trustee on behalf of the unsecured creditors of Business B. What are your findings?

11. A management consultant corporation wishes to offer its services to CA firms that do not have specialized consulting divisions. Each CA firm would retain the corporation and would be billed for services rendered by the corporation to the firm's clients at an hourly rate. The firm would then add a charge for its reviewing services and in turn bill its clients. Each CA firm would be kept fully informed of consulting work done for clients and a member of the firm would assist in the work one day a week.

Explain in detail why this arrangement does or does not violate the Rules of Professional Conduct.

12. An auditor makes an agreement with one of his clients that the amount of his audit fee will be contingent on the number of days required to complete the engagement. What is the essence of the rule of professional ethics dealing with the contingent fees, and what are the reasons for the rule? Is this auditor violating the rule?

13. Bill Jamieson, a recently qualified CA, is in the process of leaving the employ of a large firm of chartered accountants to go into public practice on his own. He is quite worried about how he will build up his clientele. He asks his former audit partner why the profession prohibits all forms of advertising and to give him some advice on how he should build up his practice. Describe in detail the response of the audit partner.

The Auditor's Responsibilities

When a chartered accountant in public practice accepts an engagement as *auditor* of an organization he assumes a set of significant responsibilities with respect to the performance of that audit engagement. Other responsibilities, some similar, some different, are assumed when a practising chartered accountant accepts engagements to provide other non-audit services to his clients (whether audit clients or non-audit clients). The purpose of this chapter is to examine solely those responsibilities which are related to an audit engagement. The auditor's responsibilities encompass three distinct levels:
• moral responsibilities,
• professional responsibilities,
• legal responsibilities.
Moral responsibilities are a matter of conscience. They can be applied only by the individual himself. Professional responsibilities are those specified and enforceable by the profession. Legal responsibilities are those arising from statute, contract, or common law and are enforceable by the courts.

Moral responsibilities

Except for an occasional technical or administrative detail, most professional and legal requirements are designed to embody in an enforceable standard, to the extent practical, certain morally desirable objectives. For example, it is a morally desirable objective that in examining audit evidence an auditor arrive at the wisest and most impartial conclusion within his abilities. Such an objective, however, is too personal to be enforceable. Professional requirements partially embody this objective in the concepts of competence, objectivity and due care. The concept of objectivity in turn is embodied in part in specific professional and legal provisions which prohibit or restrict ownership by the auditor of shares in the audited organization, even though a shareholding auditor might still have arrived at a wise and impartial conclusion. The rule makers obviously believed that the chance of biased opinions would be minimized by investment prohibitions or restrictions. Whether or not an individual auditor believes share ownership would have biased his conclusions, he has a moral responsibility as a member of society to observe specific professional and legal provisions once established.

At the same time, it is clear that mere observance of the letter of the law is not enough. Absence of a shareholding interest does not in itself assure an impartial, objective conclusion. The auditor has a moral responsibility not only to observe specific professional and legal requirements but also to comply with the *spirit* underlying both sets of requirements as well as with such further precepts as his conscience dictates.

Thus, moral responsibilities include and extend beyond all professional and legal responsibilities. In the performance of an external audit, the auditor's moral responsibilities are to users of the financial statements, to the audited organization and its shareholders and management, to his profession, and to the public. In the rare situations where a conflict appears between one professional or legal requirement and another, the auditor in finding a resolution will be guided by pertinent professional or legal advice together with his own moral concept of right and wrong.

Professional responsibilities

Enforceable professional responsibilities consist of the provincial Rules of Professional Conduct discussed in Chapter 3. Enforcement is exclusively in the hands of the provincial Institutes and Order. Certain of these rules of professional conduct, however, make reference to the accounting standards and auditing standards of the profession, which standards in turn are influenced by the Accounting Recommendations of the CICA Accounting Research Committee and the Auditing Recommendations of the CICA Auditing Standards Committee. The former Recommendations, relating to accounting principles, disclosure, and statement presentation, place no direct responsibility per se on the auditor, but they provide many of the *established criteria* in relation to which his opinion on the financial statements must be formed. The latter Recommendations, relating to fundamental auditing procedures, objectives and reporting, have a direct bearing on the auditor's work. Among the Auditing Recommendations, the most fundamental are *generally accepted auditing standards*. These standards and their relationship with provincial rules of professional conduct, are discussed later in this chapter.

Legal responsibilities

Ideally, legal responsibilities should constitute a minimum standard which professional responsibilities exceed. In practice, the relationship is not that simple. From time to time a statutory responsibility is introduced to legislate what was previously solely a professional requirement, but sometimes to go beyond professional requirements. From time to time professional requirements are promulgated to acknowledge an existing legal standard, but more often to go beyond legal standards. Court cases may at times extend the auditor's legal responsibilities beyond what many members of the profession consider reasonable; in such cases the profession may sometimes seek legislative amendments, though, of course, being bound by the case law standard until such amendments, if any, are made. The courts will often turn to, though they are not necessarily bound by, professional pronouncements in interpreting a legal standard of due care. Thus, the relationship between professional and legal responsibilities is one of complex interaction.

Legal responsibilities of the external auditor arise from one or more of the following sources:

- statutes, as interpreted by common law,
- contract, as governed by common law,
- tort, as governed by common law.

Each of these three sources of legal responsibility is discussed below. A more comprehensive discussion of legal liability is contained in the next chapter.

4.1 Statutory responsibilities

The vast majority of external audits in Canada are governed by requirements of general corporation statutes at either the provincial or federal level — hence the term "statutory audit". Provincial and federal corporations acts provide the authority for the incorporation of most companies in Canada and generally set the requirements for their activities. For example, all such acts require the company to prepare annual financial statements, require disclosure of at least certain specified items in such financial statements, and require an annual meeting of the shareholders. The corporations acts also contain a number of specific provisions pertaining to the external auditor's responsibilities and rights.

One of the most recently revised corporations acts in Canada is the Canada Business Corporations Act of 1975. Because it reflects such recent legislative thinking, because it applies to some of the largest companies in Canada, and because it may well serve as a model for future revisions to provincial legislation, this federal act is extensively quoted in the following discussion of statutory responsibilities. The reader is cautioned, however, that significant differences exist among the various provincial acts at present. In addition, a federally incorporated company is governed by the provisions of the previous Canada Corporations Act until it elects to "continue" under the new act (which it must do no later than 1980). When performing an audit of an incorporated company, the external auditor should refer to the appropriate general business corporations legislation having jurisdiction over that company's operations or, in the case of certain specialized industries, to the relevant special legislation (e.g., the Bank Act, the Loan and Trust Companies Act). In cases of doubt as to the interpretation of statutory responsibilities the auditor should seek competent legal advice.

4.1.1 Appointment of auditor

All corporations acts in Canada contain mandatory audit provisions, though varying exemptions are provided for certain classes of company. Mandatory audit provisions begin with the requirement to appoint an auditor. In the Canada Business Corpora-

tions Act the relevant provision is as follows:

156.1 Subject to section 157 [exempting certain small companies], shareholders of a corporation shall by ordinary resolution, at the first meeting of shareholders and at each succeeding annual meeting, appoint an auditor to hold office until the close of the next annual meeting.

When a public accountant accepts such an appointment as auditor he enters into a contractual arrangement to provide audit services for a fee. Because the external auditor is appointed by the shareholders the external audit is sometimes referred to as the "shareholders' audit" — a term which might suggest that the audit contract exists between the auditor and the shareholders. Indeed, many auditors view their ultimate "client" as being the shareholders — and in practical terms this view is reasonable, for shareholders are usually the principal users of the financial statements and of the auditor's report. Moreover, background papers to the federal act stated that one of its purposes was to strengthen the auditor's role as an appointee of the shareholders. Nonetheless, technically, in the opinion of some lawyers, the contractual relationship exists between the auditor (an independent contractor) and the corporation itself, the shareholders acting as agents of the corporation in appointing the auditor.

Section 157 of the federal act exempts a corporation from appointing an auditor, and thereby from the mandatory audit requirement, where (a) the corporation has not distributed securities to the public, (b) the corporation together with its affiliates has gross revenues of $10 million or less and assets of $5 million or less, and (c) an annual resolution to this effect has been passed unanimously by the shareholders. There are significant variations in these exemption requirements among the provincial acts. For example, in Ontario exempted corporations must have gross revenues of $1 000 000 or less and assets of $500 000 or less. In some provinces, small companies are not exempted from the audit requirement but are permitted to appoint non-independent auditors. In some other provinces there are no exemptions.

4.1.2 Responsibility to be independent

Most corporations acts in Canada contain certain rules with respect to the qualification of an auditor. In the federal act these rules are as follows:

155.1 Subject to subsection (5) [which provides for a court exemption order in certain cases], a person is disqualified from being an auditor of a corporation if he is not independent of the corporation, any of its affiliates, or the directors or officers of any such corporation or its affiliates.

155.2 For the purposes of this section,
a) independence is a question of fact; and
b) a person is deemed not to be independent if he or his business partner
  i) is a business partner, a director, an officer or an employee of the corporation, of any of its affiliates, or of any director, officer or employee of any such corporation or its affiliates,
  ii) beneficially owns or controls, directly or indirectly, a material interest in the securities of the corporation or any of its affiliates, or
  iii) has been a receiver, receiver-manager, liquidator or trustee in bankruptcy of the corporation or any of its affiliates within two years of his proposed appointment as auditor of the corporation.

Some provincial acts, such as the Quebec act, merely prohibit the auditor from being a director or officer of the corporation. Other acts, such as the Ontario act, prohibit the ownership of *any* securities of the corporation (as opposed to the prohibition only of a *material interest* in the federal act). As discussed in Chapter 3, the profession's Rules of Professional Conduct already prohibit *any* investment in shares, bonds, notes, etc., of the audited corporation.

A discussion of the terms *objectivity* and *independence*, together with reasons for preferring the former as more clearly denoting the attribute desired of auditors, was discussed in Chapter 3. By explicitly introducing the term independence and defining it as a question of fact, the federal act has assigned the determination of certain auditor qualifications to future courts. The British Columbia act is similar in this respect. It is to be hoped that the courts will be influenced, in such determination, by the profession's standards of objectivity; it seems probable that they will.

Under the federal act an auditor who becomes disqualified under the foregoing rules must resign as soon as he becomes aware of his disqualification and, if he does not, he can be removed by court order.

4.1.3 Responsibility to report

Generally the corporations acts require:
a) the auditor to report,

b) the auditor to make such examination as will enable him to report, and
c) the directors to present the auditor's report, together with the corporation's financial statements, to the annual meeting of shareholders.

Some provincial acts, such as those of Ontario and British Columbia, deal explicitly with each of (a), (b) and (c) above. Other acts, such as those of Quebec and Nova Scotia, provide only for (a) and (c), leaving the auditor's responsibility to make an examination to be inferred from his explicit responsibility to report. In the federal act, on the other hand, the statutory provisions deal explicitly with (b) and (c), leaving the auditor's responsibility to report to be inferred from his explicit responsibility to make an examination for that purpose. The relevant provisions in the federal act are respectively:

163.1 An auditor of a corporation shall make the examination that is in his opinion necessary to enable him to report in the prescribed manner on the financial statements required by this Act to be placed before the shareholders ... [a subsequent provision states that the auditor's report need not cover the comparative figures for the preceding year]

149.1 Subject to section 150 [which permits the government "Director" to waive individual prescribed disclosure requirements in certain cases], the directors of a corporation shall place before the shareholders at every annual meeting
a) comparative financial statements as prescribed ... ;
b) the report of the auditor, if any; ...

It should be noted that although Section 163.1 exempts the comparative figures from audit some audit responsibility is *implied* by the auditor's opinion as to consistency. In the United States, in contrast, auditors must ordinarily report *explicitly* on both current and comparative figures.

Form of report

Some provincial acts, such as those of Ontario and British Columbia, require the auditor to state in his report whether in his opinion the financial statements *present fairly* the financial position of the corporation and the results of its operations for the period under review in accordance with *generally accepted accounting principles* applied on a basis *consistent* with that of the preceding period. As well as requiring an opinion on the balance sheet and income statement these acts also call for an opinion on the statement of changes in financial position (source and application of funds) where such a statement is presented. Other provincial acts, such as those of Quebec and Nova Scotia, require an opinion only on the balance sheet (although in practice coverage of the income statement as well is customary) and use the older terminology of "true and correct view" (although the more modern terminology of "present fairly" is sometimes held to meet the spirit of these statutory provisions).

In contrast, the revised federal act of 1975 eliminated any details as to the form and contents of the financial statements or of the auditor's report, leaving these to be prescribed by regulation (for the stated purpose of facilitating more timely revisions). The relevant regulation with respect to the auditor's report is as follows:

> **Reg. 44** The financial statements referred to in section 149 of the Act and the auditor's report referred to in section 163 of the Act shall, except as otherwise provided by this Part, be prepared in accordance with the recommendations of the Canadian Institute of Chartered Accountants set out in the CICA Handbook.

By introducing, for the first time, a statutory reference to professional pronouncements on accounting and auditing, the federal act achieved the desirable objective of eliminating many inconsistencies between legal and professional standards. In the past, statutory provisions have frequently reflected the substance of the profession's recommendations, but with an inevitable time lag. Of course, the new federal legislation places an implicit responsibility on the CICA to ensure that appropriate, clear and carefully researched recommendations are issued on a timely basis.

In addition to expressing an opinion on the financial statements as such, the auditor is also required, under certain provincial acts, to report on certain other matters as well. For example, the Ontario act requires the auditor to make such additional statements in his report as he considers necessary if the financial statements are not in agreement with the accounting records, or if he has not received all the information and explanations he has required, or if proper accounting records have not been kept, so far as appears from his examination.

The auditor's responsibility to report calls for the exercise of careful professional judgment. The distinction between circumstances which justify an unqualified opinion and those which call for a reservation of opinion is frequently not clear cut. Value judgments are required in deciding upon the appropriate form of opinion in any given case and, where reservations are required, skill is required in expressing such reservations in a fair, clear and objective manner to the intended readers. As a skilled professional, the chartered accountant engaged as auditor has an implied responsibility to prepare his report with due professional care.

The concepts of fairness, generally accepted accounting principles, and consistency and the CICA audit reporting recommendations are discussed in Chapters 17 and 18.

4.1.4 Responsibility to report subsequently discovered errors in financial statements

A few corporations acts impose an explicit responsibility upon the auditor to take certain actions should he become aware of a material error or misstatement after issuance of the audited financial statements. Under the federal act the auditor's explicit responsibility is to inform the company's directors. The relevant federal provision is:

> **165.7** If the auditor or former auditor of a corporation is notified or becomes aware of an error or misstatement upon which he has reported, and if in his opinion the error or mis-statement is material, he shall inform each director accordingly.

Related provisions call for the directors in such circumstances to prepare and issue revised financial statements or otherwise inform the shareholders of the error or mis-statement. Moreover, any director or officer of the company becoming aware of any error or mis-statement must forthwith notify the auditor and the audit committee.

In a few provincial acts the responsibility is stated slightly differently. The British Columbia act requires, upon discovery of a material mis-statement, that the directors amend the financial statements, that the auditor amend his previously issued audited report, and that the directors mail the amended statement and report to shareholders. The Ontario act is similar but also provides that should the directors fail to mail the amended statement and report to shareholders within a reasonable time, the auditor shall do so if he considers amendment to his previously issued report necessary. Most provincial acts, however, do not at present explicitly define any responsibility with respect to subsequently discovered errors.

In the United States, the *Yale Express* case in 1967 raised the question of legal responsibility (under U.S. securities legislation) for the reporting of subsequently discovered errors. In response to this case the AICPA issued a specific pronouncement (now Section 561 of Statement on Auditing Standards No. 1) which calls for actions by the auditor beyond that prescribed by the above Canadian legislation – for example, failing disclosure by the directors, notification by the auditor to each person known by him to be relying on the financial statements (including regulatory agencies). To date no similar professional pronouncements have been issued in Canada, although consideration of the subject in due course seems probable.

It should be stressed that in none of the foregoing legislation or pronouncements is there any stated or implied obligation on the part of the auditor to conduct any further enquiry or audit after issuance of his audit report except when new information comes to his attention which may affect that report. Post-audit information is discussed in Chapter 18.

4.1.5 Responsibility to make an examination

As previously discussed the federal act establishes an explicit responsibility to make an examination:

163.1 An auditor of a corporation shall make the examination that is in his opinion necessary to enable him to report in the prescribed manner on the financial statements required by this Act to be placed before the shareholders ...

A similar explicit responsibility is provided for in the Ontario and British Columbia acts.

Clearly, the auditor must make an examination before reporting on the financial statements. The words "in his opinion" (newly introduced in the federal act) indicate that the nature and extent of the examination must be a matter of judgment. In exercising this judgment and in carrying out the examination the auditor has an implicit responsibility to use due professional care. Due professional care is both a legal concept (established in case law) and a professional concept (incorporated in generally accepted auditing standards).

Under the federal act the purpose of the required examination is specifically to enable the auditor to report on the financial statements. The auditor may have various secondary objectives for his examination (such as to enable him to provide his client with useful advice on accounting, internal control, taxation, financial planning, and other matters) but such objectives are not a part of his *explicit* statutory responsibilities. Whether *implied* legal responsibilities include such secondary objectives is debatable. Implicit responsibilities derived from statutes can only be established by the courts. Some lawyers consider that an extension of responsibilities by the courts is unlikely when the purpose of the examination has already been explicitly defined in the statute, as in the federal, Ontario, and British Columbia acts. According to this view, an auditor's failure to observe a deficiency in internal control leading in turn to significant losses by his client may be unfortunate but, if the deficiency itself did not affect the accuracy of the financial statements or the reliability of his opinion thereon, no breach of statutory duties has occurred.

The position is less clear under those provincial acts which do not explicitly define a responsibility to make an examination but leave all such responsibilities to be inferred from the holding of the statutory office of "auditor" or from the statutory responsibility to make a report. It was under such an act that the *Pacific Acceptance* judgment of 1970 in Australia suggested that there was a "duty to audit" over and above the examination necessary to form the opinion required by the statute. The case involved certain fraudulent transactions. The Supreme Court of Canada in the *Guardian Insurance* case in 1941 considered a similar problem as the Dominion Companies Act 1934 did not place any specific responsibility on the auditor to make an examination but left such responsibilities to be inferred from the statutory responsibility to make a report. Here the conclusion was that the auditor's duties in a statutory audit were those and only those imposed by the statute.

Nonetheless, there is some difference in legal views as to whether an auditor carrying out a statutory audit has some "duty to audit" which imposes upon him obligations in addition to those which he undertakes in performing a statutory audit with requisite degree of skill and care. It is probably fair to say, however, that any suggestion of an additional "duty to audit" over and above the opinion-forming examination would be strongly opposed by the Canadian profession because of (a) the difficulties of defining the precise additional purpose, its timing, and its materiality criteria, (b) the very high social cost involved in prescribing such audits, and (c) the undesirability of removing from management the prerogative of choosing the extent of desired services beyond the attest function. With the enactment of the new federal act it seems unlikely that the trend in Canadian law will be in the direction of such an additional, nebulous "duty to audit".

In making an examination for the purpose of forming an opinion on the financial statements, the auditor must obviously consider what constitutes sufficient appropriate audit evidence in each particular circumstance. If he fails to examine sufficient appropriate audit evidence, assuming it is available, the courts may determine that he has not fully met his statutory responsibility to make an examination. Such failures could, for example, include the failure to perform customary audit procedures in use throughout the profession, failure to probe suspicious circumstances with extra care, failure to examine readily available external evidence to corroborate the representations of management and employees. A further discussion of audit evidence is deferred until Chapters 6 and 10.

To ensure, as far as possible, that audit evidence will be available the federal act provides the auditor with a statutory right to information and access to records.

164.1   Upon the demand of an auditor of a corporation, the present or former directors, officers, employees or agents of the corporation shall furnish such
a) information and explanations, and
b) access to records, documents, books, accounts and vouchers of the corporation or any of its subsidiaries as are, in the opinion of the auditor, necessary to enable him to make the examination and report required ... and that the directors, officers, employees or agents are reasonably able to furnish.

Similar statutory rights are provided in most of the provincial acts.

Reliance on other auditors

Sometimes the audit evidence available includes the reports of other auditors with respect to investees. Such evidence is particularly important in the case of subsidiary companies whose accounts are consolidated with those of the auditor's client and in the case of investments in effectively controlled companies accounted for on the equity basis. The appropriateness of relying on such evidence is specifically recognized in the new federal act:

163.2   Notwithstanding section 164 [which provides for access to subsidiary records],
a) an auditor of a holding corporation may reasonably rely upon the report of the auditor of a body corporate that is a subsidiary of the holding corporation if the fact of his reliance is disclosed in his report as auditor of the holding corporation; and
b) an auditor of a corporation may reasonably rely upon the report of the auditor of a body corporate that is not a subsidiary of that corporation but is, as prescribed, effectively controlled by the corporation, if the fact of his reliance is disclosed in his report as auditor of the corporation.
163.3   For the purpose of section 163.2 reasonableness is a question of fact.

The Ontario and British Columbia acts provide for reference to the reports of subsidiary auditors but are less specific as to the reasonableness of reliance thereon. Most provincial acts are silent on the issue. Auditors generally recognize certain procedures as being desirable to confirm that reliance on another auditor's report is reasonable in the circumstances.

Reliance on other auditors, and the procedures desirable to justify such reliance, are discussed at greater length in Chapter 17.

4.1.6 Responsibility to attend meetings

Meetings of shareholders

The federal, Ontario, and British Columbia acts give the auditor the right to attend shareholders' meetings. Furthermore they provide that the auditor can

be required to attend. The relevant sections of the federal act are:

162.1   The auditor of a corporation is entitled to receive notice of every meeting of shareholders and, at the expense of the corporation, to attend and be heard thereat on matters relating to his duties as auditor.

162.2   If a director or shareholder of a corporation ... gives written notice ... the auditor or former auditor shall attend the meeting at the expense of the corporation and answer questions relating to his duties as auditor.

166   Any oral or written statement or report made under this Act by the auditor or former auditor of a corporation has qualified privilege.

It is clear from these provisions that the channels of communication between the auditor and the shareholders are not restricted to the auditor's written report. Of course, in the vast majority of cases all significant differences of opinion between management and auditor are satisfactorily resolved by adjustment of the financial statements (including note disclosure), by investigation of further evidence which may change preliminary conclusions, or by both. In the few cases where there remains a reservation in the auditor's mind this reservation can usually be fully conveyed by the wording of his report. Indeed the auditor has a duty to express any such reservations in a clear understandable manner within his report. Nonetheless, the law recognizes that circumstances may arise where the auditor may wish (and may even have an implied responsibility) to make certain clarifying statements at the annual meeting. As a minimum, he has the responsibility to answer any questions relating to the audit, to his audit procedures, or to the basis for his audit opinion (though not, of course, questions regarding management policies unrelated to his audit of the financial statements). The provision for *qualified privilege* protects the auditor from the laws of libel and slander in the performance of his audit duties. At the same time, it might be argued that the auditor has an implied responsibility to be forthright in his communications.

Audit committee meetings

The federal, Ontario, and British Columbia acts require the appointment of an audit committee to review the audited financial statements, give the auditor the right to attend and to call audit committee meetings, and provide that the auditor can be required to attend such meetings. The relevant sections of the federal act are:

165.1   Subject to subsection (2) [providing certain exemptions], a corporation described in subsection 97(2) [one that has issued securities to the public] shall, and any other corporation may, have an audit committee composed of not less than three directors of the corporation, a majority of whom are not officers or employees of the corporation or any of its affiliates.

165.3 An audit committee shall review the financial statements of the corporation before such financial statements are approved under section 152 [by the directors].

165.4 The auditor of a corporation is entitled to receive notice of every meeting of the audit committee and, at the expense of the corporation, to attend and be heard thereat; and, if so requested by a member of the audit committee, shall attend every meeting of the committee held during the term of office of the auditor.

165.5 The auditor of a corporation or a member of the audit committee may call a meeting of the committee.

Other meetings

The Ontario act also gives the auditor the right to attend and be heard at meetings of the board of directors on matters relating to his duties as auditor.

4.1.7 Responsibility to hold office

The external auditor is appointed by shareholders to hold office until the next annual meeting or until his successor is appointed. During this period his statutory responsibilities take precedence over any contractual or other arrangements between the auditor and management. It has sometimes been suggested, therefore, that when an auditor comes into conflict with management or the directors his premature resignation (before expiry of his term of office) could be inconsistent with the best interests of the shareholders and with his statutory responsibilities to them. An Interpretation of the Rules of Professional Conduct summarizes this problem as follows:

> In summary, the auditor of a company is appointed to represent the shareholders and has a duty to them, he should never lightly resign his appointment before reporting and should not resign at all before reporting if he has reason to suspect that his resignation is required by reason of any sharp practice, impropriety or concealment, which it is his duty to report upon. Subject to that general statement, however, there may be exceptional circumstances in a particular case which would justify his resignation and this will be a matter of individual judgment in each case.

The federal act provides for the possibility of an auditor resigning (and, in the case of a loss of independence, imposes a duty to resign). It also provides for the possibility of the shareholders removing an auditor from office.

158.1 An auditor of a corporation ceases to hold office when
(a) he dies or resigns; or
(b) he is removed pursuant to section 159.

159.1 The shareholders of a corporation may by ordinary resolution at a special meeting remove from office the auditor ...

The act, however, provides the auditor resigning or being removed from office with the right to have a written statement circulated to the shareholders.

162.5 An auditor who
(a) resigns,
(b) receives a notice or otherwise learns of a meeting of shareholders called for the purpose of removing him from office,
(c) receives a notice or otherwise learns of a meeting of directors or shareholders at which another person is to be appointed to fill the office of auditor, whether because of the resignation or removal of the incumbent auditor or because his term of office has expired or is about to expire, ...
is entitled to submit to the corporation a written statement giving the reasons for his resignation or the reasons why he opposes any proposed action or resolution.

162.6 The corporation shall forthwith send a copy of the statement ... to every shareholder ...

Similar provisions are contained in the Ontario and British Columbia acts. Such provisions provide shareholders with some protection in those rare cases where an unscrupulous management wishes to conceal a matter to which the auditor, had he remained in office, would have drawn attention in his report. The auditor's statutory right to have a statement circulated to the shareholders might be argued to imply a responsibility on his part to exercise that right when in his opinion it is in the shareholders' best interests to know the circumstances. (In the United States a more explicit provision calls for both a registered company and its retiring auditor to inform the Securities and Exchange Commission separately of all matters of dispute or contention during the previous two years.)

To reinforce these measures, the federal act also requires a succeeding auditor to request a written statement from his predecessor.

162.7 No person shall accept appointment or consent to be appointed as auditor of a corporation if he is replacing an auditor who has resigned, been removed or whose term of office has expired ... until he has requested and received from that auditor a written statement of the circumstances and the reasons why, in that auditor's opinion, he is to be replaced [an additional provision permits a succeeding auditor to be appointed if such a request is unanswered after fifteen days].

Such a requirement, which is not presently contained in any of the provincial acts, goes considerably further than the profession's rules of professional conduct. These rules, as discussed in Chapter 3, merely require the prospective successor to enquire of the incumbent auditor as to circumstances which might influence his decision whether or not to accept the engagement. Interpretations of these rules state that the retiring auditor should reply as a matter of professional courtesy but with care to avoid confidential disclosures without the client's consent. The new federal act, in contrast, by calling for "a written statement of the circumstances and the reasons why, in that auditor's opinion, he is to be replaced" may well impose a duty of candour overriding professional confidentiality. In cases of doubt a retiring auditor should, of course, seek legal advice.

Under the federal act, when a vacancy in the office of auditor occurs between annual general meetings, the vacancy can be filled by the shareholders, the directors (unless the articles of the company prohibit it), or by the court.

4.1.8 Responsibility under provincial securities legislation

A provincial securities act applies to companies who issue securities to the public or whose shares are listed on stock exchanges within that province. Thus a federally incorporated company with shares listed on the Montreal, Toronto, and Vancouver stock exchanges must meet the statutory provisions of the Canada Business Corporations Act and of the Quebec, Ontario, and British Columbia Securities Acts. The provincial securities acts impose statutory responsibilities on auditors with respect to (a) audits of financial statements contained in prospectuses accompanying issues of new securities and (b) audits of the ongoing annual financial statements. Responsibilities with respect to prospectuses are discussed in Chapter 19.

Generally the securities acts do not deal with the appointment, qualifications, or removal of auditors – these matters being left to the corporations acts.

They do, however, impose on the auditor a responsibility to make an examination and a responsibility to report. In the Ontario Securities Act, for example, the auditor is required to make such examination as will enable him to make the required report and in his report he is required to state whether in his opinion the financial statements present fairly the financial position of the corporation and the results of its operations for the period under review in accordance with generally accepted accounting principles applied on a basis consistent with that of the preceding period (wording virtually identical to that contained in the Ontario Business Corporations Act). Under the Ontario Securities Act the auditor is also required to report if the financial statements are not in accordance with the requirements of that act (which may, of course, differ from or extend beyond the requirements of the corporations act under which the company was incorporated). Where the securities act and corporations act conflict, the provincial securities commission is empowered to resolve the difference. Where the securities act requires information additional to the corporations act the company may either (a) prepare its shareholder statements to meet both the securities and corporations acts or (b) file with the provincial securities commission a copy of the shareholder statements meeting the relevant corporations act together with supplementary information to meet the additional requirements of the securities act. In the latter case, the auditor is required to report to the commission on the adequacy of the supplementary information filed.

4.2 Contractual responsibilities

The act of engaging a chartered accountant in his professional capacity, whether it is to request accounting advice or the preparation of financial statements, to appoint him as auditor, or to arrange for any other professional services on a fee basis, establishes a contractual relationship between the client and the accountant. This is true whether or not the contract is reduced to writing.

Common law (derived from court cases) requires that in fulfilling a contractual engagement, a professional must carry out his work with the care and skill to be fairly expected from a practitioner of reasonable competence. This is the legal concept of due professional care. While simple to state, it can lead to great difficulties of interpretation in any particular case. One of the common difficulties arises from uncertainty or ambiguity as to the terms of the contractual engagement. For this reason, many accountants feel it is desirable to document the agreed terms

of any professional engagement in an engagement letter. The significance of a letter however, varies depending on whether it relates to a statutory audit, a non-statutory audit, or a non-audit engagement.

4.2.1 Statutory audit engagements

Once an auditor has been appointed pursuant to provisions of a corporations act, his statutory responsibilities cannot be abridged or modified by contract (whether or not such contractual revisions were to be approved by management, the directors, or the shareholders).[1] The auditor must fulfill his statutory responsibilities in full. He can, however, assume *additional* contractual responsibilities within his role as auditor if that is the wish of both contracting parties.

It is because of the possibility of implied additional contractual responsibilities that many auditors feel engagement letters for statutory audit engagements are desirable. The purpose of such a letter is to clarify whether the auditor's duties are to be limited to his statutory obligations and, if not, to define any additional contractual duties he is to undertake. A principal concern of many auditors is to ensure that they do not inadvertently assume any additional contractual responsibilities with respect to the detection of fraud. If the management of a particular client had always let it be known that they considered it was the auditor's business to catch any defalcations, however caused and of whatever size, it might be argued that the auditor's silence on this issue implied consent and thus created a contractual responsibility where none existed before. For this reason, suggested letters of engagement commonly refer to the fact that audit procedures cannot necessarily be expected to disclose defalcations and other irregularities.

The formal engagement letter approach

The CICA has not as yet issued recommendations on the subject of audit engagement letters. However, a special committee of the Ontario Institute in 1972 issued some suggested wording for such letters.[2] A typical example of an engagement letter (based largely on the Ontario suggested wording) is as follows:

May 15, 1977

Chairman of the Audit Committee,
A. Smith Company Limited,
Any City,
Canada.

Dear Sir:

It is desirable to have a clear understanding of the terms of my engagement as auditor for your company. This letter summarizes my understanding of the terms of my engagement as discussed with the Audit Committee on May 10, 1977.

My statutory function as auditor of your company is to report to the shareholders whether, in my opinion, the annual financial statements present fairly the financial position, results of operations and changes in financial position in accordance with generally accepted accounting principles consistently applied. I will conduct a sufficient examination to discharge fully this statutory obligation to the shareholders. In particular, and in accordance with generally accepted auditing standards, my audit will include an examination of the accounting system, internal controls, and related data. My assessment of the reliability of the accounting system and internal controls will affect the nature, timing and extent of my further auditing procedures.

Because the audit examination will be planned and conducted primarily to enable me to express a professional opinion on the annual financial statements, it will not be designed to identify and cannot necessarily be expected to disclose defalcations and other irregularities. Of course, their discovery may still result from my examination and should any significant ones be encountered, they will be reported to the appropriate person in your company.

In properly organized accounting systems, reliance is placed principally upon the maintenance of an adequate degree of internal control to prevent or detect errors and irregularities. If I believe that it is desirable and practicable to make important improvements in the system of internal control, I shall bring these to your attention. [While the last sentence reflects common usuage, an alternative wording may be preferable and is suggested in the next example.]

The foregoing comments deal only with my statutory obligation as your company's auditor. I am always prepared upon instructions to extend my services beyond these required procedures. In particular, with regard to taxation, management accounting, or other areas in which I am regularly involved professionally I shall at all times be available for advice or assistance.

I understand that the above terms of my engagement as auditor shall remain operative until amended.

Yours truly,

John Doe,
Chartered Accountant

We agree with your understanding of the terms of your engagement as auditor of the company as set out in this letter. [An alternative to this signature is suggested in the next example.]

A. Smith Company Limited

May 17, 1977   per   B. Brown
Chairman, Audit Committee

The above wording (a) confirms the auditor's responsibility to discharge his statutory obligations, (b) makes reference to generally accepted auditing standards and the requirement therein to study internal control, (c) undertakes a responsibility to advise the client of irregularities encountered and of suggestions for improvements in internal control, and (d) confirms that no additional contractual obligations with respect to defalcations are to be assumed. Of course, if further contractual obligations were to be undertaken (whether with respect to fraud detection, systems work, preparation of tax returns, or other matters) they would be specified in the letter. Procedures for coordinating the audit planning with the client's accounting staff and internal audit department might also be included if desired. Some practitioners believe that it is unnecessary to request the client to sign and return such a letter provided that a sentence is added requesting the client to inform the auditor of any disagreement he has with the matters outlined in the letter.

One problem, however, with the foregoing type of engagement letter is that the reference to defalcations may appear to be defining the extent of the auditor's statutory obligations. As already stated, the auditor has no power to limit contractually any responsibilities already imposed by statute; nor do the directors or the audit committee have any authority to agree to a limitation. The problem is that nobody really knows exactly what the statutory responsibilities are or how far they extend. The question of statutory responsibilities with respect to fraud detection is discussed in Chapter 5. Those who favour the foregoing type of engagement letter argue that its intent is not to limit whatever may be the statutory responsibilities – witness the undertaking to fully discharge such responsibilities – but to prevent the inadvertent assumption of any additional contractual obligations with respect to fraud detection or any other matter.

The two-letter approach

Some auditors feel that a preferable way of meeting the objectives of clarifying the terms of the engagement is to (a) issue a formal letter accepting the statutory appointment as auditor and (b) issue an informal letter, for the client's information, describing the auditor's basic approach to the audit. Examples of such letters (requiring adaptation in each particular circumstance) are as follows:

a)

May 15, 1977

Chairman of the Audit Committee,
A. Smith Company Limited,
Any City,
Canada.

Dear Sir:

I hereby accept the appointment as auditor of your company under the Canada Business Corporations Act and look forward to being of service to you and your company.

As we agreed, I will also assist in the preparation of the company's annual income tax and certain other government returns and provide advice on tax and other matters from time to time, as agreed.

Yours truly,

John Doe
Chartered Accountant

Any additional contractual obligations would be added to the foregoing letter.

b)

June 15, 1977

Chairman of the Audit Committee,
A. Smith Company Limited,
Any City,
Canada

Dear Sir:

Following my review of audit plans at the meeting of the Audit Committee on June 10, 1977, I thought it might be useful if I summarized in writing, for your information, the principal points which were covered.

In conducting my audit of your company my objective will be to discharge my statutory function of reporting to the shareholders whether, in my opinion, the annual financial statements present fairly the financial position, results of operations, and changes in financial position in accordance with generally accepted accounting principles consistently applied. To meet this obligation, and in accordance with generally accepted auditing standards, my audit will include an examination of the accounting system, internal controls, and related data. My assessment of the reliability of the accounting system and internal controls will affect the nature, timing and extent of my further auditing procedures.

Reflecting this study of and subsequent reliance on internal control my audit for the year will be divided into two principal components. In the 'interim audit', which I expect to perform principally during the months of July and October my objective will be to study and evaluate the accounting system and internal controls as well as conducting certain tests of transactions. In the 'financial statement audit', which I expect to perform principally during the months of November and January my objective will be to examine audit evidence related to the assets, liabilities, revenues, and expenses reported on your company's financial statements, placing appropriate reliance on internal controls identified during my earlier visits. This audit evidence will include observation of your company's stocktaking procedures on November 30 and confirmation of accounts receivable at the same date.

Because the audit examination will be planned and conducted primarily to enable me to express a professional opinion on the annual financial statements, it will not be designed to identify and cannot necessarily be expected to disclose defalcations and other irregularities. Of course, their discovery may still result from my examination and should any significant ones be encountered, they will be reported to the appropriate person in your company.

In properly organized accounting systems, reliance is placed principally upon the maintenance of an adequate degree of internal control to prevent or detect errors and irregularities. In the event that my audit reveals significant weaknesses in internal control for which I believe improvements are desirable and practicable, I shall bring these weaknesses to the attention of the appropriate person together with any recommendations I may have.

In planning the detailed audit work I will meet with your company's accounting staff and internal audit department in early July in order to ensure the maximum degree of coordination in our procedures. I expect to be in a position to discuss my audit report and findings with your committee at its scheduled meeting on March 10, 1978.

If you have any questions about, or disagreements with, any of the above matters I would be pleased to discuss them with you further. Also, of course, I would be pleased at any time to undertake additional assignments as they might be required.

Yours truly,

John Doe
Chartered Accountant

Advocates of the two-letter approach argue that the first letter (formal acceptance of the statutory engagement) achieves the desired limitation of any unintended contractual extensions without belabouring the contentious area of fraud and without presenting the unattractive image of what some see as a negatively worded letter seeking an advance release for audit deficiencies. The second informal letter then achieves the objective of precluding any misunderstandings as to the auditor's approach to his audit while not requiring any formal response from the company or its audit committee.

There is little doubt that the subject of engagement letters will command renewed attention by the Canadian profession in the future. In the meantime, the two-letter approach just described is, in the writer's view, worthy of careful consideration.

The foregoing two-letter approach also includes a reference to reporting significant weaknesses in internal control. This reference differs somewhat from the Ontario committee wording illustrated previously, but is consistent with the interim audit reporting responsibilities discussed in 9.1.3.

4.2.2 Non-statutory audit engagements

When audits are performed for proprietorships, partnerships and other unincorporated organizations in Canada, where there is no statutory responsibility to have an audit performed, the nature of the services to be performed by the external auditor depend entirely on the agreed contract. It is even more important in these cases, in order to clarify the understanding between the external auditor and his client, that an engagement letter be issued.

In this case a one-letter approach is satisfactory. Suggested wording, adapted from the second letter in the two-letter statutory example, shown in 4.2.1, follows:

May 15, 1977

To the Partners of H. Jones & Company,
Any City,
Canada

Dear Sirs:

Following our discussion of May 10, 1977, I thought it would be useful to have a clear understanding of the terms of my engagement as auditor of your partnership. This letter summarizes my understanding.

Although no statutory function is prescribed for partnerships, since you wish to obtain an unqualified audit opinion if possible, I therefore propose to report to the partners whether the annual financial statements present fairly the financial position, results of operations, and changes in partners' capital in accordance with generally accepted accounting principles consistently applied. To meet this objective and in accordance with generally accepted auditing standards, my audit will include an examination of the accounting system, internal controls and related data. My assessment of the reliability of the accounting system and internal controls will affect the nature, timing and extent of further auditing procedures.

[The paragraph "Reflecting this study of and subsequent reliance on internal control . . . . accounts receivable at the same date.", with appropriate modifications, could be inserted here if desired.]

Because the audit examination will be planned . . . . appropriate person in your company.

In properly organized accounting systems, ... any recommendations I may have.

The foregoing comments deal only with the requirements leading to an audit opinion on the annual financial statements. In addition, I am to prepare the personal tax returns for the partners. You will be relied upon to provide me with the information required to prepare the returns, to examine the returns carefully when I have completed them, and to file them by the due date. Of course, I can take no responsibility for the correctness of the information supplied, other than to the extent I have expressed an opinion on the financial statements of the partnership which will be attached to the returns.

I am always prepared upon instruction to extend my services to other areas in which I am involved professionally (e.g., tax planning, management accounting, systems work) should this be desired.

If you have any questions about, or disagreements with, any of the above matters I would be pleased to discuss them with you further. I appreciate the opportunity to be of service to your partnership.

Yours truly,

John Doe
Chartered Accountant

In some circumstances, where the auditor is performing special audit or other services, the terms of his engagement may be covered in a transmittal letter attached to his final report or in the final report itself (see 19.3). In such cases, a separate engagement letter is unnecessary.

4.2.3 Duty to advise of encountered irregularities and control suggestions

It will be noted that an auditor issuing an engagement letter of some of the types previously described is assuming a contractual commitment to advise his client of any significant errors or irregularities he encounters in the course of his examination and of any important improvements he believes it is desirable and practicable to make in the system of internal control. Advice on such matters has long been an automatic part of most auditors' work and in some countries, such as the United States, is called for as a part of regular professional responsibilities. The auditor, of course, must realize that if he undertakes this commitment and then fails to advise his client as promised, he exposes himself to possible liability for losses suffered as a consequence of this failure.

In the *Pacific Acceptance* judgment of 1970 in Australia it was suggested that a "duty to warn" arose directly out of the statutory responsibilities. The judge commented that:

> The auditors perform their duty to the company and safeguard the interests of the shareholders by making communications properly called for, to the appropriate level of management or the directors, during the course of the audit, with an appropriate report to the shareholders at the annual general meeting. They do not perform such duty if, having uncovered fraud or having suspicion of fraud in the course of the audit, they fail promptly to report it to the directors and perhaps in the first instance according to the circumstances immediately to management.

In the earlier *Guardian Insurance* case in Canada in 1941 reference was made to the auditor's duty to tell the directors of suspicious circumstances encountered. In any event, most auditors would acknowledge a responsibility to advise clients promptly of significant irregularities *encountered in the course of the examination.*

It is important to emphasize the last seven words. An irregularity of $10 000 may be completely immaterial to the financial results of a large corporation. It is not a part of the auditor's normal objective to search for $10 000 irregularities if these are immaterial to the financial statements. Nonetheless, if, in the course of his audit work directed toward an expression of opinion on the financial statements, he fortuitously encounters a $10 000 irregularity (as well may happen), he has an obligation to advise his client immediately of his findings. This obligation to advise his client of an observed irregularity does not by itself imply any obligation to find such an irregularity in the first place. It is important, of course, that discovered defalcations are reported to the appropriate level. Having regard to the *Guardian Insurance* case it would seem prudent for the auditor to ensure that any significant defalcations are reported to the directors or at least to the audit committee.

4.2.4 Non-audit engagements

If a chartered accountant is hired by a client to prepare unaudited financial statements it is important that the client have a clear understanding of the nature of the services being rendered and, if the client is a limited company, that the work being performed would not fulfill statutory audit requirements. If an accountant is to be hired to provide purely accounting and not audit services it is, of course, essential that he not be appointed as auditor. Once an accountant is appointed as auditor his statutory responsibilities cannot be limited by any contractual provision.

Because of the ever-present danger that the terms of an oral contract to provide accounting services will be misunderstood or misinterpreted by one of the parties or by the courts, it is crucial that the contract be documented in the form of an engagement letter. Engagements involving unaudited statements are discussed in Chapter 20.

4.3 Responsibilities in tort

In law, a tort is a private or civil wrong. The law of torts in most jurisdictions is not a written statute but rather an accumulation of landmark decisions by the courts. The significance for the auditor is that responsibilities in tort arise independently of and may extend beyond his statutory and contractual responsibilities.

For many years the law of torts was restricted to physical actions that caused injury or damage. Examples were a vendor's sale of defective merchandise, or a house owner's failure to shovel ice off the sidewalk. There might be no statutory requirement to shovel the sidewalk, and certainly no contract between the house owner and the injured party, and yet the house owner had a responsibility in tort, based on the doctrine of 'foreseeability', for the latter's injury. Originally, the law of tort did not hold persons liable for words or negligent misrepresentation. Today, auditors may be held liable to limited groups of third parties (financial statement users) for negligent misrepresentation in their reports.

The concept of due professional care can thus be seen to be fundamental to responsibilities under each of statute, contract, and tort. The professional standard of due care was discussed in Chapter 3; the legal standard is discussed in Chapter 5. Additionally, Chapter 5 reviews the history of the law of tort as it pertains to the auditor's legal liability.

4.4 Generally accepted auditing standards

Generally accepted auditing standards reflect the profession's perception of current auditing objectives. As such they are not absolute and unchanging truths. Auditing is utilitarian in purpose; its objectives are therefore those which are perceived to have social utility at a particular point in time. Generally accepted auditing standards today reflect the objectives of auditing as recognized by the profession over the last few decades. In Chapter 1, the historical development of auditing objectives was reviewed, including the decision by the Securities and Exchange Commission in 1941 to require a reference in U.S. auditors' reports to generally accepted auditing standards and the adoption by the membership of the AICPA in 1948 of a definition of such standards. Since that time similar standards have been adopted by the accounting profession in several other countries, including New Zealand and Canada, and their substance has been incorporated in professional pronouncements in the United Kingdom.

4.4.1 Generally accepted auditing standards in Canada

Generally accepted auditing standards were introduced formally in Canada during the 1960's – first in the code of ethics of the Quebec Institute (now the Quebec Order) and subsequently into the Rules of Professional Conduct of all the provincial Institutes. In 1975 a set of generally accepted auditing standards was adopted by the Auditing Standards Committee of the CICA. It seems likely that in the near future the previous listings of such standards in the provincial rules will be replaced by a simple reference to the CICA standards.

The generally accepted auditing standards adopted by the CICA (and incorporated in Section 5100 of the CICA Handbook) are as follows:

GENERAL STANDARD
The examination should be performed and the report prepared by a person or persons having adequate technical training and proficiency in auditing, with due care and with an objective state of mind.

FIELD WORK STANDARDS
1. The work should be adequately planned and properly executed. If assistants are employed they should be properly supervised.
2. There should be an appropriately organized study and evaluation of those internal controls on which the auditor subsequently relies in determining the nature, extent and timing of auditing procedures.
3. Sufficient appropriate audit evidence should be obtained, by such means as inspection, observation, enquiry, confirmation, computation and analysis, to af-

ford a reasonable basis to support the content of the report.

REPORTING STANDARDS
1. The scope of the auditor's examination should be referred to in the report.
2. The report should contain either an expression of opinion on the financial statements or an assertion that an opinion cannot be expressed. In the latter case, the reasons therefor should be stated.
3. Where an opinion is expressed, it should indicate whether the financial statements present fairly the financial position, results of operations and changes in financial position in accordance with an appropriate disclosed basis of accounting, which except in special circumstances should be generally accepted accounting principles. The report should provide adequate explanation with respect to any reservation contained in such opinion.
4. Where an opinion is expressed, the report should also indicate whether the application of the disclosed basis of accounting is consistent with that of the preceding period. Where the basis or its application is not consistent, the report should provide adequate explanation of the nature and effect of the inconsistency.

The division of the standards into three classes – the general standard, the field work standards and the reporting standards – reflects the three aspects of the auditor's responsibilities: what he is, what he does, and what he says. The standards are not intended to prescribe detailed auditing procedures. Auditing *standards* relate to the quality of work to be performed, to the objectives to be attained, and to the suitability of the auditor's report. Standards are intended to be universal. Auditing *procedures*, in contrast, are the specific steps performed by the auditor to attain his objectives in a particular audit engagement. Procedures can be expected to vary with the circumstances.

The Introduction to Auditing Recommendations in the CICA Handbook states:

> Among the Recommendations issued, GENERALLY ACCEPTED AUDITING STANDARDS, Section 5100, constitute the basic professional standards with which, in the Committee's view, the auditor should comply when reporting upon financial statements. In exercising his professional judgment as to the procedures required for adherence to such basic standards, the auditor should have regard to the other Auditing Recommendations in the Handbook.

Applicability of the standards

Subject to the general exclusion of banks, insurance companies and not-for-profit organizations, which are not presently covered by Handbook Recommendations, the eight auditing standards apply to all engagements in which the objective is the expression of an opinion on financial statements. The general and field work standards are also applicable to other types of attest engagements (where an opinion is expressed on assertions other than financial statements). Indeed, the general standard concepts of competence and due care are clearly applicable to any professional engagement which a chartered accountant undertakes.

Comparison of Canadian and U.S. standards

There would appear to be no major differences in intent between generally accepted auditing standards in Canada and in the U.S. Nonetheless, there are certain differences in the specific wording. The two countries' standards are compared in Figure 4.a. To some extent these differences reflect merely differences in organization – differing relationships between the national and provincial or state bodies, between standards and ethical rules, and between the locations of auditing and non-auditing pronouncements. To some extent as well the differences reflect an attempt to resolve possible sources of confusion or misinterpretation which have been identified over the years since 1948, when the U.S. standards were first issued. The U.S. standards were adopted by a direct vote of the AICPA membership and, like the Canadian constitution, cannot easily be changed. The Canadian standards, on the other hand, are a committee Recommendation (albeit one that is intended to be more basic than other Auditing Recommendations) and can be modified from time to time to reflect perceived changes in the interpretation or emphasis of different auditing objectives. Some of the differences in the two sets of standards are discussed on the following pages.

4.4.2 Relationship to Rules of Professional Conduct

As indicated in Chapter 3, there is a close relationship and a degree of overlap between the Rules of Professional Conduct adopted in all provinces and generally accepted auditing standards as pronounced by the CICA. The wording of related rules and standards are compared (together with the U.S. standards) on Figure 4.a. Analysis indicates five types of the relationship between the provincial Rules of Professional Conduct and the CICA generally accepted auditing standards. These five types are tabulated in Figure 4.b.

1. *Requirements which are laid down in the Rules of Professional Conduct and repeated in Generally Accepted Auditing Standards solely for completeness*
   Rules 202, 203, and 204 establish professional requirements with respect to due care, competence, and objectivity. As discussed in 4.4.3, the repetition of these concepts in the general standard is solely in the interests of completeness and is not intended in any way to override or modify the provincial Rules.

2. *Requirements laid down in the Rules of Professional Conduct which call for observance of the auditing standards of the profession*
   Generally accepted auditing standards are recommendations of the CICA Auditing Standards Committee. The CICA has no jurisdiction with respect to the enforcement of such standards. Enforcement and discipline are provincial matters. By calling, however, for compliance with the auditing standards of the profession, Rule 206.2 calls for observance of the field work and reporting standards of the CICA, subject to any departures justified to the satisfaction of the relevant provincial Institute or Order. The Interpretations under Rule 206.2 refer to "generally accepted auditing standards" but not specifically to the CICA pronouncements on such standards, which they pre-dated. Now that the CICA standards have been pronounced, it is likely that the Interpretations under Rule 206.2 will be modified in due course to make specific reference to them.

   Likewise, Accounting Recommendations are recommendations of the CICA Accounting Research Committee. The CICA has no jurisdiction with respect to the enforcement of such recommendations. By calling, however, for compliance with the accounting standards of the profession, and furthermore specifically referring to the CICA Recommendations, Rule 206.3 in effect calls for observance of such Recommendations, subject to justified departures. The safety valve provided by the exception for justified departures means that the provincial Institutes and Order retain for themselves, as constitutionally they must, the final decision as to what is justified. It can be expected in practice, however, that the Recommendations will in most circumstances prove persuasive.

3. *Requirements which are primarily laid down in Generally Accepted Auditing Standards and repeated in the Rules of Professional Conduct for emphasis*
   A number of Rules duplicate specific provisions of the Standards, or of accompanying Auditing Recommendations. For example, Rule 206.2(1) on sufficiency of information to justify an opinion duplicates the substance of the third field work standard on sufficient appropriate evidence. Rule 206.2(3) on denials of opinion duplicates part of

Comparison of Canadian and U.S. Generally Accepted Auditing Standards and Provincial Rules of Professional Conduct

1975 Recommended Uniform Rules of Professional Conduct	Generally Accepted Auditing Standards CICA Handbook, 1975	Generally Accepted Auditing Standards SAS 1 — United States
202. A member or student shall perform his professional services with integrity and due care.	**General standard** The examination should be performed and the report prepared by a person or persons having adequate technical training and proficiency in auditing, with due care and with an objective state of mind.	**General standards** 1. The examination is to be performed by a person or persons having adequate technical training and proficiency as an auditor. 2. In all matters relating to the assignment, an independence in mental attitude is to be maintained by the auditor or auditors. 3. Due professional care is to be exercised in the performance of the examination and the preparation of the report.
203. A member shall sustain his professional competence by keeping himself informed of, and complying with, developments in professional standards in all functions in which he practises or is relied upon because of his calling.		
204. A member who is engaged to express an opinion on financial statements shall hold himself free of any influence, interest or relationship, in respect of his client's affairs, which impairs his professional judgment or objectivity or which, in the view of a reasonable observer, has that effect.		
206.2 A member shall not express an opinion on financial statements examined by him. (1) if he fails to obtain sufficient information to warrant an expression of opinion, or (2) if he has not complied in all material respects with the auditing standards of the profession, or (3) if the exceptions or qualifications to the opinion are sufficiently material to nullify the value of such opinion.	**Field work standards** 1. The work should be adequately planned and properly executed. If assistants are employed they should be properly supervised. 2. There should be an appropriately organized study and evaluation of those internal controls on which the auditor subsequently relies in determining the nature, extent and timing of auditing procedures. 3. Sufficient appropriate audit evidence should be obtained by such means as inspection, observation, enquiry, confirmation, computation and analysis to afford a reasonable basis to support the content of the report.	**Standards of field work** 1. The work is to be adequately planned and assistants, if any, are to be properly supervised. 2. There is to be a proper study and evaluation of the existing internal control as a basis for reliance thereon and for the determination of the resultant extent of the tests to which auditing procedures are to be restricted. 3. Sufficient competent evidential matter is to be obtained through inspection, observation, inquiries, and confirmations to afford a reasonable basis for an opinion regarding the financial statements under examination.
205. A member or student shall not sign or associate himself with any letter, report, statement, representation or financial statement which he knows, or should know, is false or misleading, whether or not the signing or association is subject to a disclaimer of responsibility.		
206.1 In expressing an opinion on financial statements examined by him a member shall not (1) fail to reveal any material fact known to him which is not disclosed in the financial statements, the omission of which renders the financial statements misleading, or (2) fail to report any material misstatement known to him to be contained in the financial statements.	**Reporting standards** 1. The scope of the auditor's examination should be referred to in the report. 2. The report should contain either an expression of opinion on the financial statements or an assertion to the effect that an opinion cannot be expressed. In the latter case, the reasons therefor should be stated.	**Standards of reporting** 4. The report shall either contain an expression of opinion regarding the financial statements, taken as a whole, or an assertion to the effect that an opinion cannot be expressed. When an overall opinion cannot be expressed, the reasons therefor should be stated. In all cases where an auditor's name is associated with financial statements, the report should contain a clear-cut indication of the character of the auditor's examination, if any, and the degree of responsibility he is taking.
206.3 Subject to item (3) of rule 206.2 a member shall not express an opinion on financial statements examined by him which are not prepared in accordance with the accounting standards of the profession unless such opinion is suitably qualified; without limiting the generality of the foregoing, if a member expresses an opinion without qualification or exception that financial statements are presented in accordance with generally accepted accounting principles and if such statements depart in any material respect from the recommendations of The Accounting and Auditing Research Committee of The Canadian Institute of Chartered Accountants or its successor(s), such departure must be capable of justification as proper in the particular circumstances.	3. Where an opinion is expressed, it should indicate whether the financial statements present fairly the financial position, results of operations and changes in financial position in accordance with a disclosed basis of accounting, which except in special circumstances should be generally accepted accounting principles. The report should provide adequate explanation with respect to any reservation contained in such opinion. 4. Where an opinion is expressed, the report should also indicate whether the application of such disclosed basis of accounting is consistent with that of the preceding period. Where the basis or the application thereof is not consistent, the report should provide adequate explanation of the nature and effect of the inconsistency.	1. The report shall state whether the financial statements are presented in accordance with generally accepted accounting principles. 2. The report shall state whether such principles have been consistently observed in the current period in relation to the preceding period. 3. Informative disclosures in the financial statements are to be regarded as reasonably adequate unless otherwise stated in the report.

Interpretations of Rules of Professional Conduct

204/1- 28 (Many specific interpretations with respect to objectivity)
206/3 (List of General and Field Work Standards)

Figure 4.a

Relationship Between Rules of Professional Conduct and Generally Accepted Auditing Standards

1. Requirements which are laid down in the Rules of Professional Conduct and repeated in Generally Accepted Auditing Standards solely for completeness
   - Rules 202, 203, and 204 on due care, competence, and objectivity
   - the general standard

2. Requirements laid down in the Rules of Professional Conduct which call for observance of the auditing standards of the profession
   - Rule 206.2(2)
   - calls for observance, in effect, of the field work and reporting standards (subject to justified departures)
   - Rule 206.3
   - calls for observance in effect, of the Accounting Recommendations of the CICA (subject to justified departures)

3. Requirements which are primarily laid down in Generally Accepted Auditing Standards and repeated in the Rules of Professional Conduct for emphasis
   - Rule 206.2(1) on sufficiency of information
   - third field work standard on sufficent appropriate evidence
   - Rule 206.2(3) on denials of opinion
   - second reporting standard (and more specifically thereunder, Auditing Recommendations, par. 5500.57)
   - Rule 206.1 on reservations for inadequate or inaccurate disclosure
   - third reporting standard (and more specifically thereunder, Auditing Recommendations, par. 5500.33)
   - Interpretation 206/3 on the general and field work standards
   - general and field work standards
   - Interpretations 206/6 and 206/7 on the accounting standards of the profession
   - third reporting standard, which makes reference to generally accepted accounting principles, subject to any definition of the latter term contained in Accounting and/or Auditing Recommendations

4. Requirements within the Rules of Professional Conduct which overlap but have wider applicability than provisions in Generally Accepted Auditing Standards
   - Rules 202 and 203 on due care and competence apply to all professional work
   - the general standard addresses itself only to attest engagements
   - Rule 205 on false and misleading statements applies to audits, non-audits, and non-practising members
   - third reporting standard applies to attest engagements (though similar provisions in CICA Handbook, Sec. 8100 extend a responsibility to accounting engagements)

5. Requirements within the Rules of Professional Conduct which are not covered in Generally Accepted Auditing Standards but which affect the conduct of the auditor in planning, executing, and reporting upon his work
   - a large number of Rules including 201 (reputation), 207-210 (confidentiality), 213 (unlawful activities), 300-306 (relations with fellow members), and others

Figure 4.b

the second reporting standard (and more specifically thereunder, Auditing Recommendations par. 5500.57). Rule 206.1 on reservations for inadequate or inaccurate disclosure duplicates part of the third reporting standard (and more specifically thereunder, Auditing Recommendations par. 5500.33). Interpretation 206/3 on general and field work standards duplicates the substance of the corresponding CICA standards, which it pre-dated. Interpretations 206/6 and 206/7 on the accounting standards of the profession overlap the substance of the third reporting standard (referring to generally accepted accounting principles). Many of these overlapping provisions arose because the Rules of Professional Conduct pre-dated the CICA Generally

Accepted Auditing Standards. Now that Rule 206.2(2) enforces, in effect, such standards it can be expected that a few of the specific Rules and Interpretations will be withdrawn as redundant, particularly the recitation of field work and reporting standards. A few overlapping Rules will no doubt be retained, however, in order to provide emphasis or greater certainty or in order to preserve some flexibility, such as the safety valve for justified departures.

4. *Requirements within the Rules of Professional Conduct which overlap but have wider applicability than provisions in Generally Accepted Auditing Standards*

Rules 202 and 203 on due care and competence apply to all professional work whereas the general standard addresses itself only to attest engagements. Rule 205 on false and misleading statements would necessarily be met by every member complying with the third reporting standard; but Rule 205 applies not only to audits but to unaudited financial statements and to non-practising members (e.g. chartered accountants in industry responsible for the preparation of financial statements) as well.

5. *Requirements within the Rules of Professional Conduct which are not covered in Generally Accepted Auditing Standards but which affect the conduct of the auditor in planning, executing, and reporting upon his work*

It must be remembered that there are many Rules of Professional Conduct that are not related to auditing standards and yet have a direct bearing on the external auditor's conduct of an audit engagement. For example, an auditor could fulfill all auditing standards in the sense of communicating clearly an opinion justified by sufficient appropriate evidence carefully evaluated and yet, by breaching the Rules on confidentiality (207 to 210), fail to meet all his professional responsibilities to his client. Other Rules which affect the auditor's conduct are those respecting reputation (201), unlawful activities (213), relations with fellow members (300 to 306), and many others.

4.4.3 The general standard

The examination should be performed and the report prepared by a person or persons having adequate technical training and proficiency in auditing, with due care and with an objective state of mind.

The general standard is concerned with the personal qualities of the auditor, his qualifications, his relationship with his client, and with the general quality of his work. Embodied in this standard are the three auditing concepts of *competence, objectivity,* and *due care.* These concepts are subjective and require a considerable application of professional judgment.

As already stated, they merely repeat the substance of three of the provincial Institutes' Rules of Professional Conduct. Indeed, paragraph 5100.04 in the CICA Handbook states:

The general standard in paragraph 5100.02 is intended to express the spirit of the related rule(s) of professional conduct of each provincial Institute or Order, to which rule(s) the auditor is referred.

Furthermore, the CICA letter accompanying the preceding re-exposure draft of these standards commented that the general standard related to ethical matters within the jurisdiction of the provincial Institutes and Order and that accordingly it was the intention "not to deal further with this topic in the Auditing Recommendations Section of the CICA Handbook, other than including the . . . one general standard in paragraph 5100.02 in the interest of completeness".

It is clear then that the CICA general standard is not to be interpreted as setting any more stringent or less stringent standard than that defined in the detailed Rules of Professional Conduct and accompanying interpretations. The concepts of competence, objectivity and due care were discussed at length in Chapter 3. The same three concepts are contained in the three general standards in the U.S. The only significant difference in wording is the use of the phrase "objective state of mind" in the Canadian Standard to refer to that quality described as "independence in mental attitude in the American standard". Reasons for perferring the term 'objectivity' to 'independence' were discussed in Chapter 3.

4.4.4 The field work standards

The first field work standard

The work should be adequately planned and properly executed. If assistants are employed they should be properly supervised.

It is fundamental that good field work requires adequate planning, careful execution, and proper supervision. The substance of this standard is identical to that of the corresponding U.S. standard. (The addition, in the Canadian standard, of the words "and properly executed" reflects terminology previously adopted in Canadian codes of ethics but undoubtedly implied in any case). Planning, supervision and review are discussed in Chapters 15 and 16.

The second field work standard

There should be an appropriately organized study and evaluation of those internal controls on which the auditor subsequently relies in determining the nature, extent and timing of auditing procedures.

Chapter 1 introduced the idea of an interim audit, in which internal control is studied and evaluated, followed by a financial statement audit, in which the verification of assets, liabilities and income components is completed, placing reliance on internal control where appropriate. The second field work standard expresses this idea. Its intent does not differ from the corresponding U.S. standard. Use of the phrase "those internal controls" indicates that internal control is not necessarily one unitary system but a set of many different controls; the auditor may well rely on some and not on others. Use of the phrase "appropriately organized study" indicates that the degree of organization and depth of the study of a given control may vary with the degree of reliance to be placed on that control; where the reliance is minimum a more curtailed study may suffice, where the reliance is substantial a more complete study (including compliance testing) may be required. The phrase "relies in determining" emphasizes that the study of controls is not carried out as an end in itself but rather to justify the reliance placed on control when designing and evaluating other (substantive) auditing procedures to support the expression of opinion on the financial statements. Use of the phrase "nature, extent and timing" emphasizes that each of these three aspects of audit procedures may be influenced by the observed quality of the system of internal controls. These relationships are discussed at length in Chapter 6, with respect to theory, and in Chapter 9, with respect to practice.

The third field work standard

Sufficient appropriate audit evidence should be obtained, by such means as inspection, observation, enquiry, confirmation, computation and analysis, to afford a reasonable basis to support the content of the report.

Most of the auditor's work consists in gathering, examining and evaluating audit evidence to arrive at an opinion on the financial statements. It is fundamental that the audit evidence gathered be of the right quality and quantity to justify that opinion. The third field work standard expresses this concept in terms of "sufficient appropriate audit evidence" (having the same intent as the U.S. expression "sufficient competent evidential matter"). Use of the phrase "audit evidence" emphasizes that evidence for audit purposes is not restricted to admissible evidence in the legal sense. The Canadian standard provides a slightly longer list of basic audit techniques but the phrase "by such means as" indicates that this list is not intended to be all-inclusive. The phrase "basis to support the content of the report" (in contrast to the U.S. phrase "basis for an opinion") recognizes that upon occasion the report

may properly contain a denial of opinion, which denial in turn must be warranted by the implications of the evidence examined or the insufficiency of the evidence available. The phrase "reasonable basis" implies that neither absolute assurance nor precise accuracy is usually obtainable. These relationships are discussed at length in Chapter 6, with respect to theory, and in Chapter 10, with respect to audit evidence and audit techniques.

4.4.5 The reporting standards

A few very brief comments on the reporting standards are set out below. These standards, and audit reporting in general, are dealt with at greater length in Chapters 17 and 18.

The first reporting standard

The scope of the auditor's examination should be referred to in the report.

This standard does not call for a detailed description but at least a reference to the scope of the auditor's examination – as is commonly included in the scope paragraph of the short form audit report. The Canadian standard corresponds to the last sentence of the U.S. fourth reporting standard. The U.S. standard with its phrase "if any" was intended to cover as well the case of disclaimers of opinion on unaudited financial statements. The Canadian standards, in contrast, do not address themselves to unaudited statements (these being covered separately in Section 8100 of the CICA Handbook).

The second reporting standard

The report should contain either an expression of opinion on the financial statements or an assertion that an opinion cannot be expressed. In the latter case, the reasons therefor should be stated.

This standard refers to the whole objective of the audit process: the expression of opinion. The Canadian standard corresponds to the first two sentences of the U.S. fourth reporting standard. The U.S. phrase "taken as a whole" implies that the opinion does not address each figure on the financial statements separately but rather the entire presentation of financial information taken together. It seems fair to conclude that the same sense is intended by the Canadian standard and that the phrase "taken as a whole" was omitted solely to avoid any inferred prohibition of an opinion being expressed on one statement (such as the balance sheet alone) when circumstances so demand.

The third reporting standard

Where an opinion is expressed, it should indicate whether the financial statements present fairly the financial position, results of operations and changes in financial position in accordance with an appropriate disclosed basis of accounting, which except in special circumstances should be generally accepted accounting principles. The report should provide adequate explanation with respect to any reservation contained in such opinion.

This standard recognizes that an audit opinion must indicate the degree of correspondence of the financial statements with an agreed-upon set of established criteria (appropriate disclosed basis of accounting). It goes on to add that, except in special circumstances (special purpose statements), those established criteria are "generally accepted accounting principles". Substantially the same result is accomplished in the U.S. standards somewhat differently. The U.S. first reporting standard, to which this standard corresponds, refers exclusively to "generally accepted accounting principles" but par. 620.04 of Statement on Auditing Standards No. 1 states that the first reporting standard does not apply to special purpose statements (such as cash basis statements) which do not purport to present financial position or results of operations. The Canadian standard also incorporates the word "fairly" which has traditionally been used in the audit reports of both countries. The relationship of "fairness" to "generally accepted ac-

counting principles" is discussed in Chapter 17.

The U.S. third reporting standard calls, in effect, for a reservation of opinion in the event of inadequate financial statement disclosure. No corresponding Canadian standard was issued on the grounds that the sense was already contained in the Canadian third reporting standard; a reservation of opinion is required if generally accepted accounting principles are not met and such principles in Canada clearly include disclosure of "any information required for fair presentation" (CICA Handbook, par. 1500.05).

The fourth reporting standard

Where an opinion is expressed, the report should also indicate whether the application of the disclosed basis of accounting is consistent with that of the preceding period. Where the basis or its application is not consistent, the report should provide adequate explanation of the nature and effect of the inconsistency.

Accounting presentation necessarily involves many choices from among alternative acceptable accounting methods or valuations. Such choices must be made using careful judgment. Because a subjective element is necessarily present in all such judgment, this standard recognizes the importance of at least exercising that judgment in a consistent manner so that successive years' financial statements will be comparable. This standard corresponds to the U.S. second reporting standard.

4.5 Audit committees

Reference was made earlier in this chapter to the statutory requirements to appoint audit committees under the federal, Ontario, and British Columbia acts. The growth of audit committees in Canada was in part a result of several highly publicized corporate failures in the 1960's – the largest of which was the bankruptcy of Atlantic Acceptance. Concern was expressed following these failures that (a) the rights of minority shareholders should be better protected, (b) the responsibilities of directors should be better defined, and (c) communication between the directors and the external auditor should be improved. Each of these objectives, but most particularly the third, could be more easily met if a special committee of the directors was specifically charged with the responsibility of reviewing the audited financial statements, on behalf of the directors, to see that they properly presented the financial information on which all shareholders would be relying. Accordingly, in the late 1960's the Ontario Select Committee on Company Law, the Hughes Commission on Atlantic Acceptance, and a special committee of the CICA all

recommended that corporations acts require the establishment of audit committees. These reports also describe in varying degrees the purposes and responsibilities of such committees. It can be expected that other provinces will in due course follow the federal, Ontario and British Columbia precedents in requiring audit committees. In the meantime, many companies that have not been so required by statute have voluntarily accepted audit committees as good business practice – a practice also well accepted in the United States. Those audit committees required by statute have frequently found it useful to perform additional functions beyond the minimum statutory requirements.

Statutory requirements

Provisions vary slightly from jurisdiction to jurisdiction. Those in the federal act were quoted earlier in this chapter. In summary, the common features are:

1. A corporation with publicly traded securities is required to have an audit committee elected annually from its Board of Directors.

2. The minimum size of the committee is three, and half or more of its members must be "outside directors" (directors who are not officers or employees of the corporation or its affiliates); the rationale is that outside directors may be more objective in their assessment of the financial statements and of the responsibility to shareholders than management directors.
3. The committee is required to review the financial statements before they are submitted to the full Board of Directors.
4. The auditor has the right to appear before and be heard by the committee at any meeting.
5. The committee may require attendance by the auditor at any or every meeting.
6. The auditor or any committee member may call a meeting of the committee.

Audit committee objectives

Although the statutory requirements may be limited to those summarized above, a useful set of objectives for an audit committee would include satisfying itself that:

1. The audited financial statements present fairly the financial position and results of operations and that the auditors have no reservations about them.
2. There are no unresolved issues between the management and the auditors that could affect the audited financial statements.
3. Where there are unsettled issues that do not affect the audited financial statements (e.g. disagreements regarding correction of internal control weaknesses, or the application of accounting principles to proposed transactions) there is an agreed course of action leading to the resolution of these matters.
4. Generally, there is a good working relationship between management and the auditors.
5. There are adequate procedures for review of interim statements and other financial information prior to distribution to shareholders.

Operation of an audit committee

As a minimum an audit committee must meet once a year to review the annual audited financial statements, usually a few days prior to the meeting of the Board of Directors which will formally approve the statements. It is common for both representatives of the external auditors and representatives of financial management to be invited to this meeting. Usually, but not always, the chairman of the committee is one of the outside directors. A common practice is for the chairman to ask financial management to discuss the financial statements (which are, after all, the representations of management and the directors),

commenting on results for the past year, new items in the statements, significant changes from the prior year, and so on. The auditors may then be asked for any comments they have concerning the financial statements. This request gives the auditors an opportunity to refer to any contentious matters of accounting presentation, to any areas where justifiable alternative accounting methods exist of which the committee might wish to be aware, and to any disagreements they have not been able to resolve with management. Of course, it is to be expected that the auditors will have reviewed all such matters with management beforehand and in the vast majority of cases all contentious points will have been satisfactorily resolved prior to the audit committee meeting.

Finally, the chairman may ask the auditors to review their audit report, explain any reservations (in the rare cases where reservations exist), and perhaps provide committee members with an overview of the audit work performed. Committee members are then usually given an opportunity to direct questions to financial management or to the auditors respecting either the financial statement presentation or the audit work. Such questions may include questions concerning areas of judgment (such as the adequacy of the allowance for doubtful accounts, obsolescence and warranty provisions), clarification of accounting policies (such as foreign exchange translation, consolidation policies, equity accounting), and identification of major audit procedures performed (such as with respect to accounts receivable, inventories, fixed assets, review of internal control). A common procedure is for the committee to ask the auditors, with management absent, whether they received full cooperation and all the information they required from management; likewise it is common for the committee to ask management, with the auditors absent, whether they are satisfied with the performance and conduct of the auditors and whether they would recommend their re-appointment for the coming year. The final result of the audit committee's deliberation will usually be a recommendation to the Board of Directors that the audited financial statements (including the summary of accounting policies and the accompanying notes) be approved. Only the British Columbia act, however, actually requires a report by the audit committee.

In addition to the foregoing procedures, some audit committees have undertaken additional functions including some or all of the following: (a) a review of the terms of engagement (and the engagement letter) of the external auditors; (b) a review of the major recommendations which the auditors may have made during the year on internal control, accounting, and other matters; (c) questioning of the external auditors as to their assessment of the company's internal control, as to any defalcations encountered by them in the course of their audit, and as to the integration of their work with the activities of the internal audit department; (d) a review of any other audited financial statements apart from the annual shareholder statements (for example, statements in prospectuses); (e) a review of the unaudited quarterly financial statements (possibly with the external auditors present not as auditors but as accounting advisers); (f) a review of the external auditors' fees; (g) a review of other information appearing in the company's annual report such as supplementary schedules, price-level adjusted statements, financial forecasts (if any), and the president's and/or directors' report to the shareholders.

Depending on the extent of these additional functions chosen, an audit committee may meet from once to four times a year. Where more than one meeting is held per year, it is often convenient to allocate one meeting to a major review of accounting policies, another to a major review of the auditor's work, another to the auditor's recommendations etc.

Importance of audit committees to the auditor

The development of audit committees in Canada in recent years has been welcomed by the accounting profession. On the one hand, it has helped the directors to discharge their responsibility of issuing and approving proper financial statements. At the same time, it has strengthened the independence of the auditor by giving him a forum in which to bring important matters to the attention of the directors. Additionally, it has given the auditor a valuable opportunity to have the quality of his professional services observed by the outside directors of his corporate clients.

4.6 Reference material

Canada Business Corporations Act (1975).
Provincial corporations act of the reader's province.
CICA Handbook – Auditing Recommendations, Section 5100, "Generally accepted auditing standards".

AICPA Statement on Auditing Standards No. 1, Sections 110 and 150, "Responsibilities and functions of the independent auditor" and "Generally accepted auditing standards".

4.7 Questions and problems

Review and discussion

1. State the responsibilities of an auditor upon accepting an audit engagement.
2. During the course of your interim examination of Correct Co. Ltd., you discover that the prior year's financial statements contained a material error. What is your responsibility to report this error?
3. What is an auditor's responsibility with respect to the detection of fraud and other irregularities?
4. Describe the purpose and content of engagement letters. In what respects should statutory and non-statutory engagement letters differ?
5. Discuss the reasons for the field work standards of generally accepted auditing standards.
6. What are the typical duties and objectives of audit committees?
7. What is meant by the term "due care" in carrying out an audit engagement?
8. Describe the relationship between rules of professional conduct and generally accepted auditing standards.

9. Why is it necessary to review and evaluate the internal control system of a small audit client?
10. In an auditor's report, the auditor is required to comment on the consistency of accounting principles with respect to those followed in the previous year. How may an auditor do this if he is performing an audit for the first time?

Problems

1. During his audit of B. Cement Co. Ltd., CA discovered a "paid cheque" made out to "cash" in the amount of $25 000 and endorsed by the controller and the vice president sales. When he discussed this item with the controller (also a chartered accountant), the controller closed his office door and told him it was a payment to an unidentified individual to ensure that B. Cement would get the contract for a new office complex. The controller further stated, "This kind of thing is common in the construction industry – besides the amount is not material to the financial statements, so you should not worry about it."

a) As CA, what are your moral, professional and legal responsibilities to the client?

b) What responsibilities, if any, do you have with respect to the attitude of the controller, a fellow CA. How would you resolve them?

2. The audit of XYZ Ltd. was near completion. The draft financial statements of the Company were under review by their auditors, Taylor, Barton & Co. In her review, Barbara Taylor, the audit partner, noticed that the Company did not comply with certain statutory information requirements. She then phoned the president of XYZ and told him that the provincial statutes required remuneration of officers and directors to be disclosed (usually in a note to the financial statements). The president replied that some of the minority shareholders get very upset when they see how much some of the executives are paid. He went on to say, "If the government insists on that information we will issue them a separate set of statements at a later date."

a) What are Barbara Taylor's responsibilities in this situation?

b) What should be her reply to the president of XYZ?

3. Dreher, Robinson & Co., Chartered Accountants, recently became auditors of Safety Pin Ltd. All the proper procedures had been followed with respect to the resignation of the previous auditors. During the current year's audit Dreher discovered that a series of material errors of the prior year had escaped the attention of the former auditors.

a) What are Dreher's responsibilities to his client, to his profession, and to the previous auditors?

b) What procedures should Dreher follow in this situation?

4. Lionel, Watson & Co., Chartered Accountants, recently rendered an unqualified opinion on the financial statements of Walters Manufacturing Ltd. Subsequent to issuing this opinion it was discovered that Walters' largest customer (Fly by Nite Ltd.) went bankrupt just before Walters' year-end. At the time of the bankruptcy, Fly by Nite was indebted to Walters for approximately $75 000 (25% of the net profit of Walters). It was not expected that any of this amount would be recoverable. Mr. Lionel phoned the president of Walters to discuss the situation. Mr. Walters stated that he did not want to adjust the financial statements as they had already been sent out to the shareholders. His proposal was to treat the loss as an expense of the following period, disclosing it as an extraordinary item.

a) What are Lionel's responsibilities to the shareholders of Walters Manufacturing?

b) What should Lionel's response be to Mr. Walters' proposal?

5. Hampton, Campbell & Co., Chartered Accountants, have been the auditors of Nation-Wide Sporting Goods Ltd. for a number of years. Recently the brother of Mr. Jones, the audit partner in charge, was appointed Vice-President and General Manager of Nation-Wide.

a) Does this pose an independence problem for Mr. Jones?

b) What procedures should Mr. Jones follow in this situation?

6. (CICA adapted) The president of R Ltd. (a small distribution company with 35 employees) has just telephoned F. Jones CA to ask if he would "do an audit of the company". The president explained that R Ltd. has applied for a substantial bank loan and was informed that the bank would require audited financial statements of the company. F. Jones' name had been selected by the president from a list of local firms supplied by the bank.

The president indicated that the company had never had an audit, that he was not sure what the audit would involve and what benefits to the company and himself would result. He asked Jones to come to the company's offices to discuss the terms and arrangements for the engagement with him and other officers of the company.

a) Jones intends to explain carefully to the officers of R Ltd. the extent and limits of the responsibilities he would assume if he accepted the audit engagement. What points would he make?

b) What other matters would Jones want to discuss at the meeting?

7. During the audit of XYZ Co. Ltd., CA noted a number of different problems including internal control weakness, generally accepted accounting principles not being followed, monetary errors and deficiencies in statement presentation. As a result of discussions with management, and subsequent adjustments, CA was able to resolve most of the problem areas so that there would be no material misstatements in the financial statements (to be issued in two weeks).

a) What are CA's general responsibilities and specific responsibilities in this circumstance to the directors of XYZ, to the shareholders, and to the audit committee?

b) What procedures would you follow in order to complete the engagement? (Assume that the audit committee meeting was to take place the following week.)

c) What do you feel is the role of the audit committee in this situation?

8. (CICA adapted) In each of the following four unrelated circumstances, explain what course of action the CA should follow in order to discharge his professional and ethical responsibilities:

a) CA is employed by a firm of chartered accountants practising in a small town. Early in 1976, he reviews with the principal shareholder the draft 1975 financial statements of G Ltd., a building contractor. CA notes that the company's deteriorating cash position is so serious that he believes that the company is facing bankruptcy.

CA subsequently reviews the draft 1975 financial statements of K Ltd., also a client, and notes that the company has a large overdue account receivable from G Ltd., against which no allowance for doubtful accounts has been provided. When CA questions the owner of K Ltd. on the collectibility of the account, he is convinced that the owner is not aware of the actual financial condition of G Ltd.

b) CA is approached by J, an insurance agent, with the following proposal. When counselling his clients on the purchase of Key Man Life Insurance, CA will refer his clients to J. In return J will pay CA 10% of his commission on all policies sold through such referrals. In addition, J will undertake to refer to the CA certain of his clients who require estate planning services. J points out that he has a similar arrangement with X, another chartered accountant, and that, in fairness to all concerned, he will refer to CA only those clients for whom CA offers a lower fee than that offered by X.

c) CA is in charge of the audit of P Ltd., a public company. CA is asked by an economist, who is doing research for a thesis on the financial operations of firms in the same industry as P Ltd., if CA would contribute any information or views on the financial operations of P Ltd. The economist promises to keep confidential any information received from CA.

d) R Ltd. is a small mining company whose principal shareholders are actively promoting the company's shares. CA, the auditor of the company for several years, is in the company's offices before the year-end conducting a test of transactions when he discovers a copy of a set of interim financial statements recently prepared and apparently sent to the company's bank. These were prepared by the company's accounting staff without CA's knowledge. They are clearly marked "unaudited" and CA's name does not appear on them. A quick scrutiny reveals that the statements appear to overstate net income by a material amount.

9. The President and other senior officials of Terminal Motors Limited, a public corporation with a December year-end, have become increasingly upset with the quality of service provided by their auditors, Bright, Sharp & Co. In September the poor quality of the management letter issued at the conclusion of the interim audit brings matters to a head. In that letter Bright, Sharp & Co. are critical of a number of allegedly poor accounting practices. The President resolves to replace the auditors immediately. He asks Bright, Sharp & Co. for their resignation. They refuse.

a) How should the President proceed in getting rid of the former auditors (the President and other officers hold 40% of the shares)?

b) Assuming that Bright, Sharp & Co. had in fact provided a good service over the years and that their observations in the management letter were correct, state the various courses of action which they might follow.

Legal Liability

Recent years have seen a dramatic increase in litigation involving public accountants. Partly this increase reflects the growth of "consumerism" in the modern world. If someone has been hurt, or suffered a financial loss, someone else is surely to blame. And the someone else, particularly if it is a large firm with substantial assets and insurance coverage, may appear profitable to sue. In a great number of cases, one of such parties sued has been a firm of public accountants. For reasons discussed later in this chapter, the current wave of litigation has been most pronounced in the United States. But important cases, including both the oldest and some of the newest, have occurred in the United Kingdom as well. Nor have other countries, such as Australia and Canada, been entirely exempt from the current trend.

The vast majority of engagements undertaken by public accountants are completed quietly and uncontentiously to the satisfaction of all parties concerned. The publicity surrounding the significant number (though actually a small proportion) of engagements ending in litigation has, however, made legal liability a most topical, if unwelcome, subject of interest among public accountants today. The purpose of this chapter is to review briefly the legal liability of the public accountant (particularly in the role of auditor) making reference to a few of the important court cases involved. Detailed references and annotations are not attempted; for these the reader should turn to publications such as those listed in 5.7. This review, for purposes of a general audit text, must necessarily be superficial as well as subject to the untutored perspectives of a non-lawyer. Moreover, each of the court cases cited relates to particular statutory and case law which can vary importantly from country to country and, even within the same jurisdiction, from year to year. Principles applied in the United States may not be applicable to a similar situation in Canada. Principles applied in a leading case of the past may since have been overtaken by legislative amendment or a subsequent decision. In any specific circumstance encountered in practice the reader must of course seek competent legal advice.

The legal responsibilities of an auditor have been reviewed in Chapter 4 under the headings of *statutory responsibilities, contractual responsibilities*, and *responsibilities in tort*. The specific responsibilities will vary depending on the precise provisions of the relevant statute or contract as well as on the general case law interpreting the statute or governing the contracts or torts. If the auditor fails to discharge these responsibilities properly he may become legally liable to certain parties. The majority of errors of commission or omission which expose a public accountant to legal liability fall under the *law of negligence*. Negligence results in the failure to perform a legal duty or the failure to perform that duty with the requisite standard of care.

Whether the duty is statutory, contractual, or one in tort may affect the technical nature of the action brought against the auditor. An action for negligence brought by third parties will generally be an action in tort whereas one brought by the auditor's client will generally be for breach of contract. The differences relate to the origin of the duty of care; the parties to whom that duty extends; the timing, nature, and extent of available remedies; the availability of certain defences (such as contributory negligence); and the jurisdiction of the court involved. Nonetheless, the substance of any such case turns on the question of negligence – and this chapter therefore begins with a review of the law of negligence and the related legal standard of due care.

Occasionally, actions of the practising public accountant go beyond mere negligence and expose him to the charge of fraud or to the charge that he has participated in a fraud. The charge of fraud may be made in connection with a civil suit (between private parties) or in a criminal suit (between the crown and defendant).

The chapter concludes with a brief overview of the current trend of litigation in the United States and a review of its parallels to, or differences from, possible future developments in Canada.

5.1 The law of negligence

Negligence in common usage means "the want of proper care or attention". In law, however, its definition is more restrictive than mere carelessness. A man without dependents may invest his funds recklessly and hurt only himself; this is not legal negligence. But if a paid investment counsellor gives careless advice he may be liable to his injured client for his professional negligence.

5.1.1 Elements of negligence

In law, liability for negligence arises where the following four elements are present:

1. a legal duty of care,
2. a breach in that duty of care,
3. proof that damage has resulted,

4. a reasonably proximate connection between the breach of duty and the resulting damage.

In negligence litigation under common law the burden of proof that these four elements are present falls upon the plaintiff. He need not establish this proof beyond all reasonable doubt, as in the case of criminal proceedings, but he must at least point to a preponderance of evidence.

Legal duty of care

The professional concept of due care has been discussed in the previous two chapters and is required both by the Rules of Professional Conduct (with respect to all professional services) and by generally accepted auditing standards (with respect to auditing services). If an auditor is required to justify his auditing work before the Discipline Committee of his provincial Institute, it is this professional standard of due care to which he must refer. Parallelling this concept is the legal concept of due care. Implicit in the legal duty of an auditor to report is a duty to report with due care. Implicit in the legal duty to make an examination is the duty to examine with due care. If an auditor is called upon to justify his professional work before the courts, it is this legal standard of due care to which he must refer.

The two concepts are not inconsistent. In most areas they overlap and complement one another. In assessing whether or not a chartered accountant has measured up to the legal standard of care the courts will give consideration to accepted standards of practice within the profession and particularly to the authoritative pronouncements of the profession. The close relationship between the professional and legal standards is recognized in the AICPA Statement on Auditing Standards No. 1 which quotes from *Cooley on Torts* as to the meaning of due care:

> Every man who offers his service to another and is employed assumes the duty to exercise in the employment such skill as he possesses with reasonable care and diligence. In all these employments where peculiar skill is prerequisite, if one offers his service, he is understood as holding himself out to the public as possessing the degree of skill commonly possessed by others in the same employment ... But no man, whether skilled or unskilled, undertakes that the task he assumes shall be performed successfully, and without fault or error. He undertakes for good faith and integrity, but not for infallibility, and he is liable to his employer for negligence, bad faith, or dishonesty, but not for losses consequent upon pure errors of judgment.

Nonetheless, the legal concept of due care is not necessarily identical to the professional concept. The legal concept is influenced both by legislative provisions and by past decisions in the courts. Such provisions and decisions may on occasion reach beyond previous professional standards – or address specific matters on which professional pronouncements are silent. But the auditor who does not comply with the professional standards adopted by the profession may have grave difficulty in demonstrating that he employed the degree of skill to be expected under the law.

Breach of duty of care

Identifying a breach of a legal duty of care (whether that duty arises out of statute, contract, or tort) necessarily involves defining the requisite standard of care. In defining this standard the law looks to neither the highest nor the lowest standards which may exist in practice, but rather appeals to the concept of the "reasonable man" or the "prudent practitioner".

Proof that damage has resulted

Carelessness of the auditor in fulfilling his legal duties does not in itself give another party a right of action. The other party must have suffered damage as a result of that carelessness. Nonetheless, a proven breach of the duty of care in the absence of proof of damage may still result in some portion of the legal costs of an action being awarded against the negligent auditor.

Proximate connection

An auditor might carelessly issue a clear opinion on distorted financial statements and a shareholder might subsequently suffer financial losses when the distortions become known. Nonetheless, if that shareholder never saw the distorted financial statements, and never placed any reliance on them, there might be no connection between his loss and the auditor's carelessness – in which case, the auditor might argue that no liability for negligence should arise. In cases where a shareholder received and read such statements he will ordinarily be able to establish the element of reliance.

Defences

Defences to allegations of negligence first attempt to demonstrate that one of the four necessary elements are missing. Failing this, the defendant attempts to establish the plaintiff contributed to the damage.

5.1.2 Duty of care to clients

In a non-statutory engagement the public accountant's client is the person (if a sole proprietor), partnership, association, or company which appoints him. The relationship between the public accountant and his client is a contractual one and the accountant's role is that of an independent contractor rather than agent or employee. In a statutory audit, as discussed in the previous chapter, the company to be audited is sometimes similarly held to be the public accountant's client and the relationship between the accountant and that company to be again essentially a contractual one wherein the statutory duties may in essence become a part of the contract. For the moment we shall consider only the accountant's duties to his contractual client – and later turn to his duties to other parties, such as the shareholders of the audited company and third parties, who may read his report.

Some lawyers believe that express contractual terms can override statutory provisions vis-a-vis the company itself (though not vis-a-vis its shareholders). In view of the sweeping liabilities to third parties in tort, however, the precise definition of contractual duties in a statutory audit may be academic. For all practical purposes, therefore, the chartered accountant should proceed on the basis that statutory duties cannot be restricted, although additional duties can be imposed, by contract.

As discussed in Chapter 4, the chartered accountant also has a duty of care in tort that is independent of the agreement between the parties. A duty in tort may arise whenever one person's relationship to another is such that his actions or omissions could reasonably be expected to cause injury to that other person or his property.

The distinction between contract or tort as the origin of duty to a client is not of great moment for the auditor but does have some consequences. It may affect the measure of damages and the time period permitted under the statute of limitations between failure to perform the duty and commencement of an action.

Duties in audit engagements

The contractual duties owed to a client in most audit engagements seem clear. They are to perform with due care the necessary examination to enable an opinion to be expressed on the financial statements and to express that opinion using due care. However, attendant responsibilities to these primary duties are not always clear. Some of the additional responsibilities with respect to independence, subsequent discovery of errors, attendance at meetings, etc., have already been discussed. But other questions arise. Does the auditor have the duty to check for minor fraud in the absence of a specific request that he do so? Is the chartered accountant negligent in failing to detect a material fraud in the performance of a normal audit examination? What duties attach to other ancillary services provided by the chartered accountant in conjunction with his audit – the preparation of tax returns, accounting advice, management consulting, etc.? These questions will be con-

sidered under the heading "legal standards of care" later in this chapter.

Because of the possibility of implied *additional* contractual responsibilities (over and above statutory ones) the importance of committing the terms of the contract to writing (in an *engagement letter*) has already been suggested. In non-statutory audit engagements the terms of the auditor's engagement are determined wholly by contract, whether expressed or implied.

Duties in non-audit engagements

When a practising chartered accountant is engaged to provide other professional services than auditing there is always the danger that audit responsibilities will be later inferred. In an English case an accountant was held liable for negligence in failing to detect a fraud perpetrated by the bookkeeper of a firm of solicitors. The accountant's defence that he had been hired only to balance the books and prepare the financial statements was dismissed when the plaintiff testified that the terms of the engagement included checking for fraud. These terms had been agreed orally with the defendant's former partner, now deceased, thirteen years before the fraud was perpetrated and before the defendant even became a partner!

In another English case an accountant was held liable for damages, owing to an employee fraud, where his understanding again was that he was employed only to balance the books and prepare financial statements without audit. In his summing up to the jury, the judge stated that they could not presume, merely because of the absence of an audit certificate, that a complete audit had not been contracted for.

The best known recent example of the later inference of audit responsibilities occurred in 1965 with *1136 Tenants* v. *Rothenberg* case in the United States. In this case a realty agent orally retained a CPA firm to prepare financial statements for an apartment cooperative for an annual fee of $600. The CPAs' accompanying transmittal letter stated that the financial statements had been "prepared from the books" and that "no independent verifications were undertaken thereon". The courts awarded some $200 000 damages to the client corporation for the CPAs' alleged failure to audit and discover defalcations by the managing agent. It was following this case that more explicitly worded disclaimers of opinion on unaudited statements were called for by professional pronouncements both in the United States and Canada.

These cases amply demonstrate the need for a clear understanding between client and accountant as to the terms of the engagement. The importance of an engagement letter for all non-audit engagements has already been suggested.

5.1.3 Duty of care to shareholders in a statutory engagement

There is little question as to the auditor's responsibility to shareholders. In a statutory engagement the shareholders appoint the auditor and the auditor's report is addressed to the shareholders. As previously discussed, the federal, Ontario and British Columbia Corporations Acts give the auditor the right to be heard at shareholders' meetings and provide that he can be required to attend and answer questions relating to his duties as auditor. The background papers to the federal act emphasized the auditor's role as an appointee of the shareholders. It can reasonably be argued that there is a fiduciary relationship between the auditor and the shareholders whatever the nature and terms of any contractual relationship between the auditor and the company itself. In the view of some lawyers, this fiduciary relationship gives to the shareholders the same legal rights as if they were contracting parties with the auditor. Again, however, in view of the sweeping liabilities to third parties in tort, the precise definition of fiduciary duties to shareholders may be academic. For all practical purposes, the auditor's statutory duties are owed both to the company and to its shareholders and an auditor may be liable to both for any negligence in the performance of such duties.

5.1.4 Duty of care to third parties

As the purpose of auditing is to add credibility to financial statements, it is clear that many persons other than the client itself will be placing reliance on the auditor's work and his report. If the work is performed or the report prepared negligently, many persons may suffer financial harm. It is important therefore to consider what duty of care an auditor owes to *third parties* with whom he has neither a contractual nor a fiduciary relationship.

In general, there are three possible origins of a duty of care to non-contracting third parties. First, the duty of care may be created by statute (as already discussed with respect to shareholders). Second, there may be legal means whereby the third party can make himself a party to the contract. Third, and most important, circumstances may be such as to create a relationship between the auditor and a third party which imposes upon the auditor a duty of care directly to that third party under the laws of tort.

Subrogation of contractual rights

Certain limited classes of third parties can become parties to the contract by a subrogation of rights of the client. Thus, an insurance company which pays a fidelity claim for embezzlement of a client's assets may have acquired the right to sue the auditor for breach of contract in negligently failing to detect that fraud.

Unrecognized parties to the contract

Sometimes apparent third parties can by circumstance and legal decision be made parties to the contract. Thus, in an English case where a bank requested an audit of a client before approving a loan, the court found that the chartered accountant had a contractual relationship with the bank regardless of the fact that the corporate client paid the audit fee.

Development of the law of torts

For many years in English law the defence of "privity of contract" was absolute against third party charges of negligence. In 1883, however, the *Heaven* v. *Pender* case introduced into the law of torts the first concept of a duty of care to third parties:

Whenever one person is by circumstances placed in such a position with regard to another that everyone of ordinary sense who did think would at once recognize that if he did not use ordinary care and skill in his own conduct with regard to those circumstances he would cause danger and injury to the person or property of the other, a duty arises to use ordinary care and skill to avoid such danger.

This general formula was further refined in England by the "foreseeability test" introduced in the *Donoghue* v. *Stevenson* case of 1932. This case stated that a defendant would be negligent to third parties if he was in a position (a) to reasonably foresee certain consequences of his actions, and (b) to reasonably foresee that certain third parties would be closely and directly affected by the action:

You must take reasonable care to avoid acts or omissions which you can reasonably foresee would be likely to injure your neighbour. Who, then, in law is my neighbour? The answer seems to be – persons who are so closely and directly affected by my act that I ought reasonably to have them in contemplation as being so affected when I am directing my mind to the acts or omissions which are called in question.

Negligent misrepresentation initially distinguished

The English courts, however, initially restricted the foregoing concepts to acts which could cause injury or physical damage. The *Derry* v. *Peek* case of 1889 stated that there could be no liability to third parties for negligent language (in the absence of fraud) leading to a monetary loss. If one holds that the only contact between auditor and third party is through the words in the auditor's report, it would follow that under the *Derry* v. *Peek* concept auditor negligence to third parties could not arise.

Negligent misrepresentation extended to specific third parties

The initial exemption for negligent misrepresentation was partially withdrawn by Judge Cardozo in the *Glanzer* v. *Shepard* case in the United States in 1922. Here a weigher was held liable for a negligent misrepresentation in a weight certificate because the third party plaintiff was a specific, known buyer whose reliance on the certificate could not merely be expected but was known in advance. But in the landmark *Ultramares* v. *Touche* case of nine years later, the same judge refused to find auditors liable for negligence to creditors, even though their reliance on the auditor's report might reasonably have been foreseen, because the specific creditors to whom the report would be sent were not known to the auditors in advance:

> If liability for negligence exists, a thoughtless slip or blunder, the failure to detect a theft or forgery beneath the cover of deceptive entries, may expose accountants to a liability in an indeterminate amount for an indeterminate time to an indeterminate class.

Following the *Ultramares* case United States common law has generally been held to make auditors liable for negligence to specific, known third parties but not to plaintiffs that were merely generally foreseeable members of a large and unascertained group. In practical terms, however, these restrictions have been modified by two subsequent developments. The first was that the U.S. Securities Act of 1933 gave third parties who purchased securities of companies registered with the Securities and Exchange Commission on a primary distribution the same rights as clients – namely, the right to sue auditors for negligence. The second was a tendency for U.S. courts to find auditors guilty of "gross negligence" or "reckless disregard of facts" and to interpret such findings as fraud, for which the common law has always recognized a liability to third parties. In recent years there has been considerable question whether the *Ultramares* principles were still valid in the United States. In part such question stems from the following developments in the U.K. courts.

The first of these was the *Candler* v. *Crane, Christmas* case of 1951. While the court found the defendant-auditor innocent because of privity of contract (the plaintiff had no contractual relationship with the auditor) with the plaintiff-investor, Lord Justice Denning, in a bold dissenting judgment argued that:

> I think that the law would fail to serve the best interests of the community if it should hold that accountants and auditors owe a duty to no one but their client. . . .If such be the law, I think it is to be regretted, for it means that the accountants' certificate, which should be a safeguard, becomes a snare for those who rely on it.

Like Cardozo, however, Denning argued that the auditor should not be held liable to all prospective third parties:

> They owe the duty, of course, to their employer or client, and also, I think, to any third person to whom they themselves show the accounts, or to whom they know their employer is going to show the accounts so as to induce him to invest money or take some other action on them. I do not think, however, the duty can be extended still further so as to include strangers of whom they have heard nothing and to whom their employer without their knowledge may choose to show their accounts. Once the accountants have handed their accounts to their employer, they are not, as a rule, responsible for what he does with them without their knowledge or their consent.

Hedley Byrne decision (1963)

The second U.K. development was the *Hedley Byrne* v. *Heller* case of 1963 in which the House of Lords upheld the earlier views of Lord Denning. In this case the defendant bankers were held not liable for negligence to third party advertising agents for mistakenly giving a favorable reference as to the financial stability of the company placing the advertising orders. The absence of liability, however, arose *solely* from an accompanying disclaimer stipulating that the bankers took no responsibility for their opinions. Far more important than the judgment itself, were the additional observations of the law lords rejecting the defence of absence of privity of contract and stating that persons should be held liable for negligent misrepresentations to third parties, even though unidentified at the time, whose reliance on their statement could be reasonably foreseen.

Lord Reid rejected the *Ultramares*-type argument that there could be no liability to third parties whose names were not known in advance:

> They knew that the inquiry was in connection with an advertising contract, and it was at least probable that the information was wanted by the advertising contractors. It seems to me quite immaterial that they did not know who these contractors were . . . A reasonable man knowing that he was being trusted or that his skill and judgment were being relied on, would, I think, have three courses open to him. He could keep silent or decline to give the information or advice sought: or he could give an answer with a clear qualification that he accepted no responsibility for it or that it was given without that reflection or enquiry which a careful answer would require: or he could simply answer without any such qualification. If he chooses to adopt the last course he must, I think, be held to have accepted some responsibility for its

answer being given carefully, or to have accepted a relationship with the enquirer which requires him to exercise such care as circumstances require.

In additional observations the other lords rejected the earlier view that third party liability was restricted to actions not words:

> ... if someone possessed of a special skill undertakes, quite irrespective of contract, to apply that skill for the assistance of another person who relies on such skill, the duty of care will arise. The fact that the service is to be given by means of, or by instrumentality of, words, can make no difference. Furthermore if, in a sphere in which a person is so placed that others could reasonably rely on his judgment or skill or on his ability to make careful enquiry, a person takes on himself to give information or advice to, or allows his information or advice to be passed on to, another person who, as he knows or should know, will place reliance on it, then a duty of care will arise.

Yet the lords recognized that there must be some limit to the extension of liability to unknown third parties:

> If the mere hearing or reading of words were held to create proximity, there might be no limit to the persons to whom the speaker or writer could be liable. How wide the sphere of the duty of care in negligence is to be laid depends on the court's assessment of the demands of society for protection from the carelessness of others.

While the cited observations, on which the actual judgment did not depend, were not legally binding on future courts, they have been and will undoubtedly continue to be of immense persuasive influence throughout all Commonwealth countries and perhaps in the United States as well.

The principles enunciated in the *Hedley Byrne* decision were summarized by the Council of the Institute of Chartered Accountants in England and Wales, based on advice from counsel, as follows:

> ... third parties entitled to recover damages under the Hedley Byrne principle will be limited to those who by reason of accountants' negligence in preparing reports, accounts or financial statements on which the third parties place reliance suffer financial loss in circumstances where the accountants knew or ought to have known that the reports, accounts or financial statements in question were being prepared for the specific purpose or transaction which gave rise to the loss and that they would be shown to and relied on by third parties in that particular connection.

The Council statement then proceeded to consider specific classes of third parties. With respect to clients' creditors the statement acknowledged a liability to them if the accountant knew or ought to have known at the time that the financial statements were to be shown to bankers or other creditors in order to obtain credit or the continuance of existing credit facilities. Finally, the statement went on to present the following more contentious analysis with respect to shareholders:

In Counsel's view the object of annual accounts is to assist shareholders in exercising their control of the company by enabling them to judge how its affairs have been conducted. Hence a decision by the shareholders collectively taken on the basis of negligently prepared accounts and resulting in improper payments by or financial loss to the company could result in liability. No claim by an individual shareholder however would succeed in respect of loss suffered through his own investment decisions made on the strength of misleading company accounts supported by an auditor's report containing negligent misrepresentations, since the purpose for which the annual accounts are normally prepared is not to enable individual shareholders to take investment decisions. But if the audited accounts comprised in effect part of a document of offer, and the auditors knew or ought to have known that the accounts were intended to be so used, they could be liable to third parties for financial loss suffered through reliance on a negligent auditor's report in connection with the offer.

In at least one lawyer's opinion[1] this last analysis is "dangerously soothing". It is indeed difficult not to believe that one of the purposes of financial statements (as discussed in Chapter 1) is to assist the individual shareholder in making decisions as to the increase, continuation or disposal of his shareholdings (in addition to decisions as to how to cast his vote at the annual meeting). This is an excellent example of the fact that it is often impossible to state exactly what the law is on a particular issue. As a practical matter, auditors in Canada today would seem well advised to perform their work on the basis that they anticipate that both present shareholders and at least limited classes of prospective shareholder or lenders, in making investment or credit decisions, will be placing reliance upon their reports.

Post Hedley Byrne in the United States

A number of legal decisions in the United States since 1963 have tended to move from the *Ultramares* principle of specifically known users of the auditor's report toward the *Hedley Byrne* principle of reasonably foreseeable prospective users and some have quoted *Hedley Byrne* as a reference (though a few cases have gone the other way). One supporting case was the 1969 *Ryan* v. *Kanne* decision of the Supreme Court of Iowa:

> ... we are disposed to reject the rule that third parties not in privity of contract or in a fiduciary relationship are also barred from recovery for negligence of the party issuing the instrument upon which the third party relies, to his detriment. It is unnecessary at this time to determine whether the rule of no liability should be relaxed to extend to all foreseeable persons who may rely upon the report, but we do hold that it should be relaxed as to those who were actually known to the author as prospective users of the report and take into consideration the end and aim of the transaction.

As noted by a Canadian judge in a decision (*Haig* v. *Bamford*) given in 1976:

The approach taken in the American Restatement of Torts . . . is to permit recovery for loss suffered by the person or one of the persons for whose benefit or guidance the professional person intends to supply the information or knows that the recipient intends to supply it. A duty of care arises if the defendant accountant knows that a third party will receive his statements. This knowledge is not with regard to the specific individual, but to a limited class of which he forms a part.

Post Hedley Byrne in Canada

There have been several significant Canadian cases since 1963 involving chartered accountants and using the *Hedley Byrne* decision as an authority to extend liability for negligence to third parties.

In the *Haig* v. *Bamford* case in 1972 in Saskatchewan a prospective shareholder relied on erroneous audited statements to his detriment and subsequently lost his investment. The initial court found the auditors liable for negligence to the third party following the *Hedley Byrne* precedent. While the prospective shareholder was not known to the auditors at the time the audit report was prepared, the judge ruled that "he must be included in the category of persons who could be foreseen by the defendants as relying" on their report.

After reversal in one appeal court, the trial court finding of a duty of care was reinstated on further appeal to the Supreme Court of Canada in 1976. In rejecting the argument that auditors, to be held liable, need to have been aware of the specific identity of the prospective investor, the Supreme Court stated:

> The increasing growth and changing role of corporations in modern society has been attended by the new perception of the societal role of the profession of accounting. . . . The financial statements of the corporations upon which [the auditor] reports can affect the economic interests of the general public as well as of shareholders and potential shareholders. With the added prestige and value of his services has come, as the leaders of the profession have recognized, a concomitant and commensurately increased responsibility to the public. It seems unrealistic to be oblivious to these developments. It does not necessarily follow that the doors must be thrown open and recovery permitted whenever someone's economic interest suffers as the result of a negligent act on the part of an accountant. . . . From the authorities, it appears that several possible tests could be applied to invoke a duty of care on the part of accountants vis-a-vis third parties: (i) foreseeability of the use of the financial statement and the auditor's report thereon by the plaintiff and reliance thereon; (ii) actual knowledge of the limited class that will use and rely on the statement; (iii) actual knowledge of the specific plaintiff who will use and rely on the statement. It is unnecessary for the purposes of the present case to decide whether test (i), the test of foreseeability, is or is not, a proper test . . . I have concluded on the authorities that test (iii) is too narrow and that test (ii), actual knowledge of the limited class, is the proper test to apply in this case.

It should be noted that the potential investors in the foregoing case were a limited class since the company was a private one and could not offer securities to the general public.

In the *Toromont* v. *Thorne* case of 1975 in Ontario (under appeal as this book goes to press) it was held that the auditors owed a duty of care to a subsequent purchaser of the company, the contemplated purchase being known to the auditors before they issued their report. The judge quoted the *Hedley Byrne* precedent as establishing a duty of care whenever a "special relationship" exists between the parties. Further, it was held that various earlier cases (including the *Haig* v. *Bamford* case) had established "that accountants may be held liable to shareholders who purchased shares relying on a false balance sheet where there are special circumstances bringing the purchasers within the reasonable contemplation of the accountants". Finally, it was held that consultation with the auditors (including a review of the auditors' working papers) by accountants acting for the prospective purchaser established such a "special relationship" between the auditors and the prospective purchaser, and that a duty of care therefore arose.

Based on these decisions and based on the recognition that Canadian courts have traditionally given to landmark English decisions, it seems reasonable to conclude that under the law of torts in Canada the external auditor is liable for negligent misrepresentation to limited classes of third parties. As to how wide this liability extends in all situations it will take a number of further court decisions to test the doctrine of foreseeability before the question is settled.

5.1.5 Contributory negligence

Originally, in common law a defence of contributory negligence which established that the plaintiff did not take reasonable care in his own interest and so directly contributed to his own injury caused the plaintiff's suit to fail. This original all-or-nothing position has been modified in many jurisdictions by Contributory Negligence Acts which require the damages to be apportional where the blame is shared. For example, a recent case in New Brunswick found a defendant guilty of negligence in causing an automobile accident but apportioned 20% of the damages to the plaintiff for failing to wear a seat belt. This case, of course, involved physical injury and an action in *tort*.

It is unclear, however, whether similar apportionment of damages can be applied to negligence with respect to *contractual* duties (as owed by an auditor to his client), although it was so applied by the British Columbia court in the *West Coast Finance* case. Even if it can, there is a further complication for it may be held that an auditor was hired specifically for "the very purpose of detecting defalcations which the employer's negligence has made possible". Such was the decision in the *National Surety Corporation* v. *Lybrand* case in New York in 1939. While it was established that the plaintiff's negligence had been partly responsible for permitting a material employee fraud, the defence of contributory negligence was rejected. The very nature of the auditor's role apparently limits to some extent the applicability of the contributory negligence doctrine.

On the other hand, there have been a number of cases where a complete (rather than partial) defence of contributory negligence has been successful. In the *International Laboratories* v. *Dewar* case in Manitoba in 1933 the auditors were exonerated on the grounds that the plaintiff had been contributorily negligent in not implementing a recommendation by the auditors to improve internal control. The success of the contributory negligence defence in such cases illustrates the vital importance of reporting internal control weaknesses to the client promptly and in writing.

In the *West Coast Finance* case of 1974 in British Columbia, though later reversed on other grounds, damages resulting from failure to detect the inadequacy of an allowance for doubtful accounts were initially apportioned equally between auditor and company because the company had been contributorily negligent in not operating in accordance with usual finance company practice. The monthly list of delinquent accounts was inaccurate and administrative procedures were loose or non-existent. A few cases have indicated that the defence of contributory negligence is more likely to be successful if the plaintiff's negligence can be shown not only to have contributed to his own loss but also to have contributed to the auditor's failure to discover the problem.

With respect to actions by third parties, an auditor can plead the defence of contributory negligence if indeed such negligence is the third party's, and not solely the client's. In the more common situation, however, both auditor and client (but not the third party) may have been negligent and the third party can sue them both, jointly and severally. In such a case the auditor cannot plead the defence of contributory negligence; however, should he pay the full damages to the third party he will have a right of action against his client for a contribution in proportion to the sharing of blame.

5.1.6 The measure of damages

In English common law, damages are intended to compensate the injured party for the amount of his losses suffered as a consequence of the defendant's negligence. Key elements in the measure of damages are therefore the certainty that they have occurred, that they indeed were consequential following the negligence, and that there is reasonable proximity of consequence.

Damages that are recovered or recoverable from a fidelity company (in cases of defalcations) cannot also be recovered from the auditor – although the fidelity company may, of course, have a right of action against the auditor. Damages that would have occurred regardless of the auditor's actions cannot be recovered from him even if negligence is established. For example, a bonus paid to an employee out of overstated profits could not be recovered from the auditor when it was held that the bonus would have been paid in any case. A creditor acting on erroneous financial statements could not recover damages from the auditor when it was held that the financial statement errors, which the auditor had been negligent in not detecting, were not so large that their correction would have dissuaded the creditor from advancing credit. When a plaintiff-client has suffered no real loss, but the auditor has been negligent, the damages awarded may be limited to the amount of the audit fees.

In the *Toromont* case, although the auditors were held to be negligent in that insufficient audit evidence was obtained and no adequate check of the system of internal control was made, no damages (other than certain legal costs and the waiving of unpaid audit fees) were awarded to a third party because the judge held that the financial statements, though inadequately audited, were nonetheless fairly presented. Thus, while negligent misrepresentations were contained in the scope paragraph of the auditors' report, the third party was held to have suffered no consequential loss because a more complete audit would not have changed the opinion paragraph or the financial statements themselves.

The damages must have been a consequence of the negligence. A plaintiff who had placed no reliance on the auditor's report in the first place cannot subsequently recover his losses on the grounds of negligent misrepresentations in that report. But the reliance need not have been exclusive. If the erroneous report was merely one of several inducing causes of the damage, the injured party will have a right of action against the auditor.

Since the losses must be a consequence of the negligence, it is important to identify the time the negligence occurred; only losses subsequent to that time can be relevant. The timing is clear in the case of losses resulting from the plaintiff's reliance on misrepresentations in an auditor's report. The losses can only begin to accrue after the time of the reliance, and in any event not prior to the issuance of the auditor's report. The timing is less clear in cases where the client alleges negligent failure to perform certain audit procedures. If the inadequate audit procedures lead to a clear audit report on misleading financial statements, the auditor will be liable if and when the plaintiff acts on that misleading information. For example, auditors have been held liable to a shareholder for the loss upon realization in bankruptcy of shares purchased on the strength of overstated financial statements. Auditors have been held liable for interest on income taxes paid in an earlier year than necessary as a result of overstated income figures.

But if the inadequate audit procedures lead to a failure to detect a defalcation, the timing of that failure is more contentious. In various cases the court has determined that damages should be assessed from the time when an auditor should have detected a defalcation had the audit work been properly done. Where no other logical date can be identified the courts have tended to look to the latest date in the course of an audit when the auditor should have performed a given procedure (sometimes even the final day of the field work).

A review of the measure of damages would not be complete without a consideration of the costs of the action itself. In Canada, the successful party to an action, whether plaintiff or defendant, usually recovers a substantial part of his costs of the action from the loser. The situation is quite different in the United States where such costs, other than court fees themselves, are not recoverable. (Of course, what is never recoverable in either country is the substantial time which a successful defendant will have had to spend in his defence and the inevitable damage to his reputation, even if legally exonerated.)

In Canada, legal costs are normally based on the amount of professional time spent by the lawyers. In many provinces, a Canadian lawyer may not charge *contingent* fees (contingent upon the outcome of the case). In the United States, on the other hand, contingent fees running from one-third to one-half or more of the amount recovered are common. It is commonly thought that juries are aware of this and award gross damages in an amount sufficient to yield a compensatory net recovery to the plaintiff. This is one of the reasons why damages awarded and sought in U.S. actions are usually substantially larger than in similar Canadian cases.

5.2 Legal standards of care in the audit examination

A legal concept of due audit care has evolved from the accumulation over the past century of many hundreds of legal judgments in the United Kingdom, Canada, the United States, Australia, and other countries whose law has its roots in English common law. Many of these cases address themselves to what constitutes due audit care in the verification of cash, accounts receivable, inventory, fixed assets, etc. Almost without exception any findings by the courts in these areas have subsequently been incorporated in professional literature as accepted practice. This, of course, is not to say that every audit procedure suggested in any auditing text (including this one) is necessary in order to comply with the legal standards of due audit care. As emphasized in Chapter 1, no suggested auditing procedure in any textbook can be held out to be invariably necessary on all audits nor necessarily sufficient on any given audit. Nonetheless, most of the specific procedures discussed in court cases can be found in Volume 2, and little would be served by discussing them again here. What is more relevant here is the development of the general concept of due professional care – and particularly its application to two contentious areas: detec-

tion of fraud and reliance on representations of management and others.

5.2.1 Due care and basic responsibilities

The classic statement of the basic responsibilities of the external auditor was given in the following case in England in 1895.

London and General Bank case (1895)

While the following comments by Justice Lindley were specifically directed to the U.K. Companies Act of 1879 (requiring an audit for all incorporated banks) they have long been considered in many countries as the starting point for any consideration of due audit care:

> It is no part of an auditor's duty to give advice, either to directors or shareholders, as to what they ought to do.... It is nothing to him whether the business of a company is conducted prudently or imprudently, profitably or unprofitably. It is nothing to him whether dividends are properly or improperly declared, provided he discharges his own duty to the shareholders.

His business is to ascertain and state the true financial position of the company at the time of the audit, and his duty is confined to that ... An auditor, however, is not bound to do more than exercise reasonable care and skill in making inquiries and investigations. He is not an insurer; he does not guarantee that the books do correctly show the true position of the company's affairs; he does not even guarantee that his balance-sheet is accurate according to the books of the company. If he did he would be responsible for error on his part, even if he were himself deceived without any want of reasonable care on his part, say, by the fraudulent concealment of a book from him. His obligation is not so onerous as this. Such I take to be the duty of the auditor: he must be honest – i.e., he must not certify what he does not believe to be true, and he must take reasonable care and skill before he believes that what he certifies is true. What is reasonable care in any particular case must depend upon the circumstances of that case. Where there is nothing to excite suspicion very little inquiry will be reasonably sufficient, and in practice I believe business men select a few cases at haphazard, see that they are right, and assume that others like them are correct also. Where suspicion is aroused more care is obviously necessary; but, still, an auditor is not bound to exercise more than reasonable care and skill, even in a case of suspicion, and he is perfectly justified in acting on the opinion of an expert where special knowledge is required.

This landmark case not only influenced hundreds of subsequent cases but the development of later professional pronouncements as well. Lindley's emphasis on (a) a clear distinction between the auditor's responsibilities and those of management, (b) some limitation on his responsibility for the detection of fraud, (c) a duty to take reasonable care but not to guarantee, (d) a duty to take increased care in the presence of suspicious circumstances, and (e) the right to rely on experts where special knowledge is required, may all be found today reflected in the introductory paragraphs on "Responsibilities and functions of the independent auditor" in the AICPA's Statement on Auditing Standards No. 1.

5.2.2 Responsibility for the detection of fraud

The *London and General Bank* case had suggested an auditor could, without any want of reasonable care on his part, be deceived by the fraudulent concealment of a book from him. The *Kingston Cotton Mill* decision a year later went further:

It is the duty of an auditor to bring to bear on the work he has to perform that skill, care, and caution which a reasonably competent, careful, and cautious auditor would use ... An auditor is not bound to be a detective, or, as was said, to approach his work with suspicion or with a foregone conclusion that there is something wrong. He is a watch-dog, but not a bloodhound ... Auditors must not be made liable for not tracking out ingenious and carefully laid schemes of fraud when there is nothing to

arouse their suspicion, and when those frauds are perpetrated by tried servants of the company and are undetected for years by the directors. So to hold would make the position of an auditor intolerable.

It is important to remember the auditing environment in which these decisions were given (see Chapter 1). During the 1890's in England the prevention and detection of fraud was considered to be the primary audit objective. These decisions, while perhaps anticipating ahead of their time the more significant objective of expressing an opinion, did not suggest that the auditor had no duty to check for fraud. Rather, they placed limitations on this responsibility. He was not to be required to be infallible. The principles enunciated in these two cases were quoted with approval in the *Guardian Insurance* case in Canada in 1941. In particular the Canadian judge quoted the *London and General Bank* judgment to the effect that:

It is not sufficient to say that the frauds must have been detected if the entries in the book had been put together in a way which never occurred to anyone before suspicion was aroused. The question is whether, no suspicion of anything wrong being entertained, there was a want of reasonable care on the part of auditors in relying on the returns made by competent and trusted experts relating to matters on which information from such a person was essential.

Subsequent court decisions

In the many legal cases subsequent to the early English cases cited above, courts in many countries have re-affirmed that in the ordinary audit examination the public accountant neither warrants nor represents as fact the information in his report or in the financial statements and that the financial statements are representations of the client not of the auditor. These cases also rejected the proposition that the audit engagement represents an agreement by the public accountant to protect the client from his own failure to find errors in the books or the existence of defalcations. Apart from the recent *Hochfelder* case, none of the decisions, however, appears specifically to confirm a position that reasonable care and skill only involves procedures necessary to render an opinion, with the possible detection of fraud being purely incidental.

In the *Cereal By-Products* case in Illinois in 1956, the plaintiff, the defendants, and the expert accounting witnesses all agreed with the judge that:

It is necessary that certain examinations or checks be made which would show defalcations before the auditor could render an opinion on the balance sheets and financial statements.

The importance of this decision as late as 1956 is the implication that the auditor must perform certain procedures which are *primarily directed* to the detection of fraud. According to this decision, the detection of fraud would not seem to be an incidental objective but an essential one (although it could reasonably be argued that its necessity was not an end in itself but subsidiary to the ultimate objective of expressing an opinion – a position not necessarily inconsistent with the first of the two SAS-1 sentences quoted in the next section).

This position was re-affirmed in the English *Fomento* v. *Selsdon Fountain Pen* case of 1958:

> What is the proper function of an auditor? ... His vital task is to take care to see that errors are not made, be they errors of computation, or errors of omission or commission, or downright untruths. To perform this task properly, he must come to it with an inquiring mind, – not suspicious of dishonesty, I agree – but suspecting that someone may have made a mistake somewhere and that a check must be made to ensure that there has been none ...

and in the *Pacific Acceptance* case in Australia in 1970:

> Once it is accepted that the auditor's duty requires him to go behind the books and determine the true financial position of the company and so to examine the accord or otherwise of the financial position of the company, the books and the balance sheet, it follows that the possible causes to the contrary, namely, error, fraud or unsound accounting, are the auditor's concern ... the process of verification cannot properly be carried out except by a procedure that takes account of the possibility that the affairs examined may not be true, due to errors, innocent or fraudulent, appearing in the records.
>
> The duty to pay due regard to the possibility of fraud has been recognized by the courts and by the audit profession and by the very nature of some of their procedures, for example, the surprise nature in an unannounced cash count ...
>
> There was some debate as to whether any duty to pay due regard to the possibility of fraud was a primary duty or merely some incidental duty, but I think it is sufficient to say that the duty referred to exists, as does the consequential duty to warn, and that each is comprised within the duty to audit with due skill and care.

As already discussed in Chapter 4, the latter judgment went on to define a separate "duty to audit" over and above the examination required to support the audit opinion and a separate "duty to warn" management of any irregularities encountered over and above the duty to issue an annual report to the shareholders. For the reasons there discussed, there is some question whether a separate "duty to audit" can be read into the more specific provisions contained in most federal and provincial Corporations Acts in Canada but a "duty to warn" may well exist. Indeed, the *London Oil Storage* decision (see 5.2.3) contained a statement calling for the auditor to probe suspicious circumstances and "tell the directors of it" and the *Guardian Insurance* case in the Supreme Court of Canada in 1941 quoted this statement with approval.

Whatever the position may be in other jurisdictions an auditor will run a grave risk if, having discovered some fraud or irregularity or something which arouses his suspicions, he fails to tell the directors about it. As a practical matter most auditors, while probably rejecting the notion of a separate "duty to audit" apart from the purpose of supporting the audit opinion called for by statute, would recognize a professional responsibility to inform management promptly of irregularities encountered or weaknesses in internal control observed.

Further court cases have supported the view that while management is primarily responsible to ensure that an effective system of internal control is implemented and maintained, the auditor has a duty to warn his client of weaknesses in control detected by him during his audit. It has been held that having made such warning the auditor has discharged his duty with respect to responsibility for the detection of any fraud which may result from that weakness barring the presence of suspicious circumstances. Such were the judgments in an English case, *Catterson & Sons*, in 1937 and an American case, *Boltin, Quinn and Ivy*, in 1940.

The position of the profession

The profession has always taken much comfort in the non-detective non-bloodhound principle. Furthermore, as described in Chapter 1, auditing objectives gradually changed over the years to give less emphasis to the detection of fraud and more to an evaluation of the fairness of presentation, less emphasis to asset valuation and solvency and more to income measurement. Thus forty years after the *London and General Bank* and *Kingston Cotton Mill* decisions, the profession was stating that detection of fraud was really only an incidental objective of auditing.

Professional pronouncements in Canada up to 1976 have been silent on the issue but most Canadian accountants would probably subscribe to the somewhat ambivalent statements made in the AICPA's Statement on Auditing Procedures No. 1 (SAS-1):

> The auditor recognizes that fraud, if sufficiently material, may affect his opinion on the financial statements, and his examination, made in accordance with generally accepted auditing standards, gives consideration to this possibility. However, the ordinary examination directed to this expression of an opinion on financial statements is not primarily or specifically designed, and cannot be relied upon, to disclose defalcations and other similar irregularities, although their discovery may result.[2]

These two adjacent sentences are, to some extent, contradictory: it might be inferred from the first that it was part of generally accepted auditing standards to look for material (but not immaterial) fraud, yet, from the second, that it was not part of such standards to look for fraud at all (although one might stumble across it). However, in the *Hochfelder* v. *Ernst & Ernst* case in the United States in 1974 these sentences were quoted with approval by the court. This endorsement of the profession's position is significant.

In 1976 both the CICA and the AICPA issued exposure drafts of proposed recommendations or statements dealing in part with the detection of fraud. A discussion of professional responsibilities with respect to the detection of errors and irregularities, including a discussion of those two exposure drafts, is included in 6.8.1. The reader should refer to subsequent pronouncements.

5.2.3 Suspicious circumstances

In determining standards of care appropriate in different circumstances the courts have placed special emphasis on the auditor's responsibility to detect fraud in the event that he becomes aware of suspicious circumstances. English cases have been very specific on this point. The *Kingston Cotton Mill* decision warned:

> If there is anything calculated to excite suspicion he should probe it to the bottom.

and the *London Oil Storage* decision:

> If circumstances of suspicion arise, it is the duty of the auditor, insofar as those circumstances relate to the financial position of the company, to probe them to the bottom . . . if his suspicion is aroused, his duty is to probe the thing to the bottom and tell the directors of it and get what information he can.

Recent court decisions have re-affirmed the requirement that auditors probe deeply into areas that arouse suspicion. In the *Continental Vending* case in the United States in 1969 one implication of the decision was that, if an auditor did not conduct his examination with extraordinary care and diligence in circumstances where there was clear suspicion of a diversion of funds on the part of management, he could be held to be abetting the diversion and accordingly an accomplice to fraud.

The doctrine of probing suspicious circumstances to the utmost has been carried over into non-audit situations. In the *1136 Tenants* case (see 5.1.2) the finding of negligence in failing to detect the agent's fraud was partially supported by the argument that the working papers contained notations of missing invoices and the CPA had not probed these unusual circumstances.

The judgment in the 1970 *Pacific Acceptance* case, stressing the importance of alertness for a *pattern* of suspicious circumstances, contains one of the most contemporary statements on this question:

> If, during an audit, there are a substantial number of irregular or unusual matters encountered by audit clerks and some, singly or in combination, indicate the real possibility that something is wrong, then to separate each off into watertight compartments and pose the question whether it individually raises a suspicion of fraud and on receiving a negative reply asserting that it follows that the clerk does his duty if he does nothing further, . . . denies both the true tests of legal duty of care and of common sense . . .

> Thus, if material irregularities appear, a careful auditor can normally be expected to remember and bring into consideration other irregularities, . . . and he might be expected to go back over past working papers, even those of a prior audit clerk, to bring to mind similar irregularities but whether he should take any of these steps would depend on the circumstances, particularly the seriousness and materiality of the irregularities uncovered.

In most of the court cases dealing with negligence in recognition of suspicious circumstances, the auditor's working papers themselves contained indications that things were not as they should be. The greater danger seems to be not the failure to discover and document clues but the failure to recognize them as suspicious. A healthy skepticism remains an important audit ingredient.

5.2.4 Reliance on management and third parties

Closely related to the proposition that the auditor need not guarantee the detection of all fraud but must take reasonable care to consider its possibility, particularly in the presence of suspicious circumstances, is the proposition that the auditor is entitled to place some reliance on the representations of management and others but not without considering the availability of corroborating evidence.

In the *London and General Bank* case the judge's comment was simply:

> . . . he is perfectly justified in acting on the opinion of an expert where special knowledge is required.

The *Kingston Cotton Mill* case, ruling that the auditor was not negligent in relying on management representations concerning a grossly over-inflated inventory quantity, added:

> He is justified in believing tried servants of the company in whom confidence is placed by the company. He is entitled to assume that they are honest, and to rely upon their representations, provided he takes reasonable care.

Eight years later, in the *London Oil Storage* case, the position of allowing the auditor wide latitude in relying on management representations was re-affirmed, but with the qualification that reliance could not substitute for other additional audit procedures which might be appropriate:

> ... he is not bound to suspect [a certain employee] as being a dishonest man, he is entitled to rely upon the fact that he is the trusted official, and has known him for years, but that does not justify him not using reasonable precautions; he is not entitled to let his duty be performed on the credit of [that employee] rather than perform his own duty upon his own responsibility.

Subsequent cases have added further qualifications to the degree of reliance the auditor can place on others. In the *City Equitable Fire Insurance* case in England in 1925 the judgment allowed the auditor to accept the certificate of an outsider holding assets on behalf of the company, in lieu of personal inspection, but placed on him the responsibility of justifying his belief that the custodian was a proper and reliable person.

Recent cases have continued this trend. In the *BarChris Construction* case in New York in 1968 the court ruled the procedures inadequate in a registration statement review of uncompleted contracts when the auditor relied on the unsupported word of the company controller rather than personally examining each contract. The judgment in the *Continental Vending* case made it plain that "auditors may place themselves in jeopardy in following too easily a natural inclination to meet a client's, particularly management's, point of view" and that "an auditor should not rely on the mere representations of a client if he can check them himself". The *Pacific Acceptance* judgment had much to say on an auditor's reliance on company officials, employees and outsiders:

> An auditor may properly rely a great deal on inquiries made and explanations sought of the company's staff and management at the appropriate level, but *prima facie* this is in aid of his vouching and checking procedures and not in substitution for them. In appropriate cases it may be reasonable to go no further as a result of an explanation even although there are other documents that could be inspected ... However, ... if the existence of a document which is under the control of the company is material to the audit it is the duty of the auditor acting reasonably to examine the document for himself unless there are some specific circumstances which make it reasonable to accept something less than proof by inspection.

Furthermore, the judgment cautioned an auditor against undue "credulity" and "undue reliance on those who may err wittingly or unwittingly". He does not perform his duty if he fails to make such checks and seeks to excuse himself by saying that everyone believed that the borrower was wealthy and dependable, the manager so believed, ... "He does not satisfy himself merely by being content that management is responsible and is satisfied about the matter."

In the *Toromont* case in Ontario in 1975, auditors were held to be negligent because, among other reasons, "too great reliance was placed on mainly oral evidence from the financial management".

In the *Creighton* case in Quebec, the court noted with approval that the auditors had given a denial of opinion when, because of difficulties in obtaining answers to their queries, they concluded that they could place no faith in information received from the chief executive officer and that his influence was so pervasive that the records of the company could in consequence not be relied upon.

The trend in these cases is clear. While the auditor is still entitled to presume that management is honest, he must not accept management representations and the certificate of others without being in the position to justify such reliance in lieu of performing more objective audit procedures. Of course, in cases of reliance on third-party experts (lawyers, appraisers, etc.) there may often be no alternative audit procedures practical. The legal standard of due audit care also demands that the auditor consider carefully the interests of the respondents in the subject matter of the response.

One aspect of this topic, reliance on other auditors auditing subsidiary companies or equity-accounted investees, is discussed in 12.5.7 and 38.3.10.

5.2.5 The prudent practitioner

Reference was made in 5.1.1 to the auditor "holding himself out to the public as possessing the degree of skill commonly possessed by others in the same employment" and bringing "to bear on the work he has to perform that skill, care and caution which a reasonably competent, careful, and cautious auditor would use". Implicit in these phrases is the legal abstraction of the *reasonable man* against whose imagined conduct a defendant's actual performance will be measured by the courts. The reasonable man in law is assumed:

a) to exercise a level of judgment equal to that of his community,

b) to use with reasonable intelligence the knowledge which he has,

c) to keep up with the level of his community in both general and specialized knowledge but to be aware of his own ignorance and to perceive the risk of acting in a state of ignorance of potential hazards,

d) to possess and exercise the degree of skill possessed by the general class of people in his calling, whether he is a beginner or not,

e) to take extra precaution to avoid injury to others in areas where he has specific knowledge of problems.

Slightly higher responsibilities may be demanded of persons holding themselves out as possessing special skills. In applying the general doctrine to the case of an auditor's failure to detect innocent error or some fraudulent defalcation the test is whether the prudent auditor using reasonable skill and care and possessed of the same knowledge of the facts at the time would have foreseen the risk and taken steps to avoid it.[3]

5.3 Fraud and criminal liability

Fraud in common usage means criminal deception, use of false representation, or dishonest artifice. In law, however, its meaning must be defined more precisely. This is particularly true when its application has been seen in a few cases which to the layman would appear to be instances of honest error in judgment and not fraudulent intent. Of course, should an accountant be actively involved in embezzling funds from his client neither courts nor public opinion would have difficulty in demonstrating fraud. Most litigation where the question of fraud by the public accountant has arisen, however, has concerned an alleged fraudulent misrepresentation by the auditor (in his report) or his alleged participation in a client's fraudulent misrepresentation (in financial statements or tax returns).

5.3.1 Elements of fraud

Fraud may be the basis for either a civil action or a criminal charge. In both, however, legal fraud requires proof of an intent to deceive going beyond mere negligence. The classic definition of fraud was laid down in the landmark English case of *Derry* v. *Peek* in 1889:

> First, in order to sustain an action of deceit, there must be proof of fraud, and nothing short of that will suffice. Secondly, fraud is proved when it is shown that a false representation has been made (1) knowingly or (2) without belief in its truth, or (3) recklessly, careless whether it be true or false ... Thirdly, if fraud be proved, the motive of the person guilty of it is immaterial. It matters not that there was no intention to cheat or injure the person to whom the statement was made.

In other words, provided there is express or inferred intent to deceive (intending others to believe either an assertion one knows is false or an assertion made in reckless disregard of whether it be true or false) the motive for the deception is immaterial.

In the *Ultramares* case in 1931 Judge Cardozo supported the *Derry* v. *Peek* definition of fraud, and confirmed that a liability for fraud extends to third parties:

> The defendants owed their employer a duty imposed by law to make their certificate without fraud, and a duty growing out of contract to make it with care and caution proper to their calling. Fraud includes the pretence of knowledge when knowledge there is none. To creditors and investors to whom the employer distributed the certificate, the defendants owed a like duty to make it without fraud, since there was notice in the circumstances of its making that the employer did not intend to keep it to himself.

However, the judgment went on to extend the "pretence of knowledge" concept much farther; the auditors were held liable for fraud for certifying that the balance sheet was in agreement with the books (which they believed to be true) when in reality, undiscovered by their test inspection of 200 sales invoices, there existed 17 fictitious sales invoices totalling $700 000:

> The defendants certified as a fact, true to their own knowledge, that the balance sheet was in accordance with the books of account. If their statement was false, they are not to be exonerated because they believed it to be true.

The holding of fraud in this case, for what laymen might well have considered a mere error in judgment (or at worst negligence), turned on the argument that auditors "by the very nature of their calling profess to speak with knowledge when certifying to an agreement between the audit and the entries" and that a profession of knowledge goes beyond mere profession of belief.

Of course, there can be little question that if an auditor *deliberately* avoids certain facts which an audit examination should uncover, he places himself in jeopardy of being held liable for fraud.

> Carelessness in the gathering of facts which are stated to exist will not sustain an allegation of fraud if the representor genuinely believes in the truth of that which he asserts. But if the representor has deliberately avoided facts that would have been found on investigation, a court could conclude that he had no reasonable ground for making his statement and thus that he did not truly believe the truth of that which he asserts. One who makes a false statement honestly believing it to be true and who later discovers that it was false, or one who makes a true

statement which later events falsify, before it has been acted upon, is under a duty to disclose the truth on pain of being charged with fraud.[4]

Nonetheless, as mentioned earlier, there has been a tendency in American cases following *Ultramares* for carelessness to be equated with "gross negligence", and gross negligence with "constructive fraud" – perhaps in order to establish liability to injured third parties to whom, pre-*Hedley Byrne*, most liability for negligence did not extend. A reversal of this trend may have been marked by the 1976 *Hochfelder* decision (see 5.5).

In Canada, few if any actions against auditors have been based on alleged fraud. It seems likely that such actions would be judged in terms of the *Derry* v. *Peek* criteria – and perhaps without the American courts' tendency to see carelessness as fraud.

5.3.2 Criminal fraud

The original basis of Canadian statutes concerned with criminal fraud was the English Larceny Act of 1861, which imposed criminal liability on any corporate officer or director (which included the company's auditor) involved in the publishing of a false statement with intent to deceive. That act was used by the Crown in 1931 in the English *Royal Mail* case (*R. v. Kylsant and Moreland*) to send Lord Kylsant to prison for 12 months for making, publishing and circulating a false prospectus.

In this case, the company's financial statements for a number of years had indicated that the company was earning profits. However, the net income in fact was coming from the return of a number of secret reserves established in prior years, all of which was in accordance with accepted accounting principles of the time. The court noted that the financial statement figures did apparently disclose the financial position of the company in accordance with accepted practice but held that the net effect in the prospectus was to conceal the true facts by implying that the company was in a sound financial position and that a prudent investor could safely invest in the debentures being offered in the prospectus. In summary, Lord Kylsant, the company chairman, was found guilty of circulating a false prospectus with intent to deceive. The auditor, however, was acquitted of the charge of aiding and abetting. The judge instructed the jury that to find the auditor guilty it was not sufficient to find him civilly liable for any breach of duty but rather to find that the statement he signed "was false to his knowledge and was published by him ... with the intention that it should deceive shareholders". He would have to be found guilty of having committed a deliberate and conscious act, with criminal and wicked intent, to help the chairman deceive the public. Perhaps because other accountants had testified that they would have signed a similar audit report in similar circumstances, the jury did not find the auditor guilty.

Nonetheless, the *Royal Mail* case was a forerunner of cases which would examine the question of whether defendants could be guilty of misleading the average prudent investor by making disclosure which, though adequate by the standard of generally accepted accounting principles, could be held by the court to be deficient. This issue came to the fore in the *Continental Vending* case in 1962. In this case the auditors were found guilty of criminal indictments for a false and misleading report. Continental had (a) loaned certain funds to an affiliate which had (b) in turn loaned funds to Continental's president which were (c) secured largely by the president's shareholdings in Continental. Facts (b) and (c) were not disclosed in the financial statement. Accounting experts disagreed whether such disclosure was required by generally accepted accounting principles. The court held, however, that the adherence to professional standards was not conclusive on the question of *fraud*, but merely a factor to be weighed by the jury. It was held that the auditors knew of certain material discrepancies and were therefore guilty in not disclosing them.

In one of the many *Equity Funding* cases three auditors were found guilty in 1975 (presently under appeal) on multiple criminal counts of securities fraud and filing falsified financial statements with the Securities and Exchange Commission. Many of the company's alleged sales of insurance policies turned out to be fictitious, the result of a gigantic fraud for which several company officers, including the president, were subsequently convicted and imprisoned. In the criminal case against the auditors the question was whether they were guilty of fraud as well. It appears that apparent auditor negligence may sometimes be regarded by juries as criminal complicity.

The section of the Criminal Code of Canada which is particularly relevant to the officers and directors of a company and their possible misrepresentation of facts states:

355.1 Everyone who, with intent to defraud,
a) destroys, mutilates, alters, falsifies, or makes a false entry in, or
b) omits a material particular from, or alters a material particular in, a book, paper, writing, valuable security or document is guilty of an indictable offence and is liable to imprisonment for five years.

The section of the Criminal Code of Canada which is particularly relevant to the public accountant acting in his capacity as an external auditor giving an opinion on financial statements is as follows:

358.1 Everyone who makes, circulates or publishes a prospectus, statement or account, whether written or oral, that he knows is false in a material particular, with intent

a) to induce persons, whether ascertained or not, to become shareholders or partners in a company,

b) to deceive or defraud the members, shareholders or creditors, whether ascertained or not, of a company,

c) to induce any person to entrust or advance anything to a company, or

d) to enter into any security for the benefit of a company, is guilty of an indictable offence and is liable to imprisonment for 10 years.

Finally, the Criminal Code contains, as well, the following sweeping provisions:

115 Everyone who, without lawful excuse, contravenes an Act of the Parliament of Canada by wilfully doing anything it forbids or by wilfully omitting to do anything that it requires to be done is, unless some penalty or punishment is expressly provided by law, guilty of an indictable offence and is liable to imprisonment to two years.

There have, however, to date been few if any criminal cases involving auditors in Canada.

5.4 Other liability

The legal liability discussed in the earlier sections of this chapter has been the civil liability or criminal guilt associated with the breach of a duty of audit care or the commission of, or participation in, fraud in connection with the issuance of an audit report. A number of other sources of legal liability exist but can be given only the briefest mention here.

In the provision of all professional services, the practising chartered accountant has, for example, a legal duty of *confidentiality* or secrecy concerning his client's affairs. A few English cases have held auditors liable for breaching this duty. It has been held, however, that retention of an agent or expert to provide advice or assistance in an audit does not breach this duty – the agent or expert retained merely becomes bound by the same duty.

A number of cases have also risen concerning the auditor's duty to maintain *independence*. One such case established that no necessary conflict of interest arises merely because an auditor acts for several business competitors.

In Chapter 4, various other statutory duties imposed on auditors were reviewed. Clearly, breaches of any of these duties could give rise to legal liability.

Various cases have considered the duties of a practitioner engaged as accountant to write up the records or to prepare unaudited financial statements. Unless the engagement contract specifies additional duties, the accountant (if clearly not acting as auditor) is not generally held liable for a failure to detect fraud. However, as previously discussed, liability has occasionally arisen (as in the *Tenants* case) where there was a misunderstanding as to the terms of the engagement. Even where the engagement is clearly non-audit, some English decisions have suggested that the accountant, becoming aware of suspicious circumstances, has a duty to pursue them appropriately.

There are a number of legal cases concerned with the question of the public accountant in the preparation of tax returns and the provision of tax advice. In general, chartered accountants in Canada decline responsibility with respect to tax return information supplied by the client. In such cases, the auditor generally has no legal liability except, of course, to the extent he treats the supplied information in an inappropriate manner on the return. In the rendering of tax advisory services, however, the same standards of skill, knowledge and due care are expected of the chartered accountant as in the provision of auditing services.

5.5 Recent litigation in the United States

In recent years, litigation involving public accountants has grown dramatically in the United States. In 1976 over 500 active cases (each involving up to 25 or more law suits) were in process. Famous cases such as *Continental Vending, Yale Express, BarChris, Westec, National Student Marketing*, and *Equity Funding* have become household words to most practitioners. Canada has not been exempt from law suits against auditors but their number has been proportionately far less.

There are several important reasons for this significant difference in the extent of litigation in the two countries: (a) contingency fees (b) jury system (c) court costs (d) class actions (e) U.S. securities legislation and (f) attitude of the SEC.

Contingency fees

The system of contingency legal fees in the United States has already been mentioned. Advocates of contingency fees argue that it provides legal assistance to persons who could not otherwise afford it. At the same time, unquestionably it increases the frequency of litigation. While contingent fees have until recently been prohibited in most of Canada, six provinces now permit them in one form or another, and other provinces (including Ontario) have been studying the matter.

The jury system

In the United States trial by jury can constitutionally be, and often is, demanded by the plaintiff. Many practitioners feel that defendant-auditors are at a disadvantage when technical accounting and auditing evidence must be tried by a jury, particularly when the assets of some giant, faceless insurance company are believed available to compensate for all personal losses. For the same reason, a plaintiff may be encouraged to initiate a case in what are perceived as favorable circumstances. In Canada, there is no absolute right to trial by jury in civil cases. It is the practice of the Supreme Courts in most provinces to require an action involving technical accounting evidence to be tried by judge and not by jury.

Court costs

As discussed earlier, in the United States the costs of legal actions are normally not recoverable from the unsuccessful party. As a result, a plaintiff with contingent fees for his own costs and no risk of being saddled with the defendant's costs rarely has anything to lose in instituting a major law suit. In Canada, the prospect of having to pay the successful party's costs discourages frivolous law suits.

Class actions

A further spur to litigation in the United States is the right of a few persons to sue on behalf of an entire class. A few disgruntled shareholders can accordingly sue on behalf of all shareholders, thus increasing the total damages claimed substantially. As a result, cases which would individually be prohibitively costly to pursue may become economic for both plaintiff and lawyer. In Canada class actions have not in the past been generally possible. However, in recent years Canadian class actions begun against certain automobile manufactureres may have opened the door. Advocates of class actions believe that it can bring justice to individual parties who could not separately afford it.

U.S. securities legislation

The U.S. Securities Act of 1933 and the Securities Exchange Act of 1934 impose heavy legal liability on the auditors of companies required to file registration statements, financial statements or other materials with the U.S. Securities and Exchange Commission. The degree of liability went far beyond the common law position at that date.

In the 1933 Securities Act third parties who purchase securities of registered companies on a primary distribution are given the same rights as clients under common law, that is they may sue the auditors for negligence, in any case where the registration statement contains an untrue statement of material fact by the accountant or omits a material fact which should be stated. If the plaintiff established that such was the case, the burden of proof is on the defendant to establish his innocence through a "due diligence" defence. The certifying accountant must establish that he made a reasonable investigation and based on that investigation had reasonable grounds to believe and did believe at the time the registration statement was issued that the statements therein were true and there was no omission of material facts. This contrasts sharply with common law where it is necessary for the plaintiff to establish a preponderance of evidence that the defendant acted without due care.

The *BarChris* case in 1968 was an action under section 11 of the Securities Act of 1933 brought by purchasers of BarChris's registered debentures against the directors, underwriters and independent auditors. The auditors and most of the other defendants, subsequent to the court's ruling that the registration statement was false and misleading, were unable to provide adequate "due diligence" defences. The *BarChris* case did, however, state that misstatements should be judged on the basis of generally accepted accounting principles ("accountants should not be held to a standard higher than that recognized in their profession") – though, as already discussed, not all cases have followed this view.

Under section 18 of the 1934 Act any person who makes a false or misleading statement in documents filed under the act is liable to any person who in reliance in that statement purchases or sells securities at a price that was affected by the statement. Again, once it is established that there is a false or misleading statement, the burden of proof falls upon the accountant to demonstrate that he acted in good faith and had no knowledge that the statement was in fact false or misleading. The statute sets no requirement that the plaintiff show that he relied on the statement or that such reliance was a proximate cause of any loss, as is required for common law negligence. Furthermore, there is no need for the plaintiff to demonstrate that the defendant acted with fraudulent intent. The scope of the liability under section 18 is narrow, however, since it relates only to documents filed with the Commission (and excludes annual reports to the shareholders).

Rule 10b-5 promulgated by the SEC makes it unlawful to make any false statement of a material fact or to omit to state a material fact necessary in order to make the statement, in the light of the circumstances, not misleading.

The importance of this section is that liability can be based on any false statements, without regard to whether they were filed with the SEC. There have been only a few cases completed where accountants have been sued subject to rule 10b-5. According to the *Texas Gulf Sulphur* case in 1968 rule 10b-5 applies if a false representation would cause reasonable investors to purchase and sell in reliance thereon. In a further case, the judge stated "the allegations may be sustained on either an intentional misrepresentation or on a negligent misrepresentation".

In the *Yale Express* case in 1967, auditors had become aware of errors subsequent to the issue of audited financial statements but corrections were not made until the following year's report. On a preliminary motion, the court ruled that trial should proceed both under rule 10b-5 and common law on the grounds that an auditor had a duty to disclose "after-acquired information" rendering his original opinion false. The judge conceded that such a duty raised questions concerning to whom it was owed and how long it lasted. As the case was settled out of court these questions were never answered.

In the *Hochfelder* case in 1976, the U.S. Supreme Court made a landmark decision contrary to the previous trend toward interpreting accountant negligence as fraud. Justice Powell concluded that under rule 10b-5 investors seeking civil damages from an accountant must show that he intended to "deceive, manipulate or defraud":

When a statute speaks so specifically in terms of manipulation and deception, and of implementing devices and contrivances – the commonly understood terminology of intentional wrongdoing – and when its history reflects no more expansive intent, we are quite unwilling to extend the scope of the statute to negligent conduct.

It should be noted, however, that other sections of the Act, though less broad than 10(b), permit a civil cause of action premised on negligent behaviour. Moreover, the court decision expressly left open the questions of (a) whether similar principles apply to SEC injunctions under 10b-5 and (b) whether reckless behaviour may in some circumstances be enough for action under 10b-5. Finally, the decision does not necessarily apply to similar state laws. Nonetheless, accountants hailed the decision as marking an important turning point in litigation under the federal securities acts.

There are no direct parallels in Canada to the type of securities legislation in the United States. A few analogous rules may be found in certain statutory

requirements (for example with respect to subsequent discovery of errors – as discussed in Chapter 4). Moreover, the application of the *Hedley Byrne* principle in Canada with respect to foreseeable third parties might cast the net of legal liability almost as wide as it is under the U.S. securities legislation. Provincial securities acts make it an offence to make any statement in any report, prospectus, return, financial statement or other document required to be filed pursuant to the legislation which in the circumstances is false or misleading. But the important difference remains that the burden of proof in Canada is on the plaintiff and not on the defendant.

Attitude of the SEC

A major factor in the trend of litigation in the United States has also been the attitude of the Securities and Exchange Commission. In fulfilling what it sees as its duty to protect the public interest the SEC has played an increasingly activist role in seeking to increase the legal responsibilities of public accountants. It has initiated suits against accountants and, upon occasion, urged other parties to initiate suits. It has urged auditors to assume greater responsibilities for subsequently discovered errors, fairness of presentation, detection of defalcations, interim statements, and legality of management actions. A few examples will illustrate this trend.

In the *Yale Express* case the Securities and Exchange Commission in an amicus curiae memorandum, contended that when an auditor subsequently discovers inaccuracies in audited financial statements already issued, he owes a direct duty to the investing public to disclose the inaccuracies. Following this view, the SEC laid charges against auditors in the *National Student Marketing* case in 1972. The auditors had issued a "comfort letter" pointing out errors in previously issued *unaudited* statements and urging their correction. The letter was ignored and a merger completed on the basis of the incorrect figures. The SEC maintains that the auditors had a duty to notify the SEC or the shareholders of the merging companies. The SEC's position may, however, have been somewhat weakened by the *Gold* v. *DCL* case in 1974 where it was held that, while an auditor has a continuing duty to revise an audit report should he subsequently discover something which makes it misleading, he is not associated with and does not have a duty to control all financial information which his client may reveal from time to time.

Recently, the SEC has launched a number of suits against U.S. companies for failure to disclose bribes and other illegal payments (both within the United States and elsewhere) in their financial statements and has suggested that auditors have a responsibility to report when such disclosures are not made.

In Canada, although the provincial Securities Commissions have maintained an interest in financial reporting and in all current developments in the securities, legislative and professional fields, they have not assumed the activist role of the SEC. Nor have they adopted the same adversary relationship which many practitioners have sensed in the United States.

5.6 Public expectations

Some of the foregoing reasons for the differences in frequency of litigation between Canada and the United States may continue. Some may not. It would be foolish to assume that Canada is exempt from the trends which have so influenced another country. Certainly, one of the trends common to both countries is that of "consumerism". The desire to protect consumers (whether of goods, services, or audit reports) from all possible harm has, in the words of some accountants and lawyers, created an "expectation gap" between the levels of performance envisioned by the public accountant and expected by the public.

In part this was the reason for the AICPA in late 1974 establishing a Commission on Auditors' Responsibilities (chaired by a former SEC chairman) "to study the role of independent auditors in society, to identify auditors' responsibilities that are responsive to the needs and reasonable expectations of users of financial statements, and to recommend actions that the profession should take to assure that independent auditors discharge those responsibilities adequately". The Commission has indicated it will be seeking evidence to determine the extent to which the current "expectation gap" can be attributed:

a) in part to substandard performance of present responsibilities (perhaps reflecting on professional training, professional discipline),

b) in part to factors that influence auditors not to accept responsibilities they might reasonably assume (perhaps reflecting on professional standards, conflicting responsibilities or the legal environment), and

c) in part to users' misunderstandings with respect to the meaning of auditors' reports, the inherent limitations in accounting, the limitations of auditing methods (with respect to reliance on testing, judgment, and persuasive rather than conclusive evidence), and the limitations on the auditor's authority (authority to express an opinion on information presented rather than on the soundness of investing in a company).

The findings of this Commission will undoubtedly be of importance to the accounting professions of all countries.

5.7 Reference material

R.W.V. Dickerson, LLB, PhD, FCA, *Accountants and the Law of Negligence* (The Canadian Institute of Chartered Accountants, 1966).
"Legal Cases", edited by R.W.V. Dickerson, LLB, PhD, FCA, in current issues of CA Magazine.
Liability of Accountants (The Defense Research Institute, Inc., Milwaukee, 1972).

5.8 Questions and problems

Review and discussion

1. The burden is on the plaintiff to prove negligence in litigation. What are the conditions necessary to establish liability for negligence?
2. What defences may be used by an auditor in a negligence suit?
3. Compare an auditor's duty of care to an audit client with that to a non-audit client.
4. In accepting an audit engagement, an auditor has certain duties of care to third parties. Discuss the assumptions an auditor should make with respect to these duties. Give examples of legal precedents supporting these assumptions.
5. During the course of conducting an audit, to what degree should an auditor be concerned with the detection of fraud? To what extent can an auditor be held liable for the non-detection of a fraud?
6. Explain the legal concept of the prudent or reasonable man.
7. State the necessary elements of fraud.
8. Discuss the differences between negligence and fraud.

9. Why are there more civil actions against auditors in the United States than in Canada?
10. How does a negligence action under U.S. Securities Laws (specifically related to a material misstatement in a prospectus) differ from a negligence action in common law?
11. Describe the legal purpose of engagement letters.
12. What is meant by the terms "privileged communication" and "qualified privilege"? What recognition does the law give to the existence of privilege in the auditor-client relationship?

Problems

1. For both the 1973 and 1974 audits, Pitman, Klein & Co., Chartered Accountants, issued a "Memorandum on Internal Control" to Harlan Securities Ltd., a brokerage firm. The key area where control was weak was in the bond transfer department, where there was a large volume of bonds in "bearer" form. During the Company's 1975 annual security count it was discovered that $125 000 of "bearer bonds" were missing. Further investigation indicated the initial fraud dated back to 1974. The company then sued Pitman, Klein for $125 000 on the grounds that their procedures should have detected the fraud in the year of occurrence.
   a) What defence would you suggest for Pitman, Klein for the ensuing court case?
   b) At what point should the auditors have adjusted their substantive procedures? Give reasons to support your answer.
   c) When a CA notices that management of a client is not implementing his recommendations on internal control, what procedures should he follow?
2. Auditors in Canada are becoming more exposed to lawsuits for negligence and breach of contract. Therefore, every time a CA accepts an engagement, there is a certain risk associated with that engagement.
   a) Outline the general factors affecting the degree of risk associated with a particular engagement.
   b) How do the factors outlined in (a) relate to generally accepted auditing standards?
   c) What steps in general terms can a CA take to minimize risk on each engagement?
3. Chapin Storage Ltd. was a medium-sized warehouse storage company. Its largest customer, High-Cost Furriers Ltd., maintained a substantial amount of its inventory at Chapin's premises with an agreement that the warehouse company would carry adequate insurance on all goods it stored.

Two weeks after Chapin had received an unqualified audit report on its financial statements, its warehouse was completely destroyed by fire. It was then discovered that Chapin carried no insurance at all and had no means of compensating High-Cost Furriers and its other customers. High-Cost then sued Chapin's auditors. Its claim was based on the premise that, during their review, the auditors should have determined there was no insurance and disclosed this fact as a contingent liability.
   a) Outline the points you feel would be critical in the lawsuit.
   b) In your opinion, would High-Cost be successful in its suit? Why?
   c) What responsibility does an auditor have in evaluating such items as "adequacy of insurance coverage"?
   d) To what extent did the auditor have a responsibility to review the agreement between Chapin and High-Cost and then to disclose the fact that its terms were not being adhered to?
4. Mini-Maxi Co. Ltd. manufactured ladies' dresses and Mini-Maxi blouses. Because its cash position was deteriorating, the company sought a loan from New Fashion Retailers Ltd. New Fashion had previously extended $25 000 credit to Mini-Maxi but refused to lend any additional money without obtaining copies of Mini-Maxi's audited financial statements.

Mini-Maxi contacted the CA firm of Mohr, Mason & Co. to perform the audit. In arranging for the examination, Mini-Maxi clearly indicated that its purpose was to satisfy New Fashion Retailers as to the corporation's sound financial condition and thus to obtain an additional loan of $50 000. Mohr, Mason accepted the engagement, performed the examination in a negligent manner, and rendered an unqualified auditor's opinion. If an adequate examination had been performed the financial statements would have been found to be materially misleading.

Mini-Maxi submitted the audited financial statements to New Fashion and obtained an additional loan of $35 000. New Fashion refused to lend more than that amount. After several other investors also refused, Mini-Maxi, finally, was able to persuade Taylor Department Stores, one of its customers, to lend the additional $15 000. Taylor relied upon the financial statements examined by Mohr, Mason & Co.

Mini-Maxi is now in bankruptcy, and New Fashion and Taylor seek to collect from Mohr, Mason the money they loaned Mini-Maxi.

In your opinion:
   a) Will New Fashion recover?

b) Will Taylor recover?

c) Should the purpose of the engagement have been set out in an engagement letter?

5. The CA firm of Stuart, McIntosh & Co. was engaged by Viva Retailers Ltd. to perform an audit of its financial statements for the year ended December 31, 1976. Stuart, McIntosh decided that it would be appropriate to examine certain transactions on a test basis. A sample of 150 disbursements was used to test vouchers payable, cash disbursements, and receiving and purchasing procedures. An investigation of the sample disclosed several instances where purchases had been recorded and paid for without the required receiving report being included in the file of supporting documents. This was properly noted in the working papers by Rittinger, the staff assistant who did the sampling. Stuart, the partner in charge, called these facts to the attention of Duffield, Viva's chief accountant. Duffield told him, "Don't worry about it. I'll make certain that these receiving reports are included in the voucher file." Stuart accepted this and did nothing further to investigate or follow up on this situation.

Duffield was engaged in a fraudulent scheme whereby he diverted the merchandise to a private warehouse where he leased space and sent the invoices for the merchandise to Viva for payment. The scheme was discovered later on special investigation, and a preliminary estimate indicated that the loss to Viva would be in excess of $200 000 (this is more than material).

a) What is the liability, if any, of Stuart, McIntosh & Co. in this situation? Discuss.

b) What additional steps, if any, should have been taken by Stuart? Explain.

c) What would the liability be if the error rate in the sample were deemed to be acceptable?

6. Your client, A Company, gives a copy of its audited financial statements to its banker each year. For the most recent year-end of A Company, you have given an unqualified audit report. Subsequent to this report A Company has gone into bankruptcy and the bank will realize only 80% of a $1 000 000 loan made to A Company.

What is the legal position of the bank in suing you for the remaining $200 000?

7. During the course of your examination of B Company, you obtain the following representations and explanations from Mark Johnson, the treasurer of the Company.

a) All securities owned by the Company are correctly recorded in the accounts. The Company has good title to these securities and they are free from hypothecation.

b) I have reviewed all our accounts receivable and consider the provision for bad debts and allowance for doubtful accounts to be reasonable.

c) Sales have increased this year as a result of a concentration of our sales force in selling our new product line.

What are the legal implications of this evidence?

Theory of Auditing

A modern town-planner would not attempt to build a new city without a systematic plan based on some rational underlying theory of city structure: should people live where they work or be transported daily – and if the latter, by what means? Only then could the details of residential and commercial construction be meaningfully designed. A modern auditor should not attempt to conduct a new audit without a systematic audit plan based on some rational underlying theory of auditing: should assets be verified completely or by testing selected details – and if the latter, on what basis does one determine which ones and how many? Only then can the mechanics of individual audit procedures be meaningfully planned. That cities and audits have been known to spread from year to year without the foundation of any underlying theory, proves not, unfortunately, that foundations are unnecessary. Urban and audit sprawl prove only that we are all born pragmatists. Most of us would rather patch than plan.

To be fair, the pragmatic approach has stood the profession in good stead. If those who built the profession over the last century had not tempered their vision with practical common sense, the profession would never have achieved the important position it enjoys today. Mature common sense will continue to be as important to the profession in the future as it has been in the past. But there does come a time in a growing organization when common sense alone must be supplemented by more formal planning. When the first corner stone is being erected, town planning would be an academic luxury. When multi-million dollar subways and expressways are being designed, intelligent planning is a necessity. With the proliferation of different types of business enterprises and financial transactions encountered by the auditor today, a unified underlying theory of auditing is essential. Such a theory should provide a consistent base from which specific auditing procedures, to meet new situations, can be derived by logical deduction.

Most importantly, however, auditing theory is essential because the adequacy of auditing procedures can only be planned, and subsequently defended, on theoretical grounds. There is no alternative, empirical proof of adequacy to which the auditor can appeal. If an automotive engineer designs an unworkable engine, empirical proof of his failure is readily at hand: the car does not run. Conversely, if he is successful he need not prove his success in terms of engineering theory: the observed horsepower, rate of acceleration, and economy of fuel consumption provide immediate empirical measures of the efficacy of his design. But if an auditor performs an inadequate audit, there is no immediate empirical evidence of his failure. It is not externally observable that the audit "does not run". The fact that future events subsequently proved that the financial statements were accurate does not necessarily prove that the audit work was adequate (the fire-fighter cannot take credit for stopping the fires that never started); nor does the fact that a given set of financial statements is subsequently proved to be inaccurate necessarily prove that the audit work was inadequate (the audit conclusion may have been fully justified by the audit evidence practically available at the time). The key requirements for a proper audit are that the audit evidence gathered be reasonable in extent and intensity in view of the importance of the question at the time and, further, that it be logically demonstrable that such evidence provided sufficient support for the audit opinion expressed. The satisfaction of these requirements can be demonstrated only in terms of their consistency with a logical and coherent theory of auditing.

While certain auditing concepts have always been implicit in the work of the auditor, it has been principally from 1960 on that the profession has begun to develop an explicit theory of auditing. This chapter reviews that development briefly and outlines a view of auditing theory to-day with which normal auditing practices, as described in the subsequent chapters of this book, are consistent.

6.1 Auditing: an independent field of knowledge

The first point to be observed is that auditing is a separate, independent field of knowledge. It is not a subdivision of accounting. As a profession we have done much to obscure this point. External audits are conducted by "public accountants" not "public auditors". Achievement of technical proficiency in auditing is rewarded with the right to the appellation, "chartered accountant", not "chartered auditor". Universities in Canada have departments of accounting, not departments of auditing. The new "student-in-accounts" will find commonplace among his friends the misconception that a chartered accountant spends all his time writing up the books (with a petulant concern when the cents fail to balance).

6.1.1 Comparison with accounting

Of course, there exists a relationship between accounting and auditing. Accounting information and the accounting systems which generate it constitute much of the subject matter of the audit examination. Generally accepted accounting principles constitute the established criteria against which the presentation of the financial statements is evaluated when the auditor expresses his opinion. Clearly, the auditor must be fully proficient in accounting before he can conduct a proper examination or issue an appropriate report. In this sense, every auditor is first an accountant.

But the processes of accounting and auditing are significantly different. Definitions of accounting and auditing were given in Chapter 1. From these definitions it can be seen that accounting involves the processes of "identifying", "measuring" and "communicating" economic information while auditing involves the processes of "obtaining", "evaluating" and "communicating" audit evidence. While the two disciplines share the objective of communication, the former in assembling a coherent picture of the past economic events is essentially a *creative* process, while the latter in weighing evidence as to correspondence with established criteria is essentially a *critical* process.[1] Accounting creates an image of past financial transactions; auditing provides an objective critique as to the fidelity with which the image reflects those transactions in accordance with accepted conventions.

6.1.2 The audit process

The audit process consists of an *investigative* phase (the field work) and a *reporting* phase. In the investigative phase, the auditor gathers evidence and evaluates it; in the reporting phase, he expresses the results of his evaluation as an audit opinion. In gathering and evaluating evidence, the audit process is more closely allied to the scientific method and to the judicial process, both of which are concerned with concepts of evidence and reasonable proof, than to the accounting process, which it reviews.

The *gathering* of evidence is an *active* role in which the auditor selects techniques which will yield the most persuasive evidence in an efficient manner to either confirm or deny the financial statement assertions. The *evaluation* of evidence is, on the other hand, in one sense a *passive* role in which the auditor weighs impartially the evidence he has obtained. In the judicial process these two roles are separated: reliance being placed on the adversary system to unearth all the pertinent evidence and on the judge or jury to evaluate it objectively. In the scientific method, as in the audit process, however, the two roles are combined: the scientist and the auditor each acting both as researcher and evaluator. This combination of roles places a responsibility on both the scientist and the auditor not to select only that evidence which favours a pre-conceived conclusion but, rather, to examine all pertinent evidence, whether supportive or contradictory, which is available on a timely and economical basis.

In the audit process, as in the scientific method and the judicial process, evidence and proof are relative concepts. To demand absolute evidence and perfect knowledge would delay scientific discoveries, court decisions, and audit reports indefinitely. All three disciplines must deal with reasonable rather than perfect knowledge, with persuasive rather than conclusive evidence. The uncertainties inherent in any audit opinion are best summed up in the recognized pioneering work on auditing theory:

> No mortal man in any field of professional endeavour obtains absolute knowledge. Continuing revisions of man's descriptions of the world as he knows it are accepted in the physical sciences. Courts occasionally reverse the decisions of lower courts and sometimes modify their own positions in given areas of litigation. At best, truth is relative and not always clearly discernible. Auditors have no greater powers of discernment than others. The limitations imposed by their subject matter and the conditions under which they work must be recognized by auditors as by other professional men. A judicious conclusion resulting from a search of evidence which was reasonable in extent and intensity in view of the importance of the question and the limitations of the situation must be considered sufficient to arrive at the truth for auditing purposes. The subsequent discovery of additional evidence or a better understanding of surrounding factors might later challenge or even nullify the original conclusion. Nevertheless, the best conclusion possible at the time approaches truth as closely as can be expected in this field.[2]

Analogies carried too far can, however, be dangerous. The scientific method, the judicial process, and the audit process must all make realistic compromises between certainty of proof and practical availability of evidence; but each of the three disciplines makes this compromise differently. Thus, a prime requisite of scientific evidence is the "repeatability" of experimental results, whereas time and finances do not permit the repitition of identical audit steps. Legal evidence generally excludes hearsay evidence; yet oral discussions and enquiries, often including hearsay elements, are and should be an important part of audit evidence. In considering a theory of auditing, therefore, the influence of other disciplines may be a useful guide but in the end auditing must be developed as a rational, coherent discipline on its own.

6.1.3 Development of auditing theory

For most of this century the accounting profession in its research activities, has been primarily concerned with the identification of appropriate accounting principles. The number of important accounting matters still under consideration suggests that accounting will continue to command a major amount of the profession's time in the future. In marked contrast, the amount of professional research time devoted to auditing matters had been until recently quite limited. To some extent, this is because the quality of the audit is far less visible to the public than the quality of financial accounting. Significantly, much of what little attention had previously been given to auditing had focussed on the one visible element: the wording and reservations in the auditor's report.

In the last two decades, however, the development of a logical theory of auditing by the profession has been undertaken. The pioneering work in this field was unquestionably that of Mautz and Sharaf[3] in 1961. Mautz and Sharaf identified five *auditing concepts,* which they called: evidence, due audit care, fair presentation, independence, and ethical conduct. They did not suggest that these were the only relevant concepts (and indeed additional ones are discussed in this chapter) but their thorough, careful analysis of these five laid the groundwork for a rational examination of the discipline of auditing. In addition, their critical investigation of certain *postulates of auditing* helped to expose some of the hidden assumptions on which auditing procedures are based (discussed in this chapter as *audit assumptions*).

A more recent addition to this field has been the American Accounting Association's study, *A Statement of Basic Auditing Concepts*[4], in 1972 (referred to in this chapter as ASOBAC). This study analyzed the relationships among *audit assumptions, audit perception,* and *rational argument.* In particular, the study provides many useful insights into the possibilities of errors in audit observations, which has benefited greatly the discussion of evidence evaluation in this chapter.

In 1973 the CICA established a new Auditing Standards Committee and the U.K. Institute a separate Auditing Practices Committee. In the same year the AICPA Auditing Standards Executive Committee launched a new series of pronouncements with *Statement on Auditing Standards No. 1,* a consolidation of all previous statements. A growing number of auditing pronouncements by these bodies can be anticipated. At the same time, many accountants properly have an aversion to the spectre of detailed 'cookbook' rules. In these circumstances there is an even greater need for unifying underlying concepts. Underlying concepts have indeed begun to appear more frequently in professional pronouncements. Work on such concepts has been facilitated in recent years by both theoretical and empirical research by the academic community. University symposia on auditing methods, a phenomenon of recent years, have helped to direct this research to areas of importance to practising auditors. Finally the growing number of court cases in connection with auditors' liability has focussed increased attention on the design and quality of audit work. It seems likely, therefore, that the profession will be taking a continuing, critical look at auditing concepts in the years to come.

6.2 Overview of a theory of auditing

6.2.1 A structure of auditing theory

The components of a coherent auditing theory can be classified and labelled in various ways. The Mautz and Sharaf and ASOBAC studies each presented slightly different structures. Further modifications have been introduced into the structure of the auditing theory outlined in this chapter (while still borrowing much from those two comprehensive studies) in order to emphasize the relationships among objectives, standards and concepts and among individual concepts themselves. The relationship of auditing objectives, generally accepted auditing standards, auditing concepts, auditing assumptions, auditing techniques and procedures is shown in Figure 6.a and was outlined briefly in Chapter 1.

The purpose of a theory of auditing is to provide a rational, coherent, conceptual framework for determining the auditing procedures (and extents thereof) necessary to fulfill defined auditing objectives. The objectives themselves are defined not by auditing theory but rather, as explained in Chapters 1 and 4, by the needs of economic society and how the profession perceives those needs when establishing generally accepted auditing standards. As it is socially useful at the present time to provide attestation to historically based financial statements, generally accepted auditing standards embody this objective in their reporting and field work standards. Auditing theory today must therefore provide a logical method for complying with these standards. Tomorrow, should it become socially useful to meet some additional or alternative objectives (whether reporting on forecasts, control, management performance, or otherwise), such objectives will no doubt become incorporated in a revised set of generally accepted auditing standards. Auditing theory will then have to develop an appropriate approach to meeting those revised standards.

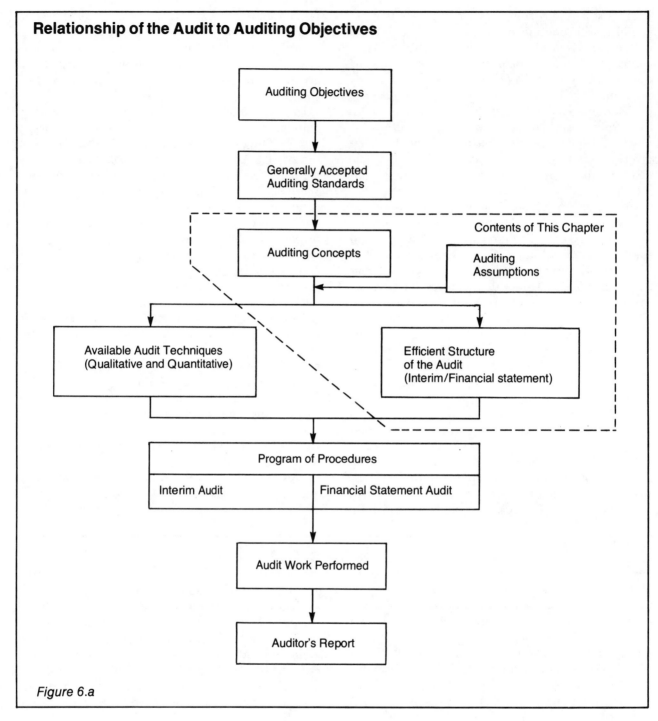

Relationship of the Audit to Auditing Objectives

Auditing Objectives

Generally Accepted
Auditing Standards

Auditing Concepts

Contents of This Chapter

Auditing
Assumptions

Available Audit Techniques
(Qualitative and Quantitative)

Efficient Structure
of the Audit
(Interim/Financial statement)

Program of Procedures

Interim Audit

Financial Statement Audit

Audit Work Performed

Auditor's Report

Figure 6.a

6.2.2 Auditing concepts

Given auditing objectives and generally accepted auditing standards to be met, auditing theory may be described in terms of a number of *auditing concepts* and their inter-relationships. Some of these auditing concepts are referred to explicitly in the standards themselves. (For a statement of the standards see Chapter 4.) The general standard, in calling for adequate training and proficiency, introduces what may be called the concept of *competence*. In calling for

an objective state of mind it introduces the concept of *objectivity*. And finally it expressly introduces the concept of *due care*. The third field work standard introduces the concepts of audit *evidence* and of *sufficiency* of such evidence. The third reporting standard expressly introduces the concept of *generally accepted accounting principles* and, by using the words 'present fairly', it introduces the concept of *fairness*.

A number of additional auditing concepts are implied by the standards. Fairness of presentation (in contrast to mechanical exactitude) implies the con-

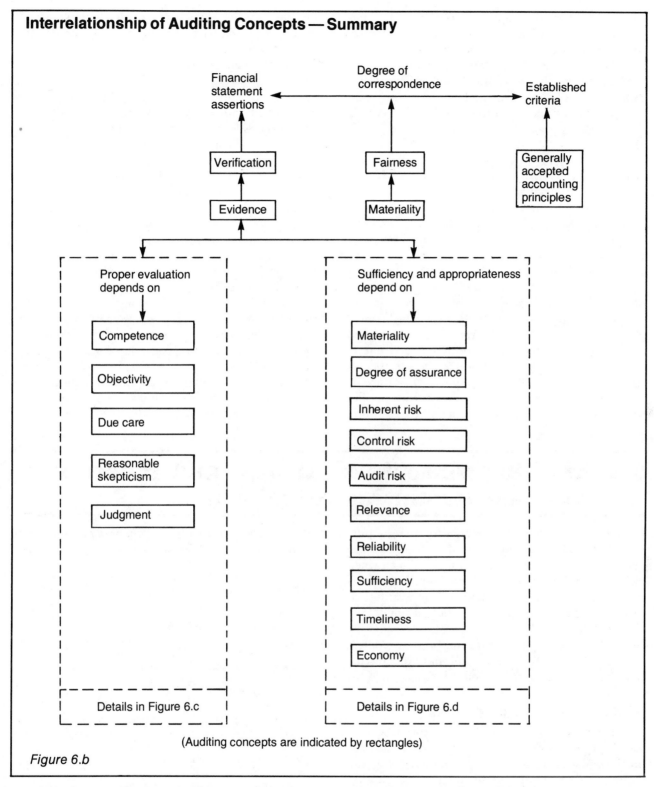

Interrelationship of Auditing Concepts — Summary

Financial statement assertions ← Degree of correspondence → Established criteria

Verification

Evidence

Fairness

Materiality

Generally accepted accounting principles

Proper evaluation depends on

Competence

Objectivity

Due care

Reasonable skepticism

Judgment

Details in Figure 6.c

Sufficiency and appropriateness depend on

Materiality

Degree of assurance

Inherent risk

Control risk

Audit risk

Relevance

Reliability

Sufficiency

Timeliness

Economy

Details in Figure 6.d

(Auditing concepts are indicated by rectangles)

Figure 6.b

cept of *materiality*. The third field work standard refers to a "reasonable basis" to support the content of the audit report. "Reasonable basis" implies that 100% certainty is not possible, and thus implies the concept of an appropriate *degree of assurance.* To be "reasonable" the degree of assurance must be limited to what can be practically achieved at a reasonable

cost and within a reasonable time; these may be called the concepts of *economy* and *timeliness.* In the general standard, the requirement of objectivity implies a concept of *reasonable skepticism.*

The obtaining of evidence and its subsequent evaluation as to sufficiency and appropriateness (third field work standard) implies the concept of audit *verification*. Appropriateness of evidence implies the concepts of *relevance* and *reliability*. By referring to a varying degree of reliance on internal control, the second field work standard implies the concept of *risk* – which may be divided into inherent risk, control risk and audit risk. Finally, by referring to an expression of opinion the reporting standards imply the overriding concept of *judgment*.

6.2.3 Summary of auditing theory

The interrelationship of these various auditing concepts, illustrated in summary form in Figure 6.b, constitutes a coherent theory of auditing, which is analyzed in the remaining sections of this chapter. In summary, auditing is concerned with evidence as to the degree of correspondence of financial statement assertions with established criteria. For general purpose financial statements, established criteria are provided by generally accepted accounting principles. These principles, however, can be identified only as general guidelines, not as detailed encyclopaedic rules. Their application to the specific circumstances of a given case requires that they be applied fairly. The concept of fairness thus implies an intelligent following of the spirit of the accounting

principle guidelines in a particular circumstance. It also implies that trivial errors can be ignored – the concept of materiality.

Gathering and evaluating evidence as to financial statement assertions can be referred to as a process of verification. The term "verification" has been used in auditing literature for many years, (though some practitioners fear mistaken inferences from its use). In an auditing context it does not imply absolute and certain proof, for, as already discussed, such proof is not practically available. It implies rather the obtaining and evaluating of sufficient appropriate evidence to warrant the expression of an informed opinion.

For audit evidence to provide adequate support for the auditor's expression of opinion, two conditions must be met: (1) the evaluation of the evidence must be properly carried out and (2) the evidence itself must be sufficient and appropriate. The former condition depends on the auditing concepts of competence, objectivity, due care, reasonable skepticism, amd professional judgment. The latter condition depends on the auditing concepts of materiality, degree of assurance, inherent risk, control risk, audit risk, relevance, reliability, sufficiency, timeliness, and economy. Each of these auditing concepts can now be examined in greater depth.

6.3 Auditing concepts of fairness and generally accepted accounting principles

In Figure 6.b, it was indicated that for general purpose financial statements, established criteria are provided by generally accepted accounting principles and that an evaluation of the degree of correspondence of financial statement assertions with such principles requires application of the concept of fairness. A full discussion of the concepts of generally accepted accounting principles and fairness is deferred until Chapter 17. The conclusions of that discussion, however, are summarized briefly below.

Generally accepted accounting principles

Arguments are presented in 17.3.1 to the effect that literal "general acceptance" is not a sound basis for the formulation of accounting principles and that indeed, the phrase "generally accepted accounting principles" today refers to a body of principles developed through a quasi-legislative process in an effort to narrow the co-existence of alternative methods of accounting for identical situations. It is also submitted that the phrase is not intended to imply a set of rigid rules to be applied mechanically to circumstances they do not fit. Rather, it is submitted that a logical

interpretation of the phrase "generally accepted accounting principles" in Canada at the present time would be:[5]

a) the Recommendations in the CICA Accounting Research Committee,
   or
b) in areas where the Recommendations are silent, those principles and practices which have, by usage or by other means, gained general acceptance in Canada or are in the spirit of existing Recommendations on similar matters,
   provided that
c) if, due to the unusual circumstances of a particular enterprise, the literal requirements of either (a) or (b) are not reasonably applicable, such adjustments are made as are consistent with the general spirit of the Recommendations, principles or practices in question.

Fairness

Arguments are presented in 17.3.2 to the effect that the concept of fairness should not be interpreted as implying a subjective set of standards overriding generally accepted accounting principles. It is submitted that such a subjective concept is not a sound basis for adding credibility to financial statements. Rather, it is submitted that the adverb "fairly" refers to a manner of applying established criteria which complies with the *spirit* of such criteria. To "present fairly in accordance with generally accepted accounting principles" is to apply such principles intelligently, judiciously and appropriately to the fact situation covered by the financial statements. It is not only to avoid rigidity with respect to trivial matters (the concept of materiality) but also to avoid applying the letter of recommendations mechanically to circum-stances where the spirit of recommendations calls for sensible adjustment.

Additional statutory requirements

Under many corporations acts the auditor has a statutory duty to report, in addition, any aspects in which the financial statements fail to meet statutory requirements (which may sometimes extend beyond generally accepted accounting principles). For this additional reporting, where it arises, "established criteria" are the provisions of the relevant statute.

6.4 Auditing concepts of verification and evidence

In Figure 6.b, it was indicated that financial statement assertions are subjected to a *verification* process which involves the gathering and evaluating of audit *evidence*.

Evidence

The audit concept of evidence refers to any relevant, reliable matter or facts obtainable by the auditor which will assist him in forming his opinion on the financial statement assertions. Auditors must generally deal with persuasive rather than conclusive evidence. As explained in 6.1.2 the concept of audit evidence must be distinguished from that of legal evidence or scientific evidence. In Chapter 10, nine different types of audit evidence are identified: (1) physical evidence; (2) concurrence of reperformances; (3) actions of client personnel; (4) statements and representations by third parties; (5) external documentary evidence; (6) accounting records and reports; (7) internal documentary evidence; (8) statements and representations by management and employees; and (9) consistency with other evidence.

Not all of these types of evidence will be available with respect to each separate financial statement assertion; those available will be present in differing quantities.

Verification

The audit concept of verification refers to the gathering and proper evaluation of sufficient appropriate evidence to warrant the expression of an opinion. It does not imply absolute proof in a mathematical sense as absolute proof is generally not available. What constitutes proper evaluation and sufficient appropriate evidence, as discussed below, involves the relationship of the concept of evidence to all the other auditing concepts. The nature of the evidence-gathering process itself varies depending upon the evidence available and the audit objective to be met. In Chapter 10, ten different auditing or evidence-gathering techniques are identified: (1) physical examination (of assets), (2) reperformance (of accounting routines), (3) observation (of activities), (4) enquiry, (5) confirmation, (6) scrutiny, (7) vouching (of source documents for transactions), (8) inspection (of other documents), (9) analysis (into components), and (10) correlation with related information. Not all these techniques will be appropriate with respect to each separate financial statement assertion.

6.5 Auditing concepts related to the proper evaluation of evidence

The first necessary condition outlined with respect to audit evidence was that the evidence be properly evaluated. The auditing concepts on which proper evaluation depends are analyzed in Figure 6.c. The evaluation process usually involves (a) certain underlying assumptions, (b) observations made by the auditor, and (c) conclusions drawn by the auditor. For example:

a) The auditor will usually assume that a signature appearing on an account receivable confirmation returned directly to him by mail represents agreement by his client's customer with the receivable amount indicated in the confirmation letter (though it does not necessarily indicate his intention or ability to pay);

b) the auditor will, say, observe that 43 out of 50 confirmation requests were returned with such signatures

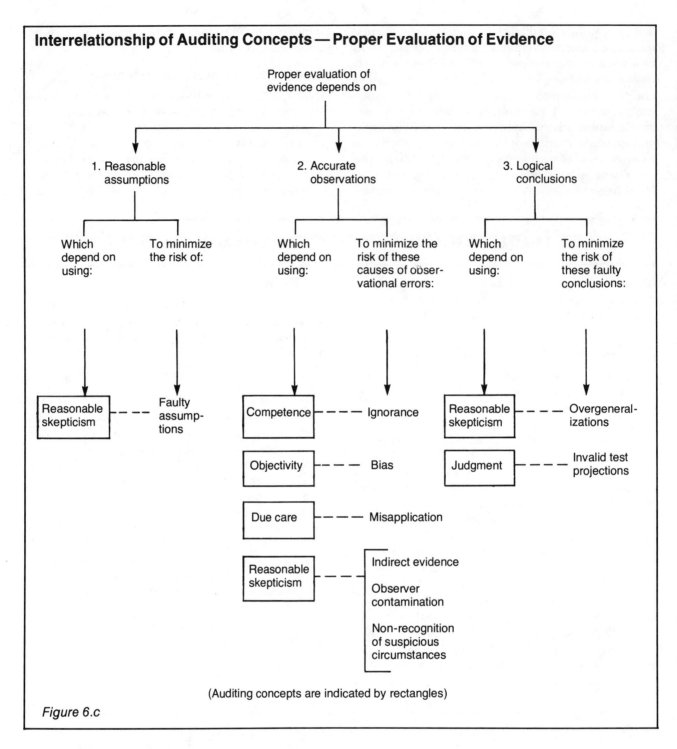

Interrelationship of Auditing Concepts — Proper Evaluation of Evidence

Proper evaluation of
evidence depends on

1. Reasonable assumptions

Which depend on using:

To minimize the risk of:

Reasonable skepticism

Faulty assumptions

2. Accurate observations

Which depend on using:

To minimize the risk of these causes of observational errors:

Competence — — — Ignorance

Objectivity — — — Bias

Due care — — — Misapplication

Reasonable skepticism — — —

Indirect evidence

Observer contamination

Non-recognition of suspicious circumstances

3. Logical conclusions

Which depend on using:

To minimize the risk of these faulty conclusions:

Reasonable skepticism — — — Overgeneralizations

Judgment — — — Invalid test projections

(Auditing concepts are indicated by rectangles)

Figure 6.c

and that the remaining 7 contained varying discrepancies which he has investigated and documented in his working papers;

c) the auditor may, say, draw the conclusion that based on this sample the total figure for accounts receivable reported on the balance sheet has been presented fairly in accordance with generally accepted accounting principles.

For the foregoing evaluation to be proper, the initial assumptions must be reasonable, the observations must be made accurately, and the conclusion must be drawn logically. Figure 6.c shows how the auditing concepts of competence, objectivity, due care, reasonable skepticism, and judgment contribute to these objectives. Of course, a number of the concepts have an overlapping effect and any diagrammatic analysis can only hope to identify some of the major relationships. Each of these concepts is now examined separately, beginning first, because of their importance, with those relating to accurate observations (centre column of Figure 6.c).

6.5.1 Competence

One of the obvious causes of observational errors is *ignorance*. An inexperienced auditor attempting to control a sophisticated computer print-out of physical inventory results is completely at the mercy of the computer operators. The operators may in fact execute all their operating procedures properly. But if they did not, the inexperienced auditor would not know the difference. His attendance in the computer room therefore adds no credibility to the inventory run, for he lacks the knowledge to make competent observations. The ASOBAC study comments that "we observe only what we know how to observe". The auditor cannot observe obsolescence in an inventory if he lacks sufficient knowledge of the business to recognize obsolescence when he sees it. Competence on the part of the auditor is thus clearly an essential condition if audit evidence is to be properly evaluated. The achievement and maintenance of competence was discussed in Chapter 3.

6.5.2 Objectivity

Another cause of observational errors is *bias*. "We are inclined to see what we want to see". The safeguard against bias is objectivity. The conditions for objectivity were discussed in Chapter 3 and the prime importance of an objective state of mind emphasized. An objective state of mind means that the auditor must be impartial and disinterested in the verdict rendered by the evidence he is examining. In reviewing the results of an accounts receivable confirmation, an impartial evaluation of the extent and results of the sample of confirmation letters might have been that a warranted conclusion as to fair presentation cannot be reached. If the auditor, however, reaches the contrary conclusion influenced by the fact that he does not want to have to extend his audit procedures, or by the fact that the client has insisted that no adjustments be made to the statements, or by the fact that he told the client three weeks ago that the audit results to date appeared satisfactory, he has failed to preserve his objectivity.

6.5.3 Due care

A further cause of observational errors is the *misapplication* of an audit procedure. Different auditing procedures have different purposes. Attempting to measure the extent of known errors with procedures designed for discovering unknown ones or attempting to investigate weaknesses with procedures designed for assessing controls is about as efficient as

attempting to use a shovel to cut wood. A particular variation of this error is the tendency to apply the most recently learned techniques everywhere. "Give a small boy a hammer and he will find that everything he encounters needs pounding." Competent and objective auditors can still make such errors through carelessness or inattention to objectives. Due care is thus another essential condition of proper evaluation of evidence.

Of course, due care is important for other reasons than ensuring that the right audit procedure is used in the right place. Any of the observational errors, unreasonable assumptions, or illogical conclusions can occur through inadvertence if due care is not continuously exercised. The professional standard of due care was discussed in Chapter 3 and the legal standard in Chapter 5.

6.5.4 Reasonable skepticism

Three further causes of observational errors all depend on reasonable skepticism for their control: the problem of *indirect evidence,* the danger of *observer contamination* of the evidence observed, and the risk of *non-recognition of suspicious circumstances.* The problem of indirect evidence is that the auditor cannot generally make direct observations of transactions as they occur. Rather he must observe what was recorded by others who did observe the transactions. It is well recognized that direct personal knowledge is more persuasive than information obtained indirectly. Unfortunately, much of the information the auditor obtains is necessarily indirect (e.g., documentary evidence, representation from other parties). In those cases it is essential that the auditor, while not ignoring indirect evidence by any means, attribute to it a degree of reliance commensurate with its lesser persuasiveness.

In those cases where the auditor can obtain direct personal knowledge through observation, he must take care that his very act of observing does not change the evidence observed (observer contamination). For example, inventory counting teams may exhibit more conscientious care when the external auditor is watching than when he is not. Thus, observations made during attendance at a physical stocktaking could, in certain cases, be misleading.

Finally, there are many audit procedures which require extension in the presence of suspicious circumstances. It is normally reasonable, in the presence of good internal control, not to observe the physical distribution of pay to employees (an audit procedure that was more common in the past when the primary objective was fraud detection). However, if wage costs show an inexplicable and material increase during the last three months, the auditor must consider whether his suspicions should be aroused and accordingly whether an extended auditing procedure is required. Of course, such suspicious circumstances will never be noticed by the auditor if he is carelessly inobservant or unduly gullible.

Closely related to the risk of overlooking suspicious circumstances is the risk of *faulty assumptions* (left-hand column in Figure 6.c). Numerous assumptions are made in the course of every audit. A few of the major ones are identified later in this chapter but it would be pointless to attempt to document all the assumptions made in each particular audit. The auditor in evaluating the audit evidence should be alert for circumstances which suggest that the underlying assumptions are unreasonable. Most of the ordinarily reasonable assumptions break down in the presence of suspicious circumstances. For example, in accounts receivable confirmation it would ordinarily be reasonable to assume that a signature on the confirmation letter indicated the existence of a bona fide client in agreement with the receivable amount indicated in the letter. However, if the amount of the receivable is unusually large, if the customer is apparently new to the client, and if the name of the customer is unknown to the auditor, the auditor would have to decide whether this underlying assumption was still reasonable or whether further, extended audit procedures (identification of the customer name in trade directories, discussion with the credit manager, etc.) might not be appropriate. This decision again demands the maintenance of an attitude of reasonable skepticism on the part of the auditor.

In drawing conclusions from his audit observations (right-hand column in Figure 6.c), one of the dangers is that the auditor will make the error of *overgeneralizing*. For example, a test deck checking programmed controls in a computer system reveals that a hypothetical $5 300 shipment to a Vancouver customer is printed out on a special credit check list, thus apparently verifying an alleged control that all sales orders over $5 000 receive a special credit review. In fact, perhaps, only domestic sales are subject to this control and through inadvertence the program design allows hundreds of foreign sales to go through each month without this control. The auditor has overgeneralized his conclusion. It would be naive to suggest there is any sure yet economical protection against the risk of audit overgeneralization. What can be expected, however, is that the auditor be aware of his risk and maintain an attitude of reasonable skepticism in drawing his conclusions.

An attitude of reasonable skepticism does not imply an obsessive suspiciousness, sensing a lurking fraud behind every innocent entry, pursuing an imagined forgery behind every document examined, or assuming the existence of a collusive conspiracy when no suspicious circumstances suggest it. The much quoted maxim that the audit "is a watchdog, but not a bloodhound"[6] conveys the proper sense. But indeed the watchdog must watch. Reasonable skepticism, then, means not the suspiciousness of the paranoic but the healthy skepticism of the scientist — a refusal to jump immediately to the hypothesis one would like to be true, should there be a reasonable possibility that it is not.

6.5.5 Judgment

Yet a further possible error in drawing conclusions from audit observations is an *invalid projection* of test results. For example, the auditor of an express company, confirming a sample of 200 freight bills receivable, finds four duplicate billings, which errors he dismisses as immaterial as they total only $800. In fact, let us say, the most likely aggregate error is 2% of total receivables, which would indeed be material. The logical fallacy in the auditor's rationalization was to confuse the immateriality of actual sample errors with the possible magnitude of total population errors. The avoidance of such invalid projections requires the disciplined use of logic together with the careful exercise of professional judgment. In many audits the use of judgment in projecting test results can be assisted by the use of statistical sampling techniques (discussed in Chapter 13). The use of such statistical techniques merely aids judgment; it does not supplant it.

Informed judgement is, of course, essential not only in drawing conclusions from audit observations, but indeed in all aspects of the audit process. It is worth repeating here a statement that was made in Chapter 1. *What constitutes an appropriate choice of auditing procedures and extents in any given engagement must be decided by the exercise of professional judgment.* No suggested auditing procedure appearing in any textbook can be held out to be invariably necessary on all audits nor necessarily sufficient on any given audit. The practitioner has a responsibility to apply those procedures which in his judgment are necessary to meet generally accepted auditing standards and to comply with the rules of professional conduct.

6.6 Auditing concepts related to the sufficiency and appropriateness of evidence

The second necessary condition previously outlined with respect to audit evidence was that the evidence examined should be sufficient and appropriate. The auditing concepts on which sufficiency and appropriateness depend are analyzed in Figure 6.d.

There are three basic factors which influence whether a particular collection of audit evidence can be considered to be sufficient and appropriate: (1) the required precision of the audit opinion, (2) the required degree of assurance of the audit opinion, and (3) the practical availability of evidence. These three factors, represented by the three main vertical divisions of Figure 6.d, are each discussed below.

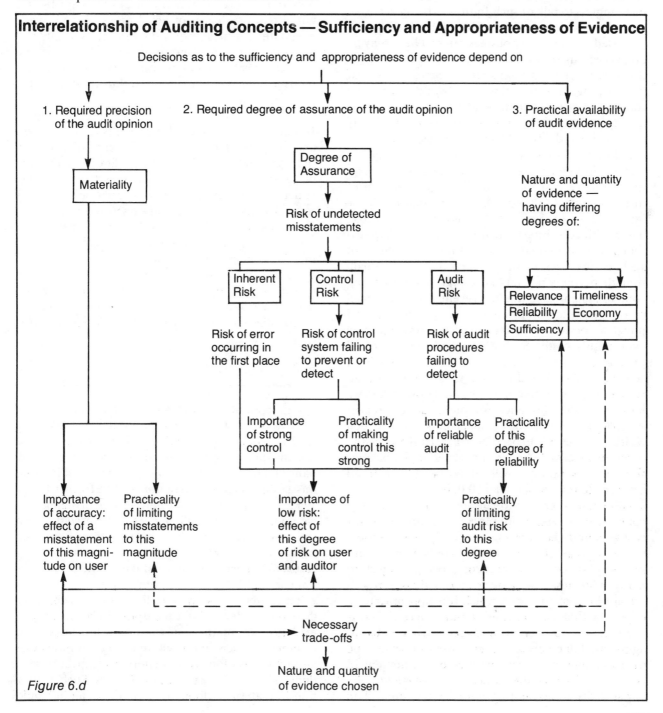

Figure 6.d

6.6.1 Required precision of the audit opinion

Absolute precision in financial statement presentation is neither possible nor its pursuit economically desirable. To start with, many figures reported on the financial statements are necessarily based on judgmental valuations (the estimate of lives of fixed assets on which to base depreciation, the allowance for doubtful accounts receivable, provisions for inventory obsolescence, warranty provisions, etc.). It is meaningless to talk of such figures as being accurate to the nearest dollar. Should $100 000 or $150 000 be provided for inventory obsolescence? There may be no precise answer to this question. All one can say is that this range constitutes a *zone of reasonableness* and that any figure within this zone would have to be considered reasonable (though persuasive evidence may exist that a $30 000 provision would be clearly inadequate and $300 000 clearly excessive).

Other aspects of the financial statement figures may be, in theory, precisely determinable, but at an unreasonable cost. For example, a good system of internal control will minimize the incidence of posting errors and cut-off errors in accounts receivable. Thus, with good internal control it can be anticipated that at any given financial reporting date the level of such errors present in the records will be small, though perhaps not nil. To design a super-strong control system that would prevent even this small error frequency or to conduct a special year-end purge to locate and correct all such errors might be exorbitantly costly. Such a cost could be out of all proportion with the small refinement in precision achieved. Why should the last $1 000 of clerical errors in accounts receivable be hunted down when we know that the allowance for doubtful accounts is subject to a "zone of reasonableness" of $50 000 width? Whatever the correction of clerical errors, the accounts receivable figure appearing on the balance sheet in this example will always be subject to an irreducible imprecision of $50 000.

Of course, such a rationale should not be used to condone unnecessary sloppiness or failure to correct easily identifiable errors. Knowledgeable readers may expect cash, largely a question of fact, to be more precisely stated than inventory, being subject to many estimates. The point is merely that there is a certain limit of precision which it is appropriate to expect of financial statements and, where the costs are excessive to prevent or correct errors which in aggregate fall below this level, it would normally be unreasonable to expect this further refinement in accuracy. This is the concept of *materiality*. Its applicability to accounting is well established. The introduction to the CICA Accounting Recommendations, for example, states:

> Recommendations also need not be applied to immaterial items. While materiality is a matter of professional judgment in the particular circumstances, the Committee believes that, as a general rule, materiality may be judged in relation to the reasonable prospect of its significance in the making of decisions by the readers of the financial statements. If the item might reasonably be expected to affect the decision, it should be deemed to be material.

The concept of accounting materiality applies not only to measurement of financial statement figures but also to the degree of detail necessary to provide adequate and meaningful disclosure. Not only is it important to communicate material data, it is also important *not* to communicate trivial data, as this tends to confuse the reader and thus frustrate effective communication.

The concept of materiality applies also to auditing. If a given set of financial statements cannot reasonably be presented with a finer degree of precision than $50 000, then clearly the audit opinion cannot be expressed with a precision finer than $50 000. Indeed, whatever the apparent accuracy of the financial statements there is always a chance that they are subject to some undetected errors. To reduce the possible magnitude of these undetected errors to infinitesimal proportions would normally increase the audit cost to astronomical levels. Thus, there is usually some required precision of audit opinion (some level of audit materiality) below which it is not reasonable to confine the total of undetected errors.

6.6.2 Materiality

An appropriate level of audit materiality is dependent upon (a) the relative importance of accuracy (which depends on the effect that a misstatement of this magnitude would have on the reader of the financial statements) and (b) the practicality of limiting misstatements of this magnitude. The former factor (sensitivity) suggests that when certain misstatements would have an unusually significant consequence on the reader (for example, misstatements of working capital when reported figures are close to violating restrictive covenants in a trust deed), the materiality limit should be lower than otherwise.

The latter factor (practicality) can be seen, in Figure 6.d, to depend in turn upon the availability of evidence within the constraints of timeliness and economy. This is not to say that on each individual audit the decision as to materiality can be varied depending upon cost and time factors. Such a variation in materiality limits from audit to audit would seriously distort the comparability and hence usefulness of all audited financial statements. Nonetheless, for a class of audit engagements taken as a whole, it is clear that cost and time factors do and should influence the materiality limit appropriate for the entire class. If it were simple and economical to audit all reported incomes within a precision of 1%, this degree of precision would no doubt be in common use by auditors and rightfully expected by financial statement users. The fact is, however, that refining materiality to such a low level would be exorbitantly costly – out of all proportion to the benefit of the refinement. Rather, a materiality level around 10% of pre-tax income (with respect to possible misstatements of pre-tax income) is a more reasonable measure of practical precisions achievable. However, for large public companies, as a class, the significance usually attached to even small changes in reported earnings per share coupled with the usually lower proportionate cost of achieving a given level of precision (a result of stronger control and the averaging effect of larger numbers of transactions) suggests the desirability of a lower materiality limit (such as 5% of pre-tax income).[7]

Deciding what is material in any particular case must be a matter for professional judgment. Many studies issued by professional accounting bodies in recent years have advocated the use of materiality guidelines to assist this judgment. In any given audit, there may be special circumstances that require the materiality limit to be high or lower than normal – and these circumstances can only be assessed judgmentally. Thus, materiality guidelines can never be rigid or mechanical rules. They can, however, provide a useful starting point in exercising judgment, and can help to establish some consistency as to how judgments are made from audit to audit or from auditor to auditor.

Materiality guidelines

The arguments in favour of materiality guidelines can be summarized briefly as follows. First, effective communication requires agreement between receiver and sender as to a common language (generally accepted accounting principles) and part of this common language should be a reasonable consensus as to materiality. Second, it is desirable that public confidence be maintained in the reliability of audited financial statements; the unguided exercise of personal judgment as to materiality can produce greatly diverse results under similar circumstances, which surely cannot inspire confidence. Third, the accounting profession has a body of knowledge which must be imparted to its recruits; as the exercise of judgment with respect to materiality is a major operational concept in the profession, it is desirable that

this concept be imparted uniformly to these recruits in their training program.

Various professional studies have advocated the use of materiality guidelines. A number of these have suggested, in effect, that materiality guidelines for income misstatements should logically be expressed as a percentage (5% to 10%) of normalized net income. Some suggested guidelines following this basis are presented as an example in Chapter 15. An alternative suggested guideline is a fixed percentage (such as 25%) of the year-to-year change in earnings; however, as discussed in Chapter 15, such a guideline does not lend itself to practical audit use. Finally, there have been advocates of disclosing materiality levels by reporting financial statement figures as ranges rather than discrete numbers.[8] Whether or not such a suggestion is adopted by the profession in the future, it is probably fair to say that the profession has not to date played a sufficient part in informing the general public of the necessary degree of imprecision surrounding most financial statement figures.

Materiality limit for a given audit

In any given audit engagement the auditor must, through the use of professional judgment and with or without the assistance of guidelines, make a decision as to what is an appropriate level of materiality in the circumstances. Of course, many individually immaterial errors could add up to a large total; once this total crosses the "materiality threshold" (or "materiality limit"), the aggregate error would normally be considered material. No materiality threshold, however, can be defined with any very exact degree of precision. For this reason, any presumptive line used by the auditor should not be viewed as a mathematically accurate measurement. Trivial breaches of the presumptive materiality limit would not normally be viewed as serious. Subject to the foregoing caveat, a materiality limit for a given audit has two uses: as a guide to audit planning, (design and extent of verification procedures) and as a guide to evaluation of audit results (the formation of the audit opinion). Both uses of the materiality limit are discussed in Chapter 11. The setting of the materiality limit itself is discussed in Chapter 15. Report reservations required in the presence of material misstatements are discussed in Chapter 18.

6.6.3 Required degree of assurance of the audit opinion

Absolute certainty in the presentation of audited financial statements is neither possible nor its pursuit economically desirable. The auditor's report adds credibility to the statements to which it is appended, but it cannot add complete certainty. Audit evidence is rarely completely conclusive. Consider, for example, the risk of undisclosed liabilities. An auditor has certain customary procedures for investigating this possibility: reviewing payments subsequent to the statement date, confirming or examining statements from the company's regular bankers and regular trade suppliers, reconciling interest expense with reported indebtedness. There are, of course, additional audit procedures that would be theoretically possible. The auditor could in theory write to every bank, financial institution, and major trade supplier in the country (or even in other countries) on the off chance of discovering an undisclosed liability to one of them. The cost of such an extension of audit procedures would be out of all proportion to the miniscule increment in credibility thereby achieved.

6.6.4 Degree of assurance and risk

Thus, it is logical that there is a certain *degree of assurance* which it is appropriate to expect of the audit opinion and, in view of the costs, and in many cases the impossibility, of increasing assurance above this threshold, it would normally be unreasonable to expect a further increment in confidence. The concept of an appropriate degree of assurance from the audit opinion can be examined in terms of the complement of such assurance: the risk of undetected misstatements remaining in the audited financial statements. This risk is in turn a product of three factors:

- inherent risk (the risk of an error occurring in the first place),
- control risk (the risk of the control system failing to prevent or detect such error – complement of the relative strength of internal control),
- audit risk (the risk of the audit procedures failing to detect such error).

The first two factors are sometimes described jointly as the concept of *relative risk:* the risk of the financial statements, prior to audit, containing misstatements. In general, however, analysis is simplified by considering each of the three factors separately.

Inherent risk

Inherent risk of error in a reported asset, for example, depends on the nature of the asset and its susceptibility to manipulation or inadvertent error. High-value low-bulk assets which are readily saleable (such as transistor radios) are more susceptible to pilferage than an inventory of sheet steel. Extension of complex price conversion factors (inventory units expressed as steel sheets of specified dimensions, prices expressed per pound) is more susceptible to inadvertent calculation errors than simple pricing factors (inventory in numbers of refrigerators, prices in dollars per refrigerator). The perceived susceptibility to manipulation or error will also be influenced by the presence of suspicious circumstances and by the nature of any past years' errors. Large unexplained inventory shortages in cycle counts during the year increase the inherent risk of error in year-end inventories. A past history of cut-off errors at prior year-ends increases the inherent risk of this year's accounts receivable being misstated. Inherent risk of error with respect to valuation is also greater when such valuation is more than usually subject to future events whose outcome at the financial statement date is necessarily uncertain.

Control risk

The relative strength of internal control is one of the most important factors affecting the total risk of error. A strong system of internal control depends on appropriate systems design (discussed in Chapters 7 and 8) and on an appropriate degree of compliance with these designed procedures. A good program of internal auditing can be an important element of internal control and, when present, decreases the risk of undetected error substantially. Conversely, recent systems changes may sometimes increase the perceived risk of error since the accuracy of the new system will not yet have stood the test of time. There is a limit, of course, to how strong it is practical to make the system of internal control. Controls cost money and each new control must be balanced by a commensurate reduction in risk of error or its cost is not justified.

Audit risk

The sources of audit risk relate to the effectiveness of the audit procedure itself (however well performed, a particular procedure might be unable to detect a given type of error), the propriety of the evaluation process (the risk of faulty assumptions, observational errors, and illogical conclusions has already been discussed), uncertainty inherent in the accounting information itself (valuations dependent upon the outcome of future events), and the risk of unexamined contradictory evidence (a particular type of which is sampling risk). These sources of audit risk can never be eliminated. But with due care and the exercise of professional judgement they can be reduced to a level commensurate with the degree of assurance required.

The risk of auditing procedures failing to detect a given error is itself usually a product of a number of individual risks each related to a separate, but overlapping, audit procedure. Thus, four specific audit procedures (confirmation, cut-off tests, scrutiny, and gross-profit analysis) all have a chance of detecting a given cut-off error in accounts receivable, supposing it exists – and conversely each is subject to a certain risk of failing to detect the error. But the joint risk of all four procedures simultaneously failing to detect the error will be the product of the four individual risks (provided that the four risks are independent) and thus will be much smaller than any of the individual risks taken in isolation. (For example, suppose hypothetically that the individual risks were measurable and each equal to 20%; the joint risk of four simultaneous failures of detection would then be only 0.16%, the joint product.) Thus, in general, more overlapping audit procedures contribute to a reduction in the overall audit risk. Nevertheless there are limits to the possible reduction. An appropriate level of audit assurance is dependent upon the practicality of limiting audit risk to a given degree. This practicality can be seen in Figure 6.d, to depend, in turn, upon the availability of evidence within the constraints of timeliness and economy.

The three risk factors (inherent risk, control risk, and audit risk) and their inter-relationships suggest a number of corollaries. For a given overall degree of assurance, the level of assurance afforded by auditing procedures taken in isolation may properly vary inversely with the level of assurance afforded by reliance placed on the system of internal control and the inherent nature of the item under examination. It is well recognized in practice, for example, that when control is weak the auditor must do more work; when it is strong he may do less. At the same time, when evidence with respect to a given item is unusually costly and time-consuming to obtain, the appropriate level of audit assurance for that item should be somewhat lower than otherwise. Conversely, when evidence is unusually cheap a higher level of audit assurance would normally be appropriate.

Some auditors are hesitant to admit a cost/confidence relationship, though as a practical matter it is usually implicit in the design of their audit programs. Yet such a relationship is both logical and in the public interest. If it were simple and economical to audit all financial statements with a 99.9% confidence of detecting any material error, such a confidence level (were it measurable) would no doubt be in common use by auditors and rightfully expected by financial statement users. The fact is, however, that improving assurance to such a near-certainty level would be exorbitantly costly – and out of all proportion to the benefit of the improvement. Within limits, therefore, an appropriate choice of audit confidence is and should be influenced by the cost of obtaining it (see also 6.6.7).

Relationship of materiality and degree of assurance

It is important not to confuse the two concepts of materiality and degree of assurance. Materiality refers to the *magnitude* of a given misstatement; degree of assurance refers to the *confidence* (degree of credibility) that such a material misstatement is not present in the audited financial statements. It should be noted, however, that the concept of degree of assurance can be expressed only in terms of a reference to materiality. It would be meaningless to talk about the degree of assurance that a 2¢ error is not present. Indeed, there is every likelihood that a number of trivial errors, not detected by the system of internal control or by the auditor's examination, *are* present in the financial statements. It is only meaningful to talk about an appropriately high degree of assurance (low risk) that a material error is not present.

To determine how high a degree of assurance (how low a level of risk) is appropriate, one must consider what effect a given level of risk that a material error has occurred should logically have on both the user of the financial statements and the auditor.

Effect of risk on user and auditor

It has been stated that the cost of audit procedures should bear some reasonable relation to the increment in credibility (reduction in risk) thereby purchased. The exact relationship, however, is not simple to define.

Consider the case of a purchaser of a business paying net book value as reported on the balance sheet (assuming asset cost were a relevant valuation for this purpose). Assume, hypothetically, that there is a 10% risk of reported net assets being overstated by $100 000 and a 10% risk of them being understated by $100 000. Mathematically, it might appear that neither purchaser nor vendor should be willing to pay for any audit cost to reduce these uncertainties; they each have a net 'expectation' of loss equal to nil and any audit cost will, on average, leave them both poorer. Yet the world does not always run on averages. In practice, both the purchaser and vendor will usually wish to pay a reasonable audit cost to reduce these uncertainties because of the consequences to them of losses of this magnitude should they occur. Like insurance, auditing is sometimes a negative-sum game whose purpose is to reduce, though it cannot eliminate, uncertainty.

The question then is: What level of uncertainty or risk should be acceptable to the financial statement reader (bearing in mind that risk reduction has a cost to the enterprise in terms of audit fees)? For the equity investor in a public company, decisions to buy, hold or sell depend on how he (or an adviser) assesses the share value in relation to the current market's assessment. An assessment of the share value can ordinarily be viewed in terms of reported or estimated earnings per share times a price-earnings multiple. To avoid a misleading assessment of share value, the investor or prospective investor therefore wants as much certainty as is practically available as to both the reported earnings per share and as to a reasonable price-earnings multiple. However, it would be uneconomic to demand a level of certainty for one of these factors out of all proportion to the level of certainty available with respect to the other. In predicting future price-earnings multiples, few investment analysts would allege that a 5% error in their prediction could be avoided with anything greater than a 50% to 75% confidence. Indeed, looking at the fluctuations of interest rates, inflation levels, and general market optimism or pessimism (on which price-earnings multiples depend) many would no doubt argue that the confidence of avoiding a 5% error was very much less. Bearing this in mind, it would seem illogical to pay the cost of achieving an extremely high (say 99%) confidence of avoiding a 5% error in the other factor, reported earnings per share. Probably a confidence level in the range of 80% to 90% would be adequate for the needs of most financial statement users. The fact that many members of the public have an unreasonable expectation that an audit provides 100% confidence of precise accuracy does not disprove the logic of the foregoing argument; rather, it evidences the inadequacy to date of the profession's education of the public.

Unfortunately, the terms of the typical audit engagement do not specify the level of confidence to be supplied (and, of course, such a level could not be measured in any very accurate sense in any case).[9] Suppose an auditor, subscribing to the foregoing arguments, saw to it that a degree of assurance of 90% (coming partly from reliance on control, partly from audit procedures) was achieved on every audit. It follows that 10% of his audits would contain errors greater (though probably not much greater) than materiality. Some portion of these errors would no doubt come to light and in some cases injured parties would contemplate law suits against the auditors for not having detected them. The dramatic increase in such litigation in recent years has been referred to in Chapter 5. Though particularly a phenomenon in the United States up to now, there is no reason to believe the trend may not be seen in Canada. The auditor in the foregoing example would, of course, hope to prove than in achieving a reasonable degree of assurance he had met reasonable standards of his profession and that the fact that in a few cases errors were thereby undetected was not evidence of negligence on his part. One would hope he would be

successful in this defence. The fact is, however, that even successful defences represent a substantial loss to the auditor in terms of the cost in professional time and the effect of the controversy on his professional reputation. Many auditors for their own protection, will conclude that a higher degree of assurance is needed – not because a lower degree of assurance would have been indefensible but merely because the disruption and cost of any such defense is best avoided. This additional desired degree of assurance will logically depend on the auditor's exposure. Thus, for companies with publicly traded shares, where there is a wide exposure, most auditors will want a relatively high degree of assurance. Were it accurately measurable it might be as high as 99%.

The purpose of this discussion has not been to suggest that degree of assurance can be measured as a percentage (only that portion relating to the risk of sampling error can be so measured) but only to argue that it would not be unreasonable for the practitioner to vary the degree of assurance (and hence the intensity of audit procedures), within certain limits, in proportion to the degree of audit exposure.

6.6.5 Practical availability of audit evidence

Infinite quantities of absolutely conclusive evidence are neither available not their pursuit economically desirable. In obtaining sufficient and appropriate evidence the auditor must necessarily be influenced by the limitations (or lack of limitations) on the quantity and quality of the evidence practically available. If one simple reconciliation can account for the total revenue level for the year (for example, reconciling interest income to average loans outstanding in a finance company) such a reconciliation should normally be considered a necessary part of 'sufficient evidence' for that audit even though in the audit of a manufacturing concern such a reconciliation may be difficult or impossible and accordingly not a necessary part of 'sufficient evidence' for the latter audit.

In general, however, decisions as to the necessity of examining a piece of evidence based on its practical availability are not as clear-cut as the case of the above revenue reconciliation. More usually the auditor is faced with a large number of different types of evidence available in varying quantities and susceptible to examination through various different auditing techniques (e.g., vouching vs. scrutiny, inspection vs. enquiry). Each type of evidence, each possible quantity, and each auditing technique for gathering it involves differing degrees of relevance, reliability and sufficiency and is subject to differing degrees of timeliness and economy. A proper choice of evidence is dependent upon the inter-relationship of these five concepts.

6.6.6 Relevance, reliability and sufficiency

The third field work standard calls for *sufficient appropriate* audit evidence. For evidence to be appropriate it must have some *relevance* and some *reliability*. The concepts of relevance, reliability and sufficiency can be illustrated by the following example.

> The auditor's objective is to verify that a $10 000 account receivable existed at December 31. He has received no reply to his confirmation request. He has, however, seen a cash receipts entry for $10 000 from that customer in February. This latter evidence is *relevant*, for it bears on the question of whether a $10 000 receivable existed. The auditor will consider the evidence *reliable* if he is satisfied that it indicates that $10 000 really was paid in February (mere enquiry would be less reliable; interception of cash receipts would be more reliable, though perhaps impractical). Even if fully satisfied as to its reliability, however, the auditor will consider the evidence *sufficient* only if it fully meets his original objective (verifying that a $10 000 receivable existed at December 31. In this example, there remains the possibility that the $10 000 February cash receipt was paying for a January sale. Depending on how he assesses this risk, the auditor may or may not decide that additional evidence (e.g., sales invoices, shipping documents) is necessary before the total evidence is sufficient to meet his objective.

Relevance

For evidence to be *relevant*, it must relate to the objective of forming an opinion on the financial statement assertions. Detailed evidence as to a company's sales strategies for the coming year may be interesting, persuasive, and (to any competitor) very valuable; but to the auditor it may be irrelevant to this year's financial statement assertions. Of course, any evidence can usually be shown to have some indirect bearing on audit objectives. Future sales strategies may indicate potential inventory losses for which provision should be made now. In each case, the auditor must decide whether the evidence is sufficiently relevant to justify the cost of examining it. If its relevance is extremely indirect, some more directly relevant evidence may be obtainable to cover the same audit question at a lesser cost.

Reliability

To be *reliable*, evidence must have some degree of trustworthiness. While recognizing that there will always be important exceptions to any generalization, useful presumptions as to the varying reliability of various types of evidence are:[10]

1. Direct personal knowledge of the auditor, gained through physical examination (of assets), observation (of activities), or recomputation is more reliable than evidence obtained indirectly (i.e., through confirmation or enquiry).
2. Evidence obtained through confirmation with or enquiry of independent third parties is more reliable than evidence obtained within the enterprise itself.
3. Documentary evidence obtained through the vouching of documents produced externally is more reliable than documentary evidence obtained through the vouching of documents produced internally.
4. When documents, accounting ledgers, accounting journals and reports, are developed (or processed) under satisfactory conditions of internal control, there is more assurance as to their reliability than when they are developed under unsatisfactory conditions of internal control.
5. Representations of company officials and employees should generally receive the least reliance of the various types of evidence available to the auditor. However, such evidence is more reliable:
   a) if it is obtained from a senior trusted official;
   b) if it is obtained from an official with a more objective view of the matter (e.g., with respect to the adequacy of allowance for doubtful accounts, the comptroller may be less knowledgeable but more objective about an account than the credit manager);
   c) if the presentation can be corroborated by the representations of a number of other officials or employees (e.g., the unanimous view of six different employees as to the workings of a system of internal control is more reliable evidence to the auditor than the view of one employee alone).

If the reliability of a given piece of evidence is extremely low, it will usually be more economical to examine some alternative, more reliable evidence as to the same audit question than to spend the time in gathering and evaluating the evidence of doubtful reliability. The varying appropriateness of the different types of evidence for varying financial statement components is discussed in Chapter 10.

Sufficiency

To be sufficient, the evidence must be persuasive to an extent which justifies the expression of an audit opinion. The degree of persuasiveness required depends on the degree of assurance required of the audit opinion, (discussed in 6.6.3). Each piece of audit evidence may have a different degree of persuasiveness. The degree of persuasiveness depends on the nature of the item being examined, the nature of the financial statement assertions implicitly being made with respect to this item (for example, assertions that $10 000 receivable exist at the year-end, that they are due from bona fide customers, that they will be fully collectible), and the relationship of the evidence to each of these assertions. Persuasiveness is also affected by the timing of the gathering of the evidence. For example, confirmations at October 31 provide less persuasive evidence as to December 31 receivables than confirmations at December 31. Nonetheless, where reliance can be placed on control and other overlapping audit tests the auditor may be prepared to accept this lesser persuasiveness in the interests of timeliness.

Increments of audit evidence pointing toward the same conclusion have a confirmatory effect and thus a joint degree of persuasiveness higher than that which any individual increment possesses in isolation. Since it is the joint degree of persuasiveness on which the audit opinion is based, sufficient persuasiveness implies the need for a sufficient quantity of evidence. Sufficient quantity, however, seldom implies an examination of all the evidence available. An auditor examining year-end accounts receivable knows that each successive amount he confirms increases the joint persuasiveness of evidence examined. He could, in theory, confirm all 10 000 accounts outstanding. Long before this point is reached, however, the joint persuasiveness will be sufficient to warrant the formation of an opinion that accounts receivable are or are not fairly presented in accordance with generally accepted accounting principles. Thus, it may be that confirmation of 200 accounts will provide the necessary assurance in a particular case. This represents the technique of *testing* or *sampling*. Properly planned, selected and evaluated, a test or sample drawn from a larger population can provide an adequate degree of assurance that a material error is not contained in that population. The relationship of desired degree of assurance and materiality to required sample size and observed sample results can be determined judgmentally (*judgmental sampling*) or with the assistance of mathematics (*statistical sampling*). Testing in general is discussed in Chapter 12 and statistical sampling techniques in Chapter 13.

Objectivity in selecting sufficient evidence

The point was made in 6.1.2 that in making a sufficient selection from among the elements of available evidence the auditor must be unbiased in his selection. That is, he must not intentionally select only that evidence which favours one particular conclusion.

And having examined the evidence, he must give due consideration both to that which appears to support and that which appears to contradict the financial statement assertions.

6.6.7 Timeliness and economy

Not only does each different type of audit evidence available have different degrees of relevance, reliability and sufficiency, but each has a different time and cost factor associated with it. A logical relationship must be maintained between the utility of audit evidence and the cost of gathering and evaluating it. This is the concept of *economy*. Additional increments of audit evidence should not be sought when the related incremental assurance thereby afforded would be out of proportion to the cost of obtaining it. The auditor should use the most economical way of obtaining, from the available evidence, a selection sufficient to support the expression of a professional opinion. In addition, for the auditor's report to be of social utility in adding credibility to the financial statements, it must be available within a reasonable time (the concept of *timeliness*). Although more persuasive evidence is usually available at later dates after the year-end (for example, with respect to discovery of undisclosed liabilities or with respect to the valuation of various contingencies), audited financial statements too long delayed do not assist the reader in making current economic decisions. The auditor must therefore usually reach a reasonable compromise between persuasiveness and timeliness of available evidence.

In addition, a compromise must often be made between the concepts of economy and timeliness themselves. The cheapest audit would usually call for all substantive verification of assets and liabilities to be performed at the year-end. When accounts receivable are confirmed and stock-taking observed at dates prior to the year-end some additional audit costs are usually involved in examining the intervening periods ('roll-forward' procedures). Nonetheless, these additional costs will often be justified in the interests of enabling the auditor to issue his report at an earlier date.

The concepts of economy and timeliness should not, however, be used to excuse a reduction in persuasiveness to such an extent that there remains no rational basis for expressing a clear opinion. To the extent that sufficient appropriate audit evidence is not practically available to remove any substantial doubt as to a financial statement assertion of material significance, the auditor must qualify his opinion or issue a denial of opinion (see Chapter 18). In the United States, SAS-1 makes the following statement concerning economy and timeliness:

An auditor typically works within economic limits; his opinion to be economically useful, must be formulated within a reasonable length of time and at reasonable cost. The auditor must decide, again exercising professional judgment, whether the evidential matter available to him within the limits of time and cost is sufficient to justify formulation and expression of an opinion.[11]

Nor should the concepts of economy and timeliness (nor difficulty and inconvenience) be used to excuse omission of an auditing procedure on which a large and essential element of audit assurance depends.

Nor, finally, should the concepts of economy and timeliness be used to excuse a reduction of required auditing work because of fee problems. The fact that an auditor has or anticipates difficulty in collecting a fair fee for the extent of work appropriate to the engagement, is not justification for performing an inadequate examination. His recourse, in the face of continuing fee difficulties, is to decline the engagement in future years – not to perform substandard work.

In summary, it is logical for the auditor to make certain cost-benefit decisions and not to seek additional evidence whose cost is out of proportion to the incremental assurance it provides – but this logic does not, merely because the auditor is unable to collect a fair fee, excuse him from gathering evidence which would have provided important and necessary assurance in relation to its cost.

Necessary trade-offs

The bottom of Figure 6.d indicates the necessary cost-benefit trade-offs that must be made in any audit. In defining an appropriate level of audit materiality, the importance of accuracy must be balanced by the practicality of limiting misstatements of this magnitude (0.1% precision is impractical). In defining an appropriate degree of audit assurance, the importance of low risk must be balanced by the practicality of limiting audit risk to this degree (99.9% confidence is impractical). In defining an appropriate selection of audit evidence to be examined, the qualities of relevance, reliability and sufficiency must be balanced by considerations of timeliness and economy. Within reasonable limits, when evidence is difficult or costly to obtain a somewhat lesser quantity may properly be deemed sufficient. Conversely, when evidence is simple and inexpensive to obtain a somewhat greater quantity should properly be demanded.

The three trade-offs are, of course, inter-related. Thus, the final decision as to what constitutes sufficient appropriate evidence will depend on the materiality level, the degree of assurance required, and on the availability of economical and timely evidence.

6.7 Efficient structure of the audit

From all the foregoing auditing concepts but particularly from the concepts of economy and timeliness can be derived, in turn, the idea of an efficient structure of the audit (see Figure 6.e). In theory, the auditor could ignore the system of internal control and obtain sufficient evidence to substantiate the reported assets, liabilities, and income components that, by itself, would justify the expression of his professional opinion. In practice, however, there are two significant drawbacks to that approach. First, in certain circumstances it is unavoidable that some reliance be placed on internal controls related to the initial recording or documentation of transactions. Subsequent audit procedures, however thorough, might be unable to detect a transaction which, because of poor controls, left no tell-tale traces behind it. Second, the cost of obtaining enough substantive evidence to be sufficient in isolation would often be prohibitive. The total audit cost can usually be significantly reduced if the auditor devotes some of his audit effort to (a) reviewing, evaluating, and verifying compliance with internal control, in effect a measure of the control risk, and then, (b) by placing

reliance thereon, demands a proportionately lesser degree of assurance from the direct substantiation of financial statement figures.

Since the concept of economy calls for the auditor to employ the most economical method of achieving adequate assurance, the division of the audit into these two components is almost universal. In this book the first component is referred to as the *interim audit* and the second as the *financial statement audit*. The interim audit usually includes a review of the system and controls, an evaluation of the system and controls, and, if warranted, verification of compliance with key controls (*compliance verification*). The financial statement audit includes the substantiation of financial statement figures (*substantive verification*), placing such reliance on controls as is warranted. In addition, some substantive verification (generally that related to transaction streams) may often be included in the interim audit while the extension of compliance verification to cover the last few months of the year is often included in the financial statement audit. The financial statement audit may often be divided into two (sometimes more) visits: pre-

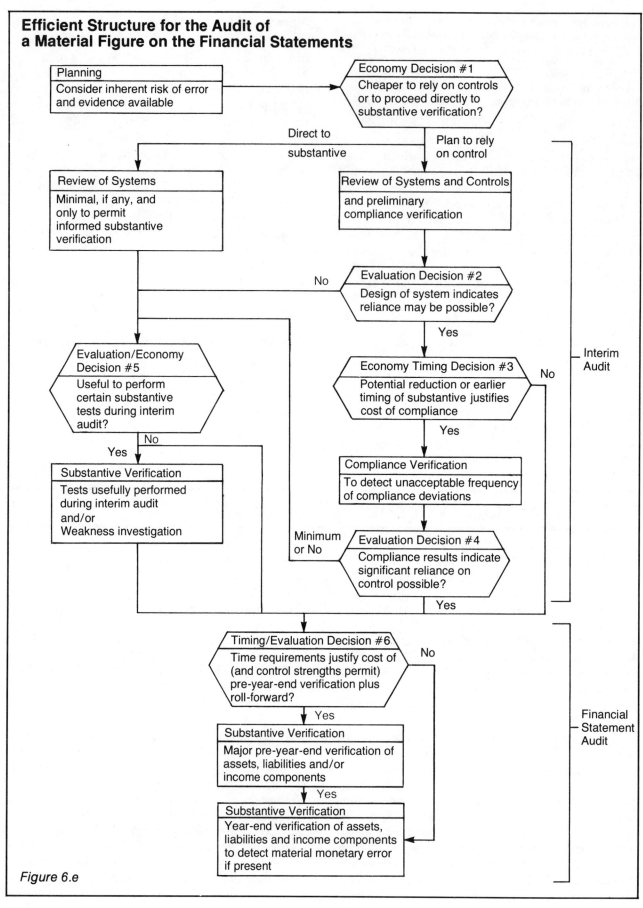

Efficient Structure for the Audit of a Material Figure on the Financial Statements

Planning

Consider inherent risk of error and evidence available

Economy Decision #1

Cheaper to rely on controls or to proceed directly to substantive verification?

Direct to substantive

Plan to rely on control

Review of Systems

Minimal, if any, and only to permit informed substantive verification

Review of Systems and Controls

and preliminary compliance verification

Evaluation Decision #2

Design of system indicates reliance may be possible?

No

Yes

Evaluation/Economy Decision #5

Useful to perform certain substantive tests during interim audit?

Economy Timing Decision #3

Potential reduction or earlier timing of substantive justifies cost of compliance

No

Yes

No

Yes

Substantive Verification

Tests usefully performed during interim audit and/or Weakness investigation

Compliance Verification

To detect unacceptable frequency of compliance deviations

Minimum or No

Evaluation Decision #4

Compliance results indicate significant reliance on control possible?

Yes

Interim Audit

Timing/Evaluation Decision #6

Time requirements justify cost of (and control strengths permit) pre-year-end verification plus roll-forward?

No

Yes

Substantive Verification

Major pre-year-end verification of assets, liabilities and/or income components

Yes

Substantive Verification

Year-end verification of assets, liabilities and income components to detect material monetary error if present

Financial Statement Audit

Figure 6.e

year-end procedures and year-end work. Conversely, in some smaller engagements both interim audit and financial statement audit procedures may be completed in one visit.

However, "economy decisions" as to the optimum allocation of audit effort between control review and substantive verification need not and should not be made only on the basis of the audit as a whole. Rather, the optimum allocation should be established for each material figure on the financial statements covered by the auditor's report. The decisions involved in making this allocation and the resulting relationships between interim audit and financial statement audit procedures and between compliance and substantive verification, are illustrated in Figure 6.e. This figure indicates the need for six different decisions, of which four arise from the concepts of economy and timeliness. Each of these six decisions is discussed briefly below (although analysis of the detailed structure of audit programs must be deferred to later chapters).

Economy decision, No. 1

The first decision is whether it is more economical to rely on controls or to proceed directly to substantive verification. Although for many statement figures in many engagements some study and reliance on controls is the optimal choice, there are exceptions. The second field work standard calls for "an appropriately organized study and evaluation of those internal controls on which the auditor subsequently relies in determining the nature, extent and timing" of substantive procedures. In those cases where it is less economical to study controls to justify such reliance, or where the auditor knows in advance that effective controls are simply not present, he should proceed directly to substantive procedures.[12] The substantive procedures must of course then be sufficiently extensive to provide adequate audit assurance in themselves. To design such substantive procedures knowledgeably it is usually necessary to conduct some limited systems review, if only to identify the types of substantive evidence available.

For example, many small businesses have only limited internal control and as a result the only reasonable audit decision may be to conduct a complete substantive program. In other cases, the decision may not depend on the strengths or weaknesses of controls at all. For instance, the income and expenses of investment and holding companies are usualy susceptible to economical substantive verification directly in conjunction with their related assets or liabilities. Even in larger manufacturing and processing enterprises with adequate systems of internal control, certain accounts (e.g., temporary investments, prepaid expenses, deferred charges, income

taxes payable) may be most economically verified by substantive procedures directly without any elaborate study of systems and controls. On the other hand, verification of cash, accounts receivable, inventories, fixed assets, accounts payable, etc. will in many engagements be more economically performed if an organized review and evaluation of systems and controls is conducted and reliance placed thereon.

Evaluation decision, No. 2

Where the decision has been made to review and evaluate systems and controls, a further decision must be made on the basis of this evaluation. Where the design of a control itself indicates that it is unreliable (or where deviations in its operation are obvious from the initial review) there is little point in wasting time with compliance verification.[13]

Economy/timing decision, No. 3

Even where the design of the control system appears satisfactory, the auditor must decide whether the cost of performing compliance verification (which is necessary before he can place significant reliance on the control) will be justified by the potential reduction in the cost and extent of substantive verification or by the potential earlier timing of substantive work thereby permitted.[14]

In many but not all audits, the cost savings from reduced extents of substantive procedures where reliance can be placed on control are enormous. In many other audits, but again not all, the requirement for timely reporting necessitates that inventory be observed, accounts receivable confirmed, etc., a month or more prior to the year-end, in which case there is no alternative but to place significant reliance on internal control for the "roll-forward period".

Evaluation decision, No. 4

The objective of compliance verification is to determine whether the frequency of *compliance deviations* (deviations from the prescribed system) is at an acceptably low level. Where compliance verification has been performed the results must be evaluated and a decision made as to whether, in the light of these results, significant reliance on control is warranted.[15]

Evaluation/economy decision, No. 5

The objective of substantive verification is to determine whether a material total of *monetary error* (errors actually distorting the financial statements) is present. Substantive verification consists of many different types including analytical review, detailed tests of balances, and detailed tests of transactions. As discussed in later chapters, detailed substantive tests of *transactions* are not always necessary with respect to every financial statement figure. Where, however, substantive transactional tests are required the auditor must decide whether they can be most efficiently conducted at the year-end (with other work on income components) or whether, as often, some should be performed during the interim audit. This is an economy decision.

Where weaknesses in control have been identified, the auditor will need to obtain assurance that no material monetary error has occurred as a result of that weakness. Sometimes this assurance can be most efficiently obtained by special substantive procedures (sometimes referred to as "compensating audit procedures" or as a "weakness investigation") performed during the interim audit. In other cases this same assurance can be more economically obtained by increasing the extent or changing the timing or nature of year-end substantive work. This is partly an economy decision, partly an evaluation decision.

Timing/evaluation decision, No. 6

From a purely economic point of view the costs of substantive verification could usually in theory be minimized by conducting all procedures at the year-end. Requirements for timeliness of reporting (as well as limitations in human resources available at one time) often require, however, that a significant amount of pre-year-end substantive verification be performed. This is primarily a timing decision. But it is also in part an evaluation decision, for substantive work several months in advance of the year-end may be unreliable if controls during the roll-forward period are excessively weak.

The foregoing relationship of compliance and substantive verification is consistent with the definitions of the respective objectives of the interim audit and financial statement audit which have already been presented in Chapter 1 (see Figure 1.d). A more complete discussion of the relationships between interim and financial statement audit and among review, compliance and substantive objectives will be found in Chapters 9 and 11. The point of the brief discussion here has been merely to indicate that the structure of the audit itself is related to auditing concepts, in particular the concepts of economy and timeliness, and the various trade-off decisions they require.

6.8 Audit assumptions

At the beginning of this chapter, Figure 6.a indicated that certain *audit assumptions* are involved in applying general auditing concepts to yield practical audit techniques and an efficient structure for the audit program. Some of the principal assumptions are the following:

1. In the absence of indications to the contrary,
   a) external evidence is more reliable than internal evidence,
   b) direct personal knowledge is more reliable than indirect evidence,
   c) good internal control reduces the probability of errors,
   d) past errors increase the probability of current errors (unless intervening systems changes have occurred),
   e) absence of past errors reduces the probability of current errors (unless intervening systems changes have occurred),
   f) the frequency of compliance deviations significantly exceeds the frequency of monetary errors.
2. In the presence of reasonable internal control, it is normally more efficient to verify the functioning of the control system and rely thereon, than to extend substantive tests to the degree necessary to avoid such reliance.

3. In the absence of suspicious circumstances, the following can generally be assumed to be sufficiently high-audit-cost low-risk situations that, in accordance with the concepts of relative risk and economy previously discussed, no special, extended audit procedures need be performed:
   a) collusive fraud,
   b) forgery of documents,
   c) management conspiracy to deceive the auditor,[16]
   d) ingenious and elaborately concealed defalcations.
   However, the auditor must be ever alert to the possibility that the foregoing conditions exist and accordingly must follow up any clue which might with hindsight be a suspicious circumstance.
4. In the absence of suspicious circumstances it can generally be assumed that confirmations and other representations received from third parties provide reasonable evidence of the existence of such third parties and of their agreement with the subject matter of the confirmation or representation.

This list is far from complete. Indeed, numerous assumptions are made in the course of any audit and it would be impossible to catalogue them in their entirety. Many of these assumptions are not readily susceptible to proof or disproof. A few are, but require a level of research beyond the scope of the individual audit engagement. In recent years there has been a growing recognition of the need for some empirical research by professional organizations. Such research could, for example, explore the efficacy of confirmation procedures under various conditions, the actual experience of good and bad control systems, the average ratio of compliance deviations to monetary errors.[17]

6.8.1 Detection of errors and irregularities

There is, and has always been, much controversy over the auditor's responsibilities with respect to the discovery of fraud. The legal implications, in particular, were discussed in Chapter 5. As also discussed in that chapter, the professional pronouncements on the subject have been somewhat ambivalent:

> The auditor recognizes that fraud, if sufficiently material, may affect his opinion on the financial statements, and his examination, made in accordance with generally accepted auditing standards, gives consideration to this possibility. However, the ordinary examination directed to the expression of an opinion on financial statements is not primarily or specifically designed, and cannot be relied upon, to disclose defalcations and other similar irregularities, although their discovery may result.[18]

As stated in Chapter 5, it might be inferred from the first sentence that it was part of generally accepted auditing standards to look for material (but not immaterial) fraud yet, from the second, that it was not part of such standards to look for fraud at all (although one might stumble across it).

It would seem more consistent with a coherent theory of auditing to start with the proposition that the objective of the auditor is to seek reasonable assurance that the financial statements are not misstated by a material amount (the conceptual framework discussed in Section 6.3 of this chapter). Material misstatements could arise as a result of innocent and inadvertent error, concealment of defalcations, unconscious bias, or deliberate misrepresentation. The nature of each such possible misstatement will, however, have a very marked effect on the degree of "reasonable assurance" that it is logical to expect from an economically useful audit (see 6.6.4). The third assumption listed above is the normal assumption implicitly made by most practitioners in most audits – and it is consistent with the concept of a reasonable degree of assurance.

The same arguments would apply equally well to a rare type of innocent error, the possibility of which could reasonably be assessed to be so far-fetched that, in the absence of indications of discrepancies, the cost of special audit procedures to hunt for such a remote possibility would be out of proportion to the small increase in credibility thereby obtained. Of course, hindsight will occasionally show that an error which seemed a remote possibility at the time actually transpired and was undiscovered by the auditor. Such hindsight is no evidence of negligence on the auditor's part, however, if the procedures he applied were reasonable in extent and intensity in view of the *relative risk* of the item in question as such risk might be reasonably assessed on the basis of known circumstances at the time.

The position discussed in the preceding two paragraphs is consistent with the CICA and AICPA exposure drafts outstanding on the subject as this book goes to press. The CICA exposure draft stated:

> In conducting an audit, the auditor recognizes that the financial statements may be mis-stated as a result of errors or irregularities. Accordingly, in obtaining sufficient appropriate audit evidence to afford a reasonable basis to support the content of his report, the auditor seeks reasonable assurance, through the application of procedures which comply with generally accepted auditing standards, that errors or irregularities which may be material to the financial statements have not occurred, or that if they have occurred, they are either corrected or properly accounted for in the financial statements. The auditor has no separate or additional responsibility to detect fraud or other irregularities. The degree of reasonable assurance achieved by the application of procedures that comply with generally accepted auditing standards would normally be higher in the case of errors than in the case of irregularities. Some irregularities, because of their nature or the manner in which they are concealed, may not be detected by auditing procedures which comply with generally accepted auditing standards.[19]

The AICPA exposure draft stated:

> Generally accepted auditing standards require the independent auditor to plan his examination to search for errors or irregularities that would have a material effect on the financial statements . . . [20]

> Independent audits provide reasonable, but not absolute, assurance that financial statements are not materially affected by errors or irregularities. The concept of reasonable assurance recognizes that, as with certain business controls, the costs of audits should bear a reasonable relationship to the benefits expected to be derived.[21]

> However, identifying irregularities resulting from collusion, forgery, or certain unrecorded transactions ordinarily is not practicable for the auditor. Reasonable reliance on the client's accounting records ordinarily is warranted and unavoidable.[22]

6.8.2 Judgment of assumptions

Most of the assumptions listed above, together with others made in the course of any audit, break down in the presence of suspicious circumstances. Therefore, as previously discussed, it is imperative that the auditor maintain a degree of reasonable skepticism tempered by experienced professional judgment in the conduct of all his work.

The AICPA exposure draft suggested the following circumstances as examples of conditions which, if not reasonably explained, might lead the auditor to question further whether errors or possible irregularities exist:

a) discrepancies within the accounting records, such as a difference between a control account and its supporting subsidiary records;

b) differences disclosed by confirmations:

c) significantly fewer responses to confirmation requests than expected;

d) transactions not supported by proper documentation;

e) transactions not recorded in accordance with management's general or specific authorization; or

f) the completion of large, unusual, or complex transactions at or near year end.[23]

Of course, for many small organizations the auditor will commonly encounter one or more of the foregoing conditions, particularly transactions not recorded in accordance with general or specific authorizations. Provided that reasonable explanations are obtained for such conditions, they do not necessarily indicate errors or irregularities. Where satisfactory explanations are not obtained however, the auditor should pursue the matter until his doubts are resolved. Other examples might include: handwritten documents when typewritten documents would have been expected, unreasonable delays by the client in providing information, and conflicting reports on important matters.

In addition, the following circumstances, though not necessarily indicating irregularities, are suggested as conditions which "might cause the auditor to be concerned about the possibility that management may have made material misrepresentation or overridden internal control procedures:"

a) operating management appears to have little regard for the need to establish and follow internal control procedures;

b) the company needs, but lacks, an internal audit staff;

d) key financial positions, such as controller, have a high turnover rate, or

d) the accounting and financial functions appear to be understaffed, resulting in a constant crisis condition and related loss of controls.[24]

Other examples which have been suggested include: operating problems (such as insufficient working capital, many lawsuits, business failures within the industry, collection problems), indicated management bias (such as a strong motivation to report a specified earnings level), or management domination by one man or a few individuals.

6.9 Reference material

General

Robert K. Mautz and Hussein A. Sharaf, *The Philosophy of Auditing* (Evanston: American Accounting Association, 1961).
A Statement of Basic Auditing Concepts, (American Accounting Association, 1972).

Audit structure

CICA Audit Technique Study, *Internal control and Procedural Audit Tests,* (1968).
AICPA Statement on Auditing Standards No. 1, Sections 320, 320A and 320B.
CICA 1976 Exposure Draft, *Internal Control,* Sections 5220 and 5230 (the reader should refer to subsequent pronouncements).

Materiality and risk

CICA Audit Technique Study, *Materiality in Auditing,* (1965).

Materiality in Accounting, (Accountants International Study Group, 1974).
AICPA Statement on Auditing Standards No. 1, Paragraphs 150.03/.05.

Evidence

AICPA Statement on Auditing Standards No. 1, Section 330.

Fraud

AICPA Statement on Auditing Standards No. 1, Section 110.
CICA 1976 Exposure Draft, *Internal Control,* Paragraphs 5215.07/.11.
AICPA 1976 Exposure Draft, *The Independent Auditor's Responsibility for the Detection of Errors and Irregularities* (the reader should refer to subsequent pronouncements).

6.10 Questions and problems

Review and discussion

1. Why is auditing theory important (a) to students, (b) to public practitioners and (c) to defence lawyers?
2. Describe briefly the similarities and the differences between accounting and auditing.
3. Evidence is an important concept in the legal, scientific and audit fields. Compare the evidence gathering process in these three fields.
4. Discuss materiality in relation to the user, the accountant and the auditor.
5. There have been improvements in audit techniques in the past, e.g., the use of statistical sampling. How do technique changes affect the audit concept of "professional judgement"?
6. What are the types of audit evidence? Give examples of each type and relate them to the verification of specific financial statement components.
7. What constitutes sufficient appropriate evidential matter?
8. What are the advantages and disadvantages of disclosing the degree of assurance achieved and the materiality limit in a given audit to (a) management and (b) shareholders?
9. Discuss briefly the three types of risk that comprise the total risk of undetected misstatements in financial statements.
10. Explain the differences between "substantive" and "compliance" verification. How are the two related?
11. What differentiates the interim and financial statement audits? How are they interrelated?
12. Differentiate between auditing standards and auditing procedures. How are they interrelated?

Problems

1. (CICA adapted) "As increasing numbers of lawsuits against auditors are demonstrating, the public accountant faces very real risks as the auditor of a corporation. In his own interest, he should be more aware of the factors that must be considered in any attempt to measure the risk of an audit engagement."

   What factors must be considered in attempting to estimate the risk of a specific audit engagement? Explain each briefly.
2. A prominent business man, who is not a chartered accountant, asks you to explain the statement – "There are many factors that affect the degree of assurance and inherent risk associated with audited financial statements." Give your answer in terms and with examples understandable to the business man.
3. Generally accepted auditing standards were introduced in Chapter 4. How do these standards specifically relate to the auditing concepts discussed under the sufficiency and appropriateness of audit evidence?
4. Relate the discussion in this chapter as to relevance, reliability, timeliness, economy and the efficient structure of the audit to the verification of sales and accounts receivable.
5. You have been asked to argue, in a debate, against the proposition: "Resolved that the public accountant should be liable to any third party for undiscovered fraud in excess of 5% of pretax income where the third party suffers damages as a result of the fraud."

   Speaking for the proposition are an eminent business man who sits on a number of audit committees, the leader of an active consumer group who purports to speak for the small investor, and a lawyer.

   Describe, in summary form, the points you would make in your presentation. Break these down as to the anticipated counter arguments that you expect each of your three opponents to make.

Internal Control

To err is human. With the best of intentions, most people make mistakes. The mistakes may be errors in the end results of their work, needless inefficiencies in achieving those end results, or both. And sometimes, without the best of intentions, a few people deliberately falsify. Any organization wishing to conduct its business in an orderly and efficient manner and to produce reliable financial accounting information, both for its own and for others' use, needs some controls to minimize the effects of these endemic human failings. When such controls are implemented within the organization's systems they are described as *internal controls* – in contrast to externally imposed controls (such as government tax audits). A requirement that supporting, approved invoices be presented to the signing officer when cheques are to be signed is an example of a familiar and important internal control.

The idea of internal control can be traced back to the stewardship of public funds in the very oldest civilizations. It has only been in the present century, however, that the importance of internal control to the external auditor has been widely recognized. In Chapter 1 the concept was introduced of a review and evaluation of internal controls during the interim audit in order to determine the extent of substantive verification to be performed both then and during the financial statement audit.

The concept is reflected in the second field work standard:

> There should be an appropriately organized study and evaluation of those internal controls on which the auditor subsequently relies in determining the nature, extent and timing of auditing procedures.

The purpose of this chapter is to describe the basic elements of internal control in preparation for subsequent chapters dealing with the auditor's review, evaluation and reliance on controls. The elements of internal control described here are relevant for organizations with either manual or computerized accounting systems. However, a computerized system calls for certain additional controls as well. Those additional computer controls are described in Chapter 8. Specific control procedures for the common major accounting systems of sales/receivables/receipts, purchases/payables/payments, etc. are described in detail in Chapter 29. Other specific controls, normally not part of major systems, but related to specific financial statement components (e.g., temporary investments) are described in Chapters 32 to 43. The purpose of the present chapter is to introduce the basic control elements from which specific control procedures can be derived in any individual case.

7.1 Introduction to internal control

While the purpose of discussing internal control in an auditing text is its importance to the external auditor, it should be made clear at the outset that internal controls do not exist for the sake of the auditor but for the sake of the organization itself and its management. No management wants to see losses suffered through error or fraud or through mistaken decisions based on unreliable financial reports. Internal control is thus an important tool by which management helps to achieve its objective of ensuring as far as practical the orderly and efficient conduct of the business of the enterprise. The fact that reliance by the external auditor on internal control, where warranted, can also serve to reduce the extent of his substantive verification is a useful by-product.

Impact of internal controls on the external auditor's work

In Chapter 6 the degree of audit assurance required was analyzed in terms of reducing to an acceptable minimum the combined effect of three different risks: (i) the inherent risk of an error occurring in the first place, (ii) the risk of internal controls failing to prevent or detect such an error, and (iii) the risk of the external audit failing to detect it. Inherent risk and audit risk are discussed in many later chapters. Control risk is related to that portion of internal control that has a bearing on the reliability of financial reporting and hence on the auditor's attest function of expressing an opinion on the financial statements. Generally, where internal controls are weak, the control risk is high and audit procedures must be intensified. Conversely, where internal controls are strong, the control risk is low and audit procedures can be reduced.

Many controls will serve both management's and the auditor's needs equally well. However, because internal control is primarily a management tool and only secondarily an aid to the external auditor, it should not be surprising that:

1. there will be some internal controls which are important to management's objectives but do not affect the attest function of the auditor at all,
2. there will be some internal controls which are as good as is practical in a certain situation from management's point of view but inadequate to permit significant reliance by the auditor.

The first point listed above implies that among the control techniques important to meet managements' objectives, there will be some of attest significance and some not of attest significance. To meet generally accepted auditing standards, the auditor must make an appropriately organized study and evaluation of those controls of attest significance on which he plans to place reliance. Testing of a control is not required where the control is not of attest significance or where, though the control could be of attest significance, the auditor finds it more economical to place no reliance on it but instead to perform more extensive substantive verification than otherwise. Notwithstanding this fact, most external auditors choose to make some limited review of non-attest controls (and of attest controls where reliance is not planned) as a collateral service to their clients. For that reason, this chapter discusses all the basic elements of internal control – not just those of attest significance. The attest or non-attest significance of various controls is discussed in Chapter 9.

The second point listed above implies that management decisions as to the level of control desirable must be influenced by cost-benefit relationships (discussed later). Sometimes a resulting control procedure will not be adequate to permit significant reliance by the auditor even though he has no practical improvements in that control to suggest to management. In such situations the auditor must plan substantive procedures that are sufficient by themselves without reliance on control.

7.1.1 Definition of internal control

Internal control may be defined as follows:

> Internal control comprises the plan of organization and all the co-ordinate systems established by the management of an enterprise to achieve management's objective of ensuring, as far as is practical, the orderly and efficient conduct of its business, including the safeguarding of assets, the reliability of accounting records, and the timely preparation of reliable financial information.[1]

The wording, "all the co-ordinate systems", emphasizes that many individual systems, each with their own controls, exist in the typical organization. A particular control in the sales system may be designed to ensure the accurate reporting of sales figures; another control in the cash receipts system may be designed to ensure that proceeds of sales are not misappropriated. Some controls will be inter-related, jointly achieving some desired control objective. Others may be independent, the nature of one neither enhancing nor diminishing the effectiveness of another. Thus, in later chapters we shall see that the auditor cannot come up with one overall assessment of internal control as good or bad, but rather

must address himself to the effectiveness of each control technique or related group of control techniques.

For a given control technique to be effective it must not only be well designed (the right control in the right place); it must function properly throughout the year (be complied with carefully by all employees involved and not bypassed when key employees are away or the workload unusually heavy).

7.1.2 Responsibility for internal control

Responsibility of management

The responsibility for establishing and maintaining adequate internal controls rests with management.

> It is management which is responsible for safeguarding the assets, ensuring that accounting data is accurate and reliable, and promoting operational efficiency and adherence to prescribed policies. The system of internal control should not be regarded as something installed purely to meet the whims of a fussy auditor, but should include the controls which management considers necessary to discharge its responsibilities. An audit does not relieve management of its responsibility and can never be considered a substitute for an adequate system of internal control.[2]

This view is reinforced by the provisions of many corporations acts requiring the corporation to ensure that proper accounting records are kept. In the Canada Business Corporations Act the relevant provisions are as follows:

> **Sec. 20(2)** . . . a corporations shall prepare and maintain adequate accounting records
>
> **Sec. 22(2)** A corporation and its agents shall take reasonable precautions to
> a) prevent loss or destruction of,
> b) prevent falsification of entries in, and
> c) facilitate detection and correction of inaccuracies in the records and registers required by this Act to be prepared and maintained.

Role of the external auditor

The external auditor is not responsible for the establishment and maintenance of internal controls. He is responsible, however, for studying and evaluating these internal controls on which he relies in determining the work necessary to support his expression of opinion on the financial statements. The phrase "relies in determining" in the second field work standard emphasizes that the study of controls is not carried out as an end in itself but rather to justify such reliance as he places on controls in his attest function. In addition, many auditors in their engagement letters (see 4.2.1.) undertake a contractual responsibility to advise management of any opportunities for practical improvements in internal control which they encounter in the course of performing their attest work. Upon occasion, of course, a public accountant may undertake a specific engagement to review internal controls either in a certain area (such as in the computer department) or throughout the organization; in such cases the required depth of his review, and his related responsibilities, will depend upon the terms of his engagement.

7.1.3 Management objectives of internal control

Management's objective of an orderly and efficient conduct of the business of the enterprise may be analyzed into a number of subsidiary objectives, the first three of which were mentioned explicitly in the foregoing definition:

1. safeguarding of assets,
2. reliability of accounting records,
3. timely preparation of reliable financial information,
4. profitability and minimization of unnecessary costs,
5. avoidance of unintentional exposure to risk,
6. prevention or detection of errors and irregularities,
7. assurance that delegated responsibilities have been properly discharged,
8. discharge of statutory responsibilities.[3]

The eight subsidiary objectives are not intended to be mutually exclusive. Each is discussed briefly below.

Safeguarding of assets

There is little point in maximizing future gains but failing to conserve the proceeds of past ones. Most systems of internal control therefore include numerous provisions to safeguard assets. The safeguarding of assets is usually understood to refer to the protection of assets such as cash, marketable securities and inventories from (a) intentional errors such as customer pilferage, employee theft, or the falsification of records in order to overstate commissions, bonuses or royalties and from (b) unintentional errors such as the accidental underbilling of customers, overpayment of suppliers, or physical loss or destruction of the assets themselves.

As explained in Chapter 9, the foregoing safeguarding controls affect the attest function of the auditor only insofar as they have a bearing on the reliability of financial reporting.

In addition, it could in theory be argued that the safeguarding of assets in a broad sense could include protection from imprudent management decisions such as selling goods at a loss, opening a warehouse in a poor location, or apying for advertising that later proves to have been ineffective. Whether control should be defined so broadly or not is a question of semantics. It does not particularly advance analysis to define every business activity as a control procedure. Usually conscious business decisions may be excluded from the types of errors covered by safeguarding controls.[4] Certainly a judgment of the prudence of business decisions made by management is not part of the attest function of the auditor provided it does not affect the fairness of presentation of the financial statements.

Reliability of accounting records

To achieve reliable financial reporting it is necessary to have reliable accounting records to start with. Controls to ensure the accurate recording of transactions are usually vital to both management and auditor. Reliable accounting records are those from which reliable financial statements can be prepared. This does not mean, however, that certain month-end or year-end adjustments may not be required to achieve proper statement presentation. For example, if the accounting system is designed to produce an entry adjusting the allowance for doubtful accounts at the year-end, the underlying accounting records month by month would not be held to be unreliable solely because they did not include such an entry. If accurate in all other respects, the accounting records would be producing the information they had been designed to produce. Of course, monthly statements prepared from such records and lacking the normal year-end adjustments would be suitable only for restricted use by management personnel who are aware of their limitations and not by shareholders or other outside readers.

What is designed to be part of the routine accounting records and what is left to be covered in year-end or quarterly adjustments will vary from enterprise to enterprise. In a larger organization, a recurring monthly entry to adjust the allowance for doubtful accounts may be an integral part of the system of accounting records. If, in such an organization, the entry, though called for by the system, was omitted inadvertently or deliberately, the accounting records would have to be judged unreliable. In such a case, adequate controls were clearly not present to ensure that the accounting records produced the information they were designed to produce.

Timely preparation of reliable information

One purpose of having reliable accounting records is to facilitate the timely preparation of reliable financial information. Reliable financial information is needed by management itself in order to make informed business decisions in operating the enterprise and by shareholders, creditors and other parties in order to make informal investment, credit and other decisions relating to their connection with the enterprise. Controls over the reliability of the financial statements provided to external users will have a direct bearing on the auditor's work. Controls over the reliability of internal management reports will only affect the auditor's work to the extent that he makes use of such reports in his audit.

Profitability and minimization of unnecessary costs

Achieving a level of profitability commensurate with the degree of risk being run is one of the foremost management objectives in most enterprises. Internal control serves this objective by minimizing unnecessary costs (guarding against unauthorized expenditures, shipments to unauthorized customers, etc.). and also be ensuring the availability of reliable information as a basis for sound business decisions.

Avoidance of unintentional exposure to risk

That this profitability is achieved in return for the assumption of some risk is fundamental to most businesses. The objective of internal control is therefore not to eliminate all risk but rather to restrict exposure to those risks consciously assumed by management. The inadvertent loss of scrap metal in a manufacturing process can usually be prevented by good internal controls over the handling and accounting for scrap. A certain level of customer pilferage, however, may be a regrettable but inevitable cost of running a retail business.

The benefits of a given control must be weighed against its cost. Fencing in stores areas is a control procedure to guard against certain types of inventory losses. Where management decides to dispense with this control because its cost is judged to be out of proportion to the risk of inventory losses, a conscious decision is being made to assume that latter risk. Management hopes the risk is remote but it is obviously not nil. If inventory losses do, in fact occur their occurrence does not mean that, from management's point of view, control was defective but merely that every consciously assumed risk may from time to time exact some penalty.

Similarly, losses due to destruction of assets can be minimized by the use of insurance. Losses due to the inadvertent failure to maintain adequate coverage could be said to reflect inadequate control. On the other hand, a conscious decision to be a self-insurer may be logical where the risk is spread over numerous separated assets. Subsequent losses which occur do not then reflect inadequate control but are the business expense associated with self-insuring (the analog of premium expense where external insurance is maintained).

Whether the conscious decision to assume certain risks and not others is made in the best possible way is another question – and as difficult to answer as judging the wisdom of any business decision in an uncertain world. That question, however, really lies outside the subject of internal control. The objective of internal control itself is to avoid the *unintentional* exposure to risk.

Prevention or detection of errors and irregularities

The prevention or detection of errors and irregularities is not a separate objective but one embodied in the objectives already discussed. It serves, however, to emphasize that while the external audit may lead to the detection of errors and irregularities the main reliance for their prevention and detection should be placed on an adequate system of internal control. For one thing, the external audit must be designed in relation to materiality of amounts in the financial statements, whereas internal control from management's point of view should be designed to reduce the risk of *any* avoidable errors or losses wherever the cost of the control is reasonable in relation to likely or possible losses in its absence.

Assurance that delegated responsibilities have been properly discharged

Internal control is one of the tools by which management achieves its objectives. Internal control is thus primarily control exercised *by* management rather than *of* management. However, the term management can be considered to comprise all levels charged with the operation of the business from the foreman or department supervisor up to the board of directors. Numerous responsibilities are necessarily delegated by each level of management down to lower levels. One of the functions of well-designed controls are to help satisfy each level of management that responsibilities it has delegated to lower levels have been properly discharged. Thus, if a certain level has been charged with the responsibility of authorizing purchases up to a certain dollar amount, a good system of internal control should include procedures to ensure that expenditures are not made for unauthorized purchases or for purchases exceeding the authorization limits.

Discharge of statutory responsibilities

Under corporations acts, the board of directors have certain defined responsibilities to the shareholders. These responsibilities usually contain either an explicit or an implied responsibility to maintain accountability to the shareholders. Internal controls can help the directors to meet this responsibility. The common requirements that certain larger transactions be approved by the board, that key management employment contracts be approved by the board or a senior committee of the board, that financial statements and the external auditor's opinion be reviewed by an audit committee of the board, and, in some cases, that the internal audit department have access to the audit committee of the board all serve this objective. In some cases statutory responsibilities are imposed upon partners in a partnership and internal control can again aid in maintaining accountability.

7.1.4 Cost-benefit relationships

The phrase "ensuring as far as is practical" in the definition of internal control indicates that absolute assurance is not possible and the level of assurance to be sought will depend upon cost. In Chapter 6 it was stated that there is a limit to how strong it is practical to make the system of internal control. Controls cost money and each new control must be balanced by a commensurate reduction in risk of error or its cost is not justified.[5]

The cost may be simply the expense of implementing the control procedure, for example, the cost of fencing in stores of raw material. It may make sense to fence in high-value low-bulk materials but not others. Or the cost may be the effect of lost business opportunities. The maximum control over bad debt losses would restrict a company's sales to only those customers with the very highest credit ratings. Usually, such a policy would unduly reduce the company's sales potential. The *optimum* credit control must therefore usually be a compromise between facilitating sales and controlling bad debt losses.

The auditor sometimes encounters situations where internal control can be improved at little or no additional cost, perhaps by a minor re-assignment of duties. In such cases the improvement is obviously desirable. In most cases, however, an associated cost is present. While it is often obvious whether the risk outweighs the cost (in which case the improvement is desirable) or the cost outweighs the risk (in which case no improvement may be practical), many borderline cases occur. It is desirable that all such cases encountered be brought to management's attention so that the cost-benefit decisions can be consciously made by management. Costs are measurable but the benefits of reducing risks are only conjectural. Is it worth spending $1 000 in control to prevent a loss of possibly up to $10 000 which may not occur anyway? Of course the costs of the control always look cheap after an actual loss has occurred. Without the benefit of hindsight the right decision in each case is not easy.

7.2 Elements of internal control

7.2.1 Methods of classifying controls

Internal controls can be classified in various ways, such as (1) by objective (safeguarding of assets, reliability of records, etc.), (2) by jurisdiction (accounting and administrative), (3) by method (preventive and detective), or (4) by general nature (organizational controls, authorization controls, etc.). Each of these classification schemes is briefly discussed. The last one (classification by general nature) is then used as the framework for the description of control elements in this chapter.

Classification by objective

The most obvious classification scheme to consider would be by control objective (such as by the eight management objectives discussed in 7.1.3). Since these objectives are not mutually exclusive, however, the same control technique would appear many times in the classification. For example, perpetual inventory records independent of the storekeeper help to safeguard inventories, to ensure accurate inventory records, to detect inventory shortages and to prevent irregularities in the handling of inventory. Thus, while it is important to understand the various overlapping objectives, classification of control techniques in this manner would be unduly repetitive.

Accounting controls and administrative controls

Another broad division of internal controls has historically been into *accounting controls* and *administrative controls*. Originally, the AICPA used the former term to describe controls primarily related to the safeguarding of assets and the reliability of the financial records and the latter term to describe controls primarily related to the promotion of operations efficiency and adherence to managerial policies and not usually of attest significance. It warned, however, that the auditor should consider the need for evaluating administrative controls where they had an important bearing on the reliability of the financial records. Subsequently, revised definitions were presented which defined administrative controls as those "concerned with the decision processes leading to management's authorization of transactions".[6] In the writer's view, the distinction between accounting and administrative controls is not a vital one from the auditor's point of view. While, generally, accounting controls are of attest significance and administrative controls not, this correspondence is not invariable. Even with the revised definitions, some administrative controls may turn out to influence the reliability of financial reporting and so be of attest significance while certain of the accounting controls may relate exclusively to the safeguarding of assets and, where this safeguarding does not influence the financial statements or the auditor's opinion, be ofnon-attest significance. The distinction between accounting and administrative controls is not used further in this book. The distinction between controls of attest and non-attest significance is discussed in Chapter 9.

Preventive controls and detective controls

Of particular relevance to the auditor is the distinction between *preventive controls* and *detective controls*.[7] Preventive controls seek to prevent the occurrence of errors or irregularities – or, more accurately, to reduce their chance of occurrence. Detective controls seek to detect such errors or irregularities as do occur – or, more accurately, to increase their chance of detection. Usually both types of control are desirable. Thus, if an accounting clerk is well instructed and properly supervised (preventive controls) and his work subjected to some type of cross-check such as reconciliation of a trial balance (a detective control) the combined chance of an error both occurring and escaping detection may be made acceptably small. In designing controls over a particular type of error (or irregularity) it is often useful to answer the two primary questions:

1. How can this particular type of error be prevented in the first place?

   If the error is due to misunderstanding, can it be avoided by better training; if due to carelessness, by better supervision; if due to fraud, by eliminating the opportunity by division of duties?

2. How can the error, if nevertheless it should occur, be detected?

   What records and accounts would the error affect? Could the effects be detected by control account reconciliation, budget variance analysis, and comparison with

prior months or can the error only be detected by double-checking the actual operation itself? If the error is accidental, what are the most likely mistakes to check for? If the error is deliberate what possible concealment might render other detective controls inoperative? How quickly is it desirable that the error be detected – is the month-end soon enough or is earlier detection important enough to justify the added cost?

As will be seen in Chapter 9, preventive and detective controls require certain differences in the auditor's approach to compliance verification. Because both preventive and detective elements are desirable in most control areas, however, the distinction between them does not itself help to define the different control areas.

Classification by general nature

Classification of controls according to their general nature is useful in describing the basic control elements desirable in most systems. Some controls relate to how people are organized (organizational controls), some to how systems are developed (systems development controls), some to how transactions are authorized (authorization controls), etc.

7.2.2 List of control elements

While any one method of classifying internal controls according to their general nature is bound to be somewhat arbitrary, the following list of basic control elements is suggested as useful:

1. Organizational controls,
2. Systems development controls,
3. Authorization and reporting controls,
4. Accounting systems controls,
5. Additional safeguarding controls,
6. Management supervisory controls,
7. Documentation controls.

The following seven sections of this chapter cover all of these control elements.

7.3 Organizational controls

The term *organizational controls* can be used to refer to controls relating to how people are organized within an enterprise.

7.3.1 Honest and competent personnel

The most obvious way to minimize the occurrence of deliberate irregularities and accidental mistakes is to hire honest and competent personnel. Even a poor system may produce good results given conscientious, able employees and even the best system may be defeated by the determined embezzler or the hopelessly incompetent. An honest group of employees is the product of proper hiring practices, insistence on a proper standard of ethical conduct, removal of dishonest employees, sensible supervision, systems which do not invite abuse, and a satisfying work environment. A competent group of employees is the product of proper hiring practices, effective training, sensible evaluation and promotion practices, removal of incompetents, workable systems, and a work environment which provides a reasonable incentive for good performance.

Responsibility for personnel, training and employee relations

Because of its importance to the overall operations of the enterprise, personnel, training and employee relations should be the responsibility of a senior executive (not more than one level below the chief operating officer in most organizations, perhaps two levels in very large organizations).

Hiring practices

The personnel department should make a careful investigation of job applicants to ensure that (a) their technical training and skills meet the demands of their specific job and (b) there are no indications of dishonesty or negligence in their past work. The department may well be assessing other important factors as well (ability to work amicably with co-workers, general deportment, willingness to travel, etc., depending on the circumstances) but the factors of relevance to internal control are competence and integrity. Technical training and skills are generally assessed through a review of applicants' education and job records, contact with former employers, one or more interviews, and, for some positions, various aptitude tests. The search for any evidence of past dishonesty or negligence may involve contact with former employers, contact with personal references,

and general assessment during interviews. To ensure that a complete record of education and work experience has been obtained, application forms commonly require the prospective employee to account for the entire time period from public school to the present. Any blanks are normally questioned as they could represent an attempt to conceal unsatisfactory employment experiences or, in the extreme, a prison term. For applicants who will have custodial responsibilities or otherwise have access to company assets, it may be appropriate to obtain a confidential credit check. Where coverage by a fidelity bond is desirable (see 7.6.4), investigation by the bonding company is another useful source of information.

Performance standards

Making it clear that a proper standard of ethical conduct is expected helps to ensure its continuation. Where, on the other hand, the company itself indulges in sharp business practices with its customers, suppliers, or the government, or where cheating on expense reports is widespread and implicitly condoned, the temptation for larger irregularities is increased. With respect to competent performance of work, many organizations have developed performance standards for labour and certain technical and clerical jobs. Where an employee knows his performance will be measured against a fair standard, he has a greater incentive than when he knows no one will know the difference anyway.

Training programs

Employees should be adequately trained in the company's procedures to be applied in their particular jobs. In large organizations this may involve formal training programs, specific job descriptions and detailed procedures manuals. Job descriptions and procedures manuals, particularly for employees with control responsibilities, help to avoid uncertainties as to what is to be done and who is responsible if errors occur. In smaller organizations, training and documentation of duties are necessarily more limited. It may be sufficient if an employee leaving or changing positions spends a few weeks initiating the new employee into the job. Alternatively or in addition, closer supervision of the new employees may be required.

Supervision

Adequate supervision helps employees to learn their jobs, forestalls many accidental mistakes and misunderstandings, and discourages dishonesty. Maintaining adequate supervision requires that work be organized in a way that leaves supervisors with sufficient time to perform their own jobs and supervise their subordinates. Many poor accounting situations can be traced back to periods where supervisors were absent or tied up in other activities.

Firing practices

Most organizations are quick to fire employees found to be dishonest. Often they are less willing, partly because competence is necessarily a subjective judgment, to terminate the services of an incompetent employee or at least to arrange a transfer to a job commensurate with his abilities. Yet in the long run, ensuring that an employee is not left with duties he is unable to discharge competently is a service both to the employee and to the organization for which he works.

Systems which do not invite abuse

It is easier to remain honest if we know we probably could not get away with anything anyway. The primary responsibility to maintain integrity must rest with each employee himself. But it is both a moral obligation and prudent self-interest on the part of employers to avoid placing temptation in front of their employees. Glaring weaknesses in control invite abuse. At the other extreme, an obsessive cross-checking of every step can sometimes be irritating to the point of provoking the very response it seeks to prevent. A judicious mixture of reasonable trust and sensible controls is probably best in most organizations.

It is easier to perform a job competently if the systems are workable and well-defined. If systems are undefined or, at the other extreme, so complex and rigid that unauthorized short-cuts are a practical necessity, one should not be surprised if things go wrong.

Evaluation and promotion practices

A contributing factor to satisfactory employee performance is the system of evaluation and promotion within an organization. Many businesses evaluate each employee annually or semi-annually (a few more often). If an employee knows that good work will be recognized and rewarded and weaknesses frankly and fairly discussed, he is more likely to be motivated to do a competent job.

In rewarding competent performance, of course, an organization must be careful not to transfer the employee to a post for which he is not trained or suited. Dr. Laurence Peter, in enunciating his theory that continued promotions are ultimately disastrous, says only half in jest of employees promoted to a new position:

But competence in that new position qualifies them for still another promotion. For each individual, for you, for me, the final promotion is from a level of competence to a level of incompetence. So, given enough time – and assuming the existence of enough ranks in the hierarchy – each employee rises to, and remains at, his level of incompetence.[8]

Work environment

Finally, honesty and a good performance are both encouraged by a satisfactory work environment, fair levels of remuneration, and the maintenance of good employee relations. Where, on the other hand, employees feel unjustly treated or bear a grudge against the company, they may be tempted, with every feeling of justification, to perform careless or even dishonest work.

Competence and integrity, a starting point

The competence and integrity of personnel are a good starting point. They do not in themselves ensure that good control will be achieved but they contribute to this goal and provide a good foundation for the controls described below. Indeed, a reasonable degree of competence and integrity is essential to the proper functioning of all other controls.

7.3.2 Segregation of functions

Next to the employment of honest and competent employees, one of the most fundamental elements of internal control is the segregation of certain key functions. The basic idea underlying segregation of functions (division of duties) is that no employee should be left in a position both to perpetrate and to conceal errors or irregularities in the normal course of his duties. The initial perpetration is almost impossible to prevent. Any employee, for example, with access to blank cheques may be able to forge a signature and embezzle company funds. But continuing embezzlement depends upon successful concealment. If the same employee maintains the cheque register and reconciles the company's bank accounts he may be able to suppress the recording of the fraudulent cheque and prevent its discovery which would otherwise occur upon reconciliation. Control against such irregularities thus involves elimination of the opportunity for concealment – by assigning the duties of bank reconciliation and cheque recording to someone independent from the employee preparing the cheque.

Functions which permit one employee both to perpetrate and conceal errors or irregularities are said to be *incompatible* functions. Of course, the segregation of incompatible functions can be circumvented by collusion. Thus the segregation of functions cannot be said to be a foolproof control. Nonetheless, an employee participating in a collusive fraud is always at the mercy of his co-conspirators and this very jeopardy is a powerful disincentive. Collusive frauds do occasionally occur and some of them make headlines. It is reasonable to assume, however, that far more frauds would occur if proper division of duties was not a common control element in most organizations.

Carried to its ultimate degree, the segregation of incompatible functions constitutes what has been called *internal check*:

> A system of allocation of responsibility, division of work and methods of recording transactions whereby the work of an employee or group of employees is checked continuously by having to be in agreement with the work of others or by being correlated with the work of other employees. An essential feature is that no one employee or group of employees has exclusive control over any transaction or group of transactions.[9]

In general, the principal incompatible functions to be segregated are:
- custody of assets from recording or reporting of the same assets or related transactions,
- custody of assets from the authorization or approval of related transactions,
- authorization or approval of transactions from recording or reporting of the same transactions or related assets.

In any individual system, careful analysis of the above three pairs of incompatible functions will usually permit an appropriate division of duties to be designed. Numerous examples of this principle can be found in the individual controls described for each major system in Chapter 29. A couple of examples will suffice here, both being of the segregation of custody and recording.

Example 1

> System: The company storekeeper is custodian of raw material inventories and supplies. He also controls the inventory requisition pads. Foremen are supposed to write up requisitions but during rush periods the storekeeper prepares them.
>
> Problem: The storekeeper could steal inventory and cover up shortages with phony requisitions. Similarly, the embarrassing results of accidental errors could be concealed by phony requisitions.
>
> Solution: The control of the unissued requisition pads can be given to the inventory control clerk who keeps the perpetual records. He should issue them to foremen only and accept for posting to his records only requisitions prepared by foremen. This does not actually prevent the storekeeper from stealing, but the resulting shortages would be detected during stocktaking when inventory counts are compared to perpetual records. Knowledge that discrepancies would be caught will discourage theft in the first place.

Example 2

> System: The accounts receivable clerk opens the mail, prepares the deposit, posts the credits to the accounts receivable ledger, prepares the monthly receivable trial balance and mails customer statements. There is no other employee with the time available to perform the cash receipts function, though less time-consuming functions could be redistributed.
>
> Problem: The accounts receivable clerk could misappropriate cash and conceal it through a variety of methods including lapping and misfooting the trial balance.
>
> Solution: Short of redistributing the cash receipts function the best solution would be to have some other person open the mail and list receipts for subsequent independent comparison to bank records. If this is not practical, an independent person should trial balance the accounts receivable at the month end, compare details to the monthly statements, and mail out the statements. At the same time the duplicate deposit slip approved by the bank should be checked to the accounts receivable postings for two or three days either side of the month-end. The comptroller should carefully review the trial balance. These procedures do not eliminate the possibility of fraud but would ensure its early detection and thus discourage its occurrence in the first place.

Extensive segregation of incompatible functions is obviously easier in large organizations where there are many more employees among whom to distribute duties. In small organizations some segregation is still possible, and important, but usually it cannot be as extensive. Compensating controls to offset this limitation in small organizations are discussed at the end of this chapter.

The need for good control does not imply that everyone steals

It is, unfortunately, not possible to explain the purpose of segregation of incompatible functions without talking in terms of potential defalcations. Of course, this does not mean that everyone is a thief, nor that instituting good control procedures is an insult to the integrity of present employees. As stated earlier, it is desirable that systems be designed that do not place temptation in front of normally well-intentioned employees. Moreover, the faithful employee of today may be succeeded by a newcomer tomorrow. Good systems design should not have to depend on the assumption that nothing could go wrong.

7.3.3 Overall plan of organization

Extending the principle of segregation of incompatible functions and introducing as well concepts of efficient administration leads to the idea of an effective organization plan for the enterprise as a whole.

Generally, reporting should be segregated from operations because one function of reporting is to provide control over operations. Where operations and reporting responsibilities overlap, operating problems may go unreported or at least be down played in information supplied to senior management.

In addition to segregating incompatible functions, the following two broad control standards should be observed:

1. Authority and responsibility should be clearly assigned to specific individuals or departments in order to provide accountability for all actions within the organization.

   When responsibility is not clearly assigned it is too easy for errors that were not anyone's fault to proliferate.

2. Within any one area of responsibility the individual or department involved should be granted as much independence as possible.

   For example, if the credit department is to be held accountable for credit management its decisions should not be allowed to be overridden by the sales department, the accounting department, and the treasury department. If everyone has a right to interfere no one can really be held responsible afterwards. Moreover, organizational independence will promote maximum internal efficiency within the credit department.

Applying these principles to the organization as a whole implies that a business should be segregated into a number of appropriate divisions, each with specific accountability, that appropriate persons should be appointed to be responsible for these divisions, that clear lines of responsibility should be established between each division and the chief executive officer, and that the coordination between different departments should be precisely defined. Effective management structure is a subject in itself, extensively treated in current business literature, and well beyond the scope of this book. The following few examples illustrate only some of the control points to be observed.

Examples of corporate organizational structures

Examples of executive level structures for three reasonably large companies are shown in Figure 7.a. So many structures occur in practice that no few examples can be said to be typical or ideal. The point to note from Figure 7.a is that separation of key functions up to a very senior level is common. Usually the separated functions, however named, include the following:

OPERATIONS

a) marketing and sales (selling the product or service)

b) manufacturing or production (making the product or performing the service)

c) personnel and industrial relations (hiring the people to make the product, perform the service, or staff the internal service departments)

CUSTODY

d) treasury (receiving, disbursing, and investing corporate cash)

RECORDS

e) comptroller (financial reports, budget analysis, accounting)

This segregation meets the basic control principle of segregating incompatible functions as well as permitting the clear assignment of authority and responsibility. It is particularly important that the operating functions (which initiate and authorize most transactions) be segregated from the custodial function[10] and the record-keeping function. It is also important that the custodial and record-keeping functions themselves be segregated up to as senior a level as possible. Treasury and comptrollership functions are sometimes separated up to one level below the president (as in Company B in Figure 7.a) and sometimes combined under a vice-president finance (as in Company C). The exact structure will depend upon the nature of the business but in any event custody of assets and record-keeping should be separated at all but the higher levels.

Automatic checks and balances

Clear separation of responsibilities within a business organization means that no one individual or department will have exclusive control over one complete business transaction. For example, the process of collecting an account receivable involves initially the acquisition of raw materials by the purchasing department, their conversion into finished goods by the production department, and their sale by the sales department to a customer approved for credit by the credit department. The involvement of each of these departments in the complete business cycle acts as a check on the others. Of course, for this automatic check to be effective the checker should not be the subordinate of the one checked. For example, the storekeeper having custody of raw materials depends on the purchaser to acquire acceptable quality and quantity of material on time. If the raw materials are not forthcoming the complaints of the storekeeper to his superior will bring the problem to management's attention – unless perhaps his superior happens to be the purchaser. Likewise, the sales manager is anxious to please customers. If product problems are causing customer dissatisfaction the complaints of the sales manager to his

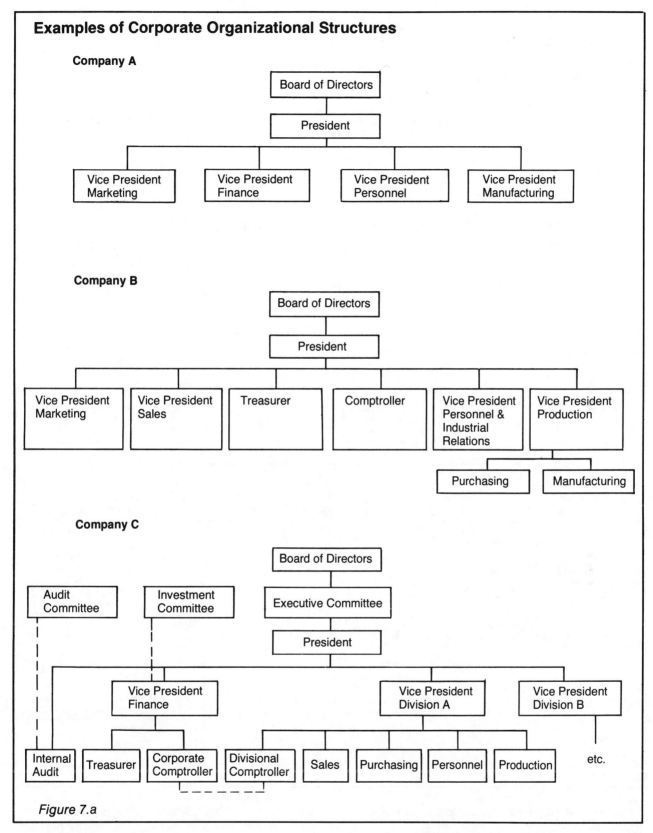

Examples of Corporate Organizational Structures

Company A

Board of Directors
President
Vice President Marketing | Vice President Finance | Vice President Personnel | Vice President Manufacturing

Company B

Board of Directors
President
Vice President Marketing | Vice President Sales | Treasurer | Comptroller | Vice President Personnel & Industrial Relations | Vice President Production
Purchasing | Manufacturing

Company C

Audit Committee | Investment Committee
Board of Directors
Executive Committee
President
Vice President Finance | Vice President Division A | Vice President Division B
Internal Audit | Treasurer | Corporate Comptroller | Divisional Comptroller | Sales | Purchasing | Personnel | Production | etc.

Figure 7.a

superior will bring the problem to senior management's attention – unless perhaps his superior happens to be the vice-president manufacturing. Analysis of the chain of command within each area of the business will indicate whether this system of automatic checks and balances can be expected to be effective.

153

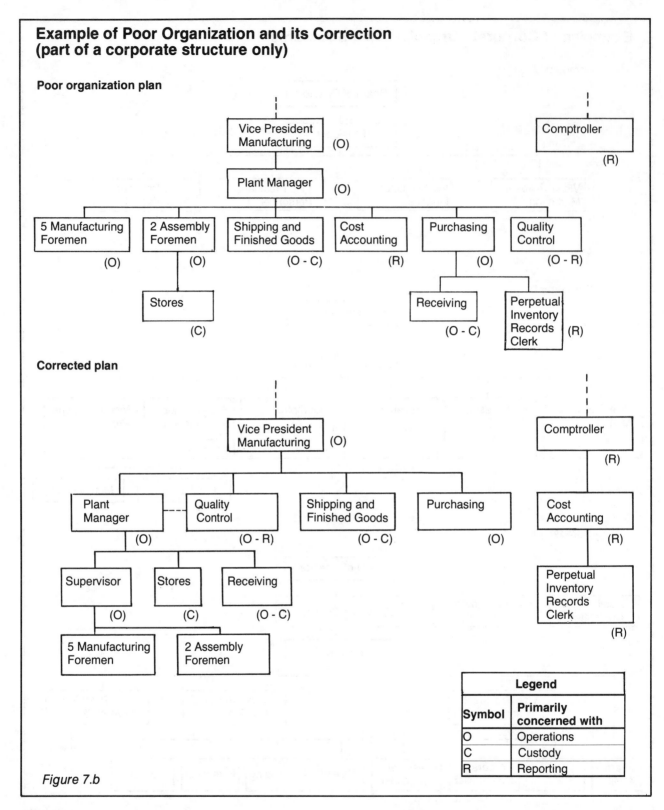

Example of Poor Organization and its Correction (part of a corporate structure only)

Poor organization plan

Vice President Manufacturing (O)

Comptroller (R)

Plant Manager (O)

5 Manufacturing Foremen (O)

2 Assembly Foremen (O)

Shipping and Finished Goods (O - C)

Cost Accounting (R)

Purchasing (O)

Quality Control (O - R)

Stores (C)

Receiving (O - C)

Perpetual Inventory Records Clerk (R)

Corrected plan

Vice President Manufacturing (O)

Comptroller (R)

Plant Manager (O)

Quality Control (O - R)

Shipping and Finished Goods (O - C)

Purchasing (O)

Cost Accounting (R)

Supervisor (O)

Stores (C)

Receiving (O - C)

Perpetual Inventory Records Clerk (R)

5 Manufacturing Foremen

2 Assembly Foremen

Legend	
Symbol	**Primarily concerned with**
O	Operations
C	Custody
R	Reporting

Figure 7.b

Example of poor organization and its correction

The control points of importance in developing an organizational structure can be seen by analyzing a poor organization plan and its correction. The top half of Figure 7.b illustrates an extreme case of poor organization. The bottom half of the figure presents a suggested correction. The corrected plan is not necessarily ideal for any given company but a comparison of the two plans at least indicates the factors to be considered.

Improving efficiency and automatic checks and balances

Problem	Solution
1. The plant manager has 11 individuals reporting to him. This number exceeds the normal "management span" that one man can effectively control. Some of them will be receiving inadequate attention. In contrast the vice president manufacturing has only 1 individual reporting to him – probably he spends his idle time interfering in the plant manager's work.	1. The 7 foremen are placed under a supervisor. For reasons explained below, certain other functions are redistributed to the vice president manufacturing and the comptroller. As a result three individuals now report to the plant manager and four to the vice president manufacturing – a number which can be controlled effectively.
2. Delays or other problems in the purchasing of materials may never get reported to senior management (the vice president manufacturing). Complaints from stores must first filter through the assembly foremen and may stop at the level of the plant manager, who will be held responsible for the very purchasing problems he should be reporting.	2. Stores is placed directly under the plant manager and purchasing is moved to the vice president manufacturing. Stores will not hesitate to report purchasing delays to the plant manager as he is no longer responsible for the problems.
3. Similarly, delays in manufactured goods reaching the finished goods area may never get reported to senior management.	3. Shipping and finished goods is moved to the vice president manufacturing to whom it can report production delays directly. This provides a check on the efficiency of the production operation, which is the responsibility of the plant manager.

Segregating incompatible functions

Problem	Solution
4. Operations, custody and reporting functions are all concentrated under the plant manager. The plant manager is in a position to conceal operating problems or irregularities by issuing instructions to cost accounting.	4. Cost accounting (a reporting function) is moved under the comptroller, who has responsibility for the reporting throughout the organization.
5. One of the jobs of the perpetual inventory records clerk should be to report inventory discrepancies which may be the result of misuse of materials, short shipments, diversion of incoming goods, or outright theft. Yet these very discrepancies could be the responsibility of his superior (the purchaser) or his co-worker (the receiver). His complaints might well be suppressed. Indeed, any reporting within the plant manager's sphere could run some risk of suppression.	5. The perpetual inventory records clerk is moved under cost accounting, now in the comptroller's department. Reporting is now segregated and acts as a check on operations.
6. Late and poorly made requisitions to stores cause production delays and should be reported by stores. Yet the storekeeper's superiors are the very individuals responsible for such requisitions.	6. Stores now report directly to the plant manager. This divides most operations and custody functions at levels below the plant manager. The two functions still overlap at the level of the plant manager himself but it is unlikely that any further division is practical. It is usually not logical for stores to report to a completely different corporate area and reporting directly to the vice president manufacturing would not usually be practical except for very specialized and sensitive inventories.

Problem	Solution
7. The purchasing agent has control of the purchasing, receiving and recording of materials. This is an extreme case of concentration of incompatible functions – perhaps the most serious weakness in internal control exhibited in this plan.	7. This problem has been solved by the changes explained above – moving the purchaser under the vice-president manufacturing, receiving under the plant manager, and the perpetual inventory records desk to the comptroller's department.
8. In rush periods there may be a temptation to cut corners in quality control. Senior management may never hear of this by-passing of control in the quality control department reports to the plant manager.	8. Quality control has been moved directly under the vice president manufacturing though obviously close liaison will have to be maintained with the plant manager.

7.3.4 Accounting/finance organization plan

Within the overall corporate structure the organization of the accounting/finance sector is particularly significant from a control point of view. The reason is that the reporting functions concentrated in the accounting/finance sector should serve as important controls over other departments but the effectiveness of these controls will depend on the segregation of incompatible functions within the accounting/ finance sector itself.

In total the functions of the accounting/finance sector can be divided into the following eight activities:

1. Comptrollership functions
   a) recording the business transactions of the company on a current basis,
   b) providing financial accounting information to management for distribution to shareholders, creditors and other outside parties,
   c) providing internal accounting information to management and to the operating departments,
   d) providing a control, as part of its reporting functions, over operating departments.
2. Treasury and finance functions
   e) receiving and disbursing company funds,
   f) custody of quick assets (cash, bank accounts, marketable securities, accounts receivable),
   g) investment of surplus cash,
   h) obtaining funds (through bank loans, debt and equity capital) to finance all corporate activities.

Because of the scope of the foregoing responsibilities, the senior executive in the accounting/ finance sector should be on a level with executives responsible for marketing, manufacturing, personnel and other operating functions. In a small company the secretary-treasurer, reporting to the president, may run the accounting department, supervise the cashier, prepare the financial statements, negotiate the bank loan, and invest idle cash. In larger organizations the comptrollership and treasury functions are usually segregated – preferably up to as senior a level as possible. A number of examples of accounting/finance organization plans are illustrated in Figure 7.c and are discussed later.

Specific control standards

Applying the previously discussed principles of segregating incompatible functions and of clearly assigning authority and responsibility, the following specific control standards can be identified for the accounting/finance sector.

1. The accounting/finance sector should have no operations responsibility, except for investments, borrowing, credit control and cash management.
2. Reporting responsibility should be centred in the accounting/finance sector, and not spread throughout the company where no one can be held responsible for the reliability of the final reports.
3. Any authorization and approval functions within the accounting/finance sector should be at a high level. Most routine authorizations and approvals come from operating departments – purchase orders, requisitions, pay authorizations etc.; if the few authorizations and approvals originating within the accounting finance sector are made at a senior level, segregation of those functions from recording and custody is facilitated.
4. Custody of cash and investments should be carefully segregated from recording and reporting functions. Any overlapping of functions should normally be restricted to the more senior levels.
5. Recording and reporting functions should be so divided among employees that there will be reasonable assurance that errors made in the normal course of their duties will be automatically detected by the accounting system.

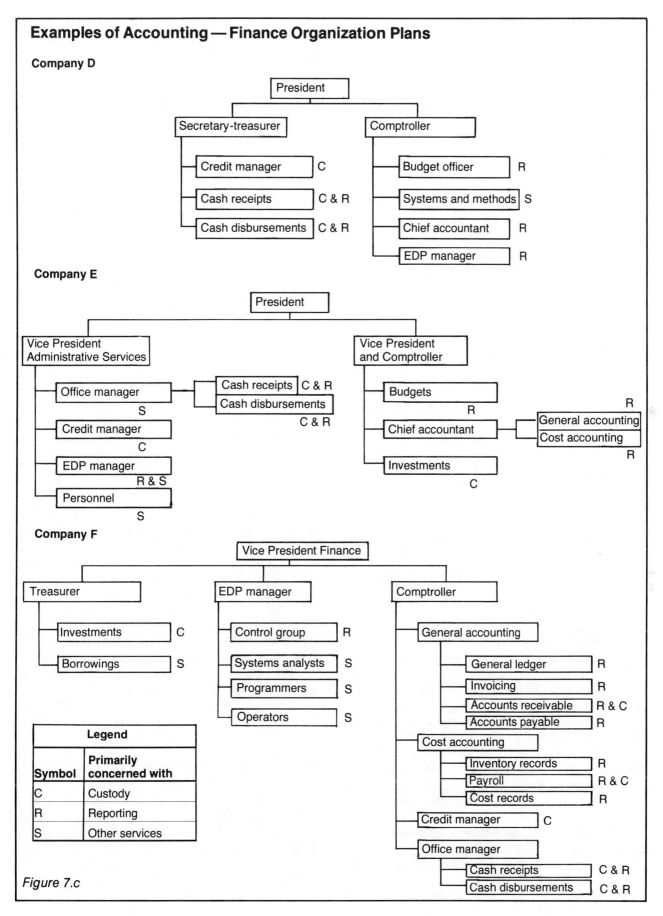

Examples of Accounting — Finance Organization Plans

Figure 7.c

157

6. The organization plan should facilitate the timely flow of information between the accounting/finance sector and other departments.

Segregation from operations

The importance of the segregation from operations is to preserve the integrity of the controls exercised over operations by the accounting/finance sector. To the extent that some operations (investments, borrowing, credit control and cash management) are necessarily carried on within the accounting/finance sector special care must be taken to segregate custody and recording functions (treasury and comptrollership functions).

Centralization of reporting responsibility

Although reporting responsibility should be centred in the accounting/finance sector some recording functions must be performed by operating departments to provide input into the accounting system. Thus, the receiver must both take custody of incoming materials and record their receipt. Usually, it is possible to design the system so that there is independent verification of input received from operating departments. For example, errors in a receiving report may be detected by comparison with packing slips or purchase invoices in the accounting department. Errors in goods shipped may be detected by customer complaints. Shortages in the stockroom may be detected by comparison with the perpetual inventory records maintained in the accounting department.

Segregation of custodial and reporting functions

Segregation of custodial and reporting functions can be accomplished by placing one senior official in charge of treasury functions and another in charge of comptrollership functions. This is illustrated by Company D in Figure 7.c, where the secretary-treasurer and the comptroller each report directly to the president. The secretary-treasurer's department is responsible for short and long range financial planning, credit approval, the custody and deposit of cash receipts, and the cash disbursements function. The comptroller's department is responsible for budgeting, accounting, financial statement preparation, and the computer function but has no custodial responsibility.

Frequently it is not practical to design an ideal plan from a control point of view, because the accounting/finance organization plan must fit into the overall corporate structure and suit the company's size and operations. In Company E in Figure 7.c

some financial and comptrollership functions are assigned to one department under the vice president and comptroller. However, some separation of functions has been achieved by assigning credit approval and cash receipts and disbursements functions to the vice president administrative services. The computer has also been placed under the vice president administrative services as it may perform complex computations for other departments, such as engineering, in addition to its computerized accounting services for the comptroller's department. Because investments and accounting remain together under the comptroller, however, it is important that the organization within the comptroller's department be designed to segregate these two functions. Control would also be enhanced if the custody of investments were shared with a responsible official from outside the comptroller's department.

In Company F in Figure 7.c a reverse arrangement shows the treasurer handling investments but shows cash receipts and disbursement functions within the comptroller's department. Nevertheless, the comptroller's department has been divided so that the accounting function in the general accounting section is segregated from custody of cash in the office manager's section. Control would also be enhanced if the second signing officer on corporate cheques were a responsible official from outside the comptroller's department.

Internal audit

In many organization plans the internal audit function will be found as part of the accounting/finance sector, perhaps reporting to the comptroller or the vice president finance. While the presence of an internal audit function, wherever it reports, is always of some control benefit, its effectiveness is generally greater if the reporting takes place outside the accounting/finance sector, and ideally to the president directly. Internal audit (see 7.8) is essentially a monitoring of the functioning of controls many of which lie within the accounting/finance sector. The monitoring is bound to be more impartial if it takes place outside the sector responsible for the controls.

Interface of accounting/finance sector with management and operating departments

Because so many of the reporting and control functions are centred in the accounting/finance sector, the organization plan must provide for efficient and timely flow of information to and from operating departments and management. The flow of information is illustrated in Figure 7.d.

Information Flow to and from Accounting/Finance Sector

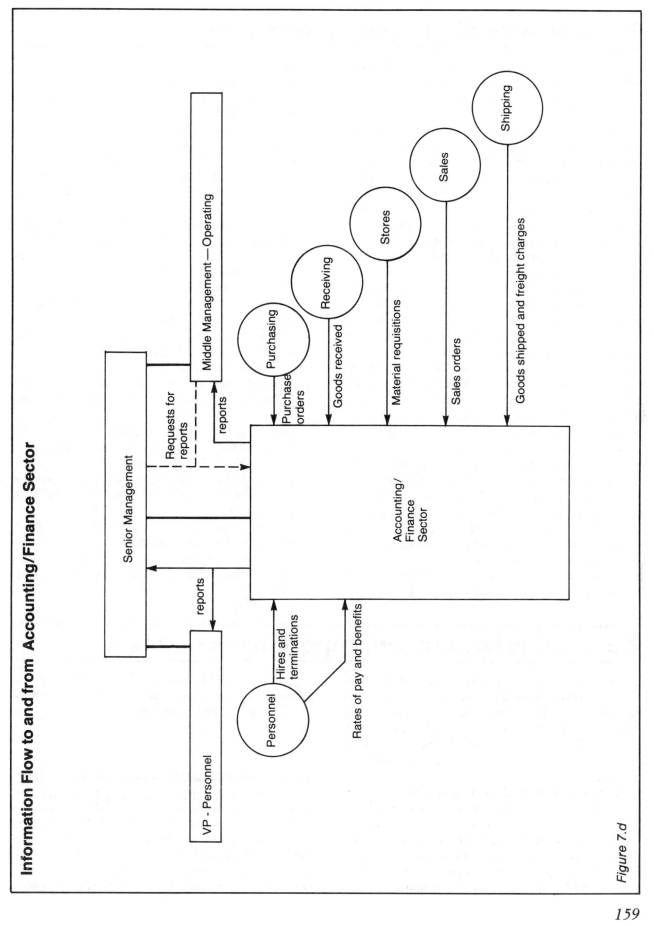

Figure 7.d

159

7.4 Systems development controls

Some individual or department should be charged with the responsibility for developing systems, approving the introduction of new systems, and approving modifications of existing systems. The formality with which this is done varies with the size of the organization. In a small office the office manager may discharge this responsibility informally and issue instructions orally. In a large organization a separate systems and methods group may have this responsibility and document their recommendations in detailed procedures manuals. With computerized systems the presence of effective systems development controls is particularly important and is discussed in the Chapter 8.

The development of new systems usually requires consultation with the operating departments (who will be affected by the new procedures), with the accounting/finance sector (who will want assurance that timely reporting and appropriate account practices are being incorporated), with internal auditors (who will want to satisfy themselves that effective controls are being maintained), and, in some cases (particularly complex computer systems), with external auditors as well.

Good systems development controls imply that:

a) certain prescribed procedures should be observed and approvals obtained before new systems or systems modifications are adopted (a clerk should not merely decide to price invoices in a different manner which seems to him to be better or easier; his suggestion should be referred to the individual or group charged with systems development since otherwise accounting principles, tax requirements, or company policies may be inadvertently violated);

b) the new systems should contain all control elements, as discussed in this chapter, which are practical in the circumstances;

c) the new systems should be designed in the most efficient manner practical (systems efficiency is not discussed directly in this chapter) – reasonable compromises between control and efficiency and between costs and benefits are usually necessary;

d) the new systems should be consistent with generally accepted accounting principles, with company policies, and with legal or governmental requirements;

e) the new systems should meet the information needs of all users involved (an individual responsible for a given operation needs detailed information to measure his own performance, guide future decisions, and gauge the performance of his subordinates);

f) where the new systems involve the acquisition or utilization of accounting equipment (including one-write boards, "whiz" machines with locked in invoice copies, cash registers, bookkeeping machines for posting ledger cards, desk-top computers, or full-fledged computer systems) a proper study should be conducted of possible alternatives, available equipment, installation timetable, etc.;

g) adequate plans should be made for the conversion of records used under the old system to records required under the new system (to avoid either omissions or inadvertent duplicate recording).

7.5 Authorization and reporting controls

The ultimate authority for entering into business transactions is governed by the owners of the business and by legal requirements. In a company, this authority is delegated by the shareholders to the board of directors, who in turn will delegate much of it to the officers of the company and other management personnel.

Fundamental to good internal control is that all transactions entered into by an enterprise should be authorized. Equally important is the proper reporting of completed transactions to the immediate supervisor of the person responsible for the transactions, to management in general, to the board of directors and to the owners of the business. Reporting controls provide management with the information needed to manage the activities of the enterprise as well as with a record of their stewardship of company assets.

7.5.1 General authorization, specific authorization, and approvals

Authorization may be general or specific. Delegation of authority to manage the business from the shareholders to the board of directors is a form of *general authorization*. Within the management structure, general authorization usually takes the form of policy statements or directives giving authority for particular classes of transactions – for example, authority to set sales prices, authority to sign contracts, authority to acquire capital assets, or authority to hire employees. With respect to transactions, general authorizations should identify the conditions under which a particular defined class of transaction should be entered into and the person or persons responsible for that class of transactions. General authorization, when contained in policy directives, is usually an integral part of the overall organization plan defining spheres of authority and responsibility.

The *fact* that general authorizations exist is an important element in the system of internal control. The *methods* by which general authorizations are established, however, may be considered as part of the policy-making process and as such outside the field of internal control itself.[11] Those methods are the responsibility of top management and the board of directors and involve establishing that the details of delegated authority are consistent with overall corporate objectives.

Specific authorization, in contrast to general authorization, is concerned with individual transactions, the particular conditions of the transaction and the parties involved in the transaction. Examples of specific authorization include authorization to purchase a particular fixed asset from a particular third party, authorization to sell product A to customer M at $100 per unit, authorization to hire a specific individual.

Controls to ensure authorization

Internal control should provide reasonable assurance (a) that authorization (sometimes general but usually specific) exists for each transaction, (b) that where specific authorizations are issued their issuance is by employees or officials acting within the scope of their general authority, and (c) that each transaction conforms with the terms of its authorization. To accomplish these three objectives it is necessary in turn (i) that general authorizations and the responsibilities for issuing specific authorizations are clearly defined, as already discussed, and (ii) that some system be established of checking that each transaction has been authorized and conforms with the terms of its authorization. The latter requirement can be met in various ways.

Often it is met by dividing the responsibilities for the specific authorization of a given transaction – one person authorizing the initiation of the transaction (such as a purchase) and a second person later authorizing completion of a transaction (such as payment of the purchase invoice). The second authorization is normally called an *approval*. Approval can be thought of as a control over the performance of the authorization function. Internal control is enhanced if the person approving the transaction is independent of the person initially authorizing it.

Sometimes the control is exercised without a specific additional approval being added. For example, the storekeeper may only accept raw material requisitions that have been properly authorized by foremen. The cheque disbursements clerk may only prepare a cheque when a properly approved invoice is submitted. The storekeeper and the clerk in these examples may not specifically add a further initial or signature to indicate that the prerequisites have been fulfilled but their insistence on the presence of the prescribed approvals and authorizations functions equally well as a control.

Occasionally authorization and approval steps may appear combined. The telephone bill may be approved by a signing officer for payment even though no prior authorizing initials appear on the bill. In effect, an implied authorization exists for the continuation of telephone services. Of course, if long distance calls exceeded the authority of the caller, detection of this infringement will depend on the thoroughness of the approval procedure.

For many transactions there may be a series of inter-related authorizations and approvals.

> For example, management may give authorization to the sales manager to establish sales prices, to salesmen to quote sales prices to their customers and write up orders, and to the credit manager to grant credit. A sales price list together with the stated policy provides general authorization for a salesman to quote a specific price to a customer for specific goods and to prepare the order. This is the initial authorization of the transaction. The credit manager reviews and approves the order for credit. The approved order provides authorization to the billing clerk to prepare the shipping documents which in turn provides authorization to the shipping department to deliver the goods. Initials on a copy of the shipping document returned to the billing clerk provide him with the specific authorization to invoice the customer. Final approval is given to the transaction on a post facto basis when the sales manager reviews all copies of the sales invoice.

Preliminary validation steps

While ultimate responsibility for the authenticity and accuracy of a transaction rests with the person who gives final approval (for example a signing officer reviewing supporting documentation paying a trade supplier) there will often be a series of preliminary validation steps necessary to ensure that all aspects of the transaction are correct.

> For example, the accounts payable clerk compares the purchase invoice with a purchase order to see that the purchase was properly authorized and the price is correct. He also compares the invoice against a receiving report to see that the goods were received in reasonable

condition and checks that the sales tax is correct and the invoice arithmetically accurate.

Preliminary validation steps are most often evidenced by initials or signatures on accounting documents. Other types of validation steps may involve ensuring the serial continuity of documents as evidence that they have been processed properly by the accounting system.

7.5.2 Budgets, responsibility reporting, management information systems

Closely related to authorization controls, which authorize an individual transaction before it is initiated, are *budgetary controls*, which in a sense authorize a whole year's transactions in terms of expected results before the year's business is begun. Budgets or forecasts provide a yardstick against which actual results can be measured and as a result of which corrective action can be taken where necessary. A budget is a detailed plan of the future, expressed in terms of money, quantities, or other values, or some combination thereof, designed to provide both control over and performance measurements of operations and other activities. The types of budgets most commonly used by normal business operations are: operating budgets, capital budgets, and financial budgets.

Operating budget

The purpose of an operating budget is to (a) forecast operating results for some future period (b) establish reasonable revenue targets to guide and encourage production and sales performance (c) establish approved expense limits to control expenditures and (d) serve as input into the financial budget to determine cash requirements. The budget should be broken down into segments according to the division of responsibilities within the organization. Comparisons of actual results will be facilitated if the budget parallels the revenue and expense accounts in the general ledger and subsidiary ledgers. Operating budgets are usually prepared in detail for each month of the coming year. Companies that practise long range planning may have operating budgets in less detail for the next five years or longer.

Preparation of the operating budget

Each individual to be held accountable for certain revenues or expenses should participate in the establishing of budget figures for his items. This participation is important both to ensure that all relevant factors are taken into account in preparing the budget and to enlist the cooperation of all employees in making the budget work. The preparation of a comprehensive operating budget would involve the following stages:

1. Preparation of a detailed sales budget (by product, geographical area, salesman, or other logical subdivision) based on past performance, current prices and price trends, new products, competition, etc. This budget should be prepared by the sales department with the assistance of marketing personnel and in conjunction with the comptroller or budget officer, who can serve as a check against excessive optimism.
2. Preparation of a production budget (quantities, prices of raw materials, direct labour costs, indirect labour costs, other manufacturing overhead) based on past performance and based on the products, volumes and time schedules called for in the sales budget.
3. Preparation of a budget for all other operating costs by department (distribution costs, selling costs, administrative costs, personnel costs, etc.) based on the sales targets established and the production levels budgeted.
4. Preparation of the total operating budget pulling together the sales, production and other cost budgets, resolving any inconsistencies between them, and adding any other revenue or expenditure accounts not already included. The final budget might be prepared by the budget officer or comptroller and should then be submitted for approval by senior management and possibly the board of directors.

Capital budget

The purpose of a capital budget is to (a) forecast required capital expenditures on equipment and property for some future period (often one to five years), (b) establish expenditure limits which, once approved, cannot be exceeded without further authorization, (c) serve as input into the financial budget to determine cash requirements, and (d) serve as input into the operating budget to determine depreciation allowances. Capital budgets would normally be approved annually by senior management and possibly the board of directors.

Financial budget

The purpose of a financial budget is to forecast the monthly and annual cash requirements to provide funds for both current operations and capital expenditures. The financial budget incorporates the projections of the operating and capital budgets. In addition, it must forecast the levels of inventories, accounts receivable, accounts payable etc. (sometimes called the balance sheet budget) and provide for dividend requirements, debt repayment obligations, etc. The final result will show, month by month, the cash surplus to be invested or deficiency to be financed. If the financing requirements are beyond the company's abilities, operating and capital budgets may have to be revised.

In the long range the financial budget is concerned with the total financing of the business, the appropriate amounts and types of debt and equity financing, a suitable debt-equity ratio, etc. Based on the financial budget the board of directors will make key policy decisions concerning dividend payments, plans for expansion of operations, and appropriate debt or share issues to the public.

Making budgets work

Once operating, capital and financial budgets are established and approved, periodic reports to management and to the departments involved must compare the actual results to budgeted figures. Major variances should be highlighted and explained. Some variances may require careful analysis to determine their cause. If variance analysis is well performed, the budgetary system can be an immense aid to management in focussing on the trouble spots requiring corrective action (often called "management by exception").

Responsibility accounting

The effectiveness of budgetary controls is increased if the organization of accounts and reports parallels the division of responsibility. If a particular revenue or expense is the net result of activities of four different departments it is hard to hold any one responsible for the final result. But if the accounts and budgets are classified in such a way that one individual or department has exclusive control over the final results of any given item, then that individual or department can properly be held accountable for the results. Personal accountability tends to ensure more realistic budgets in the first place and a greater incentive to achieving budget targets thereafter.

Management information systems

A management information system (MIS) is the result of designing and coordinating in a formal manner all the flow of budgetary, accounting, and control information to meet the information needs of management in each operating department as well as the needs of senior management and the board of directors. Management information systems are commonly broken down into various subsystems such as marketing, distribution, manufacturing, procurement, personnel, finance and control. These subsystems are not primarily concerned with the preparation of data for external reporting but rather with the provision of reliable information on which management can base day-to-day operating decisions. An organization can produce reliable financial statements without having a sophisticated management information system. Nonetheless, such a system, by facilitating meaningful management review of reported results, generally increases the reliability of all financial reporting.

7.6 Accounting systems controls

Controls at the level of an individual accounting system (such as the sales/receivables/receipts system) consist of the application to that particular system of all general control elements discussed previously.
a) organizational controls (including honesty and competence of personnel, segregation of incompatible functions, and organization plans – see 7.3),
b) authorization and reporting controls (including authorizations, approvals and budgetary controls – see 7.5).
In addition, accounting systems controls include:
• systems to ensure that transactions are initially recorded in the correct amount and period and properly classified,
• a general design of the accounts and accounting records conducive to the effective operation of the other control elements.

7.6.1 Ensuring that transactions are initially recorded

Authorization controls are designed to prevent the execution of improper transactions but they do not in themselves guard against the non-recording of authorized transactions. Approval controls may detect inaccurate recording but not unrecorded transactions. Segregation of incompatible functions is designed to prevent deliberate non-recording for fraudulent purposes but it does not in itself guard against inadvertent omissions.

To minimize the chance of non-recording of transactions, systems should provide for the recording of each transaction as close to the time of occurrence as possible. Delays may mean that the transaction is forgotten. Even if later recorded, a delayed entry will mean that records controlling assets such as cash and securities will be out of date and therefore ineffective in maintaining control over custody. Initial recording refers to the first document, record or notation evidencing the transaction. Summarization in various accounting books and reports may occur later depending on convenience and processing efficiency.

Proper forms design (discussed later), adequate training, clear instructions, and good supervision also help to ensure that early and accurate recording of transactions takes place.

Beyond the foregoing controls, management assurance that all transactions have been properly recorded must generally come from some form of detective control which would likely detect an omission were one to occur. A number of examples will illustrate the idea.

> At one extreme, comparison of paid checks returned by a bank with the recorded disbursements would reveal any unrecorded paid checks. Similarly, examination of documents supporting recorded disbursements would reveal those for which an accountability for resulting assets should be recorded concurrently. Where shipping documents are used, comparison of such documents with sales records would reveal unrecorded sales. A more indirect possibility with respect to sales is to estimate the aggregate amount that should be recorded by applying sales prices or gross profit rates to quantities or costs of inventory disposed of during a period. The degree of accuracy from such estimates depends on the variability of the pricing structure, the product mix, and other circumstances; in any event, however, such estimates ordinarily would not provide specific identification of any unrecorded sales that may be indicated. Assurance that collections on receivables are recorded rests primarily on the controls exercised over the records of receivables since these show the aggregate accountability for such collections. Accountability for collections of interest and dividends ordinarily can be established readily from securities records and independent published sources, while that for contributions from the general public ordinarily is more difficult to establish or estimate.[12]

7.6.2 General ledger and chart of accounts

The general ledger of an organization should summarize all its transactions and be designed to:
a) meet the requirements of external reporting
b) meet the requirements of internal reporting
c) reflect the allocation of custodial and operational responsibilities within the organization.

A chart of accounts is a listing of all general ledger accounts – assets, liabilities, equities, revenue, and expenses – preferably accompanied by a description of the purpose and content of each account and sometimes the expected source of input. Its function is to help the posting of transactions to the correct account in the general ledger. Use of a chart of accounts will also facilitate the coding of accounting documents and their recording in books of original entry.

External reporting requirements

External reporting requirements will usually set a minimum for the number of general ledger accounts required. The task of carrying figures from the general ledger to the published financial statements can ordinarily be fairly mechanical, though judgment is required to ensure that the statements contain all disclosures required for fair presentation in accordance with generally accepted accounting principles. There will usually be (a) a number of general ledger accounts which must be combined to make up one financial statement figure and (b) a few which require analysis into various components for disclosure on the financial statements. The former present little difficulty but the latter are inefficient. Accounts requiring analysis for statement presentation (e.g., into trade receivables, notes receivables, loans to officers, advances to employees) would be better broken into individual accounts in the general ledger in the first place.

Internal reporting requirements

Internal reporting requirements are likely to increase the number of general ledger accounts above the minimum required for external reporting. While some detail in internal reports can come from subsidiary ledgers, it is usually most efficient if important reports can be prepared directly from the general ledger. Sales analysis by broad category should be available from the general ledger. General ledger accounts should also classify costs by broad functional groupings for internal reporting purposes (for example, manufacturing costs, selling costs, and administrative costs).

Account organization by reponsibility

Finally, the organization of the accounts should parallel the allocation of custodial responsibility in order to permit responsibility accounting, as discussed earlier. If the custody of one corporate asset (such as inventories) is divided among three divisions, a separate ledger account should be maintained for each division, reflecting the portion of the inventory of which it has custody and responsibility. Alternatively a control account should be used together with subsidiary accounts for the individual divisions. The same principal applies to the division of responsibilities for operating functions. For example:

1. If there are two credit managers, one responsible for eastern sales and one responsible for western sales, there should be two trade receivable control accounts, two accounts receivable sub-ledgers, two receivable trial balances, etc.
2. If in the marketing area there are three sales managers, there should be at least three sales accounts (or some other provision for detailed sales analyses) so that each sales manager can be held accountable for the sales for which he is responsible.
3. Similarly, there will usually be a need for one, or more often a group, of general ledger accounts for each individual or department responsible for certain operating costs.

A well-designed general ledger and its related chart of accounts may often provide a useful secondary purpose in pinpointing flaws in the company's organization plan. They may indicate where undue concentration of responsibility has occurred or, more important, where there are assets, revenues or expenses for which no one has been designated as responsible.

7.6.3 Journals, sub-ledgers, balancing routines

The number, nature and design of journals and subsidiary ledgers (sub-ledgers), their allocation to various clerks, and the nature of periodic balancing routines all affect the quality of the accounting system.

Journals

Journals or "books of original entry" are used to record each business transaction. In manual systems it is usually more efficient and provides better control if similar transactions are recorded in one journal (sales in a sales journal, cash receipts in a cash receipts journal, etc., though the names of course will vary). Each journal in a manual system should be maintained on a double-entry basis so that some check on the accuracy of recording of transactions is gained from periodic balancing routines. In computerized systems, classification of transaction types and double-entry controls are equally important though their method of implementation will differ from manual systems. Where possible the system should be designed so that the person responsible for maintaining journals (and sub-ledgers) does not have access to company assets. Control over entries made in journals is afforded through balancing routines, serial continuity checks on documents recorded, and periodic comparison of the records to assets on hand. Miscellaneous entries, recorded in a general journal,

must usually be subject to additional control procedures, primarily authorization controls.

Sub-ledgers

In many accounting systems a great number of general ledger accounts require back-up detail in the form of sub-ledgers. It is most common to find sub-ledgers supporting general ledger control accounts for accounts receivable, inventory and, in larger operations, detailed expenses by cost centre. The use of sub-ledgers provides a measure of accounting control provided the persons responsible for their maintenance are segregated from those responsible for the maintenance of the general ledger.

Balancing and reconciliation routines

The accuracy and reliability of certain accounts should be periodically checked through balancing and reconciliation routines. These routines may include:

1. a check of the internal consistency of recorded transactions (double-entry control and control account balancing),
2. a check of recorded transactions against some external evidence as to the balance in an account,
3. a special review of recorded transactions at and about significant cut-off dates,
4. a comparison of recorded assets against the assets physically on hand (see 7.7.2).

The balancing of debits and credits in the books of original entry and the general ledger (double-entry control) and the agreement of sub-ledger trial balances with related control accounts is usually done monthly, but for some records may be done more frequently.

The most common example of a check of recorded transactions against external evidence is the periodic reconciliation of the general ledger cash account to the cash balance reported by the bank. Control is significantly enhanced if the function of reconciliation is segregated from cash receipts and disbursement functions. Other examples of comparing recorded balances against external evidence include the reconciliation of consignment accounts to reports received from consignees and comparison of investment accounts against reports from third party custodians of securities.

Cut-off routines

While controls may be adequate to ensure that all transactions are recorded reasonably promptly, there is always the danger that they will be classified in an incorrect accounting period due to minor delays in summarizing the initial documentary records.

It is usually desirable, therefore, to have special routines at significant cut-off dates to ensure that all transactions are recorded in the proper period. The precise routines can vary widely. A few examples are:

1. On the tenth working day of each month the accounts payable clerk reviews all unmatched receiving reports, disbursements subsequent to the previous month-end and all invoices on hand and, based on this review, prepares a journal entry to record unaccrued costs as at the previous month-end.
2. On the fourth working day of each month the accounts receivable clerk reviews all sales for the first three days of the month and the last three days of the previous month to ensure that all sales are recorded in the correct month. Adjustments are made by journal entry.
3. During the physical inventory count the receiver and the shipping clerks stamp receiving and shipping documents as pre-count or post-count for use in later reconciliations.
4. At each quarter-end the senior accountant reviews all prepaid and deferred general ledger accounts to ensure that the proper charge has been made against income and reviews all expense accounts for possible prepaid or deferred items.

7.6.4 Document design

Accounting documents should be designed to contribute to control by:
- making it simple to record the transaction correctly and completely in the first place (clear layout),
- minimizing the need for transcription of figures (multi-use documents),
- facilitating detection of lost documents (prenumbering),
- making it difficult to overlook any required validation step (use of a validation stamp).

Clear layout

If customer name, customer code, part number, quantity ordered, and date are all required on a sales order, clearly marked spaces for each of these five items should be provided on the blank form. Some information (such as a code number indicating that the transaction is a sales order) can be pre-printed on the form if required.

Multiple-use documents

Where possible accounting documents should be designed for multiple use to speed preparation and to avoid transcription errors. For example, in some companies shipping, production and sales documents can be combined into one multi-form snap set. Document sets designed for multiple use are customarily colour coded to facilitate distribution of each copy to the right department.

Pre-numbering of documents

Accounting documents for internal use are normally pre-numbered when purchased. Control features can then be built around the use of this number. A check of serial continuity of processed documents provides assurance that transactions have not gone unprocessed. Pre-numbering can also prevent fraudulent misuse of documents, particularly documents such as cheques, because the numbering system can permit control over the issuing of blank documents to responsible persons. All significant accounting documents processed internally should be subject to some degree of issue control.

Use of a validation stamp

Document design should complement the system of authorization and approvals. One method is to provide space on the face of the form for signatures or initials to be added during the accounting process. Posting copies of accounting documents should also provide space for a reference number to indicate the journal page or batch control.

Alternatively, control of the processing of internal documents can be provided by the use of a validation stamp. Validation stamps are more commonly used, however, for accounting documents originating outside the company (e.g., purchase invoices). The validation stamp should provide positions for initials as each validation, authorization or approval function is completed. Initialling makes each reviewer accountable for the particular approval he gave. A validation stamp for purchase invoices might contain spaces for (a) entering the receiving date and the voucher number, (b) initialling to indicate the checking of additions, extensions, prices, receiving slip and purchase order, and (c) initialling for final approval.

7.6.5 Cost accounting

Cost accounting is concerned with the classification, recording, analysis, and interpretation of expenditures associated with the production and distribution of goods and services. As well as providing management with information needed for decision-making (determination of sales prices, initiation and termination of product lines, etc.), cost accounting establishes a control over the entire production process. Variance analysis in standard cost systems may reveal inefficiencies or irregularities in the use of raw materials, deployment of labour and expenditure on overhead. For comprehensive information on this subject the reader should refer to the many available texts on cost accounting.

7.7 Additional safeguarding controls

Elements of internal control discussed earlier in this chapter are useful in meeting most of the eight management objectives of internal control – safeguarding of assets, reliability of accounting records, and timely preparation of reliable financial information among others. Certain additional controls are primarily concerned with just the safeguarding of assets. Such controls are described in the following sections.

7.7.1 Restricted access

Access to assets should be closely controlled and, to the extent practical, limited to only authorized personnel. Restricting access in the broadest sense could refer to restricting both (a) physical access to the assets themselves and (b) indirect access through documents authorizing the use or disposition of the assets. Restriction of indirect access has already been covered under authorization controls and under the segregation of custody, authorization and recording responsibilities; it implies in turn reasonable restriction of access to documents and accounting records. Restriction of physical access to assets involves the physical segregation of the assets themselves, the use in some cases of protective equipment or devices, a prudent but practical definition of who are authorized to have access, clear instructions as to the restricted access rules, and reasonable monitoring of their observance. Who should be authorized to have access will depend on the nature of the assets, their susceptibility to loss through errors or irregularities, and the calibre of personnel involved. While different assets warrant physical access restrictions in different businesses, three of the most common are cash, other negotiable assets, and inventories.

Cash

The handling of cash receipts should be restricted to designated cashiers who are segregated from the accounting records controlling cash balances and from the posting of accounts receivables. Access may be restricted through the use of cash registers with locked drawers, particularly in retail organizations. Where large amounts of currency are on hand, further physical protection may be afforded by locating the cashier in a separate locked teller's cage.

The disbursement of cash should be controlled through the designation of responsible company officials as signing officers. Normally, two signing officers are required to examine supporting documents before signing cheques. Where cheques are prepared by computer and signatures applied by a cheque-signing machine, it should only be the signing itself which is automated. The signing officers should still exercise the same control in examining the cheques and supporting documents (though unfortunately this requirement is not always observed). Miscellaneous cash disbursements may be controlled by the use of imprest petty cash funds maintained by designated individuals. In an imprest fund the total of cash and supporting vouchers must always equal a predetermined amount.

Additional detailed comments on cash controls may be found in 29.2.1 and 29.3.1.

Other negotiable assets

Other negotiable assets such as notes receivable and investment certificates are normally controlled by ensuring that two persons must obtain access to the assets simultaneously. This relatively simple and effective control procedure can be implemented by the use of safety deposit boxes in any bank or trust company. Alternatively, other negotiable assets may be held by third parties (for example, in safekeeping at a bank or at a security dealer). Again the signatures of two company officials should be required to release or dispose of the asset held. Additional comments on internal controls over temporary investments may be found in 37.2.

Inventories

Physical protection of inventories in manufacturing and wholesale operations can be provided through segregated locked-off storage areas under the control of responsible storekeepers and through controlled access to the plant both during and after work hours. Naturally, the degree of physical protection warranted will depend on the nature of the inventory and the frequency with which access is required for production purposes.

In retail operations physical protection of inventories can be provided through controlled access to the premises both during and after business hours (use of burglar alarms, limited issue of keys, etc.). For valuable merchandise, locked customer display cases are advisable. Most retail operations provide further physical protection of assets through the positioning of cash registers so that all customers must pass by a register on leaving the store. Larger retail operations also employ a variety of further protection measures ranging from floor walkers to the use of television cameras. Additional detailed comments on these and other physical protection controls may be found in 29.5.1.

7.7.2 Periodic count and comparison

As previously discussed, a basic control over assets is the division of responsibility between custody and recording. This division of responsibility is only meaningful where there are periodic counts or measurements of the assets and the comparison of those counts with the accounting records.

Concurrence of counts with records

The concurrence of asset counts and related accounting records provides considerable assurance as to the accuracy of both. It is, of course, possible that both asset and record contain identical errors. In the case of deliberate errors, this possibility is reduced by the segregation of custody and reporting functions, although collusion remains a possibility. In the case of accidental errors or omissions, the possibility of identical errors occurring by chance in two independent functions is usually remote. Periodic comparison, while not completely foolproof, is thus a very strong control.

Discrepancies between counts and records

Discrepancies between asset counts and related accounting records should be investigated by persons independent of both custody and recording functions. Discrepancies may indicate (a) errors, waste, losses or irregularities in the handling of the assets themselves or (b) errors, omissions or irregularities in the accounting records. Careful investigation may be required to determine which of these alternative situations exists. Once the cause of the discrepancy has been discovered, the corrective action will depend on the nature of the asset, the system in use, and the amount and cause of the discrepancy. Correction of the discrepancy itself may involve adjustment of the accounting records and/or filing of insurance claims. Preventing its recurrence may require revising procedures, improving safeguarding controls, firing dishonest employees, or measures to improve the performance of personnel.

Frequency of comparison

The frequency of asset count and comparisons will vary with the particular system, the cost of the count process, and the susceptibility to material error. Cash sales proceeds are customarily counted daily and compared with cash register tapes. A few types of inventories may also be counted daily and compared with the record (a routine common, for example, with respect to finished goods in the beverage industry). More often, however, inventories are subjected to physical examination on a less frequent basis –

monthly, quarterly, or annually. Additional comments on this control element may be found throughout Chapter 29.

7.7.3 Protection of records

Accounting records themselves represent a valuable asset requiring protection. First of all, access to accounting records should be restricted to preserve the effectiveness of the segregation of custody, authorization and recording functions. Secondly, accounting records should be carefully stored (often in fireproof vaults after working hours) to minimize the chance of loss, theft, or destruction by fire. Thirdly, in some cases back-up records may be advisable to facilitate the reconstruction of important data, such as accounts receivable by customer, in the event of accidental loss or destruction. Back-up records are particularly important in the case of computer files (where the chance of accidental loss of data may be greater) and are discussed in the next chapter.

7.7.4 Insurance

Fire, theft, liability and other insurance

In most businesses it makes good sense to carry insurance against the major insurable risks (fire, theft, liability, loss of records, business interruption, life insurance on key executives, etc.) to which the organization is exposed. In some instances, where the risks are spread over a large number of segregated assets, self-insuring may be a reasonable business decision. Decisions as to insurance to be carried and levels of coverage should be reviewed on a regular basis by senior management to ensure that coverage is kept up to date with the changing level and nature of business operations.

Fidelity insurance

Fidelity insurance provides some degree of protection against employee fraud. This protection is important because no practical system of internal control is likely to be foolproof. Frauds are a definite possibility in any organization. Indeed, recent statistics indicate that white-collar fraud is on the rise. Moreover, as explained earlier, many control elements are detective rather than preventive. Although the system of internal control may detect a fraud after its occurrence, and at least prevent its continuation, it may be impossible to obtain restitution from the employee involved. Accordingly, it is important for any organization to maintain fidelity insurance in an adequate amount covering all employees having direct or indirect access to the organization's assets.

A further benefit of fidelity insurance is the investigation the insurance company usually performs of any prospective employee to be bonded. Such investigation may reveal past indications of dishonesty or facts concerning the prospective employee's working or credit record which could have a bearing on the hiring decision.

But having the protection of fidelity insurance does not mean that other controls can be abandoned.

First of all, adequate controls are necessary to provide reasonable assurance of detecting any fraud sooner or later. Insurance is of no help for fraudulent losses that are never discovered. Secondly, controls are necessary over accidental errors, against which fidelity insurance provides no protection. In summary, an organization needs a good system of internal control including, but certainly not restricted to, adequate fidelity insurance.

7.8 Management supervisory controls

An important element in any system of internal control is careful supervision by management.

Management supervision

In small organizations (or in small departments of large organizations) a manager can have direct personal knowledge of almost every facet of the business and so maintain close *personal supervision* over all employees. The effectiveness of this supervision will depend on the competence of the manager, his familiarity with the business, and the continuity of his presence.

In larger organizations no one manager can have direct personal knowledge of every facet of the business. Supervisory responsibilities must be delegated throughout the organization. It is important, however, to retain the *involvement* of *senior officials* at key spots within the control system to provide an opportunity to detect important breakdowns in control. For example, the signing officers should be senior company officials. As well as exercising authorization control over cheque disbursements, such signing officers may for instance be in a position to assess in broad terms the overall performance of the purchases/payables/payments system.

In addition, management should exercise *overall supervision* of the business by reviewing financial reports, budget variance analyses, exception listings etc. Budgetary and reporting controls are ineffective without the active participation of senior management in the review process. Variances may require better explanation. Exceptions may call for immediate decisions as to corrective action.

From time to time management may call for special reviews of particular items such as purchasing procedures, inventory handling, payroll operations. These serve as a further instrument of control.

Monitoring of controls and detected errors

An important aspect of management supervision is the monitoring of the continuing effectiveness of all other controls. One specific method of monitoring is through analysis of all errors detected routinely by the controls within the system or by complaints from customers or suppliers. For example, the credit manager would customarily review errors found within the sales/receivables system. The nature or frequency of errors caught by detective controls may indicate that certain preventive controls are not functioning satisfactorily. Analysis and control of detected errors is particularly important in computerized systems (see Chapter 8).

Internal audit

In larger organizations the responsibility for specific monitoring of the system is usually delegated by management to an internal audit department. This department is commonly charged with the responsibility of reviewing and testing systems and controls throughout the organization and reporting their findings to both operating and senior management together with recommendations as to how control and/or efficiency could be improved. The terms of reference of internal audit departments, however, vary widely. Some are responsible for merely monitoring adherence to prescribed procedures; others for considering the effectiveness of those procedures as well. Some are responsible for considering efficiency and evaluating employee competence and performance; others for considering only control procedures. Some are responsible for covering just the financial accounting area; others for conducting *operational audits* throughout all operating departments. Some cover all areas of the organization; others just branches away from the head office location.

Whatever the terms of reference of the internal audit department, its effectiveness is improved if it reports to a very senior level within the organization, possibly the president himself. The internal audit function should ideally be segregated from the accounting sector since it will to a large extent be monitoring the activities of that sector. Where an audit committee of the board of directors exists, they may request that important findings of the internal audit department be reported directly to them.

It is important that the internal audit department hire staff with adequate training and competence for the audit work to be performed. For example, in a computerized system internal audit staff will require adequate training in computer auditing techniques.

The internal audit department should establish an organized audit program for the year. Some internal audit departments cover each area of the company each year. Many, however, cover different departments in depth on a cyclical basis over a number of years.

External audit

It was pointed out at the beginning of this chapter that in the normal statutory audit the external auditor does not have a responsibility to review internal control for its own sake but rather only to the extent that it is a means of arriving at evidence to support his expression of opinion on the financial statements. In the course of an external audit, opportunities for improvements in internal control may indeed come to light and be reported by the external auditor to his client. As a result, the management of many organizations may look on the external audit as a monitoring mechanism that assures them that internal control is satisfactory. While it is true that there is a control-monitoring element present in most external audit programs, it must be emphasized that its scope is restricted. There may be many elements of control that are not reviewed by the external auditor because they are not of attest significance. There may be others that are not reviewed because they could not be material relative to the financial statements. Nonetheless, the unreviewed controls could be important to management and it would be wrong for them to expect that they will be automatically covered by the external audit (unless the external auditor is specifically requested to take on that additional engagement).

Usually, therefore, the monitoring provided by an effective internal audit program is important for management to retain. Of course, internal and external audit programs can and should be coordinated for maximum efficiency. Use of the internal auditors' work by external auditors is discussed in later chapters.

7.9 Documentation controls

Documentation of policies and procedures is an important control for three reasons.

1. It helps to ensure that all other desirable controls are in fact established.

   For example, management may believe that clear responsibilities for authorization and approval controls exist throughout the organization. But if those responsibilities have not been documented it is more than likely that a number of important types of transactions have been left uncovered. Documentation will lead to the discovery and correction of those holes in the approval system.

2. It helps to ensure that all employees have a clear understanding of their responsibilities and of the detailed procedures they are to perform.

   Procedure manuals coupled with adequate staff training help to avoid errors through misunderstanding and therefore promote the proper functioning of all systems.

3. It safeguards the investment in systems design.

   If present employees leave or retire their procedures must be learned by new employees. Leaving all procedures unwritten with the hope that they will be passed on accurately by word of mouth is, in all but the smallest organizations, precarious. In large organizations the investment in systems design may be substantial and this investment should be protected by adequate documentation. Systems and program documentation is particularly important in the case of computerized systems and is discussed in the next chapter.

Manuals of policies and procedures

With respect to accounting systems and related procedures for authorizing, initiating, validating, approving, recording, summarizing, and reporting transactions it is useful in both large and small organizations to maintain a manual of policies and procedures. In large organizations there will likely be a series of manuals, each defining procedures for one major accounting system or class of transactions. Commonly such manuals are in loose-leaf form to facilitate up-dating. Specific employees should be assigned the responsibility of keeping procedure manuals up to date.

Larger organizations often find it desirable as well to write *job descriptions* for each position in the organization. Job descriptions clarify the overall duties and areas of responsibility of each employee. In addition, they are useful to the personnel department in searching for candidates to fill vacancies and in recommending appropriate salary ranges for each position.

7.10 Internal control in the small business

In very small businesses all the accounting routines may be performed by one, two or three persons. Frequently these persons will also have, for the sake of efficiency, both operating and custodial responsibilities. As a consequence, in most small businesses one of the most important control features, segregation of functions, is missing or severely limited. This does not mean, however, that good internal control in small business is impossible. On the contrary, in small businesses management supervisory controls can be far stronger than in large organizations because the manager can have direct personal knowledge of every aspect of the business. Usually, the controls exercised by the manager can more than offset the limitations in segregation of duties.

> ... The fact that the principal check on the work of employees lies with the manager rather than with other employees in the system should not by itself render the internal control system unreliable – in fact, direct supervision by the manager can often produce better control.[13]

Moreover, some degree of segregation of functions, though limited, can usually still be retained.

Segregation of functions

If a small business has more than four or five employees a considerable degree of segregation of duties can usually still be achieved with careful planning. For example, if two of these employees are performing accounting functions their duties should first be allocated to segregate custody of cash and recording procedures as far as possible. Then the use of non-accounting personnel should be considered in order to remove the more important incompatible functions remaining. This may involve, for example, having the receptionist open the mail and prepare the daily deposit, having the manager's secretary prepare the cheques and mail them to suppliers, etc.

Nonetheless the limitations on division of duties should be recognized. Even when there is an appearance of adequate division, the informal nature of small business operations often results in exchanges of duties at lunch times, during the busy season, or during any other emergency. In consequence, the division of duties may sometimes be more illusory than real. The key to good internal control usually remains with the manager and his exercise of supervisory control.

Use of outside services

Sometimes small businesses can significantly improve internal control by using one or more of the business services offered by outside agencies. Cash payrolls can be replaced by automatic bank transfers thereby reducing the possibility of payroll error or fraud. Invoices, the accounts receivable sub-ledger, sales analyses, and the general ledger, may be prepared by outside computer data centres thereby enhancing their reliability as well as the speed of document and report preparation.

Participation of the manager in accounting routines

An important element of control is provided by the manager's direct involvement in key points in the accounting routines. Key points include:
a) taking direct charge of the entire personnel function,
b) scrutinizing the payroll journal in detail, adding of the net-pay column, and signing of all payroll cheques,
c) being the signing officer,
d) picking up cancelled cheques from the bank and scrutinizing the returned items on the bank statement before handing them over to the bookkeeper for reconciliation (occasionally the manager might perform the bank reconciliation himself).

Further details of manager involvement in accounting routines are discussed in Chapter 29.

Budgets and operating reports

The preparation of budgets and of timely informative reports and their prompt review by the manager is a key control element. Again, the manager's close personal knowledge of the business enhances the effectiveness of this control. Periodic reports reviewed by the manager may include:
• cash and operating statements,
• sales and production summaries,
• a trial balance of accounts receivable,
• accounts payable trial balances,
• inventory summaries.

Role of the external auditor

From time to time the manager of a small business may wish to ask the external auditor to extend his work beyond the pure attest function in order to compensate for certain control deficiencies that cannot practically be cured. In these circumstances it is important for the auditor and his client to have a clear understanding of extent of the external auditor's additional contractual responsibilities. The importance of documenting such an understanding in an engagement letter was emphasized in Chapter 4.

7.11 Limitations in internal control

At the beginning of this chapter it was pointed out that absolute assurance of preventing or detecting errors or irregularities was not possible and the level of assurance to be sought from a system of internal control will necessarily depend upon its cost. Despite the importance of maintaining a good system of internal control it is worth remembering the inherent limitations in any such system. Constraints which preclude internal control from providing absolute assurance include:

1. the requirement that the cost of a control procedure not be out of proportion to the reduction in risk of error thereby achieved,
2. the fact that control systems tend to be designed to cover recurring types of transactions and may occasionally be by-passed by unusual or unanticipated types of transactions,
3. the possibility of collusion, which can circumvent controls based on the segregation of incompatible functions,
4. careless or fraudulent failure to perform certain prescribed control procedures,
5. the possibility of an employee to whom authority has been delegated (or a member of management) abusing that authority,
6. the possibility of management by-passing, or instructing subordinates to by-pass, certain prescribed controls (either fraudulently or under the pressure of time or cost constraints).

7.12 Reference material

CICA Exposure Draft of Proposed Auditing Recommendations, *Internal Control* (1976). The reader should refer to subsequent pronouncements.
CICA Audit Technique Studies, *Internal Control in the Small Business* (1976), and *Internal Control and Procedural Audit Tests* (1968).

AICPA Statement on Auditing Standards No. 1, Section 320, (The Auditor's Study and Evaluation of Internal Control).
AICPA, *Internal Control, Elements of a Coordinated System and its Importance to Management and the Independent Public Accountant* (1949).

7.13 Questions and problems

Review and discussion

1. Define internal control. Who is responsible for internal control?
2. Why must an auditor review a client's internal control system?
3. What are the objectives of an internal control system?
4. List and briefly discuss the basic elements of an internal control system.
5. Is the adequacy of the internal control system likely to vary with respect to size of the company involved?
6. Is the strength of the internal control system of the same significance in both large and small companies? Explain.
7. Discuss the difference between internal and external auditing. How can they be complementary?
8. It is common for auditors to make use of and rely heavily on standardized internal control questionnaires. What possible dangers must be guarded against in using these questionnaires as a basis for the evaluation of a system of internal control?
9. B. Grant, senior on the Friendly Finance Company Ltd. audit, has commenced his review of the internal control system. Suggest a number of sources where B. Grant might obtain the information required to complete an internal control questionnaire.
10. Individual internal controls may be weak or non-existent in specific areas of the accounting system, but compensating controls may exist. Give four examples of a weakness and a related compensating control.
11. Explain how the organization structure of a firm affects internal control. Give three specific examples of poor organization design (different from the examples in this chapter), the resulting control weaknesses, and possible solutions to strengthen control.
12. Why should the custody of cash and marketable securities be segregated from the related recording and reporting functions?

13. Discuss the purpose and the components of operating, capital and financial budgets. How do each of these contribute to good internal control?
14. How may document design contribute to internal control?
15. Explain how the documentation of policies and procedures aids effective internal control.
16. T. Nixon, manager of DHG Ltd., a small business, recently asked his auditor, George Williams, CA, "What functions should I perform to provide adequate internal controls?" Discuss some of the recommendations that George should make.
17. Absolute assurance of preventing or detecting errors or irregularities is not posssible. List six constraints which preclude internal controls from providing absolute assurance.

Problems

1. Boulton, Robertson & Co., Chartered Accountants, were the auditors for T Ltd. During his review of the system of internal control Jack Boulton encountered several major weaknesses. At the end of his review he concluded that T's system of internal control was utterly ineffective.
   a) What are Jack Boulton's responsibilities to his client in this situation?
   b) As the auditor of T what alternatives does Jack have?
   c) Is it possible to give an opinion on the financial statements where there are a number of major system weaknesses? Discuss in detail.
   d) How could an audit committee help in this situation?
2. (AICPA adapted) The president of Universal Builders Ltd. has requested that your firm (local chartered accountants) assist them with an internal control problem. His Company is establishing a branch in Freeze-Point, N.W.T. which, due to the geographical location, is to operate independently of the other branches. The branch is to have three clerical employees to perform the following functions:
   a) Maintain the general ledger
   b) Maintain the accounts payable ledger
   c) Maintain the accounts receivable ledger
   d) Prepare cheques for signature
   e) Maintain the disbursements journal
   f) Issue credits on returns and allowances
   g) Reconcile bank accounts
   h) Handle and deposit cash receipts
   There is no doubt as to the ability of any of the employees. The president requests that you assign the above functions to the three employees in such a manner as to achieve the highest degree of internal control. (It may be assumed that these employees will perform no other accounting functions than the ones listed and that any accounting functions not listed will be performed by persons other than these three employees.)

   State how you would distribute the above functions among the three employees and discuss the reasons for your choice. Assume that, with the exception of the nominal jobs of the bank reconciliation and the issuances of credits on returns and allowances, all functions require an equal amount of time.
3. (AICPA adapted) The second "field work standard" in the CICA's "Generally accepted auditing standards" states that there should be an organized study of internal controls. The most common approaches to reviewing the system of internal control include the use of questionnaires, narrative descriptions, flowcharts and combinations of these methods.
   a) What is the CA's objective in reviewing a client's system of internal control?
   b) What are the advantages and disadvantages of each of the approaches mentioned above?
4. Average Warehouse Ltd. was a medium sized distributing company which was owned 100% by Fred Allan. His right-hand man and good friend, Bill Hull, headed up the operations of the Company and also supervised all the accounting. Fred did not enjoy Canadian winters, so for six months of each year he lived in Mexico, keeping warm and making the odd business deal. As Fred was not actively involved in the operations of the company he told Bill that, in addition to his $25 000 annual salary, he would also give him 15% of the company's net profit. Fred felt confident that his company was in good hands.
   a) What basic problems of internal control exist in this situation?
   b) As the company's auditor, what procedures could you follow in this situation?
   c) Assuming that you (as the company's auditor) were going to issue an internal control letter, to whom should it be addressed?
5. B is preparing to operate a small wholesale business in which he will employ two office workers and three warehouse attendants. Although he realizes that an extensive system of internal control is impossible because of the size of his staff, he is anxious that the system adopted provide as many control measures as possible. He is aware that mechanical control devices, such as cash registers, for safeguarding the assets will assist in achieving his purpose.

   List eight other points, not having to do with

division of duties, which should be introduced into the accounting and operating procedures in order to provide some degree of internal control.

6. Almost Anything Ltd. has a chain of department stores across Canada and its annual audit is approaching. The Company has developed a reasonably competent internal audit department. The audit partner of the job has instructed you (as the audit senior) to visit the head office of Almost Anything and to assess the effectiveness of the internal audit department.

    a) What are the main differences between the work of internal auditors and external auditors in terms of objectives?

    b) What is the purpose or objective of the external auditor "assessing the effectiveness" of the internal audit department?

    c) Outline the approach you would take in reviewing the work of the internal audit department, keeping in mind your purpose or objective as stated in part (b).

7. (CICA adapted) Saturn is the owner and president of a small company, Saturn Ltd., which retails marine engines and parts for the engines. The company also provides servicing for engines sold. Saturn actively manages the business and his employees include a small office staff, a stockkeeper, and several mechanics.

    Saturn is anxious to install a system of internal control which would ensure accuracy and reliability of accounting data, provide automatic checks of accounting data, and provide statistical and physical controls to safeguard company assets against defalcations or other irregularities. However, he doubts that such a system of internal control is feasible for his small company and limited staff. The company does not have an independent auditor.

    Saturn has requested a chartered accountant to outline the features of a system of internal control over inventory and sales of engines, parts and service which could be used by a small company like Saturn Ltd. He also wants the chartered accountant to indicate in general terms what control each feature would provide, without designing an actual system of internal control.

    Prepare a letter (in good form) to Saturn which provides the information requested.

8. (CICA adapted) CA is employed by M & Co., Chartered Accountants. He is senior in charge on the audit of a new client, Colour Clothing Store Ltd.

    Colour Clothing Store Ltd. is owned by three men, Messrs. Green, Brown, and Lemon. Only one of the owners, Mr. Green, is active in the business — the other two live and work in another city. Mr. Green operated the business as a proprietorship until a few years ago, when he incorporated it and obtained additional capital for store improvements by issuing shares (20% each) to Brown and Lemon. In addition to Mr. Green, the store employs three sales clerks and Miss Blue, the cashier-bookkeeper. Miss Blue has worked for Mr. Green for many years.

    CA and the partner responsible for The Colour Clothing Store Ltd. examination have agreed that one of the first things CA should do when he starts work on the examination is to evaluate internal control.

    a) Why would the CA bother to evaluate the internal control of this small company?

    b) What particular features of internal control would the CA enquire into in the circumstances described above? Do not give detailed procedures.

9. Jerry Chrysler, CA, is the recently appointed comptroller of Nic-Pic Ltd., a medium-sized company. His initial job is to evaluate and improve upon the internal control system of Nic-Pic. The first area of review is the organizational structure, internal control procedures and personnel in relation to the accounting records and reports.

    Describe the steps, in chronological order, that Chrysler should take in his review. Do not go into details of accounting procedures.

Internal Control — Computer Systems

The last two decades have seen a phenomenal growth in the use of computers by business and government in a wide variety of data processing applications. On the one hand, the size and complexity of the most advanced installations has increased. On the other, technological improvements have brought economical systems within the reach of growing numbers of smaller businesses. A company can now lease a small business computer for less than $1 000 per month.

Computer systems, both large and small, require adequate systems of internal control if management's objectives are to be achieved. The basic objectives of internal control are, of course, unchanged by the method of processing. Therefore, the elements of internal control described in Chapter 7 continue to be applicable when a computer is introduced. But computerization brings the need for certain additional controls or sometimes new methods of achieving the previous controls. The purpose of this chapter is to describe these additional controls.

8.1 Introduction to computer controls

An understanding of computer controls requires first some understanding of computer concepts. For chartered accountants involved with computer systems as part of management, as EDP consultants, or as internal or external auditors, guidance as to the level of knowledge they may require can be found in the CICA special report, *Competence and Professional Development in EDP for the CA (1973)*.[1] An explanation of computer concepts is beyond the scope of an auditing textbook.[2] Certain characteristics of electronic data processing (EDP) can be identified, however, which have a particular bearing on control.

8.1.1 Characteristics of computer-based systems

Areas affected by the computer involve not only the physical operation of the computer hardware itself but also many interacting manual procedures – the preparation of input, the writing of computer programs, the distribution of output, etc. The term "computer-based system" is often used to convey the sense of this interaction.

A computer-based accounting system may be defined as any accounting system which uses a general-purpose digital computer to perform some of the basic accounting processes. The basic processes computerized might, for example, include the pricing or preparation of sales invoices, the preparation of cheques, the posting and trial balancing of general or subsidiary ledgers, or the processing of payrolls. To these basic processes may be added the preparation of any number of related management reports, sales and cost analyses, budget analyses, monthly financial statements, etc. The *degree* of computerization may vary from very simple systems where most of the procedures are still performed manually to very complex ones where most of the procedures are performed by the computer. Each computer application may be performed separately or applications may be *integrated* in order to share common data files. The mode of processing may be "batch-oriented", where like transactions are processed together through the system in discrete "batches", or "transaction-oriented", where transactions are processed individually through the use of on-line terminals connected to the computer. The computer facilities themselves may be in the form of mini-computers, in-house conventional computers, "over the counter" outside data centres, or large computer utilities with remote job entry.

The characteristics of computer-based systems which most directly influence internal control are:

1. internally stored programs,
2. machine operation,
3. high speed,
4. rigidity,
5. reliability,
6. invisible recording,
7. high cost.

1. *Internally stored programs.*
   Computerized processing is guided by internally stored programs which of necessity are highly detailed. The very detail creates a risk of error. Special controls over the development and implementation of programs are required to ensure that all reasonable situations have been anticipated. Errors occurring as a result of incorrect programming will tend to be patterned or systematic rather than random as in manual operations.
2. *Machine operation.*
   Although the computer is largely run by its internally stored program, certain manual operations are required as well to start the machine, load the program, mount tape files, etc. There is always the danger of inadvertent operator error or improper operator intervention.
3. *High speed.*
   Electronic speed permits computer systems to process massive volumes of data rapidly. By the

same token, of course, with inadequate controls the potential for rapid proliferation of errors is aggravated by the presence of a computer.

4. *Rigidity.*

The computer cannot handle situations which have not previously been anticipated (i.e. for which it has no programmed instructions). This rigidity requires a greater discipline on the part of users. For example, detailed instructions are required as to exactly how input forms are to be prepared, how errors are to be corrected, etc.

5. *Reliability.*

A properly controlled computer system offers a higher level of system reliability than a well controlled manual system. Electronic hardware is not prone to fatigue, carelessness, boredom, or dishonesty. However, electronic reliability must not be mistaken for system infallibility since human error can creep in during input preparation, output interpretation, programming and operating.

6. *Invisible recording.*

The information recorded in magnetic data files (tape, disk or drum) is invisible to the human eye. This factor reduces the opportunity for visual editing and, in some cases, increases the opportunity for undetected defalcation.

7. *High cost.*

Computerized processing is generally more expensive than analogous manual methods. Control over the deployment of costly EDP resources is therefore important.

8.1.2 Impact of the computer on the elements of internal control

In Chapter 7, seven elements of internal control were identified. The computer characteristics just discussed influence the method of achieving each of these seven elements. A brief review of these seven elements suggests, in turn, a few different categories for the classification of computer controls.

1. *Organizational controls.*

The normal requirement for employee competence is especially important, and sometimes difficult to achieve, because of the technical nature of EDP and the high cost of EDP resources. The impact is not limited to the EDP department but extends as well to user departments, internal auditors, and management.

The normal importance of segregation of functions is increased because of the centralization of many operations within the EDP department. This centralization must be compensated for by segregating the EDP department from other functional areas and by segregating functions

within the EDP department itself. The new aspects of *organizational controls* are described in 8.3.

2. *Systems development controls.*

The normal importance for controls over the development and modification of systems is increased by the complexity and detail in computer systems. The introduction of new EDP applications must be carefully controlled as well as the design of systems and the writing of computer programs for each such application. The new aspects of *development controls* are described in 8.4. A logical extension is the need for controls over the acquisition or modification of the computer facilities themselves. Because of their importance, they are classified separately as *pre-installation controls* and are described in 8.2.

3. *Authorization and reporting controls.*

Authorization controls may be exercised by the computer in applications where it initiates transactions (e.g., initiation of purchase orders based on pre-defined minimum re-order levels). Validation or approval controls may likewise be exercised by the computer (e.g., credit approval based on pre-defined credit limits). Because these controls thus form an integral part of the processing cycle in a computer-based system, they are more convenient to evaluate as one of the aspects of *processing controls* (see 8.6).

4. *Accounting systems controls.*

Ensuring the accuracy and completeness of data must likewise be an integral part of the processing cycle and thus represents another aspect of *processing controls* (see 8.6). Control over completeness may be based on programmed controls (built into the program logic) or based on the recording and reconciliation of control totals. Document design is also important.

5. *Additional safeguarding controls.*

The normal requirement for restricting access to certain assets can be extended to the computer room itself, for access to the computer may provide indirect access to other assets through the ability to initiate cheques (cash) or shipping orders (inventory). The normal importance of protecting records is increased in computer systems because of the centralization of data and requires proper storage and "back-up" protection. Because the controls involve the physical operation and protection of the computer itself, they are more convenient to evaluate as aspects of *operations controls* (see 8.5).

6. *Management supervisory controls.*

The normal requirement of monitoring controls in force extends to computer systems and indicates the desirability of a thorough management audit of the EDP function on a periodic basis.

Management monitoring controls are discussed in 8.7.

7. *Documentation controls.*

The normal importance of documentation controls is increased in computer systems because of the magnitude of the investment in systems design and program logic. The new aspects of *documentation controls* are discussed in 8.8.

8.1.3 Classification of computer controls

The classification of computer controls, as just discussed, in comparison with the control elements covered in Chapter 7, is summarized in Figure 8.a. *Processing controls* tend to be different for each application. For example, programmed limit checks essential in a payroll application may not be required in a sales analysis application. All other controls, which together may be termed *computer environment controls*, tend to be constant for most applications within the same installation. They provide an underlying reliability to the organizing, programming, operating and documenting functions based on which the specific processing controls required in each individual application can be planned.

The classification of computer controls used in this chapter corresponds closely to that in the CICA Study, *Computer Control Guidelines* (1970).[3] The CICA Study divided each type of control into a number of different *control objectives*. For example, organizational controls (II) were divided into objectives relating to *segregation of functions* (II-D) and *deployment of resources* (II-E). Under each objective were described a number of individual *control techniques*[4], some or all of which, depending on the circumstances, might be required to meet that objective. A similar arrangement is adopted in this chapter with three minor exceptions. One is that various types of controls applicable to outside data centres have been grouped for convenience with analogous controls for in-house computers. The second is the arrangement of some of the details of processing controls. The third is that management monitoring controls have been included as a control element; though not covered in *Computer Control Guidelines* they were recommended, in effect, in the subsequent CICA Study, *Computer Audit Guidelines* (1975). The reader will find *Computer Control Guidelines* a useful additional reference when analyzing computer controls. While all the control elements are covered in the present chapter, the CICA Study provides a more detailed discussion — particularly with respect to those elements, such as pre-installation controls, which are not of direct attest significance. A table of concordance of the classification used in this chapter with the CICA Study is shown in Figure 8.b.

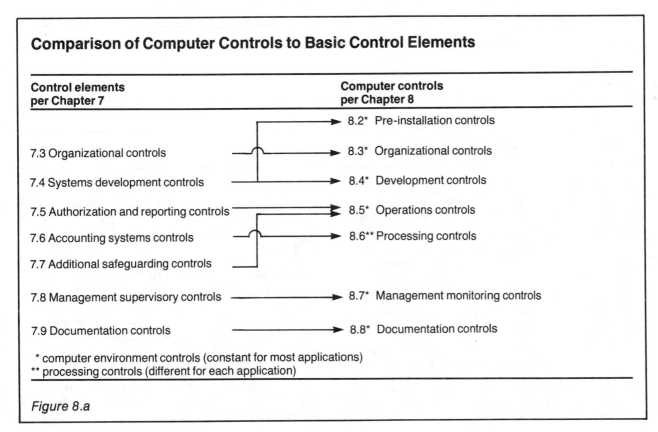

Comparison of Computer Controls to Basic Control Elements

Control elements per Chapter 7	Computer controls per Chapter 8
	8.2* Pre-installation controls
7.3 Organizational controls	8.3* Organizational controls
7.4 Systems development controls	8.4* Development controls
7.5 Authorization and reporting controls	8.5* Operations controls
7.6 Accounting systems controls	8.6** Processing controls
7.7 Additional safeguarding controls	
7.8 Management supervisory controls	8.7* Management monitoring controls
7.9 Documentation controls	8.8* Documentation controls

  * computer environment controls (constant for most applications)
 ** processing controls (different for each application)

Figure 8.a

8.2 Pre-installation controls

Although computational power per dollar has been steadily improving with each new generation of equipment, most computer facilities remain expensive. Not only are the acquisition or rental costs of the hardware itself substantial but, in addition, a major investment is required in systems design, programming, and staff training. Mistakes in acquiring EDP equipment or lack of preparedness for its arrival can be costly. The objectives of pre-installation controls therefore are:

- to ensure that a computer is ordered only if it is likely to produce greater benefits than other processing alternatives;
- to ensure selection of suitable facilities and services;
- to ensure that a pre-installation plan is prepared against which results and progress can be measured.[5]

Where, instead, the organization intends to use the services of an outside data centre, analogous controls are required to ensure that the services are really needed and to select the most suitable data centre facilities.

8.2.1 Steering committee and feasibility studies

A proposed acquisition of a computer, like any major capital investment, should be carefully studied in advance. Detailed studies, however, themselves involve a major investment of time and effort. To avoid the unnecessary completion of detailed analyses, the CICA Study suggested a two-stage approach. A *preliminary survey* would first be conducted under the direction of a senior *management committee*. The preliminary survey would identify the major areas where computer processing could be applied and its likely costs, benefits and other impacts. If the preliminary study indicated that the use of a computer appeared warranted, a more detailed *feasibility study* would be carried out. The feasibility study would be conducted under the direction of a *computer steering committee* containing more technical specialists than required for the previous management committee but, because of its importance, containing senior management representation as well. The report at the conclusion of the feasibility study should cover the detailed computer applications proposed, systems and organizational changes required, estimated computer usage, comparisons of in-house facilities versus outside data centres, recommendations, and, if a computer is recommended, the general equipment characteristics and estimated costs, benefits, and other impacts. It is desirable that the feasibility study not include an analysis of specific manufacturers or models at this stage since the identification of the general equipment characteristics is likely to be more objective in its absence.

8.2.2 Selection of facilities

Where a decision has been made to acquire a computer and the feasibility study has identified the equipment characteristics required, a list of appropriate *selection criteria* (equipment type, cost, staff requirement, delivery date, software support, languages available, etc.) should be prepared and given to each potential supplier. The *suppliers' proposals* can then be evaluated in a systematic manner using these criteria. Simulated applications (*bench mark problems*) may sometimes be submitted to each supplier and their suggested programs tested thereon to help compare the efficiency of the different computers. Before final selection, the prospective contractual arrangements with the supplier should be carefully reviewed. Technical assistance, equipment maintenance, and software support should be clearly defined.

8.2.3 Pre-installation plan

To ensure that all preparations have been completed by the time the computer arrives, a detailed list of pre-installation tasks should be made. Such tasks include the recruitment and training of staff and the design and preparation of the computer site. The use of network diagramming techniques (such as PERT) can facilitate planning and subsequent monitoring of the many inter-dependent steps.

8.2.4 Outside data centres

When the feasibility study indicates, instead, the desirability of employing an outside data centre, selection criteria should be prepared for evaluating prospective data centres. It is important to investigate the financial stability and reputation of the data centre as well as its hardware configuration. It is also important to establish whether the data centre or the user will have title to the programs and computer files – particularly if there is a possibility of conversion to in-house facilities in the future. Contractual arrangements with the prospective data centre should therefore be carefully reviewed before the final selection is made. Companies considering the use of outside data centres often do not have employees with the required technical skills to complete the feasibility study or to evaluate the prospective data centres. In such cases it may be desirable to retain an independent EDP consultant.

8.3 Organizational controls

The effects of concentration of functions and high EDP cost have already been mentioned. The objectives of organizational controls therefore are:

- to provide effective control over the concentration of functions in the EDP department;
- to ensure that management exercises effective control over deployment of computer resources.

Where an outside data centre is used, additional procedures are necessary to ensure that both it and the user are appropriately organized to maintain proper security and control.

8.3.1 The EDP organization plan

The EDP organization plan should cover both the relationship of the EDP department to other departments and the separation of functions within the EDP department itself.

Independence of the EDP department
Generally, the EDP department should be separated from the functions of:
- initiation and authorization of transactions;
- the physical custody of assets.

To the extent that the computer serves an accounting purpose, it is a part of the comptrollership function. As discussed in 7.3.5, it is important in *any* accounting/finance organization plan to have the comptrollership functions segregated from the treasury and finance functions up to as senior a level as possible. This segregation is even more crucial when some or all of the comptrollership functions are computerized. Where the comptroller's department is in fact adequately segregated from treasury and finance, where the computer serves exclusively an accounting purpose, and where the comptroller is a senior executive position, it may be suitable for the EDP department to report to the comptroller. An example is provided by Company D in Figure 7.c.

Where the computer serves other purposes in addition to accounting ones or where the installation is large or complex, it may be desirable for the EDP department to report to a senior executive other than the comptroller. Examples are provided in Figure 7.c by Company E, where it reports to the vice president administrative services, and by Company F, where it reports to the vice president finance. In these cases the EDP department functions as a separate service department responsible for the processing and recording of data on behalf of other departments (including the comptroller's department), who in turn are responsible for the initiation and authorization of transactions and for the custody of assets.

In certain situations, it may not be practical to separate the EDP department completely from the incompatible functions of transaction initiation, transaction authorization, and custody of assets. The computer system itself may be used to check the authorization of transactions and/or to initiate transactions. For example, a computerized purchasing system may automatically initiate purchase orders based on predefined inventory re-order levels. A computerized accounts payable system may automatically check suppliers' invoices to a file of authorized purchase orders and to a file of receiving reports. A computerized disbursements system may prepare company cheques (possibly signed by the use of signature plates during the computer run, though preferably under the control of the signing officer). In these three examples the EDP department has some involvement in purchase initiation, purchase authorization, and, indirectly through access to cheques, custody of cash.

In such cases, the normal separation of the EDP department is to some extent weakened. This weakening should be compensated for by accounting systems controls operating outside the EDP department (for example, bank reconciliation procedures) and by appropriate division of duties *within* the EDP department itself.

Division of duties within the EDP department

Within the EDP department the following functions should be segregated:
- systems and programming (systems analysts and programmers),
- computer operations (machine operators),
- data control (control clerks).

The reason for segregating programming and operating is so that no one person will have the ability to both (a) write or revise a program and (b) run the program with live data. Thus, computer operations should be a separate unit within the EDP department, and computer operators (who have access to live data) should ordinarily not have access to detailed program documentation nor the ability to modify the programs they use. Systems analysts and programmers, on the other hand (who necessarily have access to computer programs), should not have access to, or the ability to make changes in, the live data being processed.

It is also desirable to establish a data control group within the EDP department but independent of the other EDP functions (see 8.5.1).

Control may be further improved by the use of a computer file library under the charge of a librarian independent of the operators. Thus, while operators would continue to have access to live data, the access would be restricted to scheduled runs at scheduled times, limiting the opportunity for improper changes to other files. Where library control of all issues and receipts of files is judged too cumbersome and costly in relation to the risks covered, it may still be desirable to implement library control with respect to sensitive files.

Figure 8.c shows a typical organizational structure for a medium size EDP installation having appropriate division of duties between systems and programming, computer operations and data control.

Of course, the particular structure adopted for the EDP department must fit the size and nature of the particular organization.[6] In smaller EDP installations, for example, it may be impractical to achieve a complete division of duties. Computer programmers may on occasion be required to perform operating functions, operators to perform data control functions, etc. In such situations, the lack of division of duties within the EDP department should normally be compensated for by increased management supervision of EDP activities and by an increased review, by the user departments, of all computer output reports.

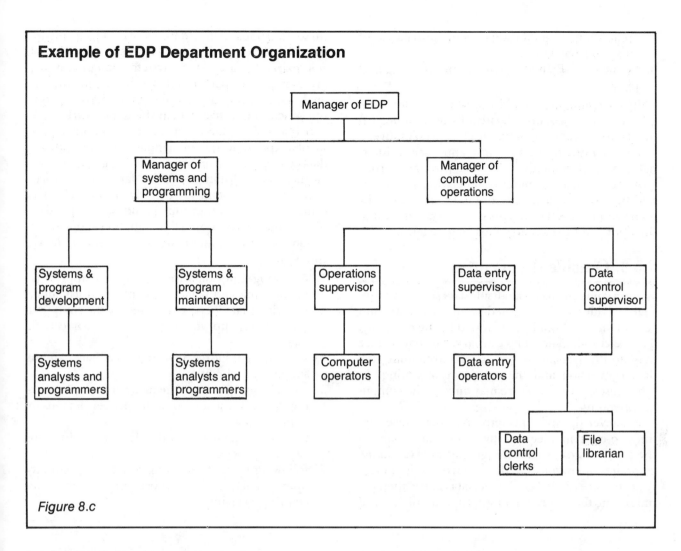

Example of EDP Department Organization

Manager of EDP

Manager of systems and programming

Manager of computer operations

Systems & program development

Systems & program maintenance

Operations supervisor

Data entry supervisor

Data control supervisor

Systems analysts and programmers

Systems analysts and programmers

Computer operators

Data entry operators

Data control clerks

File librarian

Figure 8.c

8.3.2 Deployment of EDP resources

In order for management to exercise effective control over the deployment of costly EDP resources, it is important that the EDP function report to a sufficiently senior level and that a vehicle exist for ongoing review of EDP activities.

Reporting level

The level of the executive to which the head of the EDP department reports will, of course, vary depending upon the size of the entity and on the degree of computerization. In each of the examples illustrated in Figure 7.c, the reporting level was one level below the president. Published studies have continually stressed that, where computer installations have been unsuccessful, a common reason has been a lack of executive concern and a view that EDP was too technical for management and best left to the specialists. An EDP department which grows to be the private empire of one user department is less likely to make objective decisions for the good of the company as a whole. This risk is another reason for

the desirability of the EDP department functioning as a separate service department to serve all other departments. In that case, the executive to which the EDP department reports should have a rank at least equal to that of the heads of the user departments.

EDP steering committee

The desirability of an EDP steering committee during the pre-installation stage was mentioned in 8.2.1. Management control of the EDP function is improved if such a steering committee is continued after installation to fulfill the following broad functions:

1. to establish long-term objectives and plans for the EDP activity;
2. to ensure that appropriate standards are established to guide the EDP department in the development, documentation, implementation and operation of EDP systems;
3. to establish priorities to govern the development of EDP applications;
4. to review and approve proposals for major new

applications, modifications and purchases of computer hardware;
5. to monitor EDP department progress against plans.

Such a committee should consist of a senior management representative, heads of the user departments affected, a senior financial representative, a senior data processing specialist, and a senior internal audit representative. Whether through participation on such a committee or otherwise, it is important that user departments and internal auditors be involved in the development of new systems and in the approval of revisions to existing systems.

8.3.3 Outside data centres

When a company uses an outside data centre, certain EDP activities will be assumed by the data centre and certain ones will still be performed by the company. The exact split of activities can vary. The data centre may do the systems design and programming, the data conversion and the computer operating. In other cases, the data centre may only do the computer operating.

Whatever the split, it is important that there continue to exist an adequate division of duties among the functions of systems design and programming, computer operations and data control. If all of these functions are carried out by the data centre, then it is important that there be an appropriate division of

these functions at the data centre. The company should make enquiries to determine that such a division exists. In cases where systems design and programming are performed by the company, its analysts and programmers should not have access to the processing of live data at the data centre.

It is also desirable to have one person or department responsible for all regular dealings with the data centre. Having one co-ordinating group helps to ensure that all dealings with the data centre are carried out in a consistent and orderly fashion. The data centre co-ordination group should be independent of the functions of transaction initiation and authorization and of the custody of assets. It should be responsible for:

1. reviewing input data for appropriate approvals,
2. maintaining and balancing control information,
3. ensuring that all errors rejected by the computer are followed up and any necessary corrections made,
4. ensuring that source departments adhere to input submission schedules,
5. receiving output from the data centre and ensuring that it is distributed to the proper persons or departments,
6. reviewing charges from the data centre for processing services,
7. following up and reporting to management any operational problems associated with the data centre processing.

8.4 Development controls

The investment in systems and programs frequently represents over one half of total EDP expenditures. In addition, where accounting procedures are computerized, development and maintenance of effective systems and programs will be critical to the accuracy and reliability of the accounting records.

The objectives of development controls, therefore, are:

- to ensure that an application is converted to the computer only if it will produce greater benefits than any other alternatives,
- to ensure the development of effective systems and programs,
- to ensure that systems and programs are effectively maintained.

Development controls are equally necessary whether processing is done on an in-house computer or at an outside data centre.

8.4.1 Feasibility studies and long-term plans

As a first step in ensuring the cost-effectiveness of computer applications, management should establish long range plans governing the overall use to be made of EDP within the organization. Such plans would necessarily be broad in scope and would outline the long-term management information requirements which are of most importance to the overall organization and those requirements which would be most likely to benefit from the use of EDP. The long-term EDP plans would then provide a framework within which individual proposals for new computer applications could be evaluated.

Feasibility studies are desirable not only when a decision is being made whether or not to acquire a computer (pre-installation controls) but also whenever a decision is being made whether or not to add a proposed application to an existing computer system (development controls). A senior steering committee, previously described, should be responsible for setting up the study team, establishing appropriate terms of reference and reviewing and approving the study results.

The group performing the feasibility study itself should include senior systems personnel together with representatives from all user departments which would be affected by the proposed application. In cases where employees with the required technical skills do not have the time available or where the conflicting interests of different departments make an objective study particularly important, it may be desirable to retain an outside EDP consultant.

The contents of the feasibility study[7] depend on the terms of reference established by senior management but may include:

1. Application objectives – These would include the functions to be performed by the proposed application. Problems associated with the current procedures may also be included.
2. Alternatives considered – The various processing alternatives to accomplish the application objectives should be analyzed in detail. Each alternative should be discussed in terms of the degree to which it meets the objectives, its estimated costs and its potential cost savings or other benefits.
3. Study conclusion – The study team should present its recommendation as to the most "cost-effective" alternative together with the reasons.
4. Preliminary development plan – It is desirable to include also a preliminary development budget and schedule for consideration and approval by the EDP steering committee or senior management.

In reviewing each feasibility study report, the steering committee (or senior management) should consider the proposed application in the light of long-term EDP plans and other priorities. Often there are competing needs of different functional areas for the same EDP resources. It is the responsibility of management to select from among these competing priorities, those applications which exhibit the greatest cost/benefit advantages.

It follows that the development and maintenance of long-term EDP plans is itself an important control procedure. Equipment and systems changes must often be scheduled to occur gradually over a period of years. Long-term plans are necessarily broad in scope and should outline the long-term requirements for management information. Such requirements should be ranked according to their importance to the company as a whole and to the likelihood of benefits from computerization.

8.4.2 Development of effective systems and programs

The development of reliable systems and programs requires, as a starting point, the segregation of incompatible functions already discussed under organizational controls. If programming and operating functions or if EDP and custodial functions overlap, the risk of improper or fraudulent systems and programs being developed is increased. In addition, the development of effective systems and programs requires proper standards, user participation, appropriate approvals, adequate testing, and control over conversion and implementation.

Systems and programming standards

Because of the complexity of systems development and the number of individuals likely to be involved in it, proper systems and programming standards should be established defining each individual's responsibilities and a standardized and consistent manner for their fulfilment.

Such standards should include, for example:

1. the necessary stages of systems development and the approvals required at each stage,
2. the requirements for project management – e.g., budgets and schedules, manpower plans,
3. the conventions to be used in system design and programming – e.g., required content and format of system design specifications, standard naming conventions for programs and files, programming languages to be used, program design conventions,
4. the requirements for system and program testing and implementation,
5. the requirements for system and program documentation.

Systems and programming standards should be adequately documented and should be approved by senior management. Systems and programming activities should be closely supervised by the management of the EDP department to ensure adherence to the standards.

User participation

The prospective user of a new system is usually the person most familiar with the requirements to be met. It is therefore important that users be actively involved in the systems development process.

1. User participation should commence at the stage of general system design. The user should define the detailed requirements of the system (input transactions, format and frequency of output reports, control procedures, etc.).

2. At the conclusion of the system design, the user should review the system specifications to ensure that his requirements have been properly interpreted by the systems analyst.
3. The user should generally be involved in systems tests (sometimes called "user acceptance tests") to ensure that the system, as programmed, accurately reflects the original system specifications.
4. The user should also be involved in the actual conversion and implementation of the new system to ensure that any new master files have been accurately prepared, that the cut-off in processing between the old and new system is proper, and that user personnel have been adequately trained.
5. The user may also be requested by management to participate in a post-implementation review to ensure that the new system is operating without problems.

It is desirable to include a representative of the internal audit department on the development team. He should review the specifications to ensure the adequacy of proposed controls. Consultation with the external auditor is also desirable.

When the new system is one with financial or accounting significance, it is also desirable to have a representative of the accounting department on the development team. He should review the specifications to ensure the appropriateness of the accounting principles incorporated.

Approval at each stage

The development of new computer systems normally involves a number of discrete stages such as: the definition of user requirements, detailed systems design, programming, testing, training, implementation, and a post-implementation review. It is normally desirable for management and user approval to be obtained after each stage. This procedure facilitates the early detection of problems before they are too widespread to be corrected easily.
- Management should review and approve each proposed system at the feasibility stage prior to systems design.
- Management should monitor the development process by comparing actual results to budgets and schedules at the conclusion of each major stage.
- Users and internal auditors should review and approve the detailed systems specifications prior to program coding.
- User management should review and approve system test results, training programs and conversion plans prior to final implementation.

System and program testing

Comprehensive testing procedures are usually essential to ensure that the systems and programs developed are effective and accurately reflect the original specifications.

Systems and programs should generally be tested in the following stages:
1. Program testing – involves the testing of each individual program module, usually by the programmer, to ensure that the logic operates properly.
2. System testing – usually performed by the systems analyst, involves the testing of the various computer programs in the required sequence, to ensure that related programs operate properly together.
3. User acceptance testing – performed by or in conjunction with the user, involves a comprehensive testing of all system functions to ensure that the developed system meets all of the user's specifications. The acceptance tests should include all phases of the system (both manual and computer) and should include test transactions specifically designed to violate control procedures incorporated in the programs.
4. Pilot and/or parallel testing – is performed by operations personnel but in conjunction with the user. Parallel tests involve the processing of all transactions both by the old and the new systems for a period of a month or two and a comparison of the results. Pilot tests involve the testing of the new system in a manner which simulates live operating conditions. For example, the test data should be live data with volume representative of actual operating conditions. In either case, operations personnel should use the new operating procedures for purposes of the test.

The test results should be reviewed by the development team. Once the team is satisfied that the new system accurately reflects the system specifications, the system can be scheduled for implementation.

Conversion and implementation

At some point, the old system procedures must be discontinued and the new system procedures introduced. The change-over will frequently require the creation or conversion of master files. For example, a payroll master file containing employee names, addresses, and rates of pay, may have to be converted from the format used in the old system to that required by the new system. Conversion errors are a frequent source of subsequent problems. It is essential that there be adequate controls over the conversion and implementation of new systems to ensure:
- the completeness and accuracy of the initial master files;

- a proper cut-off of the processing of transactions at the date of the change-over.

For example, the conversion procedures should provide for the computation of control totals (record counts, hash totals or dollar totals) on the old and new master files and the balancing or reconciliation of these totals on conversion. For critical master file information (e.g., employee pay rates, vendor names and addresses, accounts receivable balances) the details of the new master file should be printed out for visual review and a test performed of selected master file records from the new file back to the old (or to source documents).[8]

Usually the reconciliation of transaction control totals will ensure an accurate cut-off at the conversion date. In the absence of such control total reconciliations, however, a detailed test of transactions should be performed around the conversion date to ensure that no transactions have been duplicated or omitted during processing. Where parallel testing is performed, any cut-off errors will usually be evident from comparison of the parallel results.

8.4.3 Maintenance of systems and programs

Most systems and programs require revisions from time to time to reflect new business conditions or new information requirements. The ongoing process of revising existing systems and programs, often called "maintenance", may have major effects on the system of internal control. Accordingly, maintenance should be subject to the same general controls as govern the development of new systems.

Some changes involve a substantial overhaul of the original system specifications, require a significant amount of redesign and reprogramming, and have a major effect on the user. If good development controls are in force there is little danger that such major changes will not be properly controlled. At the other extreme, are those changes which are more of an "optimizing" nature, do not involve any change in the original system specifications, and are "transparent"

to the user. An example would be a change in program structure made solely to reduce run time. There is a much greater danger that such minor changes will escape proper testing and review and that accidental logic errors or deliberate irregularities will thereby be introduced without detection. Between these two extremes, lies a wide range of systems and program revisions of varying significance.

All changes to systems and programs, however minor, should be subject to certain minimum control procedures. These minimum procedures would include the following:

1. All proposed changes should be authorized in advance.
2. User personnel should review and approve each change and ensure that appropriate testing has been completed before the change is implemented. To ensure that user departments are made aware of all system and program changes, some organizations make it a practice of allocating the cost of systems and program maintenance to user departments. A further benefit of such cost allocations is that it forces user departments to re-assess the cost/benefit relationships continuously and to request the elimination of reports which are unnecessary or which have a cost out of proportion to their utility.
3. Operations personnel should be prevented from making changes to programs, however minor.
4. All systems and program changes should be adequately tested to ensure that each change has been properly made and that no other program logic has been accidentally altered.
5. All changes should be approved before implementation. The operations section should ensure that only properly approved programs are employed in actual processing.

The above minimum control procedures should be supplemented as necessary by additional user and senior management involvement in cases where the prospective changes are minor.

8.5 Operations controls

Operations controls involve controls over physical operations in the computer room and closely related activities. EDP operations include the receipt and recording of input from source departments, the conversion of source data into machine-readable form, the operation of the computer during processing of the data, the storage and retention of computer files, and the distribution of computer output to

user departments. These activities are complex. Inadvertent errors or omissions can easily occur if proper controls are not established. In addition, because of the concentration of data processing functions in the EDP department, controls must be provided to prevent or detect the fraudulent manipulation of computer processing by operations employees themselves. Finally, the centralization of valuable data and costly equipment aggravates the possible consequences of its loss, destruction, or unauthorized use.

The objectives of operations controls, therefore are:

- to prevent or detect accidental errors during processing by the EDP department,
- to prevent or detect fraudulent manipulation of data during processing by the EDP department and to prevent misuse of classified information,
- to provide security against accidental destruction of records and to ensure continuous operation.

These control objectives apply to any operations activity, whether processing is done on an in-house computer or at an outside data centre. The user of an outside data centre may, however, find it necessary to supplement the operations controls at the data centre to ensure the completeness and accuracy of data centre processing and the security over his data and/or programs.

8.5.1 Prevention or detection of accidental errors during processing

Data control group

A data control group should be established to control the flow of data into and out of the EDP department and to control the correction of errors encountered. While the data control group is commonly attached to the computer operations section, it should be independent of actual machine operation, data conversion, and other functions within that section. Its responsibilities should include:

1. the receipt of input from source departments, the follow-up of input not yet received, and the recording of control information in a control log for subsequent balancing;
2. the review of input for appropriate authorizations;
3. the monitoring, commonly through the use of an error log, of errors and exceptions rejected by the computer to ensure that appropriate corrections are made and that unwarranted frequencies of errors are investigated;
4. the balancing and reconciliation of totals on master files to ensure that the proper versions of the master files were used during processing;
5. the balancing or reconciliation of computer output totals to previously recorded input totals;
6. the review of computer output for any obvious processing errors;
7. the distribution of computer output on scheduled distribution dates to the appropriate user departments.

It is desirable for the control group to record and balance control totals, as just suggested, even if a user department maintains, as it should, an overall control on data submitted to and received back from the EDP department. The extent of the control group's procedures, however, may be influenced by the nature of user department controls and may therefore vary from one application to another.

Standard procedures

Standard operating procedures should be documented in up-to-date manuals used by all operations personnel. The procedures should cover the functions of:

- data control,
- data conversion,
- computer operating,
- file control and storage.

The contents of procedure manuals are outlined in 8.8. Procedures should cover not only normal operating conditions but also procedures for handling abnormal events such as out-of-balance conditions and computer halts and recovery.

Supervision of operations

To ensure that operations personnel adhere to standard operating procedures at all times, even in peak periods, vacations, or periods of employee illness, EDP operations activities should be carefully supervised. The exact form of supervision may vary from installation to installation. Some steps which may be included are:

1. personal observation of operators by the supervisor on a regular or test basis;
2. answering of operator queries;
3. a regular review of control total reconciliations prepared by the control group;
4. a regular review of error statistics maintained on data conversion and on computer operations activities;
5. a periodic review of control logs (maintained by the data control group), operator logs (maintained by each operator), and library records (showing the issue and return of files) to determine that they are being maintained in prescribed form and do not indicate any unusual or improper actions or omissions;
6. a regular review of the console printout for abnormal or unusual processing problems to ensure that appropriate corrective action was taken or for evidence of unusual or improper actions taken;
7. a review of operations statistics summarizing overall operating performance (e.g., productive time against down-time, number and percentage of reruns, number and percentage of late jobs, analysis of operations problems by cause).

Software controls

Most computer systems employ "operating systems" to control and monitor computer operations activities. Such a system, which is a collection of computer programs normally supplied by the equipment manufacturer, performs a variety of functions designed to streamline and control the operation of the computer. Although operating systems vary widely in their capabilities, the following are examples of typical functions performed:

1. providing messages to the operator – for example, to indicate the physical device assignments for the mounting of tape and disk files or to indicate the devices which are not ready for processing;
2. monitoring hardware functions such as file reading and writing so that any detected hardware malfunctions can be flagged;
3. providing standard utility programs such as compilers, sorting routines, and file copying routines;
4. checking internal file labels on a tape or disk file to ensure that the correct file has been mounted;
5. providing a printed log, normally via the console typewriter, of operations activity (e.g., jobs run, time on and off the computer, details of processing problems);
6. providing, in more sophisticated operating systems, (a) an automatic scheduling of computer jobs based on pre-assigned job priority levels, (b) comprehensive statistics on operations performance, and (c) the ability to handle two or more application programs simultaneously (multiprogramming).

The use of an operating system increases the efficiency of computer processing by reducing the set-up time required by the operator. More importantly from a control point of view, it eliminates many operator decisions and the related chances for error.

It is important to note, however, that the operating system is just a collection of computer programs, though usually highly complex ones. While such programs are normally supplied by the computer manufacturer, it may be necessary in some cases to make modifications to suit the particular requirements of the user. Revisions to operating systems should be subject to the same development controls as revisions to any programs (see 8.4.3).

8.5.2 Prevention or detection of fraudulent manipulation or misuse of data

Although the risk of fraudulent manipulation of data and misuse of classified information cannot be eliminated entirely, the introduction of adequate operations controls helps to minimize such risks.

Many of the operations controls over accidental errors just discussed provide effective control over fraudulent errors as well. For example:

1. The control total reconciliations performed by the data control group provide some protection against the fraudulent suppression or insertion of data during processing.
2. Careful supervision is an obvious preventive measure against improper operator intervention. A careful review of console printouts could disclose indications of such an intervention, had it occurred.
3. Library control of files restricts the operator's access to files other than for scheduled runs of the day.
4. Operating systems limit the opportunity of operator intervention or at least flag such intervention clearly so that its propriety can be later reviewed.

Four additional control procedures are restriction of access to program documentation, restriction of access to the computer room, rotation of operators or joint operation on sensitive applications, and the bonding of key EDP personnel.

Restricted access to program documentation

The desirability of segregating operations and programming functions has already been discussed under organizational controls. More specifically, the operator's access to program documentation should be restricted to the basic outline needed to control operations, correct computer halts, etc. He should not have access to the detailed logic diagrams or source programs which could facilitate manipulation of the data being processed.

Restricted access to the computer room

Access to the computer room, to computer files, and to blank forms (such as cheques) should be restricted to authorized personnel and the restrictions communicated to staff and enforced. Those permitted access should not be involved in the initiation of transactions or the custody of assets.

Rotation, joint operation and bonding

The technique of rotation of operators or joint operation is not common in practice but could be important in the processing of particularly sensitive runs such as payroll. An alternative might be to have an informed representative of the payroll department in attendance during processing. Bonding of EDP employees, as with any fidelity insurance, does not forestall fraud by existing employees. It may sometimes prevent the hiring of an employee with a record of past dishonesty. In any case, it protects the company in the event of loss, provided the fraud itself is eventually discovered.

Controls outside the EDP department

Some of the control over possible EDP manipulation must come from controls outside the EDP department. For example, for a cheque disbursement application, it may be prudent to ensure that sufficient outside controls exist, such as controls over the signing of cheques, numerical control over cheque forms, and bank reconciliation procedures, to make the detection of any fraud by the EDP department likely, were it to occur. Such outside controls form a part of *processing controls* (see 8.6).

8.5.3 Security against destruction of records and equipment

Considerable loss and disruption could often result from the inadvertent or willful destruction of EDP files, programs or equipment. The risk of accidental or intentional destruction of EDP resources may be minimized through techniques such as the following:

1. All files and programs should be stored in a safe location when not in use. Magnetic media such as tapes and disks are very sensitive to excesses of humidity, temperature and air pollution and storage facilities should accordingly be protected from such excesses.
2. The computer room itself should be physically protected from fire, flood or vandalism. This protection may include the location of the computer room in a remote area, the use of locks, and the installation of fire detectors and automatic extinguishers.
3. Computer hardware, like magnetic files, is sensitive to excess humidity, temperature or pollution and the computer room should accordingly be controlled to the manufacturer's specifications.
4. Computer hardware components do wear out or become unreliable with age. It is important to adhere to the manufacturer's recommended schedule of preventive maintenance.

8.5.4 Procedures to ensure continuous operation if preventive security measures fail

In addition to the preventive security measures described above, there should exist a second line of defence to enable timely recovery in situations where the preventive measures fail and files, programs or equipment are damaged or destroyed. Recovery procedures should be designed to cope with both minor and major problems. Minor processing problems may simply require reprocessing and some minor reconstruction of records. Major problems, such as the catastrophic destruction by fire of several files and equipment components, may require substantial reconstruction of data and the use of alternative processing facilities for a temporary period.

Contingency plans

It is desirable for an organization to establish and document a plan of procedures to be followed in the event of various contingencies. The plans would include, for example, the persons responsible for carrying out the various recovery steps, applications to be given top priority in reconstruction, alternate manual procedures to be followed during the recovery period, detailed steps to be carried out in reconstructing files.

It is likely that certain applications will be more sensitive to processing delays than others. For example, a union payroll application would probably be more critical to delays than would a general ledger application. The contingency plans should therefore assess the impact of processing problems on each application and establish priorities to govern the attention to be given to each system during the recovery period.

File back-up

Back-up copies of all master files should be maintained to enable reconstruction in the event that the current version is destroyed. For master files which are updated sequentially, a few previous generations of master files, together with a copy of the intervening transactions used to update them, provide short-term back-up automatically. A common method is the "grandfather-father-son" method whereby the current file and two immediately past generations are kept. On the other hand, for master files which are updated directly (e.g., random access or indexed disk files), back-up is not produced automatically. Such files must therefore be periodically copied onto tape or another disk to provide the required back-up copy.

In most cases several back-up copies are maintained. Certain of these copies should be maintained in a safe off-site location to provide for recovery in the event that all copies of the file at the computer facility are accidentally destroyed. For example, several weekly back-up copies of a master file may be maintained on-site at the computer facility and the month-end back-up copy may be stored off-site. The specific file back-up arrangements depend upon the cost and time required to reconstruct, the availability of the intervening transaction details, and the method and frequency of updating. Usually such arrangements must be decided upon separately for each application.

Program back-up

Back-up copies of computer programs (including the operating system) must be maintained to enable timely recovery in the event that the operational copy of the programs is destroyed. Most installations maintain several copies of the operational program libraries (on magnetic tape or disk) with at least one copy stored off-site. The frequency of program back-up will depend on the frequency of program changes. For example, if many program changes are made daily, the program libraries should be copied to a back-up copy each day.

In addition to back-up copies of the operational programs, there should also be back-up copies of the "source" programs (programs in the form written by the programmer) and the related program documentation (e.g., logic diagrams). Such back-up will enable normal maintenance to be continued on these programs in the event that the original copies of the source programs and documentation are destroyed.

Hardware back-up

Alternate computer hardware facilities should be available in the event of prolonged machine failure. It is usually desirable to make formal arrangements for standby equipment to ensure that sufficient time will be made available for both reconstruction and regular processing. To ensure that the back-up hardware facility remains compatible, the equipment should be tested periodically.

Insurance

As a final line of defence against potential losses arising from the destruction of files, programs and computer equipment, consideration should be given to acquiring special insurance coverage for EDP losses.

Cost versus exposure

The cost of back-up and recovery procedures must be carefully weighed against the likelihood of problems occurring and the costs which would be thereby avoided. Where the consequences of equipment failure would be unusually serious, more elaborate and costly back-up will be desirable. For example, certain large organizations with on-line systems (banks and airline companies) maintain duplicate computer systems so that in the event that one system fails the on-line systems may be switched to the alternate system immediately.

8.5.5 Security and confidentiality of data processed at an outside data centre

The general security and recovery controls just discussed apply as well to processing performed at an outside data centre. The user should ensure that the data centre has adequate security and recovery procedures in effect and preferably should request covenants to that effect in the formal contract signed with the data centre. In some cases the user may wish to visit (or have his auditor visit) the data centre to review the security procedures in effect and ensure that they are being consistently applied.

In certain cases, it may be appropriate for the user company to duplicate or supplement the back-up and recovery procedures in effect at the data centre. For example, for critical applications the company may maintain back-up copies of the master files on company premises. In other cases it may be necessary to maintain a full back-up and recovery capability independent of the data centre's procedures, including an arrangement with an alternate data centre for standby services, so that processing could be transferred on a timely basis to the alternate facility.

There is the additional concern that confidential information maintained at the data centre may be disclosed to third parties causing embarrassment and/or financial loss. The data centre, should have appropriate controls to prevent such disclosure. However, where the disclosure of confidential information might be particularly detrimental (e.g., executive payroll, selling prices) the user may choose to identify such data by means of codes rather than descriptions. In some cases, it may be prudent to have a company official present at the data centre during the processing of confidential information.

8.6 Processing controls

A complete cycle of computer processing involves the receipt of input from source departments, the actual processing on the computer, and the distribution of output to user departments. Specific controls employed in a particular application, such as customer billing, throughout this processing cycle can be described as *processing controls*. They may be made up of different components including *hardware controls* (controls built into the equipment), *input and output controls* (controls exercised primarily by the source and user departments and by the data control group), and *programmed controls* (controls built into the program logic). As the CICA Study pointed out, it is impossible to evaluate the adequacy of each of these components in isolation because one type of control can substitute for another. For example, visual editing (an output control) can be replaced by computer editing (a programmed control). All one can ask is whether, taken together, the processing controls fulfill certain essential objectives.

The CICA Study defined the objectives of processing controls as:

- to ensure the completeness of data processed by the computer,
- to ensure the accuracy of data processed by the computer,
- to ensure that all data processed by the computer is authorized,
- to ensure the adequacy of management trials.

Many of the individual control techniques, however, which serve the completeness objective serve, at the same time, the accuracy and authorization objectives.

In this chapter the objectives of processing controls are instead subdivided as follows:[9]

Master file controls

- to ensure that the most current version of the master file (including the most recent master file changes) is used during processing,
- to ensure that critical master file information is complete, accurate and authorized.

Data controls

- to ensure that all data processed by the computer is complete, accurate and authorized and that output is distributed to the proper persons or departments.

Error controls

- to ensure that all errors and exceptions are reviewed and that required corrections are re-entered into the system.

Management and audit trails

- to ensure that an adequate trail of processing can be traced to meet the information needs of management and to answer reasonable queries of customers, suppliers, employees, government, regulatory agencies, and auditors.

The types of master file controls, data controls, error controls, and management and audit trails commonly encountered are reasonably standard and are described in the following sections. The specific details as to how a given processing control (such as control totals) is employed will vary from application to application – unlike computer environment controls, which tend to be constant for all applications. A payroll application may require control totals on many key fields. A sales analysis application may require only one overall control total. In evaluating processing controls for an application in a specific major systems area (such as sales/receivables/receipts) the reader must consider the possible computer processing controls within the context of specific control procedures applicable to that systems area. Specific control procedures by major systems area are described in Chapter 29.

Under each objective in the following sections are listed a number of control techniques. Not every control technique is necessarily essential to fulfill the objective in a given case. Because both processing and environment controls are ultimately concerned with the same final objective of ensuring accurate output, a few of the processing controls described in the following sections overlap with the environment controls already discussed.

8.6.1 Master file controls

Master files contain permanent or semi-permanent information as opposed to transaction files which contain only current and temporary data. Master files are of two types: those which contain relatively constant information (such as price lists) and those which contain accumulating balances (such as accounts receivable or general ledger files). Both types must be updated periodically with transaction data and both types are used from time to time as a reference source for information needed during the processing of transactions. The first type, however, is updated infrequently but used in processing transactions extensively. For example, product selling prices stored in the product master file may be revised only twice a year but may be used daily, in conjunction with sales transaction data, for the preparation of sales invoices. The second type is updated frequently but may or may not be used in processing transactions. For example, the accounts receivable master

**Simplified Example of a Reconciliation of
Control Information For a Master File (in a payroll system)**

	No. of Records	Hash total on pay rates	Agreed to master file update report (√)
Totals on previous processing cycle	5 627	92 684.50	√
Changes this period:			
Add new hires	12	210.50	
Rate changes (net)	—	122.00	
Deduct terminations	(4)	(64.50)	
Totals on this processing cycle	5 635	92 952.50	√

Figure 8.d

file may be updated weekly. It may in turn be used in checking credit limits for incoming sales orders. The general ledger master file would not, however, normally be used in processing transactions.

For either type of master file, its completeness, accuracy and authorization of its data is of critical importance since such data will either be used repetitively during processing (product prices, customer discounts, employee pay rates, etc.) or will represent important accounting balances (accounts receivable balances, accounts payable balances, inventory balances, general ledger balances, etc.).

Controls to ensure that the most current version of the master file (including the most recent master file changes) is used during processing

The control techniques to achieve this objective may include:

1. The maintenance and balancing of master file control information on each processing cycle.
   The user (or the EDP control group) should maintain master file control information (e.g., the total number of master file records, a hash total on pay rates, a control total on receivable balances) which is subsequently balanced on each processing cycle to similar control information produced by computer. The user carries this control information forward from one processing cycle to the next, thereby ensuring that the proper version of the master file was used. Figure 8.d shows a simplified example of a control reconciliation for a payroll master file.
2. The use of internal and external file labels.
   The master files should be *internally* labelled by the application programs or the operating system. Such internal labels may include the version

number, the data created as well as control information (number of records, hash totals, etc.). The application programs or the operating system would be designed to check the label information during processing to ensure that the proper file was used.

Master files may also be labelled *externally* with respect to file name, version number and date created and the computer operator may be instructed to check such information prior to processing to ensure that the correct file is mounted.

3. The use of the librarian to control master file usage.
   Where the installation has a file librarian, the library control procedures covering the use of master file should help ensure that the proper version of the master file is released for processing.

Controls to ensure that critical master file information is complete, accurate and authorized

The control techniques to achieve this objective may include:

1. The authorization of changes by appropriate officials.
   Changes to master file information should be authorized by an appropriate officer of the organization. For example, changes to customer credit limits might be authorized by the credit manager; changes to product prices by the marketing manager; and, changes to vendor names and addresses by the purchasing manager.

   Such approval would usually involve the officer reviewing the source document for the master file change before processing and indicating his approval by signing or initialling the document.

193

2. The checking of authorization by the control group before processing.

To ensure that all master file changes have been authorized, the EDP control group should review the source documents for evidence of approval prior to processing. Any source documents which have not been approved should be returned to the approving officer for his authorization.

3. The balancing of control information upon updating the master file.

Control information should be maintained in the source department (e.g., number of updates by type, hash total on pay rate,) and these control totals should be balanced to the computer-produced update report to ensure that all updates submitted (*and no others*) were processed.

4. The printing out and checking back of master file changes to source documents.

To ensure that all master file changes were accurately converted to machine-readable form and accurately processed, the details of master file changes processed by the computer should be printed out and checked back to the source documents by the authorizing department.

5. The printing out of key information periodically for visual review.

As a further control on the accuracy and authorization of master file data, it is generally desirable for critical information to be periodically listed in hard copy form for visual review by the source department. For example, the payroll master file might be periodically listed and agreed to current personnel records to ensure the accuracy of employee names and pay rates.

8.6.2 Data controls

Data controls refer to the controls over the processing of regular input transactions (other than master file transactions) and over the distribution of output reports. A computer system will typically include several input transaction types and several outputs. A sales and accounts receivable system, for example, may include as inputs: sales transactions, back-order transactions, credit transactions, cash receipt transactions and accounts receivable adjustments. Primary accounting outputs for the same system may include: sales invoices, credit notes, a monthly sales summary, customer statements and an aged trial balance of accounts receivable. In addition, the computer system may automatically generate certain transactions (such as an interest charge on overdue accounts receivable).

Controls to ensure that all data processed by the computer is complete, accurate and authorized and that output is distributed to the proper persons or departments

The control techniques to achieve this objective may include:

1. The initial recording of each transaction on a specially designed and identified form.

The importance of an organized method to ensure initial recording of transactions and the benefits of good document design were discussed in 7.6.1 and 7.6.4 with respect to any system. In a computer-based system the increased rigidity makes the discipline imposed by standard forms even more essential. Pre-printed or pre-coded forms can help to reduce recording or conversion errors. So can turn-around documents in machine-sensible form. Identification codes are useful to permit correction of later out-of-balance conditions.

2. The existence of a data control group which is independent of data authorization and computer operations.

A fundamental control in the handling of input and output by the EDP department is the existence of a separate data control group (see 8.5.1).

3. The use of control totals and the balancing of output to input.

The use of batching (assembling similar documents in groups) and of batch control totals is perhaps the most common control technique in batch processing systems. Control information should be established by the source department (e.g., total number of transactions, sequential batch number, hash or control total on one or more fields, such as on "hours worked") preferably as close to the point of initial recording as possible.

This control information is usually recorded in a control log to permit subsequent balancing to the eventual computer output. Overall control totals should be maintained by the user department. More detailed control totals may be used by the data control group throughout the various stages of computer processing for the purpose of inter-run balancing. The critical step for overall completeness and accuracy of processing, however, is the reconciliation of final output control totals with the initial input totals. Reconciling items will generally represent data rejected by the computer during processing, and such items must be controlled to ensure that appropriate corrections are re-entered into the

**Simplified Example of a Control Total Reconciliation
for a Transaction File (in a payroll system)**

	No. time cards	Hours	Net pay
Input control totals (per batch control log)	465	14 260	
Payroll calculation run:			
Transactions read	465	14 260	
Transactions rejected	1	40	
Transactions processed	464	14 220	248 682
Payroll report run:			
Cheques printed	464		248 682
Payroll register	464	14 220	248 682

Figure 8.e

system (see 8.6.3). Figure 8.e shows a simplified example of a control total reconciliation for a payroll system.

In some cases control total reconciliation can be performed automatically by the computer and only out-of-balance conditions printed out for investigation.

4. User review of output.

In some cases, user review of the eventual computer output may be sufficient to detect incomplete, inaccurate or unauthorized data. Such errors could be detected by the users of the output reports through their knowledge of the approximate results which the reports should disclose. However, the reports must be in sufficient detail, and the reviewers must have sufficient knowledge, to permit the recognition of an unusual transaction or result.

In very sensitive applications it may be worth having output listed in detail and visually checked, by the source or user department, back to source documents. This technique is costly, however, and is more commonly restricted to master file changes (see 8.6.1).

5. Adequate computer editing of input transactions.

Input transactions should be edited by the computer to the maximum extent practical in order to ensure the completeness and accuracy of the input data. It is not appropriate for EDP personnel to omit editing controls on the grounds that input errors are someone else's fault. The computer can best serve the organization as a whole if it detects and flags as many input errors as possible. A wide range of editing tasks may be performed from routine "physical" edits (e.g.,

numeric fields must be numeric) to more complex "logical" edits such as range tests (e.g., customer number must be between 10 000 and 99 999) and limit tests (e.g., line item gross profit must be greater than 10%). Computer editing replaces the visual scrutiny lost when many visible records are converted to magnetic form. As a form of automated scrutiny, the elements of computer editing are the same as those described for any scrutiny in 10.4.1. Computer edits should be performed as close as possible to the beginning of processing to reduce the risk of inaccurate data being partially processed and thus requiring a subsequent correcting transaction.

6. The key verification of important data fields.

Some input data is initially converted to machine-sensible form, such as punch cards, by a keying operation. "Key verification" is the re-keying of some or all of each input source document by a second operator to check the accuracy of the original keying. Key verification may be applied to all data fields, or to selected data fields within the record. This control may complement or replace other data control techniques. Where an important field is not otherwise controlled (such as by a control total), key verification will usually be desirable.

7. Adequate hardware controls.

Hardware controls include controls such as parity checks, read-after-write checks, overflow checks, character validity checks, printer timing checks. The hardware controls built into most computer components give them a high, though not absolute, degree of reliability. The extent of hardware controls varies with manufacturer and model. Where hardware controls are less extensive, other controls within the system may have to be increased.

8. Software control procedures.
   Control features in certain software programs such as operating systems (see 8.5.1) or input/output control systems may be useful in detecting some types of input errors.

9. The use of self-checking digits on key codes.
   Errors in the manual transcribing of key codes such as account numbers, customer numbers, and product codes during input preparation can be detected by the use of self-checking digits (mathematically determined suffixes whose consistency can be rechecked by the computer).

10. Computer anticipation control.
    In some cases the computer program can be designed to anticipate the normal sources of daily, weekly or monthly input and to print exception reports where expected input is not received. Where input transactions are serially numbered their continuity can be checked by the computer.

11. User anticipation of output reports.
    User departments should have procedures to identify the output reports to be received, to mark off the reports when received, and to follow up missing reports. Anticipation controls help to ensure that all output is appropriately distributed.

12. The reconciliation of processing cut-off.
    Inaccurate monthly statements sometimes result from all the transactions for a whole week or for an entire batch arriving late and being inadvertently excluded from processing. Control total reconciliations should be reviewed to ensure the accuracy and consistency of processing cut-off.

13. The use of cross-addition, arithmetic and overflow tests.
    Cross-addition and arithmetic tests are commonly incorporated in program logic to provide a check on computer calculations performed. For example, if loan interest is being computed loan by loan, the computer can check that the total interest agrees with total loans times the interest rate. Overflow tests, whether programmed or incorporated as a hardware or software control, are important to ensure that computations have not produced results exceeding the register or storage space allotted to receive them.

8.6.3 Error controls

Computer edits and other programmed controls generally result in either the rejection of transactions from further computer processing or in the flagging of transactions as possibly erroneous. It is essential that such errors and exceptions be followed up and corrections made where necessary. Failure to do so will result in either incomplete or inaccurate processing.

Controls to ensure that all errors and exceptions are reviewed and that required corrections are re-entered into the system

The control techniques to achieve this objective may include:

1. The use of an error log to control outstanding errors.
   In many systems an error log is used to record transactions (or batches of transactions) which have been rejected by the computer. This log may be maintained manually, or alternatively may be a copy of the computer-produced error list. Corrections are marked off in the log (or on the error list) when the correction has been re-entered. The error log should be reviewed periodically to ensure that all open items are being followed up. Usually this is the task of the data control group.

2. The maintenance of the outstanding error log by the computer.
   As an alternative, records of rejected (or exceptional) data awaiting review and correction may be maintained by the computer as a file of outstanding errors. Reports of outstanding errors can be regularly produced for follow-up and correction, and can continue to be reported until they are corrected.

3. Well defined procedures and fixed responsibilities for error correction.
   There should be a well-defined system of procedures and fixed responsibilities for correction of errors and re-entering of corrections. Unless such procedures and responsibilities are well-defined there is a risk that error correction will be carried out incompletely.

4. The validation and control of error corrections in the same way as regular input.
   Error corrections should re-enter the regular input stream and be subject to the same control total procedures, computer edits, output balancing, etc. Where error corrections bypass the regular controls there is a danger that errors made in the correction process itself will escape detection.

8.6.4 Management and audit trails

Management and audit trails are necessary to meet the normal queries from management and others for supplementary information in addition to that provided in the primary output reports.

Controls to ensure that an adequate trail of processing can be traced to meet the information needs of management and to answer reasonable queries of customers, suppliers, employees, government, regulatory agencies, and auditors

The control techniques to achieve this objective may include:

1. The maintenance of the detailed documents or file records which support a total or summary amount in a form which facilitates their accessibility (e.g., hard copy, microfilm, machine-readable form).
2. The unique identification of each document and file record to permit accessibility (e.g., document number, unique record keys, batch numbers).

8.7 Management monitoring controls

In 7.8 an important element of internal control was identified as management's monitoring of the continuing effectiveness of all other controls. Such monitoring is particularly important in computer-based systems because of the complexity and technical nature of many of the required computer controls and the greater risks created, due to the centralization of processing, in the event of their absence.

The management audit

The CICA Study, *Computer Audit Guidelines*, suggested that periodic management audits are essential to management's control over the EDP function.

> The purpose of the management audit should be to provide management with an overview of its data processing operations and to identify any deficiencies which may cause unsatisfactory performance (e.g., operations which do not provide a satisfactory level of reliability, efficiency and cost-effectiveness). A major advantage of a management audit is that it complements the essential communications link between the electronic data processing function and senior management.[10]

As the Study pointed out, it would be wrong to assume that the external auditor's review of internal control for attest purposes will automatically provide this monitoring element. The external auditor's review is necessarily designed in the light of financial statement materiality and the attest significance of various controls. Controls of non-attest significance (pre-installation controls, documentation controls, etc.) will normally receive a cursory review and even controls of attest significance may not be pursued in

the depth that would be necessary to identify all areas of importance to management. A proper management audit should build upon the work of the external auditor but go much further. Specific management audit procedures are suggested in *Computer Audit Guidelines*.

Guidelines

A management audit may be conducted by a separate group of data processing personnel (if they are sufficiently independent to provide an objective opinion), by internal or external auditors (if they have had sufficient specialized training in computers and computer controls), or by a joint task force of the foregoing groups.

Such a management audit may be variously described as a computer audit, an audit of the EDP function, or an operational audit. Or it may be divided into components such as a security review (checking controls over damage, loss, manipulation or abuse of computer data), an efficiency review (evaluating the efficiency and cost-effectiveness of the computer processing), and a control analysis (analyzing all other controls, such as those against accidental input or processing errors). However it is named, a periodic management audit of the computer function is an essential element in management's overall control system.

That this element is missing in the major computer installations of many companies should be a matter of concern to those companies' managements – and to their auditors.

8.8 Documentation controls

The importance of documentation controls discussed in 7.9 is increased in the case of computer-based systems because of their complexity and the magnitude of the investment in their design. Adequate computer documentation is important to:

1. provide management and other interested parties

with a clear understanding of systems concepts, processing and output and to ensure that systems adhere to management policy and objectives,
2. provide operating and user personnel with a clear description of their procedures and responsibilities with respect to systems,

Documentation Controls

Purpose	Suggested contents
Systems Documentation (normally prepared by systems analysts—may be assisted by users and others)	
To provide management and other parties with a clear understanding of systems To provide a reference source for systems analysts responsible for maintenance of systems To serve as a basis for review of accounting and internal control by auditors	(a) List of approved revisions (b) Problem definition (c) General systems description (d) General systems flow chart (e) Special treatment for exceptions (f) List of programs required (g) Program specifications (h) Description of source documents and method of conversion (i) Constants, codes and tables (j) Input format and descriptions (k) Output formats and descriptions (l) File control procedures (m) Audit and management trails (n) Test data specifications (o) Conversion procedures and schedule (p) User, source department and control group instructions.
Program Documentation (prepared by programmer)	
To provide a reference source for programmers responsible for program maintenance	(a) List of approved revisions (b) Program specifications (c) Program narrative description (d) Logic diagram and/or decision tables (e) Constants, codes and tables (f) Input and output formats (g) File formats and descriptions (h) Source program listing (i) Linkage editor map of object program (j) Operating instructions.
Documentation of Operating Instructions (normally prepared by systems analyst — may be assisted by programmer)	
To provide computer operating personnel with a clear description of their procedures and responsibilities with respect to systems	(a) Program number and name (b) Brief description of the purpose of the program (c) Schematic of the operation (d) Input, output formats (e) Special operating instructions (f) List of messages, programmed halts, and corrective action (g) Recovery and restart procedures (h) End-of-job instructions, run-to-run balancing procedures, etc. (i) Estimated normal run time and permitted maximum run time.
Documentation of File Control Procedures (normally prepared by systems analyst jointly with user)	
To provide file control personnel (e.g., librarians) with a clear description of their procedures and responsibilities with respect to systems	(a) Indexing instructions for all files (b) File retention procedures for each class of file (c) Logging procedures for daily file usage.
Documentation of Data Conversion Procedures (normally prepared by systems analyst)	
To provide data conversion personnel (e.g., keypunch operators) with a clear description of their procedures and responsibilities with respect to systems	(a) Keypunching and other data conversion instructions (b) Standards and performance expectations.

Figure 8.f

Purpose	Suggested contents
Documentation of Data Control Procedures (normally prepared by systems analyst jointly with user)	
To provide data control personnel with a clear description of their procedures and responsibilities with respect to systems	(a) Source of input and disposition of output (b) Procedures for reconciliation and/or balancing of control information (c) Schedule of due dates for output reports (d) Anticipated error conditions and action to be taken.
Documentation of User Procedures (normally prepared by systems analyst jointly with user)	
To provide user personnel with a clear description of their procedures and responsibilities with respect to systems	(a) Documents or data to be forwarded to data processing (b) Controls to be established over input (c) Approvals required on input documents (d) Input schedule to be adhered to (e) Coding rules to be followed (f) Period-end cut-off procedures to be observed (g) Reports and output documents to be received (h) Output schedule (i) Error codes and messages and error correction procedures (j) Control balancing procedures.

Figure 8.f (concluded)

3. provide a reference source for system analysts and programmers responsible for systems and program maintenance,
4. serve as a basis for the review of internal controls by internal and external auditors.

The objectives of documentation controls are therefore:

- to ensure that adequate documentation exists and is effectively controlled.
- to ensure that all systems are adequately documented.
- to ensure that all programs are adequately documented.
- to ensure that instructions to all data processing and user personnel are adequately documented.

The format and content of each area of documentation must be suited to the needs of its user. For example, program documentation must be in a form which will facilitate the maintenance of programs by programmers. Operating instructions must assist the operator in running the computer. User documentation must assist the user in preparing input forms correctly and using output reports efficiently.

The following areas of documentation may be identified:

- systems,
- programs,
- operating instructions,
- file control procedures,
- data conversion procedures,
- data control procedures,
- user procedures.

Figure 8.f presents in tabular form the purpose, responsibility for, and suggested contents of, each type of documentation.

Documentation standards

It is important that documentation be prepared in a standardized fashion within the organization. Standardized program documentation, for example, permits one programmer to update a program originally written by another programmer.

The specific documentation standards adopted should, of course, be suited to the particular organization. There are, however, certain standards and conventions, such as flow charting symbols, which have been standardized within the EDP industry, and these should be used where possible.

Documentation standards should be published and included as part of the overall EDP standards. Documentation should be reviewed by senior EDP personnel to ensure that it has been prepared in accordance with the standards.

Maintenance of documentation

For documentation to be effective, there should be procedures in effect which ensure that the documentation is updated every time a change is made to the system. Such procedures may include, for example, a periodic review by the EDP systems supervisor.

199

8.9 Computer controls in the small business

As mentioned earlier, the dramatic decrease in the cost of computer hardware and the growth of mini-computers and outside data centres has brought computer processing into the systems of many small enterprises. For example, many banks provide payroll processing services on a basis which is economical for companies with even a relatively small number of employees. Many small business computers can be purchased for less than $50 000 or rented for less than $1 000 per month. Many of these smaller computer systems come with pre-programmed accounting packages (such as accounts receivable, accounts payable, payroll, general ledger, etc.) and thus a large investment in the development of systems and programs is often unnecessary.

One might at first think that inexpensive computer systems would differ little from manual systems in their impact on control. In fact, however, even small computer systems are often complex and, with the possible exception of processing speed, they have most of the characteristics of larger computer equipment. For example, small computers may have operating systems much like larger computers, on-line storage facilities, and high level languages such as COBOL. Applications developed for small computers can thus be just as complex as applications developed for large computers, and can include on-line updating, teleprocessing, use of data base management systems, and internally generated transactions.

Small computer systems, therefore, are distinguished primarily by their relatively low cost and slower processing speed. It is just as important for a small computer system to incorporate adequate controls as a large one. At the same time, however, small computer systems are more likely to be found in smaller businesses where there is less opportunity to achieve an adequate division of duties and to have formal standards and procedures for system design, programming, and operations. Where it is found impractical to provide adequate control in all the areas discussed earlier in this chapter, the deficiencies must be compensated for in other ways. Compensating controls may include, for example:

1. Increased management supervision of EDP activities. Senior management may have to take a more active role in EDP than would be necessary in larger organizations.
2. Increased processing controls exercised by source and user departments (such as control total balancing, review of computer output, checking of detailed computer calculations).

3. Increased reliance on outsiders such as consultants and external auditors (to perform feasibility studies, internal control reviews, etc.).

Pre-installation controls

Pre-installation controls are just as important for small organizations making use of EDP, since the computer costs, while smaller, will be significant relative to the organization. The selection of suitable equipment or services may, in fact, be more difficult due to the wide range of mini-computers and data centres available. Small organizations should therefore, prior to the acquisition of computer processing facilities, undertake a feasibility study with the same degree of senior management involvement as in large organizations.

Many smaller organizations may not possess sufficient EDP expertise "in-house" to be able to carry out such studies on their own and will wish to retain independent EDP consultants for this purpose.

Organizational controls

A small company will often be unable to arrange for adequate organizational controls within its EDP department. The department may consist of only a few individuals and there may exist a necessary overlap of duties and responsibilities. Computer programmers may be required to operate the computer on occasion and the computer operator may fulfill certain data control or file control responsibilities. This lack of segregation of functions should normally be compensated for by:

- Increased management supervision of EDP development and operations. (For example, the EDP manager should regularly review and approve all system and program changes and should directly supervise computer operations.)
- Increased user control of applications (control totals, output review, attendance during sensitive runs, etc.).

Development controls

In some cases, the small organization may make use of pre-programmed accounting packages sold or leased by equipment suppliers or independent software suppliers. The company will not then need a permanent systems and programming staff. Users should be involved during the feasibility study and implementation stages, however, to ensure that such packages will satisfy their particular needs and are implemented in a planned and controlled manner.

In other cases, the organization itself will design and program its own systems and programs. A highly formalized set of systems design and programming standards may not be practical. Nevertheless, senior management should ensure, through supervision and review of EDP development activities, that proper development and programming procedures are being followed. Such procedures would include: the involvement of users in the design, testing and implementation of systems; the involvement of accounting and audit personnel in the development and implementation of systems with financial significance; and procedures for the testing and conversion of systems.

In some cases, the management of a small organization may call upon the external auditor to perform a review of new systems, prior to implementation, to ensure that they contain adequate controls.

Operations controls

The likely lack of division of duties in the EDP department should normally be compensated for by increased supervision of computer operations by the EDP manager. To the extent possible, computer operators should be independent of the custody of assets (including signature plates and cheque forms).

Security and back-up considerations are generally of equal importance in small installations as in large ones.

Processing controls

Controls which ensure the completeness, accuracy and authorization of data processed are, of course, of critical importance in all EDP systems, regardless of size. However, in smaller installations, because computer *environment* controls are less formal, *processing* controls for each application take on increased significance. Where possible, processing controls should be exercised by the user, rather than by the EDP department. For example, control total reconciliations should generally be performed by the user.

In cases where there is an inadequate division of duties within the EDP department, users should perform a more extensive review of computer output, including the test checking of computer computations on each processing cycle.

Management monitoring controls

A periodic management audit of the computer function is as important for a small organization as for a large one.

Documentation controls

Although formal standards for systems and program documentation will generally not be practical in smaller installations, all systems and programs should be adequately documented. Since a smaller company is likely to employ only one or two programmers, adequate documentation is essential to prevent disruptions when a programmer leaves the company's employ.

8.10 Computer controls in advanced EDP systems

The control techniques discussed in this chapter are generally appropriate for the vast majority of computer installations and applications. The presence of advanced EDP processing methods does not affect the existing control objectives, but will have an impact on the particular control techniques employed to satisfy those objectives. The purpose of this section is to outline, in general terms, the characteristics of advanced EDP systems and their related impact on the control techniques required.

On-line systems

In on-line systems the user interacts *directly* with the computer system and with his own data. The user will thus perform many functions which were previously the responsibility of the EDP department (e.g., data conversion, error correction, scheduling of computer processing). The processing will tend to be "transaction-oriented" rather than "batch-oriented".

Thus, transactions may be completely processed at or near the point of transaction origination.
As a result:

1. There will be fewer people involved in the processing of transactions (one person may initiate, approve and process transactions). Thus, less reliance can be placed on division of duties as a control technique, and more reliance must be placed on programmed controls (computer edits, password authorization, etc.) to ensure the completeness, accuracy and authorization of the data processed.
2. Batching and control total techniques may disappear. Accordingly, more reliance must be placed on programmed controls to ensure the completeness of data processed (sequential numbering of transactions, internal balancing, etc.).
3. Conventional management trails may disappear. Thus, on-line systems should normally provide a

machine-readable transaction log to facilitate analysis of processing and reconstruction in the event of accidental or intentional destruction of files.

Telecommunications

Telecommunications facilities are used extensively in advanced systems to collect data from regional points for processing at a central location and for the distribution of output from the central location back to regional points. Such data collection and distribution is usually highly complex and is controlled principally by system software. In so-called "distributive systems" computer processing (or "intelligence") is distributed among several remote terminals and a central processor, so that some processing is performed locally and some centrally.
As a result:
• Special control techniques may be required to prevent/detect transmission errors, line problems, etc.
• Special control techniques (e.g., passwords) may be required to prevent unauthorized access to data.
• Source documents may be widely dispersed geographically and thus management trails may be difficult to retrace from a central location.

Data base management

In traditional processing (non-data base systems), each application has its own unique set of data. Generally, the *physical* storage of the data corresponds to some *logical* relationship (e.g., customer A's records are followed by customer B's records). Application programs are *data dependent*. That is, the application programs require that the data have certain predefined *physical* characteristics (record size, record format, sequence, etc.). Any change in the physical characteristics of the data requires a change to the programs which use such data. Finally, more than one user may have to maintain essentially the same data independently (*data redundancy*).

Advanced data base management techniques are designed to alleviate the two problems of data dependence and data redundancy. Such systems attempt to separate the *physical* management and storage of data from the *logical* use made of the data by individual application programs.

Generalized software programs (collectively referred to as the data base management system or DBMS) are used to handle all physical storage and manipulation of data. The DBMS translates the requests of application programs for *logical* data into the *physical* location of such data, retrieves the requested data and presents it to the application program in suitable format.

Application programs are no longer data dependent, thus reducing the need for changes to programs as a result of changes made to the physical data base. In addition, data items need be stored only once and several users are permitted access to the same data.
As a result:
• Increased reliance must be placed on programmed controls to maintain the logical relationships within the data base (completeness and accuracy).
• There is an increased risk of unauthorized access to data (i.e., one user obtaining improper access to another's data). Thus, increased reliance must be placed on software controls to ensure the authorization of data processing.
• Data base management creates a need for a new function, *data base administration*. This function should be responsible for controlling access to the data base (e.g., maintenance of passwords), dealing with conflicts between users, and establishing back-up recovery procedures.

In general, advanced EDP systems will increase the importance of having adequate computer controls.

Pre-installation controls

Advanced systems will typically involve huge commitments in terms of time and resources. The consequences of uneconomic deployment are obviously much greater. Advanced systems will also typically have a much broader impact on the organization (i.e., many users will interface with EDP). It is thus important that the impact of advanced systems be considered for the whole organization.

Organizational controls

Because of the large investment and broad impact, it is important to ensure that there is adequate senior management involvement in EDP.

In certain advanced systems (e.g., on-line systems) the user may initiate, authorize and process transactions. Thus, there is a need for special software controls to compensate for this lack of division of duties.

Development controls

Since users will tend to interface directly with the EDP system, it is important that users be involved in the design, testing and implementation of such systems. The development of advanced systems is complex and will typically involve several system analysts and programmers. Thus it is essential to have appropriate systems design and programming standards.

Operations controls

Operations activities in advanced systems are complex and increased reliance will generally be placed on system software (operating systems, teleprocessing software, DBMS, etc.) to monitor and supervise operations. There continues to be a need for standard operating procedures and well-trained staff. Security, back-up and recovery procedures are even more critical as well as more complex.

Processing controls

In general, increased reliance must be placed on software controls to ensure the completeness, accuracy and authorization of data being processed and to ensure the adequacy of management trails. Examples of such controls are comprehensive computer edits, computer-maintained error/suspense files, computer balancing of control information, and password controls.

Management monitoring controls

Because of the increased complexity, a periodic management audit is particularly important to ensure the continuing effectiveness of controls. Such an audit will require a considerable degree of specialized training and the development of sophisticated auditing techniques.

Documentation controls

Again because of the increased complexity, adequate system and program documentation is essential.

8.11 Reference material

CICA Study, *Computer Control Guidelines* (1970).
Gordon B. Davis, *Auditing and EDP* (AICPA: 1968).
AICPA, Statement on Auditing Standards No. 3,

The Effects of EDP on the Auditor's Study and Evaluation of Internal Control, (1974).

8.12 Questions and problems

Review and discussion

1. List and discuss seven characteristics of computer-based systems which influence internal control.
2. Discuss the advantages and disadvantages in a large organization of the EDP department reporting to:
   a) the Comptroller (who reports to the V.P. Administration),
   b) the Vice President of Finance,
   c) the President.
3. Within an EDP department, what functions should be segregated? Why?
4. In many EDP departments, machine operators train to become computer programmers and then systems analysts. What are the implications of this job progression on internal control?
5. What is a data centre co-ordination group? What should be its responsibilities? What functions should it not perform? Why?
6. Why are standards required for systems development and computer programming? Give examples of such standards.
7. What is the purpose of testing systems and programs? Describe the four stages of testing commonly used.
8. What are the objectives of operations controls?
9. Discuss the responsibilities of the data control group. What EDP functions should be segregated from the data control group? Why?
10. I. Beem, Manager of the EDP department of Reed-n-weep Co., is responsible for supervising the computer operations personnel. The computer room operates three shifts daily. Suggest some of the methods he may use to supervise his staff properly.
11. Discuss control techniques that will minimize the risk of accidental or intentional destruction of EDP resources.
12. Reed-n-weep Co.'s management committee has asked I. Beem, the EDP manager, what would be the procedures should there be a partial or complete failure in the computer system.

    Outline, with a few brief comments on each, the points that should be included in I. Beem's report.
13. What are the four types of processing controls and the objectives of each?
14. Outline techniques which may be used to ensure adequate data control.
15. What is the purpose of an error control log?
16. Small businesses sometimes have their own computer facilities or service bureau arrangements. As mentioned in Chapter 7, there are compensating controls which can be instituted in a small business to offset the lack of individual

systems internal controls. What compensating controls should be considered in setting up an EDP function in a small business? Consider all phases of the EDP installation.

Problems

1. (CICA adapted) Sophisticated Ltd. has been adhering to a company policy of increasingly computerizing the financial accounting and management information records. The comptroller of Sophisticated recently approached N. Henderson, CA, with a problem which was affecting this policy. He indicated to Henderson that the Data Processing Department personnel were becoming flippant and arrogant, that they appeared to see their department as being separate from the rest of the company and beyond reproach. The comptroller suggested that this situation points out the need for greater control over compliance with management policy, better safeguards against possible destruction of data and an overall review of the computerization policy.

Accordingly, the comptroller asked Henderson the following questions:
   a) What methods should be used for continuous monitoring of the operations of a Data Processing Department to ensure compliance with management's policies and objectives?
   b) What steps could be taken to ensure that only authorized use is made of the computer?
   c) What procedures could be used to ensure the adequacy of security and protection of confidential data such as customer lists, executive payrolls, etc?
   d) What steps could be taken to guard against malicious destruction of magnetic records?
   e) What procedures should be implemented to ensure that development efforts are made only for the most worthwhile systems?

   What would be Henderson's replies to the above questions?

2. You are a member of Sure Co. Ltd.'s EDP steering committee. This committee had been requested to conduct a feasibility study with respect to computerizing the inventory control system of Sure Co.

   The study was completed two weeks previously, and the management committee of Sure Co. has authorized the data service centre alternative.

   Since you are a member of the EDP steering committee and dealt specifically with the data service centre alternative, the management committee has authorized you to negotiate the contract. You are to present it to the board for final approval in two weeks time.

What features would you ensure be stipulated in the contract between Sure Co. Ltd. and the service centre?

3. Mary DeSoto, accounts payable supervisor, working for a large used car, wrecker and used parts company for the past ten years, has been informed by the comptroller, O. Hudson, CA, that the manual accounts payable system will be replaced in 10 days time by a computerized system which the company has gone to considerable expense to develop. O. Hudson points out that the new system is much easier, processing time will be reduced and the system has been documented in great detail, Mary DeSoto is given a procedural manual outlining the new system and is told to learn the system and train her employees accordingly. She is assured by the comptroller that her job will be less time consuming but it will still be very important. Four of her seven employees have been given their termination notices effective in two weeks.

   Mary considers the situation and tenders her resignation the next day.
   a) What should Hudson have done differently in his dealings with Mary DeSoto?
   b) What should the company's computer steering committee have done?

4. (CICA adapted) A Wholesaling Ltd., a company in the hardware, plumbing and electrical supply business, has sales offices and regional warehouses across Canada. The company has had a data processing department at its head office for many years. The department has grown from a small unit-record installation through a second-generation computer until, during the current year, the company took delivery of a new third-generation machine.

   The computer has a 128K core and a disk operating system. Four tape drives, two disk drives (one a spare), a high-speed printer and a card reader/punch are hooked to the computer. The installation is operating reasonably well, though the computer has been down somewhat more than expected and the printer has had a number of problems. Because the department personnel are still getting used to the new machine, operator intervention in production runs (through the console typewriter) has been frequent, but this situation is expected to correct itself before long.

   The department's other data processing equipment consists of various old but serviceable unit record machines and more than a dozen new key punches and verifiers. Some of the computer's data input is prepared at the computer centre, but the company's sales branches and warehouses also prepare data input, using key-operated machines which prepare magnetic tape directly. The tape reels are mailed to the computer centre by each branch and warehouse. (These keytape machines were installed at the same time as the new computer – previously the sales branches and warehouses had prepared their data on punched paper tape, sending the paper tape to the centre for processing just as the magnetic tape is now processed.) The information from the branches and warehouses is transferred to accumulating "transaction" tapes at the computer centre, for later use in updating master files.

Most of the department's personnel have been with the company for several years, but the two programmers and the departmental manager joined the company in the current year. The programmers have been occupied mainly in changing the company's programs over to the new computer configuration; they have had little time to devote to developing new programs. (The computer is used almost entirely for routine accounting processing; a major reason for the acquisition of the new computer was to expand its use into the provision of management information.)

Because the new computer is much faster than the previous one and because the company has not yet developed programs or systems to utilize its capabilities fully, the company uses it only about 50 hours a week. A small unrelated computer services company (in which the new data processing department manager has an interest) is therefore allowed to use the installation during evenings and on weekends, paying by the hour for the approximately 25 hours a week it uses the installation.

a) What problems have been or may have been created for A Wholesaling Ltd. by allowing the computer services company to use the installation and how could each problem be overcome?
b) Outline a set of procedures that would ensure that the information on the accumulating "transactions" tapes is accurate and complete.
c) Assume that you are the auditor of A Wholesaling Ltd. Given the above situation, explain briefly the particular aspects of your work that should be emphasized in your audit examination for the current year. Do not give detailed procedures, and ignore the matters you referred to in parts (a) and (b) above.
5. (CICA adapted) CA is comptroller of W. Ltd., a medium-sized diversified manufacturing company with several manufacturing plants and sales offices and an administrative head office. The company has been approached by IMR Ltd., a computer manufacturer, with a proposal that a computerized system be installed to handle all the company's accounting, production, inventory, sales and other records. Several of the company's senior managers, including CA, are interested in the proposal because the company's records (some of which are produced by unit-record equipment) are scattered throughout the company's plants and offices and do not provide the rapid, timely control information that the managers would like to have.

A task force, of which CA is a member, has been established to determine the feasibility of installing a computer. If it is decided that a computer is feasible, the task force will then complete the detailed system design.
a) How should the task force go about determining the feasibility of installing a computer system for the company?
b) What matters likely to be within the comptroller's jurisdiction should be considered in the detailed system design?
6. (CICA adapted) CA has been the auditor for a number of years of R Ltd., a large merchandising concern which carries over 50 000 different items in inventory. During the current fiscal year the company has completed the installation of a sophisticated computer system for inventory control.

The computer system utilizes magnetic disks which facilitate random access processing. All pertinent data relating to individual items of inventory are carried on the magnetic disks.

The system is equipped with fifteen remote inquiry terminals, distributed at various locations throughout the operations. Using these terminals, employees can inquire into the computer system to determine the current status of any inventory item. An inquiry is entered into the system with a typewriter which is hooked into the computer. The inventory is relayed back instantaneously on the same typewriter. The inventory records on the disks are updated via the remote terminals as stock movements occur.
a) Describe the effect of the new computer system on CA's present audit approach, which was developed for use with the previous manual system.
b) Without describing the techniques involved, outline the steps CA should take before developing new audit procedures for the computerized inventory control system.

The Interim Audit

The concept of an efficient structure of the audit, leading to the common division of the annual audit into two major components, referred to in this book as the *Interim audit* and the *financial statement audit*, was introduced in Chapter 6. In most engagements such a division permits overall audit objectives to be fulfilled in the most efficient and timely manner. The purpose of this chapter is to discuss the objectives, underlying concepts, basic elements, and various methods of organization of the first component, the interim audit. A detailed step-by-step description of interim audit procedures may be found in Chapters 24 to 30.

9.1 Objectives of the interim audit and relationship to internal control

9.1.1 Primary objectives of the interim audit

Taken together, the interim audit and the financial statement audit must fulfill the primary objectives of the audit as a whole. How these objectives should be divided between the interim audit and the financial statement audit components is a question of efficiency. While some internal controls on which reliance is to be placed can be reviewed at any time, others should be observed while they are operating. The underlying accounting records, which provide some evidence supporting the financial statements, are produced throughout the period covered by the statements and can be verified either after or during that period. Where audit work can be done during the year, however, this timing is usually desirable since client deadlines and the seasonal peaking of audit workloads often do not permit leaving all verification to the year-end. Accordingly, a useful division of objectives is to assign to the interim audit the objectives of reviewing and evaluating most systems and controls, determining the accuracy and reliability of the accounting records, and conducting some substantive verification, while leaving most substantive procedures for the financial statement audit. Primary objectives of the interim audit can therefore be defined as:

1. To determine
   a) through a review and evaluation of the accounting system and other relevant internal controls, and
   b) through either compliance verification of the existence, effectiveness and continuity of operation of those controls on which reliance is to be placed or substantive verification of internal evidence,
   the accuracy and reliability of the accounting records and the appropriateness of the accounting methods followed, and thus to provide a basis for planning the timing, nature and extent of substantive procedures necessary to support an opinion of the financial statements; and
2. To perform those substantive procedures which can most usefully be commenced at an interim date.
   These objectives are illustrated diagrammatically in Figure 9.a.[1]

The four basic elements

The primary objectives imply, in turn, four basic elements in any interim audit:
- review,
- evaluation,
- compliance verification,
- substantive verification.

Each of these four elements is discussed in one of the following sections of this chapter.

The *review* element consists in ascertaining what the accounting systems are. *Evaluation* includes deciding what reliance may properly be placed on internal controls. Where controls are identified as reliable and the auditor plans to place reliance on them, he must obtain evidence corroborating their existence and functioning through *compliance verification*. Alternatively, where controls are not reliable, or where it is not economical to conduct the compliance verification necessary to justify reliance, the auditor may be able to make a preliminary assessment of the accuracy and reliability of the accounting records through *substantive verification* of internal evidence (documents, books of account, and other records). In addition, it may be useful to start, during the interim audit, certain further substantive procedures otherwise required in the financial statement audit.

Relationship to internal control

The first three elements of review, evaluation and compliance verification are all related in part to internal control. That relationship is reflected in the second field work standard:

> There should be an appropriately organized study and evaluation of those internal controls on which the auditor subsequently relies in determining the nature, extent and timing of auditing procedures.

The term "study" in the standard comprehends both review and compliance verification.

> The study to be made as the basis for the evaluation of internal control includes two phases: (a) knowledge and understanding of the procedures and methods prescribed and (b) a reasonable degree of assurance that

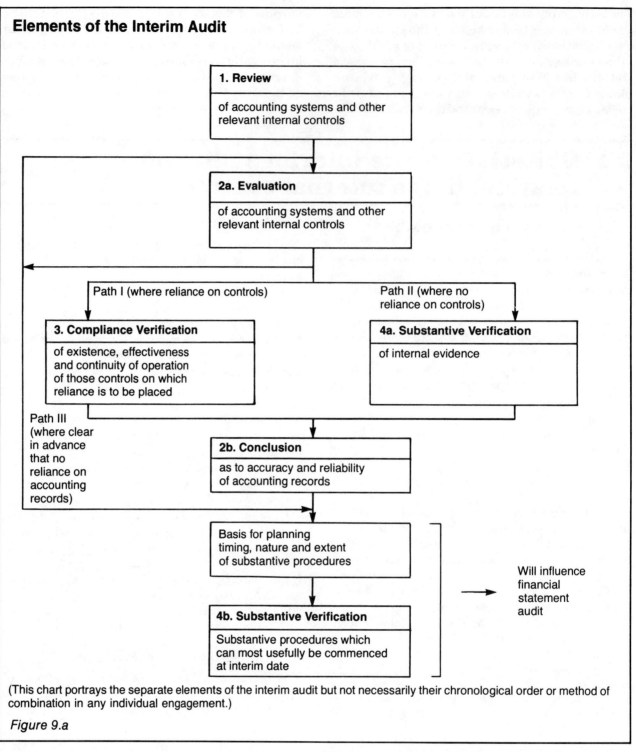

Elements of the Interim Audit

1. Review

of accounting systems and other relevant internal controls

2a. Evaluation

of accounting systems and other relevant internal controls

Path I (where reliance on controls)

Path II (where no reliance on controls)

3. Compliance Verification

of existence, effectiveness and continuity of operation of those controls on which reliance is to be placed

4a. Substantive Verification

of internal evidence

Path III (where clear in advance that no reliance on accounting records)

2b. Conclusion

as to accuracy and reliability of accounting records

Basis for planning timing, nature and extent of substantive procedures

Will influence financial statement audit

4b. Substantive Verification

Substantive procedures which can most usefully be commenced at interim date

(This chart portrays the separate elements of the interim audit but not necessarily their chronological order or method of combination in any individual engagement.)

Figure 9.a

they are in use and are operating as planned. These two phases of the study are referred to as the review of the system and tests of compliance, respectively. [2]

Compliance verification is related exclusively to internal control. Review and evaluation relate not only to specific controls but also to accounting systems and accounting records in a broader context, as will be discussed. The fourth element, substantive verification, is not related directly to internal control

or to the second field work standard but rather to specific figures on the financial statements and to the third field work standard. Nonetheless, it is influenced by the results of the evaluation of internal control.

Relationship to risk

In Chapter 6, the total risk of undetected misstatements in the financial statements was analyzed into inherent risk, control risk and audit risk. The elements of review and evaluation include some assessment of the inherent risk. The elements of review, evaluation and compliance verification lead to an assessment of the control risk. The element of substantive verification requires the choice of an appropriate level of audit risk so as, when combined with inherent risk and control risk, to yield an acceptably low level of total risk.

Audit strategies

The four elements, review, evaluation, compliance verification and substantive verification, do not occur as separate, mutually exclusive steps in the interim audit. Some degree of compliance verification is inevitably combined with review. Evaluation involves each of (a) evaluation of internal control as reviewed, (b) assessment of the results of compliance verification, and (c) assessment of the results of substantive verification. Substantive procedures may on occasion be combined with compliance procedures to become dual-purpose procedures. The question of the relative emphasis to be given to each of these four elements, the best method of performing each element, and the manner in which the four elements should be combined is one of audit strategy.

Audit strategies naturally tend to be a matter of individual preference. Considerable variation exists within the profession. Indeed, such variation is a healthy situation, for it means that new approaches are continually being explored. Unlike accounting principles, where some restriction of alternatives is an essential goal in the interests of clarity and comparability, there is less need for auditing procedures to be uniform from practitioner to practitioner. Auditing objectives remain the same, but the methods of achieving them can vary.

To cover these differences adequately, each section of this chapter dealing with one of the four elements discusses the alternative means of its performance. Then, at the end of the chapter, different audit strategies for combining these four elements are considered. Three different strategies, (a) a systems-oriented approach, (b) a data-oriented approach, and (c) in rare cases, omission of the interim audit stage entirely, are each discussed and criteria for choosing among them depending on the surrounding circumstances are suggested.

9.1.2 Secondary objective of the interim audit

While the primary objectives of the interim audit are directed toward the attest function of expressing an opinion on the financial statements, most auditors combine certain collateral services with their regular annual audit work. During the review and evaluation stages of the interim audit the auditor may observe

(1) an expenditure control which could be improved by segregating the functions of ordering and approval, (2) a billing system which could be made more efficient by using order-invoice multiple documents, (3) cash flow projections which could be improved to facilitate financial planning, (4) savings which could be achieved by changing the basis of accruing interest income for tax purposes, or (5) an accounting presentation which could be made more meaningful by segmenting income results by line of business. Passing on such observations to management can be a useful and inexpensive by-product of the review and evaluation work required to meet the primary objectives in any case.

Thus, a secondary objective of the interim audit can be defined as:

> To identify opportunities and provide timely suggestions for improvements in internal control, systems efficiency, financial or tax planning, and accounting methods to the extent that such identification and provision can be combined conveniently with the procedures required under the primary objectives or to the extent that such suggestions are requested by the client.

While the primary objectives (which contribute to attest function) are mandatory, the secondary objective (providing useful suggestions) is discretionary unless specifically covered in the terms of the auditor's engagement. It is important to distinguish between the two sets of objectives. No amount of useful suggestions for improving systems efficiency will compensate for a deficiency in the auditor's examination to support his opinion on the financial statements. Conversely, careful substantiation of the audit opinion will not in itself ensure, for example, that useful tax suggestions have not been overlooked. No amount of reporting of control deficiencies to the client will compensate for failure to allow for such deficiencies in designing the audit program. Conversely, designing the audit program to allow properly for observed control deficiencies will not compensate for failure to report those deficiencies to the client.

Procedures serving the discretionary secondary objective which are additional to those already required under the mandatory primary objectives can be classified into three types:

1. the reporting to management of opportunities for improvements (but not necessarily methods of achieving those improvements) which were identified in the course of the examination required to meet the primary attest objectives.
2. the additional work to identify other opportunities for improvements apart from those already identified in the course of the attest work,
3. the additional work to develop useful suggestions with respect to opportunities for improvements already identified.

Reporting of opportunities already identified

Where opportunities for significant improvements have already been observed, and where some improvement appears desirable and practicable (although finding the specific remedy may call for further study), most auditors would as a matter of course report the opportunities to management. The system for handling back-orders may be unnecessarily cumbersome. Control of scrap sales may warrant further study. Though the best cure may not be immediately evident, pointing out the disease observed is itself a worthwhile service. The incremental cost is negligible (mere documentation of the points observed). Clearly, it makes good sense to provide this service. Reporting of opportunities for practicable improvements would usually be omitted only where the points were completely trivial or where the auditor's observations might not be meaningful because the matter lies outside his field of competence.

Where the auditor is not sure whether any improvement is practicable, he may still wish to draw the point to management's attention so that it can be investigated. This is particularly true in the case of control deficiencies. Even where no improvement seems practicable (because the cost of control appears to outweigh the risk of error), it may be desirable to document the control deficiency so that management can consciously make the cost/risk decision involved.

Identification of additional opportunities

In most audit engagements, there are some enquiries so closely related to the systems review required for attest purposes that even though the additional enquiries do not affect the audit opinion they may be convenient to include as part of the regular annual audit. Such enquiries might, for example, include a review of insurance coverage, a consideration of tax planning points, or a brief survey of program documentation in a computer system. These enquiries are not required for compliance with generally accepted auditing standards but they can provide a useful service to management at a negligible cost. Of course, the extent of the search for other opportunities for improvements will depend upon what is useful and desired in the circumstances. Most annual audits include a certain number of such enquiries.

Developing suggestions

In many cases, the method for improving a particular element of internal control, systems efficiency, financial or tax planning, or accounting will be obvious

and the auditor will not only report the problem but suggest the cure. In other cases, useful suggestions can be developed with a minimum amount of additional work and most auditors would undertake this additional work as an integral part of their audit program. In yet other cases, however, the development of useful suggestions may require considerable investigation. The auditor may then merely report the problem, recommending its investigation. Usually he would then undertake the additional study of its solution only if specifically requested by the client.

Again, it is important to distinguish additional services provided under the discretionary secondary objective of the interim audit from the attest procedures required under the mandatory primary objective.

> Although constructive suggestions to clients for improvements in internal control incident to an audit engagement are desirable, the scope of any additional study made to develop such suggestions is not covered by generally accepted auditing standards. The scope of an auditor's study pursuant to a special engagement will depend upon the terms of the engagement. [3]

Internal control/management letter

The secondary objective of the interim audit leads to the common and desirable practice of issuing an internal control/management letter to the client at the conclusion of the interim audit. The preparation, review and issue of such letters are discussed in Chapter 19.

9.1.3 Additional reporting responsibility of the auditor

While the secondary objective of the interim audit has been described as discretionary, certain responsibilities of the auditor beyond the expression of an audit opinion are important to observe.

Responsibility to report significant errors or irregularities encountered

As discussed in Chapter 4, if the auditor encounters significant errors or irregularities in the course of his audit he has a duty to report them to his client. This duty does not imply that the auditor is responsible for *finding* all errors or irregularities. Some errors or irregularities may not be of a nature or amount which affect the fairness of presentation of the financial statements. Audit procedures required under generally accepted auditing standards are not directed to the discovery of such items, although their discovery may sometimes occur during the audit.

Even errors or irregularities which do affect the statement presentation to a material extent may in some cases have arisen from events whose occurrence was properly judged by the auditor to be remote. As discussed in Chapter 6, the audit cannot provide absolute assurance that all material distortions of the financial statements have been detected. Rather it is designed to provide a reasonable degree of assurance. In deciding what is a reasonable degree of assurance in any individual case, the auditor must consider the imminence or remoteness of the risk of error or fraud as well as the strength of related internal controls (see 6.8.1). Situations will occasionally occur where the remote event did in fact occur or where the reasonable level of audit assurance, being less than absolute assurance, did not lead to the detection of the misstatement. Provided that the auditor's procedures were properly designed, in the light of circumstances known at the time, to provide a reasonable level of audit assurance, such situations are not evidence of negligence on the auditor's part.

> The subsequent discovery that fraud existed during the period covered by the independent auditor's examination does not of itself indicate negligence on his part. He is not an insurer or guarantor; if his examination was made with due professional skill and care in accordance with generally accepted auditing standards, he has fulfilled all of the obligations implicit in his undertaking. [4]

But whether or not the auditor's examination could reasonably have been expected to detect certain errors or irregularities, if it does in fact detect them the auditor has a duty to report them to his client.

Responsibility to report suspicious circumstances encountered

The auditor's professional duty extends beyond reporting actual errors and irregularities to reporting suspicious circumstances suggestive of fraud.

> Where the auditor encounters irregularities, or specific circumstances that make him suspect that fraud or other irregularities may have occurred, additional auditing procedures may be necessary. Such procedures would be necessary if the circumstances indicate that the irregularity could be material and therefore affect the auditor's opinion. In practice the auditor may reach an understanding with the client that the client would carry out part of the detailed investigation work, subject to the auditor's review. If, on the other hand, the circumstances indicate that the irregularity could not be material and therefore would not affect the auditor's opinion, he may simply refer the matter to the proper representatives of the client with the recommendation that it be pursued to a conclusion. Where the circumstances are such that the auditor suspects that fraud or other irregularities have occurred, he should notify the client on a timely basis. [5]

Responsibility to report significant weaknesses in control where improvement is practicable

Whether the auditor's professional responsibility also extends to the reporting of weaknesses in internal control is a matter of opinion. In the writer's view, where the auditor has encountered significant weaknesses in control during the course of his audit, and where he believes that improvement is practicable and desirable, he should recognize a professional duty to report those weaknesses to his client.

Again, this duty does not imply that the auditor is responsible for finding all weaknesses in internal control. But where the auditor's examination has in fact detected significant and curable weaknesses, he should report them to his client. As stated in Chapter 4, many auditors issue engagement letters in which they undertake a contractual responsibility for such reporting.

This responsibility does not go as far as all possible work contemplated under the discretionary secondary objective discussed earlier. Under that objective an auditor might, at his discretion, decide that it was desirable to report minor weaknesses as well as significant ones, to report apparently incurable weaknesses as well as curable ones, to search for control weaknesses unrelated to his audit opinion, and to report opportunities for improvements outside the field of internal control. Whatever an auditor decides under this discretionary objective, however, he should recognize a reporting responsibility with respect to significant errors, irregularities, suspicious circumstances, or curable control weaknesses already encountered.

The additional reporting responsibility just discussed may be stated as follows:

> To advise the client of any significant errors, irregularities or suspicious circumstances encountered and, to the extent that improvement appears desirable and practicable, of any significant weakness observed in the system of internal control.

9.1.4 Accuracy and reliability of accounting records

The primary objectives of the interim audit, as previously defined, focus on the determination of the accuracy and reliability of the accounting records. Depending on the circumstances, this determination may be made either (a) by performing compliance verification of the existence, effectiveness and continuity of operation of those controls on which reliance is to be placed or (b) by performing substantive verification of internal evidence (documents, books of account, and other records). A given interim audit may include one or both of these methods (the choice was discussed in 6.7). Where it is possible to gain reasonable assurance that the accounting records are accurate and reliable, by whichever method, the persuasiveness of evidence sought through the later substantive verification of each financial statement figure can be reduced - though not eliminated. Of course, where the conclusion concerning the sales accounting records has come from substantive tests of sales transactions it is not necessary to repeat the same tests in substantiating the sales figure on the income statement; nonetheless, additional substantive verification of sales will generally be required through scrutiny and analytical review as well as through overlapping verification of beginning-of-year and year-end assets.

In some engagements, of course, the accounting records will be found to be inaccurate or unreliable. In such cases a very high degree of persuasiveness must be sought in the substantive verification of each financial statement figure. More usually, the inaccuracy or unreliability is restricted to a certain area of the records and the very high degree of persuasiveness is then required for the substantive verification of only the statement figures related to that area.

Effect of internal controls on the auditor's evaluation of the accounting records

The foregoing discussion shows that internal controls will have an influence on the auditor's evaluation of accuracy and reliability of the accounting records when both of the following conditions are present:

1. the internal controls in question have a material effect on the accuracy and reliability of the accounting records
2. the alternative of performing sufficient substantive verification to avoid the need for reliance on controls is not available, too slow, or more costly than performing compliance verification of the controls.

Internal controls of attest significance

Internal controls that affect the accuracy and reliability of the accounting records may be said to be of *attest significance* because they have a potential impact on the auditor's attest procedures. Controls of attest significance will have an actual impact on the auditor's attest procedures when the effect of the controls on the accuracy and reliability of the accounting records is material and the auditor chooses to or must place reliance on them. In Chapter 7 it was explained that the responsibility for establishing and maintaining adequate internal controls rests with management

and various management objectives of internal control were identified. Some of these objectives include or affect the accuracy and reliability of the accounting records, in which case the interests of management and the attest objectives of the auditor overlap. Other management objectives of internal control (such as minimization of unnecessary costs) do not affect the accuracy and reliability of the accounting records. Controls serving solely these latter objectives may be said to be of *not-of-attest significance*. The auditor's interest in such controls arises solely from his role as adviser (discretionary secondary objective) and not from his role as auditor (mandatory primary objective).

9.1.5 Analysis of internal controls by attest and not-of-attest significance

In sections 7.3 to 7.9 seven basic control elements were discussed. An analysis of the attest or not-of-attest significance of each of these control elements follows.

Organizational controls

The honesty and competence of personnel and the segregation of incompatible functions are of direct attest significance. To the extent that the overall plan of organization and the accounting/finance organization plan are an extension of these concepts they are likewise of attest significance. However, many organizational controls are designed to improve efficiency. Controls exclusively for this purpose will not be of attest significance.

Systems development controls

Systems development controls in manual systems are usually not of direct attest significance. Here the auditor usually places reliance on the final systems in operation and not on the methods for developing such systems in the first place. Of course, he will want his client to develop good systems and therefore to have adequate systems development controls. But if he has verified the operation of the final system it is not necessary, for the purpose of meeting attest objectives, to evaluate the adequacy of systems development controls. In larger computer systems it may sometimes be desirable for the auditor to place reliance on certain systems development controls (usually controls over computer program changes). In these cases (discussed in Chapter 27) the systems development controls in question will be of attest significance.

Authorization and reporting controls

Authorization and reporting controls are generally of attest significance. Proper authorizations and approvals add assurance that the recorded transactions are legitimate and properly accounted for. Budgetary controls add assurance that bookkeeping errors will be detected through variance analysis and corrected. Authorization and reporting controls serve other management objectives as well - limiting wasteful expenditures, avoiding risky transactions, etc. Usually they do not serve these latter objectives exclusively but rather jointly with the objective of ensuring accurate records.

Accounting systems controls

Most accounting systems controls are of direct attest significance. Of particular importance are controls to ensure that all transactions are initially recorded. If such controls are lacking the auditor must find more persuasive substantive evidence than otherwise as to the completeness of recorded transactions. Sometimes such other evidence is available. Examples are (a) the independent reconciliation of sales or purchase volumes with confirmations obtained from a few customers or suppliers accounting for most of the company's business and (b) the reconciliation of rental income with the contractual provisions of long-term leases. In many cases such evidence is not available. Where controls over the initial recording of transactions, generally or in a certain significant area, are inadequate and the auditor lacks an alternative means of gaining assurance as to the completeness of recorded transactions, he will be unable to express a clear opinion.

Additional safeguarding controls

The safeguarding of assets does not as such affect the accuracy of the accounting records. Accordingly, additional safeguarding controls are not directly of attest significance. If the auditor has verified inventory at the balance sheet date, the fact that poor safeguarding controls leave inventories open to the risk of pilferage does not invalidate the year-end financial statement presentation. Permitting poor safeguarding controls may be an imprudent decision on the part of management but it does not in itself misstate the balance sheet. Nonetheless, situations may often occur where certain safeguarding controls become indirectly of attest significance. If the auditor verifies cash, accounts receivable or inventories at dates prior to the year-end he may have to place some reliance on safeguarding controls to ensure that assets have not been lost or stolen in material amount between the verification date and the year-end. Moreover, where there could otherwise be a chance of asset losses so great that they would require disclosure as a "subsequent event", the auditor may have to place reliance on safeguarding controls for the period between the year-end and the date of his audit report.

Management supervisory controls

Many management supervisory controls are of attest significance. The supervisory function performed by senior officials acting as signing officers is certainly of attest significance. In large organizations an internal audit function can influence the external auditor's work significantly. In small organizations, the close personal supervision exercised by the manager of the business may influence the external auditor's work where controls through division of duties are necessarily limited.

Documentation controls

Documentation controls are generally not of direct attest significance. Indirectly, documentation may affect the auditor in that the absence of clearly documented instructions may lead to errors in the performance of other control procedures. However, if the auditor has been able to satisfy himself that a given control procedure has operated effectively throughout the year, he need not, for attest purposes, study the adequacy of its documentation. Permitting poor systems documentation may be an imprudent decision on the part of management but it does not in itself misstate the financial statements.

Auditor interest in controls of not-of-attest significance

This analysis is not intended to imply that the external auditor is indifferent to whether his client maintains adequate controls which are of not-of-attest significance. In his role as adviser (discretionary secondary objective) he will be alert for opportunities for improvements in such controls. But his discretionary review, verification and evaluation of these controls can be less rigorous than his review, verification and evaluation of attest controls on which his work as auditor (mandatory primary objective) depends.

9.1.6 Reasons for audit reliance on internal controls

While not all internal controls are of attest significance and while not all controls of attest significance may warrant audit reliance, it is common in most audit engagements for the auditor to place reliance on at least some controls. Reasons which would influence the auditor to place reliance on the review, evaluation, and compliance verification of a particular control are given in the five following cases. The importance of each of these five reasons varies from engagement to engagement.

1. Reducing substantive verification as to existence and ownership

Reliance on certain controls may enable the auditor to reduce the extent of (or the quality of evidence sought in) the substantive verification of the existence and ownership (or incidence) of recorded assets (or liabilities). [6] Extensive substantive verification will usually still be required, but less than what would have been required without reliance on control. For example, confirmation of accounts receivable with customers and reconciliation of accounts payable with suppliers' statements are important audit steps whatever the system of internal control. Where the related controls are strong, however, it may be possible to reduce the number of confirmations or suppliers' statements selected. Cash counts and detailed checking of year-end bank reconciliations provide better quality evidence as to the existence of reported cash than do more restricted procedures. Where the related controls are strong, however, the more restricted procedures may be warranted.

This reason for placing reliance on controls, where warranted, applies to most engagements. An exception is where reported assets and liabilities consist of so few individual accounts that 100% examination is both convenient and desirable.

2. Reducing substantive verification as to completeness

Reliance on controls over the initial recording of transactions may enable the auditor to minimize the extent of substantive verification of the completeness of recorded assets and liabilities. [7] In the presence of good control, substantive procedures for undisclosed assets, such as unbilled shipments, can usually be limited to analytical review procedures. Because of the usually greater risk of undisclosed liabilities (and the greater harm usually caused by these misstatements when they occur), certain detailed substantive procedures for detecting undisclosed liabilities are common even when control is good; where control is poor such procedures would usually need to be increased.

This reason for placing reliance on controls, where warranted, applies to most engagements. An exception is where some simple form of external evidence (such as reconciliation of membership fee revenue with the number of members in a club) permits ready verification of the completeness of recorded transactions.

3. Reducing substantive verification as to valuation

Reliance on controls over cost records or other detailed accounting records may enable the auditor to minimize the extent of substantive verification of asset and liability values derived from those records. [8] Thus, the verification of the value of manufactured goods will be influenced by the extent to which the auditor can rely on the accuracy with which material, labour and overhead costs were correctly allocated to production throughout the year and are fairly reflected in unit costs or standard costs maintained by the cost department.

This reason for placing reliance on controls, where warranted, applies only to engagements involving cost systems (manufacturers and processors rather than wholesalers and retailers) or those involving other asset or liability values derived from detailed accounting records.

4. Relying on accounting records during "roll-forward" periods

Reliance on the accuracy and reliability of the accounting records is required during the "roll-forward period" between the date of pre-year-end verification of assets and liabilities and the year-end. Inventories may be counted several months before the year-end. Accounts receivable are often confirmed one or two months before the year-end. Other possible pre-year-end verification is discussed in Chapter 11. Although special roll-forward procedures are required to provide additional substantive evidence of the continuing accuracy of the accounting records during these periods, considerable reliance on internal control is usually essential. In fact, where control is poor the auditor may not be in a position to express an unqualified opinion unless all important assets and liabilities are verified at the year-end itself.

This reason for placing reliance on controls, where warranted, applies to most engagements where management chooses to do pre-year-end physical stocktaking or where an early reporting deadline requires that the auditor perform pre-year-end verification of important assets or liabilities.

5. Limiting substantive verification of income components

Reliance on certain controls may enable the auditor to limit his substantive verification of major income statement components to analytical review, scrutiny, enquiry, and comparison. The fact that verification of the opening and closing balance sheets for the year provides considerable assurances as to the year's reported net income means that less persuasive substantive evidence as to the income components themselves can suffice provided that internal control is adequate. Where internal control is poor, however, detailed substantive tests of documentary evidence supporting sales, purchases and expenses may be required.

This reason for placing reliance on controls, where warranted, applies to many engagements. Exceptions are (a) where the cost of performing the review, evaluation and compliance procedures is greater than the additional cost of more extensive substantive verification of internal evidence or (b) where economical third party evidence as to income statement components is readily available. The degree of reliance on controls will also vary depending on the degree of detail disclosed in the income statement. Where revenues and expenses are analyzed in some detail, and particularly where operating results are segmented by line of business, the need for reliance on internal controls will usually be greater.

Varying impact of the five reasons

In a few cases, the inapplicability of all the foregoing factors will eliminate the need for an interim audit entirely. For a privately owned investment company, for example, sufficient substantive verification can normally be performed directly at the year-end with little or no reliance on internal control. In such engagements a brief review of internal control can be included in the year-end work and no interim audit visit is necessary. Usually, however, these five reasons (or their absence) do not apply to the engagement as a whole but to the verification of particular financial statement figures within the engagement. Thus, for example, the foregoing reasons for interim audit work may be present in the case of receivables and payables but absent in the case of temporary investments, prepaid expenses, accrued liabilities and share capital.

9.2 Review of accounting systems and other relevant internal controls

The objective of the review element is to ascertain what the accounting systems are and to identify internal controls which may have a bearing on either the primary or secondary audit objectives. The review element usually contains two components (a) gaining overall familiarity and (b) identifying specific systems and controls.

Gaining overall familiarity

Gaining overall familiarity with the client's business, organization and systems is a necessary preparation for a more detailed identification of specific systems, procedures and controls.

> The auditor should have sufficient knowledge of the business carried on by the enterprise to know (a) the types of transactions normally conducted by it, and (b) what its accounting records are and what they are designed to record. [9]

Gaining overall familiarity involves enquiries (or updating of the answers to past enquiries) as to:

1. the nature of the business,
2. the overall plan of organization,
3. the accounting/finance organization plan,
4. the organization of other departments having a pervasive effect on the auditor's work (such as the internal audit department and the EDP department),
5. where applicable, general information as to the computer environment.

These enquiries may be supplemented by a review of industry data and various client summaries and or-

ganization charts, if they exist. The auditor may document the result of his enquiries by writing narrative notes, preparing organization charts, and/or answering preprinted questionnaires. Narrative notes and organization charts are probably the most common but questionnaires may be useful, particularly in documenting information as to the computer environment.

Identifying specific systems and controls

The purpose of identifying specific systems and controls is:

1. where reliance will be placed on the accuracy and reliability of the accounting records, to provide the basis for a formal evaluation of systems, controls and records, or
2. where reliance will not be placed on the accuracy and reliability of the accounting records, to provide the knowledge necessary for designing a coherent program of substantive procedures without that reliance.

This level of review procedures will include:

1. identification of procedures and controls related
   a) to each major accounting system (such as sales/ receivables/ receipts),
   b) to specific types of transactions (such as fixed asset purchases),
   c) to specific accounts (such as inventory).
2. where reliance will be placed thereon, a more intensive analysis of the activities of the internal audit and EDP departments.

In planning his audit, the auditor should make himself aware of the existence or non-existence of internal control systems on which he might intend to rely in determining the nature, extent and timing of other auditing procedures.

For each internal control system on which the auditor intends to rely, he should identify in an organized manner the particular internal controls within that system. [10]

Combination with other audit elements

In practice, the review element does not occur in complete isolation. The enquiries and direct observation included in the review process already constitute some degree of compliance verification. Other types of compliance verification such as the scrutiny of document files or the tracing of a few transactions of each type throughout the system can be conveniently combined with review procedures if the auditor wishes. More extended compliance or substantive tests of transactions may sometimes be combined with review procedures. To the extent that the review is intended to provide a basis for evaluating controls, the gathering of systems information may be guided by the nature of the evaluation questions to be ultimately answered. In this case, review and evaluation procedures are closely connected. Which other audit element is most closely combined with the review element, depends on which method of conducting and documenting the review is chosen by the auditor.

Four methods of review

The following four methods are common:

1. gathering information from tests of transactions,
2. seeking answers to questionnaires,
3. preparing or updating narrative systems notes,
4. preparing or updating flow charts.

It is rare, however, for only one of these methods to be used. Most practitioners use a combination of two or more of them, though the particular combination will depend on the preference or policies of the individual practitioner or firm. A discussion of each of these four methods follows.

9.2.1 Gaining information from tests of transactions

As a method by itself (where no reliance is placed on accounting records)

The least formal method of ascertaining the nature of the client's systems and controls is simply to start testing the transactions entered in the accounting records. If the auditor spends enough time checking the records he cannot help but learn something

about what is going on. On some (usually very small) engagements this may be the most direct and sensible approach. On other engagements, however, it may not be the most efficient method of gathering systems information.

Where tests of transactions are performed *exclusively* to meet review objectives (ascertainment of what the systems are), their extents can be considerably less than extents required to meet compliance or substantive objectives. This situation can arise when it is apparent that reliance cannot be placed on the accuracy and reliability of the accounting records (Path III in Figure 9.a). Here, transactional tests may be performed merely to gain enough information about the business and the systems that sensible substantive procedures can be designed later to substantiate each figure on the financial statements. Such transactional tests may consist of both (a) a reperformance of certain bookkeeping routines (recording, posting, trial balancing, summarizing, etc.) and (b) an examination of documentary evidence underlying the transactions recorded. The extents should be large enough to give the auditor the information he is seeking as to the systems, nature of operations, and different transaction types. Testing 10 or 20 or 30 items may be sufficient for this purpose in some cases (although as discussed in Chapter 12 such extents would usually be far too low to fulfill compliance or substantive test objectives). In other cases the reperformance of bookkeeping procedures related to a given book of original entry may need to cover an entire month in order to provide adequate systems knowledge of the different types of recurring transactions.

In combination with substantive verification (where no reliance is placed on controls)

More commonly, tests of transactions will not serve review objectives exclusively. For example, they may be designed to provide substantive verification of the accuracy and reliability of the accounting records in cases where little or no reliance is to be placed on internal control (Path II in Figure 9.a).

Combining review tests and substantive tests of transactions poses certain difficulties, however. As discussed later, the proper planning of substantive tests to establish the accuracy and reliability of accounting records requires a certain degree of systems knowledge to decide how far back one should trace the chain of documentary evidence supporting each entry. Advance planning cannot be done if the required systems information is itself being derived from the testing results. Either the auditor must conduct the review tests separately first or else employ some other review technique as well. These difficulties may not be significant in repeat engagements, provided that major systems changes have not occurred since the prior year.

In combination with compliance verification (where reliance is placed on controls)

Alternatively, review tests may sometimes be combined with compliance tests of transactions where reliance is to be placed on internal control (Path I in Figure 9.a). In the writer's view, this combination, *in the absence of other review techniques,* is not desirable[11] for several reasons.

First, tests to acquire systems knowledge may need to cover a broad range of transactions whereas compliance tests should be focussed on those specific controls on which reliance is to be placed. Attempting to combine the two may mean that either the range of the former is improperly narrowed or that of the latter unnecessarily broadened. Second, tests of transactions tend to focus on what was done rather than who did it. They do not, therefore, provide a very efficient means of ascertaining division of duties, information which will be needed to evaluate internal control properly. Third, tests of transactions deal with the accuracy of recorded transactions but provide no indication of the controls to ensure that all transactions were recorded in the first place, information which will again be needed to evaluate internal control properly. Fourth, and most importantly, tests of accounting procedures are by their very nature more directed to the procedures themselves than to controls. Many important controls are not evident from an inspection of the accounting documents alone. Thus, there is a danger that important controls not revealed by review tests will not be relied upon (which is inefficient) or that significant control deficiencies not revealed by review tests will not be allowed for (which is dangerous). Finally, information on controls obtained through tests of transactions alone is usually difficult for a subsequent reviewer of the audit working papers to assess and thus an important check of the quality of the audit work performed is lost.

Accordingly, when review tests are being conducted to ascertain what the client's controls are, other review techniques should usually be employed at the same time.

In combination with other review techniques

Tests of transactions for review purposes can be combined with, and indeed make a useful addition to, any of the other review techniques (questionnaires, narrative systems notes or flow charts). In such cases it is usually the other review technique which provides the principal and most coherent source of systems information and the review tests are added to ensure that the auditor does not waste time evaluating a "blueprint" system which never existed in practice or an out-of-date description of the system. To achieve this purpose, testing a very limited number of transactions *of each type* can suffice. Indeed, it can be argued that one example of each type of transaction is sufficient for this purpose. In the systems-oriented audit approach described at the end of this chapter the testing, instead, of four or five transactions of each type is suggested at the review stage merely to avoid the danger of the auditor mistaking particular conditions noted on one document for the general rule. In either case the one or the few transactions tested at the review stage can be noted in a column beside questionnaire answers or in the margin beside narrative systems notes or along the bottom of flow charts.

9.2.2 Seeking answers to questionnaires

As a method by itself (where reliance is placed on controls)

Internal control questionnaires are primarily a tool to aid the auditor in evaluating internal control, as discussed later, but they can also be used as a means of gathering systems information in the first place. Standardized internal control questionnaires consist of specific control questions requiring "yes", "no", or "not applicable" answers. The control questions may be structured by major account balance (sales, cash, fixed assets, etc.) or by major accounting subsystem (e.g., accounts receivable and customers' deposits). Where the questionnaire is to be used as the primary means of gathering systems information, the questions must necessarily be detailed and quite numerous. While the size and exact structure of standardized questionnaire varies with the individual practitioner or firm, a typical one, taken from the AICPA *Case Studies in Internal Control*, No. 2 (1950), is 164 questions long. A portion of that questionnaire is shown in Figure 9.b.

The questionnaire is completed as one of the first steps in the interim audit through enquiry of company officials and employees, a scrutiny of the accounting records and documents, and a review of company procedure manuals, if they exist.

In combination with other audit elements

Where detailed internal control questionnaires are used, the review and evaluation elements of the interim audit are closely connected. Some distinction may still occur in that the obtaining of questionnaire answers may sometimes be delegated to audit assistants but the answers obtained evaluated by more senior audit personnel.

The review and evaluation elements can also be combined with compliance verification by providing a column on the questionnaire to document the verification performed with respect to each answer obtained. The computer control evaluation guide presented in the CICA Study, _Computer Audit Guidelines_ (1975), represents an example of this combination. When this combination is used, care must be taken to ensure that time is not wasted performing compliance verification of controls on which reliance is not ultimately placed. Alternative means of coordinating review, evaluation and compliance verification are discussed later in this chapter.

Advantages and potential abuses of the questionnaire approach

There can be little doubt that some form of questionnaire is useful for evaluation purposes. Whether or not questionnaires are the best means also of gathering information on systems and controls in the first place is largely a matter of individual preference. Certainly, detailed internal control questionnaires have been widely and successfully used for many years throughout the profession to gather systems information. As an information-gathering technique, their use has the advantage of ensuring that important controls and important control deficiencies will not be overlooked (a problem when exclusive reliance is placed on tests of transactions as a source of information on controls).

Three potential abuses of questionnaires as an information-gathering technique may be mentioned,

Accounts Receivable and Customers' Deposits

1. Are the duties and functions of the accounts receivable bookkeepers or person supervising such bookkeepers completely segregated from the following duties or functions:
_____ (a) Handling any cash or performing any work on cash records?
_____ (b) Opening incoming mail?
_____ (c) Mailing or delivering statements to customers?
_____ (d) Ageing of accounts receivable?
_____ (e) Checking customers' statements to accounts receivable ledgers?
_____ (f) Investigation and follow-up of delinquent accounts receivable?
_____ (g) Settlement of accounts receivable items in question?
_____ (h) Approving the write-off of bad accounts?
_____ (i) Approving:
_____ (1) Discounts?
_____ (2) Allowances?
_____ (3) Refunds?
_____ (4) Other credits?
_____ 2. Are accounts receivable detail ledgers balanced with the control account each month?
_____ 3. Are accounts receivable ledgers balanced to the control account at frequent intervals by someone other than the accounts receivable bookkeeper?
_____ 4. Are the accounts aged regularly?
_____ 5. Are the aged accounts reviewed by an official?
_____ 6. Are detail ledger-keepers rotated occasionally?
_____ 7. Are monthly statements sent to all credit customers?
_____ 8. Is a check made to determine that no statements are mailed to the address of the accounts receivable bookkeepers other than statements of their own accounts?
_____ 9. Are detail balances occasionally confirmed by the customers directly to some employee not in the accounts receivable department?
_____ 10. Are bad debts controlled after their write-off?
11. Is approval of an official obtained for:
_____ (a) Write-off of bad accounts?
_____ (b) Discounts in excess of regular rates?
_____ (c) Allowances or adjustments?
_____ (d) Refunds?
_____ (e) Other credits?
_____ 12. Are all credit memos prenumbered?
_____ 13. If credits are for returned goods, do routine procedures provide for a check of receivers?

(From AICPA *Case Studies in Internal Control, Number 2 (1950)*)

Figure 9.b (concluded)

though they can be avoided with adequate training, care and supervision:

1. The very length of a detailed questionnaire can be a temptation to give it perfunctory treatment, such as:
   a) copying answers from last year's questionnaire,
   b) treating the completion of the questionnaire as a separate chore rather than an integral part of the audit,
   c) completing the questionnaire at the end of the audit (when the answers are better known) rather than at the beginning (when the answers can be used to determine the nature and extent of further auditing procedures).
2. The structure of a questionnaire can be a temptation to search for acceptable answers to questions rather than a coherent understanding of the underlying system:

a) Answers may be entered mechanically without adequate consideration of the importance of the question to overall audit objectives on the particular engagement.
b) Glib answers may be accepted from client personnel without sufficient investigation to establish that the auditor's understanding of the system is correct.
c) Incorrect answers entered by junior audit staff are difficult for a file reviewer to detect because inconsistencies in the piecemeal description of the system are not readily apparent.
3. The inflexibility of a standardized questionnaire may create difficulties when applied to an individual organization
   a) Junior audit staff may waste time searching for answers to standard questions which are irrelevant to that organization.

b) Alternatively, and worse, numerous standard questions may be answered "not applicable" because on the surface they appear inapplicable when analogous questions (for example, in terms of "services supplied" rather than "goods shipped") should really have been considered and answered.

The third potential abuse can be avoided on very large engagements by designing a questionnaire tailor-made for that particular client. This method is a good one, but usually too costly for medium-size and smaller engagements. In some cases a specialized questionnaire for a particular industry (such as stockbrokers, banks, or insurance companies) may be useful, although this solution may be difficult for auditors with smaller practices.

To point out potential abuses is not to categorize a method as impractical. Where the auditor uses a questionnaire as an information-gathering tool he will find it an advantage to be well aware of any potential abuses so that he can prevent them.

9.2.3 Preparing or updating narrative systems notes

As a method by itself

An alternative method of obtaining systems information is merely to start questioning the employees involved or reviewing procedure manuals they are supposed to follow and then to summarize the findings in narrative systems notes. In repeat years it is, of course, only necessary to update the prior year's systems notes. Systems notes describe the transactions of each type, how they are initiated, what documents are processed by whom, what approvals are required, and what accounting entries finally result. Systems notes may be maintained in separate systems files, together with copies of the client's standard documents, and carried forward for continued use in the audits of many successive years.

Advantages and disadvantages of narrative systems notes

Narrative systems notes have the advantage that they provide the auditor with a more coherent understanding of the system he is reviewing. At least in smaller systems, inconsistencies and omissions in the information obtained will be readily apparent and can be corrected. Thus, systems notes may provide a better foundation for the auditor's subsequent evaluation of controls.

Particularly in larger systems, however, narrative systems notes have a number of disadvantages. The component parts of a systems description extending over many pages may be difficult to integrate mentally. The inter-relationship between procedures described on different pages which may be of significance for control purposes, may not be apparent from merely reading the notes. Inconsistencies or omissions in the description of complex systems may be hard to detect. Annual updating may be cumbersome. Finally, the tendency many of us have to describe things in terms which seem clear to ourselves but ambiguous to others (as well as in handwriting which is indecipherable to most) can aggravate the foregoing problems.

Accordingly, preparing systems notes may be an efficient review technique for smaller systems or for isolated features in larger systems. It is less likely to be efficient for the complete documentation of larger systems or for the complexities common in computerized systems.

In combination with other review techniques

Mention has already been made of the possibility of supplementing narrative systems notes with limited review tests to ensure that the procedures described are actually in operation.

Limited narrative systems notes may also be a useful supplement to reviews conducted primarily by questionnaire or flow chart. In such cases, they may be used to describe systems features not specifically referred to in standardized questions on a questionnaire or to describe alternatives or exceptions inconvenient to include in flow charts of the major systems.

9.2.4 Preparing or updating flow charts

As a method by itself

Preparing or updating flow charts is an alternative to preparing narrative systems notes. Like narrative systems notes, flow charts are intended to provide the auditor with a coherent understanding of the system he is reviewing and thus to provide a foundation for his subsequent evaluation of controls.

Advantages and potential abuses of the flow chart approach

The advantages of a flow chart are the conciseness and clarity of a pictorial presentation. The use of flow charts minimizes the amount of narrative explanation required and thereby achieves a condensation of presentation of the client's system not possible in any other form. A flow chart gives a bird's-eye view of the system and can also provide an efficient method of documenting the auditor's checking of the system. It

Simplified Examples of Narrative and Flow Charting Review Methods

Narrative Description of Portion of Sales/Receivables System

When a shipment is made, the shipping department prepares a sales form. This form is in three copies. The first copy is sent out with the goods to the customer as a packing slip. The second copy is forwarded to the billing department. The third copy is sent to the accountant. When the billing department receives the second copy of the shipping order it uses the information thereon to prepare a two-part sales invoice. The second copy of the shipping order is then filed numerically in the billing department. The first copy of the sales invoice is sent to the customer. The second copy of the sales invoice is forwarded to the accountant. The accountant receives both the third copy of the shipping order and the second copy of the sales invoice. Periodically he matches these together and files them alphabetically by customer name. Before doing so, however, he uses the second copy of the sales invoice to post the sales entry in the subsidiary accounts receivable ledger.

Flow Chart of Portion of Sales/Receivables System

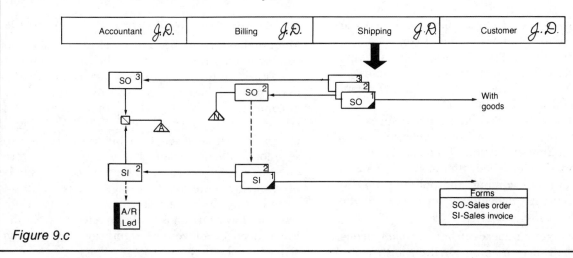

Figure 9.c

is more effective than the narrative approach in revealing inconsistencies or omissions in the systems information obtained. Flow charts make it easier for the auditor to integrate mentally the related parts of a complex system and to analyze the relationships between different procedures or transactions. They provide a discipline in the recording of systems information which facilitates the use of that information by other members of the audit team, by the file reviewers, and by next year's audit staff. Updating is also simplified.

An example of a flow chart of a portion of a sales/receivables system, compared to a narrative description of the same system, can be seen in Figure 9.c. Words have been reduced to a minimum. Yet at the same time the diagrammatic presentation will be immediately clear to most readers. Moreover, if an important piece of systems information had been omitted the omission would usually be readily detected by a review of the flow chart.

For example, if a description of the processing of the third copy of the sales order had been omitted (a point which in this case is vital to the control over unbilled shipments because of its matching with the sales invoice) the omission would have been apparent in the flow chart in Figure 9.c. The SO3 would have been left hanging in

mid-air. Such loose ends can be readily detected and corrected on flow charts. The same omission in the narrative description at the top of Figure 9.c would not have been as obvious.

Various methods of flow charting have been in use by auditors for a number of years. If flow charts are to be understood by different members of the same audit team it is, of course, important that they all use one standardized approach. The particular approach chosen may depend on individual or firm preference but is is desirable that it lend itself to the auditor's particular objectives. (Some forms of charting may be useful for efficiency studies or EDP systems design but not for the auditor's purposes.) One form of flow charting developed specifically for audit use, and similar to that illustrated in Figure 9.c, is described in detail in Chapter 25.

As with other review approaches, the primary source of knowledge of the systems information documented on the flow charts comes from enquiry of company officials and employees. To ensure that this information is obtained at first-hand from the employees actually performing the procedures charted (and not second-hand from other employees, who cannot know for sure what is actually done in practice), the flow charting approach illustrated in Figure 9.c provides for the audit staff member to initial beside the employee names at the top of the relevant chart columns.

Three potential abuses of flow charting as an information-gathering technique may be mentioned, though they can be avoided with adequate training, care and supervision.

1. The fact that flow charting requires the learning of symbols, charting conventions, and methods of enhancing chart clarity, (all described in Chapter 25) leaves the possibility, if these skills are not learned, of charts being badly or confusingly prepared.
2. The precision of flow charts can be temptation to get into excessive detail beyond what is necessary for the subsequent evaluation of control.
3. The mechanics of flow charting can be a temptation to make the flow charts an end in themselves rather than subservient to the objective of permitting an informed evaluation.
   a) If poorly controlled, charting may spread into areas of the system not of relevance to the subsequent evaluation of internal control.
   b) If poorly controlled, time may be wasted in elaborating, refining, and polishing the flow charts rather than moving on to the evaluation stage of the audit.

The first potential abuse can be controlled through adequate advance training, written instructions, chart examples, and on-the-job supervision. The second and third potential abuses can be controlled through detailed time budgets to define the degree of intensity expected in the preparation or updating of each chart, through on-the-job supervision, and through advance reference to questionnaires, evaluation guides or check lists as described later.

Again, to point out potential abuses is not to categorize a method as impractical. Where the auditor uses flow charting as an information-gathering tool he will find it an advantage to be well aware of any potential abuses so that he can prevent them.

In combination with other audit elements

Mention has already been made of the possibility of supplementing flow charts with limited review tests to ensure that the procedures described are actually in operation. These review tests can be conveniently documented on the flow charts themselves, as described later in this chapter. Flow charting is improved if it is closely coordinated with the subsequent evaluation stage. If some type of control questionnaire, evaluation guide or check list is to be used during the evaluation stage, reference to this form during the review process will help to ensure that the flow charting is being directed to areas that will indeed be of control significance in the subsequent evaluation.

9.3 Evaluation

The objectives of the evaluation element of the interim audit are:

1. to evaluate the accounting systems, other relevant internal controls, and the accuracy and reliability of the accounting records,
2. to evaluate the suitability of accounting methods used,
3. to evaluate, for purposes of reporting to management, internal controls (whether of attest or not-of-attest significance), systems efficiency, financial or tax planning, accounting methods, or other matters of potential interest to management to the extent encountered in the course of the audit examination.

The first two of these objectives relate to the mandatory primary objective of the audit as a whole; the third, to the discretionary secondary objective.

The auditor should make a preliminary evaluation of the internal control systems in order to determine:
a) whether he still intends to rely on each system of internal control on which his tentative audit strategy was based,
b) which internal controls within each system he intends to rely on, and the appropriate compliance procedures,
c) necessary auditing procedures to compensate for an identified weakness or absence of internal controls within each system. [12]

The evaluation of accounting systems can itself be divided into two stages, as shown in Figure 9.a. One stage usually precedes extensive compliance or substantive verification and the other stage follows it. The first stage can be described as the evaluation of the accounting systems and other relevant internal controls as ascertained during the review stage:

1. This evaluation represents element 2a in Figure 9.a and will be present in every audit except where it is clear in advance that no reliance can be placed on the accounting records (i.e., except for Path III in Figure 9.a).
2. This evaluation would include identification of particular controls on which the auditor wishes to rely

provided that the results of compliance verification of these controls is satisfactory (Path I in Figure 9.a).

3. This evaluation would also include identification of areas where the auditor wishes instead to rely on substantive verification of internal evidence provided that it is satisfactory (Path II in Figure 9.a).

4. The reason for this evaluation element being separated from the final evaluation of the accounting records (element 2b in Figure 9.a) is that it is usually desirable to evaluate the *design* of the systems and controls before extensive compliance and substantive verification is performed. This preliminary evaluation is useful to avoid applying compliance procedures, for example, to controls on which reliance is ultimately not placed. After compliance and substantive verification has been performed, a final evaluation of the *functioning* of the systems and controls can be made.

The second stage can be described as the evaluation of the accuracy and reliability of the accounting records:

1. This evaluation represents element 2b in Figure 9.a and will be present in every audit except where it was clear in advance that no reliance can be placed on the accounting records (i.e., except for Path III in Figure 9.a).

2. This evaluation would be based on the previous evaluation following the review stage together with an evaluation of either or both of the results of compliance verification (Path I) and substantive verification of internal evidence (Path II).

In this section of the chapter, objectives (2) and (3) and the first evaluation stage of objective (1) are discussed. The second evaluation stage of objective (1) is discussed in 9.4 for compliance verification and in 9.5 for substantive verification.

9.3.1 Evaluation of control strengths and deficiencies

A conceptual approach to evaluation

Controls that relate to the accuracy and reliability of the accounting records are effective, in relation to the attest objective of the auditor, if they substantially reduce the risk of a material total of undetected errors or irregularities. A logical approach to evaluating the effectiveness of controls is for the auditor to ask himself, "What can go wrong?" with respect to each type of transaction, group of transactions, or related assets. In particular, the auditor should proceed as follows.

1. Divide the total systems into convenient areas for analysis - perhaps by individual transaction type (e.g., sales) and individual asset (e.g., accounts receivable) or by major accounting system (e.g., sales/receivables/receipts).

2. Consider the types of errors or irregularities which could possibly occur within each area (e.g.,

"lapping" is a possibility in the sales/receivables/receipts area but not in the purchases/payable/payments area).

3. Consider the control techniques or groups of control techniques usually necessary to provide reasonable assurance of preventing or detecting such errors and irregularities.

For example, to provide reasonable assurance of preventing or detecting unbilled shipments it is normally necessary to have (a) some independent follow-up of the serial continuity of shipping slips or sales order numbers, (b) segregation of shipping and billing functions from cash receipts, (c) control of access to the shipping area, (d) control over non-routine types of sales such as scrap, fixed assets, etc., (e) adequate data and error controls if computerized systems are used as well as good overall controls such as controls to ensure employee competence and effective budgetary controls. If these control techniques are not all present, the probability of material error or irregularity may not be confined to an acceptable minimum. Because certain general controls (such as controls to ensure employee competence and budgetary controls) may affect most or all systems areas it is usually efficient to evaluate these general controls first.

4. Determine which of the foregoing control techniques have been identified in the review process and whether any indications of unsatisfactory functioning of these controls have been encountered.

5. Consider whether the specific control techniques identified are in fact sufficient and necessary to provide reasonable assurance of preventing or detecting the foregoing errors or irregularities in the particular system under examination.

Some control techniques commonly necessary may not be essential in this particular system. Alternatively, special control techniques not commonly necessary may be required.

6. Evaluate any apparent control deficiencies identified in the foregoing steps to determine whether such apparent weaknesses could in fact allow a *material* total of errors or irregularities to occur.

7. Evaluate apparent control strengths identified in the foregoing steps to determine whether it is necessary or efficient to place audit reliance on such control strengths (as opposed to planning more persuasive substantive verification not depending on such reliance) and identify exact control procedures on which reliance is to be placed so that the nature and extent of required compliance verification can be established.

In one instance, four control techniques may all be essential to the prevention of material error, and compliance verification must be applied to each of the four if reliance is to be placed on the joint control. In another instance, five control techniques may be present but only three may be essential to the prevention of material error and compliance verification need only be applied to each of these three. The other two control techniques may be directed to less material errors or to the earlier detection of errors which the first three controls would have eventually caught in any case. These last two control techniques may be desirable for the client to have but not essential to the attest objective of the auditor.

8. Summarize conclusions respecting control strengths and deficiencies in the most useful manner for integrating with further interim audit procedures and/or the planning of financial statement audit procedures.

Three methods of evaluation

Three methods of applying the foregoing conceptual approach to evaluation could be considered:
• evaluation by studying results of tests or narrative systems notes,
• evaluation by use of flow charts,
• evaluation by use of questionnaires or evaluation guides.
A discussion of each of these three methods follows.

9.3.2 Evaluation by studying results of tests or narrative systems notes

It has been suggested earlier that, where reliance is to be placed on controls, tests of transactions as a review technique to gather information about those controls is not an effective procedure *in the absence of other review techniques*. It follows that evaluation of control solely by studying the results of such tests is likely to be equally ineffective. The results of transactional tests reveal the accuracy or inaccuracy of a certain sample of documents or records but not necessarily the related controls, which may not be evident from an inspection of the documents or records alone. Important control strengths or deficiencies not revealed by the tests may therefore be improperly ignored in the evaluation.

Nor can good control be inferred from the accuracy of the documents tested. Even if the test extents were large enough to provide direct assurance that no material error had occurred, such tests would, in effect, be substantive in nature and bypass any reliance on control (since they could not assume what they were setting out to prove). The only valid inference from favourable results of such tests would be *either* that controls were good or that the errors guarded against had never occurred in the first place. Even if this were the basis for a conclusion on control alone (which it is not), the conclusion, having already bypassed control, would come too late to be of any use as a basis of reliance.

In summary, while the study of test results may be a possible method of assessing the accuracy of accounting records where no reliance is to be placed on controls (Path II in Figure 9.a), it is not desirable as the sole method of evaluating controls where reliance is to be placed on them (Path I in Figure 9.a).

Evaluation of control by studying narrative systems notes is a slight improvement but, in the writer's view, usually still inadequate. Narrative systems notes may give the auditor a more coherent understanding of the systems and of many of the controls and thus provide a foundation for the evaluation. But they do not assist in the evaluation process itself. If the notes are incomplete the auditor could easily overlook important control points or whole control areas. Moreover, controls which depend upon division of duties or upon the relationship of different procedures in the system are difficult to evaluate by the study of narrative systems alone.

9.3.3 Evaluation by use of flow charts

While flow charts are principally a review technique to gather systems information, they can serve as an important evaluation tool as well. If the charting method illustrated in Figure 9.c is used, the division of the chart into columns by employee or department highlights the division of duties and makes it easy for the auditor to see where incompatible functions have not been segregated. Moreover, the flow charts indicate the relationships between different document flows, on which many elements of internal control depend. In analyzing the charts the auditor should ask himself for each step in the system:

> What would happen if this one step were omitted or performed incorrectly, either by accident or intent? Would the omission or error be detected automatically by the system?

If it would be detected, the internal control is satisfactory. If not, there is an apparent weakness.

> For example, in the system charted in Figure 9.c, what would happen if the second copy of the sales order went astray after leaving the shipping department with the result that no sales invoice was prepared? The unbilled shipment would be detected by the accountant who would have an SO_3 unmatched with any SO_2. But what would happen if the shipping department misplaced both the SO_2 and SO_3 together immediately after preparation? The omission would be not readily apparent from the accountant's SO_3 — SI_2 file, for he keeps it in alphabetical order. Thus, this particular error is not under control and unbilled shipments could occur. The cure, of course, is for the accountant's file to be kept in numerical order and its serial continuity periodically checked.

In such a manner the auditor on the job can pinpoint specific control strengths and deficiencies and the file reviewer has the information readily available to assess the correctness of this evaluation.

Nonetheless, it is always possible that the auditor may overlook some desirable control technique which should be present but is not. In addition, a few types of controls (restricted access to assets, controls to ensure employee competence, etc.) may not be discernible on the flow charts themselves—although the auditor should have observed these controls in the process of preparing or updating the flow charts. For these reasons, flow charts as an evaluation tool should normally be supplemented by some form of questionnaire, check list, or control evaluation guide, as discussed in the next section.

9.3.4 Evaluation by use of questionnaires or evaluation guides

Questionnaires for both review and evaluation

A type of detailed internal control questionnaire for use both for gathering systems information in the first place and then evaluating it has already been illustrated in Figure 9.b. To facilitate evaluation these questionnaires are usually arranged so that "yes" answers indicate control strengths and "no" answers indicate possible control deficiencies. The absence of one control technique, however, may be compensated for by some other control. As a result, not all "no" answers will indicate actual control deficiencies. Accordingly, many questionnaires provide columns for explaining "no" answers. Some questionnaires may also be arranged to distinguish between major and minor control deficiencies, to classify controls between those of attest and not-of-attest significance, and to provide space for documenting the source of the auditor's information. The use of questionnaires for both review and evaluation purposes has proved effective on many engagements.

Evaluation guides to supplement other review and evaluation techniques

Questionnaires may also be used to supplement the evaluation of systems information gathered by other review techniques such as flow charting. When questionnaires are used for this purpose they need not have the length or detail required of questionnaires used for information gathering in the first place. Rather they can take the form of concise reminder lists, check lists, or evaluation guides. Moreover, when the purpose of such an evaluation guide is recognized as analysis rather than *assembly* of systems information, its usefulness can be improved by

analyzing individual control techniques into groups according to the primary control question to which they relate.

Such an evaluation guide is illustrated in Figure 9.d. It focuses on one major systems area, sales/receivables/receipts and within that area identifies eleven primary control questions, such as whether there are adequate controls to prevent/detect goods being shipped but not invoiced. These are the essential control elements that must be covered by any adequate system of internal control—although the precise *mechanics* by which they are achieved may vary from system to system. A number of the more usual mechanics of control are listed as "consider" points (independent follow-up of serial continuity of shipping slips, segregation of shipping and billing from cash receipts, control of access to shipping area, etc.).[13] Ultimately, it is each primary control question which the auditor must answer and whether all or only some of the individual "consider" points are necessary (some may be inapplicable) is a decision calling for experienced judgement.[14]

In the writer's view, the combination of (a) flow charts for review and initial evaluation and (b) internal control evaluation guides for further analysis and final evaluation is a particularly useful one for medium-sized and larger engagements. It is also consistent with the conceptual approach to evaluation previously described.

> Questionnaires are not usually designed to readily identify the accounting system; they emphasize controls. Flow charts, on the other hand, are a means of identifying the accounting system. Therefore, the best and most useful record of identification is the combination of questionnaire and flow chart. This ensures that the benefits of each form are obtained and that the evaluation and tests which follow are based on an identification which has taken into account both the accounting system and its control points.[15]

The questionnaire approach, the combined flow chart/evaluation guide approach, and other combination approaches can all be used successfully and, in the end, the choice among them must be made by each individual practitioner or firm.

Weakness evaluation schedules

Not every apparent weakness identified on questionnaires or evaluation guides may be of material significance. Some auditors use separate "weakness evaluation schedules" to analyze the significance of observed deficiencies (step 6 in 9.3.1). An example of such a schedule is illustrated in Chapter 26 (Figure 26.e).

225

INTERNAL CONTROL EVALUATION GUIDE –
SALES/RECEIVABLES/RECEIPTS

Evaluation
(Yes, No, N/A, Not Material)

ARE THERE ADEQUATE CONTROLS TO PREVENT/DETECT:

1. GOODS BEING SHIPPED BUT NOT INVOICED?
Consider –
- (a) independent follow-up (or computer checking) of serial continuity of shipping slips or sales order numbers?
- (b) shipping, billing segregated from cash receipts?
- (c) control of access to shipping area?
- (d) non-routine sales: scrap, fixed assets, consignment, employee sales, "direct" shipments from supplier to customer?
- (e) adequate DATA controls (e.g. control over quantities ordered, shipped and invoiced)?
- (f) adequate ERROR controls (e.g. follow-up of unshipped or uninvoiced orders)?

Yes

2. GOODS BEING SHIPPED TO A BAD CREDIT RISK?
Consider –
- (a) credit approval prior to shipment?
- (b) adequate ERROR controls (e.g. follow-up and approval of credit reject list)?
- (c) adequate customer MASTER FILE controls (e.g. changes to customer credit limits)?

Yes

3. INVOICE ERRORS OCCURRING?
Consider –
- (a) pricing, quantities, extensions checked or if computerized, reasonability tests on pricing?
- (b) standard price list, exceptions approved or, if computerized adequate price and customer MASTER FILE controls?
- (c) cancellation of source documents to prevent duplicate invoicing?
- (d) adequate DATA and ERROR controls (e.g. follow-up of pricing exception report)?

No

4. SALES BEING INVOICED BUT NOT RECORDED IN THE ACCOUNTS?
Consider –
- (a) independent follow-up (or computer checking) of serial continuity of sales invoices?
- (b) shipping or sales order numbers matched to documents processed through posting to receivables or through entry in sales summary?
- (c) billing segregated from receivables?
- (d) billing total direct to general ledger posting source?
- (e) billing total reconciled with total receivable postings?
- (f) simultaneous posting of sales journal and accounts receivable?
- (g) reconciliation of subledger to control account?
- (h) adequate DATA and ERROR controls?

Yes

5. SALES BEING INVOICED BUT NOT COSTED?
Consider –
- (a) independent follow-up (or computer checking) of serial continuity of costing copy of sales invoice?
- (b) costs extensions checked or, if computerized, reasonability tests on gross profit?
- (c) adequate DATA controls (e.g. quantities costed agreed to quantities invoiced, prices agreed to standard costs)?
- (d) adequate ERROR controls?

Yes

6. RECEIVABLES BEING CREDITED IMPROPERLY?
Consider –
- (a) prenumbered credit note approval independent of receivables clerks?
- (b) proper support for credit notes?
- (c) independent approval of bad debt write-offs?
- (d) adequate price and customer MASTER FILE controls?
- (e) adequate DATA controls (e.g. cancellation of source documents, self checking digits, key verification)?

Yes

7. PAYMENTS BEING RECEIVED AND NOT DEPOSITED?
Consider –
- (a) cashier and receivable ledger functions, separated?
- (b) cheques stamped "for deposit only" when mail opened, bank accepts only for deposit?
- (c) mail receipts direct to cashier, listed, or control totals taken immediately?
- (d) deposits checked, deposited promptly?
- (e) control over branch deposit accounts?
- (f) independent reconciliation of daily deposit total to accounts receivable postings and cash sales?

Yes

8. THE OCCURRENCE OF "LAPPING"?
Consider –
- (a) receivable trial balancing, ageing, review, follow-up of delinquent accounts independent of receivables clerks?
- (b) checking and mailing of statements independently of receivables clerks?
- (c) customer queries followed up independently?

Yes

9. OVERDUE ACCOUNTS ESCAPING ATTENTION?
Consider –
- (a) aged trial balances?
- (b) independent follow-up?
- (c) cash receipts applied against unpaid invoices?

Yes

10. CASH SALES PROCEEDS BEING MISAPPROPRIATED?
Consider –
- (a) locked-in register invoice copy or prenumbered receipts?
- (b) independent balancing of proceeds with sales records?
- (c) control over drivers' collections C.O.D. sales, etc.?

Not Material

11. MISCELLANEOUS RECEIPTS BEING MISSED?
Consider –
- (a) set up as receivable or independent check of collections?

Not Material

Figure 9.d

9.3.5 Degree of reliance on internal control

As previously explained (step 7 in 9.3.1), not every control technique found to be present will need to be relied upon by the auditor. Therefore, after control has been evaluated it is necessary for the auditor to determine which specific control techniques it is necessary or efficient for him to rely upon.

What degree of reliance can properly be placed on a given control? And should that degree be fixed or can it vary from one control to another?

Reliance less than absolute

As to the first question, it seems reasonable that a considerable, though not absolute, degree of reliance should be appropriate for at least some controls, provided that it is known that they are operating effectively throughout the period in question. Well-designed and properly functioning controls provide considerable assurance that accounting records are being prepared accurately. It would be illogical not to take this considerable assurance into account by placing considerable reliance on these controls. Indeed, were such considerable reliance not justified, it would hardly be a sensible audit strategy to conduct a thorough study of internal controls in the first place. But the reliance cannot be absolute. In the end, evidence of good control is only indirect evidence of the absence of material errors. There is always the possibility that through inadvertence or intent, certain transactions bypass the control system. Therefore, substantive verification of the resulting financial statements is always required. The second field work standard does not call for reliance on internal control to *replace* substantive procedures but rather to be used as a basis for determining the nature, timing and extent of substantive procedures required. Where *considerable* reliance on control is warranted, that reliance should significantly reduce the extent, advance the timing, and/or alter the nature of the substantive procedures otherwise required.

Degree of reliance can vary

As to the second question, it seems clear that some controls provide greater assurance of preventing or detecting material error than others. Competent, well instructed and supervised employees performing shipping and billing routines carefully, and with a proper division of duties among them, clearly reduce the risk of billing errors. It would be illogical for the auditor to distinguish between this first case and a second, where incompetent employees are issuing bills carelessly, with no segregation of incompatible functions, and every indication of frequent mistakes

and omissions. And yet the first situation may lack a proper follow-up of matched orders and invoices. Under the circumstances, considerable reliance on control over unbilled shipments in the first case would not be justified; but neither would the risk of material unbilled shipments be as high as in the second case. Logically, then, different degrees of reliance on control may be justified in different cases. As the control risk is gradually reduced (through greater control), the constraints on the audit risk can be gradually relaxed (through greater reliance on control) so as to maintain a constant joint risk of undetected material error.

As a practical matter, however, too many gradations of the degree of reliance on control could not be meaningfully distinguished by the auditor. It is suggested that the degree of reliance appropriate to place on any given control be assessed as considerable, minimum or none. Where *minimum* reliance on a control is warranted, the auditor should plan (with respect to related assets, liabilities and income components) substantive procedures that are reasonably sufficient in themselves taking into account the inherent risk of error. Minimum reliance should allow some reduction in the extent of substantive procedures and some minor changes in their nature. It should not allow radical changes in the timing of asset and liability verification nor substantial changes in the extent or nature of the procedures.

The second standard of field work calls for an appropriately organized study of controls on which the auditor relies, the term "study" comprehending both review and compliance verification. It is reasonable that where considerable reliance is to be placed on a control the degree of compliance verification should be commensurately thorough. In this book, such controls will be designated as "key" controls. Where only minimum reliance is to be placed on a control some compliance verification should be performed but it is logical that the degree of assurance demanded from this verification be correspondingly less.

Identifying key controls on which considerable reliance will be placed

If these concepts are accepted by the auditor, it follows that after evaluating controls, he should specifically identify those key controls on which considerable reliance will be placed, and those on which only minimum reliance will be placed. In making these decisions he will want to weigh the cost of the reasonably persuasive compliance verification required for key controls against the reductions in substantive verification that reliance on such key controls will permit (see 6.7).

Some auditors identify key controls in an extra column added to the internal control questionnaire or evaluation guide. An example of such identification is illustrated in Figure 26.d.

9.3.6 Evaluation of suitability of accounting methods

At the same time as evaluating internal control, the auditor should evaluate the suitability of the accounting principles and methods employed. Particular attention should be paid to changes which may have affected the consistency of reported figures.

None of the review and evaluation techniques previously discussed are perhaps ideal for evaluating accounting methods, although they should all give the auditor some knowledge of the methods in use. Nonetheless, it is easy to overlook accounting matters when assessing clerical accuracy, transaction flows, division of duties, approvals, and other controls. Now that it is general practice for a summary of accounting policies to be included in the financial statements, the auditor will usually prepare or update a working paper schedule listing significant client accounting policies and methods in a comparative form from year to year. It is a good idea for the auditor to review this schedule at the beginning of the interim audit so that he can be alert for deviations from prescribed policies during the course of his work.

9.3.7 Evaluation of non-attest controls, efficiency, and financial and tax planning

One of the objectives of the evaluation stage, listed earlier, was to evaluate, for purposes of reporting to management, internal controls (whether of attest or non-attest significance), systems efficiency, financial or tax planning, accounting methods, or other matters of potential interest to management to the extent encountered in the course of the audit examination.

Non-attest controls

Evaluation of controls beyond those necessary for attest purposes can be reviewed and evaluated by the same techniques previously discussed for attest controls. Usually, however, the thoroughness of the review and evaluation will be considerably less. For example, some review tests of non-attest controls may occasionally be done in order to identify the nature of the controls in operation or the opportunities for improvement.[16] Some questions on non-attest controls are commonly incorporated in most internal control questionnaires, though in less detail

than for attest controls. Most non-attest controls would not be covered on audit flow charts, although flow charts can be extended to cover such controls in special assignments for that purpose.

Systems efficiency

Identification of inefficiencies is not particularly easy from a review of tests of transactions. Internal control questionnaires do not usually cover efficiency points, since their identification is, after all, not the primary audit objective. Efficiency questionnaires can, of course, be developed but usually auditors would use them only on special assignments for that purpose. Whereas control questions such as "Are receiving accounts payable and purchasing functions segregated?" can be answered relatively briefly, efficiency questions such as "Do purchasing procedures optimize the levels of inventory carrying costs, inventory ordering costs, and production delay costs?" can be answered only after considerable study, which may be outside the auditor's field of competence. More modest questionnaires highlighting simple and common opportunities for improvements in efficiency may sometimes be desirable.

The flow charting approach perhaps most readily yields some efficiency points as a free by-product of the audit effort. Redundant document copies, unnecessary records, needlessly duplicated files, unused information on documents, cumbersome routing of paper flow, and unnecessary delays in transaction flows can usually be readily spotted on the flow charts. Of course, these are not the only inefficiencies which may exist in the client's systems, but they are ones which can be identified with no additional work beyond that required for the attest objective.

Financial and tax planning

Because of the control impact of budgets and management reports, where they exist the auditor will usually include in his interim audit a review of the budget preparation, some testing of the build-up of monthly management reports from the general ledger, and some analysis of budget variances. All the review methods previously discussed can be adapted to this purpose where desired. This review and testing will often lead in addition to identification of opportunities for improvements in the organization's financial planning.

As part of the review and evaluation of accounting systems, the auditor will have to give consideration to the controls over the payment (on purchases) and the levying, collection and subsequent remittance (with respect to sales) of federal and provincial sales taxes. Of the four techniques for gathering systems information, transactional testing and flow charting are probably the most efficient in providing an understanding of how tax is levied, checked and remitted. Of the techniques for evaluating that information, however, the questionnaire approach is undoubtedly the best because of the number of technical points to be remembered in each case. Usually such questionnaires will contain questions not only related to the accuracy of the tax accounting (attest objective) but also to tax planning points (Are there alternative permitted methods of tax computation which would minimize sales tax costs?).

With respect to income taxes, the verification of tax provisions and liabilities (attest objective) is done during the financial statement audit. Most auditors, however, give some consideration to tax planning points (Are there opportunities for minimizing income taxes?) during the interim audit. Depending on the desired extent of this collateral service, the consideration may be merely an informal review and an alertness for potential tax savings or it may be an organized analysis of the large number of technical points which may apply in any given case. For the latter purpose a check list or tax planning questionnaire is desirable.

9.4 Compliance verification of controls

The objective of compliance verification is to confirm that, of the controls identified during the review stage, those chosen during the evaluation stage as ones on which reliance will be placed really exist and have functioned continuously and effectively.

> The auditor should conduct compliance procedures in respect to those internal controls on which, following his preliminary evaluation, he still intends to rely in determining the nature, extent and timing of substantive auditing procedures in respect of particular classes of transactions or balances.

> The auditor should conduct sufficient compliance procedures to gain reasonable assurance as to whether the internal controls on which he intends to rely:
> a) in fact operate in the manner identified by him in his review, and
> b) have functioned effectively throughout the period of intended reliance. [17]

9.4.1 Objectives of compliance verification

The foregoing objective can be stated as follows:

> To (a) confirm the existence, (b) assess the effectiveness, and (c) check the continuity of operation of those internal controls on which reliance is to be placed.

A set of internal controls may appear adequate on paper, but if they are not always followed in practice, if they are performed poorly, if they are intentionally bypassed, or if they were abandoned half-way through the year, the final system of control will not be reliable. Therefore, compliance verification is necessary before audit reliance on the controls is justified.

Instances of a prescribed control procedure not being followed or being performed ineffectively may be called *compliance deviations*. Examples are the failure to check and initial for the accuracy of purchase invoice extensions or the failure to reconcile control totals at prescribed dates. Of course, some compliance deviations may be trivial. The prescribed control procedure may call for an employee to prepare and sign a bank reconciliation on the 10th working day after the month-end. Instead he prepares it on the 12th working day and only initials it. The deviations are trivial and the intent of the key control itself is obviously still met. However, a reconciliation prepared two months late and without any indication of its preparer (proper division of duties thus being no longer assured) would represent a *critical compliance deviation*.

A compliance deviation is critical if it represents a failure to meet the objective of the control on which the auditor wishes to rely. The magnitude of the transaction involved does not change the nature of the control failure. Thus, the failure to check, as prescribed, the purchase price on a purchase invoice would be a critical compliance deviation if the auditor had wished to place reliance on that control. Even if the unchecked purchase invoice happened to be small, the failure to check it represents a critical compliance deviation. If there are enough similarly unchecked purchase invoices they could in aggregate represent a substantial amount and make a material total of monetary error within the stream of purchase transactions a real possibility.

Since the objective of control (of relevance to the attest function) is to prevent or detect a material total of errors (or irregularities), a control procedure can hardly be considered reliable if the frequency of critical compliance deviations is so great that material monetary error is a reasonable possibility, but it may be considered reliable if at worst only a few critical compliance deviations could have occurred. The purpose of compliance verification of a control is thus not to determine that critical compliance deviations never occur (that would require checking every purchase invoice for the entire year), but rather that their frequency is not so great as to indicate a reasonable possibility of monetary error and therefore not so great as to invalidate audit reliance on the control.

The word "determine" in the previous sentence, and the words "confirm", "assess" and "check" in the previous definition of compliance verification should not be taken to imply absolute proof but rather the achieving of an appropriate degree of assurance.

Employing the concepts just discussed, an alternative definition of the objective of compliance verification can be expressed as:

> To provide an appropriate assurance of detecting, should it exist, such frequency of critical compliance deviations as would indicate a reasonable possibility of material monetary error.

The ultimate objective of the auditor is to obtain reasonable assurance that no material aggregate of monetary error exists in the financial statements. Assessing the frequency of critical compliance deviations helps indirectly in achieving this objective. The reason is that monetary errors are more likely where control systems are operating poorly (i.e., where there are frequent critical compliance deviations). Thus, where there are few critical compliance deviations there are likely to be even fewer monetary errors. Thus, the presence of no more than a few critical compliance deviations gives the auditor evidence that internal control risk is low, which in turn means that the auditor can relax slightly the constraints on audit risk in his further auditing procedures and still arrive at an acceptably low level for the final risk of undetected errors (see discussion of risks in 6.6.4). Every auditor must decide what he considers to be an acceptable level of critical compliance deviations. A suggestion for one method of arriving at such a decision follows.

Indications of a reasonable possibility of monetary error

Since the relationship of monetary errors to materiality is the ultimate consideration, it is logical that the relationship between the frequency of critical compliance deviations and some multiple of materiality (say, 3 or 4 times; at any rate, not 50 times) should be of significance. In this book, a multiple of 3 times is suggested as a reasonable (and probably conservative) working rule for the normal case. The argument is that if the critical compliance deviations are less than triple materiality then monetary errors are probably less than materiality.[18] Of course, this conclusion is only in terms of a probability and for that reason substantive procedures will still have to be applied in some measure to all assets, liabilities and income statement components that are individually material. The extent of application of these procedures can, however, be reduced (a lower degree of assurance demanded of them) in light of the reliance placed on compliance verification.

The argument may be phrased as an analogy to smoke and fire detection. If most fires (monetary errors) are accompanied by a much larger volume of smoke (compliance deviations), then using smoke detectors (compliance verification) is an efficient, though indirect way of locating fires - more efficient than, say, using thermometers (substantive verification) exclusively. Of course, the sensitivity to be demanded of the smoke detector will depend on what one believes to be the normal ratio of smoke to fire. While an assumed ratio of critical compliance deviations to monetary errors is necessarily a subjective estimate, it is an estimate that must be made if some probability of material error is to be reduced from an observed (or projected) frequency of critical compliance deviations. A multiple of three has been suggested above. This, then, becomes the multiple of materiality against which the frequency of critical compliance deviations can be assessed.

> When the projected possible total value of those transactions which are each subject to a critical compliance deviation equals several times (such as three times) financial statement materiality, a reasonable possibility of material monetary error is indicated.

It is not suggested that any such assessment can be made rigidly. Nonetheless, for compliance verification of a control to be satisfactory, it is suggested that the auditor must be satisfied that, if the total value of transactions subject to critical compliance deviations in the exercise of this control had been more than a few times materiality, he would have had a reasonable chance of detecting this fact and therefore of rejecting reliance on the control.

Further consideration of this smoke-fire argument and the triple materiality rule as applied to compliance testing is given in Chapter 12.

9.4.2 Nature of compliance procedures

The audit procedures employed in performing compliance verification of a particular control on which reliance is to be placed may be called *compliance procedures*. These procedures may consist of observation (e.g., observing an appropriate division of duties), enquiry (e.g., asking a supervisor what he watches for and what errors he encounters in exercising supervisory control), and inspection (e.g., inspecting procedure manuals used by employees or inspecting documents checked and initialled during a control procedure). Some compliance procedures, such as checking initialled documents, lend themselves to application on a test basis (*compliance tests*); other compliance procedures, such as observing division of duties, do not.

Compliance procedures for minimum reliance

It was stated earlier than, when only minimum reliance is to be placed on a control the appropriate degree of assurance to be demanded from the related compliance verification should logically be limited. It is suggested that observation, enquiry, and, where applicable, the testing of a few instances of related documentary evidence should be sufficient for this purpose. For example, where minimum reliance is to be placed on the control exercised by a clerk checking and initialling purchase invoices, it should be sufficient to observe that he is in fact performing this function, to enquire of him what procedures he follows, and to test four or five examples of checked and initialled purchase invoices. From such tests and enquiries the auditor should be able to assess whether the employee appears competent, appears to understand what is required, is in fact performing the prescribed procedures, and is preforming them carefully. In addition, some assurance is available from the self-policing nature of a good system of internal control. If the employee is, in fact, making mistakes the mistakes will usually be caught by the work of other employees in the system - and so there will be evidence of his poor performance. If the auditor makes enquiries and limited tests throughout the system, this self-policing nature adds significantly to the assurance he obtains with respect to any one control point. The total assurance obtained will not be foolproof, but it should be sufficient to justify placing minimum reliance on that control.

It was suggested in 9.2.3 that limited tests of transactions might usefully be combined with the initial review (by either questionnaires, narrative systems notes or flow charts). Where the flow charting approach has been used the observation steps and enquiry of each employee involved will also have been completed at the same time. All these steps of observation, enquiry and limited testing represent compliance procedures (though combined with the review stage) and, provided that the results of these procedures are satisfactory, minimum reliance on the control in question should be justified.

> In order to clarify their understanding of information obtained . . . , some auditors follow the practice of tracing one or a few of the different types of transactions involved through the related documents and records maintained. This practice may be useful for the purpose indicated and may be considered as a part of the tests of compliance as discussed later in this section. [19]

Where either the questionnaire or narrative systems note approach has been used similar observations and enquiries may also have been made at the review stage; if not, they can be readily added later in order to justify placing minimum reliance on the controls in question.

Compliance procedures for considerable reliance

Where considerable reliance is to be placed on a "key" control, the appropriate degree of assurance to be demanded from the related compliance verification should be correspondingly greater. This greater assurance can be thought of as coming in part from the review and compliance procedures necessary to justify "minimum" reliance, as already discussed, and additional compliance procedures performed to boost the justified degree of reliance up to "considerable". The assurance derived from the additional compliance procedures taken by themselves should be reasonable but need not be excessive because the result of reliance on internal control is not the elimination of substantive verification but only a reduction in its extent (and/or a change in its nature or timing).

The appropriate compliance procedure will depend on the nature of the control to be verified - particularly on whether it is a preventive or a detective control (see 7.2.1). Where the control is a *preventive* control, there usually is little difficulty identifying the evidence of its existence. What is difficult is assessing its likely effectiveness as a preventive measure - an evaluation problem. For example, division of duties can be observed; a manual of instructions can be seen; good forms design can be inspected.

Where the control is a *detective* control, however, evidence as to its operation may be more difficult. The only conclusive evidence of its operation is when it detects an actual error. If the error has allegedly never occurred there is no conclusive proof that the control would have caught it if it had occurred. Nor is there even conclusive evidence (except perhaps with respect to computerized controls) that a detective control which has caught intermittent errors was really operating effectively between successive detections. The auditor can check that the proper initial is on the invoice and he can check that the invoice extensions happen to be correct, but he can never prove *conclusively* that the initialler really checked the extensions carefully and would have detected an error on that invoice had its extensions been wrong. The auditor must usually be content with the degree of *persuasive* evidence practically available at a cost commensurate with the importance of the matter to the final expression of an opinion.

There must be some direct evidence of the control itself

Even though direct evidence (such as an initial) of the operation of any detective control can only be persuasive rather than conclusive, it is important that there be at least some direct evidence of the control itself. *The fact that no monetary error is present in the item tested by the auditor is not by itself direct evidence that the detective control procedure was applied.* If the auditor can find no direct evidence of the operation of the control itself, then compliance verification is impossible and audit reliance should not be placed on that control.

This point requires some explanation. The foregoing rationale for compliance verification was based on the premise that compliance deviations will normally occur much more frequently than monetary errors and that the cheaper compliance search for a triple materiality frequency of compliance deviations will permit some reduction in the more costly substantive search for a material total of monetary error. But this premise is only useful to the auditor if the compliance deviations can be observed by him. If he can see only that portion of compliance deviations that happen to be accompanied by actual monetary errors, the rationale breaks down. In that case, he can only hunt for monetary errors directly (a substantive objective) and must design his procedures (substantive procedures) to detect a material (not triple material) total of them. No saving can be achieved by relying on internal control. Where thermometers are already checking for fire, no additional reliance can be placed on an alleged smoke detector which cannot see the smoke but only the fire itself.

It follows from the foregoing argument that:

1. Compliance procedures should be applied to the actual controls rather than merely to the accounting procedures to be controlled (though it may be desirable to apply them to *both* to confirm the effective functioning of the control).

   For example, the correct pricing of a sales invoice which is never double checked can be tested by the auditor but this test does not represent compliance testing – rather, substantive testing. No reliance can be placed on any control because there are no compliance deviations to be observed other than actual monetary errors. Thus, the absence of errors in the test does not indicate a limit for compliance deviations in the population (and therefore a *much lower* limit for monetary errors) but merely a limit for monetary errors directly. The substantive test for monetary errors must thus be concerned with a possible material total (not a triple materiality total). However, in another case, if the invoice pricing *is* double checked, the auditor may perform a compliance test to see that invoices have been initialled for checking. Here he may properly direct his search for a triple materiality frequency of missing initials. For the invoices he checks he would normally check for both the presence of the initial and the correctness of the price.

2. Compliance procedures should be applied only to those controls for which compliance deviations (apart from actual monetary errors) would be observable if they occurred.

   For example, suppose a control procedure is the filing of a shipping document, after invoicing, in numerical order

and the reporting to the chief accountant of any missing numbers. Every time the clerk fails to report a missing number the greatest probability is that a shipment has not been billed and the company has suffered a direct monetary loss. Thus, a missing number would represent both a compliance deviation and a monetary error. It is not sufficient for the auditor to do a compliance search for a triple materiality frequency of missing numbers and then place considerable reliance on the numerical continuity control. He could thereby easily overlook a material monetary error. Rather he must conduct a substantive test for material monetary error without placing considerable reliance on a control which is effectively unverifiable.[20] However, as discussed later, there may sometimes be other evidence available through observation and enquiry to confirm the existence and operation of the control.

Guidelines for choice of compliance procedures

Based on the foregoing discussion, the following sections provide some suggested guidelines for determining:

- compliance procedures to be applied to controls which leave a documentary trail,
- compliance procedures to be applied to controls which do not leave a documentary trail,
- the "reliance period" during which the continuity of operation of control should be assessed.

More detailed guidelines may be found in Chapters 26 and 27.

Guidelines for controls which leave an audit trail

1. Compliance verification of controls that leave a documentary trail should normally cover the entire reliance period.

2. If the control is itself a completed accounting routine such as (a) the trial balance of a subsidiary ledger and agreement of it to a control account, or (b) the reconciliation of a bank account, it is normally sufficient to examine the evidence of the routine (e.g., the trial balance tape or the written bank reconciliation) and to agree the key figures to the accounting records. It is normally not necessary to reperform the procedure to gain satisfactory evidence as to the presence of the control. However, in these examples, all trial balances and all bank reconciliations for the entire reliance period should normally be inspected.

3. If the control is a checking routine evidenced by initials or signatures on documents, it is normally appropriate both to examine a sample of these initialled or signed documents from throughout the reliance period and to reperform the checking procedure for which the initial or signature was applied. This is because the initial or signature by itself is less persuasive evidence of the actual

checking than a trial balance is of trial balancing. Guidance as to compliance test extents may be found in Chapter 12.

4. If the absence of the control on a given transaction would usually indicate a monetary error, compliance verification and audit reliance on the control are not appropriate.

5. In computerized systems a check of program logic (a control on which reliance may be placed) can be done by examining hard-copy output. Because of the systematic nature of programmed controls, the extent of such a sample can be substantially less than for a manually applied control.

Guidelines for controls which do not leave a documentary trail

1. If evidence of the control is directly observable, then reasonable assurance can usually be gained through one or two observations of the control together with supplementary enquiries to ensure their continued operation throughout the reliance period. This is generally the case for division of duties and for controls over physical access to assets.

2. In some cases extensive enquiries can provide evidence not available in documentary form. For example, where a key control is applied by a visual review with no initial or signature, it may still be possible to find evidence of its operation by questioning the reviewer as to his procedures, assessing his knowledge of what he is reviewing, asking about procedures when he finds errors, confirming these answers with other employees who make the resulting corrections, etc. However, when a signature or initial would in most organizations have been expected (as when an invoice is approved for payment), its unusual absence may warrant discounting other evidence available and rejecting reliance on control.

3. If the evidence of the control cannot be effectively assessed by the auditor, reliance should not be placed on the control. This might be the case, for example, for a supervisory control exercised by management where the auditor has reason to doubt management's competence or thoroughness in applying the control.

Reliance period

As part of the evaluation stage, or alternatively when designing compliance procedures, the auditor must determine the period during which reliance is to be placed on controls. This is particularly important where the required procedure will be a sample drawn from a great number of documents. There are four possible reliance periods:

1. the entire year or period under audit (true for most controls that affect net income),
2. the roll-forward period between the date of primary verification of an asset or liability and the year-end (e.g., for sales/receivables/cash controls where accounts receivable are confirmed at a pre-year-end date),
3. the last few months of the year (e.g., on costing controls where information is going to be used from the cost system to check inventory pricing at the year-end),
4. the period between the year-end and the audit reporting date (only rarely relevant because the auditor normally relies instead on substantive procedures to detect significant subsequent events - but sometimes applicable to certain safeguarding controls).

9.4.3 Evaluation of compliance verification results

Based on the results of compliance procedures, the auditor should evaluate the internal controls in order to decide the degree of reliance he will place on such controls in determining the nature, extent and timing of substantive auditing procedures. [21]

The auditor's evaluation of compliance verification results includes two types of conclusions: qualitative and quantitative. In the case of key controls, a tentative decision will already have been made to place considerable reliance on control contingent upon the results of compliance verification (otherwise compliance procedures would not have been performed). This tentative decision will be contradicted should the results of the compliance verification indicate that the *quality* of performance of the control procedure is unacceptable (due to incompetence, carelessness, misunderstanding, or any other reason). The tentative conclusion will also be contradicted if the results indicate that the prescribed control is too often not followed in practice, that is, that there *may* be an unacceptable *quantity* (e.g., triple materiality) of critical compliance deviations. The auditor's evaluation of the possible frequency of critical compliance deviations (based on the verification results) must in some cases (for example, with respect to controls such as division of duties) be made judgmentally. For controls that are verified by *tests* or *samples* further guidance on the decision as to whether there is or could be an unacceptably high frequency of compliance deviations can be found in Chapters 12 and 13.

Although the main objective of compliance procedures is to search for compliance deviations rather than monetary errors, any monetary errors encountered should be carefully assessed as to their nature, cause, and likely or possible extent.

Documentation of compliance procedures

The documentation of compliance procedures establishing minimum reliance on certain controls can often be combined with the documentation of the review stage. Observations, enquiries and limited tests can be recorded on questionnaires in an extra column, alongside narrative systems notes, or at the bottom of flow charts. (A method of documentation on flow charts is described in Chapter 26).

The documentation of compliance procedures establishing considerable reliance on key controls is usually recorded on a separate schedule. Such a schedule could indicate the key controls being checked, the compliance procedures, their extents, their results, and the auditor's conclusions.

9.5 Substantive verification

Substantive verification performed during the interim audit can be divided into two components (though they often overlap and may sometimes be performed together in practice):

1. substantive verification of internal documentary evidence to determine the accuracy and reliability of accounting records where the records are believed to be reliable but it is impossible or inefficient to place reliance on controls (Path II and Step 4a in Figure 9.a),
2. stubstantive procedures otherwise required during the financial statement audit but which can most usefully be commenced at an interim date (Step 4b in Figure 9.a).

9.5.1 Substantive procedures to establish accuracy and reliability of accounting records

Substantive test of transactions generally involve, first, a reperformance on a test basis of the principal bookkeeping routines including:

a) the entering of transactions in the books of original entry, and the adding and cross-adding of such books,
b) the posting from the books of original entry to subsidiary ledgers, the checking of the trial balances of such ledgers, and their agreement to control accounts,
c) the posting from books of original entry to the general ledger and checking of its additions and trial balance,
d) the build-up of monthly operating statements and other reports,
e) the reperformance of related balancing routines such as monthly bank reconciliations.

Second, the substantive tests of transactions involve an examination of the underlying documentary evidence from which the accounting entries were derived.

An aspect of the design of substantive tests calling for careful judgment is the decision as to how far back to trace related documentary evidence. For example, a sales entry can be checked back to a sales invoice, which in turn may have been derived from a shipping document, which in turn may have been triggered by a sales order. Moreover, each of these documents probably exist in several copies filed throughout the organization. Determining the appropriate documents and copies to be checked should be planned carefully in advance. If left to the moment of actual performance of the substantive procedures there is always the temptation to stop whenever one piece of paper can be agreed to some other piece of paper, whether that agreement is really substantiating the ultimate entry or merely checking the accuracy of some minor transcription routine along the way.

The objective of such transactional tests is to obtain reasonable assurance that the accounting records are accurate and reliable, that is, that during the course of the year they do not contain a material total of monetary error. To accomplish this objective the tests must be extensive enough that, if a material total of error had occurred, one or more instances of it would likely be detected in the tests. For important tests this is likely to mean significant sample sizes (larger, for example, than required for compliance verification of controls which may focus on a triple materiality level). Usually the tests should be drawn from throughout the whole year. Further guidance on substantive test extents may be found in Chapters 12 and 13. For less important procedures, less extensive tests may be satisfactory and sometimes these may be concentrated in one period (such as a month) provided that there is reasonable evidence through observations and enquiries that systems have not altered throughout the year. As discussed earlier in this chapter, some tests may serve a review objective instead of or as well as a substantive objective.

Transactional tests are usually recorded on a sepa-

Example of a Transactional Test Program — Sales/Receivables

	Objectives of procedures	Extent	Initial	Results
	(S) Substantive (R) Review			
Sales journal				
Post to general ledger	S + R	May		
Add and cross-add	S + R	May		
Post to accounts receivable subledger	S + R	May		
Scrutinize	S	Year		
Accounts receivable subledger				
Clear postings	S + R	May		
Add accounts	S + R	May A-D		
Trial balance and agree to general ledger	S	May 31		
Scrutinize for year	S	Active accounts		
Sales documents				
Check numerical continuity of shipping document (green copy)	S + R	5 blocks of 100		
Check details from shipping documents to sales orders	R	25		
Check quantities for customer from shipping documents to sales invoices (blue copy)	S + R	} Representative sample of 300 from year		
Check sales invoice prices	S + R			
Check sales tax	S + R			
Check adds and extensions	S + R			
Agree sales invoice to sales journal	S + R			
Check from sales invoice (green copy) to sales invoice costing copy (blue)	S + R			
Credit memos				
Check from A/R subledger (all detail) to credit memos	S + R	30 selected at random		
Check numerical continuity of credit memos	S + R	4 blocks of 25		
Examine authorization and underlying support for credit memos	S + R	30 selected at random		

Figure 9.e

rate schedule and sometimes carried forward from year to year. Such a schedule could indicate the audit procedures, their objectives (whether substantive and/or review), their extents, their results, and the auditor's conclusions. An example of a transactional test program is illustrated in Figure 9.e. Suggestions for transactional tests by major systems area may be found in Chapter 29.

In evaluating the results of transactional tests the auditor must not look solely at the size of any monetary errors encountered (which may be immaterial) but at their projected effect on the accounting population from which they were drawn. Guidance for projecting most likely and possible population errors from test results is contained in Chapters 12 and 13. Where the auditor concludes from the substantive test results that the monetary errors in the accounting records for the year could not be material, he may place reliance on these records when planning the

further substantive procedures required at the year-end to substantiate each financial statement figure. In establishing this reliance (Path II in Figure 9.a) the auditor is largely bypassing reliance on controls (Path I in Figure 9.a). However, it is important that he not overlook any controls on which reliance is unavoidable. For example, substantive tests of transactions can give assurance that recorded transactions have been recorded correctly but they often cannot give assurance that all transactions have been recorded. For this latter assurance the auditor may have to place reliance on certain controls and these controls should then be subjected to appropriate compliance verification.

9.5.2 Other substantive procedures

Substantive procedures otherwise required during the financial statement audit but which can most

usefully be commenced at an interim date can themselves be divided into two components:
1. the regular substantive verification of assets, liabilities and income statement components to determine if a material monetary misstatement has occurred,
2. substantive procedures designed specifically to compensate for observed weaknesses in internal control.

Regular substantive verification of assets, liabilities and income components

The objectives, methods and evaluation of the regular substantive verification of assets, liabilities, and income statement components are described in Chapter 11. The portion of those procedures which can conveniently be started during the interim audit are usually procedures involving (a) tests of transactions to the extent they are required and have not already been performed in establishing the accuracy and reliability of the accounting records and (b) the gathering of statistical data for analytical review.

As an example of the first type, tests of fixed asset additions could be started during the interim audit. As an example of the second type, where it is decided that analytical review of labour costs (relating costs to number of employees, volume of production, etc.) will be an important part of the substantive verification of inventories and cost of sales, statistics can be gathered and a preliminary analysis made during the interim audit. Unexplained inconsistencies will call for further investigation. An unfavourable and unexplained labour quantity variance may suggest poor control over direct labour and the possibility of 'over-booking' of piece-work. In a sense the unexplained variance, until resolved, is an apparent weakness just as much as weaknesses identified during the formal evaluation of internal control.

Substantive procedures to compensate for observed weaknesses in internal control

As discussed in 6.7, where a weakness in control has been identified, the auditor will need to obtain assurance that no material monetary error has occurred as a result of that weakness. Thus, for each observed control deficiency, the auditor should: (a) identify an already planned procedure which will detect the error, if it exists; or (b) plan a revision to the nature, timing or extent of a year-end procedure; or (c) plan special compensating procedures to be performed during the interim audit or at the year-end. Where the third alternative is employed the substantive procedures are sometimes called *compensating audit procedures* (a term used, for example, in the CICA

Study, *Computer Audit Guidelines*) or *weakness investigation procedures* (the term used more commonly throughout this book).

Whatever the timing, the possible choice of procedures includes: analysis of variance accounts, analysis of budget performance, additional intensive scrutiny of certain records, reconciliation of operating statistics, further questioning of employees, examination of documents for larger transactions for the entire year, examination of a representative sample of documents for the year, increase in the extent of year-end procedures, etc. Devising the weakness investigation which has the best chance of detecting any errors material enough to distort the financial statements should they occur is a matter for careful judgement. Extended tests of documents are not necessarily the best answer, although sometimes they may be required. An example of the documentation of weakness investigation is given in Figure 26.e.

9.5.3 Dual-purpose procedures

While compliance and substantive procedures have been discussed separately, and while their objectives, nature, and extent should generally be *planned* separately on an engagement, they may sometimes be *performed* together where both procedures are being applied to the same set of records or documents.

> For example, in the audit of an organization having a major capital expenditure program (such as a utility), the auditor may wish to place considerable reliance on authorization and approval controls evidenced on fixed asset purchase invoices. But he will also wish to conduct a substantive test of fixed asset purchases to substantiate the total additions for the year. Since the two tests are being applied to the same set of documents (fixed asset purchase invoices), one sample of these documents can be drawn and tested for both objectives together.

Where compliance and substantive procedures are performed together on the same records or documents, they are usually called dual-purpose procedures. Of course, the procedures must be adequate to meet both compliance and substantive objectives. For example, where tests or samples are involved, the sample size must be equal to the greater of the two separate sample sizes otherwise required (usually the substantive sample size).

In theory, the compliance procedures, if otherwise calling for a smaller sample size, could be applied to such a smaller sample picked randomly out of the larger substantive sample; in practice this double selection process could be cumbersome. Accordingly, when a dual-purpose sample is selected the auditor will usually apply both the compliance procedures (checking approvals etc.) and substantive procedures (vouching the supporting documentary evidence) to all items in the sample.

When a dual-purpose test is being planned, the substantive sample size (which will usually determine the dual-purpose sample size) may be established in anticipation of reliance on control. If the compliance results in this dual-purpose test later prove to be unacceptable, the auditor will not be able to place reliance on control and he may therefore have to extend his original substantive sample size correspondingly.

9.6 Interim audit strategies

Combining the foregoing elements of review, evaluation, compliance verification, and substantive verification in different proportions, three basic interim audit strategies can be identified:
• a systems-oriented interim audit,
• a data-oriented interim audit,
• in rare cases, omission of the interim audit.

9.6.1 Systems-oriented interim audit

In the systems-oriented approach, the primary emphasis is placed not directly on the *end results* of the accounting system (although an assessment of end results in the form of financial statements is of course the ultimate audit objective). Rather the primary emphasis is placed on systems and controls—on the *methods* by which the end results are ultimately produced. The rationale is that, if the methods by which the end results (financial reporting) are produced are thoroughly understood and if the checks and balances to forestall errors are found to be reliable throughout the period, then these findings will provide reasonable assurance that the results produced by the system will be accurate. This assurance will then influence the planning of the financial statement audit.

The systems-oriented approach may thus be said to audit through the system. Some end results will still be tested – in the substantive verification of areas where controls prove unreliable or where reliance on control proves uneconomical. Nevertheless, the emphasis will tend to be more on systems study and analysis and less on extensive testing.

In terms of the audit elements discussed in this chapter, the systems-oriented approach will contain extensive review and evaluation elements, extensive compliance verification, and proportionately less substantive verification.

9.6.2 Data-oriented interim audit

In the data-oriented approach, the primary emphasis is placed on direct tests of the end results of the accounting system. The rationale is that, if enough of the end results are tested and found satisfactory, then these findings will provide reasonable assurance that the other end results (books of account, general ledger, financial statements) will be accurate as well. This assurance will then influence the planning of the financial statement audit.

The data-oriented approach may thus be said to audit around the system. Of course, some study and analysis of systems will still be done (if only to provide the information to design appropriate tests) and some evaluation of controls will take place (because reliance on a few controls may be essential). Nevertheless, the emphasis will tend to be more on extensive testing and less on systems study and analysis.

In terms of the audit elements discussed in this chapter, the data-oriented approach will contain limited review, evaluation, and compliance verification elements and extensive substantive verification.

9.6.3 Omission of interim audit

In rare cases, where no reliance can be economically placed on the accuracy of the accounting records, the interim audit will consist exclusively of substantive verification. In some of these situations it is useful to perform the substantive procedures at an interim date – in which case the approach is an extreme form of the data-oriented approach. In other situations it may be more convenient for all the substantive procedures to be performed together during the financial statement audit – in which case the interim audit may be omitted entirely.

9.6.4 Criteria for choice of audit strategy

The systems-oriented approach can only be applied where a reasonably defined system and set of internal controls exist. These conditions are met in most medium and larger engagements. However, it is also possible to use the data-oriented approach on medium and larger engagements as well. In small engagements there may be no well-defined structure of control to be analyzed or relied upon and in these engagements the data-oriented approach is necessary. In very small engagements the omission of the interim audit and inclusion of all procedures in the financial statement audit may be appropriate.

In the wide range of engagements where both

systems-oriented and data-oriented approaches are possible the choice will depend on economy and on the preferences of the individual practitioner or firm. A systems-oriented approach is logical where the auditor must place or chooses to place considerable reliance on many controls. For example, where major assets and liabilities are verified at dates prior to the year-end considerable reliance may have to be placed on controls for the intervening period. Also, in many cases, reliance must be placed on controls over the initial recording of transactions. A systems-oriented audit usually facilitates the reporting of suggestions on control, efficiency and other matters to the client (secondary objective). However, the systems-oriented approach may make greater demands on staff training and supervision. Moreover, where compliance verification of apparently strong controls would be very costly, it may be more economical to bypass control and plan instead more extensive substantive tests - in which case the data-oriented approach may make sense.

Decision by systems area

The whole interim audit need not be performed in one way. It may be that the sales and receivables area has a well-structured system of internal controls to which the systems-oriented approach can be conveniently applied; payrolls, on the other hand, may be known to have poor controls and may be an area where the data-oriented approach can be most efficiently applied. In practice, there are certain financial statement components that are nearly always more efficiently verified either on a data-oriented interim audit basis or, more usually, at the year-end. These components include temporary investments (except in very large portfolios), miscellaneous receivables, prepaid expenses, fixed assets (except where there are major capital expenditure programs), deferred charges, miscellaneous accruals,

taxes payable, deferred taxes, long-term debt, shareholders' equity, depreciation, tax provision, and investment income. The remaining components can often be grouped into major systems areas such as:
• sales/receivables/receipts,
• purchases/payables/payments,
• wages and salary payrolls,
• inventory records and cost records.
The choice between systems-oriented and data-oriented approaches can then be made separately for each of these major systems areas.

Practitioners will differ in how they make these choices and no one answer is necessarily the only correct one. In the writer's view, the factors which should logically influence the decision include the following.

1. The more formalized the system and the more extensive the controls, the more likely a systems-oriented approach will be desirable.
2. Generally large volumes of transactions and complex systems (including computerized systems) will favour a systems-oriented approach.
3. However, a few sophisticated computer systems may have such complexity that analysis is difficult and a data-oriented approach may be desirable.
4. Small volumes of transactions will favour a data-oriented approach.
5. The greater the cost savings possible in the financial statement audit through reliance on control the more a systems-oriented interim audit is indicated.
6. If there are likely to be very few controls on which reliance could be placed, a data-oriented interim audit may be more efficient.
7. The checking of the general ledger and build-up of monthly management reports is usually best done using a data-oriented approach.

The criteria for making the choice of approach as part of the audit planning process are discussed further in Chapter 24.

9.7 Interim audits of computer systems

The presence of a computer does not alter interim audit objectives but it usually affects the best choice of procedures to achieve those objectives. The effects of the computer on the choice of audit procedures arise from (a) the changed system of internal control and (b) the possibility of using computer-assisted audit techniques.

As with manual systems there are two general approaches to the interim audit of computerized systems, systems-oriented and data-oriented. [22] In one sense computerization may favour the systems-

oriented approach, for the computer generally requires a more formal, rigid and reliable system. The auditor can place considerable reliance on this more rigid system if he has properly analyzed and evaluated the new types of computer controls. In another sense computerization may favour the data-oriented approach, for computerized files may permit more extensive selection, analysis, comparison and editing of data (especially with computer-assisted techniques) than possible before.

Use of a systems-oriented approach

In the writer's view, the circumstances in most computerized systems favour the systems-oriented approach. Modifications from systems-oriented audits of manual systems will be required, however, because of the different nature of the detailed controls in computer systems (as described in Chapter 8), compared to manual systems, from changes in the nature of audit trails, from the effects of increasing centralization within the EDP function, from the speed and accuracy of electronic processing per se, and from the tendency toward more complex and integrated systems. These modifications will include different methods of reviewing controls peculiar to computer systems (for example, the review of processing within the computer phase), different methods of conducting compliance procedures (for example, the verification of programmed controls), and different methods of performing substantive verification (through the use of the computer itself).

Use of a data-oriented or combined approach

Some small enterprises using a limited degree of computer services (perhaps through an outside data centre) are best audited on a data-oriented basis using techniques not much different from those in the data-oriented audit of a manual system.

At the other extreme, are the dozen or so largest and most complex computer systems in the country. Here it is possible that the sheer complexity of the system would consume so much time in systems analysis and compliance procedures that the usual payback in reliance on controls might not be worth the cost. While each case must be judged on its merits, some of these most complex engagements may favour the data-oriented approach, making extensive use of the computer-assisted techniques described in Chapter 14. Even here, however, a careful review of certain of the computer controls is usually important.

Environmental controls vs. processing controls

One element in the structure of the computer control system usually has a significant effect on the design of interim audit procedures; that is, the distinction between environmental controls and processing controls. This distinction has already been made in Chapter 8. The review of processing controls (for example, input/output controls in a payroll system, programmed controls in a billing system) is an integral part of the review of each major system involved. The review of environment controls (pre-installation, organizational, development, operations,

and documentation controls) is distinct from this and is usually best conducted before the review of individual systems. The intensity of the auditor's review of environmental controls will depend upon the degree of reliance he intends to place upon them. In some computer audits, the primary emphasis can be placed on the compliance verification of the continuous operation of a given processing control (such as a programmed control) throughout the year. In other computer audits, it may be more efficient to focus the compliance verification of the programmed control at one point of time and rely on environmental controls (such as controls over program changes) to provide assurance as to its continuous operation throughout the year. In the latter case, some compliance procedures must be applied to the environmental controls themselves in order to justify this reliance.

Analysis of computer controls by attest and not-of-attest significance

In 9.1.5 the attest and not-of-attest significance of basic control elements was analyzed. The significance of organizational, development, and documentation controls described in that section apply equally to computer systems. Computer controls not specifically discussed in that secion include pre-installation controls, operations controls and processing controls. Pre-installation controls, being really an extension of development controls, are generally not of attest significance. Uneconomic use of computer resources does not in itself impair the reliability of the financial statements. Most operations controls are of attest significance to the extent the auditor places reliance on the computer environment. However controls relating to security, safeguarding and back-up (a part of operations controls) are not generally of attest significance. Processing controls are generally of attest significance as they form an integral part of the accounting systems controls for each major system. However, the quality of management trails (a part of processing controls), while it may affect the choice of audit procedures, will not usually influence the degree of audit reliance on control.

Audit training

Most of the techniques described earlier in this chapter – flow charting, use of questionnaires, etc. – can be modified for use in audits of computerized systems. Because of these modifications, however, and because of the need for some familiarity with underlying computer concepts, it is important that the audit staff performing the work have had adequate training in the auditing of computer-based systems.

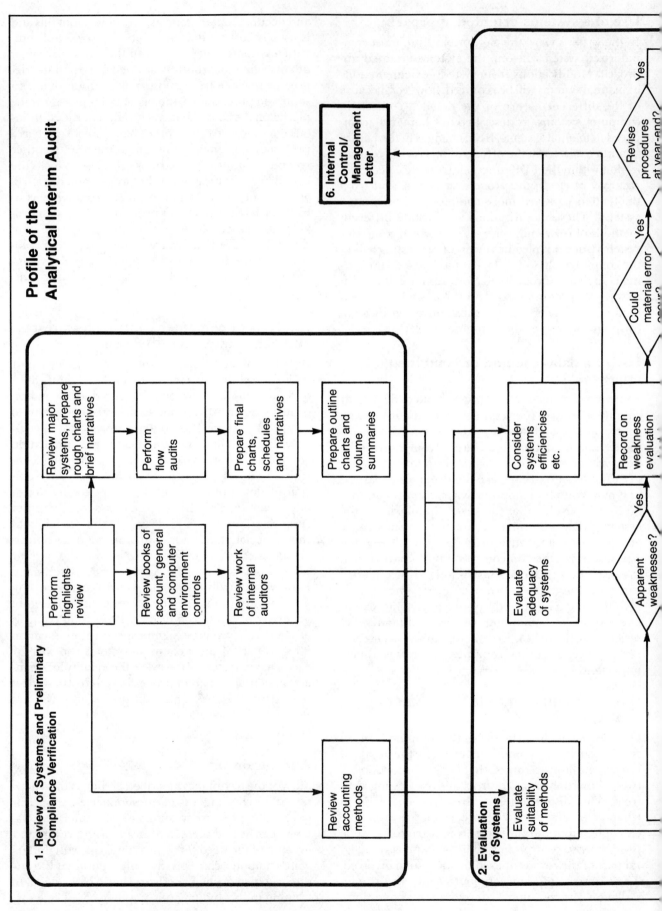

Profile of the
Analytical Interim Audit

1. Review of Systems and Preliminary Compliance Verification

- Perform highlights review
- Review major systems, prepare rough charts and brief narratives
- Perform flow audits
- Prepare final charts, schedules and narratives
- Prepare outline charts and volume summaries
- Review books of account, general and computer environment controls
- Review work of internal auditors
- Review accounting methods

2. Evaluation of Systems

- Consider systems efficiencies etc.
- Evaluate adequacy of systems
- Evaluate suitability of methods
- Record on weakness evaluation

Apparent weaknesses? Yes

Could material error occur? Yes

Revise procedures at year-end? Yes

6. Internal Control/ Management Letter

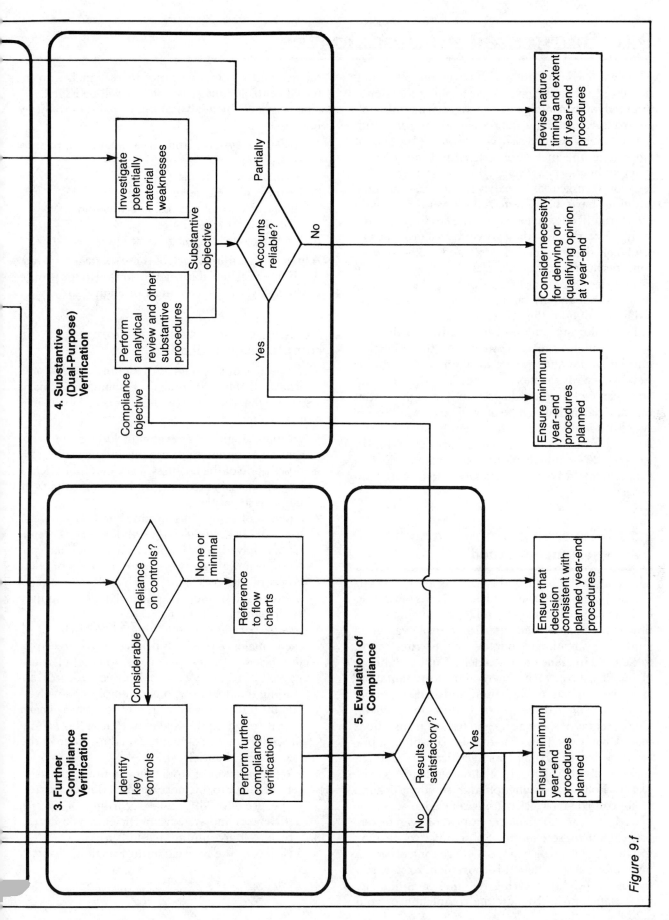

Figure 9.f

241

9.8 Suggested methodologies

This chapter is concluded with a brief outline of one suggested methodology for performing a systems-oriented interim audit and one suggested methodology for performing a data-oriented interim audit. The former is termed *analytical auditing* [23] because it emphasizes the analysis of systems and controls; the latter, *transactional auditing* because it emphasizes tests of transactions. Analytical and transactional auditing have been tested on several thousand interim audit engagements over the last fifteen years. In the writer's view, they are an efficient means of applying the systems-oriented and data-oriented concepts in practice. Nonetheless, it is clear that these can be viewed only as one set of suggestions. Many different but equally valid methodologies are in use today throughout the profession.

The following outlines are intended to do little more than list the components of the analytical interim audit and transactional interim audit. A step-by-step description of the analytical interim audit can be found in Chapter 26 – though most of the material in that chapter should be relevant to any systems-oriented approach. A step-by-step description of the transactional interim audit can be found in Chapter 28 – though most of the material in that chapter should be relevant to any data-oriented approach.

9.8.1 The analytical interim audit (systems-oriented)

The analytical interim audit makes use of (a) a combination of flow-charting and limited tests of transactions as review techniques and (b) a combination of flow chart analysis and internal control evaluation guides as evaluation techniques. In the writer's view, these combinations offer a coherent understanding of systems, a convenient method of documentation, an efficient means of evaluation, and an opportunity for identifying many useful suggestions to the client. The observations, enquiries and tests of transactions made during the flow charting also constitute a preliminary degree of compliance verification – enough for controls on which only minimum reliance is to be placed. Following evaluation and the identification of key controls on which considerable reliance is to be placed, "further compliance verification" can be performed on those controls. Substantive verification will then be performed in areas where control is weak or in other areas where it is convenient to start substantive procedures during the interim audit. Further evaluation will follow the completion of com-

pliance and substantive procedures. Finally, an internal control/management letter will be issued.

The stages of the analytical interim audit are therefore:

1. review of systems and preliminary compliance verification,
2. evaluation of systems,
3. further compliance verification,
4. substantive (dual-purpose) verification,
5. evaluation of compliance,
6. internal control/management letter.

A brief description of each of these six stages follows. Their inter-relationships are illustrated in the profile of the analytical interim audit in Figure 9.f.

Review of systems and preliminary compliance verification

The objective of this stage is to identify any relevant internal controls and to achieve some preliminary assurance that they are operating as prescribed. The basic steps include:

1. an initial highlights review (including the preparation or updating of organization charts and a description of the business, a review of the client's latest financial statements, and a general review of major systems areas),
2. a review of general accounting controls, budgets, the books of account system, and, where a computer is involved, the computer environmental controls (including the preparation or updating of a books of account chart, a schedule of management reports, and, if appropriate, a computer environment questionnaire),
3. the preparation or updating of flow charts of each major system (sales/receivables/receipts, purchases/payables/ payments, wages and salary payrolls, inventory records and cost records) including discussions with each employee involved and the tracing of four or five transactions of each type throughout the system (the latter 'flow audit' procedures are documented on the bottom of the flow charts themselves),
4. the preparation or updating of outline charts to serve as a key to the more detailed flow charts and to be used for the initial recording of control deficiencies and systems inefficiencies observed,
5. a review of accounting methods used,
6. a review of the internal audit function, if any.

Evaluation of systems

The objective of this stage is to form conclusions on those internal controls relevant to the audit. The basic steps include:

1. an analysis of information gathered during the review stage and its evaluation with the help of internal control evaluation guides,
2. an analysis of internal control deficiencies observed to consider if they could permit material errors and, if so, what weakness investigation or revision of year-end procedures should be planned,
3. a review of systems inefficiencies observed and any other matters for inclusion in the internal control/management letter,
4. an evaluation of accounting methods used.

Further compliance verification

The objectives of this stage are to determine the degree of reliance to be placed on each satisfactory control area, to identify key controls on which considerable reliance is to be placed, and to perform any necessary further compliance verification of those key controls. The basic steps include:

1. decisions as to whether no, minimum, or considerable reliance is to be placed on each major control area (each area corresponding to a primary control question on the internal control evaluation guides),
2. identification of the key controls within areas designated for considerable reliance,
3. determination of the compliance verification necessary to establish the presence, effectiveness and continuity of operation of that control and to assess whether a triple materiality frequency of critical compliance deviations could have occurred,
4. performance of that compliance verification to the extent not already included in the preliminary compliance verification.

Substantive (dual-purpose) verification

The objective of this stage is to perform those substantive procedures resulting from the need to compensate for specific control deficiencies identified during the interim audit and any other substantive procedures which can most conveniently be started during the interim audit. The basic steps include:

1. designing and performance of weakness investigation procedures where called for as a result of the earlier evaluation,
2. analytical review procedures or the gathering of statistics for later analytical review,
3. substantive or dual-purpose tests of transactions where necessary to meet final financial statement audit objectives,
4. substantive or dual-purpose tests of books of account, budgets, monthly statements, etc.

Evaluation of compliance

The objective of this stage is to evaluate the results of compliance verification and, based on this evaluation, to confirm or modify the earlier evaluation of internal control. If the results of compliance verification are unsatisfactory, it may be necessary to design and perform further substantive weakness investigation procedures.

Internal control/management letter

The final stage in the interim audit is the preparation and issue of a report to management on the results of the review, evaluation and compliance verification of the accounting systems. In addition, as indicated on the bottom of Figure 9.f, the results of the interim audit lead to decisions affecting the planning of the year-end procedures (the financial statement audit).

9.8.2 The transactional audit (data-oriented)

The transactional interim audit makes use of (a) an internal control evaluation guide as both a review and evaluation technique and (b) tests of transactions as substantive verification to assess the accuracy and reliability of the accounting records. The review of controls is less intensive than in an analytical audit (no flow charting, no tracing through of transactions of each type at the review stage, less detailed discussions) because very much less reliance is likely to be placed on internal control. Information gathered from tests of transactions, however, may be considered to serve review and evaluation objectives as well. For the few controls which may be present and on which the auditor places reliance, the related transactional tests must be designed to serve compliance objectives. After evaluation of the transactional tests, an internal control/management letter is normally issued.

The steps of the transactional interim audit are therefore:

1. review and preliminary evaluation of systems,
2. test of transactions,
3. evaluation of transactional tests,
4. internal control/management letter.

A brief description of each of these four stages follows. Their inter-relationships are illustrated in the profile of the transactional interim audit in Figure 9.g.

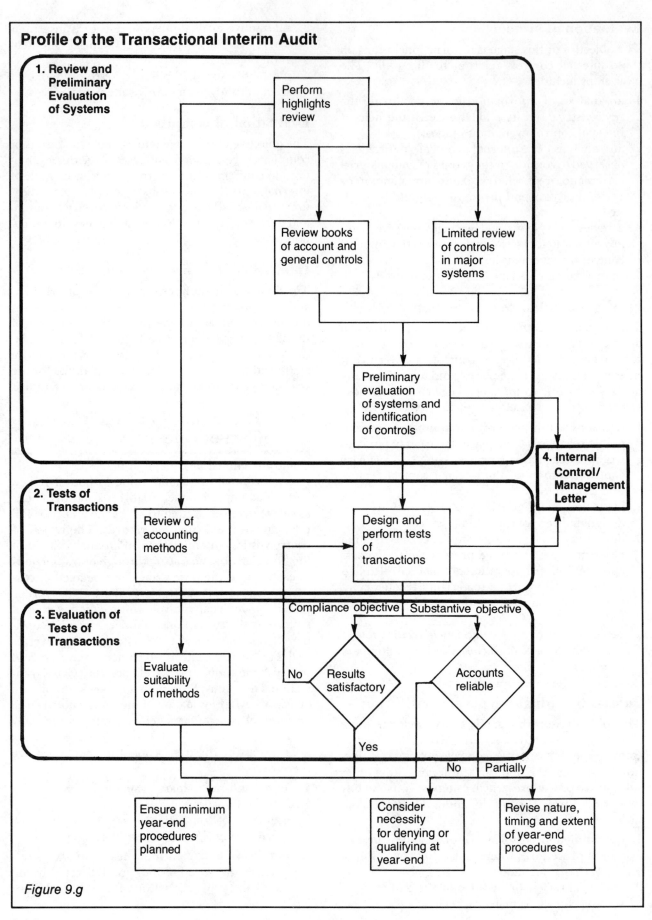

Profile of the Transactional Interim Audit

1. Review and Preliminary Evaluation of Systems

Perform highlights review

Review books of account and general controls

Limited review of controls in major systems

Preliminary evaluation of systems and identification of controls

4. Internal Control/ Management Letter

2. Tests of Transactions

Review of accounting methods

Design and perform tests of transactions

3. Evaluation of Tests of Transactions

Evaluate suitability of methods

Compliance objective

Substantive objective

No — Results satisfactory — Yes

Accounts reliable

No / Partially

Ensure minimum year-end procedures planned

Consider necessity for denying or qualifying at year-end

Revise nature, timing and extent of year-end procedures

Figure 9.g

244

Review and preliminary evaluation of systems

The objective of this stage is to identify and review relevant internal controls, make a preliminary evaluation of their adequacy, and gain sufficient knowledge of the systems in order to permit an appropriate program of transactional tests to be designed. The basic steps include:

1. an initial highlights review (including the preparation or updating of organization charts and a description of the business, a review of the client's latest financial statements, and a general review of major systems areas),
2. a review of general accounting controls, budgets and the books of account system (including the preparation of a books of account chart and a schedule of management reports),
3. a limited review of accounting procedures and controls by major systems (sales/receivables/receipts, purchases/payables/payments, wages and salary payrolls) with the help of internal control evaluation guides (particularly emphasizing management supervisory controls),
4. a preliminary evaluation of the systems with the help of the internal control evaluation guides for the purpose of designing an appropriate program of substantive transactional tests (or, in the cases where some controls will be relied upon, compliance transactional tests).

Tests of transactions

The objectives of this stage are to design and perform a program of transactional tests to assess the accuracy and reliability of the client's accounting records based on internal evidence and to determine whether the prescribed internal controls, to the extent that reliance is being placed thereon, are functioning.

The transactional test program may be structured by major accounting system, together with the books of account system. Within each accounting system the tests may be organized by primary control area. Each specific test may have one or more of review, compliance or substantive objectives. In performing the transactional tests the auditor should be alert for information on accounting methods used.

Evaluation of tests of transactions

The objective of this stage is primarily to draw conclusions concerning the accuracy and reliability of the accounting records and secondarily to evaluate internal controls that are relevant to the audit. This objective is accomplished through an assessment of the results of the tests of transactions, a review of related information gained during these tests, and a re-appraisal of the preliminary evaluation of internal control. Additionally, at this stage, the auditor may identify systems inefficiencies and any other matters for inclusion in the internal control/management letter.

Internal control/management letter

As in the analytical interim audit, the final stages are the preparation and issue of a report to management and, as indicated at the bottom of Figure 9.g, decisions affecting the planning of year-end procedures.

9.9 Reference material

Interim audits in general

CICA Exposure Draft of Proposed Auditing Recommendations, *Internal Control* (1976). The reader should refer to subsequent pronouncements.
CICA Audit Technique Study, *Internal Control and Procedural Audit Tests* (1968).
AICPA Statement on Auditing Standards No. 1, Section 320, "The Auditor's Study and Evaluation of Internal Control".
AICPA *Case Studies in Internal Control*.

Interim audits of computer systems

CICA Study, *Computer Audit Guidelines* (1975).
AICPA Statement on Auditing Standards No. 3, *The Effects of EDP on the Auditor's Study and Evaluation of Internal Control*.

9.10 Questions and problems

Review and discussion

1. What are the primary and secondary objectives of the interim audit? How do these relate to overall audit objectives and general professional objectives?

2. What are the four basic elements of the interim audit? How are they related?
3. Discuss the impact of internal controls, or lack thereof, on the auditor's evaluation of the accounting records. Why do auditors rely on internal controls?

4. Briefly describe the attest significance of each of the following controls. Use examples in your answer.
   a) Organizational controls
   b) Systems development controls
      • manual system
      • computer system
   c) Authorization and reporting controls
   d) Accounting systems controls
   e) Management supervisory controls
   f) Documentation controls

5. Define compliance and substantive verification. How are they related?

6. Discuss the purposes of testing transactions in an interim audit.

7. How does an auditor identify the key controls on which he may rely? What degree of reliance can properly be placed on a given control?

8. What are the three methods of evaluation of internal controls? Discuss the ramifications of each method and explain which method you would prefer for (a) small clients, (b) medium-sized clients and (c) large clients.

9. What are the advantages and disadvantages of the standardized questionnaire approach as a means of gathering information on systems and controls?

10. What are the advantages and potential abuses of the flow chart approach of reviewing a client's accounting system?

11. Differentiate between compliance deviations and critical compliance deviations. What is the effect of each on an audit program?

12. Identify three types of compliance procedures. How are compliance procedures related to the review stage of the interim audit?

13. Why is it difficult to find evidence of the existence of detective controls?

14. List five audit trails to be tested substantively in order to reperform, on a test basis, the principal bookkeeping routines.

15. Why should transactional tests be drawn from throughout the fiscal period under review?

16. Where a weakness is observed in internal control, what three planning decisions should an auditor make?

17. Give three examples of a dual-purpose procedure, (i.e., serving both compliance and substantive objectives).

18. In a dual purpose test, compliance test procedures should be applied to all items in the sample. However, if the tests were done separately, the sample required for the compliance test might be only one-quarter of the sample required for the dual test. Explain.

19. The Good Foam Co. is a local root brewery. It produces one brand of root beer and sells all its product to one customer (a local distributor). The sales system is sophisticated and well defined. The customer also has good accounting records and is independent of Good Foam and its external auditors.

   Suggest various different means of substantively verifying Good Foam's sales for its current fiscal year.

20. Indicate the major financial statement components that can normally be efficiently verified on a data-oriented basis.

21. Differentiate between analytical and transactional interim audits and describe conditions (using a payroll system as an example) where each approach might be the most appropriate.

Problems

1. Bob J. (a new student) and Ed S. (a recent CA) are discussing the audit approach they would take on their new client, Crooked Board Ltd. (a small lumber retailer). One of Ed's first comments was, "Before the Company's year-end we should take a look at the system of internal control to see where we can limit our procedures at the financial statement audit." Bob's immediate reaction (he was presently studying internal control and flowcharting in an auditing course) was, "That's useless – a company that small can't have any kind of system, so there is no point in conducting any kind of an audit until year-end."

   Outline the merits and shortcomings of each statement.

2. Ken Orange, CA, audit senior of Trident Co. for the 1976 fiscal year, discovered during the course of the interim audit that the following weaknesses in the system of internal control, which had been reported to management and the board of directors in previous years, were still in existence.
   a) Petty cash is not an imprest account.
   b) Suppliers' statements are not reconciled by the accounts payable clerk.
   c) Unmatched receiving reports and unmatched invoices are not investigated regularly.

   All three items have been reported by the external auditors in abbreviated form as above for the last three years. The client has indicated an unwillingness to remedy these weaknesses.
   a) What factors should be considered when reporting weaknesses and inefficiencies to management this year?
   b) What are the reasons for and against Ken Orange reporting the three weaknesses to management and the board of directors again?

3. Build All Co. is a medium-sized manufacturer of several lines of the famous widget. Eddy Frypod, CA, has been assigned as the audit senior of Build All for the current fiscal year. Eddy has met the accounting personnel and has had a tour of the processing plant and warehouse.

Eddy is very keen to perform the review element of the interim audit.

a) Suggest sources of information for Eddy to document the following:
- the nature of the business,
- the overall plan of organization,
- the accounting/finance organization plan,
- the organization of the EDP department,
- general information as to the computer environment,
- identifying specific systems and controls therein.

b) What are the advantages and disadvantages of the sources of information suggested?

4. Widget Manufacturing Limited is a medium-sized manufacturer located in South Western Ontario. Trant & Co., Chartered Accountants, were appointed auditors for their current fiscal year. R. Cleaver, CA, the audit senior on the job, has three audit assistants aiding him during the interim audit.

Trant & Co. have decided to use a systems-oriented approach during the interim audit. Cleaver, having completed the initial highlights review and review of the general accounting controls, budgets and the books of account system, has delegated the preparation of the flow charts of each major system to his audit assistants.

John Junior has been assigned the sales system, and after a general review of the system with Cleaver, he discusses the system with various members of the client's staff.

Junior talks first to Mr. Jones, an order clerk. Jones receives customer's purchase orders by mail and by phone and from that he prepares a four-part internal sales order form. Company salesmen also send him orders which they have prepared on the same forms. If the customer's orders are written, they are then filed in the customer's file. The sales order is assigned a consecutive number from the order register and the date and customer's name are entered in the order register beside that number. The sales order set is sent to the shipper, who returns the fourth copy to the second order clerk, M. Wright, after shipment.

Junior next talks to Mr. Wright. Wright enters the shipping date beside the original entry in the order register. He then files the order form in the customer's file. However, if the order was only filled partially, he holds it separately in a file by part number. He periodically checks this file of back-ordered items and, when stock is available, he initiates a new order form for the balance and files the old one in the customer's file.

Junior moves on to the shipper's office in the warehouse. The shipper, B. Smith, outlines his procedures. He initials and dates the sales orders and enters the quantities actually shipped. The first copy is sent as a packing slip with the goods. The second copy is forwarded to the billing clerk. The third copy is used as a delivery copy for in-town orders, or as a basis for preparing a three part bill of lading for out-of-town orders. If the order is in-town, the customer signs the third copy and it is returned to the shipper who files it by date. If the order is out-of-town, and once the bill of lading has been prepared, the sales order is destroyed, copies one and two of the bill of lading are sent with the carrier and the third copy, having been signed by the carrier, is filed by date.

Junior, having finished with Smith, returns to the accounting department to talk to the billing clerk, A. Clark. Clark collects the sales orders in two or three day batches, and then prepares four-part prenumbered sales invoices. These are priced from a standard price list. Retailers and dealers receive discounts of 40% and 55% respectively. The eligible dealer's list is updated by the General Manager semi-annually. The original copy of the invoice is sent to the customer. The second, third and fourth copies are forwarded to the accounts receivable clerk, the inventory records clerk and the accounting department respectively.

Clark receives supporting documents for credit notes from which she prepares four-part credit notes. The credit notes are distributed in the same manner as the sales invoices.

Clark then introduces Junior to H. Warren, the accounts receivable clerk, who describes his function. Warren posts the invoices and credit notes directly to the customer's account card in the accounts receivable sub-ledger, at the same time preparing the customer's monthly statement (a carbon copy of the ledger card). The invoices and credit notes are then filed alphabetically. At month-end, he prepares an aged trial balance in duplicate. The first copy is sent to the comptroller and the second copy is filed by Warren.

Junior then talks to the accounting clerk, T. Walker. Walker enters the invoices and credit notes in the sales journal (posting source to the general ledger) and files them numerically. Periodically he checks the file for numeric continuity.

Junior is next introduced to S. Brown, the inventory records clerk. Brown posts the perpetual finished goods inventory records (units only) from the invoices and credit notes and uses the unit standard costs, as noted in the records, to cost the invoices and credit notes. He then enters the invoices and credit notes in the cost of sales journal (a posting source to the general ledger) and files them numerically. Periodically he accounts for the numerical continuity of these files.

Junior then reviews, with other accounting personnel, the cash receipts, cash sales and credit note initiation procedures.

a) What factors should have been considered by Trant & Co. and might have influenced its decision to use a systems-oriented approach to perform the interim audit as opposed to a data-oriented approach?

b) From the facts outlined during Junior's discussions with Widget's employees, prepare a flow chart outlining the sales system of Widget Manufacturing Limited. Use the general format illustrated in the lower portion of Figure 9.c together with the following symbols.

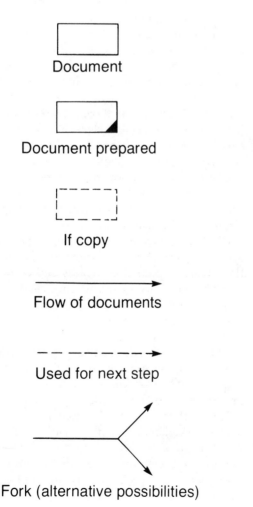

Document

Document prepared

If copy

Flow of documents

Used for next step

Fork (alternative possibilities)

Dead-end (leaves charted system)

Permanent file of documents
(alphabetically, numerically, or by date)

Serial continuity checked, unimportant, or unchecked respectively

Temporary file of documents
(alphabetically, numerically, or by date)

Attached

Destroyed

Initials

Signs

Book or ledger

Posting source

*

Keyed to explanatory note

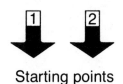

Starting points

Start your flow chart with the order clerk and, from left to right, attempt to segregate your chart into departments (in effect, the order in which Junior interviewed Widget's staff).

5. While flow charts are principally a review technique, they can also serve as an important evaluation tool. In analyzing a chart the auditor should ask himself for each step in the system, "What would happen if this one step were performed incorrectly or omitted either intentionally or accidentally? Would the error be detected automatically by the system?"

Using this approach, identify the apparent weaknesses in the sales system as outlined in problem number 4.

6. Describe how the presence of a computer affects the choice of interim audit procedures. In your discussion consider the systems-oriented approach and the data-oriented approach to computer systems controls, as outlined in Chapter 8, and the effect of these controls on audit staffing.

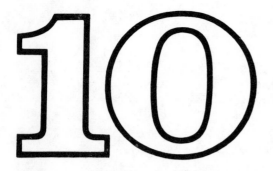

Audit Evidence and Audit Techniques

In the typical external audit, the auditor seeks *evidence* as to the degree of correspondence of financial statement assertions with established criteria. Audit verification is the process of *gathering* and *evaluating* such evidence. The nature and extent of audit evidence sought will depend upon the required *precision* and *degree of assurance* of the audit opinion, upon the *appropriateness (relevance and reliability)* and *sufficiency* of the evidence available, and upon the *timeliness* and *economy* with which that evidence can be gathered. These concepts were discussed in Chapter 6 (see particularly 6.4, 6.5 and 6.6). The purpose of the present chapter is to analyze the types of evidence available to the auditor and the types of evidence-gathering technique.

When a particular audit *technique* (such as vouching) is applied to a particular type of *evidence* (such as documentary evidence) to accomplish a particular *objective* (such as establishing the existence and valuation of fixed asset additions), the result may be described as a specific auditing *procedure* (vouching fixed asset purchase invoices). Specific auditing procedures are described in Chapters 23 to 44. The present chapter does not attempt to catalogue specific procedures, but rather to review the general characteristics of audit evidence and audit techniques.

10.1 Types of audit evidence and audit technique

10.1.1 Nature of audit evidence

Audit evidence is any perceived object, action, or condition relevant to the formation of a knowledgeable opinion on the financial statements. Perceived objects may include certain tangible assets (such as cash funds, inventories, and fixed assets), various documents, accounting records and reports, and written representations. Perceived actions generally consist of certain procedures performed by the client's employees. Perceived conditions may include the observed quality of assets, the apparent competence of employees met, the care with which procedures were seen to be performed, or an identified logical relationship with other facts known to the auditor.

Contrast with scientific and legal evidence

It is important to draw a distinction between audit evidence and evidence in other disciplines. As discussed in Chapter 6, the scientist, the judge, and the auditor must all accept evidence which is *persuasive* rather than *conclusive* but each of them may make the compromise between certainty of proof and practical availability of evidence differently. The scientist must be concerned with the possible effect of minor experimental errors when formulating exact scientific laws. Consequently, a prime requisite of scientific evidence is the 'repeatability' of experimental results within minute tolerance. The auditor is concerned with fair rather than precise measurement and this different objective does not warrant the time and cost of repetition of each audit step. Thus, evidence which would not meet scientific standards may often be perfectly appropriate for audit use. The judge must be concerned with the possible condem-nation of innocent parties. Consequently, legal evidence is defined by a number of detailed rules to give the defendant the benefit of the doubt and to require accusations to be substantiated with only the most reliable evidence (excluding, for example, hearsay evidence). The auditor is seeking reasonable evidence to support the financial statements rather than a preponderance of evidence to condemn a man to prison. Thus, oral discussions and enquiries which might not constitute legally admissible evidence for judicial purposes may quite properly be an important part of audit evidence.

Classifications of audit evidence

Audit evidence can be classified according to (a) its relevance to specific audit objectives (evidence as to existence, ownership, valuation etc.), (b) the type of logical proof it supplies (positive or negative), (c) its relationship to other evidence (underlying, corroborative, or contradictory), (d) its source (direct, indirect, etc.), (e) its nature (physical, documentary, etc.) or (f) the manner in which it is gathered (inspection, confirmation, enquiry, etc.). Each of these possible methods of classificaiton are discussed and the last three methods are then used as the basis of organization of this chapter.

10.1.2 Relevance to specific audit objectives

Overall audit objectives can be divided into *review*, *compliance* and *substantive* objectives. As was discussed in Chapter 9, compliance objectives can be further subdivided into establishing (a) the existence, (b) the effectiveness and (c) the continuity of operation of a given control. As will be discussed in Chapter 11, substantive objectives can be subdivided as well – for example, with respect to reported assets, into establishing their (a) existence, (b) ownership, (c) completeness, (d) valuation, and (e) statement presentation. Clearly, the auditor must seek evidence with respect to each of these individual objectives. Obtaining the most persuasive evidence as to the extent of a control will not compensate for failure to establish its continuity of operation. Obtaining the most persuasive evidence as to the existence and ownership of a reported asset will not compensate for failure to establish its completeness or its valuation. Audit evidence must be *relevant* to the specific objective it serves and each specific audit objective must ultimately be covered. Thus, in theory, audit evidence could be subdivided by objective.

In practice, many different types of evidence may serve a given objective. For example, the existence of reported inventories may be supported by a combination of direct examination, observation of client counting routines, review of related accounting records, confirmation of goods held by others, and pertinent enquiries. Thus, classification by objective does not itself help to identify the particular types of audit evidence Accordingly, while some references to specific objectives will be made throughout this chapter, objectives will not be used as a method of classifying evidence. For a more complete description of the specific objectives for which audit evidence must be sought, the reader is referred to Chapters 9 and 11.

10.1.3 Positive and negative evidence

Positive evidence is evidence directly supporting an assertion. For example, the reconciliation of interest expense with loans payable provides some positive evidence as to the assertion that reported loan liabilities are complete. Negative evidence is the absence of evidence, after reasonable searching for it, contradicting the assertion. For example, the failure to find, subsequent to the year-end, any repayments of undisclosed loan liabilities provides negative evidence indirectly supporting the assertion that reported loan liabilities are complete. A reply from a customer agreeing with an account receivable balance is positive evidence (positive confirmation). The absence of a reply to a request for disclosure of any disagreement with an account receivable balance is negative evidence (negative confirmation).

Positive evidence is inherently more reliable than negative evidence. Finding something right is more persuasive than merely not finding something wrong. It is always possible that not finding something wrong merely means that the auditor did not look hard enough. A repayment of an undisclosed liability may have occurred but escaped the attention of the

auditor. The customer may have discarded his monthly statement unread, thereby failing to notice serious errors in it. Because of its greater reliability, when positive evidence is practical to obtain it should be sought instead of or in addition to negative evidence. For example, positive confirmation is normally to be preferred to negative confirmation.

Sometimes, however, negative evidence is the only evidence available. This is particularly true with the completeness objective – which must generally be met by a search for undisclosed items.

In most cases, a combination of positive and negative evidence makes sense. The auditor obtains some evidence that reported results are correct (positive evidence) and then searches for and fails to find the types of error which might have occurred had the results not been correct (negative evidence).

For example, the auditor determines that the client's year-end cut-off procedures appear adequate and that gross profit trends can be accounted for (positive evidence). He checks purchases, sales, and inter-branch shipments close to the year-end (the ones most prone to inaccurate cut-off) and finds no cut-off errors among them (negative evidence).
The auditor observes during several different visits that certain divisions of duties have remained in force throughout the year (positive evidence). He searches for indications of systems changes by reviewing procedure manuals and making enquiries and finds no such indications (negative evidence).

In general, with respect to each assertion he is attempting to assess the auditor should ask himself:

1. If this assertion is correct, what evidence of its correctness should I expect to find? Have I looked for and found that evidence (its presence would be positive evidence)?
2. If this assertion were incorrect, what indications of error would likely arise (missing documents, out-of-balance conditions, inconsistent subsequent events, etc.)? Have I looked for and failed to find such indications (their absence would be negative evidence)?

While a consideration of both positive and negative evidence is important in most audit steps, classification of evidence into these two categories does not particularly further a general analysis of the different types of audit evidence available.

10.1.4 Underlying, corroborating and contradictory evidence

In any organization, the accounting records serve as a link between economic events and the financial statements or management reports. Because of this link, accounting records are often referred to as *underlying* evidence for the financial statement assertions, not sufficient in itself but a necessary component of the total evidence.

> The books of original entry, the general and subsidiary ledgers, related accounting manuals, and such informal and memorandum records as work sheets supporting cost allocations, computations, and reconciliations all constitute evidence in support of the financial statements. By itself, accounting data cannot be considered sufficient support for financial statements; on the other hand, without adequate attention to the propriety and accuracy of the underlying accounting data, an opinion on financial statements would not be warranted.[1]

Other evidence supporting the financial statements is then often described as *corroborating* evidence. The underlying and corroborating evidence taken together supply the support for the auditor's opinion.

This basis of classification has not been adopted in this chapter because corroborating evidence itself can be subdivided into some eight different types. Nonetheless, the distinction is a useful one. The importance of the evidence provided by the underlying accounting records is, in fact, the reason for the interim audit – as discussed in Chapter 9. Moreover, the accounting records, because they contain greater detail than the financial statements, serve as the focus for most verification. Thus, the auditor does not go directly from a financial statement figure (such as inventory) to a consideration of the different types of audit evidence he should seek in order to substantiate it. Rather, he goes first to the underlying accounting records, which will provide an analysis of all the different components making up the financial statement figure. How much and what inventory is held where and by whom? The very existence of this underlying detail provides some evidence of the correctness of the financial statement figure. Then, for each inventory component as revealed by the underlying accounting records, the auditor can plan the appropriate nature and extent of corroborating evidence to be sought.

Of course, the additional evidence will sometimes be found to contradict rather than corroborate earlier evidence. The auditor must take care to search for any possible *contradictory* evidence reasonably available to him and to examine and evaluate all such evidence encountered. As explained in Chapter 6, the fact that the active role of gathering evidence and the passive (in the sense of impartial) role of evaluating evidence are combined in the audit process, not separated as in the judicial process, places a responsibility on the auditor, as on the scientist, not to select only that evidence which favours a pre-conceived conclusion.

In developing his opinion, the auditor must give consideration to relevant evidential matter regardless of whether it appears to support or to contradict the representations made in the financial statements.[2]

When contradictory evidence is encountered the auditor must seek additional evidence to confirm or rebut the apparent contradiction. The additional evidence may indicate that the financial statements and underlying accounting records were materially in error and must be corrected before an unqualified opinion can be given. Alternatively, the additional evidence may sustain the initial representations and provide a satisfactory explanation for what at first appeared to be contradictory evidence. The auditor should, however, be careful not to accept glib or unsubstantiated explanations of apparent contradictions. Obviously, it should require more persuasive additional evidence to rebut apparently contradictory evidence than it would to corroborate the underlying accounting data in the absence of contradictory evidence.

10.1.5 Sources of audit evidence

Audit evidence may be classified according to its source as follows:

A. Direct personal knowledge of the auditor
B. External evidence (obtained from third parties)
C. Internal evidence (obtained from within the client's organization)
D. Overlapping evidence (the mutual consistency of different pieces of evidence obtained).

Generally, direct personal knowledge is more reliable than indirect evidence; external evidence is more reliable than internal evidence.[3] Direct observation of an item of inventory is usually more reliable evidence than confirmation from a third-party custodian, and confirmation in turn is more reliable than mere agreement with the accounting records. What degree of reliability is called for in any given audit procedure is a decision requiring the careful exercise of professional judgment.

Each of the foregoing four sources of audit evidence is covered in one of the following sections of this chapter.

10.1.6 Types of audit evidence

Within these four major divisions by source, audit evidence may be subclassified according to its nature (physical evidence vs. documentary evidence etc.). While numerous classification schemes are possible, the one adopted in this chapter distinguishes nine different types of audit evidence, as follows:

Source and type of evidence	Example of evidence
A. *Direct personal knowledge*	
1. Physical evidence	Actual inventory in the warehouse
2. Concurrence of reperformance (of accounting routines)	Concurrence of inventory extensions done by the auditor with those originally recorded on the inventory lists
3. Actions of client personnel	Careful routines followed by client personnel in counting stock
B. *External evidence*	
4. Statements and representations by third parties	Customer's agreement with an account receivable balance
5. External documentary evidence (if received directly from third parties)	Cancelled cheques obtained directly from the bank
C. *Internal evidence*	
6. Accounting records and reports	Perpetual inventory records
7. Internal documentary evidence (obtained from within the client organization)	Sales invoice copies
8. Statements and representations by management and employees	Explanations of unusual transactions
D. *Overlapping evidence*	
9. Consistency with other evidence	Concurrence of inventory counts and perpetual records with the results of a gross profit analysis

10.1.7 Types of audit technique

Finally, audit evidence can be classified according to the manner in which it is gathered, i.e., according to audit technique. Audit techniques may be either *qualitative* (what should be done) or *quantitative* (how much should be done). How much should be done is obvious in the case of an audit procedure that consists of obtaining confirmation of the one and only bank loan or of counting all the five marketable securities on hand. However, where the audit procedure consists of confirming some of the 5,000 accounts receivable balance, how much should be done is less obvious. The determination of test *extents* in such instances is a technique in itself (the technique of testing) and is discussed in Chapters 12 and 13. The audit techniques described in the present chapter are the qualitative techniques (the "what" rather than the "how much").

Some of the qualitative audit techniques are stated explicitly in the third fieldwork standard:

> Sufficient appropriate audit evidence should be obtained, by such means as inspection, observation, enquiry, confirmation, computation, and analysis, to afford a reasonable basis to support the content of the report.

While the phrase "by such means as" implies that the list given in the standard is not necessarily all-inclusive, it is possible to derive all basic audit techniques from the general ideas suggested in that list. If (a) the idea of visual "inspection" is subdivided into physical examination (of assets), vouching (of source documents for transactions), inspection (of other documents), and scrutiny (of records), (b) the idea of "analysis" is subdivided into analysis (in the sense of identification of components) and correlation with related information (as in analytical review), and (c) the idea of computation is expanded to the more general idea of reperformance (of accounting routines), one arrives at ten basic audit techniques (see top of next page).

In some cases, one technique is always associated with a particular type of audit evidence. For example, physical evidence of assets (the existence of inventory items in the warehouse) is obtained by physical examination by the auditor. In other cases, a given type of evidence may be subjected to any one of several different techniques. For example, shipping slips, purchase invoices, and employment contracts are all internal documentary evidence but the first may be scrutinized (for appropriate cut-off dates), the second vouched (to substantiate purchases), and the third inspected (for proper execution and approval). The relationships among source of audit evidence, type of audit evidence, and basic audit technique are shown in Figure 10.a.

As stated earlier, every audit technique involves the gathering of corroborating evidence related to

Basic audit technique	Example of technique
1. Physical examination (of assets)	Test count of actual inventory
2. Reperformance (of accounting routines)	Checking of extensions on inventory lists
3. Observation (of activities)	Observation of stocktaking routines
4. Enquiry	Enquiry about unusual transactions
5. Confirmation	Confirmation of accounts receivable balances
6. Scrutiny	Scrutiny of general ledger for the year
7. Vouching (of source documents for transactions)	Vouching of purchase invoices
8. Inspection (of other documents)	Inspection of lease agreements
9. Analysis (into components)	Analysis of repairs and maintenance accounts
10. Correlation with related information	Analytical review procedures on gross profit and inventory

some information in the accounting records. Each technique in Figure 10.a should therefore be thought of as including (a) the obtaining of the corroborating evidence, (b) its comparison to the underlying records and (c) the critical evaluation of the evidence and the drawing of a conclusion. Thus, the physical examination of an asset involves seeing the asset and comparing it to the records. Confirmation with a third party involves obtaining his confirmation and comparing it to the related accounting balance in the records. Vouching involves examining source documents and comparing the information on them to the related accounting records. The techniques of scrutiny and analysis shown beside accounting records and reports on Figure 10.a represent the techniques which, when applied to the accounting records, involve these records alone without reference to other sources of evidence.

Audit Evidence and Audit Techniques

Source of audit evidence	Type of audit evidence	Most closely related audit techniques*
A. Direct personal knowledge (see 10.2)	1. Physical evidence	1. Physical examination (of assets)
	2. Concurrence of reperformance (of accounting routines)	2. Reperformance (of accounting routines)
	3. Actions of client personnel	3. Observation (of activities)
B. External evidence (see 10.3)	4. Statements and representations by third parties	4. Enquiry 5. Confirmation
	5. External documentary evidence (if received directly from third parties)	6. Scrutiny 7. Vouching (of source documents for transactions) 8. Inspection (of other documents)
C. Internal evidence (see 10.4)	6. Accounting records and reports	6. Scrutiny 9. Analysis (into components)
	7. Internal documentary evidence (obtained from within the client organization)	6. Scrutiny 7. Vouching (of source documents for transactions) 8. Inspection (of other documents)
	8. Statements and representations by management and employees	4. Enquiry 5. Confirmation
D. Overlapping evidence (see 10.5)	9. Consistency with other evidence	10. Correlation with related information

*In addition, most techniques include comparison to related underlying accounting records

Figure 10.a

Composite techniques

The foregoing ten basic audit techniques are referred to here as "basic" because they represent the building blocks out of which more complex, composite techniques may sometimes be constructed. For example, the "flow audit" procedures described in Chapter 9 are a combination of reperformance of accounting routines, observation of accounting activities, enquiry of appropriate employees, vouching of appropriate documents, and scrutiny of related document files and accounting records. The computer-assisted audit techniques described in Chapter 14 may include automated reperformance of accounting routines, automated scrutiny (computer editing), and automated correlation with other data.

10.2 Direct personal knowledge

Direct personal knowledge by the auditor is usually the most reliable source of audit evidence, when it is available. Thus, when the validity of a given financial statement assertion can be verified economically through direct personal knowledge, such evidence is usually to be preferred to less reliable evidence. For example, when a share certificate can be readily examined, such examination is usually required in preference to mere reliance on a broker's purchase slip or on an accounting entry. Nonetheless, the concepts of timeliness and economy sometimes justify reliance on alternative evidence and, even where direct personal knowledge is sought, often justify limiting its extent. Direct personal knowledge about every financial statement assertion in an audit engagement would seldom be practical. But such knowledge is desirable, and commonly sought, with respect to many of the assertions.

The reliability of direct personal knowledge depends on the smallness of the risk of observational errors by the auditor (see 6.5). In certain instances this risk is high and alternative or supplementary evidence is particularly important.

The three basic techniques for obtaining direct personal knowledge as to the truth of a financial statement assertion are (a) physical examination of assets, (b) reperformance of accounting routines, and (c) observation of activities.

10.2.1 Physical examination of assets

Physical examination is applicable to the substantive verification of most assets having a definite tangible presence, such as cash, inventories, and fixed assets, and to the audit of those assets whose presence is evidenced primarily by legal documents, as are marketable securities by share and bond certificates. Cash and securities can be counted. Inventory on hand can be seen. Major fixed asset additions can be inspected.

In the case of a share investment, the actual asset is the right to participate in a certain share of the dividends or proceeds of liquidation of the investee company – a right which is not directly observable. Nonetheless, for practical purposes, the asset may usually be considered to be represented by the share certificate itself, particularly as the certificate is generally negotiable. Similar considerations apply to other negotiable instruments (including cash itself) and, to a limited extent, to other legal documents, such as mortgage agreements evidencing mortgages receivable.

Physical examination is not applicable to the audit of assets evidenced primarily by internal accounting records, such as accounts receivable, prepaid expenses, and deferred charges; nor is it applicable to liabilities,[4] revenues or expenses.

Objectives served by physical examination

Physical examination serves most directly the substantive objective of verifying the existence of an asset. It contributes as well to the verification of its valuation by establishing quantities on hand (of cash, inventory, etc.) and sometimes by establishing quality (for example, for inventory though not for share investments). It contributes to the verification of title only to the extent that (a) possession itself may be presumptive evidence of title (for example, for cash and bearer securities though not for land) or (b) that evidence of title may be seen on the asset itself (for example, for registered securities).

Importance of physical examination

In the case of tangible assets, direct physical examination is usually the most reliable source of audit evidence for at least certain objectives. Thus, actual audit examination of a pile of coal usually provides more reliable evidence as to its existence than does a purchase invoice, a management representation, or a third-party confirmation. Nonetheless, alternative evidence to physical examination may be acceptable in certain situations. The importance of direct physical examination by the auditor increases with the negotiability of the asset and its susceptibility to misappropriation or manipulation. Thus, for fixed asset additions, physical examination by the auditor is least important and may be restricted to inspection of major additions during the year or sometimes omitted entirely. For inventory, physical examination by the auditor is more important, though with adequate stocktaking routines on the client's part it may be restricted to an overall review (which establishes, for example, that a whole warehouse of inventory is not fictitious) together with limited test counts to supplement the auditor's observation of the client's stocktaking routines (see 10.2.3). For cash, unless immaterial, and for marketable securities held by the client, physical examination by the auditor is of the greatest importance.

Where assets are held by third parties, the need for physical examination by the auditor will depend on the nature of the asset, the nature of the custodian's responsibilities, the reputation and independence of the custodian, and whether the asset is earmarked or intermingled with other assets held by the custodian. Thus, the identification and examination of a quantity of wheat held in a public elevator would be neither necessary nor possible. The examination of securities and inventories held by others would, however, be desirable in some though not all situations.

Limitations of physical examination

While physical examination usually provides the most reliable evidence, its reliability is not absolute and, on some occasions, may be seriously diminished. Clever counterfeiting of cash or forgeries of cheques, share certificates or other negotiable instruments may not be detected by the auditor. For that reason, the greater the susceptibility to forgery the less the reliance which should be placed on physical evidence alone. Thus, specially designed documents, such as share and bond certificates, which would be difficult to forge, warrant greater reliance on examination than do promissory notes on plain paper. Promissory notes accordingly are usually not only examined but also confirmed with the issuer. Such confirmation would usually not be required for share investments, except in the case of "book stock" where the certificate evidences title only at the date of issue and does not itself provide assurance that title has not been subsequently transferred.

The reliablity of the evidence obtained by physical examination depends on the smallness of the risk of observational errors by the auditor (see 6.5). The auditor must know what he is examining or, where he does not, seek expert assistance or alternative evidence. Thus, the physical evidence obtained by the auditor's examination of a diamond inventory will be less reliable than the report of an independent and qualified diamond appraiser. The reliability of physical evidence is also reduced where the very process of examination could change the evidence gathered

(observer contamination). Thus, where control is known to be weak, pre-scheduled cash counts at the year-end are unlikely to detect cash shortages; the shortages would be covered over the count date. Accordingly, where control is weak, such examination may have to be done on a surprise basis.

Elements of physical examination

The elements of physical examination of an item are the identification of the item, the measure of its quantity, the assessment (in some cases) of its quality, the comparison of the physical evidence to the accounting records, the evaluation of the evidence, and the final conclusion.

Identification

In identifying the object he is verifying, the auditor must obtain reasonable assurance that he is not being confused by similar or substitute items. For example, when examining the certificate for a marketable security, the auditor must note carefully the company name, number of shares, class of shares, registration, and sometimes serial number in order to be sure he is examining the specific security recorded in the accounting records.

The identification of inventory and fixed asset items is often more difficult. The auditor requires a degree of knowledge of his client's business, a measure of common sense, and a readiness to make pertinent enquiries so that he will not confuse one product with another.

Measurement of quantity

In establishing the quantity of counted assets the auditor must ensure that his counting procedures are organized so that he will not count assets more than once, either inadvertently or as a consequence of the sleight of hand of a dishonest employee. If assets are negotiable, it is prudent for the auditor to ensure that client personnel are present during the count so that there can be no question of auditor dishonesty should shortages be found. Further, when dealing with negotiable assets it is prudent for the auditor to record his count in ink and have it attested to by client personnel so there can be no questions later as to what was actually counted. When measuring inventory quantities the auditor should take care to note the quantities unambiguously and in the same terms as those in which they are or will be recorded on the client's final inventory summary. If product A is stored in boxes of 10 units each, noting a count of 30 will be ambiguous without an indication of whether 30 units or 30 boxes were counted. In some counts the auditor, after assessing their reasonableness, must rely on client procedures for obtaining weights, tank volumes, piles dimensions, etc. In some cases, reliance must be placed in part on third-party evidence. Thus, the auditor can observe the number and weight of anodes produced by a smelter but must rely on independent laboratory analysis for a determination of their metal content.

Assessment of quality

In assessing quality, the auditor must again have a sufficient knowledge of his client's business and a readiness to make sufficient pertinent enquiries that he will not mistake one level of quality for another and will not confuse good items with damaged items. For example, if he is supposed to be counting No. 1 grade clear pine in a lumber yard he should acquire enough knowledge that he will not be misled by No. 3 grade full of knots.

Assessment of quality includes an assessment of the genuineness of the item in question. There are limits, however, as to what can reasonably be expected of economical audit procedures in this regard. The auditor would not be expected to detect a clever counterfeit or forgery and the cost of having independent experts check the genuineness of every dollar bill and share certificate counted by the auditor would be out of proportion to the small reduction in audit risk thereby achieved. On the other hand, where a tank of liquid is open to inspection, the auditor could be expected to be aware of the differences between crude oil, fresh beer, and coloured water.

In the assessment of inventory grade or quality the auditor may have to supplement his own observations with reliance on third-party evidence. Thus, the auditor may take, or observe the client's procedures to take, samples of a grain inventory and then rely on third-party analysis of its grade.

Comparison to accounting records

The comparison of the physical evidence to the accounting records may take place before or after the physical examination. Noting the alleged quantities from the accounting records on the count sheets in advance facilitates immediate comparison but may also be a temptation to count carelessly on the assumption that the book figure is probably right. Such notation may be efficient for a small security count by the auditor but undesirable for a physical stocktaking by a large number of employee count teams. Whatever the method of comparison, it is best that the agreement of counts of negotiable assets to the records be made on the spot. Inventory counts may sometimes be checked later, though in general the sooner the comparison the better. Sometimes the auditor may find it useful to select inventory items directly from the accounting records and then check the related count.

Further details on physical examination

Further details on the physical examination of assets may be found in 35.4.2 (for inventory observation), 36.3.1 (for cash counts), 37.4.1 (for security counts), and 39.4.2 (for fixed asset inspection).

10.2.2 Reperformance of accounting routines

Reperformance of accounting routines is applicable, to varying extents, to the substantive verification of nearly all assets, liabilities, revenues and expenses since the accuracy of each is usually dependent on some computation or other procedure which can be checked. The pricing and extension of inventory items can be reperformed by the auditor on a test basis to assess their arithmetic accuracy. The calculation of accrued liabilities can be repeated. Total membership revenue of an association can be recomputed from membership numbers and rates. Reperformance is also applicable to the compliance verification of many detective controls. The reconciliation of computer control totals can be reperformed to determine whether the original reconciliation was done accurately.[5]

Objectives served by reperformance

In substantive verification, reperformance such as checking prices, extensions or other computations is related principally to valuation or measurement. Reperformance of the additions of lists also helps to check the existence and completeness of listed items, since out-of-balance conditions could indicate accidental inclusions, double counting or omissions. In compliance verification, reperformance helps to demonstrate whether the original performance of a control procedure was effective. This demonstration may sometimes be direct, where it is possible to reperform a distinct control procedure itself. An example is reconstructing a control total reconciliation. But often the demonstration will be indirect, where it is only possible to reperform the underlying accounting routine which the control procedure was designed to check. An example is the repetition of payroll calculation which a second employee had initialled for checking. In some tests of the underlying accounting records, reperformance may serve a review objective as well.

Importance of reperformance

In the case of substantive verification, direct reperformance of an accounting routine by the auditor is usually the most reliable source of audit evidence as to the accuracy of its original performance. Actual audit recomputation of a large accrued liability provides more reliable evidence as to the accuracy of its accrual than does mere scrutiny of the client's schedules or mere listening to an employee explanation.

Although the concurrence of the results of the auditor's reperformance with the original results is persuasive evidence, it usually relates to only a small portion of the substantive objectives for any given financial statement figure. Thus, the nonconcurrence of the auditor's reperformance of the trial balancing of accounts receivable could indicate serious errors; on the other hand, its concurrence would be far from final verification of the existence, completeness and valuation of total accounts receivable.

There are, however, a few financial statement figures where the concurrence of recomputation *is* the primary evidence in their support. Certain general ledger accounts and their related financial statement figures are determined based on a mathematical formula or allocation. For example, depreciation is computed as a percentage of fixed assets. The allowance for doubtful accounts may be determined as a percentage of aged receivables. Construction revenue may be computed on a percentage of completion basis. In circumstances where a financial statement figure results from such a mathematical calculation, recomputation by the auditor will be the primary verification technique. Of course, he must also satisfy himself that the method of computation is appropriate and that the base data on which it is performed is correct.

In addition, there are some financial statement figures which, while not originally computed on the basis of one overall computation, can be independently checked by such a process. For example, interest income, originally determined transaction by transaction, can be verified economically by multiplying average annual rates of interest by the average level of invested funds throughout the year. The resulting answer will not be exact but should be close enough to detect material errors if present.

Limitations of reperformance

While reperformance usually provides the most reliable evidence as to the accuracy of an original computation or accounting routine, its reliability is not absolute. It is always possible that difficulties or ambiguities that led to an error in the original routine (e.g., a transcription error, misplaced decimal point, use of an inappropriate formula) will lead to an identical error in the auditor's reperformance. In any reperformance there is a danger of assuming unconsciously the same blind spots which may have been present in the reasoning of the original performer. Thus, a careless auditor might check the individual

arithmetic steps in an employee's calculation of unearned finance charges but fail to notice that the sum-of-the-years'-digits formula used in the calculation had been stated incorrectly.

The limitations of audit reperformance can be particularly serious in those situations where there are complex calculations involving a non-accounting discipline. For example, in the calculation of actuarial reserves for a life insurance company, the auditor can check the validity of the base data, can assess the reasonableness of the interest rate and other assumptions, and could, if he wished, verify the arithmetic accuracy of the reserve calculations. But he is unlikely to be able to assess, from his personal knowledge, the appropriateness of the actuarial formulas applied. Similar considerations can arise in geological computations of ore reserves as a basis for depletion entries. In such situations the auditor must place reliance on the work of other specialists. Whether, when such reliance is placed, the auditor should check the computational accuracy of the specialist's work, is a question discussed later in this chapter (see 10.3.3).

Elements of reperformance

The elements of the reperformance of a given accounting routine are the identification of the appropriate routine or computational formula to be used, the identification of the appropriate base data to be used (which data must itself usually be or have been verified by other audit techniques), the application of the routine or formula to that base data, the comparison of the audit results with the original results, the evaluation of the resulting evidence (for example, the nature, magnitude and significance of any nonconcurrence of the results), and the final conclusion.

Posting

The simplest form of reperformance is the checking that an accounting figure has been transcribed correctly from one place to another. The commonest example is the checking of postings from the books of original entry to subsidiary ledgers or to the general ledger. Similar examples include the testing of the build-up of management reports and monthly financial statements from the general ledger and other records. The reperformance of portions of the bookkeeping process usually takes place during the interim audit and can be part of the initial systems review, part of the compliance verification of controls, or part of the substantive verification of the reliability of the accounting records (see Chapter 9).

Recomputation

Any computations directly involved in the establishing of financial statement figures at the year-end are generally checked or test-checked as part of the financial statement audit. On the other hand, the arithemtic accuracy of the underlying accounting records is generally test-checked as part of the interim audit. The extent of this latter checking will depend on the auditor's assessment of inherent risk and control risk.

The double-entry system provides control over accidental addition errors in most records. In checking additions in journals, subsidiary ledgers and other records, the auditor is usually searching therefore for possible intentional errors. Misadditions could be used to conceal other errors or irregularities. The extent to which the search for intentional errors is necessary will depened on the strength of the system of internal control and on the presence or absence of suspicious circumstances. When particular totals in the records are not subject to the self-proving discipline of the double entry system, accidental errors are more likely to escape detection prior to audit, and the auditor must usually give greater emphasis to the checking of such additions, where material.

10.2.3 Observation of activities

If the auditor could economically observe all client activities having a bearing on the financial position and operating results, his need for further evidence would be very limited. For many of these activities, however, alternative auditing techniques are far more efficient than direct observation. In theory an auditor, by stationing his staff at strategic times and places, could observe a rail shipment being sent to Customer A on December 15, could observe its receipt by Customer A 1 000 miles away on December 17, could observe Customer A's cheque in payment thereof being opened in the client's mail room on January 8, and could thus conclude that an account receivable existed at December 31. But obviously the same receivable can be much more economically verified by seeking written confirmation from Customer A – or, in the event of non-response, by examining the December 15 shipping slip and the January 8 cash receipts entry. For liablities, income components and most assets, direct observation, while more persuasive, would bear a cost out of proportion to the small increment in audit assurance thereby obtained.

Nonetheless, there are some assets (notably inventory) for which observation of client activities is an important audit technique. In addition, there are some important controls (such as division of duties) that can only be verified by direct observation. Finally, observation is an important technique in gaining overall knowledge of the client's business and systems and in detecting suspicious circumstances.

Objectives served by observation

Observation of client activities generally serves a review objective (ascertaining what the systems are) or a compliance objective (establishing a basis for reliance on the activities observed). The observation of controls, such as division of duties, clearly has a compliance objective. While the classification may be less obvious, the observation of client stock-taking routines has a compliance objective as well. To perform direct substantive tests of inventory quantities on hand would usually involve far greater extents than most auditors find reasonable in practice. Fortunately, if the inventory count is well organized and properly carried out, the auditor can place considerable reliance on the client's counting procedures when planning his subsequent substantive tests from the count sheets to the final inventory summary. The observation of the stock-taking determines whether such reliance is warranted. Indeed, the few test counts usually performed by the auditor during his observation of the stock-taking are really an integral part of this compliance objective.

To the extent that audit observation includes an alertness for any suspicious circumstances, which if detected would call for additional audit procedures to confirm or deny the suspicions, observation serves a substantive objective as well.

Importance of observation

Where observation is an economical audit procedure it is important because of its high degree of reliability. Actual audit observation of a division of duties between two employees provides more reliable evidence as to the existence of that division than does an accounting procedures manual or the oral assurances of the department head. The importance of audit observation depends on the relation of audit cost to audit risk and upon the availability of alternative audit procedures. Observation of client stock-taking procedures is important because the alternative of direct substantive stock-taking by the auditor would be far more costly. Observation of shipments (as a proof of sales) is not generally important because sales can be more economically verified by documentary evidence, analytical review, and reliance on the overlapping evidence provided by the verification of the opening and closing balance sheets.

Limitations of observation

While observation usually provides the most reliable evidence as to the actual occurrence of the activities observed, its reliability is not absolute. The auditor must understand what he is observing or, where he does not, seek expert assistance or alternative evidence. As pointed out in 6.5.1, an inexperienced auditor attempting to control, through observation, a sophisiticated computer printout, adds no credibility to the validity of the resulting run if he would be unable to recognize improper operator intervention were it to occur.

Finally, as pointed out in 6.5.4, the auditor must take care that his very act of observing does not change the evidence observed (observer contamination). Inventory counting teams may exhibit more conscientious care when the external auditor is watching than when he is not. The division of duties which the auditor observed in the EDP department during his interim audit in May may break down during holiday periods in July and August or during peak pressure periods in January. Thus, the evidence obtained through observations should often be corroborated through intelligent enquiry, scrutiny, and correlation with other evidence.

Elements of observation

The elements of observation include the identification of the specific activity to be observed, the observation of its performance, an assessment of the quality of its performance, the comparison of observed activities with the procedures prescribed and with the standard of performance reasonable to expect, the evaluation of the evidence, and the final conclusion.

Observation of client counts of assets

The most common example of audit observation of client routines in counting assets is the annual or cyclical counting of inventory. Prior to the physical count the auditor may wish to tour the plant to see whether inventory items have been arranged in an orderly manner to facilitate counting and to reduce the risk of omissions or duplications. He will also wish to review in advance the adequacy of the client's detailed stocktaking instructions. In observing the actual count he will wish to note the specific count procedures followed, the care with which the count is made, the adequacy of supervision, the procedures for noting obsolescence, etc. Further details on inventory observation are covered in 35.4.2. Similar procedures may be applicable to periodic client counts of fixed assets.

Observation of internal controls

Observation is an essential technique for the compliance verification of those preventive controls, such as competence, supervision, and division of duties, for which there may be no documentary evidence

after the fact. Occasionally, observation may be the appropriate auditing procedure for detective controls as well. As explained in 9.4.2, there must be some direct evidence of the presence of the detective control itself if audit reliance is to be placed on it. The mere absence of monetary error in a document examined by the auditor is not in itself direct evidence that an alleged control procedure was applied to that document. Where documentary evidence (initials, signatures, reconciliations, etc.) is not available, observation of the performance of the detective control may be the only source of direct evidence.

Observation to gain overall familiarity

The effectiveness of many audit techniques depends on the auditor's overall familiarity with the client's systems and business operations. Much of this familiarity must be gained through alert observation during the course of the audit. While the specific activities to be observed for this purpose cannot usually be defined precisely in advance, the observation may well be as important as many of the more detailed audit steps. Thus, the auditor's observation of the daily accounting routines provides an essential context for his evaluation of either questionnaire or flow chart analysis of controls. His observation of operating procedures during a plant tour provides an essential context for his understanding of inventory categories, of the cost system, and of plant cut-off procedures.

Observation of suspicious circumstances

Closely related to the importance of gaining overall familiarity is the auditor's observation of suspicious circumstances. While making a plant tour, for example, the alert auditor may spot the presence of apparently obsolete inventory or notice an apparent lack of protection of valuable finished goods. When arriving at work he may notice employees punching two or three clock cards to circumvent the control over hours worked. In making routine enquiries of a given employee he may observe hostile or defensive answers which could be masking a fear of detection.

As discussed in Chapter 6, most of the ordinarily reasonable audit assumptions break down in the presence of suspicious circumstances. Of course, suspicious circumstances will never be noticed by the auditor if he is carelessly inobservant or unduly gullible. In the United States, a number of recent releases by the SEC have emphasized the importance of the auditor remaining vigilant for suspicious patterns of transactions, unreasonable estimates, and unusual events.

10.3 External evidence

External evidence is evidence obtained directly from independent third parties. Generally, external evidence is less reliable than direct personal knowledge but more reliable than internal evidence. External evidence may, however, be more reliable than direct personal knowledge in cases where the specialized competence of the third party is important. Because direct personal knowledge is often not available or not economically available, as discussed earlier, external evidence is frequently the most reliable evidence supporting a given financial statement figure.

The reliability of external evidence depends on the competence, trustworthiness, and independence of the third party, on the directness of the contact between the auditor and the third party, and on the effectiveness of the communication between them. Because these qualities may often be less than ideal, some supplementary evidence supporting the external evidence may often be desirable – and is essential in the presence of suspicious circumstances.

External evidence consists of oral statements and written representations made by third parties and documents received directly from them by the auditor. Auditing techniques applicable to the former are enquiry and confirmation; those applicable to the latter are scrutiny, vouching and inspection. A special case of enquiry and confirmation is reliance on the work of a specialist.

10.3.1 Enquiry of independent third parties

With the important exception of enquiries of certain specialists (discussed in 10.3.3), enquiry of third parties is a technique used only to a limited extent in most audits. Because a written response obtained by confirmation implies more care and thought on the part of the respondent than an oral response obtained by enquiry, it is a more reliable form of evidence. Since the incremental cost of obtaining this more reliable evidence from third parties is usually minimal, confirmation is generally preferable to enquiry.[6]

Enquiry of suppliers, customers, or bankers may be useful, however, to supplement or clarify confirmation results – for example, in following up queries noted by them in their responses to confirmation requests or in investigating apparent errors in their responses. Sometimes enquiry may be substituted for confirmation when earlier attempts to obtain confirmation have failed. For example, telephone enquiries of customers who have not responded to con-

firmation requests may produce satisfactory evidence that their balances were correct – not as reliable evidence as written confirmation but more reliable and often cheaper than the "alternative verification" procedures of examining shipping documents and subsequent cash receipt entries. Occasionally, enquiry of a third party may accompany other audit procedures. For example, where the auditor decides to examine, or observe the counting of, assets held by a third-party custodian, reasonable enquiries as to the custodian's procedures are desirable.

Apart from the difference in the medium of the response, the same considerations apply to enquiry as to confirmation. They are discussed in the following section.

10.3.2 Confirmation with independent third parties

Confirmation is applicable to the substantive verification of assets held by or for third parties and of balances representing a money debt from or to third parties. Such assets and liabilities commonly confirmed include: cash on deposit in banks and bank loans; marketable securities held by others (brokers, banks, trust companies, etc.) or for others; accounts receivable from debtors and accounts payable to creditors; inventories held by consignees, processors or public warehouses or held for consignors or customers; mortgages receivable or payable; and notes receivable or payable. Confirmation is generally applied as well to the accounts receivable and payable of employees, officers, directors and shareholders – and sometimes to minor amounts of company assets (salesmen's samples, company cars, etc.) held by them. While these persons would not be considered "third parties" with respect to other types of representations, such as representations concerning the financial statement preparation, they may, with some exceptions, be considered as equivalent to third parties with respect to their own personal balances with the organization. Confirmation may also be sought from third parties who, while not debtors or creditors themselves, are in a position to confirm information concerning a related financial statement figure. Such confirmations include: confirmation of long-term debt with a trustee under a trust indenture; confirmation of share capital with a registrar and transfer agent; confirmation of unexpired insurance premiums (prepaid insurance) with an insurance agent; and confirmation of guarantees, discounted receivables, and other contingent liabilities with bankers or others. In a broad sense, confirmation also includes reports requested from specialists but such cases are discussed separately in 10.3.3.

The technique of confirmation could in theory be applied to all income statement components. Sales of goods or services during the year could be confirmed with customers and purchases of goods or services could be confirmed with suppliers. In practice such confirmation is restricted to special situations such as (a) where virtually all sales have been to one or two customers or where all purchases have been from one or two suppliers, (b) where some unusual type of transaction has occurred, or (c) where there have been significant transactions with related parties. There are four reasons for this restriction.

First, many income statement components (sales, expenses, etc.) represent completed transactions which in some ways are less susceptible to error than the uncompleted transactions reflected on the balance sheet (inventory which has been manufactured but not yet sold, accounts receivable which are sales not yet turned into cash, etc.).

Second, the verification of net assets at the beginning and end of the year, together with the verification of capital transactions, provides considerable overlapping evidence as to the accuracy of reported net income for the year. Similarly, audit evidence as to opening and closing accounts receivable and as to the controls over cash receipts provides considerable assurance as to the accuracy of reported sales.

Third, the use of confirmation techniques as the primary means of verifying income statement components would be uneconomical. If 200 confirmations are required to obtain reasonable assurance as to year-end accounts receivable, the auditor might require 2, 000 confirmations to obtain the equivalent assurance as to the year's sales (the sales figure being often some ten times larger). Moreover the confirmation of sales, involving items many months past, would be more work for the customer and might well lead to lower rates of response.

Fourth, the review and evaluation of systems and internal controls provides considerable assurance as to the accuracy of reported revenues and expenses.

For these four reasons it is common, except for special situations, not to apply confirmation directly to income statement components but rather to rely on the techniques of scrutiny, analysis, and correlation with related information, supplemented, where internal control is weak, by the vouching of internal documentary evidence. Recently some practitioners have begun to apply confirmation to all very material transactions.

Objectives served by confirmation

Confirmation serves most directly the substantive objective of verifying that an asset or liability exists and is owned by or incident upon the company being audited. It contributes as well to the verification of its valuation although additional procedures will usually be necessary (for example, to assess the collectibility of accounts receivable). Its contribution to the objective of verifying completeness is limited. Confirmation of an account receivable balance is not reliable evidence of completeness since any omission would be in the respondent's favour. Confirmation of a liability balance provides some evidence of completeness. It could lead to the detection of undisclosed invoices payable to the same creditor – but not, of course, to the detection of undisclosed creditors. The principal evidence as to completeness must normally be sought from other techniques than confirmation.

Importance of confirmation

Confirmation is probably the most widely used technique for substantive verification and, where it can be applied, provides reliable evidence at a low cost. Where an asset or liability balance can be confirmed, alternative evidence would generally be less reliable (except for physical examination) and more costly. For example, for receivable balances the "alternative verification" of checking shipping documents and subsequent cash receipt entries commonly consumes three or four times the hours of confirmation. Accordingly, auditors usually exhaust every possibility of obtaining a response to confirmation requests before resorting to alternative verification.

Limitations of confirmation

The evidence obtained by confirmation is less reliable when the reputation or objectivity of the respondent is open to question. When confirming non-arm's length receivable or payable balances, the auditor may sometimes wish to supplement this evidence by vouching related documents (shipping bills etc.) or by additional enquiries or analysis. In the case of assets held by a little-known or non-arm's length custodian, physical examination is preferable to confirmation. When, in such cases, confirmation is chosen in lieu of physical examination, the auditor should satisfy himself as to the reliability of the third party and in some cases make supplementary enquiries as to his client's control procedures over the custodial function.

Confirmations will be less reliable where there are indications that the respondents did not fully understand the information to be confirmed. A further limitation in reliability is the risk that the respondent may confirm an erroneous balance, failing to notice the error. Where the respondent is a company, it is always possible that the clerk replying to the request is unaware of other information having a bearing on the balance – undisclosed items, items in dispute, counter claims, etc. Furthermore, there is always the danger that confirmation replies may be fabricated by dishonest employees. But perhaps the most serious limitation in reliability occurs when a negative form of confirmation is used.

Positive versus negative confirmations

The superiority of positive evidence over negative evidence in general has already been mentioned. A positive confirmation request asks the prospective respondent to reply noting his agreement or disagreement with the amount or information stated in the request. A positive confirmation request is usually a separate letter; it may or may not be accompanied by more detailed information such as a monthly statement of account. A negative confirmation request may be merely a sticker attached to the client's monthly statement of account. When the auditor places reliance on the absence of any reply to a specific request he implicitly makes the assumption that the debtor did not reply because he checked the confirmation form and agreed with the information shown on it. But in fact the debtor may have discarded the request unread or may still be analyzing a disagreement with it or, for some other reason, may not wish to acknowledge the debt. The assumption that he agrees with it is therefore a risky one. Because of this risk, the CICA Audit Technique Study, *Confirmation of Accounts Receivable,* in 1969 recommended that negative confirmations not be used in the verification of accounts receivable except for supplementary purposes.

> Auditors should use only positive confirmation forms for obtaining the audit assurance necessary to express an opinion on accounts receivable. The negative type should not be used for this purpose, but can be used to obtain audit assurance in addition to that required for an opinion.[7]

If the superiority of positive confirmation were obtainable only at inordinate cost, its use might not be practical. The incremental cost of sending positive requests instead of negative requests is small, however, in relation to the benefit of greater reliability. The principal additional cost is the *following up* of non-responses. *But accounts providing no response to a positive request are precisely the ones for which negative confirmation would have been unreliable.*

If, after repeated requests, a positive confirmation cannot be obtained, the auditor must resort to "alternative verification". Thus, an inherent limitation to confirmation is that it requires some third-party action which may not always be obtainable. With positive requests this limitation can be identified whereas with negative requests it can only be guessed at.

As with any audit technique, confirmation need only be applied to a sufficient sample of items to justify a meaningful conclusion about the total population of such items. While sending excess numbers of negative confirmations might take little time, excess positive confirmations could be costly. Thus, where the preferable technique of positive confirmation is used, care should be taken in selecting proper sample sizes (see Chapters 12 and 13).

Elements of confirmation

The elements of positive confirmation of an item are the identification of the item to be confirmed, the identification of the party from whom confirmation should be sought, the preparation of the confirmation request, the comparison of the confirmation request to the accounting records, the mailing of the request, the receipt of a confirmation reply, the investigation of any reported difference, the evaluation of the resulting evidence, and the final conclusion.

Prerequisites for reliable confirmation

Six prerequisites for reliable confirmation are: respondent independence, client consent, careful checking, auditor control, provision of return address, and respondent comprehension.

1. Independent respondents can be expected, in their own self-interest, to provide accurate replies to confirmation requests. While most non-independent respondents may be equally accurate in their responses, there is always the danger (a) that they themselves rely wholly on the records of the company under audit or (b) that they may be instructed by an officer of that company to provide a specified response without further checking. In either case, the confirmation provides no evidence in addition to that available from internal documentary evidence and in the latter case it may well be concealing fraud or deliberate misrepresentation. The auditor's first task is therefore to consider the independence and impartiality of the party to whom the confirmation request is being sent. Control over the risks of reliance on non-independent respondents depends on the thoroughness of the auditor's procedures for identifying related parties and auditing related party transactions (see 33.4.12).

2. The client's consent is normally obtained before seeking third-party confirmation and the consent is normally indicated on the request letter itself – by an authorizing signature, by use of the client's stationery, or both. Sometimes authorization may be implied by the inclusion of a client-prepared document, such as a monthly statement of account, with the auditor's confirmation request. Client consent is important for two reasons. First, most prospective respondents will be reluctant to reveal information about another organization without that organization's consent. Indeed, many respondents such as banks and solicitors may be prohibited from doing so. Second, a prospective respondent will be more likely to do something for an organization with which he does business regularly, than for an auditor whom he may not know. Use of requests prepared on client letterhead may therefore elicit a higher percentage response than requests on the auditor's own letterhead.

3. All pertinent information in the confirmation request should be carefully checked by the auditor prior to mailing. Descriptive information, dollar amounts, date of the confirmation, and name and address of the prospective respondent should be compared to the client's accounting records. If the address to which the confirmation is directed is a post office box number or if it appears unusual, it may be desirable to compare it with the telephone book or trade directory. It is always possible that an employee has rented a post office box, whether under a fictitious name or under the name of an actual customer, in order to intercept a confirmation request and fabricate a fraudulent reply.

4. It is important that the auditor control the selection, preparation, checking and mailing of the confirmation requests. There is always the danger that they may be inadvertently lost or, worse, deliberately suppressed by an employee wishing to conceal certain discrepancies. Thus, while the assistance of the client's clerical staff should be sought in order to minimize the costs of preparing, typing, and addressing confirmation requests, these procedures and the final mailing of the requests should be under the auditor's control.

5. It is a natural extension of the foregoing control, that the auditor be sure of receiving back any requests which cannot be delivered. Returned mail may simply indicate changed addresses, for which the request letters should now be corrected. But there is always the danger that they may represent non-existent parties and therefore fictitious assets concealing fraudulent transactions. Therefore, whether the request letter is prepared on the auditor's or on the client's letterhead, the envelope should be marked with the return address of the auditor.

6. Fundamental to reliable confirmation is the respondent's comprehension of the information requested. If the confirmation date is ambiguous the respondent may mistakenly assume that apparent differences reflect payments in transit when they may in fact reflect discrepancies. If he does not understand the information provided he may not respond at all. The auditor should therefore consider carefully the needs of the prospective respondent and provide him with clear and complete information necessary to facilitate his reply. For example, if a debtor has a voucher system, the confirmation request should be for either an individual open invoice (see 33.4.2) or a list of open invoices. Many mortgagors may be able more easily to confirm information as to the original principal, term, monthly payment, and status as to arrears or acceleration than to confirm the exact unamortized balance still outstanding. In each case, the auditor must ask himself what information the prospective respondent really needs.

Other procedures

The CICA Audit Technique Study, *Confirmation of Accounts Receivable,* suggests a number of additional procedures to overcome apathy on the part of prospective respondents.[8] These procedures are applicable to both accounts receivable and other confirmations. They include good design of the confirmation letter, provision of detailed information where helpful, provision of extra copies or bilingual forms where needed, and use of personalized letters. The provision of stamped return envelopes also facilitates response. Confirmation from the general public may sometimes be encouraged by having the client offer a small payment or credit to the respondent. Many confirmation requests are designed as turn-around forms that need merely be signed and re-mailed to the auditor. Some turn-around forms may be prepared in punched card form to permit automated matching of requests and replies by the auditor.

Example of a confirmation request

Dear Mr. Smith,   Re: XYZ Company Ltd.
In connection with our audit of the accounts of the above company we should appreciate receiving from you confirmation of your account. The company's records show an amount receivable from you of $1234.56 at October 31, 1976.

Do you agree with this amount? If you do, would you please sign this letter in the space below. However, if you do not, would you please note at the foot of this letter or on the reverse side, the details of any difference.

Would you then be good enough to return the letter directly to us in the envelope enclosed for your convenience.

Yours truly,
C.A. & Co.

Please provide our auditors, C.A. & Co., with this information.

G.E. Brown
Comptroller, XYZ Company
Ltd.

The above amount was due by me(us) at the date mentioned.

Further details on confirmation

Further details on confirmation procedures may be found in 33.4 (for accounts receivable) and in 34.4 (for accounts payable). The former section discusses as well the use of open-item (as opposed to account-balance) confirmations and the use of "either/or" confirmations.

10.3.3 Using the work of a specialist

While the auditor's training provides him with a knowledge of business matters in general and while his audit procedures should provide him with a familiarity of his client's business in particular, he cannot be expected to have the specialized skills of another discipline. On some engagements the auditor may conclude that such skills are required. In these cases he may make use of the work of a specialist. The AICPA Statement, *Using the Work of a Specialist*, states:

> In performing an examination of financial statements in accordance with generally accepted auditing standards, the auditor may use the work of a specialist as an audit procedure to obtain competent evidential matter.[9]

Objectives served by the use of a specialist's work

It is in meeting the objectives of verifying the existence and valuation of assets, rights or obligations that the work of a specialist may sometimes be required. Examples include:
1. Existence –
   a) identification of certain assets or of their condition (mineral assays, chemical analysis, determination of grade),
   b) interpretation of technical matters (legal rights, titles or obligations).
2. Valuation –
   a) valuation of assets or liabilities requiring specialized judgment (art valuations, jewellery appraisals, assessment of pending lawsuits),
   b) valuation of assets or liabilities requiring specialized calculations (computation of mineral reserves, determination of actuarial reserves, evaluation of stage of construction completion).

Importance of the use of a specialist's work

On virtually every audit engagement, reliance is placed on the specialized knowledge of the client's solicitors in identifying and evaluating contingent liablities. Difficult questions in this respect are the extent to which the client's solicitor can properly be asked to identify unasserted claims and to evaluate the probable outcome of litigation in process. These questions and a suggested wording for letters to solicitors are discussed in 34.7.2. Reliance may also be placed on solicitors in determining the title to fixed assets or the existence of charges against such title. On many engagements reliance is placed on an actuary's report in evaluating pension liabilities. On some engagements, reliance is placed on the work of other auditors (see 10.3.4). Apart from the foregoing common examples, the work of a specialist is primarily needed in engagements involving specialized industries. Examples are resource companies (geologists), life insurance companies (actuaries), jewellers and art dealers (appraisers), and construction companies (architects, engineers).

Limitations in the use of a specialist's work

The work of a competent independent specialist provided with accurate data can generally be considered reliable. The reliability may be reduced, however, where the specialist has an ongoing relationship with the client that could impair his objectivity. In such cases the auditor may wish to perform additional procedures to determine that the specialist's assumptions, methods and findings are not unreasonable or, in extreme situations, engage an outside specialist for that purpose. The reliability may also be reduced if there is evidence of incompetence on the part of the specialist or if the auditor's procedures indicate that his findings are unreasonable. Finally, the reliability of the specialist's work will be limited if he has been supplied with inaccurate data or if he has adopted assumptions which are inconsistent with the basis on which the client's financial statements have been prepared.

Elements in the use of a specialist's work

The elements in the use of a specialist's work are the selection of the specialist, a consideration of his competence and objectivity, the verification of the client data supplied to him, a review of the methods and assumptions adopted by him, the evaluation of his findings and the final conclusion.

The auditor's procedures in using a specialist's work

The AICPA Statement suggests that the auditor should attempt to obtain a specialist who is unrelated to the client but that, when the circumstances so warrant, the work of a specialist having a relationship to the client may be acceptable. In any case, the auditor should consider the professional certification of the specialist, and his reputation among those familiar with his work. In assessing reputation, it is desirable that the auditor's enquiries not be restricted to client officials but include other knowledgeable persons such as professional colleagues of the specialist.

The auditor should ensure that there is an understanding with the client and with the specialist as to the nature of the work to be performed by the latter.

> Preferably, the understanding should be documented and should cover the following:
> a) the objectives and scope of the specialist's work,
> b) the specialist's representation as to his relationship, if any, to the client,
> c) the methods or assumptions to be used,
> d) a comparison of the methods or assumptions to be used with those used in the preceding period,
> e) the specialist's understanding of the auditor's corroborative use of the specialist's findings in relation to the representations in the financial statements,
> f) the form and content of the specialist's report. . . .[10]

Except for making enquiries in the course of establishing the foregoing understanding, the auditor need not check, nor would he generally have the technical competence to check, the detailed calculations or procedures performed by the specialist. He should, however, review the specialist's findings to see that they do not seem unreasonable, such review being more extensive in the case of a non-independent specialist. Some practitioners feel that the closer the specialist's discipline approaches the field of accounting, the more intensive should be the auditor's review procedures. These practitioners would therefore argue, for example, that the auditor's review of an actuarial calculation should be more detailed than his review of a diamond appraiser's report. Current thinking regarding the auditor's relationships with actuaries in insurance company audits has yet to be resolved in Canada.

The auditor should make such tests as are reasonable to verify the accuracy of any client data supplied to the specialist as a basis for the latter's calculations.

Finally, the auditor should consider whether the specialist's findings support the related assertions in the client's financial statements. Where material discrepancies arise, the auditor may have to perform additional procedures, sometimes including obtaining the opinion of another specialist, to resolve the matter.

10.3.4 Reliance on another auditor

A particular case of reliance on the work of a specialist is the reliance on another auditor. In this case the reliance may be required not because the specialist (the other auditor) has skills not possessed by the auditor but because he has or had access to evidence not available or not economically available to the auditor. Common examples are reliance, during an initial audit engagement, on a predecessor auditor and reliance, during the audit of an investor company, on the auditor of a subsidiary, equity-accounted investee, or other major investee company. The principles discussed in 10.3.3 apply equally to reliance on another auditor. In addition, because the auditor is skilled in the same discipline as the specialist, it may be appropriate in some situations for him to conduct some review of the latter's working papers. The review of a predecessor auditor's working papers is described in 23.2.1. In the case of an investee auditor, the criteria for choosing among "basic procedures", "review procedures" and "override procedures" are discussed in 15.4.8 and the procedures themselves are described in 38.3.10.

Other examples of reliance on another auditor include reliance on another auditor's evaluation of internal controls in a public warehouse holding some of the client's goods or in an outside computer data centre processing some of the client's accounting data. Occasionally, an auditor may also place reliance on another auditor whom he has consulted in a specialized field, such as the audit of a complex computer system or an engagement in an industry with which he is not yet wholly familiar.

10.3.5 Scrutiny, vouching and inspection of external documents

Documentary evidence received directly from third parties has a greater reliability than internal documentary evidence obtained from within the client organization. The most common examples are bank statements and cancelled cheques obtained directly from the bank and creditors' statements received directly from creditors. Because of its greater reliability, such evidence requires less support by corroborating evidence. The procedures for scrutinizing, vouching or inspecting the documents themselves, however, are the same as for internal documents and are described in 10.4.

10.4 Internal evidence

Internal evidence is evidence obtained from within the client organization. Generally, it is less reliable than external evidence or direct personal knowledge. On the other hand, it is usually the most plentiful and economical evidence available. Therefore, while it is rarely sufficient by itself, some internal evidence is usually obtained for each financial statement figure. For the substantive verification of assets and liabilities, it is usually supplemented by external evidence and/or by direct personal knowledge. In the substantive verification of income components, the primary evidence is internal but it is supplemented by the overlapping evidence provided by the verification of the opening and closing balance sheets. In compliance verification, the primary evidence is also internal but it is supplemented by direct personal knowledge (e.g., from observation).

The reliability of internal evidence depends on the competence and trustworthiness of the client's management and employees, the effectiveness of the communication between those persons and the auditor, and the strength of internal controls.

Internal evidence consists of accounting records and reports, documents, and representations of management and employees. Auditing techniques applicable to accounting records and reports are scrutiny and analysis. Those applicable to documents are scrutiny, vouching and inspection. Those applicable to management and employee representations are enquiry and confirmation. A special case of enquiry is reliance on the work of internal auditors.

10.4.1 Scrutiny of accounting records and reports

As the term is used by auditors, scrutiny is a searching review of data in order to locate significant items requiring further investigation. (Some dictionary definitions of scrutiny refer to "attention to minute detail" but audit scrutiny is not used in this sense.) Significant items may be items of unusual size, of an unexpectedly high or low frequency, of a suspicious nature, or revealing inconsistencies or anomalies when compared with known information about the business. Scrutiny may be performed by visually reviewing reports, schedules, ledger pages, etc. Or it may be automated if suitable edit criteria can be specified in advance. In the latter case, computerized editing can be applied directly to magnetic tape or disk files.

Objectives served by scrutiny

Scrutiny serves essentially a substantive objective by helping to ensure that there is no undisclosed condition which, if known to the auditor, would affect his conclusions with respect to any of the other substantive or compliance objectives.

Importance of scrutiny

Most of the auditor's normal procedures are designed on the assumption that no suspicious circumstances are present. In satisfying himself that this assumption is reasonable, the auditor must usually place considerable reliance on scrutiny.

Limitations of scrutiny

When suspicious circusmstances are revealed by scrutiny, other audit procedures must be performed to resolve the suspicions – in which case, the evidence confirming or contradicting the financial statements will come from those other procedures. Where the evidence obtained by scrutiny itself is needed, is in supporting the conclusion that *no other* suspicious circumstances are present apart from those identified. As with all negative evidence, this evidence is of less than conclusive reliability. Moreover, appropriate scrutiny procedures are difficult to define precisely in any given case. The reliability of scrutiny depends on (a) the competence, experience and carefulness of the scrutinizer, (b) his knowledge of the client's business and systems, and (c) the visibility any anomaly would have in the accounting records, if it occurred. Scrutiny should not be delegated to a junior member of the audit team. Scrutiny should not be performed before the auditor has gained sufficient familiarity with the client's business and systems that he can recognize an unusual item, if encountered. Scrutiny should not be applied to those accounting records where there is little likelihood of noticing an unusual item, if it occurred. For example, visual scrutiny of a computer transaction register may be less effective than scrutiny of computer reports summarizing or grouping processed transactions in a meaningful form. Thus, the auditor must carefully think through his specific objectives in each case, before employing the technique of scrutiny.

Where scrutiny is computerized, its reliability will also depend on the completeness of the edit criteria which the auditor specifies in advance. It is always possible that the auditor will overlook a criterion which would have occurred to him had he noticed a particular item during a visual review.

Elements of scrutiny

The elements of scrutiny of an accounting record or report are the identification of the portions (columns, time periods, etc.) of the record or report to be scrutinized, the identification of criteria as to unusualness based on a knowledge of the business and systems, the perusal of the record or report, the detection of items meeting these criteria and therefore requiring further investigation, and the final conclusion.

Items to look for

The type of unusual item for which an auditor searches in his scrutiny will vary with the record or report scrutinized. For example:

1. When scrutinizing general ledger accounts, the auditor will look for unusual amounts or items from unusual posting sources.
2. When scrutinizing the general journal, the auditor will look for unusual account distributions and consider carefully the logic of all adjusting entries.
3. When scrutinizing operating reports and results, the auditor will watch for large differences between budget and actual figures or unusual differences between the current year's and prior year's amounts.
4. When scrutinizing other books of original entry, the auditor will look for unusual amounts and entries that do not follow the normal business pattern.
5. When scrutinizing inventory listings, the auditor will want to assure himself as to the reasonableness of prices, quantities and extended results.

10.4.2 Analysis of accounting records and reports

Analysis of a balance appearing in an accounting record or report is the subdivision of that balance into logical components – finding out "what is in" a given figure. Usually, analysis is merely a preliminary step preceding other auditing procedures such as detailed vouching of the larger items. Sometimes, however, analysis by itself, or analysis coupled with a few enquiries, is sufficient to demonstrate the reasonableness of a particular figure. The technique of analysis is extensively used in verifying income statement components, particularly expenses. It may also be employed in assessing miscellaneous asset and liability balances insufficient in size to warrant more detailed verification.

Elements of analysis

The elements of analysis of a given figure from an accounting record or report are the identification of the source of the details making up that figure, a review of those details, the listing and describing of large items individually and the grouping of smaller items by type into approximate subtotals, the addition of the resulting components to determine that their total corresponds (subject to approximations made) to the figure being analyzed, and the final conclusion.

10.4.3 Internal documentary evidence: some general comments

Internal documentary evidence includes two groups:
1. documents initiating in the client organization (such as sales orders, sales packing slips, sales invoices, purchase orders, receiving slips, cheques, voucher jackets, and approval forms),
2. documents received by the client from third parties (such as remittance advices, purchase packing slips, purchase invoices, and freight bills).

While the second group originated with third parties, by the time the auditor examines them in the client's files there is always the possibility that client employees or management have inadvertently lost or deliberately suppressed, altered or forged some of them. Accordingly, the second group should be considered for audit purposes as having only marginally greater reliability than internally produced documents.

The gathering of internal documentary evidence can contribute to every compliance and substantive objective. Indeed, the gathering of such evidence commonly consumes more audit time than any other audit procedure.

Limitations of internal documentary evidence

While internal documents as a group have less reliability than other types of evidence, in planning his verification program the auditor should recognize that within this group the relative reliability can vary. While the particular client circumstance will affect each case, the following generalizations are possible:

1. Legal documents which are preprinted or contain signatures of outside parties (e.g., share certificates, contracts) are usually more reliable than less formal documents.
2. Documents which contain signatures of senior management (e.g., signed minutes of meetings of the board of directors) are usually more reliable than those approved at lower levels.

3. Externally prepared documents which are on preprinted stationery or forms are more reliable than non-preprinted external documents or than internally prepared documents.
4. Handwritten source documents or source documents not on preprinted forms should be accorded little or no reliability.
5. The level of reliability accorded to documentary evidence can be increased where the documents are prepared or processed in an environment of satisfactory internal control – particularly where the auditor has performed compliance verification on the controls.

10.4.4 Scrutiny of documents

Scrutiny of a set of documents generally has the same purpose as a scrutiny of accounting records (see 10.4.1), to identify unusual items requiring further investigation. In many engagements, documents are so numerous, and their sequence of filing so haphazard, that direct scrutiny is not practical. Usually, it is more efficient to scrutinize only the accounting records and reports. Where scrutiny of documents is practical it is usually restricted to certain limited groups of key documents.

Scrutiny of a file of documents during the interim audit may serve, instead, a review objective. Its purpose is to determine that other types of transactions have not been overlooked in the auditor's review of systems.

10.4.5 Vouching of source documents for transactions

Vouching is the verification of a given transaction through the examination of the related source document. Vouching serves most substantive objectives. It provides evidence that the transaction really occurred, that the client was really a party to it, that it has been measured correctly, and that it has been classified properly in the financial statements. It does not, however, prove the completeness of reported transactions. Vouching may also serve compliance objectives, in which case it is restricted more specifically to evidence of controls exercised.

Elements of vouching

The elements of vouching of the source document for a given transaction are the critical examination of the source document, the comparison of the information on the source document to the entry in the accounting records, the investigation of any differences, and the final conclusion. In the case of sub-stantive verification, the critical examination should be directed to obtaining:
1. reasonable assurance as to:
   a) the authenticity of the document,
   b) the propriety of the transaction,
   c) the adequacy of its authorization and approval.
2. assurance as to:
   a) the correctness of any prices or rates included on the document,
   b) the mechanical accuracy of the document,
   c) the correctness of any coding (e.g. general ledger account number).

It is important that each of these elements be understood by each member of the audit team since audit programs or verification notes will usually refer to "vouching to" a particular source without repeating all the component steps involved.

Authenticity

While the auditor cannot be expected to detect cleverly forged documents, he should, in the case of externally prepared documents, be able to discern crude forgeries, misrepresentations or alterations. For internally prepared documents, the auditor should be familiar enough with the documents commonly used in the accounting system that he may detect obvious substitutions. A possible lack of authenticity may also be indicated by the nature of the information on the document.

Propriety

Assurance as to the propriety of the transaction is obtained by using common sense and a knowledge of the client's business. The auditor should ask himself if the information on the document appears reasonable in relation to the nature and scope of the business. When examining a sales invoice, the auditor should consider the reasonableness of the goods described as being sold. Are they customary products of the company? Is the customer a regular customer? Likewise, when examining purchase invoices, the auditor should consider the reasonableness of the goods or services described as purchased. Are they customary materials or services consumed by the company? Is the supplier a regular supplier? The auditor should be alert to the possibility that the purchased goods may be personal items for use by company officers or employees rather than legitimate business expenses. He also should consider the item's deductibility or lack of deductibility for income tax purposes as an aid to the verification of the income tax provision. For both sales and purchase documents he should consider whether provincial sales taxes, federal sales taxes and shipping costs have been properly included or excluded.

Authorization and approvals

The auditor must satisfy himself that the source document has been properly authorized and approved in accordance with his understanding of the system of internal control. The authorization and approvals for the purchase invoice are often evidenced by signatures or initials on the face of the document. Whether or not the auditor is placing reliance on the particular authorization, validation and approval controls, he must normally be aware of these procedures in order to vouch any given transaction. This awareness should have come from his interim audit work. When vouching a document, the auditor should also be alert for indications that his earlier internal control conclusions were incorrect or that the control system is being accidentally ignored or deliberately circumvented.

Verification of prices or rates

One or more of the source documents examined usually contains some rate or price which is to be applied to the items covered in the transaction. In some cases, vouching would include checking the correctness of the rate to some authoritative source, for example, approved rate lists for employee wages. In other cases, checking (such as to a standard price list for goods being sold or to supplier's price books for goods being purchased) might only be included in the presence of suspicious circumstances.

Mechanical accuracy

The auditor should normally satisfy himself as to mechanical accuracy by reperforming all additions and multiplications appearing on the face of the document. In some cases, this step might, in the absence of suspicious circumstances, be limited to a quick check for reasonableness.

Coding of documents

Finally, the auditor must ensure that the transaction has been recorded in the proper account or accounts. He should compare the information on the face of the document to the client's chart of general ledger accounts. Instances of miscoding can vary in seriousness. Miscoding an asset as an expense or vice versa is serious since it misstates reported income. A minor misallocation among expense accounts is less serious. On the other hand, such misallocations may concern management because of the resulting distortion in their operating reports and may affect the auditor's reliance on budgetary comparisons. Any indication of deliberate miscoding should of course be viewed as more serious.

Number of source documents to be examined

In many cases, there is no one document which, in itself, generates an entry in the accounting records. For example, the recording of a purchase in the purchase journal may be supported by a purchase invoice, a purchase order and a receiving report. It is not always necessary for the auditor to examine every document which provides some support for a given entry. He should, however, examine enough of the documents to cover all of the elements of vouching just discussed.

10.4.6 Inspection of other documents

As used in this chapter, inspection is the examination of a document other than a source document for a transaction. Documentary inspection may provide further evidence as to a transaction or group of transactions, such as the inspection of a solicitor's letter reporting on a land purchase. It may provide evidence as to an asset or liability balance, such as the inspection of a note receivable. Or it may provide evidence as to information to be disclosed in the notes to the financial statements, such as agreements and minutes.

Elements of inspection

The elements of inspection of a particular document are a critical reading of the document, the comparison of all information contained in the document with other information recorded in the accounts or known to the auditor, the investigation of any differences, and the final conclusion. Again, the auditor must obtain reasonable assurance as to the authenticity of the document. Some or all of the other elements described in 10.4.5 may apply as well, depending on the nature of the document.

Examples of documents to be inspected

Examples of documents which would normally require inspection are:
- for investments – certificates, mortgages, lawyers' reporting letters on mortgages,
- for accounts receivable – promissory notes, correspondence, credit report,
- for prepaid insurance – insurance policies,
- for fixed assets – contracts, appraisal reports, lawyers' reporting letters, lease agreements,
- for other assets – patents, licenses, royalty agreements,
- for trade accounts payables – suppliers' statements,
- for taxes payable – copies of tax returns, assessment notices, correspondence with tax authorities,

- for long-term debt – copies of notes payable, certificate stubs, mortgages, lawyers' reporting letters, trust deeds,
- for share capital – transfer register, share ledger, certificate stubs, report from registrar and/or transfer agent,
- for income statement components – purchase and sales contracts, union agreements, advertising contracts,
- general – minutes of shareholders', directors' and audit committee meetings.

Many of the above documents will be of continuing significance and the auditor will wish to obtain copies to retain in a permanent file for use in subsequent years.

10.4.7 Enquiry of management and employees

Enquiry of management and employees is applicable to almost every financial statement figure to be verified. At the same time the oral representations from persons within the organization being audited must be treated as the least reliable form of audit evidence. All representations of material consequence must therefore be corroborated by other evidence.

Importance of enquiry

Although oral representations of management and employees must be accorded a limited reliability, they are nonetheless important to the audit. While management and employees may be less objective than independent third parties, they will be more knowledgeable than anyone else concerning the operations, systems and accounts of the business. Even the most experienced auditor must ask a considerable number of questions during the course of any audit. Enquiry contributes to all review, compliance, and substantive objectives. It is a useful starting point for most other auditing procedures. Generally, it is far more efficient to obtain explanations through enquiry and then seek to corroborate them than to try to discover such explanations unguided by sifting through quantities of detailed evidence.

Limitations of enquiry

The reliability of enquiry depends on (a) the integrity of the client's management and employees, (b) the competence, experience and carefulness of the enquirer, (c) his skill and tact in eliciting the cooperation of those from whom he seeks explanations, (d) his knowledge of the client's business and systems, (e) his ability to detect inconsistencies between the explanations received and his prior knowledge, and (f) his judgment in distinguishing the important from the trivial. The first factor is, of course, the principal reason why limited reliablity must be accorded to evidence gained by enquiry. Although most managements and most employees are honest and although an assumption to that effect is normally made in the absence of any indications to the contrary, the possibility of accidental or deliberate misrepresentations suggests that corroborating evidence is desirable. Following are some general suggestions as to the reliability attributable to various representations.

1. Objectivity of the employee giving the representation.

   When making an enquiry of an official or an employee, the auditor should consider that person's objectivity with respect to the particular enquiry. For example, the comptroller may have a more objective view of the adequacy of allowance for doubtful accounts than either the credit manager or accounts receivable clerk, both of whom might be held responsible for any disclosed problems. The comptroller's objectivity might, however, be adversely affected on questions concerning the accounting principles for income measurement if a large portion of his remuneration is determined as a percentage of such income. A financial vice-president's objectivity concerning the value of a significant investment may be questioned if he was directly responsible for making that investment and there is now some evidence of permanent impairment. In each case, the responses of the official or employee may in fact be fair and impartial despite his potential conflict of interest. But it would be imprudent for the auditor not to recognize the possiblity that the responses may be biased.

2. Knowledge of the employee.

   The auditor should ensure that he is making the enquiry of the right person. Queries as to production levels and marketing strategies may be more knowledgeably answered by the production supervisor and marketing manager than by the comptroller. The auditor should resist the temptation to direct all his enquiries to accounting and financial staff merely because he has the most frequent contact with them.

3. Level of the employee in the organizational hierarchy.

   Assuming equal knowledge of the subject of the enquiry and equal freedom from a potential conflict of interest, more reliability may generally be accorded to the representations of a trusted senior official than a new junior employee. It is true that this reliability cannot usually be absolute. Cases of companies and their auditors being misled by trusted senior officials have indeed occurred. The auditor must always be alert for this possibility – though its detection is by no means assured even with the best audit procedures. If senior officers or the board of directors have concluded that reliance can be placed on a certain senior official by giving him important responsibilities, and commensurate remuneration, their confidence should have some influence on the reliability the auditor in turn attaches to that official's representations. Usually, corroborating evidence must still be sought. In a few cases, however, such as representations by the chief executive officer as to management intentions or as to the absence of undisclosed commitments, there may be little or no corroborating evidence available. In these rare cases, provided the auditor has no reason to doubt the integrity of the individual, the representations can be accepted without corroboration.

4. Representations from several sources.
   The reliability of representations is increased if the same information is obtained, as a result of separate enquiry, from two or more reasonably objective officials who are knowledgeable as to the subject matter in question. While individual misrepresentations may occasionally occur, the auditor need not normally assume that there is an organized conspiracy to deceive him.

5. Explanations consistent with the auditor's understanding.
   Increased reliability can be accorded to representations which appear reasonable to the auditor, provided that he has a good understanding of the client's business and of the industry in which it operates.

Elements of enquiry

The elements of enquiry are the identification of the question or of the missing information required, the identification of knowledgeable and trustworthy individuals to ask, the posing of the query and any necessary supplementary queries tactfully but clearly, a consideration of the explanations obtained using reasonable but not obsessive skepticism, a comparison of the explanations obtained to other information known to the auditor, and the final conclusion.

Enquiry is commonly used in four different ways in the audit: (a) as an essential component of the auditor's review of accounting systems and controls (see Chapter 9), (b) as a starting point for further substantive verification, (c) to obtain explanations of unusual items encountered during scrutiny or other audit procedures, and (d) to elicit information (such as details of confidential commitments) which may not be obtainable in any other way.

10.4.8 Confirmation with management

Confirmation with management serves the same purposes as enquiry. Similarly, it is subject to the same limitations as to reliability – except to the extent that individuals can be expected to take more care in signing their name to a written statement than in merely giving oral explanations.

It is customary to obtain written representations from management at the conclusion of the audit. Some practitioners prefer to obtain separate certificates for each major area: accounts receivable, inventories, etc. Others prefer to obtain one combined letter of representations. In whatever form, the obtaining of written representations from management serves the following four purposes:

1. to provide an opportunity for the auditor to learn from senior officials any information of which only they may be aware and which affects the financial statements (particularly with respect to commitments, contingencies, and subsequent events),
2. to ensure that senior management has given due thought to the important judgmental decisions required in choosing accounting policies, making accounting estimates, etc.,
3. to emphasize that the financial statements are representations of management and that their fair presentation is the responsibility of management (even where preliminary drafting may be done as an accounting service by the auditor),
4. to document formal representations by management concerning the title and valuation of assets, the disclosure of liabilities, subsequent events and non-arm's length transactions, and the completeness of information supplied to the auditor.

Contents of a letter of representations

Common items to incorporate in a management letter of representations include representations as to:
1. the adequacy of the description, and cut-off of accounts receivable, the extent of their hypothecation, the adequacy of the allowance for doubtful accounts, and the exclusion of consigned goods,
2. the ownership, hypothecation, and valuation of investments and the accuracy of the related income,
3. the adequacy of inventory count procedures, the basis of inventory pricing, the extent of its hypothecation, and the accuracy of inventory cut-off,
4. the propriety of fixed asset additions and disposals and the appropriateness and consistency of depreciation methods,

5. the adequacy of the provision for actual liabilities and the disclosure of contingent liabilities and major commitments,
6. the authenticity and completeness of minutes and the disclosure of non-arm's length transactions and of significant events subsequent to the year-end.

Examples of the foregoing sections of a management letter of representations can be found in 33.4.14, 37.4.6, 38.3.11, 35.4.11, 39.4.9, 34.8, and 44.2.6.

10.4.9 Reliance on internal auditors

A particular example of evidence obtained from client employees is reliance on internal auditors. An internal audit department affects the external auditor's work in two ways. The first way is the effect on internal control. Systems that otherwise would be judged as weak may be compensated for by the work of internal auditors. In this respect evidence obtained as to the internal auditors' work is similar to any evidence of internal control.

The second way is the effect on the external auditor's program if the internal auditors perform certain audit procedures on his behalf and under his supervision.

> The work of internal auditors cannot be substituted for the work of the independent auditor; however, the independent auditor should consider the procedures, if any, performed by internal auditors in determining the nature, timing and extent of his own auditing procedures.[11]

Where internal auditors perform certain procedures contributing to the interim audit or financial statement audit, the external auditor must review their competence and objectivity and supervise and review their work. Planning decisions relating to the use of internal auditors' work are discussed in 15.4.6, 24.2.6, and 31.2.4.

10.5 Overlapping evidence

Overlapping evidence is the evidence represented by the mutual consistency of different pieces of evidence obtained. It could, of course, be argued that this mutual consistency is not itself a new form of evidence but merely a confirmatory effect. As discussed in 6.6.5, increments of audit evidence pointing toward the same conclusion have a confirmatory effect and thus a joint degree of persuasiveness higher than that which any individual increment possesses in isolation. The reason, however, for treating the mutual consistency (or inconsistency) as a type of evidence in its own right in this chapter is that much important audit work is devoted exclusively to searching for it. Analytical review procedures may reveal a consistency among the accounting figures which confers a far greater reliability on the records than would normally be accorded to internal evidence. Contrarily, they may reveal an inconsistency which provides persuasive evidence of errors or discrepancies which the individual accounting records in isolation failed to reveal.

The reliability of overlapping evidence depends on the degree of consistency found (or the certainty of inconsistency revealed), the pervasiveness of the consistency, and the skill and care with which the auditor can assess the consistency. Its reliability is, however, limited to the extent that it might be possible for a dishonest employee to fabricate artificial though consistent entries and balances. The more pervasive the consistency, the more this possibility is reduced. That the possibility exists, however, is a reason why internal and overlapping evidence alone should never be considered sufficient.

Auditing techniques for gathering overlapping evidence vary from the simple correlation with related information to fully developed analytical review procedures and regression analysis. Fundamental to the evaluation of overlapping evidence is a sound knowledge of the client's business.

10.5.1 Correlation with related information

The techniques of correlating new evidence with related information is used continuously throughout the audit process. Thus, the close concurrence of a physical stock-taking with the balances recorded in perpetual inventory records provides evidence of the accuracy of total inventory far more persuasive than either stock-taking or perpetual records would provide separately. There would normally be some risk that the stock-taking had been carelessly performed and some risk that the perpetual records had been inaccurately posted. But the chance that such errors could have dove-tailed with each other so neatly as to produce an apparent concurrence item by item would usually be too remote to be taken seriously. Thus, the correlation of count results with related information (perpetual records) reveals in this case a concurrence which is itself persuasive evidence of accuracy.

Every new piece of audit evidence obtained should be correlated by the auditor with all other related information known to him. Consistencies should be noted and inconsistencies investigated.

Usually, the audit technique of correlation is only one of several techniques applied to achieve a given verification objective. Occasionally, however, it is the principal or even sole technique. For example:

- The analysis of interest costs for the year provides the only significant positive evidence that there are no undisclosed debt liabilities.
- The review of certain expense accounts, such as insurance expense, provides significant evidence that there are no undisclosed prepaids or accruals.

10.5.2 Analytical review and regression analysis

Analytical review is the systematic analysis and comparison of related figures, trends, and ratios in order to identify their mutual consistency or inconsistency. Apparent inconsistencies revealed by analytical review call for further investigation. In effect, such inconsistencies until resolved are a suspicious circumstance raising doubts as to the reliability of the previously gathered evidence.

Analytical review provides the auditor with a powerful and economical tool for gaining assurance as to the reasonableness of reported results and for isolating those accounts where unusual statistical relationships indicate that further investigation is warranted. In its special report on the Equity Funding fraud the AICPA indicated that though ingenious attempts were made to conceal the fact that certain insurance policies were fictitious by setting up fictitious premium income and acquisition expense accounts, some flaws inevitably arose in the elaborate fabrication. In certain subsidiaries the ratio of alleged commission income to alleged commission expense was seriously out of line. It is with the hope of detecting such anomalies that auditors increasingly are making use of analytical review techniques.

Objectives served by analytical review

Analytical review is a substantive procedure. It contributes to all the objectives of substantive verification, but particularly those of existence, completeness, and valuation. Fictitious insertions, inadvertent or deliberate omissions, or improper valuations if material would often be caught by well designed analytical review. Often, in fact, analytical review is the principal source of evidence available as to completeness.

Importance of analytical review

Analytical review can be applied to almost every financial statement figure. A typical example is the analysis of gross profit trends in order to provide additional evidence as to the accuracy of reported inventories. Often analytical review is cheaper than other substantive verification procedures. It is therefore often an efficient audit strategy to employ analytical review to the maximum extent possible and then to vary the required extent of other substantive procedures inversely with the degree of assurance already obtained.

Limitations of analytical review

The reliability of analytical review may be limited by the natural tendency on the part of both client employees and the auditor to search for whatever explanations are necessary to account for observed trends – and perhaps ignore explanations that "go the wrong way" or explain trends that were not in fact observed. Its reliability is also limited by the difficulty most individuals have of judging intuitively any but the most simple relationships. Thus, it is simple to realize that percentage-based sales commissions should increase in the same proportion as sales have increased. If the proportionate increases do not correspond, there is a possibility that either sales or sales commissions have been misstated. This discrepancy should be investigated. But most relationships have both fixed and variable factors, which simple ratio analysis ignores. And many results will depend on not just one but two or three different factors. Finally, the reliability may be limited to the extent that artificial, though consistent, entries are fabricated.

Advantages of regression analysis

To offset all but the last of these limitations, some practitioners have recently been exploring the use of regression analysis. Regression analysis is a means of employing mathematical techniques to determine in an objective manner the relationship among the past numbers in a series and therefore to predict the likely range in which the current number in the series can be expected to fall. If the current year's (or current month's) results fall outside that range, then an apparent inconsistency is revealed which should be investigated. The mathematical techniques provide a means of measuring the degree of correlation observed among the past numbers in the series and the degree of assurance that a current number falling outside a specified range is a result of other than random fluctuations.

The advantages of regression analysis are that (a) it serves as a discipline to ensure that analytical review is really performed, (b) it forces the auditor to identify the factors on which some accounting result should depend and therefore to focus more thought on the nature of the relationship, and (c) it helps the auditor to evaluate relationships more complex than he can easily assess judgmentally.

Limitations of regression analysis

Regression analysis is a more sophisticated technique which at once involves higher training and application costs and the opportunity for misuse through carelessness or inexperience. The auditor may be tempted to juggle numerical factors mechanically to find a high apparent correlation, which may be spurious. The concentration on past trends may divert attention from a new factor which should be influencing operating results for the first time in the current year. The computerized calculations involved may generate an aura of accuracy out of proportion to the reliability of the evidence actually obtained by this technique. Advocates of regression analysis believe that these limitations can be controlled by proper training and supervision and that they are more than outweighed by its advantages. Future years will undoubtedly see more research into the pros and cons of this techniques.[12]

Elements of analytical review

The elements of analytical review are (a) the identification of the factors on which a given accounting result should depend, (b) the determination of the approximate relationship between the accounting result and those underlying factors, (c) the prediction of what the current result should be if that relationship continued, (d) the comparison of the actual current result to that prediction, and (e) the final conclusion. The elements are in theory unchanged whether the analytical review is carried out judgmentally or whether it is performed mathematically using regression analysis. Mathematical techniques merely focus more specific attention on each of the elements separately and permit a quantification of the degree of correlation and degree of assurance obtained.

Examples of analytical review

The most rudimentary analytical review is the comparison of the current year's balances to the prior year's. Comparison for three or more years is, of course, much more reliable. Comparison and evaluation are greatly facilitated if key accounting data and ratios are tabulated in the audit working papers in graphical form. In addition to comparing current with prior years, the auditor should compare actual results with budgets and seek explanations for any variance.

More complete analytical review involves the comparison of key relationships (sales in relation to gross national product, market share, advertising budget, etc.) over a period of months or years or over a group of similar branches or divisions for the same year. Comparisons may involve statistics by geographical area and by product group, satatistics from competitors or trade associations, government statistics, analysis into components, and comparisons with related data (e.g., dollar sales with volume and price data).

Examples of analytical review procedures are described in 32.4.3, 33.4.8 and 35.4.10.

10.5.3 Knowledge of the business

Much overlapping evidence involves a comparison of the findings from individual audit procedures with the auditor's own knowledge of his client's business. Knowledge of the business is essential to analytical review as well as to many other audit procedures, such as enquiry, scrutiny and vouching. Without an adequate knowledge of the business the auditor is not in a position to distinguish between meaningful relationships and fortuitous ones, critical trends and trivial ones, reasonable explanations and invalid ones.

Gaining familiarity with the client's business was one of the first steps in the interim audit (see 9.2.1). The auditor should be aware of the manner of organization of the enterprise, the nature of its assets and liabilities, the sources of its revenues, the types of its expenses, accounting matters peculiar to the business and to the industry of which it is a part, and the concerns and matters important to a businessman in that industry.

10.5.4 Integration of conclusions

It is important that all overlapping evidence, both confirmatory and contradictory, be considered. In an engagement involving many staff members this task can be a difficult one. Frequently, different members reviewing different financial statement components and documenting their work in different working paper schedules will observe evidence which is inconsistent. If each confines his attention to his own section, the inconsistency will be apparent to none of them. It is important, therefore, that at least one member of the audit team make a final review of all the verification results and seek further explanations where the evidence gathered in different file sections seems inconsistent.

10.6 Evidence decisions

Decisions which the auditor must make regarding audit evidence can be divided into *planning* decisions and *evaluation* decisions. Planning decisions involve, for each financial statement assertion, a choice of the *nature* and *extent* of the related audit evidence to be gathered and of the *timing* of the gathering. Evaluation decisions involve (a) an assessment of the appropriateness and sufficiency of the evidence gathered and (b) a conclusion, on the basis of this evidence, as to the accuracy of the particular financial statement assertion.

10.6.1 Relationship of planning and evluation decisions

Planning decisions represent, in effect, a tentative and prospective assessment of the appropriateness and sufficiency of evidence. The auditor seeks that evidence which, provided it does not raise doubts or uncertainties unanticipated at the planning stage, will be found during the evaluation stage to be appropriate and sufficient to support an opinion. The opinion itself may be that the financial statement assertion is accurate (at least within the constraints of materiality). Or the opinion may be that the assertion is materially inaccurate. If neither of these opinions is justified, then the evidence will have proved inappropriate or insufficient and additional evidence must now be drawn – unless it is apparent, either because of the impossibility of verification or because of irremovable uncertainties inherent in the assertion itself, that appropriate and sufficient evidence is just not available.

Doubts or uncertainties which can be cured, or reduced to acceptably low levels, through the gathering of additional evidence are of two types: (a) the risk of possible (i.e., not sufficiently improbable errors indicated by the projection of tests or samples and (b) the risk of possible, though not definitely established, errors indicated by ambiguities, contradictions, unexplained conditions, or suspicious circumstances detected in the evidence gathered. A discussion of the first risk is deferred until Chapters 12 and 13. To the extent that the second risk cannot be identified until the evidence has been gathered, planning decisions cannot be foolproof and the auditor must be prepared to gather additional evidence if and when circumstances indicating such risks are encountered. Of course, likely problems or suspicious circumstances may already be known at the planning stage as a result of the auditor's knowledge of the client's business, systems, and controls or as a result of his experience in prior years' audits. These circumstances can be allowed for during planning. Other problems or suspicious circumstances may be encountered during the course of gathering the initially planned evidence. In practice, the auditor must therefore revise his planned procedures continually throughout the course of the audit as each new piece of evidence is obtained and evaluated.

10.6.2 Evidence planning decisions

In planning the nature, extent and timing of his audit procedure the auditor must consider the relevance, reliability and sufficiency of the evidence available and the timeliness and economy with which it can be gathered in relation to the required precision and degree of assurance of the audit opinion (see Chapter 6).

Decisions as to the relevance of evidence to be sought usually present little difficulty. Observation of stocktaking is relevant to the assertion that inventories exist but not to the assertion that they are valued at the lower of cost and market value. Since both assertions must be verified, the auditor must seek other evidence (from cost records, invoices, price quotations, comparisons and enquiry) as to their valuation. Choosing relevant evidence requires simply a careful analysis of the individual verification objectives to be met.

Decisions as to the reliability of evidence to be sought are more difficult. To start with, they will depend on what evidence is practically available. The existence of a piece of machinery can, in part, be verified by physical examination – physical evidence being generally the most reliable available. An intangible asset such as a patent right cannot be so verified.

Often, however, many pieces of evidence, of varying reliability, are available for a given financial statement assertion.

For example, consider the evidence available as to the ownership of land – not its existence or valuation or presentation – just the assertion as to its ownership. Among other steps the auditor can observe the land and the client's possession and use of it (direct personal knowledge) which in turn may imply ownership, he can have a special title search done (external evidence) to prove ownership, he can inspect the agreement by which the land was acquired and a lawyer's reporting letter thereon within the client's files (internal evidence), and he can correlate the alleged ownership with the insurance coverage of buildings situated on the land (overlapping evidence).

In the foregoing example, must the auditor seek the most reliable evidence available? Not necessarily. Practitioners, for instance, differ in their views as to the necessity or frequency of title searches. In many cases, a lawyer's letter in the client's files, though it is internal evidence theoretically susceptible to alteration or forgery, would be considered to be sufficiently reliable evidence in lieu of a title search.

The decision should depend first of all on the degree of overall audit assurance required. In Chapter 6 it was argued that overall audit assurance required might vary slightly from engagement to engagement (first, excess assurance might be prudent on sensitive engagements and, second, the level of assurance warranted should be influenced within limits by the cost of audit evidence available[13]). It was further argued that the audit assurance demanded of any individual audit procedure should vary significantly in inverse relation to the assurance available from internal control and from the inherent nature of the item being audited. Therefore, in deciding upon the reliability of evidence to be examined the auditor should logically consider those two factors as follows:

- the inherent risk of a material error in the financial statement assertion in question – (consider the nature of the asset, the liability or income component; the susceptibility to innocent or fraudulent error; the nature and significance of past errors observed; the current industry and economic conditions.)

- the control risk related to the financial statement assertion in question – (consider the quality and effectivness of key controls on which reliance is placed – including both the design of the control system and the results of related compliance verification; the existence and effectiveness of an internal audit program; recent systems changes which may have enhanced or diminished internal control).

Timing may also influence reliability. Confirmation of accounts receivable at October 31 does not provide as reliable evidence of the figure reported on the December 31 balance sheet as does confirmation at December 31 itself. Nonetheless, in the presence of good internal control the reliablity of the former may be sufficient, when coupled with additional review procedures during the intervening period. Where internal control is weak, however, the reliability of pre-balance sheet procedures may be insufficient and procedures such as confirmation may have to be scheduled for the year-end.

Decisions as to the sufficiency of evidence to be sought are usually the most difficult. Two aspects can be considered: (a) the number of individual items within an accounting population from which a given kind of evidence should be sought and (b) the number of different types of evidence which should be sought for any given item or assertion. The first consideration relates to test or sample extents and is dealt with in Chapters 12 and 13. The second consideration involves the question of overlapping evidence. In the example of verifying land ownership discussed earlier, should the auditor require (a) direct observation, (b) a title search, and (c) agreement and lawyer's letter and (d) a review of insurance coverage or only one of these pieces of evidence? No invariable answer can be given. Most auditors would wish to examine the agreement and lawyer's letter whether or not the other evidence was obtained as well. On the other hand, direct observation might not be considered necessary if one or more of the other pieces of evidence had been obtained.

In deciding how many pieces of overlapping evidence to seek before the joint persuasiveness should be considered sufficient to support an opinion, the auditor should consider the same factors of precision, overall assurance, inherent risk and control risk in relation to timeliness and cost, as already discussed for reliability. In addition, he should consider the degree to which the overlapping evidence is consistent or contradictory (see 10.5).

10.6.3 Evidence evaluation decisions

In evaluating the sufficiency and appropriateness of audit evidence gathered, the auditor merely updates his planning decisions for any unanticipated conditions encountered in the evidence itself.

In drawing a conclusion as to the accuracy of the particular financial statement assertion the auditor interprets evidence gathered. Often additional procedures or enquiries will be required in this process. A difference reported by a customer on an account receivable confirmation may represent an error in the client's accounts, an error in the customer's accounts, a shipment or payment in transit, a misunderstanding by the customer of the information requested, or an error by the auditor in the preparation of the confirmation request. In the end he must decide whether or not the financial statement assertion (including presentation) is materially in error. In some auditing steps, the identification of individual errors presents little difficulty but what may be complex is determining whether the accumulation of all such errors is or could be material. Projection of errors found in samples is discussed in Chapters 12 and 13. In other auditing steps, projections do not arise but the determination of what constitutes an error at all may be complex. The assessment of assertions involving accounting *estimates* is particularly difficult. Error evaluation is discussed more fully in 16.4.

10.7 Reference material

AICPA Statement of Auditing Standards No. 1, Section 330, "Evidential Matter".
CICA Audit Technique Study, *Confirmation of Accounts Receivable*, (1969).
AICPA Statement of Auditing Standards No. 9,

The Effect of an Internal Audit Function on the Scope of the Independent Auditor's Examination.
AICPA Statement of Auditing Standards No. 11, *Using the Work of a Specialist.*

10.8 Questions and problems

Review and discussion

1. What is audit evidence?
2. Discuss the usefulness of the first two methods of evidence classification described in Chapter 10.
3. What are the various objectives for which audit evidence is collected?
4. Accounts receivable balances can be verified by positive or negative confirmations. Which is preferable and why?
5. Discuss, giving examples, how underlying, corroborating and contradictory evidence are related.
6. a) Classify audit evidence according to the four principal sources and sub-classify each source according to its nature (physical evidence vs documentary evidence, etc.).
   b) Comment on the degree of reliance which can be placed on each source.
7. What are the basic audit techniques? Give examples of each (different from those listed in the chapter).
8. a) Describe the objectives of physical examination.
   b) What are some limitations of physical examination as a method of obtaining evidence?
   c) Describe the elements of physical examination.
9. Give three examples where reperformance is the primary evidence in support of financial statement figures.
10. What are the evidence objectives in the observation of activities?
11. On what does the reliability of external evidence depend?
12. Give two examples of external evidence which can simultaneously verify more than one financial statement component.
13. Why are income statement components not usually verified by confirmation? In what circumstance would confirmation of an income statement component be appropriate?
14. What are the elements of, and prerequisites for, reliable confirmation?

15. When should an auditor rely on internal evidence?
16. List five types of internal evidence and indicate the limitations of each. Give examples of an auditor's use of each type during an audit engagement.
17. "Scrutiny" is a very common term used in the audit profession.
   a) Define the term "scrutiny".
   b) What are its objectives?
   c) What are its limitations?
   d) What does an auditor look for in a scrutiny?
18. The verb "vouch", in most situations, means to give assurance or to guarantee. Discuss the meaning of "vouch" in an audit context.
19. What is the difference between vouch and inspection when used in an audit context?
20. What is the purpose of management's letter of representation? What information should it contain? What effect do you think the letter of representation would have on a chartered accountant's examination of a client's financial statements?
21. Describe the potential effect of an internal audit department on the external audit program.
22. What is the effect when new evidence confirms existing audit evidence?
23. Compare analytical review and regression analysis.
24. Why is it important for at least one member of an audit team to review the results of all verification procedures performed by all members of the team?
25. Discuss the relationship of evidence planning and evidence evaluation decisions.
26. What factors should an auditor consider in the planning process with respect to the reliability and sufficiency of available audit evidence?

Problems

1. (AICPA adapted) What would you accept as satisfactory documentary evidence in support of entries in the:

a) sales journal,
b) sales return register,
c) vouchers payable register,
d) payroll journal,
e) cheque register?

2. Smith & Co. recently acquired Green Sleeves Ltd. as an audit client. The audit senior, Robin Banks, was conducting the interim audit and planning the financial statement audit. He reviewed Green Sleeves' trial balance, which consisted primarily of the following accounts:

Petty cash	$	500
Travel advances		2 000
Cash in bank		33 278
Trade accounts receivable		476 872
Notes receivable		200 000
Inventory		322 916
Prepaid insurance		32 316
Land		1 700 000
Building, net		417 000
Furniture and fixtures, net		12 286
Goodwill		1
Trademarks		58 712
Trade accounts payable		(169 315)
Accrued charges		(200 000)
Income taxes payable		(12 010)
Notes payable		(100 000)
Mortgages payable		(302 533)
Share capital		(237 000)
Retained earnings		(689 312)
Sales		(5 612 098)
Cost of sales		1 500 032
General and administrative expenses		1 087 362
Selling expense		1 132 317
Miscellaneous expense		510 095
Interest expense		6 000
Interest income		(14 000)
Professional fees		312 017

a) What accounts might reasonably be confirmed with third parties (or verified to third-party sources)?
b) For each account so verified, describe the third party source and the details that should be confirmed.

3. Arthur Quill, CA, is the audit senior on Hi Cal Co., a medium-sized manufacturer. Quill was reviewing the accounts receivable section working papers prepared by one of his assistants. Upon reviewing the working papers, and having discussed the section with the assistant, the following points came to light.
a) The predetermined sample size of accounts receivable confirmation requests was 50. The assistant sent 60. The assistant indicated that this enabled him to accept on the first 50 confirms to be returned correctly as his sample. "This procedure will reduce follow-up time."
b) Five of the confirms requested were to affiliated companies.
c) The assistant listed the confirms to be sent by name and dollar amount. He had the client's personnel type the confirms and fill in the addresses. He obtained the confirms back from the typist, added the total dollar value of the confirms and agreed this to the total dollar value of his written requests.
d) He signed the confirms and had the client sign the confirms. He stuffed the envelopes, included a return envelope, and sent the confirms to Hi Cal Co.'s mailing room for stamps and mailing.
e) He received 59 of 60 confirms back, of which five had errors. The five plus the three smallest confirms were filed in rough work and not considered to be part of the sample. Fifty positive confirms were filed in the section – all agreed.
f) Fourteen of the confirms did not have a dated receipt of the CA firm stamped on the confirm. The assistant indicated that several confirms had been returned directly to the client, who in turn passed them on to the auditors.

Identify the shortcomings of the confirmation procedures. What can be done to rectify the situation now, and in future years?

4. Best Sellers Book Distributing Company is in the business of distributing books (novels, paperbacks, etc.) to local retail outlets such as milk stores, confectionaries, small grocery stores and several large department stores. The books are displayed in racks.

The terms of sale are as follows (for a book with a retail price of $1.00):

Cost to company	.60	(60%)
Selling price to retailer	.80	(80%)

A sale is recorded at the time of delivery; however, the retail outlet retains the right to return for full refund any books that it is unable to sell. Best Sellers in turn can return these books to the publisher. The net effect of such returns is therefore to eliminate the gross profit on the sale from the accounts of Best Sellers.

It is industry practice to overstock the book racks so as to make them more appealing to the eventual customers. That is, book racks are never left only partially full. In light of this, there are always substantial returns.

Selected income statement and balance sheet accounts for 1974 are shown below.

Summarized Financial Information

Income Statement

	1974	%	1975	%
Gross sales	$6 500 000	100.0	$7 800 000	100.0
Less actual returns	2 300 000	35.4	2 400 000	30.8
Net sales	4 200 000	64.6	5 400 000	69.2
Cost of sales (75% of net sales)	3 150 000		4 000 000	
Sub-total	1 050 000		1 350 000	
(Increase) decrease in provision for returns (See Note)	(10 000)		—	
Gross profit	1 040 000		1 350 000	
Other expenses—labour, rent, administration, etc.	720 000		950 000	
	$ 320 000		$ 400 000	

Balance Sheet

Provision for unearned gross profit on anticipated returns (1973—amount was 190 000)	$ 200 000	(Credit)
Made up of: Provision for anticipated returns from dealers	800 000	(Credit)
Provisions for returns to publishers	600 000	(Debit)

Note: In practice, sales would be reduced by $40 000 and cost of sales by $30 000 to reflect this provision in the income statements properly.

In 1975, a major management effort was made to increase efficiency and reduce the volume of returns as a percent of total sales.

The year-end figures are shown below. Best Sellers was pleased with the decrease in the return rate from 35.4% to 30.8%, and argued that the provision for future returns should be reduced.

Accordingly, they proposed a provision as follows:

	1974	1975
Provision for anticipated returns from dealers (credit)	$800 000	$600 000
Provision for returns to publishers (debit)	600 000	450 000
Net provision for unearned gross profit on anticipated returns (credit)	200 000	150 000

The effect of this provision is to increase gross profit in 1975 by 50 000, a material amount. Best Sellers argues that this reflects the 13% drop in return rate (35.4% to 30.8%) for the whole year, as well as the increased efficiency towards the end of the year.

What audit procedures would you use to substantiate the provision?

Explain in detail.

5. Typical examples of audit evidence gathered by an auditor would include:
   a) general ledger,
   b) cancelled cheques,
   c) payroll time cards,
   d) minutes of shareholders' and directors' meetings,
   e) lease agreements,
   f) actual quantities of inventories,
   g) share certificates,
   h) customer's written agreement with an outstanding invoice or account balance,

i) suppliers' statements,

j) concurrence of inventory extensions by the auditor with those of the client,

k) perpetual inventory records,

l) vendors' invoices,

m) bank statements,

n) receiving reports,

o) accounts receivable subledger,

p) sales journal,

q) journal vouchers,

r) mortgage agreement,

s) concurrence of prepaid portion of expenditure with the auditor's calculation,

t) written representation by management,

u) written representation by the client's solicitor.

Classify each of the preceding examples of audit evidence by source:

• direct personal knowledge,

• external evidence,

• internal evidence.

Indicate briefly the reliability of each piece of evidence.

6. (CICA adapted) CA has been the auditor of X Ltd., a medium-sized clothing retailer with six stores, for several years. Invoices for inventory purchases are paid by a central office and are approved for payment only after they are matched with receiving slips sent in from the stores.

Every year, CA has verified X Ltd.'s accounts receivable by direct communication. This year he plans to confirm accounts payable also. He conveyed this decision to Mr. X, the manager and principal shareholder of X Ltd., when they were making arrangements for the annual visit of CA's staff. Mr. X has never been happy about CA's direct communication with debtors but over the years had gradually accepted the need for it. When he learned that CA now planned to communicate directly with creditors, he was furious. "Why," he said, "would you want to communicate with creditors when you have statements representing over 75% of the dollar value of our payables? You've asked us to keep the statements that come in and we've gone out of our way to do so but now you're saying they're not good enough. I've gone along with you writing to our debtors because they don't send out statements, but our creditors do. What you're proposing would only serve to remind our creditors that we owe them money and there are some I don't want to remind because then we'll have to pay them faster. Anyway, I understand your main purpose in verifying accounts payable is to detect unrecorded liabilities, not that there would be any, and surely communicating with existing creditors is not going to help you do that. You're looking at subsequent invoices as it is. I can see why you have to verify accounts receivable this way, but accounts payable are completely different. Besides, it'll cost me more money because it will take you more time to do the audit."

State the points the CA would make in replying to X. Cover both theoretical and practical points.

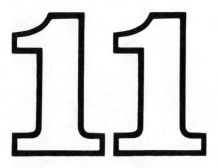

The Financial Statement Audit

The purpose of this chapter is to discuss the objectives, underlying concepts, and basic elements of the second major component of the annual audit, namely the financial statement audit. A detailed step-by-step description of financial statement audit procedures may be found in Chapters 31 to 44.

11.1 Objectives of the financial statement audit

11.1.1 Primary objective of the financial statement audit

Taken together, the interim audit and the financial statement audit must fulfill the primary objective of the audit as a whole. How these objectives should be divided between the interim audit and the financial statement audit components is a question of efficiency. As discussed in Chapter 9, the interim audit will generally have covered a review and evaluation of most systems and controls, a determination of the accuracy and reliability of the accounting records, and some preliminary amount of substantive verification. Most of the required substantive procedures, however, will usually have been left for the financial statement audit. The nature, timing and extent of these procedures will depend on the interim audit results. The purpose of the substantive procedures is to obtain and evaluate evidence as to the different assertions, discussed later, regarding the assets, liabilities, income components and other financial statement figures. The primary objective of the financial statement audit can therefore be defined as:

> To determine
> a) on the basis of the interim audit results, and
> b) through substantive verification of the existence (or occurence), completeness, ownership (or incidence or propriety), valuation (or measurement), and presentation of assets, liabilities, income components and other financial statement figures,
> the appropriate opinion to be expressed in the audit report.

The four basic elements

The primary objective implies, in turn, four basic elements in any financial statement:

1. completion and evaluation of the interim audit,
2. substantive verification,
3. evaluation,
4. formation of opinion.

Each of these four elements is discussed in one of the following sections of this chapter.

Relationship to audit evidence

The second element, substantive verification, is generally the largest component of the financial statement audit. It is most directly related to the third field work standard:

> Sufficient appropriate audit evidence should be obtained, by such means as inspection, observation, enquiry, confirmation, computation and analysis, to afford a reasonable basis to support the content of the report.

The first element involves audit evidence as well – a mixture of compliance and substantive evidence. The third and fourth elements involve the interpretation of both types of evidence as they relate to the audit opinion.

Relationship to risk

In chapter 6, the total risk of undetected misstatements in the financial statements was analyzed into: inherent risk, control risk, and audit risk. The completion and evaluation of the interim audit leads to an assessment of the control risk. Inherent risk is evaluated both during the interim audit and during substantive verification. Substantive verification in turn requires the choice of an appropriate level of audit risk so as, when combined with inherent risk and control risk, to yield an acceptably low level of total risk.

11.1.2 Secondary objectives of the financial statement audit

While the primary objective of the financial statement audit is directed toward the attest function of expressing an opinion on the financial statements, most auditors combine certain collateral services with their regular annual audit work. During the verification of fixed assets, for example, the auditor may observe a weakness in the recording of disposals which can be corrected, opportunities for improving capital budgeting, legitimate possibilities for reclassification of certain additions entitled to more favorable tax allowances, or scope for improving the financial statement presentation of fixed asset components. While many suggestions are usually made as a result of the interim audit work, some can only arise out of the financial statement audit work. In addition, the auditor may combine with his financial statement audit work, where requested, the initial drafting of the client's financial statements and the drafting or review of the client's tax returns.

Thus, secondary objectives of the financial statement audit can be defined as:

1. To identify opportunities and provide timely suggestions for improvements in internal control, systems efficiency, financial or tax planning, and accounting methods to the extent that such identification and provision can be combined economically with the procedures required under the primary objective or are requested by the client, and were not already made during the interim audit.
2. Where requested, to prepare the client's financial statements as an accounting service.
3. Where requested, to prepare the client's income tax and other government returns as a tax service.

Where the external auditor is requested to draft the financial statements, often because the client does not have staff with sufficient knowledge of current accounting practice and disclosure requirements, such drafting is an accounting service and not an auditing service. Usually the drafting of financial statements includes the calculation of various accounting estimates (for example, income taxes payable) and other year-end adjustments. The auditor may, as accounting adviser, suggest certain year-end adjustments and a certain set of draft financial statements based on the facts known to him. Client management, in accepting the adjustments and in adopting the draft statements, must consider whether their own more intimate knowledge of the business includes awareness of facts, perhaps not previously disclosed to the auditor, which would call for modifications. The financial statements remain the representations of the reporting entity and it is important that management's responsibility for making these representations fairly not be neglected when the initial drafting is done by the auditor.

While the primary objective (attest function) is mandatory, some portion of the secondary objective (useful suggestions) is discretionary – unless specifically covered in the terms of the auditor's engagement. As in the interim audit (see 9.1.2), it is important to distinguish between the two objectives. Satisfaction of one will not compensate for deficiencies in meeting the other.

11.1.3 Additional reporting responsibility of the auditor

While the secondary objective of the financial statement audit has been described as discretionary (except to the extent specifically requested by the client), a certain responsibility of the auditor beyond the expression of an audit opinion is important to observe:

> To advise the client of any significant errors, irregularities or suspicious circumstances encountered and, to the extent that improvement appears desirable and practicable, any significant weakness observed in the system of internal control if not already reported following the interim audit.

This responsibility is discussed at length in 9.1.3.

11.2 Completion and evaluation of the interim audit

An evaluation of control strengths and deficiencies and of the results of compliance verification will already have been performed as part of the interim audit itself (see 9.3 and 9.4.3). This work, however, will usually have to be extended for three reasons:

1. Systems and controls required only sporadically throughout the year, rather than daily, may not have been reviewed, verified or evaluated during the interim audit.
2. The review, verification and evaluation performed during the interim audit will have extended only up to the end of the interim audit visit.
3. Some procedures to compensate for control weaknesses observed may be best performed at the year-end.

11.2.1 Evaluation of additional control strengths and deficiencies

Major systems areas such as sales/receivables/receipts, purchases/payables/payments, wages and salary payrolls, and inventory records and cost records will generally have been covered during the interim audit. Less major systems may often be left for review at the year-end. For example, where only a few purchases and sales of marketable securities are made during the year, the review, compliance verification, and evaluation of the related internal controls will usually be combined with substantive verification of securities during the financial statement audit. (Of course, for financial institutions the purchase and sale of securities will probably *be* one of the major systems, in which case it would normally be covered during the interim audit). Examples of systems and controls which, depending on the nature of the client organization, may be deferred for review during the financial statement audit include those related to notes receivable, marketable securities, fixed assets, income taxes, long-term debt, miscellaneous assets and liabilities, and share capital.

Where the review, compliance verification and evaluation of certain systems and controls is deferred until the financial statement audit, the procedures required will still be the same as those described in Chapter 9.

11.2.2 Extension of procedures to the year-end

If the interim audit visit is completed three months prior to the fiscal year-end, it is important that the interim review, verification and evaluation be subsequently extended to cover the last three months. Indeed, the last few months of the year may be particularly important for any of three reasons:

1. The closing months of the year may contain adjustments made in preparation for the year-end. These adjustments may reflect the proper correction of errors or estimates made earlier in the year or, in some cases, the deliberate manipulation of the reported results. In either case, non-recurring adjustments or unusual transactions warrant special attention by the auditor.
2. The last few months may constitute a "roll-forward period" between the date of certain pre-year-end verification (e.g., accounts receivable confirmation or inventory observation) and the year-end. Usually, special substantive procedures are necessary to "roll" the pre-year-end verification forward to the year-end. In addition, however, particular reliance must normally be placed on the accounting records and internal controls during this period.
3. The last few months of the year may contain most of the transactions represented in the year-end balances of certain assets and liabilities. For example, December 31 accounts receivable and

payable will usually be made up primarily of December sales and purchases. To the extent that reliance is placed on internal control in verifying such assets and liabilities, the reliance is increased for the last few months.

In extending the *review* element of the interim audit up to the year-end the auditor need not normally be as thorough as in the initial review described in 9.2. Rather, he can usually limit his additional review to (a) reasonable enquiries as to systems changes since the interim audit visit together with (b) observations, scrutiny and other procedures required in the course of meeting other financial statement audit objectives. It is the extension of interim *compliance and substantive verification* which is usually the major task. Where such verification involved tests of transactions, for example, those tests should normally be extended up to the end of the year. Occasionally, where the tests have been extended to eleven months, careful scrutiny of the final month may be sufficient in lieu of further testing.

As a result of the completion of the foregoing interim audit procedures, the earlier *evaluation* of the reliability of the accounting records or of internal controls may have to be revised. Such revisions may in turn alter previous plans as to the nature, timing and extent of substantive procedures to be performed during the financial statement audit.

11.2.3 Procedures to compensate for observed weaknesses in control

As discussed in 9.5.2, control weaknesses observed by the auditor will sometimes call for special weakness investigation procedures (compensating audit procedures) to be performed either during the interim audit or at the year-end. Thus, any such procedures not already performed should be included in the financial statement audit.

11.3 Substantive verification

The objective of substantive verification is to obtain reasonable assurance that financial statement assertions individually and together correspond to established criteria within limits not exceeding materiality. But financial statement assertions can be classified (a) according to the type of financial statement figure to which they relate (asset, liability, etc.) and (b) according to the types of assertion pertinent to each such figure (existence, completeness, ownership, etc.).

11.3.1 Objectives of substantive verification

Accordingly, the foregoing objective can be stated as follows:

To provide reasonable assurance as to whether or not:
a) the existence, completeness, ownership, valuation and presentation of reported assets,
b) the existence, completeness, incidence, valuation and

Components of the Objective of Substantive Verification

Assets	Liabilities	Income Components
To provide reasonable assurance as to whether or not:	To provide reasonable assurance as to whether or not:	To provide reasonable assurance as to whether or not:
1. the reported assets really exist *(existence)* ;	the reported liabilities really exist *(existence)* ;	the reported transactions really occurred *(occurrence)* ;
2. there are not other undisclosed assets *(completeness)* ;	there are not other undisclosed liabilities *(completeness)* ;	there were not other, undisclosed transactions *(completeness)* ;
3. the enterprise really owns and has clear title to the reported assets *(ownership)* ;	the reported liabilities really incide on the enterprise and not on some other entity or person instead *(incidence)* ;	the enterprise, and not some other entity or person instead, was really a party to the reported transactions *(propriety)* ;
4. the assets are valued appropriately and accurately *(valuation)* ;	the liabilities are valued appropriately and accurately *(valuation)* ;	the income components are measured appropriately and accurately *(measurement)* ;
5. the assets are appropriately described and disclosed *(presentation)* .	the liabilities are appropriately described and disclosed *(presentation)* .	the income components are appropriately described and disclosed *(presentation)* .

Figure 11.a

presentation of reported liabilities,

c) the occurrence, completeness, propriety, measurement and presentation of transactions underlying reported income components and other financial statement figures,

correspond to established criteria within limits not exceeding materiality.

The components of this objective are shown in Figure 11.a.

The auditor's verification process encompasses both the gathering and the evaluation of audit evidence with respect to each of the five components shown in Figure 11.a. Indeed, a set of financial statements can be considered conceptually as compromising a collection of individual assertions (e.g., receivables of $1 000 000 exist as at December 31, these receivables will be collected in full, non-arm's length balances included therein are appropriately disclosed, etc.). The auditor's job with respect to each financial statement figure is (a) to recognize all the relevant assertions implied, (b) to analyze the types of audit evidence available to confirm or deny each such assertion, (c) to decide upon the appropriate levels of materiality and assurance required, (d) to gather sufficient appropriate evidence to achieve such levels of materiality and assurance, and (e) to evaluate such evidence in order to form an objective opinion as to the individual assertion in question.

Often one or two of the components of the substantive objective will be far more important than the others. For example, existence is a major component with respect to cash; ownership can be inferred from its possession and valuation is straightforward unless problems of foreign currency translation or remittance restrictions are involved. On the other hand, the existence of a new fixed asset such as a head office building will be in little doubt; but the verification of its ownership (freedom from liens or charges) and valuation may require careful work. The most difficult component is often the completeness objective. By its nature, it seldom is susceptible to positive proof. Rather, the auditor must usually be content with negative evidence – having searched for possible undisclosed items and found none. Many year-end procedures are usually designed for such a search; checking subsequent payments for evidence of unrecorded payables, checking repairs and maintenance expense for uncapitalized fixed assets, checking interest expense for evidence of undisclosed loans payable.

Monetary errors

Instances of a financial statement assertion being incorrect may be called *monetary errors*, for they result in a monetary misstatement of some portion of the financial statements. Of course, material misstatement of fact (for example, in notes to the financial statements) should also be considered even though they may not involve figures. Some practitioners may wish to classify misstatements of fact separately as *disclosure errors* but in this book they are considered to be contained within the concept of monetary errors. Some monetary errors may be trivial in amount and it is not part of the auditor's objectives to be sure of detecting such trivial errors – though their detection may sometimes occur. Rather, his objective is directed towards the possibility of a material total of monetary error.

Restatement of substantive verification objective

With the understanding that a monetary error can relate to any of the five types of financial statement assertions previously analyzed, and subject to certain qualifications to be discussed later, the objective of substantive verification can be redefined as:

> To provide an appropriate assurance of detecting the possibility of a material total of monetary error misstating reported income (or other figure in the financial statements being examined) should such a material total actually exist.

The term monetary error refers to any type of error which results, in the auditor's judgment, in a misstatement of the financial statements. Monetary errors may include (a) accidental errors (for example, an inadvertent addition error in the physical inventory, (b) differences of opinion on matters of judgment (for example, where the auditor interprets the audit evidence as indicating the allowance for doubtful accounts to be deficient while management believes the allowance to be adequate), (c) deliberate misrepresentation (for example, concealment of liabilities) or (d) fraud (for example, misappropriated cash still reported as on hand). Monetary errors do not include procedural deficiencies which are solely compliance deviations (for example, an uninitialled purchase invoice which nonetheless was accurate and valid).

Usually, the tightest constraint of materiality is upon reported income. Accordingly, the objective of most substantive verification is appropriate assurance of detecting, should it exist, a material total of income-distorting errors whether such errors arose as a result of opening net worth misstatements, closing net worth misstatements, or a combination of both. However, the auditor must not be unmindful of the possibility of material misclassification errors (whether misclassifications of assets and liabilities or misclassification of income components) which, while not distorting net reported income, do distort the financial statement presentation as a whole.

11.3.2 Precision in substantive verification

Use of a materiality limit

The foregoing definition of the substantive objective makes reference to materiality. The concept of materiality was introduced in 6.6.2. It was suggested that for any given audit the auditor should establish a presumptive materiality limit to be used (a) as a guide to planning the design and extent of verification procedures and (b) as a guide to evaluation of audit results.

The actual setting of such a limit, for the normal case, is included in the planning decisions described in Chapter 15. Assuming such a limit has been set, the question arises as to how it should be used in planning and in evaluation. To answer this question, it is useful to consider different classes of errors according to their degree of certainty.

Error classification by degree of certainty

Substantive verification procedures directed towards determining whether material income-distorting errors exist could yield any one of a number of results. At one extreme, the evidence might, rarely, be so conclusive as to the accuracy of the reported figures that the auditor is certain that no errors exist. At the other extreme, he could have found actual known errors exceeding, in total, the materiality limit. In between these two extremes lie the more usual situations found in most audits. In one case, the auditor may have found no actual errors, but the evidence to date has raised a few questions which indicate that some errors may exist; unless the possible errors are not material the auditor will usually want to seek further evidence to resolve his doubts. In yet another case, the auditor may have found some errors in his tests indicating that most likely the same proportion of errors (and possibly even a higher proportion) exists in the accounting population from which he drew his tests.

The foregoing examples show that errors indicated by the results of substantive verification may be grouped into three classes in order of increasing uncertainty: *known errors, most likely errors,* and *possible errors.* As the terms are used in this book, most likely errors include, but extend beyond, known errors: possible errors include, but extend beyond, most likely errors (see Figure 11.b).

Known errors

Known errors are errors which are actually encountered in the audit and not corrected by management. Their existence is not in doubt. The auditor has observed them directly.

Most likely errors

Most likely errors include errors which, while not conclusively proved, most likely exist, based on the audit evidence examined, and for which no provision has been made by management. The auditor has not directly observed all of these errors (apart from the

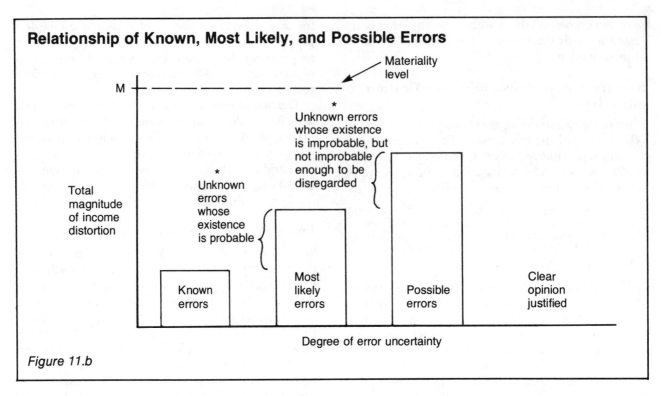

Relationship of Known, Most Likely, and Possible Errors

Materiality level

M

Unknown errors whose existence is improbable, but not improbable enough to be disregarded

Unknown errors whose existence is probable

Total magnitude of income distortion

Known errors

Most likely errors

Possible errors

Clear opinion justified

Degree of error uncertainty

Figure 11.b

component of known errors therein) but he has seen evidence indicating that their existence is probable. The most common example arises in the projection of test results: the most likely errors in a population of accounting data being the same proportion as found to be in error in a representative sample drawn therefrom (see Chapter 12). Non-testing examples, however, can occur as well, as in the following illustration:

> In a finance company, unearned finance charges have been computed individually in 5 000 individual finance contracts. Even a cursory audit review, however, reveals numerous computational errors. The auditor then estimates the most likely error in the total reported unearned finance charges by making a global calculation using other audit evidence as to the total finance paper outstanding, the average term left to run, and the average interest rate charged by major contract class. His estimate will not be exact (because of averages used) but it will not likely be seriously wrong. The difference between his estimate and the book figure will represent the most likely total error. (Alternatively, he might have estimated the most likely error by checking a representative sample drawn from the 5 000 individual calculations, but this might have been a more costly procedure in this particular instance; more costly yet would have been a detailed checking of all 5 000 calculations.)

Possible errors

Possible errors include errors which, while not probable (apart from the component of most likely errors therein), are indicated by the audit evidence examined, and within the constraints of the level of audit assurance desired, as being possible. The auditor has not directly observed all, or perhaps any, of these errors; but nor has he obtained sufficient evidence to conclude that they do not exist. Of course, almost any magnitude of error could be argued to be faintly possible if one were to imagine remote enough circumstances. But it would not be of social utility for organizations to be charged with the cost of chasing down the most far-fetched possibilities. Nonetheless, the reader of the financial statements needs something more than the mere assertion that the statements are probably acceptable. "Probably acceptable" could mean that there are barely better than 50:50 odds that a material error is not present. The reader needs, and the audit report implies an appropriate *degree of assurance* that a material error is not present. As discussed in Chapter 6, degree of assurance can be assessed in terms of its complement – the risk of undetected misstatements remaining after the audit. Thus, assuming that risks could be quantified (which, except for the specific element of sampling risk, they cannot) a 90% desired degree of assurance would correspond to a 10% permissible risk of undetected misstatements. The question then is: at this 10% permissible risk level, what errors are "possible"? If the auditor concludes that more than a material total of error is possible at this risk level, then obviously he is not in a position to give a clear audit opinion with the required degree of assurance; he must first obtain more audit evidence to confirm or deny the possibility of these "possible errors" being present.

Possible errors, in the sense used above, must therefore be understood to mean not every remotely conceivable error but rather errors whose existence is possible within the constraints of the level of audit assurance desired.[1] A common example of such possible errors arises in the projection of statistical sampling results; the possible errors in a population of accounting data (upper error limit) being the highest proportion that *could* be in error, at the specified level of sampling risk, in view of the lower error proportion actually found in a representative sample drawn therefrom (see Chapter 13).

Except for possible errors related to the sampling risk in statistical sampling applications, it is not possible for the auditor to quantify possible errors in any precise manner. Nonetheless, the concept of possible errors (exceeding the known and most likely errors) exists with respect to every verification step which the auditor performs. Possible errors exist with respect to the sampling risk in non-statistical tests and with respect to non-sampling risks in all auditing procedures (including non-sampling risks in statistical sampling applications). Possible errors do not disappear just because they cannot be precisely measured.[2] Even though no precise quantification is possible (except related to the sampling risk in statistical sampling applications), the auditor must use his professional judgment to satisfy himself that possible errors, within the constraints of an appropriate level of audit assurance, do not exceed materiality before he issues a clear opinion on the financial statements.

One materiality level or several

But one might raise the question as to whether the same materiality level should apply to all of known, most likely, and possible errors. It is tempting to argue for different levels. One can say that a bird in the hand is worth two in the bush. Surely, one might at first think, the auditor can tolerate a larger value of errors which are *merely possible* than of errors which are *known* to exist. The argument is seductive but, except for one limited case, it is, in the writer's view, invalid.

The auditor in giving a clear opinion implies that he is reasonably sure that the financial statements are not materially misstated. Suppose materiality is $20 000. If a material error ($20 000) were present and known to him, he would insist on its correction or, failing that, qualify his report. If he has not qualified his report, it must be because he is reasonably sure that such an error, which would require qualification if he knew about it, does not exist. It is not enough that he is reasonably sure that much *larger* errors (such as $50 000) do not exist. He must be reasonably sure that errors large enough to require qualification if he knew of them ($20 000) do not exist. The materiality of an error does not depend on

the degree of the auditor's knowledge about it. It is not less serious merely because the auditor is ignorant of it. If it were less serious, we should all be scrambling to become as ignorant as possible (hear no evil, see no evil, etc.).

Accordingly, it follows that, in the normal case, known, most likely and possible errors should each, in total, be contained by the same materiality limit.

Impact of materiality on substantive verification

The foregoing relationship of known, most likely and possible errors is illustrated in Figure 11.b. The excess of most likely over known errors represents unknown errors whose existence is probable. The excess of possible over most likely errors represents unknown errors whose existence is improbable but not improbable enough to be disregarded (i.e., their risk of existence is not as low as the desired degree of audit risk). If the materiality level exceeds all three of these error types (as illustrated in Figure 11.b), then obviously a clear opinion can be given. The auditor has more than adequate assurance that material errors do not exist.

This is not to say that he should be indifferent to the existence of the known and most likely errors. He should make every effort to persuade management to correct the known errors and to make an accounting provision for the remaining most likely errors, unless these amounts are completely trivial. With such adjustments the financial statements would provide what the auditor believes to be the best measurement of financial position and results. He should not seek provision for the possible errors because these errors probably do not exist and an adjustment for them would be itself erroneous and unjustified. In the end, however, the financial statements are the reporting entity's and not the auditor's. In the event that adjustments are refused, the auditor must consider his reporting responsibilities. It would be improper for him to qualify his report for known and most likely errors that were immaterial (see Chapter 18).

In some audits, however, one or more of the three different types of error may be found to breach the materiality limit. Five such cases are illustrated in Figure 11.c. In Case A, known errors breach materiality. If these definite misstatements are not corrected, the auditor would generally consider it necessary to qualify his report. In Case B, most likely errors breach materiality, though known errors do not. Here the auditor's best estimate (though not based on certain knowledge) is that the financial statements are materially in error. Unless this best

Relationship of Error Types to Materiality

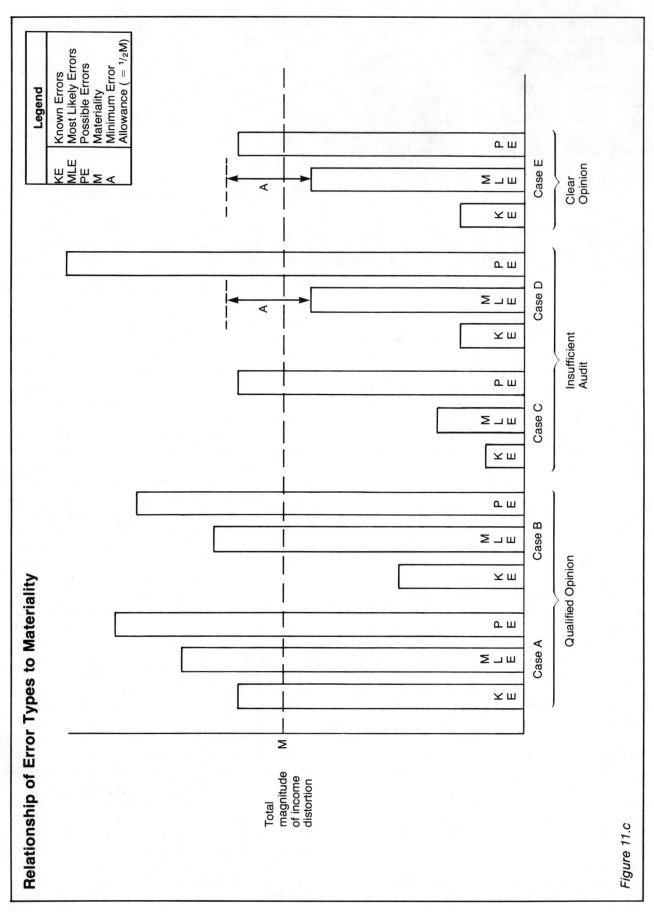

Figure 11.c

estimate is rebutted by other audit evidence, the auditor would generally consider a qualification of his report, although before such a qualification could responsibly be given he would normally have to do further work to establish *with reasonable assurance* that a material error was present. (Note that in both Case A and Case B, if management were to correct the known errors and make a provision for the remaining most likely errors, the balance of possible errors would fall below materiality and a clear opinion could be given.)

In Cases C and D possible errors breach materiality, though known and most likely errors do not. While existence of the major portion of these possible errors is improbable, it is not sufficiently improbable to be ignored (i.e., at the desired level of audit assurance these errors are "possible"). Therefore, unless these projections are rebutted by other audit evidence, the auditor would generally not consider that he could issue a clear opinion. On the other hand, it would be improper for him to qualify his report since known and most likely errors are less than materiality. The fact is that in these two cases insufficient audit work has been done. The auditor must first obtain more audit evidence to confirm or deny the likelihood of these "possible errors" before he is in a position to issue his report. Of course, with proper audit planning Cases C and D should not arise. It might be noted that even if management adjusted the statements for known and most likely errors, the remaining possible errors would still breach materiality (indicating that inadequate audit verification had been planned in the first place).

Minimum allowance for possible undetected errors

In Case E of Figure 11.c, possible errors again breach materiality while known and most likely errors do not. In this case, however, a problem becomes evident. Most likely errors are almost at the materiality level. Of course, the auditor will do his best to persuade management to correct the errors. If he succeeds, the remaining possible errors will be less than materiality and a clear opinion may be given. If adjustment is refused, however, it would at first seem that he can neither issue a clear opinion (since possible errors exceed nominal materiality) nor issue a qualification (since the most likely errors cannot be said to be material). Again, additional audit work would at first seem necessary. But the problem is that the gap between most likely errors and the materiality limit in Case E is so small that there is no practical way the auditor can, by sample extension, reduce sufficiently the magnitude of additional possible errors. Thus, if we insist that total possible errors still be

contained by the materiality limit (as in the normal case), the auditor is put in an impossible position.

All audit procedures leave a certain magnitude of undetected errors possible (possible at the risk level related to the degree of audit assurance obtained). Practical audit procedures must permit a certain *minimum allowance* for such possible undetected errors. It is submitted that it would be reasonable to allow one-half the normal materiality limit for such minimum allowance. The rationale is that reducing this minimum allowance further would, contrary to the concepts of degree of assurance and economy, lead to incremental audit costs out of proportion to the incremental gain in precision. In Case E possible errors fall within this suggested allowance and accordingly it is submitted that a clear opinion would be justified.

The role of materiality in planning substantive procedures

It follows that in the normal case the auditor must plan the extent of his substantive procedures such that, if anticipated results are in fact encountered, the evidence will indicate that known, most likely and possible errors are each in total less than materiality. Such planning necessarily involves an assumption as to what errors probably exist in the financial statements prior to audit and what degree of client correction can be reasonably anticipated for known and most likely errors subsequently indicated by the audit. If errors are expected to be minimal or client correction for all indicated errors can be anticipated, the precision demanded of the substantive procedures can be close to materiality itself. If, on the other hand, significant uncorrected errors are expected (though still less than materiality), a much tighter precision must be demanded from substantive procedures if the anticipated possible errors as a whole are still to be contained by materiality.

These relationships can only be quantified precisely in the case of statistical sampling (see 13.4.4 and 13.4.7). The concepts are nonetheless present in judgmental decisions as to audit extents as well. Messy accounts should logically require more audit work to establish that, while messy, they are not subject to a material error. Clean accounts should logically require less audit work to prove the absence of material error.

Sometimes actual errors encountered will turn out to be worse than initially anticipated and in retrospect planned audit extents will have proved insufficient. In such cases, additional audit evidence must normally be sought to obtain the reduced precision now required or, alternatively, to establish that a material error is indeed present.

A further role of materiality in planning substantive procedures is in identifying small sundry assets, liabilities or income components which are sufficiently trivial that taken together they could hardly contain a significant error even at worst.[3]

The concept of a minimum allowance for possible undetected errors has an obvious application to audit testing. It arises, however, in non-testing procedures as well, as in the following example:

> The auditor in observing a September 30 stocktaking, has discovered a clear-cut inventory error resulting in an income misstatement almost equal to materiality. He has, however, been unsuccessful in persuading management to correct the error. Normally, he would have planned to confirm receivables at October 31 and rely on a review of the months of November and December to minimize the risk of receivable errors as at December 31 year-end. Must he now shift receivable confirmation to the year-end itself on the supposed grounds that, in view of the inventory error, no further risk of possible receivable errors can be permitted at all? Clearly this would be unreasonable. On the basis of the above discussion it is still reasonable for him to confirm receivables at October 31 provided that his review of the last two months (together with his reliance on control) give him adequate assurance that possible errors in December 31 receivables do not exceed some reasonable minimum allowance.

Of course, in non-testing procedures precise quantification of the "reasonable minimum allowance" is not relevant (as quantification of the "possible errors" to be contained by such allowance is not possible). Nonetheless, the concept that some such reasonable minimum allowance must be permitted, when assessing the audit results judgmentally, is important. Without it, the auditor's substantive objectives (consistency with which is fundamental to any defence of the adequacy of his work) would not make sense. In statistical sampling procedures, on the other hand, quantification of the "reasonable minimum allowance" is relevant; the use of the one-half materiality guideline for such allowance is discussed in 13.4.4.

In most audits, however, the Case E situation does not arise.

Modified objective of substantive verification in rare cases

The normal substantive verification objective given earlier (11.3.1) presents no difficulty, if proper planning has been carried out, in the many audits where known and most likely errors (after any management correction or provision) are trivial. In rare cases, allowances must be made for a reasonable, though limited, fringe of possible undetected errors. This modification can be stated as:

> In those few cases, however, where known and most likely errors approach materiality, it is necessary, in or-

der to retain a reasonable allowance for undetected errors, to allow the limit of possible errors to exceed known and most likely errors by a limited margin (such as 50% of normal materiality).

In effect, this modification is not a change in substantive objectives but an adjustment in the determination of materiality. One of the requirements of meaningful accounting information is that it be verifiable. To be verifiable, in practice, must be interpreted to mean economically verifiable. And such an interpretation, in turn, implies that the tolerance to which statements are verified (the materiality limit) must be economically obtainable. When known and most likely errors approach what would normally be chosen as the materiality limit, confining possible but undetected errors to that normal limit is not practical. In such cases, what would otherwise be the materiality limit is not practically obtainable and the materiality limit for audit purposes should be redefined to permit the minimum allowance for undetected errors as suggested.

11.3.3 Nature of substantive procedures

The audit procedures employed in performing substantive verification of a particular financial statement assertion (such as the existence of accounts receivable) may be called *substantive procedures*. Depending on the nature of the assertion to be verified, substantive procedures may consist of any of the ten techniques applied to any of nine types of audit evidence as discussed in Chapter 10. Some substantive procedures, such as confirming accounts receivable and vouching fixed asset additions, lend themselves to application on a test basis (*substantive tests*); other substantive procedures, such as scrutiny and enquiry, usually do not. Evidence planning decisions were discussed in 10.6.2.

Effect of internal control conclusions

Where control is strong:

1. The extent of substantive tests, such as the test vouching of fixed assets, can be reduced.
2. The number of detailed steps in certain substantive procedures, such as bank reconciliation procedures, can be reduced.
3. Some substantive procedures on assets and liabilities, such as cash counts, may be able to be eliminated (unless the items involved are unusually material).
4. Major components of the financial statement audit, such as confirmation of accounts receivable and observation of physical stocktaking, can be shifted forward to a pre-year-end date in order to

accelerate the final reporting date and/or to level the monthly workloads.

5. Detailed testing (vouching) of income components can be greatly reduced in favour of scrutiny and analytical review.

Where control is weak, on the other hand, more extensive and more detailed substantive procedures are required and pre-year-end work may not be possible. Such decisions must be made separately for each major area of the accounts. Control may be excellent over accounts receivable but weak over inventory.

11.4 Evaluation

The auditor's evaluation of the results of substantive verification includes two types of conclusion – qualitive and quantitative. The first involves the decision as to whether or not a particular condition encountered represents a monetary error; the second, whether or not the known, most likely or possible total of such monetary errors exceeds materiality. Evidence evaluation decisions were discussed in 10.6.3. Error evaluation, in particular, is discussed more fully in 16.4.

Although the main objective of substantive procedures is to search for monetary errors rather than compliance deviations, any compliance deviations encountered should be carefully assessed as they may alter the auditor's previous findings on internal control and therefore the nature and the required extent of substantive procedures.

Because the evaluation of substantive verification results is influenced by the auditor's findings on internal control, the final evaluation must involve an integration of interim audit and financial statement audit results.

11.5 Formation of opinion

There are three possible outcomes to the auditor's work:

1. reasonable assurance that the financial statements correspond to established criteria within limits not exceeding materiality,
2. reasonable assurance that they do not so correspond (i.e., that they are materially misstated – with an explanation of the nature and extent of the misstatement),
3. a conclusion that such reasonable assurance is not practically obtainable (because sufficient evidence does not exist or is impracticable to obtain).

The first result gives rise to an unqualified opinion; the second, to a qualified or adverse opinion; the third, to a qualified opinion if the deficiency of evidence is not too great or too pervasive or, if it is, to a denial. Audit reporting is discussed in more detail in Chapters 17 and 18.

Of course, the appropriateness of the auditor's opinion in each of these three cases is important. He wants to avoid giving clear opinions on financial statements actually misstated by a material amount, to avoid giving qualifications on financial statements actually misstated by less than a material amount, and to avoid giving disclaimers on financial statements actually susceptible to a practicable audit and a definite opinion.

Most audit engagements result in the expression of a clear opinion. For this reason, most audit engagements are planned with this anticipation. The nature, timing and extent of substantive procedures planned are those which can be expected to yeild sufficient appropriate evidence provided unforeseen magnitudes or frequencies of uncorrected error are not encountered. In the minority of circumstances, where, because of encountering such unforeseen uncorrected errors, the auditor believes he will have to qualify his report, additional auditing procedures may sometimes be necessary to ensure that the qualification is justified – i.e., to provide reasonable assurance that he is not issuing a qualification on financial statements actually misstated by less than a material amount.

11.6 Suggested methodology

This chapter concludes with a brief outline of one suggested methodology for performing a financial statement audit. Other methods of combining and organizing the four elements discussed in this chapter are, of course, possible. The following outline is intended to do little more than list the components of the financial statement audit. A step-by-step description of the financial statement audit can be found in Chapters 31 to 44.

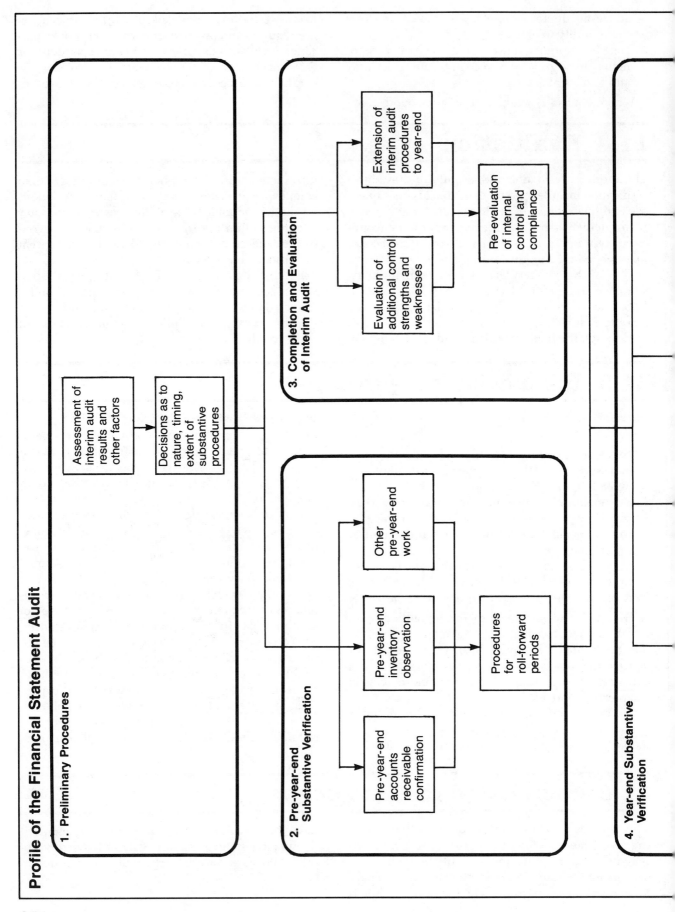

Profile of the Financial Statement Audit

1. Preliminary Procedures

- Assessment of interim audit results and other factors
- Decisions as to nature, timing, extent of substantive procedures

2. Pre-year-end Substantive Verification

- Pre-year-end accounts receivable confirmation
- Pre-year-end inventory observation
- Other pre-year-end work
- Procedures for roll-forward periods

3. Completion and Evaluation of Interim Audit

- Extension of interim audit procedures to year-end
- Evaluation of additional control strengths and weaknesses
- Re-evaluation of internal control and compliance

4. Year-end Substantive Verification

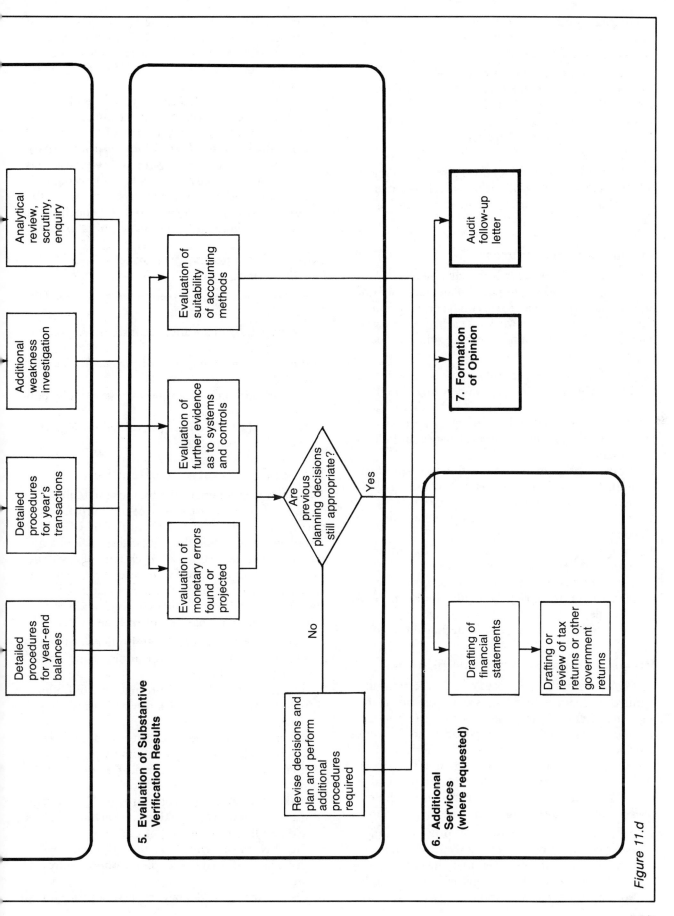

Analytical review, scrutiny, enquiry

Additional weakness investigation

Detailed procedures for year's transactions

Detailed procedures for year-end balances

5. Evaluation of Substantive Verification Results

Evaluation of suitability of accounting methods

Evaluation of further evidence as to systems and controls

Evaluation of monetary errors found or projected

Are previous planning decisions still appropriate?

No

Yes

Revise decisions and plan and perform additional procedures required

6. Additional Services (where requested)

Drafting of financial statements

Drafting or review of tax returns or other government returns

7. Formation of Opinion

Audit follow-up letter

Figure 11.d

The suggested stages in the performance of a financial statement audit are:

1. preliminary procedures,
2. pre-year-end substantive verification,
3. completion and evaluation of the interim audit,
4. year-end substantive verification,
5. evaluation of substantive verification results,
6. additional services (where requested),
7. formation of opinion.

A brief description of each of these given seven stages follows. Their inter-relationships are illustrated in the profile of the financial statement audit in Figure 11.d.

Preliminary procedures

The objective of this stage is to make detailed planning procedures based, in part, on an assessment of interim audit results and to carry out certain preliminary reviews before the work on each specific asset, liability, or income component is begun. The basic steps include:

1. planning decisions re audit emphasis and effect of the interim audit, pre-year-end verification, role of internal audit, use of statistical sampling and computer-assisted audit techniques, specialist involvement, schedule of critical dates, and client assistance,
2. the completion of an "outline financial statement audit file" to document detailed planning decisions for use on the job,
3. staffing, scheduling, work assignment, and the completion of time budgets,
4. the carry-forward of key schedules from the interim audit file and from prior years,
5. a preliminary review of operating results, minutes, accounting policies, and data for the permanent file,
6. a preliminary assessment of internal audit work.

Pre-year-end substantive verification

The objective of this stage is to perform certain substantive procedures on balances at a date prior to the year-end whenever the auditor is satisfied (a) that the advantages of more timely reporting and of work levelling are sufficient to warrant the increased cost and the lesser conclusiveness of the audit evidence obtained and (b) that the audit evidence obtainable will still be sufficiently persuasive to justify the expression of an audit opinion. The basic steps include:

1. the performance of major audit procedures such as the counting of marketable securities, the confirmation of accounts receivable, the observation of physical stocktaking, and preliminary audit work on inventory valuation,

2. the performance or planning of "roll-forward procedures" to "roll" the foregoing pre-year-end balances forward to the year-end, analyzing important transactions during the intervening period,
3. the performance of other pre-year-end procedures such as the preparation of comparative lead sheets, the advance preparation of key year-end confirmation letters (banks, long-term debt, share capital, etc.), the vouching of fixed asset additions up to date, the analysis of tax liability accounts to date, the gathering of statistics for use in the year-end analytical review, and the vouching of various revenue and expense accounts to date.

Completion and evaluation of the interim audit

This stage includes the components discussed in 11.2:

1. the evaluation of additional control strengths and weaknesses,
2. the extension of interim audit procedures to the year-end,
3. the performance of any weakness investigation left for the year-end,
4. based on the foregoing, a re-evaluation of internal control and compliance.

Year-end substantive verification

The major component of the financial statement audit consists of the performance of substantive procedures for each financial statement figure. Usually, it is convenient to divide the financial statement audit file into separate sections for each type of asset and liability, such as cash, accounts receivable, marketable securities, inventories, fixed assets, accounts payable, etc. While the procedures for each audit section will differ, common basic steps include:

1. a review of the objectives and other verification procedures elsewhere in the audit having a bearing on this audit section,
2. a review of the effect of internal control findings on this particular asset, liability or income component,
3. detailed substantive procedures with respect to account balances at a point of time (e.g., confirmation of bank balances, reconciliation of creditors' statements),
4. detailed substantive procedures with respect to transactions over a period (e.g., vouching of fixed asset additions, vouching of expenses),
5. the checking of cut-off at the year-end (and at pre-year-end verification dates, where appropriate),
6. the performance of analytical review procedures,

7. related scrutiny and enquiry,
8. the obtaining of written representations from the client,
9. the documentation of audit work performed using detailed audit programs or preprinted "verification outlines".

Evaluation of substantive verification results

Much of the evaluation of substantive evidence is made as each individual substantive procedure is completed. At the conclusion of a given audit section any errors located in that section will be accumulated, projections from tests summarized, accounting principles reviewed, and a conclusion drawn for that section and recorded in the working papers. This conclusion should be based not only on monetary errors found but also on any further evidence encountered, during the course of the substantive procedures, as to systems and controls. Where this further evidence requires the revision of earlier planning decisions, additional substantive procedures may have to be planned and performed. It is not enough, however, that each asset or liability, taken by itself, be free of material error. The auditor must be satisfied, if a clear opinion is to be given, that, for the audit as a whole, income-distorting errors have not accumulated to a material total. Thus, after the conclusion of each individual audit section (cash, accounts receivable, inventory, etc.) errors encountered and error projections made throughout the audit should be accumulated and evaluated.

Additional services (where requested)

If the auditor has been asked to draft the financial statements as an accounting service, such drafting may be partly done as each individual financial statement figure is audited and may be completed at the conclusion of the field work. If the auditor has been asked to draft the client's tax returns, a number of supporting schedules (e.g. capital cost allowance schedules) will usually be prepared during the audit of related financial statement figures. The tax returns themselves may be drafted at the same time or later, after the audited financial statements have been issued.

Formation of opinion

In the final stage the audit report is drafted, its form depending on statutory and professional requirements and the need for any reservation, consistency exceptions, explanations, or other modification of the standard wording. After final review with the client, the report is issued. At the same time, any recommendations on control, efficiency, accounting, or financial and tax planning which were not previously included in the earlier internal control/management letter (following the interim audit) can be discussed with the client and included in an *audit follow-up letter*.

11.7 Questions and problems

Review and discussion

1. What are the primary and secondary objectives of the financial statement audit? How are they related to overall objectives and to general professional objectives?
2. Give examples of internal control strengths and weaknesses which typically will be reviewed during the financial statement audit and explain why.
3. What are the objectives of substantive verification? How are substantive procedures related to compliance procedures?
4. Monetary errors consist of different types of error, with some differing effects on the financial statements. List the different types of error which are included in the concept of errors and describe how each will affect an auditor's opinion.
5. Define the term "possible errors". How does the desired degree of audit assurance affect an auditor's verification procedures?
6. Discuss the concept of "most likely errors".
7. How does a client's willingness to correct and provide for known errors and most likely errors affect the precision demanded of substantive procedures planned?
8. How do internal control conclusions affect substantive procedures?
9. What are the three possible outcomes of an auditor's substantive work and the type of opinion likely to result from each?
10. Discuss the seven stages in the performance of a financial statement audit. Assess the impact of the concept of efficiency on each stage.
11. Indicate the various specific factors that an auditor should consider when assessing inherent risk for:

    a) accounts receivable,
    b) contracts in progress,
    c) advertising expense.

    Be sure not to confuse inherent risk with control risk.

12. Describe the impact on financial statement audit procedures of a secondary audit objective — preparation of client tax returns.

13. Give the reasons why errors and irregularities should be reported to the Audit Committee or to the Board of Directors where there is no Audit Committee.

14. Why is completeness one of the more difficult audit objectives? Compare the auditor's attitude to the completeness objective for assets, liabilities, revenue and expenses.

15. Why does the audit program for pre-year-end asset verification require more senior level judgment than that for year-end verification?

Problems

1. Bob B., of Smith & Co. CA's, has completed the interim audit for Chantilly Products Limited four months prior to the company's December year-end.

   Bob attended the client's physical inventory on November 30 and circularized accounts receivable as of November 30.

   Bob and his audit assistants arrive at Chantilly's office the following January 15 to commence the financial statement audit.

   Describe the most desirable sequence of verification procedures, in your opinion. Explain the reasons for your choice.

2. Gord Clark, CA, was summarizing the total errors not adjusted by his client, Acme Investments Inc. Due to the nature and size of the client's business,

Clark was able to verify substantively many of the financial statement components 100% at the year-end. The total number of errors affecting pre-tax income were few and totalled only $10 000. The materiality limit with respect to pre-tax income was $20 000. The largest errors were in accounts receivable. There were 200 accounts receivable. Clark verified a random sample of 50 of these. The net errors in the accounts receivable sample were $5 000.

Clark was quite pleased that the total net errors in the entire audit affecting net income were only $10 000. He put the final touches on his file and gave it to his manager for review.

What should his manager conclude from the review?

3. (CICA adapted) An important part of the audit of a company is the review of the company's internal control system, during which the auditor identifies weaknesses that could affect his audit. Equally important, however, is the next step, in which the auditor evaluates the significance of each weakness (in terms of the materiality of errors that could result from the weakness) and thereby determines whether the weakness requires him to extend the scope of his normal audit procedures or employ additional procedures.

Assume that you are the auditor of X Ltd., which has annual sales of $5 000 000. One of the members of your audit staff has provided the following list of internal control descriptions and has noted what he believes to be the related weaknesses.

Staff member's internal control descriptions	Staff member's notes as to believed weaknesses
Because the company has no purchasing department, many employees make purchases. In general, employees make purchases applicable to their area of the company's operations, but it is not uncommon for employees also to make purchases of personal items through the company. A 3-part purchase order form is supposed to be used whenever merchandise is ordered: one copy to be sent to the supplier, one to be sent to the shipping/receiving clerk, and one to be kept by the individual doing the ordering. When the merchandise arrives, the shipping/receiving clerk checks the merchandise and sends the packing slips and purchase order copies to the accounts payable clerk. If he has no purchase order for the merchandise, the shipping/receiving clerk ascertains by telephone who ordered the merchandise and attaches a copy of a mimeographed form with this information on it to the packing slips.	a) No control over company's commitment to purchase goods. b) No control over employees' personal purchasing. c) Mimeographed forms are not pre-numbered.

Staff member's internal control descriptions	Staff member's notes as to believed weaknesses

Inventories are stored at various locations in the plant, usually fairly handy to where they will be used. Because the company's sales and production activities have increased so much since last year, it has occasionally used public warehouses for its overflow inventory. A material requisition form is supposed to be completed whenever material is withdrawn from the raw materials inventory and put into production, but the night shift people often seem to neglect to follow this rule. The company does not have much money invested in shop supplies so there is no necessity to use requisition forms when supplies are consumed. Also, the company often has left-over supplies (purchased for special jobs but not consumed on those jobs) that can be used to some extent on other jobs. The shipping/receiving clerk keeps perpetual inventory records (quantities) for most inventory items, but 30% of the items are not included in the records. He does physical inventory counts to check his records whenever he has time.

d) Little physical control over raw materials inventories.

e) No control over inventory of left-over supplies.

f) Shipping/receiving clerk keeps perpetual records and has access to inventories.

g) Incomplete perpetual records.

h) Casual checking of perpetual records.

When the supplier's invoice arrives, the accounts payable clerk checks the additions and extensions on it, initials it and staples the packing slip and purchase order or mimeographed form to it. He enters the invoice in his accounts payable subsidiary account for the supplier, then he sends the invoice to the manager of the department for which the employee ordering the goods works; the manager writes on the invoice the account number to which it is to be charged and then sends it to the cash disbursements department.

i) No control over managers' coding of invoices.

j) Apparent lack of price checking.

k) Managers do not specifically approve invoices for payment.

The accounts payable clerk balances his accounts payable subsidiary ledger to the general ledger control account every month and keeps track of credits due to the company for purchases returned to suppliers. Occasionally the company pays some larger suppliers round amounts of money rather than paying according to specific invoices as is its usual policy. When he has time, the accounts payable clerk attempts to reconcile suppliers' monthly statements to his subsidiary ledger accounts.

l) Accounts payable clerk balances ledger and reconciles suppliers' statements.

m) Irregular reconciliation of suppliers' statements.

For each point considered by the audit staff member to be a weakness:

i) Explain very briefly the significance of the apparent weakness, in terms of the materiality of errors that could result from it.

ii) Describe the effect, if any, of the weakness on your normal audit procedures required to form an opinion on the financial statements, in terms of any additional or extended procedures required because of it.

Set up your answer sheet in 3 columns:

Apparent weakness	Significance of weakness	Effect of weakness on audit program

4. "An auditor's responsibilities extend beyond the expression of an audit opinion." Comment on this statement, bearing in mind the auditor's legal liability as discussed (Chapter 5).

5. "The audit discipline has come a long way from verifying transactions 100%. This progress has necessitated auditors to employ their professional judgment to a high degree in both the planning and evaluation of evidence".

Discuss this statement with respect to substantive verification, economy and efficiency.

6. (CICA adapted) Y Ltd., operates a machine shop. It does custom machining, welding, fabricating and other metalwork for a large number of customers (80% of business) and also manufactures a line of metal utensils for camping and similar outdoor activities. The forecasted December 31, 1976, balance sheet is:

Assets

Cash	$	40 000
Accounts receivable		230 000
Inventories:		
Raw materials		180 000
Work in process		410 000
Finished goods		240 000
Land		100 000
Building and equipment		2 600 000
Accumulated depreciation		(1 400 000)
		$ 2 400 000

Liabilities

Bank loan	$ 300 000
Accounts payable	130 000
Equipment purchase contracts	60 000
Mortgage payable	740 000
Due to shareholder	110 000
Share capital	200 000
Retained earnings	860 000
	$2 400 000

The company had been growing slowly until early 1976, when the president, treasurer and production manager retired, turning the management over to a group of younger men, all of whom became *minority* shareholders. The new group embarked upon an ambitious expansion program. In July 1976, CA was appointed auditor and accepted the appointment after he had contacted the previous auditor and determined that the previous auditor knew of no professional reasons why CA should not accept the appointment.

On his short first visit to the company's offices, CA determined that:

1) The accounting and office staff of three clerks and a typist are supervised by the controller (one of the group of new shareholders).
2) The preparation of income tax returns, statistical reports to governments and other such documents had been done by the previous auditor and the controller expected that CA would also prepare them.
3) Perpetual inventory records are maintained for raw materials, finished utensils manufactured for stock and (on a job order basis) custom work in process. Memorandum records are maintained on the shop floor for utensils in process; these records are not tied into the general ledger.
4) Custom work reaches its peak activity in the summer and is at a low point of activity in the autumn and winter. Therefore, most of the annual production of utensils is done during the winter. Finished utensils are sold in the spring and early summer.
5) Expected sales for the year and pre-tax profits are $5 000 000 and $600 000 respectively.

Required:

a) What factors control the timing of CA's audit work on Y Ltd.?

b) How might CA take advantage of each of the following techniques in doing his audit of Y Ltd.?

- Flow charting
- Audit testing

c) Assume (i), that the company wishes to have its audited financial statements as at December 31, 1976 ready by January 20, 1977; (ii) that CA has evaluated the company's internal control and found it to be good for accounts receivable and those inventories having perpetual records but weak elsewhere; (iii) that CA has done no audit work other than to evaluate the internal control; and (iv) that it is now mid-September, 1976. Outline in general terms the work CA could do prior to December 31, 1976 to enable him to complete his work by January 20, 1977.

d) Assume that on January 15, 1977 CA was appointed auditor for the year ended December 31, 1976 and that no deadline for the completion of his work existed. What factors related to his late appointment would influence CA in determining whether he could plan to express an unqualified opinion on the financial statements as at December 31, 1976?

7. Northwest Territories Mines Limited, a large mining and primary processing company, invested $12 million over a two-year period (1975 and 1976) in the development of an ore body containing metals A and B, on the shores of the Arctic Ocean. The investment breaks down as follows:

Roads, harbour and air facilities	$ 4 000 000
Wages and other expenses in connection with delineating the size of the ore body and proving reserves	2 000 000
Primary processing facilities including both plant and equipment	4 000 000
Acquisition costs	1 500 000
Miscellaneous expenditures including both overhead costs and feasibility studies	500 000
	$12 000 000

The company acted as its own general contractor in the building of plant facilities, roads, harbour and the small airport. Ninety percent of these costs were payments to some 75 subcontractors. 75% of the plant equipment was purchased from a third party. The remaining 25% is used equipment acquired from a 60% owned subsidiary company.

Due to the depressed state of the metal market, in June 1976, the entire operation was temporarily mothballed. An independent feasibility study performed at that time indicated that the prices of metals A and B would have to increase by 10% before the project could break even and by 25% before the project would pay an adequate return on investment. The company's year-end is December 1976.

In February 1977, half way through the financial statement audit, the metal markets appear strong (a 15% increase over June 1976) with, according to management, a definite long-term upward trend. The upward trend is explained in part due to political problems in certain producer countries and in part due to the possible creation of international cartels by certain third-world metal producing countries.

Management propose to show the entire $12 million as assets with no amortization. They do not, however, at the present time intend to commence production. While positive cash flows could be derived from operations at this point, according to management, the board of directors has indicated in the minutes of a recent meeting that they intend to wait until the metal markets improve by a further 30% before beginning any production.

Develop a program for the verification of these assets as at December 31, 1976. Organize your answer under each of the five asset objectives as described in Chapter 11 (even though this will result in the repetition of some procedures). Beside each proposed procedure in the audit program, comment on the quality of evidence being sought. It is not necessary in this answer to indicate the extent of procedures, merely indicate the nature of the procedures to be performed.

Audit Testing

The technique of *testing* or *sampling* (the two terms are used interchangeably in this book) is well established in many disciplines. Geologists take diamond-drill samples to evaluate ore bodies. A 100% analysis of the entire ore body is clearly only possible after the mine is exhausted and the question no longer relevant. Doctors conduct blood tests from a sample. No patient has ever been known to insist on the marginally greater assurance available from a 100% examination. Engineers design testing procedures for maintaining quality control in a production process.

Auditors use the technique of testing to audit populations of accounting data, such as a population of receivable accounts or of payroll cheques. Although at one time 100% examination of all accounting data was the customary procedure, for more than

half a century the technique of testing has been a fundamental part of auditing practice. Indeed, from a practical point of view, there is today no economic alternative to the use of testing. The auditor, it is true, could in theory check documentary and other evidence for every recorded transaction and financial statement figure for the year. But such a procedure would, in all but the very smallest engagement, be prohibitively expensive. It would mean duplicating every step performed by the entire accounting staff over twelve months (as well as seeking other confirmatory evidence as to year-end net assets) – and the cost would come close to duplicating the total accounting expense for the year. The technique of testing, then, is essential and indeed, as explained in the following sections, is fully in accord with auditing theory and generally accepted auditing standards.

12.1   The technique of testing

12.1.1   Definition of testing

Testing is involved wherever a decision is made to apply a given auditing procedure to some (but not all) items within a group or population of accounting data or of other audit evidence. Examples are vouching a selection of fixed asset additions or confirming a selection of receivable accounts. Testing is not involved in procedures such as enquiry, review of summaries, or scrutiny of records. Nor is it involved where the appropriate decision is to examine 100% of the items within an accounting group (such as confirming the one and only bank loan or vouching the three sole security transactions executed during the year). In general, however, a substantial portion of any audit program consists of auditing procedures which can and should be applied on a test basis. It is to the testing aspect of such procedures that this chapter is directed. Although audit testing is a common occurrence, some testing concepts require careful thought. The reader will find that this and the next chapter must be taken slowly and carefully if the important points are to be understood.

12.1.2   General testing objective and sampling risk

The general objective of testing may be stated as follows:

To select certain individual items from a population on some rational basis and, by examining and evaluating the selected items and projecting the test results in some logical manner, to provide an appropriate assurance of

reaching the same general conclusion as would have been obtained by examining the evaluating all the items within the population.

It should be noted that testing makes no claim to reach a better conclusion than would be obtained through 100% examination of all items in the population. Thus, if in a 100% vouching of fixed asset additions the auditor might fail to recognize improperly capitalized expenses (through carelessness or lack of familiarity with the business), a test vouching of fixed asset additions will be subject to this same risk as well. The sources of such audit risks (here called *non-sampling risks*) were discussed in Chapter 6. They included the risk of using faulty assumptions and the risk of making inaccurate observations. Such non-sampling risks can never be eliminated; but they can be minimized by the proper application of competence, objectivity, due care, and judgment. It may often happen, of course, that the exhaustive extent and the repetitive nature of a 100% examination may induce a degree of carelessness which can be avoided through the use of testing. Clearly, a carefully performed test may provide a more reliable conclusion than a carelessly performed 100% examination. Thus, a reduction of non-sampling risk, while not the prime purpose of testing, is often one of its important by-products. Any testing procedure, however, is subject to a further risk: the *sampling risk*. Sampling risk is the risk that the conclusion derived from a test differs from the conclusion that would have been obtained through 100% examination assuming equal diligence in completion of the two types of procedures. By using an appropriate basis and extent of selection, and an appropriate basis of projecting the test results and expressing the testing conclusion, sampling risk can be reduced to an acceptably low level.

12.1.3 Specific audit testing objectives

Testing may be employed for auditing procedures directed at review objectives, compliance objectives, substantive objectives, or some combination of these.

Review tests

A review objective (ascertaining the nature of systems and controls) is seldom the only objective of a test, but it may often be a collateral objective. Generally, however, in test extents it is less onerous than the others. For that reason, review objectives, while important, need not be considered further in this chapter.

Compliance tests

The objective of *compliance tests* is the same as that of compliance verification in general (see 9.4.1):
Objective:

> To provide an appropriate assurance of detecting, should it exist, such frequency of critical compliance deviations as would indicate a reasonable possibility of material monetary error.

Suggested interpretation of reasonable possibility:

> When the projected possible total value of those transactions which are each subject to a critical compliance deviation equals several times (such as three times) financial statement materiality, a reasonable possibility of material monetary error is indicated.

An example would be a compliance test of payroll controls to see that payroll calculations had been prepared in compliance with prescribed control procedures throughout the year.

Substantive tests

Likewise, the objective of *substantive tests* is the same as that of substantive verification in general (see 11.3.1 and 11.3.2).
Objective:

> To provide an appropriate assurance of detecting the possibility of a material total of monetary error misstating reported income (or other figure in the financial statements being examined) should such a material total actually exist.

Suggested modification in rare cases:

> In those few cases, however, where known and/or most likely errors approach materiality, it is necessary, in order to retain a reasonable allowance for undetected errors, to allow the limit of possible errors to exceed known and most likely errors by a limited margin (such as 50% of normal materiality).

An example would be the test confirmation of customers' accounts to see that recorded accounts receivable actually existed.

Dual purpose tests

When verification tests are performed to fulfill both compliance and substantive objectives simultaneously, the resulting *dual purpose tests* must use a basis and extent of selection sufficient to meet both these objectives. Where the same basis of selection is appropriate for both objectives, the extent of selection should be sufficient to meet the more onerous of the two – usually the substantive objective. Of course, the extent required for the substantive objective may itself be influenced by anticipated reliance on the compliance results.

12.1.4 Materiality, error types and types of testing

The above definitions of compliance and substantive test objectives both make reference to "materiality" and to various error types. The concept, in compliance testing, of comparing the possible total of *compliance deviations* to a reasonable multiple of financial statement materiality (such as three times) was discussed in Chapter 9. The concept, in substantive testing, of analyzing *monetary errors* according to their degree of certainty into *known errors*, *most likely errors*, and *possible errors* and comparing these levels to normal materiality (with the proviso of retaining a minimum allowance, such as half of normal materiality, for the excess of possible over most likely errors) was discussed in Chapter 11. The application of these concepts of testing, and the applicability of each of three types of tests, will be examined in this chapter.

The general objective of testing above calls for a "rational basis of selection". Three such bases can be identified and each has its place in auditing:

1. *High-value item selection* – (rationale: look at the big items because the small ones aren't important);
2. *Key item selection* – (rationale: look at the risky items because that's where the errors will be if there are any);
3. *Representative selection* – (rationale: look at representative items because the others are probably just like them).

None of these three rationales is universally applicable. Accordingly, in most tests, some combination of two or all of the three types of testing will be appropriate. Where representative selection is appropriate a choice must also be made between judgmental and statistical techniques; in some such tests *judgmental representative sampling* will be appropriate and, in others, *statistical representative sampling*. The choice is discussed later in this chapter.

12.1.5 Relationship to auditing theory and generally accepted auditing standards

The relationships of auditing standards, concepts, techniques and procedures were examined as a part of auditing theory in Chapter 6. A summary of the relationships pertinent to the concept of testing may be seen in Figure 12.a.

Consistency with the third field work standard

The third field work standard calls for sufficient appropriate evidence to provide a reasonable basis for the audit opinion. Whether the evidence is appropriate (relevant and reliable) is a decision which the auditor must make in choosing the audit procedure to be performed; it does not affect the separate decision as to whether the chosen audit procedure should be applied 100% or on a test basis. Whether the evidence is sufficient, however, is a question directly related to the technique of testing.

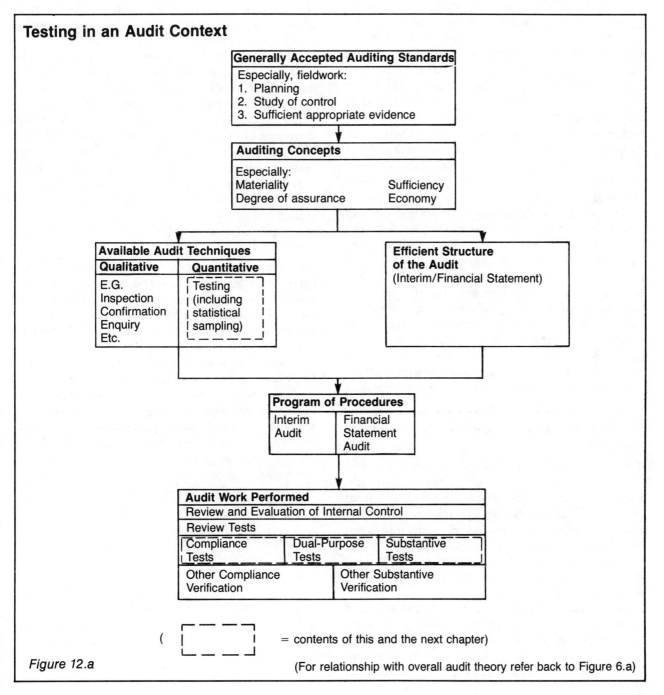

Testing in an Audit Context

Generally Accepted Auditing Standards

Especially, fieldwork:
1. Planning
2. Study of control
3. Sufficient appropriate evidence

Auditing Concepts

Especially:
Materiality   Sufficiency
Degree of assurance   Economy

Available Audit Techniques

Qualitative	Quantitative
E.G. Inspection Confirmation Enquiry Etc.	Testing (including statistical sampling)

Efficient Structure of the Audit
(Interim/Financial Statement)

Program of Procedures

Interim Audit	Financial Statement Audit

Audit Work Performed

Review and Evaluation of Internal Control

Review Tests

Compliance Tests	Dual-Purpose Tests	Substantive Tests
Other Compliance Verification		Other Substantive Verification

(⌐ ¬ = contents of this and the next chapter)

Figure 12.a   (For relationship with overall audit theory refer back to Figure 6.a)

Sufficiency of evidence depends on the inter-related auditing concepts of degree of assurance, materiality and economy. It was observed in Chapter 6 that additional increments of audit evidence should not be sought when the related incremental assurance thereby afforded (with respect to the possibility of material statement distortions) would be out of proportion to the cost of obtaining it. The auditor should use the most economical way of obtaining, from the available evidence, a selection sufficient to support the expression of a professional opinion.

When a 100% examination is replaced by testing, assuming equal diligence in performance in either case, the overall degree of audit assurance is reduced slightly by the introduction of sampling risk. In compensation, a very substantial saving in audit cost is achieved. By the proper application of testing techniques the additional element of sampling risk can be made very small. Elimination of this small sampling risk (non-sampling risks would still remain) would be out of proportion to the substantial cost of increasing the audit extent to a 100% basis. The auditing concept of economy indeed demands that society not be charged these additional costs when a reasonable basis for an opinion has already been afforded by testing.

Therefore, provided that it is properly applied so as to limit sampling risk to an acceptably low level, the technique of testing is fully in accord with auditing theory and with the third field work standard. With respect to high-value item selection, key item selection, and judgmental representative selection, the assessment of the sampling risk must be made judgmentally (as indeed must the assessment of *non*-sampling risks on all occasions). With respect to statistical representative selection, the assessment of sampling risk can be made mathematically. Both methods of assessment are suitable in their respective places.

Consistency with the second field work standard

The second field work standard calls for a "study of those internal controls on which the auditor subsequently relies in determining the nature, extent and timing" of substantive procedures. From this standard has been derived the relationship between compliance verification and substantive verification. The objectives of compliance and substantive testing given above are in turn consistent with these concepts.

As complaince testing is a part of the study of control comprehended in the second field work standard, it follows that the degree of assurance to be obtained from compliance tests should be commensurate with the reliance to be placed on them in planning substantive procedures. Furthermore, the standard implies that the determination of the extent of substantive tests should be influenced by the results of the auditor's study of internal control. Provided that these inter-relationships are observed, the technique of testing is fully in accord with the second field work standard.

Consistency with the first field work standard

The first field work standard calls for proper planning of the audit work to be performed. Proper planning implies a rational determination of what constitutes sufficient evidence to provide an appropriate degree of assurance of detecting material statement distortions, if present. While such determinations are implicit in the planning of all audit work, a number of the planning decisions must be made more explicitly when testing is used. To the extent that the technique of testing forces a more explicit consideration of decisions as to materiality, degree of assurance, etc., it lends further objectivity to the planning process called for by the first field work standard. While this increased objectivity is greatest in applications where statistical sampling is appropriate, it is present to some degree in all audit testing.

Conclusion

In summary, testing is consistent with auditing theory and generally accepted auditing standards. Indeed, except where the number of items in a population of accounting data (or of other audit evidence) is very small, it would be improper not to employ testing in performing the audit work.

A statement made in Chapter 1 is repeated here. *What constitutes an appropriate choice of auditing procedures and extents in any given engagement must be decided by the exercise of professional judgment.* This and the next chapter provide certain suggestions as to the determination of audit test extents. These should be viewed solely as guides to, and not substitutes for, professional judgment.

12.2 Choice of type of substantive testing

Because substantive tests are more directly related to the formation of an opinion that the financial statements are not materially distorted, they will be discussed before compliance tests. The following analysis of high-value, key-item and representative selection, while not always stated explicitly, is believed by the writer to be consistent with most current auditing practice. Of course, before deciding on any of the following types of test the auditor should first determine whether the audit procedure in question is necessary at all and, if it is, whether it is one that lends itself to application on a test basis.

12.2.1 High-value item selection

Where high-value item selection is necessary

High-value item selection means a selection of all items in the population over a certain dollar amount (e.g., all receivable accounts over $5 000, all expense charges over $10 000. At the very least this should include all items (in any population) over the 'materiality limit' for the audit as a whole. In most tests, however, some lower dollar threshold should be used and all items over this threshold selected for audit.

Where high-value item selection is sufficient (together, with key items, if any)

In most tests, high-value item selection should be supplemented by representative selection since knowledge of the accuracy of the high-value items does not necessarily permit a conclusion as to the accuracy of a material total of low-value items. However, high-value items selection (together, if appropriate, with key-item selection) should suffice by itself where one of the following conditions prevails:

a) The number of high-value items selected approximates the number of selections that would have been made had representative selection been used and the auditor is willing to make the subjective judgment that the proportionate accuracy of the low-value items is not significantly different from the proportionate accuracy found in the high-value selections. For example, in a small audit, 40 expense items over $2 000 might cover 70% of the total repairs and maintenance expense; the other 30% is still a material total but there might be every reason to believe they are similar in relative accuracy to the 70% already examined. However, where the 70% is covered by only 2 items, the 2 items would represent too small a sample to permit drawing any reliable conclusion about the remaining 30% and some representative sample should be drawn from this remainder.

b) After covering the high-value items, the total value of the remaining low-value items is trivial (e.g., receivables total $80 000 but the 3 largest accounts represent $75 000 of this, the remaining total of $5 000 being far less than the materiality limit).

c) The test involves income components only, internal control is adequate and there are satisfactory overlapping audit procedures (e.g., comparison, analysis, review, etc.). The reason is that considerable additional assurance as to reported net income is provided by the substantive procedures applied to beginning-of-year and year-end net assets.

Where high-value item selection is inapplicable

High-value item selection is inapplicable only in those cases where the population items are all of a relatively uniform immaterial size (e.g., residential cable television receivables).

12.2.2 Key item selection

Where key item selection is necessary

Key item selection means the selection of all items falling within certain specific categories judged to be particularly risk-prone (e.g., suspicious or unusual items, items already known to contain errors, items with a history of error in past years, overdue accounts, apparent anomalies). Wherever it is practical to identify and locate reasonably limited numbers of risk-prone items, key item selection is desirable unless the risk-prone items are trivial in aggregate. The location of key items may often be a by-product of scrutiny (whether visual scrutiny or computer-assisted editing).

Where key item selection is sufficient (together with high-value items)

In many tests, key item selection should be supplemented by a representative selection of the regular (less risky) items. For example, in a particular audit the auditor may wish to confirm, as key items, all seriously overdue accounts because of his concern as to the indication of possible items in dispute; but he will certainly want to confirm an adequate representative sample of the regular, current accounts as well. However, key item selection should suffice (together with high-value item selection) where one of the following conditions prevails:

a) Errors, if they exist in the population at all, are almost certain to be evidenced by the discovery of errors among the key risk-prone items. In such cases, if these more risky items are found to be satisfactory, the auditor may conclude that the less risky items in the population are probably satisfactory as well. For example, transactions within a few days of the year-end are most likely to contain cut-off errors if such errors have occurred at all. If the auditor finds these transactions have been treated properly, he may often conclude that the less risk-prone transactions further from the year-end have probably been treated satisfactory as well. Of course, any such conclusion is subject to some risk and should be made with care (not relied on, for example, where there is reason to believe that significant in-transit shipments may be outstanding for several weeks).

b) After covering the high-value and key items, the remainder of the population is trivial.

Where key item selection is inapplicable

Where a very large number of population items fall into a higher risk class, key item selection of all of them may be uneconomic. Instead, it may be preferable to draw a representative sample from this higher risk segment of the population, the proportionate extent of the representative sample being greater for this higher risk segment than for the remaining segment of the population. For example, new mortgages receivable written during the year may warrant proportionately more intensive sampling than older mortgages receivable carried forward from prior years.

Key item selection is also inapplicable in those tests where it is not practical to identify or locate risk-prone types of item.

12.2.3 Representative selection

Where representative selection is necessary

Representative selection, whether made *statistically* or *judgmentally*, means a selection of a sample which the auditor believes will be typical of the population from which it is drawn – a miniature replica of the population containing, hopefully, the same proportions of errors of various types as the population as a whole. The likely 'typicalness' of the sample is achieved by (a) giving every potential sampling unit an appropriate chance of selection, avoiding any systematic bias, and (b) making the sample size large enough that any chance departure from typicalness is unlikely to be of significant extent. If the items in this typical replica are found to be satisfactory the auditor would normally conclude that the entire population is satisfactory.

Representative selection is appropriate in cases where errors, if they exist in the population, could reasonably occur in any item thereof, that is, in cases where high-value item selection and key item selection are not sufficient (see above). Where high-value items and key item selection has initially been judged sufficient but serious errors have been discovered in these items, the possible need for representative selection should be reconsidered.

Where representative selection is sufficient

Where representative selection is employed it should be supplemented by high-value item selection (provided large items exist) and by key item selection (provided limited numbers of risk-prone items can be identified and located).

Where representative selection is inapplicable

It is nearly always possible to apply the technique of representative sampling. Its application is unnecessary, however, in those cases (discussed above) where high-value item selection and/or key item selection suffice.

12.3 Choice of type of compliance testing

Of the three identified bases of selection, only key-item selection and representative selection are appropriate for meeting compliance objectives, as high-value item selection is primarily directed at the substantiation of a particular financial statement figure.

Key item selection will generally be applicable wherever it is practical to identify and locate reasonably limited numbers of items that the auditor judges to be particularly risk-prone to compliance deviations. Where vast numbers of risk-prone items are evident, considerable reliance on control would usually not be warranted and compliance tests would accordingly not be involved.

Key item selection is rarely sufficient in isolation. If considerable reliance is to be placed on a particular control then normally the auditor will require assurance that the control has operated effectively throughout the year for the regular items as well as the specifically risk-prone items.

Representative selection, whether made statistically or judgmentally, is generally appropriate in all cases where compliance tests are being performed. It should be supplemented by key item selection (provided limited numbers of risk-prone items can be identified and located).

12.4 Criteria for method of representative selection

Where it is decided that representative selection is appropriate, a further choice must be made between judgmental and statistical techniques. Audit use of statistical sampling in the accounting profession is widespread and growing, but by no means universal. There are some practitioners who prefer the use of judgemental sampling in all circumstances. In fairness to those practitioners it should be pointed out that statistical sampling, while fully consistent with generally accepted auditing standards, is not required by such standards. In the writer's view, however, there are circumstances which favour the use of statistical techniques and others which favour the use of judgmental techniques; it would be logical to use the technique favoured by the circumstances surrounding a particular representative test. It is this viewpoint which is developed below.

Statistical and judgmental techniques both meet the requirements, but with varying objectivity

Two requirements of representative selection have been mentioned:

1. giving every potential sampling unit an appropriate chance of selection, avoiding any systematic bias,
2. making the sample size large enough that any chance departure from "typicalness" is unlikely to be of significant extent.

Both of these requirements can be met by either judgmental or statistical techniques – but with varying degrees of objectivity. Which level of objectivity is appropriate in the circumstances will depend upon the factors of relative risk, cost and timeliness.

The first of the above requirements (unbiased chance of selection) can be met either (a) by employing statistical methods to draw a random sample or alternatively (b) by employing judgment to draw a sample (usually by haphazard[1] selection) which the auditor believes will *approximate* an unbiased (statistically random) sample. The second requirement (sufficient size) can be met either (a) by employing statis-

tics to compute the mathematical odds of departures from typicalness and thus to compute the sample size required to yield acceptably low odds or alternatively (b) by employing judgment to choose a sample size which the auditor believes will *approximate* an appropriate (statistical) sample extent.

In its method of meeting the above two requirements, statistical sampling provides greater objectivity than does judgmental sampling. This does not mean that judgmental sampling has no objectivity at all. If used in conjunction with the rule-of-thumb guidelines as to sample size suggested later in this chapter, it does contain some element of objectivity. But the level of objectivity provided by statistical techniques is greater. Specifically, what is more objective in statistical sampling is:

- the method of relating the planned sample size to the desired conclusion,
- the method of drawing the sample,
- the method of relating the achieved conclusion to the actual sample results.

At the same time, this greater objectivity does not mean that statistical sampling is mechanical and devoid of judgment. Indeed, statistical techniques require that the judgment calls be made much more consciously and explicitly and this is a further advantage to their use.

The greater objectivity is sometimes but not always worthwhile

If the benefits of the greater objectivity could be shown to be always trivial, then statistical sampling would have no place in auditing and judgmental sampling would always be used. As explained in the following chapter, however, judgmental sampling can lead to risks of either overauditing or underauditing. These risks vary in amount depending on the nature of the population being tested and on other factors. But if these risks can be reduced by the use of statistical sampling, one must consider at what cost this reduction is achieved. The greated objectivity of statistical sampling has a cost in terms of set-up time (planning, reviewing important judgment calls re confidence levels, initial staff training, etc.) and sometimes in terms of sample selection time (applying random selection techniques). This cost will vary from audit to audit and will generally be higher in first-year applications than in repeat years. In many audits, with experienced staff, the cost is very small (if indeed there is any extra cost) and well worth the increased protection afforded by greater objectivity. Even in those cases where the cost is somewhat larger, it will often be that the risks that can be reduced by using the more objective technique are important enough to justify its use. But certainly there will always be some audit tests where the cost of formally applying statistical sampling techniques would be out of proportion to the benefits of greater objectivity available. In these latter cases, judgmental sampling is the appropriate method to use.

The choice of sampling technique will vary

The foregoing concepts indicate that the choice between statistical and judgmental sampling may well vary from test to test. To assist in making this choice the following criteria are suggested. They are applicable to both substantive and compliance testing, though some differences in test design for compliance vs. substantive purposes are discussed later in this chapter. Where these criteria are used, a given audit engagement may well include statistical sampling for certain tests and judgmental sampling for others. Sometimes practitioners have expressed concern that any use of statistical sampling would be taken as an admission that it should have been used on all tests and if not to be used universally they would be safer never to touch it. This concern is unnecessary. Far from exhibiting inconsistency, a rational variation of audit technique with varying conditions is, it is submitted, fully consistent with the auditing concepts of degree of assurance and economy.

12.4.1 Criteria for statistical representative sampling

It is suggested that statistical sampling should be employed for representative testing where the auditor concludes that the benefits of the greater objectivity in determining extent, selection and evaluation are significant in relation to the additional cost, if any. Factors favouring such a conclusion are:

1. The "set-up time" and selection time are reasonable in relation to the time required to verify the selected items and follow up discrepancies, etc.

(more likely to be true for large tests than for very small ones).

2. The most extensive part of the test (high-value plus key item plus representative) is the representative sample.

3. The verification steps for each sample item are reasonably definable in advance (e.g., confirmation, inspection, checking to supporting documents, calculation).

4. Records of the entire population are reasonably accessible for purposes of making the selection (although, even where they are not, statistical sampling may be desirable if there would otherwise be a serious risk of omitting inconvenient records).

5. The drawing of the statistical sample is facilitated by computerized records (although computerized records are certainly not essential to the use of the statistical sampling techniques suggested in the next chapter).

12.4.2 Criteria for judgmental representative sampling

It is suggested that judgmental sampling should be employed for representative testing where the auditor concludes that the cost of statistical sampling would be out of proportion to the benefits of the greater objectivity in determining extent, selection and evaluation obtainable therefrom. Factors favouring such a conclusion are:

1. The set-up time and selection time of a statistical sample would be out of proportion to the time required to verify the selected items and follow up discrepancies, etc. (more likely to be true for very small tests).

2. The planned selection of key items or high-value items is so extensive that it is more efficient to select the small representative sample judgmentally.

3. The verification step for each sample item is difficult to define or predict in advance and depends more upon a judgmental evaluation in each case.

4. The drawing of a statistical sample would be complicated by records which are not reasonably accessible (although there may be a risk in omitting inconvenient records and this risk must be guarded against).

5. The drawing of a statistical sample would be complicated by the record format (e.g. the records are unusually cumbersome to count or add through in making the statistical selections).

12.4.3 Comparison of judgmental and statistical sampling

The justification for drawing a judgmental representative sample of, say, 100 receivable accounts is that the auditor believes that any material frequency of error which would have been discovered by him had he confirmed *all* receivable accounts will, with an appropriate degree of assurance, be discoverable by error indications found in the sample of 100 confirmations. If this belief is not held, then clearly the judgmental sample of 100 confirmations is not large enough.

For example, if the auditor believes a population error frequency of a 1 in a 1 000 would represent a material error, then clearly his sample size of 100 confirmations would not be sufficient. Common sense indicates that the great majority of the time a sample of 100 drawn from such a population would contain no error at all. The absence of error in such a sample would accordingly provide no real evidence that a material error was not present. (If an observer reports that he has has seen no wolves among the sheep, his report provides no evidence if we know he was too far away to see a wolf in any case.)

On the other hand, where an error frequency of 1 in 20 would represent a material error frequency in accounts receivable, a sample size of 100 confirmations could be expected to produce several errors. Common sense indicates that not finding any errors at all would provide some sort of evidence that a material error is not present in the population.

The audit risk of finding less than a specified number of errors in a sample, when there is really a material frequency of error hiding in the population, is exactly what statistical sampling measures (by computing the mathematical odds involved). Given the same criteria as to materiality and required degree of audit assurance, an appropriate judgmental estimate and a rigorous statistical calculation must arrive at the same approximate sample size. There is no rationale by which one could demonstrate that a sample size of 50 was adequate for a judgmental sample but that 100 was required for a statistical sample using the same criteria. Should such a discrepancy appear, it must be that the judgmental estimate was in error and that really a sample size of 100 was required for both methods.

Judgmental representative sampling and statistical representative sampling are based on the same logical foundations. *Statistical sampling theory is merely a method of stating explicitly certain considerations which are and have always been implicit in any judgmental representative testing by auditors.* The only difference between the two methods is the degree of rigorousness in drawing the sample randomly and in computing the sampling risk to determine that it is acceptably low. It is perfectly reasonable to forego this greater degree of rigorousness in circumstances where the cost outweighs the benefit. But one foregoes this rigorousness hoping to achieve, with less cost and formality, the same approximate sample size and evaluation that statistical sampling would have yielded. It is not right to hope for a smaller sample size when judgmental sampling is used. To do so would be hoping for a poor use of judgment.

Because judgmental representative sampling and statistical representative sampling are based on the same logical foundations, many aspects of sample planning, selection, and evaluation are common to both. These common aspects are discussed in the present chapter. The additional requirements for statistical sampling are discussed in Chapter 13. Similarly, because judgmental representative sampling can be thought of as an approximation to the more rigorous method of statistical sampling, some of the following suggestions for judgmental procedures are intended to parallel the more rigorous techniques described in Chapter 13.

12.5 Judgmental representative sampling (substantive)

Any representative testing involves four chronological steps:
(a) making planning decisions, (b) selecting sample items, (c) verifying sample items and (d) projecting sample results.

The key planning decisions, apart from the choice between judgmental and statistical techniques, which has already been discussed are:

1. error definition,
2. population definition,
3. choice of degree of assurance,
4. determination of sample extent.

These four planning decisions are discusssed below, followed by a discussion of selection methods and exaluation. Verification procedures (the 'what to do' rather than 'how many') need not be reviewed here as they are discussed throughout the rest of the book.

12.5.1 Error definition

In any form of representative testing, errors found in the sample are not so much important in themselves as important because of their *projecting effect* in drawing conclusions about the population. If 200 receivable accounts are selected out of 20 000, each selected sample item represents, in a sense, 99 possibly similar items in the population. Thus, if one of the selected accounts proves to be the result of a duplicate billing which the customer properly rejects, the significance is not the one duplicate billing (which by itself may be immaterial) but the fact that the odds are that there are 99 or so similar duplicate billings within the whole population (which in aggregate may be material).

Because of this important projecting effect of each sample error, it is important for the auditor to define in advance exactly what he means, and what he does not mean, by 'error'. This is really only asking that the auditor clearly decide the objective of his test before he begins it. On the basis of the objective of substantive tests and assuming materiality is expressed as a proportion of normalized pre-tax income, a reasonable definition of a sample error is:

> The amount of overstatement or understatement of pre-tax income arising from any condition (whether accidental or intentional) observed in a particular sample item except for exclusions specified in advance (where such exclusions are to covered by other audit procedures).

Such a definition will automatically exclude errors (such as receivable postings made to the wrong account) which, while perhaps evidence of careless bookkeeping, do not result in a distortion of reported income.

Exclusions specified in advance

Exclusions may be specified in advance when they represent types of error that will be more fully evaluated in some other procedure elsewhere in the audit. For example, if the auditor is test confirming accounts receivable at October 31, he may know that there are going to be a certain number of cut-off errors. It may be logical to exclude any discovered cut-off errors from his definition of sample errors if he is planning to perform separate audit procedures to verify the accuracy of cut-off at December 31. Obviously, counting both October and December cut-off errors together would be double-counting. Of course, the excluded cut-off errors at October 31 can still be separately projected as supplementary information; if the projections appear out of line they might lead the auditor to intensify his year-end cut-off tests.

The auditor should avoid changing his definition of sample error *after* the sample results have been observed. The dangers of post-verification changes in error definition can be illustrated by the following example:

> The auditor concludes that a 3% population error frequency would be material and determines that a sample size of 100 receivable confirmations would be appropriate. Unknown to the auditor, a material population error frequency really does exist, and indeed, 3 sample errors are found (being accounts for customers Brown, Green and White). The auditor, naively, concludes that there is something wrong with the B's, G's and W's and accordingly verifies these sections of the receivables ledger 100% (finding in the process 20 more errors). He then notes that apart from 23 errors (immaterial in total) found in the B's, G's and W's (which he has covered 100%) the sample revealed no other errors. Excluding errors to B, G and W accounts from his definition of sample error, he triumphantly, though mistakenly, concludes that a material total of error does not exist in accounts receivable. The fallacy, of course, is changing the error definition *after* (and as a result of) his observation of the sample results.

Errors already corrected

Generally, it is reasonable to exclude automatically from the definition of sample error any error already detected and corrected within the regular accounting system before the audit test commenced.

> For example, in test confirming, during late November, receivable accounts dated October 31, the auditor encounters a pricing error that was corrected on November 10 as a result of routine account reviews by the credit department. Such a condition need not normally be projected as a sample error. The auditor is interested in assessing the accuracy of the final product of the accounting system (including all important control elements therein).

It is important, of course, if such exclusion is made, to be sure that the detection and correction of the errors were independent of the audit and not a result of or in anticipation of the auditor's tests. If correction was independent, then other errors like them in the population were probably similarly caught and corrected by the system. An individual error corrected *after* audit detection, on the other hand, merely adjusts for the individual sample error itself and leaves uncorrected the other errors like it which probably exist in the population.

Where exclusions are made because of automatic correction by the accounting system, the auditor should give some consideration to the likely time-lag of correction. In the above example, the auditor will want to make sure that in the December 31 financial statements due provision has been made for December receivable errors found during the routine credit department reviews in January.

Errors which do not misstate the financial statements

The suggested definition of a sample error excludes conditions which do not misstate the financial statements (since the auditor's opinion relates to the accuracy and presentation of the financial statements). It is not always simple to determine, however, whether certain conditions misstate the financial statements or not.

For example, assuming that physical stocktaking was done at the year-end, do unbilled shipments of $10 000 worth of goods during the year misstate the financial statements?

Situation A:

The answer is yes if management chooses to locate and bill the unbilled shipments and if collection of these billings is likely. Until corrected, the unbilled shipments represent an understatement of income and receivables.

Situation B:

The answer is no if management cannot or chooses not to locate and bill the unbilled shipments or if collection of late billings would be unlikely in any case. The $10 000 loss is being accepted as a cost of doing business and this cost has already been reflected in the financial statements.

Suppose, now, that in making a representative test of shipping documents to sales invoices as part of his regular work, the auditor encounters three sample items representing unbilled shipments totalling $100 and that his projection of most likely unbilled shipments for the population of the whole year's shipping documents is $10 000. Is this situation A or situation B? In such a case, the auditor should report his audit findings (results and projections) to management.

Situation A:

Should management decide to locate and bill all unbilled shipments for the year, then the $10 000 does represent errors (estimated) and the three sample items should be projected as errors. Of course, if, as sometimes, the location and correction of the actual individual errors throughout the whole population is then completed by management prior to issue of the financial statements, adjustment can be made for the actual total error found and the need for projection disappears.

Situation B:

Should management decide that it is not worth the cost (or perhaps the poor customer relations) to locate and bill all such unbilled shipments for the year, then the $10 000 does not represent errors and the three sample items should not be projected as errors (whether or not these three individual sample items alone are now billed). If the management decision to abandon possible recovery appears to be a straightforward business decision it is not the province of the auditor to second guess it. Of course, should the circumstances arouse his suspicions as to the honesty of the officials involved, he should pursue his concerns with more senior management or even the audit committee or board.

Conditions similar to that illustrated in the above example include the following:

1. Distributions by the enterprise which are receivables (Situation A) if management can and chooses to identify and recover them but are expenses (Situation B) if they do not:
   - goods shipped or pilfered (or services supplied) but not invoiced (whether through inadvertence or collusion),
   - payments expensed (or funds misappropriated) for services not received (whether through inadvertence, such as a duplicate payment, or collusion);

2. Receipts by the enterprise which are liabilities (Situation A) if third parties can identify and seek restitution and/or if management can and chooses to identify and offer restitution but are revenues (Situation B) if they do not (assuming no material violation of accepted business practice):
   - goods or services received but not billed by supplier (whether through inadvertence or collusion),
   - goods or services invoiced but not provided (whether through inadvertence, such as a duplicate billing, or collusion).

Since the determination of error in the foregoing situations depends on management's decision, it is desirable, where the amounts are significant, for the auditor to have management's decision documented in his working papers or the annual written representations obtained from management. Moreover, since management's decision can only be properly made in the light of known or apparent conditions, the determination of which situations represent misstatements of the financial statements (and therefore monetary errors according to the previous definition) can usually only be made *after* the sample results have been obtained. It would usually be inadvisable, for example, for the auditor to omit tests otherwise required (in accordance with his assessment of materiality, relative risk, etc.) merely on the grounds that he thinks the errors to be found would possibly be accepted by management as either a cost of doing business or a windfall gain. For all he knows, if his sample were to indicate a significant frequency of such errors, management might well decide that recovery or restitution was essential – in which case, the projected sample errors will have represented true monetary errors distorting the financial statements. In addition to these *attest* considerations, a reasonable degree of testing to discover errors, even when they do not affect the financial statements, may be a useful service to management if their discovery can permit systems improvements to prevent their recurrence.

12.5.2 Population definition

The general objective of testing is to reach the same general conclusions as would have been obtained by examining all items within the population from which the sample was drawn. It follows that testing, as such, cannot directly yield a conclusion for items outside the defined components or time period of the population. For example, a sample of fixed asset purchase invoices drawn from the first six months of the year cannot yield a testing conclusion as to the fixed asset additions for the year as a whole. A pricing test applied to a sample drawn from finished goods alone cannot yield a testing conclusion as to the pricing of raw material and finished goods as a whole.

This restriction does not mean that certain *non-testing* conclusions cannot be properly drawn, in certain cases, for components outside the population subjected to testing. For example, the auditor may select a sample of receivable confirmations as at October 31. The testing conclusion, as such, can only relate to the population of October 31 receivables. Nonetheless, this evidence, together with 'roll-forward procedures' for November and December and reliance on internal control, may justify the judgmental formation of an audit opinion on the December 31 financial statements. Similarly, the auditor may select a representative sample of fixed asset additions for the first eleven months of.the year. The testing conclusion, as such, can only relate to the first eleven months' additions. Nonetheless, this evidence, together with high-value selection, key-item selection, and scrutiny for the month of December, may justify the judgmental formation of an audit opinion on the December 31 financial statements.

Less audit risk is involved when the testing conclusion itself relates directly to the financial statement figure being substantiated. Thus, whenever possible, substantive tests of transaction streams (such as fixed asset additions) should be selected from a population consisting of the whole twelve months' transactions. This selection is usually possible with careful planning. Sample selections from the early months can be examined earlier in the year and those from the final months at the conclusion of the audit. In the rare cases where the population for a substantive test of transactions does not consist of the whole twelve months, the auditor must satisfy himself that other audit procedures adequately limit the risk in judgmentally extending his opinion to cover the year.

Definition in advance

Because of the foregoing considerations, it is important that the audit clearly define in advance the components and time period of the population from which his representative sample is to be drawn and then ensure that all items in the population have an appropriate chance of selection.

The auditor should avoid changing his definition of the population *after* the sample results have been observed. The dangers of post-verification changes in population definition can be illustrated by the same example used in 12.5.1 (assuming the auditor, in that example, were at the end to exclude the B, G and W accounts from the population). The player cannot change the rules of the game after he finds he does not like the score. In rare circumstances an exception to this prohibition may be justifiable:

> Suppose, in the same example, all three sample errors occurred in Division B of the company and on investigation it turns out that controls have completely broken down in that division. If Division B is subsequently investigated with more intensive audit procedures, and if there is reasonable evidence that the same control breakdown has not occurred in other divisions, it may be justifiable to exclude Division B and the three related sample errors from the initial sampling conclusion.

In such exceptional cases the auditor must exercise great care to avoid the danger of merely "explaining away" sample errors he does not like.

12.5.3 Degree of assurance

The concept of degree of assurance was discussed in Chapter 6. It was argued that overall audit assurance required might vary slightly from engagement to engagement (first, excess assurance might be prudent on sensitive engagements and, second, the level of assurance warranted should be influenced within limits by the cost of audit evidence available[2]). It was further argued that the audit assurance demanded of any individual audit procedure should vary significantly in inverse relation to the assurance available from internal control, from the inherent nature of the item being audited, and from overlapping auditing procedures (see Figure 6.d). When determining the degree of audit test assurance sought in a particular substantive test, the auditor should logically consider those factors as follows:

1. the inherent risk of error in the population being tested – (consider: nature of the asset, liability or income component; susceptibility to innocent or fraudulent error; frequency, value and nature of past errors observed; current industry and economic conditions);
2. the control risk – (consider: the quality and effectiveness of key controls on which this substantive test places considerable reliance – including both

the design of the control system and the results of related compliance verification; the quality of internal control on which minimum reliance is placed; the existence and effectiveness of an internal audit program; recent systems changes which may have enhanced or diminished internal control);

3. the amount of assurance available from overlapping audit evidence – (consider: nature and quality of evidence available in overlapping audit procedures; overlapping procedures already performed during interim audit or those planned for financial statement audit; direct overlaps such as related tests, year-end reconciliation, scrutiny and analytical review; indirect overlaps such as evaluation of computer environmental controls, etc.);

4. the overall level of audit assurance required – (consider: nature of engagement; cost of audit evidence available).

Through a consideration of the foregoing factors the auditor should be able to decide whether the degree of audit test assurance appropriate for this substantive test should be:

1. *minimum* – (the minimum assurance – still a moderately high level – which one would demand of any test given the need for performing a particular procedure at all – usually it would indicate considerable reliance being placed on good or very good key controls together with low inherent risk of error and moderate or extensive overlapping audit procedures);

2. *normal* – (the average degree of assurance one would likely demand of a given procedure – usually it would indicate some reliance being placed on good or adequate internal control together with average inherent risk of error, though poor control might be tolerable in situations of low inherent risk and/or extensive overlapping audit procedures);

3. *considerable* – (a relatively high level of assurance – usually it would indicate poor internal control, high inherent risk of error, and/or few if any overlapping audit procedures).

The choice of the degree of audit test assurance will in turn affect the extent of the sampling work required, as described in the following section.

12.5.4 Determination of sample extent

A moment's reflection will indicate that if an auditor wishes to have a reasonable assurance of detecting a material error within a population of accounting records, he must on average select at least one, and probably two or three or four, record(s) within each material subdivision of that population.

For example, suppose that the auditor is doing a substantive test drawn from a large population of small fixed asset purchase invoices. Suppose further that he has decided that the materiality limit for this engagement is $4 000. We may imagine that the population is divided into hypothetical bundles of invoices totalling $4 000 each. To be reasonably sure of detecting a $4 000 error (such as a total of $4 000 of invoices that really should have been expensed) the auditor must on average select at least one invoice from each bundle. Otherwise wholly erroneous bundles (each containing a material error) could be completely missed. Even selecting one invoice per bundle would only be a sufficient test for a material error that occurred solely in the form of a wholly erroneous bundle. It could well miss a $4 000 error that was spread in pieces over several bundles. To be reasonably sure of catching the latter situation, it would be necessary to select more than one invoice per bundle. How many more is the question. Intuitively one would conclude that a large number of selections per bundle should not be necessary.

It follows, from the reasoning in the above example, that *the auditor should on average select more than one accounting record (but not a large number) within each material subdivision of the population he is testing.* Obviously the more selection points he makes the surer he will be of detecting a material error if it exists. Thus, the average number of selection points per material subdivision should logically vary with the degree of audit assurance required from this particular substantive test.

Beyond the general intuitive reasoning given above, more precise definition of required sample extents can only be arrived at by appealing to statistical arguments. Such arguments indicate that the average number of selection points per material subdivision should be between 2 and 6 depending upon the degree of audit assurance required. These considerations can be applied to develop a rough rule of thumb to guide the auditor's judgment in determining the *approximate* extent of substantive judgmental representative tests. The desirability of such a guideline is that it enables judgmental decisions as to sample extent in relation to sampling objective to be made with some degree of consistency.

The following guideline is suggested:

(i) Classify the degree of audit assurance required from each particular substantive test as considerable, normal or minimum on the basis of the criteria outlined in 12.5.3.

(ii) Choose an appropriate 'judgmental factor' (representing the number of selections on average required within each material subdivision) as follows:

Degree of audit assurance		Factor[3]	
		Where a few uncorrected errors are anticipated	Where client will provide for or correct all projected errors
considerable	=	6	4
normal	=	4	3
minimum	=	3	2

(iii) Estimate population dollar value after deducting any high value items or key items already selected.

(iv) Compute rough rule-of-thumb sample size as equal to[4]

$$\frac{\text{net population dollar value}}{\text{materiality (in dollars)}} \times \text{judgment factor}$$

(v) The sample size selected should be reasonably close to this rule-of-thumb guideline.

For example, if "normal" audit assurance is desired for a population of fixed asset purchase invoices which (after deducting high-value items and key items already selected) totals $60 000 and materiality is considered to be $4 000, then the rule-of-thumb sample size would be $(60\,000 \div 4\,000) \times 4 = 60$. Something in the neighbourhood of 60 should be chosen as the sample size in this case.[5]

12.5.5 Selection method

To draw a judgmental representative sample which avoids the risk of bias (and the risk of perhaps systematically omitting those very items where most of the errors may be concentrated) the selection method should usually be a reasonable approximation to random sampling methods. This generally means making some sort of haphazard selection of sample items throughout the entire extent of the population in question.

Risks of a block sample

Selecting a group or block of adjacent items (a *block sample*) would not represent such a haphazard selection and should therefore, in most cases, be avoided. Use of a block sample, such as confirming all accounts receivable from D to F, or vouching all fixed asset additions for the month of May, is based on the implicit assumption that any monetary errors (which the substantive test is designed to detect) will be spread fairly uniformily throughout the whole population. Were the assumption of uniform error spread valid, then it is true that one block sample of 100 items would be just as likely to catch an error as any other block sample of 100. But the assumption of uniformity is usually very risky. For example, it may well be that the posting clerk handling letters R to Z in

the accounts receivable ledger has made far more errors than all the other clerks together. In such a case, most block samples will be misleading (because most of them will miss section R to Z and its cluster of errors completely). In contrast, a haphazard sample spread throughout the entire ledger makes no assumption as to uniformity (and in this example, will most likely catch one of the errors clustered in R to Z if there is a materiality quantity of them).

In rare cases the assumption of uniformity may be justifiable. The doctor, in effect, takes a block sample of his patient's blood because there is ample evidence that the composition of arterial blood is reasonably uniform throughout the body. Where the auditor is satisfied that a material quantity of error (which is what he is testing for) would, if it existed, be spread uniformly throughout the whole population, a block sample may be justifiable. In a few cases it may be reasonable to assume uniformity throughout a given month though not throughout the entire year. In such cases it may be acceptable to draw the sample in twelve blocks, one from each month. Since haphazard selection of an equal number of sample items throughout the entire population is always safer than block selection, block samples (whether by year or by month) should only be used where the risk of non-uniformity in the distribution of population errors is very small and the saving in selection time substantial.

Two types of haphazard sample

In selecting a haphazard sample, two alternative selection methods can be distinguished: (1) a tendency to favour selection of bigger items (value-oriented selection) and (2) a selection of large and small items with indifference as to size (neutral selection). Each of these methods is discussed below.

Value-oriented selection

Over the years, many judgmental tests by auditors have tended to pick proportionally more of the large items than the small ones. It is commonplace to find that the average sample item value is, as a result of this tendency, considerably higher than the average population item value. This intuitive approach to favour the more important items is perfectly logical. Over a certain dollar threshold, of course, *all* high-value items should be selected. Even beneath this threshold, however, in drawing a representative sample it usually makes sense to favour the larger items to an appropriate extent. Since the objective of substantive verification is to determine whether or not a material dollar value of monetary error is contained in the financial statements under audit, it is logical that for most substantive representative testing a value-oriented selection method should be used.

Various methods of making a value-oriented selection could be considered. One method is suggested by the rationale which was used in developing the previous rule-of-thumb guideline for sample extents. Asking the auditor to select on average a few (2 to 6) population items within each material subdivision of the population implies not only a method of calculating sample extent but also a method of sample selection wherein equal groups of dollars receive in aggregate the same average chance of selection. In the $60 000 population of fixed asset purchase invoices in the previous example, it can be argued that every dollar is equally important and therefore each of the 60 000 individual dollars should have an equal chance of selection (or, in other words, a $1 000 invoice should have about ten times the chance of selection of a $100 invoice).

A suggested rule-of-thumb guideline for selecting substantive judgmental representative samples on a value-oriented basis is therefore as follows:

1. remove (or mark off) high-value and key items for separate selection,
2. roughly divide the remainder of the population into material subdivisions (each subdivision containing an approximately material amount),
3. within each such subdivision select 3, 4 or 6 sample items depending on whether minimum, normal or considerable audit assurance is required (see 12.5.4),
4. in selecting the sample items within each subdivision, make a haphazard selection of a few larger items and a few smaller items being guided approximately by their relative proportions by total value within the subdivision (for example, if larger items make up more than half of the value of the subdivision more than half the selections should be made from these larger items).

The above rule-of-thumb guideline is not intended to be a precise mechanical routine but merely an approximate guide to judgment. It is suggested, however, that the practice of dividing a population approximately into material divisions during the selection process is a fairly convenient method to use.[6] An example of such a selection from a trial balance of receivable balances is illustrated in Figure 12.b.

Neutral selection

In some cases it is difficult to conduct a substantive representative test using value-oriented selection. Such cases arise where the population from which the selections are being made does not indicaate monetary values. An example is a case where, having identified that there is a major weakness in control over billing all shipments, the auditor has decided to conduct a substantive test of shipping documents to estimate the dollar-extent of unbilled shipments for the year. Because the test must logically be drawn *from* shipping documents (and checked *to* sales invoices) and because the shipping documents themselves may be unpriced, the auditor may have to make a neutral selection: that is, a haphazard selection of shipping documents for the year regardless of their value. Generally, neutral selection is favoured where it is safe to assume that error values are independent of book values and likely each to be less than some specified dollar amount (see 13.2.1).

In making a neutral haphazard selection the auditor may pick one document at a time at haphazard invervals through a file of documents, or choose, say, two items per page throughout a list of such documents, etc. The risk in any judgmental selection is that some *bias* will be introduced into the selection method (such as never selecting the first or last items on any page, never selecting hard-to-reach documents at the back of a file, etc.). Sometimes it is convenient to minimize this risk by using an 'interval sample' (or 'systematic sample'): picking a haphazard start near the beginning and every 40th item thereafter (or every 70th document, or the balance at every 10th inch down a trial balance tape, etc.). Interval sampling of records or documents is still subject to a slight risk (the risk of some periodicity in the population); for judgmental testing, however, it would be an acceptable selection method (and an improvement over simple haphazard selection).[7]

12.5.6 Evaluation

Known errors, most likely errors, and possible errors are concepts explained in Chapter 11. The evaluation of high-value and key-item selections involves only known errors, since such testing methods have no projecting effect. The evaluation of representative testing conceptually involves all three error types. The projection of possible errors is not quantifiable for other than statistical sampling applications. However, the sample extents suggested previously should normally be adequate to ensure that such possible errors do not exceed materiality given that most likely error projections are not found to be substantial. Therefore, as a practical matter, the evaluation of judgmental representative tests involves the observation of the known errors and the projection of the most likely errors.

Observation of known errors

One aspect of the observation of known errors is simply the accumulation of their aggregate value so

Substantive Judgmental Representative
Testing — Example of Value-Oriented Selection
(Materiality is $4 000, normal assurance desired)

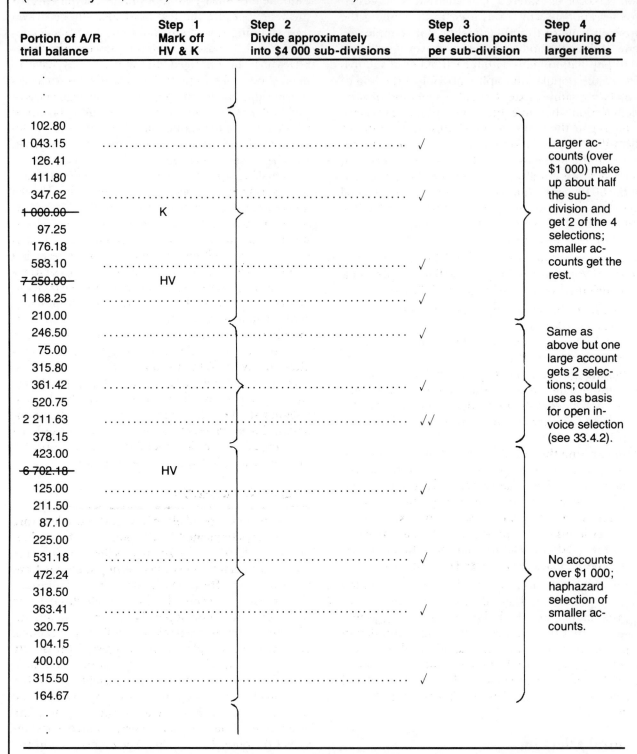

Portion of A/R trial balance	Step 1 Mark off HV & K	Step 2 Divide approximately into $4 000 sub-divisions	Step 3 4 selection points per sub-division	Step 4 Favouring of larger items
102.80				
1 043.15			√	Larger accounts (over $1 000) make up about half the subdivision and get 2 of the 4 selections; smaller accounts get the rest.
126.41				
411.80				
347.62			√	
~~1 000.00~~	K			
97.25				
176.18				
583.10			√	
~~7 250.00~~	HV			
1 168.25			√	
210.00				
246.50			√	Same as above but one large account gets 2 selections; could use as basis for open invoice selection (see 33.4.2).
75.00				
315.80				
361.42			√	
520.75				
2 211.63			√√	
378.15				
423.00				
~~6 702.18~~	HV			
125.00			√	
211.50				
87.10				
225.00				
531.18			√	No accounts over $1 000; haphazard selection of smaller accounts.
472.24				
318.50				
363.41			√	
320.75				
104.15				
400.00				
315.50			√	
164.67				

Note: This example has been constructed so as to illustrate many selection points on one schedule. In practice, the average account size is likely to be smaller relative to materiality and the selection points accordingly spaced farther apart.

Figure 12.b

that, in the event they are not corrected, the auditor may compare the total to materiality in the course of forming his audit opinion on the financial statements. In addition, however, it is important that the auditor consider the *nature* and *cause* of any errors discovered in his sample. While the test projection of most likely errors is itself blind to the cause of sample errors, the auditor may often be able to gain additional evidence judgmentally by an investigation of the particular errors encountered. One error may indicate a *breakdown in control* that may have implications for other procedures elsewhere in the audit. Another error may indicate a *systematic* mistake in pricing sales invoices or applying overhead to inventory, etc., the extent of which the auditor may now be able to assess more precisely by other procedures.

Projection of most likely errors (value-oriented selection)

The logical method of projecting most likely errors from a judgmental representative sample depends on the method (value-oriented or neutral) by which the sample was selected and on the assumptions underlying that method. If the selection method favoured the larger items (value-oriented selection) such that each population *dollar* had roughly an equal chance of selection, then we can think of a sample of 100 items as really being a selection of 100 individual dollars out of the population. In that case, the most likely average *percentage* error per population dollar will be the same as the average *percentage* error for all of the 100 selected sample dollars. In other words, *the most likely percentage of population dollar errors will be the average percentage error per sample item*. An example of such a projection is illustrated in Figure 12.c. In this example, the average percentage error per sample item is 1.7% and accordingly the most likely total error in a population of $200 000 is $3 400.[8]

Projection of most likely errors (neutral selection)

On the other hand, if the judgmental sample was drawn disregarding item size (neutral selection) such that each population *item* had a roughly equal chance of selection, then *the most likely average dollar error per population item will be the average dollar error per sample item*. An example of such a projection is illustrated in

---

Sample Projection when Large Items were Favoured in Selection

Out of a sample of 100 items drawn from a population of $200 000, 4 sample items were found containing errors as follows:

	Book value	Error	Error percentage	Direction
Step 1.	$ 400	$200	50%	overstatement
	$1 000	($100)	(10%)	(understatement)
	$ 500	$500	100%	overstatement
	$ 200	$ 60	30%	overstatement
Step 2.	Total percentage error		170%	overstatement
Step 3.	Average percentage error per sample item			
	$= \dfrac{170\%}{100} = 1.7\%$			
Step 4.	Most likely population error = 1.7% × $200 000 = $3 400 overstatement.			

Explanation of steps:

1. Compute the percentage value of the error (percentage of book value) for any sample item containing an error as defined.
2. Add up all the error percentages so obtained, appropriately netting overstatements and understatements.
3. Divide this total percentage by the total number of all sample items (with or without error) to get the average percentage error per sample item.
4. Multiply this average percentage error by the total population dollar value (excluding high-value and key items). The result is the most likely value of total error in the population (apart from errors found in high-value and key items).

Figure 12.c

Figure 12.d. In this example, the average dollar error per sample item is $3.50 and accordingly the most likely total error in a population of 1 000 items is $3 500.[9]

It should be noted that it would be improper to use the value-oriented method of projection for a sample drawn by neutral selection or the neutral method of projection for a sample drawn by value-oriented selection.[10]

The problem of duplicates

In evaluating test results, it should be recognized that if valid items happen to be included in the population more than once it may be extremely difficult to detect the duplications directly through normal test extents. The reason for this is that, supposing there to be a material value of such duplicates, the sample can normally be expected to include *one* of the paired items but not *both* members of the same pair. The sample size required to provide a reasonable chance of detecting at least one complete pair (original and related duplicate) is usually excessively large and uneconomic. Therefore, where the risk of possible duplicates is of concern, evaluation of sample items should include a scanning of the population for similar or identical items. For example, when examining a sample of inventory items, similar items in the population that could possibly be duplicates should be investigated at the same time.

12.6 Judgmental representative sampling (compliance)

The objective of a compliance test is not to search directly for monetary errors (the sample size would generally be insufficient to be sure of detecting these even if a material total were present) but rather to search for critical compliance deviations (likely to be present in greater quantities than actual monetary errors). The general rationale discussed in Chapter 9 was that if it could be economically established that the projected possible total value of transactions each subject to a critical compliance deviation did not exceed several times (such as three times) financial statement materiality, then it was likely that monetary errors did not exceed materiality and less extensive substantive tests for such possible monetary errors would accordingly be justified.[11]

Some practitioners may have different views as to what reasonable upper limit of possible compliance deviations should be breached before reliance on control should be rejected. Such different views would require slight modification of the following discussion (which is based on the triple materiality rationale).

12.6.1 Error definition

Although the objective of a compliance test is to search for critical compliance deviations and not directly for monetary errors, nonetheless both types of conditions may be encountered in the results of a compliance test. Accordingly, it is desirable to define both conditions so that their evaluation can be appropriately considered. The following definitions are suggested:

Critical compliance deviation:
A critical compliance deviation is a condition observed in a particular sample item which evidences a departure from a key control procedure on which the auditor had wished to place considerable reliance. Normally a key control is one in whose absence the occurrence of a non-trivial monetary error would, in the auditor's judgment, probably not have been caught elsewhere in the control system. For example, if a shipping document is not matched against a related sales invoice as prescribed, and if indeed it had represented an unbilled shipment, there might be no other control that would have detected the occurrence of such a monetary error. (If there had been another control which would have detected the monetary error then the first control might not have been considered "key".) A critical compliance deviation may or may not be accompanied by an actual monetary error in the same sample item (the unmatched shipping document may or may not have been an unbilled shipment on *this* occasion). Of course, an actual non-trivial monetary error (not subsequently found and corrected) would generally be evidence of a critical compliance deviation as well.

Monetary error:
The amount of overstatement or understatement of pre-tax income arising from any condition (whether accidental or intentional) observed in a particular sample item (same definition as for substantive tests but without any exclusions for errors covered by other audit procedures). Some monetary errors may be so trivial that they can be ignored (such as a few cents rounding difference in the extension of a $100 purchase invoice).

According to the foregoing definitions, the classifications of critical compliance deviations will overlap with the classification of monetary errors (the former including, but not being limited to, the latter). The evaluation of each of these conditions is discussed in 12.6.6.

12.6.2 Population definition

The clear definition of the components and time period of the population to be tested is important for the same reasons as discussed for substantive tests in 12.5.2. The time period should be that during which considerable reliance is to be placed on the related control. Often, where major pre-year-end verification is planned (e.g., pre-year-end confirmation of receivables or observation of inventories) the period of considerable reliance will be the roll-forward period only. In other cases, where the control affects only a balance sheet account, many of the later months of the year may be of particular control significance. In yet other cases, it may be important that compliance tests of transaction streams (such as sales, purchases, and payroll transactions) be selected from a population consisting of the whole twelve months' transactions. With careful planning, it is usually possible to extend compliance tests to cover the full twelve months in such cases.

12.6.3 Degree of assurance

In Chapter 9 it was pointed out that the degree of assurance required for compliance tests can be minimized because:

1. Minimum reliance can be placed on the auditor's review and evaluation procedures even in the absence of further compliance testing.
2. The result of reliance on internal control is not the elimination of substantive tests but only a reduction in their extent and/or a change in their nature or timing.

Therefore, it is reasonable that a relatively minimum level of assurance be demanded from compliance tests themselves.[12]

12.6.4 Determination of sample extent

In the rule-of-thumb guideline for substantive sample extents (12.5.4), it was suggested that, where the auditor requires only minimum assurance of detecting a *material* error, he should select *three* items within each material subdivision of the population. Where he requires only minimum assurance of detecting a *triple-material* frequency of compliance deviations, it follows that he need select only *one* item per material subdivision.[13]

The following guideline is therefore suggested for compliance testing:

1. Estimate population dollar value after deducting any key items already selected.
2. Compute rough rule-of-thumb sample size as equal to

$$\frac{\text{net population dollar value}}{\text{materiality (in dollars)}}$$

3. The sample size selected should be reasonably close to this rule-of-thumb guideline.

For example, if a population of purchase invoices totals $200 000 and materiality is considered to be $4 000, then the rule-of-thumb sample size would be 200 000 ÷ 4 000 = 50. Something in the neighbourhood of 50 should be chosen as the sample size in this case.

The above sample size guideline is computed on the basis that the auditor will accept only the compliance test as justifying the placing of considerable reliance on control (for purposes of planning substantive tests) provided that not more than one critical compliance deviation is found. By designing larger compliance samples it would be theoretically possible for the auditor to be able to accept two or more (up to some prescribed limit) critical compliance deviations and still retain reliance on control. Where compliance deviations are not infrequent, however, such larger compliance samples would not in general be as economical as the alternative of increasing planned substantive extents.

12.6.5 Selection method

For the same reasons as outlined for substantive tests, a block compliance sample is subject to significant risks of bias and should generally be avoided. Rather, judgmental compliance tests should be drawn by a haphazard selection spread throughout the whole period on which considerable reliance is being placed on the related control. A block sample of sales invoices for one week in June hardly provides evidence of the effective operation of the sales system controls throughout the year.

In a few compliance or dual-purpose tests, however, the risks of a block sample may be justified because of their value in reducing certain alternative risks. Consider the case of test posting the general ledger to check compliance with prescribed procedures for preparing and posting recurring monthly entries. One could draw a random selection of all such postings for the year. Such a sample, however, might well, by chance, cover certain types of recurring entries several times and other types not at all. In contrast, if one month is posted completely the auditor is ensured of encountering one example of each type of recurring entry. Thus, even though a month's posting represents a form of block test, in this particular case it probably represents an optimum trade-off of the various auditing risks involved. The risk that the one month's entries are atypical can usually be controlled through scrutiny of the remaining months, enquiry, and analytical review procedures.

As with substantive testing, there are two methods of selecting a haphazard sample for a compliance test – neutral selection and value oriented selection.

Neutral selection

Some practitioners believe that while value-oriented selection is desirable for substantive testing, *neutral selection* is the only relevant method for compliance testing. Their view is that compliance tests involve

procedures rather than values and that accordingly value-oriented selection is inappropriate. Advocates of this view (and a good case can be made for it) believe that neutral selection methods should be applied with the objective of detecting, if it exists, an unpriced frequency of compliance deviations (such as 2% or 5% or 10%) which exceeds what they judge to be acceptable levels.

Even where practitioners prefer a value-oriented selection (favouring larger items) there are certain cases where such a method is impossible because monetary values are not indicated in the population. An example is checking the approvals on employee clock cards in a factory payroll system. Such situations probably arise slightly more often than in the case of substantive tests. In such situations, neutral selection on a haphazard basis may be made in the same manner as described in 12.5.5.

Value-oriented selection

In the writer's view, however, a *value-oriented selection* is more appropriate for compliance tests in those many instances where the transaction streams being tested are quantified in monetary terms. This view is based on the argument presented in Chapter 9. When the value of transactions subject to critical compliance deviations equal several times materiality, the pre-audit risk of a material monetary error is increased to the point where considerable reliance on control is not justified.

The rationale for the sample extent guideline again implies a method of sample selection: selecting one item within each material subdivision of the population being tested. Suggested procedures are therefore as follows:

1. Remove (or mark off) key items for separate selection.
2. Roughly divide the remainder of the population into material subdivisions (each subdivision containing an approximately material amount); the use of page totals can facilitate this division.
3. Within each such subdivision select one sample item.
4. In selecting the one sample item within a given subdivision, select haphazardly a larger item or a smaller item on the basis of whether larger or smaller items in total comprise more than half the value of the subdivision.[14]

Again, the above guideline is not intended to be a precise mechanical rule but merely an approximate guide to judgment.

The above method is particularly convenient to apply in practice. No arbitrary decisions are required as to whether sales must be classified, say, into product A sales and product B sales with, say, a com-

324

pliance test of 60 items being performed separately on each or whether it is sufficient merely to do a compliance test of 60 items on sales taken as a whole. Following the above method, each component of sales (if there are several components) will automatically receive its proportionate extent of testing in relation to its materiality, since the auditor will merely go through the entire sales stream selecting one item within each 'material subdivision'. Indeed, the auditor need only divide the total year's transactions streams between those subject to key controls (which are worth confirming with compliance testing) and those not (on which reliance will not be placed in any case). Through the former transaction streams (which may be a mixture of sales, receipts, purchases, disbursements and payrolls – in some cases intermingled) the auditor selects one sample item in every materiality division (e.g., one item every $4 000).

12.6.6 Evaluation

Critical compliance deviations

The main objective of the compliance test, as suggested in this book, is to establish that the projected possible total value of transactions, each subject to a *critical compliance deviation*, does not exceed triple materiality. The compliance sample size suggested was based on achieving this objective provided *not more than one* critical compliance deviation is found in the sample. Therefore, if this sample size is used, reliance on the control system should be rejected (for purposes of planning substantive tests) if more than one critical compliance deviation is encountered. If just one critical compliance deviation is found the auditor can usually plan for reliance; however, the nature and cause of the compliance deviation encountered should be investigated first.

Monetary errors

While it is not the principal objective of the compliance test to hunt for monetary errors, nonetheless the auditor should not ignore those he happens to encounter. The most likely error rate of monetary errors should be projected (using methods similar to those for substantive tests). Where the most likely monetary error equals or exceeds materiality, even though not more than one critical compliance deviation has been found, the auditor should reject reliance on control. Furthermore, even where the auditor rejects reliance on control (usually because several critical compliance deviations have been found) he should not ignore the projection, if any, of most likely monetary errors from his compliance sample. These most likely monetary errors, unless duplicated in substantive test projections, should be accumulated as part of the auditor's total audit findings affecting his final opinion.

Non-critical compliance deviations

In addition, it is always possible that in examining the documents selected for his compliance test of a key control, the auditor will notice a departure from a non-key control. It is not generally necessary to evaluate such *non-critical* compliance deviations in any formal manner, although the auditor should judgmentally take into account all information that comes before him.

12.7 Planning and control

The proper use of the technique of testing requires many judgmental decisions to be made during the planning stage: definition of errors the auditor is searching for, definitions of the boundaries of the population he is testing, choice of selection method, decision as to degree of assurance required, and determination of sample extent. The exercise of further judgment is required during the evaluation stage: projection of monetary errors and compliance deviations, investigation of the causes of error conditions, and evaluation of the acceptability or otherwise of the final results. If audit assistants are used in the conduct of this work, it is desirable for review procedures to take place where these key judgmental decisions can be subjected to a second opinion. There are two points where such review should most desirably occur: one, upon completion of the planning for audit tests; the other, after evaluation of the test results. As a practical matter, however, it will often be necessary for the review of both aspects to take place at the conclusion of the field work.

Review of audit test planning is facilitated if the important planning decisions are appropriately documented in the working papers. Different practioners will have different preferences as to format. Whether preprinted forms are warranted will depend on the size of the engagement and the relative importance of the particular test. Some suggested working paper forms are provided for illustrative purposes in Figure 12.e (planning decisions for substantive representative tests) and Figure 12.f (planning decisions for compliance representative tests). These forms assume that the choice of high-value, key item and/or representative testing (itself an important planning decision) has already been made.

Example of Planning Form for Substantive Representative Tests

(To be used to determine the extent, population and method of selection where substantive representative testing is appropriate.)

Client _ABC Limited_ **Year-end** _December 31, 1976_

a)	Population(s) to be subjected to representative test (description, components and date or time period)	Sales: Shipments Nov.-Dec.	Fixed assets: Additions+disposals Jan.-Dec.	A/R: Balances Oct. 31
b)	Audit test objectives	Completeness (continuity)	Cost + existence (vouching)	Existence (confirmation)
c)	Errors affecting pre-tax income excluded from error definition since covered by other procedures	Related under-statement of sales and A/R unless adjusted	None	Bad debts Cut-off Coding
d)	High-value threshold (See 12.2.1.)	$ 25 000	$ 25 000	$ 11 600
e)	Estimated population dollar value		Additions 500 000 Disposals 100 000 = 600 000	
	Total	3 250 000	600 000	2 600 000
	Less high-value and key item	(350 000)	(465 000)	575 000
	Net	2 900 000	135 000	2 025 000
f)	Criteria 1, 2, 3, 4, 5 — see 12.4 — which favour: Statistical representative (SR) Judgmental representative (JR)	1, 2, 3 / 4, 5	1, 3, 4, 5 / 2	1, 2, 3, 4, 5
g)	Choice of SR or JR (for SR complete appropriate form — see Chapter 13, Figure 13.1)	JR	JR	SR

Remainder of Form for JR only

h)	Approximate materiality (see 15.4.2)	90 000	90 000	
i)	Audit assurance			
	A) Consider (See 12.5.3)			
	• overall level of audit assurance required	High	High	
	• inherent risk of error	Moderate	Moderate	
	• internal control risk	Poor	Adequate	
	• overlapping audit procedures	Minimal	Minimal	
	B) Choice of assurance level (considerable, normal, minimum)	Considerable	Normal	
	C) Related "judgmental factor":			

	Where a few uncorrected errors anticipated	Where client will provide for or correct all projected errors
considerable	6	4
normal	4	3
minimum	3	2

		6	4	
j)	Representative sample size $\frac{\text{Estimated net population \$ value}}{\text{Materiality \$}} \times$ judgment factor	$\frac{2\,900\,000 \times 6}{90\,000}$ = 193	$\frac{135\,000 \times 4}{90\,000}$ = 6	___ × ___ = ___
k)	Method of selection: Value oriented (VO), or neutral (N), and give reasons	N $ values not available	VO $ values available	
l)	Estimated total sample size (HV + K + R)	211	26	
m)	File reference (where test carried out)	Interim Audit VII	H	

Figure 12.e

326

Example of Planning Form for Compliance Representative Tests

(To be used to determine the extent, population and method of selection where compliance representative testing is appropriate.)

Client _ABC Limited_   **Year-end** _December 31, 1976_

	Sales	Inventory Purch.	Expense purch.
a) i) Transaction stream to be tested			
ii) Verification steps to be performed on items in each sample (organize in verification sequence)	a) Entry in sales jnl. b) Invoice c) Sales order d) Credit approval e) Quantities/prices f) Extensions/adds g) A/R entry h) Perpetual inventory entry	a) Purchase jnl. entry b) Invoice c) Purchase approval d) Qty./price e) Extensions/adds f) A/P entry g) Perpetual inventory entry	a) Purchase jnl. entry b) Invoice c) Purchase approval d) Qty./price e) Extensions/adds f) Distribution g) A/P entry
b) i) Population period to be tested (i.e., for which reliance to be placed on system)	Nov. – Dec.	Nov. – Dec.	Jan. – Dec.
ii) Estimated gross dollar value less key items	$ 3 200 000	$ 1 900 000	$ 4 200 000
c) Method of selection desirable Value-oriented (VO), or neutral (N) (and give reasons)	V.O. Dollar value for sales invoices readily available	V.O. Dollar values for purchases readily available	V.O. Dollar values for purchases readily available
d) Criteria 1, 2, 3, 4, 5 — see 12.4 — which favour:			
A) statistical representative (SR)	1, 2, 3, 4	1, 2, 3, 4, 5	1, 2, 3, 4, 5
B) judgmental representative (JR)	5		
e) Choice of SR or JR	SR	SR	SR
f) Materiality (see 15.4.2)	90 000	90 000	90 000
g) Sample size $\frac{\text{Estimated net population \$ value}}{\text{Materiality \$}}$	$\frac{3\ 200\ 000}{90\ 000} = 36$	$\frac{1\ 900\ 000}{90\ 000} = 21$	$\frac{4\ 200\ 000}{90\ 000} = 47$
h) i) Select sample, perform verification steps and record specific conclusion on Schedule of Futher Compliance Procedures	Ref: See VIII-2	Ref: See VIII-3	Ref: See VIII-5
ii) Number of critical compliance deviations found in sample	None (✓) 1 ( ) 2 or more ( )	None ( ) 1 (approval) (✓) 2 or more ( )	None ( ) 1 (✓) 2 or more ( )
i) Describe any monetary errors discovered and project MLE — record in III for transfer to III of the financial statement audit file (unless duplicated in substantive test projections)	None	None	One small pricing error. Client paid $10.90/unit; should have been $10.40 MLE = $\left(\frac{.50}{10.90} \times 90\ 000\right)$ = 4 128 Not material Reported to controller

Figure 12.f

12.8 Reference material

CICA Audit Technique Study, *Internal Control and Procedural Audit Tests* (1968)
AICPA Statement on Auditing Standards No. 1, Section 320A "Relationship of Statistical Sampling to Generally Accepted Auditing Standards" and Section 320B "Precision and Reliability for Statistical Sampling in Auditing".

12.9 Questions and problems

Review and discussion

1. Define "testing" in an auditing context.
2. Compare the risks involved in 100% examination to the risks related to testing of the same population.
3. Identify and briefly discuss the three audit testing objectives.
4. Name and describe three bases of selection in audit testing.
5. What determines the sufficiency of audit evidence?
6. Explain how substantive and compliance testing and generally accepted auditing standards are interrelated.
7. Under what conditions is high-value item selection alone sufficient?
8. How does one determine a high-value threshold?
9. The materiality of client X is $10 000. In a substantive test, the high-value items tested included all amounts over $5 000. Why may it be necessary to test the low-value items as well?
10. Why is it usually necessary to supplement key-item selection by a representative selection of the other items?
11. Why is high-value item selection usually not used in a test with a purely compliance objective?
12. Discuss the criteria for determining which method of representative selection, i.e., judgmental or statistical, is most appropriate.
13. What are the four steps in representative sampling?
14. Define "sample error". Why is it important to define what an error is at the planning stage rather than after the sample results have been observed?
15. Describe the types of error often encountered which do not misstate net income.
16. Explain why it is important to define the components and the time period of the population to be tested.
17. What factors should an auditor consider when determining the degree of audit assurance sought in a particular substantive test?
18. Define block sampling. What are the risks involved?
19. Compare value-oriented selection and netural selection.
20. Discuss briefly the logic of using value-oriented selection in a compliance objective test.
21. What is the rule-of-thumb guideline for determining the sample extent for a compliance test? Discuss the logic of this guideline.

Problems

1. (CICA adapted) Describe the advantages and limitations of statistical sampling as a technique for use by an auditor.
2. G. Ward, CA, approaches the audits of clients who have well defined systems of internal control in a systematic manner. He evaluates the internal controls of the system and performs compliance procedures on the key controls on which he intends to rely. He feels assured at this point that no significant errors are possible and accordingly, when no errors are found, he performs no further tests in these areas. At year-end, he relies upon the results of his compliance procedures and, in some cases, he performs no substantive procedures in areas where he has assessed the internal control to be exceptional – e.g., fixed assets and purchases/payables.

   Ward feels that this is warranted because he should be able to perform less auditing of a system which has a good internal control than of one which does not.

   Discuss the strengths and weaknesses of his approach.
3. (CICA adapted) During a staff training meeting, you were asked the following questions:

   a) Audit procedures appear to concentrate on detecting overstatement of assets and understatement of liabilities, in other words, overstatement of shareholders' equity. Why is an auditor not equally concerned with understatements of shareholders' equity?

   b) What is the usefulness and the limitation of the

phrase included in auditors' reports "in accordance with generally accepted accounting principles", when the reported operating results of a company can vary significantly with the adoption of alternative applications of accounting principles?

c) When testing transactions, what are the principal disadvantages of the block test, such as a test of one or two months' transactions? Under what conditions is a block sample appropriate rather than a pure random sample?

d) If errors of relatively small amounts are found in an audit test, why can't the auditor ignore such errors without further work on the basis that the errors are immaterial relative to the financial statements?

Give answers, with explanations, to each of the above questions.

4. CDAG is a radio station on the coast of British Columbia. The station derives its revenue from local and national advertisers. It has the largest listening audience of all stations in its area, and in fact, has been so successful that CDAG manages to sell over 95% of its available advertising time at its standard billing rate. The time not sold is generally in the 12.00 – 6.00 a.m. time slot.

The revenue and income history of CDAG is as follows:

	1977 Estimate	1976	1975
Sales	$390 000	$379 000	$381 000
Net income	60 000	50 000	43 000

Dave Laing, CA, of Fraser & Associates, Chartered Accountants, is the audit senior of CDAG for the 1977 fiscal year. The approved materiality limit for CDAG is $6 000 for 1977.

One of the areas tested by Laing in the sales system were the controls, to ensure that all services performed were invoiced. A summary of his compliance test procedures in this area follows.

Extent – 65 items. This was determined by dividing the total population by the material limit ($390 000 ÷ $6 000=65).

Selection of sample – Laing selected three different days in the year randomly and within each day selected three blocks of time, each within one of the three major programming segments. Within each of the resulting nine blocks he selected 7 or 8 advertising spots.

Due to the nature of CDAG's business, the test is very time consuming. It involves checking from the daily program log to the broadcast order and then to the sales invoices in order to ensure that the sale is invoiced at the proper billing rate and for the proper length of time.

Laing spent approximately 20 hours on this test. The total time spent on interim audit testing was 75 hours. He feels that if he had chosen his sample of advertising spots totally randomly, the time would have doubled.

Based on the adequacy of internal control (the conclusion resulting from no errors in the interim audit sample), substantive procedures on sales at the year-end were limited to a comparison of monthly revenue figures to budget and figures of prior years. Where monthly figures did not seem appropriate a review of detailed sales analyses by day and by each major programming segment of the day, combined with enquiry of management, appeared to provide a satisfactory solution.

a) Outline the weaknesses in Laing's interim audit approach to the verification of sales.

b) Suggest an alternative approach (Hint: The maximum number of advertising spots per hour is regulated and monitored by a government bureau).

5. Bill Davies, in his test of 120 inventory prices (10 high-value, 10 key items, 100 other), discovered 7 errors as follows:

Inventory item	Type of test	Book value	Audited value
1	Key item	$ 420	$4 200
520	Representative	$ 34	$ 17
541	Representative	$1 460	$1 314
1 376	Representative	$ 430	$ 211
1 480	Representative	$ 176	$ 514
715	Representative	$ 20	no value
320	High value	$6 800	$8 020

The total inventory book value is $450 000, high-value items $75 000, key items $5 000, other items verified $42 000.

Determine the most likely inventory error in dollars:

a) assuming the representative sample was value-oriented,

b) assuming the representative sample was a physical-unit sample.

Statistical Sampling

The technique of statistical sampling is well established in many disciplines. Economists use it for estimating interim census and GNP data, sociologists for surveying public opinion, engineers for quality control on a production line and airlines for estimating inter-airline settlements of joint fares. A growing number of businesses use statistical samples for various accounting purposes: estimating physical stocktaking adjustments, and allowances for obsolescence in inventories and doubtful accounts to facilitate the timely preparation of financial statements. Internal and government auditors use statistical testing in their programs of both financial auditing (such as test confirming mortgages receivable) and operational auditing (such as estimating the frequency of production order delays).

External auditors have used statistical sampling to varying extents over the past twenty years to meet either substantive or compliance objectives. Indeed, statistical sampling is merely a particular form of representative testing in which mathematics is employed to assist judgment in the planning, selection and evaluation of the sample. As such, it can be used wherever representative testing is appropriate, provided the benefits of the greater objectivity in determing extent, selection and evaluation are significant in relation to any additional cost.

Audit use of statistical sampling in the accounting profession is widespread and growing, but by no means universal. As stated in Chapter 12, there may be some practitioners who prefer the use of judgmental sampling in all circumstances and it was pointed out that statistical sampling, while fully consistent with generally accepted auditing standards, is not necessarily required by such standards. In 12.4, however, the writer's view was expressed that the choice between statistical sampling and judgmental sampling in varying conditions should be made on the basis of certain suggested criteria. This chapter is consistent with that viewpoint.

Requirements of a statistical sampling plan

As was stated in Chapter 12, any representative testing involves four chronological steps:

1. making key planning decisions,
2. selecting sample items,
3. verifying sample items,
4. projecting sample results.

As a form of representative testing, every statistical sampling application must have each of these four chronological steps. In addition, a suitable statistical sampling plan should provide the auditor with:

a) a rational basis of making the key planning decisions required by the plan and consistent with the

selection and evaluation methods to be used,
b) a valid but convenient method of selecting sample items consistent with the planning decisions already made and with the evaluation method to be used,
c) a method of projecting sample results and determining the level of audit assurance achieved which, within meaningful limits of accuracy and provided the planning and other judgmental assumptions are safe, is either rigorous or somewhat conservative (on the safe side).

Statistical sampling plans

To meet the above three requirements, various different statistical sampling plans have been proposed and are in use among auditing practitioners. This chapter discusses the various different plans briefly. Because a general auditing textbook cannot properly take the space to discuss each specialized technique at length, Sections 13.3 to 13.6 concentrate on one of these techniques - *dollar-unit sampling*. The dollar-unit technique is suggested as a well-tested and practical approach for use in both substantive and compliance verification. In the writer's view, for reasons described later, the dollar-unit technique best meets the above three requirements. It is recognized, however, that other approaches may also accomplish the auditor's objectives and that views on the desirability of each of the various techniques can differ.

Scope of this chapter

Space does not permit coverage of every detailed aspect of even one statistical sampling technique (such as dollar-unit sampling).[1] It is hoped, however, that both student and practitioner will find this chapter, while necessarily too short to serve as a complete manual of instructions, a useful introduction to this rapidly expanding field. Many of the concepts require careful thought and the reader will find that this chapter must be taken slowly and carefully if the important points are to be understood.

The chapter assumes familiarity with the general approach to representative testing given in Chapter 12. If this general approach is to be enhanced by the introduction of statistical techniques, it is first necessary to understand a few statistical terms and concepts. These are covered in Section 13.1. Based on this foundation it is possible to examine and compare seven different sampling plans. These are discussed in Section 13.2. A more in-depth analysis of dollar-unit sampling concepts is then given in Section 13.3. With this considerable but necessary preparation, it is possible to consider the application of dollar-unit sampling to substantive tests and compliance tests (see Sections 13.4 and 13.5); these sections build upon and parallel the framework of planning, selection and evaluation methods outlined for all representative tests in 12.5 and 12.6. The chapter concludes with an example of a planning form to aid the practitioner in documenting the seven key planning

decisions required. Additional background on sampling theory is provided for the interested reader in Chapter 22. That chapter, however, can be omitted with no loss in continuity as far as the practical application of the suggested techniques is concerned.

13.1 The technique of statistical sampling

Statistical sampling is involved wherever mathematical techniques (statistics and probability theory) are used to measure the risk that a sampling conclusion will differ from the conclusion that would have been obtained by examining and evaluating all the items within a given population. Because conflicting sets of terminology are found throughout the literature, the principal terms used in this chapter are described in the following paragraphs.

13.1.1 Statistical sampling terminology

In statistical sampling a *sample of sampling units* (such as accounts, invoices, line-items, or individual dollars) is selected from a *population* of such sampling units. For probability theory to be applicable, the selection must be made *randomly* – that is, on the basis of chance. Probability theory merely measures the mathematical odds involved in this chance. Various random selection methods are possible (unrestricted, stratified, cluster, etc.) but for the moment we shall simply call any such sample a *random sample*. Two general sampling situations can be distinguished – *attributes sampling* and *variables sampling*.

13.1.2 Attributes and variables sampling

An *attributes sampling* situation arises when one is dealing with the *rate of occurence* or *frequency* of items in a population having a certain attribute, such as the wearing of a hat. The attribute either exists or does not. A person is either wearing a hat or is not. He cannot be wearing half a hat. There is no in-between situation. Examples of attributes sampling situations are: estimating the frequency of defects in ball bearings on a production line, the frequency of obsolete items in an inventory, or the frequency of errors in a file of documents or in a group of receivable balances.

A *variables sampling* situation, on the other hand, arises when one is dealing with variations in some measurement possessed by every member of a population. For example, everyone has a height, but individual heights vary. Indeed, an infinite number of

different height measurements are possible (as opposed to the two-value yes-or-no situation in attributes sampling). A variables sample drawn from a city can estimate the *average* height of its citizens based on the average height in the sample. Examples of variables sampling situations are: estimating the average diameter of ball bearings on a production line, the average invoice dollar value of a group of puchase invoices or the average invoice gross profit percentage of a group of sales invoices.

In attributes sampling, the results of a random sample are expressed as sample frequency or, in auditing, a *sample error rate* (e.g., one unbilled shipment in a sample of 100 shipping orders would be a 1% sample error rate). The sample error rate is also the *most likely error rate* in the population because a random sample is likely to be representative of the population. Such rate is merely the statistical estimate of the *most likely errors* already discussed with respect to judgmental representative sampling. Of course, the true but unknown *population error rate* may differ from this most likely error rate. The auditor can, however, if he has chosen the *sample size* properly, have a predetermined level of sampling *confidence* (sometimes called 'reliability') that the true population error rate does not exceed a determinable *upper error limit*. The upper error limit is merely the statistical quantification of the *possible errors* already discussed judgmentally in Chapter 9. Sampling confidence, the complement of *sampling risk*, is merely the statistical quantification of the *degree of assurance* previously discussed (e.g., if sampling risk is 5% then sampling confidence is 95%).[2] The spread between the most likely error rate (sample error rate) and the upper error limit is called the *precision*.[3]

For example, as shown later, with a 1% sample error rate in a random sample of 100, the auditor would estimate most likely errors as 1% and could have 95% confidence that he would have detected more errors had the population rate exceeded 4.75% (the precision in this case being 3.75%). The foregoing terms are illustrated in the first part of Figure 13.a.

In variables sampling, the results of a random sample may be expressed as a sample average (e.g., the average invoice value in a sample of 100 invoices

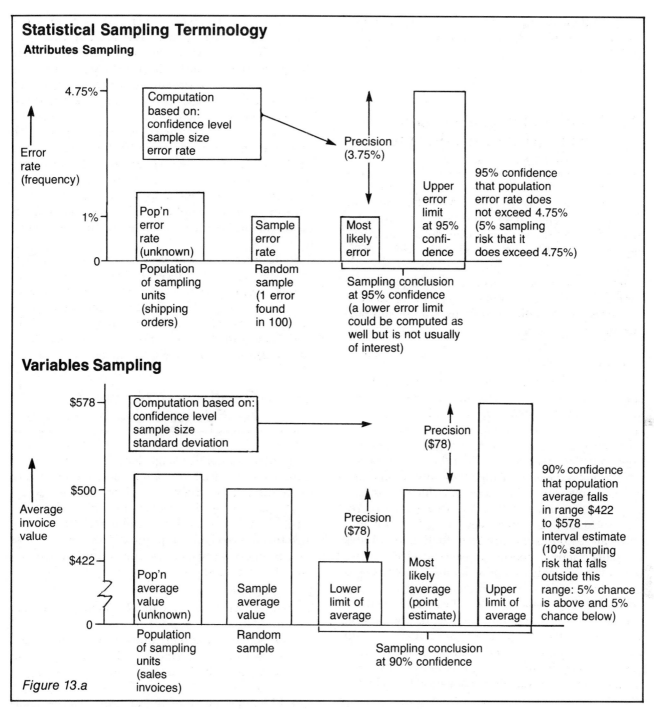

Statistical Sampling Terminology

Attributes Sampling

Error rate (frequency)

4.75%

1%

0

Computation based on:
confidence level
sample size
error rate

Precision (3.75%)

Pop'n error rate (unknown)

Sample error rate

Most likely error

Upper error limit at 95% confidence

95% confidence that population error rate does not exceed 4.75% (5% sampling risk that it does exceed 4.75%)

Population of sampling units (shipping orders)

Random sample (1 error found in 100)

Sampling conclusion at 95% confidence (a lower error limit could be computed as well but is not usually of interest)

Variables Sampling

Average invoice value

$578

$500

$422

0

Computation based on:
confidence level
sample size
standard deviation

Precision ($78)

Precision ($78)

Pop'n average value (unknown)

Sample average value

Lower limit of average

Most likely average (point estimate)

Upper limit of average

90% confidence that population average falls in range $422 to $578 — interval estimate (10% sampling risk that falls outside this range: 5% chance is above and 5% chance below)

Population of sampling units (sales invoices)

Random sample

Sampling conclusion at 90% confidence

Figure 13.a

might be $500). The sample average is also the most likely population average. The auditor can, if he has chosen the sample size properly, have a predetermined level of sampling confidence that the true population average falls within the range of this most likely average plus or minus a specified precision. For example, in a certain case the sample results might indicate that the auditor can be 90% confident that the population average invoice value falls in the range of $500 (the sample average) plus or minus $78 (the precision). The most likely average of $500 is sometimes called a *point estimate* and the range from

$422 to $578 an *interval estimate*. The foregoing terms are illustrated in the second part of Figure 13.a.

In attributes sampling for error frequency, the precision gap to be computed in the evaluation stage depends mathematically on confidence level demanded, sample size used and sample error rate observed. In variables sampling for invoice average value, the precision range to be computed in the evaluation stage depends mathematically on confidence level demanded, sample size used and the variability of invoice values observed in the population, this variability being measured by the *standard devia-*

333

tion (a mathematical measure of a typical amount by which an individual invoice deviates from the average).

13.1.3 Applicability of attributes and variables sampling to auditing

Both attributes and variables sampling techniques are in use by auditors today. While the later sections of this chapter suggest a preference for a particular form of attributes sampling (the dollar-unit technique), it should be recognized that various arguments are possible in support of a preference for either attributes and variables techniques. The applicability of these techniques depends upon their consistency with audit test objectives (both substantive and compliance).

Substantive tests

The objective of substantive tests is to provide an appropriate assurance of detecting the possibility of a material total of monetary error should such a material total actually exist. Monetary errors occur with a relatively low frequency in most accounting populations, but their magnitude when they occur varies. Only a few receivable balances typically contain any monetary errors but the few errors which occur may vary from, say, 10c to $10 000. At first glance, therefore, substantive test objectives do not fit neatly into either an attributes or a variables situation. Attributes sampling is most simply used to measure frequencies not values. Variables sampling is most simply used to measure averages of some variable possessed by every unit of the population. What the auditor needs, in contrast, is a technique of measuring the varying values of low-frequency errors. Both attributes and variables sampling methods can be adapted, however, to meet the unique requirements of the low-frequency-varying-value error situation faced by auditors.

Attributes sampling can be adapted to yield dollar values by one of the techniques of 'stratified boundary pricing', proportionate sampling, or dollar-unit sampling. Variables sampling can be adapted to the audit situation either by 'difference and ratio methods' or alternatively by 'mean-per-unit' ('direct-extension') methods.

Compliance tests

The objective of compliance tests has been suggested as that of providing an appropriate assurance of detecting a multiple materiality value of

transactions each subject to a critical compliance deviaton should such a total value actually exist. Expressed in this form, the compliance objective offers the same sampling difficulties as the substantive objective. Compliance deviations typically occur with low frequency, though not usually as low as for actual monetary errors. When compliance deviations occur, however, the value of the transaction subject to the deficiency may vary, say, from 10c (in which case the deficiency hardly matters) to $10 000 (in which case the deficiency may be very worrisome indeed). To meet this type of compliance objective, either attributes or variables sampling would have to be adapted in one of the manners listed above for substantive tests.

Some practitioners, however, as discussed in Chapter 9, would state the objective of compliance tests as simply assessing the frequency of compliance deviations without regard to the value of the transactions in which they occur. Auditors with this view would find classical attributes sampling (without the need of adaption) suitable for their objectives.

13.1.4 Relationship of precision, confidence and sample extent

It was pointed out previously that precision computed in the evaluation stage depends on three other factors: confidence level, sample size, and error rate (or, in the case of variables sampling, standard deviation). Actually, all four factors, including precision, form a mathematically inter-related set. We may picture this inter-relationship graphically (see the first part of Figure 13.b) by imagining a constant-size pie carved into four slices:

1. sample size
2. sample correctness rate (the frequency of correct sample items)
   - Of course, we usually think in terms of sample error rate (the frequency of incorrect sample items) and will do so throughout the rest of this chapter.
   - The only purpose in referring to the complementary measure, correctness rate, at the moment, is to illustrate the inter-dependence in the pie diagram.
   - For variables sampling, this pie sector could instead be thought of as the degree of uniformity in sample items—that is, as the inverse of the sample standard deviation.
3. sampling risk
   - Sampling risk will sometimes be referred to throughout the rest of this chapter and is useful here in illustrating the inter-dependence in the pie diagram.

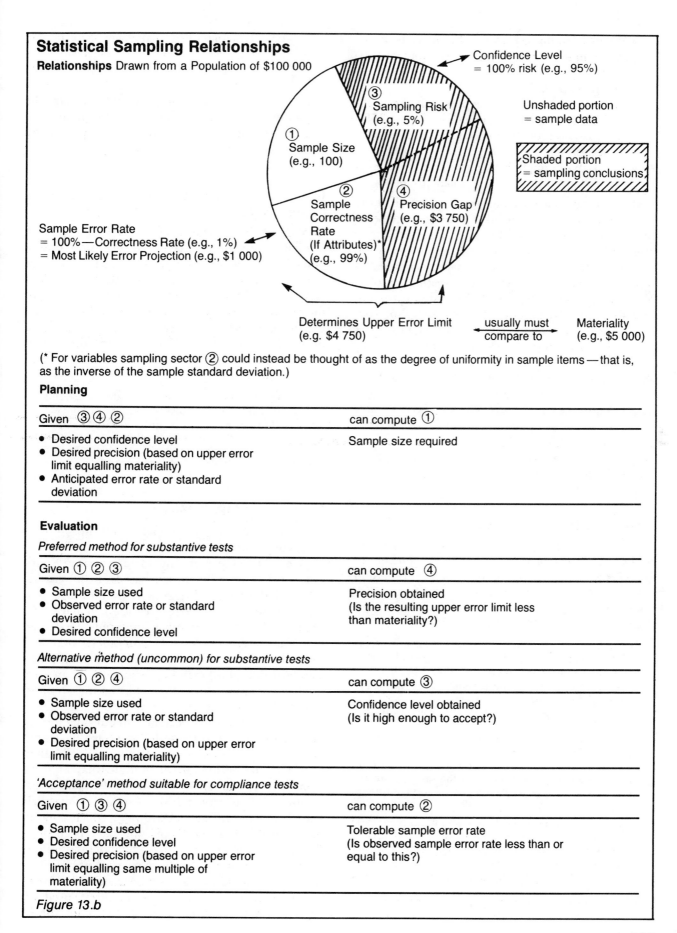

Statistical Sampling Relationships

Relationships Drawn from a Population of $100 000

Confidence Level
= 100% risk (e.g., 95%)

③ Sampling Risk (e.g., 5%)

Unshaded portion
= sample data

Shaded portion
= sampling conclusions

① Sample Size (e.g., 100)

② Sample Correctness Rate (If Attributes)* (e.g., 99%)

④ Precision Gap (e.g., $3 750)

Sample Error Rate
= 100%—Correctness Rate (e.g., 1%)
= Most Likely Error Projection (e.g., $1 000)

Determines Upper Error Limit
(e.g. $4 750)

usually must compare to

Materiality
(e.g., $5 000)

(* For variables sampling sector ② could instead be thought of as the degree of uniformity in sample items — that is, as the inverse of the sample standard deviation.)

Planning

Given ③ ④ ②	can compute ①
• Desired confidence level • Desired precision (based on upper error limit equalling materiality) • Anticipated error rate or standard deviation	Sample size required

Evaluation

Preferred method for substantive tests

Given ① ② ③	can compute ④
• Sample size used • Observed error rate or standard deviation • Desired confidence level	Precision obtained (Is the resulting upper error limit less than materiality?)

Alternative method (uncommon) for substantive tests

Given ① ② ④	can compute ③
• Sample size used • Observed error rate or standard deviation • Desired precision (based on upper error limit equalling materiality)	Confidence level obtained (Is it high enough to accept?)

'Acceptance' method suitable for compliance tests

Given ① ③ ④	can compute ②
• Sample size used • Desired confidence level • Desired precision (based on upper error limit equalling same multiple of materiality)	Tolerable sample error rate (Is observed sample error rate less than or equal to this?)

Figure 13.b

335

- More often, however, we will think in terms of the complementary measure, sampling confidence.
4. precision gap
   - In attributes sampling, the precision gap is initially measured as a frequency rate (e.g., 3.75%) but is usually more usefully converted to a dollar projection (e.g., $3 750).
   - In variables sampling, the precision gap is usually measured directly as a dollar projection.

If any one pie slice is made larger, one or all of the remaining slices must shrink.[4] Such arrangements are illustrated in Figure 13.c. Thus, a larger sample size leads to a lower sampling risk, a finer precision gap, or, if the former are to remain unchanged, a lower tolerable sample correctness rate (higher tolerable sample error rate). This relationship is reasonable for with more audit work a *better* sampling conclusion should be obtained (more assured, more precise, or both). Conversely, a lower sampling accuracy rate (higher sample error rate) leads to a higher sampling risk, a broader precision gap, or, if the former are to be maintained unchanged, a larger required sample size. This relationship is reasonable for, with worse sampling results, a *worse* sampling conclusion should arise (less assured or less precise) unless one compensates for this by more work. In short, if any three factors are given, the fourth may be computed.

Precision/confidence pairs

It follows that for a given set of results (sample size and sample error rate) the sampling conclusion can be expressed as any of a number of pairs of precision (or the related upper error limit) and confidence level. This relationship again is illustrated in Figure 13.c.

> For example, having found 1 erroneous dollar in a sample of 100 dollar-units drawn from a population of $100 000, the auditor may properly conclude that:
> 1. he is 80% confident the population errors do not exceed $3 000, or
> 2. he is 95% confident the population errors do not exceed $4 750, or
> 3. he is 99% confident the population errors do not exceed $6 640.
> In each case the most likely population error rate remains the same: 1% (as found in the sample) but the upper error limit varies depending on the confidence level.
>
> Similarly, having found 0 errors in a sample of 100 dollar-units, the auditor may properly conclude that:
> 1. he is 80% confident the population errors do not exceed $1 610, or
> 2. he is 95% confident the population errors do not exceed $3 000, or
> 3. he is 99% confident the population errors do not exceed $4 610, etc.

> In each case the most likely population error rate remains the same: 0% (as found in the sample) but the upper error limit varies depending on the confidence level.[5]

In general, given constant sample results, the higher the error limit one postulates, the greater the confidence one can have that the true population error rate does not exceed this limit.

Relationship to degree of assurance and materiality

Confidence level in statistical tests is one component of total audit assurance required. Precision, on the other hand, directly influences the computation of the upper error limit which, in the case of monetary errors, should normally not exceed materiality or, in the case of compliance deviations, should not exceed such level as would indicate a reasonable possibility of material monetary error. These relationships of confidence level and precision are well documented in professional pronouncements:

> Although 'precision' and 'reliability' are statistically inseparable, the committee believes that one of the ways in which these measurements can be usefully adapted to the auditor's purposes is by relating precision to materiality and reliability [confidence level] to the reasonableness of the basis for his opinion.[6]

Planning sample sizes

The use of the statistical inter-relationships in planning sample sizes is illustrated in the second part of Figure 13.b. One planning factor, desired confidence level, must be chosen based on the criteria affecting the required degree of assurance in general. Another factor, desired precision, or at least the related tolerable upper error limit, must be chosen based on materiality. A final factor, anticipated sample error rate (or, in variables sampling, anticipated standard deviation) can, however, only be an educated guess. From these three factors the required sample size can then be computed.

The uncertainties associated with guessing the anticipated sample error rate (or standard deviation) affect only the planning process, not the final evaluation. The final evaluation will indicate what sampling conclusion is mathematically justified by the actual sample results observed. If the planning estimate has been overly pessimistic, the sampling conclusion will be acceptable but more work will have been done than has proved necessary in the light of hindsight. If the planning estimate has been overly optimistic, the sampling conclusion may well be unacceptable (i.e., not persuasive enough) and the sample size used will have proved insufficient in the light of hindsight. In

Examples of Statistical Sampling Relationships

| Starting from the case shown in the pie diagram in Figure 13.b: | A larger sample size will lead to:
A lower sampling risk (higher confidence) | A finer precision gap: | Or, if the former are to remain unchanged, a lower tolerable sample correctness rate (higher tolerable sample error rate): |

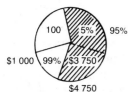 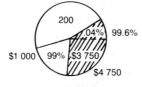 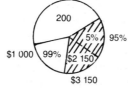 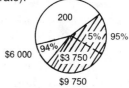

This is reasonable for with more audit work a 'better' sampling conclusion should be obtained — more assured, more precise, or both.

| Conversely, starting from the same initial case: | A lower sample correctness rate (higher sample error rate) will lead to:
A higher sampling risk (lower confidence) | A broader precision gap: | Or, if the former are to be maintained unchanged, a larger required sample size: |

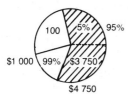 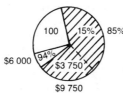 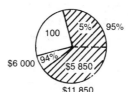 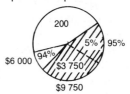

This is reasonable for with worse sampling results a 'worse' sampling conclusion should arise — less assured or less precise — unless one compensates for this by more work.

Precision and confidence go in pairs. For example, having found 1 erroneous dollar in a sample of 100 dollar-units drawn from a population of $100 000, the auditor may properly conclude that:

| He is 80% confident population errors do not exceed $3 000 | Or he is 95% confident population errors do not exceed $4 750 | Or he is 99% confident errors do not exceed $6 640 |

 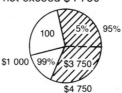 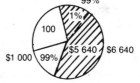

In each case the most likely population error rate remains the same: 1% (as found in the sample) but the upper error limit varies depending on the confidence level.

Similarly, having found 0 errors in a sample of 100 dollar-units, the auditor may properly conclude that:

| He is 80% confident population errors do not exceed $1 610 | Or he is 95% confident population errors do not exceed $3 000 | Or he is 99% confident population errors do not exceed $4 610 |

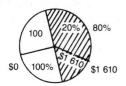 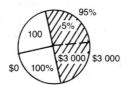 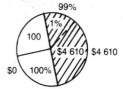

In each case the most likely population error rate remains the same: 0% (as found in the sample) but the upper error limit varies depending on the confidence level.

Figure 13.c

337

the latter case, unless other audit evidence is obtainable, it may be necessary to extend the original sample size.

Evaluating sample results

The statistical inter-relationship used in planning may be used in evaluating sample results, as illustrated in the second part of Figure 13.b. For substantive tests, there are two possible alternative methods. Under either method, one factor is the actual sample size used and another is the observed sample error rate (or, in variables sampling, the observed standard deviation). Under the usual method of evaluation, a final factor is then the desired confidence level (from the planning phase) and from these three factors are computed the resulting precision and the related upper error limit. If the resulting upper error limit is less than materiality, the sampling conclusion is generally acceptable. If the computed upper error limit, on the other hand, exceeds materiality, the sampling conclusion may either (a) provide adequate evidence only that super-material errors *much* larger than materiality are not present (in which case further audit work must be considered in order to provide the desired assurance that material errors are not present) or (b) provide some affirmative evidence that material errors *do* exist (when the projection of most likely errors also exceeds materiality).

Under the alternative method of evaluation, the final factor could be taken as the desired precision (from the planning phase) and from these three factors could be computed the resulting confidence level. If the resulting confidence level equals or exceeds the degree of assurance desired from this test, the sampling conclusion would generally be acceptable. If the computed confidence level, on the other hand, were to fall below the desired level, the sampling conclusion might either (a) provide insufficient evidence that material errors are not present (in which case further audit work must be considered) or (b) provide some affirmative evidence that material errors *do* exist (when the confidence level as to their non-existence falls below 50%).

While both methods of evaluation are theoretically valid, the second method does not lend itself as readily to the accumulation of most likely and possible errors projected by different tests (of inventories, receivables, fixed assets, etc.) throughout the audit. The first method will therefore be the one described for substantive tests in this chapter.

For compliance tests, yet another method of evaluation is often convenient. One factor is again the sample size used. Another is the desired confidence level (from the planning phase). A final factor is the desired precision level (also from the planning phase). From these three factors a tolerable sample error rate is computed – indeed, this rate would usually have been precomputed in determining the required sample size during planning. If the observed sample error is less than or equal to this tolerable rate, the sampling conclusion is generally acceptable (reliance on control is warranted). If the observed sample error rate exceeds the tolerable rate, the sampling conclusion would be unacceptable (reliance on control would be rejected). In the suggested procedures for compliance testing illustrated in this chapter and in the previous one, the tolerable sample error rate is set at one critical compliance deviation per test.[7] Other test designs are of course possible.

13.1.5 Consistency with generally accepted auditing standards

Professional literature on statistical sampling has customarily included reasons why such sampling can be considered consistent with generally accepted auditing standards – and in particular with the three standards of field work.[8] Many of the reasons advanced apply, in fact, to all testing, whether statistical or judgmental, and these reasons have already been discussed in Chapter 12. Specifically, in 12.1.5 it was argued that testing was justified because the auditor should not seek additional increments of audit evidence, such as by going to a 100% examination, when the related incremental audit assurance was out of proportion to the cost of obtaining it. To show that the specific addition of statistical aids to the general technique of testing is consistent with the field work standards and with auditing theory, it is similarly necessary to show that the incremental assurance provided by these aids is in reasonable proportion to the cost of obtaining it. This incremental assurance available from the use of statistical sampling consists of assurance (a) that bias has not been introduced into the selection of items to be tested and (b) that the sample size is really sufficient to achieve the degree of assurance desired and warrant the sampling conclusions expressed. If the risks of biased selection, of insufficient or excessive sample size, and of incorrect conclusions in judgmental testing were trivial in all applications, then the use of statistical sampling in auditing would be inconsistent with the concept of economy.

Assurance that bias is avoided

It happens, however, that these risks in judgmental testing can in some applications be very real. With respect to selection there is a natural human tendency to favour (perhaps unconsciously) easily accessible selection points. If the less accessible population items happen to be the very ones in error (indeed their very inaccessibility in some engagements may be related to their being in error), the sample bias could lead to seriously misleading conclusions. It is also possible that judgmental selection will avoid, say, the first and last items on any page on the grounds that such items do not *seem as random* as others. Of course, a true random sample will select such items some of the time. If there is some systematic reason for initial or final items on each page being more error-prone, a judgmental test avoiding them could again lead to misleading conclusions. There may also be an instinctive tendency in a judgmental test to make proportionately more selections at the beginning when the auditor is fresh than towards the end when he is tired.

Assurance that sample size is sufficient

Far more important, however, is the assurance which statistical sampling provides that the sample size is really sufficient to warrant the conclusions expressed. Whatever the abilities of human judgment in assessing qualitative factors such as relative strength of internal control or reasons for a given error encountered, these abilities are noticeably less in assessing quantitative factors such as how much testing is enough or how high might an error frequency really be. Our common sense seems to be less than perfect when it comes to assessing odds (a deficiency not unrelated to the popularity of lotteries). For example, if an average group of people are asked to estimate the chance of obtaining 3 heads out of 6 tosses of a fair coin, the most common (and indeed intuitive) answer is 50% – though a wide range of answers within the group can be expected. In fact, the chance is only 31%.[9] If groups of auditors are asked how many receivable accounts must be confirmed to provide a high degree of assurance of detecting a material error if present, similar discrepancies are likely. *The most important benefit which statistical sampling offers is the reduction, through the use of mathematical aids to judgment, of this risk of overauditing or underauditing.*

Of course, where the incremental benefit of converting testing techniques to a statistical basis is disproportionately costly, then the use of statistical sampling would not be justified despite these risks. Undoubtedly there are numerous audit tests where this is the case and where the use of judgmental testing is accordingly the only responsible course to follow. But there are also many other audit tests where there is no additional cost to statistical sampling or where the cost is slight in comparison to the benefits of the greater objectivity in determining extent, selection and evaluation by statistical means. In these latter cases, the use of statistical sampling is fully in accord with the third field work standard. Suggested criteria for making this cost-benefit decision were given in Chapter 12.

This does not mean, however, that where statistical sampling is warranted, it should be used mechanically and thoughtlessly. It is a guide to judgment, not a substitute for it. *In the end, it is the auditor's responsibility to choose those tests, test extents and testing techniques which in his professional judgment are sufficient to satisfy generally accepted auditing standards.*

13.1.6 Objective of statistical sampling in auditing

Based on the foregoing discussion, the objective of statistical sampling in an audit context can be defined as follows:

> To employ random selection procedures and statistical evaluation techniques in representative[10] testing (whether for compliance or substantive objectives) so as to eliminate the risk of bias and so as to permit quantification of the sampling confidence achieved wherever this greater objectivity is warranted. Quantification of sampling confidence in turn helps the auditor to ensure that he has obtained sufficient assurance and that the extent of his work is consistent from engagement to engagement.

An additional by-product is that statistical sampling focusses increased attention on audit planning in general.

It is assumed in the rest of this chapter that any statistical representative sampling will, on the basis of the criteria outlined in Chapter 12, be supplemented by high-value and key-item selection where appropriate.

13.2 Types of statistical sampling in auditing

The purpose of this section is to provide a brief introduction into the following types of sampling plans:

Attributes sampling plans

1. physical-unit attributes sampling (classical attributes sampling) ⎫
   ⎬ neutral selection (disregarding value) followed by attribute-type evaluation
2. stratified attributes boundary pricing ⎫
3. dollar-unit sampling (cumulative monetary amount sampling) ⎬ all being types of value-oriented selection with attribute-type evaluation
4. proportionate attributes sampling ⎭

Variables sampling plans

5. difference and ratio methods ⎫ neutral selection followed by variables type evaluation applied to errors
   ⎬

6. mean-per-unit method (direct extension method) ⎫ neutral selection or, if stratified, partly value-oriented selection followed by variables-type evaluation applied to item values
7. stratified mean-per-unit method ⎭

Other refinements and modifications exist[11] but the above list covers most of the principal types either in use or similar to ones in use by auditors today. Some practitioners believe that all or several of these seven plans should be deployed by the auditor, the choice of plan for any given test depending upon observed conditions in the sample or in the related systems or controls. Others believe that one plan can serve all or most of the auditor's sampling requirements – though opinions differ, naturally, on which that plan is. In the writer's view the technique of dollar-unit sampling (or similar plans) may be conveniently used in all *audit applications* except those few cases where the population to be tested is not quantifiable in dollars and, in certain cases, where very high error-to-book-value ratios exist (over 100%). Dollar-unit and similar plans (such as cumulative monetary amount sampling) probably account for the largest number of individual substantive statistical sampling applications in North America today. Because there are good arguments in support of various different preferences, however, many practitioners may wish to have some general knowledge of each of the techniques. Accordingly, each of the above sampling plans is discussed briefly below. The mathematical theories underlying attributes and variables sampling in general are introduced (also necessarily briefly) in Chapter 22.

13.2.1 Physical-unit attributes sampling

The term "physical-unit attributes sampling" is used in this chapter to mean an attribute sampling plan in which the sampling unit has been defined as an account balance, a purchase invoice, a line-item on a sales invoice, or any other constituent of the accounting population which has some real or physical significance. This is the classical type of attributes sampling.

For example, if an auditor decides that it is necessary to vouch a random sample of 50 fixed asset purchase invoices, he must make 50 random selections out of the entire population of fixed asset purchase invoices for the year giving every invoice an equal chance of selection. (Sample size determination and methods of random selection are discussed later.) Should he find no errors at all in his sample, he can have 95% sampling confidence that the number of fixed asset purchase invoices containing errors does not exceed 6.0%. Such an evaluation may be made using the attributes evaluation table in Figure 13.d (the derivation of this table is explained in 22.1.2) as follows:

$$\text{Upper error limit frequency} = \frac{\text{UEL cumulative factor}}{\text{Sample size}}$$
$$= 3.00 \div 50 = 6.0\%$$

Had he instead found one error in his sample, the upper error limit frequency would have been $4.75 \div 50 = 9.5\%$.

In forming an opinion on fixed asset additions for the year the auditor must then decide whether he has obtained adequate assurance that a material total of monetary error has not occurred. Such a decision requires some method of "pricing" the 6% upper error limit frequency projected from his sample. In

Attributes Evaluation Table (Cumulative)

UEL Cumulative Factors

Low confidence levels			Number of errors found in sample	High confidence levels		
80%	85%	90%		95%	97.5%	99%
1.61	1.90	2.31	0	3.00	3.69	4.61
3.00	3.38	3.89	1	4.75	5.58	6.64
4.28	4.73	5.33	2	6.30	7.23	8.41
5.52	6.02	6.69	3	7.76	8.77	10.05
6.73	7.27	8.00	4	9.16	10.25	11.61
7.91	8.50	9.28	5	10.52	11.67	13.11
9.08	9.71	10.54	6	11.85	13.06	14.58
10.24	10.90	11.78	7	13.15	14.43	16.00
11.38	12.08	13.00	8	14.44	15.77	17.41
12.52	13.25	14.21	9	15.71	17.09	18.79
13.66	14.42	15.41	10	16.97	18.40	20.15
14.78	15.57	16.60	11	18.21	19.68	21.49
15.90	16.72	17.79	12	19.45	20.97	22.83
17.02	17.86	18.96	13	20.67	22.24	24.14
18.13	19.00	20.13	14	21.89	23.49	25.45
19.24	20.13	21.30	15	23.10	24.75	26.75
20.34	21.26	22.46	16	24.31	25.99	28.04
21.44	22.39	23.61	17	25.50	27.22	29.31
22.54	23.51	24.76	18	26.70	28.45	30.59
23.64	24.63	25.91	19	27.88	29.68	31.85
24.73	25.74	27.05	20	29.07	30.89	33.11
.	.	.	.	.	.	.
.	.	.	.	.	.	.

Where: upper error limit frequency $= \dfrac{\text{UEL cumulative factor}}{\text{sample size}}$

or, for dollar-unit sampling:
upper error limit dollars $=$ UEL cumulative factor $\times$ average dollar sampling interval

Source: Computed from cumulative Poisson Formula values (see brief explanation in 22.1.2)
(For conservatism the above computations were made to three decimal places and, in rounding to two places, rounded always upwards).

Figure 13.d

some cases it may be reasonable to assume that the average value of all individual errors existing in the population of fixed asset purchase invoices (including invoices improperly capitalized, incorrectly priced, etc.) would not exceed the average popula- tion invoice value. If this assumption were valid, the 6% frequency could be applied to total reported dollars of fixed asset purchases (say, $3 000 000) and the upper error limit projected as $180 000 (which the auditor can then compare to materiality). Of course, the $180 000 is not directly a statistical projection. Rather it is the combination of a statistical upper error limit frequency (6%) and a judgmental pricing assumption (average error would not exceed average invoice value). There is nothing wrong with such a combination (auditing is filled with judgmental assumptions) providing there are grounds for believing the judgmental pricing assumption is reasonable. In a few engagements, such grounds exist. In many others, however, they do not. For all the auditor knows, the larger purchase invoices may be the very ones that happen to be in error (whether accidental or deliberate), in which case a 6% numerical frequency of errors might have a value far in excess of $180 000. Therefore, for many substantive tests, physical-unit attributes sampling cannot, without some modification, be considered to give reliable conclusions in dolllars. Of course, where dollar values are not readily obtainable for population items, physical-unit attributes sampling may be a logical method to employ – and corresponds to "neutral selection" as described in Chapter 12. Generally, physical-unit attributes sampling is appropriate when the auditor can safely make the assumption that error values are independent of book values and will not likely exceed some specified dollar amount, such as the average invoice value.

Some practitioners, including the writer, believe similar considerations apply to compliance testing. In that case, physical-unit attributes sampling would be appropriate only where it is reasonable to assume that the average value of physical units subject to compliance deviations does not exceed the average value of all physical units. Other practitioners prefer compliance evaluations to be always made in terms of non-monetary frequencies; they will find physical-unit attributes sampling to be the appropriate technique on all occasions. In any case, it is the logical technique to use where monetary amounts cannot readily be assigned to the documents (such as shipping orders) covered by the compliance test.

13.2.2 Stratified attributes boundary pricing

Physical-unit attributes sampling can be modified to permit dollar conclusions without the risky "average-value" pricing assumption used in the previous section. One method is to "price" the upper error limit frequency at the maximum invoice value instead of at the average invoice value. Assuming, for example, that high-value items over $1 000 have already been selected and examined 100%, this method would involve pricing possible errors in the rest of the population at the high-value threshold of $1 000. Certainly no error of overstatement could exceed this $1 000 limit. Even if a $999 invoice should have been completely expensed, the overstatement error would be only $999. While such upper boundary pricing is safe (in terms of not missing a material total of error when present), it is usually impractical; the inflated projections would usually be astronomical. To make the method practical, it is necessary to stratify the population items by value.

Consider the example in Figure 13.e in which a population of 10 000 fixed asset purchase invoices (totalling $3 000 000) has been stratified into 5 strata, random samples drawn separately from each stratum as indicated, and no errors found in any of the stratum samples. For the moment, the reader should merely take the sample size in each stratum as given, and follow through the resulting conclusions.

In the middle stratum, for instance, a sample of 14 containing no errors yields, using the evaluation table in Figure 13.d for 95% confidence, an upper error limit frequency of $3.00 \div 14 = 21.4\%$. Such a frequency of errors among the 840 invoices in that stratum would represent 180 possible erroneous invoices. If the amount of each of these 180 errors were $1 000 (the maximum possible – being the upper boundary for this stratum) the upper error limit value for this stratum would amount to $180 000.

It may be demonstrated mathematically that in this stratified attribute sample (where no errors were found), the $180 000 upper error limit for each stratum is concurrent, that is, the combined upper error limit for the whole population is still $180 000.[12] It can now be seen that in fact the sample sizes within the individual strata were set so as to produce these identical, concurrent upper error limits. Thus, in this case, the stratified sample of 86 items provides a reliable conclusion (with 95% confidence) that had errors in the population exceeded $180 000 the auditor would have detected it (by finding at least one sample error). Such a conclusion avoids the risky average-pricing assumption required with classical physical-unit attribute sampling. Indeed, by making the *worst* assumption (that error values are equal to upper boundaries) some degree of inefficiency is introduced. Physical units with values significantly less than their related stratum boundaries will be over-sampled. The conclusions will be safe, but larger sample sizes than necessary will have been used.

This inefficiency can be reduced by increasing the degree of stratification[13] (although there is a cost associated with the time required to do the stratifying). Were the number of strata in Figure 13.e to be successively increased it would be found that stratified sample size would be successively reduced from

Stratified Boundary Pricing

(A)	(B)	(C)	(D)	(E)	(F)	(G)	(H)	(I)	(J)
Upper stratum boundary	Number of invoices	Stratum value	Sample size number	Sample size %	Sample errors	UEL factor for 95% confidence	UEL% =G/D	UEL number = B x H	UEL $ =I x A
$10 000	120	$ 600 000	20	16.67%	0	3.00	15%	18	$180 000
3 000	240	300 000	12	5.00	0	3.00	25	60	180 000
1 000	840	500 000	14	1.67	0	3.00	21.4	180	180 000
500	2 000	700 000	17	.83	0	3.00	18	360	180 000
200	6 800	900 000	23	.33	0	3.00	13.2	900	180 000
	10 000	$3 000 000	86						$180 000

Figure 13.e

86 down to a minimum of 50. Various methods of stratifying exist (both manually and by computer) but their description is beyond the scope of this chapter.

The stratified boundary pricing example illustrated in Figure 13.e involved no sample errors. When sample errors are discovered, the upper error limit for each stratum separately can still be computed using the appropriate factors from the evaluation table in Figure 13.d but the combination of these stratum limits to arrive at a conclusion about the population involves, in that case, some additional considerations (discussed in 13.3.4).

13.2.3 Dollar-unit attributes sampling

Another method in which classical attributes sampling can be adapted to yield reliable conclusions in dollars is by changing the customary definition of sampling unit. In dollar-unit sampling,[14] the sampling unit in the population is defined not as being an individual invoice or an individual receivable balance (i.e., a physical unit) but rather *as being an individual dollar*.

For example, suppose the auditor is sampling from the $3 000 000 of fixed asset purchase invoices in the preceding examples. Instead of viewing this as 10,000 different invoices of varying sizes from which he is going to make a random selection, he would think of it instead as representing 3 million individual one-dollar bills spread out on a table. If he draws a random sample of 50 of these individual dollar bills and finds therein no errors at all, then sampling tables (Figure 13.d) tell him that he can be 95% sure that there is not more than a 6% frequency of incorrect dollars among these 3 million individual

dollar bills $3.00 \div 50 = 6\%$. But no longer is there any problem as to how to price this 6%. If there were a 6% frequency of incorrect dollars (i.e., at worst, coming from purchase invoices which should have been expensed rather than capitalized) the aggregate error would be $180 000. As a result of his dollar-unit sample of 50 the auditor could therefore be 95% confident that total fixed asset additions were not overstated by more than $180 000.

It should be noted that this conclusion requires no assumption as to the pattern or distribution of errors among the invoices, other than the assumption that any given invoice cannot be overstated by more than its reported book value, i.e., that the proper amount to capitalize cannot have been less than nil. There is no assumption that the average size of errors in the population will be equal to the average invoice size, since the errors may well be clustered in the largest invoices. Nor is there any assumption that the average size of errors in the population will be equal to the average size of errors, if any, found in the sample. A very important point about dollar-unit sampling, then, is that it is no longer possible for a very large error of overstatement to escape undetected (the needle in the haystack problem); in effect, such an error is broken up into its constituent dollars, which, if there are a material number, will have a substantial probability of at least one being detected.

Drawing a dollar-unit sample

In order to draw a random sample of 50 individual dollar bills, the auditor must give each of the individual 3 million one-dollar bills an equal chance of selection (rather than giving each invoice, regardless of size, an equal chance of selection). Of course, when he selects an individual dollar he does not verify that particular dollar by itself. Rather, it acts as a hook and drags a whole invoice with it. On this basis it can be seen that a $2 000 invoice will have about twice the chance of selection as a $1 000 invoice because it contains twice as many dollar-unit hooks by which it may potentially be fished out for audit verification. But it *should* have twice the chance of selection because it is possible (merely because of its doubled size) that it could contain twice as big an overstatement. In effect, in dollar-unit sampling every transaction gets a chance of selection approximately proportionate to its size – each bigger item gets a bigger chance because it is more important and each smaller item gets a smaller chance because it is less important.

In physical-unit attributes sampling (where, say, every invoice out of 10 000 invoices is to be given an equal chance of selection) the auditor, in choosing a sample of 50, must on average select every 200th invoice. Although the mechanics of making this selection *randomly* are discussed later, 200 may be called in this case the *average sampling interval*. In dollar-unit attribute sampling (where, say, every dollar out of 3 million dollars is to be given an equal chance of selection) the auditor, in choosing a sample of 50, must on average select every 60 000th dollar. In this case, $60 000 may be called the *average sampling interval*. The procedure of adding through population dollars progressively (which can be accomplished either manually or by computer) is slightly more work than mere counting procedures that an unstratified physical-unit sample requires but, on the other hand, is simpler than the procedures for drawing most types of stratified samples. In any case, the auditor usually wishes to verify the addition of the accounting population, whether it be a summation of fixed asset additions or a trial balance

of receivable accounts. Procedures for making the dollar-unit selection randomly are discussed later in this chapter.

Comparison to stratified boundary pricing

If the stratified boundary pricing example illustrated in Figure 13.e were progressively substratified, the total sample size would be progressively reduced, eventually reaching a minimum of 50. It will be observed that 50 is the sample size required by dollar-unit sampling in the identical situation. Thus, *dollar-unit sampling is equivalent to boundary-priced physical-unit sampling with a maximum degree of stratification*. It can be seen in Columns E and A of Figure 13.e that, for any stratum, the *sampling fraction* (percentage of sample invoices to population invoices) is directly proportional to the upper boundary of the stratum. In the limit, when dollar-unit sampling is reached, the chance of selection of each invoice is approximately proportional to its size.

Comparison to physical-unit attribute sampling

The unstratified physical-unit sampling example also used a sample size of 50 in the same situation. The two samples of 50 should not be confused, however, for they are considerably different. This difference can be seen in the following table. Although neither sampling plan is drawn on a stratified basis, the contrasting profiles of the two samples can be seen by observing how much of each sample would, on average, have fallen into each stratum previously discussed:

Upper stratum boundary	Number of invoices	Stratum value	Average sample allocation by stratum	
			Dollar-unit sample	Physical-unit sample
			1 selection every $60 000	1 selection every 200 invoices
$10 000	120	$ 600 000	10	1
3 000	240	300 000	5	1
1 000	840	500 000	8	4
500	2 000	700 000	12	10
200	6 800	900 000	15	34
	10 000	$3 000 000	50	50

It can be seen that the dollar-unit sample of 50 contains far more of the larger invoices than does the unstratified physical-unit sample of 50. In contrast, nearly all of the physical-unit selections (88%) are concentrated in the bottom two strata of small invoices, which constitute only about half the population by value. It is the favouring of the larger invoices (value-oriented selection) which permits the dollar-unit conclusion to avoid the risky 'average-pricing' assumption that was required when unstratified physical-unit sampling (neutral selection) was used.

13.2.4 Proportionate attributes sampling

Based on the foregoing discussion, it might seem logical to adopt a sampling plan whereby the chance of selection of each physical unit was made *exactly* proportional to its reported book value. Such a plan is called *proportionate sampling* and has indeed been used in other disciplines and perhaps also in auditing.[15] Thus, in the previous example, instead of giving every dollar a 1/60 000th chance of selection, proportionate sampling would give a $1 000 invoice exactly a 1/60th chance of selection and a $2 000 invoice exactly a 1/30th chance of selection. The two methods are not quite identical. Nonetheless, most forms of proportionate sampling (several exist) have the same *approximate* effect as dollar-unit sampling.

Despite theoretical attractiveness, many proportionate sampling methods may pose some minor disadvantages – difficulty in applying rigorous selection methods without a computer, somewhat more complex evaluation formulas, greater complexity for teaching, and slight unpredictability in sample sizes. Dollar-unit sampling, it is suggested, offers a simpler, convenient, and more readily understandable method of accomplishing the same general objectives. Because there are slight differences, practitioners may have preferences.

13.2.5 Variables sampling (difference and ratio methods)

One method in which variables sampling has been used to estimate errors for audit purposes is that of *difference and ratio estimates*.[16] Here the situation is defined as being one of a population of error amounts – the amount of error in each item. Every population item is considered to be in error, even if for most items the dollar amount of the error is zero.

Of course, in a typical sample of 200 receivable confirmations, most of the error values would be zero (the items involved were correct), but three or four error values might be, say, $5 or $10 or $25. In the difference method, all these values are averaged together to produce an average error per receivable confirmation of, say, 20c. Using this average, together with the individual sample error values, the auditor computes a *standard deviation*.[17] From this standard deviation, together with the 200 sample size used and, say, the 90% confidence level desired, the auditor computes, or looks up in variables sampling tables, the *precision* he has obtained.[18] For example, the computed precision might be 15c around this 20c point estimate. Projecting this per-account average onto the total population of, say, 10 000 accounts, the auditor will conclude that he has a 90% confidence that the total population error falls in the range $2 000 ± $1,500. If he is only interested in the upper error limit, as usually, he will conclude that he has 95% sampling confidence that population errors do not exceed $3 500.

Computations for the ratio method are similar except that each sample error is expressed as a ratio of the book value of the account in which it occurs. The difference and ratio methods may also be applied on a stratified basis.

One problem which difference and ratio methods may encounter is the instability of their estimates of the standard deviation. In the foregoing example the 15c precision is based on the *standard deviation of observed error values* (most of which values are zero). Rigorously, the precision should be based on the *standard deviation of the whole population of errors*. Since the latter quantity is unknown, it is customary in variables sampling to assume that the standard deviation of the sample is an adequate estimate of that of the population. This assumption may not be made consciously and perhaps may be unrecognized by some users; it is, however, implicit in the method of evaluation used. While the assumption is valid for most non-audit uses of variables sampling (and for some audit uses as well where large numbers of sample errors of all sizes are found), it may break down when the method is applied to a common audit situation of testing for infrequent but possibly large errors. To assume that the variability of the two or three small errors discovered is typical of the population *is precisely to assume that there are no large errors in the population* - which is assuming at the start what the auditor should be setting out to prove.

It is a simple matter to construct hypothetical populations containing infrequent but large errors (we may call them "outliers") where the auditor would usually fail to detect a material error using difference or ratio methods. One such example is illustrated in 22.2.5.

To reduce this problem it is wise to adopt certain protective measures:

a) stipulate a minimum number of sample errors (various users stipulate 1, or 3, 5, 8 or 20) before relying on the projections,

b) use the method only when the risk of outliers can be considered remote.

The use of these protective measures implies the development of alternative, "fall-back" sampling methods to be employed where the stipulated conditions are not met (e.g., where no sample errors are found). Some practitioners obtain additional protection by employing the mean-per-unit method (discussed below) for sample size planning and the difference or ratio method only for sample evaluation; such a procedure avoids excessively small sample sizes which could sometimes result from the use of the difference or ratio method alone. Advocates of the difference and ratio methods argue that with the use of such protective measures, the risk of erroneous conclusions is not great enough to be of concern. Although the writer has a preference for the convenience of the dollar-unit approach, the use of difference and ratio methods combined with adequate protective measures can certainly be justified and is the preference of some practitioners.

13.2.6 Variables sampling (mean-per-unit method)

Another method in which variables sampling has been used for audit purposes is the *mean-per-unit* method (sometimes called the *direct extension* method). Here the situation is defined as being a population of corrected values – that is, the reported book values after correction of any errors therein. The corrected values of, say, a sample of receivable balances are averaged together. From the sample mean-per-unit is estimated the population mean-per-unit from which, knowing the number of accounts, the auditor can project the total population dollar value and compare it to the total book value.[19]

For example, the auditor may compute that the average value of 200 fixed asset purchase invoices in his sample (after making audit corrections, if any) is $494. Using this average, together with the individual sample invoice values, the auditor computes a standard deviation.[20]

From this standard deviation, together with the 200 sample size used and, say, the 90% confidence level desired, the auditor computes, or looks up in variables sampling tables, the precision he has obtained.[21] For example, the computed precision might be ± $50 around the $494 point estimate. Projecting this per-invoice average onto the total population of, say, 1 000 invoices, the auditor will conclude that he has a 90% sampling confidence that the total corrected population of fixed asset additions falls in the range of $494 000 ± $50 000).

Alternatively, as explained in 22.2.1, he could conclude that he was 95% confident that true fixed additions were not greater than $544 000, and 95% confident that they were not less than $444 000. If the reported book value of fixed additions happens to be $510 000, he could conclude (a) that the most likely error was a $16 000 overstatement and (b) that he had 95% confidence that total errors did not exceed a net overstatement of $66 000 and (c) that he had 95% confidence that total errors did not exceed a net understatement of $34 000. These relationships are illustrated in Figure 13.f. Of course, the auditor must then normally satisfy himself that the $66 000 and $34 000 upper limits for possible net overstatements and net understatements respectively are less than materiality.

One property of the mean-per-unit approach is that it does not directly measure accounting accuracy or inaccuracy. Indeed, in the foregoing example, it might well have been that no errors at all were encountered in the sample of 200 invoices. The fact that the sample average invoice value of $494 deviated slightly from the $510 reported population average may merely then be due to 'sample bounce' rather than any presence of monetary errors. Thus, the

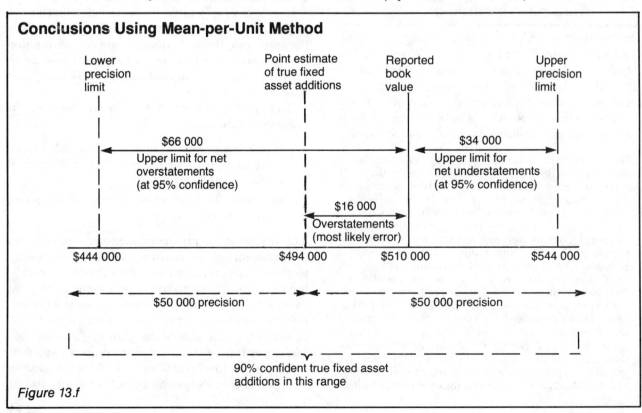

Conclusions Using Mean-per-Unit Method

Figure 13.f

$16 000 "most likely error" would in such a case not be a particularly meaningful estimate. Because of this fact, many practitioners using the direct extension method treat their conclusions as a form of *hypothesis testing* rather than *error estimation*. Thus, if the reported book value falls in a sample precision range related to materiality they accept the hypothesis that the book figure is correct. If errors found throughout the audit are few and trivial, a series of such hypothesis tests (for inventory, receivables, fixed asset additions, etc.) may be quite reasonable. Where discovered errors are larger, however, there is a real possibility that fixed asset errors, while immaterial in themselves, breach materiality when combined with inventory errors and receivable errors. Individual hypotheses tests may not always lend themselves to an estimate of accumulated possible errors throughout the engagement.

A related property of the mean-per-unit approach is that the precision, and hence the extent of work, usually depends far more on the variability of the corrected book values than on the frequency or magnitude of any errors found. It may seem strange, when the auditor is essentially hunting for errors (or attempting to establish their absence), that his conclusions and the extent of his work should be so unrelated to the degree of accounting accuracy or inaccuracy observed. The foregoing points need not, however, preclude the application of the mean-per-unit method to audit tests, if suitably designed.

13.2.7 Variables sampling (stratified mean-per-unit method)

The mean-per-unit method generally requires the use of stratification. Typically, population item values cover a wide range (such as $1 to $20 000) and the variability is accordingly so high that useful precision ranges are not obtainable unless stratification is employed.[22]

One problem, however, is that this very stratification may give rise to risks similar to those discussed for the difference method. In a population stratum containing reported item values of $900 to $1 000, the precision range expressed by the auditor will be small (because the reported values are all close together), providing no individually large sample errors are found. Rigorously, however, the precision should be based on the variability of the *correct values* rather than the *reported values* throughout the population stratum. To assume that the precision can be based on reported values (corrected only for a few small sample errors discovered) is precisely to assume that there are no large errors in that population stratum – *which is assuming at the start what the auditor should be setting out to prove.*

A further problem is that, on occasion, a selected sample can be shown to have an excessive precision range (being a function of the particular book values in the sample) even before verification of the sample items is started. There is a temptation in such a case to discard the sample and draw again rather than verify the first sample which, even if it contains no errors, will lead to inconclusive results. Discarding and drawing again, however, raises statistical problems – it is equivalent to changing one's bet retroactively after a gambling loss. The preferable, though more costly, alternative is to extend the initial sample size in order to reduce the precision range.

It is again a simple matter to construct hypothetical populations containing infrequent but large errors (outliers) where the auditor would usually fail to detect a material error using the stratified mean-per-unit method. One such example is illustrated in 22.2.6. Similar results could arise in an unstratified population that happened to have very low variability – such as residential cable television receivables.

To reduce this problem it is wise to adopt certain protective measures:

a) Stipulate a minimum stratum sample size (some users stipulate 30) regardless of how small a size the variables formulas would otherwise have permitted – of course, this stipulation has an associated cost.
b) Avoid the temptation to discard samples which, prior to audit, have large precision projections – rather, sample extension may be required.
c) Use the method only when the risk of outliers can be considered remote.

Advocates of mean-per-unit methods argue that with the use of such protective measures, the risk of erroneous conclusions is not great enough to be of concern. Of course, where the risk of extreme outliers is considered to be significant, some alternative methods must be employed. Among sampling methods attributes plans may provide some protection against outliers – but only up to a specified limit, such as the reported book value of the item containing the error. Among non-sampling methods scrutiny, enquiry and analytical review procedures may be of assistance.

Although the writer has a preference for the convenience of the dollar-unit approach, the use of the mean-per-unit method combined with adequate protective measures can certainly be justified and is the preference of some practitioners. In addition, in *accounting applications*, where statistical sampling is being used by the client, or by the auditor as an accounting service, to establish accounting figures for a population for which no meaningful book values exist, the mean-per-unit method is the logical approach.

13.3 Dollar-unit sampling concepts

The general principle of dollar-unit sampling has been described briefly in terms of the definition of the sampling unit as an individual dollar. The example given (in 13.2.3) was for a sample of 50 fixed asset purchase invoices in which no errors were found. Here, the auditor has 95% confidence that at worst 6% (or 180 000) completely fictitious dollars might exist in the population. Each one of these 180 000 potentially incorrect dollar-units was assumed to be 100% overstated (that is, each such dollar-unit was assumed to belong to a 100% overstated invoice, such as one that should have been expensed). No such errors were found, but to be conservative the auditor assumed that these *worst* errors could exist – worst, assuming that no invoice could be overstated by more than 100% of its reported value.

13.3.1 Evaluation of sample errors

In practice, of course, the auditor may find, and must evaluate, some sample errors. Suppose he finds one error resulting from a $1 000 invoice which should have been expensed. It is logical then to consider each of the 1 000 dollar-units therein (including the dollar-unit selected therein for his sample) as being 100% overstated. Referring to the sampling table in Figure 13.d, the auditor could have 95% sampling confidence that there is not more than a 9.5% frequency of incorrect dollars among the 3 million individual dollars in the population 4.75 ÷ 50 = 9.5%,

i.e., that total fixed asset additions were not overstated by more than $285 000.

The upper error limit of $285 000 may be analyzed into the following components:

	A UEL factor	B Frequency for sample size 50 = A ÷ 50	C Value for a $3 000 000 population = B × $3 000 000
Basic precision	3.00	6.00%	$180 000
Most likely error	1.00	2.00%	60 000
Precision gap widening	.75	1.50%	45 000
Upper error limit	4.75	9.50%	$285 000

The *basic precision* of $180 000 corresponds to the precision (and upper error limit) that would have been obtained had no sample errors been found. The *most likely error* of $60 000 is the auditor's best estimate of the probable error in the population (not a very precise estimate, but still the most likely situation based on projecting his 2.00% sample error rate). The *precision gap widening* of $45 000 represents the amount by which the precision gap has now widened (from $180 000 to $225 000) as a result of finding one sample error.[23]

Since the values in column C above were obtained by dividing initially by the sample size (50) and then multiplying by the population value ($3 000 000), the calculation can be shortened by merely multiplying by the *average sampling interval* ($60 000):

	UEL factor	×	Average sampling interval	=	Dollar conclusion
Basic precision	3.00	×	$60 000	=	$180 000
Most likely error	1.00	×	60 000	=	60 000
Precision gap widening	.75	×	60 000	=	45 000
Upper error limit	4.75		60 000		$285 000

To facilitate this method of evaluation it is useful to retabulate the UEL factors from Figure 13.d in incremental form in terms of basic-precision and precision-gap-widening factors. Such a retabulation is presented in Figure 13.g.

Thus, for example, for 95% confidence the first few cumulative and incremental factors may be compared as follows:

Errors in sample	Cumulative factor per Figure 13.d	Increments	Portion of increments reflecting most likely error	Basic-precision and precision-gap-widening factors per Figure 13.g
0	3.00	3.00	—	3.00
1st	4.75	1.75	1.00	0.75
2nd	6.30	1.55	1.00	0.55
3rd	7.76	1.46	1.00	0.46

As explained in the following sections, the one page table of incremental factors in Figure 13.g may be used for all evaluations of sample errors, thus representing a considerable condensation from the multi-page tables frequently presented for audit use in sampling literature.

13.3.2 Tainted dollar evaluation

Of course, not all sample errors discovered by the auditor will turn out to be 100% errors as was the error in the $1 000 invoice above. For example, if a dollar-unit in our previous sample of 50 leads us to an

---

Attributes Evaluation Table (Incremental)

Basic-Precision and Precision-Gap-Widening Factors

Low confidence levels			Errors found in sample, ranked in declining tainting percentage	High confidence levels		
80%	85%	90%		95%	97.5%	99%
1.61	1.90	2.31	Basic precision	3.00	3.69	4.61
.39	.48	.58	1st	.75	.89	1.03
.28	.35	.44	2nd	.55	.65	.77
.24	.29	.36	3rd	.46	.54	.64
.21	.25	.31	4th	.40	.48	.56
.18	.23	.28	5th	.36	.42	.50
.17	.21	.26	6th	.33	.39	.47
.16	.19	.24	7th	.30	.37	.42
.14	.18	.22	8th	.29	.34	.41
.14	.17	.21	9th	.27	.32	.38
.14	.17	.20	10th	.26	.31	.36
.12	.15	.19	11th	.24	.28	.34
.12	.15	.19	12th	.24	.29	.34
.12	.14	.17	13th	.22	.27	.31
.11	.14	.17	14th	.22	.25	.31
.11	.13	.17	15th	.21	.26	.30
.10	.13	.16	16-20th	.21	.24	.29
.09	.11	.14	21-25th	.18	.21	.25
.08	.10	.13	26-30th	.16	.19	.23
.08	.09	.11	31-40th	.15	.18	.21
.07	.08	.10	41-50th	.13	.15	.18

Method of calculation (for dollar-unit sampling):
Total precision-gap-widening $ (PGW)
= average dollar sampling interval x PGW factor for 1st error
                              x tainting % for 1st error
                              + PGW factor for 2nd error
                              x tainting % for 2nd error

                     +   .   .   .
                        .   .

Source: Analysis of increments in the cumulative Poisson factors in Figure 13.d

Figure 13.g

invoice having a reported book value of $5 000, which upon subsequent investigation should have been correctly capitalized as $4 000, we clearly have a $1 000 error of overstatement. We may think of this $1 000 error of overstatement as being evenly distributed through the $5 000 book value, so that each dollar of reported book value can be considered "tainted" by 20%, including the dollar-unit selected therein.

We shall define the tainting, then, as the ratio of the error amount (whether overstatement or understatement) to the reported book value of the physical

unit (invoice) in which it occurred.

How is a 20%-tainted dollar-unit to be evaluated? In the previous section we observed that one 100%-tainted dollar-unit in the sample raised the upper limit from $180 000 up to $285 000 – an increase of $105 000. It is intuitive that the discovery instead of one 20%-tainted dollar-unit in the sample should raise the upper limit by only 20% of that increase ($21 000) – or, in other words, from $180 000 up to 201 000.[24] The two evaluations can be contrasted as follows:

| | | | Average | | If one 100%-tainted error | | | If one 20%-tainted error | | |
	UEL factor	×	sampling interval	×	Tainting percentage	=	Dollar conclusion	×	Tainting percentage	=	Dollar conclusion
Basic precision	3.00	×	$60 000	×	100%	=	$180 000	×	100%	=	$180 000
Most likely error	1.00	×	60 000	×	100%	=	60 000	×	20%	=	12 000
Precision gap widening	.75	×	60 000	×	100%	=	45 000	×	20%	=	9 000
Upper error limit	4.75		60 000				$285 000				$201 000

Evaluation of One Sample Error

Basic precision

It will be noted that in either case the *basic precision* has been priced at a tainting percentage of 100%. This pricing allows for the fact that 100% errors are still possible in the population whether or not any are found in the sample. It would be unreasonable to expect that the discovery of sample errors, however small, could ever lead to an upper error limit lower than that arising for an error-free sample ($180 000). Maintaining the basic precision at $180 000 establishes the floor we would intuitively expect. Sample errors will raise the final upper error limit higher than this floor – how much higher depends on the number and tainting percentages of the sample errors.

Most likely error

The *most likely error* of $12 000 is merely a projection of the sample error value rate found. One

20%-tainted error out of 50 sample items represents a 2% frequency of 20% errors or, in other words, a net value rate of 0.4% – which, in a $3 000 000 population projects to $12 000. Obviously the most likely error of $12 000 is only 20% of the most likely error when one 100%-tainted error is found.

Precision gap widening

The *precision gap widening* of $9 000 again represents the amount by which the total precision gap has increased as a result of finding one 20%-tainted error. It is similarly only 20% of the precision gap widening when one 100%-tainted error is found.

Extension to several sample errors

If, instead of merely finding one 20% sample error, the auditor had found three overstatement errors having 25%, 80% and 10% taintings, his evaluation would be:

	UEL component × factor		Tainting percentage	×	Average sampling interval	=	Dollar conclusion
Basic precision	3.00	×	100%	×	$60 000	=	$180 000
Most likely error							
• 1st error	1.00	×	80% = .80				
• 2nd error	1.00	×	25% = .25				
• 3rd error	1.00	×	10% = .10				
			1.15	×	60 000	=	69 000
Precision gap widening							
• 1st error	.75	×	80% = .60				
• 2nd error	.55	×	25% = .14				
• 3rd error	.46	×	10% = .05				
			.79	×	60 000	=	47 400
Upper error limit							$296 400

In making such an evaluation, sample errors *must be ranked in order of declining tainting percentage*. Since the precision-gap-widening factors decline for each successive error (as may be observed in Figure 13.g), such ranking produces the highest upper error limit of all possible sequences.[25]

Conservatism

As explained in Chapter 22 there is some degree of conservatism contained in upper error limits projected from tainted sample errors using the tainted dollar evaluation method just described. That is, at the chosen confidence level the upper error limit will be slightly overstated or, conversely, for the computed upper error limit the confidence level achieved will be really slightly higher than the level chosen. The degree of conservatism is seldom sufficient to cause difficulties in practice (in the form of significantly excess audit work). In the few cases where this conservatism might present problems, it is possible to eliminate much of it by the use of a cell-method of evaluation to which brief reference is made in 13.3.5.

13.3.3 Offsetting errors

Understatements as well as overstatements

The foregoing discussion of dollar-unit sample projections has been in terms of overstatements. Similar projections can and should also be made for understatements. Just as an overstatement equal to the reported value of a population item was defined as a 100% overstatement, so an understatement equal to such reported value would be analogously defined as a 100% understatement. For example, if a $500 account receivable should really be nil (i.e., it is fictitious), the error is a 100% overstatement; if it should really be $1 000, the error ($500) is a 100% understatement. In practice, it is common to find that the most frequent errors of either over – or understatement encountered are taintings of less than 100%. However, it will be obvious that with respect to understatements it is always possible that the population may contain understatement taintings exceeding 100% (e.g., a $500 account that should really be $2 000).

In some cases, of course, it is possible for overstatements to exceed a 100% tainting as well. For example, it may be that a reported $500 receivable balance should really be a credit balance of $200 (i.e., overstated $700, or 140% of the reported book value). In practical applications, assurance with respect to undisclosed credit balances is most usually obtained through non-sampling means (verification procedures for undisclosed liabilities), and accordingly for most sampling work 100% is the maximum tainting that need be assumed for overstatements. For understatements, however, the situation is somewhat different.

Risk of understatements

It is important to keep in mind that no sampling plan (statistical or judgmental) can be relied upon to detect a material error when it is confined to a few items understated by substantial multiples of their reported book values. The evaluation method for dollar-unit sampling just described provides protection against 100%-size haystack needles (which some sampling plans do not) but it does not provide complete protection against 200%-size needles.[26] Nor does any sampling plan provide protection against understatements caused by items completely missing from the population; of course, this latter situation is not a deficiency of sampling per se (100% examination of the population would be subject to this latter risk).

The fact that there are certain haystack-needle risks associated with understatements (which risks, like many other audit risks, can only be assessed judgmentally) does not mean that the auditor should abandon understatement projections when he is sampling. If the sample results themselves indicate a material upper limit for understatements, the auditor cannot ignore this evidence of error merely because there is some judgmental risk that things might be even worse. If you catch a 20-pound fish in your net it is illogical to throw it back again merely because there is some chance that an even larger one has already escaped. Rather, the auditor should make the most reasonable projections possible in the light of known circumstances while at the same time carefully assessing judgmentally the haystack-needle risks associated with any sampling for understatements. In addition, audit assurance may often be obtained by examing related "reciprocal" populations for overstatements. For example, understatements in December 31 payables may be often detected by testing for overstatements in payments expensed in January – though there still remains the risk of December payables being still unpaid at the end of January.

When basic precision is 'priced' at 100%, dollar-unit sampling is making the assumption that, on average, errors not found do not exceed the book values of population items in which they occur. In most audit situations this is a reasonable assumption to make because, on average, larger errors tend to occur in larger items and smaller errors in smaller items. Should the assumption be incorrect in a particular engagement, however, the true risk will exceed the stated sampling risk. Where there is reasonable evidence that the 100% assumption is incorrect, allowance can be made (with a related audit cost, of course) by pricing the basic precision at 200%, 300% or more or by including an additional physical-unit sample of the smaller book values. These adjustments are discussed in 13.4.3.

Combining overstatement and understatement projections

If both overstatement errors and understatement errors are to be projected from sample results a proper method of allowing for the offsetting effects must be considered. The following approach is suggested as the most suitable:

1. Compute separate projections of gross overstatements and gross understatements:
   - compute the most likely error and upper error limit of gross overstatements (ignoring understatements),
   - compute the most likely error and upper error limit of gross understatements (ignoring overstatements).
2. Net the two most likely error projections to arrive at the most likely net error.
3. Reduce each gross upper error limit by the gross most likely error in the opposite direction to arrive at the net upper error limits.

These rules are illustrated in the following example:

	Most likely errors	Upper error limits
Gross errors:		
• overstatements	10 000	30 000
• (understatements)	(8 000)	(25 000)
Net errors:		
• overstatements	2 000	22 000
• (understatements)		(15 000)

If receivables most likely contain $10 000 of gross overstatements and $8 000 of gross understatements, then the most likely net error is a $2 000 overstatement. If the gross upper error limit for overstatements in receivables is $30 000 but the most likely gross understatement is $8 000, then the *net* upper error limit for overstatements is $22 000 (just as it would have been had there been no understatements but instead a management entry correcting $8 000 of the projected overstatements).

It can be shown mathematically that the above approach provides a reasonably close approximation to rigorous (and more complex) computations in all but the most extreme situations (it is not recommended where the gross most likely error in either direction exceeds twice the materiality limit, particularly where, at the same time, taintings over 100% can occur.

It should be noted that it would be *invalid* (a) to net the sample errors themselves and project merely the net error onto the population, or (b) to net the two gross upper error limits to arrive at a net upper error limit.

13.3.4 Combining results of different samples

Provided that the same confidence level is appropriate to be used throughout, attribute sampling makes no assumption as to the homogeneity of the population being sampled or as to the location of errors therein.[27] Thus, if the auditor is using an *average sampling interval* of $60 000 (selecting one item on average every $60 000) throughout receivables, inventories, and fixed asset additions, it is perfectly valid to consider the three segments as forming one global population out of which one sample was drawn (using the same average sampling interval throughout). The combined sample errors for all segments can therefore be used to make combined projections (most likely errors and upper error limits) as to the global population. The same principle can also be extended to include sampled liability populations (such as deposit liabilities of a financial institution) *provided* that error direction is consistently defined. A consistent direction can be conveniently achieved by defining each error in terms of its overstating or understating effect on pre-tax income.

Thus, it is often possible to combine directly the sample results of all substantive statistical tests used throughout the audit. Of course, this does not prevent separate statistical conclusions also being drawn with respect to each of receivables, inventories, fixed assset additions, etc., taken in isolation. Sometimes, since these separate conclusions are usually available, it is convenient to use a simple approximation rule instead of recomputing the global projections (which would involve a reranking of the error taintings, etc.). The approximation rule is simply:

Dollar-unit sampling conclusions can be combined by considering the *basic precision* components to be concurrent and the *most likely error* and *precision-gap-widening* components to be additive.

An example of this rule is as follows:

	Basic precision (concurrent)	Most likely error (additive)	Precision gap widening (additive)	Upper error limit (cross-add of final components)
Receivables	$180 000	$54 000	$39 600	$273 600
Inventory	180 000	15 000	11 400	206 400
Combined	$180 000	$69 000	$51 000	$300 000

It is shown in 22.3.2 that this approximation rule is always slightly conservative – that is, it overstates the combined upper error limit if anything. It is always possible to eliminate this conservatism by making the global computations (involving reranking the errors, etc.) but in most engagements the differences are not significant enough to require this refinement.

Combination at different confidence levels

Of course, not all statistical tests in a given engagement will necessarily employ the same confidence level. The auditor may perhaps use an 80% confidence level for receivables where he has found excellent conditions of internal control and a 99% confidence level for inventories where he is aware of serious control weaknesses. It is suggested that the same approximation rule be applied in such cases to combine basic precision, most likely error and precision-gap-widening components each as computed at its appropriate confidence level.[28]

Combination of all audit results

The principles just discussed, together with the principles for projecting offsetting errors previously discussed, permit a convenient method of accumulating the projections of both net overstatements and net understatements arising throughout the various sampling applications in a given audit. This method is illustrated in the working paper example in Figure 16.g.

13.3.5 Cell-method evaluation

Later in this chapter a selection method known as *cell-method selection* is suggested. In cell-method selection the population is divided into constant-width cells and one random selection point taken within each cell. The *cell width*, in dollars, corresponds to the *average sampling interval* previously discussed. It can be shown mathematically that the tainted dollar evaluation method already described provides conservative (safe) projections of upper error limits[29]

whether the selection method used is unrestricted random sampling of dollar-units or cell-method sampling of dollar-units. Therefore, with cell-method selection, the evaluation methods previously described continue to be safe and convenient. At the same time, however, cell-method selection permits an alternative evaluation method to be used in those few cases where the conservatism in the regular tainted dollar projections is excessive (i.e., where it would otherwise lead to unnecessary additional audit work). *Cell-method evaluation* eliminates much of this conservatism.

A brief introduction to the theory of cell-method evaluation is given in 22.3.6. In this chapter it will suffice merely to quote an example. Assuming a desired confidence level of 95%, cell width of $60 000, and 3 sample errors of 60%, 15% and 8% taintings, cell method evaluation would yield an upper error limit of $229 800.[30] In contrast the previously described method of tainted dollar evaluation for the same sample results would have given $264 000. It can be seen that cell-method evaluation produces a lower upper error limit, having eliminated much of the conservatism in the regular tainted dollar evaluation method. Whether the difference is significant, bearing in mind the necessary imprecision in choosing materiality limits, will depend upon the particular engagement.

Suggested use

As a practical matter, the following procedures are suggested. Cell-method *selection* is suggested for use whenever dollar-unit sampling is used. In the many engagements where the upper error limits evaluated using the regular tainted dollar evaluation method do not (after allowing for management adjustments for known and most likely errors) breach materiality, the refinement of cell-method *evaluation* is unnecessary. In those few engagements where there is a significant breaching of materiality and where it appears possible that this breaching may merely be a result of conservatism in the regular evaluation method, the auditor may (before making a final decision as to the need for additional audit work) recompute upper error limits using cell-method evaluation.[31]

13.3.6 Advantages of dollar-unit sampling

The advantages of dollar-unit attributes sampling may, in the writer's view, be summarized briefly as follows:

1. It avoids the difficulties of converting classical attributes frequency conclusions into dollars while at the same time avoiding risks associated with reliance on variables estimates of standard deviations.
2. It does not require the use of a computer; most forms of variables sampling do. While many dollar-unit sampling selections are indeed computerized (simply because the population items themselves may be recorded in computerized files), many more remain on a manual basis.
3. It results in an efficient sample size. When the auditor employs dollar-unit sampling, stratification into numerous strata by value is not required since the same effects have been achieved automatically by the dollar-unit technique.
4. It solves the problem of the large needle in the haystack – by chopping up the needle into individual dollars which then occur with a sufficient frequency to be detected. Large errors clustered in a few large accounts, difficult to detect by other sampling methods, are easily detected by dollar-unit sampling.
5. Planning decisions, as explained later, result in determination of an appropriate average sampling interval in dollars rather than an absolute sample size. This permits sample selection to be started even before the total value of the final population is known – a procedure which is particularly convenient during the interim audit or in use by internal auditors on a continuous basis.
6. Because it provides direct projections of most likely and possible errors, it permits an integration of sampling and other conclusions throughout an individual engagement. (Variables sampling does not always lend itself as easily to the accumulation of projected errors on related tests.)
7. It is consistent with rough rule-of-thumb guidelines which can be developed to aid practitioners in determining approximate sample sizes where judgmental testing is appropriate (as suggested in Chapter 12). This in turn permits a measure of consistency to be achieved between judgmental and statistical sample extents used by the same practitioner on different tests. Such consistency is not generally possible with variables sampling.
8. It results in the required extent of audit work being related to the relative accuracy of the client's records. Error-free accounts can be sampled more cheaply than error-laden accounts. This is a reasonable and defensible relationship. (With variables sampling the required extent depends on factors such as item-to-item variability in size, unrelated to the accuracy of the accounts.)
9. Finally, dollar-unit sampling is, in the writer's view, considerably easier to teach to audit staff. The sampling mechanics, concepts and evaluation methods are relatively simple. Procedures for optimum stratification, stratified evaluation, and standard deviation computations are not involved.

It is only fair to add that the advocates of other sampling plans may not agree with all of the foregoing points and may urge additional points in support of their preferences. Absolute truth seems elusive in this field. In the end, each practitioner or firm must make a judgment as to which arguments appear persuasive.

The application of dollar-unit sampling techniques in practice is reviewed in the remaining sections of this chapter.

13.4 Application of dollar-unit sampling to substantive tests

The use of representative sampling for substantive tests has already been described in Chapter 12. Included there was a discussion of error and population definition, degree of assurance, determination of sample extent, selection method, and evaluation (see 12.5). Most of these points continue to apply when the representative sampling is done statistically. The following sections discuss only the additional points which arise with the introduction of statistical methods.

13.4.1 Error definition

With respect to error definition, no additional points arise with the introduction of statistical methods. The points discussed in 12.5.1 for all representative tests remain equally important. Moreover, the definition there given of sample errors in terms of income overstatements and income understatements is essential if the method of combining statistical samples from assets, liabilities and income components described in this chapter is to be applied.

13.4.2 Definition of population and physical-unit

With respect to population definition, the points discussed in 12.5.2 continue to apply. When dollar-unit sampling is applied it is often convenient to define a population, such as accounts receivable, to include related balances, such as miscellaneous and employee receivables. In this way, one average sampling interval can be extended throughout the whole set of accounts without undue time being wasted on the sundry balances in isolation. However, where the sundry balances are subject to a higher degree of risk they may require segmentation so that a higher level of sampling confidence can be used for them (see 13.4.5).

With respect to the physical-unit to be verified, however, it is necessary in dollar-unit sampling to decide on a definition in advance of verification. Although in statistical terms the *sampling unit* in dollar-unit sampling is an individual dollar, it has already been explained that each selected dollar acts as a hook to fish out a particular physical-unit (account balance, invoice, etc.) for verification. If the 753rd dollar in a particular fixed asset work order has been selected, possible physical-units to be verified might be the entire work order, the whole material or labour component in which the dollar falls, or the particular fixed asset purchase invoice in which the dollar falls. Generally, the auditor should choose whichever of these physical-units can be most economically verified to yield persuasive evidence related to the audit objective. For example, verification of an invoice payable does not yield persuasive evidence that other unrecorded liabilities to that same supplier do not exist. In this case, supplier account balance is a more appropriate choice of physical unit. On the other hand, the risk of undisclosed invoices receivable is not normally very great.[32] Accordingly, open invoice receivable can be an appropriate choice of physical-unit for receivable confirmation. Since the choice will affect the book value involved, the computation of the tainting percentage of any error discovered and hence the sampling conclusion, the choice should be made in advance of verification in order to avoid bias.

Application to accounts receivable open-item confirmation

In some cases (the most common being accounts receivable), the definition of physical-unit may occasionally be changed *after* sample selection but *before* final verification. In 33.4.2 the suggested method for receivable confirmation is a combination of account-balance and open-item confirmation –

sometimes with the use of an either/or type of confirmation request. Dollar-unit sampling may be readily applied to this method. In effect, dollar-units are selected from the population of receivable account balances. The account balances in which the selected dollars fall determine the customers from whom confirmation is to be requested. If confirmation of the whole account balance is possible, such confirmation will, of course, verify the selected dollar-unit at the same time. If confirmation of the whole account balance is not possible (because it appears unlikely from the outset, or because the customer refuses a request for balance confirmation, or because the customer chooses the open invoice option offered in an either/or request), the auditor may change his definition of physical-unit to be the open invoice in which the selected dollar fell. This is perfectly valid because verification of the account balance has not as yet been effected. If the open invoice is now confirmed (or, failing response, verified by alternative verification), the originally selected dollar-unit will finally have been verified. Where a customer, in replying to an either/or confirmation request, happens to confirm the accuracy or inaccuracy of *both* the account balance and the open invoice, the auditor should generally decide *in advance* that the account balance will be considered as the physical-unit.

Treatment of debit and credit physical-units

In some cases (the most common being accounts receivable), both debit and credit physical-units occur. The debits and credits can be considered to be asset and liability populations which happen to be intermingled. Using the rationale previously discussed for drawing a global sample out of the separate asset and liability populations, it follows that an appropriate dollar-unit sample can be selected from an intermingled population by adding through all physical-units regardless of sign (debit or credit). Thus, in those few cases where computerized accounting records provide an open-item analysis of each receivable account, a dollar-unit sample can be selected from the grossed-up population (debit items plus credit items) at the outset.

In the more common case, the auditor must make his initial dollar-unit selections from a population of net account balances (grossed-up only to the extent that both debit and credit net balances occur). He may then wish to convert a few of the selected accounts to an open-invoice basis. When he does so, any selected accounts containing both open invoices and open credits will required special treatment.

For example, suppose a $1 000 net balance is composed of $1 500 open invoices and $500 open credits (totalling

355

$2\,000$ on a gross basis). If it is now desired to change the definition of physical-unit from account balance to open item, only the first $1\,000$ dollar-units in the grossed-up total of $2\,000$ have so far had a chance of selection. To give the second $1\,000$ dollar-units an equal chance of selection it is necessary to choose randomly one further selection point among the second $1\,000$ dollar-units.

In general, to the extent that the grossed-up total of an account exceeds its net book value, each dollar-unit in the excess should be given a chance of selection equal to $1 \div$ net book value if the account is to be converted to an open-item selection basis.

13.4.3 Sample type and error size-limit

Explicit decisions as to error size-limit are required with the introduction of statistical techniques (although the same decisions are implicit in all representative tests). In the dollar-unit rationale discussed earlier in this chapter it was argued that it was reasonable to assume, in most applications, that population errors could not often, or significantly, exceed the reported book value of the physical unit in which they occur. This may be stated explicitly as an *error size-limit assumption* of 100%. Where such an assumption is reasonable, basic precision should be priced at a 100% tainting – as illustrated in all the previous examples. Certainly the assumption is safe for most overstatements (a $200 invoice cannot be overstated by more than $200). Indeed, *in a few cases*, it may be appropriate to lower this error size-limit assumption (say, to 50% or 25%) *provided that* internal control or overlapping audit procedures can be relied upon to prevent or detect errors larger than such fraction of the book value. For example, low error size-limit assumptions may be justified in confirming mortgages receivable carried forward from prior years provided that reasonable assurance is available from other sources that there have been no undisclosed principal prepayments. Of course, the continued reasonableness of any error size-limit assumption must be carefully considered should larger errors be observed in the sample results (or in prior years' sample results).

Protection against understatements

As already discussed, all sampling plans are exposed to the risk of large understatements. With basic precision priced at a 100% tainting, dollar-unit sampling does provide protection against understatements up to a certain size (such as a $5\,000$ book value that really should be $10\,000$) – which some other sampling plans do not. In *rare* cases, an error size-limit assumption of 200% or more may be appropriate if larger understatement taintings are considered reasonably possible.

Another method, however, of providing protection against understatements may be more efficient. In the few cases where a serious risk of larger understatement taintings exists, the greater portion of the risk may be confined to the smaller reported book values. Protection against this risk may be obtained by forming a *lower physical-unit stratum* in which all items are given an equal chance of selection (proportional to the upper boundary of this stratum) regardless of how small their reported book values may be. In choosing a stratum boundary of, say, $500, the auditor is in effect assuming that items with book values $500 or under could scarcely contain errors of more than $500 (another form of error size-limit assumption). Such a lower physical-unit stratum can be conveniently integrated into dollar-unit sampling selection merely by *deeming* all items under $500 (including items of nil value) to have a $500 value when adding through the population to pick one selection point within each cell-width.

It is important that the regular dollar-unit sampling be continued above this stratum boundary. It would be dangerous to abandon large item selections by concentrating exclusively on the small items. Of course, there is a cost in adding such a lower stratum to a dollar-unit sample and the auditor will want to be satisfied that the risk of a *material total* of understatement errors consisting exclusively of taintings over 100% is sufficient to justify the increased sample extent. In the majority of audit applications, the writer believes that the risk of a material total of taintings over 100% is too remote to justify this cost. However, just as it was possible to construct hypothetical populations where variables methods without protective measures were subject to problems (see 13.2.5 and 13.2.7), so it is possible to construct a hypothetical population containing taintings over 100% (or over the auditor's error size-limit assumption) where dollar-unit sampling is subject to problems if a lower physical-unit stratum is not taken.

13.4.4 Precision objectives

Explicit decisions as to precision objectives are required with the introduction of statistical techniques (similar decisions are implicit though not quantifiable in judgmental representative tests). Precision objectives can be defined in various ways. Indeed, the source of much controversy as to statistical audit sampling methods stems not from mathematical issues but from differing views on the appropriateness of various precision objectives to the auditor's needs.

Alternative Precision Objectives

A. Precision gap to be reasonably small relative to the most likely error projected (a result common in difference and ratio variables sampling)

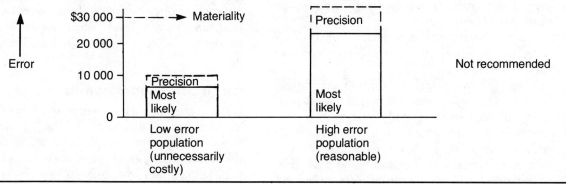

B. Precision gap to be a constant size regardless of the most likely error projected (a result common in mean-per-unit variables sampling)

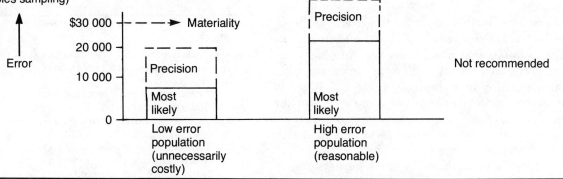

C. Precision gap to vary so as to maintain an upper error limit equal to materiality (possible in dollar-unit sampling but not recommended)

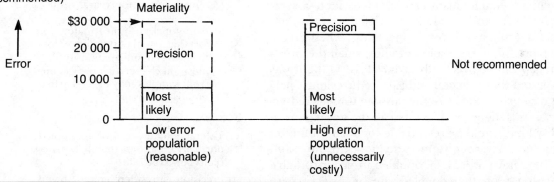

D. Precision gap to vary so as to maintain an upper error limit equal to materiality in most cases but subject to a minimum precision gap of half materiality (possible in dollar-unit sampling and recommended)

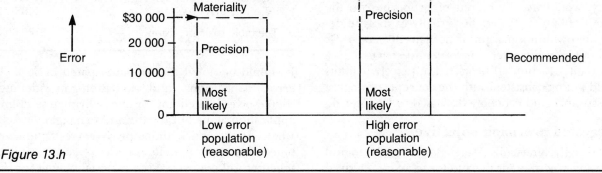

Figure 13.h

357

Alternative precision objectives

In theory the auditor could choose his desired precision gap in dollars to be:

A. reasonably small relative to the most likely error projected (a result common in difference and ratio variables sampling),

B. a constant size regardless of the most likely error projected (a result common in mean-per-unit variables sampling),

C. varying so as to maintain an upper error limit equal to materiality (possible in dollar-unit sampling but not recommended),

D. varying so as to maintain an upper error limit equal to materiality in most cases but subject to a minimum precision gap of half materiality (possible in dollar-unit sampling and recommended).

These four alternative choices are illustrated in Figure 13.h.

Remembering that the smaller the precision gap is, the larger are the sample size and audit cost, the writer submits that it is unnecessary to obtain any precision which results in an upper error limit less than materiality (as in alternatives A and B). When all the auditor wants is reasonable assurance that the financial statements are not misstated to a material extent, it seems inappropriate to incur and charge the cost of proving more.

Alternative C, on the other hand, permits organizations whose financial statements contain few or no errors to be audited more cheaply than those whose statements contain many errors. It is easier to assemble sufficient audit evidence that the former do not contain a material error. Nonetheless, when errors are plentiful, there is a limit to how small the precision gap can be practically reduced. In 11.3.2 it was suggested that practical audit procedures must permit a *minimum allowance* for possible undetected errors. It was suggested that one-half the normal materiality limit would be reasonable for such minimum allowance. As a rough approximation, attribute sample sizes must at least be doubled in order to halve precision (more than doubled when many errors are found). To double the sample size, in order to reduce the precision from $1/2$ materiality down to $1/4$ materiality, would usually be out of proportion to the benefit obtained. Materiality usually cannot be determined within a margin of perhaps 30% or 40%. To double audit extents in order to shave a 25% materiality fraction off projected upper error limits would not be consistent with the concepts of degree of assurance and economy discussed in Chapter 6.

Suggested precision objective

Accordingly, alternative D is suggested as the logical precision objective for the auditor to adopt. Desired precision should be chosen so as to maintain an upper error limit equal to materiality in most cases but subject to a minimum precision gap of half materiality. This alternative is consistent with the objective of substantive verification discussed earlier in this book. Since viewpoints differ on this matter, however, the practitioner must decide which precision objective is consistent with the overall objective of his own auditing.

Audit precision planning

If the precision objective suggested above is adopted, the auditor can estimate his 'tolerable basic precision' (needed in planning sample size) by subtracting from dollar materiality an estimate of the most likely error projections and precision-gap-widenings anticipated. This estimate is illustrated in the following example:

a) Materiality limit for this engagement	$300 000
b) Most likely error conclusions anticipated for the audit as a whole (net of client corrections)	
i) Actual population errors (after deducting anticipated client provisions or corrections) which, prior to beginning the audit, the auditor believes most probably exist, distorting the reported income figure (net overstatement or net understatement, whichever is greater) based on system knowledge, prior years' results, etc.	50 000
ii) Additional cushion to allow for fact that actual population errors may exceed anticipation in (i) most likely error projections from samples may exceed actual population errors	20 000
	70 000
c) Tolerable total precision gap (need normally not be less than half materiality, or $150 000)	230 000
d) Precision-gap-widening anticipated for the audit as a whole on the basis of past experience (depends on average size of taintings and degree of offsetting errors)	50 000
e) Tolerable basic precision	$180 000

It should be noted that the anticipated most likely error conclusions and precision-gap-widenings should be estimated not for one individual sampling application alone but for the audit engagement as a whole. If the anticipations prove correct, the combined upper error limit for all applications taken together will not exceed the materiality limit for the engagement. In the above example, the tolerable basic precision of \$180 000, in conjunction with other planning decisions, can then be used to compute required sample sizes (or, more simply, the required average sampling interval) for all statistical sampling applications throughout the particular engagement. The cushion illustrated in the above calculation is discussed in 13.4.7.

In anticipating net most likely errors, estimated client corrections will have a substantial effect. If the client agrees to correct all known errors encountered and provide for all most likely errors projected as a result of the audit, a much larger basic precision can be tolerated and correspondingly smaller sample sizes used.

In anticipating precision-gap-widening the size and direction of anticipated errors must be considered. Where a few large errors (50% to 100% taintings) are historically common, precision-gap-widening may amount to some significant fraction of most likely errors as in the foregoing example (the factors towards the top of Figure 13.g will give some indication[33]). In the many engagements where errors, whether or not numerous, can all be expected to have small taintings, the precision-gap-widenings will be a much smaller fraction of most likely errors, or even negligible. In the few applications where numberous errors in both directions can be anticipated (e.g., some inventory applications), larger precision-gap-widenings should be allowed for.

In many audits where dollar-unit sampling is employed, the foregoing considerations mean that tolerable basic precision need be set no lower than half materiality and may, where few uncorrected errors are anticipated, be set somewhere between half and full materiality (with a resulting reduction in sample size).

13.4.5 Confidence level

With respect to confidence level (degree of assurance), no new concepts arise with the introduction of statistical methods that have not already been discussed in the previous chapter for all representative tests. The factors influencing the choice of confidence level, described in 12.5.3, remain equally important. The only difference is that statistical methods permit precise confidence levels to be specified (80%, 95%, etc.) rather than merely judgmentally graded ones such as minimum, normal, or considerable.

In choosing what precise confidence level to specify, a practitioner must first decide what permissible range of confidence levels is rational to con-

sider. It is important to remember that sampling confidence is only one component of total audit assurance. Other components come from the inherent nature of the population under audit, the strength of internal control, and the evidence from overlapping audit procedures. Bearing this in mind, together with the discussion in Chapter 6, it seems reasonable to conclude that sampling confidence levels need never be greater than 99% and often can be significantly lower.

In statistical terms, the other sources of assurance apart from the auditor's sampling conclusion, can be described as *prior probabilities*. The prior probabilities thus include the probabilities that (a) error did not occur in the first place, (b) internal control would have prevented or detected it anyway, and (c) overlapping audit procedures would have detected it. These prior probabilities, when combined with reasonable sampling confidence, should yield a high *posterior probability* that no material error is present.[34]

It follows that an auditor who uses a sampling confidence of 90%, will not be signing erroneous audit reports 10% of the time. When there is reasonable evidence of favourable prior probabilities (good internal control, etc., as assessed during the interim audit), sampling confidence of 90% will yield a far higher posterior probability (probably 99% or more – in which case erroneous audit conclusions will only occur 1% of the time or less). When prior probabilities are even more favourable (excellent internal control), even lower sampling confidence (such as 80%) will still yield the same consistently high posterior probability of no material error. Conversely, when prior probabilities are less favourable, higher sampling confidence (such as 99%) will be needed to retain the desired posterior probability of no material error.

How low can sampling confidence appropriately be? In mathematical theory there is no lower limit. For any set of prior probabilities one cares to assume, one can compute mathematically the sampling confidence required to obtain any specified level of posterior probability. Theoretically, there could be situations where the prior probabilities were so good that only 20% sampling confidence was required. In practical terms, however, such an extreme would not make sense. It must be realized that evidence as to favourable prior probabilities, such as internal control, is necessarily subjective and imprecise. There should be a limit to the amount of reliance the auditor should place on such subjective and imprecise evidence. Were there no such limit, the whole financial statement audit could be eliminated under conditions of excellent internal control. Stated another way, there should be a minimum level below which the sampling confidence for a substantive test should not be reduced, however excellent the apparent system of control and however low the indicated frequencies of compliance deviations.

Decision as to minimum confidence level

Various auditors will differ on what they feel this minimum level of sampling confidence should be; various levels advocated have been 50%, 60%, and 80%. In the writer's view, a minimum level of 80% would be about the right choice for the following reasons. The auditor should not place so much reliance on prior probabilities as to reduce his sampling confidence to trivial proportions. If the risk of error is really so slight that one needs only a 50:50 chance of catching it in a given audit test, it can be questioned whether that particular audit test is really necessary. To some extent the auditor has the worst of both worlds if he admits the seriousness of the risk of error by planning a particular audit test in the first place, but then uses a confidence level with a very low chance of catching the error. (It would not be very logical for the tightrope walker to use a thin string as a safety strap merely because he is fairly sure he will not fall anyway; if he is sure enough, he needs no safety strap at all; if not, he needs more than a thin string.)

In the end, however, *The auditor must make his own decision as to what confidence level in his professional judgment, is sufficient to meet generally accepted auditing standards.*

Guidelines as to choice of confidence level

Based on the premise of an 80% to 99% range of possible confidence levels, the guidelines shown in Figure 13.i are suggested as a guide to judgment in selecting the specific confidence level appropriate for a particular test.

Because such guidelines can only be treated as a guide to and not as a substitute for judgment, and because human judgment is subjective and will vary from auditor to auditor, one might worry that discrepancies in the judgmental choice of confidence level would destroy the whole purpose of adopting rigorous statistical techniques. If sample sizes could vary by several orders of magnitude depending on

---

Guidelines for Choice of Confidence Level

Conditions requiring 99% or 97.5% confidence (considerable)	Conditions indicating 95% confidence (normal-high)
Several (or sometimes even one) of the following:	Either the following:
1. High overall level of audit assurance required —great sensitivity and/or low testing cost	1. High overall level of audit assurance required —great sensitivity and/or low testing cost
2. High inherent risk of error —nature of item susceptible to error —errors found this year or in prior years were frequent, material in value, and/or serious in nature —current industry or economic conditions suggest high inherent risk	2. High or moderate inherent risk of error —nature of item susceptible to error —some errors found this year or in prior years
3. High control risk —key controls non-existent, ineffective or not relied upon or serious compliance deviations found —no internal audit involvement —recent major systems change.	3. Usually moderate control risk —considerable reliance placed on adequate key controls with acceptable results from compliance verification —but can be high control risk (poor control) if low inherent risk of error or great assurance from overlapping audit procedures
4. Low assurance from overlapping audit procedures.	4. Usually some assurance from overlapping audit procedures.
	Or the following:
	1. Low overall level of audit assurance required —low sensitivity and/or unusually high testing cost
	2. Moderate or high inherent risk of error —nature of item susceptible to error —some errors found this year or in prior years
	3. High control risk —key controls non-existent, ineffective or not relied upon or serious compliance deviations found
	4. Usually some assurance from overlapping audit procedures.

Figure 13.i

360

the choice of confidence level this worry would be justified. However, the relationship between confidence level and sample size is such that if a certain sample size were required for 95% confidence, then to achieve instead 99% confidence the sample size would have to be increased by about 50% whereas to achieve instead 80% confidence the sample could be reduced by about 50%. No one could pretend that confidence levels can be chosen objectively to within one or two percentage points. Nonetheless, it should be possible to distinguish between very high confidence and very low confidence with reasonable objectivity. Accordingly, while planned sample sizes cannot be viewed as being perfectly precise determinations, within a reasonable margin (perhaps 10% or 20% or so) they should be able to be objectively determined.

Segmentation

Sometimes one level of confidence is not appropriate for the whole population. For example, in confirming mortgages receivable in a given engagement it might be appropriate to sample new mortgages writ-

ten during the year, and never before tested, with a 95% confidence while older mortgages, carried forward from prior years and supported by the accumulated assurance from prior years' tests, might warrant a lower confidence level such as 80%. In such situations the auditor should divide the population into two segments, sampling more intensively from one segment and less intensively from the other.

13.4.6 Top stratum cut-off

It has been stated that stratification into numerous strata is unnecessary in dollar-unit sampling because the same effects are achieved automatically. Nonetheless, as a practical matter, one simple form of stratification is suggested: a 100% top stratum (the largest items) in which all items will be verified 100%. This is really nothing other than *high-value selection*, which, as suggested in Chapter 12, should usually accompany any form of representative testing.

Wher dollar-unit selections are being made by the cell-method (for example, selecting one random point in each cell-width of $50 000), it will be obvious

Conditions indicating 85% or 90% confidence (normal-low)	Conditions permitting 80% confidence (minimum)
Either the following: 1. High overall level of audit assurance required —great sensitivity and/or low testing cost 2. Usually moderate inherent risk of error —some susceptibility to error —some small errors found this year or in prior years 3. Usually low control risk —considerable reliance placed on good key controls with good results from compliance verification —conclusion will be helped by an effective internal audit program —no recent major systems change 4. Moderate assurance from overlapping audit procedures. Or the following: 1. Low overall level of audit assurance required —low sensitivity and/or usually high testing cost 2. Usually moderate inherent risk of error —some susceptibility to error —some small errors found this year or in prior years 3. Usually moderate control risk —considerable reliance placed on adequate key controls with acceptable results from compliance verification —but can be high control risk (poor control) if low inherent risk of error or great assurance from overlapping audit procedures 4. Usually moderate assurance from overlapping audit procedures.	Generally the following: 1. High or low overall level of audit assurance required —if high level required (i.e., great sensitivity and/ or low testing cost) the following factors must be at favourable end of range —if low level sufficient (i.e., low sensitivity and/or unusually high testing cost) the following factors may be at less favourable end of range 2. Usually low inherent risk of error —usually little susceptibility to error —usually errors, if any, found this year or in prior years were few, trivial in projected value, and not serious in nature 3. Low or very low control risk —considerable reliance placed on good or very good key controls with good results from compliance verification —conclusion will be helped by an effective internal audit program —no recent major systems change 4. Moderate or great assurance from overlapping audit procedures.

Figure 13.i (concluded)

that items over \$50 000 would usually be selected in any case. Nonetheless, it will normally simplify the selection and the subsequent evaluation if all items over \$50 000 are first removed from the population as a separate top stratum and the remainder of the population then subjected to regular dollar-unit sampling. The *top stratum cut-off* should thus generally be set equal to the sampling cell-width or average sampling interval.

13.4.7 Determination of sample extent

Whereas in judgmental representative testing sample extent can only be chosen judgmentally (though the choice can be guided by the rule-of-thumb guidelines discussed in Chapter 12, with the introduction of statistical methods an objective determination is possible. First the "tolerable basic precision" should be determined, the appropriate error size-limit assumption made (usually 100%), and the desired confidence level (and related basic precision factor from Figure 13.g) chosen, all as discussed in previous sections. The required average sampling interval (or cell-width) can then be computed from the following formula:[35]

Average sampling interval equals:

$$\frac{\text{Tolerable basic precision in dollars}}{\text{Basic precision factor} \times \text{Error size-limit assumption}}$$

For instance, using the tolerable basic precision of \$180 000 as calculated in the sample in 13.4.4 (and based on \$300 000 materiality), making an error size-limit assumption of 100%, and choosing a desired confidence level of 95% (for which the related basic precision factor in Figure 13.g is 3.00), the required average sampling interval (cell width) would be:

$$\frac{\$180\,000}{3.00 \times 100\%} = \$60\,000$$

Once the required average sampling interval is known, sample size will depend directly on population size (after removing top-stratum and key-item selections). For example, if the same sampling interval of \$60 000 is being used throughout \$12 000 000 accounts receivable and \$6 000 000 fixed asset additions (assuming the same confidence level is appropriate for both), the sample size for receivables (200) will be twice that for fixed assets (100). This is, of course, logical since the receivables are twice as big. Thus, dollar-unit sampling results in a rational allocation of audit effort over the various financial statement figures to be audited. Moreover, by expressing required sampling extents in terms of sampling intervals it permits sample selection to be started even when, as frequently happens, the total

value of the final population will not be known until later in the audit. This advantage is particularly important, for example, when substantive tests applied to transaction streams are being started during the interim audit. Indeed selections can be made routinely month by month for subsequent verification at the auditor's convenience.[36]

Dependence upon anticipated errors

The foregoing basis of sample size planning is dependent, as is any method of sample size planning, on the outcome of the final sample results. If the anticipated most likely error conclusions and precision gap widenings allowed for in determining tolerable basic precision are borne out by the sample results, an adequate sample size will have been achieved. For instance, in the foregoing example with materiality of \$300 000 and an average sampling interval of \$60 000, suppose that in total one 80%, one 25%, and one 10% errors are found; the evaluation will turn out to be:

	Planned	Actual[37]
Basic precision	\$180 000	\$180 000
Most likely error	70 000	69 000
Precision gap widening	50 000	47 000
Upper error limit	\$300 000	\$296 400

Since the actual upper error limit does not exceed materiality, an adequate sample size has been obtained to support an audit opinion that the financial statements are not materially misstated.

If the final sample results indicate most likely errors exceeding \$70 000 (though still less than materiality) the final upper error limit may exceed materiality and, unless the client corrects or provides for the most likely errors in the accounts, the auditor will not have done sufficient work to support an audit opinion that the financial statements are not materially misstated. In retrospect he should have selected a larger sample (smaller sampling interval) to start with; but he can remedy his forecasting error by extending his sample size now. Sample extension is discussed in a later section.

Conservative planning assumptions

Because of the dependence of planned sample size on anticipated most likely error conclusions, it is desirable for the auditor to be conservative (i.e. slightly pessimistic) in his planning assumptions. Referring back to the planning computation of tolerable basic precision in 13.4.4, it will be noted that the auditor's best guess (based on other evidence, past experience, etc.) of the actual population errors existing is \$50 000. Certainly he must allow for at least that amount in his sample size planning. It would be invalid to take a discovery sample (the minimum possible size) hoping to be "lucky" and to not find any sample errors. That would be hoping to be deceived by the sample – if he really believes at the outset that $50 000 errors exist.

But, if this is really his best guess, is allowing for $50 000 enough? The answer is no for two reasons. First, any advance guess as to population errors is necessarily imprecise. Reasonable deviations from his best guess should be allowed for. Second, a population error of $50 000, does not mean that his sample results will yield a most likely error projection of exactly $50 000. Although such a conclusion would, of course, be the *most* probable (if the underlying population error really were $50 000), projections of $40 000 or $60 000 would also be *fairly* probable merely due to sample "bounce". Some reasonable allowance for sample bounce should therefore be made as well.

These two reasons indicate the need for an additional "cushion" in the auditor's planning assumption. In the foregoing example the cushion provided was $20 000, and thus the total allowance made for most likely error projections amounted to $70 000. In retrospect this cushion proved its worth, for the actual projection of most likely errors (illustrated above) turned out to be $69 000. Whether this $69 000 represents an accurate estimate of a population really containing $69 000 error (in which case his cushion was needed for the first reason) or whether it represents an over-estimate, due to sample bounce, of a population really containing $50 000 error (in which case his cushion was needed for the second reason) the auditor will never know. What he does know, however, is that he can be 95% sure that he would have detected errors exceeding $296 400 had they been present – and because this limit is less than materiality an audit conclusion as to fair presentation (at least in this respect) is warranted.

The choice of an appropriate "cushion" must be made by the exercise of judgment. While it is possible to determine statistically the size of the cushion required for the second factor (to restrict the risk of sample bounce to any desired, specified level) no such precise determination can be made for the first factor (the risk of anticipating a lower population error rate than really exists). As a practical matter, the writer doubts that any precise analysis of the sample-bounce component of the cushion is useful when it may often be over-shadowed by the population-misforecast component. Indeed, many auditors would find it difficult to distinguish between unconscious pessimism built into their forecast of the $50 000 and the separate additional cushion of $20 000. In effect, the auditor in his planning deci-

sion is anticipating that the most likely error projections will not exceed $70 000 and that, if they do, he will be prepared to extend his sample size.

A few generalizations, however, are possible about the size of the planning cushion needed. One is that, if the auditor really believes that many 100%-tainted errors exist in the population, he should be prepared to tolerate at least one (and perhaps more) in his sample. In the previous example, the planned average sampling interval was $60 000. If one 100%-error were to be found in the sample this in itself would immediately yield a $60 000 most likely error projection. Thus, if many 100%-errors are believed to exist it would be inconsistent for the allowance for most likely error projections to be less than $60 000. The $70 000 allowance in the foregoing example meets this condition. Of course, in some applications 100% errors may be judged sufficiently unlikely that the auditor can ignore this condition in his sample size planning, knowing, however, that if he later encounters one in his sample he will have to extend his sample size.

Avoidance of excessive conservatism in planning

If the auditor is reasonably conservative in his planning assumptions, he will probably reach acceptable conclusions on most engagements (provided an acceptable conclusion is warranted) and only have to resort to sample extension in a few. Excessive conservatism in planning should be avoided, however, as it results in needlessly large sample extents on most engagements merely to forestall unpleasant surprises on the few.

13.4.8 Selection method

The need for unbiased selection for any representative test was discussed in Chapter 12. With the introduction of statistical methods this need must be met more rigorously – by employing random selection techniques.

Random numbers

Random selection requires, in turn, the use of *random numbers*. Random numbers can be obtained from published *random number tales* or, in computerized systems, through the use of *random number generators*.

A small extract from a set of random number tables is shown in Figure 13.j. The random digits are grouped in fours by column purely for convenience. To select a series of random numbers the auditor would take a random start in the table and then read down the column (actually, in any *pre-defined* direction). Thus, a series of 3-digit random numbers might begin 038, 594, 526, 991 . . . as marked.

Extract from Random Number Tables

Column No. → 01	02	03	04	05 . . .
Row No.				
0246 2185	9765	5796	9095	0469
0247 1637	7939	2831	0385	1060
0248 9895	8140	6582	5946	4249
0249 7741	5415	2579	5262	2526
0250 8303	3420	1586	9915	3367

Source: Herbert Arkin, *Handbook of Sampling for Auditing and Accounting*, 2nd Ed. (McGraw-Hill, 1974) Appendix A, page 224.

Figure 13.j

Various selection techniques

Using random numbers, in one form or another, various techniques for making a random selection of dollar-units are possible. Those discussed briefly below are:

1. unrestricted random selection,
2. varying interval selection,
3. fixed interval selection,
4. cell-method selection.

The first and second are rigorous but a little cumbersome. The fourth is rigorous and also convenient; it is suggested here as the desirable method. The third method is a convenient approximation to the others and is also a reasonable method to employ.[38]

Unrestricted random dollar-unit sample

Suppose the auditor wishes to select a random sample of 50 dollar-units out a $3 000 000 population. He could take, after a random start in a set of random number tables, the first 50 7-digit random numbers falling in the range 1 to 3 000 000 (random numbers over 3 000 000 would merely be ignored). Each of these 50 numbers would then represent one of the 3 000 000 dollar-units in the population (counting from the beginning). To facilitate location of each selected dollar, the 50 random numbers could then be sorted into ascending order and the intervals between successive sequenced numbers computed. The resulting 50 sampling intervals (which, of course, will average to $60 000) would indicate the successive distances which the auditor must add through the population to arrive at each successive dollar-unit

selection point. Each of the $3 000 000 dollar-units has had an equal chance of selection and each selection point is independent of the location of other selection points. Such a selection method yields an *unrestricted random dollar-unit sample*. The tainted dollar evaluation method described in 13.3.2 can be applied to such a sample.

There are a few practical disadvantages to this selection method, however. The first is the minor nuisance of having to sort the selected random numbers. The second and more important is the need to know the population value accurately before selection can begin (often this value is not known accurately during the planning stage).

Varying interval sample

These two disadvantages can be overcome by using a *varying interval sample*. Since the intervals between adjacent selection points in a pure random sample are distributed exponentially, it is possible to compute (from random numbers taken from a table) a series of randomly exponentially varying intervals averaging to whatever average sampling interval is desired.

Again, while this method has been widely used, there are minor practical disadvantages. One is the need to obtain or compute exponentially varying random factors (these can be done by computer or tabulated for later use by audit staff). Another is the unpredictability, usually within a small range, of the resulting sample size (this unpredictability does not result in any theoretical deficiency but is occasionally a minor nuisance in practice).

Fixed interval sample

The simplest, and the most widely used method in dollar-unit sampling or similar plans, is fixed interval selection, for example, picking a random start (using a random number not exceeding the sampling interval) and every 60 000th dollar-unit thereafter. This method is not equivalent to a pure random sample in that it is exposed to the risk of periodicity in the population. While this exposure could be of significance in the fixed-interval selection of physical-units (every 60th account number might come at the start of a new tray of account cards and be assigned to special types of customer), the risk of periodicity *in dollar-units* must be so infinitesimal that many practitioners feel that fixed-interval selection is the preferable method to use in dollar-unit sampling. Of course, its use should be avoided in those cases where population items all have the same book values (e.g., cable television receivables).

Cell-method dollar-unit sample

A practical sampling method which retains mathematical rigour but is also convenient to use is cell-method selection. Under this method the foregoing population of $3 000 000 would be divided into 50 cells of $60 000 width each and a dollar-unit selected randomly within each cell. Where the cell-method selection is to be made manually (by adding machine or comptometer) the example in Figure 13.k describes the procedures to be followed and the type of working paper which might be prepared.

These procedures are relatively simple to program. Thus where computerized selection is to be used, a random number generator can compute the random numbers as required, list automatically top stratum items exceeding the specified top stratum cut-off and key items meeting certain edit criteria, and provide for segmentation, sample extension, or a lower physical-unit stratum where desired. This does not mean, however, that computerization is required for dollar-unit selection. While computerized selection may be common in the largest engagements, merely because the population items happen to be recorded in computerized files, most dollar-unit applications in practice involve and readily lend themselves to manual selection methods.

Advantages of cell-method selection

As already explained, when cell-method selection is used, the regular tainted dollar evaluation method is still applicable. However, where desired, cell-method evaluation can be employed to eliminate much of the conservatism in the former method.

Other advantages of cell-method selection are the following:
1. The sample is distributed fairly evenly across the entire population.
2. When miscellaneous items (sundry receivables, prepaids, etc.) are sampled in a group (as one population), the sample is distribed over the categories in direct proportion to size.
3. It will often provide a more reliable "most likely estimate" than an unrestricted random dollar-unit sample (the two methods are equal if error distribution is uniform but cell-method has an advantage should error distribution happen to be non-uniform – though neither method makes any assumption as to error distribution apart from always assuming "worst" situations).

While cell-method selection is more rigorous than fixed-interval selection, the many practitioners who view the risk of periodicity as remote – certainly a reasonable viewpoint – can consider fixed-interval selection to be a practical approximation to cell-method as well.

Use of page totals or cumlative totals

All the methods of dollar-unit selection described above involve addition of the population. In computerized applications, or where the population addition must be checked for audit purposes in any case, these selection methods involve little extra work. However, short-cuts are possible. Where population records are listed on a large number of pages, additions for selection purposes can be reduced to a minimum if page totals are available. In most cases page totals can be arranged through advance planning with the client. Where page totals are used, the addition of the pages in which the selected dollar-units fall, together with addition of the grand total from page totals, will at the same time constitute a sufficient test of population additions. Where page totals themselves are not available, frequent subtotals throughout the population will still be a help.

In some situations arrangements can be made to have each population record show both its own book value and the cumulative population total to that point. In such cases dollar-unit selections can be made without any additions; testing the incremental addition of each item selected for the sample will at the same time constitute a sufficient test of population additions.

Two-stage selection to minimize additions

An alternative short-cut is available when all population items are of a relatively small size – a situation where addition of the entire population is particularly onerous. Consider the previous example where

50 items were to be selected out of a $3 000 000 population by using an average sampling-interval of $60 000. Suppose that no population item exceeds $500 (or that the few which do can be examined 100%). In the first stage the auditor gives every population item a deemed value of $500, thereby selecting

---

Cell-Method Selection

A. Working Paper

Cell width $60 000   Population total $2 991 237

| | (1) | (2) | (3) | (4) | (5) Selected item | | (6) |
| | | | | | | | |
Selection number	Random number	Cell width multiples	Cumulative selection points	Sampling intervals	Identification No.	Amount $	Positive subtotal after selection
1	23 817	—	23 817	23 817	A 463	1 260	389
2	14 069	60 000	74 069	50 252	A 780	4 081	2 160
3	40 705	120 000	160 705	86 636	B 221	980	23
4	32 116	180 000	212 116	51 411	B 376	476	217
.	.	.	.	.	.	.	.
.	.	.	.	.	.	.	.
.	.	.	.	.	.	.	.
50	27 641	2 940 000	2 967 641	34 270	Y 411	1 649	1 376
End balance	—	—	—		—	—	(23 596)

Proof of total: $2 967 641
                    23 596
                  $2 991 237

B. Explanation

a) 50 random numbers between 1 and 60 000 are taken from random number tables and listed in column (1).

b) Successive cell width multiples are listed.

c) Addition of (1) and (2) gives the cumulative selection points throughout the approximately $3 000 000 population.

d) Differences between successive points in (3) provide the individual sampling intervals.

e) The adding machine (or comptometer) operator subtracts the first sampling interval from 0 producing a negative subtotal of $23 817. Population items (excluding top stratum items and key items which should already have been marked off) are then added (ignoring cents) until the subtotal flips positive. The item whose addition caused this flip represents the first selection and is recorded (account A463 for $1 260).

f) The positive subtotal at this point is then recorded ($389). This represents the distance by which the true selection point has been 'over-shot'. The actual selected dollar-unit is the 389th from the back end of account A463 or, in other words, the 871st dollar in the $1 260 account. In case it is subsequently decided to change the definition of physical-unit to open invoice it is important to keep a record of this selected dollar-unit.

g) The operator then subtracts, from the positive subtotal of $389, the next sampling interval of $50 252 —thereby creating a new negative subtotal. Population items are again added until the subtotal flips positive and the second selection point is recorded, and so on.

h) When, in infrequent cases, the subtotal is still positive after subtracting the next interval, a second selection point must be recorded in the previously selected item (double-hits are rare and occur generally only for large items). A further interval is then subtracted and population addition then continues.

i) At the end of the population if the final subtotal reads $23 596 negative, the population total should equal $2 967 641 + $23 596, or $2 991 237. Thus, the population addition is checked at the same time as the sample is selected.

j) As an alternative to the subtract-and-add method, the auditor may simply add population items watching for when each cumulative selection point is crossed.

k) If the cell-method is to be made by computer, the print-out need only show columns (4), (5) and (6) (or equivalent information).

Figure 13.k

1 item in every 120 ($60 000 ÷ $500 = 120) throughout the whole population. In effect, the first-stage sample is a physical-unit sample which involves mere counting rather than addition of the population. In the second stage the auditor treats the first-stage sample as a population and draws a dollar-unit sample of 50 items therefrom by using a $500 fixed interval after a random start. This two-stage method achieves the same type of selection as a one-stage dollar-unit sample.[39] The advantage, of course, is that less than 1% of the population needs to be added (instead of 100%). Naturally, when this short-cut is used the sample does not provide a proof of the total population additions and the auditor must check this by other means.

13.4.9 Evaluation

The method of projecting *most likely errors* in a dollar-unit sample is effectively the same as that for any value-oriented selection, as described in Chapter 12. With the introduction of statistical methods, however, it is possible to quantify as well the upper limit of *possible errors*, subject to a specified confidence level. When the method of tainted dollar evaluation (described earlier in this chapter) is used, a working paper format similar to that shown in Figure 13.1 is convenient. In this example the average sampling interval of $6 000 times the factor of 4.61 corresponding to 99% confidence yields a basic precision of $27 700. Net most likely errors project straightforwardly to a net understatement of $3 800. These two components, together with the computed precision gap widenings, yield net upper limits of $25 300 in the overstatement direction and $36 100 in the understatement direction.

The resulting components of basic precision, net most likely errors, and precision gap widenings can also be combined with similar components from other dollar-unit sampling applications in the same engagement using the approximation rule described earlier. The combination of these conclusions for the audit as a whole is discussed in 16.4

If most likely errors exceed materiality

In general, if the most likely errors for a sampling application, or for the audit as a whole, exceed materiality (by more than a trivial amount) the auditor would normally have to insist on correction of, or provision for, such errors or, failing that, qualify his report. Of course, most likely error projections from tests do not represent completely conclusive evidence of material error and sometimes other evidence may be available to rebut the presumption of material error. For example, a global reconciliation of inventory units produced, sold and on hand may provide evidence that the total of unbilled shipments could not be material despite the projected estimates of an audit sample. It should also be recognized that the most likely estimate projected from most audit samples is quite imprecise; indeed, as discussed earlier a small precision gap is usually not warranted. Thus, while the best guess as to population error may be that it is most likely $80 000, it may also be quite possible that it is only $40 000 (or conversely maybe as high as $120 000). Upon occasion, if there is a reason to doubt the validity of a most likely error projection, and other evidence bearing on the question is not available, the auditor may wish to extend his original sample to obtain more persuasive evidence as to the most likely error rate. It is not economic, however, to make a general practice of extending all samples that exhibit material most likely error projections in the hopes that unpalatable results will disappear. The most probable situation, of course, is that the extended sample will yield a most likely error rate close to that initially projected.

If upper error limit exceeds materiality

In general, if upper error limits exceed materiality (by more than a trivial amount), but most likely errors are less than materiality, the auditor will normally have to do further audit work in order to obtain more persuasive evidence that material errors do not exist. It is, of course, already improbable that material errors exist (since the most likely error projection lies below materiality) and accordingly qualification of his audit report would not be justified; but is is *not sufficiently improbable*, without further work, to justify a clear opinion. One exception already discussed is that a minimum precision gap of one-half materiality should always be permitted. Thus, in rare cases, upper error limits might be acceptable up to 1¹/₂ times materiality – materiality limits being an imprecise judgment in any case.

With proper audit planning, unacceptably high upper error limits accompanying immaterial most likely errors should be avoidable most of the time. When, on occasion they do arise, the auditor has a number of alternatives. If management agrees to correct or provide for the most likely errors, the upper error limit will be reduced – perhaps to acceptable levels. Alternatively, there may be other audit evidence available which confirms the improbability of material errors sufficiently that the final audit conclusions are acceptable. More usually, if the upper error limit is unacceptably high (after management adjustments, if any) the auditor will have to

Dollar-Unit Evaluation Working Paper

Physical unit Identification number	Book value	Audit value	Effect of error on pre-tax income Overstating	Understating	Tainting percentage Overstat.	Understat.	Error ranking O/S	U/S	PGW factor from Figure 13.f	Tainting x PGW factor O/S	U/S
A 423	$1 000	$ 900	$100		10%		2		.77	7.7%	
F 218	500	675		$(175)		(35%)		2	.77		(27.0%)
L 106	4 000	4 400		(400)		(10)		3	.64		(6.4)
M 247	3 000	2 550	450		15		1		1.03	15.6	
R 351	1 000	1 400		(400)		(40)		1	1.03		(41.6)
S 067	500	510		(10)		(2)		4	.56		(1.1)
U 023	500	510		(10)		(2)		5	.50		(1.0)
. . .	. . .	. . .	. . .	. . .	. . .	. . .	. . .	. . .	. . .	. . .	. . .
			$550	$(995)	25%	(89%)				23.3%	(77.1%)

Basic precision
factor for 99%
confidence (per
Figure 13.g)

$6 000
x
4.61
x
100%
=
$27 660   BP

Average sampling interval $6 000

$6 000   x   23.3%   (77.1%)   = $1 398 $(4 626)   PGW

$1 500 $(5 340)   Gross MLE
$(3 840)   Net MLE

Components of net upper error limits	Overstating pre-tax income	(Understating) pre-tax income
	$27 700	$(27 700)
	(3 800)	(3 800)
	1 400	(4 600)
	25 300	(36 100)

BP   Basic precision
MLE Net most likely errors
PGW Precision gap widenings
Net upper error limits

Figure 13.l

extend his sample in order to reduce the precision gap. Sample extension is discussed in the next section.

Other considerations

The comments made in the previous chapter with respect to investigating the *cause* and *nature* of sample errors and to searching for *duplicates* are equally applicable to statistical sampling.

When a statistical sample is being evaluated the auditor should also review all the planning decisions originally made (error definition, choice of confidence level, error size-limit assumption, etc.) to make sure that nothing discovered in the sample results, or elsewhere in the audit, should now lead the auditor to revise any of those decisions.

In a few cases it may be appropriate to employ physical-unit attributes, sampling where it is safe to assume that error values are independent of book values and will not likely exceed some specified dollar amount, such as $500. In such cases, the *most likely error* projection will be simply the average error value per sample item times the number of population items – and is the same as the method for projecting any neutrally selected sample as described in Chapter 12. The *upper error limit*, on the other hand, will, in this example, be the upper error limit frequency (determined from Figure 13.d) times the number of population items times $500.

13.4.10 Sample extension

Sample extension is the process of increasing the original sample size in order to reduce the precision gap (and hence the upper error limit) even if the most likely error estimate remains the same. With adequate audit planning sample extension is rarely required; circumstances can arise, however, where it is appropriate.

When a sample is extended, the original sample results are retained but additional selection points are examined in order to increase the total sample size. *It would be invalid to discard the initial sample results (merely because they were unpalatable) in the hope that a fresh sample might yield a more palatable result.* This would be shooting the messenger instead of coping with the bad news. Samples can be extended but not replaced.

In planning the total sample size of an extended sample (initial size plus extension required), exactly the same planning decisions and sample size computations are required as discussed previously. The initial sample results, of course, now provide better evidence as to what should be planned as "tolerable

basic precision" – and sometimes as to what other planning decisions (error size-limit assumption, confidence level) are now appropriate. As a practical matter, however, the writer suggests that it is rarely worthwhile extending a sample to less than double its original size. For example, assume that a sample size of 100 containing 2 errors yields a most likely error of $20 000 and an upper error limit $63 000 at 95% confidence – which is judged unacceptable because materiality is $50 000. A doubled sample size of 200 (which is likely to contain 4 errors) will yield a most likely error of $20 000 (unchanged) and an upper error limit of $46 000 (which would be acceptable). If the anticipated required extension to achieve acceptable evidence is less than doubling, the auditor should reconsider whether his present conclusions are really serious enough to warrant sample extension at all.

Thus, if in his initial sample the auditor had selected one item per $10 000 cell-width throughout the population he should normally consider selecting an additional item per $10 000 cell-width should sample extension now be required.

Providing for possible sample extension

If the auditor believes that a certain sample size should prove adequate but recognizes that there is an off-chance that higher-than-anticipated error frequencies could call for a larger sample size, he can provide for this possibility in advance. In other words, he can make all the dollar-unit selections required for the possible doubled extended sample but then use only half of them as his initial sample. In the unlikely event that sample extension proves necessary, he will have the remaining selection points in reserve and need not add the populaton a second time to obtain them. Such a procedure is more logical than verifying all the items in the doubled sample size in the first place just to be on the safe side. There is no point charging all clients twice the necessary audit fee in these areas just to be able to avoid the need for sample extension on those few engagements where discovered errors turn out to be much higher than anticipated.

When providing for possible sample extension in the above manner the auditor should ensure that the half initial sample is randomly selected out of the total extended selection points. This could be conveniently done, for example, by drawing total extended selection points as a cell sample using a $5 000 cell-width and then randomly choosing one out of each pair of adjacent selection points. The result will be a valid cell sample with a $10 000 cell-width (but convertible later, if necessary, into a cell sample of twice the size, having a $5 000 cell-width).

13.5 Application of dollar-unit sampling to compliance tests

The use of representative sampling for compliance tests has already been described in Chapter 12. Included there was a discussion of error and population definition, degree of assurance, determination of sample extent, selection method, and evaluation (see 12.6). Most of these points continue to apply when the representative sampling is done statistically. The following sections discuss only the additional points which arise with the introduction of statistical methods.

13.5.1 Sample type

It was suggested in Chapter 12 that value-oriented selection be used for representative compliance tests wherever possible, as it gives some indication as to whether a multiple materiality level of transactions, each subject to a critical compliance deviation, could exist. Accordingly, it follows that, when statistical methods are introduced, *dollar-unit attributes sampling* represents an appropriate technique for compliance testing.

In some situations, however, (such as testing shipping orders) it may be difficult to attach monetary values to the population from which the sample is being drawn. In such cases, if statistical methods are desired, *physical-unit attribute sampling* should be used. There are, as mentioned previously, some practitioners who believe that the objective of compliance testing should always be expressed in a non-monetary form; such practitioners would therefore find physical-unit attributes sampling to be the appropriate statistical technique on all occasions.

13.5.2 Error, population and physical-unit definition

With respect to error and population definition, no additional points arise with the introduction of statistical methods. The points discussed in 12.6.1 and 12.6.2 for all representative compliance tests remain equally important. The additional requirement, in statistical applications, to define the physical-unit in advance is the same as discussed earlier in this chapter for statistical substantive tests.

13.5.3 Confidence level

In Chapter 12, it was argued that because of the partial nature of the dependence on compliance tests, it is reasonable that a relatively minimum confidence level be demanded for the compliance tests themselves. Accordingly, it is suggested that 80% confidence level be used for compliance testing aimed at detecting a multiple (such as triple) materiality level of transactions subject to critical compliance deviations. However, this is a point on which each auditor must exercise his professional judgment as opinions differ.[40]

13.5.4 Determination of sample extent and selection method

The guideline for determining compliance sample sizes, based on accepting no more than one critical compliance deviation in the sample, and described in 12.6.4, applies equally to statistical compliance samples. Indeed the formula there given:

$$\text{Compliance sample size} = \frac{\text{Net population dollar value}}{\text{Materiality (in dollars)}}$$

is derivable directly from the dollar-unit sampling concepts discussed earlier in this chapter and is equivalent to using an average sampling interval (cell width) equal to materiality.[41] The selection of one item within each material subdivision (cell width) of the population as described in Chapter 12, therefore, also applies equally to statistical compliance samples. For example, if a compliance sample were being selected out of a transaction stream of $1 000 000 in an engagement where materiality was $10 000, the auditor would select a dollar-unit sample of 100 items – one selection point within each $10 000 cell. Statistical selection methods for dollar-unit compliance samples are the same as described earlier in this chapter. (Where a physical-unit compliance sample is required because of the absence of dollar values, the analogous selection method involves dividing the population into cells by number of items rather than by value.)[42]

13.5.5 Evaluation

The evaluation considerations discussed in 12.6.6 for all representative compliance tests continue to apply when dollar-unit sampling techniques are used. In statistical terms, when more than one critical compliance deviation is found the upper error limit of such deviations will exceed triple materiality at 80% confidence and therefore, based on the criteria suggested earlier, not warrant the placing of considerable reliance on that control.

13.5.6 Sample extension

Where an unacceptably high upper error limit for compliance deviations has been found in a compliance sample, it would be theoretically possible to extend the compliance sample in order to reduce the precision gap and hence the upper error limit to a level justifying the placing of reliance on control.

While this may be appropriate in rare cases, it is not suggested as a general practice. Usually, compliance testing is economical where the auditor believes that critical compliance deviations are exceedingly infrequent. Where the initial sample results already indicate that they are not that infrequent it is generally more economical to reject reliance on control immediately and use an appropriately high confidence level for planned substantive tests rather than waste time extending compliance tests that even then may, in the end, lead to rejection of control reliability.

13.6 Planning and control

Planning decisions common to all tests, whether statistical or judgmental, were discussed in Chapter 12 and included:

1. Choice of selection method (high-value, key-item, and/or representative),
2. Choice of selection method for representative tests (judgmental or statistical),
3. Error definition,
4. Population definition.

The additional planning decisions required when statistical techniques are applied are, as discussed in this chapter:

1. Definition of physical-unit,
2. Choice of sample type and error size-limit assumption,
3. Decision as to tolerable basic precision,
4. Choice of confidence level,
5. Decision as to 100% top stratum cut-off,
6. Decision as to provision for possible sample extension,
7. Planned mechanics of selection.

Review of statistical sample planning is facilitated if these seven decisions are appropriately documented in the working papers. Different practitioners will have different preferences as to format. One suggested type of planning form for statistical substantive tests is illustrated in Figure 13.m. This example covers only the additional seven planning decisions required with the introduction of statistical techniques and is therefore intended to supplement the general planning form for substantive representative tests described in the previous chapter (see Figure 12.e). Alternatively, some practitioners may

---

Example of Planning Form for Statistical Substantive Tests

(Purpose: To summarize the major judgment decisions made in planning statistical sampling applications throughout the financial statement audit.)

Client _ABC Limited_   Year-end _December 31, 1976_

Statistical substantive tests planned	Accounts receivable	Inventory	
1. Physical-unit – Fixed – describe – Variable (depending on ease of verification) – explain	(confirmation) – Account balance or open item.	(pricing, extensions) line-item –	
2. Sample type (usually DUS if dollar values available)	DUS	DUS	
Error size-limit assumption _____% of book value	100 %	100 %	%
Give reasons why errors must nearly always be under this % (if not appropriate for smaller items consider lower physical-unit stratum and explain)	Error not expected to exceed 100% of book value	Overstatement restricted to 100%; will scrutinize for unusual understatements	

Figure 13.m

3. Approximate materiality (see 15.4.2)	$ 90 000	$ 90 000	$_____
Deduct:			
Most likely error conclusions anticipated for the audit as a whole (net of client corrections)			
i) Actual population errors (net of anticipated corrections) believed most likely	$ 49 000	$ 49 000	$_____
ii) Additional cushion to allow for misforecast or for sample bounce	$ 5 000	$ 5 000	$_____
Tolerable total precision gap (need not be less than half materiality)	$ 45 000	$ 45 000	$_____
Deduct:			
Precision-gap-widenings anticipated for the audit as a whole	$ 10 000	$ 10 000	$_____
Tolerable basic precision	$ 35 000	$ 35 000	$
4. Factors influencing choice of confidence level			
i) Overall level of audit assurance required	High	High	
ii) Inherent risk of error	Moderate	High	
iii) Internal control risk	Moderate	Low	
iv) Overlapping audit procedures	Moderate	Considerable	
Choice of confidence level (see 13.4.5)	95 %	90 %	%
Basic precision factor (see Figure 13.g)	3.0	2.3	
Resulting sampling interval $$\frac{\text{tolerable basic precision}}{\text{basic precision factor} \times \text{error size limit}}$$	$ 11 600	$ 15 200	$
5. 100% top-stratum cut-off (if lower than average sampling interval, explain)	$ 11 600	$ 15 200	$
6. Sample extension provided for (Yes or No)	No	No	
If yes, specify initial average sampling interval (generally half that in #4)	N/A	N/A	
7. Sample to be selected by:			
Selection method: cell method? fixed interval? other?	Cell method	Cell method	
Selection process: manual? computer program?	Computerized	Manual	

Figure 13.m (concluded)

find it more convenient to combine the forms illustrated on Figures 12.e and 13.m when statistical substantive tests are being planned. For compliance tests the plannning decisions are sufficiently close for both statistical and judgmental tests that the planning form already illustrated in Figure 12.f should be suitable.

Importance of review of planning decisions

As with all testing, but particularly because of the additional seven decisions required above, it is im-portant that statistical sampling plans be subjected to a second opinion, preferably before execution. Some firms may find it useful to develop *audit test specialists* to assist in this review as well as to provide advice to other audit staff when particularly complex situations are encountered. Most of the questions commonly arising in statistical applications relate not to the statistical methods but to the judgmental planning decisions and the definition of the audit objective of a given test. Indeed, the focussing of increased attention on these important judgment calls is one of the important by-products of the use of statistical sampling.

13.7 Reference material

Statistical audit sampling in general

AICPA Statement on Auditing Standards No. 1, Section 320A (Relationship of Statistical Sampling to Generally Accepted Auditing Standards) and Section 320B (Precision and Reliability for Statistical Sampling in Auditing).

CICA Audit Technique Study, *Statistical Sampling in an Audit Context* (1972) by Giles R. Meikle, CA.

Herbert Arkin, *Handbook of Sampling for Auditing and Accounting*, 2nd. Ed. (McGraw-Hill Book Company, Inc., 1974).

Dollar-unit sampling

R. J. Anderson, FCA, and A. D. Teitlebaum, PhD, *Dollar-unit Sampling - A Solution to the Audit Sampling Dilemma (CA Magazine*, April 1973).

A. D. Teitlebaum, PhD, *Dollar-unit Sampling in Auditing* (paper prepared for presentation to the December, 1973 National Meeting of The American Statistical Association – copies available on request from the author, McGill University, Montreal).

D. A. Leslie, CA. *Monetary-unit Sampling in Auditing* (International Journal of Government Auditing, April 1975)

13.8 Questions and problems

Review and discussion

1. When should statistical sampling be used as an audit tool?
2. What are the advantages of statistical sampling over judgmental representative selection?
3. What are the seven key planning decisions to be made when a statistical sample is being considered?
4. Define the following terms:
    a) population
    b) random
    c) attributes sampling
    d) variables sampling
    e) sampling confidence
    f) precision
    g) point estimate
    h) interval estimate
    i) standard deviation
    j) error rate
5. Describe the applicability of attributes and variables sampling to auditing.
6. From what factors can the required dollar-unit sample size be calculated?
7. Explain the effect on dollar-unit sampling results of poor estimation of the anticipated error rate.
8. Describe the relationship between statistical sampling and generally accepted auditing standards.
9. How does statistical sampling affect professional judgment?
10. What do the terms "stratify the population" and "segment the population" mean?
11. Discuss the advantages of dollar-unit sampling over other attribute sampling plans.

12. State the advantages and disadvantages of the following methods of variables sampling:
    a) difference and ratio methods,
    b) mean-per-unit method,
    c) stratified mean-per-unit method.
13. Describe the components of the dollar-unit sampling upper error limit (giving a specific example).
14. Briefly describe the concept of tainted dollar evaluation with respect to dollar-unit sampling.
15. What are the consequences of greater than 100% errors in dollar-unit sampling for both overstatements and understatements?
16. Discuss how overstatement and understatement errors can be projected in dollar-unit samples.
17. Briefly explain the difference between cell-method selection and unrestricted random sampling.
18. Discuss the concept of possible errors and its application to statistical sampling.
19. How does an auditor estimate tolerable basic precision when using dollar-unit sampling?
20. Describe how a sampling confidence of 90% can yield a posterior probability of no material error of 99% or more.
21. What are the various factors that an auditor should consider in making his decision as to the confidence level to be used in sampling?
22. Identify and briefly describe the four techniques for making a random selection of dollar-units.
23. Briefly describe two shortcuts available in random selection of a dollar-unit sample.
24. Discuss alternatives which are available to an auditor in the event that statistical sampling results indicate:

a) the most likely errors are in excess of the materiality limit,

b) the most likely error is small but the upper error limit is in excess of materiality,

c) the most likely error is 75% of materiality and the upper error limit is in excess of materiality.

25. How can an auditor provide for sample extension at the planning stage?

Problems

1. (AICPA adapted) The eight following items apply to random sampling for attributes, a sampling technique often employed in transaction testing. Assume that all samples are to be drawn from large populations and select the best answer for each item.

1) If all other factors specified in a sampling plan remain constant, changing the specified confidence from 90 per cent to 95 per cent would cause the required sample size to:

a) Increase.
b) Remain the same.
c) Decrease.
d) Become indeterminate.

2) If all other factors specified in a sampling plan remain constant, changing the specified precision from 8 per cent to 12 per cent would cause the required sample size to:

a) Increase.
b) Remain the same.
c) Decrease.
d) Become indeterminate.

3) If all other factors including the upper error limit specified in a sampling plan remain constant, changing the estimated error occurrence rate from 2 per cent to 4 per cent would cause the required sample size to:

a) Increase.
b) Remain the same.
c) Decrease.
d) Become indeterminate.

4) In the planning of a sample at a specified confidence level and upper error limit, the fact that the anticipated occurrence rate in the sample was 2 per cent rather than 4 per cent would cause the sample size to:

a) Increase.
b) Remain the same.
c) Decrease.
d) Become indeterminate.

5) In the evaluation of the results of a sample, the fact that the occurrence rate in the sample was the same as the estimated occurrence rate would cause the precision of the sample estimate to:

a) Increase from planned.
b) Remain the same as planned.
c) Decrease from planned.
d) Become indeterminate.

2. (AICPA adapted) Select the best answer for each of the following items.

1) A CA may use different sampling programs to estimate different characteristics of a population. For example, from a sample of the dollar amounts of unpaid invoices he could estimate the total dollar value of a population of unpaid invoices. To test internal control a CA might sample the population of unpaid invoices to estimate the number (or rate) of errors in the population. Sampling for the number of errors is known as:

a) Sampling for variables.
b) Sampling for attributes.
c) Stratified sampling.
d) Random sampling.

2) Which of the following is an application of sampling for attributes?

a) Estimating the total dollar value of accounts receivable.
b) Estimating the reliability of a sample estimate.
c) Estimating the precision of a sample estimate.
d) Estimating the percentage of sales invoices with totals of less than $10.

3) In a random sample of 1 000 records a CA determines that the rate of occurrence of errors is 2 per cent. He can state that the error rate in the population is:

a) Not more than 3 per cent.
b) Not less than 2 per cent.
c) Probably about 2 per cent.
d) Not less than 1 per cent.

4) From a random sample of items listed from a client's inventory count a CA estimates with 90 per cent confidence that the error occurrence rate is between 4 per cent and 6 per cent. The CA's major concern is that there is one chance in twenty that the true error rate in the population is:

a) More than 6 per cent.
b) Less than 6 per cent.
c) More than 4 per cent.
d) Less than 4 per cent.

5) If from a particular random sample a CA can state with 90 per cent confidence that the occurrence rate in the population does not exceed 20 per cent, he can state that the occur-

rence rate does not exceed 25 per cent with:
a) 90 per cent confidence.
b) Greater confidence.
c) Equal confidence.
d) Less confidence.

6) If a CA wishes to select a random sample which must have a 90 per cent confidence level and an upper precision limit of 2 per cent, the size of the sample he must select will decrease as his estimate of the:
a) Anticipated occurrence rate increases.
b) Anticipated occurrence rate decreases.
c) Population size increases.
d) Anticipated reliability of the sample increases.

7) If a CA selects a random sample for which he specified a confidence level of 99 per cent and upper precision limit of 5 per cent and subsequently changes the confidence level to 90 per cent, the sample produces an estimate of:
a) Higher precision limit and more confidence.
b) Higher precision limit and less confidence.
c) Lower precision limit and more confidence.
d) Lower precision limit and less confidence.

3. The following tentative planning decisions for a statistical representative substantive test of accounts receivable balances were made prior to commencing the interim audit of ABS Limited based on the prior year's assessment of internal control and an estimate of most likely errors expected in the current year. Normal cut-off routines are planned for the confirmation date; however, no cash count will be performed.

- Materiality · · · · · · · · · · · · · · · · $100 000
- Most likely error · · · · · · · · · · · · 30 000
- Tolerable basic precision · · · · · 60 000
- Confidence level · · · · · · · · · · · · · 95%
- Sample extension required · · · · · No
- Segmentation required · · · · · · · · No
- Population   Accounts receivable at December 31 – $2 000 000 (480 accounts)
- Physical unit of verification   Account balance
- Top stratum   5 accounts totalling $450 000
- Key items   3 accounts over 90 days old ($16 000)

a) Assuming a 100% pricing assumption, calculate the average sampling interval using the dollar-unit technique.
b) Describe (without extensive calculation) the

impact on your audit program of the following three unrelated circumstances encountered during the interim audit of ABS Limited.

i) An important division of duties has broken down because the receptionist no longer lists cheques received. The accounts receivable clerk now opens the mail, lists cash receipts, and prepares the daily bank deposit.
ii) The credit manager has been very ill and the absence of collection effort has allowed the age of accounts receivable to deteriorate to the point that 30% by dollar value are over 90 days.
iii) You learn that many of the customers, including all the accounts in top stratum, will be unable to reply to the account balance request because of the nature of their accounting systems.

4. In evaluating the results of a statistical sample of inventory items which were test priced, Linda Willis, CA, noted that the net most likely error projected exceeded the anticipated error. When added to other errors discovered during the audit, the total exceeded the estimated most likely errors plus cushion that was determined when the statistical sample was planned.

a) How are the audit conclusions for the statistical sampling application and the audit as a whole affected?
b) What alternatives are available to Ms. Willis where the overall audit conclusion is unacceptable?

5. A CA wishes to test compliance with the control which ensures accuracy (pricing, additions, extensions, and coding expiry date for deferred revenue calculations) of pre-numbered sales invoices for subscription sales of a magazine publisher. The information is prepared originally by the salesman in the field, then checked by a clerk who initials the invoices indicating approval for subsequent processing. Each invoice also includes a key verification stamp indicating that the computer input has been double checked. Computer controls, verified in a separate test, account for the numerical continuity of the invoices. CA has compiled the following information:

- Materiality · $ 10 000
- Average invoice value · · · · · · · · · · · · 10
- Maximum invoice value · · · · · · · · · · 50
- Annual invoice volume   200 000 invoices (filed in approximate numerical order in 22 file drawers)
- Sales register   5 500 pages

a) Calculate the required dollar-unit sample size.

b) Assuming that computer-assisted audit techniques are not possible and that each page in the sales register has a sub-total, describe in detail the most efficient method of sample selection.

c) Given the same circumstances as in (b) except that page sub-totals are not available, describe in detail, showing calculations, a two stage physical-unit/dollar-unit selection (ensure that your answer describes the specific population from which the selection is made).

6. A CA wishes to test compliance with the control that ensures that all goods shipped by Client Company Ltd. are invoiced. The control procedure being tested is the matching in the sales order department of a copy of the invoice to an open sales order and filing it by sales order number. Open sales orders are followed up weekly.

CA would like to draw a statistical representative sample of shipping documents from the shipping department files for this test. Since the population of shipping documents from which the sample is to be drawn is not priced, dollar-unit selection is not possible. CA is considering possible use of a physical-unit sample. CA has compiled the following information:

- Materiality $ 40 000
- Annual invoice volume   100 000
- Estimated annual value of
  shipments   5 000 000

a) What compliance sampling interval would CA use in this compliance test?

b) Assuming the average unbilled transaction value which could remain undetected is the average invoice value, how could CA arrive at an average sampling interval in units?

c) What physical-unit sample size would be required for the compliance test contemplated by CA?

7. Bleeper Manufacturing Limited is a privately owned medium-sized manufacturing concern which produces equipment for use in automobile assembly and repair. Bleeper makes 1 800 different products with unit prices in inventory of from $5 to $250. Total inventory value at the year-end is $1 200 000. The company is largely capitalized by common shares.

The evaluation of internal control over pricing the physical inventory at the year-end is good, and analysis of manufacturing variance accounts indicate standard unit costs approximate actual.

Materiality has been determined as $30 000, with tolerable basic precision set at $21 000, and an error size limit of 100%.

a) What size sample would you select for tracing standard costs from the physical inventory listing to unit cost records? You will need to select a confidence level. Give reasons for your choice and show your calculations.

b) In practice, the product unit cost information for the prior year is nearly always available. If the statistical representative sample is supplemented by a careful comparison of unit costs year to year and investigation of unusual variations, it is reasonable to assume undiscovered pricing errors would not exceed 40% of reported book values. What effect would such an assumption have on the sample size computed in (a)?

8. From the following information determine the net most likely error and net upper error limits misstating pre-tax income.

- $6 518 000 accounts receivable population
- dollar-unit statistical sample
- cell width – 46 000
- confidence level – 90%
- error size limit assumption – 100%
- no key items or high-value items
- book values of accounts in error – $6 000, $3 250, $10 000
- audited values of accounts in error – $4 000, $2 600, $8 000 respectively

9. From the following information determine the net most likely error and net upper error limits misstating pre-tax income.

- $2 000 000 inventory population
- dollar-unit statistical sample
- no key items or high-value items
- confidence factor – 3.00
- basic precision – $30 000
- error size limit assumption – 50%
- book values of items in error – $500, $2 000, $200, $800
- audited values of items in error – $625, $1 500, $280, $780

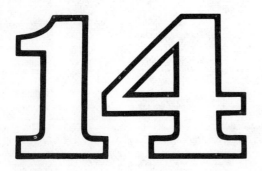

Computer-Assisted Audit Techniques

Parallelling the rapid growth of computer processing in business and government has been the growth of computer-assisted auditing. Not only can computers automate the recording, calculating, summarizing and reporting steps involved in accounting; they can automate many of the processes by which the auditor checks the functioning and the results of the accounting system. For example, the auditor can use the computer to select receivable samples for audit confirmation, check payroll calculations for arithmetic accuracy, or edit inventory balances for unusual items or amounts. The use of the computer to automate certain audit functions is known as *computer-assisted auditing*. A number of different computer-assisted audit techniques (CAAT's) exist. The purpose of this chapter is to introduce them.

The use of one of these techniques to automate a specific audit step may be called a computer-assisted *application*. A number of possible applications are suggested throughout Chapters 24 to 39. Of course, audit objectives are not altered by the use of the computer as an audit tool. Therefore, any application (whether for revenues, expenses, receivables, inventories, etc.) should be designed and evaluated within the context of the normal audit objectives and procedures described for that section of the audit.

Computer-assisted auditing is a highly technical subject. It requires specialized training and considerable experience in order to be used effectively. Most audit staff, even after basic training in EDP auditing, will require specialist help when using computer-assisted audit techniques. It is not the intention here to discuss all the detailed skills and procedures required in a given computer-assisted application. Rather, the purpose is to describe the important underlying concepts, to indicate the more commonly used techniques, and to identify the major planning, control, and documentation points to consider when using these techniques. In addition, the chapter covers a number of techniques, which, while primarily in use by internal auditors, should be of interest to the external auditor to the extent that he coordinates his work with, and places reliance on, internal audit procedures.

14.1 Introduction to computer-assisted auditing

It is important at the outset to draw a distinction between computer-assisted auditing and the audit of computerized systems. The former may serve as a part of the latter but it is not the whole of it. The auditor of a computerized system must include all the procedures required in the review, evaluation, and compliance verification of the changed system of internal control created by the computer. The changed system of internal control was described in Chapter 8. The interim audit of such a system was discussed briefly in 9.7 and is described in detail in Chapter 27. Many of the audit procedures involved in the review, evaluation and compliance verification of computer controls will be manual procedures – observation of activities, inspection of control logs, vouching of input documents, etc. – though a few may make use of computer-assisted techniques. On the other hand, computer-assisted techniques may be applied to automate procedures, such as receivables confirmation, whose primary objective is to substantiate an asset rather than to check computer controls. Clearly, no amount of sophisticated use of computer-assisted techniques will make up for a failure to review and evaluate computer controls of attest significance. Similarly, the most thorough auditing of the computer controls will not compensate for lost opportunities to improve audit efficiency or effectiveness through the use of computer-assisted techniques.

14.1.1 Advantages and disadvantages of computer-assisted auditing

Computer-assisted auditing has been one of the major growth areas in the profession. A tenfold increase in the number of computer-assisted applications over a five-year period has been a typical experience of many practitioners. An element of glamour still surrounds the use of flashing lights and spinning tape drives to replace laborious manual checking. However, as with any sophisticated tool, the use of computer-assisted auditing does not offer automatic benefits. The benefits accrue only when the technique is used with proper care, intelligence and foresight. At the same time, computer-assisted applications make many demands upon the auditor – demands of time, knowledge and experience. When these demands are not met, the use of computer-assisted auditing may results in a loss of efficiency and the risk of erroneous audit conclusions. It is useful, therefore, to consider the advantages and disadvantages of using computer-assisted techniques.

Advantages of computer-assisted techniques
1. Improvement in audit extent
Computer-assisted techniques may enable the auditor to increase audit extents and thus reduce or

eliminate sampling risks. It may be convenient to check more items using the computer than would be practical manually. For example, it would usually take no longer for the computer to check all the extensions in an inventory file than to draw and check a sample of extensions. Thus, audit assurance can be increased with no increase in processing time and the set-up time involved in sample size planning can be saved. In other cases, the sample extents called for by proper sample planning may be readily achievable with computer-assisted techniques while, because of the more cumbersome accessibility of data in voluminous pages of "hard copy", they might be inordinately costly if selected manually.

2. *Performance of otherwise impossible procedures*
Sometimes gaps in the hard-copy audit trail make conventional manual procedures impossible. The only way of matching a shipping order to a related sales invoice may, in some systems, be through the use of computer-assisted techniques. In practice, gaps in the audit trail are fairly rare. Usually they occur only in more sophisticated computer systems. Even where a hard-copy audit trail still exists, however, its retracing may have been made considerably more difficult by the method of organizing computer input and output. Computer-assisted techniques may overcome this difficulty.

3. *Elimination of tedious work*
A third advantage often noted is that computer-assisted auditing relieves the auditor of much tedious work and, as a result, permits him to focus his energies on the important judgment areas of the audit.

4. *Savings in audit costs*
Perhaps the most commonly anticipated advantage is the potential for cost savings compared to manual procedures. While there is no question that computer-assisted auditing can be economical, cost savings are by no means an automatic byproduct. In many cases, the saving in time would be more than offset by the additional time taken to prepare and test the application, attend the computer processing, and evaluate the print-out. It is important to review the anticipated costs and savings carefully for each proposed application. Net cost savings may only materialize if repeated use over a number of years can be anticipated. Of course, cost/benefit considerations are not necessarily the overriding factor. In many cases, the use of the computer can provide a more effective verification than could be performed manually.

5. *Increased discipline*
While rarely mentioned as a justification for an application, an important byproduct is the increased discipline forced on the auditor when he uses the computer. Audit objectives must be clearly and pre-

cisely defined. For example, in a computer edit for obsolescence the auditor cannot adopt a "wait and see" attitude, as he can in a visual review, as to what constitutes obsolete inventory. Criteria must be specified in advance. This need for advance decisions often leads, in turn, to a re-examination of the underlying audit objectives. As with the discipline imposed by statistical sampling, such a re-examination can have benefits extending far beyond the particular application in question.

6. *Enhancement of systems knowledge*
An additional byproduct of the use of computer-assisted techniques is enhanced knowledge of the computer systems on the part of the auditor. In any audit of a computer-based system there is always the danger that the auditor, through lack of familiarity, will give only token acknowledgement to the presence of the new computer controls. By becoming a computer user himself, the auditor is forced to acquire a much greater knowledge of EDP principles and operations. This knowledge in turn will improve his review and evaluation of controls throughout the computer systems.

Disadvantages of computer-assisted techniques

1. *Training requirements and set-up costs*
The use of computer-assisted techniques requires adequate training and an investment in acquiring or developing suitable techniques, instructional manuals for their use, and specialist resources (within the firm or via outside consultants). On some audit engagements the set-up costs in terms of specialist time, program design, computer time, etc. might outweigh the benefits.

2. *Danger of non-integration*
There is a danger that the specialized nature of computer-assisted applications will lead to their being divorced from the rest of the audit, run by specialist staff unfamiliar with overall audit objectives in a given engagement, and evaluated in isolation from other audit results. To be effective, computer-assisted audit procedures must be fully integrated in the audit program as a whole.

3. *Control requirements*
Reliable use of the computer as an audit tool requires elaborate controls over programs, files, operation of the computer, and output. Without adequate controls, the computer-assisted techniques may provide less reliable audit evidence than the manual procedures they replaced.

4. *Risk of over-emphasizing techniques*
One of the real dangers of computer-assisted auditing has always been the tendency to emphasize

technique over objective. The literature is replete with the latest variations on each particular technique. While new developments are often of real interest from a technical point of view, the audit objectives may sometimes be overlooked. The enhancement of technique can become an end in itself. As a result, certain computerized tests may be performed merely because they are now possible – though they may be unnecessary. Audit extents may be increased out of proportion to their value merely because computers can process volumes of data. Applications which are wasteful of audit time and computer resources may be carried out merely because, to the specialist, they seem more interesting. To guard against this risk, the contribution of any computer-assisted technique to the ultimate audit objectives must be carefully defined and evaluated.

Evaluation of advantages and disadvantages

The balance of advantages and disadvantages will be different for each prospective application. It is as dangerous to apply computer-assisted techniques indiscriminately as it is to ignore the proper opportunities for their use. Suggested procedures for

evaluating the net advantage or disadvantage in any particular case are described in 14.5.

14.1.2 Distinction between substantive and compliance techniques

Computer-assisted audit techniques may be classified broadly into two groups: those which serve a substantive objective and those which serve a compliance objective. The classification is somewhat arbitrary since occasionally one technique may serve either objective or both at once. Generally, computer-assisted audit techniques serving a substantive objective involve the use of the auditor's own programs to *process client data*. The data would be extracted from client data files, subjected to various logical tests by the computer, and/or printed out for further review, analysis or verification.

Computer-assisted audit techniques serving a compliance objective generally involve the use of test data (or, in some cases, a special program) to *test client programs*. The purpose is usually to verify the design of certain computerized accounting procedures or the functioning of certain programmed controls.

14.2 Computer-assisted audit techniques for substantive verification

Techniques for using the auditor's programs to process client data files can be called *data-oriented techniques*. Usually, but not always, data-oriented techniques are used for substantive verification (an exception is the use of statistical selection techniques in drawing samples for compliance verification).

14.2.1 Scope of data-oriented computer techniques

In general, the auditor should consider a data-oriented technique in those cases where large volumes of data must be analyzed or summarized or where more complex or sophisticiated calculations are required than can easily be performed manually. More detailed points to consider in deciding when to use a data-oriented technique are described in 14.5.

The actual mechanics of carrying out an application can be quite complex, involving a number of man-days to plan, test and process the application. When stripped of its complexities, however, the typical application consists of (a) reading a client data file, (b) selecting or summarizing data based on certain

criteria, (c) performing certain calculations on all data or on the selected data, (d) sorting the resulting information into a logical sequence, and (e) printing reports for audit follow-up.

Most data-oriented techniques can be classified into one of four categories:

- statistical selection of records,
- summarization or addition of data files,
- key item selection of items meeting certain criteria,
- mathematical calculations.

Statistical selection

Statistical selection, whether based on the dollar-unit approach described in Chapter 13, on a stratified variables estimation approach, or on some other method, lends itself readily to computerization. Computerized selection is particularly useful where large volumes of data must be processed and where manual selection would be cumbersome and time-consuming. The computer may also be used to project statistically the sample results discovered – though computerized projection is not necessary with the dollar-unit approach.

Summarization of data

Summarization of voluminous data is often useful to the auditor. Individual pieces of data may be of little interest. They become relevant only when summarized with similar data to provide a picture of the total population under review. For example, an ageing analysis of an individual account may be unimportant. When the ageing of the complete accounts receivable file is summarized, however, it can provide a basis for verifying the allowance for doubtful accounts. Of course, the summarized report will be only as reliable as the criteria on which the summarization was based. If these criteria were poorly chosen, the resulting report could be irrelevant or misleading. In addition to or instead of arithmetic summarizations, the auditor may use the computer to summarize data in the form of graphs or histograms.

Key item selection (computer editing)

The computer may be used to make both key item and high-value selections (see 12.2). The selection criteria may be specified singly (e.g., all balances over $5 000, all balances for special customers, all balances over three months old). Or they may be specified in multiple sets (e.g., invoices for product 23 sold by branches A and B from January to June).

Key items may be defined as only those exhibiting some specified illogical relationship (e.g. negative inventory balances, gross profit levels under 5%) or as all items *other than* those meeting a specified logical relationship (e.g., cash receipts entries other than those coded for crediting to accounts receivable or to specified miscellaneous revenue accounts). Key item selection can also be used to compare two sources of information and produce a listing of exceptions. Audit exception reporting allows the auditor to concentrate his efforts on those items which are large, unusual or sensitive.

Mathematical calculations

Performing mathematical calculations by computer is often useful when large volumes of data must be processed for simple but time-consuming computations, such as checking depreciation rates or inventory pricing. It may be useful for smaller volumes of data as well where the calculations themselves are numerous or complex, such as the calculation of principal and interest on mortgages. Large-volume simple calculations are usually processed in a batch environment. Low-volume complex calculations may often be processed using timesharing programs.

Mathematical calculations may also be included in the definition of criteria for key item selection. A further application of the mathematical power of the computer is in the use of regression analysis to replace judgmental analytical review (see 10.5.2).

Programs available

While the types of data-oriented technique which can be applied cover a wide range, the programs employed in these applications are generally one of three types: custom-written programs, generalized audit software or generalized commercial software. Following is a discussion of the capabilities, constraints, advantages and disadvantages of each of these alternatives.

14.2.2 Custom-written programs

Custom-written programs are those developed specifically for a particular computer-assisted application. Occasionally, a program can be designed so that it can, with minor modification, be adapted for use on other audits; more often each program is specific to one engagement.

The major advantage of a custom-written program is that it is tailored to meet particular audit requirements with maximum efficiency, bearing in mind the client's computer configuration and file formats. It avoids the constraints and the processing inefficiencies which are inherent in generalized software.

On the other hand, it is costly to write. Preparing and testing new programs is a time-consuming task. The audit requirements must be translated into logic flow charts indicating the input files, the computational steps and the output reports. The logic steps must be coded in a programming language. The resulting code must be keypunched. The keypunched code must be entered into the computer and compiled, i.e., converted into machine-sensible form. And finally, the program must be subjected to testing and debugging prior to audit use. In subsequent years, whenever there are changes in the audit requirements, the computer system, or the data file formats, it is likely that much of this process will have to be repeated.

The auditor must weigh the processing economies against the development costs in choosing a custom-written program in place of generalized software. With the growing versatility of the latter in recent years, the use of custom-written programs has declined. They still, however, have a place. In many cases, the use of "user-oriented" programming languages such as RPG (in a batch-processing environment) or BASIC and APL (in a timesharing environment) can significantly reduce the development and maintenance costs of these applications. In other cases, a custom-written program can be used as a supplement rather than an alternative to generalized software. Its use would then be confined to non-standard client file structures, unique audit requirements or specialized reports not easily includable in the generalized routines.

The auditor has three alternatives for developing a custom-written program.

- He may develop it himself.
- He may use a client programmer, or hire an outside programmer, to write it.
- He may use or modify an existing client-written routine.

The auditor-written program requires that the auditor have a good working knowledge of EDP concepts and computer programming. However, where the auditor has sufficient knowledge and time available, this approach may be the most efficient. The auditor has the best appreciation of the audit requirements and can thus avoid any misunderstandings in communicating these requirements to another programmer. Auditor preparation does not change the necessity for adequate testing of the program to ensure that it correctly performs the functions intended. Development time will of course depend on the complexity of the program as well as on the degree of skill which the auditor can bring to the task.

Where the auditor uses the services of a client programmer or an independent programmer, he must in either case define carefully the sequence of instructions required and become directly involved in the testing and debugging of the program before audit use. The auditor's tests must ensure not only that the program is performing the audit processes as required but also that no additional logic has been inadvertently or deliberately added to the program. For this reason, it is important that, when a client programmer is used, he be independent of the systems area under audit.

Finally, in certain instances, the client's own programs with or without minor modifications, may be used to perform audit functions. For example, the ageing of accounts receivable or the analyzing of inventory obsolescence can usually be handled by existing client routines. While this approach may be less costly in terms of program development, it is more difficult to control. The auditor must review the detailed logic steps of the program to ensure that his audit requirements can, in fact, be met by the client's program. As would be the case with other custom programs, test data must be prepared and processed against the client program to ensure the accuracy of the processing logic. In most cases, the auditor would also need to establish that no fraudulent instructions had been entered into the program. The use of a test deck is not an adequate protection against such fraudulent insertions. Test data will only verify those logic paths specifically selected for testing. The possibilities for additional logic paths, such as a special routine called into play only when a certain account number is read, are numerous. To prove their absence by using test data is just not feasible with any degree of confidence. While a review of program code could, in theory, solve this problem, it should be recognized that such a review, for all but the simplest programs, is very complex. Computer programs contain many "housekeeping" steps as well as numerous branching instructions. The way such instructions are designed depends, in large part, on the preferences of the programmer. As a result, to review program code written by someone else is time consuming and requires a high degree of skill. Partly for this reason, the use of client programs, while at first glance the easiest approach, has found only limited application by auditors.

In summary, custom-written audit programs have a definite but limited use. Successful application depends upon the skill and care which the auditor can provide. Generally, their use has been decreasing in recent years with the improvement of generalized software.

14.2.3 Generalized audit software

Generalized audit software consists of programs written for audit purposes by a number of accounting firms to process a wide range of client data files on many different computer installations. Many different generalized routines may be combined together as components of one "software package". The demand for these packages grew from the early audit use of custom-written programs. The high cost of custom programming and the similarity of audit functions from engagement to engagement prompted the logical move to generalization. Generalized audit software relieves the auditor of the burden of extensive programming. While a knowledge of EDP concepts is certainly still required, the auditor no longer needs as much detailed technical knowledge in order to use computer-assisted auditing.

Typical functions included in a generalized audit software package are:

- statistical selection,
- summarization/addition of data,
- key item selection,
- mathematical calculations,
- updating of files,
- printing.

Some specific examples of the use of each of these audit functions are shown in Figure 14.a.

Each software package is organized in a somewhat

**Examples of Audit Functions
which can be Performed Using Generalized Software**

Function	Example
1. Statistical selection	
(a) Dollar-unit samples	Select a sample of fixed asset additions
(b) Physical-unit samples	Select a sample of shipping orders
2. Summarization/addition of data	
(a) Specified fields within an individual record	Total the inventory contained by location in a record
(b) Records within a file	Total the accounts receivable file, summarize the file according to audit location
(c) Bar charts (histograms)	Compute and plot the frequency of different magnitudes of accounts receivable balances
3. Key item selection	
(a) Items outside prescribed limits (i.e., exceptions)	Identify accounts receivable balances over 90 days old
(b) Items with specific characteristics	Identify the current year's mortgages
(c) Items with unusual characteristics	Identify negative inventory quantities
(d) Records on two files which do not match	Compare two payroll master files for changes
4. Mathematical calculations	
(a) Add/subtract specified fields	Verify ageing totals for an accounts receivable file
(b) Multiply specified fields	Verify extensions of price by quantity in an inventory record, compute gross profit ratios
(c) Divide specified fields	Verify calculations of unit prices of inventory items
5. Updating of files	
(a) Update master file with transactions	Post subsequent payments to accounts receivable
(b) Match items verified with outstanding list	Match inventory counts to perpetual records, confirmations returned to initial requests, cheques cashed to cheques issued
6. Printing	
(a) Confirmation letters	Print confirmation requests for accounts receivable
(b) Audit listings/reports	List a file of fixed asset additions, list items identified in "data selection"

Figure 14.a

different fashion. Two basic approaches are common. In one approach, various control statements are prepared by the auditor based on the requirements of his application. These are read by one of the routines in the package and converted into a table. The table is used by another routine (usually written in COBOL) to generate a program to accomplish the various audit procedures. In the other approach, narrative forms which define the computer installation, the data files, the required audit functions and the various values or parameters are completed and keypunched. These specifications are then loaded into the system and are accessed by the package during execution.

While generalized audit software packages, once developed, may be used far more economically than writing new custom programs each time, the initial development of a package is a major undertaking. Numerous technical decisions must be made in planning the package. One decision is the types of computer on which the package is to be able to operate: the particular manufacturers, the minimum memory size required, and the number of peripheral devices such as tape and disk drives needed. Another decision is the types of data file which the package is to be able to process: fixed, variable, indexed sequential or random. A third is the number of audit functions which are capable of being performed in one pass of the file. Each of these decisions will affect not only the cost of developing the package but also the level of technical knowledge required to use the package and its adaptability to different audit situations. The development of an all-purpose generalized software package can cost anywhere from $250 000 to well over $1 000 000. In addition, the packages must be continually updated to meet changing audit requirements or changing technology.

14.2.4 Generalized commercial software

Generalized software packages for use by auditors are not restricted, however, to software developed by public accounting firms themselves. Other possibilities are: (a) generalized commercial software packages, (b) utility programs, and (c) generalized timesharing programs.

Generalized commmercial software packages

Apart from the selection of statistical samples, all of the functions shown in Figure 14.1 are basic functions included in most commercial packages designed for a much broader market. Most computer installations have a need for a generalized data retrieval package to supplement their own in-house programming resources and to permit special requests for information from management to be quickly and inexpensively met. Because these packages perform many of the functions required by auditors, they have found a growing use in computer-assisted auditing as well. There are literally dozens of these packages on the market today. Some of the better known ones include DYL-260, CULPRIT, EXTRACTO, MARK IV and DATA ANALYZER.

The major advantage of these packages for the auditor is cost. While commercial packages are expensive to develop, they service a much wider clientele than do audit packages alone. As a result, they can be purchased or leased for a fraction of their development cost.

Their major disadvantage is that they often lack a few specialized functions required by the auditor. The most obvious lack is usually a statistical sampling routine. In addition, some other requirements, such as special confirmation print routines, may be difficult to meet with commercial software. This disadvantage has been reduced in recent years, as certain commercial software houses have developed special audit versions of their software packages. Alternatively, some accounting firms use commercial software packages for those audit functions which are similar to the data retrieval requirements of their clients and confine the development of in-house audit software to those specialized audit requirements, such as statistical sampling or regression analysis, not

readily available on the commercial market. In this way, the development cost of generalized audit software can be reduced to a fraction of what it would otherwise be.

Because many of the commercial software packages have been designed for use by EDP personnel, they require a fairly good understanding of EDP concepts. As with generalized audit software, however, the level of required expertise varies from package to package. Some software houses have tried to ensure that client accounting personnel can code their own information requests with a minimum of reliance on the EDP department. Generally, such packages are as easy to use as the simpler audit packages.

Utility programs

Computer manufacturers offer a number of standard "utility programs" for handling various simple functions required in virtually every computer installation. These functions include sorting, file merging, disk-to-printer listings, and card-to-tape or tape-to-tape copying. In many computer-assisted audit applications the auditor will have occasion to use a utility program as a small part of his total procedures (for example, to copy an active client file for use in later audit analysis). In rare cases, the use of a utility program may be the sole computer-assisted procedure – for example, in listing an intermediate file to bridge a gap in the hard-copy audit trail or sorting a client file into a more convenient sequence for verification.

Generalized timesharing programs

Generalized timesharing programs have been developed, for the most part, by companies offering centralized timesharing computer facilities accessible through terminals in their customers' offices. Among their customers are a growing number of public accounting firms. Many of the timesharing programs include analytical calculations such as mortgage amortization, return on investment, discounted cash flow, and buy-or-lease analysis, which can be used by the auditor in verifying client calculations, performing analytical review, or assessing the carrying values of assets or investments.

Although these programs are developed independently of the client, the auditor must take care that they have been adequately tested and he must ensure that he is using the routines correctly. Unlike data retrieval software, where the auditor can usually tell if something is amiss by a simple scan of his output, erroneous results resulting from the incorrect use of a timesharing program may not always be so obvious.

14.2.5 The trade-off concept

After reviewing the various types of generalized audit and retrieval packages available, the question facing the auditor is which package to lease or buy in order to meet his audit needs. There is no easy answer to this question. Software selection involves a series of trade-offs when comparing one package with another. In general, the more capabilities and the greater flexibility provided, the more complex the package is to use and the more knowledgeable the auditor must be about EDP techniques.

At the low end of the scale, a package would have tight limitations on the format and number of data files which could be processed and on the number of functions which could be performed on any one pass. At the same time, however, it would require only limited computer memory and only limited EDP knowledge on the auditor's part. The audit requirements would be defined by completing a series of narrative form checklists. When keypunched, the coded responses would cause the appropriate audit functions to be executed. Control cards used to instruct the computer as to the sequence of routines to be run and the peripheral devices to be used would be largely pre-coded.

At the other extreme, a sophisticated package would provide a broader array of audit functions, impose fewer limitations on the types of files which could be processed and permit a fairly complex combination of audit functions to be performed on any one pass. At the same time, however, larger hardware and computer memory would be required and the auditor would have to have an extensive knowledge of EDP. Many of these packages would require at least some programming to be done – usually in COBOL.

In between these two extremes are many degrees of capability and complexity. Each package has its particular strong and weak points. One may have excellent report-writing capabilities while another's strength is multiple-file handling.

The auditor must, therefore, carefully consider his requirements. The number of audit functions performable in a single pass is usually an important consideration. Even a relatively simple task such as confirming accounts receivable can involve a number of different functions – sampling the balances to be confirmed, summarizing the open invoice file for account balances, combining the account balance and the name and address records, and printing the confirmation requests. If each function requires a separate pass, computer running costs for the application can quickly soar.

Another feature to consider is the audit control generated by the package. The auditor will wish to ensure that appropriate control totals, record counts, and print-outs of erroneous records are generated in order to establish that the correct data files were used and that all the information was processed. Some packages have better controls than others.

Another consideration is the editing performed by the package on the coding or specifications provided by the auditor. Ideally, the package should edit the audit functions and selection criteria for validity and consistency and also should provide clear and comprehensive edit messages to aid the auditor in identifying and correcting specification errors.

Finally, the availability of software support from the supplier of the package is important. Problems and questions are bound to arise, at least during the initial period of use. The users' manual provided by the supplier should be reviewed in detail. Some manuals are oriented to the unsophisticated user; others are oriented to the EDP professional and are technically complex to use.

14.3 Computer-assisted audit techniques for compliance verification

Techniques for using test data or special programs to test the client's regular accounting programs can be called *systems-oriented techniques*. Usually, but not always, systems-oriented techniques are used for compliance verification.

14.3.1 Scope of systems-oriented computer techniques

Systems-oriented techniques are not used to nearly the same extent within the profession today as are data-oriented techniques. The reason is that most computer controls can be verified more easily by visual inspection. The accuracy of programmed balancing of control totals, can be verified by checking control totals manually to batch logs. Programmed edit routines can be verified by visually reviewing error reports. Computer program logic can be verified by manually reperforming the logic procedures and agreeing the recalculated results to the computer output.

Generally, the auditor would consider a systems-oriented computer technique only where complex computer processes of audit significance are performed, where accounting transactions are generated internally and cannot be easily checked manually, where gaps occur in the audit trail, or where unusually significant audit reliance is being placed on some computer routine. The number of cases where these conditions occur is still relatively small. However, the growth of sophisiticated computer systems such as on-line processing or data base systems is likely to increase the use of computer-assisted routines for compliance verification. In these advanced systems many more of the controls are software controls, which lend themselves to computer-assisted verification. Less reliance is placed on the manual or traditional computer controls, for which manual verification has in the past been available.

The auditor usually requires even greater knowledge to use a systems-oriented computer technique than a data-oriented one. Not only does the auditor need to know the mechanics of the particular technique and the detailed format of client data files, as he does with data-oriented techniques, he must also have a detailed understanding of the client's computer programs which are to be checked.

Many of the systems-oriented computer techniques in use today are of primary interest to *internal* auditors. They are discussed in 14.4. Two techniques, however, are of more direct interest to external auditors: test decks and automatic flow charting.

14.3.2 The test deck approach

The test deck approach can be defined as the use of test data (whether on card, tape or disk) to verify certain controls or accounting processes on which audit reliance will be placed. Its major applications are for compliance purposes (a) to verify computer edits, by using invalid data which the edit routines should reject or (b) to check complex program calculations such as would be found in life insurance systems, by using valid data. Specific instances include overcoming audit trail gaps, verifying control total balancing routines and checking the accuracy of internally generated transactions.

Test decks may occasionally be used for a substantive purpose – validating a client program to be used as a custom-written audit program in some key year-end calculation or summarization (see 14.2.2).

Whatever the audit objective, the use of a test deck involves the following steps. Test data, covering each of the logic paths to be verified, is prepared first. The test data is then processed against one or more of the client's programs. Finally, the resulting output is agreed in detail to the auditor's precalculated results.

Sources of test data

One of the major tasks of any test deck application is determining where to obtain the relevant test data. There are a number of possible sources. The auditor may obtain actual historical data previously processed through the system or he may use the programmer's original test data, if it has been preserved. Or, he may prepare his own test data based upon an analysis of the conditions to be tested. Finally, a number of software packages, called "test data generators", have been recently developed which can generate large volumes of test data from a definition of the test conditions. These packages can be of particular use where sophisticated systems with a wide range of erroneous and valid conditions are involved. Most of these packages will also produce output reports and control totals of the resulting test data.

Limitations and disadvantages of test decks

In spite of their usefulness, test decks have a number of limitations.

1. The test deck approach is used to *verify* specific aspects of the system under audit; it is not a technique for *reviewing* the system, (discovering what it does). The auditor must understand the system *before* beginning his test deck application if it is to be successful.

2. A test deck application is performed at a particular point in time. Without other audit assurance, it would be dangerous to extend the conclusions to cover the entire period under audit. The auditor should either re-run his application periodically throughout the period under review or evaluate, verify and rely on controls over program changes.

3. The purpose of a test deck is to verify that certain conditions are being handled properly. It can provide persuasive evidence that accidental programming errors have not occurred. It does not, however, provide evidence that fraudulent programming errors have not occurred. Fraudulently inserted program steps designed to manipulate isolated transactions (of a particular code or for a particular customer) would not be revealed by a test deck unless fortuitously the deck happened to include one of those isolated transactions. Therefore, if the auditor is concerned about the possibility of fraudulent programming errors (as he might be in the case of a payroll application) the test deck approach will not be appropriate.

4. To ensure that the program tested is in fact the operational one, the test deck should simulate actual operating conditions. Such a simulation

would require that test data be processed through the data conversion stage, through each of the computer processing stages, and through final output distribution without the test data being in any way distinguishable from live data. In practice, such a complete simulation is rarely, if ever, possible. Planning with the EDP personnel is required prior to a run – which may mean that the processing will receive special and unusual attention. In many cases, only a small portion of the system is of particular audit interest and accordingly the test deck begins at some point part way through the processing cycle. Finally, the physical attendance of the auditor may add to the artificiality of the run.

5. The auditor must ensure that his test data does not permanently distort the master files affected by his application. He may sometimes solve this problem by running a set of reversing transactions after the run. Alternatively, and preferably, he can copy the whole or a portion of the master file and run his test against the dummy copy.

Test decks versus historical results

In a sense, the past month's or past year's transactions can be thought of as constituting one enormous test deck. As long as each type of transaction and each logic path is tested by a comparison of historical input documents and output reports, it can be argued that running a current test deck proves nothing further. With respect to programmed controls, the review of historical results can include examples of transactions violating each programmed control on which audit reliance is to be placed and their comparison to computer error reports; again it can be argued that running a current test deck proves nothing further. Since the checking of historical results may be simpler than the design and running of a test deck, the former is often the preferable approach (see Chapter 27).

However, on occasion, audit reliance must be placed on a programmed control which has never been exercised because, allegedly, violating conditions have never been encountered (see 27.3.3). To prove the existence of such a control, a test deck may be required – but it can then be limited to a test of the specific programmed control in question.

In more advanced systems the checking of historical results may be difficult. A transaction type occurring ten times a month may be buried amid thousands of more common transactions and therefore difficult to locate and check. In such cases a test deck may be more efficient. Test decks may likewise be the better approach for on-line systems and for checking certain internally generated transactions.

In summary, the test deck approach can be a useful technique for the auditor provided he appreciates the limitations of the approach and has a thorough understanding of the system under review.

14.3.3 Automatic flow charting

Special software has been developed which can generate, from the client's source program code, a flow chart of the logical sequence of steps within a program. It is limited to certain programming languages. The major commercial use of automatic flow charting is to supplement the program documentation within an EDP installation. The possible audit use of the technique is to interpret the computer programs actually in use so that their propriety can be verified.

Since the logic flow chart is generated from the *source* program, the auditor needs some way to satisfy himself that it corresponds to the actual *object* program in operation. A common method is to recompile the source program and compare the resulting object program with the one in use.

To use automatic flow charting effectively, the auditor should define the specific controls or procedures he wishes to review using this technique. To attempt to review an entire system or even a whole program using this technique is both difficult and time-consuming. The volume of output produced from a documentation approach for the whole system would be too voluminous to be adequately reviewed within the time constraints of an external audit. While automatic flow charting may indeed be feasible where only a pin-pointed area of the computer logic is to be verified, the auditor must consider whether tests of past processing or the use of a test deck would not also be feasible and perhaps more economical.

14.4 Computer-assisted audit techniques for internal audit use

A number of other computer-assisted techniques, while occasionally of use to the external auditor, tend to be applied primarily by internal auditors.

The major difference between these techniques and those discussed previously is one of timing. The techniques of most use to the external auditor tend to be one-time applications. Even though the application may be run at different times over the course of the year (for example, the sampling of cycle billings on different days of a month) or may cover an entire year's transactions (for example, an analysis of all expense transactions), the client data file or program being audited is frozen at a point in time while the auditor conducts his review. By contrast, most of the techniques described in the following sections are performed in a "continuous audit" environment. Audit evidence is extracted concurrently with the regular processing of the accounting transaction stream. A few of the techniques, while not continuous auditing applications, are ones which are too time-consuming to be of major use to the external auditor. Because of lower materiality criteria and wider management audit responsibilities they may, however, be of use to the internal auditor.

14.4.1 Relevance to the external auditor

Even though these techniques may be rarely used by the external auditor directly, they can affect his work for two reasons. First, the internal audit function is itself an important element of internal control within the organization. To the extent that the internal audit department is using computer-assisted techniques to monitor or audit computerized systems on a continuous basis, the external auditor can put greater reliance on the accounting results produced by those systems than would otherwise be the case. At the same time, to justify such additional reliance, the external auditor must be able to review and evaluate the internal audit use of these techniques.

Second, the external auditor, in his role as adviser to his client, may be expected to consult with and assist the internal auditor in implementing these techniques. The external auditor should, therefore, have an awareness of their capabilities, advantages and limitations.

14.4.2 Outline of commonly used techniques

The following techniques are currently used by only a small percentage of internal audit groups, even within the larger companies. Although the concepts are fairly simple, their successful implementation requires a good deal of both time and technical knowledge. Their application is basically limited to large integrated systems.[1]

Integrated test facility

As computer systems become more complex and integrated, the integrated test facility (ITF) approach is gaining in popularity. Also referred to as the mini-company or model office approach, it enables the auditor to duplicate, on a small scale, the system of processing which takes place for the company as a whole.

An ITF is merely a sophisticated extension of the test deck approach. Selected transactions are mixed with live data and processed through the various phases of the system. The output is then compared with the previously calculated manual results. This approach allows the auditor to monitor the performance of the system continuously.

The ITF is a sophisticated audit approach which requires time and skill to develop. Once developed, however, test transactions can be processed using the normal company procedures which apply to all regular transactions entering the system.

The major advantages of an ITF are:

1. The technique provides continuous monitoring of the system under review. When program changes, even minor ones, are made, the test data can be rerun to determine the impact of the changes on the system.
2. Because the ITF is run as a regular part of the processing operations, it overcomes much of the artificiality (abnormal conditions, point-in-time limitation) of the normal test deck approach.
3. The technique is useful for highly integrated and on-line systems. Such systems are the very ones which are most difficult to audit by conventional means.

The major disadvantages of an ITF are:

1. Special procedures must be developed to ensure that the test transactions do not affect the company's financial reporting or operations. For example, precautions are needed to ensure that

the live master files are not permanently changed or that goods are not shipped as a result of the ITF use.

2. As with any test deck approach, the ITF is not a conclusive test for faudlent manipulation of programs.

Program simulation

The accuracy of program logic in a simple program can be checked manually be tracing input to output and recalculating any extensions, additions or other calculations involved. In a complex program the manual retracing and recalculation may no longer be possible. In such circumstances, it may be necessary to prepare a special program to duplicate the alleged processes of the regular production program in order to prove their validity.

Program simulation (sometimes referred to as *parallel simulation*) is the technique of replicating the basic program logic of a given program through the use of a special program or generalized software. The auditor must first define the program functions to be verified, ensure that he has a thorough understanding of those functions, and then obtain a representative set of input and output from past processing of the production program. The input is then processed by the simulated program and the results are compared to the earlier production program output. Any discrepancies would then be analyzed.

The success of this technique will be influenced by the complexity of the program being simulated and by the ability of the audit software to duplicate the functions being reviewed.

Tagging

A large system could well have thousands of different logic paths available to it. As a result, it may be very difficult to predict exactly what will happen when a certain transaction is entered into the system. Tagging (also called Snapshot) provides an audit trail for a transaction as it flows through a computer system.

A transaction is identified or "tagged" using a special code and the transaction is traced as it flows through the system. The end result is a printed audit trail.

In order to use this technique, programmed logic must be entered into the computer system to detect the tagged transactions and to print out the audit trail.

The technique can be utilized:

a) to predict the particular processing path which a transaction, as yet unprocessed, will take,
b) to test a new program or system,
c) to determine why a particular transaction was processed in a specific manner,
d) to tag transactions randomly in order to check the quality of output.

Tagging can also complement the ITF approach. For example, if a transaction was not processed as expected through the ITF, a similar transaction can be tagged and tracked through the system to determine how the transaction was processed.

Concurrent auditing (SCARF)

Concurrent auditing is the process of automatically selecting transactions for review during live processing. It enables the auditor to become aware of potential problems as they occur rather than on the more traditional after-the-fact-basis. SCARF (Systems Control Audit Review File) is probably the best known technique using this approach.

To use SCARF, the auditor must first define his audit criteria, i.e., those transactions which he wishes to follow up. They might consist of key item selections (for example, overrides of credit limits) as well as a random sample of regular transactions. Once the criteria have been defined, the auditor must work with systems personnel to develop the appropriate routines and to add the code into the regular processing stream.

Once operational, any transactions which meet the auditor's criteria are written onto a special file and periodically, say weekly, listed for review and follow-up.

14.5 Application considerations

The use of a computer-assisted audit technique requires several important planning decisions, special procedures to maintain control, and adequate methods of documentation.

14.5.1 Planning considerations

The more important planning considerations are the following:

1. A review of the economic feasibility should be performed before each application. Such a review is essential to ensure that computer-assisted techniques are used only where they will be effective and economically feasible. The two most common reasons for using computer-assisted techniques are (a) a net saving in audit costs, or (b) at reasonable cost, a better quality audit.

In either case, a careful calculation of expected costs or savings should be made beforehand. Such a calculation may indicate that computer-assisted auditing is justified – in which case the calculation can serve as a budget during the application. Or it may indicate that conventional manual procedures are preferable. An example of a feasibility summary is shown in Figure 14.b. Estimated savings generally consist of reduced audit staff time. Estimated costs consist of computer time, keypunching costs, the time of computer audit specialists, etc.

2. At the time of reviewing the economic feasibility, the auditor should determine the technical feasibility of the proposed application. Both the hardware and software requirements must be considered. For example, an RPG program can only be run on a computer with an RPG compiler. Each generalized software package has constraints with regard to computer models, memory size and number of peripheral devices required.
3. The auditor must decide on which computer to run the application. The client's own computer would normally be the logical choice. Indeed,

---

Feasibility Summary
Computer-Assisted Audit Application

Client: ABC Limited

Proposed date of application: September 30, 19–

Brief description of application: inventory analysis

Reasons for using computer:
(a) more effective audit ☒
(b) audit savings ☒
(c) unable to do manually ☐
(d) reduce tedious staff work ☐
(e) client relations ☐

Cost and savings estimate:

First year savings:

Audit staff time	$ 1 200
Other	
Total savings	$ 1 200

First year costs:

Planning	$ 300
Coding	150
Application testing	300
Documentation	100
Keypunching costs	10
Computer rental	150
Attendance at processing	50
Other	
Total costs	$ 1 060

Net First Year Savings (Investment)   140

Future savings (only if application likely to be re-usable for unchanged client system)

$ 1 200 for 2 years   2 400

Future costs

$ 500 for 2 years   1 000

Net Future Savings (Investment)   1 400

Total First Year and Future Savings (Investment) $ 1 540

Figure 14.b

many clients have blocks of unused time available on their equipment, which could be used for such applications. The advantages of using the client computer are apparent: little if any additional cost to the client, availability of personnel who have knowledge of the system, and retention of all client data files on the premises. A byproduct is that client personnel can observe the auditor's work. If the auditor is proficient at his task, his proficiency may help to elicit the cooperation he needs from client EDP personnel in other areas of his audit.

When the client's computer is not available, or when the auditor's application will not run on the client's computer, some other computer must be arranged. In some cases, the auditor will have his own computer and it may be able to process the application; in other cases, computer time can be purchased from an outside data centre. Of course, in the last case, extra precautions are required to ensure that the confidential nature of the client data files is protected.

4. The auditor should always arrange for duplicate copies of client data files to be used for testing and processing. The use of duplicates avoids any danger of damaging or destroying a data file which could be costly to re-create.

5. For test deck applications, the auditor should consider the following additional points:
   a) the effect of the test deck on any master file involved,
   b) the way in which test data will be obtained or developed,
   c) the importance of the inevitably artificial operating conditions which exist during the running of a test deck,
   d) the possibility of avoiding, in a large system, numerous programs not of audit significance (e.g., by starting the test deck part way through the processing cycle),
   e) the importance of the unavoidable risks of fraudulent program manipulation, which test decks cannot detect.

14.5.2 Control considerations

Audit integrity of every computer-assisted audit application should be maintained by the use of appropriate control procedures. A checklist is useful to ensure that no important control is overlooked. An example of an audit control checklist is shown in Figure 14.c. The major considerations are discussed below:

1. Each individual application should be tested in advance. Testing ensures that valid specifications have been used and that these specifications will cause the application to be processed in the desired manner.

2. The auditor should attend and observe the actual computer processing of the application, even if he does not operate the computer himself. The purpose of this attendance is:
   a) to ensure that correct data files are used,
   b) to ensure that the actual test data and specification cards are used,
   c) to ensure that the prescribed operating instructions are followed,
   d) to note for subsequent verification any unplanned operator actions performed during processing as a result of unexpected processing problems (such as unreadable data file records),
   e) to control the audit output,
   f) to maintain physical control over the audit programs.

3. The auditor should control the client data files, his own specification sheets and cards, the test data, and his audit programs throughout the application to ensure that there is no substitution or tampering.

4. The audit control information generated by the application must be balanced where applicable to the client's control information.

5. When custom programs are used which were not prepared by the auditor, he must:
   a) review the documentation of the program logic,
   b) review the program code,
   c) test the program with test data.

14.5.3 Documentation considerations

Adequate documentation in the working papers is necessary to:

1. serve as sufficient audit evidence supporting the audit opinion,
2. provide sufficient information to allow a second review of the application and of the results obtained,
3. provide guidelines to organize and plan the application in a subsequent year.

Documentation which is important for all applications includes:

1. Justification for the application – the potential costs and benefits to be anticipated and a benchmark for deciding upon completion whether the anticipated benefits have been realized.
2. Written description of the application – a summary of the application undertaken and the results obtained, including the purpose, the particular software used, the files processed, procedures

Audit Control Checklist
Computer-Assisted Audit Application

	Yes	No	Explanation if No

A. All applications

1. A feasibility and estimated time analyses was prepared. ☑ ☐
2. The application was tested in advance. ☑ ☐
3. Duplicate copies of the client data files were used for testing and processing. ☑ ☐
4. A computer audit specialist was in attendance and supervised all processing. ☐ ☑ *Application performed on auditor's computer-Specialist, therefore, did not attend the line run.*
5. Physical control and custody was maintained over client data files throughout the application. ☑ ☐
6. Physical control and custody was maintained at all times over all computer-assisted auditing material (including documentation, specification sheets, programs, punched cards, tapes, disks, etc.) ☑ ☐
7. Inter-run control totals have been balanced and recorded on the control total worksheet. ☑ ☐
8. Control totals have been reconciled to client totals and recorded on the control total worksheet. ☑ ☐
9. The application has been adequately documented in the working papers. ☑ ☐
10. The application included a selection of data records for audit verification purposes to ensure the validity of the file contents. ☑ ☐

B. Generalized software applications only

1. Specification sheets have been agreed in detail to JCL listings and parameter listings. ☑ ☐

C. Custom programs only

I New programs
1. Detailed procedures were prepared defining the precise logic to be followed by the programmer in writing the custom programs. ☐ ☐ } N/A
2. The accuracy of the program logic was verified, including:
   a) a review of the programmer's documentation. ☐ ☐
   b) a review of the source coding, JCL and operating instructions. ☐ ☐
   c) the preparation and processing of test data by the program and agreement to predetermined results. ☐ ☐
3. The program was controlled from commencement of verification to completion of application, including:
   a) control over program compilation. ☐ ☐
   b) control over program cataloguing. ☐ ☐
   c) control over JCL and program execution. ☐ ☐
4. Arrangements have been made to maintain physical control over the programs and related materials until the next audit application.
   Describe control procedure:

} N/A

II Existing programs
1. The programs and related materials were under our physical control from the previous application to commencement of the current application. ☐ ☐
   Describe control procedure:
2. Arrangements have been made to maintain physical control over the programs and related materials until the next audit application. ☐ ☐
   Describe control procedure:

Prepared by _G. Black_   Date _October 23, 19–_

Figure 14.c

for attendance at processing, arrangements with the client for computer time and file copying, and an outline of unusual processing problems.

3. User instructions – an outline of any special instructions, such as for balancing procedures, and the use of turnaround documents.

4. Systems flow chart – a schematic presentation of the application including, for each program, the input (master files, data files, parameter cards), the routine being run and the output (files and printouts).

5. Specification forms – the various specification and coding forms used to run the application (to be retained in the working papers).

6. Computer console listing – a copy of the console listing in order to provide:
   a) documentation of the jobs run,
   b) a record for later review of any problems encountered and the action taken,
   c) in some cases, a record of control totals generated during the run.

7. Printer listing – generally the primary working paper in the audit file and serving to provide:
   a) a list of the detailed items generated,
   b) a series of control totals generated at the end of each routine,

c) documentation of the JCL, program options and parameter values used.

8. Control total worksheet – a single spreadsheet to combine the control totals spread over a number of runs and printouts and thus to provide a useful summary of the inter-run balancing.

Additional documentation which is important for custom programs includes:

1. Program flow chart – usually prepared by the auditor as a guide, for the programmer or for himself, in coding the program.

2. Source deck – the card deck containing the audit program to be run, kept under the auditor's control during processing and retained by him for use the next year.

3. Source listing – the listing of the source program provided during the compilation or translation of the source deck into machine-sensible form.

4. Object deck – the card deck produced during the compilation and actually used in running the application (because an object deck is not subject to direct verification, the auditor must ensure that the source deck under his control was used to produce the object deck from which the application was run).

14.6 Reference material

CICA Study, *Computer Audit Guidelines* (1975), Chapter XVI.

Jancura, Elise G., *Audit & Control of Computer Systems*, Petrocelli Books, 1975.

Porter, W. Thomas, Jr., *Auditing Electronic Systems*, Wadsworth Publishing Company Inc., 1966.

Pinkney, Anthony, F.C.A., *An Audit Approach to Computers*, The Institute of Chartered Accountants in England and Wales, 1966.

Dorricott, K.O., Appraising Computer-Assisted Auditing Techniques, *CA Magazine*, August, 1975.

14.7 Questions and problems

Review and discussion

1. Discuss briefly the advantages and disadvantages of computer assisted auditing.

2. Identify the four categories into which most data-oriented techniques can be classified.

3. There are generally three types of computer program that can be used in computer audit applications. Identify the three types and indicate the advantages and disadvantages of each.

4. Systems-oriented techniques are not used to audit clients' accounting programs to the same extent as data-oriented techniques. Briefly explain why this is so and suggest circumstances where systems-oriented audit techniques would be appropriate.

5. Describe the uses of a test deck.

6. What are the advantages and disadvantages of using a test deck as a systems-oriented audit technique? Suggest circumstances where a test deck would be used.

7. What are the basic differences between computer-assisted audit techniques used by internal auditors and by external auditors? Suggest instances where computer-assisted audit techniques employed by the internal auditor may be useful to the external auditor.

8. An integrated test facility (ITF) is becoming more popular as a computer-assisted audit technique. What are the advantages and disadvantages of an ITF?

9. Indicate how the following computer-assisted audit techniques are used by internal auditors:

   a) program simulation,
   b) tagging,
   c) concurrent auditing.

Problems

1. C. Potter, CA, is the computer audit specialist for Well, Buros and Honey Chartered Accountants. He has been requested, by a client partner, to aid the audit staff in the verification of a client's accounts receivable and inventory using computer-assisted audit techniques.

   a) What factors will Potter review in deciding what type of data-oriented technique should be employed?
   b) If a custom-written program is applicable, what factors should be considered in determining who should develop the program?
   c) If a generalized commercial software package is applicable, and Well, Buros and Honey do not have a package available, what factors should be considered by the audit firm in deciding which package should be leased or purchased?

2. J. Wallace, CA, is the audit manager for Complicated Systems Inc. (CSI) which has recently implemented a computerized accounting system. A conversion audit has been performed and no problems were encountered. Wallace is currently planning the financial statement audit for the current fiscal year.

   a) What points should be considered in order to determine whether or not to use computer-assisted audit techniques?
   b) If a computer-assisted audit technique is warranted how will Wallace's staff control its use, and what documentation should be maintained?

3. Big Wholesaler Limited is a medium-sized wholesaler of health and beauty aids, confectioneries and tobacco products. As at the previous fiscal year-end Big has added a perpetual inventory control system to its computerized accounting system. Big's external auditors, Green & Co., Chartered Accountants, observed the previous year's inventory count and performed their inventory verification procedures. Big adjusted all counts and values per Green & Co.'s findings.

   Big set up the agreed upon inventory on the master file of the new inventory control system. The information contained in the master file consists of:

- product number
- description
- size
- sale unit
- quantity on hand
- cost per unit
- total value on hand
- supplier code number
- date of last sale
- quantity sold during fiscal year
- minimum re-order point
- economic order quantity

   The purchase and sales systems were integrated with the inventory control system to automatically update the inventory.

   Monthly, Big's personnel count a portion of the inventory and compare it with the inventory record. All differences during the year were immaterial, and were attributed to normal shrinkage. Differences have not been adjusted.

   For the year-end inventory, Big has printed two copies of count books. One book is for Big's inventory counts and one is for Green & Co. The information printed in the books includes:

- product number
- description
- size
- sale unit

   On each product line, Big's personnel will record the quantity by sale unit counted by the Big's personnel. The books will then be keypunched into the computer system and processed against the current master file. The quantity on hand will be adjusted to reflect the actual count.

   The computer will then print out the adjusted inventory and a listing of every required adjustment, for an individual product, that is over $500. These items will be followed up by Big's personnel. When all discrepancies have been satisfactorily cleared by Big's personnel, the final necessary adjustments will be made to the general ledger.

   Green & Co. have a generalized audit software package that is adaptable to Big's computer system.

   You are the audit senior from Green & Co. responsible for Big Wholesaler Limited.

   a) What effect does the computerized inventory control system have on the audit plan?
   b) What procedures are required with respect to the opening inventory?
   c) How can a generalized audit software package be used to assist in the verification of Big Wholesaler Limited's inventory?

4. (CICA adapted) CA is the auditor of A Co. Ltd., a large manufacturing company with several plants

across Canada. The company has used electronic data processing equipment since 1963 to process most of its accounting information and presently has two third-generation computers at its head office.

In prior years A Co. Ltd. had never recorded accrued vacation pay in its accounts but instead had recognized the expense when vacations were taken by the employees. For the year ended December 31, 1976, however, the company decided to set up the liability at that date for accrued vacation pay.

The company employs approximately 2 400 employees, each of whom is a member of one of four unions. Employees' entitlement to vacation pay is based on length of service (calculated from the month of employment) and various other factors according to the terms of each union contract.

Complete personnel information for all employees is maintained on a payroll master file tape which is updated daily. An "Employee Status Report" containing all master file details for specified employees is produced daily on a request basis.

A specially written computer program was used to determine the amount of accrued vacation pay. This program extracted the relevant data from the payroll master file tape as at December 31, 1976, calculated the amount of accrued vacation pay for each employee, recorded the details on an output tape, and printed a summarized report showing only the grand total of the accrued vacation pay.

a) How could an audit trail be provided to enable CA to perform tests of the details of the accrued vacation pay? What practical difficulties may arise?
b) Explain briefly how CA could use a "test deck" to check the accuracy of the computer program.

5. (AICPA adapted) Peter Rogers, CA, has examined the financial statements of the Kismo Manufacturing Company for several years and is making preliminary plans for the audit for the year ended June 30, 1977. During this examination Mr. Rogers plans to use a set of generalized computer audit programs. Kismo's EDP manager has agreed to prepare special tapes of data from Company records for the CA's use with the generalized programs.

The following information is applicable to Mr. Roger's examination of Kismo's accounts payable and related procedures:
1) The formats of pertinent tapes are as follows:

a) Master file – vendor name
- vendor code
- record type
- space
- blank
- vendor name
- blank
- card code 100

b) Master file – vendor name
- vendor code
- record type
- space
- blank
- address – line 1
- address – line 2
- address – line 3
- blank
- card code 120

c) Transaction file – expense detail
- vendor code
- record type
- voucher number
- blank
- batch
- voucher number
- voucher date
- vendor code
- invoice date
- due date
- invoice number
- purchase order number
- debit account
- product type
- product code
- blank
- amount
- quantity
- card code 160

d) Transaction file – payment detail
- vendor code
- record type
- voucher number
- blank
- batch
- voucher number
- voucher date
- vendor code
- invoice date
- due date
- invoice date
- purchase order number
- cheque number
- cheque date
- blank

- amount
- blank
- card code 170

2) The following monthly runs are prepared:

- cash disbursements by check number,
- outstanding payables,
- purchase journals sorted by account charged and by vendor.

3) Vouchers and supporting invoices, receiving reports and purchase order copies are filed by vendor code. Purchase orders and cheques are filed numerically.

4) Company records are maintained on magnetic tapes. All tapes are stored in a restricted area within the computer room. A grandfather-father-son policy is followed for retaining and safeguarding tape files.

Required:

a) Explain the grandfather-father-son policy. Describe how files could be reconstructed when this policy is used.

b) Discuss whether company policies for retaining and safeguarding the tape files provide adequate protection against losses of data.

c) Describe the controls that the CA should maintain over:

- preparing the special tape,
- processing the special tape with the generalized computer audit programs.

d) Prepare a schedule for the EDP manager outlining the data that should be included on the special tape for the CA's examination of accounts payable and related procedures. This schedule should show the:

- client tape from which the item should be extracted,
- name of the item of data.

15

The Audit Team, Planning and Supervision

Although a thorough knowledge of audit objectives, evidence and techniques is essential to the conduct of any audit engagement, an effective audit requires more. It requires that the work be planned, controlled and reviewed in an organized manner. This requirement is expressed in the first field work standard:

> The work should be adequately planned and properly executed. If assistants are employed they should be properly supervised.

Taken together the functions of planning, control and review can be described as *engagement manage-*ment. Just as the auditor's clients must manage their business operations effectively if they are to prosper, so the auditor must manage audit engagements effectively in order to fulfill audit objectives properly and efficiently. The purpose of this chapter is to introduce the elements of engagement management and to discuss (a) the responsibilities of different members of the audit team, (b) general planning decisions, and (c) the control of field work. Review is discussed in Chapter 16. Specific planning and review steps for the interim audit are described in more detail in Chapters 24 and 30 and for the financial statement audit in Chapters 31 and 44.

15.1 Engagement management

Effective management of an audit engagement requires a clear conception of the engagement as a whole. While the field work stages of interim audit and financial statment audit are the two largest components, other important stages include (a) planning *prior* to the interim audit, (b) review and planning *between* the interim and financial statement audits, and (c) review, reporting and post-audit events *after* the financial statement audit. The resulting seven audit stages were introduced briefly in 1.5.

Effective management also requires that these seven audit stages be conducted within an organized administrative framework. Six basic elements in such a framework are:

1. the assignment of competent personnel,
2. an organized approach,
3. adequate planning,
4. adequate control of field work,
5. effective reporting to reviewers,
6. adequate review.

15.1.1 The six basic elements of engagement management

While the basic elements of engagement management can be inferred from the first field work standard, further authoritative guidance has not as yet been issued by the CICA. In the United States, AICPA Statement on Auditing Standards No. 4, *Quality Control Considerations for a Firm of Independent Auditors* (referred to in this chapter as the AICPA Statement), offers some suggestions.

Assignment of competent personnel

An effective audit requires competent auditors. The professional obligation to acquire and maintain competence was discussed in 3.2.3. A sole prac-titioner must assess his own competence for assignments he undertakes. Within an accounting firm there should be adequate policies for *hiring, professional development*, and *advancement*. Hiring policies may include requirements as to academic results and, for more advanced positions, as to practical experience. The AICPA Statement refers also to the need to ensure that personnel joining a firm through merger or acquisition become familiar with that firm's procedures. Professional development policies may include presentation of in-house training courses or required attendance at outside courses, such as those presented by the provincial Institutes and Order. The distribution of up-to-date technical information to audit staff and careful attention to on-the-job training are also important. Advancement policies may include periodic formal appraisals of an assistant's work, organized plans for gradually increasing the responsibilities assigned, and careful review of prospective promotions. Other desirable policies involve reasonable performance standards, realistic firing practices, and a proper work environment (see 7.3.1).

Assuming that competent personnel have been hired and developed within an accounting firm, there must be assigned to any given engagement a selection of personnel who have the levels of knowledge and experience required for the various sections of that audit. Each engagement will demand different levels both in the field work and in the planning and review. On the very simplest engagement, a student-in-accounts with a few months' experience may be able to conduct the field work if adequately supervised. The most complex engagement may require the combined work of several CA's with broad general experience, numerous assistants at different levels, and, in technical areas, CA's with specialist training in taxation, testing, computer auditing, or the particular industry. *Assignment* policies include the early identification of staff levels required and the use of time budgets to identify the hours required at each level.

An organized approach

An effective audit requires so many procedures to be coordinated and so many technical points to be remembered, that an organized approach is essential. The overall division of the audit into stages such as those introduced in 1.5 is one aspect of organization. Another aspect is the development of standard procedures, clearly explained in audit manuals, to guide staff in the conduct of each stage. The use of standard file structures for working papers is also a help, as is the development of standard audit forms (e.g., checklists, questionnaires, verification outlines). Excessive rigidity in prescribing audit procedures or their documentation must, of course, be avoided as it is likely to (a) stifle initiative in overcoming apparent problems and (b) lead to superficially uniform procedures being applied mechanically with inadequate attention to varying circumstances. Nonetheless, where different persons will be working on the same engagement, either together or over successive years, some measure of standardization is essential. Chartered accountants and students working on any audit for the first time must be able to find information contained in the file working papers quickly.

Adequate planning

Planning is a prerequisite for any complex activity. The degree of planning necessary on any audit will vary with its complexity, the level of competence of the persons performing the field work, their past exposure to the same client, the degree of guidance furnished by manuals and standard forms, and the degree of supervision available. At one extreme, the sole practitioner may plan and execute his own procedures on the spot. His need for a *formal* plan is limited but he nonetheless must make reasoned planning decisions as to his approach and the procedures to be performed. At the other extreme, an audit firm undertaking a large engagement will normally want a formal and more detailed plan because the most senior professional level will not be present throughout all the field work. The planning process allows the more senior levels to bring their knowledge and experience to bear on important audit decisions in advance. Planning is discussed in detail in 15.3 and 15.4.

Adequate control of field work

Adequate control of field work is required to ensure that work performed on the job meets the standards of the practitioner or firm and complies with gener-

ally accepted auditing standards. Many of the other elements contribute to control: careful planning in advance, an organized approach throughout, and review afterwards. A further element of control is the use of time budgets. The foregoing may be the only means of control in the case of a sole practitioner. However, where two or more persons perform the field work, the additional element of *supervision* becomes important. Supervision refers to the on-the-job guidance, monitoring, and assistance of other members of the audit team by the person charged with the direct responsibility for the field work (called, in this book, the *audit senior*). Closely related to supervision are arrangements for *consultation* with individuals having specialized knowledge. In many cases, staff on the job can resolve their questions by consulting with the audit senior, who has more training and experience. In some engagements, however, the audit staff or the audit senior will need to consult with specialists within their firm (or, in the case of sole practitioners, in other firms having specialists). The AICPA statement refers to the desirability of an audit firm designating senior qualified personnel to provide advice on accounting or auditing questions in general, maintaining a technical reference library, and developing research staff to handle practice queries. Control of field work is discussed in detail in 15.5.

Effective reporting to reviewers

A prerequisite for adequate review is that audit work and audit results be reported to reviewers in a comprehensible fashion. On many audits there may be one hundred or more individual working papers. In some audits they may number in the thousands. For a meaningful review, some summarization of key results, conclusions and controls is essential. The use of *reporting and control schedules* for this purpose is described in Chapter 16.

Adequate review

Adequate review of field work is required to ensure that work performed on the job has met the standards of the practitioner or firm and has complied with generally accepted auditing standards. Review includes both individual *engagement reviews* prior to release of the related audit reports and periodic *quality control reviews* to ensure that the quality of a firm's auditing work is being maintained. The former may involve several different levels of review depending on the nature of the engagement. Engagement reviews are discussed in Chapter 16. Quality control reviews may involve reviews conducted within an individual office by its own staff, reviews performed by travelling quality control teams within a firm, or a "peer review" requested by professionals outside the firm. In Canada, some practitioners make use of the "practice advisers" of the provincial Institutes or Order to perform limited peer reviews. In the United States, a recent development has been major peer reviews requested by one national firm of another. In 1976 the AICPA established a major voluntary quality control review program for CPA firms with SEC practices. Further use of peer reviews in Canada is under study in some provinces.

15.1.2 The impact of practice structure, policies and procedures

The managing of any individual audit engagement will, of course, vary with the nature of the engagement itself: its size, its complexity, the peculiarities of the industry, etc. But it will also vary with the structure, policies and procedures of the individual accounting firm. Various alternatives may be equally effective. What is important, is that the planning, control and review of an individual engagement be organized within the context of firm-wide procedures.

Practice structure

Most firms assign a group of clients to each partner so that continuity at a senior level will be maintained on successive annual audits for the same client. The method of assignment of personnel below the partner level, however, varies. Some firms use the *staff system* whereby professional personnel are organized into specific staffs, each staff responsible for one group of clients and reporting to one partner and manager/supervisor. Other firms use the *pool system* whereby personnel for each engagement is drawn from the entire professional pool and any chartered accountant or student may work for many partners, managers or supervisors during the course of a year. Both methods have their advantages but the choice will influence the manner in which individual engagements are managed. For example, under the staff system each manager or supervisor must ensure that a student is not given too narrow a selection of assignments, which would restrict his development and ultimately his competence – perhaps less of a danger under the pool system. Under the pool system, the manager or supervisor must ensure that supervision of the field work takes into account the specific strengths and weaknesses of each member of the audit team assigned – perhaps less of a problem under the staff system.

Some firms assign certain specialists a "line" function. For example, tax specialists may perform or review the verification of taxes payable. Computer audit specialists may perform or review the verification of computer controls. Other firms assign the same specialists an advisory "staff" function. For example, audit personnel would consult tax or computer audit specialists when they have difficult tax or computer questions to resolve. Some firms may assign certain specialists different roles in different circumstances. For example, a computer audit specialist may have a mandatory, line function in conducting any computer-assisted applications but only a consulting, staff function in answering queries with respect to the review of computer controls. No one pattern is necessarily the best. But the pattern adopted will affect the level of staff training required, the degree of detail in firm manuals, the design of audit checklists, and the levels of supervision and review required.

Policies

In designing policies to ensure adherence to generally accepted auditing standards and the rules of professional conduct, each firm may adopt its own specific rules regarding objectivity, staff training, confidentiality, use of audit manuals and standard forms, levels of review required, etc. At a more detailed level, firm policies may include policies as to the general approach to interim audits, test extents, computer auditing, statistical sampling, initial engagements, reliance on other auditors, etc. Again, these policies will influence the manner in which individual engagements must be planned, controlled, and reviewed.

Procedures

Individual procedures may also vary with respect to the organization of working paper files, the required contents of such files, methods of documenting verification planned and performed, the design of questionnaires, verification outlines, etc. These variations will likewise affect the nature of planning, control and review.

15.2 The audit team

The audit team assigned to a particular engagement is usually made up of individuals with different levels of training and experience. These levels may be variously named in different firms. For purposes of this book, four functional levels can be identified, whatever their titles. They are:

1. Reviewers – responsible for participating in the planning, for conducting the review, and for approving the issue of the audit report (their titles may be partners, client partners, audit partners, principals, managers, or supervisors and usually, in medium size and large practices, at least two review levels are involved);
2. Audit seniors – responsible for participating in the planning, for conducting and/or supervising the field work, for reviewing the work of their assistants, and for reporting the results to the reviewers (their titles might be staff seniors, senior staff accountants, etc. and they might or might not have already obtained their CA certificates);
3. Audit assistants – responsible for conducting assigned sections of the field work under the supervision of the audit senior, each assistant also being responsible for supervising the work of any assistants under him (the titles of audit assistants might be staff accountants, intermediates, juniors, etc.; usually they would be students-in-accounts each working towards a CA though some of them might be audit technicians not working towards professional designations);
4. Specialists – responsible for planning, conducting, reviewing or merely consulting on specialized areas such as taxes, computer auditing, testing, regulatory requirements (they may be full-time specialists or audit partners or managers with part-time specialist responsibilities).

On a large engagement, all four levels will likely be required. On many engagements, specialists may not be required but the other levels will be present. In smaller engagements, some of the functional levels may overlap – a manager serving as both audit senior and reviewer or an audit senior taking on review responsibilities. For a sole practitioner without assistants, the three levels of assistant, senior, and reviewer are combined.

Examples of typical audit teams which might be assigned by three different audit firms to four types of engagement are shown in Figure 15.a. Of course, other patterns would be possible as well. The purpose of the figure is not to suggest a preferred staff composition in any given case, but to illustrate the diversity of possible audit teams that can occur. This diversity must be matched by corresponding variations in the required procedures for planning, control and review.

15.2.1 Responsibilities of audit assistants

Every chartered accountant commences his professional career as an audit assistant. In the interval between joining a firm and being promoted to manager or supervisor with responsibility for a number of clients, he may be an assistant on twenty to fifty audit engagements and senior on just as many.

Specific assignments

The specific assignments of an audit assistant in a given engagement are generally (a) to review and evaluate certain major accounting systems in an interim audit and (b) to verify certain assets and liabilities in a financial statement audit. At the beginning he may be merely assisting other staff members in charge of the various audit sections. Later he may be "section senior" himself on simpler sections, such as payroll in the interim audit or prepaid expenses in the financial statement audit, while assisting other section seniors in more complex sections. Still later he may be section senior himself on complex sections, such as sales/receivables/receipts or inventories. In each case he has a responsibility to ensure that he understands the audit objectives to be met, the verification procedures to be performed, and any firm policies with respect to auditing methods and working papers. The work he performs should be carefully documented in accordance with such policies.

Background knowledge required

To perform the specific task assigned to him the audit assistant requires adequate background information and advance preparation. Procedures for obtaining this background include:

1. discussion with the audit senior in advance,
2. a review of the financial statements and of working papers, internal control questionnaires, organization charts, and planning decisions related to his assignment,
3. a re-reading of related sections of his firm's manual or an auditing textbook when assigned a particular section *for the first time*,
4. a tour of the client premises to meet key employees with whom he will be involved.

Examples of Various Audit Teams

Audit Firm / Client	Small firm X (one office) 3 partners, 3 other CA's, 2 technicians	Regional firm Y (offices in 3 cities) 7 partners, 8 managers, 1 tax manager, 9 other CA's, 23 students-in-accounts, 5 technicians	National firm Z (offices in 10 major Canadian cities and affiliates abroad) 7 senior partners, 74 audit partners, 19 specialist partners, 120 audit managers, 50 specialist managers, 220 audit CA's, 10 specialist CA's, 580 students-in-accounts, 25 technicians
Retail store A (one location) 100 hour audit	1 partner	1 partner 1 manager 1 audit senior (non-CA)	1 manager 1 audit senior (non-CA)
Small manufacturer B (one location) 300 hour audit	1 partner 1 audit assistant (technician)	1 partner 1 manager 1 audit senior (CA) 1 audit assistant	1 partner 1 manager 1 audit senior (CA) 2 audit assistants
Larger manufacturer C (one factory plus ten retail outlets in two provinces) 1 000 hour audit	1 partner 1 audit senior (CA) 2 audit assistants (CA's) (occasional consultation with outside computer specialist)	1 partner 1 manager (serving as senior) 3 audit assistants (one a CA) 1 tax specialist (CA)	1 partner 1 manager 1 audit senior (CA) 3 audit assistants 1 tax specialist (CA) 1 computer audit specialist (CA)
International conglomerate D (parent company, 5 Canadian subsidiaries, 5 foreign subsidiaries) 8 000 hour audit			Parent company and two subsidiaries: 1 senior partner 2 partners 3 managers 2 audit seniors (CA's) 6 audit assistants 2 tax specialists 1 computer audit specialist 1 audit test specialist Each of 3 subsidiaries: 1 partner 1 manager 1 audit senior (CA) 3 audit assistants 1 computer audit specialist 5 foreign subsidiaries: various affiliated audit firms

(This figure shows typical examples of audit teams which might be assigned by three different audit firms to four types of engagement. Of course, other patterns would be possible as well. The point is only to illustrate the diversity of possible audit teams and therefore the diversity of the required procedures for planning, control and review.)

Figure 15.a

Relationship with the rest of the audit team

The audit assistant has a responsibility to cooperate with other members of the audit team in a professional manner. Audit engagements are complex undertakings and can be completed effectively and efficiently only if all members of the audit team work together in harmony.

Relationship with client employees

In his relationship with client employees, the audit assistant must remember that he is a representative of his firm. The impression he gives will be the impression the client's staff receives of the firm and of the profession. He must therefore ensure that he is courteous in his dealings, careful in his appearance, and competent in his work. Potential pitfalls to avoid are (a) a lack of preparation, (b) a patronizing attitude, (c) the aggravation of employee misconceptions of the auditor's role, and (d) a loss of objectivity.

Foolish questions and a lack of understanding of the business are understandably irritating to client staff. A failure to acquire the background information previously outlined will not only lead to poor audit work, which could yet be detected during review and corrected, but also will give the client a general impression of incompetence, which may take long to repair. The audit assistant should therefore ensure that he has done his homework *before* he questions client employees in the course of his work.

The new audit assistant will be dealing with junior members of the client's staff. Many of them may lack the educational training or the career opportunities of the audit assistant. Yet they perform necessary and important functions in the client's organization and they should expect to be treated with respect. Condescension is both discourteous and, in its effect on client cooperation, damaging to the efficiency of the audit.

The profession still has much to do in explaining its role to the public. The new assistant will discover that many employees may have distorted conceptions of the role of the auditor – some seeing him merely as a nuisance, others as a spy hunting for dishonest expense reports. When seeking information, each member of the audit team, including the newest assistant, must be prepared to explain courteously and concisely to a reluctant respondent that the information requested is not to attack the honesty or competence of the employee but to assist the auditor in forming an independent opiniom on the financial statements as a whole.

While a friendly attitude is important, the audit assistant must guard against developing such close friendships as would lead him improperly to accept glib answers from a client employee without corroborating evidence.

Professional development

Finally, the audit assistant has a responsibility to upgrade his professional knowledge and to learn from his experience as fast as he can. Therefore, while being obedient to the directions of the more experienced members of the audit team, he should not carry out instructions blindly without understanding their purpose. If he is confused or uncertain as to why certain procedures are performed he should ask the audit senior for clarification.

15.2.2 Responsibilities of the audit senior

Generally, within a year of joining a public accounting firm, or of working for a sole practitioner, a student-in-accounts will be given full responsibility for the field work on a smaller engagement. In his first few jobs as audit senior, he will be subject to close supervision by his supervisor, manager or partner and he will likely not have any assistants to supervise himself. Within one to two years, the student will normally be given responsibilities for the field work of medium sized clients where he has assistants to supervise during the field work. At the same time, the degree of supervision of his own work by his manager, supervisor or partner will decrease. Within a year after obtaining his CA, an individual working for a larger public accounting firm will normally be given responsibility for the field work, and to a certain degree the planning, of the largest engagements. The field work on such engagements may require five to ten audit assistants and often specialist help as well.

Qualifications and personal characteristics

The audit senior (assuming at least two years' experience) should strive to have the following qualifications:

1. a comprehensive knowledge of:
   a) generally accepted accounting principles and generally accepted auditing standards,
   b) modern business organizations, business practices, financing and internal control,
   c) auditing techniques, types of audit evidence, and the overall theory of auditing,
   d) such quantitative audit techniques (for example, statistical sampling) as are used by his firm;

2. a basic knowledge of:
   a) computer controls and the use of computer-assisted audit techniques,
   b) tax law and economics;
3. technical skill and sound judgment in applying the foregoing knowledge to the normal situations encountered in public practice;
4. the ability to:
   a) lead, organize, and supervise others, whether they be audit assistants, specialists, client internal auditors or other client employees,
   b) communicate effectively, both orally and in writing,
   c) recognize problems, uncertainties, insufficiency of audit evidence, or suspicious circumstances;
5. the personal characteristics of integrity, tact, courtesy, reliability and self-discipline.

Specific assignments

On a particular engagement the audit senior will normally be assigned the following specific responsibilities:

1. to assist the reviewers in making general planning decisions,
2. to prepare or participate in the preparation of a detailed audit program,
3. to organize and implement the general audit approach used by his firm,
4. to interpret the audit plan and control all aspects of the field work, including all verification procedures throughout the interim and financial statement audits,
5. to review the work of his assistants,
6. to draft the internal control/management letter, the audit report, the financial statements (if called for as part of the engagement), the tax returns (if requested), and any other required reports or opinions,
7. to summarize and report the results of the field work to the reviewers,
8. to answer or follow up queries of the reviewers.

Since these responsibilities span all six elements of engagement management, the audit senior's role is critical to the successful conduct of any audit.

Relationship with client employees

Because the audit senior is in charge of the field work on the client's premises, he has the primary responsibility for maintaining good day-to-day relations with client employees. Generally he will be the senior audit representative in contact with most employees – accounting staff, inventory clerks, personnel in receiving, shipping, production, sales, etc. – as well as having numerous dealings with the more senior client officials with whom his manager/supervisor and partner also deal. While nothing must impair the objectivity with which the opinion on the financial statements is formed, in the vast majority of cases the attainment of audit objectives and the maintenance of good client relations are compatible and indeed mutually beneficial. Good client relations increases the efficiency with which the audit can be performed and improves the quality of the other services which the auditor can provide. Attention to the following points may help to promote good client relations.

1. The audit senior should keep key client personnel in the accounting/finance sector (the comptroller, the chief accountants, etc.) regularly informed of current and planned audit activities and any special requests the audit team may have.
2. He should ensure that interference with the client's daily routines is kept to a minimum. For example, the payroll system should not be flow-charted on the day of the biggest payroll of the month.
3. He should ensure that the time of client employees is not wasted answering needless questions because he or his assistants are inadequately prepared or because the documentation in the working papers has been inadequate. Sometimes, of course, the repetition of previous questions is unavoidable when controls are being reviewed, but in these cases the audit staff should indicate that they are familiar with the previous routines and that their objective is to identify any subsequent changes which have occurred.
4. He should ensure that he and his assitants are courteous to client employees at all times. He must be ready to explain concisely, where necessary, the reason why certain information is being requested.
5. Normally, better relations will be retained if the audit senior and his assistants adopt the client's working hours. Of course, they should conform to any client rules governing general office routines.
6. The audit senior should take a genuine interest in the client's operations and in being of service to the client's employees. He should encourage his assistants to do likewise.
7. At the same time, he should exhibit a pride in his profession and a loyalty to his firm. The attest function is an important and useful service. But if the audit senior apologizes for "having to waste an employee's time" or for "having to follow a stupid procedure because the firm requires it", he will hardly elicit the client's respect or cooperation.

Relationship with audit assistants

The audit senior must ensure that the work of each audit assistant contributes effectively and efficiently to the overall audit objective for a given engagement and, at the same time, to the ongoing professional development of that assistant. These tasks require leadership on the part of the senior – not so much to motivate his assistants (most students-in-accounts are already highly motivated) as to channel that motivation. An interested assistant may want to pursue an audit point beyond the limits required by materiality and reasonable assurance; his excessive pursuit must be restrained without dampening his interest. Another assistant may be impatient for greater challenge at the expense of careful completion of the work he has been assigned; he must be made to see the importance of objectives and potential difficulties of his assigned task as well as being assured of his advancement to greater responsibilities as fast as his performance and experience permit. Attention to the following points may be useful to the audit senior in his leadership role.

1. He should ensure that all audit assistants understand the objectives of the engagement and of their sections of it as well as being familiar with the client's operations. No assistant should be allowed to perform a procedure which he does not understand. Misunderstanding can lead to mistaken conclusions, wasted time, or careless performance.

2. He should keep his assistants up to date on the progress of the audit. Brief meetings of the audit team at the beginning and end of each working day are a good idea.

3. When problems are encountered which require discussion with the client, he should include in the discussion the audit assistant responsible for the related section of the audit.

4. During the field work, at its conclusion, or at some other appropriate occasion, the audit senior should let each assistant know of his evaluation of that assistant's work. Demonstrating a genuine interest in an assistant's progress obviously encourages the best performance. Pointing out strengths and weaknesses helps the assistant to improve. Some firms, particularly where the pool system is used and senior/assistant combinations vary from job to job, ask the senior to complete a formal evaluation report at the conclusion of each engagement. The importance of regular staff evaluation was discussed in Chapter 3.

Relationship with reviewers

Throughout the field work, it is important for the audit senior to keep the reviewers (partner, manager,

or supervisor) informed of the progress of the audit and of any important points discovered or unforeseen difficulties encountered. Any anticipated overruns of budgeted time should be reported immediately so that the reviewer can consider (a) whether unnecessary audit procedures are being performed or alternatively (b) whether additional audit hours are indeed justified, in which case the related fee increases should be discussed with the client promptly. Discovered frauds, other major irregularities, or suspicious circumstances should likewise be reported immediately since it is usually the reviewer's role to report these matters to the client and to consider their impact on the audit work. Other unforeseen circumstances or problems may affect the planned audit work as well. The audit senior should assess such circumstances and problems and propose any audit modifications he believes are required – rather than merely leaving the solution to the reviewer. At the same time, he should recognize the limitations in his own experience and not implement his proposed modifications without seeking reviewer approval and, where required, assistance from various specialists.

Professional development

The demands on the position of audit senior in terms of leadership, tact, technical knowledge, and organizational ability are onerous. Most people are less than ideal in one or more of these aspects. The audit senior has a responsibility to upgrade his professional knowledge and managerial skills as fast as he can, learning from his experience, from the criticisms of reviewers, and from the reactions of assistants and client employees. He must keep current with technical developments (a) by reading information distrubuted by his firm, professional pronouncements, and professional magazines, (b) by attending firm training courses or professional development seminars provided by the provincial Institutes and Order, (c) by discussion with his colleagues, and (d) by application of such newly acquired knowledge in his day-to-day work.

15.2.3 Responsibilities of reviewers

After a number of years' experience as an audit senior, a chartered accountant will normally be assigned review responsibilities. The title accompanying such responsibilities will vary depending on the size and organization of the firm and the experience and qualifications of the individual. As mentioned earlier, possible titles may be supervisor, manager, principal or partner.

Responsibilities of reviewers as a group

Whatever the titles, the responsibilities of the reviewer or group of reviewers assigned to a particular engagement are the following:

1. to maintain general contact with the client,
2. to ensure that objectivity is maintained unimpaired,
3. to establish the objectives of the engagement (including the approval of engagement letters and the discussion of services with the client),
4. to make the general planning decisions,
5. to participate in or approve the detailed audit programming,
6. to coordinate the scheduling of the audit work with client activities and requirements,
7. to assign the audit senior, assistants, and specialists required to perform the field work,
8. to supervise the audit senior and answer queries raised by him during the course of the field work,
9. to ensure that audit assistants are being properly supervised and trained,
10. to review all working papers,
11. to discuss and resolve all contentious points in auditing, accounting, taxation or other areas, seeking appropriate specialist assistance where required,
12. to review and approve internal control/management letters, audit reports, audit follow-up letters, and any other written communications prior to issue to the client,
13. to review, and often to participate actively in, special work and non-attest services,
14. to bill the client for services rendered.

Where two or more levels of reviewer are involved on the same engagement, the foregoing responsibilities may be allocated among them depending on the policies of the particular firm. For example, where a partner and manager together constitute the review team, the partner may delegate steps 4, 5, 6, and 7, as well as portions of the other steps (such as the review of more detailed working papers) to the manager. Review procedures are discussed in Chapter 16.

Responsibilities of the audit partner

While the exact allocation of detailed duties between (a) audit partners and (b) other reviewers will vary with the individual firm, certain partner responsibilities are invariable. When the partnership name is signed on an audit report, all partners of that firm become legally responsible for it. The audit partner directly involved on the engagement therefore owes a professional responsibility to his partners to ensure that generally accepted auditing standards and the rules of professional conduct have been adhered to. While every chartered accountant and student involved in the engagement has a professional responsibility to discharge his own work competently and with due care, the final responsibility for the audit as a whole rests with the audit partner. It is the partner who will generally be called to answer for any deficiencies discovered by a professional conduct committee or by a court. Where the audit partner has delegated some of his review responsibilities to other reviewers (supervisors, managers, principals), he must satisfy himself that the delegated responsibilities were properly discharged. This requirement remains even when the entire review responsibilities have been delegated (as in case A/Z in Figure 15.a).

In some larger engagements, several audit partners may share partner responsibilities.

Finally, of course, the partners of a firm collectively are responsible for the development of the firm policies and procedures necessary to promote effective engagement management (see 15.1.2). In practice, this responsibility is commonly delegated in turn to various partner committees with technical, advisory, policy, or management roles.

15.2.4 Specialists

A firm may decide to develop part-time or full-time specialists in fields such as taxation, computer auditing, audit testing, general auditing research, accounting research, regulatory requirements, business valuations, acquisitions and mergers, or specific industries (banks, stockbrokers, insurance companies, resource companies, etc.). If a firm engages in, or has affiliated firms engaging in, the practice of management consulting, EDP, or trustee in bankruptcy work, the personnel in these fields may also provide specialist assistance to the audit team when required. Sometimes specialist functions may have to be established for a temporary period to cope with, or to help clients cope with, specific legislative or economic developments. An example was the introduction of anti-inflation legislation in Canada in 1975.

As discussed in 15.1.2, specialists in a given firm may have a "staff" function, "line" function, or both. The allocation of responsibilities between specialists and other audit staff, "generalists", will depend on firm policies. Generally, a specialist's responsibilities are:

1. to maintain technical proficiency in his area of specialization by attending advanced training sessions, reading specialist literature, conferring with colleagues in his specialty, and applying his technical knowledge in practice,
2. to perform or participate in the performing of such audit procedures (verification of tax liabilities, application of computer-assisted techniques, etc.) as prescribed by firm policies,
3. to participate in the planning or review of such procedures where prescribed,
4. to assist audit staff in resolving questions or problems arising on a particular engagement and involving his area of specialization,
5. to undertake special client assignments related to his specialty.

15.2.5 The sole practitioner

By definition a sole practitioner does not have partners – but he may have employees. Where employees are used on an engagement, the same considerations of engagement management and composition of the audit team apply as already discussed. Where a sole practitioner practises without assistants, the audit team is simply himself. The question of work assignment, of supervision, and of delegation of responsibilities does not then arise. However, the other aspects of engagement management – an organized approach, adequate planning, control through time budgets, and adequate review – remain just as important.

15.3 Planning the audit

Good planning serves two objectives:

1. to ensure that effective audit procedures will be performed (the first field work standard),
2. to ensure that those procedures are designed and performed efficiently.

While an auditor could comply with generally accepted auditing standards without being efficient, significant inefficiencies cannot long be continued without loss of reasonable fee/cost recoveries or loss of clients. Most auditors will therefore wish to meet both planning objectives. The first involves:

- meeting essential requirements in timing and synchronizing certain audit steps,
- avoiding auditing deficiencies which would be impossible to correct later.

The second involves:
- choosing the optimal timing of audit steps,
- avoiding auditing deficiencies which would be costly to correct later,
- simplifying review,
- levelling staff workloads,
- maintaining good client relations and reasonable fee/cost recoveries.

A discussion of these factors follows.

15.3.1 The importance of planning

Timing requirements

Even if the auditor is an experienced sole practitioner, with no assistants to supervise, planning for certain timing requirements is essential. If he arrives to begin the audit in early November only to find that physical stocktaking was completed in September, an effective audit may no longer be possible. If he confirms accounts receivable in October only to discover subsequently that control is so weak that he should have verified cash and marketable securities at the same time, an effective audit may again no longer be possible.

> The timing of the performance of auditing procedures involves the proper synchronizing of their application and thus comprehends the possible need for simultaneous examination of, for example, cash on hand and in banks, securities owned, bank loans and other related items. It may also require an element of surprise, establishment of audit control over assets readily negotiable, and establishment of a proper cutoff at a date other than the balance sheet date.[1]

Planning for optimal timing is desirable to improve efficiency or to advance reporting dates. Some audit steps will be inefficient if performed in the wrong order. For example, an audit assistant should not normally be assigned to perform extensive transactional tests before internal control has been evaluated; there is too great a danger that some of his tests will later prove to have been unnecessary and that others may have to be repeated with modifications. Accounts receivable should not normally be confirmed as late as December 31 if completion of the audit is desired by January 15; insufficient time would be left for receiving replies, sending out second requests, and performing alternative verification. Some audit steps are not subject to critical timing constraints. For example, the verification of inventory cost records to be used for pricing year-end inventories can be performed any time between the interim audit review of costing systems and the year-end work on pricing. Its precise scheduling can therefore be based on convenience, staff availability, and efficient coordination with other audit visits.

Avoiding auditing deficiencies

Planning for the purpose of avoiding auditing deficiencies arises primarily when assistants are employed. Where assistants are not employed and provided that planning for the timing requirements just discussed has been done, additional planning may be unnecessary. Thus a sole practitioner performing the audit of a small client, known to him for years, may be able to leave many detailed planning decisions to be made on the spot during the field work. Where less experienced assistants are employed, however, such an approach could permit auditing deficiencies which, though later detected during review, might no longer be curable. For example, it may be impossible later to compensate for the omission of certain audit steps during the observation of physical stock-taking. Even where subsequent correction is possible, it may be very costly – as well as a strain on auditor-client relations. Going back later to extend inadequate sample sizes or to perform omitted procedures is less efficient than drawing adequate sample sizes and performing the proper procedures in the first place. It may, in addition, prevent reporting deadlines from being met. Of course, where review indicates that the audit procedures have been excessive, the excessive verification cannot be undone and that cost is lost.

Simplifying review

Thorough planning simplifies later review in two ways: (a) by preventing most of the deficiencies such a review would otherwise have to detect and (b) by reducing the need for an eleventh-hour evaluation of detailed audit programs. Working papers which are incomplete, full of descriptions of unnecessary procedures, or sprinkled with invalid conclusions take far longer to review than complete, concise and logical working papers. It is more efficient to prevent deficiencies through careful planning than to detect and correct them through later review. To the extent that a reviewer participates in this planning, he can shift much of his review back to the planning stage. His planning procedures thus serve as an advance review. Planning, conducted before the audit, is constructive where after-the-fact review can only be critical. The experience and judgment of the reviewer will have a greater influence on the effectiveness of the audit if they are used to modify and improve audit steps before they are performed. His subsequent review can then be restricted to determining that agreed upon procedures were in fact performed and that the results obtained have been properly interpreted.

Levelling staff workloads

One of the difficulties in managing a public accounting practice is the seasonal nature of the work. Many audit firms find that more than 50% of their chargeable time is devoted to clients with calendar year-ends. Peak demands for audit time thus occur in the early winter and again at the deadlines for filing personal and corporate client tax returns. The peaking has been aggravated by demands for more and more timely financial information and the consequent moving of field work deadlines closer and closer to the year-end. A partial solution has traditionally been staff overtime. Most practitioners and students anticipate a reasonable number of overtime hours during peak periods. But changing social values have placed limits on how far this solution can be exploited. Another partial solution is to attempt to persuade a few more clients to switch their fiscal year-ends to correspond to low points in their business cycles. Where a seasonal pattern is pronounced, such a switch can reduce the client's own accounting costs and, as well, alleviate the auditor's peaking problem. But many such companies have already adopted low-point year-ends. For other companies, the benefits are often not enough to justify the inconvenience of a change. At one time, the hiring of temporary help during peak periods was also a partial solution. The growing complexities of accounting, auditing, computerized systems and taxes have made this solution generally unworkable.

The answer therefore has to be the planning of significant pre-year-end work. The inclusion of substantive procedures during the interim audit and the verification of major assets (such as accounts receivable and inventory) at pre-year-end dates has already been discussed in Chapters 9 and 11. The shifting of substantive procedures back to earlier dates usually increases total audit costs and may increase audit risks. To limit cost increases and to control audit risks, careful advance planning is essential.

Maintaining good client relations and reasonable fee/cost recoveries

An inefficient audit is a more costly audit. The result is either an excessive fee which the client may some day refuse to accept or an inadequate fee/cost recovery for the auditor. The former may lead to loss of clients. The latter will lead to lower remuneration of partners and/or employees of the audit firm and ultimately to the retention of less capable personnel. Even if total audit fees are not objectionable, observation of inefficient or non-productive work by audit staff, resulting from poor planning, is understandably irritating to the client.

Audit inefficiency can have a spiralling effect over

a series of years. If excessive audit costs have led to fee difficulties, the auditor may in future years be tempted to cut services to the attest function alone, eliminating "frills" such as systems suggestions and tax advice. As the client observes services dropping his natural reaction will be to exert increased fee pressure in subsequent years, which leads to further reduction in services, and so on. Careful advance planning can identify and cure the inefficiencies which start such a vicious circle.

Audit costs in general have risen over the last few decades because of:

- significant increases in salaries for students-in-accounts and chartered accountants and the raising of educational entrance requirements for the profession,
- the more senior staff mix and higher in-firm training costs required by the growing complexities of accounting, auditing, computerized systems, and taxes.

These increased costs make it even more important that the maximum efficiency possible be obtained through adequate planning and that any anticipated audit or fee problems be discussed with the client well in advance.

Advance planning can also serve to identify additional services which a client may need and which could be combined with attest procedures with little extra cost.

Differences in clients and audit teams

Each audit client is unique. The audit of a steel fabricator and the audit of a hospital are as different as their products. In addition, there can be radical differences in the systems of internal control, the competence of employees, and the degree to which accounting systems are automated. That each engagement is unique and presents a new challenge is one of the attractive features of public practice. It does mean, however, that the knowledge and skills learned on one job cannot always be readily transferred to the next. Thus, advance planning is important to convey information to members of the audit team new to a particular engagement. With the raising of entrance requirements and the simultaneous shortening of the elapsed time between new student and manager or supervisor level, staff continuity on individual engagements has inevitably declined. Whereas at one time three members out of a four-man audit team might typically have had experience on the same engagement in prior years, today it is not uncommon for three of the four to be new to the engagement.

Moreover, on any one engagement there may sometimes be a significantly different mix of staff levels on the audit team from year to year. One year, the audit team may consist of two average, though inexperienced, students because at the scheduled times they are the only persons available. In the next year, there may be a team of four, headed by an experienced CA, scheduled to complete the field work in a much shorter time. One year, the audit senior may be technically brilliant but a poor communicator. Another year, the senior may be a good organizer but require more specialist assistance. Careful and flexible planning is essential to allow for these different staff mixes from year to year.

Three levels of planning

Audit planning can be broken down into three levels: general planning, detailed program planning, and scheduling. The first involves the more fundamental decisions concerning the overall approach to the audit engagement. The second refers to decisions as to specific verification steps. The third involves the detailed arrangements for the various audit visits to the client's premises over the course of the year.

15.3.2 General planning

Although the audit senior will usually provide some input, general planning is normally the direct responsibility of the more senior levels of the audit team — the reviewer or reviewers. Before he can make intelligent planning decisions, a reviewer must be acquainted with the client's business — its products, its general policies, its management, the industry — and with the terms of the audit engagement. Thus, the first step in the planning process can be called "orientation to the audit environment". Other general planning steps include:

- decision re materiality,
- decision re overall audit assurance,
- decisions re approach and emphasis,
- decisions re detailed program planning and approvals,
- decisions re internal audit and other client assistance,
- decision re overall timing,
- decision re reliance on other auditors,
- selection of staff,
- review of fees and additional services.

These general planning decisions are discussed in 15.4.

15.3.3 Detailed program planning

Detailed program planning refers to decisions as to specific verification steps, whether these decisions are made in advance of, or during, the field work. Of

410

course, some decision is implicitly made before any detailed verification step is performed. But the formality of, responsibility for, approval of, and documentation of program planning decisions can vary from engagement to engagement or even from section to section within the same engagement. Thus, while the general planning decisions should be made explicitly on all but the smallest engagements, the extent of explicit program planning will not be so uniform. The possible alternatives are:

- a detailed written audit program,
- no detailed program,
- an abbreviated written program,
- the use of pre-printed checklists (as program substitutes).

The policies of the individual audit firm will affect which alternative or which combination of alternatives is chosen for any particular engagement. In particular, the nature of staff training and the nature of, and policies governing, the use of a firm audit procedures manual will have a major effect.

Detailed written audit programs

A detailed written audit program provides a comprehensive plan for the conduct of an audit by specifying each verification step to be performed during the field work. Normally, the specification of each step will include a description of the evidence to be gathered, the technique to be used in gathering it, and, where it is to be applied to less than 100% of the items in the accounting population involved, the test extent and method of testing to be used. In addition, the specification may include an estimate or budget of the required audit time (or time may be budgeted for groups of verification steps taken together). Space may be provided for the auditor to initial as he completes the step and, where necessary, to record his conclusions.

The purposes of a detailed audit program are to:

1. describe the essential audit verification steps to be completed,
2. provide control by means of a detailed and continuous comparison of actual to planned work, of actual to budgeted hours, and of actual to anticipated conclusions,
3. assign specific responsibility for the proper completion of each verification step by means of initialling,
4. facilitate review of the completed audit work (a quick scanning can identify planned but uncompleted steps),
5. provide an organized basis for planning subsequent years' verification procedures, as the program can be reused by adding columns,
6. provide documentary evidence that the audit has

been performed in adherence with generally accepted auditing standards.

One advantage of a detailed audit program is that it combines the documentation of planning with the documentation of the actual audit work performed. Documentation of audit work performed is discussed in Chapter 16. Detailed written audit programs may be used (a) for some or all sections of the compliance and substantive work in the interim audit and (b) for some or all sections of the substantive work in the financial statement audit. An example of a portion of a detailed program for the former was shown in Figure 9.e and for the latter is shown in Figure 16.b.

The most important advantage of a detailed written program is that it is tailor-made to the needs of the particular engagement. Unusual but necessary steps which might have been overlooked in a standardized checklist can be incorporated clearly in the detailed program. This advantage is of more importance for specialized industries and large complex engagements than for others.

A further advantage is that a detailed written program permits all verification plans to be reviewed and approved prior to execution.

A disadvantage of detailed written audit programs is their cost of preparation. Of couse, this cost is limited to years when extensive changes in the program are required because of changes in the composition of assets and liabilities or in the client's systems or business operations.

Another disadvantage of such programs can be their very length and detail, which can discourage participation in, or approval of, program planning by reviewers. If program planning is delegated to too junior a level, the advantage of bringing experienced judgment to bear on planned procedures prior to their execution is lost.

A further disadvantage is the risk of omitting a standard step in the middle of a sequence of procedures. Such an omission (for example, failure to specify control of the mailing of accounts receivable confirmation requests) can nullify the whole sequence. This risk is particularly great when new professional developments or new firm policies call for additional or modified audit procedures on a given audit section for all clients. If the detailed audit program is carried forward from the prior year, the necessary addition or modification may be missed.

A final disadvantage is the risk that allegedly complete and tailor-made programs may stifle initiative on the part of the audit staff. Procedures may be performed mechanically to fill up the program with initials without retaining an alertness for changed conditions which may call for steps not anticipated by the program preparer.

That several potential disadvantages exist does not

mean they need occur on a particular engagement. With careful staff training, due care, and supervision such disadvantages can be minimized. Most practitioners will find that on at least a few engagements (e.g., in particularly large engagements or ones related to specialized industries) the advantages of detailed written programs outweigh their disadvantages. Some practitioners use them on most or all of their engagements.

When an auditing firm uses detailed written programs for *all* audit engagements, the degree of detail in any auditing procedures manual tends to be restricted. In such cases, audit staff refer to the programs rather than manuals for detailed guidance.

No detailed program

At the other extreme, after the general planning decisions have been made, audit staff may be sent out to do the field work without any advance written program at all. Audit staff in such cases are not without guidance, however. The prior year's verification notes become the *de facto* program for the current year, subject to such changes as the audit staff conclude are appropriate. In addition, audit procedures manuals will usually provide detailed guidance. The actual audit program finally performed will, of course, be documented in the current year's verification notes. An example of such verification notes, when advance written programs are not used, is shown in Figure 16.e.

One advantage of the no-program approach is its cheapness. Provided that auditing mistakes are not made which require costly reworking, the no-program approach is the most economical. A further advantage is the freedom it allows the audit staff to use initiative in solving auditing problems.

The disadvantages are that no prior approval of plans by more experienced levels is possible. If the audit staff are inexperienced, important steps may be inadvertently omitted or unnecessary steps may be performed. Audit test extents chosen may be deficient or excessive. There is a risk of last year's program being slavishly followed when, in fact, it requires modification to meet changed conditions, new professional developments, or new firm policies. Of course, any auditing deficiencies could be caught and cured during review but last minute corrections may lead to an inefficient and costly audit.

In spite of these disadvantages, where there is an experienced audit team the no-program approach will often be feasible. Careful staff training, due care and supervision are important. Most practitioners will find that for at least the most minor sections of each audit the no-program approach makes sense. Some practitioners may find it feasible on a wider

selection of sections or even for complete engagements.

Abbreviated written programs

A reasonable compromise between the time-consuming and mechanical nature of a detailed written program and the dangers of having no detailed program can be the development of an abbreviated written program. The degree of detail in an abbreviated program would be based on the expected experience of the audit team and the quality of other guidance available to them in audit manuals or elsewhere. The reviewer and/or the audit senior can identify for particular segments of the audit the more critical verification decisions and prepare brief notes that comment on these areas. For example, an abbreviated program for the confirmation of accounts receivable could be as follows:

1. Do a positive confirmation of trade accounts receivable as at November 30th.
2. Count cash and perform normal follow-up procedures as at the same date because control over cash receipts/receivables is inadequate.
3. Select all accounts for confirmation over $5 000 and a haphazard sample of 100 accounts under $5 000.
4. Follow all other standard confirmation procedures including those related to the trial balance and the follow-up of confirmations as described in the audit manual.

When this approach is followed, the fleshed-out audit program will be documented in the working papers as each verification step is completed in the same fashion as for the no-program approach (see Figure 16.e). If these more detailed notes are prepared, it would be normal not to initial each of the limited steps described in the abbreviated program.

The advantages of the abbreviated program approach are that it is tailor-made to the specific engagement, though not in elaborate detail. It facilitates higher level review of the key programming points in advance without cluttering the review with excessive detail. It is reasonably cheap. Because it makes no pretense to provide all the detailed instructions, it encourages the audit staff to use their initiative and judgment in applying the broad directives to the circumstances of the specific engagement.

One disadvantage is that it does not combine the documentation of the programming with the documentation of the work actually performed. But the principal disadvantage is, as with tailor-made detailed programs, the risk of omitting a standard step in the middle of a sequence of procedures. Again, this risk is particularly great when new professional developments or new firm policies call for additional or modified audit procedures on a given audit section for all clients.

The potential disadvantages can be limited through careful staff training, due care and supervision. Some practitioners find abbreviated programs (sometimes called "audit plans") a very efficient approach.

Use of pre-printed checklists

Regardless of the variety of client cirumstances, many verification steps are reasonably standard on most audit engagements. This standardization is found particularly in the substantive verification of assets and liabilities – which commonly consumes more than half the total field work time. Not only are the verification steps themselves reasonably standard, but generally they are most efficiently completed in a specified logical sequence. Accordingly, standardized checklists have been developed by many practitioners to eliminate the need for excessively detailed written programs while still providing reasonably detailed guidance. Such checklists serve the additional function of providing for documentation of the verification procedures actually performed with an initial or a few words of explanation in contrast to the more detailed and repetitive verification notes required in the no-program approach. In effect, the checklist provides a basic outline of the work to be performed and the auditor can expand it or modify it as required to accommodate the details of the particular engagement. As a result, such checklists are sometimes called *verification outlines*. An example of a verification outline for accounts receivable confirmation is shown in Figure 16.c.

An important advantage of verification outlines is that they reduce the risk of key procedures being omitted inadvertently. As accounting, auditing, and tax requirements become more complex it is increasingly easy for an important step to be overlooked. For example, the auditor may check all aspects of the measurement, classification, presentation, and cut-off of income components but overlook the routine step of considering related-party transactions. Standardized outlines can be readily up-dated when new professional developments or firm policies occur with some assurance that the modifications will be incorporated in all applicable audits. Standardized outlines can facilitate the review of program planning. The reviewer need not concentrate on remembering all the standard required steps to see that they have been covered but can concentrate on thinking of the special circumstances in a given engagement which should call for modifications in the normal routines.

Another advantage is that verification outlines can focus attention on the key decisions required in the program planning.

For example, in Figure 16.c, five key decisions are highlighted:

1. Determination of the confirmation date
2. The decision as to whether to count cash
3. The basis of selection of accounts for confirmation
4. The possible inclusion of other non-trade receivable items in the confirmation
5. The extent of related work to be performed on the records at the same date.

The first of these decisions can be made by the senior or reviewer and documented on the face of the verification outline. Similarly, the internal control conclusions can be noted in advance of the field work and a pencil notation made as to whether cash is to be counted or not (second decision). The third decision can be documented on the same form or referenced to a standardized planning form for judgmental or statistical representative tests (see Figures 12.e and 13.1). The fourth decision requires a brief planning note. The extent of related work (fifth decision) will normally be the same as the extent of confirmation and the basis of the work to be done at the circularization date could be noted in pencil on the face of the verification outline. Alternatively, all of these five decisions could be documented in written form in planning notes and cross-referenced to the verification outline. To the extent that fairly standardized procedures are not to be performed, the questions could be struck off the verification outline or marked non-applicable during the detailed planning. Additional verification steps required could be added to the verification outline or included in written planning notes.

A further advantage is that the documentation of planning and the documentation of verification work actually performed are integrated but at a lesser cost than the use of detailed written programs.

A disadvantage of standardized checklists is that their length and degree of detail may encourage a rigid and mechanical approach. Audit staff may fill in the blanks without giving adequate thought to the answers. Accustomed to a highly structured approach, audit staff may become less able to cope with unusual situations. This danger can again be reduced by careful staff training, due care and supervision. Indeed, it can be argued that by eliminating the need to remember recurring detailed steps, verification outlines can free staff attention to focus on the unusual.

Another disadvantage is that developers of the checklists may be tempted to try to cover every possible variation in planning decision required – a trial in which they are bound to fail. Standardized checklists should be designed instead to cover the most commonly recurring points while encouraging audit staff to consider carefully the few additional variations which may arise in any given audit.

Finally, standardized checklists, while cheaper than detailed written programs, are more costly than the no-program approach. If they are used on very small engagements or on relatively minor sections of any engagement they may inflate audit hours and working papers unnecessarily.

Many practitioners find that some form of standardized checklist is useful for program planning on most sections of most engagements. Most firms using them, however, make optional the use of many of the checklists so that they will not be used where clearly inapplicable. Their use is commonly supplemented by additional guidance in audit procedures manuals. Such audit manuals may also provide criteria for deciding when the use of various checklists is desirable.

In the writer's view, verification outlines of the type illustrated in Figure 16.c are the most efficient planning tool for the financial statement audit component of most engagements. Further examples of such verification outlines are illustrated in Chapters 32 to 42. In interim audits, verification outlines of a somewhat different type may be useful in organizing and documenting large groups of procedures. Examples are illustrated in Chapters 26 and 29. On small engagements, on minor sections, or for unusual items, the no-program approach, however, is preferable. For very complex or specialized engagements, for weakness investigation procedures, and for compliance procedures, detailed written programs are more efficient. Practitioners will have different preferences as to approach and each alternative can be workable if properly used by carefully trained and supervised audit staff.

Use of audit manuals as a planning tool

Several references have already been made to audit manuals. Most large firms and many regional and local firms have developed their own audit manuals. Such manuals are an important tool in detailed program planning. In addition, they provide a means of conveying to professional staff the firm's policies and practices.

An audit manual generally provides a condensation of authoritative auditing literature and outlines basic auditing procedures for the review, evaluation, and compliance verification of internal control, and for the substantive verification of financial statement figures. It usually also provides guidance in the preparation of the audit report, the internal control/management letter, and other types of communication. The content of the auditing procedures sections will depend on the firm's choice of detailed written programs versus pre-printed verification outlines or checklists. If the firm makes use of pre-printed verification outlines or checklists, the auditing procedures will generally be discussed in the same order as on the related forms. As well, the manual will sometimes provide brief explanations of, and reasons for, the suggested auditing procedures.

Often, however, reliance will be placed on in-firm staff training programs, professional pronouncements and studies, and auditing textbooks to provide explanations so that the audit manual itself can be more concise.

Responsibility for detailed program planning

Detailed program planning is usually the direct responsibility of the audit senior – to be done within the broad parameters established in the general planning decisions. However, the reviewers may participate in some of the more critical programming decisions and they will often wish to review and approve the detailed plans before the field work is begun.

15.3.4 Logistical planning

Logistical planning is normally the responsibility of the audit senior or his immediate superior. It involves making arrangements with the client as to the dates for audit visits, asking the client to arrange office space, making travel arrangements if the client is out of town, and gathering together all the materials to be used on the job (e.g., a locked box for working papers, prior year's working papers, audit manuals, stationery).

15.3.5 Timing of planning

On a recurring audit, most of the general and detailed planning decisions can be made prior to the interim audit, based on information about the client's sytems gained in prior years. At the conclusion of the interim audit, additional decisions can be made and plans modified based on interim audit findings. The planning of a few year-end procedures, however, such as inventory observation, will have to wait until specific plans are made by the client. Many auditors prefer to leave all or most of the detailed planning for the financial statement audit until the completion of the interim audit. This arrangement permits the detailed year-end plans to be reviewed in conjunction with the interim audit working papers.

On an initial audit, or where there have been major changes to the client's business or systems, planning for the financial statement audit must wait until the conclusion of the interim audit. Planning for the interim audit in such situations will normally have to be done in two stages – planning of the review and evaluation of control after preliminary orientation, and planning of compliance and substantive procedures after the review and at least a tentative evaluation of the systems have been made. The timing of planning procedures will, of course, also be affected by the overall timing of the whole audit (see 15.4.7).

15.4 General planning decisions

Preceding detailed program planning must come certain fundamental decisions as to the overall approach to the audit engagement. These general planning decisions, while they may sometimes be combined with one or more aspects of program planning, usually warrant the attention of senior reviewers before more detailed programming decisions can logically be made.

For the guidance of audit staff on the job and as a starting point for future years' planning, it is useful to document the general planning decisions made.

The documentation may take the form of a series of planning notes. Alternatively, some practitioners find it convenient to use a pre-printed *planning memorandum*, which identifies the key general planning decisions to be made and allows for additional explanations to be appended where required. An example of a portion of such a planning memorandum is shown in Figure 15.b. The planning memorandum may be updated and carried forward each year.

Example of a Portion of a Planning Memorandum—Audit Environment

Client *ABC Limited*   Year-end *December 31, 1976*

---

1. Who is the real client? (and to whom do we have responsibilities?)
   Consider:

   ☐ proprietor;   ☐ partners;   ☐ management;

   ☑ controlling shareholders;   ☑ the investing public;   ☐ important minority interests;

   ☑ regulatory or government agencies (identify *– Canadian – Stock exchanges and securities commission – U.S. Securities and Exchange Commission*   );

   ☐ bankers or other lenders (identify _____);

   ☑ parent companies or other auditors (identify *parent company auditors XYZ & Co., Certified Public accountants*   );

   ☐ potential purchaser (identify _____);

   ☐ other (identify _____).

2. Affiliates and related audits

   (a) Affiliates we audit and their relationship:
       ABC Distributing Ltd. – 100% owned subsidiary

   (b) Affiliates we do not audit (indicate relationship, identify auditors):
       ABC International Ltd. (parent company – 70% interest), audited by XYZ & Co., Certified Public Accountants

   (c) Related audits (e.g., pension plan):
       ABC Limited Employee Pension Plan
       ABC Employee Charitable Contributions Organization

3. Terms of engagement and reporting requirements

   ☑ General purpose financial statements and short form audit report

   Special purpose financial statements:

   ☐ with long-form report

   ☑ non-consolidated legals (where general purpose is consolidated)

   ☐ for filing with tax returns

Figure 15.b

☐ interim statements

☐ for prospectus

☐ other (describe)

☐ Preparation of tax returns (federal, provincial and other)

☑ Review of tax returns

☑ SEC reports

☐ Other reports and returns (describe) _____

☑ *Preparation of management letter* _____

☐ _____

Other terms of engagement (e.g., detection of immaterial fraud, preparation of management letter, etc.) – describe
Assistance with anti-inflation forms. In-depth study of computer systems in 1977. Personal tax returns for senior executives.

4. Geographic location of major assets (where multiple locations):

Significant asset components	Approx. value	Location
Inventory (plant)	$35 000 000	Toronto
Inventory (company owned warehouse)	12 000 000	Vancouver
Inventory (company owned warehouse)	10 000 000	Montreal

5. Characteristics of business operations of greatest significance to the audit (e.g., considerable non-arm's length dealings; large foreign currency activities; large forward purchases; long-term fixed price contracts)

  – all domestic sales of ABC brand name lines are made through ABC Distributing Ltd. which accounts for approx. 40% of total sales
  – foreign sales are made through foreign mfrs. agents and account for approx. 25% total sales
  – large foreign exchange transactions

6. Areas of recurring error or disagreement

  – provision for warranty claims
  – inventory obsolescence allowance
  – allowance for doubtful accounts

7. Most sensitive or difficult areas to audit (e.g., inventory valuation, estimated future costs, deferred revenues, etc.)

  – pricing of non-arm's length sales to ABC Distributing Ltd.

8. Other factors of possible consequence (e.g., fluctuating purchase/selling prices in the industry; other industry factors; considering going public; major financing under consideration; large turnover in accounting staff; prolonged labour strike; change in distribution of financial statements; biases of management; etc.)

  – declining foreign exchange rates in several European countries accounting for a significant proportion of the company's foreign sales
  – possible issue of debentures next year.

9. Significant factors in maintaining good client/audit staff relations with this client (e.g., close adherence to client's working hours, restricted access to sensitive client records, problems to be discussed only with comptroller, etc.)

  Information relating to the compensation of executive personnel is considered confidential and should be discussed only with those persons directly responsible for processing the information. Absolutely essential for the staff to keep employee office hours.

Figure 15.b (concluded)

416

15.4.1 Orientation to the audit environment

The first step is to identify the circumstances of the client and the express or implied terms of the audit engagement.

If the reviewer is new to the engagement, he can obtain general background information by scanning correspondence files, reviewing notes describing the client's business and organization charts in the prior year's interim audit file, reading the engagement letter, studying the prior year's financial statements, reviewing the prior year's audit budget and time summary, and, in some cases, scrutinizing key verification sections in the prior year's financial statement audit file. The new reviewer will most likely want to have a preliminary meeting with key client officials. In that meeting, the terms of engagement and required reporting dates should be carefully considered. If the reviewer is already familiar with the client, this process of orientation may be very brief. On an initial engagement, on the other hand, knowledge of the client will have to be gained through special meetings in advance of the field work and early review of some of the preliminary interim audit steps (see Chapter 23).

In any case, summary information as to the circumstances of the client and the nature of the audit engagement can be documented in a planning memorandum as illustrated in Figure 15.b. The following comments relate to that figure.

1. Who is the real client and to whom does the auditor have responsibilities?
The identification of the principal users of the financial statements and of the auditor's report is important (a) in determining the materiality of different matters and amounts, (b) in determining an appropriate level of audit assurance, and (c) in identifying possible biases in accounting judgments. Although the auditor cannot predict all conceivable future uses which his report may have, and although he must meet professional and legal standards for any report he issues whatever the identity of its potential users, nonetheless it is reasonable that he take into account all circumstances known to him at the time he makes the judgment decisions involved in any audit. The significance of a given uncertainty or imprecision may be entirely different where financial statements are prepared primarily for a prospective purchaser, than where they are prepared for a bank, a parent company, or a sole proprietor.

Identifying the client to whom the auditor has a direct legal relationship is usually no problem. In most statutory audits, the relationship is with the incorporated entity and the shareholders of the company. Common examples of third parties who may be relying on the statements are regulatory bodies (e.g., bodies regulating hospitals, radio and television companies, stockbrokers), bondholders, banks, and other creditors. In larger, publicly traded companies the whole financial community may be relying on the financial statements in making investment decisions – or on financial analysts who in turn rely on the statements.

2. Affiliates and related audits
Identification of affiliates and their relationship to the client is important so that the auditor can ensure that (a) the method of accounting for intercompany investments is appropriate in the circumstances, (b) the audit staff will be alert for the presence of related party transactions, and (c) auditing procedures performed on the various related companies are properly co-ordinated. Identification of affiliates audited by other auditors is important as well so that additional procedures occasioned by reliance on, or by, those other auditors can be properly planned.

3. Terms of the engagement and reporting requirements
Additional terms of the engagement or reporting requirements extending beyond minimum attest responsibilities will naturally affect the timing and scope of the auditor's procedures to be planned.

4. Geographic location of major assets
Where significant assets are located in more than one place, their nature and dollar value by location will give the reviewer and audit senior some perspective as to the allocation of audit time, the necessity for out-of-town work, and the feasibility of cyclical coverage of certain locations.

5. Factors of consequence to the audit
The next four items in Figure 15.b call for the documentation of specific factors influencing the detailed programming decisions: areas of greatest audit significance, areas of recurring error, areas of greatest difficulty or sensitivity, etc. The identification of these factors will also help the audit senior in preparing detailed time budgets.

6. Client relations
The reviewer will often be aware of a number of points which are especially important to good relations with a given client. One client may be particularly anxious that accounting matters be discussed only with the comptroller because they are so confidential; another, just as anxious that most matters be resolved at more junior levels because they take so much time. It makes good sense to note these particular preferences in the planning memorandum or in planning notes so that the audit staff can act accordingly. This portion of the planning memorandum can be updated and carried forward annually.

15.4.2 Decision re materiality

The concepts of audit precision and materiality were discussed in 6.6.1 and 6.6.2. It was suggested that a materiality limit or threshold be established for each audit engagement by the exercise of professional judgment, perhaps with the assistance of guidelines. Since a number of individually immaterial items could add up to a material total, the materiality limit must be applied cumulatively rather than item by item.

Importance at the planning stage

A materiality limit for a given audit should be used:

1. as a guide to planning the nature and extent of verification procedures,
2. as a guide to assessing the sufficiency of audit evidence gathered, evaluating the audit results encountered and determining the appropriate audit opinion to express.

It is the first use which requires that the materiality limit itself be one of the earliest general planning decisions made. As discussed in 9.4.1, compliance verification procedures must be planned to provide an appropriate assurance of detecting, should it exist, such frequency of critical compliance deviations as would indicate a reasonable possibility of material monetary error. As discussed in 11.3.1, substantive verification procedures must be planned to provide an appropriate assurance of detecting the possibility of a material total of monetary error misstating reported income, or misstating other figures, should such a material total actually exist. Since the definitions of compliance and substantive objectives both involve the concept of materiality, a decision on materiality must precede any program planning for either the interim or financial statement audit. The materiality limit chosen will affect:

1. judgmental decisions as to the nature and quality of audit evidence to be gathered in non-test procedures,
2. judgmental or statistical decisions as to sample extents for test procedures (see Chapters 12 and 13),
3. decisions on the job as to what constitutes immaterial items which do not warrant exhaustive verification steps but which may be passed over with some reasonable overview procedures.[2]

Materiality guidelines

The arguments in favour of using some set of normal materiality guidelines to assist in establishing the materiality limit for a given audit were summarized in 6.6.2. In choosing materiality guidelines, one must decide (a) whether they should be absolute amounts or relative proportions, (b) the base to which any relative proportions should be related, and (c) the magnitude of the guideline amounts or proportions.

Absolute amounts as guidelines

It is hard to imagine serious advocacy of guidelines based on absolute amounts. A $50 000 error which would be catastrophic in a small family-run business would be trivial in the financial statements of a major oil company. Occasionally, materiality criteria based on absolute amounts are suggested by regulatory agencies or others – for example, with respect to the disclosure of questionable payments. Whatever the applicability of such criteria to *known* errors (and such applicability is contentious) they cannot, in the writer's view, be applied to normal audit objectives which include the obtaining of assurance regarding *most likely* and *possible* errors. To obtain reasonable assurance of detecting errors exceeding in total some absolute dollar limit for all clients would (a) leave the financial statements of smaller clients subject to a risk of errors which might exceed their reported income while (b) forcing on larger clients the cost of astronomical audit samples to search for proportionately minute errors.

Possible bases for relative guidelines

Studies in various countries have supported the view that materiality guidelines should be relative proportions of some appropriate base. The choice of base has however, been less uniform. For assessing the materiality of an error in a particular financial statement figure, possible bases include (a) the individual figure itself, (b) some grouping of assets, liabilities or income components in which it occurs, (c) total net assets or gross assets, and (d) some measure of revenue or earning power. The first can usually be dismissed as unworkable. Obviously, it is unreasonable to ask for assurance that the figure for prepaid expenses is accurately stated within 5% of itself if the whole figure happens to be immaterial. A result of the second alternative is that its materiality would depend on the degree of classification in the financial statements. Financial statements with less detail, fewer groupings on the income statement, or no current/long-term division on the balance sheet would yield broader measures of materiality. Some degree of variation with level of detail is logical, but defining materiality solely in these terms may contradict the idea of assessing the financial statements "taken as a whole". The third alternative would usually yield an excessively broad measure of materiality. If net assets were misstated by 10%, most readers would usually agree that the financial statements were materially in error, but much smaller misstatements of net assets might still be substantial in relation to net income.

Generally, if the magnitude of an income-distorting error is gradually increased, it becomes material relative to reported income long before it becomes an important distortion of the balance sheet. For example, a $20 000 overstatement of a $500 000 inventory is hardly likely to be judged material relative to inventory, working capital or net assets but it may indeed be material relative to a $100 000 income figure. Because the tightest constraint of materiality is generally upon reported income, it is most useful, in the writer's view, to express normal materiality guidelines relative to operating results.

For not-for-profit organizations the magnitude of operations is generally best gauged by either total revenues or total expenses – the difference between the two in any one year being usually minor or arbitrary or the result of accidental surpluses or deficits which may be reversed in future years. For profit-oriented enterprises, however, most readers of the financial statements will attach primary importance to profitability and some measure of profitability is accordingly a logical base for materiality.

Possible measures of profitability

Actual net income, however, may fluctuate widely from year to year. Should materiality be halved, and audit costs doubled, in a year when income temporarily dips from $200 000 to $100 000? Does materiality vanish in a break-even or loss year? Clearly, actual net income is not a suitable materiality base. It was largely to avoid these problems that the CICA Audit Technique Study, *Materiality in Auditing* (1965) suggested instead the use of gross profit as the base. Since that time various other studies have expressed a preference for "normal" or "normalized" net income as the base. Indeed, the CICA Study itself reasoned from a normal net income base in deriving its percentage guidelines relative to gross profit. If, as is usually the case, errors would have a tax effect, this effect may be allowed for by relating materiality to normal pre-tax income. In the writer's view, normal pre-tax income, after eliminating non-recurring, unusual, and certain non-arm's length items, is the most logical base on which to relate materiality for profit-oriented enterprises.[3]

Another base which is sometimes suggested is the year-to-year change in income. Some have suggested, for example, that instead of materiality being measured as, say, 5% of income it should be measured as 25% of the increase or decrease in income from the prior year. The argument is that trends are

important and that any significant misstatement of a trend must be judged material. There are two objections to this argument:

1. It is unreasonable that materiality should be reduced to trivial proportions (and audit costs soar) whenever the year-to-year change in income is small. The audit costs of companies with smooth and gradual earnings trends should not, for example, be made far higher than those of companies whose earnings fluctuate erratically from year to year.

2. The precision with which an audit opinion can be formed on a year's reported income is in part a function of the audit materiality limit used in designing the verification of both the opening and closing balance sheets – because an undetected $40 000 error in an opening balance such as inventory may be distorting the current year's income statement. If there is a $40 000 imprecision in the audit opinion on the opening balance sheet, the imprecision in the opinion on the current year's income cannot be reduced below $40 000 even if audit materiality for the closing balance sheet is tightened up to $20 000. If audit materiality is based on "normal" net income, the effect of the opening balance sheet does not present a great problem since "normal" net income is not subject to dramatic and unexpected fluctuations as actual income may be. But if audit materiality is based on the year-to-year change in income, the balance sheet at one year-end would have to be audited with a precision based on predicted income changes in the following year if the defined level of materiality is later to be achieved in that following year. Basing the extent of audit work on such future predictions is just not feasible.

Thus, whatever the applicability of year-to-year criteria to *known* errors (and such applicability is contentious) they cannot again, in the writer's view, be applied to normal audit objectives which include the obtaining of assurance regarding *most likely* and *possible* errors.

Should all organizations have the same guidelines?

A much debated question is whether materiality guidelines should be less stringent for the small business. The CICA Study argued that the operations of larger organizations, compared to smaller ones, are generally the net result of a larger number of individual transactions and, statistically, one would expect a reduction in the influence of random fluctuations on the net result. A 5% growth in a monthly business net income from $2 000 to $2 100 might well be put down to mere chance (the timing of particular orders, etc.) whereas even a 2% change in some component of the gross national product involves economists for weeks in explaining its significance. It follows that incomes of large organizations are usually measurable, and auditable, with a finer relative precision than incomes of small organizations – though at the extreme of the very smallest, this comparison may not hold true. In general, then, less stringent materiality guidelines would seem reasonable for small and medium size organizations than for gigantic ones.

Other differences in guidelines may also be appropriate to consider in certain situations. The incomes of companies with very large asset-to-income ratios, such as in many financial institutions, are harder to measure with the same relative precision used for other organizations. It could be argued that slightly broader guidelines relative to income would be appropriate for these cases. One of the requirements of meaningful accounting information is that it be verifiable. To be verifiable, in practice, must be interpreted to mean economically verifiable. And such an interpretation, in turn, implies that the tolerance to which statements are verified (the materiality limit) must be economically obtainable.

Income errors and classification errors

Monetary errors distorting the financial statements may be classified into two groups:

• errors which misstate net income and net assets,
• classification errors among balance sheet components or among income components which do not misstate net income or net assets (they may or may not misstate key groupings of items such as working capital or gross profit).

The foregoing discussion has dealt with income-distorting errors. The tolerance for mere classification errors would usually be somewhat larger. Thus, a $40 000 misstatement of net income might be judged as material where a $40 000 misclassification between accounts receivable and inventory might not be. How much greater the tolerance for a classification error can be will depend upon its nature. A misclassification between accounts receivable and inventory, which misstates neither working capital or the current ratio, may be less serious than a misclassification between inventory and fixed assets, which misstates both, or between inventory and accounts payable, which misstates the ratio. A misclassification between selling expenses and administrative expenses, which does not misstate gross profit, may be less serious than a misclassification between selling expenses and cost of sales, which does. Since the circumstances vary so greatly, it seems best to leave the materiality of classification errors to be determined by judgment in each particular case – restricting the use of guidelines, therefore, for the more stringent materiality limit usually required for income-distorting errors.

Suggested materiality guidelines

The following presumptive materiality guidelines are suggested for audit use:[4]

For profit-oriented enterprises:
a) 5% of normal pre-tax income where normal pre-tax income exceeds $2 000 000,
b) 5% to 10% of normal pre-tax income where normal pre-tax income is less than $2 000 000 (the transition from 5% to 10% being gradual rather than abrupt) or where there is not widespread public ownership.

For not-for-profit organizations:
$\frac{1}{2}$% of normal gross revenues

Subject in either case to:
a) consideration of relationships to individual income components or balance sheet components which may occasionally require a tighter materiality constraint:
  • for all items (for example, when stringent dividend restrictions related to working capital exist and are in danger of violation)
  • or for certain sensitive items (such as loans to and remuneration of officers and directors);
b) judgmental evaluation of any other circumstances which justify a departure from the normal guidelines.

In estimating normal pre-tax income the auditor may consider past years' results, current interim results, and current forecasts. He should then eliminate non-recurring items which should not affect the overall level of materiality or audit effort. Examples would be (a) unusual gains or losses, (b) non-recurring items such as start-up expenses, reorganization costs, or the effects of a strike, and (c) items classed as extraordinary on the income statement. Prior years' trends may provide a further indication of what a normal ongoing level of pre-tax income can be expected to be. Where current results are believed to be not typical and where meaningful prior trends are not available, the auditor may apply industry experience to estimate normal pre-tax income as a percentage of sales or as a percentage rate of return on assets employed. Such a procedure may be reasonable, for example, where a company is still in the development stage or where its earnings are temporarily depressed relative to industry averages. Finally, in some cases certain non-arm's length transactions, such as abnormally high salary to the owner, unusual royalties or management fees to a parent company, or unusual transfer pricing of goods bought from, or sold to, affiliates, may increase or reduce reported income from what it would otherwise be. Usually it would be reasonable to eliminate these effects, which may be similar to profit distributions, in estimating normal pre-tax income for purposes of applying the foregoing materiality guidelines.

Judgment, subsequent review and documentation

It must be stressed that, in the end, the materiality limit must be a judgment decision by the auditor taking into account all the surrounding circumstances. The reasonable achievability[5] of a proposed materiality limit must be considered as well as the interests of various financial statement users. For a very small client broader materiality limits than suggested by the guidelines may be necessary; in many cases it is desirable to discuss such limits with the client. For clients with high asset-to-income ratios broader limits may also be justified. Industries with tranditionally narrow profit margins can present problems in assessing materiality. For not-for-profit organizations the decision may be the most difficult of all. Directors of a charitable organization, for example, may often have precision expectations more stringent than those suggested by the foregoing guidelines. The auditor may find it prudent, therefore, to discuss his planned materiality with the organization's management, board of directors or audit committee. The advantage of guidelines is in providing, for each engagement, a consistent starting point to which the auditor may then make adjustments to allow for special circumstances.

Any materiality limit determined during the planning stage must be viewed as tentative. At the conclusion of the audit the circumstances affecting its determination should be reviewed again. Further information obtained during the audit may warrant a revision of the tentative materiality limit chosen earlier. For example, the need for occasional adjustment to provide a minimum allowance for undetected errors was discussed in 11.3.2.

The reasons for adopting a particular materiality limit should be documented in the working papers – for example, in the planning memorandum.

Allowance for possible undetected errors (precision)

If the materiality limit is to contain known errors, most likely errors, and possible errors projected as a result of the audit (see 11.3.2), it is useful to estimate in advance the known and most likely errors that can reasonably be expected. This estimate will indicate the portion of the materiality limit that is expected to be available to cover possible undetected errors. Normally, the magnitude of this remaining portion will directly influence the extent of audit work required. The influence can only be assessed judgmentally for many auditing procedures, but for statistical tests it should be specifically determined as the sampling "precision". Planning for "precision" and "tolerable basic precision" where dollar-unit sampling is employed was discussed in 13.4.4. The choice of precision and tolerable basic precision would usually be made at the same time as the materiality decision so that all compliance and substantive tests throughout the audit can be designed in accordance with this choice.

Determination of materiality limits and precision for decentralized accounting units and entities in corporate groups

For clients with decentralized operations and accounting units within the same legal entity, the materiality limit should be chosen based on the normal guidelines for the entire reporting entity. This materiality limit can be used by the audit staff in the verification work in each division of the entity. It is inappropriate to determine an overall materiality limit and chop it up in pieces for the various divisions. The result of such an approach would be excessive auditing. Similarly, sampling "precision" and "basic precision" should be planned for the entire group. In planning these quantities, there must be deducted from the overall materiality limit the expected total of known and most likely errors for all divisions taken as a group.

Where a legal entity is part of a corporate group and the auditor is not reporting separately for that legal entity, then the materiality limit and the basic precision for the legal entity may be determined as if it were a division. This situation will be rare in Canada because most incorporated entities, other than the very small, are required by law to have an audit. In the more common case, the auditor will be issuing a separate report on the financial statements of each legal entity. In that case, it is not appropriate to determine a materiality limit on normalized consolidated pre-tax income and then use that limit to audit the separate accounts of the parent company, subsidiary companies and other investee companies. If that were done, the precision objectives on most of the subsidiary and other investee companies would be far too broad to permit separate opinions on each of them. Nor would it be appropriate to determine materiality based on consolidated normalized pre-tax income and then chop it up and apportion it to the individual reporting entities. Rather, the auditor should first determine a materiality limit, and sampling precision, for each subsidiary and other investee company individually, based on the normal materiality guidelines outlined above. (Occasionally, when a subsidiary is wholly owned, a somewhat broader materiality limit may be justified than the normal guideline on the basis of the limited use made of financial statements.) Second, he should determine a materiality limit, and a sampling precision, for the consolidated statements as a whole. Third, for each reporting entity to be audited he should choose the more stringent of (a) the individual limit and precision or (b) the consolidated limit and precision − generally, the former.

15.4.3 Decision re overall audit assurance

The overall level of audit assurance with respect to a given item on the financial statements is a combination of:

a) the assurance available from the inherent nature of that item,
b) the assurance available from internal control and from the auditor's compliance procedures with respect to systems affecting that item,
c) the assurance available from the auditor's substantive procedures for that item.

Therefore, by deciding upon the overall level of audit assurance required and by then analyzing the three contributing sources of assurance, the auditor can determine the nature and extent of both compliance evidence and substantive evidence to be sought. It was argued in Chapter 6 that, for two reasons, the overall level of audit assurance itself could properly vary within certain narrow limits. First, excess assurance might be prudent on sensitive engagements where the auditor's exposure is greater than normal. Second, the level of assurance warranted should be influenced within limits by the cost of audit evidence available.[6]

The decision as to the sensitivity of the engagement is an important planning decision which should be made before the field work is started. The auditor's exposure will usually be considered to be greater on the audits of companies with publicly traded shares and sometimes also on the audits of any organizations (such as certain charities) where there is a widespread public interest or concern. Some practitioners develop standard criteria for classifying engagements into various categories according to sensitivity − the classification in turn affecting levels of review and approval required, perhaps the basis of staff allocation, and the choice of confidence levels on individual tests. Whether formal classifications

are used or not, the decision as to the overall level of audit assurance required should usually be made or approved by the most senior level of reviewer involved on the engagement. The decision should be documented, either in a planning memorandum or elsewhere.

It is difficult to address the subject of audit exposure without someone incorrectly inferring that "the auditor is willing to do a second-rate job where he can get away with it." Such a result is not the intention. Rather, as discussed in 6.6.7, the auditor must seek a reasonable level of assurance as a minimum on all engagements but will usually wish to seek an even higher level on sensitive engagements, not because the lower level would have been indefensible, but because the disruption and cost of any such defence is best avoided.

The decision as to audit cost, to the limited extent to which it influences the overall level of audit assurance sought, must usually be made at the more detailed program planning stage. However, certain broad conclusions can sometimes be drawn during general planning. For example, if the company inventories are scattered over twenty locations in the far north, the extent of cyclical observations of stock-takings at these locations may, because of their cost, be somewhat less than would have been chosen for more accessible locations − provided that other procedures, such as analytical review, confirm their reasonableness and provided that there are no suspicious circumstances.

The effect of the planning decision as to overall audit assurance on the detailed planning of individual verification steps is discussed in 10.6.2 with respect to the reliability and sufficiency of evidence in general, in 12.5.3 with respect to test assurance on judgmental tests, and in 13.4.5 with respect to confidence level on statistical tests.

15.4.4 Decisions re approach and emphasis

The next general planning step involves decisions as to the emphasis on and approach to interim audit work, as to areas requiring special attention during the financial statement audit, and as to the nature and extent of pre-year-end substantive procedures.

Emphasis on and approach to the interim audit

The relative emphasis to be placed on the interim audit depends on:

a) the extent to which substantive procedures can be shifted back to an interim date to reduce year-end peaks,

b) the extent to which it is necessary or desirable to place reliance on internal controls.

Five reasons for placing audit reliance on internal controls were discussed in detail in 9.1.6.

Possible interim audit strategies are:

a) a systems-oriented interim audit,
b) a data-oriented interim audit,
c) in rare cases, omission of the interim audit.

Criteria for choosing among these strategies were discussed in 9.6.4.

The reasons for emphasizing the interim audit and for choosing one strategy rather than another vary in importance from audit to audit and from section to section within the same audit. Typical interim audit sections suggested in Chapter 9 were:

• sales/receivables/receipts,
• purchases/payables/payments,
• wage and salary payrolls,
• inventory records and cost records,
• books of account and general.

At the general planning stage the auditor should consider the relative importance of the interim work and the best strategy for its performance separately for each of these, or similar, sections.[7]

Where all or most of the major systems are to be reviewed and evaluated using a systems-oriented approach, an additional decision is the extent of the review of computer environmental controls. At least a limited review will always be required. In certain cases, a more extensive review and evaluation is warranted. Factors influencing the decision are: the size of the computer installation, the complexity of the computer applications, and the importance to management of advice on computer matters.

Emphasis in the financial statement audit

Final decisions as to areas requiring greater or lesser emphasis in the financial statement audit must await completion of the interim audit, which may disclose unsuspected control weaknesses or strengths. Nonetheless, on a recurring engagement preliminary decisions can be made. In areas where reliance on control is not anticipated, more extensive substantive procedures will normally be planned and more of them may have to be scheduled for the year-end itself rather than earlier. Other factors influencing the emphasis on different areas include:

a) management emphasis (any apparent bias towards achieving particular results),
b) past problem areas encountered,
c) changes in basic conditions or operations from prior years.

Nature and extent of pre-year-end procedures

As discussed in 11.6, pre-year-end substantive verification apart from substantive procedures included for convenience with the interim audit, include:

a) major procedures such as accounts receivable confirmation or inventory observation at pre-year-end dates,
b) related "roll-forward procedures",
c) other procedures such as the advance preparation of key year-end confirmation requests and the gathering of statistics for year-end analytical review.

The third category has little effect on total audit time and can usually be left for the audit senior to plan. The first two categories, however, generally increase total audit time in return for an earlier reporting date. Moreover, if roll-forward and cut-off procedures are not carefully planned, the level of audit assurance can fall seriously. For these reasons, the decision to perform major pre-year-end procedures is usually made by the reviewer. In addition, the reviewer may wish to review the more detailed plans covering the coordination of procedures at the pre-year-end dates, the extent of roll-forward procedures, the adequacy of separate analytical review of the roll-forward period, and any special procedures to be applied to the related year-end balances.

Further details in later chapters

Further details of the foregoing general planning decisions, and their relationship to more specific program planning, are described in later chapters under the following headings:

24.2.1   Decision re relative emphasis on interim audit
24.2.2   Decision re interim audit approach
24.2.3   Decision re extent of review and evaluation
24.2.4   Decision re extent of review of computer environment
24.2.5   Decision re impact of control evaluation
24.2.7   Decision re statistical sampling and computer-assisted audit techniques
24.2.10 Co-ordination with financial statement audit procedures
31.2.1   Decision re audit emphasis and effect of interim audit
31.2.2   Decision re major pre-year-end verification
31.2.3   Decision re other pre-year-end procedures
31.2.5   Decision re statistical sampling and computer-assisted audit techniques.

15.4.5 Decisions re detailed program planning and approvals

While detailed program planning itself is usually the direct responsibility of the audit senior, a reviewer should usually make four general planning decisions:

a) the nature, extent and timing of the detailed program planning,
b) the choice among a detailed written audit program, no detailed program, an abbreviated written program, and pre-printed checklists (see 15.3.3),
c) the degree of reviewer and specialist participation in program planning,
d) the extent and timing of the review of the audit senior's program planning prior to the field work.

These decisions will depend upon the nature of the audit approach used, the timing of the field work, the competence of the audit senior, and the policies of the individual firm. A brief outline of the categories of program planning to be considered follows.

For a systems-oriented interim audit, possible program planning includes:

1. specific decisions as to the scope of review and evaluation for each major system, distinguishing more important and less important areas,
2. identification of controls to be relied upon (normally on an evaluation guide or questionnaire),
3. a written program of compliance verification with respect to those controls,
4. a written evaluation of the potential materiality of control deficiencies and a written program of substantive procedures (weakness investigation) to compensate for them,
5. a written program or summary planning notes as to other substantive procedures,
6. decisions on the extent of tests (really a part of 3, 4, and 5).

On an initial engagement, the first category must await preliminary field work and the rest must await the results of the review and evaluation. Two stages of reviewing program planning are therefore desirable. On a recurring engagement preliminary decisions can be based on the prior year's results and program planning notes restricted to necessary changes. Two stages of reviewing program planning may still be desirable to cover later program changes resulting from changes in controls.

For a data-oriented interim audit, possible program planning includes:

1. specific decisions as to the scope of review and evaluation (normally on an evaluation guide or questionnaire),

2. a written program of transactional tests (including for each test its objective: review, compliance, substantive or multiple-purpose),
3. decisions on extent of tests (really a part of 2).

The previous comments with respect to initial and recurring engagements are also applicable.

For a financial statement audit, possible program planning includes:

1. detailed decisions as to major pre-year-end verification,
2. specific points to be covered during inventory observation and verification of cut-off,
3. specific verification decisions for each audit section (on brief planning notes, pre-printed verification outlines, or detailed written programs),
4. decisions on extent of tests (really a part of 1 and 3).

On an initial engagement, most of these decisions must await completion of the interim audit and usually both these decisions and the interim audit file will be reviewed together. On a recurring engagement preliminary decisions can be based on the prior year's results and made at the same time as the interim audit decisions. Revisions to plans resulting from the interim audit can be reviewed at the same time as the interim audit file. Inventory observation and cut-off verification are special cases since detailed planning must await completion of the client's planning – often long after the interim audit.

The degree of program planning and the level and timing of review and approval of the plans will be affected by the degree of specialist involvement, internal audit participation, and client assistance. For example, if computer-assisted audit techniques are to be used, it may be desirable to have detailed plans for their use prepared by, or with the assistance of, a computer audit specialist and approved by the reviewer before the field work starts. If internal auditors are to perform procedures on behalf of the external auditor, detailed programs or instructions should usually be prepared and approved in advance.

15.4.6 Decisions re internal audit and other client assistance

Client assistance such as in the preparation of schedules, typing of confirmation requests, and assembling of requested invoices is usually left for detailed planning by the audit senior. Such assistance is essentially clerical and may be provided by accounting personnel, internal auditors, or others. While this assistance is an important aid to audit efficiency, it does not generally require a significant degree of reliance on the quality of employee work – since the results will be directly checked by the audit staff.

In contrast, reliance on audit procedures performed by internal auditors involves important judgmental evaluations and may have a major impact on the extent of the external audit program. For this reason, general planning decisions as to the degree of reliance to be placed on internal audit work should be made or reviewed by a senior reviewer.

As explained in 10.4.9, an internal audit department affects the external audit in two ways:

1. its effect on internal control (systems that would otherwise be judged as weak may be compensated for by the work of internal auditors),
2. its performance of specific audit procedures which external auditors would otherwise have to perform.

Evaluation of the first effect is really an integral part of planning the reliance to be placed on internal control and the approach to be taken to the interim audit (see 15.4.4). Evaluation of the second effect includes consideration of:

a) internal audit preparatory work (such as systems notes or flow charts) which facilitates the external auditor's work,
b) compliance or substantive procedures, either planned by internal auditors for their own purposes or specifically requested by external audit staff, which can justify a reduction in the compliance or substantive procedures in the external audit program.

Degree of reliance being placed

Use of flow charts or systems notes prepared by internal auditors may not in itself imply any significant reliance as the external auditor can independently check their accuracy through discussions with employees and the performance of compliance verification. Reliance on compliance or substantive procedures performed by internal auditors, however, implies considerable reliance on their competence and objectivity as well as on the care with which they performed the particular procedures in question. Reliance on internal audit procedures to compensate for control deficiencies also implies reliance on internal auditor competence, objectivity and care, though often less reliance than in the case of specific compliance and substantive procedures.

Preliminary general decisions

Based on prior years' experience, the reviewer can usually make two preliminary decisions prior to the interim audit field work:

1. the degree of reliance which would be justified by the apparent level of competence, objectivity and

care brought to the internal audit work (should this degree be minimal the planning, of course, need proceed no further),
2. the extent to which it would be economical to rely on internal audit work after allowing for necessary planning, supervision, review, and evaluation (where reliance is evidently uneconomical the planning need proceed no further).

For initial engagements these decisions can only be made after some of the field work has been completed.

If, as a result of these preliminary decisions, reliance is to be placed on internal auditors' work, specific procedures can be planned to assess their competence and objectivity and the care with which their work was performed. These may be left to the audit senior or may be specified by the reviewer.

Planned review of competence, objectivity and care

Assessment of the internal auditor's competence may include a review of hiring policies, degrees or diplomas held, training programs, and the observed quality of their work and reports. Assessment of their objectivity may include a review of their organizational independence, their terms of reference, and the evident frankness or cautiousness of their reports. Assessment of the care with which their work is performed may include supervision of their work, comparison of their findings to external audit findings, and specific tests of their procedures.

Specific decisions

Where general reliance can be placed on the internal auditors' work because their competence, objectivity and carefulness have been established, decisions must be made as to the specific areas of reliance and the further work necessary, if any, to warrant specific reliance. Usually such decisions will be part of the detailed program planning left for the audit senior. However, where extensive use of internal auditors is to be made to perform compliance and substantive procedures, the reviewer may wish to review the overall plans for:

1. maintaining overall control of the planning, timing, nature and extent of the entire audit program supporting the external audit opinion,
2. supervising, testing and reviewing the internal auditors' work,
3. maintaining a satisfactory portion of each key area of the audit to be performed directly by external audit staff.

Further details in later chapters

Further details on the planning for reliance on internal audit work may be found in 24.2.6 (with respect to interim audits), in 31.2.4 (with respect to financial statement audits), and in 26.1.2 (with respect to the review of competence, objectivity, and care).

15.4.7 Decision re overall timing

While day to day timing will be planned by the audit senior, the overall blocks of time required must be determined at the general planning stage, so that the reviewer can assign available staff efficiently. The major constraints on timing are the need to:

1. complete the field work before the date on which the audited financial statements are required (while, depending on the jurisdiction, the statutory deadline may be six months and the tax deadline three months after the fiscal year-end, the client's own deadline may be to issue financial statements to shareholders within two months or even one month),
2. coordinate certain verification procedures with client activities (for example, inventory observation with the client's stocktaking),
3. observe during the fiscal year those controls on which reliance is planned but which do not leave reliable documentary evidence of their existence and therefore cannot be verified afterwards (for example, division of duties),
4. schedule audit work so that appropriate audit staff, including specialists, will be available at the right times to handle the needs of both this client and all other clients of the auditor,
5. coordinate the necessary review procedures with field work scheduling.

For some very small clients, where significant reliance is not being placed on controls, it will be best to schedule all of the field work, except perhaps for inventory observation and cash counts, at a date subsequent to the year-end. For small clients where a data-oriented interim audit is performed, it may be best to schedule the field work in two stages, the interim audit at some convenient date during the year and the financial statement audit after the year-end. For medium-size and large audits where a systems-oriented interim audit is performed, it may be best to schedule the interim audit in two stages, the first stage early in the year for the review and evaluation of internal control and the second stage at a later date when more of the transactions for the year are available for compliance and substantive verification. For large clients, the financial statement audit may sometimes be scheduled after the year-end but more commonly, to meet client deadlines, in two visits, one immediately before the year-end for pre-year-end verification and one shortly afterwards for the remaining verification.

Further details in later chapters

Further details on scheduling may be found in 24.3.1 for interim audits and in 31.3.1 for financial statement audits.

15.4.8 Decision re reliance on other auditors

Where a client has investments in subsidiary companies or other investees and these investments are consolidated or accounted for by the equity method but audited by other auditors, the primary audit evidence as to investee results will be the financial statements audited by the other auditors. However, additional procedures are generally required to justify and/or to supplement the reliance on such evidence.

Agency relationship

Sometimes the investee auditors act as agents for the investor auditor. A practitioner's relationship with his agent (or any office of the agent firm) will be similar to his relationship to any office of his own firm. At the planning stage he will want to ensure that there is no impediment to objectivity and that his agent will be supplied with sufficient instructions to identify the work required. The practitioner will normally have satisfied himself as to his agent's competence and standards of work at the time the agency relationship was established. If the agent will be conducting an appropriate review of the field work, it may be unnecessary for the investor auditor to perform further review procedures – though they may be desirable in certain cases. Where further review procedures are considered desirable, their overall extent should be determined during general planning.

Non-agency relationship

Where the investee auditor does not act as an agent of the investor auditor, the former's report represents a type of third-party evidence which should normally be supplemented by some additional procedures by the investor auditor. The extent of these additional procedures will vary depending primarily (a) on the materiality of the investment, (b) on his opinion of the reliability and competence of the investee auditor and, as well, of the particular office of the investee audit firm performing the work and of the partner in charge of the assignment, and (c) on the degree of risk or uncertainty inherent in the underlying entity.

A classification of the possible additional procedures into three levels is suggested:

1. Basic procedures – consisting of enquiries as to the reputation and standing of the investee auditors, direct contact with them, the receipt of suitable representations from them, and a careful review of the audited financial statements received from them;
2. Review procedures – consisting, in addition, of participation in the planning of the investee audit, a visit to the investee auditors in most cases, and a review of their working papers;
3. Override procedures – consisting, in addition, of certain audit procedures performed directly by the investor auditor on the investee records.

These three levels of procedures are described in detail in 38.3.10.

At the general planning stage, the reviewer must decide which of these three levels is appropriate so that the specific procedures may be planned and arrangements made with the other auditors well in advance. The following criteria for choosing among these three levels are suggested.

Suggested guidelines for choice of procedures

Basic procedures would usually be necessary, *as a minimum*, in all reliance situations except where the total assets and revenues subject to such reliance are minor – for example, up to 5% of total assets and revenues or, where the investee auditors and partner involved are well known and well regarded by the investor auditor, possibly up to 10%. Where, according to this criterion, basic procedures are not required, it is usually sufficient to obtain and read the audited investee financial statements.

Basic procedures alone would generally be sufficient where the assets and revenues subject to reliance do not exceed a modest proportion of total assets and revenues – for example, 10% to 20% depending on the various firms, offices and partners on whom reliance is placed, the inherent risk associated with the various investees and other circumstances. Where a subsidiary is, for instance, in the real estate or construction business and the investee auditors are not well known to the investor auditor, a limit around 10% might be as much reliance as the auditor would wish to tolerate without going beyond the basic procedures. On the other hand, he might be satisfied with only the basic procedures as high as 20% where he is relying on an experienced partner in a major office of a firm well known to him and the investee is a reasonably stable manufacturing concern.

Basic procedures may also be sufficient in themselves in some years of higher percentage reliance provided the investor auditor has had a close and ongoing relationship with the investee auditors and past experience has shown their work on the particular client to be thorough and reliable. However, in such cases he should usually not allow more than three or four years to elapse without performing some review procedures. When a significant change occurs in the circumstances (such as the partner in the other auditing firm changing), basic procedures would normally not be sufficient.

Review procedures would usually be appropriate where the assets and revenues subject to reliance exceed a modest proportion of total assets and revenues – such as 10% to 20%. The extent of review procedures should increase as the degree of reliance increases. It may be appropriate to employ some review procedures on a rotational basis over a period of years.

Override procedures should be considered when the assets and revenues subject to reliance exceed a significant proportion of total assets and revenues – for example, 20% in the case of little known auditors and high risk companies or 40% in the case of well known auditors and low risk companies. Moreover, in cases of lesser reliance, if the basic or review procedures raise serious doubts or problems about the financial statements or the work of the other auditors, override procedures will be required to resolve those doubts and problems if a clear opinion is to be given. At the planning stage such decisions can only be based on past years' experience or known developments in the current year. If unanticipated problems are later encountered, the plans must be revised.

Sometimes the investor auditor may not be granted access to investee records (sometimes, for example, in the case of non-subsidiaries). Where the auditor believes override procedures were necessary but are impossible because of lack of access to investee records, he will usually have to qualify or deny an opinion because of the limitation in scope. The implications of such limitations should be discussed with the client during the planning stage. It should be noted that, if the auditor finds evidence during an overriding examination that the investee financial statements are materially inaccurate, a qualification as to limitation in scope would not be adequate. Specific exception as to the matters in question would have to be taken in his report.

Where the assets and revenues subject to reliance represent most of the total assets and revenues, the auditor must give careful consideration as to whether, even with override procedures, he is in a position to express an opinion on the investor financial statements.

Implied agency relationship

The possibility of an implied agency relationship (where the fact of reliance is not disclosed in the auditor's report) is discussed in 38.3.10. To the extent the auditor accepts implied agency relationships, he may wish to choose review in preference to basic procedures or override in preference to review procedures. Moreover, the review or override procedures he conducts should generally be more extensive, given the same relative materiality, than those just discussed.

15.4.9 Selection of staff

Staff should be assigned to the field work who are competent for the level of work required and available at the times scheduled. Selection of staff includes the choice of the audit senior, audit assistants, and specialists.

1. The audit senior should be selected with particular care. If possible, except for the smallest engagement, he should have had previous experience with the client as either senior or assistant. An audit senior unfamiliar with the client will usually require increased audit time to complete the work properly. As well, continued use of new audit seniors is bound to be irritating to the client.
2. The audit senior should be available for both the interim audit and the financial statement audit. A loss in continuity between these two components of the audit will generally result in increased time and may in some cases yield erroneous audit conclusions.
3. To the extent possible, the audit assistants should also be available for both the interim audit and the financial statement audit. The knowledge of the client and the system of internal control obtained by audit assistants during the interim audit will improve the efficiency of their work on the financial statement audit.
4. Sometimes personality conflicts cause problems between client employees and audit staff. Where difficulties have arisen in the past, changes in the staff composition should be considered.
5. The terms of engagement and the technical demands of the audit should be considered carefully and specialist assistance arranged where required.

15.4.10 Review of fees and additional services

At the conclusion of the general planning it is useful to draw up a general time budget for the engagement as a whole. Such a general time budget is useful, first,

as a guide to the audit senior when he prepares more detailed budgets during program planning and, second, as a forecast of time values for billing purposes. A general time budget might, for example, identify the following components:

1. planning,
2. interim audit,
3. review and planning,
4. financial statement audit,
5. review and meetings with client,
6. other services.

Within each component, times would generally be estimated separately for reviewers, audit senior, audit assistants and specialists.

Review of fees

The review of the time values projected from such a time budget at the planning stage is useful to identify potential fee problems before the work has been done. First, of course, the reviewer should be satisfied that the projected fee is reasonable. Sometimes a review of budgeted time values will indicate a disproportionate allocation of audit costs to certain components of the audit. The cost of the interim audit may, for example, be out of proportion to the anticipated degree of reliance on internal control. Where the cost of all or a portion of the audit appears unreasonable to the reviewer, the earlier general planning decisions should be reconsidered. Of course, *necessary* audit work must not be cut back merely because the reviewer anticipates billing problems. But if he believes the audit assurance being gathered is out of proportion to its cost, then either unreasonable assurance and materiality objectives have been set or inefficient audit strategies have been adopted for meeting those objectives. Improvement in the definition of objectives and the choice of audit strategies is the principal benefit of this advance fee review.

A second and obvious benefit is the identification of legitimate cost increases which should be discussed with the client in advance. Good client relations depend on advance warning of anticipated costs instead of last minute surprises. Sometimes cost increases can be overcome by arranging for additional client assistance or further internal audit involvement. Alternatively, cost increases can sometimes be combined with expanded collateral services which keep the audit as a whole an economical package of services from the client's point of view.

Review of additional services

A review of all non-attest services to be provided is also an important planning step. The extent to which systems recommendations, particularly computer systems recommendations, should be researched (as opposed to mere identification of control weaknesses and inefficiencies), the extent to which financial and tax planning points should be investigated in detail, and the extent to which insurance coverage, cash management, and inventory policies might be analyzed will vary from client to client. It would be foolish to waste time reviewing computer installation plans when the client has a competent task force doing exactly such a review or to neglect considering such a review when the client has no personnel to perform it. The reviewer should identify the client's needs and wishes and tailor the selection of additional services accordingly. Of course, substantial expenditures of time on non-attest services should not be undertaken without full discussion with and approval by client management in advance.

Additional services to be considered may also include those of personal interest to client management: executive compensation studies, preparation of personal tax returns, personal tax counselling, and estate planning. Such work requires advance planning both with the corporate client and the individual executives concerned to define the specific services desired and to establish a basis of billing for them which is fair to both the company and its management.

15.5 Control of field work by the audit senior

Once the planning is complete, control of the audit passes into the hands of the audit senior. His task is to ensure that work performed on the job meets the standards of his firm and complies with generally accepted auditing standards. The audit senior maintains control over the field work by:

1. ensuring that he is completely familiar with the client's business, employees, systems and operating results,
2. ensuring that all audit assistants have sufficient familiarity with client operations to perform their work effectively,
3. allocating the work to his assistants in a logical manner,
4. interpreting general and detailed planning decisions to his assistants,
5. supervising his assistants' work and answering their questions,
6. using detailed time budgets to monitor daily the progress of the work,
7. performing certain key verification procedures himself where these procedures require senior judgment or where they serve to coordinate the work performed by various assistants,
8. reviewing in detail the verification procedures performed by his assistants and by specialists.

15.5.1 Orientation to the audit environment

To control the field work effectively, the audit senior must first be familiar with the client's business, employees, systems and operating results.[8] This familiarity can be gained through:

a) prior years' experience as audit senior or assistant on the same engagement,
b) participation in planning and review of all planning notes or memoranda,

c) review of the prior year's financial statements and working papers,
d) review of correspondence and permanent files,
e) preliminary highlight reviews:
   • for an interim audit, an updating of a description of the business and organization charts and an overview of systems changes (see 24.4),
   • for a financial statement audit, a preliminary review of operating results (see 31.4).

Audit assistants also require some familiarity with the engagement as a whole. One assistant may encounter evidence pertinent to an audit section handled by another assistant. The significance of such evidence may escape the first assistant if he is not aware of the overall audit approach. Even within his own section, an assistant's work will be less effective if he does not see it within the context of the whole audit. The audit senior can help assistants to develop a broader view by:

• holding a pre-audit conference of the entire audit team and progress meetings during the course of the audit,
• introducing new assistants to client employees with whom they will be dealing and taking them on a tour of the client's premises,
• ensuring that assistants read the description of the business, organization charts and other general notes in the working papers,
• including assistants, where possible, in any meetings which he has with client officials.

15.5.2 Allocation of work to assistants

The allocation of work to assistants by 'the audit senior involves: first, the selection of the assistant responsible for each specific section of the work (designated in this book as the section senior); secondly, the allocation of other assistants to assist the section seniors; and, finally, the interpretation of planning decisions to the section seniors and, where necessary, the development of more detailed programs for them.

The purpose of dividing the audit work into sections is partly for administrative efficiency but, more importantly, to permit intermediate conclusions to be drawn for each logical component of the work. If assistants merely performed lists of detailed procedures and the audit senior evaluated all the results in one step prior to drafting the audit report, there would be too great a danger of key procedures or findings being overlooked. Rather, it is better (a) in the interim audit, to draw together, first, conclusions about control over individual major systems such as sales/receivables/receipts and (b) in the financial statement audit, to draw together, first, conclusions about the presentation of major financial statement figures, such as inventories. Each section senior is usually given the responsibility of performing alone or of performing and supervising the work in his particular section and drawing together the conclusions for that section. The audit senior can subsequently integrate the sectional conclusions to arrive at the overall audit opinion. Such a process facilitates control by introducing specific levels of accountability within the engagement.

Guidelines for work allocation

1. One person should be designated as section senior responsible for the audit of each major accounting system (in the interim audit) and of each major component of the financial statements (in the financial statement audit).
2. The audit senior should normally undertake himself (a) those verification sections which provide or require the best overall picture of the engagement and (b) those sections which provide evidence for or require evidence from a number of different sections (examples are the books of account section in the interim audit and the income section in the financial statement audit).
3. The most difficult sections should generally be assigned to the most competent staff members. However, the audit senior himself should not undertake more sections directly than will allow him time for proper control and supervision of the audit as a whole.
4. Where possible, sections should be assigned to provide the best continuity between the interim audit and the financial statement audit. For example, the section senior for the interim audit of sales/receivables/receipts should normally be assigned as section senior for accounts receivable and should do the work as well on the sales figure.

5. Work in the income section may be divided and delegated to the section seniors working on closely related balance sheet components if the audit senior provides overall co-ordination. For example, the section senior responsible for inventories should normally perform the necessary year-end work on cost of sales and gross profits.
6. Once section seniors have been assigned to all the sections, the remaining time of staff members may be allocated to those sections requiring additional assistants. A staff member may be a section senior for one section and an assistant on several others.
7. While work allocation should be based on achieving the most effective audit, the audit senior should consider as well the development of each staff member. Keeping one individual exclusively on prepaid expenses for dozens of engagements is a disservice to the individual and ultimately to the clients who will not be served by the breadth of experience they should expect.

More detailed guidelines for work allocation may be found in 24.5.1 (for interim audits) and in 31.5.1 (for financial statement audits). After work has been assigned, the audit senior should discuss with each section senior the requirements, peculiarities, and problems of his particular section. This discussion should include a review of the related planning decisions, points from the preliminary highlights review, and suggested time budgets.

15.5.3 Development and use of detailed time budgets

Every audit plan should be accompanied by a detailed time budget whether the plan is a few very general decisions or a comprehensive written audit program. The detailed time plan is normally prepared by the audit senior. It may be prepared in two stages, before the interim audit and before the financial statement audit, or in one stage at the beginning of the year. It may be prepared before the reviewer assesses the reasonableness of the fees, providing input for that assessment, or it may be prepared after such assessment, using the reviewer's overall time estimate as a starting point. Often the detailed time budget will be submitted to the reviewer for approval so that his audit experience and his knowledge of the client can be used in judging whether the proposed plan represents the most efficient allocation of audit effort.

A time budget should not be viewed as a mechanical limit to the number of audit hours to be spent. If a staff assistant has spent the budgeted 20 hours on a particular procedure but the work is still incomplete, obviously he must finish it. But if he anticipates, after the first few hours' work, that he will require a further 50 hours, it may be that he misunderstands the audit procedure or the level of detail desired by the audit senior. Or it may be that new complications have arisen which were not anticipated when the budget was prepared. In either case it is important that anticipated budget overruns be discussed with the audit senior in advance. In this way, time budgets serve (a) to guide audit staff as to the extent of detail expected and to forestall misunderstandings and (b) to identify reasons for legitimate cost increases which should be discussed with the client. While budget overruns are best discussed with the audit senior as soon as they are anticipated, the audit assistant should, at the very least, consult his senior when budgeted hours have been spent and before a large overrun itself has been incurred.

The detailed time budget will be the principal aid to the audit senior in monitoring the overall progress of the audit. Each day the senior should record the time worked by each assistant in the various sections and measure the results against budget. At the conclusion of the audit the time budget and actual results will be employed by the audit senior as an aid to analyze and explain any time excesses or savings.

Ideally, the time budget should distinguish between supervision and verification and within the verification phase it should analyze the time into small enough units to provide assistants with the most useful guidance as to the required extent of the work desired. In the extreme, each specific procedure performed throughout the audit could have a separate time budget. Such an approach may be feasible where detailed written audit programs are used. Normally, however, the amount of detail in the budget should be sufficient if it is analyzed into time units not exceeding 10 or 20 hours. Thus, for a very small audit, there may simply be a budget of 7 hours for the performance of all accounts receivable verification procedures. On the other hand, for a very large audit, a budget figure of 120 hours may be an inadequate guide to the audit assistants performing individual procedures within the accounts receivable section. In that case, further detail such as the following may be useful:

Weakness investigation of credit memo system	15 hours
Trial balance and circularization of November 30th trade accounts	15
Cut-off procedures at November 30th	5
Follow-up of confirmations including second requests	20

Verification of aged trial balance at December 31st	10
December 31st cut-off and roll-forward procedures	15
Verification of allowance for doubtful accounts	15
Freight claims receivable	10
Employee loans receivable	5
Other receivables	10
Total	120 hours

15.5.4 Verification procedures performed by the audit senior

In the audit of smaller clients, the audit senior will of necessity evaluate the more complex systems and perform the year-end substantive verification of the most difficult sections himself. On larger engagements, however, he must reserve sufficient time for supervising assistants, as discussed earlier. On the very largest engagements, supervision and control may consume nearly all the audit senior's time. Nevertheless, there are certain key verification procedures which the audit senior should usually undertake and which usually will contribute to his control of the field work as a whole:

1. The highlights review of the business and systems including preparation or updating of a description of the business at the beginning of the interim audit.
2. The review and evaluation of controls in the books of account and general section of the interim audit (because information from all other major systems leads ultimately to the books of account and because controls in this area will influence the evaluation of other major systems).
3. The review and scrutiny of the more significant reports and records throughout the audit.
4. The assessment of the competence and objectivity of internal auditors (because reliance may be placed on their work at many different points throughout the audit).
5. A preliminary review of operating results and financial position at the beginning of the financial statement audit.
6. The review of minutes of shareholders, directors, and the audit committee (because decisions made by these bodies may influence many parts of the audit).
7. The updating of information in the permanent file.

431

8. The preparation of a cut-off summary (because most cut-off procedures span two different verification sections of the financial statement audit file, often being verified by different audit assistants).
9. The preparation or updating of a summary of client accounting policies (because it requires input from various different audit sections).
10. The drafting of the client letter of representations (from individual points drafted by section seniors).

15.5.5 Review of assistants' work

When assistants are employed, review of their work by the audit senior is important to ensure an appropriate level of quality, compliance with generally accepted auditing standards, proper communication of information from particular sections to other members of the audit team, the integration of conclusions from different sections of the working paper files, and an adequate groundwork for higher level reviews. These reasons are the same as those for the higher level reviews themselves and are discussed in Chapter 16. The steps in the audit senior's review, while more detailed, parallel those described for the first level of reviewer in 16.5.

Timing of review

The timing of the audit senior's review will vary with the circumstances of the individual engagements, the degree of staff continuity, the level of staff training and competence, and the nature of problems encountered during the audit. On repeat engagements where there is extensive preplanning and there are trained assistants familiar with the client, most of the audit senior's review will be concentrated towards the end of the interim audit and financial statement audit field work. With untrained assistants, on the other hand, supervision must be close and the audit senior may well decide to review particular sections at two or three stages during the work. In many interim audits it may be useful for the audit senior to review the evaluation of internal control and the design of further compliance and substantive procedures before those latter procedures are performed. In any case, intervention by the audit senior will usually be called for when important verification problems are brought to his attention by the assistant or when audit time in a particular section appears likely to exceed budget.

The audit senior's review procedures are described in more detail in 30.1 (for interim audits) and in 44.1 (for financial statement audits).

15.6 Reference material

CICA Audit Technique Study, *Materiality in Auditing* (1965).
CICA Exposure Draft of Proposed Auditing Recommendations, *Internal Control* (1976), portions related to planning (the reader should refer to any subsequent issue of Recommendations on this subject).

AICPA Statement on Auditing Standards No. 1, Section 310, Adequacy of Planning and the Timing of Field Work.
AICPA Statement on Auditing Standards No. 4, *Quality Control Considerations for a Firm of Independent Auditors*.

15.7 Questions and problems

Review and discussion

1. What are the seven stages in the audit process?
2. List and briefly describe the elements of engagement management.
3. Outline briefly the responsibilities of the four functional levels of the audit team.
4. What qualifications should an audit senior possess?
5. Maintaining good client relations is an important aspect of the audit function. Which levels of the audit team are responsible for this aspect, and how is it achieved?
6. What are the objectives of audit planning?
7. What factors have contributed to higher audit costs for many clients in the last few years?
8. A complaint of some audit clients is that there is no continuity of audit staff on their engagement from year to year. What can be the causes of this situation? Is it a major problem? If you were an audit partner confronted with this complaint, what would be your reply?
9. What are the advantages and disadvantages of:
   a) a detailed written audit program,
   b) an abbreviated written program,
   c) the use of pre-printed check lists,
   d) no written audit program?

10. Identify the critical decisions which must be made during the planning process of an ongoing audit engagement.
11. Discuss the importance of the materiality planning decision.
12. To what extent should all audit clients be subject to the same materiality guidelines?
13. Indicate the advantages and disadvantages of discussing the materiality limit with a client.
14. Discuss the factors to be considered in establishing the materiality limit for any particular audit engagement.
15. Overall audit assurance with respect to a given item on the financial statements consists of three sources of assurance available to the auditor. Identify these sources and describe the various factors the auditor should consider in measuring the degree of assurance from each source.
16. On an initial engagement, which planning decisions must await the completion of the interim audit?
17. What factors affect the reliance that the external auditor can place on an internal audit department?
18. Identify the major constraints on overall timing of an audit engagement.
19. What factors should an investor auditor consider in deciding the degree of reliance to be placed on other auditors?
20. What purpose does a time budget and fee forecast by the various components of an audit engagement serve?
21. How does an audit senior control the field work?
22. What is the purpose of detailed time budgets?

Problems

1. Ed Green, a new audit assistant at Traher & Co., Chartered Accountants, has been given his first assignment at Big Time Inc. Green has been assigned to review and evaluate the payroll system during the interim audit.

   What should Green do to prepare himself for this assignment? Why?
2. M. Hartman, CA, is the audit senior on Davidson Manufacturing Inc. She has participated on this engagement for several years. This year, she has three assistants, all of whom are unfamiliar with the client. Accordingly she delegates the various sections of the audit to the assistants and assigns herself to be responsible for the largest and most difficult section – inventory. Comment.
3. The year-end audit of Oneida Manufacturing starts today. It is your first financial statement audit since you joined Hark & Co., Chartered

Accountants, three months ago. You have attended Hark's Interim Audit I seminar and worked on a few analytical audits. You did not work on the interim audit of Oneida.

Yesterday the manager called you and told you the following about the job:

a) The company   – Oneida Manufacturing
b) The address and how to get there.
c) The business   – manufactures gadgets
d) The size   – one of the largest client's on the audit staff
e) The staff   – senior staff accountant – Jim
                       – staff accountant +two years experience – George
                       – staff accountant – You
f) The time   – you will be there about three weeks
g) Responsibilities   – pack a bag and meet Jim there tomorrow

You arrive at 8:55 and ask the receptionist where the auditors are or will be. While she is phoning around to find out where you should go, George arrives and takes control, by leading you to the accounting department. He is able to secure an empty desk to use until Jim arrives. He tells you to "look busy" and then goes from desk to desk meeting old acquaintances. As he passes, you ask about Jim and he says not to worry since Jim never gets in until about 9:30 but he works late.

At 9:30 Jim passes with "Good Morning" and goes to the comptroller's office. He returns later and tells you to pack up and move to the board room down the hall where he will join you shortly.

About 10:00 Jim and George join you, and Jim starts "finding something for you to do". In the meantime you can get coffee.

You return at 10:30 with coffee, after getting lost in the plant trying to find the machine. George comments,"Why didn't you use the staff cafeteria down the hall?"

Jim and George finish their initial planning about the same time you finish reading the sports section of the newspaper. Jim outlines your responsibilities. You will do cash, accounts receivable, the time summary and the statistical analysis of the plant payroll.

The first section you tackle is cash. Never having completed a cash section before, you look to Jim for guidance. He says that there is nothing to it, if you follow the questionnaire and last year's file, which he hands to you together with cash count sheets for this year. He then takes off to complete another job but will be back in two or three days. In the meantime George will answer any questions.

Having successfully completed the cash section you now tackle the accounts receivable. Jim said you could do the whole section except for the bad debt allowance which he will do. A review of last year's file leads you to believe there may be an efficiency or two that you can implement, which you mention to Jim. He agrees that your suggestions might work but he does not have time now to go into it, and suggests you just follow last year's file and be on the safe side. A day or two later he comes and gets the ageing analysis, reviews it quickly and off he goes to the comptroller's office. He returns and gives you a figure for the bad debt allowance, and says he will prepare a working paper to support it.

The accounts receivable section is filed in the binder and you spend a few days vouching specific profit and loss accounts before returning to the office for a few days.

While you are sitting in the bullpen preparing lead sheets for your next job, Jim walks by and you ask him how Oneida went. He becomes visibly agitated and lets you have it. "Why didn't you reconcile the payroll account or do a transfer schedule....and it took me hours to clear the manager's notes on accounts receivable. It looks like I can't trust you to do anything right." So with all the eyes in the bullpen on you, you quietly finish the sheet you are working on and disappear for a while, to think about what went wrong.

Using this case as a starting point prepare a list of 9-12 practice points that can be followed which will help promote good on-the-job training and management. Illustrate each point with one of the deficiencies indicated in the information above.

4. You have been assigned as the audit senior of a medium-sized engagement involving the audit of an affiliated group of companies. While the engagement is free of complications as far as accounting and reporting problems are concerned, there has been a fee problem for a number of years. Every effort is made by you and the audit manager to reduce the amount of time required; you make numerous revisions to the audit approach in several areas of the audit. After the revisions have been made and reflected in the budget, both you and the audit manager are convinced that at least part of the fee problem can be cured.

One of the assistants assigned to work with you on this engagement has had approximately two years of experience and has, at one time or another during his career, worked in every area of an audit. At first you assign him, under your close supervision, to various phases of the audit of one of the companies; his performance is satisfactory. Your evaluation of him at this point is that he is probably capable of taking on more responsibility and should be encouraged to do so. Therefore, in the interest of helping him develop more fully, you assign him the entire examination of one of the companies in the group. You review the audit program with him, give him all the information that you have relative to the company and explain your reasons for letting him perform the audit on his own. The pressure of your own work does not permit you to review his work as it progresses; however, you talk with him briefly during the lunch hour each day and, from your conversations with him, you have no reason to believe that the work is not progressing satisfactorily.

He completes his assignment within the alloted time budget and asks that you review his work as soon as possible, so that he will know how well he did with his first in-charge assignment. On review, you find that he has done well in a few areas, but has failed in others. The fact that, for the most part, his working papers are virtually copies of the prior year's papers causes you considerable concern. After your review, you find that better than fifty per cent of his work will have to be redone. Your appraisal of the situation at this point is that, in order to recoup as much of the lost time and salvage as much of the work as is possible, you should do the clean-up and additional work yourself and put your assistant on work that you know him to be capable of performing. Upon completion of the assignment, you find that your time overage is just about equal to the time required in cleaning up and completing your assistant's work.

What improvements could have been made in the supervision of this engagement? (Consider both client and staff needs.)

5. Bill Jackson is thirty years old. When he was twenty-three he received his Bachelor's degree in Accounting. Upon graduation he was employed by P & P, a large national firm of chartered accountants. He remained with the firm for two years during which he received his CA. He then resigned and joined X Manufacturing Company as assistant controller.

His progress was rapid and he became controller at age twenty-seven; however, his real desire was to practise public accounting. At twenty-eight he resigned to open his own office. He obtained many bookkeeping clients and one audit client. At first, he performed all professional work himself with his wife helping him as a typist. As his practice grew, he hired a female bookkeeper named Joy Dixon. Joy is a graduate of a local business school and has ten years of bookkeeping experience.

Two years after he left X Manufacturing Company, the company became dissatisfied with the services of P & P and in October 1975 the company engaged Bill Jackson to perform the 1975 audit. Since Bill left, the company hired a new controller and an assistant controller both of whom are unknown to Bill. It was the President who remembered Bill and gave him the job. From his prior experience at X, Bill knew that the audit would require approximately 1 200 man hours. He, therefore, hired an assistant named Joe Smith. Joe is a university student in accounting, presently in his senior year, but is willing to take a semester off to get some practical experience. Joe agreed to start working for Bill on January 28, 1976 at $700 a month plus overtime. By that time he will have completed all of the accounting part of his studies, and a course in auditing. Bill also hired a new bookkeeper to assist Joy. In October, Bill gave Joy a copy of an auditing text and told her to read it before the end of January.

Bill and Joy observed physical inventories at X on December 31, 1975, and on January 8, 1976, Bill mailed all accounts receivable confirmations himself. The company has approximately 3 000 accounts receivable totalling $2 000 000. Bill mailed confirmations to all accounts having balances in excess of $1 000 and applied statistical sampling techniques to the smaller accounts. For the latter procedure Bill obtained a sampling formula from a recent textbook he read.

On the morning of January 28, 1976, Bill, Joe and Joy started the audit. Bill explained to his assistants the business of X Company in detail. He spent about four hours going over the prior year's report with them, after which he prepared an audit program as follows:

Operation	Work to be performed by
Cash counts and reconciliations	Joy
Receivables:	
• Confirmation procedures	Joy
• All other procedures	Bill
Inventories:	
• Checking in physical test counts (70% observation)	Joy
• Test check 60% of pricing	Joe
• All other procedures	Bill
Prepaid expenses (calculating ending balances and tie in to expense)	Joy

Operation	Work to be performed by
Property, plant and equipment (vouching current year additions, calculating depreciation and testing gains and losses)	Joy
Liabilities (test for unrecorded and proving balances on the books)	Joe
Capital stock and surplus (reviewing all transactions since inception)	Bill
Income and expense accounts (vouching 80% of current year expenses, testing cut-off)	Joe
Preparation of trial balance and financial statements	Bill
Examination of minutes and all important documents since inception	Bill

During the audit Bill reviewed all of Joe's work and Joe reviewed all of Joy's work. Joy performed all work involving calculations which included footing all items 100%. Joe proves to be very helpful to Bill as his workpapers are very neat and contain all the information Bill wants. He is also very good at public relations because, although originally unknown to both Bill and Joe, Joe finds that his cousin is the Production Manager of X.

To complete the job everybody works 60 hours a week. Five adjustments (which Joy posts to the books) are found, resulting in a 6% decrease in reported income. Upon completion Bill agrees all of the working papers to the trial balance, drafts the financial statements and reviews them with the controller. He prepares and issues an unqualified opinion. Upon completion of the tax returns he bills the company for a fee of $21 000 which compares favourably with P & P's 1974 bill of $30 000.

Comment on Bill's compliance with auditing standards and professional ethics.

6. Trant & Co., Chartered Accountants, were engaged to examine the financial statements of the Salem Equipment Manufacturing Company for the six months ended June 30, 1976. The company manufactures pumps and certain other types of farm machinery related to the sugar beet industry. Annual sales average $5 000 000 and are made principally to dealers throughout the country with some local retail sales. The company, in need of working capital, had obtained a loan from a small business investment company. The terms of the loan required audited financial statements at June 30, 1976.

The company's financial statements had never been audited in the past, but the books were "reviewed" each year by a local CA and unaudited financial statements were prepared. This CA's working papers were made available to Trant & Co.

They made a preliminary review of the books, prepared a time budget and quoted a tentative fee. The accountants assigned to the engagement included a senior and a staff assistant, with first-year personnel available as required. The senior was in the process of completing another job.

The audit program included, among other procedures, observation of the physical inventory on June 30, 1976 and a review of internal control and tests of transactions for the audit period immediately thereafter.

During the inventory observation, two of the warehouse personnel indicated to one of the first-year auditors that the inventory was far more accurate than any of the previous ones and that they were ordered on previous occasions to omit from the count certain of the items that were being counted in this inventory. The first-year auditor properly noted this information in the file and advised the senior.

The review of internal control disclosed that the purchasing and accounts payable function was loosely handled (purchase requisitions were not always approved, receiving reports were not prenumbered or always used, invoices were not always extended and footed, etc.). The audit program was properly expanded by the staff assistant.

During the course of this work, the senior was not able to be present on the job, but he did inquire periodically by telephone as to the problems and progress. Each time he was given the answer that all was going well. This information was passed along to the manager and the partner in charge. On one occasion, the partner was asked by the President, and principal stockholder of the company, how the work was progressing and he informed him that all was going well.

The senior completed his other assignment and then appeared on the job at the time the work was in its final stages. He was surprised to find that the time expended on the internal control work was 25% over budgeted. He was further surprised to read the comments contained in the physical inventory observation working papers and that the accounts payable work had been expanded. When the staff assistant was asked why he did not advise the senior of these matters, the assistant indicated that he realized he was over the time budget, but that the overage was not significant since he had performed only such procedures as would normally be required. He did not have the time to investigate the comment made by the warehousemen regarding the previous inventory pro-

cedures and did not realize what additional work might be entailed. He felt that he had properly extended the accounts payable work.

The senior outlined a program to review in more detail the beginning inventory. This took some additional time, but the results were satisfactory (as sometimes happens, the warehouse employees were merely disgruntled about having an audit and therefore made the comment about omitting certain items from the inventory to see how much trouble it would cause the auditors). As a result of all these happenings, Trant & Co. were able to realize only 70% of their standard rates. The audit manager and partner were outraged.

What was wrong with the communications on this engagement?

7. (CICA adapted) You have been asked to address a group of students on the use of an audit program. Outline the points which you would develop in your discussion under the following headings:

a) What is an audit program and what are its purposes?

b) What considerations should be taken into account in developing an audit program for a new client?

c) The advantages and disadvantages of using a standard audit program for all clients.

8. You are assigned to the audit of Acme Manufacturing Company for the year ended December 31, 1976. The company has been Neil & Associate's client for several years, but this is your first time on the engagement. In reviewing last year's papers and discussing the job with the manager, you find that Acme produces a line of electronic instruments for shelf stock which are sold in a diversified market on the basis of standard price lists. The company also performs work on various Canadian Government contracts, usually for specially designed systems, which utilize few, if any, of the company's stock items. Sales for the last several years have been fairly evenly divided between the two categories.

Actual audit time for last year amounted to 512 hours.

The manager gives you last year's management letter, and you take it with you on your first visit to the client's offices, which takes place on December 17. You were not able to make your visit earlier because the Department of National Revenue had been conducting a field audit of the company's tax returns until the first of December and the company's comptroller needed the remaining time to get caught up on his work, with which he is not too familiar since he has only been with Acme since May.

When you arrive at Acme's Toronto plant and headquarters, you are ushered into the office of the comptroller, Mr. Link. He makes it plain that he has little use for auditors and considers their presence a reflection on his ability. During the course of this interview you are told that Acme has two sales branches, located in Edmonton, Alberta, and Montreal, Quebec, each with a moderate inventory, and a second manufacturing and sales plant in London, Ontario. All accounting for these branches and the plant is centralized in the home office. You recall references to the foregoing in last year's working papers.

Link takes up the better part of an hour blaming the sales department for the drop in sales from last year, and complaining about the engineers spending months of work on a couple of new products they are trying to develop. There also has been a substantial turnover of production personnel, particularly warehousemen and production supervisors.

You ask for interim financial statements and are provided with the attached comparative balance sheet, income statement and schedule of manufacturing expenses. (Others omitted for case study purposes.) When you ask about Electronic Products Inc., Link tells you of an exchange of stock early in the year. He states that Electronic is now a wholly-owned subsidiary located in a relatively new plant in Saskatoon. He gives you a copy of Electronic's annual report for last year, which includes an unqualified opinion by another national firm of CA's. (Report not included in this problem.) Electronic has its own accounting staff and Link merely includes its monthly statements with those of Acme without consolidating them. Neil & Associates are to audit Electronic for the current year.

From other schedules provided you by Link, you note the following at November 30 of this year.

Accounts receivable:	Trade	Canadian Government
Current	$ 89 751	$ 43 692
30 days	75 356	48 666
60 days	58 224	1 825
90 days	21 918	31 718
Total	$245 249	$125 901

Order backlog:

Trade	$1 431 752	
Canadian Government	310 861	
Total	$1 742 613	

You discuss last year's management letter with Link and are able to ascertain that, mainly due to his efforts, accounts receivable and credit memos are now being handled satisfactorily. The accounting department now handles all matching

and approving of vendors' invoices. When questioned about the inventories, Link says that he has not had the time to make improvements in this area because he has spent a lot of time installing the company's new computerized accounting system. He says that he is designing a computerized standard cost system utilizing "direct costing" techniques, and that this should be installed by next March. Inventories for the year-end will be observed at all locations on December 28 and 29.

In response to your question, Link says that Acme requires a consolidated comparative statement and short-form report and an unconsolidated statement with report for filing with. Neil & Associates have not prepared the company's tax returns in prior years. Just as you are leaving, Link mentions that the report will be needed by February 2 instead of March 31 as in prior years.

On your return to the office you verify that the comparative figures included in the client's interim statements agree with the working papers for last year. From last year's work papers you note the following:

Accounts receivable:	Trade	Canadian Government
Current	$ 88 691	$ 63 288
30 days	55 758	34 259
60 days	44 395	1 127
90 days	12 571	–
Total	$201 415	$ 98 674

Backlog:

Trade	$ 718 512	
Canadian Government	609 472	
Total	$1 327 984	

In checking with the manager and tax specialist, you determine that Neil & Associates had never been consulted or notified concerning the acquisition of Electronic Products, Inc.

Assess, in detail, the impact on the audit of the information given, including the balance sheets, statements of income and manufacturing expenses and the prior year's management letter which follow. Your answer should identify the problems and give your suggestion on how to solve them.

Management Letter

Mr. George Smith, President
Acme Manufacturing Company,

Dear Mr. Smith:
Our examination of the financial statements of the Acme Manufacturing Company for the year ended December 31, 1975 disclosed certain weaknesses in internal accounting controls and enabled us to identify other matters which may be of concern to you.

Items which we believe should be brought to your attention are set forth below.

General

Many of the replies received in response to our request for confirmation of accounts receivable balances expressed dissatisfaction with the manner in which the accounts are handled. The problem appears to arise primarily from the company's failure to process credit memos and to communicate effectively with the customer about credits and other account differences. Several customers indicated that repeated inquiries regarding their accounts had not been acknowledged. We found, upon referring to correspondence files, that these complaints had considerable merit. It also appears that much could be done to improve the correspondence that does go out, in terms of expressing more clearly the nature of the differences being described to the customer and the company's position regarding them.

In addition to the unsatisfactory customer relations being generated by these conditions, we believe they are contributing to the slowness of collecting receivables.

Inventories

Inventory controls have not kept pace with the company's expansion. The perpetual inventory records were found to be materially inaccurate. The variations in gross profit between locations and the company's inability to explain them indicated a lack of control over inventory. As a result, it is difficult to determine the causes of inventory losses or the branch at which they occurred. We also believe this lack of accurate information is in part responsible for the excessive and unbalanced inventory stocks now on hand, as those charged with the purchasing responsibility are unaware of exact stock positions by locations.

With approximately 50% of the inventories being stored in branches, we consider it imperative that the company establish and maintain accurate perpetual inventory records, integrated with control accounts in the general records, that will permit efficient buying and fix responsibility for physical custody.

Heretofore, the company has costed out sales on a gross profit basis for purposes of interim statements. We suggest that the monthly inventory relief be summarized by item and costed out at actual to generate accurate cost data.

Credit Memos

Inventory items being returned by customers for credit are being set aside to await processing without written verification of receipt. As a result, the customer service department controls verification of receipt, inspection of equipment for defects, prepara-

tion of the credit memo and, within certain limits, the granting of the credit. Several incidents of customer claims for returns, where the company had no record, were noted. In one case the customer was able to provide proof of receipt through the trucking company. In order to establish effective controls over receipts we suggest:

1. A special receiver be prepared in duplicate in the receiving department for all customers' returns.
2. One copy of the receiver should be filed numerically in the receiving department and the other sent to the customer service department with the returned merchandise.
3. The credit memo and the receiver should be routed through the sales department for written approval before recording.

*Purchasing Department Participation
in Purchasing Procedure*

In addition to arranging for the purchase of goods, the Purchasing Department approves vendors' invoices as to agreement with purchase order terms and matches invoices with receiving reports. This procedure both weakens internal controls and delays the flow of paper work. The company has on occasion lost discounts, and month-end accounts payable balances are often materially understated because of this delay.

We suggest:

1. The responsibility for approving invoices and for matching invoices with receiving reports should be transferred to the Accounting Department.
2. Receiving reports should be sent directly to the Accounting Department by the Receiving Department.

Etcetera

Balance Sheets

Assets	Acme Manufacturing Company		Electronic Products, Inc.
	December 31, 1975	November 30, 1976	November 30, 1976
Current assets:			
Cash in bank and on hand	$ 184 066	$ 53 371	$ 195 276
Accounts receivable:			
Canadian Government	98 674	125 901	165 337
Trade	201 415	245 249	191 756
	300 089	371 150	357 093
Less reserve for doubtful accounts	(30 000)	(14 338)	(44 671)
	270 089	356 812	312 422
Deposits	17 003	22 220	15 991
Inventories:			
Finished goods	24 940	51 751	56 645
Work in process — Canadian Government contracts	138 082	218 347	95 154
Work in process — stock items	72 107	185 819	76 735
Raw materials and purchased parts	177 617	103 088	153 716
	412 746	559 005	382 250
Prepaid expenses and deferred charges	27 353	14 086	35 201
Total current assets	911 257	1 005 494	941 140
Investment in subsidiary	–	80 000	–
Net fixed assets	754 139	831 732	754 191
	$1 665 396	$1 917 226	$1 695 331

Liabilities

Liabilities	Acme Manufacturing Company		Electronic Products, Inc.
Current liabilities:			
Trade accounts payable	$ 99 939	$ 197 949	$ 475 331
Accrued payroll and deductions	22 322	20 607	29 967
Income taxes	43 004	2 743	50 504
Accrued liabilities	26 615	20 855	39 467
Notes payable due within one year	–	60 000	–
Current portion—real estate obligation	41 452	41 452	43 000
Total current liabilities	233 332	343 606	638 269
Long-term debt:			
Series "A" debentures	100 000	–	–
Series "B" convertible debentures	–	250 000	–
Notes payable	250 000	190 000	–
Real estate obligations	483 168	469 810	846 223
Total long-term debt	833 168	909 810	846 223
Total liabilities	1 066 500	1 253 416	1 484 492
Shareholders' equity:			
Convertible preferred stock, $10 par value	133 300	–	–
Common stock, $1 par value	101 308	314 608	100 000
Retained earnings	364 288	349 202	110 839
	$1 665 396	$1 917 226	$1 695 331

Statements of Income

	Acme Manufacturing Company		Electronic Products, Inc.
	Year ended December 30, 1975	11 months ended November 30, 1976	11 months ended November 30, 1976
Net Sales	$2 504 183	$1 736 520	$1 982 566
Cost of sales	1 759 295	1 227 301	1 360 967
Gross profit on sales	744 888	509 219	621 599
Operating expenses:			
Selling and shipping	413 266	331 287	329 746
Administrative	191 231	145 766	147 805
	604 497	477 053	477 551
Operating profit	140 391	32 166	144 048
Other income	6 378	3 489	3 978
Other expense	(60 792)	(46 742)	(44 083)
Income (loss) before taxes	85 977	(11 087)	103 943
Provision for income taxes	41 000	–	48 500
Net income (loss)	$ 44 977	$(11 087)	$ 55 443

Manufacturing Expenses

	Year ended December 30, 1975	11 months ended November 30, 1976
Salaries and wages:		
Executive	$ 17 435	$ 12 855
Supervision	65 011	44 161
Indirect labor	31 590	20 925
Clerical	36 685	30 134
Overtime premium	15 323	31 268
Sick leave, vacation and holiday pay	21 744	7 356
	167 788	146 699
Depreciation	65 523	60 823
Supplies	43 501	51 309
Taxes	34 924	11 434
Equipment rentals	36 539	20 190
Repairs and maintenance	24 805	31 810
Insurance	16 272	26 998
Heat, light, water and power	13 125	12 219
Test, development and research	3 388	7 911
Professional and outside services	3 666	3 325
Telephone and telegraph	3 270	2 798
Employee welfare	2 640	1 057
Travel	1 165	257
Plant rearrangement	1 865	—
Miscellaneous	935	172
	$439 406	$377 002

Working Papers, Error Evaluation and Review

This chapter covers the purpose, nature, preparation, organization, and review of audit working papers, including the documentation and review of error evaluation for the audit as a whole. The subject of working papers and review completes the discussion of engagement management which was introduced

in Chapter 15. The discussion in the present chapter is directed primarily to general principles – although a few examples of working papers are presented. A more detailed description of specific working papers and specific review procedures is contained in Chapters 24 to 44.

16.1 Working paper and general files

The files which an external auditor maintains with respect to each audit client may be classified into two main groups: working paper files and general files. *Working paper files,* the main subject of this chapter, contain the auditor's record of the plans he made, the procedures he performed, the audit evidence he obtained, and the conclusions he drew in arriving at his final report. There are normally two types of working paper file maintained for each client – a *permanent* file used over many years (see 16.2) and *current* working paper files prepared for each annual audit or other specific engagement (see 16.3). *General files,* for purposes of this chapter, include files either related to non-attest services (for example, tax files) or of an administrative nature (for example, correspondence files, fee files, report files). General files are discussed briefly in 16.1.4.

16.1.1 Purposes of working papers

The two most important purposes of audit working papers are:

- to facilitate effective engagement management,
- to provide an important support for the auditor's report.

  Three collateral purposes are:

- to provide a source of information for non-audit purposes,
- to facilitate third party review,
- to aid professional development.

Facilitating effective engagement management

The first field work standard calls for the work to be adequately planned, properly executed, and properly supervised. Good working papers are an essential component in the engagement management procedures designed to meet that standard.

The style and extent of documentation will vary from practitioner to practitioner. One practitioner may use a specific checklist to control and review certain aspects of the field work. Another may accomplish the same objective through closer personal supervision. Provided he achieves the same ultimate objective, the latter practitioner's work is not inferior

merely because he chooses not to use the checklist employed by the former. The style and extent of documentation may also vary from engagement to engagement. A large complex audit may justify the use of certain comprehensive pre-printed forms which, for a small audit, might be cumbersome and costly in relation to their value. For these reasons, no specific working paper form can be prescribed as universally appropriate. Nonetheless, in any given engagement, working papers of some sort are, in the writer's view, essential in order to comply with the first field work standard.[1] Such compliance, therefore, is the most important purpose of audit working papers – more important than the second, more widely recognized purpose of providing a defence against future questioning of the auditor's work.

In 15.1 the six basic elements in effective engagement management were identified as:

1. the assignment of competent personnel,
2. an organized approach,
3. adequate planning,
4. adequate control of field work,
5. effective reporting to reviewers,
6. adequate review.

Good working papers can contribute to each of these six elements. To what extent any specific working paper is essential to satisfy a given element of engagement management, must, however, be decided by the practitioner or firm in the context of the particular engagement.

1. Facilitating the assignment of competent personnel.

Effective assignment policies include the early identification of staff levels required and the use of time budgets to identify the hours required at each level. Identification of required staff levels is facilitated by prior years' working papers which indicate the magnitude, degree of complexity, unusual difficulties and specialist knowledge involved in each section of the audit. Time budgets are facilitated by accurate time summaries and meaningful analyses of audit performance in prior years' files.

2. Facilitating an organized approach.

A standardized structure for the current working paper files helps to provide an organized framework for the audit work. While structures will vary from firm to firm, it is desirable that within one firm a uniform structure be used. Reasonable uniformity permits several staff members or several offices to work on different sections of a single engagement in a coordinated manner. An organized file structure ensures that major areas are not overlooked. The particular structure adopted will influence the way in which individual verification procedures are grouped together and the way in which such groups are allocated to various audit assistants. Possible structures are illustrated in 16.3.2 and 16.3.3.

An organized approach is easier if a standard method of preparing individual working papers is adopted. For example, in the interim audit, many accounting systems and controls are so complex that the external auditor cannot adequately evaluate them unless they are first documented in some organized fashion. The various means – questionnaires, narrative notes, and flow charts – were discussed in Chapter 9. In the financial statement audit, an organized approach can also be facilitated by the judicious use of pre-printed working paper forms (checklists, questionnaires, verification outlines) and the use, wherever possible, of carry-forward schedules.

3. Facilitating adequate planning.

The working papers of one year provide input for the general planning decisions and detailed program planning of the next. As a means of communicating information to the next year's audit team, good working papers compensate for the inevitable limitations in staff continuity.

> Since there will not necessarily be staff continuity on a particular audit engagement from year to year, the working papers provide an important means whereby new staff on an engagement can gain an overall understanding of the client's particular organization and operations and anticipate problems which have been encountered in previous years.[2]

Documentation of the planning decisions themselves helps to ensure that (a) the planning is completed in an organized manner, (b) the planning decisions are followed during the conduct of the field work, and (c) an appropriate benchmark is available to facilitate the review.

4. Facilitating adequate control of field work.

A standardized file structure and a standard method of preparing working papers provide guidance to audit staff on the job, reduce the chance of omissions or of incorrect procedures being applied, and so contribute to the control of the field work. In addition, the current preparation of working papers by assistants during the course of the audit facilitates supervision by helping the audit senior to spot areas where assistants may be going astray.

Most importantly, working paper files provide *coherence* to the hundreds of different individual procedures comprising any given audit. They provide the linkage among the procedures performed by different levels of staff (assistants, seniors, specialists, reviewers) and performed in different but related sections of the audit. Without this coherence, adequate control of the field work would often be impossible.

5. Facilitating effective reporting to reviewers.

Standard working paper formats provide an efficient means for the audit team to communicate the results of their work to reviewers. Good working papers do not consist solely of individual details. For meaningful communication, some summarization of key results, conclusions and controls is essential.

6. Facilitating adequate review.

Well organized working papers facilitate adequate review by helping the reviewer to spot omissions, deviations which were required from normal procedures, unusual problems which were encountered, etc. One or two neglected procedures or one or two faulty conclusions can be readily identified by an experienced reviewer given well organized working papers. With poorly organized papers, however, the same problems might escape even the most careful review. Thus, good working papers almost always improve the final quality of the audit examination.

Providing an important support for the auditor's report

Working papers provide an important support for the auditor's report – both as to (a) the assertion in the scope paragraph that the examination was made in accordance with generally accepted auditing standards and included such tests and other procedures as the auditor considered necessary and as to (b) his opinion that the statements are or are not presented fairly in accordance with generally accepted accounting principles consistently applied. But working papers do not necessarily provide the *only* support.

> ... nor is there any intention to imply that the auditor would be precluded from supporting his opinion and his representation as to compliance with the auditing standards by other means in addition to working papers.[3]

Thus, hypothetically, if an auditor conducted a proper study of control and obtained sufficient appropriate audit evidence to justify the opinion expressed in his report, he would have complied fully with the second and third field work standards, even if the work itself were not fully documented. If he could demonstrate by other means that all essential audit procedures had in fact been performed, the omission of certain of those procedures from his working papers would not in itself represent a failure to comply with generally accepted auditing standards – unless the omission affected the adequacy of planning and supervision and so compliance with the first field work standard.

However, while documentation is not required by the second and third field work standards themselves, it is obviously *prudent* for the auditor to document his compliance with those standards in order to provide a store of evidence for his defence should his work ever be questioned. With the increased litigation of recent years, adequate documentation is particularly desirable. Important procedures undocumented, important points discussed orally with the client but unrecorded, or important evaluation decisions not explained, may expose the auditor to serious risk in the future. If procedures are documented, a plaintiff alleging that they were not performed might have the burden of proof of that allegation. On the other hand, if procedures are undocumented, the burden of proof that they were in fact performed may fall to the auditor.

Usually, the two primary purposes of working papers are mutually reinforcing. Thus, any working paper which prudence dictates should be prepared to support the auditor's report is usually even more valuable for the purpose of planning, controlling and reviewing the field work. Indeed, sometimes the latter purpose could be said to call for more detailed working papers than a consideration solely of a possible legal defence would have suggested. In such cases, the requirements of effective engagement management should govern.

For example, it could be argued that detailed checklists could provide plaintiff lawyers with ammunition if they can find omissions, inconsistencies, or ambiguities in the answers given. But if the auditor believes that the checklist will lead to a higher quality examination it would seem unethical to forego this benefit in order to preclude attack on matters of detail. It is better to prepare all the working papers required to achieve a high quality examination, thereby reducing the chance of lawsuits in the first place, than to constrain documentation with a nervous eye on some future courtroom.

Providing a source of information for non-audit purposes

Working paper files can be a source of information for use in providing ancillary services such as preparation of the annual income tax returns and the annual internal control/management letter. In addition, from time to time an auditor may be asked by his client for information documented in past years' working paper files. An example would be information required to answer questions raised by income

tax authorities. In preparing his working papers, the auditor can often anticipate such needs. The information of the auditor's files may sometimes provide a convenient summarization or classification of client data. The auditor should, on the one hand, avoid unnecessary duplication of the client's records and, on the other, ensure that the client's records are not in fact deficient.[4]

Facilitating third party review

Occasionally, an auditor is requested by his client to permit his work to be reviewed by a third party, such as the auditor of a parent or investor company, the auditor of a prospective purchaser, or a successor auditor of the same client. Professional ethics call for the auditor to accede to reasonable requests of this nature. In such cases, the working papers provide useful information to the third parties and permit them to satisfy themselves that a proper audit was carried out. Of course, any working paper useful for such a third party review will have been even more useful for the auditor's own engagement management.

Aiding professional development

The discipline provided by working papers helps an audit assistant to learn procedures which are new to him. The need to record conclusions encourages him to think about the purpose of the procedures performed. At the same time, the working papers he prepares help the reviewer to assess his development, point out areas in which he requires improvement, and determine when he is ready for greater responsibilities.

16.1.2 Characteristics of good working papers

The characteristics of good working papers are organization, completeness, clarity and conciseness, ease of preparation, ease of review, and integration.

Organization

Reference has already been made to the need for an organized and consistent structure. Standard methods of filing, indexing, and cross-referencing should be established. Use of a standard index helps to ensure that the working paper files are complete. One method of indexing is illustrated in the suggested structure for a financial statement audit file in 16.3.3. Thus, if the accounts receivable section were assigned the letter C, the lead sheet could be indexed as C with supporting schedules indexed as C1, C2, C3, etc. When a figure on supporting schedule C10 is entered on Schedule C, the two schedules can be cross-referenced by entering "C" after that figure on schedule C10 and entering "C10" before the same figure on schedule C. (See Figures 16.e and 16.f.) Such a system of referencing helps readers of the file to locate related information quickly.

Loose-leaf binders may be used efficiently to accumulate the working papers for the many different audit sections during the course of the field work. Standard formats for preparing common types of working paper should be established. Pre-printed forms can facilitate organization in many cases. But audit staff should be encouraged to modify standard formats when the special circumstances of an individual engagement so require.

Working paper structures and formats should be coordinated with the procedure manuals, training programs, and auditing policies of the practitioner or firm.

Completeness

Working papers should record (a) for information obtained, all relevant and material facts and their source, (b) for audit procedures performed, their nature, timing and extent, and the auditor who performed them, and (c) for audit conclusions, the conclusions themselves and, where not readily apparent from accompanying information or verification notes, the basis for arriving at those conclusions. Each working paper schedule should be headed with the name of the client, the fiscal period covered, a description of the schedule, an indication of whether it is solely for current use or for carrying forward to future years, the name of the auditor who prepared the schedule and performed the verification, the date the schedule was prepared, and the appropriate code number for indexing and cross-referencing. To save time, the client name and fiscal period can usually be affixed with rubber stamps available from the client. The name, or initials, of the auditor performing the work is important for effective review. The work of less experienced assistants requires closer review than that of more senior ones. Identification also permits each member of the audit team to be held accountable for his own work and to be fairly evaluated on his performance. Finally, identification provides better evidence at any future date that the procedures in question were actually carried out. Dating the audit schedule is important as it is always possible that a future question could turn on whether a procedure was performed before or after some particular occurrence.

Completeness of documentation can be enhanced by the use of pre-printed forms and carry-forward schedules in suitable circumstances.

Since all working papers progress through stages of incompleteness during the course of the field work, ensuring their completeness at its conclusion requires careful attention. In particular, attention should be paid to making the appropriate changes throughout the files for any last-minute revisions of the financial statement figures.

Clarity and conciseness

Working papers should be clear, concise, but complete. Clarity in the preparation of schedules requires experience and care. The important should be distinguished from the trivial. Facts and figures should be identified precisely. Ambiguous column headings, confusing explanations, and unidentified items will lead to wasted time through later questions and perhaps to mistaken conclusions.

Conciseness calls for point form notes rather than lengthy narrative. It may be aided by the use of flow charting techniques in appropriate circumstances. Conciseness also calls for avoiding complete photocopying of voluminous documents, such as trust deeds, when only key portions need be noted. In many cases photocopies merely postpone the necessary reading, extracting, evaluating and verifying to the review stage. Instead, extracts can be taken of the important passages – usually point-form extracts but, where the precise wording is critical, verbatim extracts. Extracts have the advantage that they are concise and can be conveniently filed by subject matter in the working paper files. However, if a significant number of verbatim extracts are required, it may be faster to take photocopies of the relevant pages of the documents, underlining the key passages on the copies.

Inexperienced staff may sometimes prepare unnecessary schedules or schedules in unnecessary detail. The audit senior should attempt to minimize this waste through careful supervision – in any case, he should be sure that the files are purged of unnecessary detail at the conclusion of the field work so that this detail will not be repeated in future years.

Clarity and conciseness usually require some investment of time. A second draft is usually better organized, clearer, and shorter than the first. The investment pays dividends in terms of more efficient use of the resulting schedule by other members of the audit team, more efficient review, and more efficient planning in future years. Often part of the investment can be made in the form of developing clear and concise pre-printed forms.

Ease of preparation

Working papers should be designed in a way that makes them easy to prepare. A cumbersome schedule wastes not only the preparer's time but also the time of the reviewer and next year's audit staff who try to follow its convolutions. Where possible, working papers should be coordinated with the organization and nomenclature of the client's accounts, so that extensive reorganization and retitling is avoided. Some changes, of course, may be necessary if the client's account groupings do not correspond with the financial statement presentation or if the nomenclature is confusing.

Time can often be saved by preparing multiple working papers that cover a number of similar items at the same time. For example, a columnar schedule could cover the verification procedures for the reconciliation of several different bank accounts.

The easiest method of preparation for the auditor is sometimes simply to photocopy key schedules drawn up by the client's staff in the course of their preparation of the financial statements. It is usually wasteful for the auditor to prepare his own version of summaries or analyses which the client has already prepared. In many cases, if he plans in advance, he can arrange to have additional schedules he requires prepared to his specifications by accounting or internal audit staff. Lengthy trial balances, for example, can be typed – even if the amounts must be entered by hand later. When photocopies of client schedules are used, the auditor should be sure to add to them necessary explanations, referencing, notes as to verification performed, etc. Some client schedules used by the auditor in the course of his work, such as a list of invoice numbers to help in their location, need not be retained in the working papers, if the results of the invoice examination have been suitably documented.

Ease of preparation may be enhanced, in some cases, by the use of pre-printed forms and carry-forward schedules where appropriate. Carry-forward schedules ensure that certain documents, schedules, analyses, and systems information will be used in more than one year's audit. Well organized carry-forward schedules can reduce field work time considerably. Where carry-forward schedules are retained in permanent files, current information can simply be added to them each year. When superseded schedules, no longer relevant to the current year, are removed from permanent files, they should be retained in transfer files or in some other manner (see 16.1.3) so that a complete record with respect to prior years is available for a suitable length of time. When information on a schedule in a permanent file is to be altered, a photocopy should be taken prior to alteration and retained for the same reason. Where carry-forward schedules are used in current files, they will be transferred each year from one annual file to the next. In such cases, photocopies should be taken and retained in the file from which the schedule is being transferred (unless that file as a whole is microfilmed prior to transfer – see 16.1.3).

Ease of review

Ease of review requires not only the qualities of good organization, clarity and conciseness already discussed but also: (a) logical summarization of results, (b) highlighting of important points, (c) some method of revealing any omissions. Since errors of omission are harder to spot than errors of commission, some form of pre-printed checklist is usually an important aid to review. Reporting, control and supervision schedules are discussed in 16.3.4.

Integration

Working papers are more valuable on the job and during review if they (a) help to tie the procedures performed to underlying objectives, (b) help to integrate the planning and documentation of substantive procedures with the results of the auditor's control evaluation and compliance procedures, (c) help to integrate other related parts of the audit. The mechanics of integration will depend on the audit approach, procedure manuals, and training programs of the individual practitioner or firm. Some examples of such integrating are illustrated in 16.3.

16.1.3 Ownership, confidentiality and retention

Ownership

In conducting the normal audit a practitioner is acting in the capacity of an "independent contractor" rather than "agent". Legal cases in the United Kingdom and the United States[5] indicate that, in such circumstances, the working papers belong to the practitioner and not to his client. However, where a practitioner acts as agent for another auditor, his working papers would belong to that auditor in the absence of any agreement to the contrary. In certain non-attest activities a practitioner may be acting as an agent for his client, for example in negotiations with income tax authorities, in which case papers specifically related to those activities would belong to the client.

Confidentiality

Any rights of ownership, however, are subject to the legal and professional requirements of confidentiality.

> Regardless of who owns the working papers, the auditors must respect the confidential nature of the information contained therein.[6]

The contents of the working papers must therefore not be shown to or discussed with other parties, either persons within the client's organization or others, except in connection with the proper discharge of the practitioner's duties. Thus, for example, the auditor may properly review discrepancies in accounts receivable confirmations with the credit manager or comptroller but obviously not the deliberations of the salary committee of the board of directors. The duty to maintain confidentiality was discussed in 3.2.7. Under the Rules of Professional Conduct this duty is subject to exceptions for disclosures required by the Provincial Institute or Order or by order of lawful authority. The former may arise when an investigation is being held into the conduct of an audit. The latter may arise in conjunction with civil or criminal litigation or an investigation by Revenue Canada into a taxpayer's affairs. The lawful authority would generally be represented by a subpoena issued by the courts.

Other parties may request to see or review portions of the auditor's working papers – for example, the auditors of an investor company. The practitioner should accede to such requests only with his client's permission.

Maintaining confidentiality requires the proper safeguarding of working paper files at all times. Most practitioners have formalized procedures for the physical protection of working paper files in their offices and for the limitation of access by their staff to the files. Papers are usually filed in fireproof filing cabinets when not in use. Only staff involved with the audit, with its review, or with related quality control reviews should refer to the files of that audit. Working paper files must also be safeguarded on the job. They should not be left lying around in the client's office where unauthorized employees can see them. When left in the client's office overnight, it is desirable that they be kept in a locked filing cabinet, locked box, or locked briefcase. The purpose is to protect confidential information not only concerning the client's affairs but also concerning the auditor's procedures. Knowledge of the auditor's procedures might assist a dishonest employee in concealing either careless mistakes or deliberate defalcations.

Retention

In 1970 a CICA Study Group determined that, of a sample of Canadian accounting firms of various sizes, somewhat more than half either retain their working papers permanently or microfilm them. For most files, it would seem prudent to incur the cost of permanent retention or microfilming in order to have a permanent record of the justification for the issued reports. Some working papers of a routine

nature, however, might not be worth retaining beyond six years. Where files are to be microfilmed, the date of microfilming will depend on convenience and the anticipated frequency of reference. For some working paper files, microfilming after two or three years may make sense. For files containing significant numbers of carry-forward schedules, such as systems flow charts, which will be altered in the following year, microfilming at the completion of each year's field work may be preferable.

The CICA Study Group concluded, however, that it was also permissible to have a program for the destruction of working papers (but not copies of the financial statements, auditor's reports, or tax returns). It suggested:

> As a minimum, however, all of the working papers should be retained for at least the period during which the auditors could be held liable for actions for tort or breach of contract. In Canada, this is six years, except in the province of Quebec, where the period may be up to thirty years.[7]

16.1.4 General files

A brief description of the more common *general files* (files other than audit working papers) typically maintained by practitioners follows.

Correspondence file

The correspondence file contains a record of all correspondence between the auditor and his client and any other related correspondence, but usually excludes communications that are an integral part of the audit process, for example, letters of representation, and confirmation letters.

Tax file

The tax file normally contains copies of all tax and information returns prepared by the auditor for his client, together with copies of related notices of assessment and reassessment. In addition, the file may contain tax analyses of continuing interest such as capital surplus and 1971 undistributed income on hand. Sometimes a separate tax file is kept for each taxing jurisdiction (provincial, federal, and foreign). The purpose of the tax files is to provide a permanent documentary record of the tax work performed for the client as well as an information source for future tax planning. To the extent that information in the tax file is relevant to the auditor's opinion on tax effects presented in the financial statements, it should be summarized or noted in the working papers so that the working paper files will be complete in themselves. Thus, details of assessments received might be noted in the working paper files while photocopies of the actual assessments were filed in the tax file. Copies of correspondence on tax matters may often be filed in both correspondence and tax files.

Report file

Many practitioners maintain a separate file of all annual financial statements together with the related audit reports, internal control/management letters, and any other statement or report to which the auditor has appended an opinion. The file may also contain interim unaudited statements. Such a separate file may be convenient for two reasons. Many years' statements can be conveniently seen in one place, long after the related working paper files have been destroyed or microfilmed. The statements are still available in the practitioner's office when the current working paper files have been taken to the client's premises for the annual audit.

Fee file

Many practitioners maintain a separate fee file for each client showing a summary of time worked by category of staff and a copy of current and past years' billings.

16.2 The permanent file

Most practitioners maintain two distinct types of working paper file for each client: (a) a permanent file (or historical file) used over many years and (b) one or more current files for each audit year. The allocation of working papers between these two groups of files varies from practice to practice – the difference being the extent to which information of continuing interest is maintained in the permanent file or recorded on carry-forward schedules maintained in the current files and transferred annually to the next year's files. The former method reduces the bulk of current files. The latter method may help to ensure that permanent information does not become out of date and is not inadvertently ignored in the planning or evaluation of audit verification. A preference for the latter method (the use of carry-forward schedules) was expressed by the CICA Study Group, at least with respect to operating information. However, either method, used with care, is effective. The choice will depend on the preference of the individual practitioner or firm.

16.2.1 Documents and calculations of continuing audit interest

The following documents and calculations of continuing audit interest are, if applicable, normally found in the permanent file. In each case, extracts, complete copies of the documents, or both, may be maintained. However, the filing of complete copies of bulky documents may be unnecessary where properly signed official copies of these documents are maintained at the client's office and are readily accessible to the auditor.

Letters patent

Copies or extracts of a company's letters patent, supplementary letters patent, memoranda of association, etc. are usually retained in the auditor's perma-

nent file. They should be reviewed annually by the audit senior. Not only do they establish the legal existence of the incorporated entity, but they may describe (a) its objects (the activities the company can engage in) a violation of which might necessitate an audit report qualification, (b) its authorized share capital, which is essential disclosure on the balance sheet, and (c) other matters of potential relevance to the audit. Where complete copies are retained in the file, important passages should be highlighted by underlining.

Copies or abstracts of minutes and by-laws

Minutes of directors', shareholders', and audit committee meetings are reviewed by the audit senior annually in detail to ascertain if any of their decisions are pertinent to the audit. Information of importance may include declaration of dividends, stock options, and bonuses; the auditor's appointment; approval of contracts and major expenditure commitments; appointment of officers; redemption of shares; etc. This information is usually noted in the current working paper files. Each year, however, some portion of this information will usually be of relevance to subsequent years' audits, and accordingly, should be included in the permanent file or on a carry-forward schedule. If many of the decisions are relevant on a continuing basis, the most practical approach may be to take photocopies of the minutes and include them in the permanent file. Normally, however, there will be only a few decisions of continuing audit interest and it is more efficient to make a brief written summary of them for the permanent file.

Most of the by-laws passed by the board of directors and shareholders will be of continuing relevance to the audit. Copies or extracts of these should be placed in the permanent file.

Trust deeds

Either extracts and/or complete copies of all trust deeds are usually maintained in the permanent file until their terms have expired. Most trust deeds (indentures) relate to a company issue of long-term debt. They should be reviewed carefully by the audit seniors and reviewers in the initial year and, because of their length, extracts should be made of the more important points of continuing audit interest, whether or not the complete copies are retained on file as well. In subsequent years it will normally be sufficient to review the key item in the extracts. Trust indentures normally contain a number of covenants with which the company must abide. Typical covenants include restrictions on the acquisition of new fixed assets, restrictions on the payment of dividends, and a requirement to maintain a certain balance of working capital or a certain working capital ratio. All of such covenants will be of continuing interest to the auditor since the violation of a covenant can, in some circumstances, lead to the entire debt issue becoming due and payable immediately.

Mortgages

Copies or extracts of mortgages should be maintained in the permanent file so that they can be reviewed annually to ensure that the correct description of the debt is shown on the financial statements and to ensure that the assets securing the mortgages are fully disclosed.

Major contracts

The permanent file should also contain information respecting major contracts whose lifetime exceeds one fiscal year. Information on major contracts is important because it may be necessary in the disclosure of long-term commitments and in the verification of certain financial statement components such as fixed asset additions or inventories.

Leases

Details of lease agreements should be contained in the permanent file as these also represent long-term commitments requiring disclosure. New lease agreements should be examined carefully by the audit senior to ascertain whether the substance of the transaction is, in fact, a lease or a fixed asset purchase. Extracts of the lease will usually be needed in the verification of leasehold expenditures.

Accounts and entries of continuing interest

One section of the permanent file is usually reserved for explanations of major corporate events together with the related accounting entries. These explanations serve as essential background for the annual audit of some of the accounts. Major events of continuing interest include major fixed asset purchases (particularly, if the client does not maintain a fixed asset subledger), the issue and redemption of share capital, the issue and redemption of debt, details of asset appraisal write-ups, analysis of tax components of retained earnings, purchase equations and the acquisition of subsidiary or other investee companies. Alternatively, some of this information can be kept on carry-forward schedules in the current files.

Engagement letters

Engagement letters and any other communications with the client establishing the terms of the engagement or other important aspects of the client-auditor relationship are often filed in the permanent file (though sometimes in the current files). They should be reviewed annually to ensure that all contracted services are being rendered.

16.2.2 Other schedules of continuing audit interest

In addition to the foregoing information, there is a variety of information and schedules which may be of continuing interest. Such information includes:

- description of the business and organization charts,
- internal control questionnaires or evaluation guides,
- flow charts of accounting systems,
- statistical data or graphs,
- analysis of long-term asset and liability accounts,
- summaries of accounting policies,
- details of pension plans.

Some practitioners retain some or all of this information in the permanent file. Because such information tends to go out of date quickly, other practitioners prefer to maintain it instead on carry-forward schedules in the current files. The latter choice is assumed in the description of current files in 16.3.

Where, however, the foregoing information is kept in the permanent file, it may be desirable to index the permanent file with the same codes as the current files. Thus, when conducting the review, for example, the reviewer could open the permanent file to Section D, Inventories, for inventory statistics and accounting policies, and the current working paper file to Section D, Inventories, for the current year's observation and other verification procedures.

Where the foregoing information is not contained in the permanent file, the permanent file may be indexed quite separately from the structure of the current working paper files.

16.3 Current working paper files

Current working paper files, prepared for each year's audit, commonly consist of at least two files: one concerning systems, controls and certain interim procedures, the other concerning the verification of year-end balances. To correspond with the terminology used elsewhere in this book, the former is described as an *interim audit file,* though it may also be known in practice as an interim file, current file, or procedural file. The latter is described as a *financial statement audit file,* though it may also be known in practice as a financial statement file, balance sheet file, or year-end file. In a few small audits the two files may be combined. In very large audits each file may be further subdivided. The following discussion assumes that continuing information of the sort described in 16.2.2 is included in carry-forward schedules in the current working paper files.

16.3.1 Six types of working paper schedule

A schedule[8] prepared for filing in a current working paper file may serve one or more of the following six functions:

1. planning,
2. information,
3. evaluation,
4. verification,
5. reporting,
6. control and supervision.

Frequently two or more functions are combined, the most common combinations being:
• planning/verification,
• information/evaluation/reporting,
• information/verification,
• information/evaluation/verification,
• evaluation/reporting,
• reporting/control and supervision.

Figure 16.a summarizes under the foregoing headings all the working paper schedules illustrated in both volumes of this book. Because of the number of multiple functions served by some schedules the categorization cannot be precise, but it indicates the principal functions served in most cases. The figure includes examples in both Volumes 1 and 2. In the following discussion of each function, however, specific reference is made to only the examples included in Volume 1.

Planning schedules

The purpose of schedules serving a planning function is to document both general planning and de-tailed program planning decisions. These decisions are documented for three reasons:

1. as a means of communication from the planner (the reviewer or audit senior) to the person performing the work (the audit senior or audit assistant);
2. to provide clear evidence of adherence to the first field work standard;
3. to provide the reviewer, after the field work, with a basis for comparison of the audit work performed with that planned.

As discussed in 15.4, *general planning* decisions may be documented in written planning notes or in a preprinted planning memorandum (see Figure 15.b). Where a preprinted planning memorandum is used, it is often convenient to divide it into two parts – one part containing relatively stable information which can be carried forward each year with minor modifications and the other part containing those decisions which require extensive rethinking each year.

As discussed in 15.3.3, *detailed program planning* decisions may be documented in one or more of the following ways:

• in the same preprinted planning memorandum as used for the general planning,
• on preprinted planning forms designed for specific decisions (for example, the audit control checklist for deciding whether to use a computer-assisted audit technique – see Figure 14.c),
• on preprinted verification outlines (discussed below under "verification schedules"),
• in a detailed written audit program (e.g., an interim audit written program for sales/receivables shown in Figure 9.e and part of a year-end written program for accounts receivable shown in Figure 16.b),
• in a preprinted extent of testing form (see Figure 12.e, 12.f and 13.l),
• in general written notes.

The form of documentation will determine where the plans are found in the working paper file. For example, general planning notes and preprinted planning memoranda will often be filed in a separate planning section whereas planning notes incorporated directly on verification outlines will be filed in the specific verification sections.

Information schedules

The purpose of information schedules is to document, in some coherent fashion, information concerning the client which is needed on a current or

Working Papers Illustrated in this Book

(Numbers refer to figures; 1 to 22 are in Volume 1, 23 to 44 in Volume 2)
(IA = interim audit; FSA = financial statement audit)

(Other working papers are described throughout this book but not illustrated in the figures; only those illustrated in figures are included below.)

Planning

14.c Checklist for computer-assisted audit application
15.b Planning memorandum
24.b Planning memorandum
35.a Inventory advance planning

Planning/Verification

IA Programs
9.e Transactional tests
28.b Transactional tests

FSA Programs
16.b Accounts receivable

IA Verification Outlines
26.a Books of account
26.b Purchases

FSA Verification Outlines
16.c, 33.b Receivables confirmation
33.d Accounts receivable
32.d Income statement
34.a, 35.d, 36.c, 37.d, 39.d, 41.e, and
42.a Various assets and liabilities

Planning Test Extents
12.e Substantive representative
12.f Compliance representative
13.m Statistical substantive

Other checklists
35.b, 36.a, 36.b Various

Information

General
7.a, 7.c, 8.c Organization charts

IA Systems
9.c, 25.a Narrative and flow charts
24.d Computer environment
25.e, 25.h, 25.j, 25.l Outline and other charts
25.m, 25.n, 25.o, 25.p Computer charts

FSA Statistical
32.a Sales and cost of·sales graphs
32.b Gross profit analysis
33.c, 35.c, 37.d Accounts receivable, inventory and investment statistics

Information/Evaluation/Reporting

IA Internal control questionnaires
9.b Sales/accounts receivable

IA Internal control evaluation guides
9.d Sales/receivables/receipts
26.c, 26.d, 27.d, 27.e, 28.a, 29.a, 29.b, 29.c, 29.d, 29.e, 29.f
Various major systems

Information/Verification

FSA Accounting summaries
16.d Allowance for doubtful accounts – with verification notes
32.c Expense analysis
37.a, 37.b, 38.a, 39.a, 39.b, 39.c, 41.a, 41.b, 41.c, 41.d
Various analyses and continuity schedules re investments, fixed assets and taxes

IA Flow charts (with flow audit incorporated)
25.d, 25.f, 25.g, 25.i Various

Other
16.e Lead sheet
25.k Books of account chart
44.b Summary of accounting policies

Information/Evaluation/Verification

27.a Computer environment evaluation guide

Evaluation

13.l Sample evaluation
16.g Combined sample evaluation
26.e Weakness evaluation

Evaluation/Reporting

16.f, 16.h Total error evaluation report

Verification

27.c Computer flow audit

Reporting/Control and Supervision

30.a, 30.b Interim audit reports
44.c Senior's and reviewer's questionnaire
24.c Time budget and time record

Figure 16.a

452

recurring basis by the auditor in planning and performing both verification and evaluation procedures. Information schedules may be further subdivided into five categories:

1. general information on the business (to serve as background for the review and evaluation of internal control and for orientation of the audit senior and assistants),
2. specific information on the client's systems and other related internal controls (to be used as a basis for the evaluation of controls),
3. photocopies or extracts of key documents that provide information to be used for a variety of verification purposes,
4. other information that provides specific direction to certain substantive procedures (for example, the client's routines for the inventory count, the client's cut-off routines, the client's accounting policies),
5. specific information as to year-end account balances, analyses, statistical information, etc.

General information is usually documented in a written or typed narrative prepared by the auditor. Part of the general information may come from client-prepared organization charts (see Figures 7.a, 7.c, and 8.c). In some cases, a portion of this information could be entered onto a preprinted form, perhaps as part of the planning memorandum.

Specific information on client systems and controls may be documented in written narratives or on flow charts (see Figure 9.c), or internal control questionnaires (see Figures 9.b and 9.d). As discussed in Chapter 9, flow charts usually also serve a verification function and internal control questionnaires also serve an evaluation function.

Photocopies or extracts of key documents (such as agreements) are more commonly found in the permanent file (see 16.2.1) but occasionally occur in the current working paper files as well. Other information may be documented either in written notes or on preprinted forms.

Specific information as to year-end account balances, analyses of accounts, etc. is usually accompanied by verification notes (discussed below under "verification schedules"). However, statistical information such as monthly trends, analytical ratios, and turnover and ageing statistics, can be best documented on separate carry-forward schedules. Sometimes trends are most clearly documented by the use of graphs.

Information schedules should identify the sources from which the information was obtained. In some cases it may be helpful to give the location of the related records and the employee responsible for them.

When presenting information about client operations or procedures, the word "we" should not be used when the intended reference is actually to "the client". Such usage leads to confusion as to who performed what accounting procedures. It may also expose the auditor to unnecessary risks by creating an appearance of impairment of objectivity even though no impairment in fact occurred.

Evaluation schedules

The purpose of evaluation schedules is to document the logical basis for the auditor's conclusions concerning internal control, weaknesses observed, errors encountered, sample results, and other matters requiring the exercise of judgment.

Evaluation of internal control may involve comprehensive internal control questionnaires (see Figure 9.b) or condensed internal control evaluation guides (see Figure 9.d). Evaluation guides serve a reporting function as well since they assemble in a condensed form for the reviewer the principal conclusions resulting from the study of control. As explained in Chapter 9, flow chart analysis can also contribute to the evaluation function.

The evaluation of sample results may make use of preprinted forms in the case of statistical projections (see Figure 13.1) or simply narrative schedules and calculations in the case of judgmental tests. The evaluation of errors for the audit as a whole may make use of preprinted forms (as discussed in 16.4) or simply narrative schedules and calculations. Some schedules, usually in narrative or point form, may be devoted to an evaluation of specific accounting policies – particularly in contentious areas or where difficult accounting judgments are involved.

Verification schedules

The purpose of verification schedules is to document the verification performed and the conclusions reached as a result of that verification. Some schedules consist solely of verification notes. Where a verification note is long and complicated a short summary of it will be useful to both the reviewer and future years' audit staffs. Most commonly verification is combined with one of the other functions. For example, detailed written audit programs serve a planning function in advance of the field work and then serve to document the performance of the planned procedures (see Figures 9.e and 16.b). The same combination is involved when preprinted checklists are used.

A particular type of checklist is the *verificaiton outline*. As discussed in 15.3.3, verification outlines summarize the major verification steps to be performed in a given section, serve as a valuable aid in planning, and provide a vehicle for documenting the verification performed and conclusions reached in a concise fashion. Their advantages are the encouragement of a consistent and organized verification approach and the reduction of the possibility of inadvertently omitted steps. Their disadvantage is the danger of their misuse in a mechanical and unthinking fashion. For many sections of many engagements the advantages, in the writer's view, outweigh the disadvantages. An example of a verification outline

for accounts receivable confirmation is shown in Figure 16.c.

Whatever form verification schedules take, it is desirable that the verification notes be as specific as possible. Normally, they should:

- describe the nature of the audit procedure,
- name the records to which the procedure was applied,
- identify the date or time period for which the records were checked,
- where less than 100% of the records were checked for that date or time period, describe the basis of high value, key item, and representative selections made,
- describe any errors found,
- state the conclusions (unless included on separate evaluation schedules).

Thus, wording such as:

> Traced from cheque register to paid suppliers' invoices for the month of January for all payments over $500. Inspected unpaid invoices on hand (February 18) over $200. Of the invoices checked, traced those dated December 31 or earlier to the year-end accounts payable listing. One inventory purchase for $710 not properly set up as inventory or as payable. Immaterial. Payables cut-off appears satisfactory.

is preferable to:

> Checked subsequent payments and invoices. No material errors.

In some cases, a number of the foregoing details may be clear from the context of the note and may not have to be completely spelled out. Moreover, the degree of detail given in a verification note may properly vary according to the significance of the procedure and the materiality of the item being checked.

In other cases, the verification and information functions may be combined. For example, the analysis of a particular account and the related verification steps performed may be shown on the same page. An example of this combination for the allowance for doubtful accounts is shown on Figure 16.d. This schedule combines account analysis information with the related verification. Such a combination is common for accounts for which detailed program planning in advance, whether by written program or by checklist, has not been considered necessary.

Account analysis may consist of an analysis of the change in the account balance over a period of time (a continuity schedule as in Figure 16.d) or an analysis into components at a point in time. Either or both types of analysis may be required depending on the nature of the balance to be verified and its relationship with verification steps in other sections of the audit.

EXAMPLE OF AN ACCOUNTS RECEIVABLE CONFIRMATION OUTLINE

Client __ABC Limited__   Circularization date __November 30, 19⁻__

	Answer or file reference

1. (a) If accounts receivable are confirmed at a date prior to the year-end are internal controls adequate to allow us to render an opinion on year-end accounts receivable?

Yes – compliance tests to be performed during roll-forward period – see VIII 4

   (b) During the interim audit internal control was assessed as weak/adequate/strong over the following accounts.

   (i) sales including returns   ✓

   (ii) accounts receivable _____

   — cash debits   ✓

   — cash credits   ✓

   — other credits   ✓

Strong in all areas

   (c) If cash receipt and accounts receivable controls are inadequate, perform cash count procedures at the confirmation date.

N/A
Non-trade accounts should be confirmed at year-end.

2. Consider the possibility of non-trade accounts requiring confirmation at circularization date. If so, include account balances in sampling plan.

3. (a) Confirmation date was (date on statement).   *Nov. 30*

   (b) Date of last sales invoice included in statements.   *Nov. 30*

   (c) Date of last shipment included in statements and control account.   *Nov. 30*

   (d) Date of last cash receipt included in statements and control account.   *Nov. 30*

   (e) If these dates do not coincide consider the possible effect on reliability of the confirmation procedure.

Dates coincide

4. (a) State the bases of selection of account balances and/or open-items for confirmation (i.e. high value accounts, key accounts, representative sample (judgemental or statistical; positive or negative requests).

1. High value – balances over $50 000
2. Key item – 2 disputed, 1 large write-off
3. Representative – statistical

	No. of Accounts	Account Balances

   (b) After selecting accounts, summarize extent of confirmation

   (i) Positive confirmation requested of trade accounts:

   — account balances only

   high value accounts over $_____

   key accounts

   representative sample

| | 3 | 75 000 |

   — account balances with open-item alternative

   high value accounts over $__50 000__

   key accounts

   representative sample

| | 25 | 2 462 000 |
| | 20 | 200.000 |

   Positive confirmation requested of non-trade accounts

   Sub total

| | 48 | 2737 000 |

   (ii) Negative confirmation requested

   (iii) Alternative verification on accounts selected but not confirmed at client's request.

   (iv) Accounts not specifically verified

   Total

| | 175 | 2 104 000 |
| | 223 | 4 841 000 |

5. Note basis and extent of procedures at circularization date.

   — Check trial balance to accounts receivable subledger

   — Reconcile subledger to control account

   — Check statement addresses, balances and details to subledger

   — Add (test add) trial balance

Accounts confirmed
Agrees
Accounts confirmed
100%

6. List any accounts not confirmed at client's request. Record reason and obtain signature of an official not directly concerned with accounts receivable. If such balances are significant in size pursue alternative verification immediately.

None

Figure 16.c

7. Ensure that all shipments (including direct shipments from suppliers to customers) prior to 3(c) above are invoiced with proper shipping date and included in sales, accounts receivable and customer statements; and that subsequent shipments were not so included.

Done - 1 minor error — see C23

8. Test cash receipts/accounts receivable cut-off by checking from duplicate deposit slips and cash count sheets to accounts receivable subledger. Extents noted at —

C25

9. Indicate date of mailing of second requests for positive confirmations not replying. Where customer has declined to reply due to nature of their system, attach a list of outstanding invoices to the second request.

Dec. 29

10. Where important differences are reported on returned confirmations, follow-up procedures are recorded either on face of the confirm or at —

Noted on face of confirmation

11. Perform alternative verification for accounts not confirmed at client's request, accounts where confirmation not returned, or accounts not replying with a satisfactory confirmation by:
    (a) examining evidence of subsequent payment clearly relating to open balance and seeing evidence of shipments,
    (b) verifying existence of customer through phone or trade directories,
    (c) attempt phone communication for verbal confirmation (not sufficient alone).

Done - verification recorded directly on confirmation copy

12. Results of verification of accounts selected for positive confirmation are summarized at —

C31

List confirmations received or alternative verification performed after above summary.

See C32

13. Describe results of negative confirmations (i.e. number of disputed accounts, items cleared, items not cleared, etc.)

No negatives

14. Report all differences to the client (Mr. *Clark*) regardless of apparent importance and where appropriate send a courtesy letter to client's customers.

Done

15. Give a list of customers not replying to confirmation requests to one of the client's officials (Mr. *Smith*) not directly concerned with cash receipts, accounts receivable, cash disbursements or bank reconciliations.

Done - copy

Date *Jan. 15, 19—*

B. Simpson
Section Senior

Figure 16.c (concluded)

Another type of schedule which may combine both information and verification (or at least references to verification) is the section lead sheet. The purpose of the lead sheet for a given audit section, such as accounts receivable, is (a) to summarize all general ledger accounts making up the financial statement figure to be reported, (b) to give the precise financial statement disclosure for that figure, (c) to compare the ledger account balances with the prior year, and (d) to record, summarize, or refer to outlines of, the verification performed. An example of a lead sheet for the accounts receivable section is shown in Figure 16.e. Occasionally, as shown in that figure, some element of an account balance will require reclassification elsewhere in the financial statements and the necessary reclassification (in the example, credit balances reclassified as accounts payable) can be shown on the lead sheet.

Reporting, control and supervision schedules

There are two types of reporting schedules in the working paper files. *External* reporting schedules include the draft of the internal control/management letter to be issued to the client, schedules from which tax returns are prepared, and the specific schedules from which the financial statements are prepared. *Internal* reporting schedules are those which summarize the results of the field work for the reviewer, those which document the review itself, and, in the case of the interim audit, those which summarize interim audit results of potential significance to the financial statement audit.

Many reporting schedules also have a supervisory or control function. Thus, for example, a senior's questionnaire not only aids the audit senior in his control and supervision of the audit, but also pro-

Example of Account Analysis and Verification Notes

XYZ Limited

December 31, 1976	Allowance for doubtful accounts	
	1975	**1976**
Balance per general ledger	75 000.00	ᴎ 80 000.00
Balance beginning of year	70 000.00	*1.* 75 000.00
Recoveries on debts previously written off	7 432.00	*2.* 8 317.00
Write-offs during year	(24 372.00)	C 11 (37 819.00)
Provision during year (Bad debt expense)	21 940.00	*3.* 34 502.00
Balance end of year	75 000.00	*1.* 80 000.00

Verification

1975 figures carried forward from last year's file

1. Agreed to client's general ledger
2. Examined 12 monthly reports received from Brutal Collection Service. All accounts written off are turned over to this collection service. Proceeds are net of 33¹/₃% service charge.
3. Company policy is to provide a 25% allowance against all account balances over 90 days old. We test checked client ageing schedules for 20% of accounts by sales value. $318 000 over 90 days at 25%=$79 500. All accounts over $5 000 and not collected by Feb. 5 were discussed with the credit manager. Based on this discussion we estimate that a satisfactory allowance will be $120 000. See detailed comments in support file with aged trial balance.

Figure 16.d

Example of Lead Sheet

XYZ Limited

December 31, 1974	Accounts receivable lead sheet		
	G-L account	1975	1976
Trade receivables—domestic	13-1	1 238 427.13	C5 1 432 619.40
—export	13-2	435 629.14	C5 392 638.16
Employee loans	13-3	20 230.00	C7 17 541.70
Loans to officers	13-4	18 300.00	C7 22 000.00
Freight claims receivable	13-7	64 329.40	C8 84 639.16
Miscellaneous receivables	13-8	8 329.30	C9 11 233.70
Allowance for doubtful accounts	13-10	(75 000.00)	C10 (80 000.00)
		1 710 244.97	1 880 672.12
Transfer credit balance to accounts payable		84 300.00	C5 51 730.00
Statement presentation		1 794 544.97	BB 1 932 402.12
Accounts receivable		1 776 244.97	1 842 402.12
Loans to officers and shareholders		18 300.00	ᴎ 22 000.00
Loans to subsidiary company			C6 68 000.00
		1 794 544.97	1 932 402.12

Note 8
During the year the company loaned $75 000 to officers and shareholders.
$53 000 of the current year's loan was repaid.

Figure 16.e

vides a summary report to the reviewer of how the work was completed. Some supervisory schedules also combine planning functions as in the case of a detailed time budget combined with a daily time analysis. Reporting, control and supervision schedules are discussed further in 16.3.4.

16.3.2 The interim audit file

In Chapter 9 the four basic elements of the interim audit were identified as review, evaluation, compliance verification, and substantive verification. The working papers should adequately document the auditor's completion of each of these four elements and, in addition, the related planning, reporting to reviewers, and field work control. Interim audit files are organized in many different ways to cover the foregoing elements and the method chosen will depend on the preferences and policies of the individual practitioner or firm. The method of organization will also be influenced by the choice between a systems-oriented and data-oriented approach (see 9.6). The contents of the file commonly include:

1. various reporting, control and supervision notes (such as an interim audit report to the reviewer, highlights memorandum, uncleared notes, draft of an internal control/management time budget and analysis);
2. general planning notes (such as planning memorandum covering general planning decisions);
3. evaluation notes (questionnaires or evaluation guides covering the auditor's evaluation of internal controls, his conclusions, the identification of key controls requiring compliance verification, his evaluation of control weaknesses and their effect on further audit planning);
4. verification notes covering both compliance and substantive procedures, their extents and results, the auditor's conclusions therefrom (compliance verification notes are normally arranged by major system or they may alternatively be included directly on questionnaires or on flow-charts – substantive verification notes are often arranged by asset, liability or income component for ease of later integration with the financial statement audit);
5. general information notes (a description of the client's business, organization charts, volumes of transactions, information on internal audit);
6. systems information notes or flow charts (usually divided into sections by major system such as sales/receivables/receipts; the detailed notes or flow charts for each major system may be preceded by a systems summary and a preprinted

checklist or verification outline which ensures that all relevant points have been covered – some or all of the systems information may alternatively be included directly on questionnaires).

Suggested file structures

In 9.8 two suggested methodologies for the interim audit were presented: (a) an *analytical interim audit,* a systems-oriented approach, and (b) a *transactional interim audit,* a data oriented approach. Where these or similar approaches are used, the following file structures may be convenient. However, they are offered solely as examples. Many different but equally workable file structures are in use today throughout the profession.

Suggested structure of the analytical audit file

Normally a separate analytical audit file should be prepared each year with photocopies of significant schedules left behind to document the prior year's work. Some of the analytical interim audit schedules end up being filed permanently in the financial statement audit file as indicated in the following table. The purpose of this transfer is to facilitate the relating of interim audit results to financial statement audit planning.

The suggested working papers and flow charts for use during an analytical audit are described more fully in Chapters 24, 25, 26, 27, 29 and 30.

Suggested structure of the transactional audit file

Normally the transactional interim audit file, because it is used for smaller engagements, is a continuing file reused year after year. Schedules which become superseded are filed at the end of the file. As with the analytical interim audit, the transactional interim audit file is organized so that key results are transferred to the financial statement audit file for use at the year-end.

The suggested working papers for use during a transactional audit are described more fully in Chapters 24, 28, 29 and 30.

16.3.3 The financial statement audit file

In Chapter 11 the four basic elements of the financial statement audit were identified as completion and evaluation of the interim audit, substantive verification, evaluation, and formation of opinion. The working papers should adequately document the auditor's completion of each of these four elements and, in addition, the related planning, reporting to reviewers, and field work control. While the method

Analytical Audit File

	Final disposition[5]
I Interim audit report (analytical)	(to F/S VII – interim audit results)
II Highlights memorandum	(incorporate in F/S II – highlights)
III Uncleared items and error evaluation	(to be cleared or transferred to F/S III – error evaluation
IV Internal control/management letter	(to F/S VII – interim audit results)
V Time budget and analysis	(to F/S V)
VI Planning memorandum	(to F/S VI)
VII Internal control evaluation	(to F/S VII – interim audit results)
VIII Further compliance procedures	(A/A file)
IX Substantive procedures (including) transactional audit program if any)	(A/A file or F/S verification sections)
X Internal audit department	(to F/S X)
XI Volume Summary	(A/A file)
A Description of business	(A/A file)
B Sales/receivables/receipts	(A/A file)
C Purchase/payables/payments	(A/A file)
C Wage and salary payrolls	(A/A file)
E Cost records and inventory records	(A/A file)
F Books of account and general	(A/A file)

Transactional Audit File

	Final disposition
I Interim audit report (transactional)	(to F/S VII – interim audit results)
II Highlights memorandum	(incorporate in F/S II – highlights)
III Uncleared items and error evaluation error evaluation)	(to be cleared or transferred to F/S III – error evaluation)
IV Internal control/management letter	(to F/S VII – interim audit results
V Time budget and analysis	(to F/S V)
VI Planning memorandum	(to F/S VI)
VII Revision to financial statement audit program	(to F/S VII – interim audit results)
A Description of business	(continuing file)
B – F Internal control evaluation guides	(continuing file)
B – F Transactional audit tests	(continuing file)
Superseded schedules	(continuing file)

of file organization varies from practitioner to practitioner, the variation is less than in the case of interim audit files. Normally, the individual verification sections follow the order of the figures appearing on the financial statements, preceded by a number of general sections. The contents of the file commonly include:

1. the draft financial statements (either prepared by the client or prepared in draft, as an accounting service, by the auditor),
2. various reporting, control and supervision notes (such as a review checklist or questionnaire, a highlights memorandum, a time budget and analysis, and, because of their impact on the fi-

nancial statement audit, key reporting schedules from the interim audit including the interim audit report to the reviewer, internal control evaluation guides, and weakness evaluation schedules),
3. error evaluation notes (discussed in 16.4),
4. general planning notes (such as planning memorandum covering general planning decisions as modified during the interim audit),
5. general information and verification notes (client letter of representation, extracts from minutes, verification notes covering the notes to the financial statements and changes in financial position, verification notes covering the general review of internal audit competence and programs where relied upon, verification notes on cut-off, infor-

mation and evaluation notes on accounting policies employed),

6. specific information, evaluation and verification notes by individual section (assets, liabilities and income components),

7. information notes as to the client's account ba-

lances (grouping schedules, adjusting entries, and work sheets where necessary).

Suggested file structure

The following suggested file structure is offered as an example.

Financial Statement Audit File

	Suggested contents of outline file at planning stage
I Senior's and reviewer's questionnaire	
II Highlights memorandum	Interim audit highlights
III Error evaluation	Interim audit errors; prior years' errors
IV Letter of representation	Copy of prior year's letter
V Time budget and analysis	Interim audit time budget and results; budget for financial statement audit
VI Planning memorandum	Planning memorandum and notes
VII Interim audit results	Interim audit results: interim audit report, internal control/management letter, internal control evaluation guide, weakness follow-up schedules
VIII Extracts from minutes	
IX Working papers supporting notes to financial statements, changes in financial position, long form report	
X Internal audit	Internal audit notes from interim audit; agreed program for year-end work; plans for review and testing
XI Cut-off	Cut-off summary with interim audit results and carry-forward description of client procedures
XII Other reporting forms	
XIII Accounting policies	Carry-forward schedule
Assets	
A Cash on hand and on deposit	
B Marketable securities	
C Accounts receivable	
D Inventory	
E Prepaid expenses	
F Long-term Intercorporate investments	
G Other investments	
H Fixed assets	
Other (list and index as required)	Lead sheets with prior year's figures and statement presentation
	Verification outlines with planning notes pencilled in
Liabilities	Extent of tests planning schedules
AA Bank indebtedness	Carry-forward narrative and statistical schedules
BB Accounts payable and accrued charges	
CC Taxes payable	
DD Deferred taxes	
EE Other debt	
FF Capital stock	
GG Surplus	

Other (list and index as required)
Income components
   1. Comparative statement schedules   Carry-forward comparative statement
                                                      schedules

   2. Sales analyses
   3. Cost of sales and gross profit   Carry-forward statistical schedules
       analyses
   4. Miscellaneous revenue analyses
   5. Expense analyses
   6. Extraordinary items
       Other (list and index as required)
   X Grouping schedules   Carry-forward grouping schedules
   Y Journal entries
   Z Work sheets (where necessary)

The foregoing file structure has been designed primarily with the reviewer and audit senior in mind. Sections of the file which aid the senior in his overall control of the audit (for example, the cut-off summary, minutes, and summary of accounting policies) are towards the front of the file. Sections which summarize results of the audit or otherwise have critical information for the reviewer (for example, the senior's questionnaire, highlights memorandum and overall error results) are similarly placed towards the front.

Each of the individual verification sections (A, B, C, etc.) would contain some or all of the following schedules:

1. a lead sheet with comparative figures from the prior year and suggested financial statement presentation (see Figure 16.e),
2. verification outlines summarizing the substantive verification procedures performed and conclusions reached (see Figure 16.c),
3. statistical data (trends, analytical ratios, etc. – often on carry-forward schedules),
4. explanations of major changes from the prior year or from the date of any pre-year-end work (unless explained directly on the lead sheet),
5. other information, verification and evaluation schedules (continuity schedules, analyses, confirmation letters, etc.).

The foregoing schedules should demonstrate for each section:

1. whether the examination was made in a logical, orderly and rational manner,
2. the nature of the amounts being verified,
3. the auditor's consideration of the application and consistency of generally accepted accounting principles,

4. the auditor's compliance with generally accepted auditing standards. [10]

The suggested working papers for use during a financial statement audit are described more fully in Chapters 31 to 44.

16.3.4 Reporting, control and supervision schedules

Reporting, control and supervisory schedules play an important role in maintaining effective control of the field work and in facilitating review. The use of such schedules at the front of each of the interim audit and financial statement audit files has been indicated in the suggested file structures shown in 16.3.2 and 16.3.3. The suggested transfer of many of these schedules from the interim audit file to the financial statement audit file during the course of the annual audit helps to ensure the integration of these two major components. When assessing the results of the substantive verification completed at the year-end, the reviewer has in front of him the key conclusions on internal control which must influence this assessment.

Two important reporting schedules are the highlights memorandum and a final review checklist or questionnaire.

The purpose of a highlights memorandum is to provide the reviewer with a capsule commentary on significant aspects of the systems, operations and audit results for the current year. Such a commentary should help the reviewer by:

a) guiding him to the critical areas of the audit, particularly where the key judgment decisions are involved that may warrant a second opinion by a more experienced auditor, and

461

b) updating his knowledge of the client's affairs so that a high level of service in both audit and ancillary areas can be maintained.

Contents of a typical highlights memorandum might include:

- comments on the financial position and operating results,
- comments on important systems changes,
- other information summarized from the description of business,
- comments on significant errors discovered or on disagreements as to accounting presentation,
- summary of audit time including variances from budget and comments for the future.

The highlights memorandum prepared during the interim audit may be rewritten at the year-end or merely incorporated in the year-end memorandum.

Most auditors use some form of review checklist to summarize the principal points about which both the audit senior, who has primary responsibility for the field work, and the reviewer should be satisfied at the completion of both the interim and financial statement audits. There may be one overall report covering both interim and financial statement audit phases or two separate reports. An example is given in the CICA Audit Technique Study, *Good Audit Working Papers*, pages 28 and 29. Further examples are illustrated and discussed, for the interim audit, in Chapter 30, and, for the financial statement audit, in Chapter 44.

16.4 Overall error evaluation

One of the final steps in the audit field work is the evaluation of the combined effects of all errors encountered in the audit or indicated as likely or possible on the basis of audit evidence. Individual errors within any given section of the audit should have been assessed on a combined basis during the work in that section. Projections of sample errors (see Chapters 12 and 13) should likewise have been completed on a combined basis for each individual section. Some practitioners may find it desirable to combine the working papers documenting such evaluation for a given section (for example, the statistical evaluation form shown in Figure 13.1) with the verification notes or verification outline (Figure 16.c) for that section. In that way the auditor's conclusions as to errors projected in accounts receivable tests are coordinated clearly with his final conclusions as to the fairness of presentation of the accounts receivable figure on the balance sheet.

But it is not enough to leave the evaluation of errors at the individual section level. Errors must also be evaluated on an overall basis for the audit as a whole. In the United States, recent accounting releases of the SEC have emphasized the danger of evaluating audit results on a piecemeal basis without integrating the conclusions. To gauge the combined effect of various errors it is desirable for the auditor to summarize them in one place in his working papers.

Consolidation of all errors in one section of the working paper files

In the structure for both interim audit and financial statement audit files suggested in 16.3.2 and 16.3.3, a separate section is allocated for error summarization.

During the financial statement audit, monetary errors discovered and projected should be summarized in such a section together with error summaries carried forward from the interim audit file.

The amount, nature and cause of the errors should be noted – together, where appropriate, with their projecting effect. Care should be taken to ensure that error projections from different sections of the audit are not improperly double counted. For example, the same cut-off errors might be projected both from accounts receivable confirmations examined in the accounts receivable section and from cut-off tests performed in the income statement section. The same payroll errors might be projected from transactional tests performed during the interim audit and from labour cost analyses made at the year-end.

16.4.1 Categorization of errors by type

Errors can be categorized according to:

1. the auditor's degree of knowledge of them,
2. their effect on the financial statements,
3. their nature and cause,
4. the degree of precision in their measurement.

Categorization by the auditor's degree of knowledge

According to the auditor's degree of knowledge of them, errors can be categorized as *known errors, most likely errors,* and *possible errors.* These classifications were explained in 11.3.2. Known errors may be encountered in any audit procedure. Most likely errors commonly arise in connection with judgmental or statistical representative *tests* – though they may occasionally arise in other ways, such as from analytical review procedures. Possible errors can normally be quantified only in the case of statistical tests – though analytical review performed using regression analysis may also give rise to a measurement of possible errors.

Each of these three categories of error should be summarized for the audit as a whole. The significance of material totals of known errors, most likely errors, or possible errors was discussed in 13.4.9.

Categorization by the effect on the financial statements

According to their effect on the financial statements, errors can be categorized as:

- income statement classification errors,
- balance sheet classification errors,
- opening equity misstatements,
- closing equity misstatements,
- income misstatements.

Income statement classification errors misstate (or misdescribe) certain figures on the income statement without misstating reported net income itself. A classification error is usually not as serious as a net income misstatement of the same magnitude. Accordingly, a larger total misclassification could usually be tolerated than a net misstatement – although the auditor should of course encourage correction of all errors. The seriousness of an income misclassification of a given magnitude depends on the nature of the figures and ratios it distorts. A misclassification between cost of sales and expense distorts the gross profit percentage while a misclassification between two expense categories does not. Where segmented information is presented, misclassifications among different segments may sometimes be more significant than misclassifications within one segment.

Balance sheet classification errors misstate (or misdescribe) certain figures on the balance sheet without misstating the income statement. Again a classification error is usually not as serious as a net income misstatement of the same magnitude. The seriousness of a balance sheet misclassification of a given magnitude depends on the nature of the figures and ratios it distorts. A misclassification between inventory and fixed assets distorts the amount of working capital. A misclassification between inventory and accounts payable distorts the working capital ratio though not the amount of working capital. A misclassification between cash and accounts receivable distorts neither the amounts of working capital nor the working capital ratio – though it distorts the degree of liquidity.

Because classification errors are usually less significant than income misstatements of the same magnitude, they are best summarized separately from misstatements. A convenient method is to summarize separately classification errors which (a) distort the working capital amount (b) distort only the working capital ratio (c) distort the income statement and (d) distort other financial statement figures.

Opening equity misstatements are misstatements of net worth at the beginning of the period covered by the current set of financial statements. Taken alone, opening misstatements distort current income in the *opposite* direction from the original misstatement. Thus, if opening net worth were *overstated* $50 000, and closing net worth were correctly stated, net income would be *understated* $50 000. Closing equity misstatements are misstatements of net worth at the close of the period. Income misstatements are the combined or net effect of opening and closing equity misstatements. Thus, if net worth were overstated $50 000 at the beginning of the year and overstated $80 000 at the end of the year, net income for the year would be overstated $30 000.

Equity misstatements may be differentiated according to the rate with which they are likely to reverse themselves in future periods. An error in the addition of year-end physical inventory would automatically correct itself in the following year – thus, distorting the following year's income in the opposite direction. An error in setting up a non-depreciable long-term asset, however, would tend to be perpetuated each year unless or until (a) the error was specifically corrected by the client or (b) the long-term asset was disposed of – at which time that year's income would be distorted in the opposite direction. An error in setting up a depreciable asset, on the other hand, would have a partial reversing effect on each future year's income through the misstatement of the annual depreciation charge.

The effect of opening equity misstatements, closing equity misstatements and net income misstatements on the auditor's opinion is discussed in 18.2.2. In summarizing such misstatements, a convenient method is to:

1. summarize the closing equity misstatements discovered during the course of the audit (whether such misstatements represent errors newly introduced in the current year or accumulated equity misstatements carried forward from prior years),
2. note the totals of opening equity misstatements (such totals coming from the error summary in the prior year's audit file),
3. compute net income misstatements as the combined or net effect of the foregoing two categories (making sure that opening equity misstatements are reflected in the summary in the opposite direction to their original effect).

Corrections by the client

Where an accounting population has been verified 100%, the auditor should encourage the client to correct all *known errors* – whether or not the total error is material enough to require qualification if not corrected. Where an accounting population has been subjected to representative testing, the auditor should encourage the client either (a) to provide in the accounts for the *most likely errors* projected from the audit tests[11] or, alternatively, (b) to re-examine the population 100% and correct all discovered errors (in which case the auditor may in some cases have to retest the corrected population).

Some practitioners have suggested instead, in the case of statistical samples, that the auditor should encourage correction only if the population book value (i.e., the zero-error assertion) lies outside the precision interval surrounding the auditor's most-likely-error projection and that the proposed correction should be only up to the nearest limit of that interval. Their argument is that the most-likely-error projection may be inaccurate owing to "sample bounce" and could in some cases lead the auditor to propose adjustments which would over-correct for the actual population error. Corrections to the nearest precision limit minimize the risk of such over-corrections.

In the writer's view, it is preferable, for four reasons, to encourage correction up to the most-likely-error projection and not merely to the nearest precision limit. First, it is true that correction to the nearest limit reduces the risk of over-correction; but it increases the risk of under-correction. Both risks must be controlled within reasonable tolerances. Correction to the most-likely-error projection facilitates a balanced control of both risks. Second, the client's objective and the auditor's desire ought to be to have the final audited financial statements as accurate as possible. Correction to the most-likely-error projection is consistent with that objective. Third, in the case of judgmental tests, precision ranges cannot be computed and the only corrections possible are to the most-likely-error projections. It would seem illogical for the use of statistical sampling to cause the proposal of lesser corrections than would have resulted from similar sample results in a judgmental test. Fourth, correction to the nearest limit will on average leave in the accounts an error equal in amount to the precision gap. If this error reverses itself in the following year, the inconsistency between years will on average be equal to twice the precision gap – an amount which might exceed materiality.

Corrections by the client are often made towards the end of the audit after known and most likely errors have already been summarized by the audit staff. For that reason, it is usually convenient for the error summary of closing equity misstatements to be subdivided into:

- closing equity misstatements before client corrections,
- client corrections of known errors and provisions for most likely errors (to the extent that such corrections and provisions are made),
- net unadjusted closing equity misstatements.

Showing all three figures, rather than just the third, also highlights the relative accuracy or inaccuracy of the underlying accounting system prior to auditor-proposed adjustments. However, in many engagements the auditor may be expected, as an accounting service, to propose routine adjustments to correct the accounts for purposes of financial statement presentation. Such adjustments are normally summarized on a schedule of adjusting entries (see Section Y in the file structure suggested in 16.3.3) and normally need not be repeated on the error summary.

Categorization by cause and nature

The cause and nature of equity and income misstatements may differ widely. According to their cause, errors can be categorized as the results of:

- accidental errors or misunderstandings by client employees, (e.g., an addition error – and such errors may be either random or systematic),
- defalcations or their concealment (e.g., fictitious asset balances concealing misappropriated cash),
- deliberate misrepresentations (e.g., non-disclosure of liabilities in order to overstate income).

According to their nature, errors can be categorized in two ways. First, as discussed in 11.3.1, monetary errors encountered in substantive verification can include any violation of the conditions of:

- existence or occurrence (e.g., a fictitious account receivable),
- completeness (e.g., an account payable not set up),
- ownership or incidence or propriety (e.g., goods held as consignee but incorrectly reflected as inventory),
- valuation or measurement (e.g., inadequate allowance for doubtful accounts),
- presentation (e.g., a prior period adjustment improperly classified as income).

Second, errors can be categorized as:

- clear-cut, arithmetic or mechanical mistakes (e.g., an addition error in physical inventory),
- the use of inappropriate accounting principles (e.g., failure to include overhead components in manufactured inventories),
- errors in the application of appropriate accounting principles (e.g., erroneous classification of permanent differences and timing differences in applying tax allocation principles),

- disagreements as to valuation (e.g., a difference between the auditor's and the client's estimates of required warranty provisions).

The arithmetic accumulation of all the foregoing types of error is bound to be an oversimplification. Nevertheless, it would be equally wrong to ignore their combined effect. An analogy may be drawn to the accumulation of diverse revenue and expense factors to arrive at net earnings per share. Consideration of the bottom line alone misses the complexity of the earning process and the quality of the earnings reflected in the income statement. But to avoid the computation of any bottom income line would be equally undesirable. Thus, while the error summary itself must necessarily group many diverse types of error together, ignoring the combined effect of all errors throughout the audit would be equally undesirable. The auditor, however, should be careful to assess the nature, significance and implications of each error encountered. Where suspicious circumstances are encountered, additional investigation is warranted.

Categorization by the degree of precision

According to the degree of precision in the determination of an individual error[12], that error may be categorized (a) as a clear-cut error or (b) as a disagreement with an accounting estimate. Judgmental accounting estimates pose problems when the auditor is seeking to accumulate errors encountered in the audit as a whole. The auditor's *best estimate* may be that the allowance for doubtful accounts should be about $50 000. The client has chosen $45 000. Should the difference of $5 000 be treated as an "error"? Or should the client's value be accepted as correct because it can be said to be "about $50 000".

In the writer's view, it would be unreasonable in the case of accounting estimates to treat moderate deviations from the auditor's best estimate as "errors" – thereby restricting the total of other errors which could be tolerated and, according to the approach suggested in this book, restricting tolerable "possible errors" and thus increasing planned sample extents. Rather, it would seem more logical for the auditor to determine a *zone of reasonableness* within which he would be prepared to accept any client estimate as correct. For example, he might conclude that the allowance for doubtful accounts should be somewhere between $40 000 and $60 000. In that case, the range of $40 000 to $60 000 would represent the auditor's view of a *zone of reasonableness*. The client's estimate of $45 000, falling within that zone, would be considered as correct. The $5 000 difference between the client's estimate and the auditor's *best estimate* of $50 000 would *not* be considered as a known error. However, had the client's estimate been

$30 000, the auditor would have to conclude that it was lower than the lowest value ($40 000) he felt could be reasonably justified. In that case, the distance ($10 000) between the client's estimate and the nearest limit of the zone of reasonableness should be treated as a known error and entered on the error summary.[13]

Admittedly, the determination of a zone of reasonableness can only be subjective and its precise limits (and therefore errors measured relative to those limits) are, to a minor extent, arbitrary. Nonetheless, a line must be drawn somewhere and the concept of a zone of reasonableness is submitted as a sensible compromise between (a) the rigidity of insisting on the auditor's own best estimate in difficult judgmental areas and (b) the alternative of accepting any client estimate however unreasonable.

Once a client estimate has been accepted, however, the auditor should ensure that it is made in a consistent manner from year to year. Large swings from year to year, even though within the zone of reasonableness, could lead to material misstatements of income (see 18.2.1).

Errors which depend on management decisions

Certain types of condition represent errors if management chooses to search for and correct them but represent business expenses or revenues if management does not so choose. Examples are unbilled shipments, pilferage, and duplicate billings. These situations, and the auditor's approach to them, are discussed in 12.5.1. For example, if management decides (and *only* if it decides) to write off accidentally unbilled shipments as a business expense, such conditions do not represent misstatements of the year's income. Thus, while the auditor should (a) consider the possibility of such conditions in planning his work, (b) report such conditions, when encountered, to the client, and (c) document management's decision to treat the conditions as a business expense, he need not include these expenses as income misstatements in his overall error summarization. He must, of course, consider whether any such expenses, if material, have been properly classified on the income statement.

16.4.2 Summarization of errors

Overall summarization

A possible method of summarizing errors for the audit as a whole is illustrated by the extract from a *total error evaluation report* shown in Figure 16.f. In that figure, known errors, most likely errors, and client corrections are shown separately. Opening

Extract from a Total Error Evaluation Report

Part B—Summary of Known and Most Likely Errors Affecting Pre-Tax Income and Closing Equity

Description of Errors	File Ref.	(1) Net Known Errors Overstatement (Understatement)	(2) Net Most Likely Errors	(3) Amount of Client Correction
1. Errors identified during the audit which affect pre-tax income and closing equity a) in statistical sampling applications (from the other summaries—see Figure 16.g) b) in all other areas.	III	1 193	19 604	10 000
Fixed assets (should be expense)	H	6 000	6 000	∅
Inventory re: —goods shipped not billed	D	740	6 800	740
2. Total net known and most likely equity errors in closing balance sheet before client corrections (total of all above items).		7 933	32 404	10 740
3. Effect of client corrections (and enter amount in *both* columns (1) and (2)).		10 740	10 740	
4. Net unadjusted equity errors in closing balance sheet.		(2 807)	21 664	
5. Effect of equity errors in opening balance sheet (last year's item 4 but in opposite direction).		2 600	21 000	
6. Net unadjusted errors in reported pre-tax net income of current year.		(207)	42 664	

Figure 16.f

Example of a Combined Statistical Sample Evaluation Summary

(To be used for preparation for a combined evaluation of all
statistical samples drawn throughout the balance sheet audit)

Client _ABC Limited_   **Year-end** _December 31, 1976_

| | | | Errors misstating pre-tax income [overstating (O/S) – understating (U/S)] | | | | | | |
| Applications (see Figure 13.k) | File ref. | Net known errors (found in samples) | Most likely errors [projected from samples] | | | Amount of client correction or provision (if any) | Precision — Basic precision in both directions (BP) | Precision-gap-widenings | |
			gross O/S	gross (U/S)	net O/S (U/S)			overstating	(understating)
		A	B	C	D	E	F	G	H
Accounts receivable	C	875	7 140	(∅)	7 140	5 000	± 35 000	3 215	(∅)
Inventory	D	318	20 824	(8 360)	12 464	5 000	± 35 000	10 371	(3 395)
			( )				±		( )
			( )				±		( )
			( )				±		( )
			( )				±		( )
			( )				±		( )
			( )				±		( )
			( )				±		( )
Greatest BP last year							± 32 000		
Net totals (Note 1)		1 193	27 964	(8 360)	19 604	10 000		13 586	(3 395)
Greatest BP in column F (enter in F, G, and H)							± 35 000	35 000	(35 000)
Total Precision (note 1)								48 586	(38 995)
		A			D	E		G	H

Note: 1. Carry totals in Columns A, D, and E to Part B and totals
in Columns G and H to Part C of Total Error Evaluation Report.

Figure 16.g

Extract from a Total Error Evaluation Report
Part C — Calculation of Upper Error Limits (statistical sampling only)

	(1) Largest overstatement (Least understatement)	(2) (Largest understatement) Least overstatement
(a) Net unadjusted errors in reported pre-tax income of current year (enter Part B, item 6, column (2) in both columns)	42 664	42 664
(b) Total precision in statistical sampling applications in both directions (from other summaries — see Figure 16.g) *	48 586	(38 995)
(c) Net upper error limits in reported pre-tax income of the current year (a ± b)	91 250	3 669

*Total precision is basic precision plus precision gap widenings in both directions.

Figure 16.h

equity misstatements, closing equity misstatements, and net income misstatements are also shown separately. Another part of the form would compare both closing equity misstatements and net income misstatements to materiality. The concept of establishing a specific materiality limit for the audit engagement was discussed in 6.6.2 and 15.4.2. When the final summarization of errors is being completed, the factors influencing the decision as to materiality should be reviewed again in case additional information obtained during the audit indicates the need to modify the earlier planning decision. Another part of the form would also summarize and evaluate classification errors.

Summarization of statistical sampling projections

In Figure 16.f, projected errors from statistical sampling applications are shown separately from other errors. The reason is that statistical sampling projections will likely have been already summarized on a separate sample evaluation report (see Figure 13.l). Where a number of different sampling applications are involved, it may be convenient to prepare a combined summary of such applications first and enter only the combined totals on the total error evaluation report. An example of a combined statistical sample evaluation summary, using the method of combination discussed in 13.3.4, is shown in Figure 16.g.

Where statistical sampling has been employed in the audit, it is desirable to summarize for the audit as a whole not only known and most likely errors, as shown in Figure 16.f, but also *possible errors*. Another part of the total error evaluation report can make this computation – see Figure 16.h.

Summarization of accounting estimates

It is desirable to prepare a schedule in comparative form summarizing accounting estimates and the auditor's evaluation of them. Such a schedule is desirable because of the sensitivity of reported income to the bases used in making accounting estimates and the need to highlight this sensitivity for the reviewers. Because of the potential for income misstatements due to inconsistent swings within the zone of reasonableness from year to year, it is useful for the schedule to show not only outright disagreements with the client's estimate (departures from the zone of reasonableness) but also the auditor's best estimates as well. Thus, the schedule should show for each important estimate, such as allowances for doubtful accounts, obsolescence, and warranties, (a) the client's estimate (book value), (b) the auditor's best estimate, (c) a zone of reasonableness, and (d) where the book value falls outside the zone of reasonableness, the estimated error effect on net income (distance from the book value to the nearest boundary of the zone of reasonableness).

Effect of the error summarization on the auditor's opinion

The working papers illustrated in the foregoing figures are offered as examples only. Each practitioner or firm may have a different preference as to the format of error summaries. The important point is that some overall summarization of errors be completed for the audit as a whole. It is the overall evaluation of errors, and not just their piecemeal evaluation in individual sections, which must affect the auditor's final decision as to whether a reservation of opinion must be expressed in his report. The effects of errors on the auditor's report, together with the different types of report reservation to which different types of error may give rise, are discussed in 18.2.1, 18.2.2, and 18.3.1.

16.5 Review

Adequate review was identified in 15.1 as the final element of effective engagement management. Reference was made to both *engagement reviews* and *quality control reviews*. This section deals with the former. Engagement reviews can be divided into at least two levels: (a) the review conducted by the audit senior of his own work and that of any assistants, and (b) the subsequent review conducted by a higher-level reviewer. In many engagements, each of these two levels may be further subdivided. Section seniors may review the work of assistants in a particular section, such as inventory. The audit senior may then review the work of the section seniors. The higher-level reviews may be divided among supervisor, manager, and partner levels, depending on firm structure.

The audit senior's review is an essential component of his supervision of the field work. In addition, it ensures that information obtained in one section of the audit is taken into account in other sections on which it has a bearing. Finally, it is a prerequisite to the meaningful summarization of results for higher-level reviewers. The audit senior's review was discussed briefly in 15.5.5. Both the audit senior's review and higher-level reviews are described in more detail in 30.1 and 30.4 (for interim audits) and in 44.1 and 44.5 (for financial statement audits).

The importance of review

Every audit involves a large number of (a) detailed procedures requiring skill and care and (b) detailed and general decisions requiring judgment. Review is important to minimize the risk that necessary procedures have been omitted or improperly performed and that judgmental decisions have been poorly made. Omissions or mistaken judgments may be detected by a reviewer who has more years of experience than the audit team in the field and who can also stand back from the details of the field work and see whether the major audit conclusions make sense.

The primary objectives of review are to ensure:

1. that the field work has provided a proper support for the audit report on the financial statements and that no necessary procedures have been omitted nor important conclusions overlooked,

2. that the work has been conducted and the report prepared in accordance with (a) generally accepted auditing standards, (b) any applicable statutory, regulatory or contractual requirements and (c) the policies of the individual practitioner or firm,

3. that the working papers have been prepared in accordance with the policies of the individual practitioner or firm and contain adequate documentation (a) to substantiate the work performed and the information obtained, (b) to support the conclusions reached, and (c) to evidence adherence to generally accepted auditing standards,

4. that important matters have been or are being reported to the client, including any significant defalcations, irregularities or suspicious circumstances encountered and any recommendations on internal control, systems efficiency, accounting methods, or financial and tax planning (usually in an internal control/management letter),

5. in the case of the audit senior's review, that assistants are performing their work properly during the course of the audit, taking into account relevant information from other sections of the audit, and the results are summarized in a meaningful manner for higher-level reviewers.

Secondary objectives of review are:

1. to assess the performance and progress of individual members of the audit team,
2. to update the reviewer's knowledge of the client's operations.

In conducting his review, the reviewer should be alert for (a) faulty conclusions, (b) incomplete verification, and (c) inadequate documentation. The first is perhaps the shortcoming most frequently encountered, so it should be given special emphasis.

The auditor charged with final responsibility for the engagement must exercise a seasoned judgment in the varying degrees of his supervision and review of the work done and judgment exercised by his subordinates.[14]

The work of the AICPA Commission on Auditors' Responsibilities indicated that in audit engagements which have resulted in litigation in the United States,

469

the underlying problems were almost always documented in some fashion in the working papers – though not necessarily with the appropriate conclusions being drawn. The reviewer should therefore take care to see that individual and overall audit conclusions are reasonable, that all questions raised by the audit staff have been answered, and that any doubts have been satisfactorily resolved.

Documentation of review

Because review is an essential element of engagement management and is required in order to meet the first field work standard, it is prudent to ensure that the review performed is itself documented in the working papers. Review notes are commonly arranged so that space is provided for answers by the audit senior or his assistants. The audit senior should ensure that, before the audit report is released, all review questions have been satisfactorily answered and any necessary changes or additions made to the working papers, the auditor's report, and/or financial statements. The review notes and answers should be retained in the file both as documentation and as a guide to planning and audit performance in the following year. The review process is often documented as well by the use of some form of review checklist.

Factors influencing review

The nature of, timing of, and participants in the review process will vary from engagement to engagement. The determining factors include the competence of the audit team, the size of the audit team, the client circumstances, the nature and scope of the audit plan, and the policies and practices of the individual practitioner or firm.

1. Competence of the audit team.
The intensity of the review procedures should properly vary inversely with the competence of the person or persons performing the work and the competence and experience of any prior levels of review. The audit senior may review all or part of the verification sections two, three or more times where the work is being performed by a new and untrained audit assistant. A partner in an accounting firm will make a more searching review where the files have previously been reviewed by a new audit manager than he would where an experienced audit manager was involved.

2. The size of the audit team.
The greater the number of persons participating in the audit, the less informed each one may be as to the total picture and the greater is the danger that the relevance of the work in one section to the conclusions in another may be overlooked. The audit senior should ensure the completed sections are reviewed on a timely basis so that relevant information may be transmitted to other persons on the audit team.

3. Client circumstances.
Where particular financial statement figures are difficult to verify or subject to greater than normal inherent risk and where particular internal control systems are difficult to evaluate, the audit senior, supervisor, manager and partner will want to give more attention to those sections of the file.

4. The nature and scope of the audit plan.
As explained in 15.3.1, thorough planning simplifies later review (a) by preventing most of the deficiencies such a review would otherwise have to detect and (b) by reducing the need for an eleventh-hour evaluation of detailed audit programs. Where a detailed audit plan is used and has been carefully reviewed by the reviewer in advance, final review of the completed work can usually be restricted to determining that agreed-upon procedures were in fact performed and that the results obtained have been properly interpreted. Even where a detailed audit plan has not been reviewed in advance by the higher-level reviewer, the discipline imposed by such a plan usually permits the subsequent review to be completed more quickly.

5. Policies and practices of the individual practitioner or firm.
In the final analysis, the policies and practices of the individual practitioner or firm are likely to have the greatest impact on the timing, scope and intensity of review procedures. A sole practitioner without assistants has only his own work to review. Nonetheless, it is important that, after completion of the field work, he stand back and critically assess the work performed and the conclusions reached. A practitioner with one or two assistants must normally review the work performed in reasonable detail. Where larger audit teams are involved, a variety of review patterns are possible.

Detailed review, summary review, and consultative review

Most public accounting firms have established well-defined review policies. Typically, the policies are designed to ensure that field work performed by one person is reviewed by at least two higher levels of experience. Thus, verification work performed by an assistant might be reviewed in detail by the audit senior and in broader terms by a manager or supervisor. The summarizing and reporting of results by the audit senior might be reviewed in detail by the manager or supervisor and in broader terms by the partner in charge.

As a result, review subsequent to the audit senior's review may sometimes be divided into several levels such as (a) detailed review, (b) summary review and (c) consultative review – though the terminology will vary from firm to firm. *Detailed review* would involve a reasonably detailed check of working papers prepared by the audit senior and a less detailed check of assistants' papers already reviewed by the audit senior. In addition, the detailed reviewer would usually discuss his queries with the audit senior since oral cross-examination may often reveal or resolve problems which a reading of working papers alone would not. *Summary review* would usually concentrate primarily on the internal reporting and control schedules (questionnaires, highlights memoranda, error summaries, etc.) and other key schedules (such as section lead sheets, draft financial statements, the draft internal control/management letter). The summary reviewer would usually not refer to detailed supporting schedules except in resolving contentious points. On very large engagements, it may be desirable to have a level of *consultative review* which would involve not a review of the working papers but rather a review of any draft reports to the client and discussion of important issues raised by the summary reviewer.

Where the foregoing different levels of review are appropriate, responsibility for detailed review might be assigned to a manager or supervisor, responsibility for summary review to the partner in charge of that engagement, and consultative review to a senior partner. For a very small engagements, summary review might be delegated to the manager or supervisor level while for very large engagements some detailed review procedures might be assigned to the partner level.

In-charge review, cold review and specialist review

A common arrangement is for the reviewers (partners and managers) to be the persons having direct responsibility for the client. "In-charge reviewers" are knowledgeable about the client's business and problems, have participated in the audit planning and are aware of the competence of the audit team, particularly the audit senior. This close knowledge is a definite aid in the review process.

On the other hand, there is always a danger that a reviewer will allow his intimate knowledge of the client's operations to substitute for adequate verification work. There is also the danger that reliance on the competence of a particular member of the audit team will lead the reviewer to excuse sloppy documentation. To guard against these dangers, some accounting firms have introduced a "cold" review technique. A "cold" review is a thorough review of the working paper files conducted by an experienced reviewer having little or no previous knowledge of the client's business or of the audit plan. Such a review can provide a more objective assessment as to whether the working papers, in themselves, provide adequate support for the report being given. However, there is always the danger that a cold review may overlook problems or suspicious circumstances which would have been obvious to a reviewer familiar with the client's operations. It may also be more costly to conduct.

In an attempt to obtain the best of both worlds, some review procedures call for a mixture of in-charge review and cold review. For example, some firms require manager and partner review together with pre-release review by specialists for specified areas such as taxes, computers, sampling, statement presentation and/or audit report wording. The pre-release specialist review may apply to all engagements or, more commonly, only to certain categories of engagement. Of course, pre-release review of statement presentation and audit report wording focuses more directly on possible disclosure problems than on audit deficiencies – though the latter may sometimes be revealed by the former.

Timing of review

A basic division in the timing of review is between the review of planning decisions and the review of field work. In addition, in an interim audit it is often convenient to divide the review of field work into two stages – *preliminary review* and *final review*. Preliminary review would take place after systems had been evaluated and the compliance procedures and weakness investigation planned. Final review would take place after the compliance procedures and weakness investigation had been performed. While the audit senior's review would be commonly divided into these two stages, the need for a similar division of the higher-level reviews might depend on whether the engagement was an initial or repeat engagement and on whether major systems changes had occurred since the prior year. In a financial statement audit, review more commonly takes place in one stage after completion of all the field work. However, where very tight deadlines must be set, some preliminary review stage may be required.

16.6 Reference material

CICA Audit Technique Study, *Good Audit Working Papers* (1970).

AICPA Statement on Auditing Standards No. 1, Sec. 338.

16.7 Questions and problems

Review and discussion

1. How would you characterize the difference in the contents of working paper and general files?
2. List five purposes of working paper files. Indicate the relevance of these purposes to an auditor's defence against a charge of professional misconduct.
3. In summary, how do working papers contribute to effective engagement management?
4. Why is it necessary to document compliance with the second and third field work standards?
5. Give three examples of current working paper schedules that provide a source of information for the provision of ancillary services.
6. Why should working paper schedules indicate the name of the client, the fiscal period covered, the date the work was performed, and the name of the auditor who performed the work?
7. Why do many public accounting firms use a standard working paper index?
8. Under what circumstances should an auditor disclose the contents or portions of contents of working paper files to:
   a) other auditors,
   b) the client,
   c) professional bodies,
   d) income tax authorities?
9. Describe the contents of non-working paper files normally maintained for each client by public practitioners.
10. Give five examples of contents typical of a permanent file and describe the relevance of each to the verification process.
11. Describe the various methods of documenting planning decisions.
12. What is the purpose of a working paper schedule that combines information and verification? Give two examples of such schedules.
13. Why do auditors make extensive use of carry-forward schedules? Give three examples of typical carry-forward schedules.
14. Distinguish between evaluation and verification schedules.
15. Contrast the purposes of internal and external reporting schedules.
16. Refer to the suggested analytical audit file structure in 16.3.2. Comment on the reasons for the suggested final disposition of each section.
17. What are the principal points that should be considered in designing the working paper index for a financial statement audit file?
18. When is it desirable to use worksheets to document the client's general ledger trial balance, audit adjustments, and final figures?
19. What purpose does the highlights memorandum serve?
20. Why should errors, including misclassification errors, encountered in an audit be evaluated on an overall basis?
21. Distinguish, giving examples, between the categorization of errors according to the auditor's degree of knowledge of them and the precision of their measurement.
22. Describe the inter-relationship of misstatements in closing asset and liability balances, opening equity misstatements, and income misstatements.
23. Sometimes an error may be either an income statement misclassification or an income misstatement. Give two examples of such errors and describe the factors that will determine which type of error it is.
24. Why is it desirable that the schedules summarizing accounting estimates and the auditor's evaluation thereof be prepared in comparative form?
25. Why is review of audit work important:
   a) for a sole practitioner,
   b) for the audit partner of a firm?
26. Why must the review process be fully documented?
27. Describe the factors that will influence the nature of the review process for the working papers documenting work performed by a junior staff member on a small client.
28. Distinguish between an "in-charge" and a "cold" review.

Problems

1. Three new chartered accountants, Joe, Sam and Ed, were discussing the evaluation of most likely errors in an audit. Joe stated: "When I issue my opinion, that means I am satisfied that the financial statements present fairly. It follows that the carry-forward of most likely errors to next year's overall evaluation is an admission that I was wrong. Therefore, I do not carry-forward errors to next year's evaluation."

   Sam responded: "I agree in general. However, you both know that errors in balance sheet accounts can often accumulate over a period of years to several times materiality. Therefore, when I find a large error in a balance sheet account at one year-end, I look for a compensating amount at the beginning of the year to net it off to a less than material amount." Ed commented: "Sam, I think that is like having your cake and eating it too." Describe in detail the points that Ed should make in criticising the positions of Joe and Sam.

2. Bob Jones, a new CA, has been asked by his audit partner to prepare a presentation for a staff meeting to discuss working papers. In his presentation, Bob is to address himself to the following points:

   a) What factors should affect the chartered accountant's judgment of the type and content of working papers on any particular engagement?

   b) To comply with generally accepted auditing standards, a chartered accountant includes certain evidence in his working papers: for example, evidence that the engagement was planned and that the work of assistants was supervised and reviewd. What other evidence should a CA include in audit working papers to comply with generally accepted auditing standards?

   c) How can the staff make the most effective use of the preceding year's working paper files on a recurring examination?

   d) What general principles should the staff follow in preparing and updating permanent files?

   Describe in detail the points that Bob should make in his presentation.

3. (CICA adapted). After completing certain verification work during the course of an audit examination, audit assistants prepare notes in their working papers which are reviewed by the audit senior.

   a) Describe the types of matters which should be included in such notes.

   b) Describe the main characteristics of well-prepared audit notes.

4. An audit policy directive of a firm of public accountants states that all manager and partner review queries should be cleared before the audit report is issued. Review queries are listed in the left-hand column of two column schedules. Typical kinds of review queries include:

   a) specific enquiries as to whether or not verification was performed,

   b) a request for additional information or explanation,

   c) instructions to correct certain amounts in the general ledger and financial statements,

   d) comments as to the revision of procedures in subsequent years.

   Describe in detail how an audit senior should deal with each of these kinds of review queries.

5. George Brown, CA, is preparing a combined evaluation summary for the results of two dollar-unit statistical samples (accounts receivable and accounts payable at December 31) as part of the audit of XYZ Ltd. The method of combination described in 13.3.4 is to be used. The error results are as follows:

   a) The gross most likely overstatement of accounts receivable is $9 251, with precision gap widenings in the same direction of $6 840 ($3 210 in the opposite direction).

   b) The gross most likely understatement of accounts receivable is $1 210, with precision gap widenings in the same direction of $807 ($107 in the opposite direction).

   c) The gross most likely understatement of accounts payable is $12 342, with precision gap widenings in the same direction of $9 359 ($2 411 in the opposite direction).

   d) The gross most likely overstatement of accounts payable is $3 240, with precision gap widenings in the same direction of $250 ($37 in the opposite direction).

   e) Basic precision for both applications is $50 000.

   From the above information:

   a) Compute the net most likely error in pre-tax income.

   b) Compute the upper error limits of overstatement and understatement in pre-tax income.

6. Can Can Cameras sells photographic supplies, cameras and film to retail camera shops. During the course of the 1976 audit, Frank Webster, CA, was required to evaluate the following accounting estimates made by Can Can's accountant, Sam Phillips:

   a) Inventory obsolescence
      Phillips provided for obsolesence based on future sales estimates provided by the sales department.

      From these estimates for supplies and camera equipment, Phillips established an allowance of $15 000. Frank Webster's verification indicates a range from $14 000 to $20 000 with a best guess of $18 000.

   b) Allowance for film
      The allowance for film, which has an expiry date, is based on an analysis of the film on hand at the year-end. The film is aged by expiry date and any film with less than 4 months

473

shelf life is fully provided for. The ageing for 1976 is as follows:

Months to expiry	Cost
12 months +	$20 000
0-11 months	22 000
6-9 months	28 000
5 months	10 000
4 months	9 000
3 months	4 000
2 months	2 500
1 month	2 000
	$97 500

The company has had to destroy the following film in the last two years:

1975

on hand at year-end		subsequently destroyed	
Months to expiry	cost		
4 months	$6 000	$2 000	33%
3 months	$4 000	$3 000	75%
2 months	$2 000	$2 000	100%
1 month	$1 000	$1 000	100%

1974

on hand at year-end		subsequently destroyed	
Months to expiry	cost		
4 months	$8 000	$2 000	25%
3 months	$3 500	$2 500	71%
2 months	$3 000	$3 000	100%
1 month	$1 500	$1 500	100%

c) Warranties

The company provides for warranties on supplies and cameras as a percentage of sales. This estimate has proven to be reasonable in the past; however, there is an increasing amount of warranty work, particularly for one product. The company recognized the increased warranty experience, increased its percentage allowance and provided $24 000. Frank Webster estimated the range to be from $28 000 to $58 000 and his best guess is $38 000.

Required:

a) From the data given, determine the best estimate and related zone of reasonableness for the film allowance.

b) Prepare a working paper to compare graphically, for each estimate, Sam Phillips' estimate with Frank Webster's best guess and zone of reasonableness.

c) What adjustments would you recommend to the client and why?

7. Art Walsh, CA, discovered the following situations during the 1974 audit of the Everlast Watch Company, a manufacturer of low-priced wristwatches:

a) Accounts receivable

Accounts receivable were circularized using statistical selection techniques and the error results (overstatements of income) were:

Known overstatements	$ 3 000
Most likely overstatement (net)	$14 000
Upper error limit of overstatements	$38 000
Upper error limit of understatements	$(11 000)

b) Inventory pricing

Inventory pricing was checked using a judgmental representative sample, neutral selection; 50 items out of 1 200 were tested, representing $6 000 of a total of $160 000. The total errors found were an over pricing of inventory of $300.

"Key" and "high value" items (in addition to the $160 000) worth $22 000 were checked and found to be under-priced by $1 200.

c) Fixed assets

The audit of fixed asset additions showed a missclassification in the current year of 3 delivery trucks worth $30 000 as office equipment. The trucks are depreciated over 3 years, straight line, and the office equipment over 10 years, straight line.

d) Invoicing

In the review of the sales'/receivables'/receipts' system, Frank Webster discovered that there were inadequate pricing checks on customer invoices. A weakness investigation performed using statistical sampling projected the following understatement of income:

Known understatement	$ 1 000
Most likely understatement	$ 6 000
Upper error limit of understatement	$30 000

Management has agreed to follow up and recover the $1 000 of known error in a few weeks but indicates that the cost of searching for other errors is prohibitive. They have also indicated that they will look into correcting the weakness. No recoveries have been booked.

e) Other errors

Accrued interest (payables) was overstated by $3 000. Prepaid expenses were overstated by $2 000 known and $3 000 most likely.

f) Previous year's errors

In 1975 the following errors appeared on the

Total Error Evaluation report:

		o/s (u/s) of pre-tax income	
		Known	**Most likely**
i)	accrued interest	$ 5 000	$ 5 000
ii)	inventory	$(4 000)	$(8 000)
iii)	prepaids	$(3 000)	$(3 000)

1) Prepare a summary of known and most likely errors affecting (a) closing equity and (b) pre-tax income, using as a guide Figure 16.f.

2) Calculate the upper error limits of overstatement and understatement for Everlast (assume that no statistical sampling was performed in 1975).

3) What action should Art Walsh take if the client refused to correct the errors and materiality was (a) 25 000, (b) 35 000, (c) 50 000?

Reporting Objectives and the Short-Form Audit Report

The auditing process consists of gathering and evaluating audit evidence (the investigative phase) and communicating the results to interested users (the reporting phase). Previous chapters have described the field work components of the former. This chapter and the next two chapters describe the reporting phase. Specifically, this chapter covers reporting objectives and report wording where reservations are not required. Chapter 18 covers report reservations, international reporting and post-audit information. Chapter 19 covers prospectuses, management letters and special purpose reports.

17.1 Objectives of audit reporting

In the broadest sense, audit reporting may be said to have the following objective:

> To report clearly and objectively the results of the auditor's gathering and evaluation of audit evidence.

Varieties of audit reporting

This general objective covers a variety of reports. Commonly one thinks of a written report – such as the normal annual audit report on an organization's financial statements. But some of the auditor's reporting may be oral, such as discussions with management or responses to shareholder queries as to audit matters at the annual meeting. Commonly one thinks of a statutory report to shareholders. But some of the auditor's reporting may be non-statutory and may be directed to the directors, the audit committee, management, or specified third parties. Commonly one thinks of the expression of an audit opinion. But sometimes the auditor must deny an opinion (when insufficient evidence is available) and at other times he may merely report facts (such as his reporting to management of specific errors encountered during his work). Commonly one thinks of a report on financial statements. But some of the auditor's reporting may relate to internal control, systems, income taxes, financial planning, purchase investigations, compliance with trust deed provisions, etc. In all these cases, however, the qualities of clarity and objectivity are important, if the communication is to be effective. And in all cases the content of the report must be rationally related to the extent and quality of the audit evidence examined, if the communication is to be reliable.

The various types of audit reporting are summarized in Figure 17.a. It can be argued that some of these communications are not, strictly speaking, audit reports. The definition of auditing quoted in 1.2.2 refers to ascertaining the degree of correspondence between certain assertions and established criteria. Reports on financial statements and many special purpose reports fit such a criterion. Recommendations on internal control, comments on systems, and discussion of tax planning do not. The four reporting standards apply only to expressions of opinion on financial statements. Standards for other communications have not been defined – except to the extent that they can be inferred from the Rules of Professional Conduct (professional services must be performed with integrity and due care). Nonetheless, most of the foregoing types of communication are likely to be used regularly by most auditors and in a broad sense they all form a part of the auditor's reporting function.

Objectives of audit reports on financial statements

The specific objectives of audit reports on financial statements are embodied in the four reporting standards:

1. The scope of the auditor's examination should be referred to in the report.
2. The report should contain either an expression of opinion on the financial statements or an assertion that an opinion cannot be expressed. In the latter case, the reasons therefor should be stated.
3. Where an opinion is expressed, it should indicate whether the financial statements present fairly the financial position, results of operations and changes in financial position in accordance with an appropriate disclosed basis of accounting, which except in special circumstances should be generally accepted accounting principles. The report should provide adequate explanation with respect to any reservation contained in such opinion.
4. Where an opinion is expressed, the report should also indicate whether the application of the disclosed basis of accounting is consistent with that of the preceding period. Where the basis or its application is not consistent, the report should provide adequate explanation of the nature and effect of the inconsistency.

A brief comparison of these reporting standards with the corresponding U.S. standards of reporting was made in 4.4.5. The application of these standards to the format and wording of the auditor's report is discussed in the following sections and in Chapters 18 and 19.

Types of Audit Reporting

Type of communication	Recipient	Where discussed
Short-form reports on annual financial statements – statutory or non-statutory – company, partnership, proprietor, association, government body, etc.	Shareholders (or partners, proprietor, etc.)	17 (clear opinions) 18 (reservations)
Prospectuses – report on financial statements – comfort letters – letters of consent	Directors, securities commissions, etc.	19.1, 19.2
Special purpose reports – parent company unconsolidated statements – cash basis statements – statements in accordance with buy/sell agreements or trust deeds – compliance with trust deeds, etc. – published reports on internal control – purchase investigations – other investigations	Management, directors, trustees under trust deeds, etc.	19.3
Long-form reports	Directors (or management)	19.3.5
Management letters – internal control/ management letter – audit follow-up letter	Management, and sometimes the audit committee (or directors)	19.3.7, 30.2
Reporting of subsequent discovery of errors	Directors, shareholders	18.7
Statement upon change of auditors	Shareholders (in the United States the SEC)	4.1.7
Oral reporting of points raised by the auditor	Management, audit committee, sometimes the directors (rarely, the shareholders)	4.1.6 (general) 4.5 (audit committee) 4.2.3 (irregularities)
Responses to questions directed to the auditor	Management, audit committee, directors, shareholders	9.1.3 (interim objectives) 32.4.13 (questionable payments) 44.5.3 (year-end discussion)

Figure 17.a

17.2 The auditor's standard report

The expression *short-form audit report* has long been used colloquially to refer to a brief report on a set of financial statements. The short-form report may or may not contain certain reservations and/or certain accompanying explanations. It does not, however, contain a lengthy analysis and commentary of the financial statements; reports which do contain such an analysis or commentary are usually referred to, not surprisingly, as long-form reports.

The expression *auditor's standard report* has been adopted to refer to a short-form report which is expressed without reservation or additional explanation and which relates to financial statements prepared in accordance with generally accepted accounting principles.[1]

17.2.1 Format of the report

The normal format of a short-form report consists of up to four paragraphs:

1. a scope paragraph,
2. a reservation paragraph (if required – see 18.1.3),
3. an opinion paragraph,
4. an explanatory paragraph (if required – see 17.5.10).

By definition the auditor's standard report requires neither reservation nor explanatory paragraph and so consists of simply a scope paragraph and an opinion paragraph.

> The first ("scope") paragraph identifies the financial statements reported on and contains a reference to the scope and nature of the auditor's examination. The second ("opinion") paragraph expresses the auditor's opinion resulting from that examination. [CICA Handbook][2]

A similar two paragraph format is recommended in the United States. In the United Kingdom, in contrast, the normal report consists simply of an opinion paragraph.

While most audit reports issued in Canada and the United States follow the scope/opinion format, occasionally a reversal of paragraph order is seen. Other proposals for modifying the standard report format are discussed in 17.4.

17.2.2 Standard wording

Where neither reservation nor additional explanation is required, it is desirable that a standard wording be used for the auditor's report. Such usage helps the reader to identify reservations, important explanations, and unusual circumstances when they occur. The standard wording suggested by the CICA[3] for use in Canada is:

Auditor's Report

To the Shareholders of . . .

I have examined the balance sheet of . . . as at . . . , 19.. and the statements of income, retained earnings and changes in financial position for the year then ended. My examination was made in accordance with generally accepted auditing standards, and accordingly included such tests and other procedures as I considered necessary in the circumstances.

In my opinion, these financial statements present fairly the financial position of the company as at. . . ., 19.. and the results of its operations and the changes in its financial position for the year then ended in accordance with generally accepted accounting principles applied on a basis consistent with that of the preceding year.

| City | (signed) . . . . |
| Date | Chartered Accountant |

Where a company has subsidiaries, generally accepted accounting principles require in most circumstances that its financial statements be presented in consolidated form. Where the auditor is reporting on consolidated financial statements, it is desirable that the description of the financial statements in the auditor's report include the word "consolidated". The standard wording suggested by the CICA for such cases is identical to that quoted above except that the word "consolidated" is inserted before "balance sheet", before "statements of income", and before "financial statements".[4] Prior to 1976 it was normal to refer to the consolidated balance sheet of the company *and its subsidiaries,* to the financial position of the *companies,* and to *their* operations and *their* funds. In suggesting that such a practice is no longer necessary, the CICA Handbook points out that under generally accepted accounting principles the consolidated statements are those of a single economic entity rather than a group of companies.[5]

Title of the report and addressee

The independent status of the auditor's report is most clearly indicated if the report is printed on a separate sheet of the auditor's letterhead and attached to the financial statements to which it relates. Reproduction at the foot of one of the financial statements (usually the balance sheet), while less desirable, is an acceptable practice. The report should be addressed to the persons by whom the auditor is appointed – normally the shareholders. The report on a subsidiary company should be addressed to the shareholders if it is to be laid before a shareholders' meeting – even when the only shareholder is the parent company. Special purpose reports, including parent company unconsolidated statements, would usually be addressed to the directors. For reports on a not-for-profit organization, such wording as "To the members of . . . ", "To the Trustees of . . . ", or "To the Board of Governors . . . " would be appropriate. Care should be taken to ensure that the exact name of the client is shown (correct as to punctuation, abbreviations, etc.). Under the Canada and Quebec Corporations Acts it is permissible to use either the English or French version of a company's name or a combined version.

Signature, designation and address

The auditor's signature (or, in the case of an accounting firm, the firm signature) acknowledges responsibility for the work referred to and the opinion expressed in the report. Where the author is a chartered accountant (or, in the case of an accounting firm, where all its partners are chartered accountants), the designation Chartered Accountant(s) will be used (see 3.3.4). The address is simply the city in Canada where the auditor's office is located (or, in the case of an accounting firm, the office responsible for the final review and issue of the audit report).

Date of the audit report

The audit report should ordinarily be dated at the completion of the audit field work. To avoid possible ambiguity with respect to events occurring on the audit report date itself, a prudent practice is to have the client letter of representation, incorporating representations as to subsequent events, dated and signed one day later.

Where the auditor is issuing reports both on consolidated statements and on various unconsolidated components (including the unconsolidated parent company statements), he will wish, if possible, to use the same date on all reports. If, however, it is necessary for the date of his report on the consolidated statements to be significantly later than that on the principal components, he should ensure that the letters of representation and subsequent events reviews for such components are appropriately updated. Sometimes, the audit completion and report dates for components will be later than the date on the consolidated financial statements. In these circumstances, it is important that the subsequent events reviews and letters of representation are initially completed at the time of reporting on the consolidated statements and subsequently updated when the auditor reports on the components. It is also important that file reviews for (a) the components and (b) the consolidation both be adequately documented.

If some time elapses between the completion of the field work and issuance of the statements, and as a result it is desired to put a later date on the audit report, the subsequent events review and letter of representations should be updated. In rare cases the original date for the audit report may be satisfactory, but some subsequent occurrence may require mention in the statements. In such cases, the auditor may "split-date" his report, as in the following example:

> May 15, 1977 (except as to note 3, which is as of June 10, 1977).

17.2.3 The scope paragraph

The purpose of the scope paragraph is to identify the financial statements reported on and, as required by the first reporting standard, to refer to the scope and nature of the auditor's examination.

> In the scope paragraph of a standard report, the auditor should:
> a) specifically identify the financial statements reported on; and
> b) state that his examinatnion was made in accordance with generally accepted auditing standards, and accordingly included such tests and other procedures as he considered necessary in the circumstances. [CICA Handbook][6]

Financial statements covered by the auditor's report

The financial statements reported on normally include the balance sheet and the statements of income, retained earnings and changes in financial position. If these statements are given different titles by the client, the wording of the auditor's scope paragraph should be amended accordingly. As a minimum:

> The auditor's standard report should cover all financial statements required for fair presentation in accordance with generally accepted accounting principles. [CICA Handbook][7]

Where necessary statements are omitted[8] or where it is not practicable to obtain sufficient evidence to support one or more such statements, an appropriate reservation must be expressed (see Chapter 18). If statements in addition to those suggested in the first sentence of this paragraph are required in order to meet generally accepted accounting principles or if the client wishes additional statements, not so required, to be nonetheless covered by the auditor's report, and if the auditor has indeed audited such additional statements, they should be identified in the scope paragraph. (Alternatively, they may be referenced from other statements which *are* identified in the scope paragraph.) An additional statement sometimes included, for example, is a statement of changes in shareholders' equity accounts, which may provide information otherwise required in notes. Sometimes certain elements of the principal financial statements may be sufficiently complex to warrant a separate statement, for example, a statement of long-term debt.

It should be noted that it is unnecessary to refer to notes to the financial statements (including a summary of significant accounting policies) or to supporting schedules to which the financial statements are referenced, since such material forms an integral part of the financial statements.[9] Thus, if the sales figure on the income statement is referenced to a sales analysis schedule, that schedule would be automatically deemed to be covered by the auditor's report. Supporting schedules covered by the auditor's report will, of course, require additional audit work to verify them. Moreover, the level of detail presented in such schedules may, in some circumstances, imply a greater degree of precision than the principal financial statements themselves, which may in turn influence the auditor's decision as to audit materiality for those schedules.

Supporting schedules which are not referenced from the financial statements nor identified in the auditor's report represent unaudited information and should be clearly differentiated from the audited financial statements. Otherwise, a reader might mistakenly infer that they had been covered by the audit. Supplementary schedules might, for example, include segmented analyses, current value or price-level adjusted data, key analytical ratios, or summarized per-share data. A common arrangement is to have such supplementary information, where unaudited, follow after and distinct from the audited statements, notes, and auditor's report. Sometimes such information is specifically labelled as supplementary and/or as unaudited but such labelling has not been considered necessary as long as the information is clearly distinguished from the audited financial statements. Where the supplementary schedules appear to be financial statements, the auditor must consider a specific disclaimer of opinion for such information:

> It is important that unaudited financial information which could be construed to be part of the audited financial statements be clearly differentiated. The auditor should recognize that the Recommendations of Section 8100 may be applicable . . . [CICA Handbook][10]

Scope of the auditor's examination

The wording of the scope paragraph informs the reader that the auditor has made his examination in accordance with professional standards, that he has exercised judgment in deciding what audit procedures were necessary in the circumstances to meet those standards, and that some of the procedures quite properly were applied on a test basis. This wording is intended, in part, to prevent the mistaken inference that auditing consists of a 100% check of all transactions, that it is largely mechanical and arithmetic, and that it can therefore be expected to yield precise results with absolute assurance.

17.2.4 The opinion paragraph

The purpose of the opinion paragraph is, as required by the last three reporting standards, to express the auditor's opinion on the financial statement presentation and its consistency. By definition, a standard report is applicable only when neither reservation nor additional explanation is required.

> In the opinion paragraph of a standard report, the auditor should express his opinion that the financial statements present fairly the financial position, results of operations and changes in financial position of the enterprise in accordance with generally accepted accounting principles applied on a basis consistent with that of the preceding period. [CICA Handbook][11]

The use of the phrase "in my opinion" implies that the audit conclusion is not a matter of simply identifying facts but of applying professional judgment, not a matter of "certifying" with absolute assurance but of obtaining reasonable assurance to support the expression of an opinion. As discussed in Chapter 6, the words "present fairly" imply, among other things, the concept of materiality as opposed to mechanical exactitude. Other implications of the phrase "present fairly" are discussed in 17.3.2.

In referring to "these financial statements", the opinion paragraph covers all the financial statements identified directly or indirectly in the scope paragraph. Thus, it is not necessary to repeat the list of such statements. In particular, it is undesirable to use wording such as "In my opinion these financial statements, together with the notes thereto, present fairly . . .", or "these financial statements, when read with the notes thereto . . .". The notes are an integral part of the financial statements and specific reference to them in the opinion paragraph might be misinterpreted as being a qualification of the audit opinion. If a reservation is intended, it should be more explicit (see Chapter 18).

If the scope paragraph has made reference to statements other than the most common ones, such additional statements (for example a statement of changes in shareholders' equity accounts) can usually be considered a part of the presentation of financial position, results of operations and changes in financial position. Accordingly the wording of the standard opinion paragraph usually need not be changed.[12]

Because the opinion paragraph covers all the financial statements identified, it should be interpreted as relating to the statements *taken as a whole* and not to each financial statement figure taken piecemeal. The tighter materiality limits, which may be implied when piecemeal opinions are given, are discussed in 18.2.3. While the phrase "taken as a whole" does not appear in the standard wording of the report in either Canada or the United States, it does appear in the U.S. standards of reporting. It seems fair to conclude that the same sense was intended by the Canadian standards but that the phrase itself was omitted to avoid any inferred prohibition of an opinion, with an accompanying reservation where required, being expressed on one statement alone (such as the balance sheet) when circumstances so demand.

17.3 Generally accepted accounting principles and fairness

The third reporting standard recognizes that an audit opinion must indicate the degree of correspondence of the financial statements with an agreed-upon set of established criteria (appropriate disclosed basis of accounting). It goes on to add that, except for special purpose reports, those established criteria are generally accepted accounting principles. At the same time, the Canadian standard incorporates the phrase "presents fairly". Practitioners are not unanimous in their views as to the interrelationship between fairness and generally accepted accounting principles.

17.3.1 Generally accepted accounting principles

The obvious initial difficulty is interpreting exactly what the words "generally accepted accounting principles" mean. The two principal questions are (a) whether principles should be interpreted to mean broad guiding concepts (such as objectivity, consistency, full disclosure, materiality and conservatism) or specific procedures (such as the method of eliminating inter-company profits on consolidation) and (b) whether general acceptance should be interpreted literally. As to the first question, accounting principles are now commonly defined to include not only broad principles and conventions of general application, but also "specific rules, practices and procedures relating to particular circumstances".[13]

> Accounting principles are rules which give guidance to the measurement, classification and interpretation of economic information and communication of the results through the medium of financial statements. These rules are characterized as 'principles' by the fact that no alternative rule is generally recognized as permissible for the operation to which the principle relates. Most accounting principles are relatively broad guidelines which may be implemented by two or more alternative procedures. However, this fact reflects the way that accounting theory has historically developed and is not necessitated by this definition. Under this definition an accounting principle may be a quite specific guide for action in a particular situation, provided that no alternative procedures are recognized as permissible in the same situation.[14]

As to the second question, if the appropriateness of accounting principles were to rest literally on general acceptance (that is, agreement by most preparers, auditors and readers of financial statements) then accounting principles could only be generally accepted after they had been generally used and yet could only be used provided they were generally

accepted. With this sort of chicken-and-egg conundrum, accounting principles would be permanently frozen for all time. Such a result would be clearly impractical. "Accounting principles are not static. They change and develop to meet changed conditions."[15] It follows then, that literal general acceptance is not a sound basis for the formulation of accounting principles.

Arguments against literal interpretation of general acceptance

In arguing for the rejection of this basis, R.M. Skinner, in *Accounting Principles: A Canadian Viewpoint*, presented the following reasoning:

1. Recognized clear accounting principles are necessary for effective financial reporting. Furthermore, such principles must deal with specific subject areas. . . .
2. It is unrealistic to expect the development of a 'generally accepted' consensus for the proper solution of each accounting problem, given the absence of a consensus on basic assumptions of accounting and the fact that managements, which are primarily responsible for accounting presentations, are inevitably greatly influenced by circumstances and pressures peculiar to their own situation.
3. It is equally unrealistic, given the same absence of consensus on basic assumptions, to expect that individual public accountants in the exercise of their professional judgment will arrive at similar conclusions on all, or even a majority of, difficult accounting questions.
4. Accordingly, it must follow that 'general acceptance' cannot be relied upon as a criterion for the development and selection of accounting principles. At most, acceptance is a limiting factor to the logical development of principles, not a guide.

We come then to the position that if we expect to formulate a set of accounting principles that will be consistently applied they must be formulated by some authority. In effect, someone must exercise a legislative function. . . .
We are here drawing an analogy between principles in the conduct of accounting and laws in a society. No suggestion is intended that the legislation of accounting principles would be performed by government action – quite the contrary, in fact. . . .
In the place of general acceptance as a means of deciding on accounting methods, it is urged we should substitute the authority of an accounting legislative body. Indeed this process has begun already and has come some distance, particularly in the U.S.A. with reference to the Accounting Principles Board. . . .
There is no real alternative for the profession to a clear assumption of responsibility and authority, and action to fulfil its responsibilities.[16]

Since the issue of that Canadian study in 1972, a number of further developments have taken place, involving both clearer designation of, and wider representation on, bodies having authority to establish accounting principles. In the United States, the Financial Accounting Standards Board, containing representation from both within and outside the accounting profession, has taken over the role of the Accounting Principles Board, and begun to issue Statements of Financial Accounting Standards. Rule 203 of the AICPA code of ethics, together with the related Council designation, has effectively defined FASB pronouncements as constituting generally accepted accounting principles in the United States. A 1973 accounting release by the SEC recognizes such pronouncements as constituting "substantial authoritative support". In Canada, National Policy No. 27 of the Securities Administrators has stated that, for the purposes of administering securities legislation, the administrators would regard the Accounting Recommendations of the CICA's Accounting Research Committee as generally accepted accounting principles. In 1975 the new Canada Business Corporations Act and its regulations dropped former references to generally accepted accounting principles but established a requirement that a company's annual financial statements "be prepared in accordance with the recommendations of the Canadian Institute of Chartered Accountants set out in the CICA Handbook as amended from time to time" (see 4.1.3). In the same year, the new Rules of Professional Conduct called for any departure from the recommendations of the CICA Accounting Research Committee to be capable of justification as proper in the particular circumstances (see 3.2.6).

As explained in Chapter 2, the Accounting Research Committee of the CICA has, since 1973, included in its membership representatives from other organizations. In 1974 an Accounting Research Advisory Board, drawn from the business community across Canada, was established to provide a broader public input to the quasi-legislative process of establishing accounting principles.

The question of substantial authoritative support for alternatives

The purpose of promulgating recommendations with respect to accounting principles is to make accounting communication clearer by (a) identifying the principles to be followed and (b) reducing the number of alternative methods of accounting for identical situations. Without the first, accounting could develop into a set of secret conventions undiscoverable by the reader of the financial statements. Without the second, meaningful comparisons of similar enterprises would be impossible. However, it has been argued that accounting treatment contrary to professional pronouncements can be employed

provided that *substantial authoritative support* can be found for it. Some practitioners feel that the safety valve of well supported alternatives is essential to compensate for the inevitable imperfections in any set of pronouncements. Others feel that, with the difficulty of defining substantial authoritative support, the concept can lead only to an erosion of the original purpose of narrowing alternative treatments of identical situations. The inclusion of Rule 203 in the AICPA code of ethics effectively eliminated the concept of authoritative support for contrary alternatives in the United States.

In Canada, the concept of substantial authoritative support still exists within the Rules of Professional Conduct. Rule 206.3 (see 3.2.6) refers to the *accounting standards of the profession* and the Interpretations explain that this term is intended to encompass "that body of principles *and practices* which have been generally adopted by the profession . . . taken together with the requirements of any governing act". The Interpretations further provide that:

> In determining whether financial statements are prepared in accordance with the accounting standards of the profession, the following should be considered:
> a) accounting practices recommended by the Research Committee;
> b) accounting practices that differ from those recommended by the Research Committee, to ensure that there is substantial authoritative support for alternative treatment and the departure from the Research Committee's recommendations is disclosed;
> c) accounting practices not specifically dealt with by the Research Committee but which are generally accepted for ordinary industrial and commercial enterprises, e.g., accrual accounting; and
> d) requirements of any governing act or regulation, providing however, in the rare event that there is a conflict between the accounting standards of the profession and a specific statutory or regulatory requirement the member (subject to certain exceptions for banks, insurance companies and not-for-profit organizations to which the Recommendations do not necessarily apply) is not relieved of the responsibility of making appropriate qualification in his report.[17]

Despite this reference in the Interpretations, the wording of the securities administrators' policies, the new wording of the federal corporations act, and the precedent of the United States all suggest, to this writer, that reliance on the concept of substantial authoritative support for alternatives contrary to CICA Recommendations would normally be imprudent.

Suggested preliminary definition of generally accepted accounting principles

Therefore, for the normal situation (a more general definition is offered later) it seems reasonable to conclude that generally accepted accounting principles in Canada are:

a) the Recommendations of the CICA Accounting Research Committee, or
b) in areas where the Recommendations are silent, those principles and practices which have by usage or by other means gained general acceptance in Canada.

The reader is cautioned, however, to refer to the CICA Handbook for any authoritative definition of generally accepted accounting principles. As this book goes to press, the Handbook contains no definition of the phrase.[18]

In summary, the term 'generally accepted accounting principles' refers not to principles resting literally on general acceptance but rather to principles primarily recommended by various professional or authoritative bodies and thus differing from country to country.[19] The substance is consistent with the quasi-legislative nature that Skinner recommended, although many of the questions he raised as to how such a quasi-legislative function should be organized and as to the need for a coherent set of underlying accounting postulates remain to be answered in the future. There are some who object to the use of the words "generally accepted accounting principles" to mean, as they do now, something that is not literally based on general acceptance. Maybe the future will see some modification in this phrase. In the meantime the phrase is solidly ensconced in auditing literature and usage, in trust deeds, in many contractual agreements, and in various statutes. Perhaps, like Lewis Carroll's Humpty Dumpty, we can make the words mean what we want them to mean.

17.3.2 Fairness

The opinion paragraph includes reference not only to generally accepted accounting principles (referred to in the rest of this section as GAAP) but to "present fairly" as well. The appearance of both terms in the audit opinion has suggested, in the minds of some, the existence of a dual opinion: one opinion as to conformity with GAAP and the other as to conformity with a separate standard of fairness.[20] Advocates of this view concede that application of GAAP will usually result in fair presentation but argue that, where it does not, fairness should be the overriding criterion. Certain U.S. court decisions have lent support to this view. In the Continental Vending case, Judge Friendly concluded: "The first law for accountants was not compliance with generally accepted accounting principles but, rather, full and fair disclosure, fair presentation. . . ."[21] Proponents of this view fear, in part, that accountants may hide behind mechanical and imperfect rules as an excuse for not insisting on fair disclosure. They feel, therefore, that it is important that the auditor express not only an opinion as to GAAP (which some interpret to be a set of rigid rules) but, in effect, a second opinion

as to fairness as well. Conceivably, the first opinion could be clear and the second qualified, or vice versa (what may be called a "half-qualified opinion"). The previous wording of the CICA Handbook lent some support to this interpretation by calling for an opinion (a) as to GAAP and (b) as to fairness; that wording was superseded with the issue of Section 5400, the Auditor's Standard Report, in 1976, though the two-part style may still be found in some statutes, such as the B.C. Corporations Act.

Arguments against an abstract standard of fairness

It can be argued that a separate standard of fairness is not implied by the wording of the auditor's standard report.[22] Whether it should be or not is another question. There are persuasive arguments on both sides of the issue. The imperfections and incompleteness of any set of pronouncements are strong arguments in favour of a higher standard of fairness. But one must ask whether such a standard can provide a practical method of serving readers by adding credibility to financial statements. In the writer's view, the arguments in favour of a higher standard of fairness are outweighed by the following considerations.

1. Effective communication requires agreement between sender and receiver as to a common language in which the communication will be expressed. Generally accepted accounting principles provide that language.
2. A separate standard of fairness, on the other hand, is necessarily subjective and personal. One man's private ideals of fairness may not be another's. The subjective views of the sender will not usually be known to the receiver of the communication.
3. The formulation of GAAP recommendations is necessarily a process of compromise. For such compromises to be effective in narrowing an undesirable proliferation of alternative accounting methods, it is essential that members of the profession accept the compromise, and not overrule it with a private standard of fairness.
4. GAAP change from country to country and from year to year. One day the amortization of purchased goodwill is called for by GAAP; the day before, it was not. Can an abstract standard of fairness change overnight as well? It is more likely, if an abstract standard of fairness were acknowledged, that some accountants would feel compelled to concede the statement presentation on the old basis, while no longer in accordance with GAAP, could still be considered fair. The resulting proliferation of "half-qualified" opinions would undercut the objective of narrowing

alternative methods of presentation for identical circumstances.

5. Advocates of the concept of fairness in the abstract have expressed the understandable concern that without it accountants might hide behind mechanical rules as an excuse for not insisting on proper disclosure. But with a concept of an abstract standard of fairness, there is the alternative, and perhaps greater, danger that accountants would hide behind alleged fairness as an excuse for not insisting on compliance with an appropriate but unpalatable requirement of GAAP.

6. Accounting principles are expressed in general, not detailed, terms. Most accountants share a dislike for any notion of an encyclopaedic codification of rules to fit every conceivable situation. When the CICA Accounting Research Committee issues an Accounting Recommendation, it is clear that it is not advocating its use in the rare and exceptional circumstances where it obviously does not apply. The Introduction to Accounting Recommendations states:

   In issuing Recommendations, the Accounting Research Committee recognizes that no rule of general application can be phrased to suit all circumstances or combination of circumstances that may arise, nor is there any substitute for the exercise of professional judgment in the determination of what constitutes fair presentation or good practice in a particular case.

   Thus, when an accountant exercises his judgment in recognizing that adjustment is required for an exceptional circumstance, he is doing exactly what the Committee has advocated in its Introduction. It would seem unfortunate if such compliance with Committee intentions had to be reported as a qualification that the statements were not in accordance with the GAAP principles recommended by the same Committee.

7. It seems more logical to interpret the Introduction as calling for compliance with the *spirit* rather than the *letter* of Accounting Recommendations. "Compliance with the spirit" is, in this writer's view, the sense in which the concept of *fairness* can most meaningfully be interpreted. To "present fairly in accordance with GAAP" is to apply GAAP intelligently, judiciously and appropriately to the fact situation covered by the financial statements. To present fairly is to avoid applying the letter of the recommendations rigidly and mechanically to circumstances where the spirit of the recommendations obviously calls for sensible adjustment. *To present fairly is to avoid searching for some word or sentence among the recommendations which, in isolation, could be argued to condone a particular accounting treatment when any reasonable interpretation of the framework of GAAP taken as a whole would indicate that the treatment in question is misleading.*

8. Such an interpretation would also seem consistent with the present position in the United States.

   The independent auditor's judgment concerning the "fairness" of the overall presentation of financial statements should be applied within the framework of generally accepted accounting principles. Without that framework the auditor would have no uniform standard for judging the presentation . . . [23]

   Rule 203 of the AICPA Code of Ethics prohibits the auditor from expressing a clear opinion where the financial statements do not follow pronouncements of the Financial Accounting Standards Board except in those "unusual circumstances where the literal application of pronouncements on accounting principles would have the effect of rendering financial statements misleading". In the latter rare cases, appropriate adjustments are called for, and, provided such adjustments are made, the auditor is to give a clear opinion that the statements "present fairly . . . in conformity with generally accepted accounting principles".

9. Finally, such an interpretation would seem consistent with the possiblity of different possible disclosed bases of accounting for special purpose reports (see 19.3). The concept of the degree of correspondence between the statements and some yardstick (whether GAAP or some other disclosed basis) is essential – and the phrase "present fairly" can be said to express this concept.

Suggested revised definition of generally accepted accounting principles

On the basis of the foregoing arguments, the previously offered definition of generally accepted accounting principles in Canada might be broadened to:

a) the Recommendations of the CICA Accounting Research Committee,

or

b) in areas where the Recommendations are silent, those principles and practices which have, by usage or by other means, gained general acceptance in Canada or are in the spirit of existing Recommendations on similar matters,

provided that

c) if, due to the unusual circumstances of a particular enterprise, the literal requirements of either (a) or (b) are not reasonably applicable, such adjustments are made as are consistent with the general spirit of the Recommendations, principles or practices in question.

The reader, however, is again cautioned to refer to any subsequent CICA pronouncement defining generally accepted accounting principles.

As this book goes to press the most recent CICA

485

pronouncement on the subject states:

> In the auditor's standard report, the auditor's judgment concerning "present fairly" can be applied only within the framework of generally accepted accounting principles. Professional judgment should not be influenced by personal disagreement with particular principles which are generally accepted.[24]

The importance of fairness in applying accounting principles

To suggest that fairness is not another set of standards above and overriding generally accepted accounting principles is not to imply that fairness is unimportant. As an important factor in the manner of applying accounting principles, attention to fairness involves the exercise of care and judgment in several critical areas.[25]

1. Care must be exercised in identifying those principles and practices which can be considered to have gained general acceptance in areas where the CICA Recommendations are silent. The auditor may refer, depending on the circumstances, to industry accounting practices, to pronouncements of other professional bodies and regulatory agencies, to legislative requirements, to research studies, to accounting textbooks and articles, and to pronouncements and practices in other countries or he may reason by analogy from the spirit of existing Recommendations on similar matters,
2. Judgement is required in distinguishing substance from form. Transactions should be accounted for according to their substance.
3. The auditor must consider whether within the Recommendations or, where they are silent, within the principles and practices accepted by general usage or otherwise there exist several acceptable methods of accounting for a given transaction and whether each of these is indeed acceptable in the specific circumstances in question. For example, both diminishing balance and straight-line depreciation may normally be considered acceptable practices; but the auditor must consider whether the specific circumstances of his client render either of these normally acceptable alternatives inapplicable.
4. Judgment is required in deciding whether accepted accounting principles have been applied properly.
5. Judgment is required in deciding whether informative disclosures are adequate – indeed a specific reference to fairness is contained in the very first CICA Accounting Recommendation:

> any information required for fair presentation ... should be presented in the financial statements....[26]

> But in applying this Recommendation the auditor

should consider the general framework of GAAP as suggested in the following example:

> A specific disclosure about a particular corporate condition could be made but there is no explicit Recommendation identifying this disclosure as mandatory. May the auditor waive disclosure or should he insist on it? It is suggested that he should *not merely* use the absence of a specific Recommendation as an excuse for waiving disclosure. (Certainly, if he does, the case for "fairness" to override such a cookbook approach will be strengthened.) But nor, on the other hand, should he insist on disclosure *solely* because he personally believes the matter is more important than others generally hold it to be. For example, in 1976 it would not be reasonable to insist on disclosure in the financial statements of the identity, background and experience of the company's top management team – however much the auditor might personally believe this information to be a key element affecting the company's financial position. Rather, the auditor must decide whether, within the framework and spirit of GAAP as it exists at the time, a reasonable practitioner would consider the specific disclosure to be essential for fair presentation.

6. Judgment is required in deciding whether informative disclosures are clear and neither too detailed nor too condensed. The financial statements, for example, may comply literally with applicable disclosure principles but nonetheless do so in a way which leaves a misleading impression by highlighting points of minor importance or obscuring points of major importance.
7. Judgment is required in choosing reasonable materiality limits (discussed in Chapter 15).
8. Judgment is required in identifying unusual circumstances of a particular enterprise which call for sensible adjustment of the literal requirements of accepted principles in order to be consistent with their general spirit.

In addition, there remains the overriding ethical requirement to avoid association with false or misleading statements (see 3.2.5).

The question of "preferability"

In the foregoing discussion it was suggested (point 3) that the concept of fairness should be used in deciding whether various normally alternative accounting principles are all, in fact, applicable to the specific circumstances of a given set of financial statements. If the auditor concludes that they are, then he should be prepared to accept any of these alternatives whether or not management's choice happens to coincide with his own preference.

> Specifying the circumstances in which one accounting principle should be selected from among alternative principles is the function of bodies having authority to establish accounting principles. When criteria for selection among alternative accounting principles have not been established to relate accounting methods to circumstances, the auditor may conclude that more than one

accounting principle is appropriate in the circumstances. The auditor should recognize, however, that there may be unusual circumstances in which the selection and application of specific accounting principles from among alternative principles may make the financial statements taken as a whole misleading.[27]

Some have suggested that the auditor should go beyond this position and insist on his own preference (from among acceptable alternatives) being adopted either all of the time or whenever a change of accounting principles is being made. AICPA and SEC requirements with respect to preferability in the case of accounting changes are mentioned in 17.5.1. Pushed to an extreme, the concept of preferability would extend fairness from a consideration of "what is fair" to "which is the fairest of them all". The SEC has argued, in the case of accounting changes, that investors should not be denied the benefits of requiring the external auditor to make his best judgment and report it. Although the SEC position was put forward in the context of strengthening the concept of consistency (i.e., consistency should be violated only for a better accounting principle and not merely to "manage" net income), many practitioners have expressed concern with the implications of this position. Some of the arguments against the preferability concept are:

1. The task of narrowing the number of co-existing alternative treatments for identical situations should be left to the bodies issuing pronouncements on accounting principles.

2. Where such bodies have not eliminated certain alternatives, or defined circumstances where each alternative is applicable, it is because the decision is difficult and controversial. Individual practitioners should not be asked to decide what the pronouncing bodies have been unable to decide.

3. If each practitioner makes his own judgments on preferability, there will undoubtedly be inconsistencies among the decisions of different practitioners. It is hard to see, therefore, how the preferability concept will improve the comparability of financial statements read by the general public.

Preferability judgments are not presently required within Canadian practice. However, Canadian practitioners auditing subsidiaries of a U.S. parent company registering with the SEC must be mindful of SEC requirements when issuing special purpose reports for use in the United States.

Conclusion

Controversy over the role of fairness from the point of view of practitioners, the public, and the courts is far from resolved. In the United States the AICPA established in 1974 a special commission to study the responsibilities of auditors, including those reflected in the auditor's report. Perhaps its deliberations will help to achieve such a resolution.

17.4 An historical perspective

The changes which have occurred in auditing objectives from the mid-nineteenth century to the present day were sketched briefly in 1.3. It is natural that the wording of the auditor's report should similarly have changed over this period – and further changes may no doubt be in store for the future.

17.4.1 Development of the standard report

In the early 1900's, standard report wording did not exist. In the United Kingdom and Canada, however, statutory requirements provided a partial framework. Thus, in the former, the Companies Act of 1900, which re-introduced compulsory audits, required (a) that the auditors "sign a certificate at the foot of the balance sheet stating whether or not all their requirements as auditors had been complied with" and (b) that they should further "make a report to the shareholders . . . and in every such report should state whether, in their opinion, the balance sheet referred to in the report was properly drawn up, so as to exhibit a true and correct view of the state of the company's affairs". Some practitioners[28] argued that the first requirement called for a published *certificate* of fact (analagous to our present-day scope paragraph) and the second for an oral *report* of the auditor's opinion (analagous to our present-day opinion paragraph). Whatever the logic of this argument, the two communications were generally combined in one written "certificate" and the word "certify" was commonly used within it. Sometimes, however, despite the specific wording of the act, actual certificates consisted merely of the words "audited and found correct", or the single word "certified", or even the auditor's signature unencumbered by any words. (Contemporary advocates of brevity could hardly have pruned the message further.)

In a first attempt at standardization in the United States, the AICPA in 1917 retained the word "certify" in what might be called an early two-part opinion – the auditor certifying that the statements had been made in accordance with the Federal Reserve

Board plan *and* in his opinion set forth the financial condition of the firm. But the recommended wording was far from universally used. Actual reports varied from short opinion certificates to longer descriptive certificates, the different lengths and wording tending at times to blur the distinction between explanations and reservations.

The words "certificate" and "true and correct view" were perhaps understandable at a time when audit procedures were applied on a 100% basis rather than as tests and when their principal objective was a check on stewardship and the detection of fraud. They were recognized as increasingly misleading, however, as the emphasis began to shift to an assessment of the reasonableness of financial statement presentation. Thus, when the first widely accepted form of report was proposed by the AICPA in 1934, it used the words "in our opinion ... [the financial statements] ... fairly present, in accordance with accepted principles of accounting consistently maintained by the company during the year under review, its position at ... ". In 1939, following the McKesson & Robbins case, the word "generally" was added to "accepted principles of accounting" – giving birth to GAAP – and the phrase "fairly present" was inverted so that the report now read "in our opinion ... [the financial statements] ... present fairly the position ... in conformity with generally accepted accounting principles applied on a basis consistent with that of the preceding year". In 1941, as a result of SEC requirements, the reference to "generally accepted auditing standards" was inserted in the scope paragraph. Minor modifications were made in 1947 and 1974.

Meanwhile, in Canada, practice was constrained by the Companies Act of 1934 (continuing in force until 1965) which, following U.K. precedents, called for an opinion as to whether the balance sheet exhibited a true and correct view. Thus, when the first CICA pronouncement on audit reporting was made in 1951 (Bulletin No. 6), corresponding wording was suggested for the opinion paragraph. Three years later, however, in response to new provincial legislation, a supplement was issued adopting the U.S. wording of "present fairly" when reporting under companies acts not requiring the older wording. The original Canadian bulletins, unlike the U.S. pronouncements, left conformity to GAAP and consistency in application to be implied by the absence of disclosure to the contrary. In 1959, a further revision (Bulletin No. 17) added the explicit references to GAAP and consistency – explaining that a positive statement was felt more satisfactory than dealing with such important matters by implication. The bulletin went on to comment that the expression "exhibit a true and correct view" might be interpreted as

implying a degree of exactitude which is non-existent and it recommended that, unless specifically required by statute, the words should be replaced by the more general expression 'present fairly'. Minor changes were made in 1967. In 1976 the reference to generally accepted auditing standards was added to the scope paragraph (and certain minor changes were made at the same time).

This brief historical overview indicates that some of the controversy about one-part versus two-part opinions may have been stirred up accidentally by words originally adopted for other reasons. It seems clear that the phrase "present fairly" was adopted, as argued in the 1959 CICA bulletin, to cure the misleading aura of exactitude conveyed by "true and correct view" and not to set up an abstract standard over and above GAAP. The 1934 AICPA wording seems fairly clearly a one-part opinion. The altered order in 1939 may have inadvertently raised questions which were not then contemplated.

> The reason for repositioning the reference to GAAP was to clarify the meaning of the reference to consistency. Some accountants apparently believed that "consistently maintained during the year" did not relate the principles for the current year to those for the prior year. The changed wording removed that confusion, but may have clouded the relationship between fair presentation and GAAP.[29]

It would be wrong, however to trace the controversy entirely to the accidents of historical wording. The very real questions concerning the definition of GAAP, the interpretation of fairness, and the relationship between them are ones that the profession has not yet finally resolved.

17.4.2 Proposals for modification of the standard report

The present wording of the auditor's standard report has been criticized for being too long, for being too short, or for being unclear. Some of the points of view were summarized in a study by the Accountants International Study Group in 1969:

> Auditors in the U.S. who propose clarification of the auditor's responsibility by revision of his report suggest that an expanded opinion include:
> 1) Comment that the financial statements are those of management;
> 2) Explanation that amounts in the financial statements are reasonable approximations, and are not precise calculations;
> 3) Reference to the fact that the audit was made in accordance with auditing standards established by the accounting profession;
> 4) Representation that selective tests were used and were based upon the auditor's evaluation of internal control; and

5) Opinion that the financial statements conform with accounting principles determined by the accounting profession and that such principles were consistently applied.

Other auditors in the U.S. feel, however, that an expansion of the auditor's report designed to clarify existing problems of understanding may only introduce new areas of misunderstanding. Accordingly, there is an alternative point of view in the U.S. that would reduce the auditor's report to a simple expression of opinion on designated statements, as is done in the U.K. By this course of action, some contend, the auditor's report would be simplified, would be more easily standardized among nations, and would be less subject to misunderstanding. Furthermore, it is said, the more simplified the statement of opinion, the more stated exceptions from a standard opinion would be highlighted.[30]

Possible expansion of the report

The Committee on Auditing Procedures of the AICPA worked from 1965 to 1972 on possible expansion of the wording in the auditor's standard report. Its chairman stated that "there is sufficient evidence to indicate that the present form of report ... is not really understandable" and in particular suggested the need for clarification of the meaning of fairness, generally accepted accounting principles, examination, financial statements, management responsibility and auditor independence.[31] Some of the suggestions submitted to the committee included proposals:

1. to identify the financial statements as prepared by management (including a reference to the selection of principles by management from among acceptable alternatives)
2. to discuss briefly the nature of financial statements including references to:
   a) the going concern assumption,
   b) the judgment involved in allocating costs to different accounting periods,
   c) the use of cost rather than current values,
   d) the necessity of approximations (for example, by using phrases such as "present in all material respects" or "express reasonable approximations of" in place of "present fairly"),
3. to identify the source of "generally accepted auditing standards" and "generally accepted accounting principles",
4. to include some comment with respect to fraud and irregularities,
5. to replace the word "examined" with "audited",
6. to delete, modify, or retain the phrase "and accordingly ... circumstances" at the end of the scope paragraph,
7. to prescribe a mandatory title for the report (perhaps making reference to objectivity or independence).

In the end, however, no such modifications were made by the committee – perhaps because of possible public relations implications. Perhaps, also, the potential misunderstandings were felt to have been reduced by other developments, such as the requirement to disclose significant accounting policies in the notes to the financial statements and such as the issue in 1970 of a more comprehensive pronouncement on basic concepts accounting principles.[32]

The question of improving communication in the auditor's standard report, has, however, continued. In its Statement of Issues the Commission on Auditors' Responsibilities established by the AICPA in 1974 included the questions:

> Is the auditor's report an appropriate vehicle for improving the understanding of the audit function? ...
> What changes in the wording of the report are necessary or desirable to improve communications? Should the report
> 1. Avoid technical terms and use commonly understood words to explain the auditor's responsibility? (This would probably result in a much more lengthy report.)
> 2. Explain more fully the nature of the auditor's examination, including a fuller explanation of the limitations of an audit?
> 3. Include an explanation of the division of responsibility for financial statements between the independent auditor and the management of the company?
> 4. Include an explanation of the limitations of accounting information, financial statements, and generally accepted accounting principles?
> 5. Use varied wording rather than one standard form?
> What other methods could independent auditors use to improve the public's understanding of the audit function?[33]

In this writer's view it would seem desirable for the auditor's report to make specific reference at least to the concepts of *materiality, reasonable assurance,* and *risk.* Auditors tell each other that an audit report indicates that they have obtained reasonable, though not absolute, assurance that the financial statements are free of a material misstatement and, further, that the level of reasonable assurance must depend on the perceived risk of the hypothetical misstatement in question (see Chapter 6). It would seem useful to inform the readers of this interpretation.

Possible reduction of the report

The Accountants International Study Group concluded, on the other hand, that a more condensed report, similar to the modern U.K. format, would reduce misunderstandings. They suggested a one-sentence report reading "In our opinion, the accompanying balance sheet of X Co. at ... and the related statement of ... for the year then ended are fair and reasonable."[34] An alternative one-sentence report was earlier suggested by Mautz and Sharaf: "We have examined with due audit care the data found in (name of statement or statements) and find that they present fairly (the purpose of the statement.)"[35]

Brevity, however, is not necessarily synonymous with clarity. Removing controversial words such as "generally accepted accounting principles" does not in itself resolve the controversy. It simply leaves it up to each reader to imagine, often mistakenly, the criteria by which fair presentation has been assessed.

Other approaches

Other suggested approaches to reducing misunderstandings have included proposals for:

1. supplemental statements by management in the annual report describing the nature of financial statements and the respective responsibilities of management and the auditor,
2. educational pamphlets or other materials distributed by the profession to interested users to help explain the nature of financial statements, the role of the auditor, and the limitations of an audit.

The second proposal is in part met by the CICA's 1969 publication *Audit Reports, Their Nature and Significance* (now in need of updating), which addresses such matters as the going concern concept, the responsibility for statement preparation, the need for judgment, and the meaning of individual phrases in the standard report wording. Undoubtedly, the profession has a greater role to play in public education.

17.5 Departures from the standard report (other than reservations)

Departures from the standard report may be required:

1. to express a reservation of the opinion as to whether the financial statements are presented fairly in accordance with generally accepted accounting principles (see 18.1 and 18.2),
2. to express an exception in the opinion as to consistency or to otherwise modify the wording of the report with respect to accounting changes (see 17.5.1),
3. to modify the standard wording in order to meet legislative requirements, to express reliance on other auditors or other specialists, to cover comparative figures, to refer to other information accompanying the financial statements, or to adapt the report to initial engagements or to unincorporated enterprises (see 17.5.2 to 17.5.9),
4. to add an additional explanatory paragraph to provide further information or emphasis (see 17.5.10),
5. to modify the standard wording to clarify the relationship of the financial statements and/or the auditor's report to the principles and standards of foreign countries (see 18.6).

17.5.1 Accounting changes

The fourth reporting standard requires an opinion on consistency and an adequate explanation of the nature and effect of any inconsistency. To the extent that judgment is required in selecting one of several acceptable accounting principles (such as straight line or diminishing balance depreciation) or in making accounting estimates (such as fixed asset lives, collectibility of accounts receivable, and warranty obligations), it is important for the reader to know whether such judgment has been applied consistently from year to year. Otherwise he may misinterpret comparisons with prior years and apparent trends.

It is useful to distinguish (a) the auditor's opinion as to fairness of presentation in accordance with generally accepted accounting principles from (b) his opinion as to the consistency of the application of those principles. Depending on the circumstances it may be necessary to express exceptions with respect to one of these opinions, to both opinions or to neither opinion. In this book, exceptions to the former opinion are referred to as *reservations of opinion* (see Chapter 18) while those related to the latter opinion are referred to as *consistency exceptions* or *consistency explanations*. This terminology parallels the references to reservations of opinion in the third reporting standard and to explanations of inconsistencies in the fourth reporting standard.[36]

The opinion as to fair presentation in accordance with generally accepted accounting principles

In Canada, an accounting change does not in itself give rise to a *reservation of opinion* as defined in the previous paragraph. Provided that the change is from one acceptable accounting practice to another, the opinion as to fairness of presentation in accordance with generally accepted accounting principles may be unqualified both in the prior year and in the current year; the required explanation or exception is directed exclusively to the question of consistency.

Before expressing a clear opinion as to fair presentation in accordance with generally accepted accounting principles, the auditor must satisfy himself that (a) the newly adopted accounting principle is a generally accepted accounting principle and (b) the method of accounting for the effect of the change is in accordance with generally accepted accounting principles.[37]

In the United States, AICPA pronouncements require in addition that the auditor satisfy himself that "management's justification for the change is reasonable".[38] This justification must be considered in the light of AICPA accounting pronouncements which provide that there is "a presumption that an accounting principle once adopted should not be changed . . . [which presumption] may be overcome only if the enterprise justifies the use of an alternative acceptable accounting principle on the basis that it is preferable".[39] In 1975 the SEC also laid down a requirement that the auditor state whether or not in his judgment the change of accounting principles is preferable under the circumstances. None of these specific requirements apply to Canadian practice – although a practitioner should not, of course, accept a pattern of artificial accounting changes which he considers render the financial statements misleading. Canadian practitioners auditing subsidiaries of a U.S. parent company must be mindful of applicable AICPA or SEC requirements when issuing special purpose reports for use in the United States.

The opinion as to consistency

Where there has been a significant change in accounting principle, or method of applying an accounting principle, the nature of the change *and its effect* should be described either in a note to the financial statements or in the auditor's report. In practice, detailed disclosure is almost always by way of note. Such disclosure generally indicates what the current year's figures would have been had the change not been made. Some practitioners believe it is also acceptable to indicate what the previous year's figures would have been had the change been made one year earlier.[40]

If net income reported has been affected, the disclosure should include this effect as well as the effect on earnings per share. The auditor's report would then contain a reference to the note disclosure.

In Canada it is common, though not invariable, for accounting changes to be applied retroactively.[41] Where a change has been applied retroactively, any comparative figures presented should be restated.[42] In such cases, the opinion paragraph should include a *consistency explanation* such as:

> . . . in accordance with generally accepted accounting principles applied, after giving retroactive effect to [the

change in accounting practice] referred to in Note X to the financial statements, on a basis consistent with that of the preceding year. [CICA Handbook][43]

Where, on the other hand, the change has not been applied retroactively, the opinion paragraph should include a *consistency exception* such as:

> . . . in accordance with generally accepted accounting principles. Further in our opinion, except for [the change in accounting practice] as referred to in Note X to the financial statements, such accounting principles are applied on a basis consistent with that of the preceding year.

or

> . . . in accordance with generally accepted accounting principles which, except for [the change in accounting practice] as referred to in Note X to the financial statements, have been applied on a basis consistent with that of the preceding year. [CICA Handbook][44]

It is to be presumed that, if an auditor does not consider the new accounting policy acceptable, he would qualify his opinion. Therefore, an expression of approval in his reference to a changed policy is unnecessary in Canada although it may be given if the client wishes it. Possible wording would be:

> . . . except for the change, which I approve . . .
> . . . except for the change, with which I concur . . .
> . . . except for a change to an accepted alternative method . . .
> . . . except for the change to which I do not object . . .

In the United States, however, the AICPA statements call for the concurrence to be explicit (unless the change is the correction of an error) using the words "with which we concur".

Adequate disclosure is a part of generally accepted accounting principles. Therefore, significant changes in disclosures or methods of disclosure require treatment similar to that of other accounting changes. Usually, however, mere reclassifications of items within the balance sheet or within the income statement may be considered as not sufficiently significant to require reference in the audit report, provided that they are adequately disclosed in the statements.

Sometimes changes in accounting are made which have little effect on figures currently but could have a material effect in the future – e.g., a change from the diminishing balance method to the straight-line method of depreciation for new asset additions. The CICA Handbook[45] and certain corporations acts require that such changes be disclosed in the notes to the financial statements. In the United States, reference to changes having a substantial effect only in future years is not required in the auditor's report if they are disclosed in the notes to the financial statements.[46] In Canada, audit practice is less clearly defined on this issue but some practitioners lean towards a reference in their report. In unusual cases, where a change in accounting policy is disclosed in a note, but it can only remotely be considered to be material, the auditor may wish to word his report:

> ... applied on a basis consistent in all material respects with that of the preceding year.

Changes in accounting estimates or in the nature of transactions

A change in the basis of application of an accounting principle – e.g., a change from diminishing balance to straight-line depreciation – should be distinguished from a change in the results of applying an accounting principle caused by changed conditions. For example, the depreciation rate on plant may change to reflect changes in estimated useful life, while the method – e.g., straight-line – is unaltered. Changes of the latter type, referred to as *changes in accounting estimates,* affect the comparability of financial statements from year to year and therefore may require disclosure in the statements but do not require a consistency exception in the audit report.

The adoption of new accounting principles may also be required by changes in the nature of the transactions to be reported. Such adoption does not involve the consistency standard although disclosure in the notes to the financial statements may be required.

Where disclosures in the financial statements or notes are inadequate with respect to the foregoing changes, the auditor should, as for all inadequate disclosure, qualify his opinion as to fairness of presentation in accordance with generally accepted accounting principles (see Chapter 18).

Reports following a pooling of interests

Certain circumstances, though more narrowly defined in Canada than in the United States, call for a business combination to be accounted for by the "pooling of interests" method. The proper application of that method calls for prior years' figures to be restated[47] but such a restatement does not represent a change in accounting basis requiring comment in the audit report. A failure to restate prior years' figures for a pooling would, however, introduce an inconsistency requiring exception by the auditor.

Reporting in subsequent years

Where a retroactive accounting change or prior period adjustment has previously been reported, with restatement, in an annual report, it is not necessary in future annual reports to draw attention again to the restatement.

Reporting on consistency when other reservations of opinion are expressed

Reporting on consistency in circumstances when a reservation of the opinion as to fairness of presentation must, for other reasons, be expressed is discussed in Chapter 18.

17.5.2 Comparative figures

While it is normally considered desirable for financial statements to be prepared on a comparative basis showing the figures for the corresponding preceding period,[48] audit reports in Canada generally cover only the current year's figures.

> The auditors' opinion for the current period extends to the comparative figures only if such an extension is specifically stated in their report. [CICA Handbook][49]

In the United States, in contrast, AICPA pronouncements call for the auditor to extend his opinion to the prior year's statements as well, provided that he has examined them.[50] Where a Canadian practitioner is requested to extend his opinion to cover the prior year's statements the standard report wording might be amended as follows:

> I have examined the balance sheet of ... as at ... , 19.. and ... , 19.. and the statements ... for the years then ended. My examinations were made ...
> In my opinion, these financial statements present fairly the financial position of the company as at ... , 19.. and 19.. and the results ... for the years then ended ... applied on a consistent basis during the period.

In such cases it is desirable for the headings of the statements themselves to indicate that they cover two years – rather than one year, with comparative figures for the preceding year.

Where the opinion covers two years, reservations with respect to either year should be appropriately covered in a reservation paragraph and in the opinion paragraph (see Chapter 18). Where the opinion covers only the current year, prior reservations related solely to the prior year do not affect the current year's opinion. Nonetheless, except where the matters giving rise to the prior reservations have subsequently been settled, it may be appropriate to refer to such prior reservations in a separate explanatory paragraph following the opinion paragraph.[51]

17.5.3 Initial engagements

Where the auditor undertakes an initial audit engagement replacing a predecessor auditor, and where he is able to place reliance on the report and work of that predecessor auditor, he may be able to express an unqualified opinion on the current year's financial statements. In that case, the only modification to the standard report wording will be a third paragraph explaining that the prior year's statements were examined by another chartered accountant (see 23.2.5). Where the auditor undertakes an initial audit engagement of a previously unaudited organization and where, rarely, he is able to express a clear opinion on the current year's statements, the only modification will be a third paragraph explaining that the prior year's statements were not audited; more commonly he will have to express a reservation with respect to his opinions on both presentation and consistency (see 23.3.2). Where the auditor undertakes an initial audit engagement of a new organization, the only modifications will be a reference to the period from the date of incorporation to the period-end and the omission of any reference to consistency (see 23.4.2).

17.5.4 Legislative and regulatory requirements

Corporation acts

The Companies Acts of Nova Scotia, Quebec and Saskatchewan prescribe an older form of wording for the audit report. In such cases the standard report wording can be modified as follows:

> I have examined . . . for the year then ended and have obtained all the information and explanations I have required. My examination . . . circumstances.
> In my opinion, and according to the best of my information and the explanations given to me, and as shown by the books of the company, these financial statements are properly drawn up so as to exhibit a true and correct view of the state of the affairs of the company . . . preceding year.

The wording requirements of the Newfoundland Act are somewhat different again.

The Corporations Acts of Alberta, Manitoba, Ontario, and the Northwest Territories as well as the old Canada Corporations Act (which may in some cases apply up to 1980) require the auditor to make such statements as he considers necessary where

a) the company's financial statements are not in agreement with its accounting records,[52]
b) the company's financial statements are not in accordance with the requirements of the governing Act,
c) he has not received all the information and explanations he has required,
d) proper accounting records have not been kept, so far as appears from his examination.

The foregoing deficiencies would normally require a

reservation of opinion and the statutory disclosure would be covered by the reservation.

Alberta, Manitoba, Ontario and the Northwest Territories also require the auditor to indicate the amount of any inadequacy in provision for subsidiary company losses in the unconsolidated financial statements of a holding company. Such deficiencies would likewise normally require a reservation of opinion and the statutory disclosure would be covered by the reservation. In addition, the auditor must consider whether the lack of consolidation itself requires a reservation of opinion.

Nova Scotia requires a statement by the auditor indicating how the profits or losses of subsidiary companies, in the aggregate, have been dealt with in the statements of a holding company. This information would usually be covered in a note to the financial statements to meet the standards of full disclosure. If so, the audit report requirement can be met by a third explanatory paragraph referring to that note.

British Columbia requires the auditor to state whether in his opinion due provision has not been made for minority interests in consolidated financial statements. If provision has not been made, the required reservation of opinion would automatically cover the statutory reporting requirement. British Columbia also requires that the auditor state, whether, in his opinion, certain prescribed disclosures with respect to unconsolidated subsidiaries are adequate; this requirement can likewise be met by a third explanatory paragraph, though the auditor must consider whether a reservation of opinion is required as well.

Saskatchewan requires the auditor to state whether in his opinion all the transactions of the company that have come to his notice have been within the objects and powers of the company. This opinion can be given in a third paragraph.

> Where statutory information in addition to that included in the suggested form of auditors' report is lengthy, it should be set out in a separate paragraph after the opinion paragraph, with a reference, if appropriate, to the particular governing statute which makes it necessary to provide the additional information. [CICA Handbook][53]

Other legislative and regulatory requirements

Occasionally some legislative or regulatory requirement will include a prescribed form of audit report. The introduction to the CICA's Auditing Recommendations states that:

> No Recommendation is intended to override the requirements of a governing statute.

Nonetheless, the auditor must consider whether he can properly issue a report in the prescribed form.

Some reports "may call for a certification of fact rather than an expression of opinion, may call for an opinion on matters outside the scope of the auditors' examination, may omit essential wording or may be inappropriate in some other way."[54]

The auditors should give careful consideration to the wording of any prescribed form of auditors' report and, where necessary, should insist on making appropriate changes. [CICA Handbook][55]

Cases where CICA Auditing Recommendations do not apply

The Introduction to the CICA's Auditng Recommendations states:

Recommendations are intended to apply to all types of profit oriented enterprises, unless a particular Recommendation makes a specific exemption or extension. However, pending further study, the Recommendations do not necessarily apply to the special problems of banks and insurance companies.

It follows that the four reporting standards and the various Recommendations covering report format and wording do not necessarily apply to reports on banks, insurance companies, and not-for-profit organizations. Of course, a chartered accountant is still bound by the ethical requirement to avoid association with false or misleading statements (see 3.2.5). The auditor must use his best judgment as to what form of report best meets the legal requirements and his professional responsibilities in each case.

In particular, it is usually considered appropriate to omit references to generally accepted accounting principles and consistency in the opinion paragraph of audit reports on banks and life insurance companies and to omit references to generally accepted accounting principles for general insurance companies and at least some not-for-profit organizations. The accounting for banks and life insurance companies has in the past been influenced by the objective of protecting the depositor or policyholder, which led to practices differing from those used by other enterprises. Moreover, generally accepted accounting principles have not to date been particularly clearly developed with respect to a consistent and appropriate basis of determining allowances for doubtful accounts or loans . . . a matter of substantial importance in bank accounting. In these circumstances, neither generally accepted accounting principles nor the concept of consistency have to date been considered to be meaningful. The "established criteria" to which the auditor refers in judging whether the statements of one institution "present fairly" must be implicitly the customary accounting practices of similar institutions. Interpretation 206/8 to the Rules of Professional Conduct states in part:

The form and content of financial reports of banks and insurance companies are controlled, or heavily influenced, by statute or governmental regulation. While the Research Committee is silent as to accounting methods appropriate to the circumstances of such financial institutions some accounting practices are prescribed or permitted for them by law or regulations which are different from those that would be considered normal for ordinary commercial and industrial enterprises. In these circumstances it is considered appropriate for an auditor to omit a reference to generally accepted accounting principles in his report and not to qualify his report.

The present position is as follows:

1. *Chartered banks.*
The wording of reports on chartered banks is governed by The Bank Act. References to generally accepted accounting principles and to consistency are normally omitted. However, some revisions in financial disclosures for banks were announced in the government white paper on Canadian banking legislation in 1976. In addition, the profession has been working closely with the banking community in studying report problems. As a result of these studies, a number of changes are likely and the day is closer when references to generally accepted accounting principles and consistency may prove feasible.

2. *Life insurance companies.*
Life insurance companies under federal jurisdiction are not required by law to have auditors, and there is therefore no statutory wording. Those under provincial jurisdiction may have varying statutory provisions governing their audit reports. References to generally accepted accounting principles and to consistency are normally omitted. However, the question of appropriate accounting principles for life insurance companies has recently been under study by the accounting profession,[56] by the actuarial profession, and by government. It is possible that the resolution of these studies could lead to the introduction of references to generally accepted accounting principles and consistency. A further modification from standard report wording is a common reference to reliance on actuaries (see 17.5.8).

3. *General insurance companies.*
The accounting followed by general insurance companies in Canada follows a fairly uniform pattern guided by the federal and provincial departments of insurance. A reference to consistency is therefore normal. The accounting practices prescribed, however, differ in several respects from generally accepted accounting principles. Alternative audit reporting practices include:
a) reporting on the accounting presentation as prescribed, omitting a reference to generally accepted accounting principles, but including words

such as "in accordance with accounting practices prescribed or permitted under the Insurance law of Canada applied on a basis consistent . . . ",

b) reporting, with the standard report wording, on financial statements adjusted to conform with generally accepted accounting principles (where such statements are permitted by law),

c) reporting on financial statements in the prescribed form as in (a) but with a further opinion on supplementary data or statements to adjust to the generally accepted basis.

Again, the question of appropriate accounting principles for general insurance companies has recently been under study by the accounting profession[57] and by government.

4. Not-for-profit organizations.

Some not-for-profit organizations, such as hospitals, operate on a fee-for-service basis and follow accounting methods that would be acceptable for business enterprises, with certain reasonable modifications – e.g., the use of fund accounting for restricted purpose funds. For such organizations the standard report wording is commonly used. Evidence as to generally accepted accounting principles may be provided by common usage or by various publications such as the Canadian Hospital Accounting Manual.[58]

Other not-for-profit organizations may follow accounting methods which are recognized as applicable in that type of institution but which differ from those applicable to commercial undertakings – e.g., by omission of depreciation accounting. For such organizations, auditors' reports commonly use words such as "in accordance with accounting principles generally accepted for . . . [universities, municipalities, charitable organizations, etc.] . . . applied on a basis consistent . . . ". Evidence as to accounting principles generally accepted for particular types of organizations may be provided by common usage or by various publications such as Canadian Standards of Accounting and Financial Reporting for Voluntary Organizations.

Finally, some not-for-profit organizations employ cash-basis or modified cash-basis accounting and omit substantial amounts of assets or liabilities from the statements. For such organizations, auditors' reports commonly limit themselves to the items (e.g., cash position, receipts and disbursements) presented and to the consistency of the accounting for them, but do not refer to generally accepted accounting principles nor to financial position and results of operations, since the latter words imply the use of full accrual accounting. Reporting on cash basis or modified cash basis statements is discussed further under special purpose reports in 19.3.2. Sometimes such an organization is governed by a Corporations Act which requires the auditor to report on financial

position and results of operations in accordance with generally accepted accounting principles. To fulfill the statutory reporting requirement a third paragraph may be added with wording such as:

As these statements have been drawn up on a cash basis of accounting they do not purport to be a complete statement of financial position and results of operations in accordance with generally accepted accounting principles. In particular, the statements do not show the amounts of the Association's . . . [accounts receivable, liabilities, investment in buildings and furniture] . . .

5. Cases where AICPA reporting standards apply.

Unlike the CICA Auditing Recommendations, the AICPA reporting standard with respect to generally accepted accounting principles does apply to financial institutions and other regulated organizations.[59] Under the AICPA standards, the auditor must first express an opinion relative to generally accepted accounting principles – with reservations if required. He may then, if he wishes, proceed to express a special purpose opinion relative to a prescribed basis of accounting.[60] When Canadian practitioners are reporting on special reports on financial institutions for use in the United States they must be mindful of these different requirements. On the other hand, the AICPA requirements with respect to not-for-profit organization statements[61] and statements which do not purport to present financial position and results of operations[62] do not differ significantly from the Canadian practice just discussed.

17.5.5 Other information accompanying audited financial statments

Corporate annual reports frequently contain information in addition to the audited financial statements: supplementary schedules, tables and graphs, analyses and commentaries, and narrative reports by management, the president, the chairman, and/or the directors. In some cases the auditor may be asked to express an opinion on some portion of this other information. Usually, however, he is not.

Where the auditor is asked to express an opinion

Supporting schedules which are covered by the auditor's standard report because of being (a) referenced from the financial statements or (b) specifically identified in the scope paragraph (see 17.2.3) usually can be considered a part of the presentation of financial position, results of operations and changes in financial position. In such cases no modifications in the standard report wording may be required –

though sufficient audit procedures must be performed to justify the extension of the opinion to include those supporting schedules. However, because of materiality considerations it may, in some cases, be preferable to avoid (a) referencing from the financial statements or (b) specific identification in the scope paragraph, in order to cover the supplementary schedules instead by a third paragraph as discussed below.

In some cases, certain supplementary schedules do not logically form a part of the presentation of financial position, results of operations and changes in financial position but the auditor may nonetheless be requested to express an opinion on them. If the supplementary schedules in question consist of historical financial data (as opposed to financial forecasts, qualitative commentary on management performance, analysis of business prospects or economic conditions, etc.), the auditor may accede to such a request providing he performs the necessary audit work. In such cases the examination of and opinion on the supplementary data may be covered in a third paragraph with wording such as:

> I also examined . . . [title of statement – such as "five year review"] . . . which is presented as supplementary information on pages X to Y. In my opinion the information therein is fairly presented in all respects material to the financial statements taken as a whole.

It should be noted that the reporting standards do not apply to the expression of an opinion on data other than financial statements.[63] The foregoing wording, which does not refer to consistency or a disclosed basis of accounting (which indeed may not be practical), does not therefore need to conform to those standards.

A similar type of third paragraph was suggested in the CICA Auditing Guidelines for reports on supplementary price-level restatements:

> I have also examined the supplementary general price-level restated data accompanying the above-mentioned historical cost financial statements. Uniform criteria for the preparation and presentation of such data have not yet been established and accordingly restatement procedures could vary from one enterprise to another. In my opinion the restatement procedures described in the note appended to the supplementary data have been applied in an appropriate manner in compiling such data from the above-mentioned historical cost financial statements.[64]

Where the supplementary schedules look like financial statements but do not form a part of the presentation of financial position, results of operations and presentation of financial position, it may be preferable to include a specific reference to them in both the scope and opinion paragraphs. Appropriate wording might be:

> I have examined . . . for the year then ended. I have also examined . . . [name of supplementary statement and period covered]. . . My examinations included. . . necessary in the circumstances.
> In my opinion these financial statements present fairly . . . for the year then ended and . . . [name of supplementary statement] . . . presents fairly the information set forth therein all in accordance with . . . preceding year.

Where this format is used the auditor must be satisfied that the yardstick of generally accepted accounting principles is indeed applicable to the supplementary data.

It is acceptable to report on some but not all of the supplementary historical financial data included in an annual report provided that the auditor's report makes clear the data on which he is expressing an opinion.

Where the auditor is not asked to express an opinion

Many practitioners in Canada make it a policy to read all financial information contained in the published annual reports of their clients – although such a reading cannot be considered to be either a legal or professional obligation. The situation is slightly different in the United States. The AICPA Statement on Auditing Standards No. 8 does establish such an obligation:

> The auditor's responsibility with respect to information in a document does not extend beyond the financial information identified in his report, and the auditor has no obligation to perform any procedures to corroborate other information contained in a document. However, he should read the other information and consider whether such information, or the manner of its presentation, is materially inconsistent with information, or the manner of its presentation, appearing in the financial statements.[65]

If Canadian practitioners encounter material misstatements of figure or fact or material inconsistencies between the reviewed information and the audited financial statements in the course of such a reading, appropriate correction or investigation is normally requested. The auditor is not reporting on the other information, however, and his suggestions for any revisions should logically not carry the same weight as suggestions with respect to the financial statements. Nonetheless, in extreme cases, should the auditor be aware that the information is materially false or misleading, he must consider his ethical responsibilities (see 3.2.5) and whether he should withdraw from the engagement and/or seek competent legal advice. In Canada he would not normally be considered to have a reporting obligation with respect to such problems – except to the extent of (a) any subsequent discovery that the audited financial statements were in error (see 18.7) or (b) in the event that he resigns from the engagement, his right under certain Corporations Acts to communicate the reason for his resignation (see 4.1.7). In the United States, however, the AICPA statement suggests that in at least some circumstances the auditor should consider "revising his report to include an explanatory paragraph describing the material inconsistency."[66]

17.5.6 Language translation

Because Canada has two official languages, documents containing audited financial statements are frequently published both in English and French. In such cases the Canadian auditor will normally report in English on the English language version and in French on the French language version.

In order to report in both languages, the auditor must be satisfied that both language versions of the financial statements convey the same meaning. Since the usual situation is that the statements are drawn up in one language and, when completed, are translated into the other, this requirement means that the auditor must satisfy himself that the translation is competently performed. Because the translation of technical information requires a sound knowledge of its technical nature, many practitioners prefer to do the translation of the audited financial statements and the audit report themselves rather than review the work of a firm of translators. In such cases the auditor in effect performs two functions, an audit function and a translation function. Sometimes the auditor may be asked to convey some assurance in the form of a report as to the latter function. He may do so in words such as the following:

> . . . In my opinion the French (English) translation . . . is in all material respects an appropriate translation and contains no additions or changes of substance from the English (French) language version and omits nothing of substance therein . . .

Additional problems which arise with respect to language translation in prospectuses are discussed in 19.1.1. Translation of financial statements and audit reports for use in foreign countries is discussed in 18.4.

17.5.7 Reliance on other auditors

An auditor may often be asked to report on the statements of a company which has one or more consolidated subsidiaries or equity-accounted investee companies which have not been audited by him. While such arrangements raise certain problems for the investor auditor and are usually somewhat more expensive for the client than if the investor auditor performed all the audit work himself, there may be strong reasons from the client's point of view (particularly with respect to non-subsidiary investees) why such arrangements should be continued.

The problems for the investor auditor in such situations relate to (a) the amount of responsibility he should assume for the work of the other auditors, (b) how he should report when he has relied on the work of other auditors, and (c) the amount of audit work he needs to do to satisfy himself that he can accept this responsibility. The distinction among *agency relationships, non-agency relationships* and *implied agency relationships* was discussed in 15.4.8. Criteria for choosing among *basic procedures, review procedures* and *override procedures* for justifying reliance were likewise discussed in 15.4.8 and the procedures themselves are described in 38.3.10. The present section deals solely with report modifications which may arise when reliance is placed on other auditors. It might be noted that Canadian practice is somewhat different from that in the United States because of differences in law between the two countries. For one thing, Canadian law and pronouncements refer to the concept of *reliance* whereas U.S. pronouncements refer instead to the concept of *divided responsibility*.

Agency or implied agency relationship

Where the auditor has a formal agency relationship with the investee auditor, his relationship with his agent (or any office of the agent firm) will be similiar to his relationship to any office of his own firm. No reliance on the agent should be expressed in the auditor's work and, assuming reservations of opinion are not otherwise required, the standard report wording should be used.

> Where an agency arrangement exists between the parent company auditors and the auditors of one or more subsidiary companies, the parent company auditors should not make any reference to the work or the report of the other auditors in reporting on the consolidated financial statements. [CICA Handbook][67]
> The recommendations. . . should also be applied to situations where long-term intercorporate investments are accounted for by the equity method . . . [CICA Handbook][68]

In such cases, the investor auditor takes full responsibility, so far as the investor financial statements are concerned, for the work of the investee auditors and the latter, in addition to their responsibility to the investee shareholders, owe a responsibility as agents to the investor auditor.

In some situations the investor auditor may, without a formal agency arrangement, be prepared to accept the work of an investee auditor as though he were his agent for the particular assignment. In such cases, the investor auditor again assumes full responsibility, so far as the investor financial statements are

497

concerned. The standard report wording would again be applicable. The effect of acceptance of such an implied agency relationship by the investor auditor is to forego whatever protection is provided by a reference to reliance in the audit report. Except where the investments are immaterial, the most prudent course for an investor auditor is probably to avoid such implied agency relationships.

Non-agency relationship

Where no agency relationship exists between the investor auditor and investee auditor, the CICA Handbook calls for reference to be made in the former's report, not as a qualification but in order to define the scope of the examination by stating clearly his reliance on the investee auditors.

> Where no agency relationship exists between the parent company auditors and the auditors of one or more of the subsidiary companies, the parent company auditors should refer to the work of the other auditors in the scope paragraph of their report on the consolidated financial statements. [CICA Handbook][69]
> The recommendations . . . should also be applied to situations where long-term intercorporate investments are accounted for by the equity method . . . [CICA Handbook][70]

The expression of reliance in the scope paragraph can be made using wording such as the following:

> I have examined . . . year then ended. For . . . [the investor company] . . . and for those other companies of which I am the auditor and which are consolidated or are accounted for by the equity method in these financial statements, my examination included . . . in the circumstances. For other companies consolidated or accounted for by the equity method I have relied on the reports of the auditors who have examined their financial statements.[71]

The Canada Business Corporations Act provides that such reliance can be placed provided that the fact of the reliance is disclosed:

163.2
a) an auditor of a holding corporation may reasonably rely upon the report of the auditor of a body corporate that is a subsidiary of the holding corporation if the fact of his reliance is disclosed in his report as auditor of the holding corporation; and
b) an auditor of a corporation may reasonably rely upon the report of the auditor of a body corporate that is not a subsidiary of the corporation but is, as prescribed, effectively controlled by the corporation, if the fact of his reliance is disclosed in his report as auditor of the corporation.

The word "reasonably" implies that certain conditions or procedures are necessary to justify the reliance (see 38.3.10).

Some provincial corporations acts contain different provisions. For example, the Ontario act provides that the auditor "may refer to the reports of auditors of . . . subsidiaries, but such reference shall not derogate from the duty of the auditor of the holding corporation" to express an opinion on the consolidated financial statements. Some provincial acts are silent on the issue.

Amplifying the scope reference to other auditors

The CICA Handbook calls for a *reference* to the work of other auditors in the scope paragraph and *suggests* wording for making this reference. The suggested wording expresses the fact of reliance on, but not the identity of, the investee auditors nor the extent of the figures audited by them. It may be argued that, since the reference is not intended as a qualification, there is no need to amplify it any more than the auditor would need to disclose the extent of other audit procedures he performs. Further, the provision of information as to amounts audited by others and/or the names of the other auditors or companies will not necessarily convey useful information to statement readers. As an example, a high versus a low percentage of assets/revenues/income audited by others only has meaning in relation to all the other attendant circumstances, including the relative stability or volatility of the underlying company operations and the amount of override work the investor auditor has done.

On the other hand, the auditor has no reason to resist such disclosures provided they are not misleading in form. (It could be misleading, for example, to have a statement "we have relied on the reports of A Well-Known and Co. and B Little-Known and Co. with respect to certain subsidiary companies" if the former were responsible for 1% of the figures and the latter for 25%.) Such additional information may be most readily given in a note to the financial statements cross-referenced from the expression of reliance in the auditor's scope paragraph. The auditor should have the written permission of other auditors before mentioning them by name in his audit report.

In the United States, in contrast, AICPA pronouncements provide that (a) disclosure of the extent of reliance ("division of responsibility") is required whenever reliance is expressed (b) the investee auditor may be named only when his report is also presented, and (c) a repeated reference is called for in the opinion paragraph.

> When the principal auditor decides that he will make reference to the examination of the other auditor, his report should indicate clearly, in both the scope and opinion paragraphs, the division of responsibility as between that portion of the financial statements covered by his own examination and that covered by the examination of the other auditor. The report should disclose the magnitude of the portion of the financial statements

examined by the other auditor. This may be done by stating the dollar amounts or percentages of one or more of the following: total assets, total revenues, or other appropriate criteria . . . The other auditor may be named but only with his express permission and provided his report is presented together with that of the principal auditor.[72]

The suggested references in the U.S. auditor's report are somewhat stronger than those suggested in Canada. For example, the suggested scope paragraph, among other comments, contains the phrase "and our opinion expressed herein, insofar as it relates to the amounts included for B Company, is based solely upon the report of the other auditors"; the suggested opinion paragraph contains the phrase "In our opinion, based upon our examination and the report of other auditors".[73]

Restricted access in equity accounting situations

A potential difficulty can sometimes arise with respect to equity-accounted non-subsidiary investees. Whereas many corporations acts give parent company auditors legal access to subsidiary company information, the same degree of legal authority is not granted with respect to the obtaining of information from other investees. Directors of an investee company may, in some rare situations, see dangers in giving one minority shareholder (the investor and its auditor) access to certain inside information which is not available to all its shareholders. Therefore, it is conceivable, even though effective control exists, that a situation could arise in which an investee company would be unwilling to give (or allow the investee auditor to give) to the investor auditor the information he would normally wish to have to express a clear opinion on the investor company financial statements. However, a report qualification for limitation in scope might be undesirable where the investor auditor has received audited financial statements of the investee at the appropriate date, because:

a) it might seem to reflect on the competence of the other auditors and, indirectly, on the profession as a whole, and

b) the audited financial statements of the investee do provide important audit evidence.

Accordingly it is suggested that when:

a) directors or officers of an investee company have, for reasons of valid concern, refused the auditor needed access to investee company information;

b) the auditor has received the final audited figures of the investee directly from the investee auditor;

c) the auditor has taken reasonable steps to ensure that he can be satisfied as to the objectivity and reputation of the investee auditor;

d) the auditor has satisfactorily completed "basic procedures" (including the obtaining of representations from the investee auditor, information as to intercompany transactions, etc. – see 38.3.10);

e) nothing has arisen that should arouse the auditor's suspicions as to the overall fairness of the investee financial statements;

a stronger reference to reliance, but without reservation of opinion, would be desirable. Wording for such a stronger reference might, for example, follow the U.S. style of referring in the scope paragraph to investee figures being "based solely on the reports of the other auditors" and in the opinion paragraph to "based upon my examination and the reports of other auditors". While the CICA Handbook calls for modifying the scope paragraph and suggests wording limited to modifying that paragraph, it does not expressly prohibit modification of the opinion paragraph (provided a reservation of opinion is not expressed due solely to such reliance).

There may be rare restricted access situations where the auditor does not have even reasonable assurance as to audited financial figures of an investee company. In such cases, there exists a limitation in the scope of his audit examination and, if it is significant, this limitation will call for a reservation of opinion (see Chapter 18).

17.5.8 Reliance on specialists

Using the work of a specialist as a source of audit evidence was discussed in 10.3.3. The present section deals solely with report modifications, if any, which may arise when reliance is placed on a specialist's work.

While professional pronouncements in Canada do not speak to the subject, the practice has been to make no reference to reliance on specialists' work in the vast majority of cases. Such a position seems reasonable, for the reliance on solicitors in virtually all engagements and on engineers, geologists, appraisers, and internal auditors in many engagements is but a part of the auditor's reliance on all the various sources of audit evidence contributing to his final opinion. (This argument, however, somewhat contradicts the position taken on reliance on other auditors.) The principal exception has been in audit reports on life insurance companies (not presently covered by the CICA Auditing Recommendations in any case). In such reports, it has been customary in Canada to express reliance on the actuary's work. Typical wording for expressing this reliance is:

I have examined . . . necessary in the circumstances; the . . . [liability to provide for payments guaranteed under

499

insurance and annuity contracts and the dividends to be paid to policyholders] . . . were determined and certified by . . . [the Company's actuary]. . . .

Based on my examination and the certificate of . . . [the Company's actuary]. . . , I report that in my opinion. . . .

Some practitioners have argued that complete reliance is not appropriate when, as is common, a major portion (sometimes the predominant portion) of the statement of assets and liabilities and of the revenue statement depends upon the determination of the reporting company's own actuary. These practitioners advocate a greater responsibility for verification of the actuarial reserves on the part of the auditor – which might then eliminate the need for expressing reliance. Other practitioners hold contrary views. The relationship between auditor and actuary responsibilities has recently been under study by the accounting profession,[74] the actuarial profession, and the government.

In the United States, reference to a specialist (whether actuarial or other) in the auditor's report is normally prohibited:

> When expressing an unqualified opinion, the auditor should not refer to the work or findings of the specialist. Such a reference in an unqualified opinion might be misunderstood to be a qualification in the auditor's opinion or a division of responsibility, neither of which is intended.[75]

However, reference to a specialist's findings is permitted in expressing a reservation of opinion (for example, where the specialist's findings indicate that the financial statements are materially misstated) when the auditor believes such reference will help the reader to understand the reservation.

The U.S. position avoids an apparent conflict between disclosed reliance on other auditors and non-disclosed reliance on specialists by avoiding the term "reliance". The former situation is referred to as a "division of responsibility" and the latter as "using the work". In Canada, however, the opinion of counsel referred to in the CICA Handbook section on reliance on other auditors draws a parallel between auditors and other experts[76] – so a marked distinction may be less logical. In the end, practice is likely to be most influenced by legal requirements and pragmatism.

17.5.9 Audits of unincorporated enterprises

The wording of the auditor's standard report should, with minor changes, be appropriate in reporting upon the financial statements of unincorporated enterprises such as partnerships and sole proprietorships.[77] Reporting on a not-for-profit organizations was discussed in 17.5.4.

The statements of some partnerships, such as professional firms, are commonly drawn up on a modified cash basis of accounting, in order to conform with the basis used in filing their income tax returns. The statements of some sole proprietorships are drawn up on a cash basis for the same reason. Financial statements prepared in accordance with generally accepted accounting principles must, however, normally use the full accrual basis.

Of course, it is possible to prepare financial statements on one basis for the partners' or proprietors' purposes and on another basis for tax purposes. Often, however, the partners (or proprietor) desire financial statements prepared solely on a tax basis. The third reporting standard requires the auditor's opinion to be expressed as to the conformity of the statements with "an appropriate disclosed basis of accounting, which except in special circumstances should be generally accepted accounting principles". Whether the preparation of partnership financial statements on a tax basis can be considered "an appropriate disclosed basis of accounting" other than generally accepted accounting principles is not entirely clear. If it cannot be so considered, the auditor should first express an opinion relative to generally accepted accounting principles with suitable reservations – though he may then go on to express a special purpose opinion relative to the basis of accounting employed. Special reports on cash basis and modified cash basis statements are discussed in 19.3.1. The reader should refer to subsequent CICA reporting pronouncements, under study as this book goes to press.

Under U.S. reporting standards, the requirement to express an opinion relative to generally accepted accounting principles would not normally apply to cash basis statements since they do not purport to present financial position and results of operations but would normally apply to modified accrual basis statements since they do.[78]

A sole proprietorship is merely a convenient designation for all or some portion of the sole proprietor's business activities. Net income, assets and liabilities of the proprietorship constitute income, assets and liabilities of the proprietor. Income tax is levied on the proprietor rather than on the proprietorship. Proprietorship assets may be taken to satisfy personal debts of the proprietor or non-proprietorship assets of the proprietor taken to satisfy proprietorship liabilities. The division between the affairs of the proprietorship as a business and other activities of the proprietor is often ill-defined. The resulting limitations of the financial statements of an unincorporated business, particularly the fact that they do not include all the assets, liabilities, revenues and expenses of the owners, must be disclosed in the

500

headings or notes to the statements.[79] When issuing an audit report on such financial statements, some practitioners believe it is desirable to emphasize these limitations by adding to the scope paragraph a final sentence such as:

> My examination did not cover personal assets and liabilities of ... [name of the sole proprietor] ... not included in the proprietorship statements.

Others believe that such emphasis is undesirable provided that note disclosure is adequate.

17.5.10 Other disclosures in the auditor's report

Reference has already been made to the use of a final explanatory paragraph in certain cases: disclosing statutory information (17.5.4) or commenting on comparative figures in initial engagements (17.5.3). Auditors sometimes wish to present other information or explanations as well. If such explanations preceded the opinion paragraph they might be misinterpreted as a reservation. They should, therefore, instead, be presented in an explanatory paragraph following the opinion paragraph.

> If the auditors expand their formal report to include information and explanations neither required by statute nor intended as a qualification of the auditors' opinion, the opinion paragraph should precede that containing additional information and explanations. [CICA Handbook][80]

Furthermore, the opinion paragraph should not contain phrases such as "With the explanations provided in the following paragraph, in our opinion ..." since this wording would again imply a reservation of opinion.

It should be noted, however, that a final explanatory paragraph is not appropriate for presenting information which is essential to fair presentation in accordance with generally accepted accounting principles but which was omitted from the financial statements or notes. If the financial statement disclosures are inadequate, the auditor should express a reservation of opinion and, if possible, provide the missing information in a reservation paragraph explaining the reasons for his reservation (Chapter 18).

As a result, a final explanatory paragraph in the auditor's report will generally be limited to (a) information he wishes to present but which he does not consider essential to fair presentation or (b) information already presented in the financial statements but which he wishes to emphasize. Examples sometimes suggested are situations where the auditor "may wish to point out that the entity is a component of a larger business enterprise or that it has had significant transactions with related parties ... [or where] ... he may wish to call attention to an unusually important subsequent event or to an accounting matter affecting the comparability of the financial statements with those of the preceding period."[81]

Some practitioners believe that explanatory disclosures in the auditor's report, other than those required by statute, are undesirable. They argue that, if the information is not required for fair presentation, the auditor's reasons for presenting it will be unclear to the reader and may imply incorrectly that the reader can count on similar information always being presented in the auditor's reports in like circumstances. Information repeated in the auditor's report for emphasis may imply incorrectly a duty to emphasize and may raise questions about the relative importance of other matters in the financial statements which might be considered worthy of emphasis.

Generally, it is undesirable in a short-form report to make reference to specific audit procedures performed or, unless a reservation is being expressed, to specific audit procedures omitted. For example, where the auditor has not observed inventory-taking or not confirmed accounts receivables but has satisfied himself as to inventories and accounts receivable by other means, additional disclosures in the auditor's report are neither required nor desirable. Likewise, it is neither required nor desirable for the auditor to disclose in his audit report that he has also written up the client's books of account as an accounting service, provided that he is satisfied that his objectivity has not been impaired. Where an auditor feels he must, or is requested to, disclose in a short-form report certain specific audit procedures performed, the additional disclosures should generally be made in a final explanatory paragraph and not by expansion of the scope paragraph. (For long-form reports, however, see 19.3.5.)

17.6 Reference material

CICA Handbook, Sec. 5400, The Auditor's Standard Report (the reader should refer to additional subsequent pronouncements; as this book goes to press a proposed section on Other Reporting Matters and a possible renumbering of other sections are under study).

CICA Handbook, Sec. 5500, The Auditor's Report—Other Matters (the reader should refer to subsequent pronouncements which may supersede the present Sec. 5500).

CICA Handbook, Sec. 5530, Reliance on Other Auditors.

R.M. Skinner, FCA, *Accounting Principles: A Canadian Viewpoint*. (CICA 1972).

AICPA Statement on Auditing Standards No. 1, Secs., 410, 420, 430, 530, 543, 546.

AICPA Statement on Auditing Standards No. 2, *Reports on Audited Financial Statements* pars. 1 to 8, 14, 27, 49.

AICPA Statement on Auditing Standards No. 5, *The Meaning of "Present Fairly in Conformity with Generally*

Accepted Accounting Principles" in the Independent Auditor's Report.

AICPA Statement on Auditing Standards No. 8, *Other Information in Documents Containing Audited Financial Statements.*

AICPA Auditing Research Monograph No. 1, *The Auditor's Reporting Obligation*, D.R. Carmichael, CPA, PhD.

Accountants International Study Group, *The Independent Auditor's Reporting Standards in three Nations* (1969), pars. 1 to 51.

Accountants International Study Group, *Using the Work and Report of Another Auditor* (1970).

17.7 Questions and problems

Review and discussion

1. What are the objectives of an audit report on financial statements?
2. Identify the four types of paragraph that could occur in the standard short-form report.
3. To whom should the auditor's report be addressed?
4. How should the audit report be dated? Why?
5. What is the purpose of the scope paragraph?
6. Describe the role of the CICA Accounting Research Committee with respect to accounting principles in Canada.
7. How does one determine what constitutes a generally accepted accounting principle?
8. Discuss the possibility of consolidated financial statements being presented fairly in accordance with generally accepted accounting principles when:
   a) two subsidiaries employ principles which, while conforming to generally accepted accounting principles, are peculiar to their industries and are incompatible with the parent company's principles,
   b) the audit report of one subsidiary has been qualified because of non-compliance with generally accepted accounting principles.
9. Section 1505.04 of the CICA Handbook recommends that: "A clear and concise description of the significant accounting policies of an enterprise should be included as an integral part of the financial statements." How does this recommendation aid the user of financial statements?
10. The auditor must use his professional judgment in determining whether "financial statements present fairly" the financial position and results of operations of an enterprise. What are the implications of the term "present fairly"? How does the auditor arrive at such a judgment?

11. Some people argue that it is neither possible, nor desirable, to have an international standardized audit report. Comment.
12. What would be the advantages and disadvantages of disclosing the materiality limit (a) in the audit report or (b) in the notes to the financial statement?
13. What effect should a change in accounting principle have on the auditor's report if the auditor (a) agrees with the change (b) disagrees with the change?
14. How does reliance on other auditors affect the audit report? In what situations would there be no effect on audit report wording?
15. What purpose does an explanatory paragraph serve in the body of an audit report? Give examples.
16. "I have never issued a qualified report," said Jack Smith, CA. "Such reports satisfy no one. I find it much simpler to change the financial statements if the client is using unacceptable accounting methods." Comment.
17. Identify the important representations made by the auditor in the opinion paragraph of the standard short-form report and discuss briefly their significance.

Problems

1. Identify and briefly discuss the problems with the following report.

Certificate

To the Owners of X Company Limited
We have examined the balance sheet of X Co. Ltd. as at December 31, 1976 and the statements of earnings and retained earnings for the fiscal year. Our examination was performed using such generally accepted auditing procedures and other

tests as we considered necessary in the circumstances.

In our opinion, the financial statements present fairly the financial position of X Co. Ltd. as of December 31, 1976 and the results of its operations and the source and application of its funds for the fiscal year; the statements are in accordance with generally accepted accounting principles applied on a consistent basis.

> Trant & Co.
> Chartered Accountants

January 31, 1977
Vancouver, Canada.

2. Explain, giving reasons, why auditors report their findings as an expression of opinion rather than as a statement of fact.

3. (CICA adapted) The author of a recent article stated that the auditor of a public company would be well advised to ensure not only that the client's financial statements were prepared according to generally accepted accounting principles, but also that they reflected the client's position in an adequate and understandable way from the point of view of a layman.

What comment do you have on this author's statement?

4. The following are unrelated events which occurred after the balance sheet date but before the audit report was prepared:

a) the granting of a retroactive pay increase,
b) determination by the Federal Government of additional income tax due for the prior year,
c) declaration of a stock dividend,
d) sale of a fixed asset at a substantial profit.

Explain how each of these items might have come to the auditor's attention and discuss the auditor's responsibility with respect to each of them in connection with his report.

5. An investor auditor cannot merely accept for inclusion in the investor's consolidation the financial statements of subsidiaries of which he is not the auditor without having formed some opinion as to the reliability of such statements.

a) What factors should be considered by the investor auditor in determining the extent to which he could be justified in relying upon the work of an investee auditor?
b) What should the investor auditor do in order to rely upon the work and opinion of an investee auditor for the purpose of expressing an opinion on the consolidated financial statements?

6. In giving his opinion on the financial statements,

the auditor refers to generally accepted auditing standards and generally accepted accounting principles. In each of the following situations, describe in detail the points the auditor should consider in deciding whether or not he is able to give an unqualified opinion on the financial statements as to their fairness of presentation in accordance with generally accepted accounting principles.

a) A Co. is a retailer whose sales are primarily on a cash basis. The purchases of stock are made from the parent company; hence, the only payables to non-affiliates are for service, wages, etc.

Receivables at year-end	$ 15 000
Sales for year	$1 200 000
Net income before tax	$ 350 000
Payables to third parties	$ 30 000

You have been requested not to confirm receivables or payables other than intercompany accounts.

b) B Ltd.'s financial statements do not include a summary of significant accounting policies.
c) The client, C Ltd., insists on cross-referencing detailed schedules from the financial statements but does not wish the auditor to audit these schedules since they are not essential to fair presentation.
d) The client, D Ltd., uses an industry-accepted accounting method in the preparation of its financial statements but you do not believe that the method chosen represents the best available alternative. The CICA Handbook is silent in this particular area. Had the client used the method you prefer, net income would have been materially reduced.

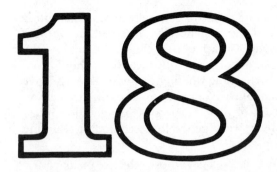

18

Report Reservations, International Reporting and Post-Audit Information

On occasion the auditor may be unable to express a clear, positive opinion as to whether the financial statements are presented fairly in accordance with generally accepted accounting principles (or, in the case of special purpose reports, in accordance with an appropriate disclosed basis of accounting). On such occasions a reservation of opinion must be expressed.

18.1 Reservations in the auditor's report

18.1.1 Circumstances requiring reservations

The circumstances calling for a reservation of opinion involve:

- accounting deficiences,
- auditing deficiencies, or
- uncertainties.

Accounting deficiencies are material departures from generally accepted accounting principles (or, in the case of special purpose reports, from an appropriate disclosed basis of accounting).[1] Such departures may be of various types:

1. incorrect valuation or measurement due to clear-cut, arithmetic or mechanical errors,
2. incorrect valuation of items requiring judgmental estimates,
3. use of an unacceptable accounting principle,
4. use of an improper or inappropriate method of applying a principle,
5. failure to disclose essential information.

Auditing deficiencies represent material departures from those procedures which, under generally accepted auditing standards, would have been required to afford a reasonable basis to support a definite opinion. Such departures may be of two types:

1. impossibility or impracticability of obtaining sufficient appropriate audit evidence,
2. restrictions on the scope of the auditor's examination.

Uncertainties concerning future events may be sufficiently material that the outcome of such events is not susceptible of reasonable estimation at the date of the auditor's report. Uncertainties may be of two types:

1. uncertainties as to specific future events which may influence the realization or settlement of one or more assets and liabilities,
2. uncertainty as to the going concern assumption.

When one or more of the foregoing circumstances are present, the auditor should express an appropriate reservation of opinion.

> Auditors should not express an unqualified opinion on financial statements where any of the circumstances set forth in paragraph 5500.29 [in effect, the foregoing circumstances] are, in their opinion, material. [CICA Handbook][2]

Terminology

The term *accounting deficiencies* follows the usage of the CICA Handbook but the Handbook classes a "disagreement on valuation" as a separate condition. In this book, incorrect valuations (whether clear-cut or judgmental) are considered to be particular types of accounting deficiency. In AICPA pronouncements, the term "departures from generally accepted accounting principles" is used instead for all deficiencies of this sort.

The term *auditing deficiencies* follows the usage of the CICA Handbook but the Handbook includes in this category uncertainties concerning future events. In this book, and in AICPA pronouncements, uncertainties are dealt with separately. The AICPA pronouncements refer to auditing deficiencies as "scope limitations" (whether caused by client imposed restrictions or by the inability to obtain sufficient audit evidence). The CICA Handbook, on the other hand, uses the term "scope limitation" to refer just to restrictions (usually client-imposed). To avoid ambiguity, the term "scope limitation" is not used in this book and *restrictions* are classed as one of the types of auditing deficiency.

18.1.2 Degrees of reservation

Three "degrees of reservation" are used in Canadian auditors' reports:

- qualification of opinion,
- adverse opinion,
- denial of opinion.

Occasionally, more than one type of reservation may be required in the same audit report – for example, an opinion might be denied on the income statement and a qualified opinion expressed on the balance sheet.

A *qualification of opinion* is a specific limitation expressed in an otherwise positive opinion. A qualified opinion is thus an opinion that the financial statements are fairly presented "except for" (or, in some cases, "subject to") certain qualifications. Qualified opinions may arise as a result of:

1. accounting deficiencies (unless they are so material that they call for an adverse opinion),
2. auditing deficiencies (unless they are so material or pervasive that they call for a denial of opinion),

3. uncertainties (unless they are so material or pervasive that they call for a denial of opinion).

An *adverse opinion* is a negative opinion, i.e., an opinion that the financial statements are not fairly presented. Adverse opinions arise in the rare cases where accounting deficiencies are too material to warrant merely a qualified opinion.

A *denial of opinion* is an assertion that an opinion cannot be expressed. Denials of opinion arise in the rare cases where auditing deficiencies or uncertainties are too material or too pervasive to warrant merely a qualified opinion.

Terminology

In this book, *reservations of opinion* (qualifications, adverse opinions or denials) refer to modifications of the opinion as to the fairness of presentation in accordance with generally accepted accounting principles while *consistency exceptions* or *consistency explanations* (see 17.5.1) refer to modifications of the opinion as to consistency. However, the term "consistency qualification" is also used by practitioners and in the CICA Handbook consistency exceptions are listed under the general heading of reservations.

In Canada, *denials of opinion* refer to situations in audit engagements where, because of auditing deficiencies or uncertainties, no opinion can be expressed, whereas *disclaimers of opinion* (see Chapter 20) refer to situations where the purpose of the engagement was to provide accounting services and not to express an audit opinion. In the United States, the term "disclaimer of opinion" is used in both senses.

18.1.3 The reservation paragraph

The second and third reporting standards (see 17.1) require that the auditor's report present adequate explanations of any reservations expressed. In the United States, explanations of all reservations (but not consistency exceptions) are required to be presented in a separate reservation paragraph. Usually, such a reservation paragraph comes between the scope and opinion paragraphs – see the report format in 17.2.1. The use of such reservation paragraphs in Canada is common but not mandatory. The CICA Handbook gives the option of providing the explanations either in an intermediate reservation paragraph or solely in the opinion paragraph.[3] In the writer's view, the use of a reservation paragraph is desirable on all occasions on which reservations (excluding consistency exceptions) are being expressed because:

a) it provides the opportunity for a clearer explanation of the circumstances giving rise to the reservation,

Types of Reservation

Circumstances requiring reservations	Degrees of reservation	Criteria	Report paragraphs affected
Accounting deficiencies	Qualification ("except for")	Materiality	Reservation paragraph Opinion paragraph
	Adverse opinion	Overwhelming materiality (or pervasiveness)	
Auditing deficiencies	Qualification ("except for")	Materiality	Scope paragraph Reservation paragraph Opinion paragraph
	Denial	Overwhelming materiality (or pervasiveness)	
Uncertainties	Qualification ("subject to")	Materiality	Reservation paragraph Opinion paragraph
	Denial (rare)	Overwhelming materiality or pervasiveness (but such criteria are contentious)	

Figure 18.a

b) it is a visually obvious departure from the standard two-paragraph format, and thus signals more clearly that the report contains something unusual.

The rest of the discussion in this chapter assumes that such a reservation paragraph is used.

The reservation paragraph should make clear whether the matter involves (a) an accounting deficiency (i.e., one as to which there is a difference of opinion between the auditor and his client and for which the auditor believes an adjustment should be made), (b) an auditing deficiency (for example, where the auditor has been unable to obtain essential information) or (c) an uncertainty that cannot presently be resolved because the outcome depends on future events.

[The reservation paragraph] should disclose the principal effects of the subject matter of the [reservation] on financial position, results of operations and changes in financial position, if reasonably determinable. If the effects are not reasonably determinable, the report should so state. If such disclosures are made in a note to the financial statements, the [reservation paragraph] may be shortened by referring to it.[4]

Explanations which the auditor wishes to include in his report solely for emphasis and without intending a reservation of opinion, should not be included in a reservation paragraph but in an explanatory paragraph following the opinion paragraph (see 17.5.10).

The types of report reservation, the circumstances giving rise to them, the criteria involved and the report paragraphs affected are summarized in Figure 18.a.

18.2 Qualifications of opinion

The elements of a qualification are:

1. an explanation of why the report is qualified (given in the reservation paragraph),
2. an indication in the reservation paragraph, where reasonably determinable, of the quantitative significance of the matter in question (including, where applicable, earnings per share effects),
3. a qualifying phrase in the opinion paragraph making clear the nature of the qualification (using the words "except for" in the case of accounting or auditing deficiencies and "subject to" in the case of uncertainties),
4. in the case of auditing deficiencies only, an additional qualifying phrase in the scope paragraph (using the words "except for").

Auditing Recommendations in the CICA Handbook state:

The auditors should give a clear expression of the circumstances which prevent them from expressing an opinion without qualification.

Where circumstances require the auditors to qualify their opinion, the opinion paragraph should be modified by wording which clearly conveys the qualification. The words "except for" should be used in expressing a qualification other than [for uncertainty qualifications and consistency explanations]. Phrases such as "with the foregoing explanation" are not considered sufficiently clear or forceful and should not be used.

The words "subject to" should only be used in expressing a qualification where the outcome of the matter giving rise to the qualification is uncertain, and is primarily dependent on future developments or future decisions by parties other than management, directors or owners.[5]

Wording such as "when read with the notes thereto" does not constitute a clear qualification of opinion and should not be used. Moreover, an improper or misleading presentation on the face of a financial statement is not cured by a note explaining that the presentation is improper or misleading. If the auditor concludes that a qualification of his opinion is required, the qualification must be expressed *explicitly* in his report.

18.2.1 Qualifications of opinion because of accounting deficiencies

Qualifications of opinion because of accounting deficiencies are relatively rare in practice. The managements of most enterprises are anxious to produce accurate and reliable information for their shareholders and other readers. In addition, few managements wish to have qualified audit reports attached to their financial statements. Thus, most accounting deficiencies discovered by auditors as a result of their work are corrected and never give rise to qualifications. Nonetheless, it is important for the practitioner to be familiar with qualification requirements both for purposes of discussing with his clients the consequences of not correcting material errors encountered and for purposes of preparing his report in the rare cases where he is unsuccessful in obtaining such correction.

In this section it is assumed that the matters giving rise to the various qualifications discussed are not so material as to call for an adverse opinion. For adverse opinions see 18.3.1.

Incorrect valuation or measurement due to clear-cut, arithmetic or mechanical errors

When the financial statements are misstated as a result of clear-cut, arithmetic or mechanical errors (such as, clerical errors in extending or adding on physical inventory listings or failure to accrue for specific supplier invoices payable at the year-end), the fact of misstatement is unlikely to be contentious. If the auditor has been unsuccessful in persuading his client to correct such errors, it is more likely that the client, while acknowledging the amount of error, believes that this amount should be considered immaterial. If, in the auditor's opinion, however, the error amount is material, he must qualify his report. Quantification of the effect of such errors will present little difficulty. For example:

> [Reservation paragraph]
> No provision has been made for invoices payable to certain suppliers in connection with services performed by them during December. In my opinion, a provision of $90 000 should have been made. Had such a provision been made, accounts payable at December 31, 1976 and administrative expenses for the year would have been greater by $90 000, net income for the year and retained earnings would have been less by $45 000, and net income per share would have been less by $2.25.

> [Opinion paragraph]
> In my opinion, except for the failure to provide for certain accounts payable as set out in the preceding paragraph, these financial statements present fairly . . . with that of the preceding year.

The auditor's report in this example thus gives a reader the information necessary to adjust key figures in the reporting entity's financial statements to a basis which the auditor would have accepted as fair presentation in accordance with generally accepted accounting principles. Provided that the prior year's figures were properly presented, the error in the current year also represents an inconsistency. However, no separate consistency exception is required since the same qualifying phrase modifies both the opinion on presentation and the opinion on consistency.

It might be noted that, in the foregoing example, were the $90 000 error to be corrected in the following year, the correction would cause a material understatement of that year's income, for which an audit qualification would again be required.

Sometimes the principal errors misstating the financial statements will not be *known errors*, but *most likely error* projections from sample results. If, in the foregoing example, the $90 000 unaccrued suppliers' invoices represented the most-likely-error projections from a sample, similar wording for the auditor's qualification would still be suitable. A number of points, however, should be borne in mind

when expressing qualifications based on sample results. These points are discussed in 18.5.

Incorrect valuation of items requiring judgmental estimates

In forming an opinion on the fair presentation of financial statements, the auditor should consider not only discovered misstatements but also any disagreements he may have about accounting estimates (such as allowance for doubtful accounts, depreciation, etc.). By their very nature, accounting estimates are subject to judgment and are therefore impossible to verify with the precision of certain other items. Nevertheless, the auditor must examine accounting estimates and be satisfied that they represent reasonable measurements and reflect the underlying circumstances and events. Where they do not, he must express an appropriate reservation in his report.

As discussed in 16.4, accounting estimates can be classified into (a) those based on some "objective" formula (e.g., inventory obsolescence computed on the basis of number of years' supply on hand) and (b) those based entirely on "subjective" judgment (e.g., inventory obsolescence based on estimated future demand). The former, while not necessarily more accurate, are objective in the sense of being based on a consistent formula and being free of any bias towards the optimism or pessimism of particular client officials. Where this type of estimate is involved, and (a) the client has departed materially from the previous formula basis, and (b) the auditor believes that past experience supports the reasonableness of the previous formula basis and that the new basis is unreasonable, a qualification similar to that illustrated for clear-cut errors will be appropriate. Quantification of the effect of the disagreement in valuation will again present little difficulty. Where, however, both the old and the new bases must be considered reasonable but the auditor believes that there are no new circumstances justifying the change, a consistency exception would be called for instead.

For estimates based solely on subjective judgment, however, any disagreements the auditor might have are harder to quantify. In 16.4 it was suggested that for each subjective estimate the auditor should calculate (a) his *best estimate* and (b) a *zone of reasonableness* in which he would normally accept the client's estimate as being reasonable. When the client's estimate lies a material distance outside this zone of reasonableness (or when such distances for various estimates, when combined with known and most likely errors elsewhere in the audit, aggregate to a material total) a qualification will be required. While the materiality of the distance from the client's figure to the nearest limit of the zone of reasonableness may be an appropriate criterion for deciding whether a qualification is required, disclosure of merely this distance (the minimum measure of the auditor's disagreement) may not always provide the best quantification of the effect of the disagreement in valuation. Rather, the auditor may often wish to express a range of values in his qualification.

For example, the auditor might conclude that an obsolescence provision of $90 000 to $130 000 (zone of reasonableness) or $110 000 (best estimate) was required when the client had provided only $50 000. If before-tax materiality is judged to be $30 000, the auditor will wish to qualify his report since he believes the statements to be misstated by at least $40 000 ($90 000 less $50 000). But disclosure of $40 000 alone would not adequately convey to the reader the auditor's opinion that the statements might be misstated by anywhere from $40 000 to $80 000. His report might therefore be phrased:

[Reservation paragraph]
Owing to discontinuance of certain model lines in the company's X division, parts inventories are substantially above quantities required for current production. In my opinion, an additional allowance in the range of $40 000 to $80 000 is required to provide for future carrying charges on slow moving inventory or losses on disposal or costs of reworking obsolete parts. Had this provision been made, income for the year and retained earnings would have been reduced in the range of $20 000 to $40 000 and net income per share would have been reduced in the range of $1.00 to $2.00.

[Opinion paragraph]
In my opinion, except for the inadequate provision for losses on parts inventories as set out in the preceding paragraph, these financial statements present fairly . . . with that of the preceding year.

A similar reporting of ranges might also be appropriate in the case of a formula-based estimate applied without change in a year in which the auditor believes that past experience or new circumstances required a change in the formula or in its application.

While the use of ranges in the foregoing types of qualification is, in the writer's view, often desirable, examples without such ranges are also in common use.[6]

Provided that the prior year's figures were properly presented, a disagreement as to the current year's estimate would represent an inconsistency as well and again the same qualifying phrase in the opinion paragraph would serve to express an exception both as to presentation and as to consistency. Occasionally, disagreement as to the manner of making judgmental estimates may give rise to a reservation as to income even though no exception, other than for inconsistency, can be taken to the balance sheet. This result can occur when there has been a significant swing from one end of the zone of reasonableness in the previous year to the opposite end of the zone in the current year. While both years may be

within the acceptable range, the swing between years may have large impact on the income statement which may not be justified. Where the auditor believes the swing is unjustified and is material his report might be phrased as follows:

[Reservation paragraph]
The company estimates the allowance for doubtful accounts by an analysis of individual customers' balances. In my opinion, this analysis indicates that the conditions of the accounts at December 31, 1976 and 1975 were essentially the same and that an allowance in the range of $30 000 to $80 000 was reasonable at either date. While the company's estimates ($75 000 at December 31, 1975 and $35 000 at December 31, 1976) were within this range, the decrease of $40 000 during the year was, in my opinion, unwarranted. Had the allowance been estimated in a manner consistent with the preceding year, income for the year would have been reduced by $20 000 and net income per share would have been reduced by $1.00.

[Opinion paragraph]
In my opinion, except for the inconsistency in the estimation of the allowance for doubtful accounts and the resulting overstatement of net income for the year as set out in the preceding paragraph, these financial statements present fairly . . . with that of the preceding year.

Use of an unacceptable accounting principle

While all accounting deficiencies have been defined as material departures from generally accepted accounting principles (and thus call for audit qualification), the clear-cut errors or incorrect estimates just discussed do not result from the specific use of an unacceptable principle. Where an unacceptable accounting principle has, however, in the auditor's opinion, been used, he must explain in his reservation what the proper principles should have been and, if reasonably determinable, their effect on the financial statements. For example:

[Reservation paragraph]
As more fully explained in note X, manufacturing overhead costs have been completely excluded in determining the carrying value of inventories. In my opinion, this basis of valuation is not in accordance with generally accepted accounting principles and an additional amount in the range of $140 000 to $180 000 should have been included in inventories at December 31, 1976. Had such an adjustment been made in 1976, and corresponding adjustments in 1975, net income for the year ended December 31, 1976 would have been increased in the range of $20 000 to $40 000, net income per share would have been increased in the range of $1.00 to $2.00, and retained earnings at December 31, 1976 would have been increased in the range of $70 000 to $90 000.

[Opinion paragraph]
In my opinion, except for the exclusion of manufacturing overhead costs from inventory as set out in the preceding paragraph, these financial statements present fairly . . . in accordance with generally accepted accounting principles. The accounting principles followed by the

company (including the policy of excluding overhead in inventory described in note X) have been applied on a basis consistent with that of the preceding year.

[Explanatory paragraph]
The financial statements for the year ended December 31, 1975 were reported on by me on March 23, 1976. My report contained a qualification, similar to that expressed in the preceding paragraphs, with respect to the exclusion of manufacturing overhead costs from inventory. In particular, the report stated that, in my opinion, had appropriate adjustment been made in 1975, and corresponding adjustments in 1974, net income for the year ended December 31, 1975 would have been increased in the range of $24 000 to $44 000, net income per share would have been increased in the range of $1.20 to $2.20, and retained earnings at December 31, 1975 would have been increased in the range of $40 000 to $60 000.[7]

Sometimes the quantitative effect of the application of improper accounting principles is difficult to determine. If the client has not made a provision for depreciation or for inventory obsolescence and has not carried out the various engineering studies which might be required to determine such provisions, it may be very difficult for the auditor to strike a figure representing what should have been provided. If he does not do so, however, his qualification loses much of its value. If at all possible it is desirable in such circumstances to indicate at least a range within which the auditor expects a normal provision would fall and, failing this, to indicate that correction of the deficiency could (or would) have a material effect, if such is true. The CICA Handbook suggests that, when an improper procedure is used, the auditor's report should "if possible, give an indication of the effect which, in their opinion, the use of the proper procedure would have had on the statements."[8] It would seem logical to interpret the phrase "if possible" in the sense of "if reasonably determinable", the phrase used in AICPA pronouncements (see 18.1.3). The AICPA pronouncements further provide that, if the effects are not reasonably determinable, the auditor's report should so state. A similar practice, while not mandatory in Canada, would seem desirable.

If, however, the quantitative effects of the use of an incorrect accounting principle are so uncertain that the auditor cannot tell whether, if these effects were known, his opinion would be unqualified, qualified or adverse, he is not in a position to express any definite opinion. In these circumstances, a denial of opinion should be given (see 18.3.2).

Use of an improper or unfair method of applying a principle

Generally accepted accounting principles include both the principles themselves and the methods of applying them. Thus, an improper method of applying a principle is really another example of the use of improper principles just discussed. Nonetheless, in forming audit conclusions it may often be convenient to evaluate separately the broad principles applied and their specific method of application. A general principle, acceptable in itself, may have been applied in an unacceptable manner. For example, tax allocation principles may have been used but with incorrect methods of distinguishing timing differences and permanent differences. In such cases the result can be considered a departure from generally accepted accounting principles and a qualification similar to the preceding example would be appropriate.

The acceptability of the method of applying a general principle brings in, as well, the concept of fairness. The definition of generally accepted accounting principles suggested in 17.3.2 included the concept of making such adjustments as are consistent with the general spirit of the Recommendations, principles or practices in question where, due to the unusual circumstances of a particular enterprise, their literal requirements are not reasonably applicable. Where such adjustments are made in appropriate circumstances, no qualification is required in the auditor's report. In the United States, the AICPA Code of Professional Ethics requires disclosure of the adjustment and, if practicable, its approximate effects, as well as the reasons why compliance with the literal requirements would have resulted in a misleading statement; however, such disclosures are presented in a separate explanatory paragraph and do not represent a qualification nor give rise to a qualifying phrase in the opinion paragraph.[9] In Canada such non-qualification disclosures in the auditor's report may also be required (see the next section) but not their quantitative effects. Indeed, the usefulness of disclosure of the quantitative effects can be debated – for if the statements, as adjusted, provide a fair presentation in the circumstances, of what relevance to the reader is the disclosure of the quantitative adjustment required to get back to an unfair presentation?

On the other hand, if the unique circumstances requiring adjustment from the literal application of some general Recommendation are present but the adjustment is *not* made, the financial statements should *not* be considered to be presented fairly in accordance with generally accepted accounting principles and a qualification should be expressed.

Failure to disclose essential information

When the financial statements fail to disclose all the information essential for fair presentation in accordance with generally accepted accounting principles, the auditor should qualify his opinion for the deficiency and disclose in his reservation paragraph "such additional information as [he considers] necessary in the circumstances."[10] For example:

[Reservation paragraph]
These financial statements do not disclose the existence at December 31, 1976 of options granted to officers of the company of 5 000 common shares of the company, exercisable at a price of $10.00 per share at any date prior to December 31, 1980.

[Opinion paragraph]
In my opinion, except for the failure to disclose the existence of options referred to above, these financial statements present fairly ... with that of the preceding year.[11]

The extent of the disclosures to be made by the auditor requires the exercise of careful judgment. The auditor should not grasp at unrealistic figures just because they have been stated somewhere. For example, a company might be sued for $5 000 000 in damages in a case where the maximum expectation of a damage award even if the client did lose the case would be $100 000. To quote the higher figure of the amount of the suit could be just as misleading as omitting reference to the suit.

CICA Accounting Recommendations presently require *disclosure* of departures from the Recommendations.[12] This requirement is echoed in the present Auditing Recommendations:

Where financial statements reported on by the auditors depart from a recommended accounting treatment or statement presentation, and the departure is not disclosed in notes to the financial statements, the auditors should make such disclosure in their report.[13]

Where the auditor concludes that such a departure means that the financial statements are not presented fairly in accordance with generally accepted accounting principles, the foregoing disclosure requirement will be met automatically by his reservation paragraph. Where, on the other hand, he concludes that, because of the unique circumstances of the reporting entity, the literal provisions of a general recommendation are not applicable, the departure in itself should not give rise to a reservation. But the Accounting Recommendations call for this departure, if material, to be disclosed in the notes and the absence of this disclosure might be considered a failure to disclose essential information. The foregoing Auditing Recommendation should therefore, in the writer's view, be interpreted as calling for a reservation as to inadequate disclosure provided that the auditor concludes that such inadequacy is material (since recommendations "need not be applied to immaterial matters").

If some minor rule has not been followed because it quite obviously does not fit the unique circumstances of the reporting entity (it being acknowledged in the Introduction that no rule suits all circumstances), the auditor may well decide that non-disclosure of this technical departure is not material. If, on the other hand, the unique circumstances call for modifications in the application of a broader rule, non-disclosure of this modification might well be judged as material – not because the departure is wrong but because the reader is left uninformed as to important conditions properly affecting the comparability of the financial statements with those of other entities.

The CICA Handbook calls for the auditor's report to cover all financial statements required for fair presentation in accordance with generally accepted accounting principles (see 17.2.3). Such statements normally include the balance sheet and the statements of income, retained earnings and changes in financial position. The auditor should not accept an audit engagement with respect to annual financial statements unless he understands that the client is willing to have him examine and report upon the full set of basic statements necessary for fair presentation of financial position, results of operations and changes in financial position. Where it turns out that an essential financial statement is omitted, the auditor should qualify his report. For example:

[Scope paragraph]
I have examined the balance sheet ... and the statements of income and retained earnings for the year ... in the circumstances.

[Reservation paragraph]
The company declined to present a statement of changes in financial position for the year ended December 31, 1976. Presentation of such a statement summarizing the company's financing and investing activities and other changes in its financial position is, in my opinion, required by generally accepted accounting principles.

[Opinion paragraph]
In my opinion, except that the omission of a statement of changes in financial position results in an incomplete presentation as explained in the preceding paragraph, these financial statements present fairly the financial position ... and the results of its operations for the year ... with that of the preceding year.[14]

Some practitioners consider that, while a statement of changes in financial position is required by generally accepted accounting principles in the United States, it is not presently required in all cases in Canada.[15] Furthermore, the materiality of any omission must be assessed by the auditor. The foregoing example assumes that the auditor has concluded that such a statement was necessary and its omission material.

The foregoing example does not mean, however, that it is impossible to give an unqualified opinion on a balance sheet when the auditor finds he has to qualify or deny an opinion on the income statement (as may happen in some initial engagements). Nor does it mean that the auditor cannot accept a *special purpose* engagement to report on one statement alone (see 19.3).

Sometimes the auditor may wish to disclose certain information in his report for emphasis rather than because of any deficiency in the disclosures in the financial statements. In such cases the information should not be included in a reservation paragraph but in an explanatory paragraph following the opinion paragraph (see 17.5.10).

18.2.2 Materiality with respect to qualifications for accounting deficiencies

All decisions as to the need for report reservations must be made in the light of materiality.

Materiality of misstatements of reported income

The concept of determining a materiality limit for a particular audit engagement by reference to some measure of earning power was discussed in 15.4.2. Where income-distorting errors exceed what the auditor considers to be this limit, a reservation would normally be required. Reported income for the current year can be distorted as a result of either or both of (a) newly-introduced misstatements of closing equity and (b) reversals, during the current year, of misstatements of opening equity. Many equity misstatements in the preceding year are automatically reversed in the current year and affect the current year's income in a direction opposite to that of the initial income impact. For example, inventory understatements at the end of the preceding year cause understated income in that year but carry forward and overstate income in the current year. Other equity misstatements in prior years may only be reversed if and when they are specifically corrected (such as accumulated errors in computing accumulated depreciation) or if and when the asset or liability containing the error is disposed of or liquidated. Both newly introduced equity misstatements and reversals of opening equity misstatements should be considered in deciding whether the current year's income is sufficiently distorted to require an audit reservation.

For example, in Case 1 in Figure 18.b the equity misstatement at the end of the previous year and the equity misstatement at the end of the current year are both slightly less than materiality. However, in the current year, the reversing nature of the prior year's error is in the same direction as the new equity misstatement and, as a result, the current income misstatement substantially exceeds materiality. Failing client adjustment, an audit reservation would normally be required.

Materiality of misstatements of closing equity

If the auditor considered exclusively the foregoing effects on reported income in judging the need for audit reservations, the situation could arise where a material misstatement of closing equity was accumulated over a series of years in immaterial annual increments. It could even be argued that the total equity error, while material in relation to income, was not material in relation to the much larger balance of accumulated equity. By this argument, such a situation could be accepted without audit reservation.

Relationship of Equity and Income Misstatements
(materiality = $50 000)

	Case 1	Case 2	Case 3	Case 4	Case 5
Previous year: Closing equity misstatement	$ 40 000	$ 40 000	$ 80 000	–	$ 45 000
Current year: Effect of reversal of the opening equity misstatement on current income	$(40 000)	$(40 000)	$(80 000)	–	$(45 000)
Closing equity misstatement	(40 000)	80 000	–	$45 000	15 000
Misstatement of current year's income	$(80 000)	$ 40 000	$(80 000)	$45 000	$ 60 000

(Note: The closing equity misstatement in the previous year is assumed to be of a type, such as an inventory error, which reverses automatically in the following year.)

Figure 18.b

The trouble with this reasoning, however, is that some or all of the accumulated errors may suddenly be reversed (either by specific correction or by disposal or liquidation of the misstated asset or liability) causing a material distortion in the current year's income. It would be hard for the auditor to resist the correction of conditions he agrees are errors and impossible for him to undo the effects of a disposition or liquidation. Thus, he would seemingly be faced with a material distortion yet perhaps precluded from expressing a reservation.

The solution is for the auditor to insist strongly on the correction of, or provision for, a material (in relation to income) misstatement of closing equity, whether due to income misstatements introduced in one year or accumulated in annually immaterial amounts over a series of years. Where such provision is not made, the auditor should seriously consider qualifying his report, but such consideration should be influenced by judgment of all the surrounding circumstances.

For example, in Case 2 in Figure 18.b the auditor should consider a reservation in his report because of the materiality of the closing equity misstatement even though the misstatement of the current year's income is less than material. If adjustment or reservation for Case 2 is ignored, the situation may lead in a subsequent year to Case 3 – where current income is materially misstated and yet there are no newly introduced errors to which the auditor can take exception.

Desirability of encouraging correction of misstatements which are less than materiality

The auditor should strongly encourage his client to correct or provide for misstatements (known and most likely errors) which are less than materiality. Although reservations are only appropriate where materiality has been breached, it should be the client's objective (and certainly the auditor's desire) to have the financial statements reflect the financial position and results of operations as accurately as possible. Also, serious future problems may be created when misstatements are not corrected but are allowed to accumulate over a period of years.

For example, in Case 4 in Figure 18.b the misstatement, entirely introduced in the current year, is slightly less than materiality. While the auditor may not feel justified in expressing a reservation for its presence, he should certainly encourage his client to correct it. If it is not corrected, it may in a subsequent year lead to Case 5, where even a small error introduced in the current year results in a material misstatement of current income and calls for an audit reservation.

It is desirable for the auditor to explain to his client that the failure to correct or provide for misstatements in the year of occurrence may severely restrict the amount of new uncorrected errors that can be tolerated in the succeeding year and that this restriction (because of its effect on planned audit precision) will increase the extent of future audit work.

Error evaluation

To permit the foregoing decisions as to reservations to be made, the auditor must be aware of the totals of various categories of error for the audit as a whole. In 16.4 the summarization of opening equity misstatements, closing equity misstatements, classification errors, and current income misstatements was discussed, as well as the analysis and evaluation of such errors in terms of known errors, disagreements on accounting estimates, most likely errors and (in the case of statistical samples) upper error limits.

18.2.3 Qualifications of opinion because of auditing deficiencies

In this section it is assumed that the matters giving rise to the various qualifications discussed are not so material or pervasive as to call for a denial of opinion (for denials of opinion see 18.3.2).

Impossibility or impracticability of obtaining sufficient appropriate audit evidence

If the auditor has been unable to obtain sufficient appropriate audit evidence to warrant the expression of a definite opinion, he should set out the nature of the information he has been unable to obtain and qualify both the scope and opinion paragraphs accordingly. His qualification should deal with the possible accounting effect of the auditing deficiency, as well as the deficiency itself.

Essential audit evidence may be unavailable owing to accidental destruction, as in the following example:

[Scope paragraph]
I have examined ... then ended. My examination ... necessary in the circumstances, except as explained in the following paragraph.

[Reservation paragraph]
Because of a fire in the custodian's premises, I was unable to count the bearer securities relating to investments, shown on the balance sheet in the amount of $50 000, and I was unable, by other means, to verify the existence of the investments represented by such securities.

[Opinion paragraph]
In my opinion, except for the effect of any adjustments

which might have been required had I been able to count the securities, these financial statements present fairly ... with that of the preceding year.[16]

The customary wording of the qualification in the scope paragraph is less than ideal theoretically, though as a practical matter its intent is clear. In Canada the third field work standard calls for sufficient appropriate audit evidence to be obtained "to support the content of the report". The report may contain a clear opinion, a qualified opinion, an adverse opinion or a denial of opinion; in each case the evidence obtained should justify the report given. If the auditor completes the work necessary to support a qualified opinion, he has therefore complied with generally accepted auditing standards.[17] Thus, strictly speaking, it is unnecessary for him to take exception to his assertion of such compliance in the scope paragraph. The same point can be argued with respect to the phrase "procedures ... necessary in the circumstances". Really, the intent of the scope exception is that, *except for* the specified deficiencies, the auditor's examination included all the steps which would, under generally accepted auditing standards, have been necessary in the circumstances to express a definite opinion – "definite" here meaning unclouded by any auditing deficiency (though possibly containing reservations with respect to accounting deficiencies).

Essential audit evidence may also be unobtainable where there is a serious inadequacy in the accounting records or in internal controls (particularly controls over the initial recording of transactions). If it is impossible or impracticable to overcome this inadequacy by "compensating audit procedures", a reservation must be expressed:

[Scope paragraph]
I have examined ... necessary in the circumstances, except as noted in the following paragraph.

[Reservation paragraph]
Owing to inadequate internal control over cash receipts and the recording of revenues from cash transactions (as to which I have reported separately to the Directors), revenues were not susceptible of complete verification by audit procedures.

[Opinion paragraph]
In my opinion, except for the effect of any adjustments which might have been required had I been able to verify revenues, these financial statements present fairly ... with that of the preceding year.

While inadequacies in the accounting records may sometimes be the result of accounting deficiencies (the adoption of inadequate accounting methods), the immediate cause of the qualification is the absence of essential audit evidence, an auditing deficiency.

In certain organizations, internal control deficiencies may be difficult to avoid. For example, some charitable organizations may receive significant revenues from sources which are not verifiable within the environment of controls practical for such organizations to maintain. Where the auditor feels that the organization has as good a system as could be expected given its size, he may wish to soften the foregoing type of qualification somewhat along the following lines:

[Scope paragraph]
I have examined ... necessary in the circumstances, except as noted in the following paragraph.

[Reservation paragraph]
In common with many charitable organizations, the association reports an amount for donation revenue which is not susceptible of complete verification by audit procedures. Accordingly, my verification of revenue from this source was limited to a comparison of recorded receipts with bank deposits.

[Opinion paragraph]
In my opinion, except for the possibility of adjustments had donations been susceptible of complete audit verification, these financial statements present fairly ... with that of the preceding year.[18]

The timing of the auditor's work may sometimes preclude the obtaining of sufficient appropriate audit evidence. The most common example is that of an initial examination where the auditor may be unable to verify the correctness of the inventory at the beginning of the year and, sometimes, the consistency of application of accounting principles with the preceding year. In such cases the auditor may, depending on the circumstances:

a) express a clear opinion on the balance sheet but a qualified opinion on the income statement and on consistency,

b) express a clear opinion on the balance sheet but a denial of opinion as to the income statement and consistency,

c) express a qualified opinion or a denial of opinion as to all the financial statements.

Examples of report reservations for initial engagements are given in 23.2.5 and 23.3.2.

Restrictions on the scope of the auditor's examination

Where a restriction has been imposed by the client on the scope of the auditor's examination or where the auditor has agreed with the client to conduct an examination subject to certain scope restrictions, he should disclose the nature of the restrictions and qualify both the scope and opinion paragraphs accordingly. For example:

[Scope paragraph]
I have examined ... in the circumstances except as explained in the following paragraph.

[Reservation paragraph]
As instructed, I did not request confirmation of amounts owing to the company by its debtors, and I have not been able to satisfy myself as to these amounts by other auditing procedures. Adjustments, if any, which might have resulted from verification of these accounts could affect both financial position and results of operations.

[Opinion paragraph]
In my opinion, except for the effect of any adjustments which might have been required had I been able to obtain confirmation of these accounts, these financial statements present fairly ... with that of the preceding year.

In statutory engagements, however, it may not be legally permissible for the auditor to accept restrictions which infringe on his statutory duties. Where acceptance of restrictions is not legally permissible but restrictions are in fact anticipated, the practitioner should not accept appointment as statutory auditor. Where such restrictions are imposed during the course of the engagement, the auditor must qualify his report accordingly and normally would not stand for reappointment at the next shareholders' meeting.

Questions as to scope of examination may sometimes arise with respect to small subsidiaries or other closely held companies. Under some Corporations Acts certain small closely held companies may not have to be audited (see Chapter 4). Most Acts, however, do not have such exemptions. Where a practitioner has been appointed a shareholders' statutory auditor under the provisions of a Corporations Act, he has a legal duty to carry out a full scope audit examination. The auditor cannot normally accept client-imposed limitations where he has this duty. Materiality decisions must be made in relation to the individual reporting entity in question and not in relation to some larger consolidated group of which it may be a member.

Sometimes a parent company with a number of small wholly-owned subsidiaries will choose to have such subsidiaries not appoint statutory auditors but merely permit the parent company auditor such access to subsidiary records as he requires in order to fulfill his statutory obligations to report on the parent company consolidated financial statements. In that case, the parent company auditor will make all his materiality decisions in relation to the consolidated financial statements. The extent of his resulting work on subsidiary records will then be considerably less than it would have been had he been undertaking separate audits of each subsidiary's financial statements. Where a parent company proposes to have one or more subsidiary companies dispense with the statutory appointment of auditor, the parent company may wish to recommend that his client seek legal advice as to the risk of penalties. Where a parent

company auditor is examining subsidiary records solely as part of his statutory audit of the parent company, and has not been appointed auditor of that company's subsidiaries, his examination of subsidiary records will normally not be sufficient to permit him to express any form of audit opinion on the subsidiary financial statements.

18.2.4 Qualifications of opinion because of uncertainties

In this section it is assumed that the matters giving rise to the various qualifications discussed are not so material or pervasive as to call for a denial of opinion (for denials of opinion see 18.3.2).

Uncertainties as to specific future events

Occasionally, an auditor is "unable to form an opinion on the fairness or adequacy of an item in the financial statements because of an uncertainty which cannot be resolved at the date of [his] report."[19] Current practice and pronouncements in North America call for the auditor's report to disclose the uncertainty (or to refer to a note containing such disclosure) and express the audit opinion as being subject to the outcome of the matter in question. No qualification is expressed in the scope paragraph. For example:

[Reservation paragraph]
As disclosed in Note X, a petition in bankruptcy has been filed against a major customer of the company. Although the company has made provision for estimated losses, no information is available at this date as to the portion of the account receivable which may ultimately be collected.

[Opinion paragraph]
In my opinion, subject to the determination of the ultimate loss, if any, on the account receivable referred to above, these financial statements present fairly ... with that of the preceding year.[20]

It should be noted that generally accepted accounting principles require that the uncertainty be appropriately disclosed in the financial statements or accompanying notes [21] – including, in the foregoing example, the dollar amounts involved. If the disclosure in the financial statements is inadequate, the auditor must not only express a "subject to" qualification with respect to the uncertainty but also an "except for" qualification with respect to the inadequacy of the disclosure. In that case, the omitted information would be presented in the auditor's reservation paragraph (see 18.2.1). The importance of full disclosure is worth emphasizing. It is tempting for an auditor to think that once he has flagged an item by a "subject to" qualification he has no further responsibility with respect to it. Recent court cases in the

United States have held that the auditor is indeed responsible for a further qualification in such cases if the disclosure was inadequate.

Qualifications for uncertainty are not required when the auditor "concludes that there is only a minimal likelihood that resolution of the uncertainty will have a material effect on the financial statements."[22] Nor are they required when the outcome of the uncertainties is susceptible of reasonable estimation at the date of issue of the financial statements.[23]

Uncertainty as to the going concern assumption

A particular type of uncertainty exists where there are serious doubts whether an enterprise will continue as a going concern. Recorded asset amounts and liability classifications in particular may have to be very different if the going concern assumption cannot be sustained. The problem is difficult since the auditor cannot forecast the future and should not give the public the impression that he can evaluate entity viability as part of his opinion. Also, an erroneous or premature going concern qualification could have unfortunate consequences for a company and its shareholders – the self-fulfilling prophecy. On the other hand, it can be argued that the auditor does have a responsibility to qualify his opinion where there are extraordinary uncertainties as to continuation of the enterprise and therefore as to the appropriate basis of financial statement presentation.

In general, going concern qualifications are rare, and confined for the most part to situations where specific events have taken place which strongly indicate that an entity may not be able to continue. Such events would include the making of a receiving order or an event of default under a credit agreement (other than a mere technical breach). However, significant going concern uncertainties may exist in the absence of such specific events. These uncertainties may be the result of a combination of circumstances and prospects – including sustained heavy losses and urgent capital requirements in the near future to meet debt obligations, with no definite prospects for obtaining needed capital or for a return to profitability.

Circumstances which may, but do not necessarily, indicate that an enterprise may not continue as a going concern include:

a) circumstances involving liquidity problems (such as recurring operating losses, working capital deficiency, worsening debt/equity ratio, preferred dividend arrears, selling goods below cost to generate cash, new restrictions on important remittances from foreign affiliates),

b) circumstances involving management, customers or operations (such as departure of key members of the management without satisfactory replacement, loss of a key franchise, failure of a major customer or supplier, a long-lasting strike, excessive development expenditures in relation to likely future earnings, the occurrence of fire or other disasters not adequately covered by insurance, expropriation of important foreign subsidiaries, pending legal proceedings which could result in judgments not possible to meet, uneconomic long-term leases or other obligations).[24]

The assessment of the foregoing types of circumstance requires careful judgment.

> ... in the absence of evidence to the contrary, the auditor should assume that the entity is a going concern ... However, the auditor does not assume that liquidation is impossible. Although he plans his examination as if the assumption were true, his mind is not closed to the possibility that in a given examination the going-concern assumption may be false. He remains alert to any indication in the present examination that liquidation may be imminent.[25]

An example of a going concern qualification follows:

[Reservation paragraph]
The company has incurred significant operating losses over the past three years. In addition, the results of the current year's operations have produced a working capital deficiency and the company has experienced recent difficulties in obtaining financing. While the company's ability to continue as a going concern is dependent upon achieving a satisfactory resolution of these problems, the accompanying financial statements have been prepared on the assumption that the company will continue as a going concern.

[Opinion paragraph]
In my opinion, subject to such adjustments as would be required should the company be unable to resolve the problems referred to in the preceding paragraph, these financial statements present fairly ... that of the preceding year.

The foregoing type of qualification is appropriate only if the reporting entity is in fact a going concern both at the balance sheet date and at the date the auditor completes his examination, but there are doubts about its continuation as such. If, in fact, the entity is no longer a going concern, its financial statements should be prepared on a liquidation basis. If they are not so prepared, the auditor should express a reservation because of an accounting deficiency (see 18.2.1). Where statements are properly prepared on a liquidation basis, that basis should be adequately disclosed in the statements or notes. Some practitioners believe that it is also desirable to refer to that basis in the auditor's report.[26]

Differing views with respect to the reporting of uncertainties

Some practitioners argue that, when the financial statements provide full disclosure of the circumstances of a given uncertainty, and the auditor has no suggestions to make for how the statements might be improved, it is illogical to require him to express a reservation in his report. The financial statements, it is held, present the clearest picture possible in the circumstances and a reservation would imply some criticism or objection when, in fact, none is intended. If the reader needs to be warned about the importance or the magnitude of the uncertainty, the place for this warning is in the financial statements (in order to meet the requirements of full disclosure), not in the auditor's report. If it is argued, in rebuttal, that the disclosure of uncertainty may be hidden from the reader by being buried in pages of detailed notes, the answer is to improve the note presentation to highlight the more important issues – rather than to resort to the auditor's report to cure a deficency in the note presentation. Advocates of this viewpoint, of which the writer is one, therefore argue that it would be preferable for professional pronouncements to eliminate "subject to" qualifications and to call for an unqualified opinion where (a) proper provision has been made for probable losses capable of estimation and (b) full and clear disclosure has been made of all other unusual uncertainties.[27]

A further argument for this position can be made on practical grounds. All business enterprises are subject to various types and degrees of uncertainty. The segregation of a particular set of uncertainties as requiring "subject to" qualifications is bound to be somewhat arbitrary. For example, all accounting estimates (such as of the collectibility of normal trade receivables, of inventory obsolescence, of fixed asset lives) are fraught with uncertainty. But such uncertainties, even if material, are not considered to be of a type calling for qualification. Other uncertainties are considered to be obvious to the financial statement reader and again not to call for qualification. It is obvious that, if oil is not subsequently discovered, deferred drilling or exploration costs presently deferred as an asset may prove worthless; if mineral prices suddenly decline, deferred mining development costs may be worth little; if new products are not accepted, deferred product development and advertising costs may be valueless; if the world economy experiences a major financial collapse or if world war breaks out, the carrying values of many long-term assets will be questionable. But unusual uncertainties associated specifically with a particular enterprise (for example, a lawsuit or imminent liquidity problems) may be considered to require a "subject to" qualification. Decisions as to what constitutes an "unusual" uncertainty may not be made with consistency by different practitioners.[28]

Other practitioners argue that at least an unqualified opinion should be justified, assuming full disclosure in the financial statements, in cases where the resolution of the uncertainty will not lead to a furture adjustment of the financial statements of the current period. AICPA pronouncements point out that the resolution of an uncertainty may:

> (a) result in adjustment of the financial statements as to which [the auditor's] report originally was modified, (b) be recognized in the financial statements of a subsequent period, or (c) results in a conclusion that the matter has no monetary effect on the financial statements of any period. [29]

The present pronouncements call for a "subject to" exception in each of these cases. Some practitioners argue, however, that a "'subject to" exception is logical only for an uncertainty that could result in case (a). In the other cases, if the current period's financial statements are never going to require adjustment, in what sense can the auditor be uncertain as to the fairness of their presentation? As discussed in 18.7, events subsequent to the balance sheet can be classed into two groups:

a) those providing additional evidence of conditions existing at the balance sheet date and therefore requiring adjustment, *up to the date of issue of the financial statements*, of accounting estimates inherent in those statements,

b) those representing occurrences subsequent to the balance sheet date which may, *up to the date of issue of the financial statements*, require disclosure in the financial statements but do not require adjustment of the accounting estimates inherent in those statements.

Uncertainties created by the occurrence of the second type of subsequent event (such as a third-party claim initiated, and related to an accident occurring, after the balance sheet date) will not give rise to subsequent adjustments of the current period's statements and so, it could be argued, do not warrant a "subject to" qualification. Uncertainties with respect to the anticipated occurrence of the first type of subsequent event (such as the awaited settlement of a lawsuit in process at the balance sheet date) may or may not give rise to a subsequent adjustment of the current period's statements depending on the extent to which they were contingent upon subsequent actions beyond the control of management.[30]

Other practitioners argue, on the other hand, that "subject to" opinions are necessary in order to emphasize the uncertainties, even if they have been fully disclosed in the financial statements.[31] They believe

517

that when a major uncertainty overhangs the reported financial position of an enterprise, there is something misleading soothing about an auditor's report which expresses an unqualified opinion.

Whatever the practitioner's personal views on this subject, on this subject, he should follow current professional pronouncements in his reporting practices so that readers of auditors' reports will be able to count on some measure of consistency in evaluating comparable situations. Current pronouncements call for "subject to" exceptions for those uncertainties for which the outcome is not susceptible of reasonable estimation at the date of issue of the financial statements.[32]

18.3 Adverse opinions and denials of opinion

In certain circumstances a qualification does not provide an adequate reservation of the auditor's opinion and an adverse opinion or denial of opinion should be given.

18.3.1 Adverse opinions

As with qualifications for accounting deficiencies, adverse opinions are rare in practice because the auditor is usually successful in persuading his client to make the necessary correction. When he is unsuccessful, an adverse opinion is called for when the auditor positively disagrees with the client's accounting, and correction of the matter would have made an overwhelming change in the picture presented by the financial statements. A denial of opinion would not be adequate in these circumstances because an opinion is held "that one or more of the statements do *not* present fairly" and should be expressed.

> When the auditors' disagreement as to the fairness of presentation is so material that in their judgment a qualified opinion cannot be given, an adverse opinion should be given. [CICA Handbook][33]

An adverse opinion is the most serious type of reservation which an auditor can express. However, criteria for identifying the rare circumstances in which an accounting deficiency is "so material" as to call for an adverse opinion rather than a qualified opinion are not clear. Some practitioners believe the question is one of magnitude (e.g., if net income is 20% misstated a qualified opinion would be appropriate; if 70% misstated, an adverse opinion would be appropriate). Others believe the question is also one of pervasiveness (e.g., if one figure alone is misstated a qualified opinion might be appropriate; if every figure is misstated because an incorrect accounting basis has been used, an adverse opinion might be appropriate).

When an adverse opinion is given, *all* the significant reasons giving rise to it, and not just some of them, should be disclosed in the auditor's report. As with qualifications for accounting deficiencies, the quantitative effect, on the financial statements, of the matters giving rise to the reservation should be disclosed if reasonably determinable.

> Whenever the auditors issue an adverse opinion, they should disclose the reasons for the disagreement which led to the opinion, usually in a paragraph between the scope and opinion paragraphs of their report. Although the description in the auditors' report of the disagreement may be shortened by reference to a note containing adequate detail, the point of disagreement and the fact of disagreement must be set out wholly in the auditors' report. The effect on the financial statements of the matters giving rise to the adverse opinion should be set forth in the auditors' report, or in the notes to the financial statements with a reference, in the auditors' report, to the note. [CICA Handbook][34]

An example of an adverse opinion follows.

> [Reservation paragraph]
> As explained in note X to the financial statements, no depreciation has been provided on fixed assets since the year ended December 31, 1974. If depreciation had been provided on a consistent basis at normal rates in subsequent years, the loss for the year ended December 31, 1976 would have been increased by $130 000 ($6.50 per share) and accumulated depreciation and deficit at December 31, 1976 would have been increased by $240 000.
>
> [Opinion paragraph]
> Because of the materiality of the amounts of omitted depreciation as described in the preceding paragraph, I am of the opinion that these financial statements do not present fairly . . . in accordance with generally accepted accounting principles.[35]

It might be noted that when the adverse opinion applies to all the financial statements, as in the foregoing example, it is customary to omit a reference to consistency. Technically such an omission may violate the literal requirements of the fourth reporting standard. However, it can be argued that it complies with the general spirit of the reporting standards, for a reference to consistency would be immaterial in comparison to the overwhelming accounting deficiency indicated by an adverse opinion. Moreover, a reference to consistency, even though grammatically covered by the earlier phrase "do not present", might create a superficial resemblance to the wording of a qualified opinion paragraph, which could be misleading.

Sometimes an adverse opinion may relate to only one financial statement (such as the income statement) while the other statements are given either clear or qualified opinions. In such cases, it is customary to place the adverse opinion first in the opinion paragraph, followed by the remaining opinions (the latter including references to consistency). [36]

If it is clear that the financial statements are sufficiently misstated to warrant the expression of an adverse opinion, although the quantitative effects of the misstatements cannot be precisely determined, an adverse opinion should still be given. Indeed, if the difficulty of quantification arises out of the pervasiveness of the accounting deficiencies, many practitioners would consider the situation to be exactly one of the rare cases where an adverse opinion is definitely called for. The auditor should disclose in his reservation paragraph that the quantitative effects are not reasonably determinable – though, if possible, he may wish to state that the effects are estimated at least to exceed a specified amount.

If, however, the quantitative effects of the misstatement are so uncertain that the auditor cannot tell whether, if these effects were known, his opinion would be unqualified, qualified or adverse, he is not in a position to express any definite opinion. In these circumstances, a denial of opinion should be given (see 18.3.2).

18.3.2 Denials of opinion

A denial of opinion is an assertion that no opinion can be expressed on one or more of the financial statements taken as a whole. A denial of opinion is called for when:
1. there has been a auditing deficiency so serious that the auditor cannot form an opinion on the statements taken as a whole, or
2. an uncertainty exists:
    a) that could lead to an overwhelming change in the picture presented by the financial statements, and
    b) the possible effects of the uncertainty on the financial statements cannot be clearly seen by statement readers.

Where circumstances are such that the auditors have no basis for an opinion or are unable to indicate clearly how, and to what extent, the statements may be misleading, the auditors should report, giving their reasons, that they are unable to express an opinion as to whether the statements present fairly the financial position, the results of operations, and/or [the changes in financial position]. [CICA Handbook][37]

The phrase "are unable to indicate clearly how, and to what extent, the statements may be mislead-

ing" could be said to apply also to an accounting deficiency which is so significant and of such a nature that the auditor cannot reasonably determine its quantitative effects and therefore cannot tell whether, if such effects were known to him, his opinion would have been unqualified, qualified or adverse. In such circumstances, a denial of opinion is required. Ultimately, however, it is not the accounting deficiency in such a case that triggers the denial, but rather the impractability of obtaining sufficient appropriate audit evidence to determine its quantitative effects. The absence of such evidence is an auditing deficiency. For this reason, it seems logical to categorize the immediate causes of denials as being simply (a) auditing deficiencies or (b) uncertainties.

In Canada, a denial of opinion (when deficiencies encountered during an audit engagement prevent an expression of opinion) should be distinguished from a disclaimer of opinion (where the terms of the engagement do not call for an expression of an audit opinion on the financial statements).

When a denial of opinion is given, all the significant reasons giving rise to it should be disclosed in the auditor's report. In the United States, AICPA pronouncements provide further that, even though a denial has been given, the auditor "also should disclose any other reservations he has regarding fair presentation in conformity with generally accepted accounting principles or the consistency of their application." [38] The CICA Handbook does not specifically call for such disclosure in connection with denials of opinion. However, since the Handbook calls for public accountants to disclose any known departures from generally accepted accounting principles in the case of unaudited financial statements with which they are associated (see Chapter 20), it seems logical that the same disclosures should be made in connection with denials of opinion in audit engagements.

Denials for auditing deficiencies

An example of a denial of opinion resulting from an auditing deficiency is:

[Scope paragraph]
I have examined ... necessary in the circumstances, except as noted in the following paragraph.

[Reservation paragraph]
In accordance with management's instructions I did not observe the taking of physical inventory as at October 31, 1976, and my other audit procedures were not sufficient to satisfy me with respect to the inventory stated at $300 000.

[Opinion paragraph]
In view of the possible material effect of any adjustments which might have been required had I been able to perform a complete verification of inventory, I am unable to express any opinion as to whether or not these

financial statements present fairly . . . for the year then ended.

As stated earlier, however, in statutory engagements it may not be legally permissible for the auditor to accept restrictions which infringe on his statutory duties. It might be noted that, when a denial of opinion is expressed, it is customary to omit references to generally accepted accounting principles and to consistency. If there is no basis of forming an opinion at all, the particular accounting basis relative to which such an opinion might have been expressed becomes irrelevant. Moreover, recitation of the references to generally accepted accounting principles and consistency might create a superficial resemblance to a qualified opinion paragraph, which would be misleading. (However, see the earlier comments concerning known departures from generally accepted accounting principles.)

Criteria for telling when an auditing deficiency is sufficiently serious to call for a denial of opinion rather than a qualified opinion are not entirely clear. Some practitioners believe the question is one of magnitude (e.g. if components affecting 20% of net income are unverifiable, a qualified opinion might be appropriate; if affecting 70% of net income, a denial of opinion might be appropriate). Others believe the question is also one of pervasiveness (e.g., if one figure alone is unverifiable a qualified opinion might be appropriate; if every figure is unverifiable because of a pervasive auditing deficiency, a denial of opinion might be appropriate).

Denials for uncertainty

Many practitioners believe that where the uncertainty, however material, relates to isolable figures or disclosures in the financial statements, the reader is better served by a "subject to" qualification confined to the particular items in question rather than a general denial which casts doubt on every item in the statements. For example, an unfavourable decision in a large lawsuit in process against a company could significantly affect the picture presented by the financial statements. However, one would expect that the issue, the amounts involved, and the accounts which could be affected could be clearly expressed to the reader so that a qualified opinion rather than a denial would normally be appropriate.

In the United States, AICPA pronouncements encourage the choice of the "subject to" qualification for all uncertainty situations but do not prohibit the use of denials:

> The Committee believes that the explanation of the uncertainties and the qualification of the auditor's opinion contemplated by this Statement should serve adequately to inform the users of the financial statements. Nothing in this Statement, however, is intended to preclude an auditor from declining to express an opinion in cases involving uncertainties.[39]

Other practitioners believe that an uncertainty, such as doubt as to the continuation of the entity as a going concern, may so overshadow the picture presented by the financial statements that no opinion, however qualified, may properly be expressed. An example of a denial of opinion for uncertainty follows:

> [Reservation paragraph]
> As described in Note X to the financial statements, the company has guaranteed bank loans of an affiliate up to $ . . . . Since the affiliate has incurred substantial losses during its most recent fiscal period, the company may be called upon to honour its guarantee. In such event, the management has indicated that there would be a serious question as to the ability of the company to continue operations, unless significant additional funds were provided. Should the company be required to liquidate its assets, it is possible that it would not be able to realize its investment in accounts receivable, inventories, fixed assets and deferred charges without substantial losses.
>
> [Opinion paragraph]
> In view of the possible material effect on the financial statements of the matters discussed in the preceding paragraph, [I am] unable to express an opinion as to whether or not the accompanying financial statements present fairly . . . for the year then ended.[40]

As with qualifications for uncertainty, the standard scope paragraph is not modified.

If professional pronouncements continue to recognize both or either of (a) denials of opinion for uncertainty and (b) "subject to" qualifications for uncertainty as appropriate in some circumstances, it would seem desirable to establish clearer criteria as to when each type of reservation should be used.

18.4 Other reporting related to reservations

Three other considerations closely related to report reservations are:

a) reliance on another auditor's report which contains a reservation,

b) whether "piecemeal opinions" may or should be given in conjunction with adverse opinions or denials of opinion,

c) whether or not "negative assurance" may be given where a positive expression of opinion is precluded.

18.4.1 Reliance on another auditor's report which contains a reservation

Where an auditor is placing reliance on another auditor's report (see 17.5.7) and that report contains a reservation, the auditor must decide whether the subject of the reservation is of a nature and materiality which requires a corresponding reservation in his own report. Where it is, the auditor may wish, in this reservation paragraph, to refer to the other auditor's report (with permission) when explaining the reasons for his own reservation. In some cases, however, a matter giving rise to a reservation with respect to an investee company's statements may have been adjusted for, or may be immaterial, in the investor company's statements, in which case no corresponding reservation is required. In some regulatory filings the full reports of investee auditors are required to be included, in which case the investor auditor may wish to make some reference as well to investee reservations which have been adjusted for, or are immaterial, in the investor company's statements.

18.4.2 Piecemeal opinions

Occasionally, when an adverse opinion or denial of opinion is rendered, it may be useful to give what is called a "piecemeal opinion" as to compliance, with generally accepted accounting principles, of those items in the financial statements unaffected by the adverse opinion or denial. The rules to be observed in giving piecemeal opinions are set out in the CICA Handbook:

Piecemeal opinions should be used:
a) cautiously;
b) only in conjunction with adverse opinions or denials of opinion;
c) only where the effects of the reservations causing the adverse opinion or denial of opinion can be related to specific items;
d) only with respect to items which are significant, either individually or as a group ...
A piecemeal opinion should not contradict or outweigh a denial of opinion or an adverse opinion. When a report containing a piecemeal opinion is given, the wording must make it clear that no overall opinion as to financial position, results of operations and/or [changes in financial position] is intended and the auditors should indicate clearly the limitation of their opinion to the individual items covered.

When expressing a piecemeal opinion, the auditors should identify specifically the items covered by that opinion.[41]

The overall opinion should be stated first (scope, reservation, and opinion paragraphs) and the detailed opinion stated subsequently, preferably in a separate paragraph. For example, after a denial of opinion due to inability to verify instalment accounts receivable, the auditor might word a piecemeal opinion as follows:

[Piecemeal opinion paragraph]
In my opinion, however, cash, inventories, fixed assets, other assets, liabilities (other than income tax and deferred income on instalment contracts), and the share capital of the company at December 31, 1976 are presented fairly in the balance sheet, the miscellaneous income and the expenses (other than bad debt expense and income taxes) for the year then ended are presented fairly in the income statement, and the items comprising source of funds (other than current operations) and application of funds are presented fairly in the statement of changes in financial position, all in accordance with generally accepted accounting principles applied on a basis consistent with that of the preceding year.[42]

Use of broad phrases such as "in all other material respects" or "all other accounts" should be avoided as they might imply an overall, qualified opinion where none was intended.

In giving a piecemeal opinion, the auditor must take note of the inter-relationships among accounts. For example, if an overall opinion is denied because of lack of verification of the closing inventory, one could not report positively on cost of sales, income tax or net income for the year. Even after excluding directly related accounts, the auditor will often have to perform additional audit procedures to satisfy himself that the specific accounts covered by the piecemeal opinion are not indirectly tainted by the matters giving rise to the adverse opinion or denial. Also, more extensive work is usually required on the specific accounts covered by the piecemeal opinion for the further reason that the measure of materiality must normally be related to such accounts individually and so will be reduced from that which is appropriate for an overall expression of opinion on the financial statements taken as a whole.

Even with the best of precautions, however, there is always the danger that piecemeal opinion will be misinterpreted as an overall opinion and thus overshadow the adverse opinion or denial expressed. For that reason, in the United States the AICPA has prohibited the use of piecemeal opinions.[43] The subject is presently under study in Canada. Many practitioners believe that a piecemeal opinion is undesirable following an adverse opinion.

18.4.3 Negative assurance

Denials or qualified opinions on reports with wide distribution should not be tempered by expressions of "negative assurance" – i.e. expressions such as "nothing has come to my attention which would give me reason to believe that these statements are not fairly stated". While the CICA Handbook does not contain an explicit prohibition of negative assurance in these circumstances, a presumption that such assurance should not be given can be inferred from the fact that (a) it does expressly prohibit negative assurance with respect to annual unaudited financial statements (see Chapter 20) and (b) it limits negative assurance in connection with prospectuses to certain restricted circumstances (see Chapter 19). In the United States negative assurance, except for certain letters to underwriters, is expressly prohibited in reports on financial statements purporting to present financial position, results of operations or changes in financial position.[44] The possible use of negative assurance in special purpose reports is discussed in 19.3.

18.5 Degree of assurance with respect to reservations

All decisions as to the need for report reservations must be made in the light of the degree of assurance reasonable to obtain. When the auditor expresses an opinion without reservation, it should mean that he has obtained a high degree of assurance that the financial statements are not materially misstated. Much of this book has been directed toward the audit procedures required to meet that objective.

Assurance with respect to reservations for accounting deficiencies

Similarly, when the auditor expresses a reservation because of an accounting deficiency, it should mean that he has obtained reasonable assurance that the financial statements *are* materially misstated. He does not wish to issue numerous needless reservations.

Sometimes the auditor's assurance that the statements contain a material error is very high. When several *known* errors aggregate to a material amount, the only risks in concluding that a reservation is warranted (failing client adjustment) are (a) that the auditor has mistakenly classified or quantified the items described as known errors and (b) that he has failed to detect significant existing errors in the opposite direction. In such cases, these risks are usually far lower than the audit risks inevitably associated with audits in which a clear opinion is expressed.

At other times, the auditor's assurance that the statements contain a material error cannot be as high. When *most likely* errors projected from sample results exceed a material amount, there is a presumption that, failing client adjustment, a reservation is warranted. But if the client refuses an adjustment, the auditor must remember that there is always the possibility that the financial statements are really misstated by less than a material amount and only exhibit a material most-likely-error projection owing to "sample bounce". He will normally wish to do some further work, such as increasing his sample size, to establish with an appropriate level of assurance that a material error is present (or alternatively to establish that it is not). The level of assurance required to support the need for a reservation can, however, in the writer's view, be considerably less than that called for to support a clear opinion. The reason can be seen in the following example.

Suppose materiality is $50 000 and the auditor's sample results show a most-likely-error projection of $55,000. Unknown to him, however, the true error in the population is only $45 000 (the deviation in his sample projection being due to "sample bounce"). If he persuades his client to adjust for the $55 000 apparent error and then issues a clear opinion, the statements will actually contain a $10 000 error. But this error is immaterial. Indeed, provided that the sample *upper error limit*, after deducting the client adjustment, is less than materiality, he has a very high degree of assurance that any final error in the adjusted statements will be immaterial. Suppose, instead, the client refuses to adjust the statements and the auditor qualifies his report, stating the amount of his disagreement to be $55 000. To what extent is the reader misled? Is he misled because the audit report is qualified when, had the auditor known the true error to be $45 000, a clear opinion would have been acceptable? No. In effect, the reader is misled only in mentally adjusting for an alleged $55 000 error instead of the true $45 000 error—a distortion of $10 000, which is immaterial. Indeed, the reader's position is not markedly different whether the client adjusts for the alleged $55 000 error or whether the auditor reports that he should have adjusted. In either case, the auditor wants to have a high degree of assurance that the alleged error is not materially different from the true error.

This example indicates that the high degree of assurance the auditor usually seeks (for example, in choosing sampling confidence levels) should be related to (a) the assurance that the *amount* quoted in his reservation is not itself materially misstated, rather than to (b) the assurance that the reservation itself is strictly required. The *former* high degree of assurance will be automatically provided if the auditor has planned his sample sizes properly, that is, if the audit precision (upper error limit less most likely error) is less than materiality. The *latter* assurance could, from the reader's point of view, be argued to be irrelevant.

522

However, because of (a) the effect on client relations and (b) the risk of devaluing important reservations by "crying wolf" too often, most auditors will wish to have some reasonable degree of assurance that statement errors do, in fact, breach materiality before issuing a reservation.

As a practical matter, in supporting proposed reservations it is suggested that, if most likely errors exceed materiality only moderately, some sample extension or alternative audit procedure, is desirable – and may also help to convince the client of the need for adjustment. If, however, most likely errors exceed materiality substantially, the risk of the reservation being unnecessary is already low and no further audit work or sample extension should be required. Where the excess is substantial it may sometimes occur that audit precision itself exceeds materiality. In such a case, the auditor cannot be sure that the amount quoted in his reservation is fairly stated within material bounds. While he could extend his sample to reduce the precision range, the more reasonable solution in such cases is usually to quote a range of values in quantifying his reservation (as previously illustrated).

Assurance with respect to reservations for auditing deficiencies or uncertainties

When the auditor expresses a reservation because of an auditing deficiency or because of an uncertainty, it should mean that he has concluded that reasonable assurance as to whether the financial statements are or are not materially misstated is just not practically obtainable. He will wish to minimize the risk of drawing such a conclusion when, in fact, sufficient evidence to support a definite opinion was available but overlooked. While no precise means of measuring this risk are possible, the auditor will wish to take reasonable steps to limit it by carefully exploring the possible sources of audit evidence before issuing a "subject to" qualification or a denial.

18.6 International reporting

Financial statements are read by shareholders, creditors, governments, regulatory agencies, and others. For many Canadian companies, partnerships, and proprietorships, such readers are all organizations or individuals resident in Canada and the question of foreign accounting and auditing standards does not arise. For some Canadian companies, however, such readers include organizations or individuals resident in other countries as well. In such cases, the following questions arise:

1. Which country's accounting principles and auditing standards should be used?
2. Should the nationality of the principles and standards used be identified?
3. Should the differences between the various countries' standards be disclosed?
4. If more than one version of the financial statements are issued, should the existence of the other versions be disclosed?

In discussing these questions it is useful to distinguish between *primary financial statements* and *secondary financial statements*. [45] The former are prepared to satisfy the reporting requirements of the company's country of domicile. The latter are prepared specifically for use in another country and may differ from the primary financial statements in form, disclosure, currency, language, accounting principles and (with respect to the acompanying audit report) auditing standards.

18.6.1 Primary financial statements

Accounting principles and auditing standards to be used

Statutes or regulations normally require that the primary financial statements of a company incorporated in a Canadian jurisdiction, and prepared for issuance to its shareholders, be prepared in accordance with Canadian "generally accepted accounting principles". The statutory auditor, in reporting on such statements, should therefore conduct his examination and prepare his report in accordance with Canadian "generally accepted auditing standards" which includes expressing his opinion in relation to Canadian "generally accepted accounting principles". This requirement continues to apply even if the company is 100% owned by foreign interests. The wording of the auditor's report should also follow the form used in Canada. If a company insists on following accounting principles accepted in a foreign jurisdiction and the effect of applying such principles is significantly different from the effect of applying those acceptable in Canada, the auditor should express a reservation in his report. Having given an opinion relative to Canadian principles, the auditor may, if it is desired, express an additional opinion relative to foreign principles. This additional special-purpose opinion, if given, would usually be presented in a separate paragraph following the primary opinion paragraph.

The CICA, in conjunction with the Certified General Accountants' Associations of Canada and the Society of Industrial Accountants of Canada, is a member of the International Accounting Standard Committee (IASC). The objectives of the IASC are "to formulate and publish in the public interest, basic standards to be observed in the presentation of audited accounts and financial statements and to promote their worldwide acceptance and observance". The IASC has issued a few accounting pronouncements to date, some of which contain differences from CICA Accounting Recommendations. The CICA has undertaken to study these differences and, unless there is a fundamental disagreement or unless Canadian circumstances require a different position, to conform its Accounting Recommendations to the IASC pronouncements. However, until such time as new or revised Recommendations are issued, reference should be made to the existing ones (together, in areas where they are silent, with principles and practices which have by usage or by other means gained general acceptance in Canada) in determining Canadian "generally accepted accounting principles". The preface to the IASC pronouncements states that they do not override local pronouncements. [46]

Disclosure of the nationality of the principles and standards used

It is not mandatory for any Canadian company to state that the "generally accepted accounting principles" it has used are Canadian nor for its auditor to state that the terms "generally accepted auditing standards" and "generally accepted accounting principles" used in his report refer to Canadian standards and principles. The reader should be expected to draw this inference, in the absence of explicit disclosure to the contrary, from the fact that the financial statements are issued in Canada by a company incorporated in Canada and are accompanied by an auditor's report bearing a Canadian address. (Some practitioners argue that this inference should also be triggered by the Canadian form of auditor's report; however, the differences between the Canadian form and that used in some other countries such as the United States are slight and are unlikely to be noticed by a reader who has failed to observe the auditor's address.)

Nevertheless, disclosure of the nationality of the principles and standards used, while not mandatory, may be desirable where a company is reporting in an international environment. With respect to disclosure by the company, CICA Accounting Recommendations suggest:

> For companies that report in an international environment it is desirable to disclose the fact that they have followed accounting principles generally accepted in Canada in preparing their financial statements. [47]

With respect to disclosure by the auditor, CICA Auditing Recommendations suggest:

> When the terms "generally accepted auditing standards" and "generally accepted accounting principles" are used in an auditor's report issued in Canada, there is a presumption that the terms refer to Canadian practice. It is therefore not necessary to explicitly modify either phrase with the words "Canadian" or "in Canada". However, such modification may be desirable when the auditor is reporting on financial statements of an enterprise operating in an international environment or having substantial foreign ownership, or on financial statements expressed in a foreign currency. [48]

The study, *International Financial Reporting*, suggested a similar disclosure where "the auditor believes a reader of the primary financial statements might mistakenly infer that the accounting principles or auditing standards followed were those of another country"[49] – including cases where the address on the auditor's report is outside the company's country of domicile.

Disclosure of differences from other principles and standards

Except where the primary financial statements are specifically prepared to meet reporting requirements in other countries as well as in Canada (discussed in the next two paragraphs), it is not common to disclose differences between the Canadian principles and standards followed and those of other countries. However, such disclosure may be desirable in some cases. CICA Accounting Recommendations suggest that for companies reporting in an international environment it is desirable for the financial statements to disclose conformity with IASC pronouncements (i.e., where these coincide with Canadian principles) or to identify deviations from IASC pronouncements (but not necessarily their effect).[50] Because this disclosure is suggested as desirable rather than essential to fair presentation, the auditor should encourage his client to make it but would not need to qualify his report solely for its absence.

Sometimes primary financial statements are specifically prepared to meet reporting requirements in other countries at the same time as meeting those of Canada. For example, a Canadian company which is registered with the SEC in the United States may prepare one set of primary statements to meet both Canadian and U.S. requirements. Where no conflict in accounting practices is involved, joint compliance may be achieved by meeting the more restrictive accounting requirements and the more comprehensive disclosure requirements in each case – in the example in the preceding sentence, normally those of the

United States. Where there is a conflict in accounting practices, the financial statements may show a second net income and/or retained earnings figure (usually in the notes). In this case the notes would usually disclose the details of significant differences which would have resulted from the use of the other country's accounting principles. Statements prepared on the basis of Canadian principles together with the disclosure of such differences are normally acceptable, for example, in Canadian filings with the SEC.

Where the financial statements contain disclosure of differences from another country's principles and standards (including usually an assertion that all such significant differences have been disclosed), the auditor must satisfy himself that the disclosures are factually correct. To satisfy himself on this matter he must be familiar with the other country's principles and standards or seek professional assistance from those who are. If the disclosures are false or misleading, the auditor, as with any significant misstatements of fact, must express a reservation in his report. Apart from such reservations, if any, or the implied satisfaction in their absence, the auditor reporting on primary financial statements would usually express his opinion solely in relation to Canadian "generally accepted accounting principles". However, a further opinion in relation to the other country's principles is permissible (provided the third reporting standard is first met by an opinion in relation to Canadian principles) and is suggested in the study, *International Financial Reporting*.[51] Such a further opinion is often given in the form of a separate letter to an investor company or to its auditor where the latter have specifically requested assurance as to conformity with foreign accounting principles and auditing standards and where permission to issue such a letter has been given by the Canadian company.

Disclosure of the existence of secondary financial statements

When primary financial statements have been issued to shareholders of a Canadian company and separate secondary financial statements have been prepared for distribution in another country, it is not customary to make reference in the primary statements to the existence of the others (though the converse reference is normal – see 18.6.2). The presumption is usually that, if the primary statements have complied fully with Canadian requirements, statements drawn up on a different basis are not relevant to the readers of the primary statements. However, if the secondary statements contain more complete disclosure of certain matters, the company's directors may wish to consider whether similar disclosures should be made to all the company's shareholders. Some auditors are

also concerned about having two different sets of audited financial statements both in wide circulation. Their concern is that an individual might later allege that he had relied on Audit Report A to his detriment because he had not been informed of Audit Report B. Provided Audit Report A met proper legal and professional standards the auditor's reporting is justified; he does not, in any case, control the distribution of his reports. Nevertheless, where secondary statements are to be widely circulated, some auditors prefer to avoid the possibility of confusion by (a) conforming the degree of disclosure in the two statements to the extent possible and/or (b) cross-referencing each audit report to the other (if both are issued at the same time).

Primary financial statements of a non-Canadian company

Where a Canadian auditor reports on the primary financial statements of a company incorporated in another country, he should form and express his opinion in relation to the accounting principles and auditing standards of that other country. His report wording should then follow the standard form used in that other country. (If his report shows a Canadian address, a specific reference to the nationality of the standards and principles followed is desirable.) To complete such an engagement the auditor must be familiar with the other country's principles and standards or seek professional assistance from those who are. It may be debated whether the Canadian auditor can be exempt from Canadian "generally accepted auditing standards" in such a case. Common sense would suggest that, if he is reporting on a company incorporated in the United States, he should follow U.S. reporting standards where these differ from Canadian ones but that he should probably seek to comply with the more stringent of the two sets of general and field work standards. The general and field work standards do not differ significantly between Canada and the United States; a number of differences of detail exist, however, between U.S. independence standards and Canadian Rules of Professional Conduct with respect to objectivity.

18.6.2 Secondary financial statements

Secondary financial statements which meet foreign reporting requirements

If primary financial statements have already been issued to a Canadian company's shareholders, secondary financial statements specifically prepared for filing or publishing in another country represent special purpose statements. According to the third

525

Canadian reporting standard, the audit opinion on such statements can be expressed in relation to "an appropriate disclosed basis of accounting" – which could be generally accepted accounting principles in another country.

Where, in order to comply with the other country's accounting principles, the secondary statements differ from the primary statements in both form and substance, it would be normal for the Canadian auditor to:

a) form and express his opinion in relation to the accounting principles and auditing standards of the other country,

b) disclose the nationality of those principles and standards in his report,

c) refer in his report to the existence of the primary statements prepared in accordance with Canadian principles,

d) summarize in his report the applicable differences between the two sets of principles (or refer to a note containing such a summary).[52]

An example of a typical report wording for secondary statements to be filed in the United States follows. Principal changes from the standard Canadian wording are (a) the standard U.S. reference to two years, (b) minor differences (italicized) to conform with standard U.S. wording, (c) disclosure of the nationality of the accounting principles and auditing standards, (d) an additional third paragraph.

> The Board of Directors of X Canada Limited
>
> I have examined the balance sheets of X Canada Limited *as of* December 31, 1976 and December 31, 1975 and the *related* statements of income, retained earnings and changes in financial position for the year then ended. My examinations were made in accordance with auditing standards generally accepted in the United States of America and, accordingly, included such tests *of the accounting records* and *such* other *auditing* procedures as I considered necessary in the circumstances.
>
> In my opinion, the financial statements *referred to above* present fairly the financial position of X Canada Limited *as of* December 31, 1976 and December 31, 1975, and the results of its operations and the changes in its financial position for the years then ended, in *conformity* with accounting principles generally accepted in the United States of America applied on a consistent basis.
>
> I have also reported on March 10, 1977 to the shareholders of X Canada Limited on the published statements of the company for the same period prepared in accordance with accounting principles generally accepted in Canada. The significant differences between accounting principles accepted in Canada and those accepted in the United States of America so far as concerns these financial statements are summarized in Note 1.

The secondary financial statements will often be translated into the currency of the other country where they are to be filed or published. In such cases, it seems logical that the auditor's opinion as to

conformity with the other country's accounting principles would automatically include the basis of translation used. (However, some practitioners prefer to express their full opinion on only the Canadian dollar figures – restated to conform to foreign accounting principles – and limit their opinion on the foreign currency figures to the accuracy of the translation in accordance with a basis disclosed in the notes.) The secondary financial statements may sometimes be expressed in a language other than English or French. In such cases, the auditor should satisfy himself as to the appropriateness of the wording, disclosures, and technical terminology used.

To report on such secondary statements the Canadian auditor must be familiar with the other country's principles and standards (and, where different, its language) or seek professional assistance from those who are.

Although the reference to foreign accounting principles may be consistent, as stated earlier, with the provision for "an appropriate disclosed basis of accounting" contained in the third Canadian reporting standard, it may be that in order to conform to foreign reporting practices the auditor's report will depart in other respects from Canadian reporting standards or CICA Auditing Recommendations. Again it may be debated whether the Canadian auditor can be exempt from Canadian "generally accepted auditing standards" – since these have a stated application to all reports on Canadian financial statements (including special purpose reports). Common sense would again suggest that, provided that a reference is made to the existence of the primary statements, the auditor should follow the foreign reporting standards where they differ from Canadian ones but should seek to comply with the more stringent of the two sets of general and field work standards (where such foreign standards exist).

Secondary financial statements which do not meet foreign reporting requirements

Occasionally secondary financial statements are prepared which are:

a) identical in basic form to the primary financial statements issued to a Canadian company's shareholders and have not been adjusted to conform with the accounting principles of another country,

b) differ from the primary financial statements only in that translated foreign currency figures are shown in addition to Canadian dollar figures and/or in that the statements have been translated into a language other than English or French.

Such statements may be circulated as a convenience to foreign readers but they do not purport to be anything other than a translation of the primary statements.

Where the only difference from the primary statements is the addition of translated foreign currency figures, the auditor would normally form and express his opinion on the Canadian dollar figures in relation to Canadian accounting principles and auditing standards. Disclosure of the nationality of these principles and standards would seem desirable. Often the auditor may have to limit his opinion on the foreign currency figures to the accuracy of the translation in accordance with a basis described in the notes.

Where the secondary statements have been translated into another language, the auditor would again normally form and express his opinion on the Canadian dollar figures in relation to Canadian accounting principles and auditing standards. In this case, disclosure of the nationality of these principles and standards is particularly important in order to avoid misinterpretation. In addition, the auditor should satisfy himself as to the accuracy of the language translation before permitting his name to be associated with the translated statements. It should be noted that the foregoing considerations call for the auditor's report to be modified in certain respects and not to be merely a language translation of his report on the primary statements.[53]

Some practitioners believe that "convenience only" translations may be misleading to users and should be avoided. The reader should refer to any subsequent pronouncements on this subject.

Where significant differences exist between Canadian and foreign principles and standards, secondary statements which are mere translations are not appropriate for use, without adjustment, by the auditor of a foreign investor company in forming his opinion on foreign statements which consolidate or equity account for the Canadian company. The study, *International Financial Reporting*, suggests that where the investee auditor knows that his report is to be so used by the auditor of a foreign investor, he should form and express his opinion in relation to the foreign principles and standards.[54]

18.7 Post-audit information

In rare cases, after the issue of his audit report, an auditor may become aware of information indicating that the financial statements were or may be materially misstated.

Subsequent discovery of information indicating possible material error

The auditor's standard report makes reference to the examination on which his opinion was based. A reader can properly assume that, as far as evidence as to the financial statement assertions are concerned, this examination extended up to the date disclosed on the audit report but not beyond.

> After he has issued his report, the auditor has no obligation to make any further or continuing inquiry or perform any other auditing procedures with respect to the audited financial statements covered by that report, unless new information which may affect his report comes to his attention. [55]

However, if new information comes to the auditor's attention which indicates that the previously issued financial statements may have been materially misstated, he may have certain professional and legal responsibilities. The auditor's legal responsibilities under certain corporations acts in Canada were outlined in 4.1.4. The auditor should refer to the specific act covering the reporting entity in question and seek legal advice where appropriate. Not all corporations acts impose specific legal responsibilities with respect to subsequent information. Most practitioners, however, would consider that they had certain professional responsibilities where they believe previously issued and audited statements are misleading. Such responsibilities are not defined in Canadian pronouncements and while AICPA pronouncements[56] offer useful suggestions they are not necessarily required practice in a Canadian context.

For newly discovered information to be of possible concern to the auditor in this connection it must:

a) relate to facts existing at the date of the auditor's report and not to subsequent developments or events (a strike begun a month after the issue of the financial statements may have an important bearing on the company's current operations but it does not affect the fairness of presentation of the past year's statements),

b) not concern merely the final determination or resolution of matters already disclosed as a contingency in the statements or already covered by a reservation in the auditor's report (the amount of the final settlement of a long-outstanding lawsuit may be important corporate news but if the lawsuit was properly disclosed in the statements and if, at the time that it was the subject of a major uncertainty, it was covered by an appropriate audit reservation, there is no need to adjust and re-issue the past year's statements),

c) be of a nature that would have led the auditor to

investigate it had he been aware of it at the time of issuing his report (information which would reasonably have been regarded as incorrect or as immaterial at the time would not require investigation either before or after issue of the auditor's report).

Where information meeting the above criteria comes to the auditor's attention, the AICPA pronouncements suggest that the auditor should discuss the information with management and/or the board of directors and take steps to determine whether it is reliable and whether the facts existed at the date of his report. If he (a) concludes that the financial statements and/or his report would have been affected by such facts had they been known and (b) believes that readers are currently relying or likely to rely on the statements and would attach importance to such facts, it is suggested that he advise his client to disclose the newly discovered facts to such readers. Disclosure could take the form of a revised set of financial statements and auditor's report or, if the revision relates to prior periods, appropriate disclosure in current financial statements about to be issued. However, if such revisions must await the outcome of a prolonged investigation, it would be desirable to inform such readers that the previous statements should not be relied on pending the results of the investigation.

Should the client refuse to make the foregoing disclosures, the AICPA pronouncements suggest that the auditor should inform the client, each member of the client's board of directors, any regulatory agencies involved, and readers known to the auditor to be relying on the statements, that his report should no longer be relied upon.

Issue of an updated audit report

Occasionally, the auditor may be requested to update his audit report on past financial statements. For example, when the report and statements are being included in a prospectus (see Chapter 19), such up-

dating, while usually not necessary, is sometimes requested. When the auditor advances the date on his audit report, he should conduct a normal subsequent events review, as in any audit engagement, up to the date of the audit report now to be issued. Normally, information which would lead to a revision of the previously issued statements (other than revisions to meet regulatory or underwriting requirements or to disclose important subsequent events during the intervening period) would have to meet the criteria outlined in the previous section. Thus, although accounting estimates are usually based on the best judgment available at an audit report date, on updated reports the estimates would usually not be adjusted to the second report date unless the estimates at the earlier report date could properly be considered to be erroneous in the light of facts existing at that earlier date. Where an auditor issues an updated audit report on financial statements containing significant revisions from those covered by his earlier report (other than revisions representing solely the disclosure of important subsequent events during the intervening period), and where the readership of the two reports is likely to be significantly different, he will wish to consider any responsibilities he may have to the readers of the earlier report.

Re-issue of an audit report (not updated)

Occasionally, the auditor may be requested to reissue his audit report, for inclusion in a prospectus or long-form report, in circumstances in which it is not considered necessary to update his report or to conduct a further subsequent events review. If, in such a case, an important subsequent event is known to have occurred between the date of the original audit report and its reissue, it may be disclosed in a note in the financial statements marked as unaudited.[57] The reissued audit report would then bear the same date as the original report. Alternatively, if the disclosure of the subsequent event is audited but the original audit report is not otherwise updated, the report may be split-dated (see 17.2.2).

18.8 Reference material

CICA Handbook, Sec. 5500, The Auditors' Report – Other Matters (the reader should refer to subsequent pronouncements which may supersede the present Sec. 5500; as this book goes to press proposed sections on Reporting Reservations and Other Reporting Matters and a possible renumbering of other sections are under study).
AICPA Statement on Auditing Standards No. 1, Secs. 545, 561.
AICPA Statement on Auditing Standards No. 2, *Reports on Audited Financial Statements*.

AICPA Auditing Research Monograph No. 1, *The Auditor's Reporting Obligation*, D.R. Carmichael, CPA, Ph.D. (1972).
Accountants International Study Group, *The Independent Auditor's Reporting Standards in Three Nations* pars. 52 to 99.
Accountants International Study Group, *Going Concern Problems* (1975).
Accountants International Study Group, *International Financial Reporting* (1975).

18.9 Questions and problems

Review and discussion

1. Identify the broad categories of circumstance which require a reservation of opinion in the auditor's report.
2. Describe the three "degrees of reservation" used in Canadian auditors' reports.
3. The auditor of X Co. Ltd. has discovered pricing errors of $5 000 in his pricing tests of X's inventory. The most likely error is $25 000. Management of X has expressed an unwillingness to adjust beyond the known errors. The materiality set by the auditor for X Co. Ltd. is $15 000. Discuss the alternatives available to X Co.'s auditor.
4. How do disagreements in subjective judgment between management and the auditor affect the audit report?
5. Arm and Arm, a law partnership, has appointed B. Grant, CA, as the firm's auditor. Arm Sr. has indicated to Grant that a statement of changes in financial position will not be prepared and, accordingly, will not be reported on by Grant. Arm's partner concurs with this approach. Will this affect B. Grant's audit report? If so, how?
6. How does materiality affect a company's audit report?
7. Why should an auditor encourage his clients to correct misstatements which are less than materiality?
8. The president of Low Key Inc. has requested you, the company's auditor, not to confirm the outstanding trade receivables with its customers. You are able to verify the accounts receivable by alternate means, i.e., subsequent payments and review of shipping documents, invoices, etc. How will this situation affect your audit report?
9. It is often impracticable to verify the donation revenue of charitable organizations. How does this situation affect the audit report?
10. DDIC Corporation has been sued for $2 000 000 by a major competitor with respect to a patent infringement. DDIC's legal counsel is of the opinion that the company will win the case and suffer no losses. How would this situation affect the audit report?
11. If, in Question 10, legal counsel feels that the company would settle for $100 000 in the near future, and the company has refused to provide for any liability for this dispute, how would the audit report be affected?
12. Discuss why going-concern qualifications are reasonably infrequent.
13. There are differing views in the accounting profession with respect to the reporting of uncertainties. Briefly outline these views, and describe the CICA position on this subject at this time.
14. Under what conditions would an adverse opinion be given?
15. Distinguish between a denial of opinion and a disclaimer as these terms are used in Canada. What corresponding terms are used in the United States?
16. What are the dangers associated with piecemeal opinions?
17. The suggestion has been made that the level of assurance required to support an audit report reservation (when the auditor believes that a material error is present) can be less than the level of assurance required to support an unqualified, clear opinion (when the auditor believes that no material error is present). Discuss the reasons for this suggestion.
18. Distinguish between primary financial statements and secondary financial statements in international reporting situations.
19. In an international reporting situation, what would a Canadian auditor normally do when the secondary financial statements differ from the primary financial statements in both form and substance?
20. What is the purpose of the Accountants International Study Group?
21. When an auditor becomes aware of information, subsequent to the issue of a company's audit report, which indicates a possible material misstatement of the issued financial statements, what are his responsibilities?

Problems

1. (CICA adapted) As auditor of the public company in each case, you are confronted with the following unrelated situations. Assume that amounts are to be considered material in each instance. For each of these situations:
   a) What additional information, if any, would it be desirable to provide in either the financial statements or the accompanying notes? Give your reasons.
   b) Assuming that no further information is disclosed in the notes, indicate, with reasons, whether you would consider it necessary to discuss a reservation in your audit report and draft any reservation you consider necessary.
      1) Two weeks before the end of the fiscal year, R. Ltd. obtained a bank loan, which

was repaid one month later. It appears that the additional cash was not specifically required for operating purposes during the one month period. You also note that the year-end ratio of current assets to current liabilities was 2:3, and without the bank loan it would have been 1:2. For statement presentation, the directors propose including the cash obtained from the bank loan with other cash balances in the current assets' section, and including the bank loan in the current liabilities as a separate item designated as "bank loan-secured".

2) For many years S Ltd. has carried a substantial life insurance policy on the life of its president. During the current year a loan was obtained from the life insurance company on security of the cash surrender value of that policy. It is the intention of the directors to repay the loan out of the eventual proceeds of the policy and, for financial statement purposes, they propose deducting the amount of the loan from the policy's cash surrender value. The net amount would be shown as non-current asset – "cash surrender value of life insurance, less loan outstanding".

3) T Ltd. is a growing public utility. To provide funds for additional plant and equipment, it usually issues general mortgage bonds each year under an existing trust deed. At the fiscal year-end, the company has a large bank loan which was borrowed for interim financing of plant additions. The directors propose classifying this loan as a non-current liability, because it is their intention to pay off the loan from the proceeds of a further bond issue within approximately six months. The item is to be captioned "bank loan".

2. (CICA adapted) C.A. is the auditor of F Ltd., which has a December 31 year-end. On January 31, C.A.'s staff completed the field work for the year 1976. On February 15, C.A. is in the process of completing his auditor's report dated January 31, 1977 when he becomes aware of a material subsequent event which occurred on February 10. Management prefers not to disclose the subsequent event. What factors should C.A. take into account before signing his report?

3. (CICA adapted) Generally accepted accounting practice recognizes that the balance sheet is a quick snapshot at a point in time, but the reality is that the operations of an enterprise are continuous. Therefore, the balance sheet should reflect the effects of some events which occur after the balance sheet date. Subsequent events may be reflected in the balance sheet (and thereby the income statement), in accompanying notes, or not at all.

a) Describe the criteria you would use in determining whether and how to report in the financial statements events occurring subsequent to the date of the balance sheet.

b) Apply the criteria from part (a) to each of the following unrelated situations, indicating the reasoning you would use to determine whether and how each event should be reported in the December 31, 1976 financial statements.

i) On February 15, 1977, X Ltd. acquired for cash the inventory and plant of a smaller competitor. The acquisition required most of X Ltd.'s cash, which had amounted to 15% of its assets as at December 31, 1976.

ii) About 10% of the consolidated sales of Y Ltd. have been made by a particular subsidiary (which is not wholly-owned). The financial situation of that subsidiary has deteriorated recently, and on February 15, 1977, the directors of the subsidiary decided on a voluntary liquidation (agreed to by the parent, Y Ltd.). Though the liquidation would take some time, the directors expect that the shareholders would ultimately recover the book value of their shares. The financial statements of Y Ltd. are prepared on a consolidated basis.

iii) On February 15, 1977, Z Ltd.'s largest customer, which had been responsible for 30% of Z Ltd.'s sales, signed a long-term purchase contract with a competitor of the company. The customer informed Z Ltd. that it intended to purchase no more of the company's products.

4. (CICA adapted) Describe the correct disclosure in the financial statements of X Ltd. at December 31, 1976 in each of the following circumstances. Then comment on the necessity of including a qualification in CA's audit report, if the disclosure is not adopted by management.

a) In the course of his annual audit of the accounts of X Ltd., as at December 31, 1976, the auditor confirmed contracts receivable and discovered that of the billings submitted to Y Ltd. in 1976, $300 000 was in dispute. The balances receivable from Y Ltd. according to the books of X Ltd. at December 31, 1976 and February 28, 1977 were $410 000 and $620 000 respectively. Y Ltd. advised X Ltd. on February 28 that, in accordance with the terms of the contract, an amount equal to the total disputed billings would be withheld until a settlement was reached. As a starting negotiating position, Y Ltd. claimed that no portion of the $300 000 is payable. Negotiations were in process during March but the outcome was uncertain when CA completed his audit. The undisputed amount of $320 000 was paid in March. The management of X Ltd. has informed CA that in its opinion no loss will be sustained as a result of the dispute. $300 000 is material.

b) The same conditions apply as in (a), with the exception that the terms of the contract do not provide for the withholding of funds by Y Ltd., and by the end of the audit, no payments on the $620 000 had been received.

5. (CICA adapted) In each of the following situations, CA is the shareholder's auditor of Y Ltd. and its wholly-owned subsidiaries. This public company is a medium-size manufacturing concern and has no internal audit department.

a) Mr. X, the comptroller of Y Ltd., a chartered accountant and a former member of CA's firm, has asked CA to confine his interim audit to specific areas. He feels that these are the areas in which internal control is weak and tells CA that he has checked all other areas and found them satisfactory. Mr. X is very emphatic about keeping the fee at the present level, as CA will only be auditing these designated problem areas.

What reply (with reasons) should CA give to the comptroller?

b) The consolidated profit of Y Ltd. and its subsidiaries for the year ended December 31, 1976 is $490 000. During the audit of X Ltd., one of the subsidiaries, CA notices that there is $5 000 of inter-company profit in the inventory. The net profit of X Ltd. for the year ended December 31, 1976 is $25 000. There was no adjustment on any of the organization's financial statements for this profit and management refuses to allow any change in the statements.

What disclosures (with reasons) should CA give in his report on (i) X Ltd. and (ii) Y Ltd. consolidated?

c) In his review of the preliminary draft of the 1976 annual report, CA notices that the president states in his message to shareholders that: "the financial statements show an increase in operating profits of 120%." CA checks this and finds that "operating profits" have increased by only 50%, whereas "net

profit" increased by 120%. The difference was due to profit on disposal of marketable securities held by Y Ltd.

What action should CA take (with reasons)?

d) In a press release, the company stated that its consolidated profit for the first quarter ended March 31, 1977 was $754 000. Although CA had nothing to do with the preparation of this figure, he knows that it does not include a loss of $150 000 on the winding up of an unsuccessful division of the company.

What action should CA take (with reasons)?

6. Prepare an appropriately worded audit report for each of the following unrelated situations. (Note: If a standard scope or opinion paragraph is to be used, this may simply be indicated without writing it out in full. If reference is made to a note in the report, then the note should also be included as part of your answer.)

a) You have relied on other auditors in preparing the consolidated financial statements of ABC Ltd. The subsidiaries audited by the other auditors account for 15% of consolidated assets and income.

b) Because of a fire in the company's vault, you were not able to count $100 000 of bearer securities owned by the company (normal pretax income is $500 000). You have not been able to satisfy yourself as to their existence by other means.

c) In auditing the consolidated financial statements of X Ltd., you become aware of certain subsidiaries which are having financial difficulties. It has come to your attention that these subsidiaries are in default of agreements with their banker and that the bank is considering calling its loans. The parent company (X Ltd.) has guaranteed these loans. In discussing this situation with the company president, you learn that the company will not be able to meet its obligations under the guarantee unless additional funds are advanced to the company. The president does not think the company can raise the additional capital required.

d) Y Ltd. is a new client. The accounts were previously reported upon by another auditor. You have not been able to satisfy yourself as to opening inventory quantities.

e) In your audit of X Ltd., you have concluded that internal control in all areas is inadequate. Because of these poor controls, you have not been able to satisfy yourself as to the completeness of sales, receivables, expenses and accounts payable.

f) The company leases a major portion of its

fixed assets under "financial lease" arrangements. In past years the company has exercised its purchase options at the end of the lease term. The company accounts for these leases as operating leases.

g) The company has valued its long-term investments at cost. In your opinion, there has been a material permanent decline in the market value of these securities of approximately $100 000.

h) You have issued to the directors of a company a set of statements which are to be used in filing the income tax returns. The accounts of subsidiaries have not been consolidated in this statement.

7. Draft an appropriately worded audit report and any related necessary notes for A Co. Ltd. Also, give reasons why the items (b)-(h) are, or are not, referred to in your report or in the notes. Following are the facts:

a) Materiality $100 000

b) Subsequent to the year-end, one of the customers, B, went bankrupt. This customer is also an audit client of yours. A Co. is not aware of the bankruptcy and has not provided for this account in its allowance. The allowance for this account would cause the allowance for doubtful accounts to be beyond the zone of reasonableness.

Allowance per books	$30 000
Zone of reasonableness	
without B	$27 000 – 37 000
Your best guess without B	$32 000
Best guess with B	$54 000

c) The company acquired certain wholly-owned subsidiaries after April 1, 1974 but does not amortize the excess ($500 000) of their purchase price over the fair value of their identifiable net assets.

d) Other known errors understating net income – $35 000

Most likely errors understating net income – $75 000

e) The company has paid dividends which exceed the maximum allowed under loan agreements with the bank. The bank has confirmed in writing to you that it is aware of the default and that it does not intend to exercise its option to call the bank loan.

f) The company has made loans to an officer (who is also a director) for the building of a house. The amount of the loan is $125 000. This amount is disclosed with other items under the caption – "other long-term investments – at cost".

g) The company has changed its method of valuing inventory from FIFO to a moving weighted average.

8. a) A company has several subsidiaries which are all wholly-owned. During a planning meeting, the president states that he does not wish an audit report for certain subsidiaries in the current year (assume, that because of size exemptions, audits are not required by the relevant Business Corporations Acts). He states that he feels that you, as auditor, can give an unqualified opinion on the consolidated financial statements even though reports are not issued to all subsidiaries (certain of which contain material amounts of assets). Give your response to the president's comments.

b) In your review of the minutes of one of its subsidiary companies (federally incorporated), you subsequently discover that you have been appointed as auditor of the company and you realize that there are active non-voting preferred shareholders. What course of action should you take in this situation?

Prospectuses, Management Letters and Special Purpose Reports

This chapter covers (a) the variations in report wording and additional audit procedures involved in prospectus engagements, (b) the format and wording of special purpose reports, (c) long-form reports, and (d) the internal control/management letter.

19.1 Reports on financial statements in prospectuses

Corporations and Securities Acts in Canada require that a prospectus or offering circular accompany most public offerings of new securities for sale or exchange (primary distributions) and, in certain circumstances, public offerings of a large block of existing securities for resale or exchange (secondary distributions). The prospectus is designed to provide the prospective purchaser with more extensive, more detailed, and perhaps more current information than he would normally find in the last published annual report of the company whose securities are being offered. Copies of the prospectus must not only be provided to prospective purchasers but generally filed with and approved by a provincial Securities Commission in advance.

Included in a prospectus are audited financial statements, usually covering the last several years' operations, and sometimes either audited or unaudited statements of more recent interim periods. The public accountant who is engaged by the directors of the issuing company to report on the audited financial statements included in the prospectus is usually the statutory auditor of the company – a situation which is assumed in the remainder of this chapter. (Where he is not the statutory auditor, he may be designated in the prospectus as the "reporting accountant".) The financial statements included in a prospectus should be prepared in accordance with generally accepted accounting principles. As mentioned in 17.3.1, National Policy No. 27 of the Securities Administrators of Canada has stated that, for the purposes of administering securities legislation, the administrators would regard the Accounting Recommendations of the CICA's Accounting Research Committee as generally accepted accounting principles.

In addition to financial statements, the prospectus generally contains a description of the company and its operations, an analysis of its capitalization, a description of the terms of the new securities being offered, information as to the intended use of the proceeds of the new issue, identification of material contracts of the company, and certain information as to the company's officers and directors. Various Corporations and Securities Acts specify detailed requirements for the contents of the prospectus. If a company's shares are listed on stock exchanges in several different provinces in Canada, the company will have to meet the requirements of several Securities Acts, several provincial Securities Commissions, and the relevant Corporations Act. Fortunately, the requirements are reasonably similar from province to province. If the securities are to be offered to residents of other countries it will be necessary to meet as well the requirements of foreign regulatory bodies, such as the SEC in the United States, The Stock Exchange in the United Kingdom, or the various stock exchanges of continental Europe.

The auditor undertaking a prospectus engagement should familiarize himself with the applicable legislative and regulatory requirements. This chapter covers only his general professional responsibilities.

19.1.1 The auditor's report

Prospectuses filed with the Securities Commissions of British Columbia, Alberta, Saskatchewan, Manitoba, Ontario, and Quebec generally include a balance sheet, and statements of income and retained earnings for the five fiscal years and the part of a fiscal year, if any, from the end of the last completed fiscal year to the balance sheet date. Though not presently required by the Acts it has been increasingly common in recent years to include a statement of changes in financial position as well. Professional requirements call for the balance sheet in a prospectus to be reasonably recent, normally not more than 120 days prior to the date of the preliminary prospectus.[1] Thus, where a prospectus is issued midway through a fiscal year, a balance sheet at an interim month-end will normally be required. Where this interim month-end balance sheet is audited, it will generally be the only historical balance sheet presented (comparative figures at the previous fiscal year-end or at any earlier date not being given). Where an audited interim month-end balance sheet is presented, the statements of income, retained earnings and changes in financial position for the related "stub period" would similarly be audited, though unaudited statements would suffice for the corresponding stub period of the preceding year. An example of a typical auditor's report in such a case follows (assuming no reservation is required):

To the Directors of X Company Ltd.

I have examined the balance sheet of X Company Ltd. as at March 31, 1977 and the statements of income, retained earnings, and changes in financial position for the five years and three months then ended. My examination was made in accordance with generally accepted auditing standards, and accordingly included such tests and other procedures as I considered necessary in the circumstances.

In my opinion, these financial statements present fairly the financial position of the company as at March 31, 1977 and the results of its operations and the changes in its financial position for the five years and three months then ended in accordance with generally accepted accounting principles applied on a consistent basis.

There are a number of cases where a statement of changes in financial position is omitted in prospectuses. This omission seems inconsistent with the position that annual financial statements must normally include a statement of changes in financial position if they are to provide a fair presentation in accordance with generally accepted accounting principles (see 17.2.3 and 18.2.1). Although the omission is sufficiently customary (and consistent with present CICA Recommendations with respect to prospectuses) that it must be considered acceptable, it would seem desirable to include such a statement. Where a statement of changes in financial position is not included, the wording of the foregoing scope and opinion paragraphs should be amended accordingly. Likewise, the scope paragraph would be amended if other audited statements are included or if the statements are differently titled by the client.

In the case of a mining or industrial company that is in the promotional, exploratory or development stage, the Acts normally require inclusion of a statement of changes in financial position or statement of cash receipts and disbursements in lieu of the statements of income and retained earnings.

Some Acts provide for certain *unaudited* financial statements to be presented in a prospectus provided that such statements are made up to a date not more than 90 days prior to the date of the preliminary prospectus and provided that audited statements are presented as of the end of the most recently completed fiscal year. Where these provisions apply, the audit report in the foregoing example could instead cover a balance sheet at December 31, 1976 and the remaining statements for the five years then ended. Unaudited balance sheet figures would then be presented as at March 31, 1977 and unaudited figures for income and for changes in financial position would be presented for the three-month periods ended March 31, 1977 and March 31, 1976. While the auditor does not report publicly on such unaudited figures he may be required to provide a "comfort letter" to regulatory authorities (see 19.2).

Consistency explanations

Where a particular retroactive accounting change, not previously introduced in an annual report, is made at the time of issue of a prospectus, and all previous years' figures are correspondingly restated, the auditor's report in the prospectus would contain a *consistency explanation* similar to that discussed in 17.5.1. However, where a retroactive accounting change or prior period adjustment has previously been reported, with restatement, in an annual report, it is not necessary to draw attention to the restatement in any future prospectus – even though some of the earlier restated years included in the prospectus may not have been covered in that annual report.

Pro-forma statements and combined statements

Where it will be of assistance to readers in understanding the nature and effect of the proposed transactions contemplated in the prospectus (e.g., issue of the offered securities and acquisition of another company with the proceeds or by a share exchange), a pro-forma balance sheet is normally presented, showing the financial position as if the proposed transactions had already taken place. Frequently, the pro-forma figures are merely presented in adjacent columns beside the historical statements. In such situations, the auditor's report is often presented in tabular form, as follows:

I have examined the balance sheet and pro-forma balance sheet of X Company Ltd. as at March 31, 1977 and the statements of income, retained earnings and changes in financial position for the five years and three months then ended. My examination . . . in the circumstances.
In my opinion:
a) The accompanying balance sheet presents fairly the financial position of the company as at March 31, 1977;
b) The accompanying pro-forma balance sheet presents fairly the financial position of the company as at March 31, 1977, after giving effect to the transactions (or changes) described in note 1;
c) The accompanying statements of income, retained earnings and changes in financial position present fairly the results of operations of the company and the changes in its financial position for the five years and three months ended March 31, 1977;
all in accordance with generally accepted accounting principles applied on a consistent basis.[2]

Some practitioners question whether a pro-forma statement can properly be said to present the *financial position* after giving effect to specified transactions — perhaps *pro-forma financial position* after giving effect to the specified transactions would be a more logical terminology; however, the former usage is common.

Occasionally, the foregoing tabular report is divided into two separate reports, one accompanying the balance sheets and the other one accompanying the remaining statements.

Where one business is acquiring another, or where two or more businesses are being merged, a combined statement of income and a combined statement of changes in financial position will normally be presented, unless the results could be misleading in the light of conditions that are likely to prevail following the acquisition or merger.[3] The auditor's report on such statements could be worded as follows.

> I have examined the combined statement of income and combined statement of changes in financial position of X Company Ltd. and Y Company Ltd. for the five years and three months ended March 31, 1977. My examination . . . in the circumstances.
>
> In my opinion, the accompanying combined statements present fairly the combined results of operations and the combined changes in financial position of the two companies for the five years and three months ended March 31, 1977 in accordance with generally accepted accounting principles applied on a consistent basis.

In some cases it may be desirable to make adjustments to reflect retroactively changes that will take place as a result of the merger. In such cases, the statements would be described as pro-forma combined statements.

In those situations in which "pooling of interest" accounting is appropriate, the combined statements would be described instead as pro-forma consolidated statements – that is, they would treat the companies involved as though they had been a consolidated group throughout the period reported upon.

Report reservations

Where report reservations are required owing to accounting deficiencies, auditing deficiencies, or uncertainties, the same considerations apply as for reservations in annual reports (see Chapter 18).

> If an unqualified opinion on the financial statements in the prospectus cannot be expressed, the recommendations set out in THE AUDITORS' REPORT – OTHER MATTERS Section 5500 should be followed. [CICA Handbook][4]

Prohibition of opinion on forecasts

For many years auditors have been precluded from expressing an opinion on forecasts for fear that a reader of the prospectus would infer from such an opinion a greater degree of reliability than any predictions of the future can possibly have.

> The auditors should not express an opinion on any forecast earnings figures which might be contained in a prospectus. [CICA Handbook][5]

In recent years, however, the question of financial forecasts has been receiving further consideration (see Chapter 21). As this book goes to press the question is under study by the CICA and by the Ontario Securities Commission. The reader should refer to any subsequent pronouncements.

Preliminary prospectuses

In some jurisdictions, a *preliminary prospectus* must be filed with the Securities Commission in advance of the final prospectus. After reading the preliminary prospectus, the Commission may issue a *deficiency letter* setting out adjustments or additional disclosures which they believe are required to be made either in the financial statements or in the body of the prospectus before the final prospectus can be approved by them for release. In particular, if there are proposed reservations in the auditor's draft report and if any statement adjustments are possible which would remove the need for such reservations, those adjustments will normally be required by the Commission.

The preliminary prospectus is a formal filing, signed by officers of the company and by the underwriter. However, it is not final for the purpose of use by prospective investors as it may still be incomplete or be subject to revision as a result of completion of the audit (if still incomplete) and/or as a result of Commission deficiency letters. For that reason, it is desirable that the auditor's report, if included in the preliminary prospectus, not be signed and that the auditor's name not appear in the signature position of his report. The CICA Auditing Recommendations[6] suggest that, provided that a sufficient amount of the audit work has been completed, it is desirable to include a draft unsigned audit report in the preliminary prospectus, particularly where audit reservations are proposed. They suggest further that issuance of the final signed audit report should be withheld until the date the final prospectus is signed by directors and underwriters.

Reporting on the translation of financial statements and related data

Because Canada has two official languages, prospectuses are frequently published both in English and French. The translation of the financial statements and auditor's report in an annual report was discussed in 17.5.6, together with type of special report an auditor might sometimes give to provide assurance as to any translation function he has fulfilled himself. Similar considerations apply to the translation of the financial statements and auditor's report contained in a prospectus.

The auditor may also be prepared to give an opinion on the translation of financial tables in the prospectus closely related to the financial statements, e.g., capitalization table, interest and asset coverage tables, dividend record. In such cases, in addition to the report discussed in 17.5.6, the auditor might add a paragraph such as the following:

> Further, in my opinion the items listed below which appear in the body of the French (English) language version of the said prospectus are translated from the English (French) language version in such a way as to be consistent in meaning with both the English and French language versions of the financial statements and notes thereto which I have translated ...

Normally auditors do *not*, however, perform the translation of other material in a prospectus (i.e., material other than the financial statements, closely related financial information, and the audit report). Translation of such other material might easily be beyond the auditor's sphere of professional competence. Nevertheless, underwriters, solicitors or clients themselves often want reassurance on the translation of all the material in the prospectus because they are legally responsible for the content of both language versions of the document. Not unnaturally they sometimes ask the auditor to furnish such reassurance, reasoning that, if he is willing to translate financial statements, he should be willing at least to report on the competence of translation of other material. It is suggested that the auditor should not, however, accede to such requests because:

1. He does not hold himself out as expert in translation in general.
2. There are no practical standards by which one could test an assertion such as "the translation is complete and accurate" or "the translation is not capable of differing interpretation from the [other language] version".

19.1.2 Additional auditing procedures

Apart from (a) the inclusion of five years' operating results, (b) where applicable, the inclusion of proforma statements, and (c) any other specific legislative or regulatory requirements, the financial statements included in a prospectus do not differ from regular annual financial statements. Accordingly, except for procedures occasioned by these differences, the required audit procedures will be the same as in an annual audit.

Where the audited historical statements to be included in a prospectus relate solely to fiscal year-ends or fiscal years and were previously audited by the auditor, he will, with some modifications, be re-

issuing past opinions. Additional required auditing procedures in such cases include the following:

1. a review of any changes made or required to be made to meet professional requirements[7] or the requirements of Securities Acts or Securities Commissions (for example, the disclosure of earnings available to service the securities being offered);
2. a review of any revisions of prior years' statements included in the five-year period reported upon which may be required to:
   a) effect retroactive changes in accounting principles for consistency with the most recent statements,
   b) allocate any "prior period adjustments" to the particular years to which they relate,
   c) correct any misstatements indicated by audit evidence examined subsequent to the dates of the original audit reports on those prior years and up to the date of the auditor's report in the prospectus (however, prior accounting estimates would not be adjusted unless they could properly be considered to be erroneous in the light of facts existing at the dates of the original reports – see 18.7);
3. where the date of the auditor's report in the prospectus is to be later than the date of his original report on the balance sheet, a review for the intervening period of subsequent events including management's proposals with respect to transactions related to the current offering of securities. (Where possible, most practitioners prefer to retain the date of their original report on the balance sheet and handle any subsequent events disclosed in the prospectus statements either by split-dating their report as described in 17.2.2 or by an unaudited note as described in 18.7).

Where the audited historical statements to be included in a prospectus include statements relating to an interim month-end or interim period then ended, the auditor will not normally have previously audited such statements. Therefore, in addition to the foregoing procedures, a regular audit of the latter statements must be performed. The final audit opinion must be based on a proper study of controls and sufficient appropriate audit evidence and thus implies completion of the normal interim audit and financial statement audit components. However, if a previous audit had been completed only a few months earlier, some of the earlier procedures might, in the presence of adequate controls, serve as suitable pre-balance sheet verification. For example, if the auditor had audited the December 31, 1976 balance sheet and, in so doing, had observed stocktaking and confirmed accounts receivable at

November 30, 1976, the latter work, when accompanied by adequate roll-forward procedures, might contribute to the evidence necessary to form an audit opinion on the March 31, 1977 statements. If the intervening period were too great, all major audit procedures would have to be repeated. In either case important period-end procedures (including, for example, verification of cut-off and key period-end confirmations), some review of controls in the current period, and scrutiny and analytical review for the current period would all be essential. Auditing figures for a period less than a year also raises materiality questions whose resolution is not entirely clear.[8]

Where audited pro-forma or combined statements are or should be included in a prospectus, additional required auditing procedures include the following:

1. examination of a signed underwriting agreement and evidence of firm commitments from responsible parties with respect to the proposed transactions reflected in the pro-forma statements,

2. a review of subsequent events to ascertain whether any such events should also be reflected in the pro-forma presentation,

3. where a combined income statement for a proposed acquisition is presented (not pro-forma), a review of management's representations and other available information as to intended transactions to ascertain whether a combined statement could be misleading in the light of conditions likely to prevail following the acquisition. (Factors such as future debt charges on debt incurred to finance the acquisition and high depreciation charges based on effective cost to the acquiring company, which are not reflected in the combined historical figures, can be disclosed by notes, but the auditor must seek reasonable evidence to determine (a) whether the note disclosure is adequate and (b) whether, even with such note disclosure, the combined statements could be misleading and pro-forma statements therefore required.)[9]

4. where a pro-forma combined income statement for a proposed acquisition is presented, a review of the propriety of the pro-forma adjustments made and verification of the calculations.

19.1.3 Procedures with respect to unaudited financial statements

When an auditor is associated with unaudited financial statements with the exception of those in prospectuses and with certain other exceptions, he must issue a disclaimer of opinion (see Chapter 20) so that the reader will not misinterpret his association. A

document containing solely unaudited statements but with a public accountant's name attached might otherwise lead a reader to infer mistakenly that the reason for the accountant's association was the conducting of an audit. In the case of a prospectus containing both audited and unaudited financial statements, however, this reason for a possible misinterpretation is not present. The reader can see that the public accountant's involvement with the prospectus was to express an opinion on the audited financial statements. Provided that any unaudited statements are clearly distinguished, he has no reason to infer that the auditor's report covered more than the scope paragraph described.

> Where unaudited financial statements are included in a prospectus they should be clearly described as such. [CICA Handbook][10]

Accordingly, no specific disclaimer of opinion is required.

The CICA Recommendations with respect to procedures required for most unaudited financial statements (see Chapter 20) do not specifically apply to unaudited statements contained in prospectuses but other CICA Recommendations prescribe procedures, indeed more onerous ones, for such cases:

> The auditors, before allowing their name to be associated with a prospectus containing unaudited statements should at least:
> a) be generally satisfied with the reliability of the accounting records;
> b) review the unaudited financial statements and compare them with those for the corresponding period for the previous year and with the latest audited financial statements;
> c) obtain explanations for substantial variances and unusual items;
> d) review minutes and make enquiries as to major commitments and contingent liabilities;
> e) make enquiries as to any events subsequent to the completion of the last audit examination which could have a material effect on the financial position or net income; and
> f) make enquiries as to whether the accounting principles and practices followed in the preparation of unaudited statements are consistent in all material respects with those followed in the preparation of the audited financial statements contained in the prospectus.
> The steps included in [the preceding] paragraph, with appropriate modifications, should also apply in connection with the comparative figures for the equivalent broken period of the immediately preceding year which may be included in the statement of earnings.[11]

19.1.4 Procedures with respect to other information in the prospectus

The normal practice of reviewing other information in documents containing financial statements was discussed in 17.5.5. In the case of prospectuses, the CICA Recommendations impose a specific professional responsibility to conduct such a review:

> Although the financial information included in a prospectus is the representation of the issuer, the auditors should ascertain that such statements and information conform with the requirements of the applicable Corporations and Securities Acts and that the standards of disclosure in the financial statements conform with Recommendations contained in Section 4000 and other Sections of this Handbook.
>
> The auditors should review the entire prospectus in its final form to satisfy themselves that the contents, insofar as they relate to matters on which they might reasonably be expected to have knowledge as a result of their examination, are presented fairly. Unless given an opportunity to review the prospectus, they should not consent to the use of their opinion therein.[12]

It is not desirable, however, for the auditor to provide any form of report on the results of such a review – except, if requested, a report restricted to schedules or tables consisting of historical financial data. As discussed in 17.5.5 for annual reports, the auditor may, if he has done the necessary work, express an opinion on such schedules or tables. In the case of supplementary schedules or tables in prospectuses, the auditor's report, if required at all, is more commonly in the form of negative assurance provided to limited readership (for example, underwriters or the board of directors). Opinions or negative assurance with respect to qualitative commentary contained in the text of the prospectus is undesirable, however, because there are no objective criteria by which its fairness of presentation can be independently assessed and such assessment might in any case involve matters to which the auditor's professional competence has little relevance.[13]

19.1.5 Reliance on other auditors

Just as in the case of annual financial statements, an auditor may often be asked to report on financial statements included in a prospectus which involve reliance on the reports of other auditors with respect to consolidated or equity-accounted investees. In general, the considerations with respect to expression of reliance on such other auditors in the scope paragraph will be the same as those discussed in 17.5.7. The choice of and performance of basic procedures, review procedures or override procedures for justifying that reliance will be generally the same as discussed in 15.4.8 and 38.3.10. Some of the additional auditing procedures described in 19.1.2 may have to be performed by the investee auditors, for example, the review of investee records with respect to subsequent events up to the date of the investor

auditor's report in the prospectus. The investor auditor should satisfy himself that such procedures were performed. Likewise, where a review of unaudited financial statements is required as described in 19.1.3, the investor auditor must satisfy himself that such review was performed as well for the investee statements:

> Where auditors have relied on other accountants in respect to audited financial statements, they should request the other accountants to carry out the review of the unaudited statements contemplated in paragraphs 7000.22 and 7000.23 [see 19.1.3] and report to them, unless they have carried out this review themselves. [CICA Handbook][14]

19.1.6 Audit reports covering only part of the period

Sometimes the statements of income, retained earnings and changes in financial position cover a number of years before the present auditor was engaged. With respect to the effect of those prior years on the figures of subsequent years audited by the present auditor, reliance may be placed on the work of a predecessor auditor – though no expression of reliance is customary (see 17.5.3 and Chapter 23). However, with respect to the prior years' statements themselves, included in the prospectus, reliance on a predecessor auditor would *not* be appropriate. The reason is that reliance on another auditor may be appropriate only when he has performed *part* of the work with respect to a given year's financial statements, not when he has performed *all* of it.[15] One alternative, therefore, is for the present auditor to report on the years audited by him and the predecessor auditor to report on the earlier years.

Audit reports by both present and predecessor auditors

In such a case the report of the present auditor would cover the balance sheet and that portion of the other statements audited by him:

> I have examined the balance sheet of X Company Ltd. as at March 31, 1977 and the statements of income, retained earnings and changes in financial position for the three years and three months then ended. My examination . . . in the circumstances.
>
> In my opinion . . . on a consistent basis.
>
> City   B. Black
> May 10, 1977   Chartered Accountant

The report of the predecessor auditor would cover the earlier portion of the other statements:

> I have examined the statements of income, retained earnings and changes in financial position of X Com-

pany Ltd. for the two years ended December 31, 1973. My examination . . . in the circumstances.

In my opinion . . . on a consistent basis.

City   A. White
April 4, 1974   Chartered Accountant

Occasionally, the present auditor issues a separate report on the balance sheet and the two auditors issue a combined report on the remaining statements with their period of responsibility being indicated beside their signatures. This practice, however, is less common.

In either case, the predecessor auditor, before consenting to the use of his report, will normally need to have some assurance as to the possible effect on his report of events subsequent to the date on which he last had knowledge of the client's affairs. Such assurance could be obtained by means of a letter from the present auditor, as follows:

> Mr. A. White
> Address
> Dear Sir:
> In reply to your request, I advise that my examination of the financial statements of X Company Limited for the three years and three months ended March 31, 1977 did not disclose any events, transactions or adjustments subsequent to December 31, 1973 which, in my opinion, would have a material effect upon the statements of income, retained earnings and changes in financial position for the two years ended December 31, 1973 or would require mention in notes thereto (except as stated in notes to the financial statements included in the draft prospectus dated May 10, 1977 furnished to you).
>   B. Black
>   Chartered Accountant

In the absence of such a letter, the predecessor auditor in the foregoing example would normally wish to conduct a subsequent events review before permitting the use of his reports on 1972 and 1973 to be included in a prospectus dated May 10, 1977. Should his audit report itself be updated to May 10, 1977, which is uncommon, the subsequent events review (in the absence of the foregoing letter) would be essential.

Audit report by the present auditor alone

Another alternative is for the present auditor to perform a sufficient audit review of the earlier years so that he can express his own audit opinion on the income and changes in financial position of those years. Ordinarily such review requires considerably less work than would an opinion given at the time, because subsequent periods would have provided confirmatory evidence of trends in earlier periods, and also would probably have uncovered some types of error, had they occurred, in the earlier years. In addition, the present auditor's initial audit examina-

tion (see Chapter 23) should already have included some work, e.g., review of propriety of fixed asset balances carried forward, that would tend to confirm the accounting in earlier years. The present auditor should consult with the previous auditor and review his working papers to obtain additional evidence to supplement his own direct examination of the past accounting records.

Whether it is possible to obtain sufficient evidence to permit the present auditor to express his own opinion on prior periods will depend on the circumstances. Obtaining adequate assurance as to past inventories and as to the cut-off between past accounting periods may be difficult. However, the lesser significance of the very earliest periods to the prospectus reader should logically mean that less stringent levels of assurance and limits of materiality would be appropriate. Where the present auditor concludes that sufficient evidence is not obtainable by him, dual reporting, as described earlier, should be used instead.

19.1.7 Reports on registration statements filed with the SEC

A Canadian practitioner may sometimes be requested to permit his report to be included in a registration statement for filing with the SEC when his client is offering securities to United States residents. While his general responsibilities will remain the same as previously described, a number of specific responsibilities are described in some detail in U.S. securities legislation and regulations. For example, Section 11(a) of the Securities Act of 1933, as amended, imposes "responsibility for false or misleading statements, or for omissions which render misleading the statements made, in an effective registration statement" on every accountant who has with his consent been named as having certified any part of the registration statement.[16] Section 11(b) provides that no person shall be liable if he sustains "the burden of proof" that as regards any part of the registration statement purporting to be a copy of a report from himself as an expert "he had, after reasonable investigation, reasonable ground to believe and did believe, *at the time such part of the registration statement became effective* [italics added], that the statements therein were true and that there was no omission."[17] Because of the reference to the effective date of the registration statement it is necessary for the auditor to "extend his procedures with respect to subsequent events from the date of his report up to the effective date or as close thereto as is reasonable and practicable in the circumstances."[18] This extension is an exception to the normal concept that the auditor has no responsibility for performing audit work subsequent to the date of his report. However, the AICPA pronouncements suggest that, as a practical matter, for the period subsequent to the date of his report the auditor may rely, for the most part, on enquiries of company officials and employees.

In addition, the various considerations regarding international reporting discussed in 18.6 would apply.

19.2 Comfort letters and letters of consent

A "comfort letter" is a letter in which the auditor tells the recipient that the auditor is not aware of any significant errors in statements of his client's financial position or results of operations or of deterioration in his financial position, although the auditor is not, at the time of writing, in a position to make an audit report on the said statements. There are at least two situations in which comfort letters are commonly provided:

1. At the time of filing the preliminary prospectus, certain provincial Securities Commissions require a comfort letter with respect to the statements upon which the auditor will eventually be reporting.
2. In relation to unaudited statements included in prospectuses or elsewhere, Securities Commissions, underwriters, or other interested parties may request a comfort letter from the auditor that would disclose any knowledge he had of events subsequent to the latest audited statements that might make the unaudited statements misleading.

A "letter of consent" is a letter, usually required by Securities Commissions, in which the auditor consents to the use of his report in the prospectus or other document in which it is included. The letter establishes that the auditor knows his report is being used in a public document. In some cases (see 19.2.3) a comfort letter type of assurance may be combined with a letter of consent.

19.2.1 Comfort letters for preliminary prospectuses

A comfort letter does not provide an audit opinion but it does give "negative assurance". The auditor should be satisfied that he has done enough work to warrant such assurance.

> The auditors should sign a comfort letter only when their examination is complete or is sufficiently advanced for them to be able to give the required assurance. [CICA Handbook][19]

If the auditor's examination has not progressed to the point where the auditor can properly provide negative assurance, he would normally inform the Securities Commission accordingly; the Regulations under the Ontario and Alberta Securities Acts, for example, provide that the auditor may make such statement as the circumstances require and as is acceptable to the Commissions.

Comfort letter where the field work is not complete

Where the auditor's field work is not complete, but sufficiently advanced to warrant negative assurance, the following form of comfort letter is common:

> The Securities Commission
> City and Province
>
> Dear Sirs: Re: X Company Ltd.
>
> I refer to the preliminary prospectus of the above company dated May 10, 1977 relating to an issue of [description of security].
>
> The following financial statements are included in the preliminary prospectus:
> > Balance sheet as at March 31, 1977;
> > Pro-forma balance sheet as at March 31, 1977;
> > Statement of income for the five years ended December 31, 1976 and the three months ended March 31, 1977;
> > Statement of retained earnings for the five years ended December 31, 1976 and the three months ended March 31, 1977;
> > Statement of changes in financial position for the five years ended December 31, 1976 and the three months ended March 31, 1977.
>
> I am engaged in an examination of the above statements. Because my examination has not yet been completed, I am unable at this stage to express an opinion on these financial statements.
>
> However, based upon the information I now have and the audit procedures I have carried out, I have no reason to believe that the financial statements do not present fairly the financial position of the company as at March 31, 1977 and the results of its operations and changes in its financial position for the five years and three months ended March 31, 1977.
>
> The pro-forma balance sheet of the company is not complete as the information necessary for its completion is not yet available. Accordingly, I am unable to comment thereon. [This paragraph is unnecessary, of course, where pro-forma statements are not to be prepared.]
>
> This letter is solely for the information of the Securities Commission(s) to whom it is addressed and is not to be referred to in whole or in part in the prospectus or any other similar document.[20]

The foregoing customary wording does not make reference to generally accepted accounting principles or to consistency – in part because such phrases might make the negative assurance too similar to standard audit report wording, which would be misleading.[21] Nonetheless, the auditor should not provide such assurance if he believes that there have been departures from generally accepted accounting principles or undisclosed inconsistencies in their application during the period.

Comfort letter where the field work is complete

In some cases the auditor's examination of the financial statements may have been completed at the time of filing the preliminary prospectus and he could quite properly sign the auditor's report included therein. There is always the possibility, however, that one or more of the Commissions may suggest changes in the financial statements. Accordingly, the normal practice is to withhold signature of the auditor's report until Commission comments have been received and, in the meantime, issue the following type of comfort letter:

The Securities Commission
City and Province

Dear Sirs: Re: X Company Ltd.

I refer to the preliminary prospectus of the above company dated May 10, 1977 relating to an issue of [description of security].

The following financial statements are ... March 31, 1977.

I have completed my examination of the above statements. However, I am withholding my signature from the auditor's report thereon pending receipt of the comments which may be issued by the Commission's staff on the financial statements.

Based upon my examination and the information I now have, I have no reason to believe that the financial statements do not present fairly the financial position of the company as at March 31, 1977, the pro-forma financial position at that date and the results of its operations and changes in its financial position for the five years and three months ended March 31, 1977.

This letter is solely ... document.[22]

If the pro-forma balance sheet figures are not complete the changes and additional paragraph previously suggested would be appropriate. In addition, the second sentence of the third paragraph might be expanded to include the phrase "pending receipt of (i) the information necessary to complete the pro-forma balance sheet; (ii) the comments which ... "

19.2.2 Comfort letters for unaudited statements and other financial information

The type of comfort letter filed with a preliminary prospectus in the normal case will be superseded shortly by an audit report. It is considerably less important than a comfort letter on unaudited figures, errors in which may not come to light for some considerable time if ever. The auditor, therefore, should consider his responsiblility very carefully in the latter situation.

Obviously his responsibility in connection with such a comfort letter is much less than in connection with an audit report, because he is not asked to perform the procedures that substantiate his normal opinion. On the other hand, he must take some responsibility to justify the comfort letter no matter how it is worded. Probably the primary justification for the practice of requiring comfort letters is that the auditor usually is fairly knowledgeable about his client, and with this background of knowledge and the relationships he has built up with the client's management and employees, and by making certain inquiries, there is a chance he might spot trouble even without doing an audit. Thus the person who asks for a comfort letter receives no real assurance as to the current state of affairs, but has at least improved his chances of knowing if something is wrong.

In the circumstances, the auditor runs considerable risk that greater reliance may be placed on his comfort letter than is justified. To lessen this risk:

1. The auditor should ensure that he has completed all the necessary procedures called for when he is associated with a prospectus containing unaudited statements (see 19.1.3). In addition, it is prudent for him to obtain written representations from senior client officials of whom he has made enquiries and to scrutinize available accounting records relating to the unaudited periods to the extent practical.

2. Since the foregoing procedures fall far short of an audit, the letter should make it clear that the assurance given in the comfort letter is not based on an audit.

3. Any assurance given should, where possible, be expressed in the form of *negative assurance* to emphasize its tentative, imperfect nature.

    For example, phrases such as "insofar as I know from my limited review, in my opinion the financial statements present fairly ... " express positive assurance and should not be used. Phrases such as "I made a review and found nothing wrong", while technically in a negative form, may imply that anything wrong would have been found if it existed and likewise should not be used. The preferable construction is of the form "nothing came to my attention as a result of my limited procedures which would give me reason to believe[23] that the financial statements do not present fairly ... ".

4. Comfort letters should be furnished only to people who can reasonably be expected to understand the nature of an audit examination and the much lesser degree of reliability afforded by a

543

comfort letter. It follows, also, that a comfort letter should be furnished only on the understanding that it not be given public circulation:

A comfort letter in respect of unaudited statements should only be issued on the understanding that it is for the sole use of the regulatory authority to whom it is addressed. [CICA Handbook][24]

Where unaudited interim figures are included in a prospectus, the Ontario Securities Act and a number of other provincial Acts require that the auditor file with the Commission such advice relating to those figures as may be required by the Commission. The letter outlined below is the form of comfort letter suggested in the CICA Handbook.[25]

The Securities Commission
City and Province

Dear Sirs: Re: X Company Ltd.

I am the above company's auditor and under date of May 23, 1977 I reported on the following financial statements included in the prospectus relating to the issue and sale of [description of security]:

Balance sheet as at December 31, 1976;

Pro-forma balance sheet as at December 31, 1976;

Statement of income for the five years ended December 31, 1976;

Statement of retained earnings for the five years ended December 31, 1976;

Statement of changes in financial position for the five years ended December 31, 1976.

Also included in the prospectus are the following unaudited interim financial statements:

Balance sheet as at March 31, 1977

Pro-forma balance sheet as at March 31, 1977

Statement of income for the three months ended March 31, 1977 with comparative figures for the three months ended March 31, 1976

Statement of retained earnings for the three months ended March 31, 1977 with comparative figures for the three months ended March 31, 1976.

Statement of changes in financial position for the three·months ended March 31, 1977 with comparative figures for the three months ended March 31, 1976.

I have not made an audit of any financial statements of the company as at any date subsequent to December 31, 1976 or for any period subsequent thereto. The purpose, and therefore the scope, of my audit for the year ended December 31, 1976 was to enable me to express my opinion as to the financial statements as at December 31, 1976 and for the year then ended but not as to the financial statements for any interim period within such year. Therefore, I am unable to and do not express any opinion on the financial position as at any date subsequent to December 31, 1976 or the results of operations or changes in financial position for any period subsequent to that date or on any of the unaudited interim financial statements contained in the prospectus.

I have, however, made a limited review, but not an audit, of the interim financial statements of the company referred to above, have read the minutes of meetings of shareholders, directors and the executive committee to May 23, 1977 and have had consultations with and have made enquiries of officials of the company having primary responsibility for financial and accounting matters of the company as to transactions and events subsequent to December 31, 1976, and on the basis of such procedures nothing has come to my attention which would give me reason to believe:

a) that such unaudited interim financial statements were not prepared in accordance with accounting principles and practices consistent in all material respects with those followed in the preparation of the audited financial statements contained in the prospectus (except as noted in the prospectus);

b) that such unaudited interim financial statements do not present fairly the information purported to be shown thereby;

c) that any material adjustment of such unaudited financial statements is required or that any adjustments have been reflected therein other than those necessary for a fair presentation of the financial position as at March 31, 1977 and of the results of operations and changes in financial position for the three-month periods ended March 31, 1977 and March 31, 1976.

It should be understood that the procedures and enquiries referred to in the preceding paragraph do not constitute an audit and therefore they would not necessarily reveal material changes in the financial position of the company and in the results of its operations or inconsistencies in the application of generally accepted accounting principles.

This letter is solely for the information of the Securities Commission(s) to whom it is addressed and is not to be referred to in whole or in part in the prospectus or any other similar document.

While the foregoing wording is customary, and is in part required to meet the provisions of securities legislation and regulations, it may be less than ideal. For one thing any non-accountant reader cannot but be struck by the number of disclaimers of opinion (at least four). It may be that multiple disclaimers are considered to provide added legal protection to the auditor, but business readers exposed to such letters (as can occur when comfort letters are requested by underwriters or by the company's board of directors) may often feel that"the lady doth protest too much". Further, the wording of subparagraphs (a), (b) and (c) provide greater elaboration than even an audit opinion provides – elaboration which seems redundant. Presumably, if the unaudited statements omitted necessary adjustments or contained unnecessary ones, they would no longer present fairly the information they purported to show nor be consistent with the audited statements. Finally, the omission of a reference to generally accepted accounting principles (except indirectly in the penultimate paragraph) may, as in the previous examples of comfort letters, leave the phrase "presents fairly" rather isolated – contrary to the emphasis on a one-part opinion introduced in the 1976 revisions of the CICA Handbook (Section 5400).

The signed comfort letter covering unaudited financial statements should be issued on the same date as the final prospectus.

Finance companies which are required to file annual financial statements with the Ontario Securities Commission are obliged to submit returns of additional financial information. Comfort letters commonly used in connection with such returns make reference to specific legislative and regulatory provisions, report that the auditor has read the annual reports prepared in accordance with those provisions, and contain a paragraph such as the following:

> Certain of the information contained in the reports, to the extent that it did not come within the scope of my regular annual examination of the financial statements, is not within my knowledge. However, insofar as I know, from such examination, in my opinion, the information contained in the foregoing reports is presented fairly.

Such wording is in positive form rather than negative. While such a form is in general undesirable, it is presently called for by securities regulations and the provincial Securities Commissions insist on it. Although a practitioner should not sign prescribed forms having unacceptable wording (see 17.5.4), the foregoing wording is not sufficiently objectionable to warrant an outright refusal in these circumstances. The profession has been attempting to obtain appropriate regulatory amendments.

19.2.3 Comfort letters for registration statements filed with the SEC

In the United States, it has become customary for underwriting agreements to specify that the independent public accountants, prior to the closing date of the agreement, shall submit a "cold comfort letter" to the underwriters in a form satisfactory to them. Such letters are designed to provide negative assurance to underwriters which they may wish in support of their own statutory requirement to make a "reasonable investigation" of financial data not "expertized" (covered by an auditor's report) in connection with registration statements filed with the SEC under the Securities Act of 1933. The accountant's comfort letter is not, however, required by the SEC itself.

Comfort letters to U.S. underwriters generally include one or more of the following: (a) a statement as to the independence of the accountants, (b) an opinion as to whether the audited statements comply with legislative and regulatory requirements, (c) negative assurance as to whether the unaudited statements comply with such requirements and are fairly presented in conformity with generally accepted accounting principles on a basis substantially consistent with the audited statements, (d) negative assurances as to changes in selected financial statement items during a period subsequent to the date of the latest financial statements in the registration statement. Detailed guidance can be found in AICPA pronouncements.[26] In recent years similar comfort letters have occasionally been requested by Canadian underwriters.

19.2.4 Letters of consent

A letter of consent is usually required by statute when an opinion of an expert (such as an auditor) is quoted or reproduced in a document such as a prospectus, statement of material facts or takeover bid circular.

The consent letter may be quite short. It should do at least four things:

1. Identify by description the document, e.g., prospectus, in which the auditor's report is to appear.
2. Identify the auditor's report (addressee and date).
3. Identify explicitly the statements or other information upon which the auditor is reporting.
4. Express the auditor's consent to the use of his report.

In addition, the letter of consent should refer to any reservations in the auditor's report.

> Where there are qualifications in the auditors' report, the letter of consent should make reference to such qualifications. [CICA Handbook][27]

Finally, the letter may contain other information required by the governing statute.

Letters of consent accompanying final prospectuses or statements of material facts

A number of the provincial Securities Commissions require that a letter of consent signed by the auditors be filed with the Commission at the time of filing a *final* prospectus or statement of material facts. A letter of consent should *not* be filed with a preliminary prospectus. A typical wording designed to meet the requirements of the Securities Acts of Ontario and certain other provinces follows.

> The Securities Commission
> [usually all provincial Commissions involved should be addressed in the same letter]
>
> Dear Sirs: Re: X Company Ltd.
>
> I refer to the prospectus of the above company dated May 23, 1977, relating to an issue of [description of securities].
>
> I hereby consent to the use in the above mentioned prospectus of my report dated May 23, 1977 to the directors of X Company Ltd. on the following financial statements:
>
> Balance sheet as at March 31, 1977;
> Pro-forma balance sheet as at March 31, 1977;

Statement of income for the five years ended December 31, 1976 and the three months ended March 31, 1977;

Statement of retained earnings for the five years ended December 31, 1976 and the three months ended March 31, 1977;

Statement of changes in financial position for the five years ended December 31, 1976 and the three months ended March 31, 1977.

I report that I have read the prospectus and that the information contained therein which is derived from the audited financial statements contained in the prospectus or which is within my knowledge is, in my opinion, presented fairly and is not misleading.

This letter is solely for the information of the Securities Commission(s) to whom it is addressed and is not to be referred to in whole or in part in the prospectus or in any other similar document.

It should be noted that the penultimate paragraph provides comfort with respect to other information, apart from the financial statements, contained in the prospectus. The wording of this paragraph is not ideal since it expresses positive rather than negative assurance and uses the phrase "presented fairly" without any reference to established criteria as to how such information should be presented. Nevertheless, the wording is prescribed by statute and the provincial Securities Commissions insist on it. Again, the foregoing wording is not sufficiently objectionable to warrant an outright refusal to sign it in these circumstances. The profession has been attempting to obtain appropriate statutory amendments. The assurances given in this paragraph make explicit the auditor's obligation to read the entire prospectus. However, whether or not such explicit assurances are given, the CICA Auditing Recommendations call for the review procedures prescribed in 19.1.4 to be performed:

Where a letter of consent to the use of their report is required from the auditors reporting on financial statements included in the prospectus, the auditors, in addition to the normal audit work, should carry out the steps outlined in paragraphs 7000.03 and 7000.04 [quoted in 19.1.4] before issuing such a letter.[28]

Other letters of consent

A brief form of letter of consent used where there are no special statutory requirements is illustrated below. This type of letter is commonly used in connection with a takeover bid circular.

To XYZ Co. Ltd.

I consent to the use in the Circular forming part of your Offer dated March 19, 1977 to purchase common shares of ABC Co. Ltd., of my Auditor's Reports dated February 27, 1977 respecting the financial statements of XYZ Co. Ltd. which appear on pages 21 and 24 respectively of the schedule to that Circular.

Generally, the more precise identification of the financial statements by name, as illustrated in earlier examples, is preferable but the reference to page numbers is acceptable if there are no other statements or financial information on those pages which could cause confusion as to the figures on which the auditor is reporting.

Letters of consent to the SEC

The SEC requires that a letter of consent signed by independent public accountants be filed when their reports are used in a registration statement or offering circular under the Securities Act of 1933.

19.3 Special purpose reports

For purposes of this chapter, special purpose reports are taken to mean any reports issued by an auditor other than (a) short-form reports on annual financial statements for shareholders (or partners or proprietors) of profit-oriented enterprises or (b) reports in prospectuses. Accountants' comments issued by public accountants associated with unaudited financial statements are not included because they are not issued "by an auditor" (see Chapter 20) – however, the dividing line between non-audit engagements and certain types of special purpose engagement is somewhat arbitrary. On practical grounds, reports on not-for-profit organizations (introduced in 17.5.4) are treated as special purpose reports in this chapter because it seemed convenient to consider here the problems of reporting on cash-basis and modified accrual-basis statements which are sometimes, though not always, appropriate for such organizations. Though similar considerations might be argued by some to apply also to reports to the shareholders of banks and insurance companies, such reports are not classed as special purpose reports in this chapter (they were discussed in 17.5.4).

Special purpose reports may be divided into three broad categories according to whether the audit objective is:

1. to provide credibility to assertions made by others,
2. to provide limited credibility to assertions made by others,
3. to provide information or an evaluation based on an investigation or on other findings in an audit.

The first category consists of *attest engagements* in which, as in a regular annual audit, the auditor attests

Special Purpose Reports

(Reports other than short-form reports on annual financial statements for shareholders or reports in prospectuses)

Audit objective	Type of engagement or report	Examples	Where covered
To provide credibility to assertions made by others	1. A full audit of complete financial statements for special purposes	Non-GAAP statements ● cash basis, modified accrual basis ● prescribed forms ● parent company unconsolidated statements ● buy/sell agreements, trust deeds ● secondary statements for foreign countries	(19.3.1)
	2. A full audit of specific elements of financial statements for special purposes	GAAP statements (various) Balance sheet only Sales as a basis for rental computation Grant applications Election expenses	(19.3.2)
To provide limited credibility to assertions made by others	3. Limited audit procedures for special purposes	The question of negative assurance The question of forecasts	(19.3.3)
To provide information or an evaluation based on an investigation or on other findings in an audit	4. Long-form reports 5. Reports on compliance 6. Reports on internal control	To management With contractual terms, laws, regulations To management To the public	(19.3.4) (19.3.5) (19.3.6) (19.3.7)
	7. Investigations	Purchase investigations Valuations Fraud investigations Insurance loss investigations Credit approval investigations	(19.3.8)

Figure 19.a

to the fairness of presentation of financial statements or other assertions made by another party (generally, his client). His report, however, may differ from that of a regular annual audit because (a) the financial statements are drawn up on a basis other than generally accepted accounting principles or (b) only specific elements of financial statements are presented.

The second category, if it does or should exist, is a matter of some contention. Some practitioners believe there is a need in certain circumstances for what might be called a "partial attest engagement" – less than an audit but more than a review of unaudited statements.

The third category does not involve an attestation of the representations of others but rather the provision of information or the auditor's evaluation of certain findings. The information or findings may have been obtained in conjunction with a regular attest audit (as is the case in long-form reports, most reports on compliance with contractual or legal provisions, and reports on internal control) or as a result of specific investigations.

These categories and the various types of engagement in each are summarized in Figure 19.a. Frequently there is some overlapping. For example, regular annual reports in some jurisdictions may include references to compliance with certain statutory requirements. Long-form reports generally include a short-form audit opinion on the financial statements. The report on a purchase investigation may include an audit opinion on the financial statements of the prospective investee as well as an evaluation of other matters. To simplify the discussion, however, each type is discussed separately in the following sections.

The whole area of special reporting is in need of clarification. In particular, the establishment of broad underlying principles consistently applied to all special reports is desirable – rather than detailed rules for each type of report, which are complex to apply and which inevitably lead to inconsistencies difficult to defend. The reader is cautioned to refer to subsequent pronouncements on the subject of special reports. As this book goes to press a possible Handbook section on Special Purpose Reports is under study by the CICA,[29] a separate CICA Research Study on Negative Assurance is in progress, and an AICPA exposure draft on Special Reports is under further review.

Prescribed forms

With respect to any of the three categories of special reports the practitioner will sometimes encounter legislative or regulatory prescription of audit report wording. Just as for general purpose reports (see

17.5.4), the auditor must consider such prescribed wording carefully and, where necessary, insist on making appropriate changes. The auditor should not make prescribed assertions which he feels are unjustified or which are outside his function, competence or responsibility.

19.3.1 Full audits of complete financial statements for special purposes

Except in cases where no CICA Auditing Recommendations necessarily apply (banks, insurance companies, and not-for-profit organizations), generally accepted auditing standards apply to all audit reports on financial statements.[30] Therefore, the work must be properly planned and supervised, an appropriate study of internal controls must be made, and sufficient appropriate audit evidence must be obtained to support the content of the report. In addition, the auditor's report should refer to the scope of his examination, express (or, where necessary, deny) an opinion on the financial statements, and express an opinion as to consistency. In these respects a special purpose report is no different from the normal short-form report. The third reporting standard, however, provides that in special circumstances the audit report need not be expressed in relation to generally accepted accounting principles but can be expressed in relation to "an appropriate disclosed basis of accounting". The CICA Handbook suggests that such a different basis of accounting may be appropriate, for example, "in financial statements prepared in accordance with regulatory legislation or with contractual requirements such as may be set out in trust indentures or buy/sell agreements".[31] Thus, in these circumstances it is unnecessary for the auditor to express a qualified or adverse opinion solely because the statements do not conform with generally accepted accounting principles; they were never intended to so conform. Rather his opinion will be as to whether the statements conform to the disclosed basis of accounting which they purport to use.

If the special circumstances referred to can be considered to include reports on not-for-profit organizations, there would be no great difficulty in meeting, for such reports, generally accepted auditing standards and other applicable CICA Auditing Recommendations. Therefore, while practitioners are not obliged to, it is assumed here that many will choose to, apply the reporting standards to their reports on not-for-profit organizations.

Special purpose audit reports on complete financial statements should use the normal scope paragraph discussed in Chapter 17, including the reference to generally accepted auditing standards. The addressee of the report will not, however, be the shareholders but the party engaging the auditor – for example, the directors of the reporting company, the management or directors of a prospective purchaser, a creditor, a trustee for debt holders, or members of a not-for-profit organization. Where an appropriate disclosed basis of accounting is used which differs from generally accepted accounting principles, the auditor should form and express his opinion in relation to that basis of accounting. While the Recommendations in CICA Handbook Section 5500 (The Auditors' Report – Other Matters) do not necessarily apply to reports "rendered for special purposes", common sense suggests that all such Recommendations, which pre-dated the third reporting standard, should continue to be applied but with the substitution of the appropriate disclosed basis of accounting for generally accepted accounting principles. [32] Thus, unqualified opinions, reservations of opinion, consistency exceptions and consistency explanations would all be formed and expressed in the manner discussed in Chapters 17 and 18, but relative to the disclosed basis of accounting.

Special purpose statements not in accordance with generally accepted accounting principles

For example, the provisions of a financing agreement might call for major note holders to receive audited financial statements of the borrowing company prepared on an unconsolidated basis and deviating from generally accepted accounting principles in other specified respects in order to exhibit more clearly and perhaps more conservatively the security for their notes. The auditor's opinion paragraph in such a case might read:

> In my opinion, these financial statements present fairly . . . in accordance with the provisions of Article 4 of the Financing Agreement dated May 23, 1969 applied on a basis consistent with that of the preceding year.

Five additional matters to be considered are:

1. the appropriateness of the disclosed basis of accounting and the adequacy of information disclosure,
2. whether or not disclosure that the statements are not in accordance with generally accepted accounting principles is desirable,
3. whether or not reference should be made to the existence of other versions of the financial statements,
4. how consistency should be interpreted in the context of special purpose reports,
5. whether or not reference should be made to the special purposes for which the report is intended.

Appropriateness of the disclosed basis of accounting and adequacy of information disclosure

In theory, the disclosed basis of accounting in a special purpose statement could be whatever the preparer and reader of the financial information have agreed (in a contract, trust deed, etc.) is meaningful to both of them. How the word "appropriate" should be interpreted in "appropriate disclosed basis of accounting" remains to be considered in future CICA pronouncements. If knowledgeable preparers and readers agree by contract that a certain basis is appropriate to their needs, the auditor would not normally consider that he should second guess their decision. [33] But the readers are not always parties to the decision. If the statements of a not-for-profit organization followed faithfully a basis of accounting fully disclosed in the notes, but the auditor believed that the basis was inappropriate and would mislead the readers, he would wish to express a reservation in his report to the effect that the disclosed basis of accounting was, in his opinion, inappropriate in the circumstances.

The basis of accounting used should, of course, be adequately disclosed – usually in the notes to the financial statements. If the basis was defined in an agreement or other document to which the reader of the statements has access, the notes may merely make reference to that agreement or document and a similar reference may be made in the auditor's opinion paragraph – as in the foregoing example. If the notes themselves spell out the basis of accounting, the auditor's opinion paragraph could instead contain the phrase " . . . in accordance with the basis of accounting described in Note X applied on a basis consistent with . . . ".

The AICPA 1976 exposure draft on Special Reports suggested that the disclosed basis should be a comprehensive and reasonably definite set of criteria applied to all material items in the statements (for example, a cash basis, an income tax basis, a basis prescribed by regulatory authority, a customary basis for not-for-profit organizations). The basis used should still be adequately described in the notes to the statements. It may be that a "comprehensive" basis is not intended by the AICPA to include a basis defined simply to be generally accepted accounting principles except for specified differences. An agreement to purchase a business, however, might often define the basis of accounting (for audited statements to be used for determining the purchase price) in terms such as (a) inventory at a certain agreed figure (b) warranty liability based on a certain agreed formula (c) generally accepted accounting principles in all other respects. In Canada, such a basis, if adequately disclosed, would be acceptable as a framework in relation to which the auditor's opinion could be expressed.

Where a disclosed basis of accounting is defined in terms of generally accepted accounting principles with specified exceptions, the exceptions usually relate to methods of accounting measurement or valuation rather than details of information disclosure. Thus, the auditor can usually judge the adequacy of information disclosure in relation to generally accepted accounting principles. Where, however, the disclosed basis of accounting is spelled out independently (either in the notes or in an agreement, law, regulation or document to which the notes are referenced), it is unlikely that the description of the basis of accounting will specify in detail what types of information disclosure are to be made. It would be unreasonable to omit important information merely on the grounds that generally accepted accounting principles did not apply and the disclosed basis of accounting did not specifically identify the disclosure as required. The CICA Handbook suggests that:

> The auditor would express a reservation of opinion on financial statements which did not disclose information appropriate and adequate in the circumstances.[34]

It would seem reasonable to judge the adequacy of information disclosure in relation to generally accepted accounting principles except where the disclosed basis of accounting specifically provides an exception or where the purpose of the statements indicates that the information would be irrelevant to the reader.

The question of disclosure of departures from generally accepted accounting principles

Some practitioners believe that it is sufficient for the financial statements in the preceding example to disclose the accounting basis used as being "in accordance with the provisions of Article 4 of the Financing Agreement" and for the auditor's opinion paragraph to contain a similar reference. Other practitioners believe that the notes to the financial statements should specifically disclose that they are not prepared in accordance with generally accepted accounting principles and should disclose the respects in which they differ. Some practitioners believe that such disclosures should be repeated for emphasis in the auditor's report – not as reservations but as explanations. The AICPA exposure draft, for example, suggested a second paragraph that:

i) States or, preferably, refers to the note to the financial statements that states the basis of presentation.
ii) Describes or, preferably, refers to the note to the financial statements that describes how the basis of

presentation differs from generally accepted accounting principles or, if applicable, states that generally accepted accounting principles have not been established. The monetary effect of such differences need not be stated.
iii) States that the presentation is not intended to be in conformity with generally accepted accounting principles. [35]

A similar recommendation has been under study by the CICA and may be included in the forthcoming CICA exposure draft on special reports, in process of being issued as this book goes to press. It might be noted that such an explanatory paragraph, by coming prior to the opinion paragraph, deviates from the normal scope/reservation/opinion/explanation order discussed in 17.2.1

The question of reference to other financial statements

Some auditors are concerned about having two different sets of audited financial statements both in wide circulation. A similar point with respect to international reporting was discussed in 18.6.1. Therefore, when one set of audited statements has been prepared for a company's shareholders in accordance with generally accepted accounting principles and another set is prepared for some special purpose on a different basis, some auditors prefer to make reference in their report on the latter set to the existence of the former.[36] The desirability of a cross-reference is greater if the special purpose report is to be given wide distribution or if its special purpose might not be recognized by a reader.

The interpretation of consistency in special purpose reports

Because the fourth reporting standard applies to special purpose reports, a reference to consistency is necessary for any recurring reports. Thus, in the earlier example, where special statements are prepared each year for a company's noteholders, the auditor's opinion includes a reference to consistency with the accounting basis used in such special reports in previous years. A similar reference is appropriate for annual reports for not-for-profit organizations, reports on annual cash-basis statements, etc.[37]

For one-time special reports, such as a report under a buy/sell agreement, a reference to the consistency of application of a special disclosed basis of accounting would be meaningless (just as in a general purpose report for the first year of a company's operation). In some cases, however, a buy/sell agreement, after identifying certain specific exceptions, might call for the statements to be prepared in accordance with generally accepted accounting principles as they have been applied by the company in its regular annual financial statements in the past. In such cases, the reader may wish a specific opinion on consistency, which could take the following form:

> In my opinion, these financial statements present fairly ...in accordance with the accounting basis prescribed in Clause 3 of the purchase agreement dated May 23, 1976 between A Co. Ltd. and B Co. Ltd. Furthermore, in my opinion, this accounting basis, except for the treatment of inventories, warranty liability, and depreciation as prescribed in Clause 3, has been applied in a manner consistent with that used in the financial statements for the preceding year issued to the company's shareholders.

The question of a reference to the special purpose

Some reports contain wording restricting their distribution (as in comfort and consent letters to securities commissions) and this wording may state or imply the purpose for which the report was prepared. Occasionally, one sees reports which contain a specific reference in the opinion paragraph, such as "...these statements present fairly...for the purpose of ... ". Such an approach is useful in putting readers on guard that the methods of computation and the levels of materiality, etc. assumed may not be appropriate to other purposes. However, the auditor may well, in so doing, be expressing an implied opinion that the information does meet the purposes set out, when in fact he cannot be sure of user needs (in particular, with regard to error tolerances). [38]

Financial statements prepared on a cash basis or modified accrual basis

Cash-basis or modified accrual-basis (sometimes called modified cash-basis) accounting may be appropriate in some instances for not-for-profit organizations or other special purpose reports. On the other hand, for some not-for-profit organizations generally accepted accounting principles are appropriate (see 17.5.4). Where cash-basis or modified accrual-basis accounting is used and is appropriate, the auditor's opinion paragraph should *not* refer to financial position, results of operations, or changes in financial position, since these words imply the use of full accrual accounting. For example, for cash-basis statements the opinion paragraph might read:

> ...present fairly the cash position of XYZ Association at December 31, 1976 and its receipts and disbursements for the year then ended on a basis consistent with that of the preceding year.

In the foregoing example, the reference to cash position and receipts and disbursements may be considered sufficient identification of the accounting basis used. For modified accrual-basis statements the opinion paragraph might read:

> ... present fairly the recorded assets and liabilities of XYZ Association as at December 31, 1976 and its revenue and expenses for the year then ended on the modified accrual [or modified cash] basis of accounting described in note 1 to the financial statements applied in a manner consistent with that of the preceding year.

The auditor should also satisfy himself that the financial statements have not been misleadingly titled. Where cash-basis accounting is used, terms such as "balance sheet" or "statement of income" may be misleading since they imply accrual accounting. The AICPA exposure draft suggested terms such as "statement of assets and liabilities arising from cash transactions". Where the modified accrual-basis is used, the terms "balance sheet" and "statement of income" are, however, often used. In such cases, some practitioners believe that it is desirable not only to refer to the accounting basis in the opinion paragraph, as previously illustrated, but to emphasize the difference by a reference as well in the scope paragraph. An example would be:

> I have examined the balance sheet ... for the year then ended, which has been drawn up on the modified accrual [modified cash] basis of accounting described in note 1 to the financial statements. My examination ...

As previously stated, the AICPA exposure draft suggested, in addition, a middle explanatory paragraph. For cash basis statements an example would be:

> As more fully described in Note X, the Company's policy is to prepare its financial statements on the basis of cash receipts and disbursements; consequently, the financial statements do not include certain assets, liabilities, revenue, and expenses. Accordingly, the financial statements are not intended to present financial position and results of operations in [accordance] with generally accepted accounting principles.[39]

In Canada, such an explanatory paragraph, if used, would preferably follow the opinion paragraph (see 17.2.1).

Parent company unconsolidated statements

At the present time, subsidiaries are normally required to be consolidated only for financial statements prepared for issuance to shareholders. A parent company may also prepare unconsolidated statements for issuance to taxation authorities, creditors or for other special purposes. Because of the restriction in the scope of the CICA Recommendations on consolidation, the latter statements may also be said to be in accordance with generally accepted accounting principles.[40] Some practitioners feel that a standard audit report wording is therefore justified, provided that the report is addressed to the directors or some party other than the company's shareholders (and assuming that consolidated financial statements have indeed been issued to the shareholders). Other practitioners feel that it is undesirable to have two different audited statements in circulation both allegedly presented in accordance with generally accepted accounting principles. Those practitioners therefore believe that it is desirable to modify the report wording for the parent company unconsolidated statements along the following lines (italics added for emphasis):

> I have examined the *unconsolidated* balance sheet of . . . and the *unconsolidated* statements of income, retained earnings and changes in financial position for the year then ended, *prepared on the cost basis of accounting for the investment in subsidiaries and effectively controlled companies*. My examination . . . in the circumstances.

> In my opinion, these financial statements present fairly, *on the cost basis of accounting for the investment in subsidiaries and effectively controlled companies*, the financial position . . . and the results of its operations and the changes in its financial position for the year then ended in accordance with generally accepted accounting principles applied on a basis consistent with that of the preceding year.

The foregoing wording seems desirable as long as unconsolidated statements can be said to be in accordance with generally accepted accounting principles. A more logical solution, however, might be for the CICA Handbook to define generally accepted accounting principles as always requiring consolidation (except for the rare situations described in Handbook par. 3050.07). Parent company unconsolidated statements would then be special purpose statements prepared in accordance with a "disclosed basis of accounting" which could be described in the notes. The opinion paragraph would then refer to the notes in the manner previously illustrated.[41] If the auditor felt that an explanatory final paragraph was needed, it might be worded along the following lines.

> As described in note 1, these financial statements are prepared on the cost basis of accounting for the investment in subsidiaries and effectively controlled companies, instead of on a consolidated and equity basis. In this respect only the financial statements are not intended to be in accordance with generally accepted accounting principles. Consolidated financial statements for the same period have been prepared for issuance to the shareholders, and have been reported on by me under date of March 17, 1976.

Special purpose statements in accordance with generally accepted accounting principles

Not all special purpose statements are prepared on a different basis of accounting. A buy/sell agreement may specify that the purchase price of a business will be adjusted in a specified manner based on financial statements of that business prepared in accordance

with generally accepted accounting principles. Where special purpose statements are prepared in accordance with generally accepted accounting principles, the auditor's report would normally still refer to the agreement prescribing the basis of accounting and would commonly refer to generally accepted accounting principles as well. For example:

> In my opinion, these financial statements present fairly . . . in accordance with generally accepted accounting principles and with the provisions of Clause 3 of the purchase agreement dated May 23, 1976 between A Co. Ltd. and B Co. Ltd. applied on a basis consistent with that used in the financial statements for the preceding year issued to the company's shareholders.

19.3.2 Full audits of specific elements of financial statements for special purposes

A special purpose report may cover a specific element of the financial statements only – for example, one statement alone (such as the balance sheet), one figure alone (such as reported sales), or a component of one figure (such as reported sales for one branch or store). Although generally accepted auditing standards apply in full only to audit reports on financial statements (which can be taken to mean complete sets of financial statements), the general and field work standards are also applicable to other types of attest engagements[42] – which should logically include engagements to express an opinion on specific elements. The work must be properly planned and supervised. An appropriate study must be made of internal controls on which the auditor relies but such controls may be fewer than in the case of an audit of a complete set of financial statements. Sufficient appropriate audit evidence must be obtained to support the content of the report. In making decisions as to audit evidence, the auditor must remember that materiality with respect to a specific financial statement element alone may be far more restrictive than for a complete set of financial statements taken as a whole. Furthermore, the normal overlapping evidence available during the audit of a complete set of financial statements will not be readily at hand and the auditor must compensate for its absence by more extensive procedures than the same element would warrant as an individual part of a complete audit. For example, in verifying sales in a complete audit the work on cash, accounts receivable, inventories, and gross profit analysis may provide considerable overlapping evidence. Where the auditor is auditing the sales figure alone he must usually do some work in related areas in order to obtain sufficient evidence as to the accuracy of reported sales. He must also be satisfied that the items not covered by his audit could not materially affect the element on which he is reporting. Commonly, however, a special purpose report on a specific element will follow a regular annual audit of the financial statements as a whole. In that case the last concern about the scope of examination does not arise, though the question of a different materiality limit is still applicable and may have a significant effect on the extent of work.

The reporting standards do not necessarily apply to audits of other than complete financial statements. However, common sense suggests that the general ideas underlying the first three reporting standards should be applied. The scope of the auditor's examination should be referred to, with a reference to generally accepted auditing standards. In a few cases the auditor may wish to report in more detail on the specific auditing procedures performed – usually in a separate paragraph following and amplifying the scope paragraph. (Some practitioners believe, however, that a listing of auditing procedures is undesirable when a full audit of the element in question has been undertaken since the auditor has accepted the responsibility of choosing and carrying out those procedures which are necessary in the circumstances; a listing of procedures might seem to place an onus on the reader for judging the sufficiency and appropriateness of the tests.) The report should express (or, where necessary, deny) an opinion on the identified elements and the opinion should be expressed in relation to an appropriate disclosed basis of accounting. A reference to consistency might or might not be meaningful.

An example of a special purpose report on a statement of gross sales (for the purpose of computing rentals) follows:

I have examined the statement of gross sales (as defined in the lease agreement dated March 4, 1974, between A Co. Ltd., as lessor, and B Co. Ltd. as lessee) of B Co. Ltd. at its Main Street store, [City], [Province], for the year ended December 31, 1976. My examination was made in accordance with generally accepted auditing standards, and accordingly . . . in the circumstances.

In my opinion, the accompanying statement of gross sales presents fairly the gross sales of B Co. Ltd. at its Main Street store for the year ended December 31, 1976 in accordance with the provisions of the agreement referred to above. [43]

Those practitioners who believe that disclosure of specific procedures is desirable might, in the foregoing example, insert the following middle paragraph:

Specifically, I examined weekly cash reports for the year submitted by the store manager. Those reports contained information as to gross sales, cash register readings, sales taxes, remittances made by the store manager, returns and allowances, discounts granted, and other information. I compared the monthly summary of those reports with the general ledger, and for selected days in each month I compared the daily net cash receipts shown in the weekly cash reports with the company's bank statements. [44]

As previously stated, some practitioners believe that the middle paragraph is better omitted.

From time to time audit reports may be required on financial data included in applications for government grants. A common format for an auditor's report in such a case is as follows:

I have examined the application for grant under the [name of Act] of A Co. Ltd. for the year ended December 31, 1976. My examination was made in accordance with generally accepted auditing standards, and accordingly . . . in the circumstances. The determination of what constitutes [class of items presented] was made by the company based on its interpretation of the [name of Act] and Regulations thereunder.

In my opinion, having regard to the [name of Act] and Regulations thereunder, the application for grant presents fairly the amount of [items presented] listed therein for the year ended December 31, 1976 determined on a reasonable and appropriate basis of accounting consistent with that of the preceding year.

The foregoing wording, while adapted from a form suggested by various past CICA subcommittees on government-prescribed reports, may not be fully consistent with the subsequently issued third reporting standard in that it does not specifically express an opinion in relation to the provisions of the Act (a "disclosed basis of accounting"). The problem is that an opinion explicitly in relation to the provisions of the Act may involve a legal interpretation, which would be outside the auditor's sphere of competence (hence, the limitation expressed in the last sentence of the scope paragraph).

A better solution might be for the notes included in the grant application to provide an adequate description of the accounting basis employed, including the factual assertion that company management believes the disclosed basis to comply with the Act and Regulations. The auditor's opinion paragraph would then express an opinion in relation to the accounting basis disclosed in the notes.

Further examples of special purpose audit reports on financial information may be found in the CICA Auditing Guidelines, *Audit of a Candidate under the Canada Elections Act* (1974) and *Auditor's Considerations when Supplementary General Price-level Restatements are Published in an Annual Report* (1975). The suggested report in the election expense guideline expresses a positive opinion that the return "presents fairly the information contained in the accounting records . . . in accordance with the accounting treatment required by the Act and the Guidelines issued by the Chief Electoral Officer" but contains an explanation that the extent of omissions is not susceptible of practicable determination and that "the Act does not require me to report, nor was it practicable for me to determine, that the accounting records include all transactions relating to the candidacy". The suggested report in the price-level guideline expresses an opinion on compilation but points out that uniform criteria for presenting price level data do not yet exist (see 17.5.5).

19.3.3 Limited procedures to provide limited credibility for special purposes

A full audit (an attest engagement) involves compliance with the general and field work standards and the performance of the tests and other procedures considered by the auditor to be necessary in the circumstances. Its objective is to add audit credibility to the financial data reported upon. An accounting engagement in connection with unaudited financial statements does not involve auditing procedures or standards – though certain other procedures and standards for such engagements have been established (see Chapter 20). Its objective is to prepare or assist in the preparation of financial statements or, on occasion, to add accounting credibility based on a limited review. Some practitioners believe that there is a need in certain circumstances for the auditor to provide limited audit assurance – something beyond · the level of a non-audit review but less than a full audit. Such limited procedures would clearly not warrant the expression of a positive opinion that the statements "present fairly" as in a normal audit report. Rather, it has been suggested, the conclusions should take the form of "negative assurance".

It was stated earlier (see 18.4.3) that negative assurance was *not* appropriate following denials or qualified opinions in full audit engagements. Negative assurance in comfort letters with respect to the special cases of preliminary prospectuses and unaudited statements contained in prospectuses was discussed earlier in this chapter (see 19.2.1 and 19.2.2), but its use was restricted to reports issued to regulatory authorities, who can be expected to understand the much lesser degree of reliability it provides. For most engagements involving unaudited financial statements (but not engagements relating to unaudited interim statements of public companies) any expression of negative assurance following the practitioner's customary disclaimer of opinion is presently prohibited (see Chaper 20). Whether or not this prohibition should be interpreted as applying also to engagements where the auditor has undertaken to

perform limited audit procedures is not entirely clear.[45] Some examples of negative assurance for special purpose limited audits have been seen occasionally in practice. Wider use of such negative assurance, if wider use is desirable at all, will likely depend on future pronouncements in this area, to which the reader should refer.

Practitioners advocating the use of negative assurance for engagements involving limited procedures usually suggest that it be restricted to knowledgeable users who agree to the limitations and who are in a position to appraise their significance. Since the accountant is not performing all the procedures he considers necessary in the circumstances to warrant a positive opinion, the user must be in a position to assess how much less is acceptable for his purposes. Examples of knowledgeable users might be the reporting company's management or board of directors, a parent company's management or auditors, and various securities commissions. The accountant would want to be satisfied that the distribution of his report will be restricted to named parties and might wish to refer to this restriction in the report itself. Since the engagement would be held out to involve more than a non-audit review, it should include such non-audit review procedures (see Chapter 20) together with additional procedures. The additional procedures should be sufficient to reduce the risk of undetected material misstatement significantly from the level associated with a non-audit review – though not to the level to be expected from a full audit. Advocates of this position usually suggest that, to undertake an engagement involving limited procedures, the accountant would need a certain basic knowledge of the reporting entity's accounts. Such knowledge might be obtained from a prior or current year's audit, a review of a predecessor auditor's working papers, or additional review and verification procedures. If such knowledge indicated that the reporting entity's accounts were unreliable, the expression of negative assurance would not be appropriate.

One example of the use of negative assurance following limited procedures occurs in reports on assets held in trust for others. Legal firms, in particular, usually hold trust assets for their clients. The auditor ordinarily cannot give a positive opinion on the trust assets because of restrictions placed on his examination (principally on correspondence with the firm's clients) and because of the nature of trust funds themselves. If the practitioner considers his report with respect to the trust section of a legal firm's balance sheet to be a special purpose report, he might word it along the following lines:

> My examination of the "Trust Section" of the balance sheet at March 31, 1977 was limited to the following procedures:

1. The cash balance was reconciled with a certificate obtained from your bankers as at February 28, 1977.
2. Securities shown on Schedule A, held in a safety deposit box at the bank, were counted on February 28, 1977. Coupon interest on bonds held in bearer form was traced to deposits in the firm's trust bank account.
3. The trial balance of the clients' trust ledger was checked at February 28, 1977 and scrutinized at March 31, 1977. At your request I did not apply to clients for confirmation of funds or securities entrusted to the partnership.

It will be appreciated that the nature of trust fund receipts is such that an audit examination cannot give assurance that all trust assets received have been recorded in the trust records. However, nothing came to my attention in the course of my examination that would indicate errors or omissions in the trust records.

Also, in my opinion, the method of keeping the trust accounts and segregating the clients' trust funds meet the requirements of [rules of the provincial law society].

Some practitioners, however, consider the trust fund situation to be simply an auditing deficiency and therefore calling for a denial of opinion with no accompanying negative assurance.

Where negative assurance is expressed in a special purpose report, some practitioners believe that a disclaimer of opinion should accompany the assurance. This practice is not universal, however.

An alternative suggested for reports following agreed-upon procedures less than a full audit is to list the procedures and the results found but express no opinion or assurance at all.[46] The reader must then decide how much reliance he will attach to the particular procedures performed.

Another instance of the suggested use of negative assurance, though very controversial, has been in connection with forecasts or projections (see Chapter 21).

19.3.4 Reports on an investigation or on other findings in an audit – general principles

Generally accepted auditing standards do not specifically apply to non-attest reporting. However, the Rules of Professional Conduct continue to apply to a practitioner's work. Accordingly, certain general principles seem desirable to observe:

1. The auditor should not accept an engagement or issue a report requiring professional competence which he lacks.

For example, the auditor should not express a legal opinion, an actuarial opinion, an engineering opinion, or a geological opinion. Such opinions require skills outside the public accountant's field. He should not word his report in a way which might seem to be predicting the future. Nor should he express an opinion on computer procedures, complex tax matters, or on business valuations unless he has acquired and maintained the necessary competence in those fields (as many practitioners have). These restrictions do not, however, preclude the auditor from pointing out an apparent legal problem, for example, and suggesting that his client seek competent legal advice.

2. If there is any danger of the client misunderstanding the nature of the work he is doing, he should be on record in writing as to what responsibilities he is assuming (engagement letters were discussed in 4.2.1 and 4.2.2).
3. The work should be adequately planned and properly executed. If assistants are employed they should be properly supervised.
4. Sufficient procedures should be performed to afford a reasonable basis to support the content of the report.

The procedures required will depend on the nature of the report. If the auditor is reporting facts such as "I found the following errors" or "The major components of this account balance can be summarized as follows", it is necessary, but usually straight-forward, to ensure that the facts are correct. If the auditor is expressing a positive opinion such as "in my opinion the method of keeping the trust accounts meets the requirements of . . ." he must have gathered sufficient appropriate audit evidence to justify that opinion – a standard similar to an attest engagement. If the auditor is making a recommendation such as "purchase orders should be approved by Mr. X" or "controls should be established over scrap sales" he should have made a sufficient study of the systems in question for the recommendation to appear a sensible one in the circumstances. But such recommendations are by the nature less formal than expressions of opinion on financial presentation and the evidence required can normally be less extensive. If the auditor is presenting an evaluation (such as of the value of a business or of the strength of a system of internal control) he should have gathered enough facts to afford a basis for making the evaluation. However, such evaluations involve a different type of subjective judgment from that involved in attestation and such evaluations therefore cannot be directly compared to the process of verifying financial statement assertions.

5. The auditor should normally refer in his report to the scope of the work he has undertaken.

A reference to generally accepted auditing standards would normally not be appropriate. However, it is desirable that he give some indication of the character of the work on which his report is based. If his report arises out of other findings (such as points on internal control) made during an audit examination of financial statements, his report could indicate that fact.

6. The facts reported, conclusions expressed, recommendations made, or assurance given should be phrased in a manner commensurate with the persuasiveness of the evidence on which they are based.

Factual matters may simply be reported. If the auditor has performed a thorough examination of matters susceptible of reasonably objective determination, a formal expression of a positive opinion may be warranted. In other cases, it may be appropriate to express conclusions in the form of negative assurance. Some prescribed forms may provide for a formal certification (e.g., that the auditor physically inspected certain share certificates). However, the auditor should only certify to facts or transactions of which he has first hand knowledge. In most instances, certification is not possible and the auditor's report should instead express an opinion or, where appropriate, negative assurance. Recommendations should be made where the auditor has reasonable grounds for believing them to be desirable. In other cases, it may be appropriate merely to identify specific items as requiring further study. Evaluations should be based on the auditor's best judgment of the underlying conditions but where major uncertainties are involved they should be identified.

7. Negative assurance should only be given where distribution of the report containing it is limited to people who can be expected to understand the significance of the limited nature of the work performed and the responsibility assumed.

Four types of special purpose reports are discussed in the following sections:

1. long-form reports,
2. reports on compliance with contractual, statutory or regulatory requirements,
3. reports on internal control,
4. investigations.

19.3.5 Long-form reports

Most commonly, the term *long-form report* is used to describe a report which contains not only the auditor's short-form report on the annual financial statements but also additional details and analyses of various financial statement items, supplementary schedules, statistical data, explanatory comments and other information.

Today, long-form reports are probably prepared on only a minority of audit engagements. On some engagements, however, they provide a useful source of summarized information and commentary to management, to owners, and, occasionally, to banks or credit agencies. Usually, where a long-form report is issued to management, the normal short-form is issued separately to shareholders. Occasionally the long-form report is the only report prepared. In either case, the long-form report normally includes the short-form report and is accompanied by the related financial statements. Since the short-form portion of the report has already been discussed in Chapters 17 and 18, it is the remaining sections of the long-form report which are considered here.

There is no set format for a long-form report. Typical contents, however, might include:

- key income and balance sheet statistics and ratios,
- per-share statistics,
- analyses of all major balance sheet accounts (e.g., bank balances, investment details, receivables ageing, inventory components, fixed asset and depreciation analyses, accounts payable components, long-term debt schedules),
- analyses of all major income accounts (e.g., sales by category, cost of sales components, expense analyses, tax details),
- explanatory comments on significant transactions or events during the year.

One of the problems with long-form reports has been possible ambiguity as to the responsibility the auditor is taking for the financial and other information presented (apart from the audited financial statements themselves). If the auditor does not intend his short-form audit report to cover all the data in the long-form report, he should ensure that the audited financial statements themselves are not referenced to the supplementary data (see 17.2.3 and 17.5.5). However, the supplementary data may be referenced to the audited financial statements. The supplementary data included in the long-form report should not be necessary for a fair presentation in accordance with generally accepted accounting principles. If it *is* necessary, the presentation of the audited financial statements taken alone is deficient and the short-form auditor's report should contain an appropriate reservation. The explanatory comments contained in the long-form report should not represent reservations of opinion but merely explanations.

In the United States, AICPA pronouncements call for the auditor to give a clear-cut indication of the responsibility, if any, which he is taking for the data in the long-form report.

... because the usual short-form report covers only the basic financial statements, the auditor should clearly establish his position regarding the other data in the long-form report. This may be accomplished, for example, by an explanation that:

a) his examination has been made primarily for the purpose of formulating an opinion on the basic financial statements, taken as a whole, and

b) the other data included in the report, although not considered necessary for a fair presentation ... are presented for supplementary analysis purposes, and either (1) that they have been subjected to the audit procedures applied in the examination of the basic financial statements and are, in his opinion, fairly stated in all material respects in relation to the basic financial statements, taken as a whole or (2) that they have not been subjected to the audit procedures applied in the examination of the basic financial statements, stating the source of the information and the extent of his examination and responsibility assumed, if any.[47]

Such an explanation could be given in a preface to the supplementary data in the long-form report. Possible wording might be as follows:

The following information is not an integral part of the basic financial statements and is presented for supplementary analysis purposes. It has been subjected to the audit procedures applied in my examination of the basic financial statements and, in my opinion, is fairly presented in all respects material to the financial statements taken as a whole.

In Canada, such explanations are not always used in long-form reports. Their use, however, would seem desirable.

The AICPA pronouncements also suggest that the auditor should take care that in his long-form report he does not make *factual* representations with respect to financial information rather than express an *opinion* on management representations.

Occasionally, long-form reports include details of auditing procedures performed in the course of the examination of the basic financial statements. For the reasons discussed in 19.3.2, some practitioners believe that such inclusion is undesirable. Others believe it can be useful and informative to readers of the statements.

19.3.6 Reports on compliance with contractual, statutory or regulatory requirements

Auditors are frequently asked to provide reports as to compliance with contractual, statutory or regulatory requirements. For example, bond indentures may contain covenants with respect to maintenance of working capital, payments into sinking funds, payments of interest, or restrictions on the sale or pledging of certain assets.

In a few cases, compliance with the requirements is susceptible of reasonable verification during the auditor's regular examination of the financial statements. In such cases, the opinion paragraph of his special purpose report on compliance may give a positive opinion:

In my opinion, the provisions of the 1973 Trust Indenture relating to the issue of the company's Series A Debentures have been complied with.

One of the difficulties of providing a positive opinion as to compliance, however, is the absence of a clear yardstick as to materiality. When the auditor expresses a positive opinion on financial statements he implies that he has obtained reasonable assurance of detecting a material total of misstatement, should it

exist (guidelines as to materiality were discussed in Chapter 15). The assurance sought by third parties with respect to compliance, however, is often as to whether *any* contravention has occurred.

In many cases, a regular audit examination cannot provide sufficient assurance that every infraction would be detected – although it provides *some* assurance. In such cases the opinion paragraph would normally provide only negative assurance:

In making our examination of the financial statements of the company taken as a whole, nothing came to our attention that indicated that the company was in default with respect to the terms, covenants, provisions, or conditions contained in the Loan Agreement of May 23, 1974.

Some practitioners would add a second sentence to the foregoing opinion paragraph:

However, it should be noted that our examination was not directed primarily toward obtaining such knowledge.[48]

A preceding scope paragraph would usually refer to the auditor's examination of the financial statements and perhaps the date of his report thereon.

Other examples of special purpose reports on compliance include reports providing negative assurance with respect to answers on prescribed questionnaires for Canadian mutual funds, negative assurance with respect to the tax deductibility of certain costs reported in government grant applications, and negative assurance as to non-contravention (by a lawyer) of rules and regulations of a provincial law society.

19.3.7 Reports on internal control and other matters

An auditor issues reports on internal control in the following circumstances:

1. commonly to management in connection with his regular annual audit (usually together with recommendations on systems efficiency, accounting matters and tax and financial planning),
2. occasionally, to management or others as a result of a special study,
3. occasionally, to other auditors or to regulatory agencies,
4. in rare circumstances, to the public.

Reports to management in connection with the regular annual audit

The importance of the auditor's recommendations to management with respect to internal control, systems efficiency, accounting matters and tax and financial planning has been discussed in earlier chapters. Most such recommendations are commonly incorporated in an *internal control/management letter* at the conclusion of the interim audit. Indeed, the secondary objective of the interim audit was defined in 9.1.2 to be:

> To identify opportunities and provide timely suggestions for improvements in internal control, systems efficiency, financial or tax planning, and accounting methods to the extent that such identification and provision can be combined conveniently with the procedures required under the primary objectives or to the extent that such suggestions are requested by the client.

and an additional reporting responsibility was defined in 9.1.3 as:

> To advise the client of any significant errors, irregularities or suspicious circumstances encountered and, to the extent that improvement appears desirable and practicable, any significant weakness observed in the system of internal control.[49]

Additional points encountered during the course of the financial statement audit may be incorporated in an *audit follow-up letter*.

Usually, an internal control/management letter or an audit follow-up letter takes the form of one or more memoranda accompanied by a covering letter. The contents of the memoranda themselves are discussed in 9.1.2 and 30.2. The present section is concerned solely with the covering letter.

The covering letter is normally addressed to the most senior executive officer that can be expected to take an interest in the subject; an alternative is to address the letter to the most senior financial official with a copy to a more senior executive officer. Often it may be appropriate to summarize the major points separately for the more senior levels, with additional explanations and less major recommendations being included in memoranda to lower management levels. Ordinarily, the level of the addressee should be higher than the level of the individual responsible for the matters discussed in the memorandum. The auditor may be asked to circulate the most major recommendations, after their discussion with management, to the audit committee of the board of directors.

Points to be included in a covering letter will depend on (a) the nature and seriousness of the recommendations being made, (b) the client's understanding of both the importance and the limitations of internal control, (c) the degree to which the recommendations have already been discussed, as is desirable for all but the most confidential recommendations, with junior officials, and (d) the auditor's relationship with his client. An elaborate recitation of "boilerplate" in a covering letter may be out of place for officers who are fully aware of the context in which the recommendations are being made. On the other hand, many practitioners feel that certain points should be covered to avoid the danger of the letter or memorandum being misconstrued at a later date. Points which have been suggested as important to communicate, in some fashion, to recipients of the auditor's internal control/management letter include explanations that:

1. the recommendations arose out of the normal audit work related to an expression of opinion on the financial statements and do not constitute a complete report on internal control for management purposes based on an exhaustive study,[50]
2. the normal audit work would not necessarily detect all internal control weaknesses,
3. notwithstanding any control weaknesses mentioned, the audit procedures were as extensive as necessary for the auditor to report on the financial statements,[51]
4. the suggestions and comments outlined concern systems only and are not intended to reflect on the competence or integrity of the client's personnel (if such is the case),
5. there are inherent limitations to any system of internal control,
6. there is always the risk of future deterioration in present controls.

Many of the foregoing points can and should be communicated orally. In some cases it may be prudent, however, to refer to some of them in the covering letter. An example of such a letter, covering the first four of the above six points, follows.

Mr. A. Stonehill,
President,
XYZ Limited,
Address   October 15, 1976

Dear Mr. Stonehill:

I have recently completed the interim portion of my audit for the year ending December 31, 1976, during which I reviewed your company's system of internal controls. The purpose of my review was to provide a basis for determining the nature, timing and extent of other auditing procedures necessary for expressing an opinion on your company's financial statements. Accordingly, my review of any given control was limited, depending on its materiality, its relevance to financial reporting, and the degree of my anticipated reliance, if any, on it in forming my opinion on the statements. Such a review would not necessarily disclose all weaknesses in the system nor all matters which an in-depth study might raise.

However, my review did reveal a few conditions which I believe to be material weaknesses and a number of other instances where I believe improvements could be made in your company's controls, systems efficiency, accounting procedures, and tax and financial planning. While I am satisfied that my audit procedures will be sufficient to enable me to report on the statements, the suggested systems changes would, in my opinion, strengthen the protection of your company's assets as well as achieving other operating improvements. The points are covered in the accompanying memoranda and have been discussed with your comptroller, Mr. Steinberg, and with certain other officials. Their preliminary views on certain of the points are indicated in the memoranda as well. The suggestions and comments made concern systems only and are not intended to reflect on the competence or integrity of your personnel.

You mentioned that you would like to send a copy of the most major points to Mr. Montpierre, the chairman of the audit committee, and I have enclosed an additional copy for that purpose.

Should you wish to discuss any of the matters at greater length, I should be glad to provide you with further explanations. You may wish to consider particularly the suggestions concerning purchasing routines.

The letter would of course be modified to fit the circumstances of the individual client and some of the foregoing points might be omitted if the auditor was satisfied they had been adequately communicated in other ways (or in similar letters in the recent past).[52]

Reports to management following a special study

Where the auditor has been asked to undertake a special study of internal control (whether for the organization as a whole or for some specific area, such as the EDP function), his reporting will generally be more formal than in the case of the annual internal control/management letter. The report should:

1. describe the scope of the study, the areas covered and not covered, and the procedures performed (and in particular whether the scope included both a review of the system and procedures to check compliance with the identified controls).
2. explain that the suggestions and comments outlined concern systems only and are not intended to reflect on the competence or integrity of the client's personnel (if such is the case),
3. explain that there are inherent limitations to any system of internal control and that there is always the risk of future deterioration in present controls,
4. state the auditor's conclusions and any recommendations for changes (or for further investigation).

Reports to other auditors or to regulatory agencies

Occasionally, an auditor may be asked to provide a report on internal control to another auditor. One example might be a report to the auditor of a parent or investor company who wished to prepare for that company's management a summary of control points throughout a consolidated or affiliated group. Sometimes an auditor is asked to report on internal control

to a regulatory agency – though this practice is more common in the United States than in Canada. The foregoing reporting considerations, depending on whether the report arose out of a regular annual audit or a special study, would continue to apply.

Sometimes an auditor is asked to report on controls in common systems used by or on behalf of other parties. An example might be the report by the auditor of a data centre to various data centre users (or their auditors) seeking assurance as to the controls over the processing of their data. In such cases, the question of materiality is particularly difficult. A weakness which may appear trivial in the circumstances as viewed by the data centre auditor, unfamiliar with the systems and transactions of a given user, may be of critical importance to that user because of an unusual concentration of transactions of a particular type in his business. Contrarily, an apparently serious data centre weakness may be offset by user controls of which the data centre auditor cannot know.

As a result of these difficulties, one suggestion made has been that the report of the data centre auditor (or any other accountant engaged for the purpose of making such a report) merely express an opinion as to whether or not the systems and controls conform to the data centre's written description of them and disclaim an opinion as to the adequacy of the controls with respect to the data centre or any of its users. A reservation would be expressed if controls represented to be in existence were not in fact operating. An additional explanation would be given where a control was not represented to be in existence but would, in the auditor's judgment, be desirable.[53]

A possible further example of an inter-auditor report is the report of the auditor of a custodian of pension fund assets to the auditor of a specific pension fund. Such reporting raises the same difficulties concerning materiality and overall evaluation of control. The subject requires further study by the profession.

Reports to the public

Reports on internal control issued to the public are not common. In the view of many practitioners they are undesirable – particularly because they may lead readers to attribute an unwarranted degree of reliability to unaudited interim financial statements (on the mistaken assumption that a good system of internal control will guarantee accurate interim figures). AICPA pronouncements summarize the arguments for and against public reporting, conclude that it is the responsibility of management and/or relevant regulatory agencies to decide whether audit reports on internal control should be circulated to the public, but state that an auditor should not authorize such a report to be issued to the general public in a document that includes unaudited financial statements.[54]

Where the auditor reports to the public (e.g., large numbers of shareholders) on the internal controls within his client's systems, he will usually have already completed his audit and issued his audit report on the financial statements. His report on control will often refer to his regular audit report. The points previously mentioned in connection with internal control/management letters should be covered in his report – perhaps at greater length than is needed in reports to management, regulatory agencies, or other auditors. In addition, it may be desirable to emphasize that controls provide reasonable but not absolute assurance of achieving their objectives, and that the level of assurance will depend on management's analysis of the costs and benefits associated with any given control. The AICPA pronouncements provide an example of a possible public report on internal control.[55]

19.3.8 Investigations

Auditors may be called on to perform various types of special investigations:

- a purchase investigation (investigation of a prospective business to be purchased),
- a business valuation (for a prospective purchaser, for the prospective vendor, for tax planning purposes, for expropriation purposes, etc.),
- a feasibility study (such as for the proposed acquisition of EDP equipment),
- a fraud investigation (to evaluate the extent of a discovered fraud),
- an insurance loss investigation (to evaluate the extent of some loss for which an insurance claim is being made),
- a credit investigation (on behalf of a prospective lender or as assistance to the prospective borrower in seeking financing),
- a practice investigation (peer review of another practitioner's work on behalf of a provincial Institute or Order).

Each investigation may have different terms of reference and may call for different procedures and reporting. The general principles outlined in 19.3.4 should be observed. Sometimes an investigation may be an isolated engagement; sometimes it may be a specific extension of procedures requested in conjunction with an annual audit. Space does not permit an analysis of each type of investigation but, as an example, the major points involved in a purchase investigation are outlined below.

Purchase investigations

The terms of reference will vary from one purchase investigation to another. Certain terms may be embodied in the purchase agreement between the buyer and seller; others may be established by the buyer, sometimes based on the auditor's suggestions. Depending on the terms of reference established, some or all of the following points (and sometimes others) may be considered in drawing up the program for the investigation.

1. General –
   - Exact name of the company (according to the letters patent).
   - Nature of the business (disclosing recent major changes).
   - Locations (with a description of the operations at each location).
   - Present ownership.
   - Brief history (noting prices and circumstances of previous transfers of ownership of the business).
   - Position in the industry.
   - Fiscal year-end.
   - Affiliates
     - description
     - interest therein
     - who the minority shareholders are

2. Proposed offer –
   - Principals (vendors and purchasers and their interests)
   - Auditors, solicitors and bankers (for both vendors and purchasers)
   - Details of offer (consideration to be exchanged by vendor and purchaser, offer date, closing date, etc.)
   - Special points to consider:
     a) Whether purchasers should get assets (if a premium over book value is to be paid) or shares (if the price is less than book value).
     b) Whether there is a potential designated surplus.
     c) Advantages of issuing redeemable preference shares, notes payable, etc. as against only common shares.

3. Examination and report –
   - What examination is required, and at what date.
   - What restrictions there are on the examination (secrecy, time limit, etc.).
   - Reliability of the data available.
   - What report is required (rough outline of form).

4. Financial –
   - A review and analysis of the audited financial statements for at least the past five years, and

the interim statement to the latest date available.

- A review of the letters patent, by-laws, shareholders', directors' and management committee minutes for unusual items for the last several years.
- A brief summary of all litigation during the past five years that resulted in any substantial loss to the company. Include all litigation still pending.
- A consideration of sources of profits and losses (products, locations, departments, etc.), for example:

  a) Management's estimates of sales and profits for the next five years, including new products and capital requirements and comments of management thereon, including important contrasts with the past. Industry indices that have some relation to the company's general business activity.

  b) Current order backlog with comparable figures for at least one prior year.

  c) Analysis of dollar and/or unit sales for at least two years, preferably five, on the following bases: by products or major product groups and including parts and service; by geographical territory; by method of distributions; by month; by users accounting for roughly 80% of sales.

  d) Analysis of gross profits by products or major product groups for at least two years, preferably five. If standard costs are used, an outline of the standards procedures.

  e) Analysis of cost of sales for at least two years, preferably for five, to indicate direct labour, material, factory overhead, any other charges normally made to cost of sales. Details of factory overhead, if available.

  f) Analysis of charges by selling and advertising, engineering, and general administrative expenses. If engineering expense is normally a part of factory overhead, these charges will have been included under item (e) above.

  g) Bad debt write-offs and inventory obsolescence practices.

  h) Comments on any unusual charges such as royalties received, interest payments, capital gains, etc. under other income and other deductions.

- A consideration of balance sheet items, for example –

  a) Current assets – convardism and consistency of valuation; reasonableness of inventory quantities and total of outstanding accounts receivable.

  b) Liabilities – present line of credit (and possible limits), security given to banks, contingencies.

  c) Present working capital and requirements (budget and source and application of funds).

  d) Fixed assets   – appraisal values
  – insurance coverage
  – efficiency
  – room for expansion
  – major additions in recent years
  – depreciation policy.

  e) Funded debt – redemption provisions, restrictions and covenants in trust deeds.

  f) Contractual obligations under pension plans, leases, employment contracts, union agreements, material and fixed asset purchase contracts, etc.

  g) Reserves – disclosed and hidden.

  h) Capital – sufficiency – share options – special conditions attaching to shares.

  i) Available credit reports on business.

  j) Estimated liquidation value.

  k) Book and market value (if any) of shares and reasonableness of price in relation to market price of shares of similar companies.

5. Taxes –
- Consideration of:
  a) Date to which taxes are assessed.
  b) Tax cushion and contingencies.
  c) Accumulated depreciation per books and per tax department,
  d) If assets are to be purchased, the tax payable on recaptured capital cost allowances.
  e) Loss carry-forward.
  f) Undistributed income.
  g) Designated surplus.

6. Personnel –
- Chief personnel – pertinent data including position, age, length of service, competence, salaries, bonuses and other benefits, employment contracts, etc.
- Labour situation – unions and contracts, labour relations, pension plans and other benefits and cost thereof, labour rates and comparisons with other local rates, number of employees at various locations, how much technical training is required, etc.
- Organization chart.
- Important effects on the business and its personnel if the purchase of the business is completed.

7. Purchasing –
- Chief suppliers and their reliability.
- Government policy towards the industry

(tariffs, subsidies, etc.).
8. Marketing –
   - Outline of sales organization and methods of distribution.
   - Salesmen's compensation arrangement.
   - Tabulation of geographical sales coverage; number of sales, service, or other personnel assigned; and names and addresses of manufacturers' representatives, agents, distributors, jobbers and dealers.
   - Copies of standard sales agreements used.
   - Schedule of discounts extended to various levels of distribution.
   - List of major competitors, their market shares, and prospects of each, trade names, research position, new markets, etc.
   - Complete set of catalogues, price lists of past five years.
   - Important contracts (in existence, under negotiation, running out).
9. Engineering –

- Brief resume of status, training of engineering personnel.
- List of principal company products that have been contributed by this engineering group.
- Market introduction date of each important product line.
- Outline of development programs underway.
10. Patents –
   - List of patents and applications, including number, expiration date, products covered, and significance.
   - Name and address of patent counsel.
   - Schedule of all royalty agreements, including name of licensor, or licensee, royalty rate, prepayments made, terms of agreement, and product covered.

As stated at the beginning of this section, not all of the foregoing points will be relevant in every purchase investigation. Other points may also warrant attention.

19.4 Reference material

CICA Handbook, Sec. 7000, Prospectuses.
CICA Exposure Draft of a Proposed Auditing Recommendation, *Auditor's Report on Special Purpose Financial Statements Prepared on an Appropriate Disclosed Basis of Accounting other than Generally Accepted Accounting Principles* (1976). The reader should refer to

any subsequent pronouncements.
AICPA Statement on Auditing Standards No. 1, Secs. 518, 610, 620, 630, 640.
AICPA Exposure Draft of Proposed Auditing Statement, *Special Reports* (1976). The reader should refer to subsequent pronouncements.

19.5 Questions and problems

Review and discussion
1. What is the purpose of a prospectus?
2. List the usual components of a prospectus.
3. What purpose does a preliminary prospectus serve?
4. Why is it desirable for the auditor's report, if included in a preliminary prospectus, to be unsigned, and for the auditor's name not to appear in the signature position of his report?
5. If an auditor is willing to translate the financial statements in the prospectus from French to English or vice versa, why should he not translate all the other material in the prospectus?
6. Where an auditor is in effect reissuing his past opinions in a prospectus, what additional audit procedures should be performed?
7. What additional audit procedures are required when audited pro-forma or combined statements are to be included in a prospectus?
8. Why is a disclaimer of opinion unnecessary for unaudited financial statements included in a

prospectus?
9. In what situation would two auditors issue a combined report in a prospectus?
10. Why is it necessary for an auditor to extend the review of subsequent events from the date of his report to the effective date of the registration statement when such statement is to be filed with the SEC?
11. Give a specific example of when a pro-forma statement might usefully be included in a prospectus.
12. What is the purpose of a "comfort letter" and when does an auditor issue one?
13. When issuing a comfort letter for unaudited statements, what procedures should the accountant perform?
14. State the differences between "letters of consent" and "comfort letters".
15. Give examples of three types of "Special Purpose Reports".
16. What five items should be considered by an audi-

tor when issuing a special purpose report?

17. If a parent company with several subsidiaries has prepared only unconsolidated financial statements, how does this fact affect the audit report?

18. Discuss briefly the relationship of materiality (a) to an audit of specific elements of financial statements on which a separate report is to be given and (b) to an audit of a complete financial statement.

19. To whom may a report providing limited audit assurance be distributed?

20. Discuss how "limited" procedures should be disclosed to the readers of financial information.

21. Outline the general principles to be followed by an accountant when preparing a report on an investigation.

22. What items is it desirable to include in the covering letter accompanying an internal control/management letter and why?

23. List six types of special investigations an auditor might be requested to perform.

24. Identify and briefly discuss the factors an accountant should consider in a purchase investigation.

Problems

1. The Vice-President, Finance, has informed you, the company's auditor, that XYZ Limited is issuing a prospectus, for a debt issue, which is to be filed with various Provincial Securities Commissions.

   The draft prospectus has been prepared. It contains the audited balance sheet as at December 31, 1976, an unaudited balance sheet as at June 30, 1977, and statements of income, retained earnings, and changes in financial position for the five years ended December 31, 1976, and the six months ended June 30, 1976 and 1977. The notes to the statements as drafted are those notes which appeared in the 1976 statements.

   During 1976 the company changed its method of depreciating buildings from the declining balance method to the straight-line method. This change was adopted retroactively and was reported in the annual report for the year ended December 31, 1976. This change caused the only audit report reservation in the past five years. The change has been worked back through the income statements for the entire period covered by the prospectus.

   a) Describe the changes necessary in the notes to the financial statements as presently drafted.

   b) Prepare a draft report to be included with the filing of the preliminary prospectus.

2. Bob White has been the auditor of High Style Limited, a federally incorporated company with a July year-end, for three years. Prior to this, he provided accounting services, including the preparation of unaudited statements, and tax advice. In recent years the company has experienced a high rate of growth through the acquisition of subsidiaries, all of which are presently audited by Bob White.

   In December 1976, the President of High Style asked Bob to come to a meeting at which he informed him that the company would be making its first public offering of shares next April. The bulk of the offering would be treasury stock with the proceeds to be used to finance further expansion. An audited January 31, 1977 balance sheet and six months income statement would be required for this purpose. In addition, the President would expect considerable advice and assistance through the entire process of going public. The President asked Bob to give him a very tentative fee quotation for this service.

   After reviewing the prior year's working paper files and financial statements for High Style and its subsidiaries for the past five years, Bob phoned the President with a fee estimate of $50 000. The President was shocked; all he was asking for was a six month statement and some other help and the regular audit fee, which included a full range of tax services, for the immediate preceding year was only $35 000 for the consolidated group.

   Assuming that Bob's estimate was fair, outline the points that he might include in a letter to the President explaining his fee estimate.

3. The Discipline Committee of your Provincial Institute has asked you to develop a peer review program for use in the review of medium-sized CA firms that provide auditing, accounting and tax services. Prepare a review program which would take about 100 hours to perform which reviews adherence to the general and field work standards of the profession. It is not necessary in your answer to describe all the specific details of the items you would look for in the review, if any, of working paper files—merely the highlights of such an element of your program.

4. Ace Trucking Limited has been your client for a number of years. It provides public commercial vehicle services in and between four major cities in Western Canada. Internal control is excellent, sales reports are prepared on a daily, weekly and monthly basis, and operating statements prepared monthly reflect a fairly reliable measurement of operating results. The business is seasonal in nature; therefore, the number of truck drivers employed varies from week to week.

In 1977 a wildcat strike of the inter-city truck drivers closed operations for two weeks. Ace locked out its local delivery drivers, who were in the same union, but retained all other employees throughout the strike period. The Vice-President, Finance, of Ace has asked you to audit and report on the cost to the company of the wildcat strike. The report would be used as the basis of a court action against the union. He has prepared the following estimate of costs:

Estimate of sales loss (4% of actual sales for the year as audited)	$400 000
Less related direct costs (4% of drivers' salaries and benefits for the year)	(100 000)
Claims for perishable goods lost (to the extent not covered by insurance)	50 000
	$350 000

a) Describe the deficiencies, if any, in the above claim for costs.

b) Describe the procedures you would employ to determine and audit a statement of costs for purposes of the court action.

c) Describe, in general terms, the nature of your report.

5. (CICA adapted) Mr. DM has inherited BW Limited, an amusement park in a resort area near a large city, and has come to you for advice on changes which should be made in the management control and information systems presently in operation. The elderly gentleman who previously prepared the annual financial statements and tax returns for the 15 years the park has operated died four months ago, shortly after Mr. DM inherited the park. Mr. DM will not require a full audit examination of the company by you, but wants you to prepare unaudited financial statements for him in the future. Mr. DM has made all the records available to you for your current investigation.

Mr. DM has noted that while the amusement park as a whole has shown a modest profit over the past three years, profits have been steadily declining. In examining the operating statements, prepared at the company's fiscal year-end of July 31, he has not been able to discover the reasons for this decline.

Your examination of the records and your other review procedures reveal the following background information:

The amusement park operates 5 months a year from May to September and has four main sources of revenue:

- general admissions;
- amusement rides;
- two food outlets, one a busy food booth, the other a cafeteria;
- a parking lot.

There are separate revenue and detailed expense accounts for each of these areas; in the case of the rides, there is a further breakdown of this information for each ride.

All employees handling cash are bonded.

a) *General Admissions*
Admission to the well-fenced grounds, at $1.00 for adults and 50¢ for children, is by way of pre-printed tickets bought from a cashier at the gate and handed to a gate-keeper on the way in. The number of adult and child tickets is reconciled with the cash turned in daily by the office staff. Since the tickets are then destroyed to prevent their being reused, the preprinted numbers are not accounted for.

There are approximately 5 000 admission tickets given free to local youth organizations each year. No accounting has been made of this in the books of account. These tickets (which are identical to the tickets sold but are overprinted "FREE") are deducted from the total tickets turned in on the ticket reconciliation.

b) *Amusement Rides*
Admission to the rides is gained by depositing money in cash-collecting boxes similar to those used on municipal buses for the collection of fares. The boxes are set up at the entrance to each ride, and the ride operators are responsible for ensuring that people are not allowed on a ride unless they have put their money in the box. The ride operators are given the incentive to promote their particular rides on the midway and to show a profit for them by being paid, in addition to their wages, a commission of 7% of their gross sales. No other employees in the park obtain commissions.

The revenue is collected, as is all park revenue, by outside security men at the close of business each day.

c) *Food Outlets*
Purchasing of food and supplies has been handled for years through an outside purchasing consultant, who acts for other clients in the food business and offers better prices through bulk-buying, and who has a thorough knowledge of the trade. He is paid a commission of 5% of the cost of the goods he purchases. When the consultant submits his invoices for reimbursement, these are checked by the office staff to pre-numbered receiving reports prepared and signed by the head

564

cook at each location showing the quantity received each day; when these are reconciled and the numbers accounted for, payment is made to the consultant.

Analysis of the gross profit percentage of each outlet for the past few years shows some fluctuation, but the total remains stable for the two outlets and the internal difference is explained by the office staff as being from food transfers between outlets.

Staff may eat at either outlet in the amusement park free of charge; no record is made of this.

d) *Parking Lot*

The parking lot is used primarily by visitors to the park. Revenue is controlled by pre-numbered time-tickets, which the office staff reconciles daily with cash and for which all numbers are accounted; issue of new time-tickets to the parking lot from the office is also strictly controlled. The lot is very closely supervised by the parking foreman, a long-time employee who has never missed a day of work.

e) *General*

The park produces its own electricity for the operation of various rides on its midway. All other power used is purchased from the local public utility. Each building and ride has a separate meter showing the amount of electricity used and its source.

An account in the general ledger called "non-revenue assets" contains the cost of the electrical generating plant and machinery, and the employees' living quarters. These staff quarters are small bungalow-type dwellings and the $50 received monthly from each of the sixty units throughout the full year is merely intended to offset repairs and maintenance. Furniture in the houses is owned by the tenants. Since the "non-revenue assets" were not considered by the company to be related to any of the sales areas, no depreciation has been recorded in the books. All direct expenditures for these overhead areas, including the cost of electricity bought from outside as well as the rental income credits from cash received, are posted to one "general expenditure" account, which is deducted on the financial statements in total from the total departmental income of the other areas in arriving at income before income taxes.

All the other assets are in separate ledger accounts, with sub-ledger accounts for individual rides. Depreciation is calculated for each asset and charged to the appropriate department.

Areas which are not mentioned in detail, including the accounting offices, have been found

by you to have satisfactory internal control and information systems.

Required:
1. Prepare a memorandum for Mr. DM in a 2 column format—suggested change or improvement, reasons.
2. Draft the covering letter to DM.
3. How would your report in (1) and (2) differ if it was being issued to the company banker?

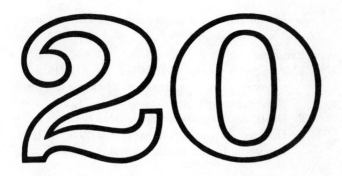

20

Association With Unaudited Financial Information

The subject of unaudited financial information may seem out of place in a textbook on auditing. However, the questions of what responsibilities, standards, procedures and reporting apply to non-audit engagements are sufficiently related to the analogous questions with respect to audits that they are usually included in any comprehensive treatment of auditing topics.[1]

A public accountant's practice may include a number of types of non-audit engagement: tax assistance, insolvency work, EDP services, etc. The non-audit engagements raising questions most nearly analogous to auditing matters, however, are those which involve the provision of *accounting services to clients in the preparation or review of unaudited financial information*. Most practitioners have some recurring engagements of this type. For many it constitutes a major portion, and for some, almost all of their practice. The purpose of this chapter is to consider the responsibilities, standards, procedures and reporting applicable to such accounting engagements. Unaudited financial statements included in prospectuses, however, were discussed in Chapter 19. The question of financial forecasts or projections is considered in Chapter 21.

20.1 The nature of an accounting engagement

An engagement to provide accounting services differs markedly from an audit engagement. In an audit engagement the auditor undertakes to examine financial statements (or sometimes other assertions) in accordance with generally accepted auditing standards and, based on sufficient appropriate audit evidence, to express an audit opinion on them. The auditor's report adds *audit credibility* to the representations made by management. All the other chapters of this book are directed to such engagements. In an accounting engagement, on the other hand, the public accountant's function is not to provide credibility to statements prepared by others but to perform certain accounting services, which may include:

1. providing advice to his client on accounting matters (e.g., accounting policies to be adopted, accounting procedures to be used),
2. preparing accounting records (e.g., writing up books of account manually, preparing monthly records and statements using his or a data centre's computer),
3. preparing or assisting in the preparation of unaudited financial statements or other unaudited information (either interim or annual; either for distribution to shareholders, bankers, governments, and regulatory authorities or for the client's internal use only),
4. performing a review of unaudited financial statements or other unaudited information after preparation by the client (on behalf of management, the board of directors, the shareholders or other parties).

The objective of the fourth category comes closest to sounding like a restricted type of audit (compare to limited special purpose engagements in 19.3.3). However, accounting engagements are considered to provide only *accounting credibility* – the credibility associated with an accountant who has performed his accounting work carefully, not the degree of credibility provided by an auditor who has sought corroborating evidence to support an opinion on the financial statement assertions. In an accounting engagement the public accountant does not seek to meet generally accepted auditing standards – though he may sometimes choose to perform *a few* of the same procedures as might be found in an audit. In an accounting engagement the public accountant does not express an audit opinion on the financial statements – though he may make certain comments, accompanied by an explicit disclaimer of opinion.

Unaudited financial statements versus other unaudited financial information

In the course of his work a public accountant often prepares or assists in preparing records or schedules which are not financial statements or parts of financial statements. Examples are (a) the client's books of account; (b) related schedules such as trial balances, bank reconciliations, accounts receivable listings; (c) schedules for filing in tax returns or other governmental returns, such as capital cost allowance schedules and reconciliations of net income to taxable income; and (d) various analyses for management use, such as sales analyses. It would be impractical to suggest that such records or schedules should all be marked "unaudited" (though such labelling may occasionally be employed on some schedules) or to prescribe specific responsibilities with respect to them. Accordingly, the CICA Recommendations with respect to non-audit engagements (Handbook Section 8100) do not apply to such records and schedules. In preparing such records and schedules the public accountant should, however, observe the Rules of Professional Conduct – in particular, the requirements to perform his services with integrity and due care (see 3.2.2), to sustain his professional competence related to such services (see 3.2.3), and to avoid association with any letter, report, statement or representation which he knows, or should know, is false or misleading (see 3.2.5). A practitioner's relationship to unaudited financial information (other than statements) appearing in a company's annual report accompanying financial statements he has audited was discussed in 17.5.5.

Where, however, the public accountant in Canada is involved with unaudited *financial statements,* certain additional responsibilities may apply as discussed in sections 20.2 to 20.6. Unaudited financial statements for this purpose are defined in the CICA Handbook as:

> those statements which have not been audited and which present or could be considered to present:
> a) the financial position, results of operations and changes in financial position of an enterprise or a part thereof (i.e., a complete set of financial statements); or
> b) one or more but not all of the financial position, results of operations and changes in financial position of an enterprise or a part thereof (i.e., part of a complete set of financial statements).[2]

Thus, for example, the unaudited balance sheet of one division of a company would be an unaudited financial statement – because it is a *complete* statement, though of only *part* of an enterprise. On the other hand, an unaudited statement of long-term debt and an unaudited statement of manufacturing overhead, even if titled as "statements", would be only unaudited schedules according to the foregoing definition – because they are only *parts* of complete statements of financial position and results of operations.

Engagements involving unaudited financial statements can be further divided, as discussed later in this chapter, into *review engagements* and *non-review engagements.* The former involve an enquiry-based review while the latter do not. The two types differ also in the form of communication to readers. Certain general responsibilities remain applicable to both types of engagement. The division of non-audit engagements into review and non-review categories differs from practice in the United States – where review responsibilities are not prescribed except with respect to certain engagements involving interim statements.

Situations to which the additional responsibilities do not apply

Excluded from the specific responsibilities prescribed for certain cases of involvement with unaudited financial statements are: statements in connection with an insolvency practice, interim statements to public shareholders, and comparative figures.

Unaudited financial statements in connection with an insolvency practice

Statements prepared by, or with the assistance of, a public accountant acting in his capacity as trustee in bankruptcy, receiver or liquidator, are usually prepared on a liquidation basis[3] and include other types of statement such as statements of affairs, statements of practitioner receipts and disbursements, and various financial summaries. The Bankruptcy Act imposes certain reporting obligations on a practitioner in insolvency work which may conflict with the type of reporting suggested for other non-audit engagements. The practitioner's responsibilities with respect to unaudited statements in insolvency engagements require further consideration by the profession. They are, however, beyond the scope of this chapter. The practitioner should again be guided by the Rules of Professional Conduct.

Unaudited financial information in interim reports to public shareholders

The considerations discussed in sections 20.2 to 20.5 do not necessarily apply to unaudited financial information contained in interim financial reports to shareholders of public companies. Section 8100 of the CICA Handbook specifically excludes such information pending further study. Interim financial reports to public shareholders are discussed in 20.6.

Section 8100 *does* apply to other unaudited interim financial statements. Interim financial reports are commonly in a summarized form (e.g., summarized results of operations, summarized changes in financial position and no balance sheet). It could be argued that summarized reports, being incomplete, do not represent financial statements.[4] Such an argument seems somewhat strained. To most readers of the interim reports, the reports probably "could be considered to present" results of operations, etc. and accordingly the provisions of Section 8100, subject to the considerations with respect to public companies discussed in 20.6., would apply.

Unaudited comparative figures in an audit engagement

A practitioner may be engaged to audit and report on the current year's financial statements in a case where the prior year's statements were unaudited. If the prior year's comparative figures appearing alongside the current year's audited statements were not prepared by the practitioner, he is not associated with them and need not issue accountant's comments thereon. However, the comparative figures should be clearly labelled as unaudited and, desirably, a third explanatory paragraph in the auditor's report should state that they were not examined by a public accountant (see 23.3.2).

20.1.1 The concept of association

The public accountant is not necessarily involved in every communication of financial data by his clients. However, where he prepares a set of financial statements or lends his name to such statements, other parties will associate him with the statements and perhaps accord them greater credibility as a result. For this reason, certain responsibilities are placed on the public accountant when he is *associated* with unaudited financial statements *as a whole*.

The CICA Handbook defines association as follows:

> Association with unaudited financial statements as a whole exists where the public accountant:
> a) prepares unaudited financial statements, whether or not the statements have been prepared on plain paper and whether or not they are accompanied by a transmittal letter; or
> b) uses his name or consents to the use of his name on or in connection with unaudited financial statements.[5]

Association by preparation

When the public accountant has prepared the complete set of unaudited financial statements himself, his association according to the foregoing definition is clear. However, if his services are limited to typing or reproducing the statements on the client's stationery or on plain paper, association does not exist. If his services are limited to advice on accounting matters or consultation or assistance in determining a particular financial statement figure, association again does not exist with the statements as a whole. Sometimes an engagement originally contemplated to include only limited advice grows to include assistance in determining many or all major financial statement figures. Assistance, even when extensive, does not result in association with the statements as a whole. However, the public accountant is well advised in such cases to document his services at the completion of the engagement to make it clear that they involved assistance only and not preparation of the financial statements.

Association by use of the public accountant's name

When financial statements appear on the public accountant's stationery, are accompanied by comments signed by the public accountant, or appear in a document disclosing the public accountant's involvement (with his consent), association according to the foregoing definition is clear — at least, with respect to readers of the statements or documents in which the accountant's name appears. The definition, however, leaves open the question as to whether it is possible for the public accountant to be associated with the statements with respect to one reader but not with respect to another. For example, suppose a banker asks a public accountant to perform a non-audit review of a corporate borrower's unaudited financial statements prepared by the borrower (a non-public company). The accountant will certainly be associated with the unaudited statements which he subsequently submits to the banker with accompanying accountant's comments. Presumably, however, he would *not* be associated with other copies of the statements, neither prepared by him nor bearing his name or comments, circulated by the company to its shareholders — and without such association those other copies would not need to bear a disclaimer of opinion. Were the CICA Recommendations to cover interim reports to shareholders of public companies (which, as this book goes to press, they do not), similar questions would frequently arise with respect to interim reviews conducted for management or boards of directors (see 20.6).

Responsibilities where association does not exist

Where the public accountant is not associated with a set of unaudited financial statements as a whole, he is responsible only for the exercise of due professional skill and care in the services he performs for his client. Thus, if he has given advice or assistance in accounting matters and such advice or assistance was recklessly given, the accountant cannot escape responsibility merely on the grounds that he is not associated with the statements. He remains responsible to his client for the professional services he performs. Such responsibilities would not normally extend to third parties.

The public accountant should also ensure that he has a clear understanding with his client that his services will not be communicated to third parties receiving the client's unaudited financial statements and that his name will not appear in documents containing those statements. Such communication would be inconsistent with the absence of association and could lead a reader to mistakenly infer association and to accord the statements a greater degree of credibility than may be warranted. Similarly, the accountant should not use his name or stationery when his services have been limited to typing or reproduction of the statements. If the public accountant is aware that his name is, improperly, to be communicated to others, he should advise those planning the communication appropriately:

> If the public accountant is not associated with unaudited financial statements as a whole and is aware that his name is to be used in connection with such statements, he should advise the parties responsible that he has not consented to the use of his name and request that his name not be used. [CICA Handbook][6]

569

Responsibilities when association does exist

When the public accountant is associated with unaudited financial statements as a whole, the greater credibility which readers of the statements may accord to them places certain responsibilities on the accountant (general responsibilities, reporting responsibilities, and, in many cases, review responsibilities) as described in the following sections.

> Where the public accountant is associated with unaudited financial statements as a whole, he should meet the responsibilities, as appropriate, for either a review engagement [see 20.4] or a non-review engagement [see 20.5], and should attach the appropriate communication to the statements. [CICA Handbook][7]

Association and responsibilities in the United States

In the United States the concept of association is slightly broader than in Canada. In addition to situations covered in the Canadian definition, association in the United States includes instances where the public accountant "submits to his client or others . . . unaudited financial statements where he has . . . *assisted* in preparing [emphasis added].[8] On the other hand, the defined responsibilities are less in that, except for review engagements for interim reports (see 20.6.4), the AICPA pronouncements do not require review procedures.

20.2 Terms of the engagement

The importance of a clear understanding with the client as to the terms of a non-audit engagement was discussed in 4.2.4. In some instances the client may not be sure of the services he requires. He may not understand the differences between audited and unaudited financial information both in terms of reliability and in terms of procedures employed thereon by the practitioner and attendant costs. The practitioner should help his client to understand these differences and to choose the services which best fulfill his requirements. If non-audit services are chosen, the practitioner should do his best to ensure that his client understands their limitations.

A written letter of engagement is highly desirable. The absence of such a letter contributed in part to the findings against the practitioner in the *1136 Tenants* v. *Rothenberg* case in the United States in 1965 (see 5.1.2). The CICA Handbook provides that:

> For non-audit engagements, the public accountant should reach an understanding and agreement with the client as to:
> a) the services to be provided by the public accountant;
> b) the fact that the client will supply the information necessary to permit the public accountant to carry out such services;

> c) the fact that the client will be responsible for the accuracy and completeness of such information;
> d) the fact that such services are not intended to, and accordingly will not, result in the expression of an opinion on the financial statements or the fulfilling of any statutory audit requirements;
> e) the restrictions, if any, regarding communication to third parties concerning the public accountant's involvement with the financial statements; and
> f) the anticipated form and content of the written communication to be attached to the financial statements.[9]

Where the client is a limited company and there is a statutory audit requirement, a non-audit engagement will not discharge that requirement. Where a public accountant has been appointed auditor he should not accept the limitations implicit in a non-audit engagement (see 18.2.3). Where no auditor has been appointed but the public accountant has been asked to undertake a non-audit engagement, he should refer his client to the provisions of the applicable Corporations Act. He may also wish to suggest that the client seek legal advice concerning the statutory obligations. Examples of engagement letters for review engagements and non-review engagements are given in 20.4.6 and 20.5.5.

20.3 General professional standards

Whether or not the non-audit engagement involves a review, certain general standards should be observed in all cases of association with unaudited financial statements:

> In all non-audit engagements, the public accountant should meet the following professional standards:
> a) ensure that the services are performed, and any accompanying communication is prepared, by a person

or persons having adequate technical training and proficiency in accounting, and with due care; and
> b) ensure that the work is adequately planned and properly executed and that, if assistants are employed, they are properly supervised. [CICA Handbook][10]

Such standards are the counterparts, for non-audit engagements, of the general standard and first field work standard in generally accepted auditing standards. The counterpart of the second field work standard does not exist, for there is no obligation in non-audit engagements to conduct a study of internal control. Modified counterparts of the third field work standard and of the reporting standards differ as between review engagements and non-review engagements and are discussed in the following sections.

Applying the foregoing general standards to a specific engagement to prepare unaudited financial statements, whether or not the non-audit engagement involves a review, the general responsibilities of the public accountant can be said to be:

1. to receive accounting data from the client and, using that data, to prepare draft financial statements which, to the best of his knowledge, are complete and in good accounting form (in accordance with the appropriate basis of accounting),
2. to submit the draft statements to the client (the final statements must remain the representations of the client),

3. to report to the client any accounting deficiencies in the statements of which he is aware or any unresolved problems with respect to the satisfactory completion of his engagement,
4. to attach the appropriate form of communication to the statements.

The differences between review and non-review engagements involve:

1. the intended distribution of the statements (whether a wide general distribution or a restricted distribution to certain classes of knowledgeable users for special purposes),
2. the procedures, if any, which the accountant should apply to the accounting data received from the client apart from using it to prepare the statements (whether an enquiry-based review or merely notice of any information which he should know is false or misleading),
3. the format, wording and general tone of the communication to be attached to the statements.

These differences are discussed in the following sections.

20.4 Review engagements

Most non-audit engagements where the public accountant is associated with unaudited financial statements are review engagements (the restricted circumstances in which non-review engagements can be accepted are described in 20.5). Readers of the statements may place some additional reliance on them because of the known involvement of the accountant and a limited, enquiry-based review by the accountant is a useful service in these circumstances.

20.4.1 Professional standards for review engagements

The enquiry-based review adds further *accounting credibility* to the financial statements. To be effective, the review must be coupled with some background knowledge of the business. The CICA Recommendations establish the following professional standards for review engagements:

When undertaking a review engagement, the public accountant, in addition to complying with [the general professional standards described in 20.3], should observe the following professional standards:

a) possess or acquire the amount of knowledge of the business carried on by the enterprise that a public accountant should reasonably be expected to have so that he can make intelligent enquiry and assessment of information obtained;
b) perform a review, consisting primarily of enquiry, comparison and discussion, with the limited objective

of considering whether the information provided to him relative to the financial statments and the statements themselves are plausible in the circumstances. Such a review does not require:

 i) a study or evaluation of internal controls; or
 ii) an exmaination of evidence as to representations made or information supplied to him, except where such representations or information are not plausible; and

c) determine, so far as he knows and based on information provided to him and the review carried out by him, whether the financial statements appear to be in accordance with generally accepted accounting principles (or in special circumstances the appropriate disclosed basis of accounting) consistently applied.[11]

Knowledge of the business

In order to conduct a meaningful enquiry-based review and to assess the plausibility of the financial statement presentation, the public accountant must have a reasonable background knowledge of his client's business. The accountant's knowledge of the business would not be expected to be as great as that provided by an audit base (see 9.2 and 24.4.1 for the corresponding step of gaining familiarity with the client's business in an audit). The accountant should, however, be aware of the general organization of his client's business, the principal assets and liabilities, and the main types of revenue and expense. He should also be familiar with accounting principles and procedures applicable to the business or to the industry in which it operates.

When, for example, he seeks explanation for differences from prior periods' results, he must be able to distinguish explanations which make sense from those which do not. He does not need to verify, or seek corroborating evidence for, the explanations obtained as in an audit. However, if an explanation offered is, on the face of it, incomplete, contradictory or inconsistent with the accountant's knowledge of the circumstances, he must make further enquiries and, in some cases, seek additional evidence to resolve his doubts as to its plausibility.

Review objective

The term *review*, as it is used in the CICA Handbook in connection with non-audit engagements, refers to a review consisting primarily of enquiry, comparison and discussion. It should be distinguished from:

1. the "review" called for with respect to unaudited financial statements in prospectuses, which contains certain steps such as a review of minutes and an obtaining of general satisfaction with the reliability of the accounting records (see 19.1.3) not necessarily required in a review for plausibility,
2. the "limited review" of interim financial information referred to in AICPA pronouncements, which includes a reading of minutes and more extensive analytical review procedures (see 20.6) than necessarily required in a review for plausibility,
3. the "review" of systems and controls constituting one of the four major elements in an interim audit (see 9.2),
4. the audit technique of "analytical review" (see 10.5.2), though some analytical review procedures may be included in the comparisons made during a review for plausibility.

The public accountant's objective in a review engagement is:

> the preparation, for his client, of financial statements which are plausible in the circumstances (or the review of client-prepared financial statements to consider whether they are plausible in the circumstances).[12]

The concept of *plausibility* in a non-audit engagement is to be distinguished from the concept of *reasonable assurance,* which applies to the gathering of evidence in an audit. Financial statements are plausible if they appear worthy of belief based on the information obtained by the public accountant in connection with his review. Plausibility does not, however, rule out the possibilities of undetected error or deception. (Indeed, such possibilities are present even in a full audit, but with a much lower probability).

The logic of calling for the public accountant to conduct a review as to plausibility is that such a review

is implicitly part of financial statement preparation by a conscientious chief accountant or comptroller. A chartered accountant employed as chief accountant or comptroller of an enterprise would not just enter numbers on the statements indifferent to their likely accuracy. (If he did, he would not be meeting the ethical requirement to avoid association with misleading statements – see 3.2.5 – which applies to chartered accountants both in public practice and in industry.) Rather, his inside knowledge would be used to assess the plausibility of the data he received from other sources, and to call for further explanations where he was unsatisfied. The public accountant cannot be expected to have the degree of inside knowledge of a chief accountant or comptroller. Nonetheless, to the extent that he provides a form of comptrollership service to clients lacking the necessary skills in their permanent staff, it is reasonable that he assume responsibility for making some of the assessment of plausibility which would be expected in such a service if performed by an employed chartered accountant.

Basis of accounting employed

The fact of being unaudited does not change the basis of accounting on which financial statements should be prepared. General purpose statements, whether audited or unaudited, should be prepared in accordance with generally accepted accounting principles. It should be noted, however, that generally accepted accounting principles include certain differences in presentation with respect to *interim* statements compared to annual statements. For example, in the case of *interim* financial statements sent to shareholders, Accounting Recommendations in the CICA Handbook Sec. 1750, Interim Financial Reporting to Shareholders, permit certain data to be summarized, the balance sheet to be omitted, and certain other changes to be made in adapting the annual accounting basis to the interim period. Special purpose statements, whether audited or unaudited, may be prepared in accordance with an appropriate disclosed basis of accounting (see 19.3.1).

The difference between audit engagements and non-audit review engagements is thus not in the criteria by which the statements are judged but in the degree of assurance demanded from the judging process – reasonable assurance for the former but merely plausibility for the latter.

20.4.2 Review procedures

The CICA Handbook suggests that review procedures for the limited objective of assessing plausibility should consist primarily of:

a) enquiries concerning financial, operating, contractual and other information, and consideration of information received in response thereto;

b) comparisons of the current and prior period financial information and consideration of the reasonableness of financial and other relationships; and

c) discussions with responsible client officials concerning information received and the financial statements.[13]

Generally, the enquiries and comparisons should cover as *broad* an area as in an audit (i.e., covering each of cash, receivables, inventories, investments, fixed assets, etc.) but not in the *depth* nor degree of detail involved in an audit. Many practitioners find it convenient to use certain planning forms and checklists[14] to ensure that all appropriate enquiries are made. In preparing or answering such planning forms or checklists, terms such as audit, verification and examinatnion should not be used as they are inappropriate to the limited objective of a non-audit review. In some engagements the accountant may wish to consider supplementing his enquiries with a letter of representation from management.

Procedures performed do not change the objective of the engagement

All of the foregoing procedures are also used in audit programs. Enquiry of management and employees was discussed in 10.4.7. Comparisons and correlation with related information were discussed in 10.5.1. Moreover, the accountant may sometimes perform additional procedures, similar to audit procedures, when specifically requested by his client or when the information he has obtained in the course of his review appears implausible. Some practitioners, for example, may decide to make limited checks of bank reconciliations, confirm major accounts receivable balances, and make certain other tests. The practitioner has no obligation to perform such procedures (except when specifically called for by the terms of his engagement).

The performance of some procedures similar to those in an audit does not change the character or objective of a non-audit engagement. The objective of an engagement is determined by the terms agreed to when it is accepted (or, in the case of audits, often imposed by law or regulation) and not by the nature of the procedures conducted. The objective of a non-audit review engagement is the preparation of financial statements plausible in the circumstances (or a review as to the plausibility of client-prepared statements) and this objective is not expanded to an audit objective merely because some of the procedures performed are the same as those in an audit.

The CICA Handbook provides:

> . . . if the public accountant in assessing the plausibility of information provided decides to perform additional procedures which he might also carry out in an audit engagement, this does not convert the non-audit engagement to an audit engagement.[15]

In the United States, in contrast, the AICPA pronouncements provide that, while the original purpose of the engagement is one factor in determining the nature of the engagement, other factors such as the procedures actually performed may also have an influence and could, in some circumstances, cause the nature of the engagement to change.[16]

Procedures performed to resolve doubts as to plausibility

Non-audit review engagements do not require examination of external evidence (physical inspections, confirmations with third parties), tests of accounting records or documents, or analysis of systems and controls. However, the CICA Handbook provides that the accountant may decide to supplement his enquiries with some of these procedures where he has reason to doubt the plausibility of information supplied to him.[17] This provision is rather open-ended and how far the accountant should go in performing audit-type procedures in an attempt to resolve doubts as to plausibility is not entirely clear. Certainly, if his doubts are not resolved he must report them (see 20.4.5), but how far should he go before concluding that such a report must be given? The Handbook implies he should proceed until "it is completely impractical to obtain satisfactory information".[18] To this writer, it seems reasonable to conclude that because a non-audit review is primarily enquiry-based, the accountant should only be considered to have an obligation to attempt to resolve any doubts as to plausibility by making further enquiries. In most cases, further enquiries would likely be sufficient to establish whether the information previously obtained was or was not plausible. If such further enquiries are unable to resolve his doubts, however, he should be entitled to report that a satisfactory review was impractical – for, indeed, a review of the type originally envisioned, and for which the accountant was engaged, has proven inadequate to establish plausibility. He *may*, though he need not, resort to examinatnion of external evidence, tests of records, etc. to resolve his doubts. In practice, moderate use of such procedures to resolve doubts is probably common but such use, in the writer's view, can be considered discretionary rather than mandatory. The reader should refer to subsequent pronouncements or current literature for further guidance in this difficult area. Usually, a decision to perform discretionary procedures would be discussed with the client in advance, unless already covered in the terms of the engagement. If the accountant does decide to perform certain discretionary procedures, he should perform those procedures with due care. If the results of such procedures indicate certain conclusions, the accountant should consider those conclusions in assessing the plausibility of the financial statements.

In the United States, the discretionary nature of such extended procedures would seem to be indicated by certain AICPA pronouncements:

> The certified public accountant has no responsibility to apply any auditing procedures to unaudited financial statements.[19]

though it is less clear in other pronouncements.[20]

Additional procedures performed at the client's request

A client may sometimes ask the accountant to perform certain additional procedures in what is still a non-audit review engagement. For example, if there have been discrepancies in accounts receivable, the client may ask the accountant to confirm some or all of the accounts as an accounting service (to locate balances with disagreements) and not as an auditing service to permit an expresison of opinion. There is rather a fine line between such circumstances and those in which limited, agreed-upon procedures are performed to provide limited credibility for special purposes (see 19.3.3). The distinction lies in the type of communication sought from the accountant.[21]

20.4.3 Accountant's comments

To indicate the work he has done (a review), the responsibility he is taking (by implication, due care in completing the review), and the responsibility he is not taking (no audit and no expression of opinion), "accountant's comments" should be attached to unaudited financial statements with which the accountant was associated in a review engagement.

> The public accountant's communication accompanying unaudited financial statements relating to a review engagement should clearly convey the limited nature of his involvement with the statements. The communication should be entitled "Accountant's Comments" and should:
> a) identify the financial statements;
> b) state who prepared the financial statements;
> c) indicate the source of the information used in the preparation of the financial statements when these have been prepared by the public accountant;
> d) state that a review was performed and briefly describe its nature;
> e) state that an audit has not been performed and disclaim an opinion;

> f) Not express any form of negative assurance.
> The communication should be phrased to avoid possible confusion with an auditor's report and accordingly:
> a) should not refer to the public accountant as auditor;
> b) should not use the word "report"; and
> c) should not include an opinion on the financial statements or any part thereof. [CICA Handbook][22]

Where additional explanations or modifications, as discussed later, are not required, it is desirable that a standard wording be used for the accountant's comments. Such usage helps the reader to identify important modifications and unusual circumstances when they occur. The standard wording suggested by the CICA[23] for use where the accountant has prepared the statement is:

ACCOUNTANT'S COMMENTS

I have prepared the accompanying balance sheet as at (date) and the statements of income, retained earnings and changes in financial position for the (period) then ended from the records of (name of company) and from other information supplied to me by the company. In order to prepare these financial statements I made a review consisting primarily of enquiry, comparison and discussion, of such information. However, in accordance with the terms of my engagement, I have not performed an audit and consequently do not express an opinion on these financial statements.

City   (signed) . . . . .
Date   Chartered Accountant

The standard wording suggested[24] instead where the accountant has consented to the use of his name in connection with unaudited financial statements but has not prepared them is:

ACCOUNTANT'S COMMENTS

I made a review of the accompanying balance sheet as at (date) and the statements of income, retained earnings and changes in financial position for the (period) then ended which were prepared by (name of company). My review consisted primarily of enquiry, comparison and discussion of information supplied to me by the company. However, in accordance with the terms of my engagement, I have not performed an audit and consequently do not express an opinion on these financial statements.

City   (signed) . . . . .
Date   Chartered Accountant

The foregoing standard wording does not make reference to generally accepted accounting principles or to an appropriate disclosed basis of accounting – presumably, to avoid a superficial similarity with the wording of an audit report. However, it would seem desirable that the financial statements themselves disclose by note the basis on which they have been prepared.

In addition to bearing the foregoing accountant's comments, the financial statements should be specifically marked as unaudited.

Each page of the financial statements should be conspicuously marked unaudited. [CICA Handbook][25]

Where the client has requested additional procedures to be performed he may wish to have a written report on those procedures. Such a report should not be included in the accountant's comments prepared for general distribution as it might lead a reader to attach more credibility to the unaudited statements than might be warranted.

> If the public accountant undertakes work in addition to the preparation or review of unaudited financial statements, any communication with respect to that work should not be included or referred to in the accountant's comments or in the financial statements. [CICA Handbook][26]

The separate communication of the additional procedures (for a restricted readership) was discussed in 19.3.3.

In the United States, since AICPA pronouncements do not require review procedures for unaudited statements (except in review engagements for interim reports – see 20.6.4), the standard disclaimer of opinion simply states that the "accompanying balance sheet of . . . were not audited by us and accordingly we do not express an opinion on them."[27] If the practitioner is not independent with respect to his client, AICPA pronouncements call for the disclaimer to be prefaced by a clause disclosing that fact.[28]

20.4.4 Known accounting deficiencies in review engagements

The accountant should report any accounting deficiencies of which he is aware to his client. Where they are not corrected, certain additional disclosures are required in his "Accountant's Comments".

In the case of audit engagements, reservations for accounting deficiencies (departures from generally accepted accounting principles or, for special purpose reports, from an appropriate disclosed basis of accounting) were discussed in 18.2.1 and 18.3.1. and consistency exceptions or explanations were discussed in 17.5.1. Analogous principles apply to non-audit review engagements. The differences are that:

1. In audit engagements accounting deficiencies can be categorized as either *known errors* encountered or *most likely errors* projected during the examination of audit evidence, if material; in non-audit review engagements accounting deficiencies are limited to *known errors* encountered during the conduct of the review or otherwise known to the accountant, if material.

2. In audit engagements accounting deficiencies lead to reservations of opinion; in non-audit review engagements there is no opinion being expressed in the first place but the accountant should disclose the known accounting deficiencies, if material – taking care in so doing not to imply an opinion with respect to the remaining items.

In a review engagement where the public accountant concludes that unaudited financial statements are not in accordance with generally accepted accounting principles (or in special circumstances the appropriate disclosed basis of accounting), he should request that appropriate amendment be made. Failing amendment, he should clearly disclose in his comments the fact and nature of the departure from generally accepted accounting principles and, if known, the effects on the statements. If the effects are not readily determinable, he is not obligated to determine them but should indicate in his disclaimer that the effects were not determined. Each page of the statements should be referenced to the accountant's comments.

If the client will neither agree to the amendment, nor attach to the unaudited financial statements the accountant's comments clearly disclosing the departure from generally accepted accounting principles, the public accountant should refuse to be further associated with the statements. [CICA Handbook][29]

Disclosures of accounting deficiencies should be made in a second paragraph of the accountant's comments. For example:

Management has informed [me] that the investment in (name), a subsidiary company, is recorded at cost in the accompanying unaudited financial statements. In this case, generally accepted accounting principles require that the financial statements be prepared on a consolidated basis. The effects of this departure from generally accepted accounting principles on the accompanying unaudited financial statements have not been determined.[30]

Where unresolved problems preclude the accountant from completing a review, he should not simply dissociate himself from the statements but rather disclose the problems in his comments as just discussed. Where, however, the client refuses to attach the accountant's comments, an accountant may decide that he must dissociate himself from the statements. In that case he should write to his client explaining why he cannot continue the engagement. He may wish also to obtain legal advice as to his responsibilities, if any, to the client or to third parties. Finally, he would usually consider discontinuing his relationship with that client.

The requirements in the United States with respect to known accounting deficiencies are generally similar to the Canadian ones just described.

20.4.5 Inability to complete a review

Occasionally, the accountant may be unable to assess the plausibility of the financial statements because certain figures are based on very broad estimates. Such a situation may occur, for example, with respect to some interim statements where it is not economic for the client to make the accounting determinations required at a year-end. A similar situation may occur where it is impractical for the accountant to resolve doubts as to plausibility which have arisen during the course of his review (see 20.4.2). The accountant should report unresolved problems to his client. In addition, certain disclosures are required in his "Accountant's Comments", as discussed in the following paragraphs.

The inability to complete a review in a review engagement is analogous to an auditing deficiency or an uncertainty in an audit engagement. The differences are:

1. In an audit engagement, the deficiencies or uncertainties are those which remain unresolved after a full program of audit procedures; in a review engagement, the deficiencies or uncertainties are those which remain unresolved after an enquiry-based review. Thus, an uncertainty remaining after a review engagement might be resolvable were a full audit to be performed, but the accountant is not obligated to perform a full audit to resolve deficiencies or uncertainties encountered in a review.
2. In an audit engagement, what constitutes a deficiency or uncertainty is defined in relation to the objective of obtaining reasonable assurance; in a review engagement, what constitutes a deficiency or uncertainty must be judged in relation to the less stringent standard of plausibility. Thus, a condition which would fail to meet the criterion of reasonable assurance were an audit opinion required, might yet be sufficiently plausible to be accepted in a review.

If, because there is an unavoidable lack of information or because it is completley impractical to obtain satisfactory information, the public accountant is unable to complete his review and is thus unable to decide whether the statements are plausible in the circumstances, he should modify his comments both to state clearly the reasons for his inability to complete his review and to convey an appropriate warning concerning information in the financial statements which may require adjustment. Each page of the statements should be referenced to the accountant's comments. [CICA Handbook][31]

Disclosure of an inability to complete a review should be made in a second paragraph of the accountant's comments. For example:

Management has informed us that the company was unable to determine physical quantities of logs and lumber on hand due to severe snow conditions at the balance sheet date. They also advise that these inventories are stated at the amount determined at the end of the previous fiscal year (date) since no reliable accounting or other records exist to make a reasonable estimate of the amount of this inventory. Accordingly, adjustments may be required which would materially affect the amounts shown for inventory, cost of goods sold, income taxes, net income and retained earnings.[32]

In the preparation of unaudited statements, particularly unaudited interim statements, accounting estimates may often be based on less precise and less objective data than used in the preparation of audited annual statements. Gross profit percentages may be estimated since physical inventory is taken only once a year. Provided that the accounting estimates are reasonable and plausible, they can be accepted in a review engagement. However, where estimates are completely arbitrary and may be subject to overwhelming error, the accountant must usually disclose an inability to complete a review, as just discussed.

Occasionally, the deficiencies and uncertainties may be more widesrpread than in the foregoing example. The accountant may wish to warn the reader that statements may not include all necessary adjustments or disclosures and thus may be incomplete. If, in the extreme, the accountant believes that the statements, even when accompanied by such a warning, could mislead a reader, he should dissociate himself from the statements.

20.4.6 Engagement letter for a review engagement

Typical wording for an engagement letter for a new engagement involving the preparation and review of unaudited financial statements by the public accountant is as follows:

Mr. A. Smith,
President,
A. Smith Company Limited,
Any City,
Canada.

Dear Mr. Smith:
Following our discussion of May 10, 1976, I thought it would be useful to summarize my understanding of the terms of my engagement as your accountant, and to outline the nature and extent of the services I will be providing.

I drew to your attention that under the [name of act] Corporations Act the appointment of an auditor is required. Should you not appoint a statutory auditor, you may wish to take legal advice concerning the relevant statutory obligations. Since I am accepting this engagement as accountant, rather than as statutory auditor, you should not record this as an audit engagement in your minutes nor at any time refer to me as being auditor of your company.

[Or, instead of the preceding paragraph, the following one.]

I understand that you are of the opinion that your company qualifies under [specific section of the Act] for exemption from the audit provision of that Act. In order to obtain this exemption it is necessary that each shareholder consent in writing to the non-appointment of auditor each year and I understand that you will arrange to obtain this consent. Since I will be accepting this engagement as accountant rather than as statutory auditor I request that you do not record this as an audit engagement in your minutes nor refer to me in any way as being the auditor of the company.

The following services are to be performed under the terms of my engagement:

1. I am to prepare, without audit, annual financial statements based on accounting records and other information which you will provide to me and discussions with you and other appropriate persons in your company. Prior to issuance, I will submit these statements to you for approval and acceptance since the final financial statements must be the representations and primary responsibility of company management. To such statements I will append "Accountant's Comments" which will normally be in the following form where the statements have been prepared in accordance with generally accepted accounting principles:

   [Form suggested in 20.4.3 would be inserted here.]

   The review outlined in the above Accountant's Comments does not involve auditing procedures such as examination of documents, physical inspections of assets (particularly attendance at physical inventory), confirmation with external parties or evaluation of internal controls. The review is therefore not designed to and would not, except by chance, disclose material errors in the financial statements nor any defalcation or irregularities should any such exist. I will not express an opinion on the financial statements.

2. I am also to provide the services set out below [modifications as necessary]. Any report with respect to such additional services will be a separate communication to you.
   • to carry out such bookkeeping services as I find necessary preliminary to the preparation of the financial statements [or description of additional bookkeeping services to be performed],
   • to carry out a limited review of your accounting methods and financial affairs, and to discuss such suggestions and recommendations as I consider appropriate with the officers or directors,
   • to prepare the necessary Federal and Provincial income tax returns with supporting schedules,
   • to examine income tax assessment notices,
   • to advise on income tax matters generally,
   • to discuss with the income tax department any matters concerning your taxes, as arranged with you from time to time.

If you have any questions regarding, or disagreements with respect to, any part of this letter, I would be pleased to discuss them with you further. I appreciate the opportunity to be of service to your company.

Yours very truly,

John Doe
Chartered Accountant

The wording in the foregoing example covers the basic points suggested in the CICA Handbook[33] together with the following additional ones:

a) the provision for the audit exemption situation (alternate second paragraph),
b) a reference to what a review does *not* include (last paragraph in point 1),
c) emphasis that the statements remain the representations of management (the accountant may suggest certain year-end adjustments and a certain set of draft financial statements based on the facts known to him; client management in accepting the adjustments and in adopting the draft statements, must consider whether their own more intimate knowledge of the business includes awareness of facts, perhaps not previously disclosed to the accountant, which call for modifications),
d) omission of the provision for client signature (in the writer's view, the requesting of such a signature may often be unnecessarily formal and can be replaced by the negative assurance obtained if the client does not report any disagreement as requested in the final paragraph).

Each practitioner must decide what form of letter best meets his requirements. In addition, any engagement letter should be personalized to relate to the circumstances of the individual client. It may, for example, be desirable to specify the deadline for completion of the assignment, the extent to which client employees will be available to assist the practitioner in certain procedures, and other details of the working arrangements.

In the case of a non-corporate client, the second paragraph or its alternate, in the foregoing example, would not be required.

In a recurring engagement the engagement letter should be reissued either annually or at least every three or four years. Where a letter is being reissued, the first paragraph of the foregoing example might be replaced with wording such as the following:

In order to avoid any misunderstandings with respect to the regular work I do for you each year, I believe it is desirable upon occasion to summarize my understanding of the terms of my engagement as your accountant.

20.5 Non-review engagements

In some non-audit engagements the review procedures called for in review engagements are not necessary for the special purposes of the users. Therefore, in certain specified circumstances these review procedures may be omitted. A common example is accounting records and monthly statements prepared on an accountant's computer from transaction data submitted by his client. Such monthly statements may be exclusively for use by management within the client's organization. It would not be worthwhile to have the accountant conduct a probing enquiry-based review with respect to each month's statements. However, the communication accompanying the statements in such non-review engagements should make the accountant's lesser involvement clear. Moreover such statements should be restricted to informed readers who will not be misled as to the extent of the accountant's involvement.

The CICA Handbook also explains that certain users (such as management in the case of monthly statements) may not need all the disclosures normally required for general use. While this point is true, the practitioner should remember that restricted disclosure does not have to imply a non-review engagement. Sometimes a review engagement may involve special purpose statements prepared in accordance with an appropriate disclosed basis of accounting and lacking some of the disclosures required by generally accepted accounting principles. Restricted disclosure, if suitable for the special purpose of the statements, is not *in itself* reason for a non-review engagement.

20.5.1 Criteria for acceptance of non-review engagements

If an accountant is preparing (a) unaudited statements with a review or (b) audited statements once a year for general distribution, it seems logical that monthly statements without a review should be permitted for a restricted set of informed readers (such as management or bankers) who have access to more information if they need it. This concept is reflected in the CICA criteria:

> In certain non-audit engagements (described as non-review engagements in this Section), the public accountant need not meet the Recommendations for review engagements set out in [20.4.1] if, in his judgment, both at the time of accepting the engagement and during the conduct of it:
> a) he has no reason to believe that the information supplied to him for the purpose of preparing the financial statements is false or misleading; and

> b) he has an understanding with the client and believes that:
>   i) the users of the statements are either within the enterprise concerned or are specific third parties who are aware of the possible limitations of the financial statements;
>   ii) no external user need place undue reliance on the statements because he could have access to further information if desired;
>   iii) the statements will be used only for the purpose agreed in the terms of engagement and will not, without the agreement of the public accountant, be made available to other parties; and
>   iv) additional statements will be prepared (usually annually) which include the period covered by the non-review statements and which are subject to either a review engagement or an audit (except that this particular requirement does not apply when the statements are to be prepared and used only for the purposes of meeting client requirements to submit information to governments and regulatory authorities).[34]

The logic behind the special exception for statements submitted to governments is not entirely clear but, as a practical matter, statements prepared solely for filing with tax returns have for many years been exempt from any review requirements – perhaps on the grounds that the government has its own staff for reviewing, and where desired auditing, tax return information.

The foregoing criteria should be agreed to by the client before the accountant undertakes the engagement.

> If the public accountant believes it is appropriate to prepare unaudited financial statements without review, the agreement with the client should also recognize the substance of the conditions to be met by both of them, as set out [in the foregoing criteria]. [CICA Handbook][35]

20.5.2 Professional standards for non-review engagements

Although review procedures may be omitted, the accountant should still perform his own work with care and, in preparing the statements, should not accept data which he knows or should know is false or misleading. The CICA Recommendations establish the following professional standards for non-review engagements:

> Because of the nature and limited objectives of non-review engagements, the public accountant is not required to meet the Recommendations set out in [20.4.1] for review engagements; however he should:
> a) meet the [general] professional standards outlined in [20.3]; and
> b) based on the information provided to him, prepare financial statements which are, so far as he knows, suitable for the purposes intended.[36]

20.5.3 Notice to reader

To indicate his very limited involvement with the statements, a "notice to reader" should be attached to unaudited financial statements with which the accountant was associated in a non-review engagement.

> The public accountant's communication accompanying unaudited statements resulting from a non-review engagement should be entitled "Notice to Reader" and should convey the nature of his involvement with the statements and the very limited responsibility he assumes. The communication should be placed on each page of the statements (or each page should be conspicuously marked "Unaudited – see Notice to Reader"). The notice to reader should:
> a) state the nature of the work done;
> b) state the restriction on use;
> c) state that the public accountant did not audit, review or otherwise attempt to verify the accuracy or completeness of the statements;
> d) employ wording which is distinctly dissimilar to that in other forms of disclaimer or report; and
> e) not express any form of opinion or negative assurance. [CICA Handbook][37]

The standard wording suggested by the CICA[38] for use in non-review engagements is:

NOTICE TO READER

This statement has been compiled solely for (indicate specific use, for example, income tax) purposes. I have not audited, reviewed or otherwise attempted to verify its accuracy or completeness.

City   (signed) . . . . .
Date   Chartered Accountant

The concept of two classes of disclaimers (accountant's comments and a notice to reader) does not exist in AICPA pronouncements in the United States. The same form of disclaimer, which includes no reference to a review, is used for all engagements (except in the case of interim statement reviews – see 20.6.4). However, where special purpose statements are prepared for internal use only and do not include all the detailed disclosures otherwise required, AICPA pronouncements call for an additional sentence in the disclaimer "to the effect that the financial statements are restricted to internal use by the client and therefore do not necessarily include all disclosures that might be required for a fair presentation in conformity with generally accepted accounting principles."[39]

20.5.4 Known accounting deficiencies in non-review engagements

Despite his very limited involvement with the unaudited statements, the accountant may sometimes become aware of known accounting deficiencies in their preparation. Unaudited statements in non-review engagements are, by definition, restricted special purpose statements. As such, accounting deficiencies would usually be gauged in relation not to generally accepted accounting principles but to an appropriate disclosed basis of accounting. The accountant should report any accounting deficiencies of which he is aware to his client. Where known accounting deficiencies are not corrected, disclosure in the notice to reader would almost inevitably overstate the degree of the accountant's involvement with the statements. In such cases, he should instead dissociate himself from the statements.

> In a non-review engagement where the public accountant is aware that there are specific accounting deficiencies which would cause the statements to be materially mis-stated for the purposes intended, he should request that appropriate amendment be made. Failing amendment, he should refuse to be further associated with the statements. [CICA Handbook][40]

20.5.5 Engagement letter for a non-review engagement

Typical wording for an engagement letter[41] for a new engagement involving the preparation of unaudited financial statements by the public accountant without a review is as follows:

> Dear Mr. Smith:
>
> I will compile, without audit, review or other verification as to accuracy or completeness, financial statements for each of the months January to November, 1976. To such statements I will append a "Notice to Reader" which, unless unanticipated difficulties are encountered, will be in the following form: [see suggested form in 20.5.3].
>
> It is understood and agreed that:
> a) these financial statements will be used only within the Company and by Mr. Black, manager of [branch and name of bank] and will not be made available to other parties without my agreement;
> b) the above users understand the possible limitations of these financial statements and need not place undue reliance on them because they have access to further information; and
> c) I will prepare without audit, but with a review, financial statements for the year ending December 31, 1976.
>
> Yours very truly,
>
> John Doe
> Chartered Accountant

In some circumstances, a more expanded engagement letter may be desirable. For example:

> Dear Mr. Smith:
> In order to avoid any misunderstandings with respect to the regular work I do for you each year, I believe it is desirable upon occasion to summarize my understanding of the terms of my engagement as your accountant.
>
> Each month I process by computer the information supplied by you and provide you with a listing of this

information, a general ledger, and financial statements in the form agreed to by you. I do not audit, review or otherwise attempt to verify the accuracy or completeness of the financial statements other than to scrutinize them from a management viewpoint and pass along to you any observations I believe to be pertinent. To such statements I append a "Notice to Reader" which, unless unanticipated difficulties are encountered, is in the following form:

[See suggested form in 20.5.3.]

You have undertaken to ensure that the accounting data supplied to me is accurate and complete. Inasmuch as I do not perform an audit on the information submitted, I may not necessarily discover mistakes that may be in the data.

Although it is obviously desirable to detect and eliminate any errors before the financial statements have been prepared, you should review your statements and other output as soon as you receive it as an additional check that there appear to have been no omissions or errors in the input. My statement scrutiny may bring to light significant errors but it is unlikely that less significant errors will be detected. If you should discover any errors in the statements, you have undertaken to advise me promptly so that I can make the necessary corrections. Of course, if material mistakes are located or suspected, I will not be able to release the financial statements until such items have been corrected or clearly noted on the statements.

It is understood and agreed that:
a) these financial statements will be used only within the Company and will not be made available to other parties without my agreement;
b) the above users understand the possible limitations of these financial statements and need not place undue reliance on them because they have access to further information;
c) I prepare without audit, but with a review, financial statements at the end of the fiscal year.

Since I am accepting this engagement as accountant, not as auditor, I request that you do not record this as an auditing engagement in the minutes of your shareholders' meetings. My services will not result in the expression of an opinion on the financial statements or the fulfilling of any statutory audit requirements. If you do not appoint auditors, you may wish to obtain legal advice concerning the relevant statutory obligations.

To assist me in checking that all information supplied to me has been accurately processed, you provide me with certain control totals each month. [Some detail should be given to identify the control information that is to be provided].

You also provide me with new cost of sales percentages [if applicable] and new values for the Management Operations Report [if applicable] whenever the existing percentages or values are changed. Until I receive new amounts from you I use the existing ones and assume that no changes have occurred.

In order to receive your interim statements promptly each month you have also agreed to supply me with all the necessary input data by the tenth working day of each month. Any delay in delivering the data to me may require me to re-schedule the computer processing and delay the delivery of the statements and other output to you.

Yours very truly,

John Doe
Chartered Accountant

20.6 Interim financial reports of public companies

The 1976 revisions made to CICA Recommendations on Unaudited Financial Statements (Section 8100) specifically excluded from its provisions unaudited financial information contained in interim financial reports required by statute or regulatory authority to be issued to shareholders of public companies. The reason for the exclusion was that widespread reporting to the public raises additional considerations which may warrant further study. Therefore, whether or not a company's regular auditor is deemed to be associated with its interim reports to shareholders, he does not presently have a professional obligation to make a review of such statements or to attach accountant's comments. On the other hand, if he chooses to conduct such a review and attach accountant's comments he is not presently precluded from expressing negative assurance therein. As this book goes to press, interim reporting to shareholders of public companies is under study by the CICA and the reader should refer to any subsequent pronouncements. The present Recom-

mendations do, however, cover reports on interim statements of non-public companies. In the United States, following an SEC release in 1975, the AICPA issued pronouncements in 1975 and 1976 providing for (a) limited reviews of interim financial information and (b) reports thereon.[42] Subject to the effect of future developments in this area, the considerations outlined in the remainder of this chapter would seem relevant to practice in Canada.

Desirability of practitioner involvement

It is desirable for the auditor to encourage his public clients to involve him in a consultation or review capacity before they issue their interim financial statements. The auditor of a company's annual financial statements can provide a useful service in assisting in the resolution of interim reporting problems. Furthermore, as a practical matter, it makes sense to identify and resolve accounting problems at an interim date rather than to face changes at the

580

year-end in an accounting practice previously established in publicly issued interim statements.

The annual auditor's involvement with respect to the interim statements may take one of several forms:

1. informal consultation on specific matters,
2. informal consulting engagement with respect to the interim financial statements as a whole,
3. formal review engagements.

It is important that the client (i.e., management, the board of directors, the audit committee, as appropriate) fully understand and be in agreement with the nature and extent of the annual auditor's involvement and the responsibilities to be assumed. In particular, the client should appreciate the limitations inherent in a consulting or review engagement. The three gradations of involvement are discussed in the following sections.

20.6.1 Informal consultation on specific matters

Some public companies may request only that their auditor be available, as accounting adviser, to consult on specific problems which may arise in the course of their preparation of the interim financial statements. In such cases, the auditor's responsibility is limited to giving advice on the particular issues raised by the client. He is not associated with the statements. His informal consultation should lead to no report on the interim statements as a whole, either written or oral. An engagement letter for such services would not be necessary.

20.6.2 Informal consulting engagement with respect to interim financial statements as a whole

Other public companies may request their auditor, as accounting adviser, to read the interim financial statements, perhaps perform certain review procedures, and report orally thereon to management. Sometimes a letter of comment might be requested on specific accounting or disclosure matters arising from the accountant's review or on which the accountant's advice is desired. It seems reasonable to conclude that an annual auditor accepting such a consulting engagement would not be associated with the statements[43] since he has not prepared them, is not lending his name to them, and is not formally reporting on them. It would be inconsistent with such informal arrangements for the accountant to report, either orally or in writing, to the board of directors or audit committee. (If such reports are desired, more formal arrangements should be made – see 20.6.3.)

An informal letter confirming the accountant's understanding of the engagement may be desirable but a formal engagement letter would not seem necessary.

The informality of such a consulting engagement may save time and be less costly than a more formal review, but it carries with it an increased risk that the accountant's involvement will be misunderstood. It is therefore especially important that the auditor take reasonable steps to ensure that mangement understands his involvement and its very limited scope.

20.6.3 Formal review engagements

Some public companies may wish to have their auditor perform a review of the interim statements, as an accounting service, and report thereon to the board of directors or its audit committee, usually in writing. In such cases it seems reasonable to conclude that the accountant is associated[44] with the interim statements with respect to the directors or audit committee though not, unless he lends his name to the published interim reports, with respect to the shareholders or other parties.

Normally, it would seem desirable for an accountant to accept a formal engagement to review and report upon published interim financial statements only when he has an audit base – that is, where he has audited the annual financial statements of the preceding year.

Review procedures

Because of the accountant's association, the review procedures described in 20.4.2 would seem desirable as a minimum. Certain additional procedures are suggested for purposes of the *limited review* described in AICPA Statement on Auditing Standards No. 10, *Limited Review of Interim Financial Information*. While the objective of the AICPA limited review is described as "to provide the accountant with a basis for reporting to the board of directors on those matters that he believes should be brought to its attention, based upon . . . inquiries and analytical procedures" rather than the CICA objective of assessing plausibility, the two objectives are not inconsistent. The additional procdures suggested in the AICPA statement are not required for Canadian review engagements but some practitioners may wish to apply them.[45] The procedures additional to the Canadian requirements include:

1. enquiring about (a) accounting systems involving the recording, classifying and summarizing of transactions for purposes of the interim statements and about (b) significant changes in internal controls since the last annual audit, which

might affect the interim statements,

2. reading the minutes of shareholders, the board of directors, and various committees of the board,
3. obtaining letters from investee accountants conducting reviews of the interim statements of significant investees.

Furthermore, some of the procedures referred to in the CICA pronouncements are spelled out in more detail in the AICPA ones. For example:

1. Comparisons are described in terms of an analytical review involving:
   - comparison of the current and immediately preceding periods and of the current and corresponding prior year periods,
   - study of the interrelationships that would be expected to conform to a predictable pattern based on past experience,
   - consideration of past types of accounting adjustment.
2. Enquiries are described in terms of enquiries[46] as to:
   - generally accepted accounting principles and consistency,
   - changes in business activities or accounting practices,
   - questions raised by the foregoing procedures,
   - material subsequent events.

Reporting to management, directors or audit committees

The recommended form of accountant's comments where the accountant has made a review of client-prepared unaudited statements was described in 20.4.3. However, such accountant's comments, by implication, are intended for reports to be circulated outside the reporting entity – reports to which the accountant is "lending his name". Such an implication is supported by the fact that a subsequent recommendation states that special reports on additional procedures performed at the client's request should not be included in the accountant's comments (by implication, for outside distribution) but rather in "a separate communication *to the client* [italics added]".[47]

Reports to management, the directors, or the audit committee can be interpreted as such a separate communication to the client and can therefore contain a list of, or reference to, the procedures performed. By inference, this separate communication to the client could also differ from accountant's comments for outside parties in other ways.[48] Specifically:

1. The reference to who prepared the statements is unnecessary since the client knows this fact.

2. Negative assurance should not necessarily be precluded, provided the distribution of the report is restricted to the client.

Accordingly it is suggested that a special report to management, the directors, or the audit committee contain the following elements:

1. identification of the interim financial data reviewed, including the name of the client, and the date of the financial statements;
2. an adequate description of the procedures performed or a reference to an engagement letter in which the procedures are listed;
3. a statement that the procedures described are less extensive than those constituting an audit, and would not necessarily disclose adjustments or disclosures which should be given effect in the interim financial information or which may be determined to be necessary as a result of the practitioner's examination of the annual financial statements;
4. a statement that, since the procedures do not constitute an audit, no opinion is expressed;
5. a description of the results of the practitioner's review – that is, a statement of matters which he feels should be brought to the attention of those to whom he is reporting, or a statement to the effect that no such matters came to his attention (a form of negative assurance);
6. an expression, if requested and if warranted by the review made, of the stronger form of negative assurance commonly used in other comfort letters ("nothing came to my attention which caused me to believe that the unaudited financial statements do not present fairly . . . " – see 19.2.2),
7. a statement that the report is solely for the information of the addressee, and is not to be quoted or referred to in any document setting forth the unaudited financial information or made available to anyone who is not an employee or a director of the company.

An example follows of report wording containing all of these elements except the sixth.

[Date – completion of procedures]

[Addressee – member of management, board of directors, or audit committee, etc. as appropriate]

I have performed the procedures outlined in my letter of [date] describing my engagement with respect to the unaudited [describe data or statements subject to review] of [company name] for the quarterly and year-to-date periods ended [date]. With respect to [subsidiary/ investee names] I read letters from other accountants reporting on their reviews of the interim financial information of such companies.

Since my review did not constitute an examination made in accordance with generally accepted auditing standards, I do not express an opinion on the unaudited interim statements referred to above.

In connection with my review, and that of the other accountants referred to above, the following [no] matters came to my attention which I believe should be reported to you:

[Matters which should be brought to the attention of the addressee(s).]

Since the procedures described above are less extensive than those constituting an audit, they would not necessarily reveal adjustments or disclosures which should be given effect in the interim financial statements, or which may be determined to be necessary as a result of my examination of the company's annual financial statements.

This letter is solely for your information and is not to be quoted or referred to in any document setting forth the unaudited interim financial information or made available to anyone who is not an employee or director of the company.[49]

It is prudent for the accountant to review the subsequent minutes of the board of directors' or audit committee meeting at which his report was presented. If he is not satisfied that they express accurately the points he made, he should write to the board to put those points on record.

The foregoing type of report would only seem appropriate for restricted reports to management, directors, or audit committees. If, for example, a report is required on interim statements for a banker, creditor, etc., accountant's comments in the form described in 20.4.3 would seem desirable (though Section 8100 may technically not apply).

Engagement letter

Because of the accountant's association, it is desirable that an engagement letter be prepared. Typical wording, subject to modification to fit individual circumstances, might be as follows:

[Client official or board of directors
or audit committee, as appropriate]
[address]

Dear Sir:

I appreciated having an opportunity to meet with you to discuss the nature of my services with respect to the company's unaudited quarterly financial statements for quarterly and year-to-date periods ending March 31, June 30, and September 30 each year. I take this opportunity to outline the nature of my services to be performed in that connection.

As discussed with you, I will perform the following procedures:

1. Read the unaudited interim financial statements and consider on the basis of information coming to my attention, whether the statements appear to meet regulatory requirements and generally accepted accounting principles.

2. Read the minutes of meetings of shareholders, directors, the executive committee and the audit committee.

3. Make an analytical review, consisting of:
   - a comparison of current interim financial information in trial balances supporting the interim financial statements with that of the immediately preceding period, with the corresponding period of the previous year, and with budgetary information for the current period;
   - consideration of the interrelationships of the above information; and
   - consideration of the types of matters that have required accounting adjustments in the preceding year or quarters.

4. Enquire concerning (a) the accounting system as it relates to the recording, classification and summarization of the interim financial information, and (b) any significant changes in the system of internal control which may affect the preparation of interim financial information.

5. Enquire of officials of the company having primary responsibility for financial and accounting matters concerning:
   - whether the interim financial information has been prepared in accordance with generally accepted accounting principles, consistently applied;
   - changes in the company's business activities and accounting practices;
   - any matters as to which questions have arisen in the course of applying the above procedures; and
   - events subsequent to the date of the interim financial statements that would have a material effect on the presentation of such information.

6. Obtain written representations from Mr. Smith, the president, and Mr. Jones, the vice president finance, with respect to the above and certain other matters.

7. Respond to such questions as you may raise with respect to accounting, disclosure, or reporting matters regarding the unaudited interim financial statements.

8. Perform such other procedures or consider such other matters as you may request.

These procedures are significantly less extensive than an audit. Among other differences, they do not contemplate a study and evaluation of internal control; tests of accounting records and of responses to enquiries by obtaining corroborating evidential matter through inspection, observation or confirmations; and other procedures ordinarily performed during an audit.

Upon completion of these review procedures, I will communicate in writing to [management, the board of directors, the audit committee].

It is understood that:
- The quarterly financial statements will be labelled "unaudited".
- The procedures set out above would not necessarily reveal adjustments or disclosures that should be given effect in the quarterly financial statements, or may later be determined to be necessary as a result of my examination of the annual financial statements.
- My report will include a statement of any matters which I feel should be brought to your attention, or a statement that no such matters came to my attention. Since my review procedures will not constitute an examination in accordance with generally accepted auditing

standards, my report will disclaim an opinion on the quarterly financial statements.

- The report is solely for the information of the addressee(s), and is not to be quoted or referred to in any document setting forth the unaudited interim financial information, or made available to anyone who is not an employee or director of the company.

If information comes to my attention which leads me to question whether the interim financial statements are materially in error or not in accordance with generally accepted accounting principles, I will inform Mr. Smith and enquire as to any further action which you may wish me to undertake.

If you have any questions or disagreements with the contents of this letter, please raise them with me. I appreciate the opportunity of continuing to be of service to your company.

The procedures listed in the second paragraph of the letter should, of course, be modified as appropriate. (For example, they might also include obtaining reports from accountants of specified subsidiaries/investees and the visiting of specified locations if accounting records are maintained at multiple locations.)

20.6.4 Public reporting to shareholders

Although the present CICA Recommendations do not cover reports on interim financial statements issued to shareholders of public companies, it would seem undesirable to adopt a contrary reporting format until Recommendations on this subject have been issued. Indeed, any public reporting by accountants on interim statements of public companies would seem undesirable until such Recommendations have been issued. If pressed, however, a practitioner should presumably be prepared to issue accountant's comments in the form described in 20.4.3, provided that the necessary review has been performed.

An exception to this position must be made where a Canadian practitioner has clients which are subsidiaries or other investees of U.S. companies or which are themselves registered with the SEC. For such clients the Canadian practitioner, where requested, would normally accept engagements in accordance with the requirements of AICPA Statement on Auditing Standards No. 10 to perform a limited review and report thereon in the recommended format[50] to a parent/investor company's management or its auditors, provided that he has obtained appropriate approvals from Canadian company management. Likewise, he would normally be prepared to issue a report to shareholders or to the SEC in the forms recommended by AICPA Statement on Auditing Standards No. 13 provided that the relevant requirements had been met. The AICPA suggested form of reporting to shareholders is as follows:

> We have made a limited review, in accordance with standards established by the American Institute of Certified Public Accountants, of (describe the information or statements subjected to such review) of ABC Company and consolidated subsidiaries as of September 30, 19x1 and for the three-month and nine-month periods then ended. Since we did not make an audit, we express no opinion on the (information or statements) referred to above.[51]

The concept of "limited review" is relatively new and the practitioner involved with U.S. reporting, particularly with respect to SEC registration statements, should refer to current AICPA pronouncements on the subject.[52]

The subject of interim reporting continues to be controversial. Some practitioners are concerned with the foregoing form of report because it may imply negative assurance without stating it; others believe that a better warning is needed as to possible undisclosed adjustments along the lines of the non-public report described in 20.6.3.

20.7 Reference material

CICA Handbook, Sec. 8100, Unaudited Financial Statements.
AICPA Statement on Auditing Standards No. 1, Sec. 516, Unaudited Financial Statements.
AICPA Statement on Auditing Standards No. 10, *Limited Review of Interim Financial Information.*

AICPA Statement on Auditing Standards No. 13, *Reports on a Limited Review of Interim Financial Information.*
AICPA *Guide for Engagements of CPAs to Prepare Unaudited Financial Statements* (1975).

20.8 Review and discussion questions

1. Contrast the nature of public accountants' association with audited and unaudited financial statements.

2. List typical accounting services provided by public accountants.

3. Certain non-attest engagements are excluded

from the CICA Handbook, Section 8100, requirements. List a few of these and explain why they are excluded.

4. In what circumstances is a public accountant not associated with a client's financial statements?

5. What are the public accountant's responsibilities when accounting services are provided, but he is not associated with the financial statements as a whole?

6. Compare in detail the importance of engagement letters for attest and non-attest services.

7. Compare the general and field work standards for audit engagements with the professional standards for non-audit review engagements.

8. What are the essential differences between a review and a non-review engagement?

9. Compare the term "plausibility" with the term "reasonable assurance" within the context of the work of a public accountant.

10. Identify the procedures an accountant employs in assessing plausibility and compare these procedures with similar ones performed on an audit engagement.

11. Under what circumstances, if ever, should an accountant resort to intensive investigation (e.g., seeking out external evidence) when he is involved in a review engagement of annual unaudited financial statements?

12. Describe the public accountant's course of action if, in a review engagement, he becomes aware of material non-compliance with generally accepted accounting principles.

13. Describe the public accountant's course of action if, in a review engagement, he becomes aware that a number of significant figures have been determined on a purely arbitrary basis by the client because no objective means of determination is practical at the interim date.

14. The example engagement letter in 20.4.6 covers several additional points which are not discussed in the CICA Handbook, Section 8100. Identify these additional points and describe the reasons why they are desirable in an engagement letter.

15. Describe, for both review and non-review engagements, the differences between accountants' reports in Canada and the United States.

16. Discuss the current position of the CICA with respect to interim statement reviews for shareholders.

17. Describe three possible levels of auditor involvement with interim reports. For each case, give reasons why you consider such involvement to be desirable or undesirable.

The Future

The purpose of this chapter is to identify and describe briefly some of the possible future developments in auditing scope, practice and technique. Some of these possible developments are the extension of trends which are already evident and which have been discussed elsewhere in this book. In these cases, the present chapter merely identifies the topic, refers to the chapter in which it is discussed, and in some cases comments on its possible applicability to the future. Other possible developments, while already much debated in the profession, represent changes which have not yet occurred (at least in Canada), which may or may not occur, and which have not been discussed elsewhere in this book. In these cases, the present chapter discusses the question at greater length.

While many future developments are possible, they are not equally probable. For example, audit reporting on management integrity may never happen. It may be an idea which is undesirable in principle and unworkable in practice. But, as an idea which has been suggested[1], it warrants the profession's attention. Only by considering possible future public expectations can the profession hope to encourage those trends which it believes desirable, to resist those which it believes both undesirable and preventable, and to prepare for those which it believes inevitable.

The profession has already conducted a number of studies of possible future developments. In 1969 the CICA established Task Force 2000 "to determine what the future role of the chartered accountant should be . . . and what policies should be established by the organized profession to allow present and future members to fulfill those roles". In the following year the *Report to the Executive Committee and Council of the CICA by Task Force 2000* was issued (referred to in this chapter as the Task Force 2000 Report). In 1974 the AICPA established a Special Commission on Auditors' Responsibilities. In the following year its *Statement of Issues: Scope and Organization of the Study of Auditors' Responsibilities* was issued (referred to in this chapter as the AICPA Commission Statement of Issues). The final report of the Special Commission is in preparation as this book goes to press and may well have a profound effect on the profession's future course of action.

Future challenges and opportunities are of particular interest to a young profession. As the Task Force 2000 Report stated:

> Almost half of the chartered accountants in Canada today will still be under normal retirement age in the year 2000; in 1990, three-quarters of today's members will not have reached the age of sixty-five.[2]

Most of today's chartered accountants will, during the course of their careers, encounter conditions markedly different from the present – including, undoubtedly, many developments not foreseen at the time of writing of this chapter.

21.1 Auditor responsibilities and public expectations

Auditor responsibilities under present legal requirements and professional standards were discussed in Chapter 4. For some time, there have been advocates for the assumption of greater responsibilities by the auditor. The growth of consumerism has, in the words of some accountants and lawyers, created an "expectation gap" between the levels of performance envisioned by the public accountant and expected by the public. Such a gap may be divided into three components:

> A gap between performance and expectations may be caused in part by substandard performance under present responsibilities, in part by users' reasonable expectations that auditors accept additional responsibilities, and in part by users' unreasonable expectations.[3]

Ensuring adequate performance under existing responsibilities

With the recent wave of litigation in the United States (and to a lesser extent in Canada), with the activist attitude of the SEC, and with the forthcoming report of the AICPA Commission, the immediate future is likely to see considerable efforts to ensure adequate performance under existing responsibilities. Some of the areas investigated by the AICPA Commission were[4]:

1. National licensing and disciplining of external auditors – perhaps less likely to be a concern in Canada,

2. Quality control reviews– Many accounting firms have internal quality control programs. Voluntary peer reviews by other firms, by institute staff, or by public review boards have been a feature of U.S. practice for the last few years. Canadian practitioners occasionally request voluntary peer review by provincial Institute/Order staff and some mandatory review programs exist, for example in Quebec, but neither practice is widespread. Widespread mandatory peer review seems likely in the United States within a few years' time though its real effectiveness may be open to question.

3. Auditor appointments – including the possibiltity of rotation of auditors on some systematic basis and the question of alleged conflicts of duty between audit and consulting services,
4. Clarification of the fairness/GAAP question – see 17.3,
5. Clarification of the responsibility for detection of fraud – see 6.8.1,
6. Clarification of the auditor's role in evaluating uncertainties – see 18.2.4,
7. Clarification of the responsibility for detecting and disclosing adverse management behavior – see 32.4.13 re questionable payments,
8. Auditing methods and techniques, including clarification of the auditor's relationship to other experts – see 10.3.3 re reliance on other experts in general, 10.3.4 re reliance on other auditors, 34.7.2 re reliance on the client's solicitors.

There has also been some suggestion that time pressures lie at the root of many of the auditing deficiencies evidenced by recent litigation. In Chapter 6 it was suggested that the concept of *timeliness* justified, to a degree, some limited reduction in audit assurance. For example, pre-year-end confirmation of accounts receivable, even when coupled with extensive rollforward procedures, is normally less conclusive than year-end confirmation, but is commonly accepted in the interests of more timely issue of the audited financial statements. But the concept of timeliness should not be used to excuse inadequate verification, failure to resolve important open questions, or failure to investigate suspicious circumstances. The future may well see a modest reversal of past trends to earlier reporting dates if it is found that unreasonable deadlines have been a contributing cause of any inadequate audit performance.

Dealing with unreasonable expectations

The future is also likely to see continued efforts by the profession to correct what it sees as unreasonable user expectations. Some of the areas investigated by the AICPA Commission were[5]:

1. Clarification of the auditor's standard report in an attempt to preclude misinterpretations or unreasonable expectations as to what an audit provides – see 17.4.2, particularly with respect to communication of the concept of materiality,
2. The legal environment – including the question of limitation on monetary damages, explored in various countries but not considered very likely in the near future.

Extension of the auditor's role

Whatever the results of the foregoing two approaches to the expectation gap, improving the performance under present responsibilities and dealing with unreasonable expectations, the future will undoubtedly see an extension of the auditor's role into new areas. Some of the possible reporting areas investigated by the AICPA Commission were[6]:

1. accounting for social costs and benefits – see 21.2.3,
2. forecasts – see 21.3.1,
3. interim and other financial information – see 21.3.2,
4. adequacy of systems, information and controls – see 21.3.3,
5. effectiveness, efficiency, competence and integrity of management – see 21.3.4,
6. non-audit reporting, including consultation and review engagements – see Chapter 20 and 19.3.3.

21.2 The effect on auditing of possible accounting developments

Auditing was defined in Chapter 1 as the process of obtaining and evaluating evidence as to the degree of correspondence between (a) assertions, such as financial statements, and (b) established criteria, such as generally accepted accounting principles. Changes in the established criteria do not change the objective of auditing – but they may affect auditing methods. Accrual accounting, for example, has called for verification steps related to non-cash assets and liabilities which would not have been required under cash-basis accounting. Current value accounting may call for yet other verification steps not now required by historical accrual accounting. The purpose of this section is not to debate the *accounting* merits of the

possible developments but to consider briefly the *auditing* implications if such developments were to occur. In extreme cases the auditing implications could in turn affect the feasibility of a given accounting proposal, if *verifiability* is accepted as one of the required attributes of meaningful accounting information (see 1.2.2).

The possible accounting developments discussed are:

1. current value and price-level accounting,
2. accounting for non-financial resources,
3. accounting for non-profit objectives.

In 1976 the CICA established a study group to investigate the objectives of financial reporting – building on the results of a similar AICPA study in 1973.[7] In the United States continuing studies of reporting objectives are being undertaken by the Financial Accounting Standards Board. It is possible that such studies may lead to fundamental revisions in accounting concepts having audit implications additional to those discussed here.

21.2.1 Current value and price-level accounting

The accounting development which seems most imminent is a move toward disclosing, either as primary or as supplementary data, the results of some form of inflation accounting. Inflation accounting, as the term is commonly used, includes both *general price-level accounting* and *current value accounting*. Both methods were discussed in a 1972 CICA Research Study.[8] It was not until the outbreak of double-digit inflation in 1974, however, that Canadian interest in these methods became significant. Strictly speaking, only price-level accounting is directed exclusively to adjustments for inflation; however, the recent interest in current value accounting has been spurred by the same inflationary distortions which price-level adjustments seek to correct. Indeed, current value accounting now seems to be the leading contender should any alternative to unadjusted historical costs ultimately prove acceptable.

General price-level accounting

As an interim measure, the CICA issued in 1975 an Exposure Draft on *Accounting for Changes in the General Purchasing Power of Money* (likely to be withdrawn) and two Guidelines, *Accounting for the Effects of Changes in the Purchasing Power of Money* (currently in process of revision) and *Auditor's Considerations when Supplementary General Price-level Restatements are Published in an Annual Report*. These documents proposed that general price-level adjustments be made by applying certain indices, such as the Gross National Expenditure Implicit Price Index, to "non-monetary" assets and liabilities. The intention was to produce supplementary common dollar financial statements, presented on a historical cost basis, but restated into units of general purchasing power. While a number of contentious accounting questions would require resolution – principally controversies over the classification of monetary and non-monetary items and the presentation of income and equity accounts – the proposed methods would present little difficulty as to auditability. The auditor would merely need to check that (a) the specified external indices had been used, (b) the adjustments

had been made in accordance with accepted principles, once established, and (c) the calculations were arithmetically correct. Transitional guidance on audit report wording (such as contained in the 1975 Auditing Guideline) would be required during the interim period until all related accounting principles were finally established and until the status of the adjusted data in relation to unadjusted financial statements was clarified. But no major changes in auditing approach would likely be required.

Auditability by itself does not, however, guarantee suitability. It now seems unlikely that pure price-level accounting will be adopted. At least eight countries have studied the method and all but one (Chile) have turned instead to a consideration of current value accounting. In Canada, few companies acted on the price-level proposals and attention is now focussed on possible current value approaches and on a CICA Discussion Paper (discussed in the next section). In the United States, an earlier exposure draft of the Financial Accounting Standards Board on price-level accounting has been overtaken by the SEC's disclosure requirements for supplementary replacement cost data, effective for the 1976 financial statements of the thousand largest registrants. In the United Kingdom, earlier price-level proposals by the profession have been overtaken by the 1975 recommendations of the government-appointed Sandilands Committee in favour of "current cost accounting" for implementation in 1978. In Australia a government-appointed committee has proposed a current value accounting system for taxation purposes and has rejected price-level accounting.

One element of general price-level accounting, however, is retained in some current value accounting proposals – the concept of "general purchasing power capital maintenance". Under this concept, shareholders' equity, prior to inclusion of the current year's income, would be restated in current dollars by applying a general price-level index. Income would be reflected only after allowing for the adjustment required to make this restatement. This element, by itself, would again present little auditing difficulty – but it relates to only one aspect of the financial statements. Individual assets, liabilities and income components would be subject to current valuations as discussed in the next section.

Current value accounting

Current value accounting seeks to reflect current values on an enterprise's balance sheet – rather than historical costs or price-level restated costs. Adjustment of carrying values to current values automatically takes inflation into account, although the purely inflationary effects may or may not be separately disclosed. Adoption of current value accounting would represent the most significant revolution in accounting since the advent of the double-entry system almost five hundred years ago. The effects would be pervasive. Ultimately, its adoption could influence not only financial statement reporting but also taxation, government economic policies, and countless contractual and statutory provisions. Its study must therefore involve a far wider forum than just the accounting profession. It is premature to predict what version, if any, of current value accounting might be adopted in Canada. The possible effect on auditing can, however, be discussed in terms of some of the current proposals.

In 1976 the CICA issued a Discussion Paper on *Current Value Accounting* and, as this book goes to press, is working on a Research Study on the practical implementations of adopting this method of accounting. Appendix I of the CICA Discussion Paper summarizes recent proposals or pronouncements on current value accounting in Australia, Germany, South Africa, the U.K., and the U.S.A. and by the International Accounting Standards Committee. Proposals in those countries call for current values to be established on the basis of *current entry prices, current exit prices, discounted cash-flow values*, or, more commonly, a choice of the foregoing depending upon their interrelationship and on the type of asset, liability or income component in question. The CICA Discussion Paper itself does not make any formal proposals but discusses the various concepts involved in the many alternatives and indicates a few very preliminary and tentative preferences. The following discussion relates only to *auditability* and not to the important accounting questions as to which of the various conflicting proposals makes the best sense, presents the fairest picture, would be easiest for reporting entities to implement, or would be best understood by readers.

Auditing current entry prices

Current entry prices (prices of assets as they enter the reporting entity) have been variously defined as the replacement costs of identical used assets where a used market exists, the reproduction costs of identical new assets, or the replacement or reproduction costs of equivalent productive capacity. The CICA Discussion Paper indicated a preliminary and tentative preference for the application of current entry prices to inventories and fixed assets and suggested the following possible sources of such data:

> Current entry prices might ideally be ascertained from current supplier prices in catalogues or price lists, quotes, etc. In certain cases, however, such prices will not be available and estimates such as the following will need to be used:

specific price indices — computed by external sources (e.g., Statistics Canada)
                            — prepared internally by the enterprise

appraisals — computed by external appraisers

management estimates — computed internally by the management group.[9]

For most raw materials inventories, current supplier prices would normally be available and would in theory present little audit difficulty. The most persuasive evidence would usually be supplier invoices covering normal order quantities of the materials in question purchased just before and just after the fiscal year-end. Where purchases close to the year-end had not occurred, reference to price lists or quotations or, in some cases, direct confirmation with suppliers would be necessary. The auditor would have to ensure that the quoted prices were consistent with the terms (price and volume discounts, tax status, etc.) normally granted to the enterprise. A practical problem, however, even if up-to-date information is available, could be the time required to assemble it. In the interest of timely reporting, an enterprise might well have to estimate current prices, or the adjustment required to historical costs, by (a) checking a statistical sample of inventory items, (b) applying global factors for recent price changes, and/or (c) projecting past price trends using techniques such as regression analysis. While experimentation would be required to determine the most practical method of making these estimates in different industries, such calculation-based estimates should prove auditable, given adequate audit planning.

For purchased finished goods, the further problem arises of allowing for model and style changes. If current price quotations included improvements or impairments in quality compared to goods actually in stock, some estimate would have to be made of the dollar effect of such changes in order to arrive at a hypothetical current cost of the inventory. In many cases such estimates would likely be made by company personnel — for example, in the engineering, production or purchasing departments. If the estimates were carefully made and documented by knowledgeable employees, the auditor should be able to review their reasonableness, just as he now reviews the reasonableness of employee estimates of obsolescence. Again, these adjustments might sometimes have to be determined for only a sample of inventory items and the results projected — but such projections should again be auditable.

For manufactured finished goods and work in process, it would be necessary as well to compute labour and overhead components at current rates.

Auditing such computations would probably require the auditor to maintain a more detailed knowledge of his client's cost system than he does at present. Changes in production methods during the current year could raise some complications, but they should not prove insurmountable.

Verification of the lower input value and net realizable value would consume more time because net realizable value would be the lower figure more frequently than under historical cost accounting. More frequently the auditor would therefore have to verify precise calculations of net realizable value. At present he may often merely seek evidence that such value, if anything, is in excess of cost.

Measurement of cost of sales on a current value basis and the separation of holding gains and operating gains would require that current entry prices be determined not just at the fiscal year-end but continuously throughout the year. The mechanics of determining these prices would undoubtedly have to involve approximations throughout the year and could present very real problems for many reporting entities. While not minimizing the importance of resolving these accounting problems, in which the auditor would wish to assist his clients, it is probably fair to say that problems of a purely auditing nature would not be excessive. The timing of auditing procedures could sometimes pose difficulties. Often, however, the auditor would be able to gauge the reasonableness of the cost-of-sales approximations when verifying year-end inventory valuation.

For fixed assets, the difficulties of auditing current entry prices would be greater. Because the time lag between historical and current costs would be longer than in the case of inventories, the impact of errors or inconsistencies in estimating current values would be far greater.

The simplest case would be where no changes had occurred in either production technology (how the plant operates) or construction technology (how the plant is built). In that case, the required estimate would be the current cost of reconstructing an identical plant in a similar manner. If the estimate were made by an independent appraiser, the auditor should be able to accept the appraiser's results if he satisfied himself that (a) the assumptions made by the appraiser were appropriate, (b) the data supplied to the appraiser was correct, and (c) the type of appraisal requested of the appraiser was consistent with the accounting policies adopted for current values.[10] If the estimate were made by client personnel, the foregoing considerations would apply and in addition the auditor would usually need to review and test the details of the appraisal calculations. If the estimate were made by applying construction cost indices, the auditor would need to check that (a) the

historical costs had been accurately classified into components corresponding to the indices used, (b) the historical cost components were correctly dated, (c) the indices used were appropriate for the purpose, and (d) the calculations had been correctly made. Auditing specific price index adjustments would require more training and experienced judgment than general price-level adjustments because of the difficulty of matching the specific index to the circumstances. Where specific price indices had been developed internally by the client, the auditor would have to check (a) the accuracy of the calculations involved in preparing them and (b) the appropriateness of their weighting.[11]

The more common, and more complicated, case would be where construction technology had changed. In that case, the current cost estimates would have to be based on construction using current methods. Where an independent appraiser was used the auditor could usually satisfy himself, by enquiry, as to whether the appraisal had indeed been prepared on the basis of current methods. Where specific cost indices were used, the auditor would have to check that appropriate *output* indices had been used. *Input* indices for individual elements of construction would usually overstate total cost increases by ignoring technological changes in the manner in which such elements are now combined.[12] The availability of appropriate output indices and the means of allowing for technological change in their absence require further study. Where suitable indices or other methods are available, however, auditability should not be a major problem.

The most complex case would be where both construction and production technology had changed. If entry prices were defined in terms of productive capacity, they would have to include an allowance for the fact that assets designed to be efficient under current technology would often have a greater capacity or a lower operating cost than the assets actually in use. How such an allowance would be made, and therefore how it would be audited, is as yet undetermined. Usually, it is suggested that the lesser operating efficiency of assets actually in use be allowed for by deducting, from the reproduction or replacement cost of more efficient assets, the discounted present value of the savings they would have yielded. Estimates of savings would require the services of engineers or other experts, either within or outside the client's organization. Marginal differences in economic productive capacity could be allowed for in the same way. This approach would not likely be feasible, however, where different orders of magnitude were involved (e.g., when a modern plant would have several times the capacity of the plant actually in use).

Two accounting questions to be resolved in valuing fixed assets concern the level of aggregation and the measurement of depreciation. The first involves the decision as to whether current entry prices should be determined for the client's productive capacity as a whole or for individual units within this total. The second, and perhaps the more difficult, concerns the bases of (a) valuing accumulated depreciation and functional obsolescence and (b) providing for annual depreciation. Until further accounting research has been done on these questions it is difficult to assess any potential auditing problems. As a minimum, however, it should be possible for the auditor to assess (a) the adequacy of the disclosure of the bases actually used and (b) the consistency of their application from year to year.

Further questions arise as to the valuation of natural resource properties. To the extent that a market can be identified for such properties it could be regarded as providing both entry and exit prices. Some of the problems of auditing such market values are mentioned in the next section.

Auditing current exit prices

Current exit prices (prices of assets as they exit from the reporting entity) are usually defined as selling prices less out-of-pocket selling expenses. The CICA Discussion Paper expressed a preliminary and tentative preference for the application of current exit prices to marketable securities and to certain categories of inventory, such as obsolete goods. For most of these assets the verification of such prices is already required in connection with historical cost statements – because of the parenthetic disclosure of market values for securities and the rule of lower of cost and net realizable value for inventory. Temporary investments without quoted market values might, where material, require the use of independent experts for valuation but an auditor should be able to place reasonable reliance on such experts in most cases.

The auditing of current exit prices for natural resource properties and related expenditures would, however, present greater difficulties. The value to be audited would presumably not be the *true* value (in the sense of the value of the resources actually in the ground), for this value would only be known in the future. Rather, the value to be audited would be the *probable* value in the eyes of a reasonable investor. For producing properties, such values might be based on discounting estimated cash flows from the proven and probable reserves determined by geologists – a practice already well established for appraisal purposes in the industry, but one subject to the auditing difficulties discussed in the next section. For exploratory properties, however, that basis is not available.

Where a market existed for the properties in question, or for similar properties, the probable value would be reflected by the price other resource companies would be willing to pay. Likely estimates of such prices, in very general terms, may sometimes be known informally within the industry, but whether such estimates can be assessed objectively is another question. Although third-party evidence is normally more reliable than internal estimates, obtaining information from prospective purchasers themselves would probably be impractical. The obvious problems would be (a) the possible disadvantage of disclosing information to third parties concerning properties the client may have no intention to sell, (b) the possible unreliability of a non-binding opinion from a third party who has no intention to buy or who knows that the client has no intention to sell, and (c) the time and cost required to obtain such opinions. The more likely alternative would be to rely on periodic appraisals by consulting geologists. In general, the accounting for, and auditability of, resource values requires much further investigation.

Auditing discounted cash flow values (economic value)

Discounted cash flow values (economic values) are simply the present value of estimated future cash flows discounted at an appropriate interest rate. The CICA Discussion Paper expressed a preliminary and tentative preference for the application of discounted cash flow values to monetary assets and liabilities. For such items the future cash flow is readily determinable, except when foreign currency risks are involved, and the principal audit question is how to assess the reasonableness of the interest rate used for the discounting. A CICA Research Study on *Imputations and Discounting* is in process as this book goes to press. Within a narrow range, the choice of interest rate is bound to be arbitrary. However, it seems reasonable to suppose that workable guidelines could be established to facilitate this choice and that the auditor in any case could assess its consistency from year to year. Allowance for foreign currency risks would presumably be part of the choice of discount rate (instruments denominated in high-risk currencies generally bearing higher interest rates); for short-term items the allowance could be based on the market for currency futures.

If discounted cash flow values were to be more widely used than in the foregoing proposals, additional problems would have to be solved. For non-monetary assets the future cash flow itself would have to be estimated. Auditing the discounted present value in such cases is tantamount to auditing a forecast – which auditors, except in the U.K., have traditionally hesitated to do (see 21.3.1). In certain limited contexts, such as in adjustments for technological changes in productive capacity as discussed earlier, a sufficiently objective basis might exist for estimating future cash flows (e.g. definable savings in operating costs). For cash flows from defined reserves of natural resources, there may or may not exist auditable bases for estimating extraction time, extraction costs, and proceeds. One problem in the latter case is whether or not allowance should be made for anticipated changes in selling prices and extraction costs – such as increases due to supply and demand factors or decreases due to technological change. Without such allowance, the current value of mines would bounce up and down with current metal prices. But *with* such an allowance, the auditor might have difficulty finding objective criteria to assess the results. Disclosure of the assumed price and cost trends might be a partial answer.

It has been suggested by some that discounted cash flow values should also be calculated for other fixed assets to ensure that their book values (for example, current reproduction costs) do not exceed their ongoing economic value to the reporting entity. The objectivity, and therefore the auditability, of such discounted cash flow values could be subject to significant problems.

Auditing combination approaches

Most current value proposals involve some combination of different approaches. One example is the proposal to use current entry prices for assets *essential* to the current operations of the enterprise and current exit prices for *non-essential* assets (the Australian basis). Another example is the concept of *deprival values* based on a set of rules for choosing among replacement cost, net realizable value, and discounted cash flow values (the U.K. basis). Most of the questions to be resolved here are accounting questions – what selection of values makes sense in what circumstances? Once these questions are resolved, the auditing task of assessing whether the established accounting principles have in fact been applied should not be impossible, though difficult audit judgments would often be required. In considering the distinction between essential and non-essential assets the auditor would have to consider the stated intentions of operating management, which might be supported by client engineers or other experts.

Conclusion as to auditability

While it is premature to pass judgment on all the auditing issues which continued experimentation with current value accounting may reveal, it seems likely that any system ultimately adopted would be able to be audited without insurmountable difficulty. Of necessity, however, a lower quality of audit evidence (less external more internal evidence) would usually have to be accepted. Wider materiality limits might also be essential. There would inevitably be a greater cost associated with the auditing, as with the accounting, of current values and the timeliness of audited financial reports might also be impeded. Whether this reduced quality of evidence and these costs and delays would be justified by the improved utility of the information produced, must be assessed during the next few years of study and experimentation. *Widespread* use of current exit prices or discounted cash flow values could present serious auditing problems. In the extreme, valuations based solely on intuitive hunches, whose consistency from year to year could not be assessed, would be unauditable; they would also be susceptible to serious manipulation. Since such extreme bases would hardly yield objective and meaningful results to readers, it seems likely that their use would be rejected. Auditors can assist in the next few years of research by helping to identify such unauditable extremes. If they do, the system ultimately adopted, if indeed any current value system is adopted, should prove auditable.

Auditors, however, must accept the fact that the auditing of current values would involve more judgmental decisions than the auditing of historical costs. When the SEC introduced its replacement cost rules in 1975 a spokesman stated: "It's time that accountants and financial types developed a greater tolerance for imprecision because that's the way the world is." It would be unfortunate if auditors resisted a rational study of the advantages and disadvantages of current value accounting by insisting on an alleged audit requirement of precise, though perhaps irrelevant, numbers.

Major effects on auditing

The following overall effects on auditing seem likely should current value accounting be adopted:

1. As in all auditing, the auditor must first be an expert accountant. Current value accounting would involve a whole new set of principles, conventions, choices and pitfalls. The auditor would have to be familiar with this new field and perhaps develop specialists to assist his staff in resolving problems – particularly during the initial years. A massive educational program would be necessary to meet this challenge.

2. The auditor would have to place more reliance on other experts – in making valuations, in identifying technological change, in applying mathematical techniques, in selecting discount rates, and in estimating cash flows. Reliance on other experts is not a new phenomenon (see 10.3.3) but it would be more widespread if current value accounting were adopted.

3. Some serious problems could be experienced in assessing the reliability of valuations of assets located in foreign countries.

4. The auditor's time would be shifted to some extent from verifying clear-cut numbers to evaluating accounting estimates. The audit evaluation of accounting estimates is likewise not a new phenomenon (see 16.4 and 18.2). Evaluating the allowance for doubtful accounts and the basis of depreciation are difficult judgment calls in every audit engagement now. With current value accounting, the audit evaluation of accounting estimates would extend to more financial statement items. This extension could increase the auditor's exposure to legal liability and some practitioners have suggested that statutory limitations to the magnitude of this liability would be essential in such an environment.

5. Coupled with the increased emphasis on accounting estimates would be the importance of assessing (a) the adequacy of the disclosure of the basis on which the estimates are made and (b) the consistency of the estimates from year to year. Evaluating such consistency would be a greater audit task than in the past since it would more often involve evaluating the consistency of the environment rather than solely that of internal operating procedures.

6. In addition, the auditor as accounting adviser could be expected to assist his client in developing the techniques to make many or all of the accounting estimates. For example, if statistical sampling and/or regression analysis prove useful in facilitating the valuation of large inventories, the auditor could perform a useful service by helping his clients apply these techniques efficiently. The responsibility for the final estimates made and the necessary judgments required would, of course, remain with the client.

7. Interim audit procedures would be expanded to focus on new types of information systems and controls related to the obtaining and generating of current value data from both internal and external sources. Evaluation techniques and compliance procedures would both be affected.

If current value accounting were to be adopted, its results might, during a transitional period, be presented as supplementary unaudited data. For example, in the United States the SEC's 1975 rules permitted replacement cost data to be unaudited but considered the auditor to be *associated* with the disclosures. Ultimately, however, unless the experiment were to be abandoned, attestation of the current value data would seem inevitable. During any experimental period, therefore, auditors would be wise to evaluate the future auditability of any unaudited

current value data presented by their clients. Were current value figures ultimately to be adopted as the primary financial statements, auditors would also have to resolve a considerable number of reporting problems with respect to legal contracts, trust deeds, and regulatory requirements based on historic cost accounting.

21.2.2 Accounting for non-financial resources

Accounting for resources which have up to now been treated as non-financial in nature is another possible development. Though less imminent than others, it could conceivably occur over the next two decades.

One such resource is people. Recent years have seen a number of advocates of human resouce accounting. The Task Force 2000 Report stated:

> Looking at the majority of today's management accounting and information systems, we find that they are concerned primarily with information relating to production, output and costs related to the organization of tangible assets. They are inadequate for the measurement of human values; they do not reflect the investment in human resources or the information required to consider alternative courses in such matters as recruiting, hiring, training and developement of staff ...

> Many believe that accounting for human resources may soon be considered as essential for the planning and control functions of management. Studies have indicated a degree of correlation between the profitability of an enterprise and the expenditure on acquisition, training and retention of human resources; cases of high personnel turnover may have a material effect on the immediate future operations of the organization, yet the effects of such losses are not accounted for. Were the accounting system to measure the value of the company's human resources and their change over a period of time, then income might reflect a more realistic measurement of managerial effectiveness.[13]

Somewhat related to human resources is the resource of knowledge. The Task Force 2000 Report argued that, with increasing technological advances, knowledge might some day replace capital as the critical resource – and, if so, ways of accounting for that resource should be found.

> The avalanche of knowledge resulting from the combination of science and technology and mass education is knowledge that is based less on experience and more on systematic, purposeful, organized information. Knowledge is becoming a central economic resource. The systematic acquisition of knowledge through organized, formal education instead of experience acquired traditionally through apprenticeship is becoming the foundation of modern enterprise and innovation ...

> New criteria must be found for measuring the effective use and development of knowledge; growing concern for knowledge as a resource by business and government organizations will require that appropriate means be developed for planning and control of its use.[14]

Other possible resources include good supplier and customer relations – usually not accounted for except when purchased from other parties (e.g. customer lists). Yet another is systems and organization.

Resources such as the foregoing are sometimes included in the catch-all concept of goodwill. Present accounting practice values purchased goodwill as an asset but expenses much of the home-grown goodwill as a period cost – an anomaly underlying many of the contentious problems in accounting for business combinations. Most proposals for current value accounting would continue this practice, at least for the time being.

Were external reporting some day to include recognition of such intangible assets, a number of difficult accounting and auditing questions would have to be resolved. It does not seem inconceivable that a rational and auditable basis could be developed for deferring portions of intangible asset costs and allocating them systematically to future periods. Converting such accounting from an historical cost basis to current entry prices might be difficult but probably not insoluble. The greatest difficulty, however, would be constraining such deferrals, should it be deemed necessary, by consideration of their ongoing value to the enterprise. A costly but unsuccessful management training program is hardly a valuable asset to the business. If its historical or current replacement cost is higher than its economic value it should presumably be written down. But the concept of auditing the economic value of goodwill would seem to lead to discounted cash flow valuations of the enterprise as a whole. It seems questionable that discounted cash flow valuations on such a widespread basis can be audited with sufficient objectivity to yield meaningful results.

One alternative would be to dispense with valuation write-downs except when there is clear evidence of a permanent impairment in goodwill value – a position similar to that now existing for the unamortized balance of purchased goodwill and, implicitly, for the undepreciated balance of tangible fixed assets. Under such circumstances, the accounting results might be auditable. At the same time, the absence of an economic value test could leave the door open to abuses. Attestation of a splurge of doubtful balance sheet values (reminiscent of the late 1920's) would hardly be a service to the public.

Should the profession turn to a study of the accounting for human and knowledge resources, presumably after the more immediate problems of current value accounting are settled, the question of auditability will have to be carefully examined.

21.2.3 Accounting for non-profit objectives

A more profound potential development could be a move to accounting for collateral non-profit objectives in a profit-oriented enterprise. The AICPA Commission raised the question of whether an auditor should report on:

> Data on a company's contributions to society and the costs to society of its operations in an annual report or a separate release.[15]

Task Force 2000 had argued more directly that:

> The realization on the part of many organizations that their activities and performance will be measured, not only in monetary terms, but also in relation to the degree of social benefit, will require a form a social accounting that recognizes a multi-goal concept. For accounting to be multi-dimensional – for it to measure performance against more than one goal or objective – it may be necessary to consider several aspects of a transaction or event simultaneously. For example, the measurement of revenues and costs in monetary terms, the measurement of employee satisfaction in terms of individual goals, and the measurement of national interest by relation to certain social standards.[16]

The idea of social benefit accounting, while already discussed for a number of years,[17] may not be accepted in the immediate future. But the growing interdependence between government and private initiative would seem inevitably to lead in this direction – perhaps not within the next decade but surely by the turn of the century. Social benefit accounting may well be introduced first in the government sector, where the planning, programming and budgeting systems (PPBS) of recent years could already be said to be laying a foundation. But its extension to the private sector and to the process of resource allocation will surely happen some day, and within the careers of the younger members of the profession today.

To reflect the broader potential application of accounting measurements, Task Force 2000 recommended:

> That the profession adopt as its goal the achievement and maintenance of the highest level of professional competence in the measurement and communication of information pertaining to the efficient allocation and effective use of resources.[18]

What effects would such trends have on auditing? One effect would be the importance of maintaining attestation as an opinion expressed relative to *established* criteria. To the extent that objective bases of measurement can be established – and surely many can – the results of social benefit accounting should prove to be auditable. It will be important to remember, however, that the quantity which is measurable will always be somewhat different, and usually less inclusive, than the quality in which the reader is ultimately interested. Measurable employment statistics, pollution results, and expenditures on extra-curricular programs provide an indication, but not a complete picture, of labour satisfaction, environmental values, and recreational benefits. In any attestation of social benefit accounting, an auditor's opinion can only be expressed within the framework of the "accounting model" or measurement model adopted. A defined framework of generally accepted accounting principles, whatever its scope, must continue to be distinguished from an abstract standard of ideal fairness (see 17.3) – just as law must inevitably fall short of ideal justice.

A second effect is the likely introduction, in due course, of other disciplines into the audit team.

Auditing itself will, undoubtedly, undergo significant technological change, and it follows from the changing nature of stewardship accounting that the accountant of the future will have to approach the auditing function from a wider perspective. The future auditor may have to have at his disposal an enormously larger inventory of knowledge and skills than he has ever needed before. It is more than a little doubtful that one man could ever obtain all the knowledge that will be required to carry out such a comprehensive form of audit, or that any one profession could embrace such a wide field. Auditing may develop into a multi-disciplinary activity and we will likely see audit teams composed of people drawn from many different backgrounds. The accounting profession could well remain as the core of the 'new auditing activity', not so much because it has preempted the field in the past, but because it has the traditional identity with the concept of independence. The quality of independence should always be the cornerstone of auditing.[19]

21.3 Other possible subjects of attestation or review

Other possible effects on auditing may arise not from accounting changes in annual financial statements but from extension of the public accountant's role to other types of communication, such as forecasts, interim financial information, and reports on internal control. In each of these areas one must first consider the appropriate form of association of the public accountant. The AICPA Commission *Statement of Issues* identified three possible forms of association: audit, review and consultation. A fourth level of limited procedures, intermediate between audit and review, has also been suggested by some (see 19.3.3). Some of the questions to be answered in deciding upon the *feasibility* of extending the auditor's role are:

1. To what extent should association with information depend on the development of relatively objective measurement standards?
2. To what extent should limits be placed on the auditor's association with information, based on
   a) some scale of the relative amount of uncertainty of such information?
   b) the availability of evidence to support the information?[20]

Some of the cost-benefit factors to be considered in deciding upon the *desirability* of extending the auditor's role are:

1. the potential consequences of inherent differences in the reliability of other forms of information as contrasted with traditional financial statements,
2. the potential effectiveness of audits in increasing the reliability of information,
3. the possibility of unwarranted reliance on the information,

4. the costs of having the information audited,
5. the potential delays in distribution,
6. the possible effects on the primary audit function,
7. the cost and benefits of institutional changes that may be necessary to implement the auditor's association with particular information.[21]

21.3.1 Forecasts

The desirability of permitting or requiring enterprises to publish forecasts and of permitting or requiring public accountants to express some sort of opinion on them has been a contentious question for many years. The traditional posture of the accounting profession has been cautious – reflecting concern that undue reliability might be accorded to forecasts with which public accountants were associated and that an unreasonable degree of legal liability might be assumed by the preparers or reviewers of forecasts. Indeed, the CICA Handbook has recommended that:

> The auditors should not express an opinion on any forecast earnings figures which might be contained in a prospectus.[22]

Securities regulation in Canada has also prohibited publication of forecasts for a prospectus or take-over bid except in rare circumstances and, where one is published, has prohibited the auditor's association with it.

In certain limited situations, practising chartered accountants are associated with forecasts. For example, those in insolvency practice often prepare (a) cash flows and operating forecasts of companies in receivership, in liquidation, or in the process of reorganization and (b) projections [23] of estimated results to creditors under alternative sets of circumstances, such as on-going operation by the debtor versus liquidation. Chartered accountants may also be asked to assist in the preparation or review of forecasts contained in applications for bank loans or for government grants. Finally, an auditor may be asked to review, on behalf of his client's management or directors, internal forecasts prepared in connection with a prospective acquisition. But normally enterprises have *not* prepared formal forecasts for wide distribution to shareholders or the public, either (a) in their regular annual reports or (b) in prospectuses, circulars issued in take-overs, or other special documents. The preparation of financial forecasts for a public company, apart from informal comments occasionally contained in presidents' reports or speeches or in corporate press releases, has instead been the task of financial analysts independent of the company and of its auditors.

In recent years this traditional position has begun to change. In the United Kingdom encouragement of published forecasts in certain situations began in 1968 and was the subject of an Institute pronouncement in 1969. Today, The Stock Exchange requires forecasts, reported upon by the auditors, to be included in a prospectus and the City Code on Take-overs and Mergers requires that, if a forecast is included in a take-over circular, it must be reported upon by the auditors or consultant accountants. Auditors rarely report, however, on a forecast given in a U.K. company's annual report. Annual reports are required to compare actual results to prior forecasts.

In the United States in 1973, the SEC issued a release changing its prior policy of prohibiting forecasts in prospectuses or other regulatory filings. The 1973 release proposed rules permitting voluntary disclosure of forecasts and requiring a company to include in its regulatory filings any forecast which it had disclosed outside of such filings "whether through financial media, financial analysts or otherwise". Certification of such forecasts by auditors was not permitted. Annual reports would be required to compare actual results to prior forecasts. The proposed SEC rules were revised in 1975 and again in 1976. Few U.S. companies had, by late 1976, chosen to issue forecasts under these new provisions. In 1975 the AICPA issued *Guidelines for Systems for the Preparation of Financial Forecasts*[24], neither advocating nor discouraging forecasts but describing systems conducive to their preparation where desired .In the same year the AICPA also issued *The Statement of Position on Presentation and Disclosure of Financial Forecasts*[25], suggesting certain standards of presentation if forecasts were issued. Neither the AICPA

Guidelines nor the Statement of Position referred to third-party review of foreceasts.[26]

In 1974 the Accountants International Study Group issued a Study on *Published Profit Forecasts* comparing the practices in the U.K., the U.S., and Canada and recommending that "in the light of U.K. experience, there should be orderly progress towards the publication of profit forecasts." [27] Critics of the use of the U.K. as a precedent have argued that U.K. profit forecasts usually cover only the fiscal year already in progress. In fact, sometimes the term profit forecast has been used in the U.K. to refer to an estimate of the year's results issued after the year-end but prior to audit. This experience, it is argued, is not necessarily relevant to current North American proposals, which suggest forecasting of the following fiscal year once the current year is half over.

In Canada, interest in the subject of forecasting was increased by the *1973 Report on Mergers, Amalgamations and Certain Related Matters* by a special committee of the Ontario Legislature. The report concluded that the advantages of published forecasts outweighed the disadvantages and that, if forecasts are published, they should be independently reviewed, probably by public accountants.

> The Committee therefore recommends, having regard to its view of the desirability of financial forecasts, that the Ontario Securities Commission institute a study of this matter with the accounting profession and members of the financial community with a view to developing necessary guidelines and regulations which will require financial forecasts reported on by the auditors of a company.[28]

Responding to this interest, and to related considerations of the Ontario Securities Commission, the CICA published in 1976 a research study on *Earnings Forecasts*, [29] referred to in this section as the CICA Study. This Study is extremely comprehensive and the reader seeking a detailed analysis of U.K. and U.S. experience, arguments for and against current proposals, suggested forecasting standards, legal considerations, the question of third-party review, and a related bibliography will find all these topics amply covered. Following this study, consideration will presumably be given to the subject by both the Accounting Research and Auditing Standards Committees of the CICA. The reader should refer to any subsequent pronouncements.

If published forecasts were to be encouraged in Canada, various statutory and regulatory provisions would presumably be revised. The CICA Study suggested that these revisions should include specific provisions to limit the liability of reporting entities, and perhaps of their directors and auditors, should subsequent operating results vary significantly, as many inevitably would, from earlier forecasts made in good faith. While there are many contentious questions with respect to the format, disclosure and updating of forecasts by the reporting entity, the following comments are restricted to the question of third-party review by a public accountant.

Association

A preliminary question is whether public accountants should be associated with forecasts at all. The special committee of the Ontario Legislature, as already stated, concluded that they should be. The Accountants International Study Group advocated association at least in the case of take-over circulars and prospectuses.[30]

The advantages and disadvantages of third-party association are discussed in the CICA Study.[31] Advocates argue that the quality of forecasts would be improved by third-party review. Critics argue (a) that forecasts are not auditable in the sense that historic financial statements are, (b) that third-party comments would lead to undue reliance being placed on the attainability of a forecast, (c) that the objectivity of a public accountant who has reported on a forecast may be, or appear to be, impaired when it comes time to report on subsequent actual results, and (d) that unattained forecasts might destroy the credibility of all published financial information. Despite the latter arguments, public accountant association with some form of published forecast seems inevitable. The public accountant does have the skill and training to add appropriately limited credibility to published forecasts and such addition would seem in the public interest provided that forecasts are avoided where inadequate systems, major uncertainties, or unusual cost-benefit relationships make their preparation or their review impractical.

The CICA Study suggested that a public accountant should be considered associated with a forecast if he prepares it or consents to the use of his name in connection with it – a similar definition of association to that used in connection with unaudited financial statements (see 20.1.1).

Compilation, principles, assumptions and levels of assurance

If the public accountant is to be associated with a forecast, the next question is what level of assurance he should provide (positive opinion or negative assurance) and whether that assurance should be restricted to the compilation and to the accounting principles used or should extend to the completeness and reasonableness of the assumptions made. The Accountants International Study Group suggested the assurance should be restricted to the compilation and to the accounting principles used but that the accountant should nonetheless review the assump-

tions and comment if any of them appeared unrealistic or if any important ones had been omitted.[32] The same position was considered as one of the questions included in the Statement of Issues of the AICPA Commission on Auditors' Responsibilities.[33] Task Force 2000, however, had hinted at a broader coverage:

> It is perhaps not inconceivable that, in the future, the accountant could lend some credibility to a forecast, or at least report on the principles and assumptions used in their preparation. This may be an activity to be performed by the accountant but probably only in conjunction with experts from other disciplines.[34]

The position adopted in the CICA Study was that the accountant should:

a) express an opinion on compilation and accounting principles,

b) disclaim an opinion as to the attainability of the forecast,

c) provide a rather indirect implication that management's assumptions are complete and not unreasonable.

The Study suggested the following form of communication: [35]

Earnings forecast review comments

To the Directors of
XYZ Company Limited

I have reviewed the accompanying August 29, 1977 earnings forecast of XYZ Company Limited for the year ending December 31, 1977. My review consisted primarily of enquiry and comparison, together with such tests of compilation as I considered necessary in the circumstances.

I do not express an opinion as to whether the actual results for the forecast period will approximate those forecasted, because the earnings forecast is based on assumptions made by management regarding future events which, by their nature, are not susceptible to independent substantiation.

In my opinion, however, this earnings forecast properly reflects the assumptions used in its preparation and is prepared on a basis consistent with the accounting principles applied in the company's financial statements for the year ended December 31, 1976.

City
August 29, 1977   Chartered Accountant

The Study goes on to explain that the words "properly reflects the assumptions" are intended to refer primarily to the compilation but to imply as well that the public accountant is satisfied that the assumptions are not unreasonable and that all important assumptions have been disclosed. The latter implication, however, does not seem entirely clear from the words.

In the writer's view, it would seem reasonable for the public accountant to provide explicit negative assurance with respect to the completeness and reasonableness of the assumptions used.[36] The CICA

Study suggests he conduct an enquiry-based review, similar to that applied in a review of unaudited financial statements, to assess the *plausibility* of the assumptions, so there should be a basis for negative assurance. Moreover, judgments as to the reasonableness of future-oriented assumptions are already required of auditors in assessing many accounting estimates in financial statements and will be even more frequently required should current value accounting be adopted. The concern, however, is that the specific expression of assurance as to plausibility might be misinterpreted as assurance as to the attainability of the forecast. This concern seems excessive after an explicit disclaimer has been given. However, it may be prudent to proceed slowly. Avoiding explicit assurance on the assumptions may be wise for the first few years – at least, with respect to reports to the public (as opposed to reports to a restricted readership such as the directors).

It would also seem more consistent with the practice of referring to specific note disclosure of an appropriate basis of accounting in special purpose reports (see 19.3.1) to have the opinion paragraph in the foregoing example contain words such as "properly relects the assumptions disclosed in the accompanying notes and is prepared . . . ".

With respect to accounting principles the CICA Study calls for the accountant to consider consistency both with principles used in the prior year and principles likely to be used during the forecast period. The suggested comments do not refer to "generally accepted accounting principles" since such principles do not presently apply to forecasts – but this position could change in the future.

Review standards

The CICA Study suggested a set of general, field work, and comment standards which would serve, for forecast reviews, as the counterparts of generally accepted auditing standards for audits. The suggested general standard was analogous to the auditing general standard – including references to proficiency, due care, and an objective state of mind.[37] The suggested field work standards were basically parallel to the auditing field work standards. The suggested second field work standard called for a study and evaluation of those forecasting procedures or systems on which the accountnat relies – the idea being that reliable forecasting requires good forecasting systems. Other suggested standards stressed the importance of the reviewer's knowledge of the company, the industry in which it operates and the general business environment and the need to consider the plausibility of the forecast and of related information provided. The suggested comment standards are best illustrated by the example of earn-ings forecast review comments previously given. The CICA Study suggested that qualified opinions should be restricted to cases where the deficiency can be rectified by disclosure in the reviewer's comments; otherwise, an adverse opinion is suggested.

Review procedures

The CICA Study suggested that the public accountant's review procedures consist of:[38]

1. preliminary considerations – including inquiries prior to acceptance of the engagement (the Study suggests forecasting systems should appear to meet the AICPA Guidelines before a review engagement is accepted),
2. issue of an engagement letter – including reference to management's responsibility for the forecast and the assumptions on which it is based,
3. initial general survey – simplified if the reviewer has been the auditor of prior financial statements of the company,
4. consideration of forecasting system and techniques – including a comparison to the AICPA Guidelines and the review of any mathematical or modeling techniques used,
5. review of assumptions – including both major assumptions disclosed in the forecast and minor or more detailed assumptions not disclosed.
6. compilation tests – including a review of the related accounting procedures (easier if the reviewer is also the auditor) and tests of the compilation and arithmetic accuracy,
7. obtaining of a general representation letter – including reference to the fact that the forecast represents management's best estimate of the most probable results for the forecast period,
8. obtaining of approval by the board – including the prior issue to the board of a long-form forecast memorandum analyzing and commenting on the forecast and its assumptions.

The foregoing review standards and review procedures are research study proposals only. With respect to both, the reader should refer to any subsequent pronouncements.

Effect on the public accountant's techniques

If third-party reporting on forecasts were to be adopted, there would inevitably be greater emphasis on the more effective use by the public accountant of analytical review procedures and mathematical techniques such as regression analysis.

21.3.2 Interim and other financial information

The auditor's association with interim financial reports was discussed in 20.6. While present CICA Recommendations do not, as this book goes to press, cover reports on interim financial statements issued to shareholders of public companies, public reporting based on "limited reviews" has begun in the United States. The subject remains controversial but the future is likely to see increasing pressure for some sort of interim reporting by public accountants in Canada. Were third-party reporting on quarterly updated forecasts to be adopted, reporting as well on the accompanying unaudited past results would seem inevitable. It is also possible that the future could see a move toward *audited* interim reports.

Quite apart from the question of what specific interim reports should be reviewed or audited is the question of whether the public accountant's association should be with specific reports or with the reporting entity in general. In recent years in the United States, the SEC has been advocating more *continuous reporting* by public companies. The argument is that continuous timely reporting would reflect the fact that "business is inherently a continuum, rather than being done in a series of discrete segments". Associated with the idea of continuous reporting has been the *auditor-of-record concept*.

> An auditor-of-record would have a continuing responsibility to assess the client's accounting decisions on a timely basis and review all public reports prior to issuance in accordance with a reasonable set of standards developed by either the public accounting profession or the SEC. Acceptance of an engagement to audit annual statements would mean automatic acceptance of the responsibility implicit in the concept.[39]

The auditor-of-record concept would seem to be an extension of the current wave of demands for more and more ombudsmen and guardians of the public interest. From one point of view, it might seem desirable that the completeness and fairness of all communications issued by a public company (including annual statements, interim statements, forecasts, disclosures under the timely disclosure requirements of stock exchanges, press releases, etc.) be subject automatically to review by an objective third-party. The possible move to some form of association with information other than the financial statements themselves (for example, information elsewhere in a company's annual report) has already been discussed in 17.5.5. The SEC has argued that all financial communications affect the market place and should therefore all maintain a basic reliability.

But the costs and delays of continuous third-party review must be weighed against the possible benefits. To assess the fairness and completeness of day-to-day disclosures by a public company the auditor would have to conduct continual and costly reviews of all corporate developments for fear that some undisclosed development had escaped his attention. In this writer's view, it seems doubtful that these costs would be warranted by the benefits. Moreover, the auditor-of-record concept could expose auditors to far more onerous legal liability than the present system of association with specified individual reports[40] – a liability which would ultimately be reflected in more protective procedures and higher costs. Finally, the spectre of the auditor as censor of all outgoing corporate information could produce an adversary relationship between auditors and their clients which would inhibit the free discussion between them of confidential information and thus impair the efficiency and effectiveness of all audit procedures. If the auditor-of-record concept were prescribed by government or regulatory authority, auditors could no doubt design appropriate procedures to operate in the new environment. But one must question whether the final result would be in the public interest. Reviews or audits of specific interim reports can be conducted without invoking the auditor-of-record concept.

21.3.3 Adequacy of systems, information and controls

The question of public reporting on the adequacy of a company's system of internal control was discussed in 19.3.7. In the view of many practitioners such reports are undesirable – particularly because they may lead readers to attribute an unwarranted degree of reliability to unaudited interim financial statements (on the mistaken assumption that a good system of internal control will guarantee accurate interim figures). Nonetheless, it seems likely that the future will see increasing pressure for this type of reporting and it is conceivable that mandatory reporting of at least significant weaknesses could be introduced relatively soon.[41]

In addition, the suggestion has been made that an auditor might report on the "adequacy of a company's information system for management decision-making".[42] This suggestion would seem less likely to be acted on in the near future. It would raise many of the problems associated with reporting on management effectiveness and efficiency (see 21.3.4).

21.3.4 Effectiveness, efficiency, competence and integrity of management

Suggestions are advanced from time to time that auditors should report on:

1. management effectiveness and efficiency (the AICPA Commission on Auditors' Responsibilities considered the subjects of economy or efficiency of operations and effectiveness of various programs or activities),
2. management competence, or
3. management integrity (the AICPA Commission also considered the question of compliance with laws and regulations not directly affecting the financial statements).

Possible moves in the third area have already been discussed in connection with the SEC's position on questionable payments (see 32.4.13).[43]

All the foregoing three areas would present serious difficulties. Auditing was defined in Chapter 1 as the process of obtaining and evaluating evidence as to the degree of correspondence between assertions and established criteria. Fundamental to the process of auditing, therefore, is that there exist established criteria. Generally accepted accounting principles constitute such criteria for most audits of financial statements. Auditing need not be limited to accounting data – but if it is extended to other fields, assuming that they remain within the auditor's own sphere of competence, established criteria must exist for those fields. Otherwise audit reports would be purely subjective and of limited use to readers wishing to compare companies audited by different auditors. It is understandable that a member of the public might sometimes think: "The auditors must have seen that management was incompetent and that the company was going downhill; why didn't they let us know?". But subjective assessments of managerial competence varying from company to company and from auditor to auditor in identical situations could do more harm than good.

The problem of subjectivity is not necessarily an obstacle to *internal* reports. Thus *operational audits* and *management audits* conducted by a company's internal auditors may well, at senior management's request, cover some or all of the foregoing three areas. But in such cases senior management has access to additional information if desired. Moreover, it can establish its own internal criteria for measuring departmental performance. Finally, some consistency is provided if all departments are subjected to review by the same internal audit group.[44] Access to additional information, internal performance standards, and some measure of consistency are *not* available, however, when such reporting is transferred to *external* reports for the public.

If external reporting on efficiency, effectiveness, competence or integrity were to be adopted, objective criteria would have to be established for measuring these attributes. It seems doubtful that meaningful and practical criteria for general use can be found.

Indeed, it can be argued that the most objective criteria of management performance are the actual results – on the presentation of which the external auditor *does* express an opinion.

In discussing a case in which the auditors were called into question for not stopping management from entering into certain business dealings which later turned out to be unsuccessful, one U.S. lawyer has commented:

> Clearly, the auditor was never intended to make decisions in the audit function on the quality of management nor should the auditor be so required. Managerial decisions require the exercise of judgment based on a myriad of existing facts known at the time the judgement is made. Unless one is living with the business on a daily basis and familiar with every detail of the operation, one is not, cannot, and should not make or be asked to evaluate those decisions. Moreover, even if the auditor believes a managerial decision is wrong, the imposition on him of the duty to alter that decision (as plaintiffs ask), would effectively usurp managerial prerogatives and raise substantial questions of independence.[45]

It seems likely, however, that the profession will have to continue examining the public's expectations in these areas carefully in the years to come.

21.4 The effect on auditing of possible economic developments

Undoubtedly auditing over the next few decades will be affected as well by important economic developments. Some of the developments which can be reasonably foreseen are:

1. the continued growth of multi-national enterprises,
2. increasing government intervention in the economy,
3. major technological innovation,
4. resource limitations and ecological constraints.

The effect that these developments may have on the role of auditing is less easy to predict.

Multi-nationalism

The continued growth of, and perhaps domination of the economy by, multi-national enterprises will increase the importance of reporting to an international readership. Some of the problems of international reporting were discussed in 18.6. The incidence of such problems is likely to increase. Auditors will more frequently be faced with a multitude of accounting yardsticks in relation to which their opinions may have to be expressed. At the same time, the pressure for development of international standards will grow (see 2.6) though the acceptance of such standards is likely to be controversial for some time. For a decade or so it seems likely that the Canadian auditor associated with multi-national clients will have to cope with generally accepted accounting principles established in Canada, the U.S., the U.K., continental Europe, Japan, and elsewhere, as well as with a growing set of pronouncements by an international body. Whether multi-national standards will ultimately give way to international ones is difficult to predict – and the outcome may well depend more on economic and political developments than on professional efforts.

The growing complexity of multi-national reporting will also create a gap between large and small enterprises. Already there have been advocates of one set of generally accepted accounting principles for large enterprises and a simplified set for the smaller. Whatever the theoretical inconsistencies, such a split seems inevitable on practical grounds and may in turn influence the manner in which auditing practices are organized.

Government intervention

The role of government planning, control and intervention in the economy seems likely to increase throughout the developed world. In any short-term period the exact degree of government intervention will no doubt be contentious. Abuses are always possible and public accountants, both individually and as a profession, can help their clients speak out against them. But in the long run, some increasing amount of government intervention would seem to be an irreversible trend. Canada will likely be no exception.

The effect of increasing government intervention is likely to be more complex legislation, more regulations, and more work for auditors. Pressure will increase for audit reporting on compliance with new laws and regulations. The profession declined such a role, perhaps unfortunately, with respect to the anti-inflation program of 1975 to 1978. But similar pressures will occur in the future (one example has been reporting requirements under the election expenses act) and increased audit reporting responsibilities in this environment seem inevitable. Increased government intervention may some day also accelerate moves to explore social benefit accounting (see 21.2.3).

Technological innovation

It is commonplace to observe that we live in a world of rapid technological change. Continuing advances in computer technology will undoubtedly have an impact on auditing methods (see 21.6.1). The very organization of accounting data in large enterprises is likely to change dramatically under the impact of data base concepts, information theory, and decision theory – with corresponding changes in the auditor's approach to selection, retrieval, and review of stored data. Gradual progress to electronic funds transfer (the chequeless society) may change the very nature of "cash" and its verification. Similar changes may affect the nature and verification of marketable securities with the move to integrated markets and central depositories. The transition to a *post-industrial society*[46] with its increasing emphasis on service industries (versus primary and secondary industries) will change the auditor's mix of clients. It will also perhaps raise additional accounting and auditing problems not contemplated in the traditional manufacturing model implicit in so much past accounting and auditing thought. The rapidity of technological change will complicate the auditor's evaluation of fixed asset values and depreciation – as asset lives become progressively shortened by obsolescence. Perhaps the greatest impact on the auditor's role will come as one of the minor side-effects of major breakthroughs (perhaps in energy technology, perhaps in communications) which may restructure economic society in ways we cannot imagine at present.

Resource limitations and ecological constraints

In the last generation the world has suddenly come up against the limitations of a finite planet. Oil and mineral resources are not inexhaustible. Agricultural land is not available in limitless supply. Population growth will further aggravate the problems created by urbanization and pollution. Whether the doomsday projections of the early studies of the Club of Rome are valid or the recent more tempered studies of regional disparities, it is clear that ecological constraints will increasingly play a major role in both governmental and corporate planning. Central to the problem of planning in the face of ecological constraints is accurate and reliable measurement and communication of what those constraints are – an area in which the disciplines of both accounting and auditing could conceivably make an important contribution. The importance of ecological factors may well be reflected in revised bases of accounting which could in turn affect auditing methods in ways not yet foreseeable.

Task Force 2000 expressed its view of the possible opportunities as follows:

> It sees exciting opportunities for the accountant and an expanded role for accounting as a vital tool in the problem-solving activity. Problems – such as pollution, urbanization, food supply and others – related to our

quality of life, give rise to a need for application of accounting to new fields – fields that urgently require new criteria, methods of quantitative measurement and accountability. By developing its knowledge in such activities as management accounting and the information function, forecasting, financial statement reporting, auditing and the attest function, taxation and accounting for human resources, social costs and benefits, and the quality of life, the Profession will be an important resource of society – its central role being the performance of service based on professional knowledge in accounting.[47]

21.5 The practice of auditing

The effects of a number of future developments are likely to involve the overall practice of auditing rather than individual auditing procedures.

21.5.1 Recruitment in a time of change

To meet the challenges of the future, the accounting profession will have to maintain an aggressive program of recruitment. Exploding knowledge requirements will call for increased study prior to entry into the profession and will place a premium on finding candidates with both the necessary educational qualifications and the capacity for professional development. Changing social values will challenge the profession to provide such candidates with work which fully utilizes their potential. Already the profession has moved far in this direction.

The days of tedious checking of months of invoices have been replaced by more sophisticated sampling methods and systems analysis. At the same time, competition for trained chartered accountants will continue, both from industry and from an increasingly dominant government sector.

A positive factor, however, will be the growth in the number of women entering the profession and advancing to senior positions in it. Presently representing 38% of the total work force, women account for only 1% or so of total Institute membership and even less of its senior positions. That the proportion will change dramatically is evidenced by the fact that, among new student registrants in the profession, women make up more than 15% and, among the recruits in the larger offices of some national accounting firms, more than 30%. The overdue addition of this resource to the ranks of the profession, including its senior ranks, paralleling anticipated increases in corporate ranks as well, will make a major contribution to the profession's future achievements.

21.5.2 Knowledge explosion and specialization

A serious problem which tomorrow's practitioner must face is coping with the exploding body of professional knowledge. The growing volume of professional pronouncements with which the practitioner must be familiar is a case in point. In the auditing area alone the AICPA has been issuing some 6 statements a year (whose implications for Canadian practice a chartered accountant cannot ignore) and the CICA perhaps half that many. Projected to the year 2000, the practitioner could be faced with over 200 auditing pronouncements – and undoubtedly a far larger number of accounting ones with which he must be equally familiar! It is to be hoped that such pronouncements will be based on broad underlying concepts and not encyclopaedic lists of arbitrary rules. But whatever their format, the trend toward producing more guidance on countless new problem areas is unlikely to be reversible. Yet the results will be far beyond the capacity of any one practitioner to absorb.

Inevitably this trend will lead to increased specialization (see 15.2.4). Indeed, Task Force 2000 recommended that the attest function itself should become a specialty and be recognized as a separate accredited activity of the accounting profession.[48] New ways may have to be found of retrieving and communicating specialist knowledge within any one accounting firm. The traditional pattern of dwindling generalists supported by increasing batteries of specialists may become increasingly unworkable. Interdisciplinary teams will become more common. Future computer technology may also provide some assistance in grappling with the immense quantities of information with which practitioners will have to work. One can imagine central Institute data banks with remote access terminals providing a better answer some day than vast quantities of printed paper stacked in each practitioner's office.

Further pressure toward specialist accreditation may ultimately prove irresistible (see 3.4.6). The rapidity of change and the problem of obsolescent knowledge will undoubtedly increase the importance of continuing education programs. The controversial question of mandatory professional development was discussed in 3.2.3. However it is dealt with at the present time, this question will undoubtedly return.

Advances in educational techniques and learning theory may also help tomorrow's practitioners to keep current with the flood of changing knowledge.

21.5.3 The regulatory and legal environment

Government regulation of all types is likely to increase and the professions will not be exempt from this trend. The increasing government policing of all professions in Quebec was discussed in 2.2.3. Similar proposals have recently been under study by the Ontario government. In the United States, the Department of Justice has been reviewing the structure of the accounting profession. The pressures of consumerism will intensify this trend and all professions can expect to live under more constant public scrutiny than in the past.

Other government regulations could affect the profession as well. In recent years studies have been undertaken of a possible transfer of securities regulation from the provincial to the federal level, although such proposals have many outspoken critics. If the U.S. experience is a reliable indication, any such development could have profound effects on the Canadian profession.

Present trends of increasing legal responsibilities and litigation are likely to continue. In the United States, where the wave of litigation has been the most intense, a lawyer has commented:

> I believe that the scope of the auditor's liability will be increased dramatically in the next decade and the correlative responsibilities imposed upon the auditor will show a commensurate growth. This responsibility will increase as a result of three fundamental facts. First . . . the pecuniary desire of the lawyer to plow new fields, to obtain new sources of revenue. Second, the misconception of the auditor's function universally shared by the user of his workproduct. Unfortunately the general public and even many of the courts and people, whom you expect to know, consider the auditor a guarantor or insurer of the financial statements. This misconception is as much the public's fault as it is the auditor's fault. The profession as a whole has been very lax in its attempts to educate the public as to what its role is; and in fact, as several commentators have suggested, may have permitted the public to bask in false delusions. Third, and the only ligitimate reason I see for the increase and expansion of the auditor's responsibilities, all professionals are being asked to assume greater responsibilities with respect to the performance of their duties. I do not fault this. In fact I praise it and feel it is a desirable result. I also believe that as a whole the profession is continually attempting on its own to achieve this result. Where I do disagree, however, and where I do see potential problems for the auditor in the next decade, is the extent and bounds to which these responsibilities may be pushed as a result of a combination of all three factors.[49]

Moreover, some of the reasons for differences between the U.S. and the Canadian experience – the relative absence in Canada in the past of contigent fees and class actions suits – may well disappear (see 5.5).

21.5.4 The small practitioner

In an environment of growing complexity, knowledge explosion, specialization, and multi-nationalism the small practitioner will face certain problems – but not ones without solution. Task Force 2000 suggested that small accounting firms:

> will have to learn to make greater use of experts in other disciplines in the future if they want to be involved in complex problem-solving activity. More extensive working relationships could be developed between small accounting firms and firms of other professions or disciplines in an effort to provide an integrated approach to service.[50]

It may also be necessary for associations of small firms to be formed to pool their individual research, educational, and specialist resources. Some such associations already exist – for example, the Associated Accounting Firms International, which contains both U.S. and Canadian members – and their number is likely to increase. With increasing specialization among individual firms, referrals will become more and more common (see 3.5.2). The problems of the small firm will be to organize such *external* relationships efficiently – just as the problems of the large firm will be to overhaul its *internal* communications efficiently.

21.5.5 Autonomy of the Canadian profession

A very real question is whether the Canadian profession will be able to retain any degree of self-determination. In an age when international professional bodies will likely assume increasing importance, too narrow a nationalistic view is hardly desirable. Nonetheless, to the extent that national organizations continue to play an important role, as they surely will, one might hope that the Canadian profession will be able to retain an identity and make its own contribution. Whether such a hope is naive or not depends on one's view of the survival of Canada as a country. It is fashionable to forecast the integration of Canada into the U.S. economy:

The development of an integrated North American economy appears inevitable, implying continental economic planning, customs union, free capital flows, continental labour force mobility, wage parity, integration of the educational systems ... Canada will retain quasi-sovereignty. Canada's national identity will still survive, despite further erosion of sovereignty resulting from economic integration. Her status may be similar to that of Monaco in relation to France.[51]

Similar opinions were expressed by Task Force 2000:

It is not possible, nor may it even be desirable, to develop Canadian educational facilities independently of developments in the United States ... Canada's research and development activities are not suggestive of a country directing itself towards independent status. ... There is no question that Canadian management style is foreign-dominated and does not exhibit a peculiar Canadian entrepreneurial quality ... It would appear, on the basis of our situation today and our present trends, that Canada will proceed on a path which will bring it closer, if not completely, to North America economic integration. It would also appear that social and political integration might follow closely behind.[52]

If these projections are realistic, Canadian practitioners might be wasting their time to worry about the structure, development, pronouncements, and contributions of the Canadian profession. The decisions would soon all be made elsewhere.

But economic projections can be subject to the fallacy of assuming that all human behaviour is determined by economics. On purely economic grounds many countries would not exist at all. Toynbee has argued that many nations have flourished more because of the challenges with which they were faced than the natural advantages which they inherited. In the end, national identity probably depends more on will than on means. This is hardly the forum to discuss whether, as one might hope, Canadians are likely to exhibit a will to continue as a separate nation. But were they to do so, a major problem to be faced by the Canadian profession would be how to maintain an autonomous viewpoint when it is unlikely to be able to compete with the research budgets, training expenditures, and volume of pronouncements of its colleagues in the United States.

One possibility could be specialization. Rather than attempting to tackle every new problem from scratch – repeating the work of the profession in the United States, the United Kingdom, Australia, and elsewhere – the Canadian profession could focus its limited resources on researching selected problems. The Canadian profession has made a significant contribution to accounting and auditing developments in the past. There is no reason that it cannot continue to do so in the future in grappling with several individual subjects of importance. The advantages of a smaller population can sometimes be greater flexibility and greater ease in reaching a consensus. The Canadian profession should exploit these advantages. With an intelligent mixture of self-development and international cooperation, the Canadian profession can make an important contribution to future auditing developments worldwide, maintain an environment in which future Canadian practitioners will find career satisfaction, while at the same time making rational use of the ideas, research efforts, and pronouncements developed in other countries.

21.6 Auditing methods, techniques and research

The future developments of auditing techniques will perhaps not be as revolutionary as some of the possible changes discussed earlier in this chapter. However, present developments in a number of technical areas are likely to continue:

1. computers,
2. statistical sampling,
3. regression analysis and other mathematical techniques.

21.6.1 Computers

Computer-assisted auditing techniques were discussed in Chapter 14 and the application of interim audit procedures to computer-based systems is dealt with in Chapter 27. Many of the developments on the horizon are discussed briefly in these chapters. A summary of some of the likely characteristics of future systems and their impact on the auditor is shown in Figure 21.a.

21.6.2 Statistical sampling

Statistical sampling techniques were discussed in Chapter 13 and supplementary material is included in Chapter 22. Increasing volumes of data and competitive pressures on audit costs are likely to lead to the expanded use of such techniques in the future. The possible effect of current value accounting on sampling applications was mentioned in 21.2.1. In any event, increased use of statistical sampling by business for making *accounting estimates* seems likely in the future and the public accountant will be expected to assist his clients to apply these techniques efficiently. The expanded use of statistical sampling

Possible Future Computer Technology

Characteristics	Audit Impact
1. In future systems, fewer, if any, people will be involved in the processing of transactions. e.g., —automatic cash dispensing systems —automatic funds transfer systems from one organization to another.	Increased reliance will have to be placed on programmed controls to compensate for lack of division of duties, visual reviews, etc.
2. In future systems, there will be reduced use of traditional source documents such as vouchers, master file change forms, and cheques.	Possible problems may arise for the auditor in finding evidence of the satisfactory operation of controls. The auditor may have to test for compliance in "real time".
3. In future systems, there will be much greater reliance on "non-application" software such as operating systems, telecommunications software, and data base management systems.	The auditor may have to review, evaluate and verify very complex systems. There may be an implied responsibility for the auditor to review the contents of the data base for conditions requiring investigation rather than just extracting specified data for the audit. The auditor will require a high level of EDP expertise. He will probably require very sophisticated computer-assisted audit techniques (tagging, SCARF, ITF, — see 14.4.2).
4. Future systems will be "transaction-oriented" or "event-oriented" rather than "batch-oriented". Transactions will be completely processed at or near the point of origination.	The auditor will not find conventional control total techniques on which he can rely to ensure the completeness of data processed. Increased reliance will have to be placed on programmed controls to ensure completeness and accuracy. The management/audit trail will be less visible and computer-assisted techniques may be required to verify processing. The auditor will be required to review advanced systems *before implementation* to ensure that they are auditable.
5. In future systems, there will be powerful high-level programming languages available to the end user to enable him to design and program his own applications.	The auditor may have to contend with a proliferation of application programs. It may be difficult for the auditor to determine the consistency of program operation when changes can so readily be made. Programming systems will have to be designed to prevent the use of erroneous programs. The auditor will probably have to make use of high-level languages to prepare audit programs and may execute audit programs in an interactive mode.

Figure 21.a

606

for accounting estimation may raise some difficult auditing questions as well. How should the statistical precision on the client's accounting estimates be combined with the statistical precision on the auditor's audit tests? This question and others may require considerable further research.

Research into audit sampling methods in general is likely to continue both by the profession and by the academic community. Refinements and improved methods will no doubt be developed in the coming decades. Specialists in the field will have to work hard to stay current with new ideas and changing methods.

21.6.3 Regression analysis and other mathematical techniques

The application of regression analysis to analytical review procedures were discussed briefly in 10.5.2. This is a new field and much more research and experimentation may be required before the technique is widely used (though some accounting firms are using it now). The trend toward some form of association with interim financial statements will probably increase interest in the use of regression analysis. A possible application in current value accounting was also mentioned in 21.2.1. But the greatest impact of regression analysis would probably be on review procedures should public forecasting be adopted (see 21.3.1).

Research into regression methods may focus on practical methods of helping the auditor select useful independent variables and meaningful correlations. Possible methods of combining regression analysis results with statistical sampling conclusions may also be explored. Probably this research will extend to the audit application of other mathematical techniques as well – particularly, financial modeling techniques but perhaps also decision theory analysis.

21.6.4 Research

Whatever the direction of future auditing developments, it will probably be marked by much more auditing research than has taken place in the past. Task Force 2000 concluded that the profession conducted far too little research and development – though its activities have been increased since the date of that conclusion. As mentioned in 6.1.3, it has only been in the last two decades that significant attention has been given to auditing concepts (beginning with Mautz and Sharaf) and only in very recent years that these concepts have begun to be supplemented by both theoretical and empirical research. The widespread participation of the academic community in the United States in auditing research has been a major contribution as have been the symposia on auditing methods held by various U.S. universities. The future is likely to see an increasing interest in auditing research by the Canadian academic community. There remain a great many questions that practical research could help to resolve. Some suggested topics, for example, were listed in an AICPA Auditing Research Monograph, The Auditor's Reporting Obligation in 1972.[53] More recently an accounting firm has published a book, Research Opportunities in Auditing.[54] A few of the suggested research subjects are:

1. techniques of analytical review,
2. methods of internal control evaluation,
3. effectiveness of individual auditing procedures (such as confirmation),
4. weighing of audit evidence,
5. techniques of engagement review,
6. reliance on other experts,
7. criteria for evaluating uncertainties,
8. quality control techniques,
9. materiality criteria.

In addition, most of the topics discussed earlier in this chapter require further research.

21.7 Conclusion

At the beginning of this chapter it was suggested that most of today's chartered accountants will, during the course of their careers, encounter conditions markedly different from the present. The potential effects of current value accounting, accounting for non-financial resources, social accounting, forecasts, the expanding role of attestation, the development of new mathematical techniques, the effects of advanced computerization, and the explosion of technical knowledge requirements may all have a profound impact on the future practice of auditing. Undoubtedly other important developments, not presently foreseen, will occur as well. Many of the future developments seem likely to involve greater uncertainties, less conclusive audit evidence, and wider precision ranges thatn auditors have dealt with in the past – but such results may be the price of expanding the horizons of financial reporting. For tomorrow's practitioner it will be a time of many new challenges. For the profession as a whole it will be a time of new opportunities. For those interested in participating in these developments, the profession will provide an exciting and rewarding environment in which to make a contribution.

21.8 Reference material

Report to the Executive Committee and Council of the CICA by Task Force 2000 (1970).
The Commission on Auditors' Responsibilities, *Statement of Issues: Scope and Organization of the Study of Auditors' Responsibilities* (AICPA, 1975).
Robert H. Kidd, C.A., CICA Research Study, *Earnings Forecasts* (1976).

The Corporate Report, A discussion Paper prepared by a working party drawn from six major U.K. and Irish accountancy bodies (published by the Accounting Standards Steering Committee of The Institute of Chartered Accountants in England and Wales, 1975).

21.9 Review and discussion questions

1. Comment on the reasons for the formation of such groups as Task Force 2000 and the Special Commission on Auditors' Responsibilities.
2. Describe the nature of, and the most significant symptons of, the expectation gap which exists between the public accountant and the public he serves.
3. How do changes in established accounting criteria (e.g., from historical cost basis accounting) affect the audit process?
4. Distinguish between the objectives of price level and current value accounting.
5. Why would the wide-spread adoption of current value accounting be the most significant revolution in the field since the advent of the double-entry bookkeeping system?
6. Compare the nature of audit evidence normally gathered with respect to the valuation of manufactured inventories priced on an FIFO basis with the audit evidence which might have to be gathered with respect to the valuation of similar inventories priced at current entry prices.
7. Why might wider materiality limits be appropriate for the examination of statements prepared on a current value basis?
8. Comment on the major effects on the audit process of the wide-spread adoption of current value accounting (criticize the points in 21.2.1, section "Major effects on auditing"). How might these effects influence the auditor's objectivity?
9. Compare the problem of auditing an asset dollar amount for human resources (consisting of training costs and acquisition costs) with the problems of auditing fixed assets and accounts receivable.
10. What are the concerns of the profession with respect to the attestation of forecasts?
11. Give the arguments for and against a positive opinion on assumptions and consistency with respect to a forecast (as opposed to giving negative assurance).

12. If third-party reports on forecasts and on interim reports are given by the external auditor, what impact would there be on audit techniques in general? (Relate your answer to the suggested review program in 21.3.1 for forecasts and to the probable audit program for quarterly reports.)
13. What would be a major difficulty in having audit reports comment on management effectiveness, management competence, or management integrity?
14. How might resource limitations, ecological restraint, and increasing government regulation affect public accountants vis-à-vis (a) a large multi-national manufacturing client and (b) their profession?
15. In what specific ways might the current knowledge explosion in auditing, accounting, and other fields of knowledge relevant to the attest function, affect the traditional audit process in the future?

22

Supplement on Statistical Sampling Theory

The purpose of this chapter is to serve as a supplement for the interested reader who wishes an introduction to the mathematical theories underlying attributes and variables sampling in general and dollar-unit sampling in particular. Readers who find the general explanations given in Chapter 13 adequate for their needs, as it is hoped many will, may omit the present chapter without loss of continuity. Those, however, who wish some demonstration of a number of the assertions made in Chapter 13 may find the present chapter of help. Every effort has been made to present the demonstrations in layman's language rather than Greek-letter equations. Necessarily the scope must be limited. More extensive explanations of classical attributes and variables sampling (though usually not of the Poisson attributes tables and analysis of "outlier" risks included here) can be found in numerous statistical texts. Literature on dollar-unit sampling theory (apart from the articles and papers referred to in 22.4) is limited; the brief introduction in this chapter is offered as a stop-gap measure.[1]

22.1 Introduction to attributes sampling theory

22.1.1 The odds of unlikely samples

The mathematics of attributes sampling in auditing is based on the odds of selecting a sample containing far fewer errors proportionately than the population from which it was drawn. Consider the case illustrated in Figure 22.a. A population of 600 sampling units contains 18 errors (3%). A sample of 100 sampling units is drawn randomly therefrom. Of course, the most probable sample would contain 3 errors (3%) but there is some chance that it might contain 2 or 4 errors, etc. The sample shown in Figure 22.a is obviously very unlikely, for it contains no errors at all. But exactly how unlikely is this sample result?

Computing the chance of an unlikely sample

To compute the chance of this sample result being produced from such a population, we must compute the chance of drawing 100 error-free items in a row. Immediately prior to the first draw, the population contains 582 error-free items in total. The chance of drawing an error-free item on the first random draw is thus 582/600. Immediately prior to the second draw, the population contains 581 error-free items out of 599 items in total. The chance of drawing an error-free item on the second random draw is thus 581/599. The chance of drawing 100 error-free items

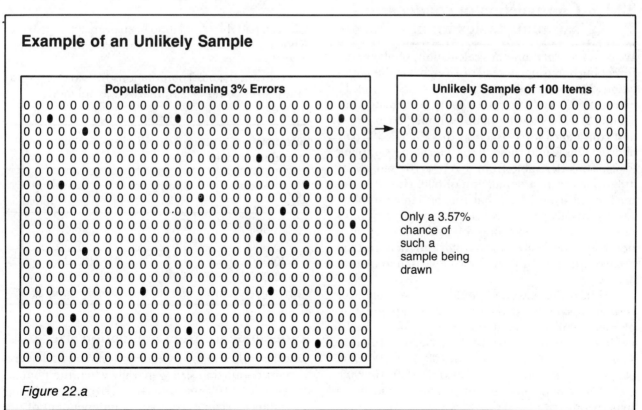

Example of an Unlikely Sample

Population Containing 3% Errors

Unlikely Sample of 100 Items

Only a 3.57% chance of such a sample being drawn

Figure 22.a

in succession is thus:

$$\frac{582}{600} \times \frac{581}{599} \times \frac{580}{598} \ldots \ldots \times \frac{483}{501} = 3.57\%$$

In other words, the chance of drawing an error-free sample of 100 from a population of 600 containing 3% errors is only 3.57% – very unlikely indeed.

Interpretation of sample results

Suppose that, from another population of size 600, but containing an unknown frequency of errors, we have just drawn an error-free random sample of 100. What can we conclude? First of all, there is a fair probability that the unknown population contains no errors at all; this is, in fact, the *most likely error* frequency (the same frequency as found in the sample). But clearly, the population might contain a few errors and by chance we did not encounter any of them in the sample. By the foregoing computation, however, we know that had the unknown population error frequency been as high as 3%, there would have only been a 3.57% chance (the *sampling risk*) of drawing an error-free sample. In other words, we can be 96.43% confident that had the unknown population contained an error frequency as high as 3% we would have detected it (by finding a sample error-rate higher than the zero-sample-error-rate we actually observed). At a *confidence level* of 96.43% the *upper error limit* is therefore 3%.

22.1.2 Construction of condensed sampling tables for attributes

We could repeat numerous calculations similar to the foregoing but using, instead of 18 errors in the population (3%), other values such as 19 errors (3.2%), 17 errors (2.8%), etc. The results could be tabulated in a sampling table showing pairs of upper error limits and confidence levels (such as the 3%/96.43% pair above). This would show all the alternative sampling conclusions derivable from a zero-error sample of 100 drawn from a population of 600. (It will be remembered from 13.1.4 that for the same sampling results various pairs of confidence and upper limits are possible.) By searching this table for the confidence level he desires, the auditor can then find the related upper error limit (for comparison to materiality, etc.).

Such a table, however, would only be usable for zero-error samples of 100 drawn from a population of 600. Similar computations could therefore be made and tabulated for 1-error, 2-error, 10-error samples, etc., for sample sizes of 100, 150, 200, 500, etc., for populations of 600, 1 000, 10 000, 100 000, etc. The compilation of such tables (known as hypergeometric tables) provides a perfectly accurate

evaluation tool for the auditor but requires numerous pages and frequent interpolations by the auditor when the exact conditions desired are not tabulated.[2] Fortunately, if two minor and *conservative* (i.e., on the safe side) approximations are allowed, considerable simplification of such tables is possible.

First simplification

The first simplification can be made by ignoring the minor effect of even substantial variations in the population size. That this effect is indeed minor can be seen from the following calculations. Suppose, in the foregoing illustration, that the population had been 6 000 instead of 600, and still contained a 3% error rate (180 errors). The chance of drawing an error-free sample of size 100 would have been computed as:

$$\frac{5820}{6000} \times \frac{5819}{5999} \times \frac{5818}{5998} \times \ldots \ldots \times \frac{5721}{5901} = 4.64\%$$

Had the population instead been 600 000 and still contained a 3% error rate (18 000 errors) the chance of drawing an error-free sample of size 100 would have been computed as:

$$\frac{582\,000}{600\,000} \times \frac{581\,999}{599\,999} \times \frac{581\,998}{599\,998} \times \ldots \times \frac{581\,901}{599\,901}$$

which, to the limits of five figure accuracy, equals

$$.97000 \times .97000 \times .97000 \times \ldots \times .97000$$

$$= (.97000)^{100} = 4.75\%$$

Clearly, had the population been even larger (such as 6 000 000), the chance would still have worked out to 4.75%.

Accordingly, our computations for varying population sizes could be summarized as follows:

Summary of rigorous calculations for varying population sizes

Population size	Sampling risk	Sampling confidence
600	3.57%	96.43%
6 000	4.64	95.36
600 000	4.75	95.25
6 000 000	4.75	95.25
(error-free sample of 100, upper error limit of 3%)		

Independence from population size

It will be noted in the foregoing summary that over a certain population size (generally when the population is at least 100 times the sample size), the sampling confidence becomes completely independent of the population size provided the upper error limit is expressed as a frequency rather than an absolute amount. Even below this level, the effect of variation in population size is trivial unless, for example, the sample consists of half the entire population, which is unusual. This independence from population size is often puzzling to newcomers to sampling. It may, however, be understood in the following sense: one need take only one swallow to determine how salty the ocean is (i.e., what *frequency* or *proportion* of salt occurs therein); the size of the required swallow is not dependent on the size of the ocean (although marginally greater assurance would be theoretically possible if one drank half the ocean and thus significantly reduced the size of the remaining population to be estimated).

It can also be noted from the foregoing summary that (for the same upper error limit percentage and same sample results) the sampling confidence for a large population is *slightly less*, if anything, than the sampling confidence for a small population. Thus, if an auditor were always to use evaluations appropriate for large populations he might sometimes slightly understate the sampling confidence he had obtained – but this would at least be on the conservative or safe side. Of course, gross understatements would be undesirable as they would lead the auditor to do more work than necessary. However, as can be seen, the understatements of confidence are trivial in amount. Indeed, as explained in Chapter 13, the judgmental decision as to desired confidence level cannot be said to be meaningful within one or two percentage points. Thus, while it is theoretically possible to make the *finite population corrections* to allow for small populations, as a practical matter it is suggested that the auditor ignore such trivial adjustments and use evaluations based on large populations.

The compilation of large-population tables (known as binomial tables) provides a somewhat more concise evaluation tool for the auditor.[3] However, yet further simplification is possible.

Second simplification

The second simplification consists of using a mathematical approximation. The previous binomial calculation:

$(.97000)^{100} = 4.75\%$ sampling risk for a 3% upper error limit can be conveniently approximated by the Poisson formula:

$e^{-100 \times 3\%} = e^{-3} = 4.98\%$ (where e is the symbol for a particular number used in many areas of higher mathematics and equals approximately 2.718).

The comparison of these two calculations can be summarized as follows:

Effect of Poisson approximation

	Sampling risk	Sampling confidence
Binomial calculation (rigorous for large populations, slightly on the safe side for small populations)	4.75%	95.25%
Poisson approximation (always an approximation on the safe side)	4.98	95.02

(Error-free sample of 100, upper error limit of 3%)

Once again it can be shown (the proof, however, is beyond the scope of this text) that, in relevant ranges for audit use, the Poisson approximation is always on the safe side although, as can be seen in the foregoing, the difference is usually small.

Effect of the two simplifications on evaluation

If both these simplifications are made, the confidence level obtained with respect to a specified upper error limit will always be slightly understated, as demonstrated in the following summary:

Effect of both simplifications on confidence level

Population size	Computed rigorously (hypergeometric)	First simplification (binomial)	Second simplification (Poisson)
600	96.43%	95.25%	95.02%
6 000	95.36	95.25	95.02
600 000	95.25	95.25	95.02
6 000 000	95.25	95.25	95.02

(Error-free sample of 100, upper error limit of 3%)

Alternatively, for a specified confidence level the computed upper error limit will be slightly overstated by these simplifications. Either discrepancy is in a conservative (safe) direction for the auditing conclusion.

Effect of the two simplifications on sample size planning

If desired confidence level and upper error limit are specified, the computed sample size necessary to achieve these results will be slightly overstated, as demonstrated in the following summary:

Effect of both simplifications on (a) sample size and on (b) sample size times upper error limit

Upper error limit frequency	Rigorous (hypergeometric) For population size of:				First simplification (binomial)		Second simplification (Poisson)	
	10 000		50 000					
	(a)	(b)	(a)	(b)	(a)	(b)	(a)	(b)
10%	29	(2.90)	29	(2.90)	29	(2.90)	30	(3.00)
5%	58	(2.90)	58	(2.90)	59	(2.95)	60	(3.00)
3%	98	(2.94)	98	(2.94)	99	(2.97)	100	(3.00)
1%	294	(2.94)	297	(2.97)	298	(2.98)	300	(3.00)
0.5%	580	(2.90)	594	(2.97)	598	(2.99)	600	(3.00)
0.3%	948	(2.84)	987	(2.96)	997	(2.99)	1 000	(3.00)

(95% confidence and error-free samples in each case)

Again the differences can be seen to be always in the safe direction and generally trivial in amount.[4]

The foregoing summary exhibits a remarkable feature: for a specified number of sample errors (in this case 0), the product of the upper error limit times the sample size is almost constant – and when the Poisson approximation is used the product *is* constant. This product represents the most likely number of sample errors one would have expected had the true error rate in the population been equal to the upper error limit. Thus, the Poisson approximation permits condensing the whole of the foregoing table into one line:

Upper error limit frequency × sample size = 3.00
(for 95% confidence and 0 sample errors)

In brief, if you would have expected three sample errors, had the upper-error-limit frequency really existed, but you found no sample errors, you can be 95% sure the population error rate is not as great as the upper error limit.

Extension to one or more sample errors

While the preceding calculations were for the case of 0 sample errors, similar calculations can be made for 1, 2, 3, etc. sample errors. For example, for a sample size of 100 and a population error frequency of p:

The risk of drawing 0 sample errors
$= e^{-100p}$
(the same formula quoted previously)
while the risk of drawing 1 sample error
$= 100p.e^{-100p}$
(the analogous formula for 1 sample error)
So, the risk of drawing 0 or 1 sample errors
$= (1 + 100p)e^{-100p}$
When $p = 4.75\%$ this risk works out to
$$(1 + 4.75)e^{-4.75} = 5.0\%.$$

In other words, if the population really contains a 4.75% error rate there is only a 5% chance of a sample of 100 yielding as few as one sample error. Therefore we can say, having discovered only one sample error, that the upper error limit is 4.75%. And again we can express the result for all possible sample sizes in one line:

Upper error limit frequency × sample size = 4.75
(for 95% confidence and 1 sample error)
Similar calculations would derive the following results:

Number of errors in sample	Upper error limit frequency sample size
0	3.00
1	4.75
2	6.30
3	7.76
.	.
.	.
.	.

(For 95% confidence)

If we use the term "UEL cumulative factor" to describe the product of the upper error limit frequency times the sample size, and if we repeat similar calculations for other confidence levels besides 95%, we can construct a table beginning:

UEL Cumulative Factors

Number of errors in sample	80% confidence	95% confidence	99% confidence
0	1.61	3.00	4.61
1	3.00	4.75	6.64
2	4.28	6.30	8.41
3	5.52	7.76	10.05
.	.	.	.
.	.	.	.
.	.	.	.

Where upper error limit frequency = $\dfrac{\text{UEL cumulative factor}}{\text{sample size}}$

For example, for a sample of 200 containing 3 errors, at 95% confidence, UEL frequency = $\dfrac{7.76}{200} = 3.9\%$

Completing this table for more confidence levels and sample errors results in the complete tabulation shown in Figure 13.g. This represents a remarkably convenient one-page condensation of the eighty-page attributes sampling tables otherwise required.

22.1.3 Interrelationship of sample size, confidence, sample error rate, and upper error limit

In Chapter 13 the interrelationship of sample size, sampling confidence, sample error rate, and projected upper error limit was explained in general terms (see Figure 13.b). This interrelationship can be demonstrated in terms of the table and formula just discussed.

a) Given: desired confidence level (95%)
   desired upper error limit (2%)
   anticipated sample error rate (3 errors)
   One can compute:
   required sample size = $\dfrac{7.76}{2\%}$ = 388

b) Or given: sample size used (250)
   observed sample error rate (2 errors)
   desired confidence level (80%)
   One can compute:
   upper error limit frequency = $\dfrac{4.28}{250} = 1.7\%$

22.1.4 Independence from error distribution or population distribution

It should be observed that in the foregoing discussion no assumption was made as to the distribution of errors in the population being audited, nor as to the distribution of population item values, nor as to the homogeneity of the population. Provided that the same confidence level is appropriate throughout, it does not matter whether all the large items are clustered at one end of the population or sprinkled randomly throughout, whether all the errors are clustered in one section of the population or spread uniformly throughout, whether all population items were processed by the same clerk or by several clerks, or even whether some of the population items are receivable balances and others inventory units. All that attributes sampling theory says is that if there is a certain proportion of income-distorting errors somewhere in that population, a random sample of a given size will have calculable odds of encountering a specified number of them. The process of making a *random* selection is equivalent to shuffling the population. The top ten cards would constitute a random sample from a deck if the deck had first been randomly shuffled. Because the deck is going to be shuffled anyway (random selection is equivalent to shuffling) the order in which the deck happens to be, prior to sampling, does not matter.

615

Comparison to variables sampling theory

It may also be observed in the foregoing discussion that, unlike variables sampling as later discussed, computations for attributes sampling do not depend upon the *normal distribution*, normality of sampling means, normality of the underlying population, stability of estimates of the standard deviation, etc.

While a very few sampling texts have tabulated 'normal curve approximations' to attributes formulas (i.e., normal curve approximations to hypergeometric formulas), such approximations often deviate from the rigorous values on the risky side (unlike the Poisson approximations which are always conservative). For use in attributes sampling such 'normal curve approximations' are therefore best avoided.

22.2 Introduction to variables sampling theory

22.2.1 The tendency for 'normal curve' distribution of sample averages

The mathematics of variables sampling is based on the tendency for sample averages (from numerous random samples of equal size drawn from the same population) to be distributed in a certain pattern referred to as the *normal curve*. The larger the sample size, the greater this tendency (central limit theorem). For example, even if invoice values in a population of purchase invoices are distributed in a *non-normal* or *skewed* distribution (as illustrated in the left half of Figure 22.b and as is common in accounting populations), the distribution of sample averages from many random samples drawn therefrom will tend to be *normally distributed* (as illustrated in the right half of Figure 22.b). About half of all possible samples will tend to overestimate the true population average of $500 and about half will tend to underestimate it – which is why the bell-shaped "normal curve" at the right is symmetrical.

The width of the normal curve can be characterized by a quantity known as the *standard deviation* (explained below). The shape of the normal curve is such that 68.3% of all possible sample averages fall within a range of the true average ± 1 standard deviation, 90% within ± 1.65 standard deviations, 95% within ± 1.96 standard deviations, etc. Of course, a typical sample average will likely be much closer to the true population average of $500 than is a typical individual invoice (which is why the right-hand curve is much narrower than the left-hand one). Exactly how likely it is to be closer will depend on the sample size. The distribution of sample averages of samples of size 1 000 will obviously be much more tightly clustered around the $500 mark than a distribution of sample averages of samples of size 10. Indeed, according to the central limit theorem,

Standard deviation of sample averages (right-hand curve)

$$= \frac{\text{Standard deviation of population (left-hand curve)}}{\sqrt{\text{Sample size}}}$$

Interpretation of sample results

Of course, in practice the auditor does not take repeated samples from the same population but rather *only one sample*. Nonetheless, in the example illustrated in Figure 22.b, of all the samples the auditor might have taken, 90% would have had averages falling within the range indicated in the right-hand curve. Accordingly, there is a 90% chance that his one audit sample average is within this range. One commonly summarizes this conclusion by stating that the auditor can be 90% confident that the true population average is not more than 1.65 standard deviations away from his sample estimate. In terms of the standard deviation of the population, his audit precision is therefore:

Precision (for 90% confidence)

$$= \frac{1.65 \times \text{Standard deviation of population}}{\sqrt{\text{Sample size}}}$$

$$= \frac{1.65 \times \$312}{\sqrt{100}}$$

$$= \$51$$

He can be 90% confident that the population average will lie within a range of ± $51 around the average found in his sample Of course, there is a 10% chance he is wrong (a 5% chance that the population average is really above this range and a 5% chance that it is really below). Thus, in this example, should the auditor only be interested in the upper limit, he could conclude with 95% confidence that the population average did not exceed his sample average (the most likely value) by more than $51.

Estimating the population standard deviation

The foregoing computations were based on the standard deviation ($312) of the population – but, of course, the auditor does not know this standard deviation (unless he has examined the population 100%). It is common practice to estimate the population standard deviation from the sample values in the manner illustrated in Figure 22.c. It will be noted in

Relationship of Sample Average to Underlying Population

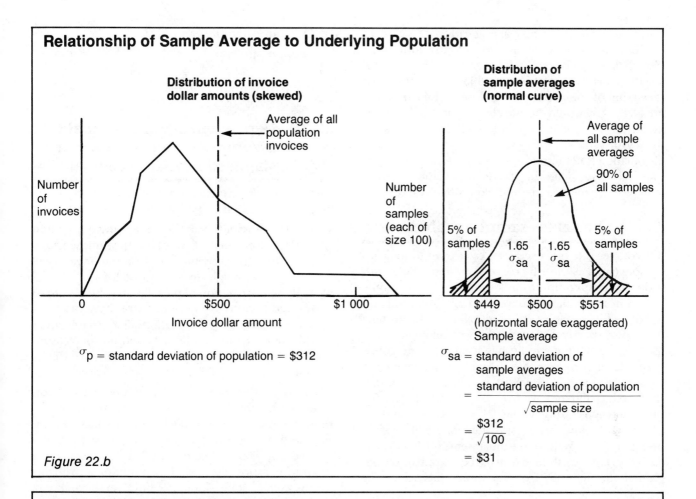

Figure 22.b

Variables Sampling Calculations

Individual invoice values within the sample		Sample average	Deviation from average	Squared deviations
1.	$ 410	$494	− $ 84	7 056
2.	223	494	− 271	73 441
3.	1 160	494	+ 666	443 556
4.	581	494	+ 87	7 569
.	.	.	.	.
.	.	.	.	.
.	.	.	.	.
100.	476	494	− 18	324
Totals	$49 412		ϕ	9 089 192

Average $\dfrac{49\,412}{100} = \$494$

Adjusted average $= \dfrac{9\,089\,192}{(100-1)} = 91\,810$

Square root of adjusted average $= \sqrt{91\,810} = \$303$

An unbiased estimate of the standard deviation of the population ⟶

Sampling conclusion: 90% confident population average lies in range $\$494 \pm 1.65\,\sqrt{\dfrac{303}{100}}$ i.e., in range $\$494 \pm \$50$

(Formula is: precision in dollars $= \pm \dfrac{t}{\sqrt{\text{sample size}}} \times \sqrt{\dfrac{\text{sum of squared deviations in sample}}{(\text{sample size} - 1)}}$

where t is a tabulated factor depending on confidence level)

Figure 22.c

this figure that the sample average of $494 is close to the population average (unknown to the auditor) of $500 – it would be purely fortuitous if it were identical. Similarly, his estimate of $303 for the standard deviation of the population is close to the true value of $312 – it would be purely fortuitous if it were identical. For many populations, the minor discrepancy in estimating the standard deviation of the population is not important. But clearly if it were not possible to estimate the standard deviation reasonably well, the above method would be invalid.

22.2.2 Variables sampling tables

Of course, it is not necessary each time to look up factors (such as the 1.65 corresponding to 90% confidence), or to compute the square root of the sample size. These calculations have been precomputed and tabulated in variables sampling tables.[5] The auditor need only specify the standard deviation he has computed, the sample size he has used, and the confidence level he desires, and the tables will provide the resulting precision (sometimes called sampling error) he has obtained. Conversely, he can specify the precision and confidence he desires and the standard deviation he anticipates, and the tables will provide the sample size required. Adjustments for *finite population corrections*, though not large, can also be obtained automatically from most such tables.

22.2.3 Interrelationship of sample size, confidence, sample standard deviation, and precision

The interrelationship between sample size, sampling confidence, sample standard deviation, and precision (see Figure 13.b) can be demonstrated in terms of the calculations and formula just discussed.

a) Given: desired confidence level (95% one-sided = 90% two-sided)
desired precision of estimate of invoice average (± $40)
anticipated sample standard deviation ($400)

One can compute:

$$\text{required sample size} = \left(1.65 \times \frac{\$400}{\$40} \right)^2 = 272$$

(Or look it up in tables.)

b) Or given: sample size used (250)
observed sample standard deviation ($386)
desired confidence level (99% one-sided = 98% two-sided)

One can compute:

$$\text{sampling precision} = \pm \frac{2.33 \times \$386}{\sqrt{250}} = \pm \$57$$

(Or look it up in tables.)

22.2.4 Dependence upon 'normality' assumption and accuracy of standard deviation estimate

The validity of variables sampling calculations of the type just described rests upon two assumptions:

a) that the distribution of the underlying population is not so abnormal (skewed) nor the sample size so small that the distribution of sample means will not be reasonably close to normality,

b) that the distribution of population values is not so skewed (by the presence of extreme values) that the estimate of the population standard deviation calculated from sample data will not be reasonably close to the true population standard deviation.

For most of the conditions commonly met in audit practice the first assumption is reasonably safe – though it may break down where very small stratum sample sizes occur in a highly stratified sample of a skewed population. For many of the conditions met in audit practice the second assumption is probably safe as well. In some situations, however, it can break down as illustrated in the following sections.

22.2.5 Extreme example where difference method is unreliable

Difference and ratio estimation are described briefly in 13.2.5. An example will illustrate the difficulties to which the difference method (and, to a lesser extent, the ratio method) is occasionally prone. Suppose that an auditor has confirmed all receivable balances individually exceeding $5 000 (high-value selection) and is left with a remaining population of 10 000 receivable balances totalling $1 000 000, from which he draws a sample of 100 balances (one every 100). Suppose that, unknown to him, the 10 000 balances contain the following errors of overstatement:

200 errors averaging $1 each	= $	200
20 errors averaging $3 000 each	=	60 000
		$60 200

Typically, his sample of 100 balances will contain 2 of the $1 errors (since he is choosing one account per 100) and none of the $3 000 errors (indeed, about 80% of the time, choosing one per 100, he would find

618

none of the 20 $3 000 errors). He will compute his typical sampling conclusion as follows:

Sample item	Error value
1	$1
2	1
3	0
4	0
.	.
.	.
.	.
.	.
.	.
100	0
Total	$2
Average error per sample item	2¢

Unbiased estimate of the standard deviation of the population (computed as in Figure 22.c)   14¢

Sampling conclusion (ignoring finite population correction):

90% confident that population average error

lies in range $2¢ \pm 1.65 \dfrac{14¢}{\sqrt{100}}$

i.e., in range $2¢ \pm 2.3¢$

The auditor would therefore typically conclude that he had 90% confidence that the average error per account lay in the range $2¢ \pm 2.3¢$ or, for 10 000 accounts, that total population error lay in the range $200 \pm $230. But in fact, far from being right 90% of the time (as his stated confidence implies), he will be right only about 20% of the time. Indeed, his conclusion will usually be seriously in error – for the true population error is $60 200! His mistaken conclusion was based on the smallness of the errors he found in his sample ($1 each) and ignored the possible size ($3 000 each) of undiscovered errors. Statistically, the problem arises in assuming that the 14¢ standard deviation of the sample of differences is close to the standard deviation of the population of differences. In fact, the correct standard deviation of the population of differences in this example is $223.20. Had he used this correct (but to him unknown) standard deviation in his evaluation his conclusion would have been expressed as the range $200 \pm $368 000 (which range does indeed contain the true population error).

Nature of the problem

The problem thus is one of estimating the standard deviation of the population. If his sample contains no $3 000 errors (as is most likely), his computed standard deviation estimate will be around 14¢ and thus far too low. If, rarely, his sample contains one $3 000 error, his computed standard deviation estimate will be about $500 and thus somewhat high. Since his standard deviation estimate depends directly on whether he discovers a large error or not in his sample, he can hardly argue, from the smallness of a particular sample's standard deviation, that large population errors do not exist.

As explained in Chapter 13, advocates of the difference and ratio methods believe that in many cases the risk of 'outliers' (the $3 000 errors) being present is remote and that, where it is not, certain protective measures can help to prevent the auditor from making the sort of mistake just illustrated.

22.2.6 Extreme example where stratified mean-per-unit method is unreliable

The mean-per-unit method is described briefly in 13.2.6 and 13.2.7. An example will illustrate the difficulties to which the stratified mean-per-unit method is occasionally prone. Suppose that an auditor wishes to confirm a sample drawn from a large department store's 2 000 000 receivable balances which vary from $10 up to $2 000 (after removing high-value selections). Because of the large variability, the population requires extensive stratification. While a sample will be drawn from each stratum, we will confine our attention to the stratum of 100 000 accounts between $900 and $1 000, from which the auditor draws a sample of 100 balances (one every 1 000). Suppose that, unknown to him, the 100 000 balances contain 500 fictitious accounts recorded in error during a recent computer conversion and totalling $500 000. Over 60% of the time he will not catch any of these 500 errors in his sample, for he picks only 1 item in every 1 000. The stratum values are as follows:

	True value	Reported value
99 500 valid accounts @ average value of $945 =	$94 027 500	$94 027 500
500 invalid accounts @ average value of $945 =	ϕ	472 500
	$94 027 500	$94 500 000

Failing to find any errors, the auditor computes his sampling conclusion as follows:

Sample item	Audited value of account balance
1	$920
2	990
3	940
4	960
.	.
.	.
.	.
.	.
.	.
100	930
Average value of audited account balance	$945
Unbiased estimate of the standard deviation of the stratum (computed as in Figure 22.c)	$28.90

Sampling conclusion: 80% confident that stratum average lies in range

$$945 \pm 1.28 \frac{28.90}{\sqrt{100}} \text{ i.e., in range } \$945 \pm \$3.70$$

The auditor would therefore typically conclude that he had 80% confidence that the average stratum value lay in the range $945 ± $3.70 or, for 100 000 accounts, that total stratum value lay in the range $94 500 000 ± $370 000 (i.e., from $94 130 000 to $94 870 000). But in fact, far from being right 80% of the time (as his stated confidence implies), he will be right less than 40% of the time. His conclusion will usually be in error – for indeed the true population error of $472 500 lies outside his $370 000 precision range. The monetary discrepancy in this case is not large proportionately, but the misstatement of sampling confidence level is substantial.

His mistaken conclusion was based on the low variability of the reported book values in the stratum (standard deviation $28.90), a low variability that had been obtained by the very process of stratification, and ignored the possible greater variability created by large undiscovered errors (500 errors averaging $945 each). Statistically, the problem arises again in assuming that the $28.90 standard deviation of the sample is close to the standard deviation of the whole stratum. In fact, the correct standard deviation of the true values in the whole stratum in this example (assuming a uniform distribution of balances from $900 to $990 except for the 500 nil amounts) is $72.70.

Nature of the problem

Once again, the problem is one of estimating the standard deviation of the population stratum. If his sample contains none of the fictitious accounts (as is most likely) his computed standard deviation estimate will be around $28.90 and thus be far too low. If his sample does contain one of the fictitious accounts, his computed standard deviation estimate will be about $99 and thus be slightly high. Since his standard deviation estimate depends substantially on whether he discovers a large error or not in his sample, he can hardly argue, from the smallness of a particular sample's standard deviation, that such large population errors do not exist.

Again, as explained in Chapter 13, advocates of the mean-per-unit method believe that in many cases the risk of outliers (the $945 errors) is remote and that, where it is not, certain protective measures can help to prevent the auditor from making the sort of mistake just illustrated. Indeed, mean-per-unit projections (with such protective measures where necessary) may be the only practical approach for *accounting* applications, where sampling is being used to estimate the total of some population for which no total recorded book value exists. For *auditing* applications, however, where the auditor is searching for errors in recorded book values, the alternative of applying attributes sampling exists and the practitioner must decide which method most efficiently and reliably meets his audit objectives.

22.3 Introduction to dollar-unit sampling theory

The basic concepts of dollar-unit sampling were described in 13.3. The purpose of the sections which follow here is to provide a brief explanation of the theory underlying:

1. the tainted dollar evaluation method described in 13.3.2,
2. the approximation rule for combining sample results described in 13.3.4,
3. the rule-of-thumb guidelines for judgmental representative tests described in 12.5.4,
4. control of the risk of false alarms,
5. control of the risk of extreme understatements,
6. the cell-method of evaluation referred to in 13.3.5.

For a more extended treatment of these and other aspects of dollar-unit sampling the reader is referred to the sources listed in 22.4.

22.3.1 The tainted dollar evaluation method

The evaluation of dollar-unit discovery samples (those containing zero sample errors) follows directly from the classical attributes sampling theory described earlier in this chapter – the only novel feature being the definition of the sampling unit as an individual dollar. No modifications to long established theory are required. It is only when sample errors are encountered that additional theoretical considerations arise.

One way of continuing with classical methods

Actually, it is possible to cast dollar-unit sampling in a mould to which classical evaluation methods can be applied straightforwardly without modification. Instead of considering a $1 000 overstatement error found in a $5 000 invoice as "tainting" each of the 5 000 component dollars by 20%, one could instead decide in advance that any discovered error was to be allocated to the front-end of the physical-unit in which it occurred.

It can be readily seen that this allocation method involves a classical attributes sampling situation – every dollar in the field is either correctly stated or false, even when only an invoice or account is only partially misstated, because the errors are assigned to specific dollars. It would be perfectly valid for the auditor to use such an approach, applying the sampling table values in Figure 13.d directly to the number of dollar-unit errors discovered.[6] (It must be remembered, of course, that, as in the above illustration, not every discovered error will turn out to be a dollar-unit error for projection purposes using this method.)

While such an approach is perfectly valid (indeed the simplest to explain in classical attribute terms), it does not make maximum use of the sample information available. It ignores any errors that do not happen to be "scored" as dollar-unit errors. As a result, repeated samples drawn from the same population will lead to a greater variability in sampling conclusion than in the tainted dollar evaluation method – although both will yield the same average conclusion in the long run. Since such variability can lead to undesirable variability in the extent of audit work necessary to audit identical situations, the tainted dollar evaluation method is suggested as the preferable approach.

Modifications to classical methods when the tainted dollar evaluation method is used

With the tainted allocation method it is necessary to determine how the projections of various possible taintings should be combined. In 13.3.2 a method was described whereby the discovery of one 20%-tainted dollar-unit in the sample would increase the upper error limit over that for a sample having no sample errors by only 20% of the increase which the discovery of one 100%-tainted sample error would have caused.[7] While the result may seem intuitively reasonable, one must properly ask if it is indeed valid. To examine this question, consider the same example of a sample of 50 fixed asset purchase invoices drawn from a population of $3 000 000, in which sample the auditor has found one 20%-tainted overstatement and desires 95% sampling confidence as to his conclusion. To be on the safe side in evaluating this sample one must ask: what is the worst (i.e., highest error value) hypothetical population condition which, if it existed, would not have produced, 5% of the time, sample results equal to or better than those actually observed?

Clearly such a worst hypothetical population:

a) could not contain more than 9.5% (4.75/50, see Figure 13.d) combined frequency of errors of all taintings, for, if it did, sample results as good as only one error (our actual case) would have occurred less than 5% of the time,

b) could not contain more than a 6.0% (3.00/50, see Figure 13.d) combined frequency of errors of all taintings over 20%, for, if it did, sample results as good as only one 20% error (our actual case) would have occurred no more than 5% of the time.

If we wish to identify a worst hypothetical population, we should imagine a population containing a 9.5% frequency of errors, the maximum permitted by constraint (a). Various hypothetical populations could fit this assumption, some of which are as follows:

Hypo-thetical population type	Combined frequency of taintings		Total combined frequency
	over 20%	20% and under	
A	0	9.5%	9.5%
B	1%	8.5	9.5
C	2	7.5	9.5
.	.	.	.
.	.	.	.
.	.	.	.
G	6	3.5	9.5

Clearly, as one moves down this table the total error *value* in the population increases (since taintings 20% or under are replaced by equal frequencies of taintings over 20%). However, population type G is the furthest down one can go in the table, since a 6% frequency for taintings over 20% is the maximum permitted by constraint (b). Thus, the *worst* hypothetical population (i.e., the one having the highest possible error value consistent with constraints (a) and (b) above) must be one with a 6% combined frequency of taintings over 20% and a 3.5% combined frequency of taintings 20% and under (a population of type G). Of all the populations of this type, the one having the highest (worst) error value, is clearly that in which the 6% frequency of taintings "over 20%" is composed solely of 100% taintings (the maximum possible) and the 3.5% frequency of taintings "20% and under" is composed solely of 20% taintings.

The error value of this worst population is:

Tainting	Upper error limit frequency		Upper error limit value rate	Error amount in $3 000 000 population
100%	6.0%	(3.00/50)	6.00%	$180 000
20	3.5	(1.75/50)	0.70	21 000
	9.5%	(4.75/50)	6.70%	$201 000

Thus, we may say that $201 000 is the error value in the 'worst' population possible which satisfies both constraints (a) and (b) individually. In the regular tainted dollar evaluation method, $201 000 would be taken as the *upper error limit* for this example. Actually, it can be shown to be slightly high, which is conservative. By satisfying constraints (a) and (b) individually, no credit was taken for the *joint effect* of these two constraints. For the one-sample-error case it can be shown mathematically that the correct *worst* upper limit in this example should really be $181 500[8] rather than $201 000. (Conversely, it can be shown mathematically that the true sampling risk of the $201 000 error rate is not 5%, but only 3.6%).[9,10]

It should be noted that by always assuming the worst situation, dollar-unit sampling places no reliance on any probable distribution of error sizes or of item values (as does variables sampling). Thus, although the worst situation chosen will, of course, vary with the sample results found, there is no variables risk or normal-curve assumption involved in dollar-unit sampling.[11]

22.3.2 The approximation rule for combining sample results

An approximation rule for combining sample results was described in 13.3.4. By this rule, "basic precisions" within different sampling conclusions were taken as concurrent while "most likely errors" and "precision gap widenings" were added. A demonstration of the validity of this rule is shown in Figure 22.d. There it can be seen that while the global evaluation of receivables and inventory taken together would yield an upper error limit of $296 400, the approximation rule for combining the separate receivables and inventory evaluations yields a slightly higher upper error limit, $300 000. By being slightly higher, the approximation rule is on the safe side. Indeed, it can be shown mathematically that the approximation rule is always conservative, if anything, relative to the global evaluation. (Examination of Figure 22.d will indicate that the reason for this is that the precision-gap-widenings are, in fact, not quite additive and adding them is therefore conservative.)

Combination at different confidence levels

In 13.3.4 it was suggested that the approximation rule also be applied to combine sampling projections made at different confidence levels. The separate sample evaluations should *not* be converted to equal confidence levels for combination purposes since the differences in sampling confidence level reflect real differences in the other associated risks (inherent risk of error, control risk, effect of overlapping audit procedures). To convert dissimilar situations to identical confidence levels would yield either misleadingly high upper error limits (if low-risk situations were restated at a needlessly high level of sampling confidence) or misleadingly low upper error limits (if high-risk situations are restated at an unjustifiably low level of sampling confidence).[12]

22.3.3 The rule-of-thumb guidelines for judgmental representative tests

In 12.5.4 some rule-of-thumb guidelines were suggested for determining approximate sample sizes for judgmental representative tests where the testing

Demonstration of Validity of Approximation Rule for Combining Sample Results
(95% confidence, all errors are overstatements)

	UEL component factor	×	Tainting percentage	×	Average sampling interval	=	Dollar conclusion
Separate Evaluations							
Receivables							
Basic precision	3.00		100%		$60 000		$180 000
Most likely error							
− 1st error	1.00		80%				
− 2nd error	1.00		10%				
			90%		60 000		54 000
Precision gap widening							
− 1st error	.75		80%	.60			
− 2nd error	.55		10%	.06			
				.66	60 000		39 600
Upper error limit							$273 600
Inventory							
Basic precision	3.00		100%		60 000		$180 000
Most likely error							
− 1st error	1.00		25%		60 000		15 000
Precision gap widening							
− 1st error	.75		25%	.19	60 000		11 400
Upper error limit							$206 400
Global Evaluation							
Basic precision	3.00		100%		60 000		$180 000
Most likely error							
− 1st error	1.00		80%				
− 2nd error	1.00		25%				
− 3rd error	1.00		10%				
			115%		60 000		69 000
Precision gap widening							
− 1st error	.75		80%	.60			
− 2nd error	.55		25%	.14			
− 3rd error	.46		10%	.05			
				.79	60 000		47 400
Upper error limit							$296 400

Approximation Rule for Combining Separate Evaluations

	Basic precision (concurrent)	Most likely error (additive)	Precision gap widening (additive)	Upper error limit (cross-add final components)
Receivables	$180 000	$54 000	$39 600	$273 600
Inventory	180 000	15 000	11 400	206 400
Approximation of global	$180 000	$69 000	$51 000	$300 000

Figure 22.d

623

objective was substantive. The derivation of these guidelines can be explained using the formula for computing dollar-unit sample extents explained in 13.4.7.

1. *Where a few uncorrected errors are anticipated*

$$\frac{\text{Net population dollar value}}{\text{sample size}}$$

= Average sampling interval

$$= \frac{\text{Tolerable basic precision in dollars}}{\text{Basic precision factor} \times \text{error size-limit assumption}}$$

In the typical audit, total "most likely error" projections (after client corrections or provisions) do not exceed one-third materiality. If sample taintings are small, this means "tolerable basic precision" can usually be as high as two-thirds materiality. Thus, on a typical audit:

Sample size

$$= \frac{\text{Basic precision factor} \times \text{net population dollar value}}{2/3 \times \text{materiality (in dollars)}}$$

This can be restated as:

Sample size

$$= \frac{\text{Net population dollar value}}{\text{Materiality (in dollars)}} \times \text{Judgment factor}$$

where judgment factor

= basic precision factor ÷ 2/3

2. *Where the client will provide for or correct all projected errors*

On the other hand, in those audits where it is anticipated that the client will provide for or correct all projected errors, virtually all the materiality limit can be reserved for basic precision and the 2/3 factor is unnecessary.

In that case, the judgment factor equals the basic precision factor

Related confidence levels

Accordingly, the related confidence level in statistical terms would be:

Degree of audit assurance	Anticipated errors (net of corrections and provisions)	Judgment factor prescribed in 12.5.4	Related basic precision factor	Related confidence level
Considerable	Up to one-third materiality	6	4.0	98%
Normal	Up to one-third materiality	4	2.7	93%
Minimum	Up to one-third materiality	3	2.0	86%
Considerable	None	4	4.0	98%
Normal	None	3	3.0	95%
Minimum	None	2	2.0	86%

Since these statistical confidence levels are reasonably consistent with those suggested in Chapter 13, it follows that the rule-of-thumb guidelines should result in judgmental sample sizes not too dissimilar from what statistical sample extents would have been. Of course, practitioners having different views as to what range of levels of sampling confidence is appropriate will wish to adjust these guidelines correspondingly.

22.3.4 Controlling the risk of 'false alarms'

In audit sampling it is common to identify two types of risks – the risk of the auditor erroneously accepting a population containing material errors (what we

have been calling the *sampling risk*) and the risk of erroneously rejecting a population containing immaterial errors (which we may call the *false-alarm risk*).[13]

It should be recognized, however, that "rejection" in auditing is not a sudden death situation (as when a quality control inspector rejects a production lot of ball bearings). Rather rejection means concluding that upper error limits are unacceptably high and (provided most likely errors are immaterial) that further audit work must be done to reduce the precision gap. If this further audit work consists of extending the sample to the point where the upper error limit is acceptable, the concept of any 'false alarm risk' disappears. It is true that to the extent that the computation of upper error limits under the tainted dollar evaluation method contains some degree of conservatism the final sample sizes will be slightly larger than they really need be. In practice, however, the degree of conservatism is not usually sufficient to have a significant effect on the extent of audit work; in the few cases where it is, much of the conservatism can be removed through cell-method evaluation.

The false-alarm risk (of having to later extend the sample size) can be reduced to any desired degree by taking a larger sample size to start with. Over a series of audits the minimum average final sample size can be achieved by taking the smallest justifiable sample size to start with and subsequently extending whenever necessary. Frequent sample extension would be inconvenient, however, and usually average audit time can be reduced (even though the average final sample size may be slightly larger) by selecting initial sample sizes somewhat above the justifiable minimum so as to reduce the frequency of required sample extension. The desirability of building "cushions" into sample size planning was discussed in 13.4.7.

22.3.5 Controlling the risk of extreme understatements

The risks inherent in any sampling for understatements were discussed in 13.3.3. Recognizing these risks, it is still necessary for the auditor to obtain the best sampling evidence that is practically and economically available as to the possible extent of understatements. Some practitioners have felt concern that in dollar-unit sampling the existence of an understatement automatically diminishes the chance of the understated item being selected. It should be recognized, however, that the auditor wishes to express an opinion not about the population of true values but rather about the population of *reported* book values. The reported receivables, for example, are those alleged to be in existence. The auditor

wishes to express an opinion on this allegation and so should draw his sample not from the true values but from the population of reported values (as is done in dollar-unit sampling). Based on misstatements found in his sample of reported values he will reach a conclusion about the possible frequency of such overstatements and understatements (of various taintings) in the population of reported values.

The risky decision is, of course, the assumption as to the maximum tainting possible for undiscovered understatements. In theory, there is no limit to the size of possible understatements and every sampling plan must necessarily make some subjective assumption. It is precisely this planning assumption which is discussed in 13.4.3. Various methods of providing protection against large understatements, when this risk is considered to be significant, are discussed there. None of these methods are foolproof; nor is foolproof protection provided by any sampling plan.

22.3.6 Cell-method evaluation

Cell-method evaluation is an evaluation method which eliminates much of the conservatism inherent in the regular tainted dollar evaluation method. It can only be used provided the sample was drawn using *cell-method selection* (one random selection point made within each constant-width cell throughout the population).

Evaluation where no sample errors are found

The basis of cell-method evaluation begins with the fact that if no sample errors are found (but 100% errors are presumed to be possible in the population) the 'worst' pattern of 100% errors to assume (that is, the hardest[14] for cell-method selection to detect) can be shown mathematically to be an even spread throughout all cells.

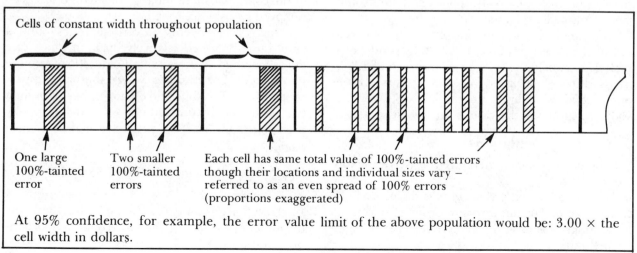

Cells of constant width throughout population

One large 100%-tainted error

Two smaller 100%-tainted errors

Each cell has same total value of 100%-tainted errors though their locations and individual sizes vary – referred to as an even spread of 100% errors (proportions exaggerated)

At 95% confidence, for example, the error value limit of the above population would be: 3.00 × the cell width in dollars.

Evaluation where one sample error is found

If, now, one sample error of T% tainting is discovered, it can be shown mathematically that one of the following two alternatives will nearly always be the "worst" pattern (i.e., hardest for cell-method selection to detect):

1. An even *spread* of the 100% errors (at a level consistent with a zero sample occurrence) together with a *load* of one cell completely with T% errors

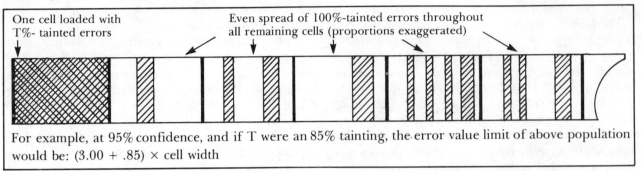

One cell loaded with T%- tainted errors

Even spread of 100%-tainted errors throughout all remaining cells (proportions exaggerated)

For example, at 95% confidence, and if T were an 85% tainting, the error value limit of above population would be: $(3.00 + .85) \times$ cell width

2. An even *spread* of the T% errors alone (at a level consistent with a one sample occurrence)

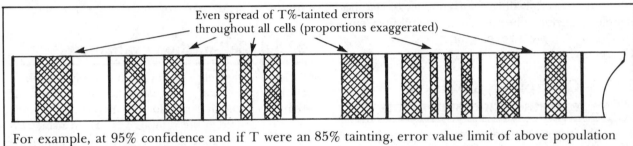

Even spread of T%-tainted errors throughout all cells (proportions exaggerated)

For example, at 95% confidence and if T were an 85% tainting, error value limit of above population would be: $(.85 \times 4.75) \times$ cell width

Evaluation where several sample errors are found

The same argument can be extended to each new sample error encountered (providing they have been ranked in order of declining tainting percentage). With each successively smaller tainting a decision must be made as to whether the 'worst' pattern involves loading errors of that tainting (leaving the previous error pattern in existence as well) or spreading errors of that tainting alone. The decision is made merely by computing both upper error limits and choosing the larger (worst).

For example, in the above one-error case, an even spread of 85% errors $(.85 \times 4.75 = 4.03)$ produces a greater potential UEL than an even spread of 100% errors with one cell loaded full of 85% errors $(3.00 + .85 = 3.85)$. Accordingly the spread of 85% errors would be chosen in this case as the "worst" pattern.

Evaluation calculations

Cell-method evaluation therefore consists of the following steps:

1. List all dollar-unit error taintings discovered.
2. Rank all dollar-unit errors in order of declining taintings (just as in the tainted dollar evaluation method).
3. List the UEL cumulative factors (from Figure 13.d) for the desired confidence level.
4. Calculate for each successive error the greater of the load or spread limits as indicated in the numerical sample at the top of the next page.

For a $60 000 cell width, the upper error limit in dollars would then be $5.87 \times \$60\ 000 = \$352\ 200$. In contrast, the regular tainted dollar evaluation method would have produced an upper error limit of $415 800 $(6.93 \times \$60\ 000)$. Clearly, therefore, much of the conservatism in the regular method has been removed by using cell-method evaluation.[15]

In many engagements, the error taintings found in audit samples are *all* relatively small, in which case the cell method involves a simple addition of tainting percentages. For instance, where the tainting percentages are 15%, 60% and 8% the upper error limit is given simply by the addition of their total to the precision $(3.00 + .83 = 3.83)$. See middle of next page.

Upper error limit in dollars = $3.83 \times \$60\ 000 = \$229\ 800$

In effect, "precision-gap-widenings" disappear and the upper error limit in dollars becomes simply basic precision plus most likely errors.

Example of Cell-Method Evaluation with Large and Small Taintings

A	B	C	D	E	F	G
Error	UEL cumulative factor per Figure 13.d	Tainting (expressed as a decimal)	Intermediate UEL (G) for previous line	"Load value" C + D	"Spread value" B × C	Intermediate UEL = greater of E and F
0	3.00	1.00			3.00	3.00
1	4.75	.85	3.00	3.85	4.03	4.03
2	6.30	.80	4.03	4.83	5.04	5.04
3	7.76	.60	5.04	5.64	4.65	5.64
4	9.16	.15	5.64	5.79	1.37	5.79
5	10.52	.08	5.79	5.87	.87	5.87
		2.48				

Example of Cell-Method Evaluation with Small Taintings Only

A	B	C	D	E	F	G
Error	UEL cumulative factor per Figure 13.d	Tainting (expressed as a decimal	Intermediate UEL (G) for previous line	Load value C + D	Spread value B × C	Intermediate UEL (greater of E and F)
0	3.00	1.00	—		3.00	3.00
1	4.75	.60	3.00	3.60	2.84	3.60
2	6.30	.15	3.60	3.75	.95	3.75
3	7.76	.08	3.75	3.83	.62	3.83

22.4 Reference material

Statistical audit sampling in general

CICA Audit Technique Study, *Statistical Sampling in an Audit Context* (1972) by Giles R. Meikle, CA
Herbert Arkin, *Handbook of Sampling for Auditing and Accounting*, 2nd Ed. (McGraw-Hill Book Company, Inc., 1974).

Dollar-unit sampling

a) Introductory:
R.J. Anderson, FCA and A.D. Teitlebaum, PhD, Dollar Unit Sampling – A Solution to the Audit Sampling Dilemma (*CA Magazine*, April 1973).
D.A. Leslie, CA, *Monetary-unit Sampling in Auditing* (International Journal of Government Auditing, April 1975).

b) More mathematical:
A.D. Teitlebaum, PhD, *Dollar-unit Sampling in Auditing* (paper prepared for presentation to the December, 1973 National Meeting of the American Statistical Association – copies available on request from the author, McGill University, Montreal).
AICPA Auditing Research Monograph No. 2, *Estimates in Sampling Accounting Populations – An Empirical Study*, by J. Neter, PhD, and J.K. Loebbecke, CPA
J.K. Goodfellow, CA, J.K. Loebbecke, CPA, and J. Neter, PhD, *Some Perspectives on CAV Sampling Plans, Part I and II*, (*CA Magazine*, October and November, 1974).
A.D. Teitlebaum, PhD, D.A. Leslie, CA, and R.J. Anderson, FCA, *An Analysis of Recent Commentary on Dollar-unit Sampling in Auditing*, (pursuant to a letter to *CA Magazine*, March, 1975 and available on request from the authors).
A.D. Teitlebaum, PhD, and C.F. Robinson, ACA, *The Real Risks in Audit Sampling* (*Journal of Accounting Research*, Vol. 13, Supplement 1975, Studies on Statistical Methodology in Auditing).

Notes

Chapter 1

1. One of two definitions given in *Terminology for Accountants*, the Canadian Institute of Chartered Accountants (CICA), 1976.
2. The three uses of accounting are discussed in *Accounting Principles: A Canadian Viewpoint*, R.M. Skinner, FCA (CICA, 1972), p. 25.
3. *A Statement of Basic Accounting Theory* (ASOBAT), American Accounting Association, 1966.
4. The following four conditions are those identified in *A Statement of Basic Auditing Concepts* (ASOBAC), American Accounting Association, 1972.
5. *Objectives of Financial Statements*, Report of the Study Group on the Objectives of Financial Statements (AICPA, 1973), p. 17.
6. The four attributes defined by *A Statement of Basic Accounting Theory* (ASOBAT), American Accounting Association, 1966.
7. *A Statement of Basic Auditing Concepts* (ASOBAC), American Accounting Association, 1972.
8. Per CICA Handbook, par. 5400.16.
9. In a sense, the auditor's client in a statutory audit is ultimately the body of shareholders who appoints him. However, as discussed in Chapter 4, the contractual relationship may legally be with the corporation itself. In any event, as a practical matter the term 'client' is commonly used to refer to the entity being audited, and is used in that sense in this book.
10. So named because they were designed to prevent "speculative schemes that had no more basis than so many feet of blue sky".
11. *Auditing Theory and Practice*, R.H. Montgomery, 1st edition 1912 (superseded by many subsequent editions, the most recent of which, the 9th edition of *Montgomery's Auditing*, was published in 1975).

Chapter 2

1. As this book goes to press, the Society of Industrial Accountants is considering a possible change of name.
2. CICA Handbook (Canadian Institute of Chartered Accountants, 1972), 'Policy Statements', p. 72.
3. CICA Handbook, 'Policy Statements', p. 72.
4. Foreword to the Recommended Uniform Rules of Professional Conduct (Inter-provincial Committee on Uniform Rules of Ethics, 1975).
5. Some provinces do not have the category of Fellow.

6. CICA Handbook, 'Policy Statements', p. 71.
7. The Chartered Accountants Act, 1956 (Statutes of Ontario), Art. 3.
8. Summarized from the CICA Handbook, 'Policy Statements', pp. 72 and 73.
9. Agreement to establish an International Accounting Standards Committee (London, 1973).
10. 'Foreword to Recommended Uniform Rules of Professional Conduct' (The Inter-Provincial Committee on Uniform Rules of Ethics), last paragraph.

Chapter 3

1. Foreword to the Recommended Uniform Rules of Professional Conduct (Inter-provincial Committee on Uniform Rules of Ethics, 1975).
2. Many practitioners in Canada, as a result of their work on Canadian subsidiaries of American companies registered with the Securities and Exchange Commission or on Canadian companies registered themselves with the SEC (because of listing on American stock exchanges), must adhere as well to the 'independence' regulations of the SEC and/or of the AICPA.
3. As explained in Chapter 4, the Canada Business Corporations Act grants oral or written statements by the auditor the status of "qualified privilege". This protects the auditor from actions for libel or slander but does not remove such statements from the purview of the courts.
4. Foreword to the Recommended Uniform Rules of Professional Conduct.
5. A more stringent position (in the writer's view, too stringent) was taken in the CICA Audit Technique Study, *The First Audit Engagement* (1974). In par. 10 of that Study it was suggested that accounting, tax and consulting services be provided by staff members other than those carrying out the audit, in order to avoid the appearance of a lack of independence.
6. The following extracts are somewhat condensed from the actual Interpretations.

Chapter 4

1. With respect to the auditor's duties to the company itself (as opposed to its shareholders) this point is open to slight question, and is considered in Chapter 5.
2. Similar wording was also suggested in Appendix E of the CICA Audit Technique Study, *The First Audit Engagement* (1974).

Chapter 5

1. R.W.V. Dickerson, LLB, PhD, FCA, *Accountants and the Law of Negligence* (The Canadian Institute of Chartered Accountants, 1966), p.92.
2. AICPA Statement on Auditing Standards No. 1, par. 110.05.
3. The concept of the "prudent practitioner" is discussed at some length in Robert K. Mautz and Hussein A. Sharaf, *The Philosophy of Auditing* (Evanston: American Accounting Association, 1961), Chapter 6.
4. R.W.V. Dickerson, LLB, PhD, FCA, *Accountants and the Law of Negligence* (The Canadian Institute of Chartered Accountants, 1966).

Chapter 6

1. The terms "creative" and "critical" were suggested by Robert K. Mautz in *Fundamentals of Auditing* (2nd ed.; New York: John Wiley & Sons, Inc., 1964), p.2.
2. Robert K. Mautz and Hussein A. Sharaf, *The Philosophy of Auditing* (Evanston: American Accounting Association, 1961), p.85.
3. Robert K. Mautz and Hussein A. Sharaf, *The Philosophy of Auditing* (Evanston: American Accounting Association, 1961).
4. *A Statement of Basic Auditing Concepts*, American Accounting Association, 1972.
5. The reader is cautioned to refer to the CICA Handbook for any recent definition of the term "generally accepted accounting principles". As this book goes to press no definition is contained in the Handbook but certain sections of the Recommendations are currently under committee review.
6. Lopes, L.J., in the *Kingston Cotton Mill* case of 1896.
7. That larger business enterprises should be audited to lower materiality levels than smaller enterprises was advocated in the 1965 CICA Audit Technique Study, *Materiality in Auditing*.
8. *Objectives of Financial Statements*, Report of the Study Group on the Objectives of Financial Statements (AICPA, 1973), p.40.
9. Some studies, such as the American Accounting Association's *A Statement of Basic Auditing Concepts*, have suggested the disclosure in the audit report of the degree of credibility added, while at the same time admitting that such a development is hardly likely from a practical point of view.
10. Compare AICPA Statement on Auditing Standards No.1, par. 330.08. Note that the U.S. standards use the term "competent" where the Canadian use "appropriate"; also the U.S.

statement uses "validity" where this book uses "reliability".
11. AICPA Statement on Auditing Standards No. 1, par. 330.12.
12. CICA 1976 Exposure Draft, *Internal Control*, par. 5220.05(d) made the same point.
13. *Ibid.*, par. 5225.14(a) made the same point.
14. *Ibid.*, par. 5225.14(b) made the same point, as does AICPA Statement on Auditing Standards No.1, par 320.55.
15. *Ibid.*, par. 5225.30 made the same point.
16. *Ibid.*, par. 5220.10 stated: "In the absence of suspicious circumstances, the auditor designs his auditing procedures on the assumption of management's good faith."
17. For suggested topics for professional empirical research in the field of auditing see: *The Auditor's Reporting Obligation*, D.R. Carmichael (AICPA, 1972), Appendix "Future Directions of Auditing Research".
18. AICPA Statement on Auditing Standards No.1, par. 110.05 (subject to amendment if the 1976 AICPA exposure draft is ultimately approved).
19. CICA 1976 Exposure Draft, *Internal Control*, par. 5215.08. The reader should refer to subsequent pronouncements.
20. AICPA 1976 Exposure Draft, *The Independent Auditor's Responsibility for the Detection of Errors or Irregularities*, par. 4. The reader should refer to subsequent pronouncements.
21. *Ibid.*, par. 6.
22. *Ibid.*, par. 18.
23. *Ibid.*, par. 8.
24. *Ibid.*, par. 12.

Chapter 7

1. CICA Exposure Draft of Proposed Auditing Recommendations, *Internal Control* (1976), par. 522.05. The reader should refer to subsequent pronouncements.
2. CICA Audit Technique Study, *Internal Control and Procedural Audit Tests* (1968).
3. Adapted from the CICA Exposure Draft, *Internal Control* (1976). The Exposure Draft presents these subsidiary objectives in a different order, however, and includes avoidance of unintentional exposure to risk as a part of safeguarding assets.
4. Inclusion of business decisions as part of "Safeguarding controls" was considered and rejected in the AICPA Statement on Auditing Standards No. 1, pars. 320.14 and 320.19. Of course, controls may cover business decisions in the sense of preventing misguided decisions based on faulty information or preventing im-

proper decisions exceeding delegated authority (both discussed later) but usually such controls would not be classified as safeguarding controls.

5. The same point is made in AICPA Statement on Auditing Standards, No. 1, par. 320.32.

6. The earlier definitions can be found in par. 320.10 and the subsequent definitions in pars. 320.27 and 320.28 of the AICPA Statement on Auditing Standards No. 1.

7. Such a division is discussed in the CICA Studies, *Computer Control Guidelines* and *Computer Audit Guidelines*.

8. Dr. Laurence ʹ. Peter and Raymond Hull, *The Peter Principle* (Bantam edition, 1972), p.8.

9. *Terminology for Accountants* (CICA, 1976).

10. The custodial function illustrated here is that involving cash. Segregation of the custody of inventory often presents greater difficulties and is illustrated in the next set of examples.

11. However, in the AICPA Statement on Auditing Standards No. 1 (see par. 320.27) such methods would be included in the definition of "administrative controls".

12. AICPA Statement on Auditing Standards No. 1, par. 320.39.

13. CICA Audit Technique Study, *Internal Control in the Small Business* (1967) p.2.

Chapter 8

1. Subsequently published in the September 1974 issue of *CA Magazine*.

2. The reader will find several good, non-technical courses on computer concepts available today.

3. The writer, who served on the CICA study group which wrote these guidelines, is grateful for the permission to adopt a similar structure for the discussion of computer controls in this chapter.

4. The CICA study also identified an intermediate category of *minimum control standards* between *control objectives* and *control techniques*. This intermediate level has been omitted in the present chapter.

5. These objectives and the objectives quoted at the beginning of the following sections are taken from the CICA Study, *Computer Audit Guidelines*.

6. Other examples of organizational structures can be seen in *Computer Control Guidelines*, pp. 29 and 30.

7. Also see *Computer Control Guidelines* pp. 18 and 19.

8. Also see *Computer Control Guidelines*, p. 43.

9. This restatement of the objectives of processing controls involves a difference in format but not of substance from those used in *Computer Control Guidelines*.

10. CICA Study, *Computer Audit Guidelines* (1975), p. 147.

Chapter 9

1. This figure covers a portion of the relationships previously analyzed in Figure 6.e.

2. AICPA Statement on Auditing Standards No. 1, par. 320.50.

3. AICPA Statement on Auditing Standards No. 1, par. 320.08.

4. AICPA Statement on Auditing Standards No. 1, par. 110.08.

5. CICA Exposure Draft, *Internal Control* (1976), par. 5215.11. The reader should refer to subsequent pronouncements.

6, 7, 8. The objectives of substantive verification as to the existence, ownership, completeness, evaluation, and statement presentation of reported assets etc. are discussed in Chapter 11.

9. CICA Exposure Draft, *Internal Control* (1976), par. 5220.02.

10. CICA Exposure Draft, *Internal Control* (1976), pars. 5220.04 and 5220.09.

11. A similar view is expressed in the CICA Audit Technique Study, *Internal Control and Procedural Audit Tests* (1968), par. 7.

12. CICA Exposure Draft, *Internal Control* (1976), par. 5225.13.

13. Examples of similar internal control evaluation guides covering all major systems in a typical business are presented in Chapter 29.

14. The concept of analyzing control into certain primary control areas each of which may be served by some or all of a group of individual control techniques was also developed in the CICA Study *Computer Control Guidelines* (1970) and incorporated in the control evaluation guide presented in the companion *Computer Audit Guidelines* (1975).

15. CICA Audit Technique Study, *Internal Control and Procedural Audit Tests* (1968), p.7.

16. For example, such limited tests were suggested for important non-attest controls in computerized systems in the CICA Study, *Computer Audit Guidelines* (1975), p. 170.

17. CICA Exposure Draft, *Internal Control* (1976), pars. 5225.17 and 5225.23.

18. Individual auditors may conclude that ratios different from 3 to 1 are appropriate in all or some circumstances. Empirical research into typical ratios of compliance deviations to monetary errors in practice would undoubtedly be of value.

19. AICPA Statement on Auditing Standards No. 1, par. 320.52.

20. This example assumes that unbilled shipments in this case do, in fact, constitute monetary misstatements of the financial statements (see 12.5.1).
21. CICA Exposure Draft, *Internal Control* (1976), par. 5225.31.
22. These approaches are discussed in the CICA Study, *Computer Audit Guidelines* (1975), p. 155.
23. The analytical approach was originally advocated in an article, 'Analytical Auditing' by the writer in *The Canadian Chartered Accountant* (November, 1963) and later in a book *Analytical Auditing*, R.M. Skinner, FCA and R.J. Anderson, FCA (Pitman: Toronto, 1966). Chapters 24 to 27 incorporate, with some subsequent modification, the techniques originally described in *Analytical Auditing* and therefore supersede that earlier book. The term 'analytical' in analytical auditing, referring to analysis of systems and controls, should not be confused with the term 'analytical review procedures' which are substantive procedures for assessing the reasonableness of business statistics, ratios, etc. as described in Chapter 10.

Chapter 10

1. AICPA Statement on Auditing Standards No. 1, par. 330.04.
2. AICPA Statement on Auditing Standards No. 1, par. 330.15.
3. See discussion of relative reliability in 6.6.6.
4. One could argue that the inspection of mortgage agreements evidencing mortgages payable represents direct physical examination of a liability. However, since the idea of observing a liability is foreign to customary audit thinking, such inspection is classified in this chapter as inspection of external documentary evidence (see 10.3.3). One could alternatively argue that the inspection of share certificates should be treated as the inspection of external documentary evidence rather than direct physical examination of an asset itself. However, as the same argument would apply to cash itself, such a treatment would be more confusing than helpful. Some symmetry must be sacrificed in the interests of convenience.
5. The checking of the arithmetic accuracy of a source document for a given transaction and the tracing of that document to its recording in the books of original entry could also be said to be the reperformance of accounting routines. For convenience, however, in the classification used in this chapter such procedures have been included in vouching. Also, as stated earlier, the comparison of corroborating evidence to the underlying accounting records has been included with the technique of gathering that evidence even though the act of comparison in some cases could be said to be the reperformance of some accounting routine.
6. This preference applies to external evidence and not necessarily to internal evidence, where the cost/benefit trade-off between confirmation and enquiry will be different (see 10.4.7).
7. CICA Audit Technique Study, *Confirmation of Accounts Receivable* (1969), Chapter V, par. 2(a).
8. CICA Audit Technique Study, *Confirmation of Accounts Receivable* (1969), Chapter IV, pars. 8 to 19.
9. AICPA Statement on Auditing Standards No. 11, *Using the Work of a Specialist*, par. 4.
10. *Ibid.*, par. 7.
11. AICPA Statement on Auditing Standards No. 9, *The Effect of an Internal Audit Function on the Scope of the Independent Auditor's Examination*, par. 1.
12. A recent report on audit use of regression analysis by Kenneth Stringer CPA of Haskins & Sells can be found in the proceedings of the University of Chicago's 1975 Conference on Statistical Methodology in Auditing – see *Journal of Accounting Research*, Vol. 13. Supplement 1975, p. 1.
13. On the basis of the argument presented in Chapter 6, a somewhat higher level of audit assurance should be demanded when highly reliable evidence is unusually cheap. Conversely, a somewhat lower level of audit assurance should be demanded (but never less than a certain minimum level) when highly reliable evidence is unusually costly. This logic should not, merely because the auditor is unable to collect a fair fee, excuse him from gathering evidence which would have provided important and necessary assurance in relation to its cost. Nor does it excuse a reduction in assurance to such an extent that there remains no rational basis for expressing a clear opinion (see 6.6.4 and 6.6.7).

Chapter 11

1. In statistical terms, the quantity referred to as "possible errors" represents that error level which, had it occurred, would have yielded as favorable audit evidence only that small proportion of the time (e.g. 10%) corresponding to the level of audit risk desired.
2. Of course, if we *could* make possible errors disappear merely by ignoring them, every auditor would have a powerful incentive to avoid the use of statistical sampling – but this would be like

turning out the lights to hide the obstacles they reveal, or shooting the messenger of bad news.

3. Such a role was suggested in the CICA Audit Technique Study, *Materiality in Auditing* (1965).

Chapter 12

1. The word "haphazard" is not used here in the sense of sloppy or careless but in the everyday sense of random; the term "random" is avoided here merely to prevent confusion with the more rigorous sense of "random" employed in the following chapter for statistical samples.

2. On the basis of the argument presented in Chapter 6, a somewhat higher level of audit test assurance should be demanded when the per-item testing cost is unusually low. Conversely, a somewhat lower level of audit test assurance should be demanded (but never less than a certain minimum level) when the per-item testing cost is unusually high. This logic should not, merely because the auditor is unable to collect a fair fee, excuse him from gathering evidence which would have provided important and necessary assurance in relation to its cost. Nor does it excuse a reduction in assurance to such an extent that there remains no rational basis for expressing a clear opinion (see 6.6.4 and 6.6.7).

3. The derivation of the above "judgmental factors" is explained in 22.3.3. The left-hand factors are based on the assumption that in the typical audit about one-third of the materiality limit may be consumed by 'most likely error' projections and that *audit precision* must therefore be limited to about two-thirds of materiality. Some auditors may prefer to make their own planning decisions as to what portion (sometimes even all) of materiality can be allocated to desired audit precision. If 'materiality in dollars' is replaced by 'desired audit precision in dollars' in the above guideline, slightly smaller judgmental factors can be used: 4, 3 and 2 for considerable, normal, and minimum assurance respectively. These latter factors (the right-hand factors) are also the appropriate ones to use if it is anticipated that the client will provide for or correct all projected errors throughout the audit – a common situation in small engagements.

4. This expression is equivalent to the product of: (number of material subdivisions in the population) and (number of required selection points per material subdivision on average). This product, clearly, is equal to the required sample size. In the numerical example following there are 15 material subdivisions of $4 000 each within the total population of $60 000. Making 4 selections on average within each of the 15 subdivisions represents a total sample size of 60.

5. This sample size would approximate that required by the dollar-unit statistical sampling techniques described in Chapter 13. (It would also approximate the sample size required by physical-unit statistical sampling in those few cases where it is safe to assume that average possible error size would not likely exceed average population item book value.)

6. The foregoing rule-of-thumb guideline results in a sample which approximates one drawn by the dollar-unit statistical sampling techniques described in Chapter 13. Indeed, dollar-unit sampling may be said to be the statistical analogue of judgmental value-oriented selection. As explained in Chapter 13, not all practitioners use statistical methods similar to the dollar-unit approach. Some use stratified variables sampling plans (which usually also favour the larger items though in a somewhat different manner). Practitioners using the latter plans may wish to modify the above suggestions for judgmental value-oriented selection correspondingly.

7. Physical-unit statistical sampling (described in Chapter 13 for cases where population dollars are not readily available) is the statistical analogue of judgmental neutral selection.

8. The reader may find the reasons for using this method of projection more apparent after reading Chapter 13. This method of projection parallels that used for dollar-unit statistical sampling as described in that chapter.

9. This method of projection parallels that used for physical-unit statistical sampling as explained in Chapter 13. Sometimes an alternative method of projection is suggested whereby the total sample error value is divided by the population book value. While this alternative method produces the same projection *on average*, it will differ in any individual case. The method suggested in the text is more logical where it is believed that error sizes can only be small and independent of book value – which is the assumption favouring neutral selection. The alternative method can be argued to be preferable where error sizes have a tendency to vary with book value – but in that case, value-oriented selection would have been the preferable testing basis in the first place.

10. The two examples given in Figures 12.c and 12.d could each have been drawn from the same population, but by different methods. Appropriately valued they each give approximately the same most likely error projection. Evaluated using inconsistent projection methods the reader will find that significantly different, and incor-

rect, projections would have resulted.

11. The rationale is based on the assumption that compliance deviations will generally outnumber actual monetary errors and that evidence of the more frequent compliance deviations can be more economically detected than evidence of the less frequent actual monetary errors (the 'smoke/fire argument'). This rationale is valid only when there indeed exists separate evidence of compliance deviations as such. Where the only available evidence of a compliance deviation is in fact the existence of a monetary error, this rationale does not function and the justification for placing considerable reliance on control (together with the need for compliance verification) may not arise. Available compliance evidence is discussed in 26.3.3.

12. In statistical sampling terms it is suggested, in Chapter 13, that this minimum assurance level be 80%.

13. A more precise derivation of this statement and the following guideline is explained in 13.5.4.

14. Again, the foregoing rule-of-thumb guideline results in a sample which approximates one drawn by the dollar-unit statistical sampling techniques described in Chapter 13. The approximation is necessarily imperfect but still results, in the writer's view, in a more appropriate test than neutral selection.

Chapter 13

1. The writer is particularly indebted to Dr. Albert Teitlebaum of McGill University for his advice in the condensation of this chapter from much lengthier existing material, although the writer alone must take the responsibility for any shortcomings of the final text. Some portions of the introductory material in this chapter originally appeared as an article by Dr. Teitlebaum and the writer in *CA Magazine* (see 13.7). The writer is grateful for the permission to reproduce and adapt such portions here.

2. Throughout this chapter the terms *assurance* and *confidence* are used interchangeably to refer to the assurance that misstatements over a certain limit are not present in the final audited statements (i.e., the assurance that bad statements will be rejected). In AICPA Statement on Auditing Standards No. 1, Sec. 320B, this concept is referred to as "reliability level". Some auditing literature (for example, the ninth edition of *Montgomery's Auditing*) uses the term confidence to refer instead only to assurance that good statements will not be rejected. That assurance is relevant when a reservation is being expressed.

Of course, the auditor wants appropriate assurance both when reservations and when clear opinions are given. In this chapter, however, confidence is used in the sense of confidence that a clear opinion is warranted. Assurance when reservations are expressed is discussed in 18.5.

3. Some writers use the term "upper precision limit" for upper error limit; that use is avoided here in order to prevent confusion with the concept of precision as the spread between most likely error rate and upper error limit.

4. The pie diagram is intended to illustrate only the *directions* of inter-related changes in the four factors and not their exact quantification. For a brief introduction to the mathematical bases for such computations the interested reader may refer to Chapter 22.

5. Where zero sample errors are planned or encountered, the sampling is sometimes referred to as *discovery sampling* or *exploratory sampling* as it involves the chance of failing to discover even one occurrence of an error. No difference in either mathematics or basic audit objectives is involved, however. A discovery sample is merely the particular case where the sample error rate is zero. If the same confidence and upper error limit are maintained, the discovery sample size represents the smallest sample size possible. If sample errors are encountered or should be anticipated, larger sample sizes will be necessary.

6. AICPA Statement on Auditing Standards No. 1, par. 320A.10.

7. Sampling plans with precomputed tolerable sample error rates or "acceptance levels" are sometimes called *acceptance sampling plans* – in contrast to plans designed to estimate population characteristics directly (called *estimation sampling plans*). The difference is one of format only, for both are based on the identical mathematical formulas. It is suggested here that the acceptance format is convenient for compliance testing and the estimation format for substantive testing.

8. For example, see AICPA Statement on Auditing Standards No. 1, Section 320A, (Relationship of Statistical Sampling to Generally Accepted Auditing Standards).

9. 20 three-head possibilities out of 64 possible six-toss sequences.

10. The term "representative" is used in this chapter, as in Chapter 12, in the layman's sense of a random sample which is likely to be typical of the population from which it is drawn – and not in the technical sense of sample selections allocated in a deliberate fashion to ensure representation

of specified factions of the population.

11. Some additional modifications can be found in the AICPA Auditing Research Monograph No. 2, *Behaviour of Major Statistical Estimators in Sampling Accounting Populations – An Empirical Study*, by Dr. J. Neter and J.K. Loebbecke, CPA.

12. While space does not permit a formal proof of that statement here, briefly it can be said that the 5% risks of failing to detect errors totalling $180 000 in each stratum (if they existed) are *alternative* risks [for the *joint* risk of failing to detect $180 000 errors in each of two strata would be $(5\%)^2$ or 0.25%]; in fact, for 95% confidence (rather than 99.75% confidence) the upper error limit remains $180 000 for the whole population.

13. An example of a ten-strata physical-unit sample with error frequencies priced, in effect, at the respective stratum boundaries is presented in the CICA Audit Technique Study, *Statistical Sampling in an Audit Context*, by Giles R. Meikle, CA (1972), pp. 25-30.

14. The technique of dollar-unit sampling was first described in the article, "Dollar-unit Sampling – A solution to the audit sampling dilemma" by R.J. Anderson, FCA and A.D. Teitlebaum, PhD (*CA Magazine,* April, 1973) and subsequently presented in more detail in other papers (see 13.7). Its practical effect is similar to the *cumulative monetary amount* sampling plan developed earlier by the firm of Haskins & Sells and the late Dr. F. Stephan of Princeton University. Somewhat similar concepts were also previously suggested by a Dutch accountant, van Heerden, in 1961.

15. Proportionate sampling may be the basis for certain portions of the H & S sampling plan, although the mathematical basis of the latter has not as yet been published.

16. A general description of this method can be found in Herbert Arkin, *Handbook of Sampling for Auditing and Accounting*, 2nd ed. (McGraw-Hill Book Company, Inc., 1974), p. 190.

17, 18. The computation of the standard deviation and the resulting precision is described in 22.2.1.

19. A general description of this method can be found in Arkin's Handbook, pp. 119-121.

20, 21. The computation of the standard deviation and the resulting precision is described in 22.2.1.

22. A general description of stratification methods for variables sampling can be found in Arkin's Handbook, pp. 162-172.

23. The statistical fact that the precision gap *widens* with increasing sample errors may be comprehended intuitively by realizing that precise estimates are easier in accurate populations; when errors abound the same sample size will yield estimates that are less precise.

24. While this statement and the following few paragraphs explain the method of tainted dollar evaluation in intuitive terms, the reader wishing a more mathematical explanation may refer to 22.3.1, where it is demonstrated that this evaluation method results in a conservative (safe) approximation to the true upper error limit.

25. In fact, the requirement for such ranking follows directly from successive application, to each new error, of the reasoning described for the one-sample-error case in 22.3.1.

26. Actually, some protection against 200%-size errors is provided but at a confidence level less than that originally specified. It is possible to adjust the dollar-unit sampling planning decisions, at a cost, to maintain the originally specified confidence level with respect to certain larger understatements as discussed in 13.4.3.

27. The absence of any assumption as to homogeneity is explained in 22.1.4.

28. The validity of this suggestion for combining mixed confidence levels is explained in 22.3.2.

29. Subject always to the unavoidable risks associated with any sampling for understatements as previously discussed.

30. This calculation can be found in 22.3.6.

31. A number of statisticians are exploring alternative methods of eliminating the conservatism in the regular tainted dollar evaluation method. These methods, when developed, may likewise be of interest in those few engagements where the degree of conservatism is large enough to present practical problems. Present experience indicates that such engagements are rare.

32. Even where there is a risk of unbilled shipments, confirmation of account balances is not a very reliable method of detecting them.

33. Where errors are all in one direction the ratio of precision-gap-widening to most likely errors will be given by the weighted average of the precision-gap-widening factors involved.

34. The reader with some introduction to statistics will recognize these arguments as derived from 'Bayesian' analysis. Although prior and posterior probabilities cannot be rigorously calculated the concepts are useful in understanding why sampling confidence should logically vary with varying circumstances.

35. This formula is merely the converse of the evaluation calculation explained in 13.3.2.

36. This "continuous" auditing approach can be useful as well for tests conducted by internal auditors.

37. The computation of these actual results was

shown in the example in 13.3.2.

38. All dollar-unit selection techniques are methods of value-oriented selection according to the terminology used in Chapter 12. In the few cases where neutral selection is appropriate because population items cannot be quantified in dollars, dollar-unit techniques do not apply and, instead, a physical-unit sample must be drawn by selecting physical-units randomly out of the whole population.

39. The chance of any dollar-unit in the population being selected in the two-stage sample = 1/120 x 1/$500 = 1/$60 000, the same chance it would have had in a one-stage dollar-unit sample selecting one item every $60 000.

40. It should be remembered that statistically confidence and precision limits go in pairs. Some practitioners have suggested the use of a 90% or 95% compliance confidence level but coupled with an unpriced upper error limit frequency of 5% or 10%. Such levels are suggested (*but only as examples*) in the AICPA Statement on Auditing Standards No. 1, paragraphs 320 B.22 and 320 B.24. In most cases, such confidence levels would not be as great as the 80% suggested above when re-expressed in relation to a reasonable multiple of materiality. It is possible indeed, that future audit research will indicate that it is safe to assume a higher multiple than 3 for the ratio of compliance deviations (in terms of transaction value) to materiality.

41. Compliance sampling interval
    = $\dfrac{\text{tolerable upper error limit (in dollars)}}{\begin{array}{c}\text{UEL cumulative factor for 1 sample error}\\ \text{and 80\% confidence per Figure 13.f}\end{array}}$
    = $\dfrac{\text{triple materiality (in dollars)}}{3.00}$
    = materiality (in dollars)

42. The same sample size as computed above may still be appropriate for such physical-unit samples, provided it is safe to make the assumption that transactions subject to critical compliance deviations are no larger on average than other transactions.

Chapter 14

1. A more detailed discussion of these techniques may be found in the monthly issues of EDPACS from July 1973 to April 1975.

Chapter 15

1. AICPA Statement on Auditing Standards No. 1, par. 310.08.

2. The third type of decision was the principal subject of the CICA Audit Technique Study, *Materiality in Auditing* (1965). Since the issue of that study, many more professional pronouncements have appeared on the subject of testing and today the first two types of decision would usually be viewed as the more important reasons for establishing a preliminary materiality limit.

3. It should be noted, however, that a pre-tax income base loses one feature which the CICA Study advocated. The CICA study pointed out that the smaller the net income is relative to sales, gross profit, etc., the harder it is to measure with the same relative precision. It could be argued, therefore, that materiality limits should be less stringent relative to net income for industries operating on narrow margins than for those on broader ones. This relationship was partially achieved by the gross profit guidelines proposed in the CICA Study. Not everyone agrees, however, that such a relationship is appropriate.

4. The reader is cautioned to refer to any subsequent CICA pronouncements on the subject of materiality or materiality guidelines. As this book goes to press, the subject of accounting materiality is under study by the Financial Accounting Standards Board in the United States and its pronouncements may in turn influence the thinking of the AICPA in the United States and the CICA in Canada on auditing materiality. In 1974 the Accountants International Study Group study, *Materiality in Accounting*, basing its conclusions largely on a 1973 Australian exposure draft, suggested various bases; among these can be drawn the inference that income-distorting errors should be judged material if they distorted income by more than 5% to 10%.

5. AICPA Statement on Auditing Standards No. 5, par. 4 states, for example, that the auditor must determine whether the financial statements are presented "within a range of acceptable limits, that is, limits that are reasonable and practicable to attain in financial statements".

6. However, this logic should not, merely because the auditor is unable to collect a fair fee, excuse him from gathering evidence which would have provided important and necessary assurance in relation to its cost. Nor does it excuse a reduction in assurance to such an extent that there remains no rational basis for expressing a clear opinion (see 6.6.4 and 6.6.7).

7. The CICA 1976 Exposure Draft, *Internal Control*, also refers to the need for planning the extent of the intended reliance on control. The reader should refer to any subsequent pronouncements.

8. The CICA 1976 Exposure Draft, *Internal Control*,

refs to the auditor's need for a sufficient knowledge of the business. The reader should refer to any subsequent pronouncements.

Chapter 16

1. Hypothetically, it is possible to imagine a limited special purpose engagement conducted by a single auditor and requiring but a small number of familiar procedures which he could conduct and evaluate without preparing any working papers (though this omission would be imprudent). For practical purposes, however, the regular annual audit, whether of a large client or a small one, whether conducted by a single auditor or an audit team, requires the preparation of working papers if it is to be adequately controlled.
2. CICA Audit Technique Study, *Good Audit Working Papers* (1970), par. II-6.
3. AICPA Statement on Auditing Standards No. 1, par. 338.01.
4. See AICPA Statement on Auditing Standards No. 1, par. 338.07: "While the independent auditor's working papers may serve as a useful reference source from time to time for his client, the working papers should not be regarded as constituting a part of, or as a substitute for, the client's accounting records."
5. Also see AICPA Statement on Auditing Standards No. 1, par. 338.06, which states in part: "Working papers are the property of the independent auditor, and in a number of states there are statutes which designate the auditor as the owner of the working papers."
6. CICA Audit Technique Study, *Good Audit Working Papers* (1970), par. V-8.
7. *Ibid.*, par. V-15.
8. Some practitioners use the term "schedules" to refer only to tabulations of figures. Others use the term more generally – as in "verification schedules" and "planning schedules". The more general sense is intended here.
9. F/S and A/A refer to financial statement audit and analytical audit files. The suggested sections for the financial statement audit file are outlined in 16.3.3.
10. Adapted from CICA Audit Technique Study, *Good Audit Working Papers* (1970), par. III-15(f).
11. As discussed in 13.4.9, correction to the most-likely-error projection is meaningful only if the resulting adjusted upper error limit (i.e., the precision gap) is less than materiality. If precision exceeds materiality, the result after adjustment will still leave the auditor in doubt as to whether the financial statements are fairly presented. Stated in another way, a most-likely-error projection surrounded by a more than material precision range is too imprecise to serve as an appropriate basis for proposing a client adjustment.
12. Precision in this paragraph is not used in the sense of sampling precision when statistical projections are made of clear-cut sample errors encountered, but rather of the precision in measuring an individual error.
13. Superficially, it might seem inconsistent to measure known errors as the distance to the nearest limit of the zone of reasonableness while advocating that, for statistical samples, corrections should be made to the most-likely-error projection and not to the nearest precision limit. The inconsistency disappears when one considers the different natures of the two precision ranges. In the case of accounting estimates, the range reflects reasonable differences of opinion which can be anticipated in the judgmental estimating process. The auditor's best estimate is not inherently better than the client's estimate if both fall within the zone of reasonableness. If numerous additional opinions were sought, the auditor's estimate might not be confirmed any more often than the client's. In sample projections, on the other hand, the most-likely-error projection *is* a measure of the population error which most likely exists. While it is true that the estimate may be slightly erroneous owing to "sample bounce", it is more likely to be accurate than any other value within the precision interval. Indeed, the chance that the true error is really as far away as the statistical precision limit is exceedingly small (the chance being measured by the sampling risk, e.g. 5%). It is reasonable, therefore, that more weight should be given to the most-likely-error projection within a sampling precision range than to the auditor's best estimate within the zone of reasonableness for an accounting estimate.
14. AICPA Statement on Auditing Standards No. 1, par. 210.03.

Chapter 17

1. See CICA Handbook, par. 5400.01. The term "auditor's standard report" is similarly used in the AICPA Statement on Auditing Standards No. 2, pars. 6 to 8.
2. CICA Handbook, par. 5400.06. References in this chapter and in the following chapters to reporting sections of the CICA Handbook are based on the wording and numbering approved by the Auditing Standards Committee as this book goes to press. A possible change in section

numbering is under study.

3. CICA Handbook, par. 5400.16.

4. CICA Handbook, par. 5400.18.

5. CICA Handbook, par. 5400.17.

6. CICA Handbook, par. 5400.09.

7. CICA Handbook, par. 5400.04.

8. Of course, occasionally a special purpose report may be requested covering only one statement such as the balance sheet. Statements covered by special purpose reports do not necessarily purport to present complete financial information in accordance with generally accepted accounting principles (see 19.3).

9. See CICA Handbook, par. 5400.07 and par. 1500.04.

10. CICA Handbook, par. 5400.07. Disclaimers are discussed in Chapter 20.

11. CICA Handbook, par. 5400.15.

12. The same point is made in AICPA Statement on Auditing Standards No. 2, par. 6.

13. CICA Handbook, par. 5400.11.

14. *Accounting Principles: A Canadian Viewpoint*, R.M. Skinner, FCA (CICA 1972), p. 29.

15. *Ibid.*, p. 19.

16. *Ibid.*, pp. 316, 368, and 369.

17. Interpretation 206/7.

18. In 1975 a CICA exposure draft of a proposed accounting recommendation, *Fair Presentation and Generally Accepted Accounting Principles*, included a definition of generally accepted accounting principles similar to the one suggested in this chapter and, like it, containing no reference to substantial authoritative support for contrary alternatives. The exposure draft was subsequently dropped, however, and further study of that subject was discontinued.

19. Compare to AICPA Statement on Auditing Standards No. 5, par. 2. "... The phrase 'generally accepted accounting principles' is a technical accounting term which encompasses the conventions, rules, and procedures necessary to define accepted accounting practice at a particular time...."

20. For example, L.G. Eckel, PhD, in "The Two-part Audit Opinion", *CA Magazine*, June, 1973.

21. U.S. Court of Appeals, Judge Henry I. Friendly, Continental Vending Case, 1969.

22. Such an implication would seem to require the insertion of "and" before the phrase "in accordance with generally accepted accounting principles".

23. AICPA Statement on Auditing Standards No. 5, par. 3.

24. CICA Handbook, par. 5400.12.

25. See also CICA Handbook, par. 5400.13.

26. CICA Handbook, par. 1500.05.

27. AICPA Statement on Auditing Standards No. 5, par. 9.

28. For example, L.R. Dicksee, FCA, in *Auditing* (5th ed., 1902).

29. D.R. Carmichael, CPA, PhD, "What Does the Independent Auditor's Opinion Really Mean?", *The Journal of Accountancy* (November, 1974).

30. Accountants International Study Group, *The Independent Auditor's Reporting Standards in Three Nations* (1969), pars. 32 and 33.

31. J.L. Roth, CPA, *The Journal of Accountancy*, July, 1968.

32. AICPA Accounting Principles Board Statement No. 4, *Basic Concepts and Accounting Principles Underlying Financial Statements of Business Enterprises*.

33. The Commission on Auditors' Responsibilities, *Statement of Issues: Scope and Organization of the Study of Auditors' Responsibilities* (AICPA, 1975) pp. 20 and 21.

34. Accountants International Study Group, *The Independent Auditor's Reporting Standards in Three Nations* (1969), par. 100.

35. R.K. Mautz and H.A. Sharaf, *The Philosophy of Auditing* (American Accounting Association, 1961) p. 202.

36. However, in the CICA Handbook, Sec. 5500, which pre-dated the reporting standards, the distinction between opinion reservations and consistency exceptions is not made. It is possible that future revisions may conform the terminology to that used in the reporting standards.

37. See CICA Handbook, par. 1500.10 and par. 3600.11.

38. See AICPA Statement on Auditing Standards No. 1, par. 546.04.

39. AICPA Accounting Principles Board Opinion No. 20, pars. 15 and 16.

40. From the reference in CICA Handbook, par. 1500.10 and 5500.48 to the effect "on the current statements" one might infer a preference for the first alternative but in some situations it may be argued that the change is most clearly illustrated and the spirit of the Handbook Recommendations best met by the second alternative.

41. See CICA Handbook, par. 3600.11.

42. See CICA Handbook, par. 1500.10.

43. CICA Handbook, par. 5500.50.

44. CICA Handbook, par. 5500.51. Note that the consistency exception should not be located as the last words in the opinion paragraph as such a practice might leave it ambiguous as to whether the GAAP opinion was being qualified as well.

45. See CICA Handbook, par. 1500.11.

46. See AICPA Statement on Auditing Standards

No. 1, par. 420.18.

47. See CICA Handbook, par. 1580.69.
48. See CICA Handbook, par. 1500.09.
49. CICA Handbook, par. 5500.23.
50. See AICPA Statement on Auditing Standards No. 2, par. 49 and AICPA Exposure Draft of Proposed Statement on Auditing Standards: *Reports on Comparative Financial Statements* (1976).
51. See CICA Handbook, par. 5500.24.
52. Note that mere reclassification or regrouping of figures on the financial statements does not mean that the statements are not in agreement with the accounting records. Also, consolidated statements may be considered to be in agreement with the books even though the eliminating and consolidating entries are not on the books of any corporate entity. Companies should, however, keep a permanent record of their consolidating entries each year, as a form of accounting record.
53. CICA Handbook, par. 5500.17.
54. CICA Handbook, par. 5500.21.
55. CICA Handbook, par. 5500.22.
56. See, for example, the CICA Research Study, *Financial Reporting for Life Insurance Companies*.
57. See, for example, the CICA Research Study, *Financial Reporting for Property and Casualty Insurers*.
58. Also see various AICPA Industry Audit Guides, such as *Audits of Voluntary Health and Welfare Organizations, Hospital Audit Guide, Audits of Colleges and Universities*, etc.
59. See AICPA Statement on Auditing Standards No. 1, par. 544.02.
60. See AICPA Statement on Auditing Standards No. 1, par. 544.04.
61. See AICPA Statement on Auditing Standards No. 1, par. 620.08.
62. See AICPA Statement on Auditing Standards No. 1, par. 620.04.
63. See CICA Handbook, par. 5100.03.
64. CICA Auditing Guideline, *Auditor's Considerations when Supplementary General Price-level Restatements are Published in an Annual Report* (1975), par. 13.
65. AICPA Statement on Auditing Standards No. 8, *Other Information in Documents Containing Audited Financial Statements*, par. 4.
66. *Ibid.*, par. 4.
67. CICA Handbook, par. 5530.10.
68. CICA Handbook, par. 5530.23.
69. CICA Handbook, par. 5530.18.
70. CICA Handbook, par. 5530.23.
71. Adapted from CICA Handbook, par. 5530.24. With the subsequent issuing of Handbook Sec. 5400, this suggested wording has the result of

relating generally accepted auditing standards exclusively to those portions of the consolidated figures examined directly by the investor auditor – although it could be argued that the basic review or override procedures performed by him on the investee auditors' work should also be comprehended by generally accepted auditing standards. The U.S. report wording differs in this respect.

72. AICPA Statement on Auditing Standards No. 1, par. 543.07.
73. *Ibid.*, par. 543.09.
74. See, for example, the CICA Research Study, *Financial Reporting for Life Insurance Companies* (1973), Chapter 22.
75. AICPA Statement on Auditing Standards No. 11, *Using the Work of a Specialist*, par. 11.
76. See CICA Handbook, par. 5530.03.
77. See CICA Handbook, par. 5400.19.
78. See AICPA Statement on Auditing Standards No. 1, pars. 620.05 and 620.07.
79. See CICA Handbook, par. 1800.05.
80. CICA Handbook, par. 5500.19.
81. AICPA Statement on Auditing Standards No. 2, par. 27.

Chapter 18

1. Throughout this chapter, accounting deficiencies are discussed solely in relation to generally accepted accounting principles but the points made apply equally, in the case of special purpose reports, to accounting deficiencies in relation to an appropriate disclosed basis of accounting (see 19.3).
2. CICA Handbook, par. 5500.31.
3. See CICA Handbook, par. 5500.33.
4. AICPA Statement on Auditing Standards No. 2, *Reports on Audited Financial Statements*, par. 33.
5. CICA Handbook, pars. 5500.33, .34, and .36.
6. For an example, see CICA Handbook, par. 5500.AIII. An objection could be raised that it is inconsistent to quote ranges in expressing a reservation but not in expressing an unqualified opinion – for indeed zones of reasonableness for accounting estimates are present in both cases. While there are some grounds for this objection, the distinction can be drawn that in the case of a reservation the auditor is explaining a disagreement as to valuation and, because of the conflicting views, quoting a range of values may be more important than where such disagreement does not exist.
7. Note that the explanatory paragraph is desirable when the prior year's report was qualified (see 17.5.2). For a further example, though without

the explanatory paragraph, see CICA Handbook par. 5500.AII(2).

8. CICA Handbook, par. 5500.46.

9. See AICPA Statement on Auditing Standards No. 2, pars. 18 and 19.

10. CICA Handbook, par. 5500.45.

11. Adapted from CICA Handbook, par. 5500.AII(1).

12. CICA Handbook, par. 1500.06.

13. CICA Handbook, par. 5500.20.

14. Adapted from AICPA Statement on Auditing Standards No. 1, par. 545.05. While one can quibble that the reservation as to incompleteness may not strictly speaking affect the opinion as to financial position and results of operations alone, the suggested wording may, as a practical matter, be considered satisfactory.

15. Note that CICA Handbook, par. 1500.03 says that such a statement is normally included and that par. 1500.05 requires the presentation of "any information required for fair presentation of financial position, results of operations, *or changes in financial position*" (italics added). Some practitioners, however, argue that the "or" means that a statement of changes in financial position is not mandatory – though if it is presented it should contain full disclosure.

16. Adapted from CICA Handbook, par. 5500.AI(2) (described there as a "scope limitation").

17. The question of whether an auditor can properly undertake an engagement leading to a qualified opinion because of a scope restriction is discussed later. All the third field work standard says, however, is that the work done must fit the report given.

18. This form of qualification, while essential in certain circumstances, has perhaps been used more widely than necessary. Many charitable organizations receive revenues from verifiable sources (United Appeal, government, large organized fund raising drives, etc.) and have adequate internal controls to permit the expression of a clear opinion. In any case, the auditor should design auditing procedures which will go as far as is practicable in giving him audit assurance. On occasion, these procedures may include confirmation with selected donors. Given a reasonable system of control, the mere fact that there is always some slight risk of an unreported donation from some member of the public should not in itself preclude a clear opinion – any more than the inevitable risk of an undisclosed depositor liability in a financial institution.

19. CICA Handbook, par. 5500.40.

20. Adapted from CICA Handbook, par. 5500AI(1) (described there as "inability to obtain essential information").

21. See, for example, FASB Statement of Financial Accounting Standards No. 5, *Accounting for Contingencies*.

22. AICPA Statement on Auditing Standards No. 2, par. 24.

23. *Ibid.*, see par. 22.

24. See Accountants International Study Group, *Going Concern Problems* (1975) pars. 12 to 21.

25. AICPA Auditing Research Monograph No. 1, *The Auditor's Reporting Obligation*, D.R. Carmichael, CPA, PhD (1972), p. 93.

26. See, for example, Accountants International Study Group, *Going Concern Problems* (1975), par. 71(2). The argument is based on the presumption that generally accepted accounting principles imply the going concern assumption and a different basis is therefore involved where that assumption is invalid. A contrary argument is that generally accepted accounting principles call for normal accrual accounting for going concerns and liquidation-basis accounting for entities in liquidation; according to that argument no separate reference is required in the auditor's opinion paragraph provided that adequate disclosure of the basis used has been made in the financial statements or notes.

27. Such a viewpoint was presented, for example, by D.R. Carmichael, CPA, PhD at the 1976 Touche Ross/University of Kansas *Symposium on Auditing Problems*.

28. For example, some practitioners consider that qualification for an uncertainty as to the going concern assumption is necessary only if the cause of the uncertainty is not readily apparent from reading the financial statements and is unnecessary if the uncertainty is obvious from financial difficulties clearly portrayed. Other practitioners argue that if the uncertainty is really obvious a qualification can do no harm; if a qualification is resisted on the grounds that it may be a self-fulfilling prophecy, then the uncertainty cannot have been all that obvious.

29. AICPA Statement on Auditing Standards No. 2, par. 26.

30. See CICA Handbook Sec. 3600 for the circumstances under which "prior period adjustments" are justified.

31. Some arguments against the use of the auditor's report as a medium for providing emphasis, however, were mentioned in 17.5.10.

32. The reader is cautioned to refer to any subsequent CICA pronouncements on this subject. Audit report reservations are under study as this book goes to press.

33. CICA Handbook, par. 5500.55.
34. CICA Handbook, par. 5500.56.
35. For a further example, see CICA Handbook, par. 5500.B(3).
36. For examples see CICA Handbook, pars. 5500.B(1) and (2).
37. CICA Handbook, par. 5500.59.
38. AICPA Statement on Auditing Standards No. 2, par. 45.
39. AICPA Statement on Auditing Standards No. 2, footnote to par. 25.
40. CICA Handbook, par. 5500.C.
41. CICA Handbook, pars. 5500.63, .65, and .66.
42. Adapted from CICA Handbook, par. 5500.D(2). Further examples are provided in pars. 5500.D(1) and (3).
43. See AICPA Statement on Auditing Standards No. 2, par. 48. Prior to 1974 piecemeal opinions had been prohibited omly in cases of a significant client-imposed restriction on audit scope.
44. See AICPA Statement on Auditing Standards No. 1, Section 518.
45. These terms were introduced by the Accountants International Study Group in *International Financial Reporting* (1975).
46. See CICA Handbook, Section 1501, "International Accounting Standards".
47. CICA Handbook, par. 1501.05.
48. CICA Handbook, par. 5400.23.
49. Accountants International Study Group, *International Financial Reporting* (1975), par. 63(b).
50. See CICA Handbook, par. 1501.05.
51. Accountants International Study Group, *International Financial Reporting* (1975), par. 63(c).
52. The same suggestion is made in Accountants International Study Group, *International Financial Reporting* (1975), par. 64(b). However, there exists a body of thought that any restatement of a set of financial statements to comply with accounting principles outside a company's country of domicile is misleading. The "single domicile" school argues that the interrelationship between the form of transactions executed and the local economic, legal and social environment makes restatement meaningless unless the very transactions themselves were to be reconstructed as they might have occurred in a different environment. While such views are not universally held, they underlie in part the reluctance of some practitioners to associate themselves, except when required by law or regulation, with any restatements of financial presentations.
53. See Accountants International Study Group, *International Financial Reporting* (1975), par. 64(a).
54. See Accountants International Study Group, *International Financial Reporting* (1975), par. 66(a).
55. AICPA Statement on Auditing Standards No. 1, par. 561.03.
56. AICPA Statement on Auditing Standards No. 1, Section 561 (Subsequent Discovery of Facts Existing at the Date of the Auditor's Report).
57. AICPA Statement on Auditing Standards No. 1, par. 530.08 suggests a caption such as "Event (Unaudited) Subsequent to the Date of the Report of Independent Auditor".

Chapter 19

1. See CICA Handbook, par. 4000.04.
2. Modified from CICA Handbook, par. 7000.12, to be consistent with the standard auditor's report introduced in 1976 in par. 5400.14 and to include coverage of a statement of changes in financial position. The tabular form may seem to separate "present fairly" a little from "generally accepted accounting principles" (contrary to the emphasis on a one-part opinion introduced in the 1976 revision of Section 5400); however, it may be a practical solution in the circumstances.
3. Many practitioners believe that combined statements in purchase (non-pooling) situations should usually be limited to the current year and prior year only since such a combination in the earlier years may not reflect realistic circumstances.
4. CICA Handbook, par. 7000.13.
5. CICA Handbook, par. 7000.15.
6. See CICA Handbook, pars. 7000.05 and .06.
7. See CICA Handbook, Section 4000 (Prospectuses).
8. For example, must three-month figures, in order to maintain the same proportionate precision relative to reported income, be audited using a materiality limit only one quarter of that for a full year? Such a position would imply that both the opening and closing balance sheets for this three-month period should be audited using such a one-quarter normal materiality limit — a result which seems impractical and unreasonable.
9. Some practitioners believe that adequate note disclosure is usually difficult, since so many financial statement figures may be affected, and that pro-forma statements are therefore to be preferred.
10. CICA Handbook, par. 7000.21.
11. CICA Handbook, pars. 7000.22 and .23.
12. CICA Handbook, pars. 7000.03 and .04.
13. A similar comment (in the context of comfort letters to underwriters) is made in AICPA Statement on Auditing Standards No. 1, par. 630.37.

14. CICA Handbook, par. 7000.24.
15. See CICA Handbook, par. 5530.21.
16. AICPA Statement on Auditing Standards No. 1, par. 710.02. Also, see the whole of Section 710 (Filings Under Federal Securities Statutes).
17. *Ibid.*, par. 710.03.
18. *Ibid.*, par. 710.08.
19. CICA Handbook, par. 7000.09.
20. CICA Handbook, par. 7000.10, modified to include coverage of the statement of changes in financial position and to exclude coverage of the pro-forma balance sheet (usually incomplete at this stage). This form of letter also conforms with the requirements of the various provincial Acts. The Handbook suggests that it is preferable for one such letter to be addressed to *all* regulatory authorities requiring it but that separate letters to each are acceptable.
21. The absence of a reference to a GAAP yardstick may leave the phrase "presents fairly" rather isolated – contrary to the emphasis on a one-part opinion introduced in the 1976 revisions of Section 5400.
22. Adapted from CICA Handbook, par. 7000.11, modified to include coverage of the statement of changes of financial position and of the pro-forma balance sheet.
23. While the construction "give me reason to believe" is suggested in the CICA Handbook, some practitioners consider the U.S. wording "caused me to believe" to be preferable (see AICPA Statement on Auditing Standards No. 1, par. 630.45).
24. CICA Handbook, par. 7000.25.
25. CICA Handbook, par. 7000.26, modified primarily to (a) express the report in the singular, (b) include coverage of the statement of changes in financial position, and (c) include illustrative dates. Again, it is preferable to have one comfort letter addressed to all regulatory authorities requiring it.
26. See AICPA Statement on Auditing Standards No. 1, Section 630 (Letters for Underwriters).
27. CICA Handbook, par. 7000.18.
28. CICA Handbook, par. 7000.17.
29. A CICA Exposure Draft of a Proposed Auditing Recommendation, *Auditor's Report on Special Purpose Financial Statements Prepared on an Appropriate Disclosed Basis of Accounting other than Generally Accepted Accounting Principles* (1976), is approved but not as yet released as this book goes to press. This exposure draft covers part, but not all, of the subject of special reports. Because the wording has not yet been released, this chapter does not contain detailed references to the exposure draft. However, the reader should refer to

this draft and any subsequent pronouncements.
30. See CICA Handbook, Introduction to Auditing Recommendations, Application, par. 1. Note that the Rules of Professional Conduct continue to apply to engagements with respect to banks, insurance companies and not-for-profit organizations.
31. CICA Handbook, par. 5100.05.
32. The only exception is that the recommended disclosure in the audit report of non-compliance with Accounting Recommendations (par. 5500.20) should logically not be applicable – but see the later discussion on this subject.
33. A particular problem however, is accounting developments which occur after the date of the contract. For example, a 1960 trust deed may call for the statements used for purposes of determining compliance with certain covenants to be prepared on an unconsolidated basis but otherwise to be in accordance with generally accepted accounting principles. At the time, unconsolidated investments would normally have been accounted for on a cost basis. Subsequently, the equity accounting basis has come to be generally accepted for certain types of investment. Is it now appropriate to adopt equity accounting for the unconsolidated investments in conformity with the literal wording of the trust deed or would this frustrate the intention of the various prescribed covenants? Perhaps the reference to generally accepted accounting principles in the trust deed should be interpreted as referring to 1960 principles – but this interpretation can also be abused.
34. CICA Handbook, par. 5100.06.
35. AICPA Exposure Draft of Proposed Auditing Statement, *Special Reports* (1976), par. 5. The reader should refer to subsequent pronouncements.
36. Such a recommendation has been under study by the CICA and may be included in the CICA exposure draft.
37. A recommendation under study by the CICA has been that a reference to consistency should be made where financial statements have previously been issued in the same special circumstances as the current special purpose statements. Such a recommendation may be included in the forthcoming CICA exposure draft.
38. A recommendation under study by the CICA has been that the purpose of the financial statements should be disclosed together with (a) the reason that the basis of accounting used is considered appropriate for that purpose and (b) an assertion that the basis may not be appropriate for other purposes. Such a recommendation

may be included in the forthcoming CICA exposure draft.

39. *Ibid.*, par. 7.

40. See CICA Handbook, par. 3050.03. As this book goes to press, the CICA is in process of issuing an exposure draft revising Section 3050 on long-term intercorporate investments. According to the proposed revision, parent company unconsolidated statements would no longer be considered to be in accordance with generally accepted accounting principles.

41. This position is suggested in the forthcoming CICA exposure draft on long-term intercorporate investments.

42. See CICA Handbook, par. 5100.03.

43. Adapted from AICPA Exposure Draft of Proposed Auditing Statement, *Special Reports* (1976) par. 13. The reader should refer to subsequent pronouncements.

44. *Ibid.*

45. In the United States, negative assurance is permitted in certain special purpose reports – see AICPA Statement on Auditing Standards No. 1, par. 518.03 and AICPA Exposure Draft of Proposed Statement on Auditing Standards, *Special Reports* (1976) footnote 1.

46. Such an alternative is recommended in the AICPA Exposure Draft of Statement on Auditing Standards, *Special Reports* (1976) pars. 14 and 15. The suggested report contains wording such as: "We have applied certain agreed-upon procedures ... solely to assist you in connection with. ...It is understood that this report is solely for your information and is not to be referred to or distributed outside the Company for any purpose". The report also contains a strong disclaimer of opinion including the words: "had we performed additional procedures ... matters might have come to our attention that would have been reported to you". A type of negative assurance, while not emphasized, is permitted: "no matters came to our attention that we believe should be reported to you". The reader should refer to any subsequent pronouncements.

47. AICPA Statement on Auditing Standards No. 1, par. 610.02.

48. See AICPA Exposure Draft on Proposed Statement on Auditing Standards, *Special Reports* (1976), par. 17. The reader should refer to subsequent pronouncements.

49. Refer also to legal responsibilities discussed in 4.2.3 and contractual responsibilities which may have been assumed in a letter of engagement (4.2.1).

50. This point is also made in the CICA Exposure Draft of Proposed Auditing Recommendations, *Internal Control* (1976), par. 5215.13. The reader should refer to any subsequent pronouncements.

51. Of course, the reporting of a control weakness to the client does not excuse the auditor from modifying his program appropriately and performing compensating audit procedures where necessary (see Chapter 9) or, in extreme cases, where a definite opinion cannot be formed, expressing a suitable reservation (see Chapter 18).

52. Note that the recommendations on weaknesses and on controls in the accompanying memorandum should *not* be omitted just because the same ones appeared in prior years' memoranda. Important recommendations should be repeated each year if they continue to be applicable. The suggestion here is only that the general matters referred to in the covering letter need not necessarily be repeated each year.

53. For a discussion and examples of this type of reporting, see AICPA Audit Guide, *Audits of Service-Center-Produced Records*, Chapter 4, Third-Party Review of Service Centers. A number of limitations in the use of such a report, however, were noted in the CICA Study, *Computer Audit Guidelines*, p. 181.

54. AICPA Statement on Auditing Standards No. 1, pars. 640.06 to .11.

55. AICPA Statement on Auditing Standards No. 1, par. 640.12.

Chapter 20

1. For example, the terms of reference of the CICA Auditing Standards Committee embrace not only auditing matters but "'non-audit' services closely related, or appearing to be closely related, to auditing and the services provided by auditors". The CICA's Auditing Recommendations include recommendations with respect to such non-audit services. Likewise, the AICPA Auditing Standards Executive Committee issues Statements on Auditing Standards which include pronouncements on non-audit engagements.

2. CICA Handbook, par. 8100.03.

3. As discussed in 18.2.4, practitioners differ as to whether the liquidation basis, applied when liquidation is indeed in prospect, is a part of generally accepted accounting principles, a special version of generally accepted accounting principles, or completely different from generally accepted accounting principles.

4. For example, CICA Handbook Section 1750, Interim Financial Reporting to Shareholders, carefully avoids the use of the term "financial statements".

5. CICA Handbook, par. 8100.13.
6. CICA Handbook, par. 8100.16.
7. CICA Handbook, par. 8100.14.
8. AICPA Statement on Auditing Standards No. 1, par. 516.03.
9. CICA Handbook, par. 8100.08.
10. CICA Handbook, par. 8100.20.
11. CICA Handbook, par. 8100.27.
12. CICA Handbook, par. 8100.23.
13. CICA Handbook, par. 8100.29.
14. A "staff example" of a checklist accompanied the original CICA exposure draft of the 1976 revisions to Section 8100, Unaudited Financial Statements. The reader should refer to any subsequently issued material, such as Guidelines, on this subject.
15. CICA Handbook, par. 8100.28.
16. AICPA Statement on Auditing Standards No. 1, par. 516.02, provides that financial statements are unaudited if the public accountant "has not applied auditing procedures which are sufficient to permit him to express an opinion concerning them". The AICPA *Guide for Engagements of CPAs to Prepare Unaudited Financial Statements*, p.5, provides that "during an engagement, the accountant may decide to perform certain procedures in order to resolve questions with which he is confronted" and that he "should evaluate whether, as a result of performing these procedures, the nature of the engagement would change".
17. See CICA Handbook, par. 8100.26.
18. CICA Handbook, par. 8100.49.
19. AICPA Statement on Auditing Standards No. 1, par. 510.02. The AICPA *Guide for Engagements of CPAs to Prepare Unaudited Financial Statements*, p. 19, states that the accountant "*may wish* [italics added] to make further enquiries or to consult the client's records to gain a better understanding of the information".
20. For example, with respect to limited reviews of unaudited *interim* financial information, AICPA Statement on Auditing Standards No. 10, par. 18, provides that, where questions arise, the accountant "should make additional enquiries or employ other procedures he considers appropriate to permit him to report informatively". Many practitioners, however, interpret "other procedures" in this paragraph to refer only to information-gathering procedures and not to corroborative procedures.
21. The reader should refer to subsequent pronouncements on special purpose reports.
22. CICA Handbook, pars. 8100.34 and .35.
23. CICA Handbook, par. 8100.37.
24. CICA Handbook, par. 8100.37, footnote 6.
25. CICA Handbook, par. 8100.39.
26. CICA Handbook, par. 8100.41.
27. AICPA Statement on Auditing Standards No. 1, par. 516.04.
28. *Ibid.*, par. 517.03. The AICPA requires such disclosure regardless of the extent of the public accountant's procedures. Of course, if an accountant is non-independent, it is impossible for him to meet generally accepted auditing standards and an engagement which might otherwise be an audit becomes a non-audit engagement.
29. CICA Handbook, pars. 8100.44 and .45.
30. CICA Handbook, par. 8100.47.
31. CICA Handbook, par. 8100.49.
32. CICA Handbook, par. 8100.51.
33. See CICA Handbook, par. 8100.A.
34. CICA Handbook, par. 8100.58.
35. CICA Handbook, par. 8100.08.
36. CICA Handbook, par. 8100.60.
37. CICA Handbook, par. 8100.62.
38. CICA Handbook, par. 8100.63.
39. AICPA Statement on Auditing Standards No. 1, par. 516.05.
40. CICA Handbook, par. 8100.66.
41. Adapted from CICA Handbook, par. 8100.B.
42. AICPA Statements on Auditing Standards No. 10, *Limited Review of Interim Financial Information*, and No. 13, *Reports on a Limited Review of Interim Financial Information*.
43. Of course, the specific Recommendations in Section 8100 with respect to association do not presently apply anyway, but it seems desirable to consider the general concept of association and, using this general concept, association would not seem to arise in informal consulting engagements.
44. Again, the specific Recommendations in Section 8100 with respect to association do not presently apply, but using the general concept of association, association *would* seem to arise in formal review engagements.
45. See AICPA Statement on Auditing Standards No. 10, *Limited Review of Interim Financial Information*, pars. 10 to 17.
46. The practitioner may wish to document the answers to such enquiries by obtaining a letter of representations from the client.
47. See CICA Handbook, pars. 8100.40 and .41.
48. Again, the Recommendations in Section 8100 do not presently apply to interim statements of public companies anyway. However, it seems desirable to adopt practices which are not inconsistent with the general concepts implied in that Section. The discussion here is intended to show that the practices suggested are not inconsistent

with those concepts.

49. The example letter is generally similar to that suggested in AICPA Statement on Auditing Standards No. 10, *Limited Review of Interim Financial Information*, par. 22, except for omission of a reference to AICPA standards and for certain minor modifications.

50. See AICPA Statement on Auditing Standards No. 10, *Limited Review of Interim Financial Information*, par. 22.

51. AICPA Statement on Auditing Standards No. 13, *Reports on a Limited Review of Interim Financial Information*, par. 5.

52. A number of auditing interpretations are under study by the AICPA as this book goes to press.

Chapter 21

1. See AICPA Commission *Statement of Issues: Scope and Organization of the Study of Auditors' Responsibilities* (1975), p. 27.

2. *Report to the Executive Committee and Council of the CICA by Task Force 2000* (1970), p. 1.

3. AICPA Commission *Statement of Issues*, p. 10.

4. See AICPA Commission *Statement of Issues*, pp. 27 to 36 for the first three areas and pp. 13 to 22 for the last five areas.

5. *Ibid.*, pp. 20 and 21 for the first point and pp. 36 to 38 for the second.

6. *Ibid.*, pp. 23 to 27.

7. *Objectives of Financial Statements* (AICPA, 1973).

8. L.S. Rosen, PhD, CA, *Current Value Accounting and Price-level Restatements* (CICA, 1972).

9. CICA Discussion Paper, *Current Value Accounting* (1976), p. 16.

10. Other procedures regularly involved when reliance is placed on experts are discussed in 10.3.3.

11. Some of the problems in index weighting are discussed in the CICA Research Study, *Current Value Accounting and Price-level Restatements* (1972), pp. 37 to 41.

12. *Ibid.*

13. *Task Force 2000 Report*, pp. 164 and 165.

14. *Task Force 2000 Report*, pp. 143 and 144.

15. AICPA Commission *Statement of Issues*, p. 24.

16. *Task Force 2000 Report*, p. 167.

17. See also *The Corporate Report* (The Institute of Chartered Accountants in England and Wales, 1975), pp. 57 and 58.

18. *Ibid.*, p. 179.

19. *Ibid.*, pp. 171 and 172.

20. AICPA Commission *Statement of Issues*, p. 25.

21. *Ibid.*, p. 24.

22. CICA Handbook, par. 7000.15.

23. The AICPA has suggested the use of the term *projection* for a presentation which shows *what would happen if* a certain course were adopted without necessarily implying that adoption of that course is probable. The term *forecast*, on the other hand, is suggested for the best estimate of the most probable future results and is used in that sense in this chapter. The SEC, however, has used the term projection in all cases.

24. The Guidelines were issued by the Management Advisory Services Executive Committee of the AICPA. Such guidelines are intended to present the Committee's recommendations as to the best practices in the area under study.

25. The Statement of Position was issued by the Accounting Standards Executive Committee of the AICPA. This committee does not have the authority to establish accounting principles, such authority resting with the Financial Accounting Standards Board (which has not as yet pronounced on the subject) and the SEC.

26. The latter subject had been under study by the Auditing Standards Executive Committee of the AICPA but as this book goes to press no pronouncement on that subject appears imminent.

27. Accounts International Study Group, *Published Profit Forecasts* (1974), par. 76.

28. *Report on Mergers, Amalgamations and Certain Related Matters* by the Ontario Select Committee on Company Law (1973), Chapter 19, "Financial Forecasts".

29. Robert H. Kidd, CA, *Earnings Forecasts* (CICA 1976).

30. Accountants International Study Group, *Published Profit Forecasts* (1974), par. 83.

31. See *Earnings Forecasts* (CICA, 1976), Chapter 16.

32. Accountants International Study Group, *Published Profit Forecasts* (1974), par. 84.

33. AICPA Commission *Statement of Issues*, p. 25.

34. CICA *Task Force 2000 Report*, p. 173.

35. CICA Research Study, *Earnings Forecasts* (1976), Chapter 18, par. 4. See the accompanying discussion in that chapter. The reader should also refer to any subsequent pronouncements.

36. The CICA Study suggests that the assumptions disclosed be classified into *internal assumptions* and *external assumptions*. Were the auditor to provide specific negative assurance, it is possible that it might be affected by this classification. For example, negative assurance might be given with respect to the *completeness* of all assumptions but with respect to the *reasonableness* of only the internal assumptions – the reader being in a position to make his own evaluation of the reasonableness of the external assumptions.

37. Note that objectivity was not considered essential for the accounting service of preparing unaudited financial statements (see 20.3) but is im-

portant for the more attest-oriented service of reviewing forecasts.

38. For further details see CICA Research Study, *Earnings Forecasts* (1976), Chapter 17 and Appendix C.

39. AICPA Commission on Auditors' Responsibilities, *Statement of Issues*, p. 26.

40. In "The Assurance Function – Auditing at the Crossroads", *The Journal of Accountancy*, September, 1974, D.R. Carmichael, CPA, PhD, commented: "Implicit responsibility – as suggested in the auditor of record concept – creates too great a chance that users of financial information will misunderstand the independent auditor's role and place unwarranted reliance on the information". He argued instead for specific association with individual reports, some on a full audit basis and others on a lesser review basis.

41. The subject is under study by the AICPA Auditing Standards Executive Committee as this book goes to press. One possibility is that management representations as to internal control could be included in the notes to the financial statements and therefore covered by the auditor's report.

42. AICPA Commission on Auditors' Responsibilities, *Statement of Issues*, p. 27.

43. In 1976 the AICPA issued an exposure draft on *Illegal Acts by Clients*, proposing that it is not the auditor's function to detect illegal acts but that when, as a result of his procedures, he believes that illegal acts may have occurred, he should investigate those matters further and seek legal advice where necessary.

44. As this book goes to press, approaches to auditing, for example, the efficiency of government expenditures (the value-for-money concept), are under study by the Office of The Auditor General of Canada.

45. Carl D. Liggio in *Dilemma or Delight? A Look at the Accountant's Litigation Today*, a paper presented at The American Bar Association National Institute in Montreal in May, 1974.

46. A term originally introduced by Daniel Bell and subsequently used by Herman Kahn and Anthony J. Wiener in *The Year 2000, A Framework for Speculation on the Next Thirty-Three Years* (New York: The Macmillan Company, 1967) to describe a state which the U.S., Canada, and a few other nations will achieve before the turn of the century.

47. *Task Force 2000 Report*, Synopsis, p. 1.

48. *Task Force 2000 Report*, p. 196.

49. Carl D. Liggio in *The Accountant's Legal Environment for the Next Decade*, a paper presented at "Accounting Colloquium III – Institutional Issues in Public Accounting" sponsored by The Arthur Young Professorship at The University of Kansas, May, 1973.

50. *Task Force 2000 Report*, p. 256.

51. J.R. Petrie, PhD, "The outlook for Canada in 30 years – implications for the accounting profession", *CA Magazine*, July, 1969.

52. *Task Force 2000 Report*, pp. 107, 110, and 111.

53. D.R. Carmichael, CPA, PhD, *The Auditor's Reporting Obligation* (AICPA, 1972), Appendix "Future Directions of Auditing Research".

54. Peat, Marwick, Mitchell & Co., *Research Opportunities in Auditing* (New York, 1976).

Chapter 22

1. The writer is again indebted to Dr. Albert Teitlebaum of McGill University for his advice in the condensation of this chapter from lengthier technical material, although the writer alone must take the responsibility for any shortcomings of the final text. The writer is working jointly with Dr. Teitlebaum on a more complete book on the theory and practice of dollar-unit sampling.

2. An example of such tables can be found in *Handbook of Sampling for Auditing and Accounting*, 2nd ed. by Herbert Arkin (New York: McGraw-Hill Book Company, Inc., 1974), Table F – some 81 pages in total but covering only three specific confidence levels.

3. The far right-hand columns in Table F of Arkin's Handbook represent such binomial values and take up less than 15% of the total table.

4. The differences introduced by the first simplification increase with increasing ratios of sample size to population size but generally remain trivial for most sampling fractions found in audit practice. The differences introduced by the second simplification increase with increasing numbers of sample errors but again generally remain trivial for most error rates found in audit practice.

5. Examples of such tables can be found in Arkin's Handbook, Tables E and G – some 16 pages in total.

6. Such an approach was suggested by a Dutch accountant, van Heerden, in a 1961 article (no English translation published) and in an unpublished paper prepared for the 1967 International Congress of Accountants in Paris.

7. This modification was first developed by the firm of Haskins & Sells but without, as far as the writer is aware, any explanation of its basis. It is hoped that the following explanation will help to fill that gap.

8. The highest-error-value population subject to

exactly a 5% risk of detection can be shown to contain 5.95% 100%-errors and 0.5% 20%-errors. For such a population the risk of a sample of 50 yielding 0 100%-errors is 5.1% and risk of yielding 0 or 1 20%-errors is 97%, for a combined risk of 5.0%. The error value in such a population amounts to 6.05%, or $181 500. For the one-sample-error case the formula for computing this correct 'worst' upper limit was described in *Dollar-unit Sampling in Auditing* by A.D. Teitlebaum, PhD (see 22.4). For numbers of sample errors beyond one, however, the rigorous results are not easily soluble.

9. The most difficult-to-detect population containing an error value of $201 000 can be shown to contain 6.60% 100%-errors and 0.5% 20%-errors. For such a population the risk of a sample of 50 yielding 0 100%-errors is 3.7% and the risk of yielding 0 or 1 20%-errors is 97%, for a combined risk of 3.6%.

10. The demonstration in this section may be considered a heuristic proof of the tainted dollar evaluation method. To date the mathematics involved in a completely rigorous theoretical proof have not been soluble. However, after a great many hypothetical numerical examples of risk calculations and a number of computerized empirical tests, no case has been found of an upper error limit determined by this method which did not yield an actual risk equal to or less than the stated risk (e.g., in the above example, equal to or less than 5%). There is ample evidence, therefore, that the tainted dollar evaluation method results in conservative conclusions.

11. Choosing the worst pattern of error in each case, in the light of actual sample results found, rather than sticking with a consistent pattern of error chosen in advance, introduces a degree of conservatism. Some statisticians have suggested that it might be possible to confine the range of possible error patterns, and thus reduce this conservatism, by making certain assumptions based on pre-sampling knowledge. At present, the only use, in dollar-unit sampling, of pre-sampling knowledge with respect to error patterns is in making the error size-limit assumption.

12. In theory, the validity of combining projections, each as calculated at its appropriate level of sampling confidence, can be explained using Bayesian analysis in terms of combining results at a consistent level of *total* assurance (posterior confidence).

13. In statistical terms, the false-alarm risk and the sampling risk are sometimes referred to as the producer's risk and the consumer's risk or as the α-risk and the β-risk – though unfortunately without uniformity as to which is meant by which when applied in an auditing context.

14. At the other extreme, the easiest pattern to detect is where 100% errors completely filled one or more cells – in which case their detection by cell-method sampling would be absolutely certain.

15. Research by a number of practitioners and statisticians is continuing both in cell-method evaluation and in other possible methods of reducing the conservatism in the regular tainted dollar evaluation method.

Consolidated index

References to Volume 1 are in regular type (e.g., 201) References to Volume 2 are in bold type (e.g., **201**)